D1271540

THE CHURCH IN THE MODERN AGE

by

GABRIEL ADRIÁNYI–QUINTÍN ALDEA VAQUERO
PIERRE BLET–JOHANNES BOTS–VIKTOR DAMMERTZ
ERWIN GATZ–ERWIN ISERLOH–HUBERT JEDIN
GEORG MAY–JOSEPH METZLER–LUIGI MEZZARDI
FRANCO MOLINARI–KONRAD REPGEN
LEO SCHEFFCZYK–MICHAEL SCHMOLKE
ANTONIO DA SILVA–BERNHARD STASIEWSKI
ANDRÉ TIHON–NORBERT TRIPPEN–ROBERT TRISCO
LUDWIG VOLK–WILHELM WEBER
PAUL-LUDWIG WEINACHT–FÉLIX ZUBILLAGA

Translated by
Anselm Biggs

CROSSROAD · NEW YORK

1989

The Crossroad Publishing Company

370 Lexington Ave., New York, NY 10017

Translated from the *Handbuch der Kirchengeschichte*

Vol. VII: *Die Weltkirche im 20. Jahrhundert*

© Verlag Herder Freiburg im Breisgau 1979

English translation © 1981 by The Crossroad Publishing Company

Printed in the United States of America

Library of Congress Cataloging in Publication Data

Weltkirche im 20. Jahrhundert. English.

The Church in the modern age.

(History of the Church; v. 10)

Translation of: Die Weltkriche im 20 Jahrhundert/

Anslem Biggs.

Bibliography: p.

Includes index.

1. Church history—20th century.   I. Adriányi,

Gabriel.   II. Biggs, Anslem.   III. Series: Handbuch

der Kirchengeschichte. English; v. 10.

BR145.2.J413   1980, vol. 10   [BR479]   270s   81-5057

ISBN 0-8245-0013-X   [270.8'2]   AACR2

CONTENTS

Preface. xi

Preface to the English Edition. xv

List of Abbreviations. xvii

SECTION ONE: THE INSTITUTIONAL UNITY OF THE UNIVERSAL CHURCH. . . 1

Chapter 1: Statistics. 1
  Statistics of the World's Population, Statistics of the World Religions,
  Proportion of Catholics. 1
    Statistics of the World's Population 1914–65. 1
    Statistics of the World Religions 1914–65. 5
    The Southward Movement of the Christian World. 9
  The Organization of the Entire Church from 1914 to 1970. 9
    Congregations, Tribunals and Offices, Commissions and Secretariats of the
    Curia (1916–68). 11
    The College of Cardinals (1916–68). 18
    Titles and Areas of Jurisdiction in the Totality of the Hierarchy of the
    Catholic Church (1916–68). 18
    Diplomatic Representations of the Apostolic See with the Nations and of
    the Nations with the Apostolic See (1916–68). 19

Chapter 2: Popes Benedict XV, Pius XI, and Pius XII—Biography and Activity
  within the Church. 21
    Benedict XV. 21
    Pius XI. 23
    Pius XII. 29

Chapter 3: Foreign Policy of the Popes in the Epoch of the World Wars. . . . 35
  The First World War and the Postwar Years: Benedict XV. 35
    Neutrality. 35
    Papal Measures of Assistance. 38
    Efforts for Peace. 39
  Between the Two World Wars: Pius XI. 47
    The Lateran Treaties of 1929. 47
      The "Roman Question" to 1926 47; The Route to the Lateran Treaties
      (1926–29) 52; After the Lateran Treaties: The Crisis of 1931 and 1938 55
    Pius XI and the Totalitarian Systems. 59
      Pius XI and the Soviet Union 60; Pius XI and National Socialist Germany:
      The Way to the Concordat with the Reich (April–July 1933) 63; *Between the
      Concordat and the Encyclical* Mit brennender Sorge *70; From the Encyclical* Mit
      brennender Sorge *to the End of the Pontificate (1937–39)* 72
  The Second World War: Pius XII. 77
    Neutrality. 79
    Efforts for Peace. 82
    Papal Measures of Assistance 88
    The Pope's "Silence". 93

Chapter 4: The Second Vatican Council. 96
  John XXIII: Summoning and Preparation for the Council. 96
  The First Session and the Change of Pontificate. 106
  Second Session (1963) and First Results. 116
  Third Session: Crisis of November and Constitution on the Church. 125

CONTENTS

Fourth Session and Closing. 135
Impact. 146

Chapter 5: The Code of Canon Law and the Development of Canon Law to 1974. 151
From the Promulgation of the Code to the Second Vatican Council. 151
  The Codification of Canon Law. 151
  The Development of the Law from 1918 to 1958. 153
    Benedict XV 154; Pius XI 154; Pius XII 156
From the Convocation of the Second Vatican Council. 158
  John XXIII. 158
  Paul VI. 159
    Organs 159; General Character 163; Individual Legislative Actions 167; Revision of the Code and of the Canon Law of the Eastern Church 173

Chapter 6: The Holy See's Policy of Concordats from 1918 to 1974. 177
Era of Concordats under Pius XI and Pius XII. 177
  To the Beginning of the Second World War. 177
    Point of Departure, Motives, and General Character 177; Individual Concordats: *With the New States 183; With the "Separation Countries" of Europe 185; With the Latin American States 189; Germany 190*
  During the Second World War. 198
  In the Postwar Period. 200
    Fate of Concordats in Socialist Countries 200; Concordats with Free Countries 203
The Agreements under John XXIII and Paul VI. 209
  The Significance of the Second Vatican Council for the Legal Relationship of Church and State. 209
  The Individual Agreements. 213
    The "Protocols" with Socialist States 213; The "Modus vivendi" with Tunisia 215; The Changes in Concordats in States Giving Preferential Status to the Catholic Church 216; Latest Concordats and Agreements with Free Countries 218

SECTION TWO: THE DIVERSITY OF THE INNER LIFE OF THE UNIVERSAL CHURCH. 229

Chapter 7: Society and State as a Problem for the Church. 229
The Social Claim to Educate and Its Bases: Natural Law and Revelation ("Question of Competence"). 232
Social Principles: Personality, Subsidiarity, Solidarity, Common Good, Universal Common Good. 236
State and State Power—Democracy. 242
The Church and the Social Errors of the Age. 248
  Socialism–Communism. 248
  Fascism–National Socialism. 253
Understanding of Peoples: "World State". 257

Chapter 8: Main Lines of the Development of Theology between World War I and Vatican II. 260
The Departure from Neo-Scholasticism in Systematic Theology. 260
  Temporal and Intellectual Presuppositions. 260
  The Turning of Dogma from "Reason" to "Living". 264
  The "Theological" Deepening of Moral Theology. 272
  From "Apologetics" to "Fundamental Theology". 277
The Evolution of Historical Theology with the Aid of the Historicocritical Method. 280
  The Progress of Church History. 280
  Overcoming Resistance to the Historical Method in Biblical Scholarship. . 283
The Rise of Pastoral Theology to a Scientific Theological Discipline. . . . 288
  The Increased Significance of General (Fundamental) Pastoral Theology. . 288
  The Catechetical Renewal. 291
  The Turning of Homiletics to Kerygmatics. 293
  The Reestablishment of Liturgy as "Theology of Worship" 295

CONTENTS

Chapter 9: Movements within the Church and Their Spirituality. 299
   The Liturgical Movement. 300
   New Awareness of the Church and the Scriptural Movement. 305
   Catholic Action. 307
   The Spiritual Exercises Movement 310
   Eucharistic Piety in Transition. 312
   Devotion to the Sacred Heart of Jesus. 315
   Devotion to Mary and Mariology. 318
   The Spiritual Development of the Orders. 321
   The Secular Institutes. 326
   Worker-Priests. 331

Chapter 10: Developments in the Clergy since 1914. 336

Chapter 11: Religious Communities and Secular Institutes. 352
   The Orders between Persistence and Change. 352
   The Rise of New Types of Communities. 355
   The Acclimatization of the Orders in Mission Lands 358
   Religious Reform under Pius XII. 361
   The Second Vatican Council and Its Effects. 364
   The Orders in the Field of Tension between Church and State. 371

Chapter 12: Educational System, Education, and Instruction. 378
   Church and Society in Their Relation to the Educational System. . . . 378
   Catholic Educational and School Doctrine. 380
   The Second Vatican Council and the Postconciliar Period. 382
   Catholic Education in the European and North American Educational Systems. 388
      Preschool Area. 389
      Primary and Secondary Spheres. 391
      Tertiary Sphere. 395
      Continuing Education (Education of Adults). 399
   Conditions for Catholic Education in Other Areas of the World. 403

Chapter 13: Information and the Mass Media. 410
   The Catholic Claim and the "Colorless Press". 411
   Film and Radio in the Early Phase. 413
   The Development of the Catholic Press in the International Survey. . . 415
   Catholic News Agencies. 427
   Radio and Television under the Restrictions of Commercial or of Public
   Control. 428
   Church Journalism in the Third World. 430
   Church and Mass Communication in Theory and Organization. 432

Chapter 14: Charity and Ecclesiastical Works of Assistance. 436
   Laying the Foundations in the Nineteenth Century. 436
   National Organizations. 441
   International Cooperation. 443
   Consolidation of Charity between the World Wars. 445
   Charity in the Totalitarian State. 447
   Assistance in Emergency and Catastrophe since the Second World War. . . 448
   Caritas Internationalis. 450
   Catholic Works of Assistance. 453

Chapter 15: History of the Ecumenical Movement. 458
   The Development of the World Council of Churches and Its Route from
   Amsterdam (1948) to Nairobi (1976). 458
   The Share of the Roman Catholic Church in the Ecumenical Movement. . . 466

Chapter 16: The Dissident Eastern Churches. 473
   The Orthodox Churches. 474
      The Four Ancient Patriarchates. 474

CONTENTS

The Orthodox Church in Georgia. 478
The Patriarchates Originating in the Middle Ages and in Modern Times. . 479
Other Orthodox Churches. 488
   In the Mediterranean Area 488; In East Central Europe and the Far East
   492
Foreign Churches. 494
The Eastern Pre-Chalcedonian National Churches. 496
The Nestorian Churches. 496
The Monophysite Churches. 497

SECTION THREE: THE CHURCH IN THE INDIVIDUAL COUNTRIES. 505

Chapter 17: The Church in Northern, Eastern, and Southern Europe. 505
The Scandinavian Countries. 505
The Baltic Countries. 507
The Soviet Union. 509
Poland. 512
Czechoslovakia. 516
Hungary. 520
Rumania. 523
Yugoslavia. 526
Bulgaria. 529
Albania. 530

Chapter 18: The Church in German-Speaking Countries. 531
Germany. 531
Austria. 549
Switzerland. 552
The Situation in the German-Speaking Area after the Second Vatican Council. 553

Chapter 19: The Church in the Benelux Countries. 557
Belgium. 557
Luxemburg. 560
The Netherlands. 561
  Period of Flowering (1919–60). 561
  Disintegration (1960–70). 564

Chapter 20: Catholicism in Italy. 569

Chapter 21: The Catholic Church of France. 583
Under Benedict XV. 584
Under Pius XI. 586
Under Pius XII. 592

Chapter 22: The Church in Spain and Portugal. 600
Spain. 600
  The Monarchy of Alphonso XIII (1914–31). 601
   The Problem of the Two Spains 601; Christian Syndicalism 603
  Second Spanish Republic and Civil War (1931–39). 604
  The Civil War (1936–39). 605
   The Red Zone 606; The National Zone 607
  Spain in the Postwar Period (since 1939). 608
   The Twofold Trend: *Traditional Generation* 608; *Critical Generation* 609;
   Institutions: *Episcopal Conference* 609; *Religious Communities* 610; *Catholic
   Action* 610; *Asociación Católica Nacional de Propagandistas* 611
Portugal. 611
  The Anticlerical Revolution (1910–26). 611
  The New Regime (1926–60). 612
  Under the Influence of the Second Vatican Council (from 1960). . . . 613

Chapter 23: The Countries of the English-Speaking Area. 614
Europe. 614
  Great Britain. 614

CONTENTS

Population 614; Organization 615; Educational System 616; Social Movement 622; Catechetical and Apologetic Work 629; Liturgical Movement 630; Journalism 631

Ireland. 632
Population 632; Political Development 633; Ecclesiastical Organization 635; Relations with the State 635; Educational System 637; Social Movement 638; Lay Apostolate 640

North America. 642
The United States. 642
Population 642; Organization 643; Educational System 645; Social Movement 650; Liturgical Movement 657; The Situation in American Society 658; The Position of the Church in International Affairs 660; Lay Movements 663; Journalism 664

Canada. 667
Population 667; Organization 668; Educational System 668; Social Movement 670

Chapter 24: The Church in Latin America. 672
Brazil. 674
Ecclesiastical Organization 674; Lack of Priests 674; Catholic Action 675; Piety 675; Too Few Priestly Vocations 676; Care of Souls 677; Catholic Universities and School 680; Newspapers, Periodicals, Means of Social Communication 681; Ecclesiastical Shortcomings 681; Religious Orders, Pastoral Cooperation 682; The Postconciliar Period 683; Formation of New Priests 684; Catholic Missions among the Indians of Brazil 684; Fraternal Associations 684

Argentina. 685
The Argentine Church after the Council 686; Difficulties within the Argentine Church 687; The Determining of the Functions of Priests 688; The "Emergency Residential District" of Buenos Aires 689; The "Priests for the Third World" United with the People 689; The Church's Functions 690

Paraguay. 690
Ecclesiastical Organization 691; Educational Institutions 691; Protests of the Bishops 691; Two Worlds Developing 692; The Function of Priests 693; Church-State Relations 694

Uruguay. 694
Ecclesiastical Structure 695; Celibacy 696; Renewal in the Light of the Second Vatican Council and of the Congress of Medellín 696

Chile. 697
In Search of a Uniform Ecclesiastical Activity 698; Attempt at a Balance 699; Christians for Socialism 699; Situation of the Chilean Church 700

Bolivia. 701
Ecclesiastical Structure 701; Human Solidarity 702; Defense of the Miners 702; Miner Priests 703; New Initiatives 703; Increase of Priestly Vocations 704; Authentic Justice and Humanization 705

Peru. 705
Educational Institutions 706; The Social Sphere 706

Ecuador. 708
School System 709; Political and Socioeconomic Position of the Church 709; First National Assembly of Ecuadorian Priests 710; In Search of an Integral Development 710; The Church Facing the New Agrarian Law 711; The Church in the Present 711

Colombia. 712
School System 713; Missions and Missionaries 713; Catholic Initiatives 713; The Voice of the Bishops 714; Agricultural Reform 715; Communist Infiltration in the University 716; The Postconciliar Church 716; The National Plan for Pastoral Care 717; Pastoral Letter to the International Eucharistic Congress 717; The Priestly Group of Golconda 717; Implementation of the Medellín Decrees 717; Birth Control 718; Land Reform and Limitation of Property 718; Catholic-Anglican Dialogue 718; Social Security for the Clergy 719

CONTENTS

Venezuela. 719
    Ecclesiastical Organization 719; Situation of the Church 720; Social
    Works 721; Care of Souls 721
Cuba. 723
    Ecclesiastical Structure 723; Pastoral Letter of the Bishops 724; The
    Economic Situation of the Cuban Church 724; The Persecuted Church
    725; The Standpoint of the Bishops 726; Decrease of the Cuban Clergy
    727
The Dominican Republic. 727
    The Concordat between the Holy See and the Dominican Republic 728;
    The Church in Public Life 729
Panama. 730
    The Situation of the Church 730; Social Revaluation 731; Religious Life
    in Central America and Panama 731; Arrest and Expulsion of Father Luis
    Medrano, S. J. 731; The Church and Reform of the National Constitution
    732
Nicaragua. 733
    Apostolic Activities 733; National Constitution 733; Activity of the
    Church 734
Honduras. 734
    The Voice of the Bishops 735; Land Occupation 736
El Salvador. 736
    The Land Problem and the Position of the Priests 737; Against the Use of
    Violence 738; Seminary for Priestly Vocations 738; The Abortion Law
    738
Guatemala. 739
    Tensions 739; Pastoral Guidelines 740; The Christian and Political
    Activity 740
Mexico. 741
    Constitution of 1917 742; New Persecution: Plutarco Elías Calles 742;
    Economic Boycott, the "Cristeros War" 742; Papal Documents 743;
    Balance Sheet of the Persecution 744; Church and State since 1940 744;
    Organization of the Mexican Church 745; Parishes and Missions, Organi-
    zation of the Clergy 746; Episcopal Documents 747; Piety of the Mexican
    748; National Plan for Common Pastoral Care 748; "Priests for the Poor"
    750

Chapter 25: The Young Churches in Asia, Africa, and Oceania. 751
The Young Churches in Asia. 753
  The Far East. 753
    China 753; Taiwan 757; Japan 758; Korea 761
  Southeast Asia. 763
    India 763; Pakistan 768; Bangladesh 769; Sri Lanka 769; Vietnam 771;
    Laos 773; Cambodia 774; Thailand 774; Burma 774; The Malay Peninsula
    775; Indonesia 775
The Young Churches in Africa. 777
The Young Churches in Oceania. 795
  Australia and New Zealand. 795
  The Pacific Islands. 796
  The Philippines. 802

BIBLIOGRAPHY. 805

INDEX. 853

PREFACE

The pretentious title of this volume* is justified by an overwhelming fact of both ecclesiastical and secular history: the Catholic Church, which has ceaselessly claimed to be universal, has actually become a world-church in our century. Restricted in antiquity essentially to the lands around the Mediterranean, cast back in the Middle Ages to the West by the encircling Islamic wall and the Eastern Schism, and still Europe-oriented in modern times despite the world-mission that had got under way, it developed in the twentieth century into a world-church. The Second Vatican Council, at which this development entered into the general consciousness, stands at the center of this volume. It does not pass over the fact that the spatial expansion, and even more the internal happenings, have created a critical situation, which shows itself in all three areas into which we have organized the matter: in the principle of unity, in the papacy, the council, and canon law; in virtually all the inner expressions of the Church's life, as much in theology as in spirituality; and finally in its members, the local churches of European and non-European countries.

We provide a cross section of the diversity of the Church's life, but our deeper motive remains the continuation of the longitudinal section which this series has striven to supply in its earlier volumes. Thus the association of this volume with the series is justified, but also its independence in so far as it offers the historical information, becoming ever more difficult, which is needed for an understanding of the present.

As the temporal point of departure there presented itself the year 1914, the outbreak of the First World War, joined to a change of

---

* The original German title is *Die Weltkirche im 20. Jahrhundert* (The World-Church in the Twentieth Century).

pontificate. More difficult was the delimitation at the other end. "The present" is an elastic concept. From the start it was not intended to understand by it the year of publication of the volume. Some collaborators have excluded the last years, mostly with regard to developments still in progress; others have included the most recent events in their presentation.

To write the ecclesiastical history of the age is more risky than to deal with the political history. The growth of the Church moves in longer waves than does that of states: the era of National Socialism, as a historical fact, is behind us; the impact of the Second Vatican Council has not yet been evaluated. The sources accessible to the historian for political history are more abundant, whereas for ecclesiastical history important complexes of sources are not yet accessible. On the other hand, the remaining material which was to be assimilated is so bulky and many-layered that only specialists are in a position to acquire a survey and thorough view, to supply the existing trends, and to join them with the earlier. Hence, of necessity the number of collaborators has been increased and the coordination made more difficult, not only for the subjects of the Church's life, but also in regard to the accounts of countries, especially those of the Third World. In none of the previous volumes of the series were the selection and the gaining of competent collaborators so difficult as in this one. What was required of them was not only exact knowledge of events, but the ability to extract the essentials from the abundance of phenomena and to present them in the brevity demanded by the nature of a handbook. Some manuscripts had to be abbreviated, but nevertheless some excesses in bulk could not be avoided. The contributions made in a foreign language had to be translated. In spite of all the efforts of the editors, a certain amount of overlapping could not be avoided, for example, when the question of concordats concluded by the Holy See and the theme of papal external policy had to be treated according to their juridical content and in their social effects, as well as in other contexts. Hence it would not be appropriate to regard such overlappings as "repetitions." We have tried, by means of cross-references in the text, to facilitate the orientation; furthermore, the list of subject matter in the Index makes possible the locating of relevant passages.

As in the earlier volumes, so too in this one the editors have sought technically to standardize the individual contributions. For this purpose a conference of the contributors, arranged by Verlag Herder in July 1975, was helpful, but of course it had to be implemented by constant correspondence. If it has still not been possible to eliminate all lack of symmetry in the arrangement and the method of citation, this does no harm to the usability of the entire work.

Finally, as regards the inner orientation of the volume, it was, as in the case of the previous volumes, the basic principle that the authors speak for themselves and especially bear the responsibility for the judgments rendered. We did not regard ourselves justified to intervene in their formation of opinion and hence could not identify ourselves with every view here expressed. However, all collaborators were united in faith in the One, Holy, Catholic, and Apostolic Church, united in the conviction that Church history, including the ecclesiastical history of the contemporary period, must follow historical method. In selection and evaluation we have held to the principle which Joseph Ratzinger very recently formulated: "On the one hand, the Church must never be separated from its concrete manifestation, but, on the other hand, it must also never be entirely identified with it."

The present text was, to this point, formulated on 28 August 1977. Still lacking was only the constantly promised chapter on the "The Young Churches"; the rest of the volume was set and made up into pages; publisher and editors counted on publication in autumn 1977. But this was prevented because the author of this chapter fell seriously ill and finally gave up. It was not easy to find a new author. We are grateful to Father Metzler for stepping into the breach and quickly composing Chapter 25. When other, equally unforeseen hindrances had happily been overcome by the beginning of 1979, production could start without interruption.

The delay in publication for one and one-half years explains why the pontificate of Paul VI was not included: when the book was ready in these parts, this Pope was still alive and hence not yet a subject of history. His death on 6 August 1978 ended an important chapter of the most recent history of the Church. Whether the short pontificate of his successor, John Paul I, elected on 26 August and dead on 28 September 1978, still belongs to this chapter or means the beginning of a new one cannot be said scientifically at this moment with sufficient assurance— for this the contours of the new are not yet sharp enough; although there is much to be said for the view that 1978 will be a very important caesura in the history of the Catholic Church.

Hubert Jedin
Konrad Repgen

PREFACE TO ENGLISH EDITION

By a sad coincidence the translation of the final volume of the *History of the Church* was completed within the week of the death of Msgr. Hubert Jedin, 17 July 1980. Perhaps more widely recognized in Europe and Latin America than in the English-speaking world, his rapport with Protestant scholars bore fruit on both sides of the Atlantic. While his *History of the Church* (formerly *Handbook of Church History*) will no doubt serve as an impressive and lasting monument to his work as a Church historian it was in a sense peripheral to the great endeavor of his life, *Geschichte des Konzils von Trient,* a definitive work that he did not complete until shortly before his death. Yet long before the appearance of the first volume of the history of the council of Trent in 1949, Jedin had established himself as an authority on the history of the Reformation and the nature of historical methodology. His biography of Seripando and his study of Albert Pigge gave him an early international reputation. No work on the Thirty Years War or Wallenstein is complete without his reference to Piccolomini's correspondence. His pioneering efforts in the study of the writings of Luther's literary opponents opened a new field in Reformation studies and helped to place the future Second Vatican Council in proper historical perspective.

Jedin's basic premise that Church history can be understood only as the history of salvation was supported by his conviction that there is a difference between Church history and the history of Christianity, since the former is rooted in faith and therefore a theological discipline. As history, it is bound to certain rubrics: it is bound to its sources and the causal connection of the facts related; hence the importance of recognizing human freedom. "There are historical guilt and historical merit but the judgment of history is not a sentence pronounced upon the Church's past."

In all of his writings Jedin sought to see and describe the past in the spirit of *veritas et caritas*. It is hoped that the reader will find this same spirit in this volume that treats a Church so different from the Church of Trent and yet a Church, not unlike that of the sixteenth century, open to the perennial exhortation: *ecclesia semper reformanda est.*

John P. Dolan

LIST OF ABBREVIATIONS

AAS   *Acta Apostolicae Sedis,* Vatican City 1909ff.
ACJF   Action Catholique de la Jeunesse Française.
ADAP   *Akten zur Deutschen auswärtigen Politik 1919–1945,* Göttingen 1966ff.
ADSS   P. Blet, R. A. Graham (from Vol. 3), A. Martini, B. Schneider, eds.: *Actes et documents du Saint Siège relatifs à la seconde guerre mondiale,* Vatican City 1965.
AfkKR   *Archiv für Katholisches Kirchenrecht,* (Innsbruck) Mainz 1857ff.
AHC   *Annuarium Historiae Conciliorum,* Paderborn 1969ff.
AHP   *Archivum historiae pontificiae,* Rome 1963ff.
D. Albrecht I, II   D. Albrecht, ed., *Der Notenwechsel zwischen dem Hl. Stuhl und der Deutschen Regierung. I: Von der Ratifizierung des Reichskonkordats bis zur Enzyklika "Mit brennender Sorge,"* Mainz 1965; II: *1937–1945,* Mainz 1969.
D. Albrecht, *Kirche*   C. Albrecht, ed., *Katholische Kirche im Dritten Reich. Eine Aufsatzsammlung,* Mainz 1976 (with bibliography).
ALW   *Archiv für Liturgiewissenschaft,* Regensburg 1950ff.
ANEC   Asociación Nacional de Estudiantes Católicos.
AnGr   *Analecta Gregoriana,* Rome 1930ff.
ASS   *Acta Sanctae Sedis,* Rome 1865–1908.
Atlas hierarchicus   *Atlas hierarchicus. Descriptio geographica et statistica ecclesiae catholicae tum occidentis tum orientis,* ed. H. Emmerich, S.V.D., Mödling 1968.

Bihlmeyer-Tüchle III   K. Bihlmeyer and H. Tüchle, *Kirchengeschichte* III: *Die Neuzeit und die Neueste Zeit,* Paderborn 1968.
Bilanz der Theologie   H. Vorgrimler and R. Vander Gucht, eds., *Bilanz der Theologie im 20. Jh.,* I–IV, Freiburg, Basel, Vienna 1969–70.

CADC   Centro Académico de Democracia Cristã.
CALA   Conferencia anglicana latinoamericana.
Catholica   *Catholica. Jahrbuch (Vierteljahreszeitschrift) für Kontroverstheologie,* (Paderborn) Münster 1932ff.
CEHILA   Comisión de Estudios de Historia de la Iglesia en América Latina.
CELAM   Consejo Episcopal Latino-Americano, Bogotá 1968ff.
CHR   *The Catholic Historical Review,* Washington 1915ff.
CIAS   Centro de Investigación y Acción Social.
CIC   Centrum Informationis Catholicum.

LIST OF ABBREVIATIONS

CIDSE   Coopération Internationale pour le Développement Socio-Économique.
CIMI   Consejo Indigenista Misionero.
CISOR   Centro de investigaciones en ciencias sociales, Caracas.
CivCatt   *La Civiltà Cattolica,* Rome 1850ff. (1871–87 Florence).
CLAR   Confoederatio Latino-Americana Religiosorum.
CNT   Confederación Nacional de Trabajo.
ComRel   *Commentarium pro religiosis et missionariis,* Rome 1920ff.
Concilium   *Concilium, Internationale Zeitschrift für Theologie,* Einsiedeln, Mainz, Zurich 1965ff.
CPA   Catholic Press Association.
CS   *Communicatio Socialis. Zeitschrift für Publizistik in Kirche und Welt,* Paderborn 1967ff.

DBFP   *Documents on British Foreign Policy,* 1947ff.
DCV   Deutscher Caritasverband.
DDF   *Documents Diplomatiques Français.*
DDI   *Documenti Diplomatici Italiani.*
DIP   G. Pelliccia and G. Rocca, *Dizionario degli Istituti di Perfezione,* Rome 1974ff.

ECQ   *Eastern Churches Quarterly,* Ramsgate 1936–64.
EKD   Evangelische Kirche Deutschlands.
EphLiturg   *Ephemerides Liturgicae,* Rome 1887ff.
EThL   *Ephemerides Theologicae Lovanienses,* Bruges 1924ff.

FRUS   *Foreign Relations of the United States. Diplomatic Papers.*

Giacometti, *Quellen*   Z. Giacometti, *Quellen zur Geschichte der Trennung von Staat und Kirche,* Tübingen 1926.
GS   *Gaudium et spes.*
GuL   *Geist und Leben. Zeitschrift für Askese und Mystik,* Würzburg 1947ff.

Hampe   J. C. Hampe, *Die Autorität der Freiheit. Gegenwart des Konzils und Zukunft der Kirche im Ökumenischen Disput,* 3 vols., Munich 1967.
Herder TK   *Das Zweite Vatikanische Konzil. Konstitutionen, Dekrete u. Erklärungen, lat. u. deutsch. Kommentare,* ed. by H. Vorgrimler et al., 3 vols., Freiburg 1966–68.
HJ   *Historisches Jahrbuch der Görres-Gesellschaft,* Cologne 1880ff., Munich 1950ff.
HK   *Herder-Korrespondenz,* Freiburg 1946ff.
HOAC   Hermandad Obrera de Acción Catòlica.
Hochland   *Hochland,* Munich 1903ff.
HPTh   *Handbuch der Pastoraltheologie,* ed. Franz Xaver Arnold et al., Freiburg 1964ff.

IKZ   *Internationale Kirchliche Zeitschrift,* Bern 1911ff.
IRA   Irish Republican Army.
ISAL   Iglesia y sociedad para América Latina.

JbCarWiss   *Jahrbuch für Caritaswissenschaft und Caritasarbeit,* Freiburg 1957–68.
JAC   Jeunesse Agricole Catholique.

LIST OF ABBREVIATIONS

JEC	Jeunesse Étudiante Catholique.
JMC	Jeunesse Maritime Catholique.
JOC	Juventud Obrera Católica.
JOC	Jeunesse Ouvrière Chrétienne.

KH	*Kirchliches Handbuch für das katholische Deutschland* 1907–43.
KNA	Katholische Nachrichtenagentur, Bonn, Munich.
KNP	Katholiek Nederlands Persbureau.
Kolping	A. Kolping, *Katholische Theologie gestern und heute. Thematik und Entfaltung deutscher katholischer Theologie vom I. Vaticanum bis zur Gegenwart*, Bremen 1964.
A. Kupper, *Staatliche Akten*	A. Kupper, ed., *Staatliche Akten über die Reichskonkordatsverhandlungen 1933*, Mainz 1969.

LJ	*Liturgisches Jahrbuch*, Münster 1951ff.
LThK	*Lexikon für Theologie und Kirche*, 2d ed., Freiburg, 1957–68.
LWB	Lutherischer Weltbund.

M	E. Marmy, ed., *Mensch und Gemeinschaft in christlicher Schau. Dokumente* (from Gregory XVI 1832 to Pius XII 1944), Fribourg 1945.
MM	*Mater et Magistra.*
MThZ	*Münchener Theologische Zeitschrift*, Munich 1950ff.
Müller	*Vaticanum secundum*, ed. by O. Müller, W. Becker, J. Gülden, 4 vols., Leipzig 1963–66.

NCE	*New Catholic Encyclopedia*, New York 1967.
NCWC	National Catholic Welfare Conference.
NRTh	*Nouvelle Revue Théologique*, Tournai, Louvain, Paris 1879ff.
NZMW	*Neue Zeitschrift für Missionswissenschaft*, Beckenried 1945ff.

ÖAfKR	*Österreichisches Archiv für Kirchenrecht*, Vienna 1950ff.
OCIC	Office Catholique International du Cinéma.
OrChr	*Oriens Christianus*, Rome 1901ff.
OstkSt	*Ostkirchliche Studien*, Würzburg 1951ff.

PIME	Pontificio Istituto Missioni Estere.
PP	*Poplurum progressio.*
PrOrChr	*Le Proche-Orient Chrétien*, Jerusalem 1951ff.
PT	*Pacem in terris.*

QA	*Quadragesimo anno.*

REB	*Revista eclesiástica brasileira*, Petropolis 1941ff.
RHE	*Revue d'histoire ecclésiastique*, Louvain 1900ff.
RHMC	*Revue d'histoire moderne et contemporaine.*
Rohrbasser	*Heilslehre der Kirche. Dokumente von Pius IX. bis Pius XII.*, ed. P. Cattin and H. T. Conus, transl. A. Rohrbasser, Fribourg 1953.
RPB I	*Die Kirchliche Lage in Bayern nach den Regierungspräsidentenberichten 1933–1943*, I: *Regierungsbezirk Oberbayern*, ed. H. Witetschek, Mainz 1966.
RPB II	II: *Regierungsbezirk Ober- und Mittelfranken*, ed. H. Witetschek, Mainz 1967.

RPB III   III: *Regierungsbezirk Schwaben*, ed. H. Witetschek, Mainz 1971.

RPB IV   IV: *Regierungsbezirk Niederbayern und Oberpfalz, 1933–1945*, ed. W. Ziegler, Mainz 1973.

RSR   *Recherches de science religieuse*, Paris 1910ff.

RSCI   *Rivista di storia della Chiesa in Italia*, Rome 1947ff.

RThom   *Revue thomistique*, Bruges 1893ff.

SEDOC   *Serviço de Documentacão*, Petropolis 1969ff.

Sic   *Sic* (periodical, ed. Centro Gumilla), Caracas 1938ff.

SOG   Solidaritätsgruppen der Priester.

SOG-Papiere   *SOG-Papiere. Mitteilungsblatt der Arbeitsgemeinschaft von Priestergruppen in der Bundesrepublik Deutschland und der SOG-Österreich*, ed. A. Schilling, Bochum 1968–73.

SPEV   Segretariato permanente del episcopo venezolano.

SSCC   Congregatio Sacrorum Cordium Jesu et Mariae.

Schmidlin   J. Schmidlin, *Papstgeschichte der neuesten zeit* I–IV, Munich 1933–39.

B. Stasiewski I, II, III   B. Stasiewski, ed., *Akten deutscher Bischöfe über die Lage der Kirche*. I: *1933–1934*, Mainz 1968; II: *1934–1935*, Mainz 1976; III: *1935–1936*, Mainz 1978.

StdZ   *Stimmen der Zeit* (before 1914: *Stimmen aus Maria Laach*), Freiburg 1871ff.

StL   *Staatslexikon*, 6th ed., ed. H. Sacher, Freiburg, 1957ff.

STO   Service du Travail Obligatoire

ThGl   *Theologie und Glaube*, Paderborn 1909ff.

TheoluPhil   *Theologie und Philosophie. Vierteljahreszeitschrift für Theologie und Philosophie*, Freiburg 1966ff.

ThprQS   *Theologisch-praktische Quartalschrift*, Linz a. d. Donau 1848ff.

ThRev   *Theologische Revue*, Münster 1902ff.

ThQ   *Theologische Quartalschrift*, Tübingen 1819ff., Stuttgart 1946ff.

TThZ   *Trierer Theologische Zeitschrift* (until 1944: *Pastor Bonus*), Trier 1888ff.

UCIP   L'Union Catholique Internationale de la Presse.

UG   A. F. Utz, J. F. Groner, *Aufbau und Entfaltung des gesellschaftlichen Lebens. Soziale Summe Pius' XII.* I, II, Fribourg 1954.

UGT   Unión General de Trabajadores.

UISG   Unio Internationalis Superiorissarum Generalium.

UMAE   Unión de Mutua Ayuda Episcopal.

USG   Unio Superiorum Generalium.

VZG   *Vierteljahreshefte für Zeitgeschichte*, Stuttgart 1953ff.

L. Volk, *Kirchliche Akten*   L. Volk, ed., *Kirchliche Akten über die Reichskontkordatsverhandlungen 1933*, Mainz 1969.

L. Volk, *Faulhaber Akten*   L. Volk, ed., *Akten Kardinal Michael von Faulhabers 1917–1945*. I: *1917–1934*, Mainz 1975; II: *1935–1945*, Mainz 1978.

WACC   World Association for Christian Communication

WiWei   *Wissenschaft und Weisheit*, Düsseldorf 1934ff.

ZAM   *Zeitschrift für Askese und Mystik*, Würzburg 1926.

ZevKR   *Zeitschrift für evangelisches Kirchenrecht*, Tübingen 1951ff.

LIST OF ABBREVIATIONS

ZKG   *Zeitschrift für Kirchengeschichte*, Stuttgart 1876ff.
ZKTh   *Zeitschrift für Katholische Theologie* (Innsbruck), Vienna 1877ff.
ZMR   *Zeitschrift für Missionskunde und Religionswissenschaft*, Berlin 1886ff.
ZRGG   *Zeitschrift für Religions- und Geistesgeschichte*, Marburg 1948ff.
ZSavRG, KanAbt   *Zeitschrift der Savigny-Stiftung für Rechtsgeschichte, Kanonistische Abteilung*, Weimar 1911ff.

The Institutional Unity of the Universal Church

CHAPTER 1

Statistics

Statistics of the World's Population, Statistics of the World Religions, Proportion of Catholics

In order to be able suitably to estimate to some degree the importance of the Catholic population of the world absolutely and relatively, in the longitudinal section of the historical development and in the geographical cross section of the present, its numerical relationship to the total world population, its relative significance in the concert of the world religions, and finally the trend of the frequency distribution in the geographical sphere—north-south drift of the Christian or of the Catholic world respectively in the course of time—must be investigated. There are no absolutely reliable numbers for all three relationships, but—according to individual continents and countries with differently developed facilities for inquiry—more or less exact estimates and approximations.

STATISTICS OF THE WORLD'S POPULATION 1914–65

For the population problem and population statistics on both the national and the international level there is an almost incalculable abundance in publications, which can scarcely be controlled by even the experts.[1] Hence, in what follows there can be offered only a strictly consolidated and necessarily simplified summary, which is as reliable as the primary source material and becomes the more problematic as one moves into the past.

The most important factor in the population development is the present still extraordinarily different rate of growth in the individual continents and countries. In general it can be said that the rates of growth in the First and Second Worlds—the Western industrialized

---

[1] A very good and concise summary is provided by the international research and information center *Pro Mundi Vita* in its publication, *Die demographische Explosion und die Zunkunft der Kirche* no. 40 (1972), 6, rue de la Limite, Brussels.

TABLE 1: WORLD POPULATION FROM 1920 TO 1965
(IN MILLIONS)

Country	Year					
	1920	1930	1940	1950	1960	1965
Africa	140	164	191	222	278	311
North Africa	46	39	44	53	66	75
Central and South Africa	94	125	147	169	212	236
America	208	242	274	329	413	460
North America	117	134	144	166	199	214
Central America	30	34	41	52	68	80
South America	61	74	89	111	146	166
Asia	966	1,120	1,244	1,381	1,659	1,830
East Asia	487	591	634	684	794	852
South Asia	479	529	610	697	865	978
Europe	329	355	380	392	425	445
Northern Europe }	115	65	68	73	76	79
Western Europe }		108	113	123	135	143
Central Europe	112					
Eastern Europe		89	96	88	97	100
Southern Europe	102	93	103	108	117	123
Oceania	8.8	10.0	11.1	12.7	15.7	17.5
U.S.S.R.	158	179	195	180	214	231
Total World	1,810	2,070	2,295	2,517	3,005	3,295

SOURCES: *UN Demographic Yearbook,* Vol. 11 (New York 1959); *UN Statistical Yearbook,* Vol. 18 (New York 1967).

states, including Japan, and the Communist lands—are indeed still positive, apart from exceptions, but decidedly lower than in the Third World—the developing countries. In the Western nations the rate of growth at the end of the 1960s averaged less than 1 percent, so that, *ceteris paribus*, their population would about double in seventy years, whereas in Asia it averaged ca. 2 percent, which would lead to a doubling in some thirty-five years.[2]

In all the developing countries the population increases by leaps and bounds. "However, it should at once be explained that the problems which confront the majority of the underdeveloped countries do not

[2] Cf. ibid., 7.

result chiefly from their high birthrate, but rather from their mortality rate, which grows less from year to year . . . . This is a quite general problem today, affecting about two-thirds of mankind: 2.056 billion Asiatics, 283 million Latin Americans, and 344 million Africans."[3]

This is above all true of the thickly populated countries of China and India. The last Chinese census was taken in 1953. Since then only fragmentary information has been at our disposal. Since the growth rate results from the birthrate less the mortality rate, a parallel development of the two rates—lowering of the birthrate by measures of population and family planning, and lowering of the mortality rate by hygienic and political health measures—will lead in time to a considerable growth. Accordingly, the results of the efforts in China for a reduction of the population growth can be evaluated somewhat as follows:

TABLE 2: THE DEVELOPMENT OF THE POPULATION IN CHINA FROM 1953 TO 1970

Year	Number of Inhabitants (in millions)	Birth Rate %	Mortality Rate %	Rate of Increase %
1953	589.7	43	29	14
1956	618.5	41	24	17
1959	649.9	38	23	15
1962	676.2	38	24	14
1965	705	35	21	14
1968	735.1	33	19	14
1970	757.3	32	17	15

SOURCE: *Die demographische Explosion und die Zukunft der Kirche,* no. 40 (Brussels: Pro Mundi Vita, 1972), p. 9.

Now as earlier, India, as the second most populous country on earth, is far from having found a solution for its population problem. "The population grew (therefore) from 356.9 million in 1951 to 498.7 million in 1966. Today India must have at least 547 million inhabitants. Hence, in each decade the population grew by ca. 100 million. According to the testimony of the population experts of the United Nations, in 1970 the population amounted to 554 million, the birthrate 42.8 percent, the mortality rate 16.7 percent, the growth rate 26.1 percent for the period 1966–70."[4]

In contrast to China, where the rate of growth was stabilized at ca. 15

[3] Ibid., 8f.
[4] Ibid., 9.

percent, in India it grew from 19 to 26 percent between 1951 and 1970.

Africa also shows high rates of growth, from 20 to more than 30 percent. Different but equally high rates of growth must be recorded for most countries of Central and South America.

The high birthrates in the countries of the Third World have led, together with a drastic decline of the mortality rates, to a very favorable age-group structure in these nations. But this is at the same time decisive for the development of the present population. "Even if there should be success in quickly and drastically decreasing the number of births per marriage in India and China, the population of these areas, just as that of most Latin American and African states, would grow further still over many decades because of their favorable age-group structure, that is, of the high proportion of young people old enough to have children."[5]

TABLE 3: POPULATION INCREASE IN INDIA FROM 1951 TO 1970

Year	Birth Rate %	Mortality Rate %	Rate of Increase %
1951–1960	42	23	19
1966–1970	43	17	26

SOURCE: *Die demographische Explosion*, p. 9.

TABLE 4: ESTIMATED POPULATION GROWTH
IN VARIOUS LANDS AND AREAS IN 1985
(in percentages)

Age	North America	Europe	USSR	East Asia	Latin America	Africa	South Asia	Oceania
0–14	28.7	24.8	26.2	31.7	41.4	45.0	42.0	30.4
15–64	61.6	63.3	64.3	63.1	54.5	52.0	54.6	60.1
65 and older	9.8	11.8	9.4	5.3	4.1	3.0	3.4	7.4

SOURCE: *Die demographische Explosion*, p. 14.

[5] "Daten der Bevölkerungsentwicklung. Überblick und Vergleich der Entwicklung in den Industriestaaten und in den Ländern der Dritten Welt: Soziographische Beilage Nr. 24," *Hk* 27 (1973) 345 ff. Mit einem Begleitkommentar von Dr. Hermann Schubnell, Direktor im Statistischen Bundesamt, Wiesbaden; here p. 346.

This development is of an importance for the Christian Churches that must not be underestimated. The outcome will be that in the next decades the Christian world will shift ever more southward and into the lands of the Third World.[6]

STATISTICS OF THE WORLD RELIGIONS 1914–65

Exact and generally satisfactory statistics of the religions of the world are no more possible to obtain than are exact statistics of the world's population. The best information comes from national censuses to the extent that these are even taken. A good survey is provided by the *U.N. Demographic Yearbook* and the *U.N. Statistical Yearbook*. For many countries of the Third World we are referred to ecclesiastical data. They are especially problematic where a large part of the baptized maintain no living relationship with the Church. Also problematic are data on the countries of the Communist world. For the statistics of the world religions it is also true that information can be only as reliable as the primary material which can be obtained from the sources at our disposal.

Here follows a summary of religious statistics according to continents.

TABLE 5: RELIGIOUS STATISTICS OF EUROPE WITH SUBDIVISIONS FROM 1920 TO 1965
(in thousands and percentages)

Region	Total Popu-lation	Cath-olics	Prot-estants and Angli-cans	Ortho-dox	Other Chris-tians	Jews	Muslims	Others
Central Europe								
1920	114,899	59,991	44,902	2,939	515	4,008	—	2,465
%	100	52.2	39.0	2.55	0.45	2.7	—	2.1
1935	127,247	67,789	46,916	4,335	1,047	4,335	—	104
%	100	53.3	36.9	3.47	0.8	3.47	—	0.62
1965	130,865	74,380	48,541	584	?	128	—	7,519
%	100	56.8	37.0	0.44	?	0.09	—	5.7
Northern Europe								
1920	15,520	30	15,320	60	20	15	—	75
%	100	0.2	98.7	0.4	0.13	0.1	—	0.48
1935	16,833	35	16,607	70	1	17	—	104
%	100	0.2	98.6	0.41	—	0.1	—	0.62
1965	20,844	80	20,495	73	?	21	1	264
%	100	0.38	98.3	0.35	?	0.1	—	1.26

[6] Cf. Table 10, p. 9.

Region	Total Population	Catholics	Protestants and Anglicans	Orthodox	Other Christians	Jews	Muslims	Others
Western Europe								
1920	104,666	55,611	46,895	—	—	552	—	1,608
%	100	53.1	44.8	—	—	0.53	—	1.53
1935	109,558	56,502	48,165	140	20	843	100	3,808
%	100	51.6	43.9	0.13	0.02	0.77	0.09	3.5
1965	126,234	64,085	39,140	260	?	1,030	250	21,372
%	100	50.7	31.0	0.21	?	0.81	0.28	16.9
Eastern Europe								
1920	43,075	12,925	3,606	22,076	6	1,437	2,850	175
%	100	30.0	8.3	51.2	0.01	3.3	6.6	0.4
1935	50,915	15,029	3,855	26,749	—	1,625	3,568	89
%	100	29.5	7.6	52.5	—	3.2	7.0	0.17
1965	54,838	13,352	4,262	29,521	?	277	3,922	3,350
%	100	24.3	7.8	53.8	?	0.51	7.1	6.1
Southern Europe								
1920	75,410	66,276	168	6,419	—	55	1,015	1,477
%	100	87.9	0.3	8.5	—	0.07	1.3	2.0
1935	82,333	73,920	184	6,689	10	213	1,255	72
%	100	89.7	0.22	8.1	0.01	0.26	1.5	0.09
1965	102,476	93,887	301	8,143	?	47	108	304
%	100	91.6	0.29	7.9	?	0.05	0.1	0.29
Total (Europe)								
1920	353,570	194,833	110,891	31,494	541	6,067	3,901	5,800
%	100	51.0	31.4	8.9	0.15	1.7	1.1	1.6
1935	388,615	213,283	115,755	38,521	1,078	7,032	4,932	8,014
%	100	60.3	32.7	10.9	0.3	2.0	1.4	2.2
1965	435,257	245,784	112,739	38,581	?	1,503	4,281	32,809
%	100	56.4	25.9	8.8	?	0.35	0.98	7.5

SOURCES: For 1920: H. A. Krose, ed., *Kirchliches Handbuch für das katholische Deutschland,* Vol. 7, 1930–31 (Cologne 1931), p. 263; for 1935: Zentralstelle für kirchliche Statistik des katholischen Deutschlands, Cologne, ed., *Kirchliches Handbuch für das katholische Deutschland,* Vol. 21, 1939–40 (Cologne 1939), p. 150; for 1965: *Atlas Hierarchicus,* 1968, p. 56 (without USSR).

The major European divisions are comprised of the following:

Central Europe: Danzig, German Reich including Saar region, Austria, Poland, Switzerland, Czechoslovakia;
Northern Europe: Norway, Sweden, Denmark, Finland;
Western Europe: Belgium, France, Great Britain and Ireland, Luxembourg, Monaco, the Netherlands;
Eastern Europe: Albania, Bulgaria, Yugoslavia, Romania, Hungary, the Baltic states;
Southern Europe: Andorra, Greece, Italy, Portugal, Spain, European Turkey.

	Total Population	Catholics	Protestants and Anglicans	Orthodox	Jews	Other Religions	Others*
*North America***							
1910	94,583	17,364	69,332	?	1,837	550	5,500
%	100	18.3	73.0	?	1.9	0.58	5.8
1950	166,000[1]	34,717[2]	72,535[3]	2,030[2]	5,433[4]	76	51,209(?)
%	100	20.9	43.6	1.2	3.3	0.04	
1966	210,357	54,171	76,743	3,406	5,944	70,089	
%	100	25.7	36.4	1.6	2.8	33.3	
Central America							
1910	25,458	23,101	1,072	?	16	732	565
%	100	90.6	4.2	?	0.06	2.8	2.2
1950	52,000[1]	42,978[2]	3,242[3]	—	47[4]	158	557(?)
%	100	82.6	6.2	—	0.09	0.3	
1966	66,830	60,408	3,892	—	112	3715	
%	100	90.3	5.8	—	0.16	5.5	
South America							
1910	48,980	47,147	463	?	6	1,340	24
%	100	96.2	0.9	?	0.01	2.7	0.05
1950	111,000[1]	94,155[2]	5,876[3]	38[2]	582[4]	431	9918(?)
%	100	84.8	5.2	0.03	0.52	0.38	
1966	152,008	137,923	6,054	480	685	5,366	
%	100	90.7	3.9	0.3	0.5	3.5	
Total Americas							
1910	169,048	87,612	70,867	?	1,858	2,622	6,089
%	100	51.8	41.9	?	1.1	1.5	3.6
1950	329,000[1]	171,850[2]	81,653[3]	2,068[2]	6062[4]	665	66,702(?)
%	100	52.2	24.2	0.62	1.8	0.2	20.2(?)
1966	429,195	252,502	86,689	3,886	6,741	79,170	
%	100	58.8	20.1	0.9	1.6	18.4	

* "Others": Denomination not available or without denomination.
** "In South and Central America there are fairly reliable statistics on religion, but it is very difficult to evaluate the various denominations in the United States": H. A. Krose, ed., *Kirchliches Handbuch für das katholische Deutschland,* Vol. 3, 1910–11 (Freiburg i. Br. 1911), p. 202.
SOURCES: For 1910: H. A. Krose, ed., *Kirchliches Handbuch für das katholische Deutschland,* Vol. 3, 1910–11 (Freiburg i Br. 1911), p. 201; for 1950: [1]*UN Statistical Yearbook,* 18 vols. (1966) (New York 1967), p. 26; [2]*World Christian Handbook,* ed. E. J. Bingle et al. (London 1952), p. 266; [3]*World Christian Handbook,* ed. H. Wakelin Coxill (London 1962), p. 243; [4]*World Christian Handbook,* ed. E. J. Bingle et al. (London 1957), p. 173; for 1966: *Atlas Hierarchicus,* 1968.

TABLE 7: RELIGIOUS STATISTICS OF AFRICA FROM 1910 TO 1960/65
(in thousands and percentages)

Year	Total Popu- lation	Cath- olics	Other Chris- tians	Jews Muslims	Hin- dus Bud- dhists	Others without Denomi- nations
1910	126,351	6,689	8,457	43,872	—	71,000
%	100	5.3	6.7	34.75	—	56.3
1950	223,000	18,193	17,495(?)	52,832	543	?
%	100	8.1	7.7	23.75	0.24	?
1960/65	317,545	31,782	33,890(?)	61,668	523	?
%	100	10.0	10.6	19.4	0.16	?

SOURCES: For 1910: H. A. Krose, ed., *Kirchliches Handbuch für das katholische Deutschland*, Vol. 3, 1910–11 (Freiburg i. Br. 1911), p. 200; for 1950: *World Christian Handbook*, ed. E. J. Bingle et al. (London 1957), pp. 162ff.; for 1960/65: *World Christian Handbook*, ed. H. Wakelin Coxill (London 1962), pp. 234ff., and *Atlas Hierarchicus*.

TABLE 8: RELIGIOUS STATISTICS OF ASIA FROM 1910 TO 1960/65
(in thousands and percentages)

Year	Total Population	Cath- olics	Other Chris- tians	Jews Muslims	Hindus Buddhists	Others without Denomi- nation
1910	828,455	12,661	19,079	155,845	624,000	16,870
%	100	1.5	2.3	18.78	75.0	2.0
1950	1,581,000	27,771	17,018	275,967	839,399	?
%	100	1.7	1.07	17.45	53.1	?
1960/65	1,831,640	43,947	22,907	355,175	501,479(?)	?
%	100	2.4	1.25	19.44	27.38(?)	?

SOURCES: as in Table 7.—For 1960/65 China is responsible for the great uncertainty.

TABLE 9: RELIGIOUS STATISTICS OF AUSTRALIA AND OCEANIA FROM 1910 TO
1960/65

Year	Total popula- tion	Catho- lics	Other Chris- tians	Jews Muslims	Hindus Budhists	Others without Denomi- nation
1910	6,633	1,244	3,997	36	70	1,286
%	100	18.7	60.2	0.54	1.0	19.3
1950	14,600	2,108	10,562	58?	?	?
%	100	14.4	72.3	0.30	?	?
1960/65	17,722	3,782	10,342	89	?	?
%	100	21.3	58.43	0.5	?	?

SOURCES: as in Tables 7 and 8.

The Southward Movement of the Christian World

It has already been mentioned in another context that the different growth rates of the population in different parts of the world will bring great problems for the Church of the next years and decades. In this context we cannot go more deeply into this.[7]

Nevertheless, one important consequence of the different growth rates should be pointed out: the inexorable shift of the quantitative center of gravity of the Christian world into more southern regions and the nations of the so-called Third World. The problem can be best illustrated with the aid of the following Table 10, which we took from the often mentioned study by *Pro Mundi Vita*.

TABLE 10: SOUTHWARD MOVEMENT OF THE CHRISTIAN WORLD, 1900–2000
(in millions and percentages; boldface = Christians)

Continent	1900 Population	1900 Christians	%	1965 Population	1965 Christians	%	2000 Population	2000 Christians	%
Europe	298	**260**	87	440	**385**	87	526	**404**	77
North America	82	**41**	50	213	**192**	90	354	**300**	85
U.S.S.R.	130	**91**	70	231	**60**	26	353	**92**	26
Total population of developed world	510			884			1,233		
Old Churches		**392**	77		**637**	72		**796**	65
Asia	902	**9**	1	1,827	**62**	3	3,457	**165**	5
Africa	118	**4**	3	306	**75**	24	768	**351**	46
Oceania	6	**3**	50	17	**13**	77	32	**27**	85
Latin America	64	**51**	80	245	**220**	90	638	**575**	90
Total population of Third World	1,090			2,395			4,895		
Churches of Third World		**67**	6		**370**	15		**1,118**	23
Total World Population	1,600	**459**	28.7	3,279	**1,007**	30.7	6,128	**1,914**	31.2
Total Non-Christians		**1,141**			**2,272**			**4,214**	

SOURCE: *Die demographische Explosion*, p. 16.

The Organization of the Entire Church from 1914 to 1970

The whole Church, as a spiritual community of believers and necessarily "visible" and as such an organized society of believing human beings within the world, needs an organization that is capable of functioning in order to be able as effectively as possible to carry out the tasks proper to it. The actual organization of the entire Church has changed in many ways in the course of history. At one time it was the

[7] If one is interested in details, one is referred to *Die demographische Explosion . . . ;* cf. there especially pp. 21ff.

result of long experience, but at another time the outcome of more or less spontaneous developments and decisions of individual Popes and/or bodies representing the whole Church, especially councils.

The central institution for the administration of the whole Church under the Pope is the Roman Curia (*Curia Romana*), by which since the end of the eleventh century the totality of the chief administrative offices and courts in Rome that act in the Pope's name for the government of the Catholic Church are designated. In the broader sense the papal household (*Familia Pontificia*) and the persons bound to participate in the papal liturgy (*Cappella Pontificia*) are also counted in the Curia. In 1588 Pope Sixtus V reorganized the Curia in order to modernize it and established as the new permanent form of authority the so-called congregations of cardinals. By the constitution *Sapienti Consilio* of 29 June 1908 (*AAS* 1 [1909], 7–19) Pius X fundamentally reorganized the Curia. Except for individual decisive changes under Pope Paul VI in 1967[8] the reorganization under Pius X still forms the basic type of the curial constitution. To the Roman Curia belong (Canon 242 of the Code of Canon Law): a) the congregations of cardinals, b) the *Paenitentiaria*, c) the tribunals and curial offices, d) various commissions of a permanent nature and most recently various secretariats. To the official staff belong the cardinals, the higher officials (*officiales maiores*: prelates), and also the lower officials (*officiales minores*), who are designated as "curiales" in the narrower sense.[9]

After the Pope, the cardinals are today the ranking dignitaries of the Catholic Church. They are his advisers and first collaborators in the direction of the entire Church, whether this be within the Curia or outside Rome, especially in the great and important metropolitan sees.[10] Hence these last likewise play a significant role within the organizational structure of the whole Church.

Finally, also counted in the organizational and functional structure of the entire Church is the whole ecclesiastical hierarchy, especially the bishops, governing *iure divino* their particular churches as ordinary shepherds in communion with the Pope and the college of their episcopal confreres.

The institutional and personal functionaries just mentioned constitute

[8] By the apostolic constitution *Regimini Ecclesiae universae* of 15 August 1967 (*AAS* 59 [1967] 885–928); cf. *HK* 21 (1967) 460ff.

[9] On individuals cf. N. del Re, *La Curia Romana. Lineamenti storico-giuridici,* 2d ed. (Rome 1952); C. A. Berutti, *De Curia Romana* (Rome 1952); *LThK* 2d ed., 6 (Freiburg, 1961), 692–94.

[10] Cf. H. W. Klewitz, *Die Entstehung des Kardinalskollegiums. Reformpapsttum und Kardinalskollegium* (Darmstadt 1957); *LThK* 2d ed. (Freiburg 1960), 1342–44.

the organization framework of the whole Church *ad intra*.[11] Externally, that is, in regard to many nations of the world and to international organizations, such as the U.N., UNESCO, and so forth, not the Church but the Holy See maintains diplomatic or quasi-diplomatic relations in the sense of active—nuncios, internuncios, and so forth—and passive—messengers, envoys, and so forth—diplomatic law. Even though this complex does not pertain directly to the formal organization of the whole Church, nevertheless at least the active agents of diplomatic relations on the part of the Holy See are not unimportant for the direction of the whole Church because of their membership in the hierarchy or in the College of Bishops respectively, and because of their actual exerting of influence on the formal members of the ecclesiastical organization, for example, cooperation in the nomination of new bishops.

CONGREGATIONS, TRIBUNALS AND OFFICES, COMMISSIONS AND SECRETARIATS OF THE CURIA (1916–68)

Congregations

Congregations are permanent bodies of the Roman Curia, collegially constituted of a certain number of cardinals, with a legally determined content of duties and powers for the government of the entire Church.[12] After Sixtus V had created a comprehensive system of fifteen congregations with defined spheres of business by the constitution *Immensa aeterni* of 21 January 1588, their number was subject to strong changes in the course of time. Around the middle of the nineteenth century there were almost thirty, and when Pius X succeeded to the papacy there were still twenty-one. In his reform of the Curia this number was restricted to eleven. At the beginning of the period here treated, under Benedict XV, there were thirteen congregations, including the special Congregation for the Fabric of Saint Peter's Basilica, which however did not belong to the general congregations of cardinals.

---

[11] From the organizational-sociological viewpoint one can name the traditional organizational framework of the Catholic Church, as regards the center of gravity, as a "line system" in which, generally with a weak reaction to the at times subordinate stages, essentially directions were given "from above to below," whereas only since the council has this traditional organizational model been gradually completed by elements of a "staff system" on different levels of the line system ("Councils" from the Priests' Council even to the "Council of the Laity" in Rome).

[12] Complete presentation in F. M. Cappello, *De Curia Romana;* V. Martin, *Les Congrégations romaines;* in addition, numerous monographs on individual congregations; cf. also E. Eichmann and K. Mörsdorf, *Lehrbuch des Kirchenrechts* 7th ed. (1953), I, 360ff.

In 1917 Benedict XV abolished the Congregation of the Index. A creation of Benedict's as an autonomous congregation was the *Congregatio de propaganda Fide pro negotiis Rituum orientalium.*[13]

Tribunals and Offices

The real courts (tribunals) of the Roman Church are only the Rota (*Sacra Romana Rota*) as the highest court of appeal (Canon 259 of the Code of Canon Law; for details see Canons 1598ff.) and the *Segnatura Apostolica* (*Supremum Signaturae Apostolicae Tribunale*) as

[13] By the motu proprio *Dei providentis* of 15 January 1917 (*AAS* 9 [1917], 529). Following the reorganization resulting from the motu proprio *Sancta Dei Ecclesia* of Pius XI of 25 March 1938 it became competent for all affairs of the Eastern Churches under the title "S. C. pro Ecclesia Orientali" (*AAS* 30 [1938], 154ff).

TABLE 11: THE CONGREGATIONS FROM 1916 TO 1968

Name Sacra Congregatio	1916 Benedict XV	1923 Pius XI	1939 Pius XII	1961 John XXIII	1968 Paul VI
Sancti Officii	exist.	exist.	exist.	exist.	since 12/7/1965 Congregatio pro Doctrina Fidei
Consistorialis	exist.	exist.	exist.	exist.	since 8/15/1967 Congregatio pro Episcopis
de Propaganda Fide pro negotiis Rituum Orientalium	exist.	exist.	since 1938 S.C. pro Ecclesia Orientali	exist.	exist.
de Disciplina Sacramentorum	exist.	exist.	exist.	exist.	exist.
Concilii	exist.	exist.	exist.	exist.	since 8/15/1967 Congregatio pro Clericis
Negotiis religio- sorum sodalium praeposita	exist.	exist.	exist.	exist.	since 8/15/1967 Congregatio pro Religiosis et Insti- tutis saecularibus

Name Sacra Congregatio	1916 Benedict XV	1923 Pius XI	1939 Pius XII	1961 John XXIII	1968 Paul VI
de Propaganda Fide	exist.	exist.	exist.	exist.	since 8/15/1967 Congregatio pro gentium Evangelisatione seu de Propaganda Fide
Rituum	exist.	exist.	exist.	exist.	exist.; after 1969 divided into the two following congregations
pro Cultu Divino	—	—	—	—	since 5/31/1969 from the previous congregation
pro Causis Sanctorum	—	—	—	—	since 5/31/1969 as the previous congregation
pro Sacramentis divinoque Cultu	—	—	—	—	since 7/31/1975 from a combination of the two previous congregations
Caeremonialis	exist.	exist.	exist.	exist.	1967; abolished
pro Negotiis Ecclesiasticis extraordinariis	exist.	exist.	exist.	exist.	1967; abolished, in hands of Secretary of State
de Seminariis et Universitatibus studiorum	exist.	exist.	exist.	exist.	since 1967 Congregatio pro Institutione catholica
Indicis	3/25/1917 abolished	—	—	—	—

SOURCES: H. A. Krose, ed., *Kirchliches Handbuch für das katholische Deutschland,* Vol. 5, 1914–16 (Freiburg i. Br. 1916), pp. 13ff.; ibid., Vol. 11, 1922–23 (Freiburg i. Br. 1923), pp. 8ff.; Zentralstelle für kirchliche Statistik des katholischen Deutschlands, ed., *Kirchliches Handbuch für das katholische Deutschland,* Vol. 21, 1939–40 (Cologne 1940), pp. 14ff.; F. Groner, ed., *Kirchliches Handbuch. Amtliches statistisches Jahrbuch der katholischen Kirche Deutschlands,* Vol. 25, 1957–61 (Cologne 1962), pp. 8ff; ibid, Vol. 26, 1962–68 (Cologne 1969), pp. 9ff. All mentioned sources refer to corresponding years of the *Annuario Pontificio.*

the highest court of administration and reversal of judgment (Canon 259; for details see Canons 1602ff.). The *Sacra Paenitentiaria,* on the contrary, is the curial court of grace for the internal forum. Since it predominantly grants pardons, it should be considered rather as an administrative office than as a court (Canon 258).[14]

Since they are charged only with duties of administration, the curial offices are merely administrative offices and, in contrast to the congregations, have not a collegial but a monocratic constitution. This was even

TABLE 12: TRIBUNALS AND OFFICES OF THE CURIA FROM 1910 TO 1968

Tribunals Offices	1916 Benedict XV	1923 Pius XI	1939 Pius XII	1961 John XXIII	1968 Paul VI
Tribunals: S. Romana Rota	exist.	exist.	exist.	exist.	exist.
Supr. Signaturae Apost. tribunal	exist.	exist.	exist.	exist.	exist.
S. Paenitentiaria	exist.	exist.	reorganized 3/25/1935	exist.	exist.
Offices: Cancellaria Apostolica	exist.	exist.	exist.	exist.	exist.
Dataria Apostolica	exist.	exist.	exist.	exist.	—
Camera Apostolica	exist.	exist.	exist.	exist.	exist.
Praefectura rerum oeconomicarum S. Sedis	—	—	—	—	8/15/1967 established
Administratio Patrimonii Apost. S. Sedis	—	—	—	—	8/15/1967 established
Apost. Palatii Praefectura	—	—	—	—	8/15/1967 established
Generale Ecclesiae Rationarium	—	—	—	—	8/15/1967 established

SOURCES: as in Table 11.

[14] For details see Eichmann-Mörsdorf, op. cit., 369ff. For historical details cf. A. Perathoner, *Das kirchliche Gesetzbuch,* 5th ed. (Brixen 1931), 147ff., 549ff.

TABLE 13: PAPAL COMMISSIONS FROM 1916 TO 1968
(list incomplete)

Name and Year of Establishment	1916 Benedict XV	1923 Pius XI	1939 Pius XII	1961 John XXIII	1968 Paul VI
Christian Archaeology (1852)	exist.	exist.	exist.	exist.	exist.
Scriptual Studies (1902)	exist.	exist.	exist.	exist.	exist.
Revision and Improvement of the Vulgate (1914)	exist.	exist.	1933 reorganized	exist.	exist.
Authentic Interpretation of the CIC (1917)	—	exist.	exist.	exist.	exist.
For Protection of the Artistic Monuments of the Holy See (1923)	—	exist.	exist.	exist.	exist.
Religious Art in Italy (1924)	—	—	exist.	exist.	exist.
Codification of Eastern Canon Law (1935)	—	—	exist.	exist.	exist.
Film, Radio and Television (1948)	—	—	—	exist.	exist.
Papal Charities (1953)	—	—	—	exist.	exist.
Historical Sciences (1954)	—	—	—	exist.	exist.
Latin America (1958)	—	—	—	exist.	exist.
Revision of the CIC (1963)	—	—	—	—	exist.
Social Communications Media (1964)	—	—	—	—	exist.
The New Vulgate (1965)	—	—	—	—	exist.
The Interpretation of the decrees of Vatican II (1968)	—	—	—	—	exist.

SOURCES: as in Table 11.

15

true, until the so-called little reform of the Curia by Paul VI in 1967, of the Chancery (*Cancellaria Apostolica*), which was responsible for the preparation and dispatching of bulls (Canon 260), the Datary (*Dataria Apostolica*), which was competent for the conferring of the lesser ecclesiastical benefices (Canon 261), the Chamber (*Camera Apostolica*), to which was entrusted the administration of the temporal property and rights of the Holy See (Canon 262), and finally the Secretariat of State (*Secretaria Status*), on which was incumbent the responsible direction of the policy of the Holy See. Alongside the Chancery, whose competence was changed by Paul VI, and the Chamber, three new offices were established on 15 August 1967: the Prefecture of the Economic Affairs of the Holy See (*Praefectura rerum oeconomicarum S. Sedis*), the Administration of the Patrimony of the Holy See (*Administratio Patrimonii Apostolicae Sedia*), and the Prefecture of the Apostolic Palace (*Apostolici Palatii Praefectura*). The competence of the Secretariat of State was again defined. It is employed for the immediate aid of the Pope in his efforts for the entire Church as well as for the individual departments of the Roman Curia. At the same time the newly created Office for Ecclesiastical Statistics (*Generale Ecclesiae Rationarium*) was incorporated into the Secretariat of State. The Datary was abolished.

Commissions

Special tasks, for the most part of a rather lengthy character, are managed by permanent commissions, partly in association with a congregation, partly independently. In the course of time their number has undergone considerable variation and most recently has been greatly enlarged.

Secretariats

Under Pope John XXIII and following the council various secretariats were established in order to assist in realizing in the postconciliar period the basic concern of the council—dialogue of the Church with the world. They are:
    —the Secretariat for Promoting Christian Unity (*motu proprio Superno Dei nutu* of 5 June 1960: *AAS* 52 [1960], 433ff.);
    —the Secretariat for Non-Christians (proclaimed in the homily of Paul VI on Pentecost 1964; *AAS* 56 [1964], 560);
    —the Secretariat for Unbelievers (established on 7 April 1965: *Annuario Pontificio* 1966, p. 1111);
    —the Council on the Laity (*motu proprio Catholicum Christi Ecclesiam* of 6 January 1967: *AAS* 59 [1967], 25ff.);
    —the Papal Commission for Studies *Ivstitia et Pax* (ibid.).

Land (Nationality)	Numbers in Year				
	1916	1923	1939	1961	1968
Italy	29	31	32	34	35
France	6	7	6	8	8
Spain	5	5	3	5	6
United States	4	2	3	6	7
Germany	2	4	4	3	5
Austria	3	2	—	1	1
England	2	2	1	2	2
Portugal	2	1	1	1	2
Hungary	2	1	1	1	1
Netherlands	1	1	—	—	2
Belgium	1	1	1	—	1
Ireland	1	1	1	1	2
Brazil	1	1	1	3	4
Poland	—	2	1	1	3
Canada	—	1	1	2	3
Czechoslovakia	—	1	1	—	1
Argentina	—	—	1	2	2
Syria	—	—	1	1	1
Colombia	—	—	—	1	1
Cuba	—	—	—	1	—
Armenia	—	—	—	1	1
Mexico	—	—	—	1	1
Ecuador	—	—	—	1	1
Uruguay	—	—	—	1	1
Venezuela	—	—	—	1	1
India	—	—	—	1	1
China	—	—	—	1	—
Japan	—	—	—	1	1
Philippines	—	—	—	1	1
Australia	—	—	—	1	1
Portuguese East Africa	—	—	—	1	—
Tanganyika	—	—	—	1	—
Switzerland	—	—	—	—	2
Bolivia	—	—	—	—	1
Chile	—	—	—	—	1
Peru	—	—	—	—	1
Algeria	—	—	—	—	1
Upper Volta	—	—	—	—	1
South Africa	—	—	—	—	1
Tanzania	—	—	—	—	1
Ceylon	—	—	—	—	1
Indonesia	—	—	—	—	1
Egypt	—	—	—	—	1
Yugoslavia	—	—	—	—	1
Total Number	59	63	59	85	109

SOURCES: as in Table 11.

The College of Cardinals (1916–68)

The Cardinals constitute the Pope's Senate and are his chief advisers and assistants in the government of the Church (Canon 230). They form a college, whose membership declined in number in the Middle Ages but was fixed by Sixtus V in 1588 at seventy, with reference to the seventy elders of the Israelites (Num. 11:26). They are divided into the orders of cardinal bishops, cardinal priests, and cardinal deacons—formerly 6+50+14. For the first time in the modern period Pope John XXIII exceeded the number seventy in the consistory of 15 December 1958. Only since Pius XII and more strongly since John XXIII, in connection with the numerical enlarging of the Sacred College, was account taken of the stronger internationalization of the College of Cardinals recommended by the Council of Trent.[15]

Titles and Areas of Jurisdiction in the Totality of the Hierarchy of the Catholic Church (1916–68)

During the pontificate of Pius XI (1922–39) there occurred a strong extension of the number of titles in the totality of the Catholic

Table 15: Existing Titles of the Hierarchy
of the Catholic Church from 1916 to 1939

Title	1916	1923	1939
Cardinals	75	70	70
Patriarchs	14	14	14
Metropolitans with residence	214	216	219
Archbishops with residence (without metropolitan rights)	—	—	36
Bishops with residence	849	874	935
Bishops in personal union	65	—	—
Permanent Administrators	9	—	—
Titular Archbishoprics and Bishoprics (without residence)	558	599	772
Archabbeys, Abbeys, Priorates and other Prelates Nullius	23	28	50
Apostolic Delegates	13	18	—
Vicariates Apostolic	172	206	292
Apostolic Prefectures	69	67	135
Missions and Autonomous Areas	—	—	19
Total Number	2,061	2,092	2,542
(Without Titles: = approximate numbers of areas of jurisdiction)	(1,503)	(1,493)	(1,770)

[15] Session XXIV de ref. c. 1.

TABLE 16: DEVELOPMENT OF JURISDICTIONAL AREAS FROM 1961 TO 1968

Jurisdictional Areas	Europe 1961	Europe 1968	Africa 1961	Africa 1968	America 1961	America 1968	Asia 1961	Asia 1968	Australia 1961	Australia 1968
Patriarchates	—	2	2	2	—	—	10	11	—	—
Exarchates	9	10	2	—	1	3	1	1	—	1
Metropolitans (without suffragans)	112	111	40	44	122	146	65	81	6	11
Suffragan Bishops	432	436	151	231	423	510	210	287	22	45
Archbishops (without suffragans)	23	27	3	2	3	1	15	22	2	2
Exempt Bishops	97	89	11	13	8	10	32	26	—	2
Exempt Prelates	7	8	—	1	52	76	7	11	—	—
Exempt Abbeys	13	10	3	3	3	3	1	1	1	1
Administrators	9	5	—	1	1	1	2	2	—	—
Vicariates Apostolic	6	6	20	19	48	41	50	18	28	1
Apostolic Prefectures	—	—	46	20	21	16	57	38	3	—
Independent Mission Areas	—	—	—	—	—	—	5	5	1	1
Ordinariates	3	3	—	—	2	2	—	1	—	—
Priorates	—	1	—	—	—	—	—	—	—	—
Total Number	711	728	278	336	684	809	455	504	63	64

SOURCES: *Annuario Pontificio,* 1961 and 1968; also as in Table 11.

TABLE 17: DEVELOPMENT OF TITLES AND AREAS OF JURISDICTION FROM 1916 TO 1968
(CONSOLIDATED FROM TABLES 15 AND 16)

Year	1916	1923	1939	1961	1968
All titles	2,061	2,092	2,542	3044*	4,205*
Areas of Jurisdiction	ca. 1,503	ca. 1,493	ca. 1,770	2191	2,441

* Without Cardinals, whose number since 1968 has fluctuated between 100 and 130.

hierarchy. In particular, the Pope erected thirty-one mission stations, 139 prefectures apostolic, 113 vicariates apostolic, twenty-three prelacies *nullius,* 110 episcopal sees, and twenty-seven archbishoprics[16]

DIPLOMATIC REPRESENTATIONS OF THE APOSTOLIC SEE WITH THE NATIONS AND OF THE NATIONS WITH THE APOSTOLIC SEE (1916–68)

The Apostolic See exercises the active and the passive diplomatic right (Canons 265ff.). It appoints extraordinary envoys for specific

[16] Cf. *Kirchliches Handbuch für das katholische Deutschland* 21 (1939–40) (Cologne 1939), 2ff.

TABLE 18: ACTIVE REPRESENTATION OF THE HOLY SEE, 1916–1968
(a) with governments and governmental agencies
(b) governments at the Apostolic See

Rank of the Representative (Apostolic See only)	1916		1923		1961		1968	
	(a)	(b)	(a)	(b)	(a)	(b)	(a)	(b)
Nunciatures	4		19		31		61	
Pro- or Inter-nunciatures	5		5		11		1	
Delegations	6		—		17		16	
Total Number	15	16	24	25	59	47	78	65

SOURCES: as in Table 11.

occasions and maintains permanent representatives in nations or in larger areas—nuncios, internuncios, apostolic delegates. By tradition the apostolic nuncio is the dean of the diplomatic corps accredited to the state in question. The internuncio holds the rank of a minister plenipotentiary. The extraordinary envoys also have diplomatic status; the delegates do not.

The Apostolic See also receives the diplomatic representatives of states, partly extraordinary and temporary, partly ordinary and permanent. They enjoy all privileges and freedoms which by international law pertain to diplomatic representatives, even with respect to Italy, in whose territory they live. All accredited representatives of the states together constitute the diplomatic corps at the Apostolic See. The representatives bear partly the title "Ambassador Extraordinary and Minister Plenipotentiary" (*Ambasciatore Straordinario e Plenipotenziario*), partly the title "Envoy Extraordinary and Minister Plenipotentiary" (*Inviato Straordinario e Ministro Plenipotenziario*).[17]

In addition, the Apostolic See maintains representation, chiefly by so-called "permanent observers," at the following international organizations: (1.) The United Nations in New York; (2.) Office of the United Nations and Special Institutes in Geneva; (3.) International Atomic Energy Office in Vienna; (4.) Organization of the U.N. for Food and Agriculture (FAO) in Rome; (5.) Organization of the U.N. for Education, Scholarship, and Culture (UNESCO) in Paris; (6.) Council of Europe in Brussels; (7.) International Institute for the Standardization

[17] Cf. U. Stutz, "Die päpstliche Diplomatie under Leo XIII. nach den Denkwürdigkeiten des Kardinals Domenico Ferrara," op. cit.; A. Verdross, "Die Stellung des Apostolischen Stuhles in der internationalen Geminschaft," *Österr. Archiv für Kirchenrecht* 3 (1952), 54–68; G. de Marchi, *Le Nunziature Apostoliche dal 1800 al 1957* (Rome 1959); *Annuario Pontificio*.

of Private Law in the Vatican; (8.) International Committee for the study of Military Medicine and Health in Tirlemont; (9.) International Union for the Official Tourism Organizations (UIOOT); (10.) International Geographical Association.[18]

Final Observation: The development of the organizational structure of the entire Church, unchanged in essence since 1914, increasingly takes into account, in almost all its institutional and personnel function-population.[19] This applies to the greater internationalization of the College of Cardinals as well as to the expansion of the ecclesiastical hierarchy in the countries of the Third World. This process of re-grouping seems to have thus far affected even the Roman Curia itself.

[18] F. Groner, ed., *Kirchliches Handbuch. Amtliches Statistisches Jahrbuch der katholischen Kirche Deutschlands* 26 (1962–68) (Cologne 1969), 16.
[19] See Table 10, page 9.

CHAPTER 2

Popes Benedict XV, Pius XI, and Pius XII
Biography and Activity within the Church*

Benedict XV

Giacomo Paolo Battista Della Chiesa was born at Genoa on 21 November 1854, the son of the Marchese Giuseppe; he had two brothers and a sister. A great-uncle was a Capuchin. After finishing his college preparatory work, from 1869 as an extern he studied philosophy in the archepiscopal seminary and then, at the University of Genoa, the laws, in which he took his doctorate in 1875. As a member of the Capranica College at Rome he studied theology and listened to the Jesuit Franzelin; on 21 December 1878 he was ordained a priest and until 1882 continued his studies in the Accademia dei Nobili. After he had finished them, he was accepted, on Rampolla's recommendation, into the Congregation for Extraordinary Ecclesiastical Affairs. In 1882 Rampolla took him along as secretary to the Spanish nunciature. In Madrid he was known to the poor as "Curate of the Two Pesetas" because of his generous alms.

When in 1887 Rampolla was appointed cardinal secretary of state, Della Chiesa became his close collaborator, first as *minutante* and from

* Hubert Jedin

21

1901 as *Sostituto* (undersecretary of state). It was a purely diplomatic career, but parallel with it went a zealous activity in the care of souls at the church of Sant'Eustachio and catechetical instruction in the Girls' Home of the Daughters of Charity, besides conferences in the boarding school at Santa Trinità. The undersecretary of state survived Rampolla's fall, because the latter's successor, Merry del Val, could not do without the experienced *Sostituto*. Only in 1907 was he named, not nuncio in Madrid, as he had wanted, but archbishop of Bologna. His episcopal ordination by Pius X in the Sistine Chapel on 21 December 1907 called forth the expression that, while he had to yield to the new course in the Secretariat of State, he still possessed the personal good will of the Pope.

Giacomo Della Chiesa was small of stature, slight, and somewhat misshapen, but of an active mind, clear thinking and clever, a finished diplomat, filled with zeal for souls. He took his removal from the Vatican well, visited the 390 parishes of his diocese, held conferences of deans, and twice, in 1910 and 1913, convoked his suffragan bishops in council. Not until seven years after his appointment as archbishop of Bologna did he receive the red hat, on 25 May 1914. When his mother complained to Pius X about the long delay, she received the reply: "Your son takes few but long steps." The prediction was verified. As he began his journey to Rome for the conclave, a fellow countryman reminded him of his predecessor at Bologna, Prospero Lambertini, who had mounted the See of Peter as Benedict XIV: "Prospere, procede, et regna" (Ps. 44:4). The Cardinal replied dryly: "My name is not Prospero, but Giacomo."

In the conclave (31 August to 3 September 1914)[1] the norms decreed by Pius X were strictly observed, the Italian state guaranteed freedom of election, the imperial German government permitted Cardinal Mercier to leave occupied Belgium. Of the sixty-five qualified electors, sixty took part in the election. Confronting each other were the "Pius Circle," as whose head ranked the influential De Lai and as whose candidate there first came forth during the conclave the former abbot general of the Subiaco Congregation, Domenico Serafini, and on the other side the circle of "progressive" cardinals, which was for Ferrata or Gasparri. At the start the most promising candidacy seemed to be that of Cardinal Maffi of Pisa, "italianissimo" and a diocesan bishop, like the last three Popes; on the second ballot he received sixteen votes, the same number as Della Chiesa, whom the German and Austrian cardinals preferred. From the fifth ballot Della Chiesa moved ahead of

---

[1] Summarized on the basis of the literary remains of Lafontaine and, for 1922, of Piffl. J. Lenzenweger in *Linzer Theol-Prakt. Quartalschrift* 1964, 51–58.

Serafini, who in the eighth ballot still obtained twenty-four votes, but the tenth ballot brought the decision: thirty-eight votes out of fifty-seven for Della Chiesa. The adherents of Rampolla had carried the day.

None of the papal garments on hand was small enough for the newly elected Pope. In memory of his great predecessor Lambertini, who had likewise come from Bologna, he called himself Benedict XV. Familiar with persons and the spirit of the Vatican because of his long activity in the Secretariat of State, from the first moment he moved with assurance and awareness of his goal. He transferred his coronation on 6 September to the Sistine Chapel, named as his secretary of state the former nuncio at Paris, Ferrata, and, after the latter's death on 10 October, Gasparri. The Pope's first pastoral word on 8 September and his first encyclical on 1 November were calls for peace.

In the next four years the world war put narrow limits on the Pope's activity within the Church. Not until after the armistice did there come the doctrinal letter on Saint Jerome (15 September 1920)[2] and the naming of Saint Ephrem the Syrian as a Doctor of the Church[3] (5 October 1920); he honored Dante on the six-hundredth anniversary of his death[4] and the founder of the Order of Preachers, Dominic, who is buried at Bologna, on his seven-hundredth.[5] The canonizations of Margaret Mary Alacoque and Joan of Arc were regarded by the French as a triumph of victorious Catholic France.

In accord with the program of Leo XIII, he founded Catholic universities at Lublin and Milan. The ecclesiastical event of the pontificate that had the widest influence was the new codification of the Canon Law, planned since the close of the sixteenth century but again and again postponed (see Chapter 5). The Uniate Eastern Churches were removed from the competence of the Congregation for the Propagation of the Faith in 1917 and a special Congregation for Seminaries was founded in 1915. The greatest merit of the skillful, diplomatically experienced Pope was that he had piloted the ship of the Church through the reefs of the First World War and was able to maintain the neutrality of the Holy See (see Chapter 3). He died on 22 January 1922.

Pius XI

Achille Ratti came from the industrial middle class of Lombardy. His father was employed as a factory manager in the silk industry. His

[2] *AAS* 12 (1920), 385–422.
[3] Ibid., 457–71.
[4] *AAS* 13 (1921), 209–17.
[5] Ibid., 329–35.

mother was Teresa Galli. Born on 31 May 1857, his parents' fifth child, he attended the private elementary school of the priest Volontieri and spent the vacations with his uncle, Damiano Ratti, provost of Asso. From 1867 he pursued his classical studies at the seminaries of Seveso, Monza, and San Carlo, but concluded them at the Milan State Lyceum. After a three-year course at the Milan seminary for priests, he went in 1879 to the Lombard College at Rome, heard lectures on canon law at the Gregoriana, where the later general of the Jesuits, Wernz, was one of his teachers, and also theology at the Roman Sapienza and philosophy at the Academy of Saint Thomas. He was ordained a priest in the Lateran on 20 December 1879.

Having returned to Milan in 1882, he worked for five years as professor of homiletics and of dogma at the seminary until in 1888 he was admitted to the College of Doctors of the Ambrosian Library. As librarian he displayed versatility and established relations with scholars of many countries, including Grabmann, Ehrhard, and Kehr; with the last named he practiced his German. In 1907 he succeeded Ceriani as prefect. The fruit of his scholarly works was the *Acta ecclesiae Mediolanensis,* with Charles Borromeo as the center, and the *Missale Ambrosianum.* As an Oblate of San Sepolcro he was active in the care of souls, and he was on friendly terms with Catholic intellectuals, such as Contardo Ferrini. His recreation was Alpine climbing, including the ascent of Mont Blanc and the Matterhorn, and journeys to Germany and France.

At the suggestion of Ehrle he became vice-prefect, then in 1914 prefect of the Vatican Library. But as early as the beginning of 1918 he was removed from this activity and named apostolic visitor in Poland, which was at that time still occupied by German and Austrian troops. By way of Munich, Vienna, and Berlin, where he called on Imperial Chancellor Hertling, he reached Warsaw on 30 May 1918. Politically much was in a state of flux: the visitor assured the bishops whom he called on and the Polish people of the Pope's good will. After the Republic of Poland had been established, he became nuncio and titular archbishop of Lepanto; on 19 July 1919 he presented his credentials to President Pilsudski.

Nuncio Ratti succeeded in restoring five bishoprics that had been suppressed under Russian rule, in seeing to the appointment of new bishops, and in bringing about the first episcopal conferences. When in August 1919 the Bolshevik armies stood before Warsaw, the nuncio remained at his post. He was able at least to mitigate the oppression of the Ukrainian Uniates but not, however, to go into the Soviet Union and Finland. Appointed apostolic visitor of the area of Upper Silesia that was subject to a plebiscite, he went to Oppeln in April 1920 and in

July also into the part of East Prussia that was subject to a plebiscite. His conduct in the struggle over the plebiscite satisfied neither side. When on 29 November 1920 Prince-Bishop Bertram of Breslau (Wroclaw), with the Pope's consent, forbade political propaganda to the Upper Silesian clergy of both nations, under threat of suspension, the Poles obtained the recall of the nuncio.

There followed a sudden rise. Appointed archbishop of Milan and cardinal on 13 June 1921, he entered his diocese on 5 September 1921 after a month of quiet recollection at Monte Cassino and immediately displayed an almost feverish-seeming activity: when visiting the monasteries and ecclesiastical institutes he sometimes preached from five to ten times a day. On 8 December he opened the Catholic University of the Sacred Heart. He held up as models of his episcopal work the two great bishops of Milan, Ambrose and Charles Borromeo, with whom he had occupied himself as a scholar. But only five months of episcopal activity were granted to Ratti in his home diocese. The death of Benedict XV called him to Rome for the conclave of 2 to 6 February 1922.[6] Fifty-three cardinals took part in it, including thirty-one Italians. At the start the same factions stood in confrontation as in the conclave of 1914. The German and Austrian cardinals—Bertram, Faulhaber, Schulte, and Piffl—at first came out for Gasparri, until now secretary of state. The candidacy of Merry del Val, which had found some response in the first five ballotings, proved to be hopeless, and so the moderate Lafontaine, patriarch of Venice, came into prominence and received twenty-three votes on the eleventh ballot; the representative of the other faction, Gasparri, obtained twenty-four votes on the eighth ballot. Neither of the parties could achieve the two-thirds majority. This reason procured for the compromise candidate, Ratti, an increasing number of votes from the eleventh ballot. He was elected on the fourteenth ballot, 6 February 1922, with forty-two out of fifty-three votes; even Maffi and Mercier were for him. He chose as his motto *Pax Christi in Regno Christi,* which was explained in his first encyclical, *Ubi arcano,* and was later enlarged on in the encyclical on the Kingship of Christ in 1925: Christianity and Church must not, as liberal laicism wished, be excluded from the life of society but must be active in it.

He was the first scholarly Pope since Benedict XIV. He was recommended by his broad knowledge, his considerable knowledge of languages and international relations, and not least his acquaintance with modern scientific investigation. But not only by these gifts. As a pious priest, he had constantly been active in pastoral care, and as nuncio he acquired experience of ecclesiastical politics. His special energy gave

[6] See above n. 1; the acts, *AAS* 16 (1924), 109ff.

promise of initiatives in many areas of ecclesiastical life. His health was excellent, his springy gait, even when he was in his seventies, made clear that he had succeeded in maintaining it by regular walks in the Vatican gardens.

"Life is action" ("La vita è azione," according to Confalonieri) was one of his maxims; another was "Don't put off until tomorrow what you can do today." Of a character like granite, "born to command" ("nato per il comando," according to Confalonieri), the formerly reserved Pope radiated inner assurance and a strong consciousness of authority. With strict objectivity and painstaking order he carried through in deliberate calmness his program of work, in which the several hours of constant reception of pilgrimages, which he addressed if at all possible in their native languages, occupied a broad, perhaps too broad, part. He did not think much of delegating the preparation of papal decisions to commissions: not entirely without reason was he reproached for an authoritarian, even autocratic, conduct of his office. The College of Cardinals was strongly deemphasized. Still another maxim: "Laws are to be observed, not to be dispensed with" (Confalonieri). Was he a fighter? It is certain that, where Christian principles and the Church's basic rights were at stake, he was as unflinching as his model, Ambrose. His devotion was "una pietà all'antica"; even at the age of eighty he held fast to the exercises of piety with which he was familiar from his seminary days: the breviary, the rosary, visit to the Blessed Sacrament, retreats. Lest even the suspicion of nepotism should appear, he received his relatives, not in his private apartments, but in the official reception halls.

The pontificate began with a surprise. Pius XI, as he called himself, because he was born under one Pope Pius and had come to Rome under another Pope Pius, imparted the blessing "Urbi et Orbi," customary at the proclaiming of the election, from the external loggia of Saint Peter's Basilica, thereby indicating that he intended to move toward a solution of the Roman Question. Even before his coronation on 12 February, he confirmed the previous secretary of state, Gasparri, in his office and thus made known that he planned to maintain the previous direction of Church government; when he sent him to Loreto as papal legate, he called him "the most loyal interpreter and implementer of his will." Even more decisively than Benedict XV, he held himself aloof from certain measures during the strife over Modernism, in which he rehabilitated Francesco Lanzoni and without advance concessions restored to Albert Ehrhard the prelatial dignity he had been deprived of. The scholarly Pope regarded the promotion of science and of serious scholarship as his peculiar duty. He had the reading rooms of the Vatican Library modernized and enlarged; he gave the purple to his predecessor in the position of prefect of the library, Franz Ehrle, and to his successors, Giovanni Mercati and Eugène Tisserant. The Oriental Institute founded by Benedict XV and the Papal Archaelogical Institute established by himself obtained sumptuous sites near Santa Maria Maggiore. For the Vatican collection of paintings he erected the new Pinacoteca. The means for all this were provided by the indemnity payments agreed to by the Italian government in the Lateran Treaties.

The Italian bishops were instructed to take care of a better preservation and organization of existing archives. In order to complete the collection of papal documents to 1198, begun by Paul Kehr, he established the *Piusstiftung* in Switzerland. Of great importance was the reform of priestly formation, into which modern scientific methods, for example, the employment of seminars and the production of scholarly dissertations, were incorporated.[7] A historical section for the completing of the processes of beatification and canonization was added to the Congregation of Rites. The Pope took into account the significance of the natural sciences, with the results of which he was completely fascinated, by founding in 1936 an Accademia delle Scienze, into which were admitted important students of science from the entire world.

The Pope exercised the apostolic teaching authority in numerous encyclicals, which in part were related to historical anniversaries. In his first encyclical of 23 December 1922[8] he admonished the victors of the world war to reconciliation of peoples. On the occasion of the ecumenical conferences of Stockholm and Lausanne he warned against vague formulas of union and urged unity in faith.[9] As "Pope of Jubilees," he liked to use historical anniversaries to consider problems of the present: on the three-hundredth anniversary of the death of Francis De Sales the connection of being in the world and loyalty to principle;[10] six hundred years after his canonization he called Thomas Aquinas the "Guide in Studies";[11] seven hundred years after the canonization of Francis of Assisi he aimed to strengthen the Franciscan spirit in the Church;[12] fifteen hundred years after the death of Saint Augustine he glorified him as a light for his contemporaries and for our age;[13] and the Jubilee of the Council of Ephesus in 1931 gave him the opportunity to strengthen devotion to Mary.

Other encyclicals recommended participation in retreats, devotion to

---

[7] Constitution *Deus scientiarum* in AAS 23 (1931), 241–84, supplemented by the encyclical on the priesthood of 22 December 1935 in AAS 27 (1935), 5–51.
[8] AAS 14 (1922), 673–700.
[9] AAS 20 (1928), 5–16.
[10] AAS 15 (1923), 49–63
[11] AAS 15 (1923), 309–26.
[12] AAS 18 (1926), 153–75.
[13] AAS 22 (1930), 201–34.

the Sacred Heart of Jesus and the rosary, or inculcated the bases of Christian education[14] and Christian married life.[15] The encyclicals on Catholic Action and against atheistic Communism[16] advanced still farther into the social field. Out of the conviction that in Fascist Italy no political but only a religious association of Catholics was possible, he sought to realize this insight in the whole Catholic world. For Italy a Central Council of Catholic Action had been appointed as early as November 1922: it supervised the activity of the organizations, of the diocesan commissions, of the youth organizations, and of the university federations. During the succeeding years Catholic Action was introduced in many countries—Spain, Portugal, Poland, Yugoslavia, Austria. In Switzerland and the Anglo-Saxon countries there were hesitations, because its basic aim had already been realized. For the same reason there existed doubts in already overorganized Germany; nevertheless, the Pope pressed for the introduction in his letter to Cardinal Bertram of 13 November 1928. That it was not to be understood as a withdrawal of the Church to a ghetto was made clear by the encyclical *Quadragesimo anno,* which attached itself directly to the social program of Leo XIII (see Chapter 7).

The "Pope of Jubilees" celebrated three Jubilee Years: the Jubilee falling according to the cycle in 1925, for which more than a half million pilgrims came to Rome; the missionary exposition organized at the same time attracted seven hundred fifty thousand visitors; the Holy Year closed with the instituting of the solemnity of Christ the King. Extraordinary jubilees were celebrated on the occasion of the Pope's golden jubilee of his priesthood in 1929 and in memory of the Incarnation and Redemption by Jesus Christ from Easter 1933 to Easter 1934; in the following year it was extended to the whole world. The world Eucharistic Congresses at Rome in 1922, Amsterdam in 1924, Chicago in 1926, Sydney in 1928, Carthage in 1930, Dublin in 1932, Buenos Aires in 1934, Rio de Janeiro in 1936, Manila in 1937, and Budapest in 1938 made people aware of the universality of the Church.

In the allocutions customary before Christmas the Pope took care to give to the College of Cardinals summaries of the most important ecclesiastical events of the year. Thus in 1923 he spoke of the aid to the populations of the Central Powers and of Russia, in 1926 and at other times of the persecution of the Church in Mexico, the menacing development in China, but also of the important happenings in Europe. He strengthened the College of Cardinals by eight members in his first

---

[14] *AAS* 21 (1929), 723–62.
[15] *Casti conubii* of 31 December 1930 in *AAS* 22 (1930), 539–92.
[16] *Divini Redemptoris* in *AAS* 29 (1937), 65–106.

creation; in the next years he filled up only with difficulty the vacancies caused by death and extended, though again only slowly, the representation of other continents in the college: in 1924 through the elevation of the archbishops of New York and Chicago, in 1930 of the archbishop of Rio de Janeiro. Not until 1935 did there follow a great promotion of twenty cardinals, but there were only two non-Europeans among them—Buenos Aires and the Syrian patriarch of Antioch. He left to his successors the step discussed by him toward a numerical internationalization of the College of Cardinals.

Noteworthy among the numerous beatifications and canonizations are those of: Robert Bellarmine, beatified in 1923 and canonized and declared a Doctor of the Church in 1930; Peter Canisius in 1925, when he was also declared a Doctor of the Church; Albertus Magnus in 1931, also a Doctor of the Church; the curé of Ars in 1925; Don Bosco, beatified in 1929 and canonized in 1935; Conrad of Parzham in 1934; Bernadette Soubirous, beatified in 1925 and canonized in 1933. In addition to many founders of religious institutes, martyrs in the missions were preferred: in 1935 John de Brébeuf and his companions, who had shed their blood in Canada in the seventeenth century; the Korean martyrs of 1839 in 1926; the Syrian martyrs of 1860 in 1926. The most imposing canonization of this sort was that of the English witnesses to the faith, John Fisher and Thomas More, in 1935.

Through all the internal ecclesiastical activity of Pius XI there runs like a red thread the awareness that the Church, to a degree never achieved before in its history, had become a World Church. This fact found expression in the extension of the international relations of the Holy See: at the end of the pontificate it maintained thirty-seven nunciatures and twenty-three apostolic delegations, and thirty-six ambassadors or ministers were accredited to the Pope.

Already marked by a mortal illness, the Pope planned an address that was to be delivered on the anniversary of the "reconciliation" with a fierce protest against the ecclesiastical policy of Fascist Italy, but he died on the previous evening, 10 February 1939. His successor was his secretary of state, Pacelli.

Pius XII

Pius XII came from a family of Roman jurists closely connected with the papacy. His grandfather, Marcantonio (1804–90), was from 1851 to 1870 deputy of the papal minister of the interior; the latter's son, Filippo (1837–1916), second oldest of ten children, was an advocate at the Rota and from 1896 consistorial advocate; as a legal adviser he participated in the codification of the canon law. By his wife, Virginia

Graziosi (1844–1920), he had two sons: Francesco, who played a role in the preparatory negotiations of the Lateran Treaties, and of whom were born the papal nephews, Carlo, Marcantonio, and Giulio; and Eugenio, the future Pope. In addition, the Pope had two sisters, Giuseppa Mengarini and Elisabetta Rosignani.

Eugenio, born on 2 March 1876, attended the state secondary school Visconti and, after finishing there, he pursued philosophy at the Gregoriana from 1894 to 1899, while he was a member of the Collegio Capranica. He studied theology at Sant'Apollinare as an extern, but at the same time for an entire year he heard lectures at the state University Sapienza, including those of the ancient historian Beloch. He was ordained to the priesthood on 2 April 1899 by the cardinal vicar of Rome in the latter's private chapel. He celebrated his first Mass in the Borghese Chapel of Santa Maria Maggiore, and on the next day a Mass at the tomb of Saint Philip Neri in the Chiesa Nuova. This procedure is informative for his later career.

Favored by Cardinal Vannutelli, a friend of his father's, after the completion of his legal studies at Sant'Apollinare (1899–1902), he entered the Congregation for Extraordinary Ecclesiastical Affairs as a *minutante* in 1904; its secretary, Pietro Gasparri, requisitioned him for cooperation in the codification of canon law. Pacelli became undersecretary in 1911 and secretary of the congregation in 1914. Parallel to this, from 1909 to 1914, he was teaching at the Accademia dei Nobili and performing pastoral work as confessor, preacher, and lecturer.

The career of the young Pacelli was exclusively carried out in the area of Rome and the Vatican until on 20 April 1917 he was appointed nuncio in Munich. Benedict XV himself ordained him as archbishop of Sardes on 13 May 1917 in the Sistine Chapel and thereby made clear that he enjoyed the full confidence of the Pope in the discussion to be undertaken by him of the aims of the war with the German government. On 26 June the nuncio conferred with Imperial Chancellor Count von Hertling and on 29 June he was received in the imperial headquarters (see Chapter 3).

After the overthrow of the monarchy, Pacelli was on 22 June 1920 made the first nuncio to the German Republic, while retaining temporarily the Munich nunciature, and, as its occupant, on 29 March 1924 he signed the Bavarian concordat. Not until 1925 did he move definitively to Berlin. The reputation and influence of the "perhaps most skillful diplomat of the Curia," as the German evangelical *Korrespondenz* put it, grew from year to year. He regularly participated in the German Catholic Days, at which he gave the address. Later he remembered with pleasure these years in Berlin.

Recalled at the end of 1929 and created a cardinal on 16 December, on 7 February 1930 he became Gasparri's successor as secretary of state, and as such he signed concordats with Baden and Austria as well as the concordat with Germany. On 25 March 1930 he was named archpriest of Saint Peter's as successor of Merry del Val. He became known to the Universal Church through legations to Buenos Aires in 1934, Lourdes and Lisieux in 1935 and 1937 respectively, and Budapest in 1938. In 1936 he visited the United States in a private capacity. And so, at the end of Pius XI's reign he was the best known cardinal, and in the College of Cardinals there was a consensus that he was preeminently qualified to guide the Universal Church through the storm of the threatening war, as had Benedict XV, who had had a similar career, during the First World War. The conclave lasted only one day, 2 March 1939: Pacelli was elected as early as the third ballot, with forty-eight out of sixty-three votes, and assumed the name Pius XII. No secretary of state had obtained the tiara since 1667. His coronation on 12 March took place, out of regard for the masses of people whom Saint Peter's could not hold, on the loggia over the principal portal. It was the first to be carried on radio. As his secretary of state the new Pope named the Neapolitan Luigi Maglione, who had been nuncio at Paris until 1935.

When in the summer of 1939 the danger of war grew more real, the Pope in a radio broadcast to the world on 24 August urged peace: "Nothing is lost through peace; all can be lost through war." The appeal was made in vain. When the new Pope's first encyclical appeared on 20 October, the Second World War had begun. While it raged, the Pope, relying on his moral authority, could only urge peace again and again and demand a just and humane treatment of the civil population in the militarily occupied areas. The information bureau set up in the Vatican collected the names of prisoners of war and the missing and supplied information on them to their families—from July 1941 to December 1946, 1,162,627 particulars were furnished. After the bombing of 19 July 1943 the Pope personally visited the severely hit city quarter of San Lorenzo and succeeded in getting the Italian government to declare Rome an "open city." In order to improve the providing of foodstuffs to the city crowded with refugees, provisions were brought from central and upper Italy in Vatican truck convoys.

Like Benedict XV after the First World War, so also Pius XII did not regard the time as suitable for filling the vacancies in the College of Cardinals until after the concluding of the armistice. In order to make of this a "living image of the universality of the Church," on 18 February 1946 he named thirty-two cardinals from all parts of the world, among them Armenian Patriarch Agagianian and the archbishops of New York, Saint Louis, Toronto, São Paulo, Rio de Janeiro, Santiago de Chile, Lima, Havana, Sydney, Lourenço Marques, and the Chinese Tien; the

Pope displayed courage by giving the purple also to three Germans: to Archbishop Frings of Cologne and Bishops Count Galen of Münster and Count Preysing of Berlin. A further step toward internationalizing the College was the promotion of twenty-four cardinals on 19 January 1953. Among them were the archbishops of Los Angeles, Montreal, Quito, Bahia, and Bombay. The proportion of Italians dropped to one-third.

In the thirty-three canonizations which Pius XII performed, French and Italians predominated, among the latter being Pius X in 1954.

Unaffected by the war was the exercise of the papal teaching office, which in several respects prepared the ground for the Second Vatican Council: the encyclical *Mystici Corporis* of 29 June 1943 on the Church,[17] followed on 30 September of the same year by the encyclical *Divino afflante Spiritu* on Holy Scripture, which encouraged the investigation of the literal sense and regard for literary forms and allowed biblical scholarship more freedom than had been permitted it during the defense against Modernism.[18] The constitution *Sacramentum ordinis* of 30 November 1947 defined as the essence of the Sacrament of Orders the invocation of the Holy Spirit through the imposition of hands; the symbolic presentation of chalice and paten do not pertain to it.[19] The bull *Munificentissimus Deus* of 1 November 1950 defined, without eliminating all the scientific difficulties, the dogma of the bodily Assumption of the Mother of God into heaven. The constitution *Sempiternus Rex* of September 1951 laid the foundation for the encyclical *Haurietis aquas* of 15 May 1956 on devotion to the Sacred Heart.[20] The encyclical *Humani generis* of 12 August 1950 basically accepted theological progress but warned against the relativization of dogmas and the all too close accommodation to the trends of the day.[21] The constitution *Sedes sapientiae* of 31 May 1956 extended the circle of theological departments of study in accord with the demands of modern pastoral work.[22]

No Pope before Pius XII treated as often and as forcibly as he in his numerous and always carefully prepared addresses to pilgrims, participants in congresses, and members of the most varied professions the general themes of Christian life—human dignity, formation of conscience, marriage and the family—and questions of professional ethics—jurists, physicians, natural scientists, and others—and referred to the

[17] *AAS* 35 (1943), 143–248.
[18] *AAS* 35 (1943), 297–325.
[19] *AAS* 40 (1948), 5–7.
[20] *AAS* 48 (1956), 303–53.
[21] *AAS* 42 (1950), 561–78.
[22] *AAS* 48 (1956), 354–64.

importance of the mass media—press, film, radio, and television. To the Lenten preachers of Rome he took care to speak on the sacraments as sources of sanctification. He remained rather reserved in regard to the ecumenical movement that grew so powerfully after the war.

But his liturgical reforms were epoch-making. Accepting the basic idea of the liturgical movement, the encyclical *Mediator Dei* of 20 November 1947 demanded the active participation of the faithful in the Sacrifice of the Mass, declared the reception of Communion to be desirable, though not necessary, and rejected the move to do away with cult forms that were unknown in antiquity.[23] The Evening Mass, granted during the war out of regard for nocturnal bombardments, was definitively allowed by the constitution *Christus Dominus* of 6 January 1953, and at the same time the Eucharistic fast was modified.[24] But perhaps the Pope's greatest deed in this field was the decree of the Congregation of Rites of 1 February 1951, which restored the Easter Vigil Liturgy. The new translation of the psalms, introduced in 1945, eliminated the translation mistakes in the Vulgate, but in the next years had to be again assimilated to the text made sacred by tradition. In September 1956 the First Liturgical World Congress met at Assisi.

Of the exhaustive legislative activity of the jurist Pope (see Chapter 5), to be singled out because of their general importance are the new decrees on the conclave and the papal election: photographic and radio apparatus could not be brought in, and television speakers and writers could not be employed; one vote over the two-thirds majority was needed to elect the Pope.[25] A step on to new ground was the constitution *Provida Mater Ecclesia* of 2 February 1947: it laid down rules for secular institutes, whose members bound themselves to the observance of the evangelical counsels without living in community.[26]

The slender, ascetically active Pope with the Roman head, who always took great care of his external appearance, was without doubt in the succession of Popes of the twentieth century the most brilliant phenomenon, admired by non-Catholics even more than by Catholics. He appeared to them as the perfect *Pontifex,* in form and looks the incarnation of the Roman Catholic Universal Church. The Romans never forgot that in the most difficult days of the war he had stayed with them and had been their single protector. Although he had three Germans in his immediate entourage—the Jesuits Robert Leiber and Augustine Bea and the former leader of the Center Party, Ludwig

[23] *AAS* 39 (1947), 521–95.
[24] *AAS* 45 (1953), 15–24.
[25] *AAS* 38 (1946), 65–99.
[26] *AAS* 39 (1947), 114–24.

Kaas—and as his housekeeper Sister Pasqualina of the Congregation of the Swiss Sisters of the Cross, and although he employed the German Jesuits Gundloch and Hürth as advisers, he was far from favoring Germany or even of pursuing a pro-German policy. Earlier than many Germans, he had recognized the threat to Christianity from National Socialism, although the threat from Bolshevism seemed to him still greater. He, and only he, piloted the Universal Church; in his hand all the strings of the Church's direction ran together. In a clearly superhuman working achievement he obtained for himself from acts the insights from which his decisions proceeded. After the death of his secretary of state, Maglione, on 22 August 1944, he appointed no successor and governed in direct contact with the heads of the two departments of the Secretariat of State, Montini and Tardini. As time passed, the College of Cardinals was more and more removed from transactions. In his relations with people he astounded them by his unerring remembrance of persons and charmed them by his amiability. His undoubted deep personal piety was strongly Marian under the influence of the apparitions at Fatima and misled opportunistic theologians to an excessive Mariology. Though viewed from without, the Catholic Church under the pontificate of Pius XII operated as a monolith in the whirlpool of the upheavals of world history, the Pope could only hesitatingly draw under the spell of his juridically stamped image of the Church the results that presented themselves and were even necessary for the accommodation to the new hour of world history. Only his successor dared to do so, and the Second Vatican Council introduced the new epoch. It must remain undecided whether he would have implemented the plans attributed to him of reorganizing the Curia and summoning a council,[27] even if the deterioration of his strength from which he suffered in his last years and which his physician sought in vain to arrest, had not impaired his activity.[28] Painful indiscretions of the physician overshadowed his last days and his death on 9 October 1958 at Castel Gandolfo.

---

[27] G. Caprile, "Pio XII e un nuovo progetto di concilio ecumenico," *CivCatt* 117, 2 (1966), 209–27.

[28] Presentation by the physician R. Galenzzi Lisi, *Dans l'hombre et dans la lumière de Pie XII* (Paris 1960).

CHAPTER 3

*Foreign Policy of the Popes in the Epoch of the World Wars**

The First World War and the Postwar Years: Benedict XV

Benedict XV has frequently been called a "political" Pope in contrast to his predecessor, who was a "religious" Pope. This is correct to the extent that Benedict XV, who was likewise a "religious" Pope, was confronted in foreign policy by problems of greater impact than was any of his predecessors since 1815. As early as the beginning of September 1914 the war had expanded beyond the boundaries of Europe and become a "world war." It soon took on proportions for which historical memory could find no comparable examples. Two-thirds of the Catholics of the time were directly involved in this war, 124 million on the side of the Entente, 64 million on the side of the Central Powers. The third of the Catholics living in countries not engaged in the war were, except for German-speaking Switzerland and Spain, under the overwhelming propaganda influence of the Entente Powers.

It goes without saying that the war, with its presumed consequences, constituted a powerful criterion for the voting of the cardinals in the conclave of 1914, which was able to take place without hindrances, but it was hardly the decisive factor. Thus, the papal electors from the Central Powers were from the start for Della Chiesa, but the ecclesiastical questions—integralism and its problems—were more important to them than political considerations.[1] The same must have been true of most other cardinals.

For the new Pope the question of the correct foreign policy course never became publicly a problem for the solution of which there would basically have been alternatives. From the first hour three points of orientation determined his answer to the challenge of the war: strict neutrality, charitable measures of assistance, and the call for peace and reconciliation.

NEUTRALITY

The basis of political neutrality can be precisely grasped in the papal allocution of 22 January 1915.[2] In it the Pope claimed for himself

* Konrad Repgen
[1] Cf. Piffl's diary for 2 and 5 September 1914 (M. Liebmann, "Les Conclaves du Benoît XV et Pie XI." *La Revue Nouvelle* 38 [1963], 45. Also J. Lenzenweger, "Neues Licht auf die Papstwahlen von 1914 und 1922," [Linzer] *Theologisch-praktische Quartalschrift* 112 [1964], 51–58).
[2] *AAS* 7 (1915), 33–36.

without restriction the right to be "summus interpres et vindex legis aeternae." He also declared in the abstract that he in no way sanctioned violations of rights but condemned them. He avoided with difficulty a concretizing and actualizing in regard to the problems which the war had raised. Hence he did not take a stand on the question of war guilt and of the infringements by German troops in Belgium or of the Russian occupation in Galicia. The war was by no means made less demanding: it was rather a "butchery" (*trucidatio*) than a fight (*dimicatio*). To intervene with papal authority into the confrontations of the warring parties was, however, neither significant (*conveniens*) nor useful (*utile*); on the contrary, the Holy See must remain neutral (*nullius partis*), however difficult this might be. Christ died for all men; the Pope is the Vicar of Christ for all men and on all sides of the war has children for whom he bears responsibility. And so he must not look at the *rationes proprias* separating them, but he must pay attention to the common bond of faith which unites them. Should the Pope act otherwise, he would not be promoting the cause of peace but further jeopardizing the interior unity of the Church. To be sure, he called emphatically and urgently for peace and reconciliation. Earlier the first encyclical (1 November 1914) had invited rulers and governments to peace negotiations: There are better means and ways to restore violated rights that war.[3]

This program, to which the Pope held firm during the succeeding years without essentially new arguments and ideas, was the opposite of a preaching crusade: incomparably moderate and temperate in goals and hence without any emotional force of enthusiasm. The war was still young, and the propaganda organs were running at full speed. At this moment few were ready to listen to the Pope; in fact, he was reproached with the charge that his peace-preaching crippled the moral power of resistance against the (unjustified) attack of the enemy among his (own) Catholics. The Pope presumably was under no illusions as to the direct effects of his appeal. But the essentially pastoral outlook enabled him to look beyond the clamor of the day.

Pius XII followed this fundamental orientation in the Second World War. It may seem today in retrospect as a sheer foregone conclusion, but it was at first nothing of the sort. To establish and stick to such a tradition required considerable and continuous efforts. Of course, in regard to ecclesiastical interests and understanding, there were no acceptable alternatives.

A withdrawing from the principle of neutrality would necessarily have meant taking one side or the other. Just as the Pope would have

---

[3] Ibid. 6 (1914), 565–81, here 567.

had to establish this morally, legally, and politically, so right and wrong, guilt and innocence were by no means one-sided, clear, and undoubted in this or that warring coalition of powers. The Pope could identify himself with none of them. But even if this should have been possible, the Vatican, in the translating of such a concept into practical political activity, would soon have run up against scarcely surmountable barriers. The papacy of the High Middle Ages had not been able to realize *in praxi* the theoretical claim to be judge of the world. Between 1914 and 1918 the word of the Bishop of Rome meant incomparably much less. Among non-Catholics the political authority of the Holy See had dropped to its nadir under Pius X.[4] Then people listened all the less to the Pope when even Catholics loyal to the Church did not collectively turn to Rome politically either predominantly or exclusively. This was especially true of the levels and groups that were then in any way "modern." Because a nationalism extending even to chauvinism was the prevailing tendency of the age, whoever wanted to obtain "contact" with his "contemporary age" could let himself be swept along easily and far by the nationalist movements. To accuse the Holy See that before 1914 it did not proceed energetically enough against this probably overestimates the possible influence of the ecclesiastical leadership and the political conduct of the faithful in purely political matters and leads ultimately to the posing of the question to which history from Gregory VII to Boniface VIII had already given a clearly negative answer. Hence, even with regard to the real ability to implement, neutrality was the only Vatican foreign policy that was available. A prudent judgment of the moral-legal situation of the military leadership and a skeptical evaluation of the readiness of the Catholics to echo the concrete political postulates of the Pope corresponded with Benedict XV's understanding of his office. This successor of Peter could and would "act [only] as the merciful Samaritan, not as judge of the world."[5] That persons, both in the camp of the Central Powers and among the Allies, again and again imputed to the papal policy prejudice or partisanship for the respective other side[6] is not a refutation of our thesis but indirectly a confirmation.

---

[4] Sali's report for 1916–22 in T. E. Hachey, *Anglo-Vatican Relations 1914–1939*, 1–72, here 4.

[5] L. Volk, "Kardinal Mercier, der deutsche Episkopat und die Neutralitätspolitik Benedikts XV. 1914–1916," *StdZ* 192 (1974), 611–30, here 628.

[6] For accusations from French and Italian circles cf. G. Jarlot, *Doctrine pontifical et l'histoire. L'enseignement social de Léon XIII, Pie X et Benoît XV vu dans son ambiance historique (1878–1922)* (Rome 1964); for the German side the paper edited by the Evangelisches Bund, "Papst, Kurie und Weltkrieg. Historisch-kritische Studie von einem Deutschen" (Berlin 1918).

As a consequence of the Vatican's neutrality and the Pope's reserve with statements containing concrete proposals, much political latitude was possible for the Catholics and their organizations in the different countries. For most of them identification with the cause of their own state, regarded as good and just, was important. Hence the Pope hardly determined the political attitude of the Catholicism of the countries and nationalities affected by or participating in the war in the specific problems which the war raised. Whether this may be regarded as a failure of papal policy is questionable, for in this regard Benedict XV probably had no wish to lead. Conversely, his neutrality was the indispensable presupposition for extensive humanitarian measures of assistance and for diplomatic activities to prevent the spread of the war and for the restoration of peace.

PAPAL MEASURES OF ASSISTANCE

Humanitarian measures of assistance fade easily and fast in historical memory. But, especially in war time, they require much patience, time, energy, and flexibility. The papal measures of help were supplied without regard to the religious, national, or ethnic membership of those affected, as the cardinal secretary of state had expressly prescribed on 22 December 1914.[7] This conduct found widely noticed recognition through the erecting of a great monument for Benedict XV at Constantinople in December 1921, hence in his own lifetime. The dedication speaks of the gratitude of the East for the Benefactor of peoples, who provided aid without distinction of race and religion.

In the First World War cruelties occurred in the Mideast which recall the Second World War, but were and are only lightly regarded by the historical memory of the Western world. For example, after the retreat of the Russians from eastern Anatolia one hundred twenty five thousand Assyro-Chaldeans were first driven into western Azerbaijan and from there back into the area of Mosul, modern Iraq, where most of them starved. Deportations and massacres among the Armenians[8] cost about 1 million human lives. A like fate was spared the Christians of Lebanon, but they too were decimated by hunger. The Pope could not prevent these happenings. But by avoiding branding them publicly, he continued in his neutral position and for this reason and by

---

[7] *AAS* 6 (1914), 7f.

[8] J. Deny, "Arminiya," *Encyclopedia of Islam,* 2d ed., I (Leiden and London 1960), 634–50, here 640f.; G. Jaeschke, "Das Osmanische Reich vom Berliner Kongreß bis zu seinem Ende (1878–1920/21)," T. Schieder, ed., *Handbuch der europäischen Geschichte* VI (Stuttgart 1968), 43, remarks that the treatment of the Armenians "was not undeserved by them." The Armenian revolts from 1890 would have simultaneously supplied motive, pretext, and excuse.

means of personal letters to Sultan Mehmed V he was able to bring about the partial halting of the massacres, to save from execution those condemned to death, and to insure that surviving children of the victims were cared for. An orphanage set up for this purpose in Constantinople received the name of Benedict XV.

On the other hand, the war in Europe was on the whole oriented in some degree to the contemporary norms of international law. Accordingly, the Vatican's measures of assistance in this sphere bore the charitable character of "normal" war care. First, from the spring of 1915, an exchange of prisoners unfit for military service succeeded by means of Switzerland, then the liberation and exchange of interned civilians, then the lodging of sick and wounded prisoners of war in neutral countries, to a total of over one hundred thousand, and finally the exchange of prisoners of war who were fathers of families of many children and the permitting of consumptive Italians to return from Austro-Hungarian prisons. In addition, collections of money prepared the way for these measures, and the Vatican's own resources were given to a total amount of approximately 82 million gold lire. Furthermore, efforts were undertaken or supported to put into motion again the postal exchange between the occupied and the unoccupied areas of a state, and, above all, corresponding institutions were established for the pastoral and charitable care of prisoners of war. Not least of all, with the help of these institutions the Vatican took part in the search for the missing. The office maintained by the German episcopate alone investigated eight hundred thousand applications, on which the state offices could give no information; one-eighth of these missing could be identified, and of these sixty-six thousand were still alive. Measured by the misery of the years-long war of attrition for soldiers and the civilian population, such measures of assistance were, to be sure, only a palliative. But in the framework of what was possible much was attempted and far more was accomplished than in the field of "pure" foreign policy.

Efforts for Peace

The Holy See's strivings for peace were first concentrated on Italy, the history of which in the period from September 1914 to the declaration of war on Austria-Hungary on 23 May 1915 is nothing other "than the history of the overwhelming of a reasonable but impassive majority by an enthusiastic or unscrupulous, but in any case tirelessly active minority," in which it was not clear "who had used or compelled whom: the active minority the government, or conversely."[9] Benedict

---

[9] E. Nolte, "Italien von der Begründung des Nationalstaats bis zum Ende des I. Weltkriegs (1870–1918)," T. Schieder, ed., *Handbuch* above, n. 8, 427.

XV was fundamentally interested in the outcome of these internal Italian struggles. It was of course unclear whether and how the Prisoner in the Vatican could at all continue the central government of the Universal Church if a state of war occurred in Italy. Besides, for the Italian Catholics loyal to the Church the Bishop of Rome had a special moral and political leadership responsibility. Finally, in the event of an Italian defeat in the Appenine peninsula there loomed the threat of a revolution from the left; in the event of an Austro-Hungarian defeat the collapse of the Hapsburg Empire and hence the end of the last great Catholic monarchy. Hence the Pope's aim was that Italy should stay neutral.

The conservative intransigents loyal to the Pope within Italian political Catholicism consistently upheld this goal.[10] The other large groups, the moderate so-called *Clerico-Moderati,* who sought a compromise with and an integration into the liberal state, conformed to all the changes of the government; they began with neutrality and ended with interventionism. The other, smaller groupings were partly for and partly against entry into the war. This variety and these oppositions were apparently accepted by the Pope without his pressing for a uniform formation of purpose in the sense of the Vatican program and carrying this through. He did not prevent substantial portions of Italian Catholicism from coming out for intervention from March 1915.

On the other hand, Benedict XV made intensive use of the traditional means of diplomacy to move the Dual Monarchy to timely and adequate concessions to Italian nationalism and to keep the Italian government from joining the Triple Entente.[11] He was unable to put across these aims, either at Vienna or in Rome. Austria-Hungary only proposed negotiable offers for Italy when the Kingdom had long before committed itself to the Entente in the London Treaty of 26 April 1915. ARTICLE 15 of the treaty, of which the Vatican learned as early as the end of 1915[12] and which the Bolsheviks published in *Izvestia* on 28 November 1917, was at first secret. By this article the Holy See was excluded from all peace negotiations. Behind it lay the traditional anticlericalism of the Freemasonic *Risorgimento* and the fear

---

[10] P. Scoppola, "Cattolici neutralisti e interventisti alla vigilia del conflitto," G. Rossini, ed., *Benedetto XV,* 95–152; A. Prandi, "La guerra e le sue consequenze nel mondo cattolico italiano," ibid, 153–205.

[11] Cf. F. Engel-Janosi, *Österreich und der Vatikan 1846–1918,* II: *Die Pontifikate Pius' X und Benedikts XV. (1903–1918)* (Graz 1960), 190–247.

[12] Proof: the acts in W. Steglich, *Friedensappell,* 27–30. The contrary claim of the Gasparri *Memoirs,* 169, is false.

that otherwise the "Roman Question" could be referred to an international conference. Attempts in 1918 to change this article failed.[13]

The legal and practical consequences for the Holy See at an outbreak of the state of war in Italy were after 1870 governed neither by international nor by Italian law.[14] Hence the government of the Kingdom had theoretically a free hand. The diplomatic representatives accredited to the Holy See by Austria-Hungary and Germany withdrew immediately to Switzerland on 24 May 1915, after the Secretariat of State had refused to accommodate them in the Vatican. In other respects the Italian government observed its unilateral obligations according to the Law of Guarantees of 1871 throughout the war and showed itself generous in some matters not regulated by that law. The Holy See's freedom of movement was, it is true, limited by the Italian state of war; for example, *Osservatore Romano* was bound by the Italian rules of censorship. But on the whole the Vatican had to deal with fewer difficulties than had been previously feared. Even during the war the Curia was able to operate as the center of the Universal Church, and the Pope could continue his foreign policy. In this field his prestige even increased: in 1915 the Netherlands and Great Britain undertook diplomatic relations with the Holy See and sent their representatives to the Vatican. Formal relations with France did not yet materialize, it is true, and in Vatican-Italian relations there persisted the coexistence traditional since 1870 of legal nonrecognition and in practice the possibility of a many-sided contact. At the beginning of the First World War there were fourteen diplomatic missions of states at the Holy See, and at the end seventeen.

After Italy's entry into the war papal foreign policy strove ceaselessly to support whatever could offer a certain prospect of bringing the warring nations to the negotiating table. In this connection the Vatican also followed unconventional routes. Thus from May 1915 to May 1916 it accepted offers of contact from Jewish personalities of France, from whom it apparently expected influence on the Jewish organizations in the Western nations and thereby again on the

---

[13] Cf. R. Mosca, "La mancata revisione dell'art. 15 del Patto di Londra," G. Rossini (ed.), *Benedetto XV*, 401–13. A new investigation by W. Steglich is expected; cf. idem, *Verhandlungen*, 407, n. 151.

[14] Cf. R. A. Graham, *Diplomacy*, 305–17. On the plans for building a Vatican State system, cf. S. A. Stehlin, "Germany and a Proposed Vatican State," *CHR* 60 (1974), 402–26.

foreign policy of the Entente Powers.[15] How difficult it was in the hate-filled atmosphere to make progress with peace probings appeared, for example, in the fact that the Pope could not get the future Cardinal Baudrillart in the fall of 1915 to bring a Vatican paper on possibly acceptable conditions of peace to the official notice of the French government.[16]

While, except in eastern Central Europe, the Catholics of all the warring countries very unselfishly carried out their duties as citizens, the Pope continued to be abstract in his frequent public expressions on peace and war,[17] though individual concrete statements positively impressed themselves on the memory, as from his address of 28 July 1915[18] the formula "that the nations not die." On the other hand the "Peace Appeal" of 1 August 1917 to the heads of the warring nations contains declarations of concrete content.[19]

The beginning of this diplomatic action went back to the turn of the year 1916–1917. It assumed concrete forms when the new nuncio at Munich, Eugenio Pacelli, on 13 June 1917 received instructions for personal soundings in Berlin.[20] He discussed this on 26 June with Imperial Chancellor Bethmann Hollweg and Secretary of State Zimmermann. The pivot was Belgium. Bethmann had earlier offered the restoration of the nation only among "real guarantees" for Germany; now he promised "complete independence" of all three great powers—a fundamental concession, for which he had not yet internal agreement. A meeting of Pacelli with Austrian Emperor Charles I on 30 June showed that the Hapsburg Monarchy apparently still maintained its readiness of May 1915 for concessions to Italy. These verbal promises of Berlin and Vienna were materially so important that the Vatican could go further with them. Belgium should be the starting point.

It was precisely on this point that the papal action become jammed. The fall of Bethmann Hollweg on 13 July 1917 contributed to this. His

---

[15] Cf. P. Korzec, "Les relations entre le Vatican et les organisations juives pendant la première guerre mondiale: la mission Deloncle-Perqual (1915–1916)," *RHMC* 20 (1973), 301–33. In this context there came about a remarkable official comment by the Holy See against anti-Semitic actions in Poland: Gasparri to the American Jewish Committee, 9 February 1916 (ibid, 320 ff.).

[16] J. Leflon, "L'action diplomatico-religieuse de Benoît XV en faveur de la paix durant la première guerre mondiale," G. Rossini, ed., *Benedetto XV,* 62–64.

[17] Texts in A. Struker.

[18] *AAS* 7 (1915), 364–77.

[19] Officially published on 1 September 1917 in *AAS* 9 (1917), 417–20; often printed since 15 August 1917. Critical text in W. Steglich, *Friedensappell,* 160–62.

[20] Content in A. Martini, *Preparazione,* 128f.

successor Michaelis was not prepared for domestic policy promises that had not been assured. The Curia could not know this, and overestimated the actual chances of success, but apparently placed itself under a portentous time pressure, because it seemingly wanted to publish it unconditionally on 1 August, the beginning of the fourth year of the war. Nevertheless the new Center-Left majority of the Reichstag on 19 July rejected the celebrated peace resolution[21] which came close to the Vatican program and had been accepted by the new imperial chancellor.

Before the Pope turned to all the powers, the concrete formulations with Berlin had to be unambiguously agreed to. To this end Pacelli on 24 July submitted in Berlin the so-called "Pacelli Punctation"[22] that had been elaborated in Rome at the beginning of July. This was a memorandum in seven points, the first four of which described concrete material regulations—freedom of the seas; limitation of arms; international arbitration; German withdrawal from France, restoration of the complete political, military, and economic independence of Belgium with regard to Germany, England, and France, and on the other hand the return of the German colonies by England—while the last three enumerated the other subjects to be treated at the peace conference—economic questions; Austrian-Italian and German-French boundaries; Poland, Serbia, Rumania, Montenegro.

This memorandum corresponded to the status as of 26 June. But now Berlin at once raised objections, especially in relation to Belgium, where again there was talk of "guarantees." The written reply, the German counterstatement,[23] was not presented until 12 August. The Vatican did not wait for it before drawing up[24] and delivering the papal peace appeal.

The "peace appeal" is a document of Benedict XV, backdated 1 August, to the heads of state of the warring nations, which the cardinal secretary of state officially[25] delivered to the powers on 9 August. The note consists of three parts: a review and recalling of the papal admonitions to peace, previously made, but in vain; a summons to the governments to reach an understanding on the points sketched in what

[21] Often printed. Critical text in E. Matthias-R. Morsey, eds., *Der Interfraktionelle Ausschuss 1917/18* I (Düsseldorf 1959), 114f.

[22] Often printed. Critical text in W. Steglich, *Friedensappell,* 133.

[23] Text in W. Steglich, *Friedensappell,* 151–55.

[24] Cf. A. Martini, *La Nota,* 418f.

[25] Since the Holy See maintained no diplomatic relations with the United States, France, and Italy, the notes for these powers were directed through the English ambassador at the Vatican. Russia and Belgium received the notes through their representatives in Rome; Germany, Bavaria, and Austria-Hungary, through the nuncios in Munich and Vienna.

followed as the basis of a just and lasting peace; a moving closing appeal to put an end to the more and more "useless carnage" (*inutile strage*) through negotiations. The crucial second part corresponded in content to the Pacelli Punctation with regard to the verbal German replies of 24 July, except for the point of Belgium.

It could not be proved at the time which prospects the Pope had assigned to his step. If one starts with the probably compelling assumption that he had reckoned on the chances of success, then one must presume that, despite the replies of 24 July, he had estimated Bethmann's promise of 26 June as capable of being revived. This would have—thus, for example, may one understand the Vatican's assessment—released so much political leverage that the Entente could scarcely have avoided serious negotiations resulting from it, step for step. Hence, because the stone which the avalanche would set in motion was the German promise of 26 June concerning Belgium, the reply of Germany to the papal peace appeal acquired special importance. It consisted formally of a note from the imperial chancellor to the cardinal secretary of state of 19 September,[26] which was followed by a confidential letter of Michaelis to Pacelli of 24 September.[27]

The note of 19 September contains various civilities but no clear acceptance of the matter of the statements of the peace appeal. An evasion of this sort, especially in regard to Belgium, had been suspected by the Curia at the latest since 12 August. Thereafter Vatican diplomacy sought persistently and ingeniously somehow to obtain, vis-à-vis the Entente, a usable German declaration of renunciation of Belgium. This policy of delimitation culminated in a letter from Pacelli to Michaelis of 30 August[28] which, with the adding of the English interim reply of 21 August to the papal note, demanded precise statements on Belgium as a presupposition "to further progress of the negotiations." Michaelis rejected such a declaration on Belgium on 24 September, since "certain preconditions" were still "not sufficiently explained." His letter was a provisional decree: the door was not slammed shut. But the papal effort at mediation had come to a halt: the precise German declaration did not come later either, so that the Curia could never again take up the thread.

The already mentioned notes of 21 and 30 August and of 24 September were published by the Germans at the end of July 1919 and

---

[26] Often printed. Critical text in W. Steglich, *Friedensappell*, 197–202, with the full, complicated history of the origin. The note was delivered to Pacelli on 20 September, published on 22 September.

[27] Often printed. Critical text in W. Steglich, *Friedensappell*, 361–63.

[28] Often printed. Critical text in W. Steglich, *Friedensappell*, 342f.

were long the subject of passionate controversies, which in the meantime cleared the way for more quiet and painstaking investigations.[29] It is firmly held today, in contradiction to Erzberger's claim in 1919, that Berlin with the German replies of September 1917 had wasted no unconditionally certain opportunities for peace. It is likewise established that Michaelis had not let himself be influenced in his treatment of the peace note by Protestant prejudices against Pope and Church. But there is today still not complete agreement on the bases and the consequences of the German decisions in September. Of course, it is known that Michaelis aligned himself in foreign policy alongside Secretary of State Kühlmann, and the latter, like Bethmann-Hollweg, wanted to give Belgium complete independence. For reasons of negotiating tactics in foreign policy and perhaps also from domestic policy considerations, Kühlmann, however, was willing to use the Vatican's mediation only at the end of a three-phased plan. First he envisaged private probings through the Spanish diplomat Villalobar in England with a declaration of German concessions on Belgium; this should be followed by German-British preliminary peace negotiations and then more formal peace negotiations mediated by the Vatican with a definitive declaration of the renunciation of Belgium. This oversubtle concept foundered in Madrid and in London. Whether a renunciation of the three-phase plan and a direct acceptance of the papal proposal was capable of being realized in Germany's domestic politics and of producing more success in foreign policy cannot be clearly stated, because here many hypotheses must be fitted together. Important, however, in this context is the attitude of the other powers to the peace appeal.

The three other Central Powers likewise replied formally to the Pope and in fact did not depart substantially from the German line;[30] Russia, France, and Italy, on the contrary, chose one of the more rude types of rejection by not replying. The answer of the United States, on 27 August,[31] was mainly conditioned by domestic policy. Wilson declared an Imperial Germany incapable of peace negotiations. British policy did

---

[29] Basic are W. Steglich, *Friedensappell* I, and V., and Conzemius, *L'offre*. To be added for French policy is P. Renouvin, "Le gouvernement français devant le message de paix du Saint-Siège (août 1917)," *Festschrift A. Latreille. Religion et Politique. Les deux guerres mondiales. Histoire de Lyon et du Sud-Est* (Lyon 1972), 287–302; for English policy, W. Steglich, "Die Haltung der britischen Regierung zur päpstlichen Friedensaktion von 1917," *Verhandlungen*, 365–409.

[30] Often printed. Critical text in W. Steglich, *Friedensappell*, 210f. (Austria-Hungary, 20 September 1917), 227f. (Bulgaria, 20 September 1917), 231–33 (Bavaria, 21 September 1917), 223–25 (Turkey, 30 September 1917).

[31] Often printed. Text in W. Steglich, *Friedensappell*, 422–24.

not conform to this denial. The English envoy at the Vatican was instructed on 21 August[32] to give an interim answer, which "to a certain degree conformed to the papal action" (W. Steglich). For reasons not clearly determinable, Paris at first attached itself to this step, and London communicated this to Rome on 23 August.[33] The London instructions of 21 and 23 August led to the Vatican's overestimating France's readiness for negotiations completely and England's considerably. On 26 August France made an about-face in regard to England and pressed for aloofness. To what extent London agreed is controverted.[34] England's actual readiness for negotiations from 30 August was probably described most precisely by Steglich, who thinks that London "wanted to defer the definitive stand until clarity had been obtained in regard to the willingness of the Central Powers to make concessions."[35]

From these relations it becomes clear how very much Pacelli had to believe at the end of August that with a German renunciation of Belgium the open sea of the peace negotiations had been reached, but also that at the end of August such a declaration would in no way have guaranteed surer success. How London would have decided if it had resulted cannot be said. Historically it must be held that the German silence on Belgium on 19 and 24 September spared the English government from finding a political reply to Germany, which it could have stuck to internally and could have subscribed to externally.

The failure of the action of 1 August 1917 did not induce the Pope to a fundamental correcting of his readiness to mediate. For example, in February 1918 Gasparri offered the Italian government mediation in special negotiations with Austria-Hungary, which also led to the formulating of corresponding plans, but because of internal Italian differences was not pursued farther.[36] But Benedict XV no longer expressed himself publicly in the further course of the war on concrete problems of peace.

The Pope did not need to observe this discretion during the Paris peace negotiations. He could, of course, exercise no influence on the content of the treaties,[37] since he was excluded from the congress as well as from the League of Nations. Nevertheless, the secretary of the Vatican Congregation for Extraordinary Ecclesiastical Affairs, Bonaven-

---

[32] Critical text in W. Steglich, *Friedensappell,* 335.

[33] Critical text in W. Steglich, *Friedensappell,* 337.

[34] The sources say nothing about it. Cf. the declarations in P. Renouvin, *Le gouvernement français,* 298, and W. Steglich, *Die Haltung,* 380.

[35] W. Steglich, *Die Haltung,* 390.

[36] Cf. F. Margiotta Broglio, 45–49.

[37] Nevertheless it was obtained that ARTICLE 238 of the Treaty of Versailles turned over the mission stations to the Vatican, cf. G. Jarlot, 440f.

tura Cerretti, stayed for some time in 1919 at the congress as the Pope's secret representative. In this way he established numerous contacts which led to the assuming of diplomatic relations with the new eastern central European nations and constituted the point of departure for the concluding of many concordats. Altogether the Vatican foreign policy worked for the most extensive possible international presence and for contractual accommodation with all nations, in connection with which it was shown to be quite prepared for concessions. For example, it was an unmistakable sign of reconciliation when the encyclical *Pacem Dei munus* of 23 May 1920[38] abolished the regulations which since 1870 had restricted the visits of Catholic heads of state who had been received at the Quirinal. This encyclical also directed the episcopate to exert itself for the promotion of a real attitude of peace among the faithful and thereby unambiguously distinguished itself from the Paris peace achievement, which was not characterized by the spirit of reconciliation. A great success of the Vatican's desire for reconciliation was the resumption of diplomatic relations with France in 1921. When Benedict XV unexpectedly died on 22 January 1922, the foreign policy presitge of the Holy See, as measured against 1914, had risen remarkably. That the number of diplomatic representatives at the Vatican had more than doubled was a clear indication of this.

Between the Two World Wars: Pius XI
THE LATERAN TREATIES OF 1929

The "Roman Question" to 1926

Also for the election of Pius XI on 6 February 1922, not primarily political but inner ecclesiastical reasons were decisive. At this moment no one could know that this political novice, who had spent his life among books and manuscripts until 1918, would conclude the Lateran Treaty and thereby bring about the most important foreign policy decision of the papacy since 1870. The agreements of 11 February 1929 sealed the end of the more than millennial history of the Papal State: at the same time they did away with the "Roman Question" that the Holy See had left open since 1870.

In the decades since 1870 there had been no dearth of deliberations, proposals, and exertions for the elimination of the "Roman Question" by reconcilation (*conciliazione*).[39] But nothing had been achieved in principle. Hence even Pius XI, in his first encyclical, *Ubi Arcano Dei,* of

---

[38] *AAS* 12 (1920), 209–18.
[39] Survey in P. Scoppola, *La Chiesa.*

23 December 1922,[40] though in a conciliatory form, repeated the legal reservation of his predecessors against the occupation of the Papal State, which had made the Pope the "Prisoner of the Vatican," and against the Italian "Law of Guarantees" of 13 May 1871.

Meanwhile, the "Roman Question" had lost its first-class significance for Italian domestic policy. This facilitated an accommodation for the Kingdom. In addition, the liberal governments had become increasingly dependent on the Catholic voters. Out of reasons of principle and tactics the leading politician of the period before 1914, Giolitti, had already substituted for Cavour's old formula of the "Free Church in a Free State" of 27 March 1861 the new view of 30 May 1904, that of "Two Parallel Lines" which never meet in a contractual arrangement but also can never collide in conflict. Under Pius X a *conciliazione* policy on this basis was not timely.

It was otherwise under Benedict XV. In an interview of 28 June 1915[41] that became renowned, Secretary of State Gasparri broke with the tradition of the inflexible policy of revindication and a little later let the powers know by diplomatic means that the Vatican sought a compromise with Italy not through political pressure but through negotiation and compromise. So long as the war lasted, there was no prospect of this, and even afterwards the exclusion of the Holy See from the peace discussions made the including of Italian-Vatican negotiations among the business of the other states impossible. However, on the periphery of the Paris conference there occurred on 1 June 1919 discussions between Cerretti and Italian premier Emmanuele Orlando on a text[42] which Gasparri had composed. It must have included: first, the demand for a material revision of the Italian Law of Guarantees of 1871; second, the renunciation of formal internationalization of the Roman Question, but assurance of the outcome or negotiations on the part of the other states through the entry of the Vatican State into the League of Nations; third, agreement of the Kingdom with the Papacy through Italian recognition of a sovereign Vatican State with an expanded territory. Differing from the arrangements of 1929, Gasparri's *appunto* certainly did not contain the demand for a simultaneous financial compensation and probably not a concordat that was to be signed at the same time.[43] Orlando accepted Gasparri's plan but could not obtain the approval of the King of Italy for it.[44] After

---

[40] *AAS* 14 (1922), 673–700.

[41] To the leading Catholic daily, *Corriere d'Italia*. Text in *CivCatt* 66, 3 (1915), 236–39.

[42] For a reconstruction of the content, cf. P. Scoppola, *La Chiesa*, 4–6.

[43] Thus P. Scoppola, 5f.; there also the differing views, to which can be added G. Martina, 119.

[44] F. Margiotta Broglio, 366f., 537f.

Orlando's fall on 19 June 1919 contacts in this affair were not broken off, but the new minister-president, Nitti, probably again ran aground on King Victor Emmanuel III.[45]

In these first postwar years there appeared many sorts of indications of the Vatican's readiness for negotiations. It was waiting, as Gasparri made clear in an interview of 29 September 1921,[46] for a statesman with whom there could be discussion of the matter. The program of the Catholic Popular Party, *Partito popolare italiano*,[47] founded on 18 January 1919, contained no direct allusion to a definitive contractual settlement of the "Roman Question" as an immediate aim, while the atheistic Fascist leader, Benito Mussolini, had departed in a famed speech in parliament on 21 June 1921[48] from his previous antiecclesiastical expressions and had signaled his readiness for reconciliation with the papacy. Thus matters stood when Benedict XV died.

The change of pontificate meant no alteration of the direction of Vatican foreign policy. This already appeared in the fact that Pius XI, contrary to tradition, left the cardinal secretary of state in office. To stress the significance of this continuity of personnel does not mean to imply that Pius XI was to a degree dominated by his bureaucracy. On the contrary, while Achille Ratti was an outsider to the Curia, he was a strong personality with a pronounced talent for independent judgment, quick grasp, and energetic action. And so the Lateran Treaties are historically his work, especially as he took a personal share in the origin of the treaty to the smallest formulation. Still, his treaty policy was completely in continuation of that of Benedict XV. Likewise, the replacing of Gasparri by Pacelli on 9 February 1930 meant no change of direction. The actual motives of the Pope for this change, over which there has been much speculation,[49] cannot be determined.

Mussolini's rule—he became minister-president on 30 October 1922—offered from the first a very confusing picture. Measures friendly to the Church stood alongside shock-troop violence. At first the Vatican reacted with a policy of the most extreme caution. No

---

[45] Thus F. Margiotta Broglio, 71; P. Scoppola, *La Chiesa*, 32.

[46] Text again in P. Scoppola, 46–51.

[47] Also G. de Rose, *Storia del movimento cattolico in Italia*, II: *Il partito popolare italiano* (Bari 1966).

[48] Extract from the text in P. Scoppola, *La Chiesa*, 52f. On the matter, cf. R. de Felice, *Mussolini il fascista*, I: *La conquista del potere 1921–1925* (Turin 1966), cited as R. de Felice II, 126f.

[49] A survey of the contemporary commentaries in *Ecclesiastica* 10 (1930), 135–39. A. Ottaviani, "Pio XI e i suoi Segretari di Stato," *Pio XI nel trentesimo della morte (1939–1969)* (Milan 1969), offers nothing more but is a very important source for the history of the two secretaries of state.

understanding on principles was sought, but on timely individual questions.[50] This was apparently the result of a secret meeting of Mussolini with Gasparri on 19 or 20 January 1923 in the residence of the president of the Banco di Roma, Carlo Santucci. In this interview there was presumably question especially of this Vatican-controlled bank, which had fallen into difficulties. Its failure, which could only mean catastrophic consequences for Italian Catholicism,[51] could not be averted without state help. Moreover, the two sides felt each other out and presumably agreed here to use the Jesuit Pietro Tacchi-Venturi for the future as go-between; his first intervention with Mussolini is demonstrable on 9 February 1923.

The Vatican's cautious reserve probably sprang first of all from the desire to avoid a frontal collision with Fascism, apparently especially because of the feared reaction on the Catholic organizational system. Only for a certain time, to the end of May 1923,[52] and not beyond a certain limit was the Popular Party defended by the Vatican. Between the end of July 1923 and the end of October 1924 the Holy See by stages removed its founder, Don Luigi Sturzo (1871–1959), from political life.[53] So long as the Vatican documents on these problematic proceedings are not accessible, it is difficult to make a correct judgment.[54] In the election campaign of 1924 the Vatican prudently acted with reserve while clearly denouncing Fascist violence.[55] On 9 September 1924 the Pope personally and publicly condemned a Popular Party coalition with the Socialists loyal to the constitution.[56] When Mussolini had successfully weathered the Matteotti crisis on 3 January 1925, there began the real construction of the Fascist regime, which lasted until 1943. It was essentially characterized by repression of revolutionary

[50] R. de Felice II, 497.

[51] The Banco di Roma was the principal bank of many Catholic organizations, financed the Catholic Press, and occasionally also aided the Popular Party, and had especially close economic relations with the Credito Nazionale and the network of Catholic Raiffeisen banks built in the nineteenth century. On the meeting between Gasparri and Mussolini, cf. R. de Felice II, 494ff.

[52] On 24 May 1923 *Osservatore Romano* still stood behind the policy of de Gasperi (R. de Felice II, 527f.).

[53] The decisive steps were: 7 July 1923, retirement as political secretary of the PPI; 19 May 1924, retirement from the directorate of the PPI; 25 October 1924, emigration to London. For the pressure which the Vatican exercised at each of these stages, cf. Sturzo to Cardinal Bourne, 15 November 1926, in F. Piva and F. Malgeri, *Vita di Luigi Sturzo* (Rome 1972), 291, n. 8.

[54] On the Sturzo problem cf. the important remarks in this connection in L. Volk, *Geschichte*, 125f.

[55] Cf. R. de Felice II, 578–89 (elections on 6 April 1924).

[56] Cf. R. de Felice II, 659ff.

radical, properly[57] Fascist elements and by concessions of Mussolini to the more conservative forces and groups that supported him, hence, in a certain sense, moderates. It was firmly established with the November decrees of 1926.

At this time there began, on Italy's part, the policy which led to the Lateran Treaties. At the beginning of 1925 the government convoked a commission for a revision of the law of Church and state; it engaged in the work of amending from February to December.[58] A former deputy of the Popular Party's center-right wing occupied the chair, and with papal permission, three canons of the Roman major basilicas belonged to the commission. The commission's final report was unanimously adopted. It made many concessions to the Church. The Italian episcopate reacted altogether positively toward it. As regards substance, the outcome of these consultations was already a piece of the Lateran Concordat of 1929. But the Pope rejected it, first orally on 26 December 1925 and then definitively by a letter of 18 February 1926 to Cardinal Secretary of State Gasparri[59] and thus produced a linking between this work of amendment and a contractual regulating of the Roman Question.

This attitude seems the more astounding since at that time there were present agreeing views on the Roman Question on both sides of the Tiber, as the Vatican knew fully. In the spring of 1925 Carlo Santucci, acting in a private capacity, had elaborated a "project" on the regulating of the Roman Question.[60] It treated the individual problems in general along the line of the Gasparri program of 1919, but deviated from it in two significant points: Santucci went into the financial problems passed over in 1919[61] and had misgivings in regard to the internationalization of the Roman Question. Santucci envisaged as the method of procedure an agreement of Italy with the Holy See on the material content but a formal regulation by a unilateral amending by the state of the law of 1871. On this point the Italian minister of justice was of another mind. He held that a regular treaty should be negotiated and included in

---

[57] "Properly" in the meaning of the period before 30 October 1922 and after 25 July 1943. On what follows, R. de Felice II, 729, as well as idem, *Mussolini il fascista* II: *L'organizzazione dello Stato fascista 1925–29* (Turin 1968), cited as R. de Felice III, 3ff.

[58] The protocols in P. Ciprotti, ed., *Atti della Commissione per la riforma delle leggi ecclesiastiche del Regno (12 febbraio–31 dicembre 1925)* (Milan 1968).

[59] Text in P. Scoppola, *La Chiesa*, 117f.

[60] Text in G. de Rosa, *I conservatori nazionali. Biografia di Carlo Santucci* (Brescia 1962), 195ff.; also F. Margiotta Broglio, 226–48.

[61] In the Law of Guarantees of 13 May 1871 the Italian state had offered to the Pope, as compensation for the papal income from the Papal State, an annual payment of 3.25 million lire, which he never accepted. Because of the subsequent decline of value, this sum was completely inadequate according to its current evaluation.

Italian legislation and announced to the foreign governments. This was an overly clear offer of negotiations. The Pope, as Santucci later experienced, is said to have expressed the view that this sort of regulation of difficult matters had probably better be left to his successor.[62]

Hence in the summer of 1925 the Holy See dropped Santucci's project and in the winter of 1925–26 rejected the acceptance of "unilateral" state legal reform. The reasons for these can be stated only hypothetically.[63] It is certain that the Curia took its time, because so much was at stake for the Church's future. The negotiations which led to the Lateran Treaties began on 5 August 1926.

The Route to the Lateran Treaties (1926–29)

The secret negotiations on the Lateran Treaties lasted two and one-half years, from 5 August 1926 to 10 February 1929, even though not continuously. Discretion was facilitated by the hardly exalted rank of the negotiators. On the Vatican side this was Francesco Pacelli, a layman, jurist in Vatican service, and brother of Eugenio Pacelli. For the discussion of the material of the concordat Prelate Borgongini Duca of the Secretariat of State was also involved. The Italian negotiator was, until his death on 4 January 1929, the state councilor Domenico Barone. Thereafter Mussolini himself, supported at the conclusion by high government officials, conducted the negotiations. The signing of the treaties and of the documents of ratification on 7 June 1929 was done on the Italian side by Mussolini, on that of the Vatican by Gasparri. The content of the negotiations was allotted to three treaties: the Lateran Treaty proper, which politically settled the "Roman Question," to which was added as Appendix IV a "Financial Agreement," and the Concordat.

The historical-legal aspect of the treaties of 1929 is discussed elsewhere, in Chapter 6. Here only the political aspect is to be treated, in which of course the details of the history of the treaty[64] cannot be debated. The route was from the start determined by the fact that both sides had, even before entering upon the official preliminary negotiations, discussed their minimum demands and had reached agreement on the essential points of the Lateran Treaty proper: Mussolini's sole condition, that the Holy See recognize the regulating of the Roman Question as definitive and thereby say "yes" to 1870, was accepted by

[62] P. Scoppola, *La Chiesa*, 111.
[63] Also R. de Felice III, 29f., 106–15, where the other hypotheses are also discussed.
[64] A useful introduction is supplied by G. Martina, "Sintesi storica," *A. de Gasperi, Lettere sul Concordato* (Brescia 1970), 113–73.

the Pope. Conversely, Italy had absolutely admitted the sovereignty of the Vatican, even though the important expression *Stato* for Vatican City was not conceded by Italy until 22 January 1929.[65] In principle the Kingdom had recognized its debts to the Holy See from ARTICLE 3 of the Law of Guarantees of 13 May 1871.

The final great material difficulties and ceaselessly numerous small detailed questions of the form of the text were settled in January and February 1929. In the school questions Italy countered a Vatican maximal program—in a draft concordat of 5 December 1926[66]—with its own minimal program of 22 February 1927.[67] The final compromise in ARTICLE 36 meant, it is true, a very solemn affirmation of the Church's principles, but drew from them only very limited consequences. And so in substance there was no agreement through a compromise. Similarly, even if it was much more favorable for the Vatican side, an agreement was reached in the complex of marriage law: when on 19 January 1929 the Italian minister of justice stated that, by the adopting of the canon law of marriage by the state, the Italian civil law was turned upside down—*sovvertimento delle norme*—the Pope on 20 January declared any concession in the substance of this point to be unacceptable; rather should *conciliazione* founder. He thereby got his way.[68] He was able to be so firm at this time also because he had immediately before lowered the financial demands already accepted by Mussolini on 14 January from 2 to 1.75 billion lire, whereby methods of payment tolerable for Italy had been worked out.[69]

If one inquires into the historical and political importance of the treaties, it is undisputed that their signing meant for Mussolini a "great, undoubted success," according to the judgment of his competent biographer, "one of the greatest which he ever gained,"[70] in which there is no doubt that the "reconciliation" of 1929 had for him only the character of a tool and was purely tactically conditioned. The significance of the treaties for the Holy See, on the other hand, is very much disputed, so that there can certainly be no talk of a "success" without limitations, even if details that can be criticized are disregarded. One must proceed from the self-understanding of the modern Church, which wants to be a pastoral Church, and from the great aims of the Pope, whose whole activity here, as also elsewhere, was apparently not

[65] F. Pacelli, *Diario*, 170.
[66] Text of ARTS. 31–41 in F. Pacelli, *Diario*, 260ff.
[67] Text of ARTS. 36 and 37 in F. Pacelli, *Diario*, 282.
[68] F. Pacelli, *Diario*, 116.
[69] 750 million lire to be paid in cash, 1 billion in Italian state loans at 5 percent (16 January 1929, F. Pacelli, *Diario*, 162).
[70] R. de Felice III, 415.

determined primarily by political goals but by the desire to create better and more effective possibilities for the care of souls.[71] Under this aspect the short-term and the long-term must be separated.

From the short-term the Lateran Treaties offered the Church undeniable advantages. The intervening of the state into the Italian Church and church administration was ended. The Vatican could cast off historically obsolete ballast and finally place the central government of the Universal Church economically on its own feet again—an advantage for the essential independence of the papacy that must be very highly evaluated. Furthermore, through the article of the concordat on the protections of associations—ARTICLE 43, par. 1—the Church obtained a powerful legal position for the defense of the Catholic organizational system. This assured their presence in the Italian world, far beyond the limits of clergy and episcopate, over which the state now lost its most extensive personal political influence. Besides, the general jubilation in the country on the sudden report of the concluding of the treaty speaks for itself. So authentic a Catholic and a democrat as Alcide de Gasperi (1881–1954), the last secretary of the meanwhile forbidden Popular Party, thought, under the immediate impression of the signing, that even Don Sturzo, if he were Pope, would have had to sign this treaty, which definitively freed the head of the Church from the burden of *temporalia*.[72] Of course, the Lateran Treaties strengthened the regime and hence the dictatorship: but this would pass. For the future, in any case, the Church should no longer be, as hitherto, constantly in search of unsuitable concessions for a solution of the Roman Question, and the solution should be obtained without the complication of an international guarantee. This outweighed all else. Problematic for the future was rather the concordat policy.

With this the second aspect is reached—long-term consequences. Precisely here opinions have been very much in conflict until today. Decisive is the question whether the Church, while letting itself be embraced by Mussolini's regime, jeopardized or sacrificed its own proper self. This did not happen. If Pius XI in the first weeks after the signing of the treaty, in favor of which he said little, hoped that Italy would now again become a "Catholic state"—in the sense of the preliberal epoch—Mussolini's arguments in May in the parliamentary debates on ratification unmistakably taught him otherwise. Two and one-half months after the signing the differences were so great that on 6 June it was still entirely unclear whether the treaties would become effective on the seventh. Ratification became possible only when both

[71] G. Martina, 134, leaves the "political" interpretation open.
[72] Letter of 12 February 1929 to S. Weber (*A. de Gaspari, Lettere,* 63).

parties joined in a dilatory formal compromise which concealed the disagreement over pinciple.[73]

In the next years Mussolini could not but recognize that the Church never unconditionally supported him—not in domestic policy and not at all in foreign policy. On the contrary, Catholic Action received a lift, especially the youth and student groups. This meant a serious hindrance to the penetrating of all of Italian society with Fascist tendencies, as Mussolini gradually became aware. Thus matters arrived at the great crisis of 1931, in the course of which the papal foreign policy advanced to the limits of its possibilities and finally had to accept a severe setback.

After the Lateran Treaties: The Crises of 1931 and 1938

Mussolini produced the crisis of 1931, chiefly from domestic policy considerations.[74] Catholic Action had gained too much ground for him. The great confrontation began in March with the accusations in the Fascist trade-union press that Catholic Action was overstepping its competence and interfering in the political-social sphere. In the background of the Fascist-Catholic journalistic polemic that now began, the government in April made demands through the diplomatic route which the Holy See rejected. At stake were two problems: the essential question of where the boundary ran between "ecclesiastical" and "extraecclesiastical," and the political question of who was to define the courses of this boundary. In the second question the Church claimed an unlimited autonomous competence. In the first question it demanded the right to have not only purely religiously oriented organizations, such as the liturgy and the administration of the sacraments, but also to be able to include the field of social Catholicism. In the Concordat Italy had recognized Catholic Action and its organizations as subject to ecclesiastical direction, so far as they "displayed their activity outside every political party for the spread and implementation of Catholic basic principles" (ARTICLE 43, par. 1).

From 19 April Pius XI publicly intervened in these confrontations.[75]

---

[73] The four drafts of the text of the communiqués in F. Pacelli, *Diario,* 151–53. At issue was the contractual law question of whether the Lateran Concordat was an integral element of the Lateran Treaty, and hence, like the latter, unchangeable, or not. Pius XI had written to Gasparri, 30 May 1929 (text in *Osservatore Romano,* 6 June 1929, then, *AAS* 21 (1929), 297–306; repeated in extract in P. Scoppola, 217–25): "Ne viene che 'simul stabunt' oppure 'simul cadent'; anche se dovesse per conseguenza cadere la 'Città del Vaticano' col relativo Stato. Per parte Nostra, col divino aiuto impavidum ferient ruinae."

[74] R. de Felice IV, 250–53.

[75] Address before the Diocesan Committee of Catholic Action of Rome (*Osservatore Romano,* 20–21 April 1931).

He placed himself before the "social" Catholic organizations, which are "legitimate," "necessary," and "irreplaceable," and in an open letter of 26 April[76] to Cardinal Schuster of Milan he bitterly assailed the Fascist education of youth, oriented to hate and irreverence. In these circumstances the grandly staged ecclesiastical demonstrations gained more special political emphasis in mid-May.[77] On 29 May Mussolini dissolved all Catholic youth and student groups by administrative measures.[78]

After useless protests and exchanges of notes, the Pope turned against this police action with the encyclical *Non abbiamo bisogno* of 29 June 1931.[79] The choice of this method of fighting was a political challenge of the first rank. In long and bitter passages the encyclical condemned the Fascist attack as clearly an injustice hostile to the Church. Mussolini's monopoly of the education of children and youth was founded on a "world of ideas which led professedly to a true and authentic deification of the state, which stands in full opposition, no less to the natural rights of the family than to the supernatural rights of the Church." The Fascist "notion of the state, which" claims "for it the young generation entirely and without exception," is "for a Catholic not compatible with Catholic teaching." The oath required of the members of Fascist organizations is "therefore, as its exists, not permitted," and hence at the least it must be taken with a *reservatio mentalis.* But the encyclical did not amount to a definitive break with the regime. It emphasized that the Pope had hitherto refrained from a "formal and express condemnation" and here too "in no sense" condemned "the Fascist Party as such." Rejected and condemned were only that part of its program and practice which are "irreconcilable with the name and profession of a Catholic."

And so the encyclical bore a contrary character: it could signify defining and signal readiness for negotiation. This ambivalence was perhaps the result of an inner-Vatican compromise between two groups with distinct notions in regard to the actual conflict.[80] In any event, as early as 23 July the Pope had entered into compromise discussions with

---

[76] *AAS* 23 (1931), 145–50.

[77] Celebration of the fortieth anniversary of the encyclical *Rerum novarum* and First General Assembly of Catholic Action of Italy. Cf. *Ecclesiastica* 11 (1931), 267–80, 290–94.

[78] R. de Felice IV, 258f.

[79] *AAS* 23 (1931), 285–312, delivered on 6 July; *Osservatore Romano* had carried the text on 5 July; F. Engel-Janosi, *Vom Chaos zur Katastrophe. Vatikanische Gespräche 1918 bis 1938, vornehmlich auf Grund der Berichte des österreichischen Gesandten beim Hl. Stuhl* (Vienna and Munich 1971), 229–55.

[80] According to R. de Felice IV, 264f., Gasparri and Pacelli belonged to the more moderate faction, Marchetti-Selvaggiani and Borgongini Duca to the more intransigent.

Mussolini, which led in September to a written agreement[81] that ended the strife and—with reference to the *conciliazione* of 1929—is frequently termed the *reconciliazione*.

The September Agreement was, of course, not a compromise without victors and vanquished, but a clear success for Mussolini.[82] The agreement described the organization and functions of the associations protected by concordat and hence meant a renunciation of autonomous ecclesiastical regulation and, with this, a definition in principle unfavorable to the Church. As regards substance, in most points the state had carried the day. Italian Catholic Action was parceled into 250 diocesan units independent of one another and had to accept a sort of prohibition of former members of the Popular Party for its leadership. Trade-union and quasi-trade-union functions were in general forbidden to it, and in its work of social formation it was virutally bound to a support of the idea of the Fascist corporate system, a few months after *Quadragesimo anno* (cf. Chapter 7). Nothing was said of the suppression of the objectionable Fascist oath. The counterconcession was that the youth groups could again exist under a new name, now patterned to purely religious aims, and with the explicit prohibition of pursuing sports—which meant renunciation of an essential part of modern education of youth.

The reason for these papal concessions was presumably that no better alternative was at hand. From 9 July the provincial prefects reported to Mussolini that the encyclical did not go over well among the people, not even the clergy: agreement and peace were desired.[83] The capacity of the clergy for a long fight with the state on the question of the Catholic system of associations was clearly slight. The ecclesiastical leadership could not ignore this. On 2 September it contented itself with the part of the education of youth which was permitted to it. It was much less

---

[81] Text often printed, most recently A. Martini, "Gli accordi per l'Azione Cattolica nel 1931," *CivCatt* 111, 1 (1960), 574–91, repeated in idem, *Studi*, 147–73, here 171; R. de Felice IV, 268f. Basic for the crisis of 1931 is A. Martini, op. cit., also idem, "Il conflitto per l'Azione Cattolica nel 1931," *CivCatt* 111, 1 (1960), 449–58, repeated in idem, *Studi*, 131–46.

[82] Thus P. Scoppola, 225f., R. de Felice IV, 269. Differing is A. C. Jemolo, *Chiesa e Stato in Italia negli ultimi cento anni* (Turin 1952), 666: "Pace di compromesso, senza vincitori né vinti." J. Schmidlin IV, 113, judges differently. An interesting report on Sturzo's opinion of 5 September 1931 in R. de Felice IV, 270f.

[83] R. de Felice IV, 263. In the 1931 annual report the English Ambassador Forbes said that the encyclical had confused the problem, since as a further climax there would have remained to the Vatican the possibility of excommunicating Mussolini or interdicting all Italy; the Pope had, in the crisis, "in many cases been badly advised" (T. E. Hachey, *Anglo-Vatican Relations 1914–1939*, here 213).

than it wanted. But this little it had to accept, if the alternative was "still less."

The long-range political expectations which in 1929 could have been attached to Catholic Action became largely illusionary through the events of 1931. It was eliminated as politically dangerous opposition for Mussolini. Whether the successful preservation of the organizational framework of Catholic Action, especially of the youth and student groups, which as late as 1933 were joined by an academic organization,[84] would alone have sufficed to prevent the advancing loss of the political importance and identity of Catholicism vis-à-vis Fascism is questionable.

The crisis of 1938 took place under changed political conditions; it was part and sequel of the gradually more open confrontation of Church and regime after the radical wing of fascism had gained ground remarkably since the foreign policy rapprochement of Italy to Germany since 1936.[85] The partial imitation of the anti-Jewish German policy by Mussolini aroused a spontaneous resistance among churchmen, to whom the Pope made it unmistakably clear that National Socialist notions of race stood in an irreconcilable opposition to the Catholic faith. Open conflict erupted in the fall, when the government amended the Italian marriage law in accord with "racial" viewpoints in a law of 17 November 1938. This meant that a marriage entered into in the Church between a baptized or unbaptized Jew and a Catholic lost its effect in civil law, which had been agreed to in ART. 34, para. 1 of the Lateran Concordat. As soon as the Holy See learned of these aims, it made use of its diplomatic means to prevent the introduction of these new forms or to modify their implementation.[86] Seemingly in this there was question "only" of a peripheral problem, for in Italy in that year that there were about three hundred thousand marriages performed in the Church in comparison to a few dozen marriages which were affected by the amendment.[87] But for the Church there were here at stake the validity and binding force of its sacramental law and its general mandate to the human race. Hence no one displayed any readiness for concession *in principiis.* The Vatican's protest notes did not, of course, prevent the Italian amendment from going into effect. To this extent the Holy See suffered another foreign policy defeat. But in regard to its intransigence

[84] On their non-Fascist function cf. P. Scoppola, 283ff.
[85] Basic for what follows is A. Martini, "L'ultima battaglia di Pio XI," *CivCatt* 110, 2 (1959), 574–91; 110, 3 (1959), 572–90, repeated in idem, *Studi,* 175–230; R. de. Felice, *Storia degli ebrei italiani sotto il fascismo* (Turin 1972), 285–91.
[86] Cf. the compilation of the Secretariat of State, *ADSS* 6, 532–36 (of 14 November 1938), as well as R. de Felice, *Storia degli ebrei,* 550–52.
[87] *Osservatore Romano,* 14–15 November 1938, repeated in P. Scoppola, 323–26.

it had churchmen on its side. In the long run this was a perhaps more important political event.

The Holy See did not exploit the 1938 violation of the Concordat to put entirely in question the treaty work of 1929.[88] For twenty years the framework was maintained. On the tenth anniversary of the Lateran Treaty Pius XI would have risked a break in a public accounting with Mussolini if death had not meanwhile overtaken him. The outline of the text of the papal address,[89] published in 1959, has pulled the rug from under this supposition. Pius XI intended before the entire assembled Italian episcopate to complain and to accuse the regime, but not to break with it. Hence the change of pontificate in 1939 meant in principle no alteration of course in Vatican foreign policy, even if a new handwriting and another political style are unmistakable. In fact, little changed—little was able to change: As the crisis of 1938 shows, the government of the Church, as soon as the sphere of the doctrinal and moral teaching was touched, could make no real concessions, even not with a dictatorship equipped with the twentieth century's techniques of power. The Church may be incapable of bringing the state or the prevailing regime to observance of the norms represented by it (which holds not only for our century), but it must insist on the validity of these norms.

PIUS XI AND THE TOTALITARIAN SYSTEMS

Opposition between the normative bases of a state and the teaching of the Church did not mean compulsion to renounce Vatican foreign policy with this state. So long as Catholic norms were not thereby sacrificed, the question of the beginning, continuing, or ending of the foreign policy activity of the Church with any state or regime was a question of expediency, in which the advancement of the possibilities of pastoral care represented the ultimate goal. In this way the lack of means of power and often the difficulty of gauging the consequences and side effects for the entire Church constituted the characteristic dilemma of papal foreign policy with reference to normative and/or *in praxi* hostile states. This dilemma appeared especially in relation to the really[90] totalitarian systems of our epoch: Bolshevik-dominated Russia and national socialist-ruled Germany. In this connection "totalitarian"

[88] On the Vatican side one spoke not of a "violation" of the concordat but of (this added) "vulnus."

[89] *Osservatore Romano*, 9 February 1959, repeated in P. Scoppola, 334–41; cf. A. Martini, *Studi*, 231–51.

[90] In contrast to the Italian "Stato totalitario" of the late 1930s.

means the claim to dispose, without limit and exclusively, of the totality of human existence, even in the sphere of conscience.[91]

Pius XI and the Soviet Union

At the Vatican there was never any question that the old ecclesiastical delimitations vis-à-vis socialism were true to a still greater degree in regard to the Communism recognized as totalitarian—not yet according to the idea, but in fact. If, nevertheless, between 1921 and 1927 the Holy See three times seriously explored whether and under what conditions formal, perhaps even diplomatic, relations could be established with the Soviet Union, it let itself be guided by the same principles which in an entirely different context Pius XI expressed on 14 May 1929 in the pointed statement: "If there would be a question of saving a single soul, of warding off a greater harm from souls, then We would have the courage to treat with the Devil in person."[92] The details of these Vatican-Soviet conversations and negotiations are knowable only in outline in the present state of research;[93] but the aims pursued in them by the Holy See and the reasons for the failure can be described sufficiently clearly.

The starting point of the first attempt was the frightful famines following the Russian civil war, which in 1921 led to extensive internationally organized acts of assistance.[94] Because of an Italian protest the Holy See could not take part in these directly and had to organize its own activity, which called for contact with Russian authorities. In this connection there appeared in Rome on 18 December 1921 a sketch signed by Pizzardo of a Vatican-Russian agreement[95] which went far beyond the technical problems of the distribution of charitable measures. In it the agents to be sent by the Holy See were designated as *missionaires,* to whom every sort of political action and propaganda was to be forbidden, but they

[91] The literature on the problem of totalitarianism is listed in Chapter 7. Especially useful in our context is H. Buchheim. *Totalitäre Herrschaft, Wesen und Merkmale* (Munich 1962).
[92] "Quando si trattasse di salvare qualche anima, di impedire un maggiore danno alle anime. Ci sentiremmo il coraggio di trattare col diavolo in persona" (*Osservatore Romano,* 16 May 1929). The contemporary translation of KIPA (*Ecclesiastica* 9 [1929], 255) weakened it to "struggle even with the incarnate devil."
[93] For what follows cf. R. A. Graham, *Diplomacy,* 349ff. Because of the details which the author obtained from the archives of the papal Secretariat of State, H. Stehle is important, although the necessary scholarly precision is missing from his presentation.
[94] Cf. H. H. Fisher, *The Famine in Soviet Russia 1919–1923. The Operations of the American Relief Administration,* 2d ed. (New York, 1935).
[95] Text in J. Kraus, 190, 192.

were allowed by treaty to set up schools and provide religious instruction (*éducation morale et religieuse*). To permit such beginnings of pastoral care and mission was an impossibility to the Bolshevik ecclesiastical policy of the time (see Chapter 17). Accordingly, the definitive agreement,[96] signed at the Vatican on 12 March 1922, strictly limited the papal mission of assistance to distributing food to the starving population and spoke of mere "agents" (*envoyés*). On the basis of this agreement, from July 1922 to September 1924 a Vatican mission composed of thirteen priests from various orders was active in several Russian cities.[97] Although the regime had on 26 February 1922 just taken a new step in the persecution of the Church by the expropriation of liturgical vessels of the churches, the Curia apparently tried to utilize even the slightest opportunities to counteract the oppression and suppression of pastoral care in Russia.

This goal becomes still clearer in the second action which occurred on the borders of the World Economic Conference of Geneva from 16 April to 19 May 1922. For the first time the new Russia had been invited again into the society of nations. The Holy See used this as an occassion to formulate in a memorandum[98] addressed to the conference general conditions to which Russia should be bound as condition of "reentry into the circle of civilized powers": full freedom of conscience, freedom of the private and public exercise of religion and worship, as well as restoration of expropriated property to the "religious corporations." What was important in this démarche, which the collapse of the conference deprived from the outside of any prospects, was not least of all its universal concern: the Vatican demands affected all religious communities, not only the Christian. The Pope did not speak only *pro domo*.

In the third attempt, which was drawn out from the winter of 1923–24 to December 1927, at stake was the concrete question of what returns the Soviet Union offered if the Vatican changed the de facto into a de jure recognition. Since the Soviet Union was then very much concerned for legal recognition by the rest of the world, the presence of a papal nuncio at Moscow would have been a great Russian success. The Vatican had, apparently from tactical reasons of negotiations, brought up the question, not of a nuncia-

[96] Text in J. Kraus, 191, 193.
[97] The Moscow leadership of the mission made use of the news associations of the German embassy in Moscow for the connection with the Secretariat of State.
[98] Text in *Osservatore Romano,* 15–16 May 1922.

ture, but of merely an apostolic delegation, hence a representative without diplomatic character.[99] The negotiations became jammed on the question of whether the Vatican conditions of 21 February 1924[100] should be the presuppositions for the erecting of a delegation or the subject of negotiations with the future delegate in Moscow. For unknown reasons the discussions were now transferred to Berlin and there continued by Pacelli. In February 1925 he negotiated with the Russian envoy Nikolai Krestinski about two Russian outlines—"theses"[101]—both of which were unacceptable to the Pope, because they implied unilateral Vatican advance concessions. In place of this, Pacelli in a note of 7 September 1925 apparently designated two points as *conditio sine qua non:* appointment of bishops and freedom of religious instruction for youth within church buildings. It was only on 11 September 1926 that the Russian government replied, offering not a reciprocal agreement but a unilateral one, hence an internal right of religion revocable by the state at any time.[102] Pacelli discussed this on 14 June 1927 with the Russian Foreign Minister Čičerin in Berlin, again unsuccessfully, because the Soviet Union would not concede religious instruction.[103] The Pope apparently wanted now to cancel the negotiations, but was induced by the nuncio in Berlin and Gasparri to one last, clearly doubtful attempt. It is contained in a communication from Pacelli of 5 October 1927.[104] Thereafter the Holy See would have been prepared, in the event that seminaries were opened and ecclesiastics could be sent from the Vatican, to appoint only such bishops and send only ecclesiastics who would be acceptable to the Bolshevik regime. Here it can be seen that there was a question of the absolute minimum possibility in pastoral care. But Moscow apparently rejected this too. Thereupon, on 16 December 1927 Pius XI directed that further discussions be stopped, so long as the persecution of the Churches lasted.[105] And there things remained. The breaking off of the negotiations with the Soviet Union by the Curia in December 1927 clearly denoted the hopelessness of a situ-

---

[99] A convenient survey of the ranks and titles of papal representatives in I. Martin.
[100] Text in F. Margiotta Broglio, 464f. (letter of Silj to Acerbo, 22 February 1924).
[101] Cf. H. Stehle, 92 (communications of the Secretariat of State).
[102] Cf. Ibid., 127f.
[103] Cf. ibid., 132f. (according to Hencke's communications).
[104] Tel. 101 Bergen, Rome, 24 October 1927 (*Pol. Archiv des Auswärtigen Amtes in Bonn: Geheimakten, Vatikan Pol. 3* [=K 012074]. Wrong date in H. Stehle, 141; ibid., 445, n. 19, another wrong date and wrong locality; hence the polemic against E. Winter, based on the false locality, is irrelevant.
[105] Cf. H. Stehle, 143 (communication of the Secretariat of State).

ation. Basically this was the same problem that was included in Hitler's long-range goals.

Pius XI and National Socialist Germany

THE WAY TO THE CONCORDAT WITH THE REICH (APRIL–JULY 1933.) Pius XI's foreign policy related to Hitler is marked in its first phase by the concluding of the concordat with the Reich. Next to the Lateran Treaties, it attracted contemporary attention as did no other concordat of the period between the wars. Its significance has again been much debated since the historical-political discussion in the early 1960s[106] of the attitude of German Catholicism to Hitler's seizure of power. After the fundamental publication of the acts in 1969[107] an unprecedentedly high state of research was achieved with a comprehensive monograph on the history of the concordat with the Reich by Ludwig Volk in 1972.

He positively confirms earlier communications of Robert Leiber,[108] according to which the Holy See exercised no influence on Hitler's gaining of powers in the spring of 1933. The naming of Hitler as chancellor on 30 January, the Emergency Decree of 28 February,[109] and the Reichstag elections on 5 March were never in question. A part of the research argues differently in relation to the yes of the Center to the Enabling Act and the not much later proclamation of the Fulda Episcopal Conference. Both groups, the Center Party of the Reichstag and the bishops, yielded, according to this view, to National Socialism, with an eye to the concordat that was being sketched, or, to put it crudely, accepted the dictatorship in return for cultural-political concessions. The sources do not uphold this view. A future concordat played no role[110] in the yes of the Center on 23 March. Likewise, an exact analysis of the origin of the bishops' statement of 28 March,[111] with which, conditionally, the prohibitions of national socialism, lasting for years, were annulled, shows that neither the Vatican nor the Berlin nunciature had exercised any influence on it. Conversely, however, it is

[106] Also U. von Hehl, "Kirche, Katholizismus und das national-sozialistische Deutschland," D. Albrecht, ed., *Kirche,* 219–51.

[107] A. Kupper, *Staatliche Akten;* L. Volk, *Kirchliche Akten.*

[108] Most recently in R. Leiber, "Der Vatikan und das Dritte Reich," *Politische Studien* 14 (1963), 293–98.

[109] The importance of this Emergency Decree can scarcely be overestimated; for Hitler's seizure of power it was at least as important as the Enabling Act (cf. K. Repgen, "Hitlers Machtergreifung und der deutsche Katholizismus. Versuch einer Bilanz," D. Albrecht, ed., *Kirche,* 6, n. 10 [with reference to Bracher]).

[110] Exact proof in L. Volk, *Geschichte,* 80–83 (also in critical evaluation of the contrary and erroneous assertions of the Brüning *Memoirs*).

[111] Text in B. Stasiewski I, 30–32; also, L. Volk, *Geschichte,* 76ff.

probably true that Hitler's declaration on 23 March of his government's friendliness toward Christianity and the Church, the subsequent yes of the Center to the Enabling Act, and the canceling of the earlier episcopal prohibitions of National Socialism on 28 May compelled the Vatican to act when the Catholic vice-chancellor, Franz von Papen, appeared on 10 April at the office of the cardinal secretary of state with the offer of concluding a concordat with the Reich and from the outset, among other items, offered in the law of education what the Curia had been unable to obtain in its negotiations since 1920 with the Weimar government.

For the Holy See there was obviously no question that it could not disregard this offer of negotiations. The widespread view that Hitler's rule would be of only short duration was not taken into consideration in the Vatican as the premise of a possible alternative. It is well attested that from the start Cardinal Pacelli was prepared for a long duration of the "Third Reich."[112] Nothing to the contrary is known as regards the Pope. True, in contrast to his secretary of state, Pius XI had in the spring of 1933 thought for a brief time that in Hitler he could perhaps find an anti-Communist defense agent.[113] This consideration was no longer present publicly on 19 May, when the bishop of Osnabrück visited him; he now fluctuated over the judgment of the internal German situation, in which pessimism apparently prevailed.[114] At the end of August he condemned the persecution of Jews in Germany in very strong words as an affront "not only to morality but also to civilization."[115]

Decisive for the Vatican's readiness for negotiations was the new dimension of danger in Germany. With the Emergency Decree of 28 February and the Enabling Act of 24 March the two "fundamental laws of the National Socialist state coming into being," as Volk puts it, were created. Now in case of need the government could itself decide whether it intended to deviate from the constitution; this deprived the Catholic Church in Germany of all previous legal protection. Hence to a hitherto unknown degree it was "in need of a concordat"; for if the previous legal assurances were refused, it had to look for others, if possible. Thus the concordat with the Reich was understood by the Holy See as a defensive weapon from the negotiations in 1933—in contrast to the Lateran Treaties.

The external course of the negotiations for the concordat with the

[112] For Pacelli's pessimism, cf. L. Volk, *Geschichte,* 63, n. 21.
[113] Also L. Volk, *Geschichte,* 64f.; also, idem, *Faulhaber-Akten* I, 745.
[114] L. Volk, *Kirchliche Akten,* 33.
[115] Kirkpatrick's report of 28 August 1933 (text in L. Volk, *Geschichte,* 217, n. 20).

Reich is not very involved. Von Papen conducted discussions in Rome from 10 to 18 April. In these was reached a preliminary draft on the part of the Church, which led on 20 April, out of consideration for changes in the Pope's wishes, to a sketch called "Kaas I" in the research. This was replaced on 11 May, not essentially altered, by the draft "Kaas II,"[116] which went both to Berlin and to the Fulda Episcopal Conference on 31 May. The desired changes of the episcopate were communicated to the government in mid-June. On 28 June Von Papen again took up his own negotiations on the Tiber, whereas he had entrusted the business of the concordat since 18 April to Prelate Ludwig Kaas,[117] who was staying in Rome. Von Papen brought along a new text outline. From 30 June to 2 July the negotiations were in the Vatican, from 1 July including Archbishop Gröber of Freiburg. On 2 July agreement was reached on a text ready for initialing,[118] which the Pope approved the same evening, but Hitler did not. The latter sought to gain time, then brought in the really appropriate Interior Ministry of the Reich, and on 5 July sent the director of the ministry, Buttmann, as a new, supplementary negotiator to Rome. On 8 July, after further negotiations, the text ready for initialing[119] was achieved and the Reichskabinett approved it on 14 July, so that Pacelli and von Papen could sign in the Vatican on 20 July.

The politically disruptive points during the three months of negotiations were until 1 July the de-politicization of the clergy (ARTICLE 32), then the protection of Catholic organizations (ART. 31). The German initial demand for a general prohibition of all partisan political activity by the clergy had been parried by Kaas in April by an extraordinarily clever counterproposal. It amounted, in a corresponding good conduct by the state, to promising by treaty a certain numerical reduction of the politically active pastoral clergy by canonical measures and actually meant "little more than nothing."[120] But at the end of June the political scene in Germany had completely changed. Like the other parties, so

---

[116] Text in A. Kupper, Staatliche Akten, 41–55.

[117] Kaas, the best German expert on the concordat, was until 6 May 1933 still chairman of the Center Party. His function in the negotiations for the concordat with the Reich cannot be clearly classified in a formal manner. The charges lodged against him in connection with the concordat negotiations (most recently in 1970 in the Brüning Memoirs, the composition of which in these passages goes back to the period after 1945) are untenable (details in L. Volk, Geschichte, 201–11; general: R. Morsey, "Ludwig Kaas," idem, ed., Zeitgeschichte in Lebensbildern. Aus dem deutschen Katholizismus des 20. Jahrhunderts [Mainz 1973], 263–72.

[118] Text in A. Kupper, Staatliche Akten, 149–63; L. Volk, Kirchliche Akten, 95–106.

[119] Text in A. Kupper, Staatliche Akten, 199–213.

[120] K. Repgen, "Das Ende der Zentrumpartei und die Entstehung des Reichskonkordats," idem, ed., Historische Klopfsignale für die Gegenwart (Münster 1974), 109.

too the Center was no more. Its dissolution was directly at hand.[121] When this was once accomplished, ART. 32 was no longer a real concession of the Church, but on the contrary a "protection of the Church against a Nazi invasion of the clergy," as Leiber's *votum* on 29 June explicitly stated.[122] When on 1 and 2 July the Vatican conceded ART. 32, scarcely anything was therefore really "sacrificed," but perhaps the opportunity to save Catholic organizations was seen. The concrete alternative to negotiations was narrowed to the concordat with the Reich—or renunciation of the organizations.

As early as April 1933 the German Catholic associations, in existence since the nineteenth century, and a greatly admired network of organizations strong in membership, were considered in jeopardy. True, they survived more intact during the following months than, for example, did the trade unions or the parties, since they were not exposed in the same degree to direct Nazi attacks and displayed a stronger willingness to assert themselves and to stay autonomous. But danger threatened them also from without. The sketch "Kaas I" had, therefore, envisaged a general article of protection for the Catholic societies, and then the Fulda Episcopal Conference had both expanded it and made it more concrete. On the other hand, according to the government's draft of the end of June a significant part of the doubtful organizations was to remain unprotected by concordat. This signified the worst, because it had meanwhile become apparent, through waves of political elimination of the opposition and police action, that now in Germany in this area also definitive facts were to be settled by force. The greatest part of the politically relevant Catholic associations were already dissolved or quite directly threatened by incorporation into Nazi units when the meetings at the negotiating table began in Rome.

And so, in this situation there was presented to the Holy See the basic question of whether there could be any negotiations at all. The issue was apparently decided by Gröber, the representative of the German bishops. On 1 July he saw only the alternative of allowing everything to

---

[121] The Socialist trade unions were brought into line on 2 May 1933, the Christian on 23 June. The SPD was forbidden on 22 June, although it had assented to Hitler's governmental declaration of 17 May. In Bavaria on 25 June 2,000 representatives of the BVP, including 200 priests, were jailed in order to accelerate the dissolution. The DNVP was dissolved on 27 June, the DDP (State's Party) on 28 June. On 29 June Brüning predicted the dissolution of the Center for 30 June; it was actually dissolved on 5 July (self-dissolution). On 4 July the BVP and the DVP had dissolved themselves. For the end of the Center Party, see R. Morsey, *Der Untergang des politischen Katholizismus* (Stuttgart 1977), a completely new edition of his basic studies of 1960; also U. von Hehl, 228f.

[122] Text in L. Volk, *Kirchliche Akten,* 86–89, here 89.

collapse or, "at least temporarily," to recover the *status quo ante*.[123] On 2 July he more reflectively posed the condition that the government publicly disavow its most recent police action—of 1 July—and offer guarantees for the future.[124] This route was followed. At the moment of initialing Hitler publicly withdrew most of the measures of 1 July against the organizations and their heads and forbade a repetition.[125] In contrast to the trade unions and the parties, therefore, the Catholic organizations continued, with some exceptions, in the summer of 1933, but of course not unassailed and also only for a while. For them the concordat with the Reich implied no concluding of peace but a pause in the struggle, according to Volk.

This is connected with the entangled story of the origin of ART. 31. The definitive formulation contained an unconditional guarantee for the Catholic associations which served exclusively religious and purely cultural and charitable ends (para. 1); the others enjoyed this guarantee, according to para. 2, only under definite preconditions. Paragraph 3 defined that the clarification of which societies should enjoy the protection of the concordat was to be regulated between the government of the Reich and the German episcopate. The concordat contained no explicit definition of the criteria and competence for this regulating. The fact that, nevertheless, the Holy See signed on 20 July was characterized by the competent expert in the Interior Ministry of the Reich as perhaps the "worst tactical blunder" of the Curia in the concordat.[126] He cannot be contradicted. Immediately after the treaty took effect the state exploited the holes and claimed the decisive competence for establishing the principles and the drawing up of the protected list. The Vatican did not accept this. The (for the Church) unsuccessful struggle over the "principles of interpretation" and over the list of protected societies constituted a substantial part of Vatican-German relations after the concluding of the concordat with the Reich.

Perhaps the Church could still have settled the unresolved problems of ART. 31 if it had made ratification dependent on this. This did not occur because the German bishops at Fulda from 29 to 31 August were of the opinion "the sooner, the better."[127] Urging this on the one hand was anxiety lest Hitler lose interest in the concordat, while on the other hand it was expected that one could make better headway with a treaty binding in law against the continuing anti-Catholic actions. The Holy

[123] Gröber to Pacelli, 1 July 1933 (L. Volk, *Kirchliche Akten*, 92f.)
[124] Gröber to Pacelli, 2 July 1933 (L. Volk, *Kirchliche Akten*, 107).
[125] Text in A. Kupper, *Staatliche Akten*, 219f.
[126] W. Conrad, *Der Kampf um die Kanzeln. Erinnerungen auf die europäischen Katholiken* (Berlin 1957), 44.
[127] Gröber to Leiber, 2 September 1933 (L. Volk, *Kirchliche Akten*, 242).

See treated lightly some hesitations in regard to the desire of the German episcopate and on 10 September the ratification took place—that of the secret appendix on 2 November.

As in the case of the Lateran Treaties, the historical significance of the concordat with the Reich can be understood only if one distinguishes between short-range and long-range consequences. Incontestably Hitler gained prestige; his propaganda interpreted the signature of the cardinal secretary of state as papal legitimation of National Socialism. This was actually false, but politically inevitable. Of course, this propaganda operated in various ways. The concrete foreign policy of the other nations was hardly affected by it. "The concluding of the concordat implied very little sympathy of the Vatican for the Nazi regime in Germany," maintained the British envoy at the Vatican in retrospect at the end of the year.[128] Equally slight was the impact on European Catholics outside Germany, somewhat stronger perhaps in Latin America, where, however, other factors were more important. More powerful was the effect on the German Catholics, even if here one must be careful of exaggeration. It was not established that by this agreement "the power of resistance of the German Catholics to a criminal regime had been broken," as was claimed on the political side in the 1950s[129] and was repeated in the following decade by a too biased historiography.[130] The concordat with the Reich probably offered a

---

[128] T. E. Hachey, *Anglo-Vatican Relations 1914–1939*, 252.

[129] Thus Thomas Dehler, chairman of the FDP Party of the German Bundestag, on 11 March 1956; cf. J. M. Görgen, *Pius XII. Katholische Kirche und Hochhuths "Stellvertreter"* (Buxheim 1964), 42. The circulation of the most important Catholic opposition newspaper, *Junge Front,* rose from 85,000 at the beginning of 1933 to 120,000 at the end, and at the time it was prohibited at the beginning of 1936 it was 330,000 (cf. K. Gotto, *Die Wochenzeitung Junge Front/Michael* [Mainz 1970], 225 f). Between the middle of 1933 and the middle of 1934 the male Catholic youth lost about one-third of its membership, but the circulation of its association journals rose rapidly; cf. B. Schellenberger, *Katholische Jugend und Drittes Reich. Eine Geschichte des Katholischen Jungmännerverbandes 1933–1939 unter besonderer Berücksichtigung der Rheinprovinz* (Mainz 1975), 178, 198. J. Artez, *Katholische Arbeiterbewegung und Nationalsozialismus. Der Verband katholischen Arbeiter- und Knappenvereine Westdeutschlands 1923–1945* (Mainz 1978), estimates that, on the other hand, the loss of membership of West German workers' unions between mid-1933 and the end of 1934 amounted to only about 8 percent. For the other situation among Catholic academicians no study has been made. For the Catholic public school male teachers (not the women teachers!), cf. H. Küppers, *Der katholische Lehrerverband in der Übergangszeit von der Weimarer Republik zur Hitler-Diktatur. Zugleich ein Beitrag zur Geschichte des Volksschullehrerstandes* (Mainz 1975).

[130] Thus G. Lewy, *Die katholische Kirche und das Dritte Reich* (Munich 1965), 109; also U. von Hehl, 238ff., as well as L. Volk, "Zwischen Geschichtsschreibung und Hochhuthprosa. Kritisches und Grundsätzliches zu einer Neuerscheinung über Kirche und Nationalsozialismus," D. Albrecht, ed. *Kirche,* 194–210.

starting point to a series of Catholic journalists, who then came forward for the easing of tensions by the building of bridges to Nazism. Meanwhile this small portion of German Catholics—in contrast to a not inconsiderable proportion of German Protestantism—sacrificed nothing of the content of faith, insisted on the Church's share in the right to issue rules in *res mixtae,* and furthermore claimed autonomy for the Catholic associations. Hence persons based on the illusory premise the expectation that the other side was ready for substantial restrictions of its totalitarian claim. This promise very quickly proved to be false. The Catholic attempts at bridge building came to an end, with a few exceptions, in the winter of 1933–34 and at the latest in the summer of 1934.

On the other hand, in the short view the concordat meant a great success for the Church. The catastrophe of the Catholic associations was literally prevented at the last minute. One who stresses the negotiating blunders in ART. 31 must also emphasize this achievement. Precisely in the period immediately after the ratification the concordat with the Reich was, for the most endangered groups, an irreplaceable help in the struggle for self-assertion. In contrast to German Protestantism, the Catholic Church in Germany could at first remain for some time what it had hitherto been. This was attentively recorded on the part of ecumenism. "The position of the Roman Catholic Church in Germany was never so strong as now," wrote its probably best expert in Germany on 30 September 1933.[131] "It stands on its principles, which were guaranteed in the concordat. Priests are free to teach old and young in their churches what they [spacing of the author] wish without encountering the possibility of any secular interference."[132]

In the long run, on the other hand, the concordat brought Hitler little, in fact no advantage at all. It did not, as was later said, get the German bishops back into line,[133] but was, on the contrary, experienced by Hitler as an irksome fetter. Precisely for this reason he had it more and more disregarded, when and to what extent this seemed fitting to

---

[131] A. Koechlin to G. Bell, 30 September 1933 (A. Lindt, ed., *George Bell-Alphons Koechlin. Briefwechsel 1933–1954* [Zürich 1969], 47).

[132] Elly Heuss-Knapp, wife of the first president of the German Federal Republic, wrote in a letter of 18 May 1933: "Our friends . . . have at least proclaimed loud and clearly that the Aryan article is impossible in the Church. I go even farther and clearly declare to everyone that I shall leave the Church on the day when it is implemented. That I will then enter the Catholic Church I do not say so clearly to everyone, but I am thinking of it" (M. Vater, ed., *E. Heuss-Knapp, Bürgerin zweier Welten. Ein Leben in Briefen und Aufzeichnungen* [Tübingen 1961], 228).

[133] Thus G. Ritter, *Carl Goerdeler und die deutsche Widerstandsbewegung* (Stuttgart 1954), 114.

him, and this was not unexpected at the Vatican.[134] But not all the rules were broken at once, and with the existence of the concordat the Church was given the possibility of complaining about and denouncing every violation. The concordat was an outstanding defense line—the cardinal secretary of state prophesied this in August 1933[135] and, now as Pope, was able to repeat it as a historical fact on 2 June 1945.[136] For the concordat with the Reich essentially helped the Church in Germany to achieve the not self-evident accomplishment of maintaining its autonomy despite Hitler's rule to such a degree that the bishops and the clergy could proclaim the doctrine of faith and morals undiminished and administer the sacraments. That German Catholicism survived the Third Reich essentially more intact than almost all other comparable large bodies was, therefore, also a long-range effect of the agreement of 20 July 1933. It "created with its guarantees the legal basis by which resistance to totalitarianism could be and was realized."[137]

BETWEEN THE CONCORDAT AND THE ENCYCLICAL *Mit brenneder Sorge* (1933–37). To maintain the administration of the sacraments and the proclamation of the faith in Germany remained, after the signing of the concordat, the chief goal of papal foreign policy. This becomes evident in the long quarrel over the "principles of interpretation" and the list of protected associations according to ART. 31.[138] The Holy See went to great pains to make up here for the failures of July 1933. It did not succeed in this, but it contributed significantly to seeing that the concluding of agreements which would have been still more unfavorable for the Church than the situation without an agreement was prevented. At the beginning of 1935 the negotiations were practically wrecked because of Nazi intransigence, even though they were not formally declared to be ended by either party. The Ecclesiastical Ministry of the Reich, established in July 1935, in September 1935 once more asked for episcopal proposals and then conducted oral and written discussions. These were tacitly interrupted by the state in the spring of 1936. The resumption on 10 December 1936 was explicitly designated as "superfluous," because a new situation had arisen.[139] The bishops would have been as ready in principle for further discussions, as

---

[134] Kirkpatrick's report of 19 August 1933 (repeated in L. Volk, *Geschichte,* 250f.)
[135] Cf. n. 134.
[136] *AAS* 37 (1945), 163.
[137] K. Gotto, "Katholische Kirche und Nationalsozialismus," *StL,* 10th ed., 10 (Freiburg 1970), 489.
[138] The ecclesiastical documents and the texts of the draft now in B. Stasiewski I–III, and D. Albrecht I.
[139] Cf. D. Albrecht I, 195, n. 7.

was also the Vatican—but only to supply no pretext to the other side for easily disavowing the obligations of the concordat.

At stake in these exhausting negotiations was whether the Church could act beyond the walls of the sacristy or not. Every ecclesiastical concession extended totalitarian rule, every intransigence raised up obstacles to the Church. In this respect the question was where to draw the line—to a certain degree a problem of judgment. In general the Curia avoided letting the German bishops have a voice in this point. Its apodictic "no"[140] to a draft[141] agreed to in June 1934 by the episcopal delegation was an exception, scarcely to be overestimated in its importance, in which the Vatican of course knew that the affected societies in Germany were entirely behind it and with its protest strengthened their position vis-à-vis the bishops. Seen in its totality, the defense line of the Catholic societies was sought relatively far to the front, although this principle constantly encountered reductions in concrete details. For example, the Holy See consistently claimed only "partisan political" activity was forbidden to the associations, as the text of the treaty said; on the other hand, the Curia insisted on a general political right of activity for the organizations, hence on involvement with basic problems of political and social life. As a consequence the assertion of rights which the Church had negotiated for itself in the concordat created a dam against the totalitarian flood. While the Church was defending its own position with the means appropriate to it, it was at the same time a general antitotalitarian factor of importance.

On another plane a like function was performed by the thick exchange of notes of the Holy See with the German government, which began on the Vatican's initiative immediately after the ratification of the concordat. "Soul and mover"—such are the words of D. Albrecht—of this exchange of notes was the cardinal secretary of state with the intimate cooperation of the Pope. In almost wearisome repetition "again and again the brutal discrepancy" of the government "from law in accord with the concordat and activity hostile to the concordat" was brought up.[142] In this connection Pacelli proceeded from the Church's Leonine neutrality in regard to all types of states. He used this start in order to define the moral minimal conditions which every form of state must realize, by which principles of natural law served as the rule of conduct. In statements of principle of great strength the notes registered charges against rule by force. "There is no regulation of the concordat which could oblige the Church to recognize state laws as

[140] First by Pacelli to Bertram, 23 July 1934 (B. Stasiewski I, 762–69).
[141] Text in B. Stasiewski I, 744–46.
[142] D. Albrecht I, p. XXI.

binding on its members which were lacking in the requisite of morally obligatory state laws, that is, conformity with the divine law."[143] A basic principle of National Socialism was sharply rejected: "Human norm is unthinkable without anchoring in the divine. This ultimate mooring cannot lie in an arbitrary 'divinity' of race. Not in the absolutizing of the nation. Such a 'God' of blood and race would be nothing other than the self-made reflection of one's own narrowness and tightness."[144] The editor of these documents has correctly established in summary that here, on the basis of the concordat, the "painful truth was for years spoken directly into the face" of the government of the Reich, "as those could not do who would also have wanted to do, and those did not do who otherwise could have done."[145]

On the other hand, it is objected that a real giving of witness would have demanded publicity "with ultimate personal risk," and this in fact was not the case in regard to statements of principle, but remained in the diplomatically internal official documents.[146] In this view the goal which the notes pursued was not entirely known. They were not only diplomatic documents of a confidential nature. The most important pieces in the exchange of notes were printed by the Holy See in three issues in 1934 and 1936 as a white paper. The government of the Reich had a suspicion of this. It had to include the constantly threatening publication of these documents in its political calculations. It was still more significant that the white papers had been transmitted to the German bishops each time, and described the line of the Vatican's formation of view and will to the German episcopate; in this way they became an essentially inner-ecclesiastical instrument of government. In addition, in 1935 the contents of two very clear notes was published in *Osservatore Romano* and from there were taken into the official ecclesiastical newspapers of the German sees.[147] This was already "publicity," if only officially. Entirely public and official was finally the encyclical *Mit brennender Sorge*. Concordat—exchange of notes—encyclical were logical steps of a uniform defensive struggle by the Church.

FROM THE ENCYCLICAL *Mit brennender Sorge* TO THE END OF THE PONTIFI-CATE (1937–39.) The encyclical *Mit brennender Sorge*, dated 14 March

---

[143] Ibid. I, 255 (10 July 1935).
[144] Ibid. I, 146 (14 May 1934).
[145] Ibid. I, p. XXIV.
[146] E. W. Böckenförde in *Der Staat* 8 (1969), 266f.
[147] L. Volk, *Enzyklika*, 175f.

1937,[148] was read in the Catholic churches of Germany on 21 March, Palm Sunday, and was immediately distributed in print in an extensive issue. It is the best known papal document of the Catholic Church's struggle with Hitler. The German bishops had given the official impetus in the traditional letter of homage of the Fulda Episcopal Conference on 18 August 1936.[149] Five of the bishops were invited to Rome for January 1936 to deliver a report: the three cardinals and two of the youngest:[150] Clemens August von Galen of Münster and Konrad von Preysing of Berlin, who belonged to the "hard" wing of the Episcopal Conference. Several discussions produced unanimity to adhere to the Concordat as far as possible; although it was disputed whether a papal encyclical would jeopardize the concordat, there was agreement that such a pastoral letter was desirable. In addition, in strict secrecy Faulhaber prepared a first draft for Pacelli on 21 January 1937.[151] Then, until 10 March, the cardinal secretary of state composed the definitive text, presumably with the collaboration of Kaas, demonstrably under the personal supervision of the Pope.

Faulhaber was an important preacher. He intended his draft as a homily. It described the most serious present dangers for the Catholic faith, proceeding first from the positive—"pure" divine faith, "pure" faith in Christ, "pure" faith in the Church, "pure" faith in the papal primacy; then, in a polemical defense against Nazi premises and methods, it warned against what would today be called "remodeling" ("no novel interpretation of holy values"). There followed an exhortation to the young as well as to the priests and the "loyal," especially the members of the associations and Catholic parents—struggle over the denominational schools.

The Faulhaber draft was a "letter for teaching and encouraging," says Volk. Pacelli added a third leitmotiv. The persecution of the Catholic Church in the Third Reich was not only described by him as a fact but it was brought back to its political bases and aims. This gave the encyclical its timely sharpness. The other side, said the Pope, has "made the reinterpretation of the treaty, the undermining of the treaty, finally the

---

[148] AAS 29 (1937), 145–67; M, 211–38. There is no Latin version of this encyclical, but an Italian translation (ibid. 145–67). Often printed, it is now best in D. Albrecht I, 404–43.

[149] Text in B. Stasiewski III, no. 315/IIa.

[150] The age of the German bishops in 1937 amounted, in numerical average, to 64 years (7 over 70, 9 between 60 and 70, 8 between 50 and 59, and 1 under 50). Von Galen was 59 years old and three years a bishop; von Preysing was 57 and four years a bishop.

[151] Text now in D. Albrecht I, 404–43; ibid, 402f., the fundamental investigations of A. Martini are discussed.

more or less public violation of the treaty the unwritten law of operation." The "visual instruction of past years" reveals "machinations which from the first knew no other goal than a war of annihilation." That this war of annihilation had its cause in the irreconcilability of Catholic faith and national socialist principles of government is worked out in copious detail. "Whoever dissociates race or the people or the state or the type of state, the executors of political power, or other basic values of the organization of the human community—which claim an essential and honorable place within the earthly order—from this secular value scale of theirs, makes them the highest norm of all, even of religious values, and deifies them with an idolatrous worship, overturns and falsifies the divinely created and divinely commanded order of things." Ideas of race, the Führer principle, and totalitarianism were thus repudiated by faith. Man has "as a personality God-given rights," which "must remain immune" to any "interference on the part of the community"; in the context of school registration there was mention of the "condition of notorious absence of freedom." In contrast to *Non abbiamo bisogno*, the encyclical of 1937 is incomparably harsher. But, as in 1931, here too the Pope did not want to burn all bridges.

The impact of the encyclical can be described only in connection with its aims. The papal pastoral letter was intended as "a word of truth and of pastoral support." In groups loyal to the Church, which were amenable to the intellectual level of the encyclical, it presumably had this limiting effect to an optimal degree. In other groups, which could hardly receive the ingenious sentence structure of this text without assistance, the theoretical understanding may have been slight, but not the solidifying effect.[152] The individual distinctions and conclusions were indeed far less important than the unprecedented fact that the Pope proclaimed publicly to the world: The Church in Germany is fighting for life and death; you German Catholics, you who are persecuted, are in the right; do not be confused; I am standing behind you.

Corresponding to the direct impact of the encyclical was the reaction of the other side, which had only learned of the imminent reading at the last minute.[153] The Nazi leadership did not make the risky attempt to suppress the reading on 21 March in the 11,500 parish churches; instead, it exerted itself for the drastic stopping of further distribution and took up massive measures of retaliation. Of these the most spectacular was a barrage of propaganda. On 6 April Hitler ordered the

[152] The *RPB* from Bavaria are ambiguous on this point; cf. *RPB* I, 211f; II, 167; III, 128; IV, 121.
[153] Cf. L. Volk, *Enzyklika*, 182–85.

immediate resumption of the trials on morals charges against Catholic religious and priests which had been halted the previous year. Thereby was inaugurated a propaganda action of unusual perfection and radical nature, the aim of which was to destroy the bonds linking the faithful to their clerical leadership.[154] Not without a very active counterdefense by the bishops and clergy did the loyalty of German Catholics endure this ordeal.

Meanwhile, the government, taking up considerations from the period before the encyclical, prepared to give notice of denouncing the concordat.[155] Into these plans there burst on 19 May a report which even further embittered German-Vatican relations. Because of an indiscretion of the press it was learned that the cardinal of Chicago, George William Mundelein, in the presence of five hundred priests of his diocese had condemned the Nazi regime and had characterized Adolf Hitler as "an Austrian paperhanger, and a poor one at that." German policy made an issue of this. It let its minister at the Holy See go ostentatiously on leave and on 29 May delivered a testy note, which demanded "redress."[156] The war of nerves against the Church was now pushed to its climax in Germany,[157] but apparently this did not greatly impress the Vatican. Its reply of 24 June[158] contained no apologies or weakening, but turned the tables and on its part again rejected the German policy. Furthermore, the Curia continued the war of notes in the previous form until in the summer of 1938 it was in practice called off, for reasons thus far unknown.[159]

Berlin's plans for denouncing the concordat were put aside, unrealized, in the fall of 1937, without the relevant motives being clearly known. Presumably Hitler, as he was about to enter upon immediate preparations for his expansionist policy, desired relative peace on the domestic policy scene, in any case not an added burden because of this action.

Until the Pope's death the situation of the Church in Germany did not improve. Quite the contrary: the prohibition of youth associations and the abolition of denominational schools were now implemented by the state. At the same time there appeared areas not covered by the concordat: Austria after the *Anschluss* of 13 March 1938 and the

[154] H. G. Hockerts, *Die Sittlichkeitsprozesse gegen katholische Ordensangehörige und Priester 1936/37. Eine Studie zur nationalsozialistischen Herrschaftstechnik und zum Kirchenkampf* (Mainz 1971), 74.
[155] Cf. D. Albrecht I, 373f., n. 3.
[156] Text in D. Albrecht II, 23f.
[157] Cf. H. G. Hockerts, 132–46.
[158] D. Albrecht II, 24–30.
[159] The view of the German ambassador to the Holy See: D. Albrecht II, 81f., n. 2.

Sudetenland from 1 October 1938. The German government refused, using legal arguments, to extend the validity of the concordat to these areas,[160] and also rejected new agreements. The positive results of the concordat in the "Old Reich," despite serious inroads precisely in 1938 and 1939, here became well known. The Holy See, like many other powers,[161] most of which were economically affected, did not lodge a diplomatic protest against the German Jewish pogrom in November 1938, whereas in the same days it pushed to its climax its conflict with Mussolini's "race legislation." In the long-run the encyclical accomplished nothing, in so far as the actual relations thereafter became, not better, but worse.

It likewise meant no turn in the ecclesiastical battle tactics of the Fulda Episcopal Conference. Preysing and Galen apparently desired this. They felt that permanent mobilization of publicity against violations of rights was a more effective method than Bertram's previous "petition policy."[162] The majority of the Episcopal Conference did not agree. Hence the putting to the test did not occur. The chances of such an attempt could be assessed with difficulty because it could not be said how long the episcopate, considering corresponding countermeasures of Hitler, could have kept the faithful on a permanent collision course. The Holy See did not meddle in these confrontations over the better defense tactics, although Pacelli would probably have been glad to see if Galen and Preysing were to be followed. Hence to this extent the encyclical was "not a caesura" (L. Volk).

On the other hand it incontestably produced a clarification whose long-term consequences must not be underestimated. Not only for foreign lands was it declared that the Catholic Church was in fact persecuted in Germany and that between Hitler and the Pope there existed an unbridgeable opposition: this clarification was of the utmost importance for the clergy and faithful in Germany. They found authentically marked here the route and the direction and indeed in the genuine ecclesiastical sphere of faith and morals, hence in an area in which the claim to obedient hearing was then undisputed. Exactly because the encyclical did not directly argue politically was it so demanding. The Church defended not its "influence" in the "world" but its *proprium*. No one could seriously challenge the legitimacy of this

[160] Also D. Albrecht II, 80f.
[161] Cf. the statement of the Germany report of the Berlin Foreign Office of 20 December 1938: *ADAP* D V, 769–73.
[162] Also basic is L. Volk, "Die Fuldaer Bischofskonferenz von Hitlers Machtergreifung bis zur Enzyklika 'Mit brennender Sorge,'" as well as idem, "Die Fuldaer Bischofskonferenz von der Enzyklika 'Mit brennender Sorge,' bis zum Ende des NS-Herrschaft," D. Albrecht, ed., *Kirche,* 35–102; W. Adolph, *Hirtenamt und Hitlerdiktatur* (Berlin 1965).

position. But by defending what was its own and by persevering in what was its own, it showed that it did not fit into Hitler's totalitarian system. Whether through a defense on a more political line the Catholic Church in Germany would have been able to retain as many people in the same degree before the intellectual accommodation to National Socialism as was possible to it according to the judgment of its Nazi enemies and the experience of contemporaries may be doubted.

When the foreign policy of Pius XI vis-à-vis Hitler is surveyed from the beginning to his death, the absence of genuine alternatives becomes obvious. What would have happened if Hitler had not unloosed the Second World War and lost no one can positively say. Everything suggests that the Catholic Church in his sphere of rule would then have fallen into a situation without hope of escape, similar to that in Stalin's Russia.

The Second World War: Pius XII

More than in 1914 and 1922, political reasons, in addition to ecclesiastical, may have been decisive in the election of Pius XII on 2 March 1939. Anything more precise is unknown.[163] The Second World War, which had already cast its shadows, by which it could be gauged that it would cause much greater spiritual and material damage than in 1914–18, brought the papacy far more difficult tasks than the first. This was very well known to the Pope, who had had experience in important political posts in the First World War. It was depressing for this austere observer that, despite the entirely correct insight, he could change so little in the course of things.

Most of Pacelli's contemporaries were of the opinion that he endured this ordeal magnificently. Apart from coarse Communist polemic,[164] after 1945 a vast increase in the prestige of the Holy See was testified to by the Protestant[165] and also by the liberal side and was referred essentially to the demonstration of the high, statesmanlike qualities[166] of

[163] The comment in D. Tardini, *Pius XII. als Oberhirte, Priester und Mensch* (Freiburg 1961), 34, is very cautiously expressed.

[164] Cf. M. M. Scheinmann, *Der Vatikan im Zweiten Weltkrieg* (East Berlin 1954). Criticism from the other side was less noticed. On the one hand, it came to a head in the charge made by the Russian Orthodox, American Protestant, and Freemason side that Pius XII, like the other Popes of the nineteenth and twentieth centuries, pursued politics and thereby failed in his ecclesiastical duty, and on the other hand in the reproof from the Jewish side (L. Poliakow) that he pursued politics too little, or even the wrong politics, and championed the Jews in Rome so little in order not to jeopardize his relations with Germany (cf. P. Duclos, 11f.).

[165] H. Hermelink, 2.

[166] Thus Sumner Wells, *The Time of Decision* (New York and London 1944), 142.

the Pope in the Second World War: "At no time since 1848 has the papacy had so good an international press as today."[167] Correspondingly it could be written at the Pope's death in 1958 that Pius XII had "brilliantly" discharged the heavy task of leading the Church through the Second World War. "In this epoch of raw force, of hatred, and of murder, the Church only gained in prestige, trust, and possiblities of effectiveness."[168] Five years later a play by the hitherto unknown German poet Hochhuth, with its serious charges against Pius XII, evoked a uniquely passionate debate in the Western world, with numerous discussions, seventy-five hundred letters to editors, and so forth.[169] The hitherto almost universal high esteem now changed in many to the opposite, even to scorn and hatred. Even a part of the literature appearing at the time and making a claim to scholarship did not hold itself far aloof from emotions, posing of problem questions, and even clear errors in method.[170] This "Hochhuth Debate" produced for scholarship a substantial profit to the extent that the Holy See at the turn of the years 1964–65 gave to a group of internationally recognized historians of the Society of Jesus[171] the task of publishing its acts and documents for the history of the Second World War. This voluminous publication appeared since 1965 and was to be completed in 1978. Research then had firm[172] ground under its feet.

As with Benedict XV, the foreign policy of Pius XII is summarized from three points of view: neutrality—exertions for peace—humanitar-

---

[167] L. Salvatorelli, *Chiesa e Stato dalla rivoluzione francese ad oggi* (Florence 1955), 139.

[168] R. Leiber, "Pius XII," *StdZ* 163 (1958–59), 88.

[169] A selection of the contemporary contributions to the discussion, not made from a scholarly point of view, in F. J. Raddatz, ed., *Summa injuria oder Durfte der Papst schweigen? Hochhuths "Stellvertreter" in der öffentlichen Kritik* (Reinbek 1963); *Der Streit um Hochhuths "Stellvertreter." Theater unserer Zeit* (Basel, Stuttgart 1963); also, cf. U. von Hehl, 236f., as well as, collectively, V. Conzemius, *Églises,* 487ff.

[170] For G. Lewy, *The Catholic Church and Nazi Germany* (New York and Toronto 1964), cf. above n. 130. Striking errors in method in S. Friedlaender, *Pie XII et le IIIe Reich. Documents* (Paris 1964). Also cf. A. Martini, "Un concerto non mai eseguito alla presenza di Pio XII," *CivCatt* 116, 1 (1965), 538–46; P. Blet, "Pio XII e il Terzo Reich," *CivCatt* 116, 2 (1965), 251–58; R. Lill, "Die Kirche und das Dritte Reich. Ein Forschungsbericht," W. P. Eckert, ed., *Judenhass—Schuld der Christen?! Ergänzungsheft* (Essen 1966), 62–64; V. Conzemius, *Églises,* 491–93; R. Graham, "Come non fare il processo 'storico,' " idem, *Il Vaticano,* 283–92.

[171] Pierre Blet, R. A. Graham, A. Martini, and B. Schneider (the last named is now deceased). They have made sure that for their edition the same rules hold as for other historical source publications (*ADSS* 1, p. IX).

[172] The doubts about the objectivity of the editors in B. Martin, *Friedensinitiativen und Machtpolitik im Zweiten Weltkrieg 1939–1942* (Düsseldorf 1974), 371ff., are not substantiated and so irrelevant.

ian measures of assistance. To these is added as a fourth the problem of his "silence."

NEUTRALITY

The reasons which had persuaded Benedict XV to opt for neutrality persisted in the Second World War. Two more were added. One was founded in Pacelli's personality. Pius XII, whom a bon mot characterized as the complete "diplomate de l'ancien régime,"[173] was by background, nature, self-evaluation, and experience an outspoken man of peace—but not at the cost of evil compromise. International law provided the other reason. In the Lateran Treaty the Holy See had assumed the obligation of holding itself aloof from the properly political problems of international politics (ARTICLE 24). This principle was, however, limited by two provisos: first, the Pope reserved the right to mediate peace in the event that both parties requested it, and, second, it had reserved the right to vindicate the moral and the ideal in every case. Tradition, circumstances, and legal situation converged in the Holy See's neutrality.

For this neutrality Pius XII, who was accustomed to think and to speak in very distinct ways, preferred the term "impartiality."[174] In this manner the political facts should be removed from the moral circumstances. "Neutrality," Pius XII declared to the cardinal of Munich, "could be understood in the sense of a passive indifference," which in a period of war such as this "was unbecoming" to the head of the Church. "Impartiality means for us judgment of things in accord with truth and justice," by which, however, in public announcements he granted "to the situation of the Church in the individual countries every possible consideration in order to spare the Catholics there hardships that could be avoided."[175] In other respects, like his predecessor Benedict XV, he declared: The Church "does not have the function of intervening and taking sides in purely earthly affairs. She is a mother. Do not ask a mother to favor or to oppose the part of one or the other of her children."[176]

The consequences of such a neutrality were observed by Pius XII "almost rigoristically," according to J. Becker. It was certainly his view, even before 1944,[177] that a war of aggression is not a morally and legally legitimate means of politics. With regard to his obligations of interna-

---

[173] W. d'Ormesson, "Pie XII tel que je l'ai connu," *RHD* 82 (1968), 21
[174] For example in the Christmas address of 1942 (cf. below n. 200).
[175] B. Schneider, *Piusbriefe,* 215 (31 January 1943).
[176] Thus in the Christmas address of 1946, *AAS* 39 (1947), 7–17; *UG* II, 1919–32. Similarly in his address of 2 June 1939, *ADSS* 1, 163.
[177] P. Duclos, 47ff., bases himself on the Christmas address of 1944 (cf. below n. 202).

tional law, before the outbreak of the war and during the war he refrained with difficulty from any explicit condemnation of many acts of aggression on the part of Germany,[178] Italy,[179] the Soviet Union,[180] the Allies,[181] and Japan,[182] and made only a much pondered exception in regard to the Benelux countries on 10 May 1940.[183] He was likewise careful to see that the Vatican did not become entangled in any crusade propaganda of one of the warring sides—neither from 1939 to 1941 against Hitler and Stalin nor, from 1941, when both the anti-Communist and the anti-Nazi crusade would have liked to appeal to a papal support. Even the term "Communism" disappeared from the vocabulary of the Holy See, and the idea of "West" was pretty much avoided from this period.[184] The maintaining of such an impartiality was very much more difficult in comparison to the First World War. It required "almost superhuman exertions" in order "to keep" the Holy See "above the strife of parties," the Pope confided to the archbishop of Cologne.[185] In this connection the integrity of the Vatican State represented the lesser, even if not a slight, problem.

The Lateran Treaty had guaranteed to the Holy See perfect independence and the possibility of communication with the rest of the world even in the event of a renewed state of war in Italy. These contractual decisions were not fully observed, but still, by and large, certain limits of flagrant violations of rights were not exceeded. The actual state of affairs depended on the general situation. Since Italy did not enter the war until 10 June 1940, the Vatican had to put up with relatively few restrictions until the beginning of the German campaign against France on 10 May 1940. Now matters underwent a change. Not only did measures such as blackouts and various other war-economy restrictions have to observed; Italy exerted strong pressures for the limiting of the Vatican's propaganda possibilities. The possibilities of communications

[178] 15 March 1939, occupation of Czechoslovakia; 23 March 1939, occupation of Memel; 1 September 1939, attack on Poland; 9 April 1940, occupation of Denmark, attack on Norway; 10 May 1940, attack on Luxemburg, Belgium, and The Netherlands; 6 April 1941, attack on Yugoslavia and Greece; 22 June 1941, attack on the Soviet Union.
[179] 7 April 1939, attack on Albania; 28 October 1940, attack on Greece.
[180] 17 September 1939, occupation of eastern Poland; 30 November 1939, attack on Finland; 4–17 June 1940, occupation of Estonia, Latvia, and Lithuania; 21 June 1940, occupation of Bessarabia; 25 August 1941, occupation of Iran.
[181] United States, July 1941, occupation of Iceland; England, 10 May 1940, occupation of Iceland, 25 August 1941, occupation of Iran.
[182] 7 December 1941, attack on the United States.
[183] Cf. J. Becker, 174f.
[184] Evidence in P. Duclos, 127–35.
[185] B. Schneider, *Piusbriefe,* 280 (3 March 1944).

by press (*Osservatore Romano*) and radio (*Radio Vaticana*) were there-upon curtailed; from the end of April 1941 *Radio Vaticana* discontinued its broadcasts on the status of the Church in Germany.[186] On the other hand, direct diplomatic contact with the powers hostile to Italy was maintained even after June 1940. When, contrary to the treaty, Mussolini withdrew their extraterritoriality, the Pope did not have them withdraw, as in 1915, to Switzerland, but gave them cramped quarters in the Vatican State, where finally a dozen representatives were lodged. Their contact with the Curia was thereby facilitated, and they were not entirely cut off from their governments; there remained radio communication and the possibilities of travel. Roosevelt's deputy, Myron C. Taylor,[187] went to Rome seven times for brief and long stays up to 1944; the English representative, Osborne, was able to journey to London and back for some time in the spring of 1943, and Archbishop Spellman of New York spent a few days in Rome. Conversely, in 1944, when Rome obtained an Allied garrison, the Holy See sheltered the diplomatic representatives of Germany, Japan, Hungary, and so forth. True, their possibilities of working were limited, but they were preserved in substance.

Hence during the entire Second World War the central authority in the Universal Church could continue to operate essentially intact and keep contact with its nuncios and the episcopate to the extent that this was not regionally and locally restricted and paralyzed, especially in the areas under German and Russian rule.[188] This was not self-evident. From the spring of 1941 the Curia reckoned with the possibility of a German occupation of Vatican City and the forcible withdrawal of the Pope;[189] it made preparations in case the central authority should no longer be capable of functioning. These measures reached their climax before and after the fall of Mussolini on 25 July 1943, which was

---

[186] Cf. P. Duclos, 32–36; *ADSS*, 4, 18–33; R. A. Graham, "La Radio Vaticana tra Londra e Berlino. Un dossier della guerra delle onde: 1940–1941," *CivCatt* 127, 1 (1976), 132–50. Compensation was sought through new means. Thus the organ *Parola di Papa* was issued as a new publication, which was sent to all Italian parish priests. According to P. Duclos, 34, n. 1, the Christmas address of 1941 was published in Italy with a circulation of 370,000.

[187] Cf. G. Q. Flynn, *Roosevelt and Romanism. Catholics and American Diplomacy, 1937–1945* (Westport 1976), 106ff.; cf. idem, *CHR* 58 (1972), 171–94.

[188] The Warsaw nunciature was not able, after the nuncio had withdrawn with the Polish government to Rumania, to be opened again; the nuncios in Brussels and The Hague had to depart in July 1940 on German orders, the nuncios in Kovno and Riga in August 1940 on Russian orders. Conversely, from 1943 there were also difficulties for the Vatican in the territories occupied by the Allies.

[189] Also R. A. Graham, "Voleva Hitler allontanare da Roma Pio XII?" *CivCatt* 123, 1 (1972), 319–27, 454–61, repeated in idem, *Il Vaticano,* 89–110.

followed on 8 September by the occupation of Rome by German troops and police. Then the foreign diplomats at the Vatican burned their papers; the Pope had a part of his documents hidden in his palace, and microfilm photographs of others sent to Washington in order to save them. The extraterritoriality of the Holy See was violated in December 1943 and February 1944 by police raids on political and racial refugees in papal buildings outside Vatican City.[190] But the Vatican state remained outside Hitler's direct clutches. The reasons for this are not evident. But it is indisputable that the Pope and his collaborators had to take this possibility into consideration on the basis of their information since 1941, and they were delivered from this anxiety only by the Allied occupation of Rome on 5 June 1944, although many restrictions and limitations were still protracted beyond the war.

Also the considerable, altogether rather successful exertions of papal policy to keep Rome as a city out of the events of the war[191] were not only conditioned by humanitarian reasons; at the same time they aimed at preserving the neutral independence of the papacy, not only for reasons of international law but still more from ecclesiastical motives. To the Pope belonged as a principal task of his office, in accord with the Church's understanding of itself, the preservation of the Church's unity. This presupposed unconditional loyalty of all Catholics, behind whichever warring front they stood, to the common Supreme Head of the Church, which could only be maintained if people knew that the Pope's independence guaranteed his impartiality. If Rome were involved in the direct action of the war, it was not to be expected that the Vatican's walls would thereafter protect its independence. Hence, as he himself wrote to the bishop of Berlin,[192] the "further[193] involvement of Rome in the war intensified to the intolerable" the excessive dangers to Church unity. This trial was spared the Church. Just as Benedict XV, Pius XII was therefore able to carry out a humanitarian, charitable activity and promote peace initiatives. In these two fields much was attempted but much or little was achieved in different ways.

EFFORTS FOR PEACE

The Pope's exertions for peace began immediately after his election and were continued to the end of the war with undiminished readiness. They took place on two different planes, in the area of teaching and in that of practical politics. In both fields the difference between the pontificates of Benedict XV and Pius XII became obvious.

[190] P. Duclos, 30f.
[191] Also A. Giovannetti, *Roma aperta città* (Milan 1962).
[192] B. Schneider, *Piusbriefe,* 291 (21 March 1944).
[193] The text alludes to air attacks on Rome.

Benedict XV developed no real doctrine of peace, no coherent system of detailed expressions on theoretical bases and aims, on practical assumptions and possibilities of a domestic and international order of peace. He had been content to admonish abstractly to peace in his public statements and put the rest aside for negotiations which should lead to a compromise. It was different with his successor in the Second World War. Already his first public announcement as Pope on 3 March 1939[194] contained the keywords of a universal program for peace. He again took up these points in his Easter homily of 1939,[195] further pursued it in his first encyclical, *Summi Pontificatus* (20 October 1939),[196] and put it in the center of his Christmas address of 1939,[197] in which the five basic conditions of a lasting international peace were discussed. All subsequent Christmas addresses, which were likewise planned with a view to the greatest possible publicity, treated pretty much in detail, and sometimes exclusively, problems of the ethics of peace—in 1940 the moral assumptions of a peaceful international order;[198] in 1941 the bases of a new international order;[199] in 1942 the basic elements of national and international community life;[200] in 1943 the moral presuppositions for a world peace among victors and vanquished;[201] in 1944 the bases of a true democracy;[202] in 1945 the Universal Church and universal peace.[203] On other public occasions, especially regularly on 2 June, he constantly returned to it.[204]

The Pope's concern was to develop the conditions, not for just any peace, but for a just and hence lasting peace.[205] On the basis of natural law he displayed the ideal of an international order which should guarantee security and existence equally to all nations and national minorities, as the personal dignity of the individual human being demanded. His view was not restricted to the legal but was directed to

[194] Text in *ADSS* 1, 97f.; *AAS* 31 (1939), 86–87.
[195] Text in *ADSS* 1, 104–10; *AAS* 31 (1939), 145–51; *UG* II, 1862–68.
[196] Draft of the parts referring to peace in *ADSS* 1, 315–23; text in *AAS* 31 (1939), 413–35; *UG* I, 5–40.
[197] Draft of the parts referring to peace in *ADSS* 1, 353–61; text in *AAS* 32 (1940), 5–13; *UG* II, 1869–82.
[198] Draft of the parts referring to peace in *ADSS* 4, 307–13; text in *AAS* 33 (1941), 5–14, *UG* II, 1824–38.
[199] Draft in *ADSS* 5, 337–50; text in *AAS* 34 (1942), 10–21; *UG* II, 1944–59.
[200] Extract in *ADSS* 7, 161–67; text in *AAS* 35 (1943), 9–24; *UG* I, 98–119.
[201] Draft of the parts referring to peace in *ADSS* 7, 732–34; text in *AAS* 36 (1944), 11–24; UG II, 1962–79.
[202] Text in *AAS* 37 (1945), 10–23; *UG* II, 1771–88.
[203] Text in *AAS* 38 (1946), 15–25; *UG* II, 2091–2105.
[204] The texts are most conveniently found in *AAS* and *UG* respectively.
[205] A concise but penetrating systematic treatment in P. Duclos, 70–103.

the economic order—distribution of wealth—and to society. Special attention was applied to the problems of disarmament. Decisively but also prudently were treated the bases of the law of treaties, by which treaties were to be maintained or, if necessary, to be revised—a recalling of the treaty of Versailles. Not least, the creating of supranational institutions with real competence was indispensable.

These instructive discussions by the Pope, in which actual everyday cases and principles were blended, clearly had a threefold aim. In the rather long run, material should here be circulated which would be further debated by the Church's social doctrine, by practical philosophy, and by the juristic disciplines.[206] Thereby Pius XII intended to provide guiding principles to the political thought of the faithful and at the same time influence concrete political decisions to the degree this should be possible. The fact that between his concepts and the peace aims of Hitler or Stalin there ran insurmountable abysses was beside the point. But there were also important differences and contradictions relative to the guiding ideas of the Western democracies. Thus on 1 September 1943 the Pope expressed himself, both from considerations of principle and for tactical reasons, against the formula of "unconditional surrender" of the Casablanca Conference of January 1943,[207] and he did not support the Atlantic Charter of 14 August 1941, which coincided with his ideas in important but not in all points.[208] The maxims of Pius XII's peace doctrine drew collectively "the consequences from the frustrated peace of 1919," according to J. Becker; its increased repetition in a harsher form should be avoided. While it had little influence on the postwar planning of the victorious powers, it did perhaps on the political development after 1945. To this degree it was not in vain.

On the other hand, with his exertions to prevent the outbreak of war and then Italy's entry into it and thereafter to bring about the ending of the conflict, Pius XII had as little success as Benedict XV, although the experience of 1914–18 must have been constantly present to the Pope, and he strove to avoid the mistakes of that period.

Three actions before the outbreak of the war must be mentioned: First, at the beginning of May 1939, probings for a five-power conference[209] for discussion and regulation of the present German-Polish and French-Italian oppositions. They found rejection among all

---

[206] A first detailed effort by an author close to the Curia: G. Gonella, *Presupposti di un ordine internazionale* (Vatican City 1942).
[207] *AAS* 35 (1943), 277–79, here 278; *UG* II, 2020–24, here 2022; draft also in *ADSS* 7, 600.
[208] Cf. *ADSS* 5, 17f.
[209] Poland, Germany, England, France, Italy.

those addressed and were canceled on 10 May.[210] Next, in close agreement with the English government, an extremely urgently formulated public appeal to reason and negotiation was presented on the evening of 24 August.[211] The essential statement came from a preliminary draft by the future Pope Paul VI and read: "Nothing is lost with peace. All can be lost with war."[212] Finally, on 30 August, there was the desperate attempt to gain Poland at the last minute for concessions to Germany,[213] which originated with Mussolini and was supported by England, as well as, on 31 August, a plea to the powers[214] for a just and peaceful solution of the conflict.[215] In a declaration personally originating with the Pope, *Osservatore Romano* on 13 September 1939 remarked that the Holy See had "exhausted all possibilities which" had offered "in any way still some hope for the preservation of peace or at least the excluding of the immediate danger of war."[216] This view was shared by the British government.[217] The collapse of the papal efforts for maintaining peace was mostly caused by the policy of Hitler, who was unimpressed by reasonable motives in the framework of a possible revision of the Treaty of Versailles. Polish intransigence in August 1939 made the German dictator's game easier.

Meanwhile, on 1 September 1939 Italy proclaimed itself "not at war." The Curia had gone to great pains to nail Mussolini down to this and for this purpose assured itself of the support of Roosevelt, who at Christmas 1939 had entered into diplomatic relations with the Pope.[218] The Vatican's internal démarches, strengthened by spectacular public happenings—on 21 December the visit of the King of Italy to the Pope;[219] on 28 December, the return visit of the Pope to the King;[220] on 5 May 1940, the Pope's homily at Santa Maria sopra Minerva[221]—and a personal letter from the Pope to Mussolini on 24 April 1940[222] were unable to keep the Italian dictator aloof from the suggestion which the victorious march of the German armies in France exercised in the way of

[210] *ADSS* 1, 139f.
[211] *ADSS* 1, 230–38 (with the different drafts).
[212] B. Schneider, "Der Friedensappell Papst Pius' XII, vom. 24. August 1939," *AHP* 6 (1968), 415–24.
[213] *ADSS* 1, 263f.
[214] To Germany, England, France, Spain, Italy, Poland.
[215] *ADSS* 1, 271f.
[216] *ADSS* 1, 303.
[217] *ADSS* 1, 299
[218] *ADSS* 1, 348f. (Roosevelt to Pius XII, 23 December 1939).
[219] *ADSS* 1, 345f.
[220] *ADSS* 1, 362f.
[221] *ADSS* 1, 437f.
[222] *ADSS* 1, 425f.

anticipation. Italy's declaration of war on 10 June 1940 confirmed the dread that had been pervading the Vatican for months.

Immediately after the French armistice of 25 June 1940 the Pope formally made preliminary soundings in England, Germany, and Italy in regard to possible negotiations for a "just and honorable peace."[223] Behind these stood the wish at least to preserve England intact, before it could be overrun by a German invasion, as a European counterweight to German hegemony.[224] When this preliminary probing found consent in none of those concerned,[225] the diplomatic possibilities of the Vatican were at first exhausted. Whether in May and June 1940 the West had lost only a battle, as Churchill and de Gaulle said, or the war, as Mussolini felt, or whether this question could not yet be answered, as presumably Pétain and Franco thought, was unclear.[226] How the Pope evaluated the views cannot be known in detail, because on that point there are hardly any sources. The editors of the papal acts warn, not by chance, that one must be cautious with judgments concerning the secret considerations of the Pope.[227] In the period between the end of the war in France and the beginning of the war in Russia he presumably placed his hopes rather on a change in domestic politics in Germany than on a military victory of England over Hitler.[228]

With the German attack on Russia on 22 June 1941 and the Japanese attack on the United States on 7 December 1941, the acts of war expanded into a global world war. At first there were no diplomatic possibilities of peace. Politically significant was a papal decision in September 1941 which, giving a theologically not unproblematic interpretation to Pius XI's Communism encyclical *Divini Redemptoris* of 19 March 1937, made it possible to overcome the hesitations of conscience of North American Catholics in regard to military support of the Soviet Union.[229] The Curia did not share the illusions in regard to Russian policy[230] which underlay later American planning for peace. "I am surprised," noted the secretary of the Congregation for Extraordinary Ecclesiastical Affairs, Domenico Tardini, on 22 September 1942, "that such clear matters are not seen [simply] by governments and by

[223] *ADSS* 1, 497f.
[224] Cf. R. A. Graham, "La missione di W. d'Ormesson in Vaticano nel 1940. Intervista inedita," *CivCatt* 124, 4 (1973), 145–48, here 146f.
[225] *ADSS* 1, 500f. (England), 501f. (Italy).
[226] Cf. *ADSS* 4, 3.
[227] Ibid. 1, 98.
[228] Cf. ibid. 4, 58.
[229] Cf. Tardini's notes of 12, 13, 14 and 15 September with the instruction to Cicognani, 20 September 1941 (*ADSS* 5, 202–6, 208f., 215–18, 240f.).
[230] Cf. Taylor's memorandum of 22 September 1942 (*ADSS* 5, 694f.).

such important politicians."[231] As though Communist Russia after victory would return like a brave little lamb into the family of European states! "If Stalin wins the war," he stated to Taylor, "he will become the lion that devours all of Europe." Neither Hitler nor Stalin could be peaceable, satisfied members of the European family of nations. In the smaller states, situated diagonally along the war fronts, people shared the Curia's anxieties since the German defeat at Stalingrad in the winter of 1942–43 and would have been glad to steer toward a compromise peace under papal mediation before Russia became overmighty.[232] The Secretariat of State saw no concrete hopes for this in the spring of 1943[233] and had to be content with opposing Allied appeasement in regard to Russia[234] with the facts known to it and the cares derived therefrom, which were proved later to be correct.[235] This did not mean relying instead on Hitler's Germany, which since 22 June 1942 rejected the Holy See as a partner in discussions and negotiations for the area outside the "Old Reich,"[236] after it had not recognized the German annexations as definitive.[237] Apart from other weighty reasons, such an attitude was forbidden as a result of the persecution of the Catholic Church in Hitler's entire sphere of dominion, worst of all in Poland.[238] "Two dangers threaten European and Christian civilization—Nazism and Communism. Both are materialistic, antireligious, totalitarian, tyrannical, cruel, and militaristic," declared Tardini to the English *chargé d'affaires* on 30 May 1943.[239] Only if the Second World War eliminates both dangers can the future Europe find peace. If either of them survives the war, "a peaceful and ordered coexistence of European nations" would be "impossible," and in the not distant future a new, still worse war would be faced.

[231] *ADSS* 5, 694, n. 2.
[232] An attempt by Switzerland was spontaneously agreed to by the diplomats of the Lithuanian and Polish governments-in-exile, neutral Spain, Greece, and Brazil against the Axis warring powers, as well as of Hungary on the side of the Axis warring powers; cf. *ADSS* 7, 225–28, 234.
[233] *ADSS* 7, 258 (instruction to the Berne nuncio, 3 March 1943).
[234] Cf. the English aide-mémoire of 4 March 1943 (*ADSS* 7, 259–61) and the note of 20 April 1943 (ibid. 7, 306–9).
[235] Cf. *ADSS* 7, 277f. (Maglione, 27 March 1943), 281f. (Tardini, 1 March 1943), 378–80 (idem, 30 May 1943).
[236] Text in *ADAP* E III, 40–42.
[237] Note of 18 January 1942 in D. Albrecht II, 116–30. For the whole problem cf. D. Albrecht, "Die Politische Klausel des Reichskonkordats in den deutsch-vatikanischen Beziehungen 1936–1943." idem, ed., *Kirche,* 128–70.
[238] The often printed, comprehensive Vatican note on these proceedings, of 2 March 1943, now (with commentary) in D. Albrecht II, 135–49.
[239] *ADSS* 7, 378.

The Vatican could not translate this insight into direct foreign policy because it lacked the means for putting it into effect and the preserving of the principle of impartiality and noninterference in domestic political problems became ever more difficult. This also determined the attitude of the Holy See toward Italy. It was able to avoid becoming involved in the preparations for the fall of Mussolini, who on 12 May 1943[240] completely shut his eyes[241] to a very clear papal hint. A firsthand document, prepared as early as June, for the King of Italy was spared the Curia through a favorable turn of circumstances.[242] The Holy See participated only on the periphery in the negotiating of the Allied armistice with Italy.[243]

It is all the more astounding to "assess the extraordinary readiness of the Pope to incur risks" as J. Becker expresses it; in the winter of 1939–40 he was in intimate contact with the German military opposition, whose ideas he sent on to England, and functioned as connecting link.[244] In 1944 also he still had contacts with this part of the German opposition.[245] Perhaps toward the turn of the years 1943–44 the Pope's expectation was based on this, that perhaps "after not too long a time" the responsible statemen would listen to the peace proposal of his 1943 Christmas address, "which then, God willing, would grow into a peace mediation."[246] This did not happen, for the opposition was unable to topple Hitler. But "another Germany" was a presupposition that could not be waived[247] for a realization of the papal peace idea by means of concrete politics in the last years of the war, although the individual details for 1944–45 are still secret until the publication of the acts of this period.

PAPAL MEASURES OF ASSISTANCE

The cruelties of the Second World War, not restricted to the military conduct of the war, by far surpassed the horizon of ideas originating in 1914–18. The Pope understood this as a challenge, which must not be

[240] Ibid. 7, 330f.
[241] Ibid. 7, 334.
[242] Cf. ibid. 7, 37–39, and especially 431–35 (report of Borgongini Duca, 17· June 1943).
[243] Cf. ADSS 7, 56f.
[244] H. C. Deutsch, Verschwörung gegen den Krieg. Der Widerstand in den Jahren 1939–1940. (Munich 1969) (English: Minneapolis 1968).
[245] P. Hoffman, Widerstand, Staatsstreich, Attentat. Der Kampf der Opposition gegen Hitler (Munich 1969), 347.
[246] Cf. the expunged passage in the letter to Bertram, 6 January 1944, in B. Schneider, Piusbriefe, 266, n. q.
[247] Also, most recently, A. Martini in CC 128, 2 (1977), 232ff.

evaded. The question was not *whether* one should help, but *how* one could. In this regard, no role was played, as also under Benedict XV, by the religious, ethnic, or national background of those concerned, and the Vatican began, it goes without saying, from its experiences with the organization of measures of help of the First World War. However, there appeared entirely new forms and types of needs of gigantic proportions, in regard to which nothing could be achieved with the hitherto customary means. Time after time this forced an effort to achieve something in new and different ways. There was no lack of readiness to assist. But there survived an oppressive difference between being willing and being able as an historical experience from this epoch, in which aid for the politically and racially persecuted became necessary as a new problem for the Western world; for it there were no regulations of international law and no precedent by which to orient oneself.

The territorial war order of The Hague of 18 October 1907, supplemented in the Geneva Agreement on 29 July 1929, had fixed clear norms for the treatment of prisoners of war and had entrusted the implementation to the International Red Cross, but this did not exclude supplementary actions of other institutions. As in the First World War, from the start the Vatican would have gladly participated in the search for the missing and in the transmission of news about prisoners of war and civilian internees to their families. Under the responsibility of the later Pope Paul VI, who was then *Sostituto,* an "information bureau" was set up in Section II of the Secretariat of State in 1939; it was directed by Msgr. Alexander Evreinoff and was competent for measures of that sort.[248] However, its possibilities of action were limited; for Germany and Russia refused and thwarted all cooperation. And so the "information bureau" had to limit its activity to the prisoners of states allied with Germany, which observed the tradional rules of war—Italy, Slovakia, Hungary, Rumania—and also, even though here not continuously accepted,[249] of the Western Allies and Japan. Corresponding to the course of the war, it developed its chief activity, whose happy impact on those affected can scarcely be overestimated, after 1943[250]

Furthermore, there was erected in November 1941, likewise under Montini's responsibility, an "Assistance Commission" (*Commissione per i Soccorsi*) within Section II of the Secretariat of State, whose secretary

---

[248] Report of activity: *La Chiesa e la guerra. Documentazione dell'Opera dell'Ufficio Informazioni del Vaticano* (Vatican City 1944).

[249] Cf., for the difficulties with England, *ADSS* 8, 12–14.

[250] The "information bureau" published a monthly bulletin, *Ecclesia*. Statistics for June 1941 to the end of April 1943 in *ADSS* 9, 603f. The acts of the "information bureau" are not generally included in the *ADSS;* cf. *ADSS* 6, 9.

was Prelate Mario Brini.[251] It was competent for the properly charitable measures, and this forced it to ever new improvisation and work techniques. In other respects, the entire well-coordinated apparatus, which the Curia and especially the Secretariat of State displayed, was requisitioned for these measures of assistance, so far as they were appropriate in individual cases. A complete history of these undertakings has not yet been written. However, the documents published in recent years, for the period to the end of 1943, make it impressively clear that a very considerable part of the diplomatic activities of the Vatican in the Second World War, despite all the daily failures, was unflinchingly put at the selfless service of these charitable exertions. The Pope intentionally insisted as little as possible on it from without, because in most cases—in contrast, for example, to the present-day possibilities of effectiveness by Amnesty International—publicity impaired or even destroyed the chances of success. This affected especially those most in need of help—the Jews. If in the official sphere of activity of the Holy See for 1939 there was still mention of Vatican aid for "persons" who "were regarded as racially non-Aryan and hence were punished by laws of certain nations," this ceased for the succeeding years, after the German ambassador at the Vatican had called Berlin's attention to it in January 1940.[252] The more Hitler's murderous grip closed on the Jews, the more laconic became the particulars from the Secretariat of State. "The Holy See did, does, and will do all that is within its power" was the stereotyped information from the Secretariat of State.[253] This was not an alibi for indifference or inactivity but the indispensable presupposition for the efforts, renewed every day and perseveringly undertaken, to bring help whenever even only the slightest opportunities presented themselves. The number of cases is legion. Here only some outlines can be indicated.

The attempts to help the politically and racially persecuted in Germany and Italy went back to the days of Pius XI.[254] They were continued under the new Pope. Once there was a question of not quite one thousand individual cases.[255] In addition, help for those wishing to emigrate required great pains, in which the German *Sankt Raphaelsverein* in Hamburg played a substantial role until its forcible dissolution on

[251] *ADSS* 6, 9.
[252] Cf. ibid. 6, 10.
[253] Cf. ibid. 9, 39.
[254] Cf. Pacelli's circular of 30 November 1938 and his telegram to Cardinal Hinsley of London and the letter of Pius XI to five American archbishops of 10 January 1939 (*ADSS* 6, 49f., 539, n. 3, 50f.).
[255] *ADSS* 6, 23.

26 June 1941.[256] Not least of all, there was a question of the effort to impede the "racial" legislation of states in the German sphere of influence or, if that was not possible, to effect modifications in the practical enforcement. In Germany, of course, influence was without prospects,[257] but not in Italy. The presence of the Holy See contributed to the fact that the Italian Jewish policy throughout the war was in very favorable contrast to the German: up to his downfall, Mussolini did not release any Jews for deportation to the extermination camps of the S.S., and the Social Republic of Salò, to the extent that it could function, preserved this orientation in principle.[258] In Rumania, supported by the stipulations of the concordat, relatively much was accomplished;[259] Hungary, despite racial legislation, treated the Jews the least inhumanely;[260] in Slovakia the Vatican chargé d' affaires had at first to limit himself to observing.[261] The curial policy had especially in view the situation of baptized Jews or of Jews married to Catholics, since they were the farthest excluded from the aid given by the organizations of believing Jews.

After the outbreak of war the worst fate first affected the Poles, not only in the German-occupied area: in the Russian-occupied part the situation was scarcely less horrible. However, this area was almost hermetically sealed off from the rest of the world. News hardly got through, and Vatican help was completely impossible. The Curia did not succeed in learning anything substantial of the fate of those deported from there—one reckons with about 2 million—not even with the aid of the diplomatic representatives of other powers in Moscow.[262]

In spite of ceaseless difficulties, the intelligence connections with the German-occupied part of Poland were better. In the winter of 1939–40 the Curia hoped to be able to help with food and clothing; but at the end of 1940 the Secretariat of State had to admit that the German authorities had intentionally and successfully boycotted the papal

[256] Also cf. L. F. Reutter, *Die Kirche als Fluchthelfer im Dritten Reich* (Recklinghausen 1971).
[257] On the visit of the German foreign minister in 1940, the most recent is M. Clauss, "Der Besuch Ribbentrops im Vatikan," *ZKG* 87 (1976), 54–64.
[258] Cf. *ADSS* 6, 22; 9, 36, as well as R. de Felice, *Storia degli ebrei*, 447–50, 463–67.
[259] Cf. *ADSS* 9, 27–32; A. Martini, "La S. Sede e gli ebrei della Romania durante la seconda guerra mondiale," *CC* 112, 3 (1961), 449–63.
[260] Cf. *ADSS* 6, 24; R. A. Graham, "Pio XII e gli ebrei di Ungheria nel 1944," idem, *Il Vaticano*, 241–48 (first in English in *Historical Records and Studies* 50 [1965], 5–26).
[261] Cf. *ADSS* 6, 24; 8, 45–47; 9, 22–27; F. Cavalli, "La S. Sede contro le deportazioni degli ebrei dalla Slovacchia durante la seconda guerra mondiale," *CC* 112, 3 (1961), 1–18.
[262] *ADSS* 6, 28f.; 8, 53–55; 9, 48–50.

initiatives.[263] Matters were otherwise in relation to the Polish refugees in other countries. In Hungary, Rumania, France, and Italy the Vatican, with the financial aid of American Catholics, could at first do something, but in Germany, on the contrary, it could do little.[264] Even in Spain, basically amenable to Vatican requests, it required very much effort and patience to assist the Polish refugees.[265]

The year 1941, in which the war essentially altered its countenance, also signified a caesura for the assistance measures of the Holy See. The restricted possibilities of emigration from Europe almost entirely ceased.[266] Vatican exertions for aid from overseas for the hungry civilian populations of Belgium and Greece were wrecked on the English blockade.[267] "Deportation" of Jews now became a new catchword of papal anxieties. To prevent it or at least to limit and restrict its volume became a chief item of papal assistance efforts, even where there was still no information on the mass-produced organized murders in the extermination camps.

In the present state of knowledge what was thereby accomplished cannot be put in precise figures, and in consideration of the situation of the sources will perhaps never be possible. One may proceed, in regard to a total number of victims, to a high of about 5 million.[268] In addition, some nine hundred fifty thousand are said to have survived.[269] The individual numbers from which this total sum is arrived at may be open to criticism, but hardly the order of magnitude. If it is estimated that, of the nine hundred fifty thousand saved, some 70 to 90 percent owed their life[270] to measures taken by the Catholic Church, as the specific numbers are also subject to discussion in this case, on the whole, however, this result must be striking. In view of the number of murdered, the number of the saved is depressingly small. But behind it

---

[263] Ibid 6, 492–96, as well as the survey, ibid, 25–28. For the further Polish policy of the Vatican, basic is ADSS 3, I. II, with detailed introduction; cf. also R. A. Graham, Il Vaticano, 207–20.

[264] ADSS 6, 29–31.

[265] Cf. ibid. 8, 64–67.

[266] Ibid. 8, 16ff.

[267] Ibid. 8, 58–64; A. Martini, "La fama in Grecia nel 1941 nella testimonianza dei documenti inediti vaticani," CivCatt 118, 1 (1967), 213–27.

[268] G. Reitlinger, Die Endlösung. Hitlers Versuch der Ausrottung der Juden Europas 1939–1945 (Berlin 1956), 573; English edition 1953; cf. I. Arndt and W. Scheffler, "Organisierter Massenmord in nationalsozialistischen Vernichtungslagern," VZG 24 (1976), 112–35. They start with a figure of more than 3 million who were killed by being gassed.

[269] P. E. Lapide, Rom und die Juden (Freiburg 1967), 185, estimates "at least a million."

[270] Thus ibid., 188; cf. 359, n. 189. J. Chevalier, 133f., accepts these figures.

stands a desire of the Catholic Church under Pius XII to stand up for every individual human life, which cannot be minimized.

In individual cases the measures differed from country to country and also changed in the course of time. On the whole it can be said that the success of the papal rescue exertions was the greater the more the political influence of the Holy See continued on the government of the territory concerned; in other words: the less direct the possibilities of Hitler's grasp were, so much the more could the Pope accomplish. In Slovakia, Hungary, Rumania, Croatia,[271] and especially in Italy relatively much succeeded. In Rome, which was characterized as typical of the alleged indolence of Pacelli in regard to the annihilation of the Jews,[272] the quick cessation of the celebrated police raid of 16 October 1943 demonstrably goes back to a personal initiative of the Pope.[273]

In summary, today it may be held that the papal measures of assistance of the Second World War, accomplished under entirely different difficulties, need not at all fear comparison with the time of Benedict XV.

THE POPE'S "SILENCE"

In the debate of the 1960s over the Pope's conduct in the Second World War there was a question of his alleged silence at the extermination of millions of Jews. In this connection the expression "silence" was supposed to suggest a reprehensible omission of possible and/or necessary actions, while the opposite—"to speak," "to say," "to protest"—referred to morally mandated sympathy, signified willingness to help, or even stood symbolically for "help." This terminology is not suited to characterize the real problem to which the Hochhuth Debate,[274] in which the picture of Pius XII was distorted into caricature, can point: It is the question in what manner a Pope is bound, by virtue of his office, to bear witness against the violation of elementary human rights, such as the genocide of the Second World War. This question was itself

---

[271] *ADSS* 9, 32–34.

[272] Thus Hochhuth (because of the Pope's avarice) and S. Friedlaender (because of the Pope's anti-Communism).

[273] *ADSS* 9, 509f. and 510, n. 2: Hudal's letter of noon, 16 October 1943 to General Stahel, who brought about the halting of the raid, was suggested by Carlo Pacelli on orders of the Pope. On the matter the most recent is O. Chadwick, "Weizsäcker, the Vatican and the Jews of Rome," *Journal of Ecclesiastical History* 28 (1977), 179–99; cf. also R. A. Graham, "La strana condotta di E. von Weizsäcker, ambasciatore del Reich in Vaticano," *CivCatt* 121, 2 (1970), 455–74; repeated in idem, *Il Vaticano*, 49–73.

[274] Cf. above, n. 169.

posed at that time;[275] he was confronted with it by others as well;[276] and even in war he knew it had to be settled "with painful difficulty."[277] The decisions of the Pope were taken neither blindly nor easily, but were pondered responsibly. For him the alternatives were not simply "to speak or keep silent." The question amounted to much more: how clear *must* be the word which was offered by virtue of office, how concrete *may* it be if the consequences are taken into account.

It was a curial tradition to speak, not of the erring, but of the errors, not of people, but of the mistakes of people.[278] Pacelli's theological conception was in accord with this tradition. It amounted to this, that the Pope had to formulate the general and the fundamental, while it pertained to the bishops to translate the principle into the concrete, on the spot, with regard for all circumstances. This suggested to the Pope to condemn the false ideological directions and the violations of rights without "directly naming their proponents or perpetrators," according to J. Becker. This was the line which Pius XII followed in his many public utterances—every expression about peace was linked with these themes.

How strong his anxiety was about whether in view of the unleashed terror he was satisfying the duties of office by this behavior can be known from that fact that he several times clearly considered proceeding beyond the general condemnations. I must utter real "words of fire" on "the frightful things which are occurring in Poland," he hurled at the Italian ambassador on 13 May 1940. Only the knowledge that the fate of the unhappy Poles would then become still worse held him back from doing so.[279] The intention of preventing worse was "one of the reasons why We impose restrictions on Ourselves in Our utterances," he wrote to the bishop of Berlin on 30 April 1943.[280] The Pope and his collaborators were, on the basis of their experiences with National Socialism, firmly convinced that a flaming papal protest would not put a stop to the murders but would increase their tempo and magnitude and at the same time destroy the remaining possibilities of diplomatic action in favor of the Jews in states such as Hungary and Rumania.

In this regard, the Secretariat of State was informed relatively early of

---

[275] *ADSS* 1, 454f.
[276] Ibid. 3, II, 633–36 (Radonski to Maglione, London, 14 September 1942). Von Preysing's inquiry of 6 March 1943 (B. Schneider, *Piusbriefe,* 239, n. 1) moved in the same direction.
[277] Pius XII to Archbishop Frings, 3 March 1944 (B. Schneider, *Piusbriefe,* 280).
[278] P. Duclos, 21, n. 5.
[279] *ADSS* 1, 455.
[280] B. Schneider, *Piusbriefe,* 240.

the manner in which the murder of the Jews was organized and, in contrast to many others,[281] trusted these reports. Communications from Jewish sources that the deportation meant for many of those affected a sure death sentence were obtained from Pressburg and Budapest[282] in the spring of 1942. In December the Polish ambassador-in-exile at the Vatican correctly concluded from the fact that the aged, sick, women, and children were deported that the aim of deportation was not "workers' camps"—whatever persons might mean by that—but places erected especially for the "killing of persons in various ways."[283] On 7 March 1943 the Vatican *chargé d'affaires* at Pressburg finally sent the report of a parish priest, who had credibly learned that deported Jews were killed by gassing; the corpses were used for making soap.[284] Perhaps this report was already on hand when the Secretariat of State on 3 April 1943 laconically telegraphed to the apostolic delegate in Washington: "The Holy See continues its exertions for the Jews," after the delegate had been asked by three rabbis to induce the Pope to a "public appeal" which might put a halt to the systematic extermination of the Jews.[285] Privately the Secretariat of State thought of this: "A public appeal would be inappropriate"; Germany had to be prevented from taking it as an occasion "to carry out even more rigorously the anti-Jewish measures in the areas occupied by it and exercise new, stronger pressures" on the Jewish policy of the satellite nations.[286] On 5 May 1943 an entry in the documents of the Secretariat of State spoke of the "frightful situation" of the Jews in Poland and mentioned "gas chambers."[287]

Against this background must be understood the sharp and impressively composed Christmas address of 1942, which proclaimed a catalogue of the inalienable basic rights of every person and thought explicitly of the "hundred thousands of persons," who, "with no guilt of their own, partly only because of their nationality or race (*stirpe*)," were delivered up "to quick or slow death" ("destinate alla morte o ad un progressivo deperimento")[288] Privately the Pope thus characterized the

---

[281] Cf. L. de Jong, "Die Niederlande und Auschwitz," *VZG* 17 (1969), 1–16, with striking examples to prove that the extermination camps first became a psychological reality when they no longer existed.
[282] *ADSS* 8, 453 (Burzio report, Pressburg, 9 March 1942); 470 (Rotta report, Budapest, 20 March 1942).
[283] *ADSS* 8, 755 (19 December 1942).
[284] Ibid. 9, 177f., n. 6.
[285] Ibid. 9, 206f., 207. n. 3.
[286] Ibid. 9, 217.
[287] Ibid. 9, 274.
[288] *AAS* 35 (1943), 23; *UG* I, 118.

purpose and reaction of this word on the extermination of the Jews: "It was brief but it was well understood."[289] In the address of 2 June 1943 he repeated his condemnation with a quite similar formulation.[290]

Hence the Pope also "spoke," but the "speaking" was not his chief or exclusive means in the struggle against Hitler's Jewish policy. After clear condemnation he followed the ethical demand of conscience, but predominant for him was the ethically responsible aspect that he must avoid choosing a form of provocation which would not bring a halt to *the* evil but would increase the evils: The extermination of the Jews could not be undone by a public appeal, but perhaps drastic retaliation against Jews, Catholics, and the Church lay in the logic of the Nazi system of government. Conversely, the papal policy preserved for the Holy See the opportunity to save the Jews in the future. As proof that this opportunity was effectively used, "the warmest recognition of his saving work" was at the time "expressed by the Jewish chief centers"[291] to the Pope.

[289] B. Schneider, *Piusbriefe,* 242 (to von Preysing, 30 April 1943).
[290] *AAS* 35 (1943), 165–71, here 167; *UG* II, 1909–17, here 1912f.; *ADSS* 7 does not contain the draft of this part of the address.
[291] Pius XII to von Preysing, 30 April 1943 (B. Schneider, *Piusbriefe,* 242). *ADSS* 9, 59–61, provides a list of the expressions of gratitude, then either in the Vatican or otherwise known, from the Jewish side.

CHAPTER 4

*The Second Vatican Council**

John XXIII: Summoning and Preparation for the Council

The convoking of the Second Vatican Council was the action of Pope John XXIII. His election, after a brief conclave (25–28 October 1958), seemed at first the solution of a transition or at least of a perplexity. But it soon became evident that it was a decisive turning point in the history of the Church.

Angelo Giuseppe Roncalli was born in Sotto il Monte (Province of Bergamo) on 25 November 1881, the fourth of fourteen children of the farmer Battista (d. 1935) and his wife Marianna Mazzola (d. 1939), and was baptized the same day by the parish priest Rebuzzini; his godfather

* Hubert Jedin

was his devout great-uncle Zaverio.[1] After attending the minor and the major seminaries at Bergamo from 1892 to 1900, he continued his theological studies at the Roman Seminary of Sant'Apollinare from 1901 to 1905, interrupted by one year of military service at Bergamo, "un vero purgatorio," as he wrote to the rector of the seminary, V. Bugarini. From his professor of church history, Benigni, he received the advice, "Read little but well"; of his superiors, the vice-rector Spolverini was closest to him. His Roman studies were crowned by the doctorate in theology on 13 July 1904 and ordination to the priesthood on 10 August 1904. After the completing of his studies, he participated in the fall of 1905 in a pilgrimage to the Holy Land. Then Giacomo Maria Radini Tedeschi, appointed bishop of Bergamo, took him along as secretary to his home diocese of Bergamo, where from October 1906 he also lectured on church history in the seminary and later on patrology and apologetics and edited the ecclesiastical journal, *La vita diocesana.* At that time he began the editing of the visitation documents of Saint Charles Borromeo in the diocese of Bergamo, the last volume of which could, however, not appear until 1957. In a memorial lecture on the occasion of the three-hundredth anniversary of the death of Cardinal Cesare Baronio he extolled the compiler of the *Annals* of ecclesiastical history as the renewer of historical studies.

After the death in 1914 of Radini Tedeschi, who as no other had formed his first priestly years, he wrote his biography. During the war (1915–18) he served as a military chaplain; it was probably the experiences then gained which induced the bishop to entrust to him, as chaplain of the seminary, the spiritual direction of the theologians returning from the field (1918–20). Then he went back to Rome for four years as president of the Italian work of the Propagation of the Faith. On 3 March 1925 he became apostolic visitor in Bulgaria and on 19 March was ordained as titular archbishop of Areopolis in San Carlo al Corso; as his motto he selected "Obedientia et Pax," Baronius's motto.

The position of the visitor at Sofia was in several respects not easy: the Queen was a daughter of the King of Italy, and hence a Catholic; the King was Greek Orthodox; the authority of the visitor over the

---

[1] For the life and character of Pope John XXIII the following especially were consulted: the notes edited by his secretary, Loris Capovilla, during the retreats and days of recollection in the *Giornale dell'Anima,* the fragment of an autobiography begun in 1959 (419–28), and the attached chronology (pp. XXXI–XLIV). A *curriculum vitae: AAS* 50 (1958), 902. On the Pope's choice of a name, Schwaiger in *AKR* 132 (1963), 7: the number XXIII presupposes that the Popes of the Pisan Obedience, Alexander V and John XXIII, were considered illegitimate, although the later Alexanders—Alexander VI to VIII—took the first named into account in their enumerations.

approximately fifty thousand Catholics was not sharply defined. He saw himself reduced to an eremitical life, which did not gratify his need for activity, and he complained of "acute, intime sofferenze." After ten difficult years he was, on 24 November 1934, named apostolic delegate in Turkey and Greece and at the same time administrator of the vicariate apostolic of Istanbul; he thereby obtained greater pastoral duties. This activity satisfied him: "I feel young in body and mind," he wrote in 1939 in his spiritual diary. The delegate paid a visit to the ecumenical patriarch on 27 May 1939, spent a rather long time at Athens, especially after Greece was afflicted by war, and visited Syria and Palestine.

When, after the retreat of the German troops from France and the victory of the Allies, General de Gaulle demanded the removal of thirty-three bishops who had been adherents of the Vichy regime, Roncalli was made nuncio to France on 22 December 1944. He achieved a compromise. After the concluding of the armistice he instituted at Chartres theological courses for German theological students who were prisoners of war. Made cardinal on 12 January 1953 and three days later named patriarch of Venice, he felt fortunate to be able to live completely his episcopal-pastoral duties. The small area of the diocese permitted him frequent journeys, including visits to the Marian pilgrimage sites of Lourdes, Einsiedeln, Mariazell, Fátima, and Czestochowa.

The new Pope's personality was stamped by his ancestral home and his spiritual instructors, Rebuzzini, Spolverini, and Radini Tedeschi; his spirituality was thoroughly traditionally Catholic. His spiritual diary indicates that he frequently read *The Imitation of Christ* and regularly made the Ignatian exercises. The rosary was a fixed ingredient of his strictly regulated order of the day: praying of the breviary, Mass, a half-hour's meditation, weekly confession. His spiritual models were Francis de Sales and Philip Neri and, as a pastor, Charles Borromeo: as regards the otherwise highly venerated Baronius, it struck him that he never laughed. The craftiness of the peasant was in him united to the humor of the peasant; of no Pope since Benedict XIV have so many anecdotes been handed down. The young professor of church history unambiguously held himself aloof from Modernism, but he still did not thereby escape the suspicion expressed concerning him in the Benigni Circle and remained convinced that positive theology must be more intensively pursued than was then usual in Italy. Different from that of Pius X, whom he revered in his lifetime as a model pastor, his outlook for the task of the mission and for union was broadened by activity in the work of the propagation of the faith and the two decades in the Middle East. The other task of the Church, to work for a "better world," was for him not an item of a program but a foregone conclusion resulting from his simple origin; the admonition of Father Lombardi to the bishops of the region of Venetia in the retreat of 1955, to be concerned for the social question, would hardly have been needed by him personally, "I am one of you," he exclaimed to the faithful of a Roman suburban community; to his brothers and sisters he gave the advice, "You do well in living even more frugally," and he himself wanted "to be born poor and to die poor." Throughout his life bound to his Bergamo homeland, as nuncio he obtained the family's original fifteenth-century house as a place of holiday and rest; he firmly repelled any advancement in status of his brothers, sisters, and nephews, who lived in modest circumstances.

Although in his youth Pope John had lived at Rome a rather long time and had then been active in the service of the Curia for almost three decades, he was no "curialist." He never regarded himself as a curial official, and constantly desired to be only a "good shepherd"; it was no accident that in the first year of his pontificate, on 1 August 1959, he devoted an encyclical to the Curé d'Ars, to him the "imago sacerdotis." Before his departure for the conclave, he had exclaimed to the seminarians of his diocese: "The Church is young, it remains, as constantly in its history, amenable to change." The statement is that of a program. As a church historian, familiar with the historical change of the Church in a constantly changing world, Pope John was convinced that the Church must adapt its preaching, organization, and pastoral methods to the fundamentally changed world, and for this he coined the much disputed notion of *aggiornamento*.[2] In an effort to realize it, he convoked the Council.

In the presence of the cardinals gathered for the stational Mass in San Paolo fuori le mura on 25 January 1959 he announced a Roman diocesan synod and an ecumenical council. This announcement was certainly prepared for by his development, but in no sense was its result. Both in private conversations and in the opening address of the Roman diocesan synod on 24 January 1960 he understood it as the challenge of God, *divinum incitamentum,* but in no way was it the implementation of a long prepared plan. There is no evidence that he resumed the project of a general council pondered by Pius XII.[3] The Pope, who had nothing

---

[2] In defining the content of *aggiornamento* one must begin with the literal meaning of *aggiornare,* which the widespread *Dizionario della lingua italiana* of Zingarelli (p. 33) gives as *mettere al corrente libri, registri.* However, there can be no doubt that in the mouth of John XXIII not only an adaptation to the age but also an inner renewal was meant, as Urs von Balthasar, Ratzinger, et al. have rightly noted.

[3] G. Caprile, "Pio XII e un nuovo progetto di concilio ecumenico," *CivCatt* 117, 2 (1966), 209–27.

more in mind than to carry out the will of God, recognized the *kairos* and followed the inspiration of the Holy Spirit.

The announcement of an ecumenical council operated as a blare of trumpets, within and almost even more powerfully outside the Church. It was forgotten that, in Catholic usage and also in canon law, "Concilium oecumenicum" was the designation of the general councils embracing the whole Church; the Pope intended to convoke a general council of the Catholic Church, but from the start, and at the beginning more decidedly than in later stages, there moved before his view a participation, somehow constituted, of the Christians separated from Rome as a first step toward Church unity; he could hardly have been thinking of a great union-council of representatives of all Christian Churches and ecclesial communities. *Osservatore Romano,* reporting the talk at San Paolo, spoke of the Pope's aim "to invite the separated communities to the quest of unity." That there was no thought of a formal invitation to the separated Churches to full participation first appeared definitively from a press conference held by Cardinal Secretary of State Tardini on 30 October 1959; in it there came forth for the first time the plan of inviting the separated Churches to send official observers.

Meanwhile, the Pope had set for the future council its task of renewal within the Church. In the first session of the Antepreparatory Commission (*Commissio antepraeparatoria*), established on 17 May 1959, he declared on 30 June 1959 that the Church strives, "loyal to the holy principles on which it is built and the unchangeable doctrine which the Divine Founder entrusted to it . . . with courageous energy to strengthen again its life and its unity, even with regard to all circumstances and demands of the day," hence both inner renewal and entry into the problems of the age. At the same time he announced in the encyclical *Ad Petri cathedram* the revision of canon law; the goal of his pontificate was the proclaiming of the truth, peace among peoples, and the unity of the Church in doctrine, government, and worship.

The preparation of the council began when the bishops—all together 2,594—and 156 superiors of religious institutes and also the Catholic universities and faculties were called upon by Secretary of State Tardini on 18 June 1959 to submit suggestions for the program of consultation. The 2,812 *postulate* thereupon sent in were sifted by the Antepreparatory Commission and turned over to the competent curial offices, which for their part composed the suggestions and admonitions (*Proposita* and *Monita*). After the sifting of the material was completed, the motu proprio *Superno Dei nutu* of 5 June 1960 introduced the proximate preparation.

The motu proprio determined for the first time the name of the future council: The Second Vatican Council. Then ten "preparatory commissions" (*Commissiones praeparatoriae*) were formed to work out the draft of decrees to be laid before the council. Nine of these were modeled, in accord with their defined purpose, but also in organization, on existing central offices of the Roman Curia: the Theological Commission was competent for all questions of the teaching office, which pertained to the competence of the Holy Office; the Commission for the Bishops and the Government of Dioceses corresponded to the Consistorial Congregation; the Commission for the Discipline of the Clergy and the Christian People, to the Congregation of the Council. The Commissions for the Discipline of the Sacraments, (ecclesiastical) Studies and Seminaries, the Sacred Liturgy, the Eastern Churches, and the Missions received essentially the same tasks as the corresponding central offices, whose heads were at the same time the chairmen of the related commissions. Only the Commission for the Apostolate of the Laity was not modeled on any congregation, because none such existed.

If these preparatory commissions are compared with the five of the First Vatican Council, important differences appear: through their chairmen and their composition they were more closely bound than the earlier ones with the central offices in which the tradition of the Curia is incarnate; they were not composed, like the earlier ones, almost exclusively of theologians and canonists, that is, *periti* who had no right to vote in the council, but included up to about one-half bishops and religious superiors, hence future council fathers with a right to vote. The first measure subjected the preparatory commissions to the strong influence of the curial official mechanism, the second enhanced its power in so far as the participation of the future council fathers made these latter familiar with the themes presumably to be discussed at the council and seemed from the start to recommend them to the *periti* for the conciliar commissions to be set up later. On an equality with the ten commissions in respect to the preparation of the schemata, as an agency of contact with the churches not united with Rome, but going beyond their competence, was the Secretariat for Promoting Christian Unity under the direction of Augustin Bea, S. J., Rector of the Pontifical Biblical Institute, named a cardinal on 14 December 1959.

The examining and coordinating of the drafts prepared in this manner was incumbent on the Central Commission, set up on 16 June 1960, to which belonged, in addition to the presidents of the commissions, the chairmen of national and regional episcopal conferences; their number rose finally to 102 members and 29 consultants; the future secretary-general of the council, Pericle Felici, acted as secretary. Since the commissions were continually expanded by the naming of new members, their total number increased at the end of 1961 to 827, two-thirds of them Europeans.

The work of the preparatory commissions in the almost two years from the fall of 1960 to the summer of 1962 suffered from the fact that no directives had been given them for the constituting of centers of gravity. It was undoubtedly an advantage that they were free in the choice and elaboration of the themes, but on the other hand it worked in favor of the strong influence of the Curia, of the Roman universities, and of the central authorities of religious institutes in the tendency that the sixty-nine schemata submitted by them to the Central Commission were rather a summary of papal statements during the last decades or, respectively, an inventory of the theology and practice prevailing in Rome rather than the hoped for advance into new areas. The Central Commission first met on 12 June 1961; this session was followed by six more. In addition to the schemata submitted to it, it also drew up the rules of procedure.

If it was possible to hear during the period of preparation that the Second Vatican Council would be the best prepared council in the history of the Church, it soon became evident that the material collected in overwhelming mass was chosen unilaterally and did not satisfy the council. Of the seventeen schemata which had been worked out by the Commission for the Discipline of the Clergy and the Christian People under Cardinal Ciriaci, not a single one was approved in this form by the council; of the six texts of the Theological Commission under Cardinal Ottaviani, after complete revision only two; of the nine of the Commission for the Discipline of the Sacraments, not even one obtained the acceptance of the council. Only the Commissions for the Sacred Liturgy, Religious, and the Apostolate of the Laity submitted each only one document, which constituted the point of departure of the corresponding conciliar decrees. Out of the five texts prepared by the Commission for Studies and Seminaries there originated through concentration and revision two conciliar decrees on the formation of priests and Christian education; the four schemata worked out by Bea's secretariat went, after amalgamation with related material of the Theological Commission and the Commission for the Eastern Churches, into the Decree on Ecumenism, and the declarations on religious freedom and non-Christian religions. Nevertheless, the work of the preparatory commissions was not in vain: it furnished a voluminous collection of material, few new viewpoints. Only at the council did these break through.

The preparatory work was kept strictly secret, so that only a small part of it leaked to the public. Thus it could hardly fail to happen that during the long waiting period a certain disappointment began to spread, especially since the Roman Diocesan Synod, which the Pope himself had opened on 24 January 1960, moved in the traditional routes and gave little notice of the desire for bold reforms and large-scale ecumenism, which appeared in numerous books and articles of theologians and lay persons. The expectations had been strained too tightly, it had not been made sufficiently clear that councils had never been revolutionary, but instead the necessary new elements had to be consciously linked with the proven old elements. But even during the years of preparation unmistakable were the voices from the episcopate that "all problems posed by the development of the world" must concern the council, according to the message of the French cardinals and archbishops of 26 October 1961, that the Church must be universal in the true meaning of the word, as Cardinal Frings said at Genoa on 19 November 1961, that a decentralization called for by Cardinal Alfrink of Utrecht and a deeper and broader ecumenical understanding, urged by Archbishop Jaeger of Paderborn, were necessary. In February 1962 Cardinal Montini of Milan demanded a discussion of the nature and function of the episcopate in unison with the Roman Pope; a deepened self-awareness, he said, would enable the Church to adapt itself to the needs of the age. But he warned against seeing in a council a healing means of miraculous and immediate effect.

Earlier than anticipated, on 25 December 1961, the council was summoned to Rome for the next year by the constitution *Humane salutis,* but still without indication of the opening date; the motu proprio *Concilium diu* of 2 February 1962 appointed 11 October of the same year as the opening day. In these documents the tasks of the council were again sketched only in very general outlines. The promulgation, surrounded with unusual solemnity, of the constitution *Veterum sapientia* on 22 February 1962, whereby Latin was imposed as the language of ecclesiastical speech and theological instruction, was in opposition to the wishes prevalent in the Preparatory Commission for Studies and Seminaries and strengthened the impression that everything would continue as before. The paving of the way for church unity was not expressly mentioned, but a step was taken in this direction when the churches and ecclesial communities not united with Rome were invited through the Secretariat for the Promotion of the Unity of Christians to send official observers to the council. The invitation met a better reception among Protestants than among the Eastern Churches. The Anglican Church, whose head, Archbishop Fisher of Canterbury, had paid a visit to the Pope on 2 December 1960, sent three representatives; the Evangelical Church of Germany sent the Heidelberg professor

Schlink; the Lutheran Reformed World Union and the Ecumenical Assembly in Geneva acceded to the invitation; on the other hand, the Orthodox patriarchs of the East reacted with hesitation. The patriarchate of Moscow agitated powerfully against the "sirens" from the Vatican. All the greater was the surprise when, on the eve of the opening of the council, it became known that two representatives of Patriarch Alexius were en route to Rome. This about-face was due to a visit to Moscow of the closest collaborator of Cardinal Bea in the Secretariat for the Promotion of the Unity of Christians, his eventual successor, Johannes Willebrands. The other dissident patriarchates later followed the Russian example.

By means of the motu proprio *Appropinquante concilio* of 6 August 1962 the Pope gave the council its agenda, the *Ordo Concilii Oecumenici Vaticani II celebrandi.*[4] It had been worked out by a subcommission of the Preparatory Central Commission under the presidency of Cardinal Roberti and his secretary, Vincenzo Carbone, and in seventy articles defined, first, the rights and duties of those participating in the council and, second, the general, and, third, the special norms for the order of business.

As at Trent and the First Vatican Council and in conformity with Canon 223, paragraph 1, of the Code of Canon Law, the right of deciding on proposals pertained only to the plenary session of the council fathers qualified to vote in the general congregations and sessions. The direction of the discussions was entrusted to the presidency, *consilium praesidentiae,* of ten cardinals appointed by the Pope. It devolved on the ten permanent conciliar commissions to draw up the drafts of decrees (schemata) to be submitted to the council and to modify them, having regard for the motions offered by the council fathers; of its twenty-four members, two-thirds were to be elected by the council, one-third and the chairman were named by the Pope. To the full members entitled to vote were added *periti,* summoned by the Pope, without the right to vote; among them were laymen; at the beginning of the fourth session they numbered 106. An entirely new category was constituted by the observers (*observatores*) sent by the churches and ecclesial communities not in communion with the Holy See; all texts were delivered to them and, like the *periti,* they were entitled to participate in the general congregations. Not yet envisaged in the agenda were the "hearers" (*auditores*), who were permitted in the *aula* of the council from the second session, and who from the third session also included women. At the head of the official machinery of

---

[4] Text in *AAS* 54 (1962), 609–31; cf. H. Jedin, "Die Geschäftsordnung des Konzils," *Herder TK* III, 610–23; critical notes by Mörsdorf, ibid. II 144f.

the council stood the secretary-general named by the Pope; to him were allotted several Undersecretaries.

The routine was as follows: The drafts submitted by the presidency were explained by one or more commentators; the general debate on the schema as a whole was followed by special debate on its individual parts. For the adoption of a text a two-thirds majority was required. Out of regard for the number of council fathers, oral intervention in the general congregations was made dependent on previous written notice and its length was restricted to ten, finally eight, minutes; the council fathers had the right to present written suggestions for changes, which were to be submitted to the commissions. The process was continued until a two-thirds majority was achieved, and the promulgating of the text could take place in the solemn session.

In the course of the very first session of the council it appeared that the *Ordo* in its existing form was inadequate to achieve concrete results in a reasonable period of time. And so it was revised on 13 September 1963, with regard for various modifying motions made by, among others, Cardinals Döpfner and Spellman: The direction of the general congregations was turned over to four moderators, again named by the Pope, and, together with the presidency, now expanded to twelve members, they constituted the Presidential Council. For the rejecting of a proposed schema now a simple majority of those present sufficed; fifty fathers could submit a new draft to the moderator, who could bring about the close of the debate by a simple majority decision; the minority in the case was protected by this, that it might have its viewpoint set forth by three speakers. The same end was served by changes in the composition and procedure of the conciliar commissions. By the side of the chairmen were two vice-presidents, who were to be named with the consent of the commission; they together determined the commentator (*relator*) or commentators.

A second modification of the *Ordo*, of 2 July 1964, went into effect during the third session. Speakers who acted in the name of at least seventy council fathers received certain privileges; the distributing of propaganda material in the *aula* and nearby required the approval of the Presidential Council.

Even in this altered form, the *Ordo* could not eliminate all defects and confusion from the routine. The relationship of the Pope to the council, severely burdened by history, led to tensions also at the Second Vatican Council. As head of the council, the Pope had the right to intervene in the procedure, and both Popes of this council made use of this right when unexpected difficulties arose. He could approve the decrees and promulgate them, but he could also refuse his assent. It was not foreseen in the *Ordo* in what form he, as a member of the council, which he was, could make known his view to the council in the course of the deliberations. Also unclarified was the question of whether a vote was necessary at the end of the general debate. Rightly was the question posed whether it was significant to permit only *placet* and *non placet* in the voting on the individual parts of a text, but *placet iuxta modum,* that is, consent with reservation, in the voting on the chapters as a whole; the opposite would have been preferable.

As regards the form of the conciliar decrees, in conformity with Pope John's wish but different from all earlier councils, the council refrained from condemning errors by means of canons with a subjoined *anathema*. The texts approved by it bear three different signs in which their authority is graduated: at the head are four constitutions—on the liturgy, the Church, divine revelation, and the Church in today's world; then follow nine decrees and three declarations. Two other forms, considered for a time, *propositiones* and *vota,* were finally not used. The council also abandoned the pastoral instructions that it had also pondered for a while.

An actual change of the procedure was under way toward the end of the council in this regard, that the real work of the council was transferred more and more to the commissions, and the general congregations were more and more filled with voting, which could be carried out far more quickly with the aid of a punch-card system than at the First Vatican Council. Still other technical contrivances contributed to overcoming the problem of sheer numbers. An especially well operating loudspeaker system assured the understanding of the spoken word in the gigantic *aula*. The otherwise inevitable losses of time, which at the last council arose from the coming and going of individual speakers, were avoided by the fact that in each section of the *aula* microphones were installed, before which they spoke. The prescribed language of the council, Latin, on the whole stood the test; an already installed device for simultaneous translation into the languages of the world was not put to use, because it proved to be impossible then to assure the necessary precision of expression.

The First Session and the Change of Pontificate

The opening session on 11 October 1962 by far surpassed in grandeur that of the First Vatican Council. Two thousand five hundred forty council fathers with the right to vote took part in it, a number not even remotely reached at any previous council. The Pope was borne through the bronze door to the entrance of Saint Peter's on the *sedia gestatoria,* but then he left it and walked through the ranks of the council fathers; the fact that on this occasion he wore, not the tiara, but the miter, had symbolic value. The rite was basically that usual since the Council of Vienne: *Veni Creator* and Mass of the Holy Spirit, celebrated by Cardinal Tisserant; enthroning of the gospel on the council altar erected in front of the presidents' table; making of the profession of faith; the conciliar prayer, *Adsumus;* singing of the gospel (Matt. 28:18–20 and 16:13–18) in Latin, Greek, Old Church Slavonic, and Arabic.

In his opening talk the Pope repeated the conviction that the summoning of the council followed an inspiration from above and indicated to the council its direction: to bring to mankind the sacred wealth of tradition in the most effective way, with regard for changed conditions of life and social structures; not to condemn errors but "fully to declare the strength of the Church's life" ("doctrinae vim uberius explicando"). The council was charged to move nearer to the unity willed by Christ in the truth ("conferre operam ad magnum complendum mysterium illius unitatis"). Overcome by the magnitude of the moment, the Pope ended with a prayer for the divine assistance.

The council assembled in the nave of Saint Peter's was the most universal in church history. Not only in accord with its mandate and claim, but in fact the Church of the twentieth century was a Universal Church. All five continents were present in their episcopates. Europe, which at the medieval councils was virtually the only continent represented, sent only a mere half of those qualified to vote—1,041; America, which was not at all represented at Trent and only weakly at the First Vatican Council, sent 956 bishops, Asia more than 300, Africa 279. The numerical superiority of Italians, which had led to voting by nations at Constance and even at Trent had produced tensions, was ended: the 379 Italian bishops made up less than one-fifth of the council fathers, but just the same the Italian curial cardinals and high curial officials exerted an additional strong influence.[5]

The order of seating was more than a formality. The presidents, and later also the moderators, had places in front of the *confessio*; on the platforms to their right sat the cardinals, to their left the patriarchs of the Uniate Eastern Churches; then followed, on both sides, first the archbishops, then the bishops according to the date of their nomination. The generals of religious institutes had places on the front balconies, the *periti* on the others. For the observers a platform was designated to the left of the presidency; for the later admitted *auditores* platforms on the other sides of the high altar. Each general congregation was opened with Mass, frequently in an Oriental or the Slavonic rite.

[5] For the statistics refer to the publications cited in the bibliography for this chapter. Although the council's four periods of meeting are often called "sessions" in accord with parliamentary usage, I reserve this term for the solemn sittings.

That the council was esteemed as a world happening appeared from the presence of almost one thousand reporters sent by the press and the mass media. During the first session they almost entirely referred to indiscretions, which only a few, for example, *La Croix* of Paris and *Il Tempo* of Rome, exploited. The reports of the press office under the Frenchman Vallainc, consisting of seven members—one each for German, English, French, Italian, Polish, Portuguese, and Spanish—were jejune, and only from the second session were its members permitted in the *aula,* and the press office was no longer subject to the secretary-general but to a conciliar commission. Thereafter the official reports were fuller in content, and the still valid rule of silence was in practice relaxed. The edited reports, partly collected, form a not to be underestimated historical source, that must of course be used with caution.

Although the superficial facts are better known than in any previous council, there were also many enigmatic incidents in this council that are either unknown or demonstrable only with difficulty. Above all, in little more than a decade after the close an unambiguous evaluation of the effects which proceeded from the council is not yet possible. What follows is not a history of the council, but only a report in which should be noted what Oscar Cullmann said: that this council must be evaluated not only from the texts approved by it, but the total council event must be considered, for its impulses are as effective as the texts.[6] These were not produced by "parties" such as modern parliaments have, but proceeded from a tension-filled struggle between "intransigent" and "progressive" forces. The former, numerically weaker group had its firm prop in the Roman Curia, the latter was composed, in addition to bishops from central and western Europe and North America, suprisingly also of council fathers from so-called mission countries. Of great significance were the national and regional Episcopal Conferences, partly constituted only at the beginning of the council.

In the first general congregation on 13 October the election of the conciliar commissions was on the agenda. In addition to the ten ballots, on each of which sixteen names were entered, the lists of those qualified to vote who had belonged to the preparatory commissions—and a majority of them were candidates of the Curia—were given to the council fathers. Against this procedure misgivings were first expressed by Cardinal Liénart of Lille, then in more detail by Cardinal Frings of Cologne: We still know too little about one another; in view of the importance of these elections it is necessary to prepare them carefully:

---

[6] O. Cullmann in *Was bedeutet das Zweite Vatikanische Konzil für uns?,* ed. by W. Schatz (Basel, n.d.), 20.

they should be postponed for a few days. The motion was passed with overwhelming approval and became a decree.

In the next days the Episcopal Conferences caucused and drew up their own election lists. The most successful among them proved to be that prepared by the cardinals of central Europe and France, because it took into consideration distinguished experts from all parts of the world. Among the 160 commission members then elected on 16 October were twenty-six from Latin America, twenty-five from North America, nineteen from Asia and Oceania, seven from Africa; Europe supplied twenty Italians, sixteen French, eleven Germans, ten Spaniards, five Poles, and twenty-one from the other countries. The power of the Italians was enhanced by papal nomination of nine, instead of originally eight, more members of each commission.

The general congregations of 13 and 16 October were the "starting point" of the council. In them it made known its wish to make its decisions according to its own judgment and conscience, not merely to approve what was suggested to or submitted to it. This self-will of the episcopate became still more clearly visible in the debate on the liturgy schema, which began on 22 October and lasted to 14 November. Previously, on 20 October, the council issued a proclamation to the world, drafted by four French bishops and presented to the council in the Pope's name, to the effect that "the message of salvation, love, and peace which Jesus Christ brought to the world and entrusted to the Church" was announced to all mankind.

The liturgy schema drafted by the Preparatory Commission had adopted the basic notion of the liturgical movement, that the Christian people should not passively attend the worship of God but actively participate in it, not only hear but pray and act together; as a consequence it recommended an extensive introduction, to be determined in detail by the respective episcopal conferences, of the vernacular in the Liturgy of the Word at Mass and in the administration of the sacraments and envisaged a reform of the liturgical books and, on specific occasions, the reintroduction of Communion *sub utraque specie.* On these questions there was enkindled the opposition between traditionalists and progressives which, in changing groupings, was to put its stamp on the council throughout its duration. For the schema were especially cardinals and bishops of countries in which the liturgical movement had spread, at their head Cardinals Frings, Döpfner, Feltin, Lercaro, Montini, and Ritter; the opponents of the draft fought the substitution of Latin by the vernacular and the intervention of the episcopal conferences in its introduction. Cardinal Ottaviani implored the assembly to bear in mind that it was moving "on holy ground" and proposed that the schema be referred to the Theological Commission, which he headed, for revision. Agreeing with him were Italian bishops, such as Cardinal Ruffini of Palermo, and prelates of the Curia, such as Parente, Staffa, and Dante, and also Americans, notably Cardinals Spellman and McIntyre, but not leading prelates from mission lands, such as Cardinals Gracias of Bombay and Rugambwa of Dar es Salaam and the Chinese Archbishop Lokuang of Tainan. Bishop Duschak, vicar apostolic of Calapan, Mindoro (Philippines), even proposed on 5 November the introduction of an ecumenical Mass, which should, as far as possible, be free from all the historical links to the events of the Last Supper; it would also be comprehensible to the faithful in the missions without historical explanations and could take its place next to the historically developed liturgy as *Missa orbis.*

And so the surprise of the first general congregation was repeated: the bishops of Latin America, Asia, and Africa, although they were in great part trained at Rome, turned out to be, in the majority, thoroughly non-curialist and non-traditionalist; their pastoral experiences drove them to the side of the "progressives." What could be foreseen only with difficulty was that the "pastoral" goal which Pope John had set for the council was accepted by the majority of the council fathers.

In the course of the debate on the liturgy many requests were presented which had long ago been discussed in the pale of the Liturgical Movement: the adapting of the Divine Office to the spirituality of the diocesan clergy; the better choice and distribution of the scriptural readings; in the ecclesiastical calendar the deemphasizing of celebrations of the saints in favor of the Christocentric Church year; a reform of the calendar with a fixed date of Easter; ecclesiastical music and Christian art. The vote on 14 November produced a large majority—2,162 to 46, with seven abstentions—for the further revision of the schema, with consideration of the suggestions for change brought forward in the debate by the standing conciliar commission under the direction of Cardinal Larraona, of whose sixteen elected members twelve were on the central European list. Even before the council dispersed, on 7 December, the new first part, composed by the commission, was approved, but with 180 reservations.

Not so clear was the outcome of the debate begun on 14 November on the schema worked out by the Theological Commission under the centralized control of its Jesuit secretary, Tromp, on the sources of divine revelation.[7] It obtained its pungency first through the fact that

[7] On the prehistory of the text submitted on 14 November, whose original form was sent to the Central Commission on 4 October 1961 and to the council fathers in modified form in the summer of 1962, cf. J. Ratzinger in *Herder TK* II, 498ff., and, for

the text submitted sought to exclude the interpretation of the Tridentine decree defended by the Tübingen theologian Geiselmann—"tradition" means that the Bible is to be interpreted by the Church, but does not represent, beside it, a second independent source of revelation—and through this intensified condemnation of the Protestant scriptural principle affected the ecumenical rapprochement. In addition, the draft was directed to damming up the penetration of modern biblical criticism into Catholic exegesis, over which a powerful controversy had erupted between professors of the Papal Lateran University and members of the Biblical Institute. In contrast to the "progressive" liturgy schema, which had evoked the resistance of the "traditionalists," now the "progressives" were the aggressors. Many fathers, including Cardinals Frings, Döpfner, König, and Alfrink, rejected the schema totally and had already prepared a new one; others, such as Cardinals Suenens and Bea and Bishop De Smedt of Bruges, demanded a complete revision and presented the principles to be taken into account. A vote on the schema as a whole, contrived on 20 November—the first of its kind—led to the result—probably as a consequence of the motion, which required a "yes" for the ending of the debate—that 1,368 council fathers voted *placet*, 822 voted *non placet;* hence the opponents of the draft did not obtain the two-thirds majority. On the other hand, it had become obvious that it could never count on adoption in its current form.

The Pope resolved the existing situation, not envisaged in the agenda, by setting up a mixed commission under the chairmanship of Cardinals Ottaviani and Bea for the further revision of the schema; in it both tendencies were represented equally. This measure, at first accepted with great skepticism, proved to be the right one: in protracted discussions a middle road was found.

In the debates over the schemata on the liturgy and revelation, the oppositions had collided harshly. Now a certain relaxing of tension showed itself in the fact that a proposal[8] prepared by the Secretariat for the Means of Social Communications and treating the mass media—press, cinema, radio, television—was submitted on 23 November. It essentially restricted itself to a fundamentally positive stance of the Church toward them, the possibilities of using them for the apostolate,

---

the especially controverted Chapter 3, A. Grillmeier, ibid., 528ff. Further literature in the bibliography.

[8] German members of the secretariat were Bishop Kempf of Limburg and, as consultors, K. Becker, K. A. Siegel, and E. Klausener. According to *Herder TK* I, 112f., the secretary was A. M. Deskur, the undersecretary of the Papal Commission for Film, Radio, and Television

and the dangers to be encountered. The schema had been only in the next to last place among the drafts sent to the council fathers in August 1962. Although the chairman of the conciliar commission, Cardinal Cento, and the commentator, Archbishop Stourm of Sens, had recommended the adoption of the text, in the debate from 23 to 26 November it encountered opposition because it one-sidedly stressed the Church's right to the modern means of communication and too little the right of persons to appropriate and correct information and did not condemn sharply enough the misuse of the mass media. Some speakers, for example, Cardinal Wyszyński and Bishop Charrière of Fribourg, demanded a theological and sociological deepening, others a stronger regard for the collaboration of the laity in this field. Cardinal Bea suggested a merger of existing Catholic news agencies into a world agency. On 27 November the council by a great majority—2,138 to 15— approved the substance of the schema, but demanded its abbreviation and limitation to instructional principles and pastoral guidelines. Apparently the theme was treated as marginal. A great part of the council fathers were not yet clear that there was a question here of a pastoral problem of the first rank; but it also took a long time in the sixteenth century before the significance of printing for Church and preaching was grasped.

In the treatment of the schema submitted on 26 November on the Eastern Churches it became clear how inadequately the preparatory work had been coordinated. The Preparatory Commission, under Cardinal Amleto Cicognani, the future secretary of state, with Father Welykyi as secretary, had, in addition to a schema *De ecclesiae unitate,* drafted fourteen brief texts, which were transmitted to the corresponding conciliar commissions, to which belonged only five members of the Preparatory Commission but all six Uniate patriarchs. The first part of the schema, which treated of the unity of the Church under one Supreme Shepherd, contained passages which, as was remarked in the debate by Patriarch Maximos IV and others, were suited rather to upset the Orthodox than to gain them. Cardinal Bea proposed that the draft be reworked with that of his Secretariat for Promoting Christian Unity and merged with a third, which originated with the Theological Commission. On 1 December the council decided, 2,068 to 36, to send it back with this version to the commission.

As early as this debate it had been said by Archbishop Heenan of Liverpool that the difference between the Roman Catholic Church and the separated Eastern Churches lay less in a discrepancy of the doctrine of salvation than in the concept of the structure of the Church.

Nature and structure of the Church were the central theme of the schema *De ecclesia,* which the chairman of the Theological Commission,

Cardinal Ottaviani, and Bishop Franič of Split, as *relator,* explained on 1 December. To no other theme were so many *postulate* appended, and no other would be so powerfully contested as this one. The draft occupying 123 printed pages linked the view of the Church, prevailing since Bellarmine, as an institution with ideas from the encyclical of Pius XII on the Church. Its twelve chapters were, as Cardinal Montini remarked in the course of the debate (1–7 December), placed side by side, not developed separately, and the doctrine of the Episcopal College was present only as a start. One of the leading minds of the traditionalists, Bishop Carli of Segni, defended the schema and used the opportunity for an emotional settlement with the "ecumenists" and "pastoralists" who, allegedly out of fear, were managing to attack dogmas and basic elements of Catholic piety as taboo. Other critics found the text too juridical and triumphal (De Smedt of Bruges) or failed to find in it a deeper treatment of the relation of Christ to the Church (Cardinal Montini) and of the doctrine of the Church as the People of God and of the Episcopal College (Cardinal Döpfner). They recommended a full revision of the schema and a rearranging of the material, so that the inner structure of the Church should precede its mission (Cardinal Suenens). Thus were the signposts for the further reworking set up, which, without a formal decree, was entrusted to the conciliar commission. The route which this draft had to travel was still far and full of potholes.

When on 8 December the Pope dismissed the council for the time being, none of the five discussed proposals was ready for publication. He comforted the fathers: "It is easy to understand that in a so broadly planned gathering a great deal of time must be devoted to achieving agreement." The public displayed disappointment over the absence of concrete results, many Catholics took offense at the "lack of unity" of the council fathers, which was in reality only the struggle, necessary in all councils, concerning the true and the right. One important result was achieved: The episcopate had learned to feel as a unity, had understood the council as its own affair and testified to its desire actively to form its decisions itself. Even if the council had not been continued, it would have left behind its mark on church history. But if it wanted to realize concrete results, priorities had to be established, the mass of current schemata had to be reduced, they had to be combined and abbreviated. The Secretariat for Extraordinary Affairs, set up in the procedure (ARTICLE 7, par. 2), had not sufficient authority for this. Such authority was given to a Coordinating Commission established by the Pope on 6 December. To it belonged: as chairman, Cardinal Cicognani, since 12 August 1961 successor of the deceased Cardinal Tardini as secretary of state, as well as Cardinals Confalonieri, Döpfner, Liénart, Spellman,

Suenens, and Urbani. The Coordinating Commission was also instructed to turn over all details relative to the revision of canon law and the regulations for implementing the conciliar decrees to the postconciliar commissions. It acquitted itself of its mandate in close cooperation with the conciliar secretariat and the conciliar commissions,[9] but also in constant contact with the whole body of council fathers, whom the Pope in a letter of 2 January 1963, not published until 8 February, had called upon for cooperation. The drafts newly formulated in this manner, which at the beginning of May were sent to the council fathers, showed almost entirely another face than the drafts of the preparatory commissions. The will for renewal of the conciliar majority carried the day: the proponents came from the previous opponents. Only now was the direction of the council definitely decided. The resumption of the discussions was proposed for 8 September 1963. Pope John was not destined to witness them. Only with great effort had he, already marked by death, continued the usual reception of the Episcopal Conferences. On 3 June 1963 he died, mourned by the whole world, almost more outside than inside the Church.[10]

In his brief pontificate John XXIII, parallel with the council and supplementing it, had in several encyclicals shown the Church new routes and again taken up some earlier trodden. The mission encyclical *Princeps pastorum* of 28 November 1959 came out for a native clergy and the lay apostolate in the missions and approved the accommodation to non-European cultures.[11] *Mater et magistra* of 15 May 1961 aimed to continue the tradition of the great social encyclicals since Leo XIII, but with some new emphases.[12] The Pope regarded as his legacy the encyclical on peace, *Pacem in terris,* of 11 April 1963.[13] Cutting deeply into the traditions of the Roman Curia were the Pope's arrangements in regard to the College of Cardinals: The suburbicarian sees received residential bishops with full authority, while their former occupants, the

[9] The Coordinating Commission held five sessions from January to March 1963; on their importance, cf. G. Alberigo in *Cultura e Scuola,* 1968, 117ff.

[10] Some memorials on Pope John are in the bibliography. Carl Burckhardt wrote in a letter to Max Rychner of 4 June 1963, hence under the direct influence of his death: "He will change much, after him the Church will no longer be the same. Perhaps at the end of his days he will come to know fear. He remains worthy of love, also worthy of admiration": C. J. Burckhardt and Max Rychner, *Briefe 1926–1965* (Frankfurt 1970), 246.

[11] *AAS* 51 (1959), 833–64.

[12] Ibid. 53 (1961), 401–64; see below, Chapter 7.

[13] *AAS* 55 (1963), 257–304; cf. E. Fogliazzo, *Papa Giovanni spiega come giunse alla Pacem in terris* (Rome 1964). The receiving of Khruschev's son-in-law, Adzhubei, after the freeing of the Ukrainian Greater Archbishop Slipyj was understood as a rapprochement to the Soviet Union; cf. also P. Camellini, *Giovanni XXIII e i communisti* (Reggio 1965).

cardinal-bishops, retained only the title. The cardinal-deacons also received episcopal ordination: on Holy Thursday 1962 the Pope personally ordained them.[14] In five consistories the Pope created fifty-two new cardinals and thereby definitively and basically exceeded the guiding number of seventy established by Sixtus V. The question was already raised of whether the College of Cardinals should retain the exclusive right to elect the Pope.

In accord with the prevailing canon law, the council was suspended by the death of the Pope. But Giovanni Battista Montini, archbishop of Milan, elected Pope on 21 June 1963 after a conclave of only two days, from the outset allowed no doubt to arise that he was determined to continue the council.[15]

Paul VI (1963–78) was, by background, spiritual makeup, and the course of his education and his life, as different as possible from his predecessor. His father Giorgio (d. 1943) was a well-to-do publisher at Brescia and had been a member of the Popular Party and deputy in parliament. The son, born 26 September 1897, had in 1916 finished his schooling at the Liceo Arnaldo da Brescia, a public school, then attended the lectures in the seminary at Brescia, after ordination to the priesthood on 29 May 1920 studied canon law at the Gregoriana in Rome, then from 1922 prepared in the Accademia dei Nobili for an ecclesiastical diplomatic career, for which a short stay at the nunciature in Warsaw in 1923 could count as his first practical introduction. From 1924 he was active for almost three decades in the papal Secretariat of State, from 13 December 1937 as undersecretary (*sostituto*). After the death of Secretary of State Maglione in 1944, he remained, together with Tardini, secretary for extraordinary affairs, the closest collaborator of Pius XII. Parallel with his activity in the Secretariat of State proceeded zealous work in the pastoral care of students and academics (FUCI or *Laureati Cattolici* respectively). He first entered upon the normal pastoral care after his surprising nomination as archbishop of

---

[14] *AAS* 54 (1962), 253–58.

[15] The personality and work of a living person are not a subject of historical scholarship; hence only a few references to available sources and literature. M. Serafian, *La difficile scelta. Il Concilio e la Chiesa fra Giovanni XXIII e Paolo VI* (Milan 1964); F. García Salve, *Vida de Pablo VI* (Bilbao 1964); C. Pallenberg, *Paul VI., Schüsselgestalt eines neuen Papsttums* (Munich 1965); A. Hatch, *Pope Paul VI, Apostle on the Move* (London 1967). On the Oratorian Bevilacqua, friend of the Montini family, in A. Fappani, *Giulio Bevilacqua, prete e cardinale sugli avamposti* (Verona 1975). The Pope's speeches in: *Discorsi al popolo di Dio* (Rome, since 1964); *Dialogo con Dio. Riflessi liturgici nei discorsi di Paolo VI* (Vatican City 1966), with preface by Cardinal Lercaro; *Cristo vita dell'uomo d'oggi nella parola di Paolo VI,* ed. by V. Levi, II (Milan 1969); V. Levi, *Di fronte alla contestazione. Testi di Paolo VI* II (Milan 1970). For the opening address of 29 September, cited below, see *Decreta,* 895–927.

Milan on 1 November 1954, where he succeeded Cardinal Schuster. From the outset he gave social impulses. At the council he was very reserved and intervened only twice; next to the outspokenly progressive Cardinal Lercaro of Bologna, he ranked as a moderate progressive, and it was as such that he was elected. He approved the course of his predecessor, but differing from him he controlled the keyboard of the Roman Curia and knew the opposition which had come out against the new course during the first session.

As early as the day after his election Paul VI announced in a radio message that he intended to continue the council and appointed 29 September as the beginning of the deliberations. On the solemnity of Peter and Paul he received about one thousand journalists and promised to improve their possibilities of information at the council. On 1 July, in a speech to the diplomatic missions that had come for the coronation on 30 June in the piazza of Saint Peter's, he took up the theme of the "Church in today's world." He showed his ecumenical attitude by sending a representative to the celebration of the Golden Episcopal Jubilee of Patriarch Alexius of Moscow. In a letter of 12 September to Cardinal Tisserant he expressed the wish that in the future more lay persons should be used as *periti* at the council and introduced a new category of participants, the *auditores*. On 14 September he appointed for the directing of the general congregations four moderators, not legates, as was originally considered: Cardinals Agagianian, Döpfner, Lercaro, and Suenens. In a speech to the members of the Roman Curia on 21 September he adhered to the principle already represented by the Popes of the Council of Trent, that the reform of the Curia was the concern of the Pope, not of the council, but at the same time demanded strict obedience from the members of the Curia. The warning was unmistakable.

Second Session (1963) and First Results

In his opening address on 29 September the Pope appointed, more precisely than his predecessor had ever done, four tasks for the council: a doctrinal presentation of the nature of the Church—whereby he advanced the schema *De ecclesia* to first place—its inner renewal, the promoting of the unity of Christians, and—in this form again new—the dialogue of the Church with today's world. For the first and now the chief task a guideline was given in the statement: "Without prejudice to the dogmatic declarations of the First Vatican Council on the Roman Pope, the doctrine of the episcopate, its tasks, and its necessary union with Peter, is to be investigated. From this will result for Us also guidelines from which, in the exercise of Our apostolic mission, We will derive theoretical and practical advantage." The collaboration of the bishops (*adiutrix opera*) in the exercise of the primatial authority, which he designated as desirable, already pointed to the future establishment of the Synod of Bishops. The inner renewal of the Church, the Pope continued, must orient it to Christ, but not as though it had abandoned him so that its traditions would have to be broken up and its life completely reorganized (*ecclesiae vitam subvertere*). In the ecumenical area another statement created a great sensation: "If any guilt in the separation is Ours, We humbly ask God's pardon and also seek forgiveness from the brethren who should have felt themselves separated from Us; for Our part, We are prepared to forgive the wrongs which have been done to the Catholic Church." This was no unconditional confession of guilt, such as that of Pope Hadrian VI of 3 January 1523, but the avowal that the causes of the ecclesiastical division lay not only on *one* side. The still existing great obstacles to union must not stifle the hope for it. The Pope greeted the observers present and then turned to those holding themselves aloof—adherents of non-Christian religions and atheists—and made mention of those persecuted for the sake of their belief.

The revised schema on the Church, which was explained on 30 September by Cardinals Ottaviani and Browne—the latter had been general of the Dominicans—was divided into four chapters: The Church as *mysterium,* its hierarchical structure, the People of God and the Laity, holiness of the Church. On the very first day of the debate Cardinal Frings moved to place the concept of "People of God" at the beginning, because hierarchy and laity together constitute the Church; furthermore, he recommended the adding of a chapter on the eschatological character of the Church and the incorporating of the text on the Mother of God into the schema.

A vote arranged for 1 October on the schema as a whole produced an overwhelming majority, 2,231 to 43, for further discussion. In the special debate, which was protracted throughout October, Cardinal Lercaro referred to the fact that *Corpus Christi mysticum* and "Visible Church" are not identical, because all the baptized belong in some way to the mystical body of Christ without their necessarily being members of the visible Catholic Church. But this very important question in the ecumenical view was soon eclipsed by the opposition which erupted in the debate on the second chapter, the hierarchical structure of the Church. It lasted from 4 to 16 October, and 127 speakers managed to be heard. The bone of contention for a minority, consisting especially but not exclusively of members of the Curia, was the doctrine that the College of Bishops, into which the individual is admitted by episcopal ordination, together with its head, the Pope, bears authority and responsibility for the whole Church. Speakers such as Cardinal Siri of Genoa, president of the Italian Episcopal Conference, Archbishop Staffa, secretary of the Congregation of Seminaries and Universities, Archbishop Parente, assessor of the Holy Office, and Bishop Carli of Segni saw in this teaching an encroachment on the papal primatial power and denied that it is based on scripture and tradition. Against them, the adherents of "collegiality," for example, Cardinals Liénart and Léger and Auxiliary Bishop Betassi of Bologna, pointed out that the papal primacy was clearly stressed in several passages of the schema, in conformity with the definition of the First Vatican Council, and the doctrine of the College of Bishops had a solid biblical basis in the mission of the Twelve and a foundation in tradition in texts of episcopal ordination and other testimonies.

A second, if not so strongly contested question was the restoration of the permanent diaconate. Since the Council of Trent the diaconate had been considered as a transitional stage to the priesthood. Now the lack of priests prevailing in many countries suggested the notion of gaining in deacons helpers for the steadily growing pastoral and charitable services. But since there was also consideration of freeing them from the law of celibacy, the proposal encountered powerful resistance, not only among clear traditionalists, so that in this question the factions were not identical with those in regard to collegiality.

The debate on the third chapter—People of God and Laity—offered the opportunity to refer to the coresponsibility of the laity, rooted in the universal priesthood and often claimed on the part of the Church, and the necessary overcoming of clericalism. There were not lacking voices which warned against an obliteration of the distinction between the general priesthood and the official priesthood of orders and saw in the "higher evaluation" of the laity a danger to ecclesiastical authority.

In the fourth chapter—the holiness of the Church—there was discussed, even if not yet in a gratifying manner, the call of all the baptized to sanctity, then the religious state and the evangelical counsels were treated in particular. There was no section on the diocesan priesthood and nothing about its goal, except perhaps in the different means of the way to holiness of religious and lay persons. Also the total picture of the Church drafted in the schema appeared unrealistic to Cardinal Bea; it did not accord with the reality of the Pilgrim Church.

The debate on the schema on the Church lasted an entire month. The question was: Which of the proposals of change should the commission adopt for the revision? Which corresponded to the will of the majority of the council? To produce clarity, Cardinal Suenens, as moderator in the general congregation of 15 October, had announced a preliminary vote on four controverted items. It did not take place. On 23 October the Presidential Council, on the motion of the moderators, decided with a bare majority the proposal of five, not four, questions: (1.) Whether episcopal ordination has a sacramental character; (2.) Whether the bishop ordained in communion with the Pope and the bishops becomes thereby a member of the *Corpus episcoporum*; (3.) Whether the College of Bishops (*Corpus seu collegium episcoporum*) is the successor of the College of Apostles and, with its head, the Pope, and never without him, possesses the highest authority over the entire Church; (4.) Whether this power is based on divine right; (5.) Whether it is fitting, in each case in accord with the needs of the Church in certain areas, to reinstitute the diaconate as a special and permanent degree of orders. The five questions did not have the character of final votes, but were related only to the future formulation of the schema by the commission.

Again a week elapsed until the five questions were submitted. The dissension was further increased by the fact that a powerful propaganda had been unleashed against the insertion, decided on 29 October with a simple majority, of the text on the Mother of God into the schema on the Church by broadsheets which were distributed in front of the conciliar *aula* or sent by mail, without any steps having been taken against their authors. Only on 30 October was there a vote on the five questions. Questions 1 and 2 were approved by a large majority, but in the case of the next three questions the number of "no" votes increased: 1,808 to 336; 1,717 to 408; 1,588 to 525. Although the opponents of collegiality and of the permanent diaconate urged that the vote was not binding, their future acceptance by a two-thirds majority now seemed as good as assured. The "October Crisis" was thereby overcome, and the general congregation of 30 October 1963 was a second climax of the council after that of 13 October of the previous year.

The confrontation over the structure of the Church naturally influenced the discussion of the schema on the pastoral office of bishops and the government of dioceses, which claimed nine general congregations from 5 to 15 November. The schema had originated in the combining of five texts of the Preparatory Commission and was submitted to the council fathers at the end of April. It was still restricted to the bishops' tasks of governing: their relation to the Roman central departments, the position of auxiliary bishops, the episcopal conferences, the boundaries of sees, and the administration of parishes; hence it proceeded from above to below, not from the local church. After its presentation by Cardinal Marella, chairman of the competent conciliar commission, it was accepted after a brief general debate, against 477 "no" votes, as the basis for the special debate. While some demanded that in the first chapter the outcome of the votes on collegiality be taken into consideration, its opponents—Ottaviani, Carli—contested the binding nature of the vote of 30 October. The chief problems were picked out: the reorganization of the Curia, the composition and rights of the episcopal conferences, the position of auxiliary bishops, and the question of an age limit for residential bishops.

Although the great majority was clear in regard to the desire that the request for reform of the Curia could be fulfilled only by the Pope, not by the council, far-reaching wishes were expressed: an episcopal council should be established in order to exercise the collegial direction of the Church (Cardinal Alfrink), and to it, so some thought, instead of to the College of Cardinals, could be entrusted the right of papal election. Many speakers indulged in complaints about the curial bureaucracy without taking into account its great importance as bearer of many centuries of traditions and experiences. The spectacular outcome of the debate was the demand made by Cardinal Frings on 8 November that, before condemning a doctrine or a book, the Holy Office must hear the relevant ordinary and the accused. Cardinal Ottaviani irritably defended his department, but the attack by the Cardinal of Cologne gave the signal for a reorganization of the *Suprema*. There had been regularly meeting episcopal conferences in Germany since 1848, and they had become usual in some other countries later, but plenary conferences of the bishops of France and Italy only very recently. The nine African episcopal conferences were constituted with a central secretariat under the leadership of Cardinal Rugambwa only at the council. Their structure and their authority had to be more precisely determined, because greater competence, for example, in the sphere of liturgy, needed to be given to them, especially the right to issue decrees binding on the members. In Germany and the United States they had hitherto got along without such a right, but it was to be expected that just this right was necessary to prevent dissension and even ruptures in certain areas, for example, the school system and trade unionism, and in dangerous situations of ecclesiastical politics.

Supported by the doctrine approved by the majority in the debate on the Church, that one becomes a member of the College of Bishops by means of ordination, the auxiliary bishops demanded an improvement in their legal position. African bishops spoke out against the naming of auxiliary bishops, because these latter jeopardized the unity of direction; also criticized was the naming of titular bishops for the sake of personal distinction. If the residential bishop is shepherd and teacher of his diocese, then would it not be desirable that, through establishing an age limit—in one comment the seventy-fifth year was given—the superannuation of the bishop could be prevented? It was easy to cite examples that a superannuated or sick bishop stubbornly refused to step down; but had not the council's Pope John been elected at the age of almost seventy-seven, and were there not men of more than eighty years among the most active and fertile in ideas among the council fathers? The list of problems touched on extended even to the complaint over the many tiny dioceses not capable of surviving by themselves and the dioceses that had become too large and tortuous around great cities and in high-population-density areas, over friction with the personal dioceses of Eastern Rites and with the military ordinariate, and finally over the lack of priests in Latin America. As hardly in any other debate the bishops spoke their anxieties and grievances from their hearts. One hundred fifty-eight fathers had spoken when the debate was closed on 15 November without a vote and the schema was referred back to the commission for further revision. Even before the session ended, the apostolic letter *Pastorale munus* of 30 November 1963 conferred on diocesan bishops forty powers of office and on all bishops, including titular bishops, a series of privileges by which the episcopal office was revaluated vis-à-vis the papal central authority and at least partly restored to its original extent.[16]

The schema *De oecumenismo,* debated from 18 November to 2 December, was, on the basis of the conciliar decree of 1 December 1962, revised and abridged by a mixed commission of members of the Secretariat for Promoting Christian Unity and of the Commission for the Eastern Churches. It treated the principles of Catholic ecumenism (Chap. 1), its actual state (Chap. 2), the relations with the Eastern and, of course only briefly, with the Protestant churches (Chap. 3), the position of the Jewish religion in the history of salvation (Chap. 4), and the principle of religious liberty (Chap. 5). Whereas the first commentator, Cardinal Cicognani, claimed to understand the ecumenical efforts of the council merely as a continuation of the tendency "of almost all councils" to restore peace and unity, the second one, Archbishop Martin of Rouen, designated it as entirely new; the third, Coadjutor Archbishop Bukatko of Belgrade, who spoke for the Eastern Churches, took a stand for improvements.[17] In the course of the debate the

---

[16] As K. Mörsdorf remarked in *Herder TK* II, 139, the text in *AAS* 56 (1964), 5–12, was altered in several passages in comparison with the original text presented to the council fathers. On the interpretation: K. Mörsdorf, "Neue Vollmachten und Privilegien der Bischöfe," *AKR* 133 (1964), 82–101; L. Buijs, *Facultates et privilegia episcoporum concessa Motu proprio Pastorale munus cum Commentario* (Rome 1964).

[17] Detailed assessment of the reports by W. Becker in *Herder TK* II, 25 ff.; on the debate, with the names of the speakers, E. Stakemeier in Müller II, 540–63.

question was posed: Just what is "Catholic Ecumenism"? Must the Church not seek union with the powerfully strengthened ecumenical movement? Does the Roman Catholic Church surrender its claim to be the true Church if it designates the separated ecclesial communities simply as "churches"?

The presentation of the common elements, just as that of the differences, in Chapter 3 satisfied neither the representatives of the Eastern Churches nor the Protestant observers. There was agreement only on this, that it was meaningless, as happened before the First Vatican Council, to invite to a return to the Catholic Church and to accentuate the existing differences, but that it was also not right to gloss over the existing doctrinal differences. The schema turned to Catholics with the invitation to make their Church a model by striving for Christian perfection; it recommended a mutual getting acquainted and dialogue, common prayer for unity but not common celebration of the Eucharist; it warned against any injury to love in the interchange. It was above all Cardinal Bea and Archbishop Jaeger of Paderborn—the latter well-known for his ecumenical work in Germany—who supplied as the guiding idea for the third chapter the stressing of the uniting elements in doctrine, piety, and Christian fulfillment. They found support from bishops from all parts of the world, for example, even from Spain, but of course also contradiction from those who already glimpsed a danger in the word "ecumenism." It remained controversial how far the collaboration of the denominations might and should go in the charitable and social sphere. The question of mixed marriages only appeared on the edges.

Despite many still unresolved problems, whose existence Cardinal Bea did not dispute, the debate left the impression that a genuine breakthrough to ecumenical thought had taken place. Strongly disputed, on the other hand, were the last two chapters of the draft, on the Jews and on religious liberty. The former seemed required by the unique position of Judaism in the history of salvation, but also operating was the motive of opposing to modern anti-Semitism a basic declaration that would correct earlier failings in the Church's behavior. Against it was raised opposition especially from bishops from Arab states, who feared from such a declaration, which would be interpreted as taking a position in favor of the State of Israel, a deterioration of their own already difficult situation and as a compromise wanted a word on Islam added.

The chapter on religious liberty had to be defended by its commentator, Bishop De Smedt of Bruges, against objections chiefly of a theological sort: that it equated truth with error. In many fathers there emerged doubts whether the last two chapters were in their right place at all. These doubts and the opposition from the Arab world declared that, although the schema as a whole had been accepted in the general voting of 21 November by a great majority, 1,966 to 86, as a working basis, there was no longer harmony on these two chapters. They continued in suspense; still powerful confrontations were imminent over both, not only their content but also their position.

In the drafts on the Church and ecumenism the council had laid hold of decisive problems of the Church's self-awareness without being able to satisfactorily solve them. Nevertheless, at the close of this second session, in *Sessio III* of 4 December 1963, two texts were adopted by vote: the Constitution on the Sacred Liturgy and the Decree on the Media of Social Communication.

The voting was done by chapters on the schema on the liturgy, which had been once more basically revised by the conciliar commission in the spring, from 23 April to 10 May 1963; the voting took place during the debate on the schema on the Church. In regard to Chapters 2 and 3—on the Mass and the sacraments—so many reservations, 781 and 1,054 respectively, were made on 13 and 18 October that they had to be reworked. Not until the final vote on the constitution as a whole on 22 November did an overwhelming majority appear: 2,158 to 19. And so it could be confirmed and proclaimed by the Pope in *Sessio III* on 4 December. Its basic idea is the "full and active participation of all the people" ("totius populi plena et actuosa participatio") in the Easter Mystery, the fundamental concept of the liturgical movement. Subordinate to it was the authority conceded to the episcopal conferences to permit great parts of the Liturgy of the Word at Mass, especially the scriptural readings and the Universal Prayer before the preparation of the gifts, to be performed in the venacular and *only* in it, hence not *also* in Latin. Latin was by no means abolished as the liturgical language of the Western Church; on the contrary, "The use of the Latin language," it is said in ARTICLE 36, par. 1, "should be maintained in the Latin Rite to the extent that special rights do not oppose this." Enhanced significance was granted to the texts of Holy Scripture and the homily that explained them, and concern for congregational singing was recommended. For special occasions the concelebration of Mass by several priests was permitted.[18]

At the end of the Constitution on the Sacred Liturgy the formula of approval and promulgation, issuing from long consultations with *periti,*

---

[18] On the formula of approval, V. Fagiolo in *Diritto ecclesiastico* 75 (1964), 370–86; G. Alberigo, "Una cum patribus," *Mélanges theologiques. Hommage à Mgr. Gérard Philips* (Gembloux 1970), 291–319. Other literature on the Constitution on the Liturgy in the bibliography.

was first used. It was based on the Church's understanding that had been gained at the council: "What is expressed in this constitution, as a whole and in particulars, has obtained the assent of the fathers. And We, by virtue of the apostolic authority entrusted to Us by Christ, approve, decree, and enact it together with the venerable fathers in the Holy Spirit and command to the honor of God the publication of what has been ordered by the council."

The rules for implementation were left to the episcopal conferences dependent on confirmation by the Holy See; the reform of the liturgical books, especially of the missal and the breviary, was entrusted to a postconciliar commission which was instituted by the Pope on 25 January 1964, shortly after the end of this session; it established numerous special commissions. The reform of the liturgy, thus introduced, broke with the rubricist rigidity of the last centuries: whether it would produce an organic further development of the liturgical heritage without substantial loss could not yet be foreseen.

Not so close to unanimity as in the case of the Constitution on the Sacred Liturgy was the assent of the council fathers to the Decree on the Media of Social Communication, greatly abbreviated by the conciliar commission under Cardinal Cento. Archbishop Stourm of Sens had explained it, as commentator, on 14 November. The new text defined the attitude of the Church to the press, theater, cinema, radio, and television, but still without seeking a theological and sociological deepening; especially missed was the elaboration of persons' *right* to information and the *duty* of state and Church to provide it. In a petition of 16 November American journalists, including J. Cogley, R. Kaiser, and M. Novak, spoke of a retrogression: they saw the freedom of journalists jeopardized. On 17 November ninety council fathers, including Cardinals Frings, Gerlier, and Alfrink, made a proposal to the commission to revise the schema again, but without success. This opposition explains the fact that in the final vote on 25 November a relatively large number of "no" votes (503) was cast against the 1,598 "yes" votes, so that for a moment it was doubtful whether the decree would be approved. But since a supplementary instruction was taken into consideration, for the working out of which more lay experts than previously were to be employed, in the session the "no" votes dropped to 164. It was noted that preconciliar vision of the Church was at the basis of this decree;[19] but if it is pondered how negatively for a long time the mass media were evaluated in ecclesiastical circles, it was

[19] O. B. Roegele in Hampe III, 349–55; also the introduction by K. Schmidthüs, *Herder TK* I, 112–15. The Pope's closing address in *AAS* 56 (1964), 31–40; also *Decreta*, 928–45.

certainly a forward step, even if it remains true that it did not yet take account of the current importance of the mass media.

In his closing address the Pope admitted that the outcome of this session did not indeed correspond to all expectations, and still many tasks had to be accomplished. He indicated, alluding to the establishing of the Synod of Bishops and the reorganization of the Curia, that the "share of the bishops in the service of the Universal Church" would be made "still more effective." With satisfaction he stated: "We have mutually gotten to know ourselves better and learned to exchange ideas"; two important decrees had been passed. But the Pope warned against interpreting the Constitution on the Sacred Liturgy arbitrarily before the necessary norms had been laid down. At the end of his talk, the Pope announced, to the great surprise of most, a pilgrimage to Jerusalem, during which a meeting with Ecumenical Patriarch Athenagoras was envisaged. It took place from 4 to 6 January 1964, followed by the world public with great attention. More than words could do, this act strengthened the ecumenical orientation of the council.

Third Session: Crisis of November and Constitution on the Church

The third session, which was opened on 14 September 1964 with a Mass celebrated by twenty-four council fathers, the first concelebration at the council, brought the climax of the council but also its most serious crisis. The commission work directed by the Coordinating Commission had in the meantime so broadly expedited six schemata than on 7 July there could be indicated to the bishops as program points of the coming deliberations: the Church, the episcopal office, ecumenism—hence the three chief subjects of the second session—revelation, discussed in the first session but tabled, the lay apostolate, and the Church in the world of today. The last-mentioned concern, the "Dialogue with the World," was touched by the Pope in the encyclical *Ecclesiam suam* of 6 August 1964, and thereby the catchword given by his predecessor, *aggiornamento,* had been made concrete; on the other hand, the Pope had warned against novelties, according to the view of which the Church must break radically with its traditions and find entirely new forms of its life. The stand against atheistic Communism and the mention of the Jewish religion and of Islam as partners in the dialogue seemed to broaden the council's program.

The Pope's opening address on 15 September,[20] however, made it clear that he, now as earlier, considered the schema on the Church as the most important subject of deliberation, and if he indicated that the

[20] *AAS* 55 (1963), 841–59; *Decreta,* 895–927.

nature and function of the episcopate as complement of the doctrine of the primacy must be clarified, this was an unmistakable sign to the opponents of collegiality to abandon their opposition, but at the same time to its adherents that there must be no undermining of the papal primacy in the extent defined in the First Vatican Council. On the basis of the preliminary votes on 30 October 1963, the commission had given to the schema on the Church a new arrangement and form, for which the Louvain professor of dogma, Philips, deserved great merit. To the schema, divided into six chapters, were added a seventh on the eschatological character of the Church and an eighth on Mariology. They still had to be debated from 15 to 18 September, and at the same time began the voting, without debate, on the first six chapters. The first two—Chapter 1: "The Mystery of the Church" and Chapter 2: "The People of God"— passed without serious opposition. But Chapter 3— "The Hierarchical Structure of the Church and the Episcopate in Particular"—was vigorously disputed. It was divided into thirty-nine sections for the voting from 21 to 30 September; on each of these the vote had to be *placet* or *non placet*. As regards the sections on the College of Bishops, which in its present form was defended by Archbishop Parente and rejected by Bishop Franič, the "no" votes mounted to more than 300: it was the influential group, which saw the papal primacy endangered in these statements. Far more numerous but differently made up were the 629 "no" votes against the conceding of the diaconal order to older married men; the concession to young men without the obligation of celibacy was rejected with 1,364 "no" votes. Although the opponents of collegiality had not by far mustered the necessary one-third for rejection, they sought in the final vote on Chapter 3, in which *placet iuxta modum* was permitted, still to put their views into the text. They may have constituted the great majority of the 572 votes with reservation, in addition to 42 "no" votes, cast on 30 September on the first part of Chapter 3. The curial opposition began to crumble, but it did not yet admit defeat. Chapter 4 on the laity was well received, as were Chapter 5 on the vocation to holiness and Chapter 6 on religious, the explanation of which was successfully defended by the commentator, Abbot Primate Gut. Chapter 7, "The Eschatological Nature of the Pilgrim Church and its Union with the Church in Heaven," drafted by Cardinal Larraona, could be substantially improved because of the debate of 15 and 16 September: the time between the Lord's Ascension and the Parousia was emphasized as the Age of the Holy Spirit, the Christocentric cult of the saints was approved. Greater resistance was evoked in the debate, from 16 to 18 September, on Chapter 8: "The Blessed Virgin Mary, Mother of God, in the Mystery of Christ and of the Church," the including of which in the schema on the Church had encountered powerful opposition and appeared to some zealous devotees of Mary to be minimalistic. The primate of Poland and some Spanish and Italian bishops desired a solemn consecration of the world to the Mother of God, some recommended the adoption of titles such as "Mother of the Church" and "Mediatrix" into the text, but Cardinals Bea and Frings raised scruples against this: One should stay on strongly dogmatic ground.

Before it came to a vote on these last chapters the opposing views collided again more severely on the second schema, which was in the program as: "On the Pastoral Office of Bishops in the Church." The submitted text had originated through the curtailing of the draft debated in the second session on the episcopal office and its combination with a draft on the form of pastoral care in March 1964, and hence, because it had been greatly altered, it had to be discussed anew, from 18 to 22 September. Bishop Carli disputed the competence and responsibility of bishops for the Universal Church, on which the text was based; other critics, for example, Cardinal Léger and several French bishops, found the text too juristic, too clerical, and not suited to today's tasks. Some individual concerns were brought forward again: the scarcely toned-down powerlessness of the diocesan bishop in regard to the exempt orders; the necessary adjustment between dioceses of few priests and those of numerous priests; the fluctuation of the population in the "wandering Church." The schema revised in this direction by the commission was once again opened up for debate, from 4 to 6 November, but so many *modi* were submitted on the first two chapters—852 on Chapter 1, 889 on Chapter 2—that the revised text could not again be presented until the close of this session.

Tensions became even sharper when on 23 September religious freedom and on 25 September the declaration on the Jews came up on the agenda; originally they had been linked, as Chapters 4 and 5, to the schema on ecumenism. Bishop De Smedt of Bruges, the commentator on the first text, could point out that 380 suggestions for change had been assimilated. Proceeding from the natural dignity of humans, the decree protected freedom of conscience in the civil sphere, even if the conscience is in error. The opponents quite rightly felt that this concept broke decisively with the medieval legal order, which required the proscription of heretics by common action of Church and state. In the debate, 25 to 29 September, Cardinal Ruffini posed the question: How can the Catholic Church, which is the true Church and bearer of the truth, abandon the fostering of this faith, wherever possible, even with the help of the state? Toleration—yes; freedom—no! Cardinal Ottaviani raised the question: Will not the concordats concluded by the

Holy See, for example, with Italy and Spain, which allow to the Catholic Church a privileged position, come to nothing through this declaration?

The draft found firm defenders above all in the American episcopate, through Cardinals Meyer and Ritter, and also in the Polish through Archbishop Wojtyla of Cracow, eventually Pope John Paul II, who understood its worth vis-à-vis Communist totalitarianism. It was perceived that the motivation and the sphere where religious freedom prevailed must be more keenly grasped in order to meet the objection that truth and error as such—not the people who defend them—are equated. The debate ended without a vote, and the text was turned over to five members of the Theological Commission for appraisal, while the Secretariat for Unity undertook the further revision.

In comparison with the "Declaration on the Jews," submitted in the second session as Chapter 4 of the schema on ecumenism, but not discussed, the text introduced by Cardinal Bea on 25 September was planned with a view to appeasing its Arab opponents[21] In this regard, Islam was expressly mentioned; in the opinion of its champions the text was diluted, because only the Jews now alive, not the people as a historical unit, were absolved from the charge of "deicide," which in the past had been raised by Christian polemicists; twenty-one fathers demanded a return to the earlier wording. Other critics desired the deepening of the accomplishment of the history of salvation (Frings, Lercaro, Heenan, Hengsbach of Essen) and the taking of other mono-theistic religions into account (König). The chief difficulty was and remained the political misunderstanding. The Arabic countries interpreted the "Declaration on the Jews" as taking a stand for the State of Israel and exerted strong pressure on the bishops of their countries and by way of diplomacy; Patriarch Maximos IV had the presumption to charge that the authors of the text were "bought." This explains why the secretary-general of the council in a letter of 8 October invited Cardinal Bea to have the text still once more examined by a group composed of three members each from the Secretariat for Promoting Christian Unity and the Theological Commission; the effort to insert it into the Constitution on the Church and thereby to take it entirely away from the Secretariat for Promoting Christian Unity misfired.

Surprisingly calmly proceeded the debate, from 30 September to 6 October, on the schema on revelation, tabled two years previously, which had received a new text from a subcommittee, on which Philips,

---

[21] Very detailed presentation of the prehistory, including the political factors, by J. Oesterreicher, who was strongly involved in the whole process, in *Herder TK* II, 404–87. The text submitted in 1964 (op. cit., 437f.) was already the third.

Ratzinger, Congar, K. Rahner, and other leading theologians had collaborated. As Bishop Franič, the second commentator, expressed it, it was not in accord with the notion of a minority of the commission, which saw in it a departure from the Tridentine decree on Scripture and tradition. In reality, it constituted its completion, gained from the deepening of the ideas "Scripture," "Tradition," and "Teaching Office," which are intimately linked and can exist only together; the theological discussion on the interpretation of the Tridentine decree was purposely left in suspense. Other disputed points were the inerrancy of Scripture and the historicity of the Gospels. As in the votes on the schema on the Church and in the debate over religious liberty, so too in this on the schema on revelation it was apparent that the great majority of the council concurred with the aims set by Popes John and Paul, and that the group which held stubbornly to the views hitherto represented at Rome was influential, numerous, but weak.

From this procedure of the council's majority resulted the fate of the nine texts which were submitted to the council between 7 October and 20 November. Two of them were sent back to the relevant commissions: on 14 October the schema, consisting of only twelve basic points, on the life and ministry of priests, and on 9 November the schema on the missions, even though on 6 November the Pope had appeared personally in the *aula* and recommended its adoption. The schema on the lay apostolate, on which Bishop Hengsbach of Essen reported, escaped this fate in the debate of 7 to 13 October, but exception was taken to the fact that it did not draw the necessary conclusions from the doctrine of the People of God; it did not adequately elaborate the proper rights of laity or also their proper responsibility and specific spirituality; for the first time a layman, P. Keegan, spoke on the matter.

The basic principles on the renewal of the life of religious, debated 10 to 12 November, and on Christian education, 17 to 19 November, seemed to many fathers to be too abstract, but capable of being developed. Better received were the twenty-two basic principles on the formation of priests, which entrusted to the episcopal conferences the creation of plans of studies and thereby the accommodation to the regional circumstances; only on the question of what authority Thomas Aquinas had to occupy in the system of teaching philosophy and theology was there a separating of minds.

The text "On the Church in the Modern World," debated from 20 October to 9 November, at first schema 17 in the original sequence in the list of drafts, later schema 13, was drawn up by a working group which had met in February 1964 at Zurich—hence it was dubbed the "Zurich Text." It had been preceded by a "Roman" draft, composed in the spring of 1963, and a "Mechlin" text in French, conceived by Belgian and French theologians[22] in September 1963 at the suggestion of Cardinal Suenens. The Zurich draft, in which the Redemptorist Bernhard Häring had a powerful share, discussed in accord with a theological foundation the ministry of the Church to the world (Chapter 2), poverty, overpopulation, and war (Chapters 3 and 4). In the course of the general debate, opened by the comments of Bishop Guano of Livorno, Cardinal Meyer demanded the deepening of the theological bases; however, the text was accepted by a large majority, 1,576 to 296, as the basis for the special debate. In it Cardinal Lercaro moved a decision on the problem "Church and Cultures," and on 9 November the layman James J. Norris submitted copious material on the questions raised. Taken into account was the fact that this document, appearing for the first time in the history of the councils, had to mature slowly so that it could correspond to the expectation of people. The encyclical *Ecclesiam suam* of 8 December 1964, which in its third part treated the dialogue of the Church with the world, encouraged further work.

A schema on the sacrament of matrimony, worked out by the Commission for the Discipline of the Sacraments with the aid of members of the Theological Commission and of the Secretariat for Promoting Christian Unity, treated in five chapters of the impediments, mixed marriages, matrimonial consent, the form, and matrimonial processes, but at the direction of the Coordinating Commission was reduced to a *votum,* which limited itself to listing the guidelines for a reform of the law of marriage.[23] Introduced by Archbishop Schneider of Bamberg, it was discussed on 19 and 20 November in the *aula,* but at the end of the general congregation of 20 November Cardinal Döpfner, as moderator, proposed, with regard to the law on mixed marriages, which in denominationally mixed countries was felt to be a great hindrance to the rapprochement of the denominations, to turn over the *votum* to the Pope in order to assure as quick a regulation as possible. The Council understood that so difficult a juridical and pastoral problem could hardly benefit in the plenary session, and a fortiori could not be solved, because the circumstances in the various countries were

---

[22] For the history of the text, C. Moeller in *Herder TK* III, 242–78, where (p. 251) the letter of the secretary general of the World Council of Churches, Lukas Visher, of 18 April 1963, on "Faith and Order" is mentioned. Somewhat simplified in Hampe III, 15ff.

[23] On the origin of the *votum* on the Sacrament of Matrimony, B. Häring in *Herder TK* III, 595; there, pp. 596–606, the text; J. G. Gerhartz, "Die Mischehe, das Konzil und die Mischeheninstruktion," *Theol. u. Phil.* 41 (1966), 376–400.

all too different. This expedient was declared for by 1,592 fathers, 427 declaring against it.

Of the nine texts debated in October and November, only one accomplished its purpose after a brief debate, 16 to 20 October—the schema on the Eastern Churches, which was promulgated in the fifth *sessio*. While the Council, seen from without, moved ahead uninterruptedly, within it the tensions had increased. On 11 October seventeen cardinals from central and western Europe and the United States, by means of a letter to the Pope, thwarted the attempt to send the two controversial declarations on religious liberty and the Jews, by outflanking the council through appeal to an alleged desire of the Pope, to new mixed commissions, from whose planned makeup the aim of the minority to alter the text in its sense was recognizable. The appeal to the Pope was successful, but the opposing faction did not admit defeat.

Chapter 3 of the Dogmatic Constitution on the Church also encountered the stubborn resistance of the most active and influential minority in the Vatican. When on 14 November a thick book with proposals for changes in Chapters 3 to 8 together with the replies of the Theological Commission was handed to the council fathers, it was preceded by a *nota explicativa praevia,* which was supposed to exclude every encroachment on the doctrine of primacy by the doctrine of the College of Bishops developed in Chapter 3. It had, to be sure, been submitted to the Theological Commission, but, as the secretary general communicated, came from a "higher authority," hence from the Pope personally. It was supposed to reconcile with the text the minority, whose *modi* that altered the meaning were not accepted by the commission, and assure its acceptance with moral unanimity. Twice, on 16 and 19 November— the latter was the day before the final vote—the secretary general declared that the *nota* was, it is true, not an element of the text, but the text had to be interpreted in its sense.

The aim underlying the *nota* was achieved: the "no" votes to Chapter 3 dropped to forty-six on 17 November, including no doubt such of the defenders of collegiality who suspected an injury to or a weakening of this doctrine; in the *sessio* only five fathers still voted *non placet.* The Pope had, therefore, achieved his purpose. The question was: Did the *nota* alter the value of the statement of the text?

One who lays both side by side impartially will answer in the negative. The *nota* stengthened the adherence to the doctrine of the First Vatican Council on the primacy, but it did not subsequently strike out anything from the direct divine origin of the episcopal office and its function and the responsibility of the College of Bishops for the Universal Church. In any case, the minority abandoned its scruples and gave up its resistance. What was doubtful was less the content than the form in which the *nota* preceded the conciliar text. But had not the Pope, as head of the council, the right to make his consent dependent on an interpretation determined in advance?

The agitation over the *nota* had not yet subsided when on "Black Thursday," 19 November, the vote published on the previous day on the Declaration on Religious Freedom was canceled by the ranking member of the presidency, Cardinal Tisserant. This was preceded by a petition to the presidency from 200 Spanish and Italian bishops, which, appealing to ART. 30, par. 2, and ART. 35 of the order of procedure, demanded more time for study of the actually significantly altered draft and the postponement of the vote. If voting took place, there could be scarcely a doubt as to its outcome: the great majority would give the draft the green light, even if it did not fully satisfy the defenders of religious freedom. When shortly after eleven o'clock the vote was to take place, Tisserant, after a conference with other members of the presidency, announced that it was prorogued—and that meant that the declaration could no longer be passed in this session. Never had the *aula* of Saint Peter's seen such commotion as at this hour: Many council fathers had left their places and were standing together in groups, excitedly discussing. Was the council's freedom endangered? American bishops hurriedly circulated a petition to the Pope, which at once obtained 441 signatures, and later about 1,000; "with all respect, but with the greatest urgency—*instanter, instantius, instantissime*—we ask that before the end of this session of the council a vote be taken on the Declaration on Religious Liberty; otherwise we lose the confidence of the Christian and the non-Christian world." Bishop De Smedt, who reported on the text, received demonstrative applause. After the close of the general congregation, Cardinals Meyer, Ritter, and Léger went to the Pope, but received only the assurance that the declaration would come as the first point on the program of the fourth session; this assurance was repeated the next day by Cardinal Tisserant.

The stormy general congregation of 19 November produced yet another surprise. The text of the Decree on Ecumenism, formulated by the commission and explained on 5 October by the commentators Martin, Helmsing, Hermaniuk, and Heenan, was, it is true, rejected by only a few fathers but almost two thousand *modi* were introduced, which had to be sifted and compiled. The fathers waited in vain for the printed definitive text, on which there was supposed to be a vote on 20 November. Then the secretary general announced that it was not yet ready, because some changes had been made; he read these changes, nineteen altogether, with the additions; they went back to a "higher authority." The Pope had sent forty suggestions for changes to the chairman of the Secretariat for Promoting Christian Unity, which because of lack of time Cardinal Bea could submit to only a few members from his closest associates, with the result that the nineteen mentioned had been worked into the text. Some were only stylistic, but others changed the sense, for example, that the Churches not in communion with Rome "seek" instead of "find" God in the Bible; however, none could be regarded as a substantial alteration. Again, only the form was strange: that a text produced with great care by a council and its competent organ, in this case the Secretariat for Promoting Christian Unity, had at the last moment been altered, not entirely over its head but still not in a form in keeping with the order of procedure. Among the sixty-four fathers who on the next day voted *non placet* not a few declared their disillusionment in this way; in the *sessio* of 21 November the "no" votes dropped to eleven.

In the fifth *sessio* of 21 November 1964, with which the third session ended, three texts could be adopted and promulgated. The constitution *Lumen gentium*[24] is in two respects the climax and center of the conciliar decrees. Historically considered, it is the climax, for it ended the Church's quest for its self-understanding which had begun at the end of the thirteenth century, had led to the reform councils of the fifteenth century and at Trent to serious collisions, and had not been brought to an end at the First Vatican Council. It is the center of the conciliar decrees, for almost all other decrees of the council must be interpreted in its light. As no other decree, it is "the work of the council itself and of its most active members," wrote Philips. As the Theological Commission had declared on 6 March 1964 with regard to all doctrinal statements of the council, it does not claim infallibility but demands acceptance in faith in accord with the measure of the subject and the form of statement. The definition of the Church as "People of God" broke with the one-sided juridical concept of an institution and the notion which practically identified it with the clergy and forced a passive role on the laity. It ended the confrontation over the relation of the papal primacy to the episcopate in the sense of an organic union of both: the College of Bishops, into which the individual bishop is admitted by sacramental ordination and receives the charisms and full authority to exercise the apostolic office, possesses, by virtue of divine right as successor of "The Twelve," power over and responsibility for the Universal Church, but only in communion with the Pope, who is its member and its head. The successor of Peter regulates the exercise of the full authority given by God by the entrusting of a specific territory

---

[24] For the extensive literature on the Constitution on the Church see the bibliography for this chapter (H. Schauf, "Zur Textgeschichte grundlegender Aussagen aus Lumen gentium über das Bischofskollegium," *AKR* 141 [1972], 5–147).

to the bishop, which can be refused or taken away. The bishop thus appointed rules the local church with full authority and responsibility, by virtue of *potestas propria, ordinaria et immediata.* The College of Bishops is a spiritual community (*communio*), not a college in the sense of Roman Law. It can exercise its authority continually only in union with its head, and here it is left undecided in which form, without possessing the right of corule (*ius congubernii*), it can be given a share in the government of the Universal Church by the Pope, but equally also whether the Pope is the source of all and every actual power of government in the Church or may intervene only subsidiarily in the interest of Church unity.

The diaconate was reinstated as a state of life. All Christians are called to holiness, but the way to it in the religious state, which complies with the evangelical counsels, is different from the way of persons living in the world. The Church feels itself less as "fighting" and still less as "triumphing," but as being on pilgrimage, looking forward impatiently to its eschatological fulfillment. The Mother of the Lord stands also in a unique relationship to the Church by virtue of her singular position in the history of salvation; she is "our Mother," but is not called "Mediatrix of salvation": the chapter on Mariology suited neither the maximalists nor the minimalists.

If the constitution *Lumen gentium* is by far the most important outcome of the council because it articulates the Church's self-awareness, it is followed at a short interval by the Decree on Ecumenism,[25] which regulated anew the relations with other Christian Churches and ecclesial communities. It proceeds from this, that there can be and is only *one* Church of Christ, but that in the Churches separated from the Roman Catholic Church, not without fault on both sides, "non sine hominum utriusque partis culpa," "the written Word of God, the life of grace, faith, hope, and charity, and other interior gifts of the Holy Spirit" are operative. The Decree on Ecumenism ended the stressing, necessary in its day at Trent, of denominational opposition by throwing into relief what is common, opening the door to mutual knowledge and understanding, and by the invitation to common prayer evoked the power which can make possible the apparently impossible, the reunion of the Christian Churches. The separating differences in doctrine and piety, more numerous in the Churches of the Protestant Reformation than among the Eastern Churches, are not denied out of a false irenicism but must be discussed in the spirit of love, as occurred in the ongoing dialogue of the observers with the Secretariat for Unity during the council. Persons were thoroughly aware that in this field a greater distance still had to be covered.

[25] Literature in the bibliography.

The third decree promulgated in the fifth *sessio,* the Decree on the Oriental Catholic Churches,[26] declared solemnly in ART. 5: "The Churches of the East, like that of the West, have the full right and duty always to be governed according to their proper principles, which are recommended by their venerable antiquity, correspond better to the customs of their faithful, and appear more adapted to care for the salvation of souls." *Orientalium ecclesiarum instituta* regulates especially practical questions of ecclesiastical communities—liturgy, administration of the sacraments, here for example the abolition of the obligation of the form in mixed marriages—but it disappointed the representatives of the Eastern Churches in ARTS. 7 to 9 on the patriarchates, the "pivot of the entire Eastern question," according to Abbot Hoeck.

Fourth Session and Closing

On 4 January 1965 the Pope, who at the beginning of December had taken part in the eucharistic congress at Bombay, appointed 14 September as the beginning of the fourth session. Meanwhile, the commissions worked more intensively than ever before on the already discussed eleven texts, five of which were sent to the council fathers at the end of May. If the November Crisis had left the impression that the Pope feared a diminution of the Petrine office, the following statements and measures showed that he still unerringly pursued the line drawn by him at the beginning of his pontificate. In an address to the College of Cardinals on 24 June 1965 he held out the prospect of the reform of the Curia and the revision of the canon law, but also the alteration, turned over to him by the council, of the law on mixed marriages and the study of birth control. In the encyclical *Mysterium fidei* of 11 September 1965 he repudiated the effort to weaken the dogma of the Eucharistic transubstantiation and stressed on various occasions that the Church has no cause to abandon good and proven traditions. "We have a Pope," was one radio commentator's summary of his impression.

On the day of the opening of the fourth session, 14 September 1965,[27] Paul VI surprised the council by the announcement that he

---

[26] Brief introduction by Abbot Johannes Hoeck in *Herder TK* I, 362f.; also, Hampe II, 637–97. The Pope's address in *AAS* 56 (1964), 1107–18, and *Decreta,* 971–91. Retrospect of the entire third session by Hirschmann et al. in Müller III/2, 897–925.
[27] The speech of 14 September 1965 in *AAS* 57 (1965), 794–805, and *Decreta,* 992–1011. The motu proprio with a German translation in the pamphlet edited by me: *Ordnung der Bischofssynode* (Trier 1968), 50–61; there, pp. 18–49, the agenda issued on 8 December 1966.

would summon a Synod of Bishops, through which the episcopate could work together for the welfare of the Universal Church. From the motu proprio *Apostolica sollicitudo* of 15 September it appeared that the majority of the members of the Synod of Bishops was to be elected by the episcopal conferences, whereby a general representation of the bishops, not of the College of Bishops as such, was assured. The Synod of Bishops is convoked, prepared, and guided by the Pope. It is "a permanent synod of bishops for the entire Church, which is directly and immediately subject to Our power," and hence not a "little council" with its own deciding power.

The fourth session differed from all the earlier ones in this, that the work of the commissions in refining the texts was in the foreground, the general congregations were to a great extent taken up with voting and were several times interrupted by rather long pauses. The council was under the pressure of time, for this session was to be the last. Without a break the still outstanding decrees were brought to a conclusion.

At the beginning of the renewed debate on religious freedom, on 15 September, the commentator, De Smedt, once again made it clear that the text did not equate truth and error and that it did not release the individual from the moral obligation of seeking and embracing the truth but merely contained freedom from religious compulsion in the civil sphere. A newly inserted passage left open the possibility of allowing to the Church a privileged position in states with an overwhelmingly Catholic population and thereby reconciled a part of the Italians, such as Cardinal Urbani of Venice, but not all opponents: In the final vote on 21 September, 224 fathers voted *non placet*. After repeated clarification of the text on the basis of *modi* submitted, the number of "no" votes on 19 November even rose to 249. In the preceding debate the Polish Cardinal Wyszyński and the Czech Cardinal Beran, only released in the spring, had indicated the importance of the declaration for the Church behind the Iron Curtain: acts of conscience could be neither commanded nor prevented by a purely human power. The Church claims for itself, as a "spiritual authority established by Christ the Lord," the freedom to proclaim the gospel to all creatures. It renounces the notion that the secular power is justified and obliged to support the Church's saving work by compulsory means; it notes that the modern state is no longer Christian, but neutral; modern society is no longer monistic, but pluralist; but it limits their rights through the natural right of the individual not to be impeded by the civil power in the following of conscience. The burning of a Hus, the principle "Cuius regio, eius et religio" are henceforth not only historically outdated according to the teaching of the Church but are basically repudiated. The impact of this decision explains why the Declaration on Religious Liberty was only ready for publication in the last session.

On the other hand, from the end of September to the end of October the five decrees which were approved and proclaimed in the seventh *sessio* on 28 October 1965 moved quickly and without great objection across the stage of the council. The Decree on the Pastoral Office of Bishops assumed the doctrine of the episcopal office explained in the Dogmatic Constitution on the Church and was oriented to practice. The curial offices and tribunals are "to be more strongly adapted to the needs of the time, the regions, and the rites," and more foreign bishops, "ex diversis ecclesiae regionibus," are to be brought into them for permanent cooperation. The right was given to the episcopal conferences to issue statutes for themselves and to make legally binding decrees with a two-thirds majority. A redrawing of episcopal sees and ecclesiastical provinces was envisaged. Bishops were authorized to appoint episcopal vicars with material or territorial competence. Fruitful, even if also difficult to realize in large dioceses, was the idea of the *presbyterium* united with the bishop as father—ART. 28: "unum constituunt presbyterium atque unam familiam cuius pater est episcopus." The final vote on 6 October yielded almost unanimity—2,161 to 14, and only two "no" votes in the *sessio*. The decree "interlocked more powerfully than any other conciliar document in the juridical order of the Church," says Mörsdorf; it would only achieve its full impact in the course of the reform of canon law.[28]

The schema on the renewal of religious life had, in the debate of the third session, 10 to 12 November 1964, incurred the opposition of several bishops, for example, Cardinals Döpfner and Suenens, but especially of the religious institutes—882 *non placet* at the close of the general debate—and so in the spring of 1965 it was again revised by three subcommissions with such success that in the final vote on 11 October there were only thirteen negative votes, and in the *sessio* only four.[29] It proceeded from the ideal of perfection developed in Chapter 6 of the Dogmatic Constitution on the Church; in its practical part it is,

[28] Introduction and commentary by K. Mörsdorf in *Herder TK* II, 128–247. There can be no doubt that the priests' councils to be set up bore no analogy to the College of Bishops. Proposals in this direction were made by J. Neumann in Hampe II, 496ff.
[29] The long and complex prehistory of the decree *Perfectae caritatis* by F. Wulf in *Herder TK* II, 250ff.; L. Kaufmann in Hampe II, 291–334. On the fundamental element, F. Wulf, "Gebot und Rat," *GuL* 39 (1966), 321ff.; S. Légasse, *L'appel du riche. Contribution à l'étude des fondements scripturaires de l'état religieux* (Paris 1966). The passage on secular institutes (ART. 11) was not inserted into the text until the fifth version, but with the remark "Quamvis non sint instituta religiosa."

like the Tridentine reform decree, a law providing a framework which did not encroach on the differences and the proper life of the orders and other religious communities, but obliged them to sift from the order's tradition what was original and essential, to improve the formation of the young members, to give them the salutary measure of freedom, to understand the, now as earlier, necessary obedience not as renunciation of their own responsibility, to live for God but likewise for people. Of course it happened, as Cardinal Ruffini had already said in the debate on 11 November 1964, that this decree would evoke "extravagant" desires for reform.

The text on the formation of priests, expanded again from. a principle to a decree, explained by Bishop Carraro of Verona, found so favorable a reception in the third session that only a few controverted points were left. The revision submitted on 11 October was accepted almost unanimously—2,196 to 15.[30] The decree *Optatam totius Ecclesiae renovationem* designated the family as "a sort of first seminary" for the vocation to the priesthood and left the preparation to the Tridentine seminary, but attached importance to the improvement of biblical and liturgical studies and of the practical pastoral instruction that was neglected in some countries. The natural virtues, *sinceritas, urbanitas, modestia,* were to be cultivated. The episcopal conferences were instructed to set up programs of study which were adapted to the intellectual and religious level of the country. A debate suggested by Latin American bishops on the law of celibacy was rejected by the Pope as "inopportune" in a letter of 11 October 1965 to Cardinal Tisserant but it invited the council fathers to express their views in writing. Shortly before, the intervention of a Brazilian bishop of Dutch descent on the eliminating of the lack of priests by ordaining laymen who had been married for five years for pastoral work in smaller congregations had been rejected by the moderators.[31]

---

[30] In the very succinct introduction by J. Neuner in *Herder TK* II, 310ff., it is maintained that the Tridentine decree on seminaries belongs "to the age of the Counter Reformation"; cf., on the contrary, my *Geschichte des Konzils von Trient* IV/2, 73ff., and the literature cited there on p. 273. The lack of previous seminary training had been deplored in the earlier debate, on 12 November 1964, by Cardinal Colombo of Milan, himself a former seminary Rector: Hampe II, 172f; cf. H. Jedin, "Das Leitbild des Priesters nach dem Tridentinum und dem Vaticanum II," *ThGl* 59 (1969), 102–24; A. De Bovis, "Nature et mission du presbyterat," *Sacerdoce et célibat. Études historiques et théologiques,* ed. by J. Coppens (Louvain 1971), 187–224.

[31] The undelivered talk to the council by Bishop Pieter Koop of Lins in Hampe II, 239ff. A glimpse of the postconciliar discussion is provided by the collective work of J. Coppens mentioned in the preceding note.

The Declaration on Christian Education, *Gravissimum educationis momentum,* was the eighth version of a text elaborated by the Commission for Studies, which after a temporary reduction to seventeen basic principles in March 1964, was again expanded and explained by Bishop Daem of Antwerp and in the debate of the third session, 17 to 19 November, ran into heavy criticism and obtained 419 "no" votes. Thereupon Archbishop Coadjutor Elchinger of Strasbourg had directed attention to the importance of the formation of teachers and pointed out the danger that the state might force its own ideology on the children in its schools. Not only was there a vote on the new version on 13 and 14 October 1965: the final vote turned out to be 1,912 to 183. In twelve principles the declaration developed the right of the individual to education, the right of parents, the desirability of denominational schools and Catholic universities, but it intimated that both, especially the last, urgently needed coordination and consolidation. Of the fact that the great majority of Catholic students attended neutral universities and that many Catholic professors taught at these, the declaration took note only in passing, in ART. 7.[32]

The Declaration on the Church's Attitude toward Non-Christian Religions, frequently called the "Declaration on the Jews" because of its principal item, was not yet able in its new form, in comparison with the earlier diluted form, to satisfy all its opponents. Then the reaction had been so strong that publication had been abandoned. The bishops of Arab countries, such as Jacobite Patriarch Jacob III, intimidated by the threats of the Arab states but supported by members of *Coetus Internationalis,* continued their resistance, and anti-Semitic pamphlets against the alleged "Jewish-Freemason Conspiracy" were distributed; on the other hand German Catholics in a petition to the Pope had intervened in favor of promulgation.[33] The form now presented for a vote endeavored to remove misunderstandings and also to gain the opponents. Their number remained mostly under 200 in the special votes on 14 and 15 October, but in the vote on the whole rose to 250; in the *sessio* it dropped to eighty-eight. The disputed expression "deicide" was dropped, but it was stated clearly that the guilt for the passion and death of Jesus must be laid neither on the Jews of today nor "on all Jews living at that time, without distinction." Urged not by

[32] Literature on the Declaration on Christian Education in *Herder TK* II, 358f; B. Dezza, "L'educazione cristiana nella Dichiarazione Conciliare," *CivCatt* 117, 1 (1966), 110–25; M. J. Hurley, *Declaration on Christian Education of Vatican Council II* (Glen Rock 1966). Both authors took part in the origin of the declaration.

[33] Cf. *Herder TK* II, 465–70; there, pp. 478ff., Excursus on the statements on Islam, Hinduism, and Buddhism with the citations of the literature. For an understanding of the Declaration on the Jews, A. Bea, *Die Kirche und das jüdische Volk* (Freiburg 1966).

political motives but by the love of Christ, the Church "deplores" anti-Semitism and "rejects every discrimination against a person, every deed of violence against him because of his race, his color, his status, or his religion." By means of this closing statement the condemnation of anti-Semitism was placed on a broader basis and made applicable to every racial discrimination. It was to become the maxim of Catholics in the approaching period of racial strife.

The far less controverted central part of the declaration applied the basic attitude of the Decree on Ecumenism, with which it had been originally united, to Islam, Hinduism, and Buddhism. Monotheism was recognized as obligatory in Islam, and in a reference to the crusades, in which Muslims had been fought with the sword as "heathens," the wish was expressed that the past be forgotten. In Hinduism the liberating "contemplation of the mystery of God" was positively evaluated; in Buddhism, the effort to become free, by means of asceticism, from this passing world. For all the world religions the principle was valid: "The Catholic Church rejects nothing that is true and holy in these religions"; it is often "the reflection of the ray of that truth which enlightens all people," where the fullness of life is to be found: in Christ. For the confrontation with non-Christian religions the declaration has no less significance than the Decree on Ecumenism for the relations with the separated Churches.

In his homily the Pope, alluding to the five promulgated texts, exclaimed: "The Church lives!" It has not grown old, but young; it does not let itself be sucked into the whirlpool of historical change, but remains constant—"semper eadem est sibique constat"; it speaks, prays, watches, rebuilds itself. The council convoked by Pope John "represents the entire Church," *totam repraesentat*. At the end the Pope recalled the persecuted Church, whose representatives were concelebrating with him.[34]

After the October meeting the last snags were quickly overcome. The Dogmatic Constitution on Divine Revelation still had to contend with the opposition of a minority, which based itself on Trent. It only crumbled when, at the personal desire of the Pope in a letter of 18 October 1965 to Cardinal Ottaviani, the inerrancy of Holy Scripture was more precisely defined[35] and the relations of Scripture and tradition

---

[34] The Pope's homily in *AAS* 57 (1965), 899–903, and *Decreta*, 1037–43.

[35] On the petition, preceding the papal letter, of conservative fathers against the expression *veritas salutaris*, too greatly restrictive in their view, cf. A. Grillmeier in *Herder TK* II, 536f.; what is meant is the truth which God might communicate to us; cf. A. Grillmeier, "Die Wahrheit der Heiligen Schrift und ihre Erschließung. Zum dritten Kapitel der Dogmatischen Konstitution Dei Verbum des Vaticanum II," *Theol. u. Phil.*

were newly formulated: "The Church does not derive assurance on all the truths of revelation from Scripture alone"; "tradition" is the living teaching office of the Church, which authoritatively interprets and complements Scripture. This formulation left to the theological schools the liberty of defining more in detail the mutual relations of the two. The doctrine of inspiration—"God speaks through men in a human way"—and the historical character of the Gospels were expressly affirmed. The study of the books of the Bible in the original languages and the ancient translations, as well as of the ancient commentaries and liturgies, and the reading of biblical translations in the vernacular were recommended. In the voting on the individual parts of the constitution on 29 October, only the passage on the relationship of Scripture and tradition got fifty-five *non placet;* the vote on the whole was 2,081 to 27, and in the *sessio* the "no" votes dropped to six. "The text joins fidelity to ecclesiastical tradition with the assent to critical scholarship and thereby opens up again to the faith the road to today," said Ratzinger.

After 29 October the general congregations were interrupted for ten days in order to allow time to the commissions for working on the *modi.* The Decree on the Apostolate of the Laity, explained on 9 November by Bishop Hengsbach of Essen, had assimilated the proposals for change submitted in the voting of 23 to 27 September, as were also those presented personally by the Pope. It received a virtually unanimous approval on 10 November.[36] If Trent had defended the priesthood of ordination, so too in the justification of the lay apostolate the general priesthood of the faithful came into its own. "In the Church there are various ministries but only one mission"; no member of the Church is only passive; all are called to cooperate actively in the building of the Body of the Church as witnesses of faith and love, in the family, in charity, in the missions—everything under the direction of the ecclesiastical hierarchy, as the authority established and ordered by God, but not intended to patronize. The council itself gave an example by the fact that it employed lay persons as *periti* on the commissions in an increased measure.

A schema *De Indulgentiis recognoscendis,* drawn up not by a conciliar commission but by the Congregation of Rites, was felt almost by all to be a disaster when it was explained by Grand Penitentiary Cento and

---

41 (1966), 161–87; G. Caprile, "Tre emendamenti allo Schema sulla Rivelazione," *CivCatt* 117 (1966), 214–31.

[36] On the history of the origin, F. Klostermann in *Herder TK* II, 587–601, supplemented by the same author's article in Hampe II, 72–87; Müller III/2, 608–74, gives the reports and several interventions during the debate in September 1964, for example, on pp. 628f. that of Auxiliary Bishop Betazzi of Bologna on the spirituality of the laity.

the regent of the *Poenitentiaria* on 9 November. The text envisaged certain simplifications in the practice of indulgences, for example, that only *one* plenary indulgence could be gained in one year, the time references in partial indulgences were suppressed, but it did not grasp the theological problem of the indulgence in its depth and was withdrawn on 13 November[37] because of the keen criticism which it encountered from the episcopal conferences which had been questioned about it.

The Dogmatic Constitution on Divine Revelation and the Decree on the Apostolate of the Laity were proclaimed in the eighth *sessio* on 18 November 1965. In his talk the Pope tried to dissipate the hesitations concerning the now imminent ending of the council's work by reference to the establishing of postconciliar agencies: the *consilia* for the liturgy, for the revision of canon law, and for the mass media; the already existing Secretariat for Promoting Christian Unity would be complemented by one secretariat each for non-Christian religions and for unbelievers; the first meeting of the Synod of Bishops was held out in prospect for 1967. The Pope asked for patience, if the necessary organizational, not structural, changes in the Roman Curia were implemented only slowly; persons wrongly held it to be an "instrumentum veterascens, ineptum, corruptum." By far most important of all was the renewal of Christian life.[38]

Until the close of the council three problem children still had to be examined: The Decree on the Missionary Activity of the Church, the Decree on the Ministry and Life of Priests, and Schema 13.

The general of the Divine Word Missionaries, Johannes Schütte, named by the chairman, Cardinal Agagianian, as vice-chairman of the Commission for the Missions, succeeded, with the assistance of newly added *periti*—Congar, Ratzinger, Seumois—at a private meeting at Nemi in the Alban Hills in drafting a wholly new schema, which was based on a theological foundation corresponding to modern mission scholarship and, in that respect, from a backward-looking had become a forward-looking document. In the debate, 7 to 12 October, Cardinal Frings had come out for the retaining of the old "classical" idea of the mission, but the Jesuit General Arrupe harshly criticized the practice of the past. There was no dearth of unresolved problems: the relations of the orders, which till now were the chief agents of missionary work, to the native clergy and of both to the Congregation for the Propagation of the Faith; financing; competition with non-Catholic missions. When

---

[37] Hampe I, 436–49; there 445–49 the opinion of the German and the Austrian episcopal conferences.

[38] *AAS* 57 (1965), 978–84; *Decreta*, 1044—57. It can hardly be denied that the tone now sounded in regard to the Curia was different from that in September 1963.

the vote was taken on the refined text, 712 fathers—most all from mission lands—expressed in their *modi* to Chapter 5 that the missionaries active on the spot should have to collaborate in the decisions of the central offices. Thereupon the contested passage was revised, so that "elected representatives" of the missionary episcopate and of the missionary orders had to be summoned to the Propaganda with a decisive vote, hence not merely as advisers.[39]

In the third session the council had also sent back to the competent commission the schema on the priesthood. At that time there prevailed the impression that priests, compared, for example, with bishops and religious, would be unduly neglected by the contracting of the schema into guiding principles. The commission worked out a new schema, which was submitted at the end of the third session and was again revised, better organized, and stylistically polished at the beginning of 1965 on the basis of 157 suggestions for change, presented in writing. Archbishop Marty of Rheims introduced it on 13 October; on 16 October the council decided to have the proposals for changes presented by Cardinals Döpfner and Léger and other speakers reworked by the commission. The vote by parts on 12 and 13 November, however, produced so large a number of *modi*—1,331 on celibacy alone—that still another revision became necessary, and on 2 December it was approved by a great majority, 2,243 to 11.[40]

Nevertheless, the decree *Presbyterorum ordinis* had by no means fulfilled all expectations. With reference to the pertinent parts of the constitutions on the liturgy and on the Church, it treated the mission of the priest, his threefold ministry, the relation of priests to the bishops, to one another, and to the laity. "Every priestly ministry shares in the worldwide mission which Christ entrusted to the Apostles"; the priest should be prepared to work in other dioceses with too few priests. Celibacy is "not demanded by the nature of the priesthood," as the practice of the Eastern Churches proved, but is "in many respects appropriate to the priesthood." The law of celibacy was approved and confirmed. "And so the council admonishes all priests who have taken

---

[39] For the origin, *Herder TK* III, 10–21; J. Glazik entitled his commentary in Hampe III, 543–53: "A Correction, Not a Magna Carta"; O. Stoffel is of a different mind, "Missionsstrukturen im Wandel," *NZMW* 31 (1975), 259–70: "The mission was pushed from the edge of the Church to the middle." Turning away from the traditional concept of mission, a layman from Togo said: "Mission is everywhere"; Hampe III, 530.
[40] For the history of the origin, J. Lécuyer in *Herder TK* III, 128–41; the strongly critical commentary on ARTS. 1–6 by F. Wulf, ibid., 141–69; on ARTS. 12–22, ibid., 198–237. Many interventions are given in *Documentation Catholique* 62 (1965), 2183–2202; 63 (1966), 329–48; J. Colson, *Ministre de Jésus Christ ou le sacerdoce de l'Évangile* (Paris 1966).

celibacy upon themselves with confidence in God's grace in a free decision according to the model of Christ, to remain faithful to it generously and with the entire heart and to persevere loyally in this state." (ART. 16).

Schema 13 evoked by far the greatest concern. For even the new draft, produced between the third and fourth sessions at Ariccia, Paris, and Louvain,[41] upon which Archbishop Garrone of Toulouse gave the report, ran into varied criticism in the debate from 21 September to 8 October—the fourteenth general congregation—because of the superabundance of general claims which it contained (Elchinger), because of the language, unclear in many passages (Frings), because of its all too optimistic evaluation of the "world" and its confidence of progress (Höffner), but especially because it said only a little on what the Church of today has to give to the world (Bishop Volk of Mainz). Cardinal König and others noted the absence of a confrontation with atheism, especially with atheistic Communism, whose express condemnation was demanded by 450 fathers in a petition to the presidency. A fortiori views were juxtaposed in the concrete problems: total war, atomic weapons, disarmament, refusal of military service, assurance of peace. The council was naturally in no position to give a clear answer to these pressing questions. The appearance of the Pope before the United Nations in New York on 4 October was, it is true, suited to make visible the Church's involvement in today's world; in the structurally conditioned problems of this organization it changed nothing.

In feverish work the commission, which had divided itself into ten subcommissions, strove to incorporate into the text the more than three thousand proposals for changes for the votes on 15 to 17 November. Even the title "Pastoral Constitution" was challenged—541 *non placet*. The most "no" votes (140) were cast on ARTS. 54 to 56 (marriage, birth control) and the section on war and peace (144). The final vote on 6 December produced, just the same, a respectable majority: 2,111 to 251.

The pastoral constitution *Gaudium et spes*, the most voluminous text

---

[41] The last phase of the history of the origin in *Herder TK* III, 266–79; there, pp. 266, n. 47, and 268, n. 74, are given the lists of priests and laity who shared in the revision of the text; pp. 273f. give the composition of the ten subcommissions. Commentary by A. Grillmeier in Hampe III, 138–56; the collective work *L'Église dans le monde de ce temps* (Paris 1967); P. Mikat, "Kirche und Staat in nachkonziliarer Sicht (1967)" in *Religionsrechtliche Schriften* I (Berlin 1974), 217–35; J. Ratzinger, "Der Weltdienst der Kirche," *Internat. Kath. Zeitschrift*, 1975, 439–54. The Central Office of Catholic Social Science of Mönchengladbach publishes *Kommentare zur Pastoralkonstitution des Zweiten Vatikanischen Konzils*, for example, A. Langner, *Die politische Gemeinschaft* (Cologne 1968).

of the council, was placed, as the "heart of the council," at the side of the three other constitutions. It aimed to be "a fundamental new definition of the relation of the Church to the world" and thereby to orient the Church to the world, and that meant to the spirit of the new epoch, from which it had held itself aloof since a century earlier in the Syllabus. This constitution was greeted with enthusiasm, but history has already proved that at that time its significance was greatly overestimated and there was hardly a suspicion of how deeply that "world" which people wanted to win for Christ would penetrate the Church. Only too confident of progress, it remained self-consciously in a static manner of contemplation without being able to give clear answers to such urgent problems as birth control and the prevention of war; entirely inadequate is ART. 58 on the relation of the Church to the cultures. Perhaps a brief "declaration," in which the Church turned *ad extra,* would have made a deeper impression than this diffuse treatise.

When the secretary general announced in the general congregation of 6 December that this, the one hundred and sixty-eighth, was the last of this council, stormy applause thundered through the halls of Saint Peter's. The council had done its work. In the ninth *sessio* on 7 December, in addition to *Gaudium et spes,* the decrees on the mission and the priesthood and the Declaration on Religious Freedom were approved and proclaimed. Once again the ecumenical orientation of the council was confirmed. In a common declaration the Pope and the ecumenical patriarch canceled the mutual excommunications of 1054. In his homily[42] during the Mass celebrated by twenty-four fathers, the Pope admitted that "not a few questions which were taken up during the council still awaited a satisfactory solution"; nevertheless, it might be said that the Council had corresponded to the goal set by Pope John. The Church had not been concerned to admire itself but to serve people, *ut homini serviat.*

On the next day, 8 December, the council was declared ended in a closing celebration arranged in the piazza of Saint Peter's. There were messages in French directed to political leaders, scholars and artists, women, the poor and suffering, workers and youth, delivered by representatives of these groups.[43] The Pope had said good-bye to the observers in an hour of devotion which deeply impressed all the participants in the basilica of San Paolo on 4 December.

[42] *AAS* 58 (1966), 51–59, and *Decreta,* 1061–77. In his radio address at Christmas the Pope again took up this idea: the council was an encounter of the Church with itself and the world.
[43] The messages of 8 December in *Decreta,* 1084–1100; ibid., 1101f., the Pope's declaration that the council is closed: "concludere decernimus atque statuimus ad omnes iuris effectus."

The Second Vatican Council was a world event. Was it an event of world history? A reply to this question would assume that one could in some way take in its effects at a glance.

Impact

In an interval of only a decade the impact of the Second Vatican Council cannot be decisively determined, but its effects can be observed. It is now established that it penetrated more deeply into the history of the Church than the First Vatican Council; in any event, its effects are comparable to those of Trent.[44] The first historians of Trent, Sarpi and Pallavicino, were not able to give a historical orientation, although they wrote more than half a century after the event: for them the council was still an object of strife, not history. It is tempting to say something similar about the Second Vatican Council. Of course, it can hardly be disputed that it represented a turning point in the history of the Church. Much began to move in it, its internal structure was loosened up, it opened itself up ecumenically and to the world. Was this movement for the business of Jesus Christ on earth gain or loss?

The verdicts differ widely. The original enthusiasm with which the council was greeted yielded to harsh criticism. The critics pointed to the perplexity in the faith which "pluralism" in theology and preaching had caused; to the constantly declining participation of the faithful in Mass; the sharply increasing number of priests and religious who abandoned their vocation; the bewildering number of "councils" which were supposed to promote the "democratization" of the Church; the weakening authority of the Pope and the bishops; the increase of mixed marriages; the "earthly messianism," to use Ratzinger's term, which throws man back to the feasible; to the new sexual morality: the influence of the Church on the world has not increased but dissipated. The fact is incontrovertible.

The "progressives," on the contrary, have to reflect that an inner process of fermentation was necessary in order to realize Pope John's

---

[44] The reserve which I professed immediately after the council I cannot yet even now abandon. The earlier observations: "Tradition und Fortschritt. Einige Erwägungen zum geschichtlichen Ort des Vaticanum II," in *Wort und Wahrheit* 21 (1966), 731–41; *Vaticanum II und Tridentinum. Tradition und Fortschritt in der Kirchengeschichte* (Cologne and Opladen 1968), with contributions to the discussion by J. Ratzinger, K. Rahner, et al. On the tenth anniversary of the close of the council Bavarian Radio arranged a broadcast series, which was inaugurated by J. Ratzinger, "Erfolge und Enttäuschungen"; from my own contribution, "Das Vaticanum II und die Konziliengeschichte," printed in *Klerusblatt* 56 (1976), 53–56, much has made its way into the following presentation. H. Helbling, *Dauerhaftes Provisorium. Kirche aus der Sicht eines Weltchristen* (Zurich 1976), attempts a balance.

aggiornamento. They do not deny that the new liturgy is experiencing its "childhood illnesses," but claim that, thanks to the vernacular, the faithful participate in it more actively than previously. "Declericalization" and "democratization" are consequences of the doctrine of the People of God: a far-reaching cooperation, even having a voice, by the laity is necessary if the Church is to fulfill its mission in today's world. Finally, the ecumenical stance has reduced denominational strife and brought about the "end of the Counter-Reformation." The positive assessment of the religious and ethical content of the ancient world religions offers to the mission positive starting points, and Europeanism has long been outdated. They rightly affirm that the undoubtedly present phenomena of dissolution are, at least partly, not to be referred to the council but to the upheavals within industrial society and in the Third World, and hence in the long-run have struck root in the turn in world history in which we stand. In an intermediate stage, which is full of uncertainty but also full of honest struggling and full of hope, there are movements and beginnings which promise new possibilities; a search for the mean appears, which gives the lie to the diagnosis of the end of the religious and paves from faith ways of new life, in which the unexhausted fertility of the Church's faith again proves itself, as Ratzinger says.

An accommodation of the opposing views is not yet in sight. It can be found only if one adheres to this: that the council, the highest authority in faith and morals, had set up binding norms, behind which one must not fall back, which one must also not go beyond or even disregard. There is no retreat back behind the council, but even less is this only an initial kindling for a total adaptation of the Church in faith, morals, and structure. Only if one holds fast to the council itself, can the compromise between tradition and progress be found, the identity of the Church in a changing world be preserved.

After the close of the Council of Trent a deputation of cardinals was instituted for the interpretation of the decrees, which later undertook the added task of promoting and supervising their implementation. The Second Vatican Council, differently from Trent, did not enact any decrees directly to be admitted to the canon law; this task was given to the Commission for the Revision of the Code,[45] set up during the council. For the interpretation of the decrees for the period from 3 January 1966 to 11 July 1967 the Coordinating Commission of the council was still competent, but on 11 July 1967 a special commission for interpretation was instituted, the *Pontificia Commissio decretis concilii*

---

[45] See below, the contribution of G. May (Chapter 5); important contribution by K. Mörsdorf, "Zur Neuordnung der Systematik des CIC," *AKR* 137 (1968), 3–38.

Vaticani II interpretandis. [46] It does not have the same authority as did in its day the Congregation of the Council, expanded into an office.

The council itself had in several places referred to the still to be issued rules of implementation (directories) and turned over other tasks—celibacy, indulgences, mixed marriages—expecially the reform of the Roman Curia, to the Pope.

For the implementation of the council, on 3 January 1966, to the three postconciliar commissions set up during the council, five others were added, whose chairmen and members were identical with those of the corresponding conciliar commission:[47] (1) for bishops and the government of dioceses; (2) for religious; (3) for the missions; (4) for Christian education; and (5) for the lay apostolate. The Secretariat for Promoting Christian Unity and the Secretariats for Non-Christian Religions and for Unbelievers were confirmed.

The reform of the curial offices was begun after the Council of Trent by Pius IV and Pius V but only completed by Sixtus V. After the Second Vatican Council the reconstruction of the Roman Curia, demanded during the debate on the Decree on the Pastoral Office of Bishops and promised by the Pope, had to wait only a year and a half. In the constitution *Regimini Ecclesiae universalis* of 15 August 1967[48] the work hitherto performed by the Curia received high praise, *egregia laude digna.* The Secretariat of State obtained the competence to coordinate the work of the congregations. Even the hitherto "Suprema," the Holy Office, was subordinated to it, obtained the name of *Congregatio de doctrina fidei,* and was instructed to declare the prohibition of books only after hearing the author, *audito auctore,* and reaching an understanding with the competent ordinary, *praemonito ordinario.* The former Congregation of the Council received the name of *Congregatio pro clericis;* the Congregation *De Propaganda fide,* the name of *Pro gentium evangelizatione seu De Propaganda fide.* The divisions at first acting as sections of the Congregation of Rites for the liturgy (*de cultu*) and canonizations (*de causis servorum Dei*) soon became independent. Entirely new was the Council on the Laity, *consilium de laicis.* The composition of the congregations was changed by the fact that seven residential bishops were assigned to each as ordinary members.

---

[46] *AAS* 58 (1966), 37–40; V. Carbone, *De commissione decretis Concilii Vaticani II interpretandis* (Naples 1969).

[47] The Paulinusverlag at Trier has published since 1967 a *Nachkonziliare Dokumentation,* 58 issues to 1977; there, as no. 2, the apostolic constitution *Paenitemini* of 17 December 1966 on the discipline of fasting and penance, ed. by O. Semmelroth (Trier 1967).

[48] *AAS* 59 (1967), 885–929; ibid., 881–84, the new structure of the congregations. For the reorganization of the Congregation for the Propagation of the Faith by the motu proprio *Integrae servandae* of 7 December 1965, cf. *AKR* 134 (1965), 479ff.

The three tribunals—the Apostolic Signatura, the Rota, and the Sacred Penitentiary—the Apostolic Chancery, and the Apostolic Camera remained in existence, but the entire economic sphere was reorganized by the establishing of a finance ministry, *Praefectura rerum oeconomicarum S. Sedis,* and of a central administration of property, *Administratio Patrimonii S. Sedis,* beside which the Prefecture of the Apostolic Palace took its place; also new was the Office of Statistics.

Three years after this reorganization of the Curia came the motu proprio *Ingravescentem aetatem,* which deprived cardinals after the completing of the eightieth year of age of the right to participate in a papal election,[49] but the right to elect the Pope remained as such in the College of Cardinals.

It far exceeds the possibilities of space here to offer even only a fleeting glance at the activity of the individual curial departments.[50] New is that at their side, not subordinate to them, appeared the Synod of Bishops.[51] So far it has had three regular sessions and one extraordinary session. The theme of the first regular session of 29 September to 28 October 1967, in which 199 synodalists took part, was: principles for the revision of the code; dangerous doctrinal opinions; seminaries; mixed marriages; liturgy. The newly composed profession of faith was published. The extraordinary session of 11 to 27 October 1969 took up the collaboration between the Holy See and the episcopal conferences and of these conferences among themselves. It was significant that at the opening of the Synod of Bishops the Pope referred the episcopal conferences and the summoning of residential bishops to the congregations to the principle of collegiality.

The second regular session of 30 September to 6 November 1971 took up in thirty-seven meetings the problems of the priestly office and of justice in the world. The third session of 27 September to 26 October 1974, in which 207 synodalists participated, dealt with the "evangelization of the world of today." It probably corresponded best

---

[49] *AAS* 62 (1970), 810–13.

[50] For what follows recourse was had to the annual (since 1965) publication *L'Attività della S. Sede. Pubblicazione non ufficiale.* As example may be mentioned the meeting of experts, summoned by the Congregation of Seminaries and Universities in Rome from 20 to 28 November 1967, which had the duty of submitting proposals for the revision of the constitution *Deus scientiarum* of 24 May 1931 on the basis of the conciliar decree *Optatam.* By making use of the proposals then elaborated, the Congregation of Seminaries and Universities on 20 May 1968 published norms for the new form of programs of study (A. Mayer and G. Baldanza, "Il Rinnovamento degli Studi philosofici e teologici nei seminari," *La Scuola Cattolica,* 1966, Supplemento 2).

[51] Establishing and statute of the Synod of Bishops along with a brief introduction in no. 12 of *Nachkonziliare Dokumentation* (Trier 1968) mentioned in n. 47.

to the meaning of the institution in so far as during it a survey was given of the status of the Church in Africa, Latin and North America, and Asia, as well as in the Second World behind the Iron Curtain. Continuity was assured by the Permanent Secretariat under the Pole Rubin, whose competence was significantly expanded in the course of time. There is no doubt that this typical fruit of the Second Vatican Council, a new thing in church history, still needs further development.

Pope Paul VI continued the form of apostolic proclamation by means of doctrinal writings, as cultivated by his predecessors. In the encyclical *Populorum progressio* of 26 March 1967 he took a stand in favor of the Third World;[52] in the Encyclical *Humanae vitae* of 25 July 1968 he again inculcated Christian principles for the reproduction of human life. He utilized the Holy Year 1975, proclaimed by him, to make stronger the union of the local churches with Rome and to inspire the pilgrims arriving in unexpectedly great numbers. For the more the idea was put across that the Universal Church lives in the member and local churches, the more urgent became their internal and external problems for the Church as a whole; the *communio ecclesiarum* is more demanding than any legal order. This structure of the Church, which can appeal to *Lumen gentium,* also sets new tasks for church history. The national and regional episcopal conferences have acquired a previously undreamed of importance.[53] The postconciliar synods organized by them give reason for a variety in ecclesiastical life which on occasion threatens its unity. Guarantor of this unity is the Petrine Office. It would be fatal to aim to prune it back to its functions in the ancient Church, and just as fatal to maintain certain claims raised in the high and late Middle Ages. The world Church of the twentieth century, in which all continents and races are on an equal footing, cannot be governed in a centralized way, as was the Church of the nineteenth century. However, it is just as certain that the centrifugal tendencies, becoming inexorably stronger, can be met only by a strong central power; an honorary precedence is inadequate for this, quite apart from the fact that it withdraws behind the dogma of the primacy. The modern means of news and communication give the Apostolic See the possibility of being abreast of all happenings in the world Church and, where necessary, of intervening in them to preserve the unity of the Church without reestablishing uniformity. The relaxing of centralization is demanded by the mission

[52] *AAS* 59, 1 (1967), 257–99; with commentary by O.v. Nell-Breuning in no. 4 of *Nachkonziliare Dokumentation* (Trier 1967); ibid., as no. 14, an edition of "Humanae vitae" with a "Word of the German Bishops on the Pastoral Situation" (Trier 1968).
[53] For the Federal German Republic, G. May, "Die deutsche Bischofskonferenz nach ihrer Neuordnung," *AKR* 133 (1969), 405–61; ibid., 3–13.

of the Church in our time; the Petrine Office further preserves the unity.

The Council of Trent would never have been able to exert its impact if it had not been carried by a wave of holiness. The impact of the Second Vatican Council will also depend on whether the Church of the twentieth century renews itself in the spirit of Jesus Christ. "The definitive decision on the historical worth of the Second Vatican Council depends on whether people realize in themselves the drama of the testing of chaff and wheat"; "whether at the end it will be reckoned among the luminous moments of church history depends on the people who transfer it into life," says Ratzinger.

CHAPTER 5

The Code of Canon Law and the Development of Canon Law to 1974*

From the Promulgation of the Code to the Second Vatican Council

THE CODIFICATION OF CANON LAW

The codification of the canon law of the Latin Church is due to the energy and initiative of Pius X. In the motu proprio *Arduum sane munus* of 19 March 1904 the Pope had made known his intention of assembling in one uniform codification the valid canon law of the Latin Church, which lay scattered in many sources of the law. The task was courageously undertaken and energetically pursued under the direction of Pietro Gasparri. The bishops of the world and consultors from the most important countries took part in the work. In the secret consistory of 4 December 1916 Benedict XV announced the completion of the project. On 27 May 1917 the Pope issued the law in which the Code of Canon Law obtained ratification—the apostolic constitution *Providentissima Mater Ecclesia*. The Code of Canon Law was promulgated on 28 June 1917 and took effect on 19 May 1918. The intended aim— to unify the fragmented law in the great and important questions of ecclesiastical life—was accomplished. The Code of Canon Law is a codification, complete in itself, of the common law of the Church of the Latin Rite. But it refers to earlier laws which retain their validity because and in so far as it mentions them (Canon 6). The Code of Canon Law is the law book of the Church of the Latin Rite, but to a certain extent it is also valid for the congregations of the Eastern Rites (Canon 1). The codification was stamped by the principles of the

* Georg May

151

greatest possible retention of the traditional and by prudent adaptation. The code thus contains no radical novelties, but only modifications suited to the age. Some archaic elements were dragged along, and certain newer developments, for example, in the sphere of the law of property and benefices, were not considered. The code accepted in the widest scope the proposals made by the fathers of the First Vatican Council and the bishops employed for consultation. It built also, in many ways, on the ideas and guidelines given by Leo XIII. Finally, some elements from the law of concordats entered the code, for example, in regard to the privileges of the clergy. The thinning, reworking, and modernizing of the vast matter of traditional norms represent an important legislative achievement. The code is the climax and conclusion of the development begun in the nineteenth century, which the Church aimed also to make through strict uniform discipline and close union with the Apostolic See into a fit tool of the Christian penetration of the earth. It is an achievement due preeminently to the work of the Catholic Church in Europe. It stands in the tradition of medieval canon law and draws upon the lines begun by Trent.

The Code of Canon Law is divided into five books; to it were attached eight older documents which, as regards content, had not been adopted into it. It is introduced by the *Professio catholicae fidei*. Its principles of classification are not satisfactory in every respect. For example, the law on ecclesiastical offices is dismembered and divided between two different books. The code aimed to be basically only an internal law book of the Church and hence omits from the codification the regulation of the relations of Church and state. It thereby considerably facilitated its implementation. The language of the code is succinct and clear, but it suffers from uncertainty in terminology. In regard to new elements in the content, the following examples are illustrative. The position of the bishops was strengthened. The inclination existing since the Middle Ages to curtail the power of the hierarchical courts between Pope and bishops is expressed in the insignificance of the metropolitans (Canon 274). The bishops are freely named by the Pope (Canon 329, paragraph 2), and in this matter he makes ever more use of the lists submitted by the bishops. For the first time, the office of the bishop's vicar general was regulated by the common law (Canons 366–71). Trent's law on the contracting of marriage was made binding on the whole Church, and the exceptions for Germany and Hungary were abolished (Canon 1094).

The code was accepted by Catholics in general with joy and gratitude; they showed themselves overwhelmingly convinced of the advantage of the reform. The enacting of the code actually strengthened the inner order of the Church. The states accepted the codification at least without delays. The upheavals after 1918 assisted the introduction of the code to a great degree. A considerable part of the Church-state law, which chained and limited the Church, broke apart. Numerous conditions based on concordat, privilege, or indult disappeared as a consequence of the cessation of states or favored subjects. More open regulations were often found in the building and rebuilding. The other religious congregations, apart from some German Protestants, raised hardly any objections to the code.

In an effort to assure the legal unity effected by the codification, Benedict XV on 15 September 1917, through the motu proprio *Cum iuris,* set up a Commission of Cardinals and gave it the task of authentically interpreting the code and incorporating in it modifications that had become necessary. It fulfilled the first part of its office, but, apart from two exceptions, it did not take up the second. At the same time the Pope decreed that the congregations of the Roman Curia should issue no new *decreta* without urgent cause, but should limit themselves to *instructiones.*

THE DEVELOPMENT OF THE LAW FROM 1918 TO 1958

It soon became clear that it was not to be supposed that scholarship and practice could get along essentially with the code. The law formulated in the code required implementation and completion by further norms. Codification did not halt the development of the law, but fostered it. The law of the code developed further powerfully, especially through the numerous authentic declarations of the Commission for Interpretation, but also through the legislation of the Popes, especially Pius XI and Pius XII and the Congregations of Cardinals. The last mentioned issued their norms under the title of *instructiones, decreta, normae, indices,* and *formulae.* The judgments of the Roman Rota,[1] published annually from 1912, and the decisions of the congregations in individual cases likewise contributed to the interpretation and further growth of the law, especially that of marriage. And the letters of admonition and of teaching of the Holy See were also of great significance for the implementation and growth of the law.

The law of the code, so far as this can be observed, on the whole made its way relatively successfully. However, it was not possible to convert all prescriptions of the code into actuality. The code left untouched the treaties made by the Apostolic See with countries and hence to that extent renounced any claim to enforce them (Canon 3). Likewise, acquired rights as well as privileges and indults granted by the Apostolic See remained basically valid (Canon 4). Hence law that was

[1] *Sacrae Romanae Rotae Decisiones seu Sententiae* I (Rome 1912).

compatible and recognized by the Holy See constituted a limit for the expansion of the new law. In view of the extensive sphere of validity of the code, one must reckon with a still stronger separation between formal and actual validity than with other codifications. New particular law, which supplemented or modified the code, was created especially by concordats. And in the enforcing of the code the bishops displayed an abundant activity at diocesan synods through the adapting and collecting of diocesan law.

Benedict XV

The remaining years of the pontificate of Benedict XV stood under the standard of the imposing, the constructing, and the maintaining of the situation of legal unity that had been achieved. The manner of appointing to episcopal sees in the United States that had been set by the decree *Ratio iuris* of the Consistorial Congregation on 25 July 1916 was extended with insignificant changes to a number of other countries.[2] The Pope undertook important changes in the constitution of the missions.[3] In view of certain radical movements in Czechoslovakia and Hungary, he several times declared, most clearly in the letter of 3 January 1920 to the archbishop of Prague, that the Holy See would never grant the abolition or modification of the law of celibacy.[4]

Pius XI

Pius XI did the chief work in legislation for the enforcing of the Code of Canon Law. Nevertheless he permitted no profound changes in the code. The norms issued by him were thoroughly worked out and adjusted to practice. A special characteristic of Pius XI's legislation was the comprehensive establishing of norms for concordats, which will be discussed below.

In 1929 the Pope introduced the codification of the canon law of the Eastern Churches, establishing a Commission of Cardinals under the chairmanship of Pietro Gasparri.[5] To two other commissions, which were set up in 1930, he confided the task of collecting the sources of Eastern canon law and elaborating drafts for the codification. The second commission was changed on 17 July 1935 into the *Pontificia*

---

[2] Canada (*AAS* 11 [1919], 124–128); Scotland (*AAS* 13 [1921], 13–16); Brazil (*AAS* 13 [1921], 222–25); Mexico (*AAS* 13 [1921], 379–82); Poland (*AAS* 13 [1921], 430–32). cf. K. Mörsdorf, *Das neue Besetzungsrecht der bischöflichen Stühle unter besonderer Berücksichtigung des Listenverfahrens* (=*Kölner Rechtswissenschaftliche Abhandlungen* no. 6) (Bonn, Cologne and Berlin 1933).
[3] For example *AAS* 12 (1920), 331–33.
[4] Ibid. 11 (1919), 122f.; 12 (1920), 33–35, 585–88.
[5] Ibid. 21 (1929), 669.

Commissio ad redigendum "Codicem Iuris Canonici orientalis."[6] From the codification of the Eastern canon law it was expected that it would consolidate the bonds among the Eastern Rite congregations on the one hand and that of these with the Latin Church on the other and produce adaptations of law suited to the day.[7] In two decrees some canons of the code were extended also to the Eastern rite communities.[8] The motu proprio *Sancta Dei Ecclesia* of 25 March 1938 subjected also the Latin rite Catholics living in the Middle East to the Congregation for the Eastern Church.

The delayed arrival of three American cardinals on the occasion of the papal election of 1922 was utilized by Pius XI as an opportunity to modify in the motu proprio *Cum proxime* of 1 March 1922 the regulation of the conclave by Pius X on 25 December 1904. According to it the legal interval for the beginning of the conclave was lengthened from ten to fifteen days, to which, by decision of the College of Cardinals, three more days at the most might be added. The motu proprio was adopted into the appendix of documents of the code. Many decrees of the Pope affected the organization and the order of the competence and of the procedure of the departments of the Roman Curia. The congregations were strongly meshed in personnel. Through the constitution *Quae divinitus* of 27 March 1935 the *Sacra Poenitentiaria* obtained a new organization; on 29 July 1934 the *Sacra Romana Rota* underwent a reorganization of its constitution and its procedure. In the carrying out of Canon 328 there appeared on 15 August 1934 the constitution *Ad incrementum* on the prelates of the Roman Curia. For the quinquennial faculties of residential bishops, reintroduced on 17 March 1922,[9] the motu proprio *Post Datam* of 20 April 1923 created a uniform formula, which was issued by the Consistorial Congregation. For carrying out Canon 296 the Congregation for the Propagation of the Faith on 8 December 1929 issued the important instruction *Quum huic Sacrae* on the relations between missionary bishops and religious superiors. In order to bring the statutes of cathedral and collegiate chapters into conformity with the law of the code, the Congregation of the Council on 25 July 1923 directed the bishops to allow the chapters an interval of six months for the adjustment of their statutes; if nothing should be done during this period, they should themselves carry out the revision. The discipline of the clergy was strictly inculcated or regulated by a considerable number of complexes of norms; in the encyclical *Ad*

[6] Ibid. 27 (1935), 306–8.
[7] Cf. A. Coussa, "De Codificatione canonica orientali," *Acta Congressus Iuridici Internationalis* IV (Rome 1937), 491–532.
[8] *AAS* 20 (1928), 195; 26 (1934), 550.
[9] Ochoa, *Leges Ecclesiae* I, 431–38.

catholici sacerdotii of 20 December 1935 the Pope had called the clergy's attention to the dignity and importance of its mission. The constitution *Deus scientiarum Dominus* of 24 May 1931, with the *ordinationes* of the Congregation for Studies of 12 June 1931 on Catholic universities and faculties[10] represented a sort of fundamental law of the Catholic system of higher education. It demanded an increase of ecclesiastical faculties and the raising of the scholarly requirements for promotions as well as the improvement of the teaching profession and the means of instruction. The Congregation of Seminaries and Universities was stripped of the right of promotion granted in Canon 256, par. 1. Under the name "Catholic Action," Pius XI called into being a lay movement united to the apostolate of the hierarchy. On 7 May 1923 appeared the decree of the Congregation of the Sacraments, *Catholica doctrina,* which in the appended bylaw exhaustively regulated the procedure in the dissolving of marriage *ratum sed non consummatum.* The instruction of the Congregation of the Sacraments of 27 December 1930 on the ordination *scrutinia* set up a detailed method for examining candidates for orders in an effort to keep out of the priesthood unsuitable or unworthy persons. The instruction of the Congregation of the Sacraments of 15 August 1936 brought, in 240 articles, detailed norms on the conducting of the annulment of marriages in the diocesan tribunals, which further developed the law of the code.

Pius XII

Pope Pius XII displayed a voluminous legislative activity in all areas. He intervened considerably more deeply into the body of the Code of Canon Law than had his predecessor. Pius XII was himself a learned canonist, who knew the history, system, and spirit of canon law. Together with his delight in responsibility and decisiveness, as well as with his gift for choosing the right collaborators, he was in a sense created to be a legislator. The legislation of Pius XII was throughout determined by the intention of coming to the aid of pastoral necessities. It was dedicated to doing justice to all realities conditioned by time and locally circumscribed. The Pope courageously faced changed conditions and took into account new insights. He carefully put his laws in the right way for legal reality. Modified norms for the Universal Church were often prepared and tested by indults for specific areas. Then they were introduced in gradual steps. The basic features of this legislation were prudent adjustment to new situations, openness to developments, foresight in changes, firmness in the fundamental, and flexibility in questions of procedure. Although the legislation of Pius XII partly

---

[10] A. Bea, "Die päpstliche Studienreform," *StdZ* 121 (1931), 401–5.

involved deeply incisive changes of ecclesiastical discipline, at no time did there exist in clergy or faithful a feeling of insecurity or of helplessness. There never was even the appearance that the Pope was pushed or subject to pressure. At all stages he remained sovereignly the master of the situation.

In the encyclical *Mystici Corporis* of 29 June 1943 Pius XII treated the fundamental relation of Church and canon law. In a happy synthesis he sketched the correlation and distinction of legal structure and supernatural life in the Church. The encyclical was a landmark for the doctrine of Church membership. On 8 December 1945 he issued the constitution *Vacantis Apostolicae Sedis.* In content it adhered essentially to the constitution *Vacante Sede Apostolica* of Pius X of 25 December 1904, but added the modification that in the future for the papal election one further vote beyond the two-thirds majority was required. Above all, Pius XII became the great legislator in the field of the law of the sacraments. In the constitution *Episcopalis consecrationis* of 30 November 1944 he clarified the role of the two coconsecrators in episcopal ordination; in the constitution *Sacramentum Ordinis* of 30 November 1947, the matter and form of the ordination of deacon, priest, and bishop. By the decree *Spiritus Sancti munera* of 14 September 1946 parish priests obtained the authorization to administer the sacrament of confirmation,[11] in the territory of their parish, to the faithful who as a result of a serious illness are in danger of death. The encyclical *Mediator Dei* of 20 November 1947 is important for the law of the sacrament-sacrifice of the Eucharist and of the liturgy in general. The constitution *Christus Dominus* and the appended instruction of 6 January 1953 reorganized the precept of the Eucharistic fast and granted to local ordinaries the power to permit the celebration of evening Mass. The motu proprio *Sacram Communionem* of 19 March 1957 brought further mitigations of the Eucharistic fast and the extension of the faculty to permit evening Mass. Many legislative acts of the Pope and his assisting agencies applied to matrimony. The premarital investigations were minutely regulated in 1941, the order of precedence of the ends of marriage was clarified in 1944, artificial insemination, apart from the permissible *adiuvatio naturae,* was rejected in 1949 and 1956. Liturgical law was permanently developed by Pius XII. The Solemn Easter Vigil was restored in 1951, the liturgy of Holy Week was reorganized in 1955, the reform of the missal and breviary was taken up in 1955. Church music obtained guidance in the encyclical *Musicae sacrae disciplina* of 25 December 1955 and in the instruction *De*

---

[11] The decree was prepared by the indult for South America of 30 April 1929 (*AAS* 21 [1939], 554–57).

Musica sacrae of 3 September 1958. The constitution *Provida Mater Ecclesia* of 2 February 1947 is in a sense the founding charter of secular institutes. To the already existing three forms of the state of perfection a fourth was added.[12] The constitution *Sponsa Christi* of 21 November 1950 and the related instruction *Inter praeclara* of 23 November 1950 brought about an adaptation of the inclosure of nuns to the times without sacrificing anything essential of the life of virginity and contemplation. The constitution *Exsul Familia* of 2 August 1952 introduced an exhaustive ordering of the pastoral care of refugees, exiles, and emigrants. Under Pius XII the codification of the canon law of the Eastern Churches reached its maturity. The following parts were promulgated: on 22 January 1949 the law of marriage; on 6 January 1950 the law of trials; on 9 February 1952 the law of religious institutes and of property as well as the stipulating of specified concepts; on 2 June 1957 the constitutional law. That this law of the diversity of the communities of the Eastern rites was adequate in every respect is not claimed. But a certain simplification was necessary. Nevertheless, it is questionable to what extent the codified law has been put into practice.

From the Convocation of the Second Vatican Council

The Second Vatican Council was an event of the greatest significance for canon law. An account of it does not fall within the scope of this contribution. Let merely this be remarked: the greatest part of the declarations and directions of the council was not directly oriented to the individual law in force, but, so far as there was question at all of legally relevant texts, a sort of legislative program or stating of principles, which had in view the ecclesiastical legislators. They were called upon to undertake a modification of canon law in accord with the spirit and the letter of the conciliar texts.

JOHN XXIII

On 25 January 1959 Pope John XXIII announced a revision of the Code of Canon Law. On 28 March 1963 he instituted a Commission for the Reform of the Code. At first the chairman was Cardinal Pietro Ciriaci. In view of the short duration of the pontificate no results could be expected from the work of the commission, especially since all the personnel were monopolized by the preparation and implementation of the council. Under John XXIII the legislation of the Holy See bore thoroughly traditional characteristics. No single decree of the Pope or of the Holy See abandons the line of continuity and of cautious change.

---

[12] Further norms for secular institutes in the motu proprio *Primo feliciter* of 12 March 1948, decree of 25 March 1947, instruction *Cum Sanctissimus* of 19 March 1948.

That the genial but indecisive impulses of the Pope had intended extensive changes is at least doubtful, considering his conservative outlook. Nevertheless, this legislation has no uniform character; it lacks planning and a dominating guidance. The Synod of the Diocese of Rome, held by John XXIII from 24 to 31 January 1960, proceeded in expressly traditional paths. It seemed to wish to impose once more the traditional church discipline firmly and sharply. The law, already challenged from 1910 to 1915, of the suburbicarian sees underwent new modifications through the motu proprio *Ad Suburbicarias* of 10 March 1961, which abolished the cardinals' right of option to the suburbicarian sees, and especially by the motu proprio *Suburbicariis sedibus* of 11 April 1962. Thereafter the cardinal bishops no longer have any jurisdiction in the see whose title they bear. It is governed rather by a residential bishop. The cardinal deacons, for whom the code already required priestly ordination (Canon 232, par. 1), in the future had to be bishops, in accord with the motu proprio *Cum gravissima* of 15 April 1962. To this higher valuation of the College of Cardinals scarcely corresponded the increase in the number of cardinals carried out by John XXIII. In the creation of 15 December 1958 the Pope for the first time exceeded the maximum number set by Sixtus V. The motu proprio *Summi Pontificis Electio* of 5 September 1962 supplemented the constitution *Vacantis Apostolicae Sedis* and changed the law of the papal election in the sense that he is elected who obtains two-thirds of the valid votes. Only in the event that the number of cardinals present is not divisible by three is a further ballot required. The turning of the Pope to the separated Christians began to appear in law. On 17 July 1961 the graduation of non-Catholics was conceded to ecclesiastical faculties.[13]

PAUL VI

Organs

Naturally, the chief role in the implementation of the Second Vatican Council devolved upon the Holy See. In numerous apostolic constitutions, motu proprio, decrees, instructions, directories, encyclicals, norms, and proclamations an exhaustive material in norms of varied obligatory force was spread through the Church, claiming to serve the carrying out of the Second Vatican Council.[14] The centralized control

---

[13] *AfkKR* 130 (1961), 485f.
[14] The rules for implementation of the decrees *Christus Dominus, Presbyterorum ordinis, Perfectae caritatis,* and *Ad gentes* were issued in the form of a skeleton law in the motu proprio *Ecclesiae Sanctae* of 6 August 1966.

lies regularly in the Congregations of Cardinals. The Secretariat for Promoting Christian Unity and at first the Commission for the Implementation of the Constitution on the Liturgy also had an important share. The episcopal conferences and the Synod of Bishops exercise a powerful influence on the shaping of papal law. By the motu proprio *Finis Concilio* of 3 January 1966 Paul VI called into being the postconciliar commissions. The authentic interpretation of the conciliar decrees was entrusted to the Central Commission. Its place was taken in 1967 by the *Pontificia Commissio decretis Concilii Vaticani II interpretandis*.[15] However, this commission interprets not only documents of the council,[16] but also the decrees issued for their execution. But other congregations likewise care for the interpretation of the conciliar decrees and the norms pertaining to them for their sphere.

The legislative acts of the Holy See in turn call forth numerous rules of implementation from episcopal conferences and from bishops. In several countries diocesan synods or synods of a new sort were held for the enforcement of the council. As the first, the Catholic Church in the Netherlands organized a so-called Pastoral Church at Noordwijkerhout from 1966 to 1970.[17] The bishops of the country, priests, and laity took part in it, and non-Catholic observers played an important role. The legal nature of the meeting remained undefined. The binding force of the decrees passed by it must not have gone beyond the character of recommendations. This new type of synod aspired to show, as the first after the close of the Second Vatican Council, how to realize and concretize the decrees and initiatives of the council in a particular Church. Its chief goal, however, was probably the creating of a changed awareness among the Dutch Catholics. Voluminous texts were enacted in six sessions, and their range extended from the concepts of authority to the Jewish question. However, they are very frequently conceptually ambiguous and theologically inadequate as well as to a great extent determined by the ideology of democracy and of hostility to canon law.

---

[15] *AAS* 59 (1967), 1003.

[16] For example, ibid. 60 (1968), 360–63.

[17] B. Cardinal Alfrink, *Kirche im Umbruch* (Munich 1968); J. C. Hampe, "Das niederländische Pastoralkonzil," *StdZ* 181 (1968), 177–95; E. Kleine, *Autorität im Kreuzfeurer* (Essen 1968); idem, *Welt zwischen Hunger und Heil* (Munich 1968); idem, *Primat des Gewissens* (Munich 1969); idem, *Glaube im Umbruch* (Munich 1970); idem, *Es geht um mehr als Zölibat* (Munich 1970); idem, *Ökumene auf dem Prüfstand* (Munich 1971); J. Strauss, ed., *Ökumenisches Modell Holland* (=*Forum-Reihe* 13) (Göttingen and Zürich 1969); J. Lortz, *Holland in Not* (Luxemburg 1970); J. Kerkhofs, "Das niederländische Pastoralkonzil als Modell einer demokratischen Kirchenversammlung," *Concilium* 7 (1971), 212–15; M. Schmaus, L. Scheffczyk, J. Giers, eds., *Exempel Holland. Theologische Analyse und Kritik des Niederländischen Pastoralkonzils* (Berlin 1972).

Opposed to individual positive regulations was an abundance of misleading and erroneous assertions. At the synod the spirit of a radical reformism was predominant, and neither the common law of the Church nor the binding teaching of the Church was a barrier against it. Experiments were unscrupulously advocated, regardless of the possible consequences. Many novelties were introduced without regard to the Universal Church. Decisive statements of faith were obfuscated or disregarded. A binding profession of faith seemed not to exist for the synod's majority. The concept of God and revelation were reinterpreted. Holy Scripture was in many passages improperly interpreted. The idea of the Church was completely deformed. Heretics and unbelievers also have a place in the "Church" described by the Pastoral Council. The sacramental and hierarchical structure of the Church was denied. The primacy was leveled, the ecclesiastical teaching office eliminated, jurisdiction reduced. The Church was sociologized and humanized. Unequivocal moral norms disappeared. Pope Paul VI in his letter of 24 December 1969[18] to Cardinal Alfrink displayed anxiety over the direction taken by the pastoral council. The bishops, however, who took part in it were in general silent in regard to the absurd statements that were contrary to the faith. Nevertheless, the episcopate wanted to avoid a break with the Pope. The Dutch Pastoral Council was at the same time the expression and cause of the crisis in which the Catholic Church in the Netherlands finds itself. As far as putting the Second Vatican Council into practice it accomplished hardly anything. In Germany, following individual diocesan synods—Hildesheim, Meissen[19]—the so-called Common Synod of the bishoprics in the Federal Republic of Germany[20] and then the so-called Pastoral Synod of the

---

[18] *AAS* 62 (1970), 66–69.

[19] F. J. Wothe, *Kirche in der Synode. Zwischenbilanz der Hildesheimer Diözesansynode* (Hildesheim 1968); G. May, "Bermerkungen zu dem Rätesystem in der Diözese Meissen nach den Dekreten I und II der Diözesansynode des Jahres 1969," *TThZ* 80 (1971), 308–15.

[20] Statute of 11 November 1969 in *AfkKR* 138 (1969), 554–56; decree of the Congregation for Bishops of 14 February 1970 for confirmation of the statute of the Common Synod of the Dioceses in the Federal Republic of Germany, ibid., 139 (1970), 150f.; pastoral letter of 16 February 1970, ibid. 139 (1970), 177–82; promulgation of the German Episcopal Conference of 22 September 1970 relating to the agenda of the Common Synod of the Dioceses in the Federal Republic of Germany, ibid. 139 (1970), 526–38. Since 1970 there has appeared the periodical *Synode. Amtliche Mitteilungen der Gemeinsamen Synode der Bistümer in der Bundesrepublik Deutschland:* cf. M. Plate, *Das deutsche Konzil. Die Würzburger Synode. Bericht und Deutung* (Freiburg, Basel and Vienna 1975); *Gemeinsame Synode der Bistümer in der Bundesrepublik Deutschland. Beschlüsse der Vollversammlung. Offizielle Gesamtausgabe* I (Freiburg, Basel and Vienna 1976).

German Democratic Republic[21] were convoked. They met in several sessions from 1971 or 1973 respectively to 1975. The first meeting of the Common Synod suffered from serious structural defects.[22] Its statutes overlooked the fact, first, that the episcopal conference possessed no general competence to legislate for all ecclesiastical matters, but only for those concerning which such competence was given it by the Apostolic See. In the area of local ecclesiastical legislation, for which the episcopal conference had no competence, the synod was instructed to have the individual residential bishops adopt the synodal material as their own. No however great majority of the members of the episcopal conference could oblige them to this. The synod was erroneously conceived. The roles within the commission were not properly distributed. The synod gave priests and lay persons a share in legislation and hence obscured the fact that legislation in the Church pertains only to the bishops by right and that priests and lay persons are restricted to advising. More satisfactory was the structure of the Pastoral Synod of the jurisdictional area of the German Democratic Republic. In it the members of the Conference of Ordinaries did not partake in the voting, according to the statute. In this way the fundamental distinction between shepherds and subjects, as well as that between legislating and advising, persisted.

The Common Synod issued numerous documents on the share of the laity in preaching, on the duties and goals of religious instruction, on the administering and receiving of the sacraments, on the importance and form of the liturgy, on the aims of youth work, on the obligation of the Church vis-à-vis foreign workers, on the Church's duties in the sphere of education, on the position of religious communities in the Church, on structures and services of pastoral care, on the protection of the personal rights of the individual within the Church, and on the coresponsibility of all the faithful for the Church's mission. In the main, they have declamatory value, but to a degree they penetrate deep into the structure of the congregations.

In Austria most bishoprics held diocesan synods. The Holy See granted the admission of lay persons under the proviso that the priests

---

[21] Statute of spring 1972 in *AfkKR* 141 (1972), 538–43; order of election of 1 September 1972 in *Kirchliches Amtsblatt für die Bistümer und die erzbischöflichen bzw. bischöflichen Kommissariate im Gebiet der DDR. Ausgabe des Bistums Meissen* 21 (1972), 33–35.

[22] W. Aymans, "Synode 1972. Strukturprobleme eines Regionalkonzils," *AfkKR* 138 (1969), 363–88; idem, "Ab Apostolica Sede recognitum. Erwägungen zu der päpstlichen Bestätigung des Statutes für die 'Gemeinsame Synode der Bistümer in der Bundesrepublik Deutschland,'" ibid. 139 (1970), 405–27; idem, "Synodalstatut—Kritik einer Verteidigung," ibid. 140 (1971), 136–46.

had at least an absolute majority on the commissions and in the plenary assembly.[23] All dioceses of the country met in the "Austrian Synodal Proceeding," which, despite extensive borrowing from the statute and routine of the German synod, did not constitute a synod.[24] The decrees of the meeting represented only recommendations to the episcopal conference. In Switzerland meetings of diocesan synods alternated with those of the Swiss Plenary Assembly.[25]

General Character

The task of implementing the Second Vatican Council was given to Paul VI, the episcopal conferences, and the individual bishops. However, several obstacles presented themselves to the converting of the directions and efforts of the council into practicable norms. First, many statements of the council were not clear as a consequence of the "pastoral" style and hence were controverted. On the other hand, the development in the Church had already actually gone on ahead of the council in many respects. Finally, a uniform desire, such as is indispensable for a harmonious legislation, was usually absent. The Church was in a leadership crisis, which adversely affected legislation to a serious degree.[26] And so the development of the law since the Second Vatican Council is basically different from the earlier. The traditional reserve and discretion of the changes were abandoned. Incisive, even radical changes took place rapidly and without preparation, often in homely dress. The haste with which norms were produced in the postconciliar period was favorable to neither their quality nor their content. Contra-

---

[23] *Leben und Wirken der Kirche von Wien. Handbuch der Synode 1969–1971* (Vienna 1972); *Im Dienst an den Menschen. St. Pöltner Diözesansynode 1972* (St. Pölten, n.d.); *AfkKR* 138 (1969), 172f.

[24] "Statut des Österreichischen Synodalen Vorgangs," *ÖAfkR* 24 (1973), 249–52.

[25] "Rahmenstatut für Diözesanssynoden," *ÖAfkR* 23 (1972), 112–15: J. Amstutz, "Zu den ecclesiogischen Grundlagen der Synode 72," *Schweizerische Kirchenzeitung* 12 (1971), 181f.; W. Künzle, J. Meili, J. Gähwiler, *Was Kann die Synode? Ein theologischer Bericht* (Olten and Freiburg i. Breisgau 1972); J. G. Fuchs, "Neuere Entwicklungen des Katholischen Kirchenrechts auf Schweizer Boden," *ÖAfKR* 23 (1972), 163–94; I. Fürer, "De synodis dioecesanis in Helvetia," *Periodica* 62 (1973), 143–48; *Liebe-Sexualität-Ehe. Die Synode Zum Thema. Zusammengestellt und Kommentiert von H. Camenzind-Weber* (Zurich, Einsiedeln and Cologne 1975).

[26] H. Heimerl, "Einige formale Probleme des poskonziliaren allgemeinen Rechtes," *ÖAfKR* 24 (1973), 139–59; G. May, "Bemerkungen zu der kirchlichen Gesetzgebung nach dem Zweiten Vatikanischen Konzil unter besonderer Berücksichtigung von Liturgie und Kirchenmusik," H. Lonnendonker, ed., *In Caritate et Veritate. Festschrift für Johannes Overath* (Saarbrücken 1973), 67–99; C. G. Fürst, "Die kirchliche Gesetzgebung seit 1958 oder Zur kunst der Gesetzgebung," H. Heinemann, H. Herrmann, P. Mikat, eds., *Diaconia et Ius. Festgabe für Heinrich Flatten zum 65. Geburtstag, dargebracht von seinen Freuden und Schulern* (Munich, Paderborn and Vienna 1973), 287–301.

dictions in one and the same law, to the law of a higher legislator, or in laws rapidly succeeding one another were not rare. Mistakes and omissions made improvements necessary. Changes in the law increased so that a growing insecurity seized upon members of the Church. Legal material grew enormously and even for the expert was not always easy to master. The voluminous production of norms was, to be sure, not only an effect of the Second Vatican Council but also a symptom of critical phenomena appearing in the Church in almost all spheres and in most countries. The trend of the legislation was regularly to adaptation and relief, adaptation not so much to changed circumstances, whose form was not subject to the power of the Church, but rather to a changed mentality, for example, to the ideology of equality and the wave of democratization, and relief not from burdens which could no longer be borne, but from obligations whose fulfilling demanded moral effort and strength of self-control, for example, in regard to the Eucharistic fast or the carrying out of the obligation of attending Mass on holy days. The trust of the legislator in the strength of men's self-determination had grown, and greater responsibility was laid on the individual. Ecclesiastical standardization withdrew from some subjects; it became grandiose. Lower courts were empowered to a great extent to deal with business hitherto reserved to higher. Full authority was ever more generously imparted to bishops and pastors, and even to chaplains. In increasing measure power of jurisdiction was turned over to lay persons.[27] Legislation was not rarely determined by external motives, not those inherent in the matter, especially with the aim of letting powerful groups do their will. In an effort to relieve the pressure on the bishops, made aware of their importance at the council, Paul VI, long before the issuing of the Decree on Bishops, granted them new faculties in the motu proprio *Pastorale munus* of 30 November 1963.[28] The standardization of the valid dispensations from the precept of the Eucharistic fast was made known orally by the secretary general of the Second Vatican Council on 21 November 1964.[29] In not a few cases modifications of the law were regularly extorted. Proceeding from the statements of specific theologians, certain circles of clerics and lay persons introduced practices and texts desired by them and placed the bishops before faits accomplis. This procedure was practiced especially in the sphere of liturgy. The bishops, sometimes after trivial resistance,

---

[27] For example, motu proprio *Causas matrimoniales* of 28 March 1971, V, par. 1, *AAS* 63 (1971), 441–46, here 443.

[28] K. Mörsdorf, "Neue Vollmachten und Privilegien der Bischöfe," *AfkKR* 133 (1964), 82–101.

[29] *AfkKR* 133 (1964), 428.

gave in, and the arbitrarily introduced methods of acting and texts were made law or permitted by the Holy See to become law. A further characteristic of this legislation was the intention of meeting the wishes or the pressure of non-Catholics. The ecumenism proclaimed by the council had turned out to be a fertile motive of many alterations of law, for example, in regard to mixed marriages, *communio in sacris,* and the reception of the sacraments. The connivance with Protestantism in the area of liturgy and sacramental law, whereby the innermost sphere of ecclesiastical life was affected, became serious. The claim for many postconciliar documents of compliance with the directions of the council could not be verified after exact examination, because either the programmatic declarations of the council were observed too imprecisely or the postconciliar norms did not remain within the clearly discernible will of the council.[30] Thus, for example, as regards the system of government by councils, which was set up in the German dioceses, it was demonstrated from many sides that it was in opposition to the conciliar directives.[31]

The particular synods sought to introduce into the life of the Church by way of legislation in the local churches all the matters which had no prospect of being taken up at the Second Vatican Council. The following examples may be cited. Confirmation should be administered to a greater degree by nonbishops. The penitential devotion should acquire a sacramental character. Remarried divorced persons should be admitted to receive Communion. The matrimonial impediment of disparity of cult and the obligation to the canonical form in contracting marriage should be abolished. The participation of Catholics in the Protestant Lord's Supper should be made possible. Also demanded were the admission of married men to the priesthood, the reinstatement of married priests in the priestly ministry, and the investigation of the possibility of granting priestly ordination to women. In the question of contraception there even appeared in the synodal statements a deviation from the Church's binding moral teaching. In the light of

---

[30] For example, M. Pesendorfer, "Zur Ausführungsgesetzgebung der Österreichischen Bischofskonferenz zum MP 'Matrimonia mixta,' " *ÖAfKR* 23 (1972), 16–33; R. Potz, "Pastoralrat und Domkapitel. Überlegungen zur Stellung bischöflicher Beratungsorgane," ibid., 69–96; G. Luf, "Allgemeiner Gesetzeszweck und Iusta Causa Dispensationis (Anmerkungen zu einem aktuellen Problem)," ibid., 97–106.

[31] K. Mörsdorf, "Die andere Hierarchie. Eine kritische Untersuchung zur Einsetzung von Laienräten in den Diözesen der Bundesrepublik Deutschland," *AFkKR* 138 (1969), 461–509; G. May, "Das Verhältnis von Pfarrgemeinderat und Pfarrer nach gemeinem Recht und nach Mainzer Diözesanrecht," H. Heinemann, H. Herrmann, P. Mikat, eds., *Diaconia et Ius. Festgabe für Heinrich Flatten zum 65. Geburtstag* (Munich, Paderborn, and Vienna 1973), 202–25; H. Socha, "Mitverantwortung gleich Mitentscheidung?" *AfkKR* 142 (1973), 16–70.

these aberrations and numerous other serious flaws, the verdict on the synods in the German-speaking lands can only be that they increased the perplexity in the Church. The critical and most urgent task of confirming the faith and intensifying devotion was not even approached by them, let alone implemented. Many decrees of the synods did not promote the carrying out of the council but worked against it or disregarded it. To the extent that they aimed to implement the council, they partly skipped over the middle portion of the still existing regulations for total church implementation. In any event the synodal assemblies encroached upon the law of the revised code. In the question of lay preaching the offense against the common law was later censured by the Holy See.[32] But this was precisely the matter which, after the Holy See had given in, became the first to be put in force.[33] Presumably the intention was to present a fait accompli which the universal legislator could not disregard. The chief significance of the synods lies in the fact that they acted as opinion-forming agents, and indeed in the demolition of dogmatic, moral, and legal ties. Practice already closely followed the perspectives which appeared at the synods, regardless of contrary law. The so-called pastoral character of many documents, which claimed to be practicable norms, frequently obscured their normative value and thereby paved the way for a dangerous legal uncertainty. Many of the *vota* issued at the synods just mentioned were useless for the further developments of ecclesiastical law because they either were too vague or bypassed reality.

Of the greatest significance for the development of canon law, then, was the raising of the episcopal conferences to a real hierarchical tribunal between the individual bishop and the Apostolic See by the Second Vatican Council. Their legislative competence was constantly growing. In this way the process of centralizing and standardizing the law by the Holy See, to be observed in the nineteenth century and the first half of the twentieth, was halted and gave place to a countermovement. The particularizing of the law increased. Peculiarities of national Churches gained greater weight, in fact were to a degree consciously promoted. The inserting of ever broader circles of persons into the process of legislation showed the enactment of norms and well-nigh leveled every legislative project. The actual incompetence of most members of synods of the new type for the treating of the questions posed is notorious. The assignment of competence and the precedence of the

---

[32] *Deutsche Tagepost* no. 3, of 5–6 January 1973, 1f.; *Klerusblatt* 53 (1973), 5–7, 288. First came the decree of the German Episcopal Conference of 18 November 1970 on the permission for lay preaching, in *AfkKR* 139 (1970), 578f.

[33] Decree on the sharing of the laity in preaching of 4 January 1973, *Amtsblatt für das Erzbistum München und Freising* no. 162, 1973, 282–92.

norms were especially not often observed by the particular legislators. The synods mentioned considered themselves competent for almost all areas of church life and interfered illicitly in the sphere of the Universal Church.

Individual Legislative Actions

The Second Vatican Council was under the aegis of a revalorization of the episcopal office. The lever for this undertaking was the principle of collegiality. According to it, the holders of the highest power in the Universal Church are not only the Pope but also the College of Bishops acting in agreement with the Pope. The episcopate logically claimed to share in the rule of the entire Church even outside the general councils. The Pope had regard for this desire in a twofold respect. First, he announced to the surprised fathers at the opening of the fourth session of the Second Vatican Council on 14 September 1965 the establishing of a Synod of Bishops. On the next day the motu proprio *Apostolica sollicitudo*[34] was published in the council *aula*. The Synod of Bishops is a central ecclesiastical institution, which represents the episcopate of the world. In accord with its nature, it is a permanent institution, but meets only on special invitation. The Synod of Bishops has fundamentally only an advisory function, but can, if the Pope allows, also issue decrees; its decrees are subject to papal confirmation. It should foster the union and cooperation between Pope and bishops, put information at disposal, bring about uniformity in questions of doctrine and in procedure within the Church as well as advise in regard to the subjects which from time to time are to be placed on the agenda. Convocation, approval of elected members, drawing up of the list of *tractanda,* and issuance of the agenda, as well as the chairmanship, belong to the Pope. Representatives of the episcopal conferences constitute the greatest part of the members. In addition, there are the Eastern patriarchs, religious, heads of the departments of the Roman Curia, and bishops, clerics, or religious nominated by the Pope for this case. Then the motu proprio *Pro comperto sane* of 6 August 1967 prescribed the admittance of seven residential bishops as full members into each of the congregations of the Roman Curia. They took part in their plenary sessions. Together

---

[34] *AAS* 57 (1966), 775–80. Also, Paul VI's *Regolamento* for the Synod of Bishops, 8 December 1966, in *AAS* 59 (1967), 91–103; announcement of the Council for the Public Affairs of the Church of 8 August 1969 on the revision of the order for the Synod of Bishops, in *AAS* 61 (1969), 525–39; announcement of the Council for the Public Affairs of the Church of 20 August 1971 on changes in the order for the Synod of Bishops, in *AAS* 63 (1971), 702–4; cf. K. Mörsdorf, "Synodus Episcoporum," *AfkKR* 135 (1966), 131–36.

with the motu proprio *De Episcoporum muneribus,*[35] issued on 15 June 1966 to implement the decree *Christus Dominus* on the pastoral duty of bishops, which gave bishops the faculty basically to dispense in individual cases from all general laws of the Church, as well as with the abolition of the fundamental irremovability of pastors by the motu proprio *Ecclesiae Sanctae* (no. 20), the aims of the bishops for the mentioned changes seemed to have been satisfied.

In connection with the stressing of the collegiality of the bishops was the diminution of privileges of the College of Cardinals. The dignity of cardinal-protector of monastic congregations was abolished as early as 28 April 1964.[36] In order to take into account the special position and the sensibilities of the Eastern patriarchs, Paul VI in the motu proprio *Ad Purpuratorum Patrum* of 11 February 1965 decreed that at their admission into the College of Cardinals these should be assigned to the *Ordo episcopalis.* The motu proprio *Sacro Cardinalium consilio* of 26 February 1965 allowed the election of the dean and subdean of the Sacred College only from among the suburbicarian bishops. The motu proprio *Ingravescentem aetatem* of 21 November 1970 dealt a severe blow to the Sacred College. It decreed that cardinals who had completed their eightieth year without more ado lost their curial offices as well as the right to elect the Pope.[37]

The Pope began the reform of the Roman Curia, desired by the council, with the Holy Office. He sought to counter the attacks on this congregation, which were made to some extent even in the conciliar *aula,* first with the change of name and of sphere of competence, prescribed in the motu proprio *Integrae servandae* of 7 December 1965, as well as the reorganization of the procedure of the department, also held out in prospect in the same document. Further steps followed. On 14 June and 15 November 1966 respectively, the *Index librorum prohibitorum* and the prohibition of books by law as prescribed in Canon 1399 were declared abolished.[38] A little later a Commission of Theologians from the various countries was set up beside the Congregation for

[35] Also the motu proprio *Episcopalis potestatis* of 2 May 1967 on the extension of faculties for the Eastern rite bishops to dispense from the general law of the Church, *AAS* 59 (1967), 385–90; cf. J. Lederer, "Die Neuordnung des Dispensrechtes," *AfkKR* 135 (1966), 415–43.

[36] *AfkKR* 134 (1965), 499.

[37] W. M. Plöchl, "Der alte Kardinal und das Recht," U. Mosiek and H. Zapp, eds., *Ius et Salus Animarum. Festschrift für Bernhard Panzram* (Sammlung Rombach n.s. 15) (Freiburg 1972), 159–70.

[38] G. May "Die Aufhebung der kirchlichen Bücherverbote," K. Siepen, J. Weitzel, P. Wirth eds., *Ecclesia et Ius. Festgabe für Audomar Scheuermann zum 60. Geburtstag* (Munich, Paderborn and Vienna 1968), 547–71.

the Doctrine of the Faith.[39] On 15 August 1967 the constitution *Regimini Ecclesiae Universae* effected the reorganization of the Roman Curia demanded by the council. According to it, the Curia remains the representative and assisting agency of the Pope and is in no relationship of subordination to the episcopate, as some bishops desired. In the structure and activity of the Curia, however, a series of changes is found. Henceforth the Pope is no longer the prefect of some congregations; he is no longer also in them, but only above them. The position of the cardinal secretary of state was strengthened, and a better communication and coordination of the individual congregations was provided for. The Secretariat of State had to assure the close union of the offices of the Roman Curia with the Pope and among themselves. The cardinals who presided over the departments of the Curia could be summoned by the cardinal secretary of state to a common meeting. A number of offices were newly instituted or confirmed respectively, especially the Secretariat for non-Catholic Christians, non-Christian religions, and unbelievers, as well as an Office of Statistics. The *Dataria* was abolished. The "Council for the Public Affairs of the Church" is competent for relations between the Church and state governments. All members of the congregations are for the future appointed for only five years, and after the lapse of this period must be again appointed, which, of course, hardly works to the benefit of willingness to accept responsibility and independence of judgment. The members of the Curia are selected from the various peoples, in each case in accord with knowledge and pastoral experience. Contact with the bishops should be maintained and their views taken into consideration. A detailed *regolamento* regulates the routine of the Curia. But the organization of the Roman Curia created by the constitution *Regimini Ecclesiae* soon underwent new changes. By the constitution *Sacra Rituum Congregatio* of 8 May 1969 the Congregation of Rites was divided and a new Congregation for Divine Worship was established. The constitution *Constans nobis studium* of 11 July 1975 abolished it again and joined it with the Congregation of the Sacraments as the new "Congregation for the Sacraments and Divine Worship." The motu proprio *Quo aptius* of 27 February 1973 put an end to the Apostolic Chancery and transferred its duties to the Secretariat of State. The instruction of the cardinal secretary of state of 4 February 1974 on the obligation of secrecy in regard to the proceedings of the Holy See, which arose from an actual incident, made known that the critical procedures in the Church did not stop at the Roman Curia.

---

[39] Preliminary statutes of the Congregation for the Doctrine of the Faith of 12 July 1969 for the Theological Commission, in *AAS* 61 (1969), 540f.

The motu proprio *Sollicitudo omnium Ecclesiarum* of 24 June 1969 again defined the duties of papal envoys.[40] The law produced a stronger differentiation of the Holy See's diplomatic representations and made provision for extraordinary circumstances in nations. The duty of legates to promote the union of the bishops with the Pope was put at the head of their obligations. On 25 March 1972 the Council for the Public Affairs of the Church issued a directive for the determining and naming of candidates for the episcopal office in the Latin Church.[41]

In taking up relatively vague statements of the Second Vatican Council a comprehensive apparatus of councils on all levels of ecclesiastical activity, from the parish to the episcopal conference, was constructed, above all in the German-speaking countries. These bodies moved beside, and in the parochial sphere partly over, the ordained shepherds. No longer the cathedral chapter, but the Priests' Council is, according to a declaration of the Congregation for the clergy, the bishop's senate for the future.[42] Many decrees aimed to promote the renewal of religious institutes or sought to master the critical conditions in them.[43] Comprehensive complexes of norms were issued for the implementation of the Second Vatican Council's Constitution on the Liturgy, beginning with the motu proprio *Sacram Liturgiam* of 25 January 1964 through the instructions of 26 September 1964, 23 November 1965, 4 May 1967, 25 May 1967, 29 May 1969, and 5 September 1970, and numerous decrees and norms, up to the Encyclical on the Eucharistic Prayers of 27 April 1973, without there being an end to this production of norms in prospect. New texts were published for the Mass, new *ordines* for the administration of the sacraments. The constitution *Missale Romanum* of 3 April 1969 promulgated the changed Roman Mass book. From 1965 the fulfilling of the Sunday obligation of attending Mass was already granted for the preceding evening. Concelebration and Communion *sub utraque* became more and more widespread.[44] The instruction from the Congregation of the Sacraments, *Immensae caritatis* of 29 January 1973, granted the faculty of permitting lay persons to administer Communion, increased the number of cases in which Communion could be received twice on the same day, and further modified the Eucharistic fast. Under specified conditions,

---

[40] W. M. Plöchl, "Das neue päpstliche Gesandtschaftsrecht," *ÖAfKR* 21 (1970), 115–29.

[41] T. G. Barberena, "Neuvas normas sobre nombramientos de obispos [texto y comentario]," *Revista española de Derecho Canónico* 28 (1972), 657–82.

[42] H. Müller, "Der Priesterrat als Senat des Bischofs," *ÖAfKR* 24 (1973), 4–17.

[43] For example, apostolic admonition *Evangelica testificatio* of 29 June 1971; decrees of 4 June and 8 December 1970, 2 February 1972; declaration of 4 June 1970.

[44] *AAS* 57 (1965), 410–12; 64 (1972), 561–63.

according to the instruction of the Secretariat for Promoting Christian Unity of 1 June 1972, non-Catholic Christians can be permitted to receive Communion in the Catholic Church. The motu proprio *Firma in traditione* of 13 June 1974 brought a new regulation of the system of Mass stipends. The motu proprio *Sacrum Diaconatus Ordinem* of 18 June 1967 created the canonical basis for the reintroduction of the permanent diaconate in the Latin Church. Because it was intended to ordain married men of mature age as deacons, there resulted the first breakthrough in the law of celibacy. The minor orders and the subdiaconate were abolished by the motu proprio *Ministeria quaedam* of 15 August 1972. Their place was taken by the ministries of reader and acolyte, which could also be bestowed on laymen who had no intention of entering the ecclesiastical state. The motu proprio *Ad pascendum* of 15 August 1972 joined entry into the clerical state with the reception of the Order of Deacon. On 17 February 1966 appeared the constitution *Paenitemini*. The penitential discipline, especially fasting, was considerably mitigated by it. A decree of the Congregation for Divine Worship of 2 December 1973 prescribed a new *ordo* of penance. The constitution *Sacram Unctionem Infirmorum* of 30 November 1973 regulated the Sacrament of the Anointing of Sick anew. The law on mixed marriage had already been mitigated in the instruction *Matrimonii sacramentum* of 18 March 1966. The decree *Crescens matrimoniorum* of 22 February 1967 eliminated the sanction of invalidity for the nonobservance of the obligatory form in the contracting of marriage between Catholics and Eastern non-Catholics. The motu proprio *Matrimonia mixta* of 31 March 1970 was a new retreat before Protestant pressures and for the first time in the history of papal regulation of mixed marriages abandoned the assuring of the Catholic upbringing of the children in mixed marriages. In issuing this law, the Pope was standing, as was rightly remarked, under "progress compulsion."[45] The instruction of the Holy Office of 5 July 1963 basically allowed cremation to Catholics. The motu proprio *Pastoralis migratorum cura* of 15 August 1969 reorganized the pastoral care of emigrants.

Numerous rules of procedure were revised or issued anew. The motu proprio *Sanctitas clarior* of 19 March 1969 rearranged the process of beatification and canonization. In view of the more and more public celibacy crisis Paul VI reasserted the celibacy of priests in the encyclical *Sacerdotalis Caelibatus* of 24 June 1967.[46] The growing number of

---

[45] K. Mörsdorf, "Matrimonia mixta," *AfkKR* 139 (1970), 349–404.
[46] *AAS* 59 (1967), 657–97. Cf. also Paul VI's letters to Cardinal Secretary of State Villot of 2 February 1970 on celibacy with regard to the discussion in the Netherlands, in *AAS* 62 (1970), 98–103.

laicizations of priests induced the Congregation for the Doctrine of the Faith on 13 January 1971 to issue new norms for the implementing of the procedure of reducing men in major orders to the lay state.[47] In implementing the motu proprio *Integrae servandae* the Congregation for the Doctrine of the Faith on 15 January 1971 issued an order for the procedure in the examination of doctrinal opinions. The motu proprio *Causas matrimoniales* of 28 March 1971 provided norms for the expediting of marriage cases in the Latin Church; the motu proprio *Cum matrimonialium* of 8 September 1973, in the Eastern Churches. The instruction of the Congregation of the Sacraments of 7 March 1972 improved the rules of processes for establishing the nonconsummation of marriage. The decree of the Congregation for the Doctrine of the Faith of 19 March 1975 reorganized the previous censorship of books. Henceforth only editions and translations of Holy Scripture, liturgical books and their translations, catechisms and theology texts are subject to it. Nevertheless, it was urgently recommended to diocesan clerics and members of the state of perfection to obtain the permission of their local ordinary or higher superior respectively for books which are related to religion and moral teaching.

More and more often was the instituting of an ecclesiastical jurisdiction over acts of administration requested. The Holy See sought to take this concern into account in a twofold way. In the process of reform of the Curia the tasks of an ecclesiastical law court for administration were assigned to the Church's supreme tribunal, the Apostolic Signatura. They are cared for by the newly formed Second Section. Recourse can be had to this if the contested administrative act was issued by a department of the Roman Curia and a law was transgressed by it. The Apostolic Signatura grants no legal protection against measures of lower ecclesiastical organs. Two drafts were elaborated in 1970 and 1972 for the establishing of a court for administrative acts on the other ecclesiastical levels. While the first draft envisaged three types of legal devices against burdensome acts of administration—recourse to the hierarchical superior, recourse to the court of administration, complaint to the regular court—the second draft proceeded from the possibility of complaint before the regular court. The promulgation of a corresponding motu proprio is still to come.[48]

---

[47] *AAS* 63 (1971), 303–8. Also, the declaration of the Congregation for the Doctrine of the Faith of 26 June 1972 to interpret the decree on the implementation of the procedure for reduction to the lay state, in *AAS* 64 (1972), 641–43; cf. F. Romita, "La perdita dello stato clericale," *Monitor Ecclesiasticus* 97 (1972), 128–36.

[48] *Normae Speciales in Supremo Tribunali Signaturae Apostolicae ad experimentum servandae post Constitutionem Apostolicam Pauli PP. VI Regimini Ecclesiae Universae* (Vatican City 1968); R. A. Strigl, "Kritische Analyse der in Jahre 1968 zur Erprobung ergangenen

On 1 October 1975 Paul VI published the apostolic constitution *Romano Pontifici Eligendo,* the new regulation of the papal election. On 5 December 1973 the Pope had posed the question of whether it was not fitting to expand the group of electors for the choosing of the Pope and to add to the College of Cardinals the patriarchs of the Eastern Churches and the members of the Council of the General Secretariat of the Synod of Bishops. Nevertheless, the above-mentioned constitution, for the sake of the freedom and independence of the proceedings, retained the election of the Pope by the cardinals, but including only a maximum of 120 (no. 33). Likewise, the conclave and the three forms of election procedure were retained. Difficulties in achieving the prescribed majority of two-thirds plus one, which are to be anticipated in view of the increasing pluralism in the Church, permit the cardinals, under specified presuppositions, to be satisfied with an absolute majority plus one or with a final ballot between the two candidates with the most votes (no. 76). With his acceptance of the election, the one chosen, if he has already received episcopal ordination, is immediately bishop of the Church of Rome and at the same time Pope and head of the College of Bishops with complete and supreme power over the Universal Church (no. 88).

Revision of the Code and of the Canon Law of the Eastern Church

The revision of the Code of Canon Law could be seriously taken up only after the close of the Council. On 20 November 1965 the *Pontificia Commissio Codici Iuris Canonici recognoscendo* began its work.[49] It worked in constant contact with the Synod of Bishops, the episcopal conferences, and the individual bishops. Since 1967 its president has been the secretary general of the Second Vatican Council, Pericle

Verfahrensordnung für die Apostolische Signature," *Ius Populi Dei. Festschrift R. Bidagor* III (Rome 1972), 79–111; G. Lobina, "Rassegna di giurisprudenza della Sectio Altera del Supremo Tribunale della Segnatura Apostolica (1968–1973)," *Monitor Ecclesiasticus* 98 (1973), 293–323; *Communicationes* 2 (1970), 191–94; 4 (1972), 35–38; 5 (1973), 235–43; 6 (1974), 32–33; P. Wirth, "Gerichtlicher Schutz gegenüber der kirchlichen Verwaltung. Modell eines kirchlichen Verwaltungsgerichts," *AfkKR* 140 (1971), 29–73; I. Gordon, "De iustitia administrativa ecclesiastica tum transacto tempore tum hodierno," *Periodica* 61 (1972), 251–378; M. Kaiser, "Einführung einer Verwaltungsgerichtsbarkeit in der katholischen Kirche?" *Essener Gespräche zum Thema Staat und Kirche* 7 (Munich 1972), 92–111; P. Moneta, *Il controllo giurisdizionale sugli atti dell'autorità amministrativa nell'ordinamento canonico* (Milan 1973); G. Lobina, *Elementi di procedura amministrativa canonica* (Rome 1973); J. A. Souto, "Algunas cuestiones básicas en torno a una posible ley de procedimiento administrativo," *Ius Canonicum* 14 (1974), 14–23; H. Schmitz, "Kirchliche Verwaltungsgerichtsbarkeit. Bericht zum Stand der gesetzgeberischen Arbeiten," *TThZ* 84 (1975), 174–80.
[49] *Communicationes* 1 (1969), 35–54.

Felici. In 1974 the commission was enlarged to fifty cardinals from twenty-five nations. Ten, later thirteen subcommissions of consultors prepare the drafts of the revised code, which are then submitted to the commission, and this in turn sends them to the bishops. Following the revision of the drafts in accord with the bishops' remarks, the individual partial codifications are presumably to be promulgated by the Pope *ad experimentum*. Since 1969 the periodical *Communicationes* has reported the aims and progress of the work. The progress of the project is slow; lacking is an energetic, uniform will. The new law book is supposed to be in keeping with the intellectual outlook of the Second Vatican Council and oriented more strongly than the code to pastoral requirements, but to retain its legal character and not be a sort of rule of faith or morals. In jurisdiction and administration the subjective rights of physical and juridicial persons are to obtain an effective protection. Sanctions are reduced to a minimum. The principle of subsidiarity is to be utilized to a greater degree. The new code should be restricted to the codification of canon law indispensible and feasible for all parts of the Church. It is the duty of the regional legislative tribunals to create norms for the respective territories. The position of the bishops is to be further strengthened. A common legal status is to be granted to all Christians, on which then are based the rights and obligations which are united with specific ecclesiastical offices and functions. The strict territorial principle of ecclesiastical organization should be modified. In the law relating to the sacraments and to penalties a better coordination of *forum externum* and *forum internum* should be undertaken. The Synod of Bishops, meeting from 30 September to 29 October 1967, expressed itself in favor of the ten principles of renewal of the canon law which Cardinal Felici submitted.[50]

The current drafts for individual books of the revised code make it obvious that the revision will be, not a new edition of the Code of Canon Law, but a new law book. The changed canon law will presumably carry to a considerable extent the marks which were presented above in their general characterization. For the canonical changes of the postconciliar period are ordinarily adopted into the revised code little or not at all modified. Tense expectations which were set for the new law must be disappointed. For example, the draft of the penal law,

---

[50] "Principia quae Codicis Iuris Canonici recognitionem dirigant," *Communicationes* 1 (1969), 77–85 (=X. Ochoa, *Leges Ecclesiae post Codicem iuris canonici editae* III (Rome 1972), no. 3601, col. 5253–57; ibid., 86–100 (of 187 present, 57 *placet*, 130 *placet iuxta modum*, but in individual points always a two-thirds majority); *AfkKR* 136 (1967), 595f.; R. Laurentin, *Le premier Synode. Histoire et bilan* (Paris 1968), 74–86; R. Rouquette, *Une nouvelle chrétienté. Le premier synode épiscopal* (Paris 1968), 89–107; F. X. Murphy, G. MacEoin, *Synode '67 Aufbruch nach dem Konzil. Eine Chronik* (Paderborn 1969), 64–91.

submitted in 1973, suffers from many, partly serious defects. The schema aims to abbreviate the penal law, to unify it, and to avoid the confusion of the external and the internal *fora*. Baptized non-Catholics are basically excepted from ecclesiastical penal sanctions. However, the practicability of the penal law which the schema envisages is doubtful, among other reasons because of the excessive extension of the competence of particular law and of the enormous number of mere authorizations of penalties. As in the code, the penal criminal law is again mixed with the law of disciplinary penalties. In addition to the technical, the draft also displays serious theological flaws. For example, the suggestion in Canon 16, par. 1, b, that excommunication not prevent the reception of the Sacrament of Penance destroys the ecclesiological connection of excommunication and the Sacrament of Penance and suffers from an inner contradiction that excommunication and reconciliation with the Church cannot coexist.

The draft of the new ecclesiastical law of marriage, sent to the bishops in 1975, must, on the contrary, despite certain weaknesses, rather measure up to the claims which must be set for a codification of this material that is theologically and canonically unobjectionable. It leaves the structure of the matrimonial law of the code untouched and in general proceeds cautiously with the integration of the law's development since 1918. The legislative competence of the episcopal conferences and the faculties of the bishops are extended, of course, to a tolerable degree. The notion and precedence of the "ends of marriage" are, however, abandoned to the detriment of the matter. The impediments to contracting marriage are strictly limited. The will to marry is again defined, the defects in knowledge are thoroughly discussed, the idea of cunning deception is reintroduced. The ability to contract marriage is treated on a grand scale. The circle of persons bound to the canonical form is drawn considerably more narrow than before. Catholics who have separated themselves formally or publicly from the Church are no longer to be bound to the canonical form of marriage (Canon 319, par. 1).

Since the death of Pius XII and in consequence of the development then getting under way the codification of the Eastern Canon Law came to a standstill. The opposition of certain hierarchs to some tendencies of the codification, the decay of discipline in the Church, the widespread hostility to law, and the effects of the Second Vatican Council were not favorable to the continuation of the codification. Account had to be taken of the new trends coming to light. And so on 10 June 1972 Paul VI set up a new Commission for the Revision of the Eastern Canon Law—*Pontificia Commissio Codici Iuris Canonici Orientalis recognoscendo*—with Cardinal Joseph Parecattil, archbishop of Ernakulam, India, for the Syro-Malabar Christians, at its head.[51] It had to revise the parts of the Eastern Canon Law that were already in force as well as those not yet published. On 18 March 1974 the Pope set two goals for the commission: to bring the Eastern Canon Law into harmony with the decrees of the Second Vatican Council and to preserve fidelity to the tradition of the Eastern Churches.[52] The commission publishes *Nuntia* as its organ of communication.

From the Second Vatican Council the project of a constitutional law of the Church, a *Lex Ecclesiae Fundamentalis,* was championed by bishops and theologians. On 20 November 1965 Paul VI referred to it in an inquiry.[53] Now, from the very beginning the Church has had a constitution in the material sense, the norms of which are scattered through the various sources of law, especially the code. A constitution in the formal sense, that is, a constitutional law, would have to assemble the norms essential and characteristic for the fundamental legal organization of the Church and prescribe the degree and limits of the legislation of each particular church. Such a constitutional law, in view of the increasing particularization of canon law, is an imperative necessity to guarantee the integration of the parts into the whole, especially to facilitate the verification of particular legislation for its compatibility with the law of the Universal Church. In 1971 the frequently improved draft of a *Lex Ecclesiae Fundamentalis* was officially submitted by the Commission for the Revision of the Code to the bishops. Of 1,306 bishops who gave an opinion on it, 593 replied *placet,* 462 *placet iuxta modum,* and 251 *non placet.*[54] The draft fulfilled the demands to remain within the spirit and letter of the Second Vatican Council, to unite theology and law, and to speak in a pastoral manner. In the ninety-five canons formulations in more than three hundred passages were adopted from the texts of the Second Vatican Council. And for the first time the draft codified basic laws of Catholics. Nevertheless, it found criticism chiefly from three areas. Some approved it basically, but wanted to see it improved in content and in legal techniques. The difficulty of examining theological statements as to their legal power to bind, or respectively, to convert them into norms, explains the variety of the proposals for correction made by members of this group. Others assented, in itself, to the notion of a *Lex Ecclesiae Fundamentalis,* but repudiated the submitted draft as impracticable. They saw in it an obstacle for developments that were under way in the Church, especially the ecumenical strivings. A third group came out

[51] *AfkKR* 141 (1972), 238.
[52] *Communicationes* 6 (1974), 14–19.
[53] *AAS* 57 (1965), 985.
[54] *AfkKR* 142 (1973), 217.

against any codification of the constitutional law of the Church. Their criticism was aimed, to a considerable degree, not only against the draft, but against the hierarchical, in fact the legal structure of the Church in general. As a matter of fact, the draft of the *Lex Ecclesiae Fundamentalis* stands clearly in ecclesiastical tradition and checks all promiscuity and arbitrariness. If the one Church of Christ is the Roman Catholic Church (Canon 2, par. 1), then there is no possibility of labeling non-Catholic ecclesial communities unequivocally as Churches. If the Pope possesses the supreme and immediate power over the Universal Church (Canon 34, par. 1), then it is inadmissible to lower his position to that of a secretary general. If the bishop is the sole legislator in his diocese (Canon 81, par. 2), then synodal committees of priests and laity cannot issue norms. If every believer in Christ had a right to this, that the liturgy be celebrated according to the prescriptions of his rite (Canon 15), then the foundation is removed from under liturgical experimentation and manipulation. Although the arguments of the opponents of the *Lex Ecclesiae Fundamentalis* are frequently at variance with one another, Paul VI showed himself to be impressed by the resistance. He had the draft withdrawn and turned over to the commission for revision.

The revised form of the *Lex Ecclesiae Fundamentalis* will presumably, in conformity with the wishes of many bishops, contain hardly any basically theological statements. The juristic character of the law should stand out more prominently, especially its binding effect in relation to the total subordinate legislation. The enumeration of the basic rights of the faithful should become more complete. The ecclesiastical organs of the Universal Church and of the particular Churches, hence also the councils, should be mentioned.

The manuscript of this chapter was ready at the end of 1974. The subsequent development could be added only to a slight extent.

CHAPTER 6

The Holy See's Policy of Concordats from 1918 to 1974 *

Era of Concordats under Pius XI and Pius XII

TO THE BEGINNING OF THE SECOND WORLD WAR

Point of Departure, Motives, and General Character

The First World War ended with a profound convulsion of the structure of states and peoples. The peace treaties in the years from 1918

* Georg May

produced no secure peace among nations, because too little justice and wisdom were inherent in them. The drawing of boundaries frequently did not agree with the ethnographical realities. Minorities were further suppressed. In the interior of many countries fermentation and unrest became chronic. In most states of Europe which began as parliamentary democracies after the First World War authoritarian regimes soon came to power. The attitude toward the Church was generally in danger in the former because of instability, in the latter because of caprice. The Church was ordinarily in a difficult position and was left to the good will of the civil partner. The constitutions of almost all countries contained a guarantee of freedom of denomination and of the practice of religion. But the text of the constitution did not ordinarily indicate as a matter of course how the relations of Church and state appeared in practice. Too much depended on its interpretation and application, on the ecclesiastical personnel, and especially on the religious feeling of the people and the spiritual power of the Church in the country in question. The legal ordering of the relations of Church and state is only one facet of the reality of this relationship. It made models and standards obligatory, according to which the mutual outlook of Church and state was to be fashioned, and only to the extent that this occurred was the relation of Church and state a legal relationship. The situation of Church-state policies must not be regarded as the legal Church-state situation. The constitution ordinarily permitted different forms of the relations of Church and state within a specific framework. Thus the constitutionally legal security of religious freedom was in many countries in sharp contrast to the legal reality. In some countries it was not taken for granted even as a private legal freedom. In so far as it was a matter of states governed by law, the Church had no interest in the surrender of a moderate involvement in the state because this assured it of favorable possibilities of acting in society. The quality of a corporation of public law seemed to the Church as the relatively best suited manner of fulfilling its mission in the sphere of state law. A number of countries decided for the constitutionally legal separation of Church and state. However, the implementation of this was subject to the greatest differences. The concept "separation of Church and state" is ambiguous and hence impracticable in a country without an interpretive addition to the description of the relation in the sphere of canon law. Separation can be recommended in order to free the Church from the pressure of the state, but also in order to weaken it as the agent of religion. Separation which a state ruled by law undertakes seeks, of course, to end the relations to religious societies as far as possible but does not forbid their effectiveness; it does not even exclude the formal legal recognition of one or several Churches as well as the making of treaties with them.

The separation legislation of many countries, it is true, consciously or unconsciously took as model the French law of 9 December 1905,[1] which was not, of course, motivated by benevolence toward the Catholic Church. On the other hand, a system of union of Church and state can be a heavy burden for a Church, compromise it, even cripple it. Even a concordat, which in itself serves the adjustment between ecclesiastical and secular interests as well as the production or promotion of a harmonious cooperation of Church and state, must operate not without conditions in favor of the Church's life. It depends too much on the manifold organizational powers and power factors within a country whether a legal relationship between Church and state brings benefit or injury to religion. The Code of Canon Law basically does not treat the relations of Church and state and touches on them only occasionally in consequence of objective connections. Law agreeable to states, even that which contradicted the Code of Canon Law, was to be maintained (Canon 3). Relations in the religiously neutral countries, for example, in regard to marriage, were taken into account to a certain extent.

The reorganization of ecclesiastical relations was an imperative necessity in many countries after the First World War. The map of Europe had been, especially in the east and southeast, profoundly altered. From the bankruptcy of tsarist Russia and of the Dual Monarchy of Austria-Hungary had arisen a large number of new states. In other countries territorial changes and alterations of state forms took place. Inflation had serious financial restratifications as a consequence. The Apostolic See sought to control the circumstances especially through the establishing of diplomatic relations with the states and the conclusion of agreements with them. In the address in the consistory of 21 November 1921[2] Pope Benedict XV (1914–22) declared that many older concordats had lost their force and practicability because of the political changes of the last years. A concordat had to be regarded as null when the legal personality of a state was no longer identical with the partner which had concluded it with the Holy See. But, he said, the Church was ready to enter into negotiations with the governments, of course without prejudice to its dignity and liberty. In this manner the Pope indicated his readiness to conclude new concordats which would take account of altered circumstances. As a matter of fact, Benedict XV's talk released a wave of concordats and other treaties, so that it is correct to speak of an Era of Concordats between the two world wars and beyond. In concluding concordats the Holy See principally aimed to assure the freedom of religious life and of the Church in general by

[1] Giacometti, *Quellen*, 272–86.
[2] *AAS* 13 (1921), 521f.

legally binding the state. It was also concerned that the state recognize the position of the Church and its organization. The law of the code had to be circulated and implemented. This was not possible without a tolerant attitude on the part of states. Likewise, a satisfactory arrangement of *res mixtae,* such as schools, religious instruction, marriage, the system of associations and institutes, as well as property could be realized only in harmony with the state. Of primary importance to the Holy See in this regard was the assuring of the religious instruction of children, especially through the guarantee of the erecting of Catholic schools. Then the ecclesiastical circumscription and organization had to be adapted to the changed political and legal circumstances. The drawing of boundaries in the peace treaties had, moreover, created numerous new problems of minorities, which included for the Church in these countries the danger of serious conflicts with the nationalistic-minded popular majorities that dominated the state. Hence, not a few concordats of the postwar period saw to the religious protection of these minorities. The Holy See regularly tried to translate the attempts and desires of governments relating to stipulations in individual points in negotiations for a concordat as comprehensive as possible. Even if the arrangement worked out was frequently not satisfactory or the content of a treaty was meagre, the mere fact that it had achieved the concluding of an agreement with a state seemed to the Holy See to be a gain. For in fact in not a few countries there was a fundamental antipathy to any making of a treaty with the Church. Under favorable circumstances there could be further building on the position reached.

On the other hand, new states endeavored to consolidate and exalt their newly won existence by means of treaties with the oldest sovereign of Europe. The esteem for the Holy See was not only not affected since the loss of the Papal State but had even increased because of the effectiveness of important Popes. Also, the Holy See wanted to help strengthen the new states with its means and hoped thereby to serve the cause of peace. The liturgical prayer for the country, for example, corroborated the union of Church and state and testified to the Church's concern for its welfare. Further, the states were interested in a visible and enduring organization of the Catholic Church in their territory, in the coinciding of the ecclesiastical circumscriptions with the national boundaries, in the appointing of loyal bishops, and in the formation of a clergy reliable in regard to the nation. The new states especially placed great value on this, that no territories or monasteries in their country should be or remain subject to foreign bishops or superiors. The Code of Canon Law, as a clearly arranged, precise source of the law of the Church, made it easy for the states to take part in the concluding of treaties with the Church. They knew to what they were obliging themselves, and the interpretation and implementation of the concordat norms were considerably facilitated.

Concordats are systems of mutual concessions by Church and state. In the majority of cases the Church is the receiving party to a greater extent than the state. Hence, after the First World War the nations whose principle of separation proceeded from an ideology hostile to the Church generally avoided the concluding of concordats. They were ordinarily made by states which conceded to the Church a position in public law.

The norms contained in the concordats are, each looked at separately, particular canon law, but, seen in context, they constitute, because of their repetition, the substratum of a common law, of the *ius concordatarium* on specific subjects. The law of concordats between the two world wars was relatively homogeneous; the legal forms and legal institutions utilized by it displayed an extensive agreement. This similarity was derived from two roots. First, in the negotiations the Church proceeded from canon law, which had fortunately just been codified, and so it constantly had basically the same point of departure. Then the effect of precedence was greatly developed in the concluding of concordats. Usually, previous concordats served to a greater or lesser degree as models for later ones.

In individual cases the Church aspired to assure, by means of concordats, a minimum of those guarantees and prerogatives which belonged to it by canon law. And so, treaties frequently repeated principles and assurances which were already expressed in the constitution of the country in question. The Church set critical importance on independence from the state in the filling of its offices. Numerous concordats logically stipulated the free nomination of the bishops by the Pope (Canon 329, par. 2). The government of the state concerned was ordinarily permitted the right, partly in place of an earlier right of nomination, to make known misgivings of a general political nature— the so-called political proviso—before the appointment of residential bishops and of coadjutor bishops with the right of succession. Then, the concordats of Pius XI as a rule contained regulations on appointments to canonries and parishes, schools and theological faculties, the supervision by the bishops of the religious and moral instruction of youth, and the liberties and legal rights of religious institutes. Teaching in the name of the Church was made dependent on the possession of the *missio canonica*.[3] A special legal protection was assured to clerics in the exercise of their office. Pastoral viewpoints induced the Holy See in

---

[3] H. Flatten, "Missio canonica," T. Filthaut, J. A. Jungmann, eds., *Verkündigung und Glaube. Festgabe für Franz X. Arnold* (Freiburg i. Br. 1958), 123–41.

some cases to agree to the prohibition of partisan political activities by clerics. The right of minorities to religious instruction in their vernacular was assured.[4] In many concordats the legal competence of ecclesiastical legal persons to acquire, possess, and administer property was recognized. In some cases concordats referred to individual canons of the code or other ecclesiastical norms explicity named. In the main, however, reference was made to the prescriptions of the code or of ecclesiastical law or ecclesiastical principles in general, for example, in the sense that questions pertaining to ecclesiastical persons or things and not expressly treated in the concordat should be regulated according to canon law. Finally, the rule was often adopted into the treaties that both parties, in the event of differences of interpretation, will effect an amicable solution in a common agreement. In this way, repudiation and break were made difficult and at the same time the door to new negotiations was kept open.

One can say that after the First World War the concordat was found in an increasing measure to be the suitable form for ordering the relations of Church and state. The territorial episcopate was regularly consulted by the Holy See in the negotiations, and its ideas and wishes were as far as possible taken into consideration. Elected representatives of the episcopate played a direct role in the negotiations. The Holy See regularly aspired to have the ratification of completed concordats take place in the Vatican.

In retrospect it must be admitted that the concordats achieved their goal only inadequately. The circumstances and the development were not to a great extent favorable to their existence and their implementation. Most were ruined by the Second World War and its sequel. In concluding them, the Holy See in general showed itself to be well informed about the situation in the individual countries. However, occasionally it seemed to have overestimated the power of the forces prepared for cooperation. Nevertheless, the concordat policy was right and necessary. By it the Holy See went on record that in its relations with nations it did not champion the view of all or nothing but in recognizing realities was ready for compromise solutions. The concluding of a treaty as such testified before the whole world to the claim and the right of the Holy See to represent the Catholic Church uppermost and definitively. The concordats also strengthened the self-awareness of the Catholics, who saw themselves cared for and protected by the supreme head of the Church and for the first time mentioned by the government of the nation. They set up signs which could not be

---

[4] T. Grentrup, *Religion und Muttersprache* (Münster 1932), 458–524; W. Hasselblatt, "Reichskonkordat und Minderheitenschutz," *Nation und Staat* 6 (1932–33), 690–95.

obliterated; they created an incontestable legal basis for the Church and in many cases prevented worse. The separation legislation of states and the concordat policy of the Holy See overcame, from different points of departure, the system of state Churches and of state supremacy over the Church and provided the Church with the autonomy for the regulating of which the Code of Canon Law stood, seen in its entirety, as one excellent instrument at its disposal.

Individual Concordats

WITH THE NEW STATES. A majority of the new nations in the east and the southeast of Europe were ready for agreements with the Apostolic See for reasons of foreign and domestic policy. Nevertheless, there were also usually obstacles to the concluding of treaties, namely laicism, exaggerated nationalism, and the negative attitude of non-Catholic religious groups, especially the Orthodox. On 30 May 1922 Pius XI concluded a concordat with predominantly non-Catholic Latvia,[5] at first for three years but with the implied prolongation from year to year on a six-months' notice. An exempt archbishopric was established at Riga. An oath of loyalty, to be made on entering office, was prescribed for the archbishop, a stipulation that was to be repeated in the following concordats.

In Poland, where the territorial boundaries were disputed until the end of 1924, the constitutional mandate to regulate the future relations of Church and state in a concordat with the Holy See could not be carried out until 10 February 1925.[6] The Polish concordat reorganized the Church in this country—five provinces of the Latin Rite with twenty-one sees, one province of the Byzantine Rite, and one archdiocese of the Armenian Rite—and especially arranged questions of the filling of offices, of religious instruction, and of Church property. In regard to Poland the Holy See showed especially generous willingness to cooperate. ARTICLE 19, Section 2, page 2 of the concordat excluded from the office of pastor all clerics whose activity jeopardized the safety

[5] A. Van Hove, "Le Concordat entre le Saint-Siège et le gouvernement de Lettonie (3. novembre 1922)," NRTh 50 (1923), 132–43; Al Giannini, "Il Concordato con la Lettonia," L'Europa Orientale 5 (1925), 653–58.

[6] A. Süsterhenn, Das polnische Konkordat vom 10. Februar 1925 (Cologne 1928); F. Grübel, Die Rechtslage der römisch-katholischen Kirche in Polen nach dem Konkordat vom 10. Februar 1925 (Leipzig 1930); H. Bednorz, Le Concordat de Pologne de 1925. Nomination aux Sièges Épiscopaux et aux Paroisses. Commentaire avec comparaison aux autres Concordats d'après-guerre (Paris 1938); R. Sobański, "Das erste polnische Plenarkonzil—seine Bedeutung für den Integrationsprozess der Bevölkerung Polens zwischen den beiden Weltkriegen," ÖAfKR 26 (1975), 143–58.

of the state. Thereby an at the time unrivaled right in the nomination of pastors was conceded to the Polish government.[7]

On 10 May 1927 a concordat with Rumania was concluded,[8] which was not ratified until 1929 because of the opposition of Orthodox circles. The Catholic Church in the nation was to be organized in one province each for the Greek and the Latin Rites, with four suffragan sees each, as well as a spiritual head for the Armenians. As in Poland, here too the state laid special importance on the national reliability of the pastors (ART. XII, par. 2). The two contracting parties reserved to themselves, by way of exception, the right to repudiate the concordat after a preliminary notification of six months (ART. XXIII, Section 2). On 27 September 1927 Lithuania made a treaty with the Holy See.[9] It gave the Church extensive rights in the school system, entrusted to ecclesiastics the direction of the register of births, deaths, and burials, and gave civil effects to the canonical form of marriage. The pastoral care of the faithful in their vernacular was assured. But there was constant friction over the interpretation of the concordat.

The government of Czechoslovakia usually showed itself to be unfriendly toward the Catholic Church and pursued a policy of petty annoyances against it. The Hus Celebration of 1925 almost led to the breaking off of diplomatic relations. On 2 February 1928 a meagre modus vivendi was arrived at.[10] It was concerned with the circumscription of dioceses and the naming of bishops. The agreement eliminated a group of points of difference and envisaged negotiations for the future. The carrying out of the regulations of the modus vivendi encountered considerable difficulties. Not until seven years after after its signing did the government fulfill the chief condition whereby the Holy See had made the defining of dioceses (ART. 1) dependent on the restoration of

[7] Cf. R. Jacuzio, "Il diritto di opposizione riservato al governo nella nomina dei parrocci," *Il Diritto concordatario* 2 (1937), 56–58.

[8] I. Mateiu, *Valoarea Concordatului incheiat cu Vaticanul* (Sibiu 1929); L. Honoré, "Une Église servante de l'État. L'Église orthodoxe roumaine," *NRTh* 56 (1929), 56–66; N.N., "De concordato inter Sanctam Sedem et Rumaniam," *Appollinaris* 3 (1930), 581–600.

[9] L. Maser, *Das Konkordat zwischen dem Apostolischen Stuhle und der Republik Litauen vom 27. September 1927 in rechtsvergleichender Betrachtung* (Lippstadt 1931); A. Ottaviani, "Concordatum Lithuanicum" *Appollinaris* 1 (1928), 53–64, 140–49.

[10] I. Pasquazi, "Modus vivendi inter Sanctam Sedem et Rempublicam Cechoslovachiae," *Appollinaris* 1 (1928), 149–55; N.N., "Der 'Modus vivendi' in der Tschechoslowakei," *Ecclesiastica* 13 (1933), 353–56; F. Kop, *Modus vivendi. Nýnêjši stav jeho provedeni* (Prague 1937); E. Hoyer, "Das Schicksal des tschechoslowakischen Modus vivendi," M. Grabmann, K. Hofmann, eds., *Festschrift Eduard Eichmann zum 70. Geburtstag* (Paderborn 1940), 373–400; D. Faltin, "La crisi della Chiesa in Ceco-Slovacchia e il Modus vivendi del 1927. L'opera del Card. Pietro Ciriaci," *Divinitas* 9 (1965), 600–605.

the church property in Slovakia. Nothing further could be achieved before the collapse of the state in 1938–39.

On the other hand, the concordat of 5 June 1933 with Austria[11] involved a comprehensive regulation. ARTICLE 30, Section 3 of the federal constitution raised specific articles of the concordat to constituent parts of the constitution and thereby gave them a constitutional character. It partly corresponded to the concordat concluded soon after with the Third Reich. The concordat promised the erecting of the bisphopric of Innsbruck-Feldkirch and of the prelacy *nullius* of Burgenland (ART. III, Par. 2) and endeavored, through prudent fostering and the promise of financial support for free Catholic schools, to create the presuppositions for the development of public Catholic schools (ART. III, Pars. 3–4). However, the government lacked the majority and the power to implement the stipulations agreed to. Above all, the subordination of marriages contracted in Church to the canon law (ART. VII) evoked the united bitter resistance of liberalism, Marxism, and National Socialism.

Tedious negotiations led in 1935 to the concluding of a comprehensive concordat with Yugoslavia.[12] But the resistance of the Orthodox Serbs[13] was so strong that it caused the fall of the government after the chamber had accepted it, because it agreed not to bring it before the Senate. In it were the important stipulations that, when the concordat became effective, contrary norms of the Kingdom of Yugoslavia should become null (ART. XXXV) and that subjects not treated in the concordat should be handled in accord with the pertinent canon law (ART. XXXVII, Sec. 1).

WITH THE "SEPARATION COUNTRIES" OF EUROPE. The ideology of separation was usually a preserve of the political left. As a consequence of it there ordinarily occurred in the "separation countries" of Europe an agreement with the Holy See only if governments of a different political orientation came to power in them. In regard to France, from

[11] A. Van Hove, "Le concordat entre le Saint-Siége et l'Autriche," *NRTh* 61 (1934), 785–803, 897–913; R. Köstler, "Das neue österreichische Konkordat," *Zeitschrift für öffentliches Recht* 15 (1935), 1–33; idem, *Das österreichische Konkordats-Eherecht* (Vienna 1937); G. Stutzinger, *Das österreichische Konkordat vom 5. Juni 1933* (Cologne 1936); J. Hollnsteiner, *Das österreichische Konkordat in seiner kirchen-und staatsrechtlichen Bedeutung unter besonderer Berücksichtigung der eherechtlichen Bestimmungen*, 2d ed. (Leipzig and Vienna 1937); E. K. Winter, *Christentum und Zivilisation* (Vienna 1956), 370–402.
[12] J. Massarette, "Um das Konkordat in Jugoslawien," *ThprQS* 90 (1937), 733–35; A. Giannini, "Un concordato mancato (Il Concordato Jugoslavo del 1935)," *L'Europa Orientale* 22 (1942), 245–69.
[13] Serbia had concluded a concordat with the Holy See on 24 June 1914, but because of the war it was not implemented.

the beginning of the pontificate of Benedict XV the Holy See pursued a policy of yielding and of concession, which in a certain respect prevailed over the separation regime. The Law of Separation had also proved to be impracticable. From the end of the First World War the élan of laicism diminished. From the resumption of diplomatic relations in 1920 the Holy See inquired of the French government before the appointing of a bishop whether there were any political objections to the candidate.[14] In the corresponding declarations of the French Council of State of 13 December 1923 and Pius XI's encyclical *Maximam gravissimamque* of 18 January 1924 on diocesan associations[15] could be seen a tacit agreement on the thorny problem of the administration of church property. The Council of State declared on 3 February 1925 that the French government and the Holy See were in agreement on maintaining the concordat of 1801 in Alsace and Lorraine.[16] In 1926 were concluded two accords with France,[17] insignificant in content but important for the atmosphere. In them were determined the liturgical privileges which belonged to the representatives of France in the countries where France still occupied the religious protectorate or in which this had been recently abolished.

In Portugal, which had again established diplomatic relations with the Apostolic See in 1918, there began under the dictatorship of Carmona a rapprochement of Church and state. The decree of 18 July 1926 annulled some of the most odious provisions of the Law of Separation of 1911. The constitution of 19 March 1933 was strongly influenced by Catholic ideology. In one and the same article it proclaimed the Catholic religion as the religion of the state, the principle of religious liberty, the principle of separation, and the maintaining of diplomatic relations with the Holy See (ART. 46). Thus no serious obstacle prevented the concluding of treaties with the Holy See. The accord of

---

[14] Cf. the aide-mémoire of Cardinal Secretary of State Gasparri of May 1921 in *Revue des Sciences religieuses* 4 (1924), 248f.

[15] Giacometti, *Quellen,* 383–86.

[16] A. Erler, "Das Napoleonische Konkordat im Elsass und in Lothringen," *AfkKR* 122 (1947), 236–78; R. Metz, "Un cas intéressant d'application du droit concordataire: La nomination d'un coadjuteur avec droit de succession à l'évêché de Strasbourg," *L'Année Canonique* 6 (1959), 179–86; idem, "Les incidences concordataires de la démission de l'Évêque de Strasbourg," *Revue de droit canonique* 17 (1967), 273–97; idem, "Les nominations épiscopales en France et plus spécialement dans les diocèses concordataires de Strasbourg et de Metz," ibid. 18 (1968), 97–121.

[17] C. Crispolti, "Gli accordi franco-vaticani sugli onori liturgici in Oriente," *Rassegna Italiana* 19 (1927), 226–30.

15 April 1928[18] reorganized the hierarchy in Portuguese India and solved the question of the patronate that as of 11 April 1929 regulated the situation in the diocese of Meliapôr.

Ever since its unification, Italy had more and more became a nation with a hostile separation of Church and state: state schools without religious instruction, abolition of theological faculties at the state universities, compulsory civil marriage. However, after the end of the First World War a slow rapprochement between the nation and the Holy See made progress. In January 1919 a Catholic party was formed with the toleration of the Holy See; in this way the principle of the "Non expedit" was canceled. In the encyclical *Pacem Dei munus* on 23 May 1920 Benedict XV abandoned the prohibition, applying to Catholic heads of states, of making an official visit to the Quirinal. The Fascist regime recommended itself to the Church through many laws and measures that were friendly to the Church in relation to school and marriage, clergy, and ecclesiastical property. Thus was the way opened for a comprehensive clearing out of the matter of conflict between Church and state. In 1929 occurred the solution of the Roman Question in the Lateran Treaties. On 11 February 1929 three agreements were signed: the political treaty, the financial settlement (as Appendix IV of the political treaty), and the concordat.[19] On 27 May

---

[18] A. Correja de Silva, "Concordatum Lusitanicum," *Apollinaris* 1 (1928), 280–95; E. Hocedez, "Convention entre le S. Siège et la République du Portugal," *NRTh* 55 (1928), 519–25.

[19] L. Laghi, G. Andreucci, *Il trattato lateranense. Commentato* (Florence 1929); N.N., "De Concordato inter S. Sedem et Italiam," *Apollinaris* 2 (1929), 458–94; H. Ferrand, "La question Romaine et les Accords de Latran," *Revue Apologétique*, 48 (1929), 569–91; A. Hagen, *Die Rechtsstellung des Heiligen Stuhles nach den Lateranverträgen* (Stuttgart 1930); K. Strupp, "Die Regelung der römischen Frage durch die Lateranverträge vom 1. Februar 1929," *Zeitschrift für Völkerrecht* 15 (1930), 531–622; Z. Giacometti, "Zur Lösung der römischen Frage," *Zeitschrift für die gesamte Staatswissenschaft* 90 (1931), 8–50; A. Giannini, *Il cammino della Conciliazione* (Milan 1946); W. von Bergen, *Der Einfluss der Lateranverträge auf die staatliche Gesetzgebung Italians mit besonderer Berücksichtigung des Eherechts* (Düsseldorf 1954); A. C. Jemolo, *Chiesa e Stato in Italia dal Risorgimento ad oggi* (Turin 1955); G. Migliori, *Codice concordatario*, 3d ed. (Milan 1959); F. Pacelli, *Diario della Conciliazione con verbali e appendice documenti* (Vatican City 1959); U. Del Giudice, *I Patti Lateranensi* (Rome 1960); F. M. Marchesi, *Il concordato italiano dell' 11 febbraio 1929* (Naples 1960); A. Martini, *Studi sulla Questione Romana e la Conciliazione* (Rome 1963); R. Motsch, *Die Konkordatsehe in Italien* (Frankfurt and Berlin 1965); W. Gamber, "Die Konkordatsehe in Italien," K. Siepen, J. Weitzel, P. Wirth, eds., *Ecclesia et Ius. Festgabe für Audomar Scheuermann zum 60. Geburtstag dargebracht von seinen Freunden und Schülern* (Munich, Paderborn and Vienna 1968), 393–404; P. Ciprotti, *Atti della Commissione mista dei delegati della Santa Sede e del Governo Italiano per predisporre l'esecuzione del Concordato (11 aprile–25 novembre 1929) e altri documenti connessi* (Milan 1968); G. Salvemini, *Stato e Chiesa in Italia* (Milan 1969).

1929 they were transformed into internal state law. In the political treaty the Italian state recognized the Catholic religion as the "sole religion of the state" (ART. 1). Likewise, the sovereignty of the Holy See was confirmed (ART. 2) and a territory of its own, Vatican City, was guaranteed (ART. 3). The neutrality of Vatican City was established (ART. 24). The person of the Pope is sacred and inviolable (ART. 8). The Holy See's active and passive diplomatic right was acknowledged (ART. 12). The Holy see declared the Roman Question definitively and irrevocably settled and recognized the Kingdom of Italy with Rome as capital (ART. 26). In the financial settlement the payment of compensation for the losses which had befallen the Pope through the events of 1870 was agreed to. The concordat complemented the treaty and brought a detailed regulation of affairs touching Church and state (45 articles). The state guaranteed to the Catholic Church its special position in Italy and the rights pertaining to this. To the Church was assured the free exercise of spiritual power, of public worship, and of jurisdiction in ecclesiastical affairs. The sacred character of Rome was acknowledged and protected (ART. 1, Sec. 1). The freedom of the filling of episcopal sees and of other offices was restored (ARTS. 19, 24, 25). No cleric could acquire or retain a post or an office in the Italian state or in a public institution or corporation dependent on it without the approval of the local ordinary. Apostate priests or those under censure must under no circumstances be employed in education or in an office or post in which they came directly into contact with the public (ART. 5). The civil effects were recognized in the sacrament of matrimony, which was regulated by the canon law. Cases of invalid marriages and the dispensation from nonconsummated marriages continued to be reserved to ecclesiastical courts and officials. Only the procedure in the separation from bed and board was conducted by the civil courts (ART. 34). Instruction in the Catholic religion was designated as the "basis and crown" of public instruction and was now envisaged also for the universities (ART. 36). The state promised a change in its legislation in order to bring it into harmony with the Lateran Treaties (ART. 29). For its part, the Church made considerable concessions. A revision of the boundaries of dioceses and their decrease in number were envisaged (ARTS. 16 and 17). In connection with the appointment of bishops the government had the right to adduce political memories (ART. 19). In the naming of pastors its right to express reservations was allowed. Especially far-reaching appeared the power likewise conceded to it, in relation to the emergence of reasons which made it seem harmful for a pastor to continue in his position, to inform the local ordinary, who had to take appropriate measures in accord with the government within three months (ART. 21). Partisan political activity was forbidden to all ecclesiastics (ART. 43 Sec. 7). The Holy See obliged itself to a condonation in regard to all possessors of church property (ART. 28). Noteworthy is the concession that the state, in the case of unfit administration of property, may proceed, in agreement with the ecclesiastical authority, to the sequestration of the temporalities of the benefice (ART. 26, Sec. 2).

The Lateran Treaties ended the decades-long opposition of the Church to a united Italy and were for both parties an honorable peace treaty. They satisfied the national will of the people and assured the Church's possibility of effectiveness. The treaties produced a solution which, as is said in the preamble of the treaty, corresponded to the justice and dignity of both sides. They were in general balanced, took account of the Catholic tradition of the people without violating the rights of the state or of other religious communities, and fulfilled the political claims without treading too near the freedom of the Church. The Holy See sought not a restoration but a new start. In it it saw the guarantee of permanence. It accommodated itself in the renunciation of the Papal State, which was overdue, and set resolutely about carrying out its universal mission from the area of a diminutive state. This was the only remaining possibility of assuring, at least in normal circumstances, the independence required for the fulfilling of its task. Of course, in the sequel there were some collisions between Church and state, which usually had their cause in the interference and usurpation of the Fascist regime. Nevertheless, Mussolini did not permit a prolonged conflict to occur, but strove constantly for an adjustment acceptable to both sides.

WITH THE LATIN AMERICAN STATES. The economic and social grievances as well as the unstable political conditions in most countries made Latin America for a considerable time the object of special concern of the Holy See. The ordinarily traditionally Catholic people often could not assert themselves against the Freemasonic oligarchies that were hostile to the Church. Thus is explained the surprising fact that relatively rarely did the conclusion of satisfactory agreements of the Holy See with Latin American nations succeed, which would either have established a system of concordats or have continued the concordats made in the past century.[20] Only Colombia was an exception: with it, between 1918 and 1928, several treaties, the most important being

---

[20] F. B. Pike, *The Conflict between Church and State in Latin America* (New York 1964); J. L. Mecham, *Church and State in Latin America. A History of Politico-Ecclesiastical Relations,* rev. ed. (Chapel Hill 1966); C. H. Hillekamps, "Staat und Kirche in Südamerika," *Hochland* 58 (1966), 409–19.

the mission accord of 5 May 1928, were concluded. Only the agreement of 1928 put an end to the uninterrupted *Kulturkampf* in Guatemala. Likewise in 1928 there came about an agreement with Peru over the naming of the bishops.[21] With Ecuador, following the decrees of the 1920s, hostile to the Church, a modus vivendi was achieved on 24 July 1937.[22] The government guaranteed freedom of instruction. State and Church joined to evangelize the Indians and to encourage them in every respect. Any political activity was forbidden to the clergy. (See also Chapter 24.)

GERMANY. The German Reich had to pay for the First World War with serious territorial losses. Through the Treaty of Versailles the Catholic Church in Germany lost the bishoprics of Strasbourg and Metz, the greatest part of Gnesen-Posen and Kulm, and a considerable part of Breslau. In the Free City of Danzig, separated from Germany, an Apostolic Administration was created in 1922, an exempt see in 1925. The German Reich changed from constitutional monarchy to parliamentary democracy. On 11 August 1919 the constitution decided upon by the National Assembly at Weimar went into force. In contrast to the situation in the German Empire of 1871 it established the competence of the state as a whole for the regulation of the relations of Church and state and of Church and school (ART. 10, nos. 1 and 2). The basic legislation of the Reich on Church and school assured to the Church for all of Germany a specific degree of freedom and potential efficacy. The ecclesio-political system of the Weimar Republic was that of an organizational separation with mutual cooperation of Church and state. The foundation of the position of religious society in the Weimar constitution was religious freedom (ARTS. 135, 136, 137, 140, 141). ARTICLE 137, Secs. 1 and 7, contains the idea of separation; ART. 138, Sec. 1, is in accord with it. ARTICLE 137, Sec. 1, declares that no "state Church" exists. Thereby the Protestant territorial church system was once and for all abolished, but at the same time the fundamental secularism, neutrality, and equality of the state were expressed. The Weimar Republic looked at the principle of separation as an institutional guarantee for the protection of the state from the power of the Church and of the Church from interference by the state and saw in it the means of restoring a liberal arrangement of the compromise. Nevertheless, the Churches continued to

---

[21] F. B. Pike, "Church and State in Peru and Chile since 1840: A study in contrasts," *American Historical Review*, 73 (1967), 30–50.
[22] J. I. Larrea, *La Iglesia y el Estado en el Ecuador* (Seville 1954).

be corporations of public law, and this status could be bestowed on other religious congregations (ART. 137, Sec. 5). In this way the importance of Churches and religious groups for the life of the people was recognized and the ability was granted them to be bearers of public competencies and rights. The granting of the right of self-determination to religious societies (ART. 137, Sec. 3) protected the liberty of the whole of ecclesiastical activity in the world, to the extent that it was regarded by the Church as necessary for "its affairs." ARTICLE 137, Sec. 3, assured to religious groups a sphere of freedom within which they could establish an independent legal power, for example, ecclesiastical power, and by means of them an independent legal order. With the system of the relations of state and Church created by the Weimar constitution the state's sovereignty over the Churches was no longer compatible, but of course it was still practiced by the government and administration of some states. The public denominational school, which was regarded by the German Catholics as a vital question, was basically guaranteed (ART. 146). Religious instruction continued in all public schools, except the nondenominational, to be a regular subject (ART. 149).

The ecclesiastical articles of the Weimar Constitution were the best that could be obtained in view of the political power situation. However, during the entire epoch of the Weimar Republic the reciprocal alienation of Church and state could not be overcome. Still, in 1920 an embassy of the German Reich was established at the Holy See in place of the previous Prussian legation. The German Catholics set great hopes on it. The legal binding force of the concordats and conventions with the Holy See surviving from the nineteenth century had become uncertain. The territorial alterations following the peace treaty necessitated an adaptation of diocesan boundaries. For these reasons, in order to exhaust the possibilities supplied by the Weimar Constitution and convert them into concrete assurances, in regard to which the concern for the Catholic denominational school was predominant, the Church endeavored to conclude a concordat with the Reich. The Weimar Republic was also basically interested in this. The Reich sought from the Holy See moral and political support against the front of the victorious powers. From time to time in 1921 the Reich government promised itself from a concordat a stabilizing influence on the German boundaries, threatened by desires for annexation in the east and desires for separation in the west. But the party constellation in the Reichstag did not go beyond drafts of a concordat. The liberal and Protestant forces, like the elements in the Social Democratic Party that were hostile to the Church, refused the conclusion of a treaty. In particular, the hurdle of the Reich School Law, that was first to be enacted, could not be overcome.

However, in view of this situation, the Holy See did not give up. Instead, it utilized the tension between the Reich and the states, produced by the federalist construction of the state, to pursue a multitrack concordat policy. The extensive independence of the states in cultural policy even gave to concordats with the states a precedence over a concordat with the Reich. From the standpoint of the Church as well as of the state Bavaria was especially suited to be the pacemaker for such agreements. The Holy See wanted to come to an accommodation with Bavaria first, because here it could most easily expect a relatively favorable concordat, which should then serve as model for the other German states. The Free State of Bavaria saw in the conclusion of a concordat a means of stressing emphatically its threatened political independence. On 24 March 1924 the concordat with Bavaria, advantageous to the Church, was concluded.[23] However, particularly because of the state's concessions in the school question it had a chilling effect on public opinion.

A concordat with Prussia of 14 June 1929[24] was, as far as concerns the meagre content, a casualty because in it there was no agreement on school, marriage, and religious institutes. Indicative of the atmosphere heated up by the Protestant side is the fact that in the negotiations and

---

[23] C. Mirbt, "Das bayerische Konkordat vom 29. März 1924," *Neue Kirchliche Zeitschrift* 36 (1925), 371–411; F. X. Kiefl, *Kritische Randglossen zum Bayerischen Konkordat unter dem Gesichtspunkt der modernen Kulturideale und der Trennung von Staat und Kirche* (Regensburg 1926); I. A. Brein, "Der publizistische Kampf um das bayerische Konkordat vom 29. März 1924 und die Verträge mit den evangelischen Kirchen," *HJ* 46 (1927), 547–54; A. Greiger, *Bekenntnisschule und Religionsunterricht nach dem Bayerischen Konkordat* (Coburg 1928); H. Zenglein, *Religionsunterricht und Religionslehrer nach dem Bayerischen Konkordat 1924* (Hassfurt am Main 1928); C. Schwarzmeier, "Das Bayerische Konkordat vom 29.3 1924 und der CIC" (Diss. Würzburg 1929); H. Rust, *Die Rechtsnatur von Konkordaten und Kirchenverträgen unter besonderer Berücksichtigung der bayerischen Verträge vom 1924* (Munich 1964).

[24] O. Zschucke, "Der Vertrag zwischen dem Freistaate Preussen und dem Heiligen Stuhle," *Deutsche Juristen-Zeitung* 34 (1929), 1097–1100; J. V. Bredt, "Das preussische Konkordat," *Preussische Jahrbücher* 217 (1929), 137–50; J. Danziger, *Beiträge zum preussischen Konkordat vom Jahre 1929* (Breslau 1930); R. Leiber, "Das Preussische Konkordat," *StdZ* 118 (1930), 17–31; A. Perugini, "Inter Sanctam Sedem et Borussiae Rempublicam sollemnis Conventio seu Concordatum," *Apollinaris* 5 (1932), 38–53; E. Wende, *C. H. Becker, Mensch und und Politiker* (Stuttgart 1959), 268–92; R. Morsey, "Zur Geschichte des Preussischen Konkordats und der Errichtung des Bistums Berlin," *Wichmann-Jahrbuch für Kirchengeschichte im Bistum Berlin* 19/20 (1965–66), 64–89; D. Golombek, *Die politische Vorgeschichte des Preussenkonkordats (1929)* (=*Veröffentlichungen der Kommission für Zeitgeschichte bei der Katholischen Akademie in Bayern*, series B, vol. 4) (Mainz 1970).

the wording of the text the term "concordatum" was purposely avoided. Nevertheless, the Prussian concordat was of importance as a political event.

In 1932 two treaties were made with the Free State of Anhalt,[25] and a concordat was concluded with Baden on 12 October 1932.[26] Although in Baden everything except a maximum program for the Church could be negotiated, the concordat obtained only a perceptibly weak parliamentary majority.

The other German states did not make concordats with the Holy See. In them the relations of state and Church were regulated according to legal decisions, for example, in Württemberg by the comprehensive law of 3 March 1924.

The three state concordats sought especially to create a new order in their territories, which were affected by the alteration of boundaries, of the form of government and of the constitution, as well as by the codification of canon law. They guaranteed the claims of the Church going back to older legal titles—endowment of sees, establishing of new sees and parishes—and the interests of the state in specific presuppositions for ecclesiastical officeholders—state citizenship, triennium—as well as the appointment to episcopal sees and cathedral chapters. Except for Bavaria, the cathedral chapters' right to elect the bishops was maintained in the German states, but was limited to a proposal of three names by the Holy See. The cooperation of the Church in the appointing of professors on Catholic theological faculties of the state universities and of posts for the teaching of religion was minutely regulated. Only the Bavarian concordat contained greater concessions to the Church in the guarantee of denominational public schools and teacher training (ARTS. 5 and 6) as well as in the awarding of the right to religious orders, eventually as publicly recognized, to maintain private schools (ART. 9). Contrary to the wishes of the Church, no settlement of the school question was included in the concordats with Baden and Prussia, but just the same in an appendix or, respectively, an exchange

[25] N. Hilling, "Die beiden Vereinbarungen zwischen dem Heiligen Stuhl und dem Freistaat Anhalt vom 4. Januar 1932," *AfkKR* 115 (1935), 457–63.
[26] A. Van Hove, "Le Concordat entre le Saint-Siège et l'État libre de Baden," *NRTh* 60 (1933), 769–82; E. Föhr. *Das Konkordat zwischen dem Heiligen Stuhle und dem Freistaate Baden vom 12. Oktober 1932* (Freiburg i. Br. 1933); E. Will, *das Konkordat zwischen dem Heiligen Stuhl und dem Freistaat Baden vom 12. Oktober 1932* (Freiburg i. Br. 1953); E. Föhr, *Geschichte des Badischen Konkordats* (Freiburg i. Br. 1958); G. May, "Mit Katholiken zu besetzende Professuren für Philosophie und Geschichte an der Universität Freiburg nach dem Badischen Konkordat vom 12. Oktober 1932," U. Mosiek, H. Zapp, eds., *Ius et Salus Animarum. Festschrift für Bernhard Panzram* (Freiburg 1972), 341–70.

of letters pertaining to the work of the treaty, the observance and implementation of the stipulations of the constitution of the Reich relevant to the school and religious instruction were promised. In Prussia, in addition to that of Cologne, the provinces of Paderborn and Breslau (Wroclaw) were created, and the sees of Aachen and Berlin and the prelacy *nullius* of Schneidemühl were newly established. The concordats with Bavaria, Prussia, and Baden followed, as regards content, similarly shaped treaties with the Protestant Churches. Concordats and ecclesiastical treaties assured the public status of the Churches by contract, thereby set them off from the group of other religious congregations of public law, and laid the foundation for a relationship of coordination of Church and state. Thus there appeared in Germany a new type of relation of Church and state, that of the "autonomous separate Church guaranteed by treaty or concordat," to quote Ulrich Stutz.

A new phase of ecclesiastical policies began when on 30 January 1933 Adolf Hitler became chancellor of the Reich. In his government's statement of 23 March 1933 he labeled the two denominations as "most weighty factors for the preservation of our nationhood" and bound himself to respect the treaties concluded with them and not to attack their rights. Most especially he promised that he intended to "allow and assure" to the Christian denominations "the influence pertaining to them" in school and education. Hitler at once made known his intention of reaching an agreement with the Catholic Church. With recourse to the preliminary work since 1920 and 1921, the concordat with the Reich was signed in Vatican City on 20 July 1933.[27] On 10

[27] A. Roth, *Das Reichskonkordat vom 20.7.1933* (Munich 1933); A. Van Hove, "Le Concordat entre le Saint-Siège et le Reich allemand," *NRTh* 61 (1934), 158–85; R. Oeschey, "Das Reichskonkordat vom 20. Juli 1933." *Bayerische Gemeinde- und Verwaltungszeitung* 44 (1934), 526–32; R. Buttman, "Das Konkordat des Deutschen Reichs mit der römisch-katholischen Kirche vom 20. Juli 1933," H. Frank, ed., *Nationalsozialistisches Handbuch für Recht und Gesetzgebung,* 2d ed. (Munich 1935), 407–24; J. Schmitt, "Ablösung der Staatsleistungen an die Kirchen unter Berücksichtigung der Weimarer Verfassung, des Reichskonkordats und der drei Länderkonkordate," *AfkKR* 115 (1935), 3–52, 341–88; G. Ohlemüller, *Reichskonkordat zwischen Deutschland und dem Vatikan vom 20. Juli 1933. Urkunden und geschichtliche Bemerkungen,* 2d ed. (Berlin, 1937); K Krüger, *Kommentar zum Reichskonkordat* (Berlin 1938); H. G. Germann, *Fünf Jahre Reichskonkordat mit der römischen Kirche* (Berlin, n.d.); W. Weber, "Das Nihil obstat," *Zeitschrift für die gesamte Staatswissenchaft* 99 (1939), 193–244; W. Hausmann, "Reichskonkordat und Weimarer Verfassung," *Nationalsozialistische Monatshefte* 10 (1939), 145–49; M. Maccarrone, *Il nazionalsocialismo e la Santa Sede* (Rome 1947); G. Schreiber, "Deutsche Kirchenpolitik nach dem ersten Weltkrieg," *HJ* 70 (1951), 296–333; F. von Papen, *Der Wahrheit eine Gasse* (Munich 1952), 313–18; E. H. Fischer, "Die politische Klausel des Reichkonkordates und ihre

September 1933 the documents of ratification were exchanged. By the law of 12 September 1933 the Reich's minister of the interior was empowered to issue legal and administrative regulations required for the implementation of the concordat. They were never issued.

The concordat with the Reich let those with Bavaria, Prussia, and Baden continue and complemented them, but in addition it applied also to those German states in which there was previously no agreement (ART. 2). And so certain assurances were given by the Reich to those Catholics who were in a hopeless minority position. The assurances of the Weimar Constitution for the freedom of denomination and worship, as for the autonomy of the Churches, were now established by treaty (ART. 1). The exercise of the spiritual functions of priests was placed under special protection (ARTS. 5 and 6). Pastoral care in public institutions was assured (ART. 28). Catholic societies were protected in a defined framework (ART. 31). The German episcopate was named in ART. 31, Sec. 3, as a partner of a definitive agreement with the government of the Reich. In this manner was taken a route heavy with consequences for the future. Nevertheless, the opportunity was neglected of making the principles of interpretation agreed to between the German bishops and the government concerning this article an integral item of the treaty in an incontrovertible manner. The decisive concessions of the state lie in ARTS. 21 to 25, in which the Church's demands in regard to religious instruction and denominational and private schools were essentially met.[28] Religious instruction was to be a

---

rechtliche Tragweite," *ThQ* 134 (1954), 352–76; W. Groppe, *Das Reichskonkordat vom 20. Juli 1933. Eine Studie zur staats- und völkerrechtlichen Bedeutung dieses Vertrages für die Bundesrepublik Deutschland* (Cologne 1956); H. J. Becker, *Zur Rechtsproblematik des Reichskonkordats,* 2d ed. (Munich 1956); E. Deuerlein, *Das Reichskonkordat* (Düsseldorf 1956); F. Schuller, "Das grundsätzliche Verhältnis von Staat und Kirche nach dem Reichskonkordat vom 20.7.1933," *AfkKR* 128 (1957–58), 13–79, 346–404; R. Morsey, "Zur Vorgeschichte des Reichskonkordats aus den Jahren 1920 und 1921," *ZSavRG,* Kan. Abt. 44 (1958), 237–67; idem, ed., "L. Kaas, F. von Papen, Briefe zum Reichskonkordat," *StdZ* 167 (1960–61), 11–30; A. Kupper, ed., *Staatliche Akten über die Reichskonkordatsverhandlungen* (=*Veröffentlichungen der Kommission für Zeitgeschichte bei der Katholischen Akademie in Bayern,* series A, vol. 2) (Mainz 1969); L. Volk, ed., *Kirchliche Akten über die Reichskonkordatsverhandlungen 1933* (=*Veröffentlichungen der Kommission für Zeitgeschichte bei der Katholischen Akadamie in Bayern,* series A, vol. 11) (Mainz 1969); idem, *Das Reichskonkordat vom 20. Juli 1933. Von den Ansätzen in der Weimarer Republik bis zur Ratifizierung am 10. September 1933* (=*Veröffentlichungen der Kommission für Zeitgeschichte bei der Katholischen Akademie in Bayern,* series B, vol. 5) (Mainz 1972).

[28] E. Dackweiler, "Reichskonkordat und katholische Schule," *Juristische Wochenschrift* 62 (1933), 2487–90; Meyer-Lülmann, "Reichskonkordat und Schule," *Der Gemeindetag* 27 (1933), 446–48; Schulte, "Die Schulartikel des Reichskonkordats," *Reichs-*

regular subject of instruction in the public schools, including the professional schools (ART. 21). The maintenance and establishment of Catholic denominational schools was assured under certain conditions (ART. 23). Equality of rights was promised to the private schools of the orders (ART. 25). The Holy See for its part held out the prospect, "on the ground of the special circumstances existing in Germany" and in view of the guarantees contained in the concordat with the Reich, of issuing decrees which forbade clerics and religious from participating in party politics (ART. 32). The "Depoliticization Article" was the *conditio sine qua non* of the government for the conclusion of the concordat. Hitler's goal was the depoliticization of the clergy in order thereby to destroy political Catholicism. It coincided with the intention of the Holy See to keep pastors out of political party involvement for pastoral reasons. Matters of ecclesiastical competence which were not dealt with in the treaty were regulated "for the ecclesiastical sphere" in accord with the prevailing canon law (ART. 33, Sec.1). In regard to the law of marriage, the German government was not ready to make any concession (ART. 26).

On the whole, with the concordat with the Reich there came into being a moderate and durable system of accommodation and cooperation between Church and state. In its essential prescriptions it was modeled on the democratic state constitution of the Weimar Republic. Only a few regulations resulted from the development toward the totalitarian one-party system, in which the German Reich found itself (ARTS. 16, 31, 32). The Holy See strove to bring the concordat with the Reich as close as possible to the most recent ecclesiastical treaties—with Italy and Austria—and thereby to achieve a type of concordat that was uniform in its fundamental lines. The drawback of the German concordat lay in the fact that it was perhaps not honestly meant by the leading statesman and in any event was not taken seriously. The treaty, just like the state concordats, was from the beginning and to an increasing degree circumvented, reinterpreted, violated, and broken.[29]

---

verwaltungsblatt und Preussisches Verwaltungsblatt 54 (1933), 821–24; J. Schröteler, "Das katholische Schulideal und die Bestimmungen des Reichskonkordats," *StdZ* 126 (1934), 145–54; F. Pitzer, *Die Bekenntnisschule des Reichskonkordats. Eine rechtsgeschichtliche Studie und zugleich ein Beitrag zum Schulrecht* (Cologne and Berlin 1967).

[29] E. Rosa, "'Condizione concordataria' o persecuzione in Germania?" *CivCatt* 89 (1938), IV, 305–18; W. Weber, "Das Reichskonkordat in der deutschen Rechtsentwicklung" *Zeitschrift der Akademie für Deutsches Recht* 5 (1938), 532–36; R. Jestaedt, "Das Reichskonkordat vom 20. Juli 1933 in der nationalsozialistischen Staats- und Verwaltungspraxis unter besonderer Berücksichtigung des Artikels 1," *AfkKR* 124 (1949–50), 335–430; W. Corsten, ed., *Kölner Aktenstücke zur Lage der katholischen Kirche in Deutschland 1933–1945* (Cologne 1949); W. Conrad, *Der Kampf um die*

The rights which were guaranteed to the Church by constitution and concordat were extensively undermined; in this matter the procedure was rather by way of decree and administrative practice than by means of legislation. The freedom of the Church's activity was severely impaired. The aim was a state corresponding to the National Socialist ideology. If at this time matters did not go so far as an annulment of the concordat, at times pushed by the minister for the churches, Hanns Kerrl, and to a full separation of Church and state, still the reasons were suited for the regime effectively to be able to effect a supervision of the Church under the existing system, and it meant to take still more certain domestic and foreign policy motives into consideration.

Things moved forward with similar, partly far worse measures of persecution in the occupied and annexed territories. In the part of Poland occupied by Germany, the so-called Government General, there occurred a furious persecution of the Church, which decimated the clergy. The Polish concordat, the Austrian concordat, the modus vivendi with Czechoslovakia, and the Napoleonic concordat in Alsace-Lorraine were considered abolished. In regard to Austria, the government of the Reich adopted the view that the Austrian concordat had been ended by the annexation of Austria to the German Reich, because the country had perished as an independent state and had lost its position as a subject of international law. In Austria there now prevailed "a situation without concordat."[30] In the Wartheland District the Church was treated as a private association. An extension of the concordat with the Reich to the newly acquired territories was rejected.

The Holy See tried to influence the Nazi regime by the diplomatic route, but, when the exchange of notes remained without effect, turned to publicity. In the encyclical *Mit brennender Sorge* of 4 March 1937 Pius

Kanzeln (Berlin 1957); A Kupper, "Zur Geschichte des Reichskonkordats," *StdZ* 163 (1958–59), 278–302, 354–75; D. Albrecht, ed. *Der Notenwechsel zwischen dem Heiligen Stuhl und der Deutschen Reichsregierung,* 2 vols. (=*Veröffentlichungen der Kommission für Zeitgeschichte bei der Katholischen Akademie in Bayern,* series A, vols. 1 and 10) (Mainz 1965–69); B. Schneider with P. Blet and A. Martini, eds., *Die Briefe Pius' XII. an die deutschen Bischöfe 1939–1944* (=*Veröffentlichungen . . . der Katholischen Akademie in Bayern,* series A, vol. 4) (Mainz 1966); B. Stasiewski, ed., *Akten deutscher Bischöfe über die Lage der Kirche 1933–1945* I: *1933–1934* (=*Veröffentlichungen . . der Katholischen Akademie in Bayern,* series A, vol. 5) (Mainz 1968); F. Pauly, "Zur Kirchenpolitik des Gauleiters J. Bürckel im Saargebiet (März–August 1935)," *Rheinische Vierteljahrsblätter* 35 (1971), 414–53.
[30] K. Scholder, "Österreichisches Konkordat und nationalsozialistische Kirchenpolitik 1938/39," *ZevKR* 20 (1975), 230–43.

XI stigmatized the interference and usurpations by the state.[31] Despite the just described hostile measures, the concordats were not entirely useless. Their existence acted, in some respects, as a restraint on the pressures, preserved for the Church one or another position for the proclamation of the Gospel, even though curtailed, and even exercised a certain influence in the concentration camps. The binding of the state to the concordats made, on the one hand, its measures of oppression visible even on the plane of international law and induced it to certain considerations, and on the other hand offered the Holy See the basis for interventions. The fact that the Holy See had, by the concluding of the concordat, recognized the Nazi government as a treaty partner could no longer be annulled. By concluding the concordat the government of the Reich had acknowledged the competence of the Holy See over the Catholic Church in Germany as legitimate in an agreement of international law. Every violation of the concordat injured the credibility of the Nazi regime.

DURING THE SECOND WORLD WAR

The approaching Second World War naturally interrupted the conclusion of concordats with the warring nations. Only with countries which lay on the lee side of world politics or could keep themselves aloof from the power struggle were a few treaties made.

In Salazar's Portugal the Church was cautiously encouraged. On 7 May 1940 the country concluded with the Holy See a significant concordat and a mission treaty,[32] which Salazar termed a "concordat of the separation of state and Church." The concordat extended the existing system of the demarcation and collaboration of Church and state in free agreement and mutual respect. The legal personality of the Catholic Church was recognized, the maintenance of diplomatic relations was agreed (ARTICLE I). A series of guarantees assured the activity and the property of the Church (ARTS. II–VII). Clerics enjoyed special protection and certain immunities (ARTS. XI–XV). Religious instruc-

---

[31] S. Hirt, ed., *Mit brennender Sorge. Das päpstliche Rundschreiben gegen den Nationalsozialismus und seine Folgen in Deutschland* (Freiburg i. Br. 1946); R. Leiber, "'Mit brennender Sorge'. März 1937 bis März 1962," *StdZ* 169 (1961–62), 417–26.

[32] A. Perugini, "De novis Conventionibus Lusitanis," *Apollinaris* 13 (1940), 205–17; P. Aguirre, "Ecclesia et Status in Lusitania secundum recens concordatum" *Periodica* 29 (1940), 289–302; A. Giannini, "Il concordato Portoghese," *Rivista di Studi Politici Internazionali* 10 (1943), 3–28; L. Scheucher, "Die Glaubens- und Gewissensfreiheit in Portugal," *ÖAfKR* 7 (1956), 211–31; B. J. Wenzel, *Portugal und der Heilige Stuhl* (Lisbon 1958); T. Kreppel, *Die Trennung von Staat und Kirche in Portugal. Das Konkordat zwischen Portugal und dem Heiligen Stuhl als Beispiel einer neuen Ordnung von Kirche und Staat* (Frankfurt 1962); L. Renard, *Salazar. Kirche und Staat in Portugal* (Essen 1968).

tion was an obligatory subject in the country's public schools, and their entire teaching had to be oriented to the principles of the Christian faith (ART. XXI). Private schools could be erected by the Church (ART. XX). The law of marriage was governed by the principle of optional civil marriage (ARTS. XXII–XXV). The state supported the missions in the overseas territories (ARTS. XXVII–XXVIII). The mission treaty envisaged the admittance of foreign missionaries to Portuguese colonies (ART. 2). Mission societies were supported by the government (ARTS. 9–14). The free operation of the missions was assured (ART. 15). With these two agreements, peace and cooperation between Church and state in Portugal and its overseas possessions seemed assured for a long time. The effects of the Second World War could not be foreseen at the time of their signing. The conclusion of the concordat of 1940 led to the revision of the present ART. 45 of the constitution on 11 June 1951.

In the 1930s the Church experienced difficult times in Spain. The republican constitution of 9 December 1931 adopted a hostile attitude toward religion and Church. In the following years there erupted a full-scale war against the church. In 1933 the Spanish government declared it regarded the concordat of 1851 as ended. Parts of the army rose against maladministration and terror, and for several years a bitter civil war raged. Chief of State Franco sought to restore the Catholic character of the nation.[33] Laws and measures hostile to the Church were annulled. On 7 June 1941 the Spanish government concluded with the Holy See an agreement on the exercise of the privilege of nomination in the appointment to episcopal sees.[34] According to it, the apostolic nuncio, after an understanding with the government, draws up a list of six qualified persons and transmits it to the Holy See. This submits to the government a proposal of three names, with regard for the list but without being restricted to it. From this the chief of state names a candidate, so far as he raises no objections of a general political nature. A concordat was envisaged.

A treaty going into the greatest detail on questions of church property came into existence with Haiti on 25 January 1940. The Holy See concluded an agreement with Colombia on 22 April 1942.[35] The greatest part consisted of the regulation of questions of marriage law

[33] J. Soto de Gangoiti, *Relaciones de la Iglesia Católica y el Estado Español* (Madrid 1940); idem, *La Santa Sede y la Iglesia Católica en España* (Madrid 1942).
[34] R. S. de Lamadrid, "El convenio entre el Gobierno espãnol y la Santa Sede," *Boletín de la Universidad de Granada* 13 (1941), 371–85; A. Giannini, "La convenzione tra la S. Sede e la Spagna per la provvista delle diocesi," *Il Diritto Ecclesiastico* 53 (1942), 137–45.
[35] J. A. Eguren, *Derecho concordatario colombiano* (Bogotá 1960).

(ARTS. 4–10), which were largely in accord with canon law. The civil registrar of marriages was present at the church wedding, without his presence being an indispensable condition for the recognition of the civil effects. The government's right of proposal in the naming of the bishops was replaced by the right to express reservations "of a political nature" (ART. 1). Thereby the traditional *patronate* was done away with.

IN THE POSTWAR PERIOD

The effects of the Second World War were much more comprehensive and profound than those of the First World War. The map of Europe was again considerably altered. In Asia and Africa the colonial epoch ended. Within many states there proceeded considerable changes, which also concerned religious law. The close union between Church and state was dissolved or at least loosened in many countries. The number of countries with a system of union of Church and state progressively declined. This was especially the case with nations having a predominantly Christian population. The order established by concordat in Eastern Europe completely broke up. The Church's concordat policy entered a new phase.[36]

Fate of Concordats in Socialist Countries

For religion and the Church the most fateful effect of the Second World War was the advance of the Soviet Union dominated by the Bolshevik Party, the strongest military power of Eurasia, as far as the Elbe, and the establishing of a Communist regime in China, the most populous nation on earth. For Communism religion is a scientifically untenable prejudice. The ecclesiastical policy of the socialist states is in accord with this notion. It has the chief goal of hastening the death of religion, viewed as inevitable, by restricting or neutralizing the Church's possibilities for influence. In the final analysis the socialist regimes aimed to exclude the Church little by little as guardian of religious faith but also as guarantor of civil liberty. The state bureaucracy moved openly or secretly into the service of the antireligious and antiecclesiastical strivings of the Communist Party. It made use of two means: tempting offers on the one hand, obstacles, prohibitions, force, and terror on the other. A falling off of the supression or persecution always sprang only from tactical viewpoints and was caused by pressure from without or unrest within. The difference between constitutional law and constitutional reality is nowhere greater than in socialist lands. It is not the constitution that is inviolable but the historical process of development. The constitution

---

[36] J. Salomon, "La politique concordataire des États depius la fin de la deuxième guerre mondiale," *Revue Générale de Droit International Public* 59 (1955), 570–623.

describes only the state of development of the revolution achieved at the time of its adoption. Basic rights in our sense are impossible systems in Soviet ideology.

There were differences in the manner and rapidity of the advance among the individual socialist countries. In general it is to be noted that the area of freedom left to the Church is the greater, the nearer the states in question are to the free West. Relatively the greatest degree of freedom of movement is possessed—or assumed—by the Catholic Church in Poland[37] and is permitted to the Orthodox Church in Rumania[38] and Bulgaria.[39] Hopeless, on the other hand, is the situation in Czechoslovakia.[40] The "Marxist Josephinism" of this country allows the Church only a narrow living space and trivial freedom of organization. Not much more favorable is the situation in Hungary.[41] The model for the socialist countries even in ecclesiastical policy is basically the Soviet Union. Since 1918 the hostile separation of the Church from the state and of the school from the Church has existed there.[42] The Church's sphere of activity is limited to worship. Correspondingly, the

[37] K. Weber, *Der moderne Staat und die katholische Kirche. Laizistische Tendenzen im staatlichen Leben der Dritten Französischen Republik, des Dritten Reiches und der Volksrepublik Polen* (Essen 1967).

[38] G. Rosu, M. Vasiliu, G. Crisan, "Church and State in Romania," V. Gsovski ed., *Church and State behind the Iron Curtain* (New York 1955), 253–99; F. Popan, Č. Draskovic, *Orthodoxie in Rumänien und Jugoslawien* (Vienna 1960); G. Podskalsky, "Kirche und Staat in Rumänien," *StdZ* 185 (1970), 198–207.

[39] G. Podskalsky, "Kirche und Staat in Bulgarien," *StdZ* 189 (1972), 112–24.

[40] F. Cavalli, *Governo Comunista e chiesa cattolica in Cecoslovacchia* (Rome 1950); L. Němec, *Episcopal and Vatican Reactions to the Persecution of the Catholic Church in Czechoslovakia* (Washington 1953); idem, *Church and State in Czechoslovakia* (New York 1955); V. Chalupa, *Situation of the Catholic Church in Czechoslovakia* (Chicago 1960); E. Schmied, "Die rechtliche Stellung der Kirche in der Tschechoslowakei," *Jahrbuch für Ostrecht* 1 (1960), 129–36; K. Rabl, "Die tschechoslowakische Verfassungsurkunde vom. 11. Juli 1960 in Theorie und Praxis," *Jahrbuch des öffentlichen Rechts,* n.s. 12 (1963), 353–416.

[41] A. Bedö, H. Kálnoky, L. LeNard, G. Torzsay-Biber, "Church and State in Hungary," V. Gsovski, ed., *Church and State behind the Iron Curtain* (New York 1955), 69–157; L. Mezöfy, "Staat und Kirche in Ungarn," *Jahrbuch für Ostrecht* 3 (1962), 249–71; A. Emmerich, J. Morel, *Bilanz des ungarischen Katholizismus* (Munich 1969).

[42] E. Jacobi, "Staat und Kirche in der Sowjetunion," *Wissenschaftliche Zeitschrift der Karl-Marx-Universität Leipzig. Gesellschafts- und sprachwissenschaftliche* Reihe 4 (1954–55), 325–344; W. de Vries, *Kirche und Staat in der Sowjetunion* (Munich 1959); J. Chrysostomus, "Kirche und Staat in Sowjetrussland. Das Schicksal des Moskauer Patriarchates von 1917–1960." *Jahrbücher für Geschichte Osteuropas,* n.s. 11 (1963), 13–16; G. Schweigl, *Il nuovo Statuto della Chiesa russa e l'art. 124 della Costituzione sovietica* (Rome 1965); G. Zananiri, *Le Saint Siège et Moscou* (Paris 1967); D. Konstantinow, *Die Kirche in der Sowjetunion nach dem Krieg, Entfaltung und Rückschläge* (Munich and Salzburg 1973).

constitutions of the so-called People's Democracies of Rumania, Bulgaria, Hungary, Czechoslovakia, Albania, and Yugoslavia carried out the separation of Church and state. It happened regularly in conscious opposition to the still considerably popular ecclesiastical situation of religion in these nations. The principle of freedom of religion and conscience, proclaimed with the separation of Church and state, nowhere benefited the Catholic Church. It was often more severely persecuted than all other religious communities. The Church lost its status in public law and as far as possible was completely excluded from public life. Everywhere there was an effort to restrict it to undertaking cult functions and to prevent every other influence on people, especially on youth. At the same time the Church was to a very great degree subjected to control. In all Socialist states there are offices for ecclesiastical affairs, which to an enormous extent interfere in the filling of ecclesiastical offices, supervise the formation of the clergy, and determine the number and capacity of the places of this formation. Where several religious groups face one another, the government tries to play them off against one another, but in every case the chief opponent is seen in the Catholic Church. In the individual Church it strives to provoke various groups against one another, in this way to introduce schism into the Church, and thus to maintain its influence over it the more effectively.

The union of the bishops with the Holy See was either thwarted or subject to control, diplomatic relations were severed, and concordats were repudiated, that with Lithuania on 1 July 1940, with Poland on 12 September 1945, with Rumania on 17 July 1948. Without any official repudiation, Czechoslovakia disregarded the modus vivendi and in 1950 broke off diplomatic relations with the Holy See, as did Yugoslavia in 1952. So long as religion was not yet extirpated, Communism tried to make use of its adherents, especially of its clergy and its institutions for its own ends. For the sake of this advantage it was even ready to aid the Churches to a certain extent. Although the socialist states almost everywhere have the means of power to carry through almost any desired measure against the Church, they were anxious for the assent, even if extorted, of the Church to their regulations. The Communists know that the most secure route to a gaining of the Catholics of a country is through Rome. Furthermore, they anticipate from the concluding of a concordat that they can win the sympathy of some Catholic circles outside the country. In case they have no success in reaching an agreement with the Holy See, they turn to the bishops. If these refuse, they approach the priests. Thus are explained not only the repeated attempts to come to an understanding with the Holy See, but also the series of agreements with the episcopate in the 1950s. The governments of Czechoslovakia and Yugoslavia sent out feelers in the direction of a concordat in 1949 and 1952 respectively. The Holy See rejected them in the case of Czechoslovakia because it regarded any agreement as hopeless, considering the situation, but it showed itself accommodating toward Yugoslavia. However, the contacts did not lead to the signing of a treaty, because Yugoslavia was not prepared to acquiesce in the Church's minimum demands. The Polish government was unwilling to apply to the Holy See. It expected the attainment of its goals from negotiations with the nation's episcopate. On 14 April 1950 and 8 December 1956 it made an agreement with the Polish bishops.[43] These treaties were not concordats but administrative agreements on the plane of domestic public law. Their content differed greatly from that of the concordats which were concluded before the appearance of socialism. In them the state endeavored to put the Church at the service of its political and economic aims. The bishop manifested a broad accommodation in order to promote the desired relaxation of tensions. But the government did not adhere to even trivial promises. Especially in the school system all concessions promised or made were again revoked. The agreements reached in Hungary, Rumania, and Czechoslovakia were considerably more unfavorable to the Church than the Polish. In Hungary the episcopate made great concessions in the agreement of 30 August 1950. It bound itself to support the policies of the government, which promised to supply subsidies to the Church for a period of eighteen years. The signing of the agreement could not prevent the further disorganization of ecclesiastical life. In Rumania an assembly of progressive clerics signed the agreement of 15 March 1951 submitted by the government. In Czechoslovakia a part of the clergy accepted the law of 14 October 1949, which unilaterally regulated the situation of the Church.

Concordats with Free Countries

The situation of the Holy See with regard to the free nations was, in general, not unfavorable after the Second World War. In the postwar period the Holy See entered into diplomatic relations with a considerable number of states, especially in Africa and Asia. On the other hand, it did not succeed in inaugurating with them an era of concordats like that after the First World War. In many countries material reconstruction following the devastation of the war occupied the foreground. In the new states of Africa and Asia Catholics were ordinarily too weak to

---

[43] L. Pérez Mier, "El acuerdo entre el episcopado polaco y el gobierno de Varsovia," *Revista Española de Derecho Canónico* 6 (1951), 185–255; *Ost-Probleme* 9 (1957), 237; K. Hartmann, "Über die Verständigung zwischen Kirche und Staat in Polen," *Aussenpolitik* 8 (1957), 571–82.

be able to effect the conclusion of an agreement with the Holy See, apart from the inner chaos and necessities of existence of many of these areas. The raw nationalism and the sensitive self-esteem of the young African states opposed the solving of occurring questions between Church and state by means of agreements and insisted on their unilateral regulation by law. Most states exercised strict control over the external affairs of the Church. The state reserved to itself the ultimate competence for decision in mixed matters. The majority of these countries have hitherto not developed their own legal system regulating Church-state relations. The relations of the religious groups to the state were still based extensively on improvisation. The instability and uncertainty of the political situation recommended to both parties, Church and state, that they avoid the conclusion of treaties, whose binding force confronted the often abrupt changes and hence could evoke tensions and conflicts. It was enough to assume diplomatic relations whereby occurring questions could be solved quickly and without complication. In other countries the traditional reasons that did not permit a concordat with the Holy See persisted. Thus, for example, the Brazilian constitutional documents of 18 September 1946 (AR-TICLE 31, no. 3) and of 24 January 1967 (ART. 9, no. 2), like that of 16 July 1934 (ART. 17, no. 3), contained the stipulation that no agreement with a church or worship group could be concluded. Certain trends in France for again achieving the state of a concordat with the Holy See were unable to materialize to the extent of concrete political treatment. Still, where concordats were concluded, they displayed a stronger individualism than those earlier entered into.

The Catholic nations of southern Europe—Italy, Spain, and Portugal—had, after bitter struggles, restored the traditional close union between Church and state. In Italy the Lateran Treaties held good after the war's end. They survived the overthrow of Fascism and of the Kingdom and were confirmed by ARTICLE 7 of the republican constitution of 27 December 1947.[44] They thereby obtained a direct constitutional guarantee. The Holy See entered into an accord with Portugal on 18 July 1950 in regard to the filling of episcopal sees in Portuguese India.[45] In it the government renounced the privilege of presentation

[44] S. Lener, "I patti lateranensi e la nuova Italia," *CivCatt* 101 (1950), II, 609–21; idem, "I precedenti legislativi e storici dell' articolo 7 della costituzione," ibid. III, 248–60; G. B. Arista, *La Costituzione Italiana,* 3d ed. (Rome 1963), 61ff., 348ff.

[45] J. Damizia, "Annotationes ad conventionem inter S. Sedem et Rempublicam Lusitaniam," *Apollinaris* 23 (1950), 261–63; J. M. Lourenço, "Portugal e a Santa Sé," *Revista Española de Derecho Canónico* 6 (1951), 171–83; A. da Silva Rego, *Le patronage portugais de l'Orient* (Lisbon 1957); B. J. Wenzel, *Portugal und der Heilige Stuhl. Das portugiesische Konkordats- und Missionsrecht. Ein Beitrag zur Geschichte der Missions- und Völkerrechtswissenschaft* (Lisbon 1958).

belonging to the president and freed the Holy See from the obligation of appointing bishops of Portuguese nationality for specified sees. Here was introduced a development which was continued by the Second Vatican Council.

The development in Spain tended toward a climax in the matter of concordats. The constitutional law of 17 July 1945 placed the profession and practice of the Catholic religion as the religion of the state under official protection (ARTICLE 6, Section 1). The private practice of worship was permitted to non-Catholic religious groups (ART. 6, Sec. 2). With this arrangement Spain returned to unity of nation and religion, which was in accord with its tradition. In Spain the Catholic religion is a part of the culture. The activity of the Protestant religious groups was logically usually opposed to both. And so the government regarded itself as justified in hindering any agitation by them. Thereby the road was staked out for the contemplated concordat. The accord of 16 July 1946 regulated the filling of nonconsistorial benefices.[46] According to it, half the dignitaries of the chapters, after nomination by the chief of state, were filled from a list of three names presented by the appropriate bishop. Before the appointing of pastors the government had the right to raise objections of a general political nature. On 5 August 1950 a convention on the pastoral care of the military was signed.[47] But these and other smaller treaties were only the introduction to the great concordat of 27 August 1953.[48] It was the climax of Pius XII's concordat policy. According to the concordat, the Catholic religion remained "the sole religion of the Spanish nation," with all the rights pertaining to it in keeping with divine

[46] L. Pérez Mier, "El Convenio español para la provisión de beneficios no consistoriales," *Revista Española de Derecho Canónico* 1 (1946), 729–75.

[47] M. García Castro, "El Convenio entre la Santa Sede y el Estado español sobre la jurisdicción castrense y asistencia religiosa a las fuerzas armadas," *Revista Española de Derecho Canónico* 5 (1950), 1107–71; 6 (1951), 265–301, 701–71.

[48] A. Giannini, "Il Concordato con la Spagna," *Il Diritto Ecclesiastico* 64 (1953), 417–49; P. Mikat, "Das spanische Konkordat," *Kirche in der Welt* 6 (1953), 323–28; S. Pappalardo, "Inter Sanctam Sedem et Hispaniam sollemnes conventiones. Adnotationes," *Monitor Ecclesiasticus* 79 (1954), 247–88; M. Useros Carretero, "A propósito de la neutralidad confesional del Estado y el Concordato español," *Revista Española de Derecho Canónico* 9 (1954), 225–39; E. F. Regatillo, "Il valore del nuovo Concordato spagnuolo per la vita religiosa della Spagna," *CivCatt* 106 (1955), II, 378–92; III, 265–76, 499–507; R. Bidagor, "Das Konkordat zwischen dem Heiligen Stuhl und Spanien," *ÖAfKR* 6 (1955), 3–13, 173–88; 7 (1956), 5–17; I. Martín Martínez *Concordato de 1953 entre España y la Santa Sede* (Madrid 1961); E. F. Regatillo, *El Concordato español de 1953* (Santander 1961); S. Alvárez-Menéndez, "El Concordato Español de 1953," *Angelicum* 41 (1964), 63–86; L. Gutiérrez Martín, *El privilegio de nombramiento de obispos en España* (Rome 1967); J. Pérez Alhama, *La Iglesia y el Estado español* (Madrid 1967).

and canon law (ARTICLE I). The prescriptions of the agreement of 7 June 1941 continued in force for the naming of residential and coadjutor bishops (ART. VII). The immune legal status of the clergy was recognized with certain modifications (ART. XVI). The state obliged itself to important financial donations to the Church (ART. XIX). Marriage contracted in accord with the prescriptions of canon law had full validity in the civil sphere (ART. XXIII). Questions of nullity and separation were the responsibility of ecclesiastical courts (ART. XXIV). In all schools the instruction was to be given in harmony with Catholic doctrine (ART. XXVI). Catholic religious instruction was an obligatory subject in the schools of every rank (ART. XXVII). In the agencies for the formation of public opinion room was assured to the Church for the presentation and defense of religious truth (ART. XXIX). The freedom of ecclesiastical universities and academies as well as the possibility of erecting schools of every kind were guaranteed (ARTS. XXX and XXXI).

By means of the concordat the Church in Spain obtained a position of imposing compactness. The Spanish concordat once again took into account the Catholic tradition of the Spanish people and created a system of the relations of Church and state in a Catholic country that must be termed, theoretically, almost ideal. A more far-reaching favoring of the Catholic Church and a more intensive collaboration of the state with it was scarcely conceivable. Nevertheless, in Spain one can speak of a system of state Church only with restrictions. For the concordat did indeed proclaim the Catholic religion as the religion of the state, but not a state Church. Even more, the free exercise of its sovereignty was expressly guaranteed to the Catholic Church (ART. II). Its independence in Spain is incomparably greater than that of Protestantism in the Scandinavian countries. In addition, the concordat did not essentially impair the individual's freedom of denomination. The concordat did not represent a capitulation of the state to the Church but the attempt, undertaken in the interests of both parties, to realize the closest possible union between Church and state. The Spanish system of the relations of Church and state, as constructed by the concordat, was based on the principle that the Catholic religion, as the sole true one, alone possessed an objective right to existence and social liberty and that consequently the adherents of the other religions had only a claim to the protection of their erroneous conscience. On the other hand, the propagation of error implied a danger for the faith of the Catholics and for public morality and hence was to be thwarted. The state has the duty of protecting and supporting the Catholic Church as guardian and proclaimer of the truth. The concordat strove to create for the Church the legal and economic presuppositions necessary or useful for the exercise of its mission. The example of the Islamic states with their system of unity was as effective in the conclusion of the concordat as was the memory of the civil war, which, in view of the reign of terror in the republican part of Spain and the atrocities of the Republicans against the Church, had here and there assumed the character of a crusade. The de-Catholicizing of the country, which the republican regime had sought, ranked as treason to the national tradition.

For the conclusion of the concordat some deliberations were decisive, which proved later to be miscalculations. The two contracting parties were not, it is true, mistaken as to the religious situation among the Spanish people. They knew of the spread of socialist, Communist, and anarchist ideologies, they knew the religious lethargy and antipathy of broad groups. They did not fail to see that in Spain there was a considerable number of persons who were or wanted to be at the same time Catholic and anticlerical, and that the liberalism disseminated especially at the universities was not pleased with a powerful position for the Church. If they nevertheless could not be deterred from allowing the Catholic religion and Church so outstanding a position, then this happened because they had confidence in the power of the Church to bring its mission convincingly and enticingly to development if only the external presuppositions for this were created for it. But they did not foresee that a decade would suffice to weaken the Church critically, and, in fact, from within, not from without. They counted on the stability of the Church and its stabilizing function for society and state. They did not suspect that this stability was based to a considerable extent on factors which could be swept away with a change of pontificate. The contracting parties also probably underestimated the publicity strength of Protestantism, which, despite numerically insignificant circumstances, was employed to the fullest extent, the mood of so-called world publicity, which was decisively determined by Protestantism, and the inclination of many states with a Protestant majority, especially the United States, to intervene on behalf of their coreligionists in Catholic lands. The concordat became the occasion for isolating Spain economically, culturally, and politically. The untiring attacks of world Protestantism against the concordat could not be without effect in the long run. They could not but gradually undermine also the power of resistance of some politicans and bishops, for whom the defense of the concordat was an obligatory responsibility. Finally, it appeared that the hope linked with the conclusion of the Spanish concordat that it could serve as model for the other Catholic countries was unfulfilled. With one exception, now to be mentioned, it remained a unique case.

With the Latin American states, to which Pius XII constantly brought his increasing care, the conclusion of treaties occurred in three cases. On 29 January 1953 a mission agreement was signed with Colombia. The government granted to the mission protection and support, among other reasons for the formation of a native clergy (ARTICLE 7). On 16 June 1954 the Dominican Republic signed with the Holy See a comprehensive concordat, which borrowed extensively from that with Spain.[49] The Catholic religion remains the religion of the state (ART. I). The patronate was abandoned (ART. V). The activity of foreign clerics and religious in the country is assured (ART. X). Until the present (1974) this was supposed to be the ultimate treaty, basically regulating all questions of common interest. On 21 January 1958 there followed, in accord with ART. XVII of the concordat, an agreement on the pastoral care of the military. With Bolivia a mission agreement[50] was reached on 4 December 1957, a treaty on the pastoral care of the military[51] on 29 November 1958. On the missionaries was laid, besides the work of evangelizing, also care for the promotion of the temporal welfare of the natives (ART. VII). In the agreements with the Dominican Republic (ART. XIX) and with Bolivia of 4 December 1957 (ART. XIV) the Church's charitable activity was taken into consideration, which was something new. In Peru the mandate of the constitution of 9 April 1933 and that of 5 September 1940 did not permit the conclusion of a concordat with the Holy See (ART. 234). Finally, a long cherished desire of Pius XII was fulfilled in Germany. The successor states of Prussia in the Federal Republic proceeded after the war, even if partly after long hesitation, on the basis of the continuing validity of the Prussian concordat. Likewise, Bavaria and Baden-Württemberg adhered to the continuing validity of the respective concordats.[52] To supplement the Prussian concordat, the state of

[49] J. Damizia, "Annotationes ad sollemnes Conventiones inter S. Sedem et Rempublicam Dominicanam," *Apollinaris* 27 (1954), 243–76; A. Giannini, "Il concordato Dominicano," *Il Diritto Ecclesiastico* 65 (1954), 288–98; P. Mikat, "Zur neuesten Konkordatspraxis des Heiligen Stuhles. Das Konkordat zwischen dem Heiligen Stuhl und der Dominikanischen Repbulik," *Die Kirche in der Welt* 8 (1955), 177–82.
[50] J. Damizia, "Annotationes ad conventionem inter Apostolicam Sedem et Bolivianam Rempublicam," *Apollinaris* 31 (1958), 220–27; F. Cavalli, "La recente convenzione missionaria tra la Santa Sede e la Bolivia," *CivCatt* 109 (1958), I, 502–16.
[51] A. Pugliese, "Adnotationes," *Apollinaris* 34 (1961), 309–12.
[52] ARTICLE 182 of the Bavarian constitution of 2 December 1946 declares that the treaties of 24 January 1925 with the Christian Churches remain in force. ART. 35, Sec. 2, of the constitution of the Saarland of 15 December 1947 recognizes the legally

Nordrhein-Westfalen and the Holy See made a treaty for the erection of the see of Essen[53] on 19 December 1956. In this way, the care of souls in the Ruhr district was united and uniformly directed.

The Agreements under John XXIII and Paul VI

THE SIGNIFICANCE OF THE SECOND VATICAN COUNCIL FOR THE LEGAL RELATIONSHIP OF CHURCH AND STATE

The death of Pius XII meant the end of an epoch in the government and politics of the Church. The most momentous happening in the pontificate of John XXIII was without any doubt the convocation of a General Council. The Second Vatican Council had a heavy impact, not only on the relations of Church and state in general but on the policy of the Holy See especially.[54] Here let reference be made to only three

---

existing treaties and agreements with the Churches. ARTICLE 23 of the constitution of North Rhine-Westphalia of 28 June 1950 recognizes as a valid the treaties with the Churches which were concluded in the former Free State of Prussia. ARTICLE 8 of the constitution of Baden-Württemberg of 11 November 1953 declares that rights and duties from the treaties with the Churches remain intact(cf. A. Erler, "Die Konkordatslage in Deutschland," *Süddeutsche Juristen-Zeitung* 1 [1946], 197–200; M. Gebhart, *Die Rechtslage des Reichskonkordates und der Länderkonkordate nach 1945* (Diss. Munich 1951); O. Born, *Das Problem der Weitergeltung des Reichskonkordats und der Länderkonkordate nach dem Zusammenbruch des Reiches im Jahre 1945* (Diss. Münster 1953); G. Ostermann, *Die Fortgeltung des Badischen Konkordates von 1932* (Cologne 1962); A. Herzig, *Die Systematik und Problematik des konkordatären Rechts in Nordrhein-Westfalen* (Cologne 1965); K. Orywall, *Die Geltung der neueren Konkordate und Kirchenverträge im Saarland* (Cologne 1969).

[53] E. Hegel, *Kirchliche Vergangenheit im Bistum Essen* (Essen 1960), 275–95; W. Haugg, *Staat und Kirche in Nordrhein-Westfalen* (Berlin, Neuwied and Darmstadt 1960); P. Mikat, *Das Verhältnis von Kirche und Staat im Lande Nordrhein-Westfalen in Geschichte und Gegenwart* (=Veröffentlichungen der Arbeitsgemeinschaft für Forschung des Landes Nordrhein-Westfalen 129) (Cologne and Opladen 1966); J. Bauer, *Das Verhältnis von Staat und Kirche im Land Nordrhein-Westfalen* (Münster 1968).

[54] A. Schwan, *Katholische Kirche und pluralistische Politik. Politische Implikationen des II. Vatikanischen Konzils* (=Recht und Staat in Geschichte und Gegewart 330) (Tübingen 1966); P. Mikat, "Kirche und Staat in nachkonziliarer Sicht," K. Aland, W. Scheenmelcer, eds., *Kirche und Staat. Festschrift für Bischof D. Hermann Kunst D.D. zum 60. Geburtstag am 21 Januar 1967* (Berlin 1967), 105–25; H. Barion, " 'Weltgeschichtliche Machtform?' Eine Studie zur Politischen Theologie des II. Vatikanischen Konzils," H. Barrion, E. W. Böchenförde, E. Forsthoff, W. Weber, eds., *Epirrhosis. Festgabe für Carl Schmitt* I (Berlin 1968), 13–59; D. Grimm, "Die Staatslehre der katholischen Kirche nach dem zweiten Vatikanischen Knozil," *Civitas. Jahrbuch für Sozialwissenschaften* 8 (1969), 11–30; P. Mikat, "Nachkonziliare Überlegungen zum gewandelten Verhältnis von Staat und Kirche," *Militärseelsorge* 14 (1972), 206–27; J. Wössner, ed., *Religion im Umbruch. Soziologische Beiträge zur Situation von Religion und Kirche in der gegenwärtigen Gesellschaft* (Stuttgart 1972).

decisive statements of the council. The declaration *Dignitatis humanae* on religious liberty demanded the freedom of religion of the individual and of groups in the state without regard to the question of truth. According to it, religious freedom is a basic human right, derived from human dignity, the striving proper to human nature for a knowledge of the truth, the different task of Church and state, as well as the goal of the state to serve the common good. The legal order must make this human right a civil right (ARTICLES 2 and 3). Hence, fundamentally the state must guarantee free possibility of activity to all religions. The only restriction on this liberty is the endangering of public order—"iustae exigentiae ordinis publici": ART. 4; "iustus ordo publicus": ART. 2; also ART. 7. The declaration takes note of the system of a state religion only as a fact based on special circumstances, without recommending it. In case it is introduced, the right of all citizens and groups to religious liberty must be recognized and preserved (ART. 6). Thus the ideal of the Catholic state seemed to have been abolished. True, in ART. 1 of the cited declaration occurs the *clausula salvatoria:* that the traditional doctrine on the moral obligation of persons and of groups vis-à-vis the true religion and the One Church of Christ remains unaffected. But this abstract allusion to a doctrine which is itself not expounded cannot prevail against the concrete statements of the articles mentioned. They became of great importance for the relationship of legal proximity of Church and state existing in some countries.

The pastoral constitution *Gaudium et spes* on the Church in today's world stressed that the Church is tied to no political system but is basically prepared for cooperation with each one. While it makes use of the temporal to the extent that its mission requires, it does not place its hope on privileges offered to it by the state authority. It would even renounce the exercise of certain legitimately acquired rights if it is established that their use jeopardizes the credibility of its witness or changed conditions of life demand another arrangement (ART. 76). These statements, which are in themselves self-evident, corresponded to a widespread mentality which saw in the depriving of the Church of earthly assurances and temporal means an opportunity for the better propagation of the faith. They supplied the signal for a movement under way in many countries, which anticipated from the sacrifice of legal positions a deepening and greater effectiveness of the Church's ministry.

The decree *Christus Dominus* on the pastoral office of bishops finally expressed the wish that in the future no more rights or privileges be conceded to heads of state to select, appoint, suggest, or designate bishops. Heads of state were asked to renounce, in agreement with the Holy See, these rights, just mentioned, which they possessed at present by virtue of a treaty or through custom (ART. 20). With this invitation was continued a development which had begun long before the council,[55] but which had been sensationally infringed in Spain because of the special circumstances.

As important as the above mentioned and other pertinent expressions and directions of the Second Vatican Council were for the relations of Church and state, all the more must one not overlook, for the understanding of the changes which have taken place in this area since the council, the development which proceeded in the Catholic Church itself from about the beginning of the 1960s. For the unity, the vitality, and the missionary élan of the Church determined its radiation to society and thereby regularly decided its influence on the state and its work. Particularly in the democratic state is the Church left to influence its members in the state to grant it freedom to move and support, which it needs for a wholesome activity. The importance of the Church in the pluralistic democratic state depends to a decisive degree on the spiritual substance, the inner strength, and the credibility which it is able to display and radiate. But the just mentioned qualities of the Catholic Church are in a state of constant and rapid retreat. The faith, the foundation of the Church and of all its activity, has been attacked and questioned for years from its own ranks. As a consequence countless Catholics are insecure, devoid of a vital conviction of the faith, and unfitted for an effective witness to the faith. The authority of Pope and bishops is gravely weakened. The clergy is to a great extent disoriented and divided. Discipline in the Church has seriously declined. Ecclesiastical laws are unashamedly transgressed and liquidated as a result of mounting disobedience. In extensive Catholic circles this worldliness and antihierarchical sentiment are widespread. In the name of pluralism the most contrary views on almost all subjects establish themselves in the Church. The holders of the teaching office contradict one another in important points. Many theologians ignore the Church's authentic doctrine. The release of diversity of opinion among Catholics by the Second Vatican Council—ART. 43 of the pastoral constitution *Gaudium et spes*—scarcely permitted any further unity of public activity of Catholics and also raised questions about the capability of function of ecclesiastical authority in the realm of politics. Subjects in which the Church appeared united grew steadily fewer. A gathering of the strengths of the Church became ever more difficult. In consequence of the enervation and disunity within the Church the influence of Catho-

---

[55] ARTICLE 1 of the concordat with Colombia of 22 April 1942; ART. I of the accord with Portugal of 18 July 1950; ART. V of the concordat with the Dominican Republic of 16 June 1954.

lics on society noticeably and constantly declined. The evidences of decay within make the Church an even weaker pole in the partnership relations with the state. They make it easy for forces which abhor the Church to ignore it or to play off hierarchy and theologians against one another. On the other hand, the well-intentioned governments show their concern whether the Church is able henceforth to measure up to its task in the forming of morals and in the education of persons. Following the example of other Christian religious groups, especially of German Protestantism and Russian Orthodoxy, in the most recent period certain elements of the hierarchy have taken part in politics, often with notable partiality. Among the members of the Church appear fanatical associations which attack the intimacy with the "authoritarian" or "capitalistic" state, but at the same time advocate the surrender of the Church to the socialist state, unite with socialist and Communist cadres, and support real or alleged freedom movements in European and non-European countries. Some groups in a sectarian spiritualism question all connections between Church and state and demand the repudiation of valid concordats. The political disunity of Catholics increases, and this condemns the Catholics in lands where they represent a minority to a status of no influence. Christian politicans to a great extent no longer have clear directions of the Church at their disposal. All in all, it must be noted that the strength of the Catholic Church has strongly declined in the last few years. The phenomena described are suited to jeopardize from within the current legal positions of the Church. A Church which no longer corresponds to the claims which are made on it and to the promises which proceeded from it loses in the eyes of citizens who measure by democratic rules the justification of occupying an outstanding position in the structure of society.

It has been correctly stated by Hans Maier "that in a democracy every right becomes obsolete if it is not maintained and renewed by vital political forces." Where the spiritual power of Christians yields, experience teaches that sooner or later constitutional guarantees for the Church break up. The Church is an essentially public power with demands on the state that cannot be renounced. But the more the strength of the faith and the moral level in the Church decline, the more the number of practicing Catholics drops, so much the less understanding do its "privileges" find in the sphere of public law. The state will be equally prepared for treaties in the long run only with a society which fulfills a significant function in the life of the people. Hence, for the concluding of concordats there are no favorable assumptions now and for an unforeseeable future. In this regard the situation in the free nations and the socialist states is not very different. Concordats are basically agreements made to last between Church and state. The present is not favorable to this permanence. Most free countries show in increasing measure critical phenomena, experience a continuing rapid change of law and partly even of institutions, and look insecurely to the future. Considering this instability there exists for the civil partner an understandable aversion to tie itself down for a somewhat long time or soon to consider new negotiations. In case of real necessity to reach an agreement, people are usually content with individual understandings, which contain a minimum of regulating content. In place of concordats there are new possibilities of collaboration of Church and state, for example, through permanent contacts or those agreed to as occasion suggests. The striving for an institutionalization of the relations of state and Church yields to a certain extent to the contentment with a functional relation. In place of the assignment and definition of rights and competencies there comes to a great extent the cooperation agreed to for a short to moderately long period. The socialist states do not necessarily intend to have a comprehensive agreement with a structure condemned to extinction, as in their view the Church is. What they are in any event prepared for is the contractual regulating of particular questions, from which they promise themselves a tactical advantage. The hopes of a gradual dying out of hostility to religion in the socialist countries have so far not been realized. Aleksandr Solzhenitsyn says, "The furious hostility against religion is what is most permanent in Marxism." To be sure, now as earlier, the Holy See ordinarily puts the greatest value on the realization of accords with the states and in this connection displays its proved flexibility. It even concludes agreements with states that are atheistic or non-Christian and is ready to enter into accords of slight range of content. The pluralistic structure of the constitutional democracies is recognized without reservation. Nevertheless, there exists, at least in parts of the Church, a widespread weariness of concordats. The enhanced self-confidence of the bishops finds expression in the demand raised in some circles that, in the future, in place of concordats should come easily repudiated particular accords, which are negotiated by the bishops and, if need be, submitted to the Holy See for confirmation.

THE INDIVIDUAL AGREEMENTS

The "Protocols" with Socialist States

Since John XXIII Vatican diplomacy has sought to prepare an accommodation with the socialist states, especially those of Eastern Europe, at the cost of heavy sacrifices and considerable advance concessions.[56] Talks were agreed upon by means of preliminary contacts on the occasion of international meetings, and it was anticipated that they would result in the contractual solution of this or that question of the Church's life. On the other side, with the Second Vatican Council and Montini's election as Pope, the socialist governments sought contact with the Holy See in order thereby to gain influence over the Church and the more easily to tie the Catholics in their sphere of power to their course. On 15 September 1964 there first came into existence a "protocol" between a socialist state, Hungary, and the Holy See.[57] In it the political condition and the oath of loyalty of the bishops were granted to the government. In 1968 it was complemented by a second agreement. On 25 June 1966 there followed a "protocol" with Yugoslavia.[58] In it the government acknowledged the competence of the Holy See to exercise its jurisdiction over the Catholic Church in Yugoslavia in spiritual, ecclesiastical, and religious questions, without prejudice to the internal order of the nation. The Holy See guaranteed the restricting of the activity of clerics to the religious ecclesiastical sphere and disapproved every type of political violence. The secular side intended by these stipulations to keep the Croatian clergy apart from the national aspirations of the people and to gain the Holy See as a confederate against the protesting Croats. Also in the "protocol" the exchange of an envoy to the Holy See and of an apostolic delegate—not of a nuncio—in Yugoslavia was agreed upon; but, going beyond Canon 267, par. 2, to the delegate pertained the duty of fostering contact with the government. However, in 1970 Yugoslavia resumed diplomatic relations with the Holy See. These "protocols" represent agreements at the lowest stage of diplomatic activity and of minimum content. They were the first fumbling steps on

---

[56] N.N., "Konkordatsexperimente im Ostblock," *Ost-Probleme* 17 (1965), 194–200; G. Simon, *Die katholische Kirche und der kommunistische Staat in Osteuropa* (=*Berichte des Bundesinstituts für ostwissenschaftliche und internationale Studien* 31/1971) (Cologne 1971); H. Stehle, *Die Ostpolitik des Vatikans 1917–1975* (Munich 1975).

[57] M. Csizmás, "Staat und Kirche in Ungarn seit 1945," *Ungarn zehn Jahre danach. 1956-1966. Ein wissenschaftliches Sammelwerk,* ed. by W. Frauendienst on the orders of the Deutsch-Ungarischer Kulturkreis (Mainz 1966), 285–322; S. Orbán, "Das Abkommen zwischen Staat und Kirche in der Volksrepublik Ungarn," *Jahrbuch für Geschichte der UdSSR und der volksdemokratischen Länder Europas* 9 (1966), 27–54.

[58] Illyricus, "Erstmals Zeit zum Atemholen. Die Entspannung zwischen Kirche und Staat in Jugoslawien," *Wort und Wahrheit* 20 (1965), 132–37; *L'Attività della Santa Sede nel 1966* (Vatican City 1967), 1272–74; *Kirche und Staat in Bulgarien und Jugoslawien. Gesetze und Verordnungen in deutscher Übersetzung. Unter Mitwirkung mehrerer Fachgenossen,* ed. by R. Stupperich (=*Schriftenreihe des Studienausschusses der EKU für Fragen der Orthodoxen Kirche* 3) (Witten 1971).

an uncertain road. The situation of the Church within the country scarcely improved in Hungary by the signing, and in Yugoslavia only insignificantly, and the alleviations obtained are constantly threatened by a change of course.

The Holy See's contacts with other socialist nations have not yet advanced to the signing of "protocols." In Poland the government is keenly interested in an arrangement with the Holy See, whereby it expects to play down the irksome primate, Cardinal Wyszyński, and to be able to bring him to submission.[59] Nevertheless, the Polish bishops want no arrangement with the government purchased by precipitate concessions. Without the concluding of a treaty but in accord with the state, Paul VI in the apostolic constitution *Episcoporum Poloniae* of 28 June 1972 organized the Catholic Church in the area beyond the Oder-Neisse line. Four dioceses—Opole, Govzow-Wielkopolski, Szczecin-Kamien, and Koszalin-Kolobrzeg—were erected; the see of Ermland was incorporated into the ecclesiastical province of Warsaw, and that of Gdansk into the province of Gniezno. On the basis of prolonged and often interrupted negotiations, four new bishops were ordained in Prague at the end of February 1973. A written agreement was not published. In May 1973 the Holy See declined when the government of Czechoslovakia offered new talks, because they appeared to be without prospects. The predominant power of the socialist nations, the Soviet Union, now as earlier, rejected institutional relations with the Holy See because it wants to conduct its religious policy according to its own discretion.

The "Modus vivendi" with Tunisia

On 27 June 1964 there came into being for the first time a treaty between the Holy See and a country where Islam is the state religion (ART. 1 of the constitution of 25 July 1957), the "Modus vivendi" with Tunisia.[60] The treaty aims to guarantee to Catholics the practice of their faith. However, the public performance of the liturgy and preaching in public are not allowed. The Church is subjected to a strict police regime. Whether the treaty, with its humiliating conditions—suppression of the archbishopric of Carthage—and the great sacrifices which

[59] K. Hartmann, "Staat und Kirche nach dem Machtwechsel in Polen," *Osteuropa* 22 (1972), 119–29; S. Lammich, "Die Rechtsstellung der römisch-katholischen Kirche in der Volksrepublik Polen," *ÖAfKR* 23 (1972), 3–15.
[60] S. Sanz Villalba, "El 'modus vivendi' entre la Santa Sede y la República de Túnez," *Revista Española de Derecho Canónico* 20 (1965), 49–56; F. Romita, "Adnotazioni," *Monitor Ecclesiasticus* 90 (1965), 15–32.

the Catholic Church accepted in it, can be of future significance for similar agreements with other Afro-Asian states is unclear.

The Changes in Concordats in States
Giving Preferential Status to the Catholic Church

The unity of the state-Church system is today more or less shaken or jeopardized everywhere in Europe. Secularism and pluralism undermined the foundations on which state religions and state churches rested. The number of countries with coordination and separation systems is increasing. The existence of a state Church now ordinarily presupposes a religiously homogeneous population with a pervasively positive attitude to religion and Church. Today this assumption is no longer present for any Church of the so-called Western World. Its members are, in a considerable number, no longer rooted in it by virtue of conviction. As a result of serious opposing views in theology and faith, its theologians and clergy are no longer united. The religious foundation of the state-Church system is, it is true, broader and more stable in the Catholic countries of southern Europe than in the Protestant nations of Scandinavia,[61] but it displays dangerous cracks and is constantly further undermined by the development of the Church since the council. It is unlikely that this system can still be maintained in the long run by constitutional legal means. Violent changes through rapidly erupting passions are not to be excluded in some countries.

Paul VI's policy seeks a loosening of the bonds which exist, especially in the Iberian Peninsula, between Church and state, and the sacrifice of those privileges of the Church which find growing criticism. It agrees with the urging, lasting for years, of the majority of the Spanish bishops for a revision of the concordat. The state has reluctantly yielded to the desire and entered into negotiations with the Holy See. The revision of the concordat should assure "independence of each other, mutual respect, and the necessary cooperation." In particular, the Church should renounce its right of nomination in the appointment of bishops. in the Council of State, and in the Council of the Kingdom, as well as the privileged position of the clergy in penal law; the government should renounce its right of nomination in the appointment of bishops. The Spanish government yielded quickly to what is regarded as an

[61] E. Berggrav, "Norwegen: Krise zwischen Kirche und Staat," *Frankfurter Heft* 9 (1954), 695–98; P. O. Ahrén, "Staat und Kirche in Schweden," *ZevKR* 10 (1963), 22–45; L. St. Hunter, ed., *Scandinavian Churches* (London 1965); G. Garonson, "Reform des Staatskirchenrechts in Schweden," *ZevKR* 15 (1970), 60–76; G. Weitling, "Kirche und Volk in Dänemark. Kirchliche Gesetzgebung und kirchliches Leben in Dänemark im 19. und 20. Jahrhundert," *ÖAfKR* 22 (1971), 85–109.

expression of the will of the Second Vatican Council. On 10 January 1967 ART. 6, Sec. 2, of the Charter of the Spaniards was changed and the principle of religious liberty was proclaimed in a word-for-word borrowing from the declaration *Dignitatis humanae*. On 26 June 1967 the law on religious liberty was adopted. On 28 July 1976, after the death of General Franco, there was signed a treaty in which Spain renounced the right of presentation of the chief of state (or king) in the filling of bishoprics, and the Holy See renounced the criminal-law privilege of the clergy (ART. XVI of the concordat of 1953). The negotiations for the revision of the concordat were quickly continued.

A development similar to that in Spain proceeded in Portugal. The law on religious liberty of 21 August 1971 and ART. 45 of the constitution revised on 23 August 1971 conceded legal equality to all religious groups. The concordat and the missionary agreement were discussed. The toppling of the authoritarian state in 1974 introduced a development which certainly intended to weaken the position of the Catholic Church. In the agreement of 15 February 1975 the Holy See, by changing ART. XXIV of the concordat of 7 May 1940, sacrificed the principle of the civil indissolubility of marriages contracted in church.

In Italy negotiations on the revision of some articles of the concordat have long been under way.[62] Without consultation with the Holy See, contrary to ART. 34 of the concordat, civil divorce was introduced in 1970. The popular referendum against it produced a serious defeat for the Catholics. At the end of 1976 the Italian government and the Holy See agreed on a document which aimed to adapt the concordat to Italian constitutional reality and the spirit of the Second Vatican Council. The Catholic religion was thereafter no longer to be the religion of the state. The restrictive stipulations against apostate priests were to be dropped. The obligations which encumbered the state because of Rome's sacred character were to be abolished.

In Ireland (Eire), whose relations with the Church posed no problem and needed no guarantee by concordat, the deletion of the so-called Church Clause from the Irish constitution (ART. 44), which granted to the Catholic Church a special status as "Custodian of the Faith which the majority of the population professed," was decided by popular vote in 1972.

---

[62] P. Ciprotti, "Divorzio e art. 34 del Concordato italiano," *Apollinaris* 40 (1967), 483–88; C. Rousseau, "Italie et Saint-Siège. Problème de la révision du concordat du 11 Février 1929," *Revue Générale de droit International Public* 39 (1968), 451–53; S. Lener, "Sulla revisione del Concordato," *CivCatt* 120 (1969), II, 432–46; III, 9–21; IV, 214–17.

Latest Concordats and Agreements with Free Countries

In the most recent period the Holy See has also signed treaties with many states. However, most of them deal only with particular questions, and not one provides a comprehensive regulation of the total complex of subjects affecting Church and state. In many agreements existing treaties were altered or expanded, in which case the adjustment meant in most cases a diminution of the Church's legal position, which had been gained through previous concordats. In some agreements references to the Second Vatican Council appear. In place of institutional guarantees there are in increasing measure guarantees of religious liberty for individuals and groups. One of the most difficult questions which confronted, now as previously, the nations of central and Western Europe in connection with the ordering of the relations of Church and state is usually the regulation of the school system, in particular the assurance of the establishment of free, nonstate, private schools. The council saw as the optimal type of school—in the declaration *Gravissimum educationis* on Christian education, ART. 9—the free Catholic school, endowed with public legal position and supported by public means. Accordingly, the Holy See strove to have the justification of the Church's maintaining its own schools and the financing of them by the state assured by treaty.

The Austrian concordat of 5 June 1933, whose further validity had at first been challenged,[63] especially by the Socialists, was continued by a series of treaties, of which especially noteworthy are those which led to the erecting of the two new dioceses of Burgenland in 1960 and Feldkirch in 1964 and gave the ecclesiastical school system financial security in 1962 and 1972.[64] In the treaty of 5 April 1962 Spain

[63] F. Jachym, *Kirche und Staat in Österreich,* 3d ed. (Vienna 1955); D. Mayer-Maly, "Zur Frage der Gültigkeit des Konkordates vom 5. Juni 1933," *ÖAfKR* 7 (1956), 198–211; L. Leitmaier, "Das verweigerte Konkordat. Staat und Kirche im neuem Österreich," *Wort und Wahrheit* 11 (1956), 169–71; J. Schmidt, *Entwicklung der katholischen Schule in Österreich* (Vienna 1958); B. Primetshofer, *Ehe und Konkordat. Die Grundlinien des österreichischen Konkordats-Eherechtes 1934 und das geltende österreichische Eherecht* (Vienna 1960); I. Gampl, "Oberster Gerichtshof-Konkordat 1933-Katholikengesetz," *ÖAfKR* 15 (1964), 126–30; A. Kostelecky, "Die Anerkennung des österreichischen Konkordates vom 5. Juni 1933 und die Verträge der Republik Österreich mit dem Heiligen Stuhl von 1960 und 1962," A. Burghardt, K. Lugmayer, E. Machek, G. Müller, H. Schmitz, eds., *Im Dienste der Sozialreform. Festschrift für Karl Kummer* (Vienna 1965), 431–41; I. Gampl, *Österreichisches Staatskirchenrecht* (=*Rechts- und Staatswissenschaften* 23) (Vienna and New York 1971).
[64] S. Sanz Villalba, "Las convenciones entre Austria y la Santa Sede del año 1960," *Revista Española de Derecho Canónico* 16 (1961), 531–39; J. Damizia, "Convenzione fra la

expressed a generous recognition of nontheological studies at ecclesiastical universities.[65] On 26 November 1960[66] the Holy See concluded with Paraguay a convention on the establishment of a military vicariate. The convention with Venezuela of 6 March 1964[67] moved generally in traditional paths. But, as earlier in the concordats with Latvia (ART. XII) and the Dominican Republic (ART. X), so also in this agreement attention was given to the activity of foreign priests and lay persons in the care of souls and in social services (ART. XIII). The patronate for the naming of bishops (ART. VI) and for the filling of capitular and parochial benefices (ARTS. VIII–X) was abolished, but in regard to the bishops, in contrast to other countries, the state's right of veto in the procedure was confirmed in accord with the political proviso. The "protocol" with Haiti of 15 August 1966 confirmed, after preliminary conflicts, the intention of the government especially to protect the Catholic Church in accord with ART. 1 of the concordat of 1860 and to guarantee its free exercise of its pastoral care in conformity with the concordat, canon law, and the Second Vatican Council. Similarly, the treaty with Argentina of 10 October 1966[68] referred in the preamble to the principles of the Second Vatican Council. It gave the Church freedom to alter the diocesan organization in the country (ART. II) and abolished the state's right of nomination to episcopal sees (ART. III). The agreement of 24 July 1968 with Switzerland led to the long desired establishment of the see of Lugano for the canton of Ticino.[69]

A new concordat with Colombia was concluded on 12 July 1973 and ratified on 2 July 1975. This is a typical postconciliar concordat with a Catholic country. In it the humane and social aspect of the Church's

---

Santa Sede e la Repubblica Austriaca al fine di regolare questioni attinenti l'ordinamento scolastico," *Apollinaris* 35 (1962), 76–115.

[65] J. Maldonado y Fernández del Torco, "El convenio de 5 de abril de 1962 sobre el reconocimiento, a efectos civiles, de los estudios de ciencias no eclesiásticas realizados en España en Universidades de la Iglesia," *Revista Española de Derecho Canónico* 18 (1963), 137–98; A. de Fuenmayor, *El Convenio entre la Santa Sede y España sobre Universidades de Estudios civiles* (Pamplona 1966).

[66] A. Pugliese, "Adnotationes," *Monitor Ecclesiasticus* 87 (1962), 385–401.

[67] S. Sanz Villalba, "Adnotationes," *Monitor Ecclesiasticus* 90 (1965), 361–76; M. Torres Ellul, "El Convenio entre la Santa Sede y la República Venezolana," *Revista Española de Derecho Canónico* 21 (1966), 485–555.

[68] R. De Lafuente, "El acuerdo entre la Santa Sede y la República Argentina," *Revista Española de Derecho Canónico* 23 (1967), 111–25.

[69] H. Kehrli, *Interkantonales Konkordatsrecht* (Bern 1968); A.W. Ziegler, "Kirche und Staat in der Schweiz," *MThZ* 19 (1969), 269–87; E. Kussbach, "Die Errichtung eines selbständigen Bistums Lugano. Übereinkommen zwischen dem schweizerischen Bundesrat und dem Heiligen Stuhl vom 24. Juli 1968," *ÖAfKR* 21 (1970), 96–114.

activity comes strongly to the fore. The ministry of the Church to the human person is expressly mentioned (ART. V). The Catholic religion is recognized only as the "basic element of the common good and of the total development of the nation," and the Church's freedom is assured in the framework of the religious freedom of the other denominations (ART. I). The independence of Church and state is strongly emphasized (ARTS. II and III). The ministry of the Church and its cooperation with the state in the area of the educational and social systems is especially stressed (ARTS. V and VI). The canonically contracted marriage remains basically subject to the Church alone, except for separation from bed and board (ARTS. VII–IX). The Church's activity in instruction and education is regulated in detail (ARTS. X–XIII). The naming of the bishops is done freely by the Pope, but in this matter there is conceded to the president of the republic a right to express reservations "of civil or political character" (ART. XIV). The immunity of clerics and religious is retained in modern form (ARTS. XVIII–XX). The Church's property is protected with noteworthy adaptations to today's circumstances (ARTS. XXIII–XXVI).

With regard to comparative law the state-Church law of the Federal Republic of Germany occupies a special place.[70] The Second World War ended with the occupation of the country by the victorious Allies. The Western occupation powers in general assured the Churches freedom of action. Immediately after the ending of the war, which the Churches had survived as intact organizations, these were sought and recognized as guarantors of a civil law order. Their position in public life seemed to be consolidated and to prepare for a new alliance of Church and state. The Churches were first restored to their former rights, but in some states with marked restrictions, particularly in the school system. In the positive law of the state Church the experiences of the period of Nazi domination were expressed in only a relatively modest measure. A fundamental

---

[70] H. Quaritsch, H. Weber, eds., *Staat und Kirchen in der Bunderepublik. Staatskirchenrechtliche Aufsätze 1950–1967* (Bad Homburg v.d. H., Berlin, and Zurich 1967); J. Listl, *Das Grundrecht der Religionsfreiheit in der Rechtsprechung der Gerichte der Bundesrepublik Deutschland* (=*Staatskirchenrechtliche Abhandlungen* I) (Berlin 1971); E. L. Solte, *Theologie an der Universität. Staats- und kirchenrechtliche Probleme der theologischen Fakultät* (=*Jus Ecclesiasticum*, 13) (Munich 1971); J. Jurina, *Der Rechtsstatus der Kirchen und Religionsgemeinschaften im Bereich ihrer eigenen Angelegenheiten* (=*Schriften zum öffentlichen Recht* 180) (Berlin 1972); U. Scheuner, *Schriften zum Staatskirchenrecht*, ed. by J. Listl (Berlin 1973); P. Mikat, *Religionsrechtliche Schriften. Abhandlungen zum Staatskirchenrecht und Eherecht*, ed. by J. List, 2 vols. (Berlin 1974); E. Friesenhahn, U. Scheuner, J. Listl, eds., *Handbuch des Staatskirchenrechts der Bundesrepublik Deutschland*, 2 vols. (Berlin 1974–75); E. G. Mahrenholz, "Kirchen als Korporationen," *ZevKR* 20 (1975), 43–76.

new ecclesio-political orientation was either prevented or made difficult both in the Federal Republic and also in many federal states because of the resistance of the socialists and liberals. In the federation, just as in the states, a beginning was made basically with the state-Church law of the Weimar Constitution, which was modified only in details. Even the capability for compromise of the Weimar solution of the relations of state and Church proved to be realistic and lasting. The Basic Law for the German Federal Republic of 23 May 1949 adopted word for word ARTS. 136–39 and 141 of the Weimar Constitution and in ART. 4 guaranteed freedom of denomination and of worship and in ART. 7 religious instruction. The constitutions of the states proceeded in a similar fashion. In this matter, in each state according to the partisan political composition of the state conventions that drew up the constitutions, certain changes and supplements were included. On the whole the states with a predominantly Catholic population granted the Church a more favorable position than did those with a Protestant majority population. Thus, for example, according to the constitution of the state of Rhineland-Palatinate of 18 May 1947 the Churches are recognized institutions for the preservation and consolidation of the religious and moral bases of human life (ART. 41, Sec. 1). The constitution of the state of Baden-Württemberg of 11 November 1953 makes a similar statement (ART. 4, Sec. 2). On the other hand the constitution of the state of Hesse of 1 December 1946 envisages a clear delimitation between Church and state (ART. 50) as well as the elimination of actions by the state by means of legislation (ART. 52). In contradistinction to the Weimar constitution, the federation no longer has any principle of legislative competence in ecclesio-political questions. However, it retains a series of legislative competencies, because the constitutional legal bases of the relations of Church and state are, now as before, federal law (ART. 140 GG). In view of this legal situation it was principally the business of the states to take the initiative in the construction and completion of the arrangement between Church and state.

If there can be no question of a fundamentally new order of the relations of state and Church, there can still be the question of a new manner of interpretation of the traditional formulas. As a consequence of the different legal constitutional framework of the Weimar Constitution, the stipulations on religious groups have experienced a change of meaning. This can be briefly summarized in the two poles: end of the state-Church sovereignty and recognition of a full public status of the Churches. The ecclesiastical treaties with the Protestant state Churches in Lower Saxony (1955), Schleswig-Holstein (1957), and Hesse (1960) accepted, recognized, and legally concretized the new interpretation of the relations between Church and state in legal theory. The claim and the task of the Churches are positively evaluated by the state and regarded as basically worthy of assistance. The coresponsibility of the Churches for the shaping of public order, even for the fate of state and society, is accepted. The achievements of the Churches for the maintenance of the moral foundations of human life, their struggle for freedom and human dignity, as well as their stabilizing function have led to the recognition of their qualification basically to take a stand on all questions of the life of the people. The assertion of overly positive rights antecedent to the state in the Basic Law forbids state interference in ecclesiastical affairs, just as it even seemed possible according to the Weimar Constitution, and gives the Church an independence such as, with this clarity, the Weimar Constitution did not. The state's traditional powers of supervision and collaboration are almost entirely abolished or placed on a contractual basis. But the state does no longer wish regularly to drop mere ties, but rather to free the Church for the carrying out of its tasks. Its position in public law is confirmed by treaty.

The relationship between Church and state existing since 1945 is, according to the prevailing view, that of coordination. Church and state face each other as independent partners in their own right, which, because of their common responsibility, regulate in fundamental harmony questions affecting each other. True, the state is not obliged by a treaty with the Church to arrange common matters. But the treaty is the adequate means in a constitutional system that expresses the independence of the Church and the secular nature of the state. Besides, the modern socially active state has created or reemphasized many relationships with the Church. Hence the number of treaties concluded with the Churches in the years since the end of the war is very high. Most of the agreements were made between the federal states on the one hand and the Protestant state Churches or the Holy See respectively, or the bishops of a state, on the other, and relatively few by the federation with the groups of Churches. In regard to the treaties, the two groups of fundamental agreements determining status and regulating individual questions must be distinguished. The number of administrative agreements with bishops is considerable, for example, for regulating the appointment of teachers of religion or of questions of property. For the first time in the history of German ecclesiastical law, after the Second World War the initiative for treaties between Church and state in the various federal states proceeded from German Protestantism. In double contrast to the practice in the period of the Weimar Republic, the treaties with the Protestant Churches were, first, not mere equalizing complements of Catholic concordats, but independent agreements developed from Protestant ideas and exigencies, and, second, they were not followed by any, or by any adequate, agreements with the Catholic Church that took into account principles of parity. All the more noteworthy is the fact that in some of these treaties, likewise for the first time in the history of German ecclesiastical law, there appear express provisos of parity, which guarantee to Protestantism equal treatment with the Catholic Church.[71]

The Catholic Church was at first hindered in the conclusion of new agreements because of its clinging to the concordat with the Reich, whose existence with legal effect and whose continued validity were challenged by leftist groups, and especially by its insistence on the school articles, which were annoying to some state partners.[72] In several federal states there were long-lasting conflicts over the school regulations. The state of Lower Saxony enacted a school law which, in the Church's view and that of the federal government, was in opposition to ART. 23 of the concordat with the Reich. The conflict was brought before the Federal Constitutional Court by the federal government. This was supposed to decide the question whether the state of Lower Saxony was obliged, vis-à-vis the federation, to observe the stipulations of the concordat with the Reich in fashioning its school law. In its verdict of 26 March 1957[73] the Federal Constitutional Court accepted both the legally effective existence and the continued validity of the concordat with the Reich, but denied the authority of the federation to hold the states to the observance of those obligations of it whose object, according to the Basic Law, falls under the exclusive competence of the states. This unfortunate and contradictory decision granted to the states, with regard to their exclusive legislative competence in questions

[71] Final protocol in ART. 23 of the Hesse treaty with the Church, final protocol to ART. 28 of the Rhineland-Palatinate treaty with the Church, ART. VI of the Hesse treaty with the Catholic bishoprics, ART. 14 of the supplementary treaty to the Lower Saxon treaty with the Church.

[72] K. O. Hütter, *Bindung der Länder an die Schulbestimmungen des Reichskonkordats von 1933. Rechtsnachfolge oder Funktionsnachfolge* (Münster 1964); F. Müller, "Landesverfassung und Reichskonkordat. Fragen der Schulform in Baden-Württemberg," *Baden-Württembergisches Verwaltungsblatt* 10 (1965), 177–81; P. Feuchte, P. Dallinger, "Christliche Schule im neutralen Staat," *Die Öffentliche Verwaltung* 20 (1967), 361–74; F. Müller, *Schulgesetzgebung und Reichskonkordat* (Freiburg, Basel and Vienna 1966); F. Pitzer, *Die Bekenntnisschule des Reichskonkordats* (Cologne and Berlin 1967); W. Weber "Die Reichweite der Bekenntnisschulgarantie in Artikel 23 des Reichskonkordats," H. Brunotte, K. Müller, R. Smend, eds., *Festschrift für Erich Ruppel zum 65. Geburtstag am 25. Januar 1968* (Hanover, Berlin and Hamburg 1968), 354–74.

[73] *Der Konkordatsprozess*, ed. by F. Giese and F. A. Frhr. v. der Heydte, 4 vols. (Munich 1957–59); C. J. Hering, H. Lentz, eds., *Entscheidungen in Kirchensachen seit 1946* IV (Berlin 1966), 46–94.

of the educational system, the legal constitutional freedom arbitrarily to exempt themselves from international law ties. By it the concordat with the Reich was annulled in essential parts. Nevertheless, the Lower Saxon school controversy became the occasion to seek a contractual solution of the open questions and to restore, to a certain extent, the equality in Lower Saxony, which was no longer protected by the Loccum Treaty of 19 March 1955, very favorable to the Protestant state Church. After prolonged discussions, which were accompanied by a passionate anti-Catholic campaign in the state, there occurred on 1 July 1965 the conclusion of the first and only concordat with a state of the German Federal Republic, Lower Saxony.[74] It continued the Prussian concordat of 1929, but went considerably beyond it in topics and statements. The treaty eliminated the splintering of the state-Church law in the state and ended the conflict between Church and state over the organization of the school system. The state guaranteed under certain conditions the maintaining and erecting of public Catholic denominational schools. The Church recognized the nondenominational school as the regular school, the denominational school as a school by request (ART. 6). In the matter of a substantial altering of the structure of the public school system, the opening of discussions in the spirit of the treaty was envisaged (ART. 19, Sec. 2).[75] The encouragement of Catholic adult education by the state was promised (ART. 9). The interests of the Church in broadcasting were taken into consideration (ART. 10). With these two regulations the attempt was made to introduce newer developments into the usual matter of concordats. The agreement went beyond the traditional friendship clauses to establish "continuing contact" on all questions of the mutual relationship (ART. 19, Sec. 1).

The Lower Saxon concordat did not give rise to other similar treaties. Other states, like Hesse and Rhineland-Palatinate, were prepared only to conclude agreements with the bishops of the state. Today there is no favorable set of circumstances in the Federal Republic for the signing of

[74] J. Niemeyer, "Kirche und Staat nach dem Konkordat in Niedersachsen," *Ordo Socialis* 13 (1965), 205–18; E. G. Mahrenholz, "Das Niedersächsische Konkordat und der Ergänzungsvertrag zum Loccumer Kirchenvertrag," *ZevKR* 12 (1966–67, 217–82; E. Ruppel, "Konkordat und Ergänzungsvertrag zum Evangelischen Kirchenvertrag in Niedersachsen," *Deutsches Verwaltungsblatt* 81 (1966), 207–12; D. Scheven, "Das Niedersächsische Konkordat," *Juristenzeitung* 20 (1966), 341–47; H. J. Toews, *Die Schulbestimmungen des Niedersächsischen Konkordats* (Göttingen 1967).
[75] As early as 21 May 1973 adjustments of various rules to changed circumstances became necessary (*AAS* 65 [1973], 643–46). The exchange of notes between the Holy See and the state of Lower Saxony of 22 December 1972 envisages the total elimination of the state denominational school system.

concordats. The erecting of new theological faculties at Bochum, Regensburg, Augsburg, and Passau or, respectively, of technical disciplines at Osnabrück and professional chairs at Saarbrücken at the state universities, as well as the extensive elimination of the denominational character of the public elementary schools and of teacher education made necessary a number of treaties of individual federal states— Bavaria, Rhineland-Palatinate, North Rhine-Westphalia, Saarland, Lower Saxony—with the Holy See. The tendency to push the denominational schools and teacher education conformable to the creed to the private level is unmistakable. Articles 23 and 24 of the concordat with the Reich became entirely obsolete through this development. Still, some states have been found ready for extensive support of Catholic private schools. The treaty with Bavaria of 4 September 1974 confirmed the possibility, already agreed to on 7 October 1968, of forming in the public elementary schools, under certain conditions, classes and instruction groups for pupils of the Catholic faith; in these the instruction and training would be governed by the special principles of the Catholic denomination (ART. 6, pars. 2 and 3). The state of Bavaria bound itself to grant financial and personnel assistance to the schools of Catholics "in the framework of the general encouragement of private schools" (ART. 8, par. 1). To the private Catholic elementary and special schools was promised, with certain restrictions, the repayment of the necessary expenditure and building costs (ART. 8, pars. 2 and 3). The accord of 15 May 1973 with Rhineland-Palatinate also assured the establishment and financing of Catholic private schools. The treaty contains generous promises of state contributions for the expenditures for building projects of Catholic schools (ART. 7) and for the assignment of state teachers to Catholic private schools (ART. 10). Essentially similar is the agreement reached on 21 February 1975 between the Holy See and the Saarland on the same subjects.

In the most recent period a new phase of the relations of Church and state in the Federal Republic seems to be under way. The Church fell into strong dependence on the movements in society. The changed public attitude reacts upon the interpretation of the norms, but now in a sense increasingly more unfavorable to the Churches. The interpretation of the rules of the ecclesiastical law is, to a great degree, dependent on the political and ideological tendencies in public life prevailing at the moment and occasionally rapidly changing. For example, since the close of the Second Vatican Council the public position, as well as the political, social, and cultural influence of the Churches in the Federal Republic, are in increasing measure questioned by teachers, party politicians, and certain organizations. The process of secularization moves after the trauma of the lost war and the "shock of the first postwar period," as Siegfried Grundmann expresses it, with new intensity.[76] An influential movement sees the Churches to an increasing degree in relation to other social forces and includes them in the associations and interest groups. This view does not let the nature of the Churches be given adequate recognition any more. The institutional relations between Church and state become weaker, they are abandoned in favor of a stronger social orientation of the two powers. The Church must engage in the process of forming the state's will less as an institution than through the presence of its faithful in society. In the administration of justice there partly exists the tendency to overstress the negative side of religious freedom, that is, less to protect liberty in the practice of religion and rather much more to assure the right of dissidents to the nonexercise of religious acts. In the course of this development religious practice is threatened with being restricted to the church building and the family sphere. The verdicts of the Bremen Supreme Court of 23 October 1965[77] and of the Supreme Court of Hesse of 27 October 1965[78] on questions of religious instruction and of prayer in school point in this direction.

Quite differently from the situation with the Western occupation zones, or the German Federal Republic, proceeded the development of the relations of Church and state in the Soviet occupation zone, or the German Democratic Republic.[79] At first the Soviet occupying power refrained from interference in the inner ecclesiastical sphere. The

---

[76] S. Grundmann, "Laizistische Tendenzen im deutschen Staatskirchenrecht?" *Festschrift Kunst,* 126–33; J. Listl, "Staat und Kirche in der Bundesrepublik Deutschland. Wandlungen und neuere Entwicklungstendenzen im Staatskirchenrecht," *StdZ* 191 (1973), 291–308; I. Gampl, C. Link, *Deutsches und österreichisches Staatskirchenrecht in der Diskussion* (=*Rechts- und Staatswissenschaftliche Veröffentlichungen der Görres-Gesellschaft,* m.s. 10) (Paderborn 1973); H. Maier, "Die Kirchen in der Bundesrepublik Deutschland," *Internationale katholische Zeitschrift 'Communio'* 2 (1973), 547–58; 3 (1974), 63–74; P. Rath, ed., *Trennung von Staat und Kirche? Dokumente und Argumente* (=rororo aktuell) (Reinbek bei Hamburg 1974). E. G. Mahrenholz (*Die Kirchen in der Gesellschaft der Bundesrepublik,* 2d ed. [Hanover 1972], 132) terms religious instruction a "foreign body" in the constitutional structure of the Basic Law.

[77] C. J. Hering, H. Lentz, eds., *Entscheidungen in Kirchensachen seit 1946* VII (Berlin 1970, 260–75).

[78] Ibid., 275–99.

[79] E. Jacobi, "Staat und Kirche nach der Verfassung der Deutschen Demokratischen Republik," *ZevKR* 1 (1951), 113–35; W. Meinecke, *Die Kirche in der volksdemokratischen Ordnung der Deutschen Demokratischen Republik* (Berlin 1952); U. Krüger, "Das Prinzip der Trennung von Staat und Kirche in Deutschland," *Festschrift für Erwin Jacobi* (Berlin 1975), 260–86; W. Meinecke, *Die Kirche in der volksdemokratischen Ordnung der Deutschen Demokratischen Republik* (Berlin 1962); C. Meyer, *Das Verhältnis zwischen Staatsgewalt und Kirche im Lichte der Glaubens- und Gewissensfreiheit in der sowjetischen*

constitution of the German Democratic Republic of 7 October 1949 in ARTS. 41–49 adopted in great part formulas of ARTS. 135–41 of the Weimar Constitution. But these regulations were essentially modified by the intensified principle of the separation of Church and state. The constitution guaranteed religious freedom (ART. 41) and guaranteed to religious groups the character of corporations of public law with the traditional right to raise money (ART. 43, Secs. 3 and 4). Religious instruction might be given by them in school buildings (ARTS. 40 and 44). But the educational system was subject exclusively to the control of the state (ARTS. 34–40). More unfavorable than the constitutional law was the constitutional reality. By means of laws and directives, as well as through administrative measures, the Church's sphere of action was ever more strictly limited and the de-Christianization of the people was pressed as planned. A relatively more trustworthy expression of the present status of the relations of Church and state is the constitution of the German Democratic Republic of 6 April 1968. It guarantees liberty of conscience and of belief and equality of rights of all citizens without regard to religious denomination (ART. 20, Sec. 1), as well as freedom of denomination and of the practice of religion (ART. 39, Sec. 1). The arranging of the affairs of the Churches and religious groups and the exercise of their activity are subject to the reservation of the constitution and of the law (ART. 39, Sec. 2). The independence of the Churches in the arrangement and administration of their affairs is no longer guaranteed. There is no longer any constitutional protection against interference in their inner sphere. There is no more word of any rights of the Churches. Ecclesiastical activity is handed over to the arbitrarily manipulable "legal decisions" of the German Democratic Republic. Churches and religious groups are, according to the 1968 constitution, no longer corporations of public law. Hence, from now on they move only in the area of private law and have lost the capacity to employ any disciplinary power. In the other fields of law also, for example, in penal law, the prerogatives accruing to the Church from its public position are eliminated. A guar-

---

Besatzungszone Deutschland (Mainz 1964); H. Bayl, "Zum Verhältnis von Staat und Kirche in der Deutschen Demokratischen Republik," *Wissenschaftliche Zeitschrift der Universität Rostock. Gesellschafts- und sprachwissenschaftliche Reihe* 15 (1966), 315–23; H. Johnsen, "Staat und Kirche in der DDR," *Im Lichte der Reformation. Jahrbuch des Evangelischen Bundes* 10 (1967), 51–70; K. Richter, "Katholische Kirche in der DDR. Wandel kirchlicher Strukturen unter den Bedingungen einer sozialistischen Gesellschaft," *Jahrbuch für christliche Sozialwissenschaften* 13 (1972), 215–45; S. Mampal, *Die sozialistische Verfassung der Deutschen Demokratischen Republik. Text und Kommentar* (Frankfurt 1972).

antee of religious instruction is absent, just as is the assurance of pastoral care in public institutions. No constitutional guarantee of ecclesiastical property exists any longer. The right of the Church to raise money has come to nothing. The public achievements are no longer mentioned. The 1968 constitution of the German Democratic Republic does, however, mention, as the sole constitution of a socialist country, the agreements as means for regulating the relations of state and Church (ART. 39, Sec. 2). It thereby makes known that it is aware of the independence of the Churches. Apparently, the leadership of the German Democratic Republic has grasped that treaties can be a useful means of socialist ecclesiastical policy. The German Democratic Republic especially has some desires relating to the Catholic Church, the fulfilling of which can be obtained only from the Holy See, for example, a new arrangement of diocesan boundaries. First contacts with the Holy See have been made. However, a concordat with substantive guarantees of the Church's activity is presumably not sought by the German Democratic Republic. It treats as nonexistent the concordats with Prussia and with the Reich. The appointment of apostolic administrators in the German Democratic Republic on 23 July 1973 took place without a treaty.

The Diversity of the Inner Life
of the Universal Church

CHAPTER 7

*Society and State as a Problem for the Church**

The period since the outbreak of the First World War (1914–18), the start of which is marked within the Church by the change in the See of Peter from Pius X (1903–14)[1] to Benedict XV (1914–22),[2] presents itself as an epoch of socio-political crises and a global inability to establish peace. During the very war itself the Bolshevik Revolution—the "October Revolution" of 1917—under Lenin was victorious in Russia. Five years later Mussolini inaugurated the Fascist era in Italy with his "March on Rome" of 28 October 1922. On 30 January 1933 there followed the subjection of Germany to the dictatorship of National Socialism through Hitler's so-called "seizure of power."

The three revolutionary movements with more or less monistic ideologies[3] ended politically in totalitarian dictatorships of nationalistic style, but with claims beyond their own national frontiers—Bolshevism: "Socialist World Revolution"; Fascism: "Mare Nostro," with claims of hegemony around the Mediterranean; National Socialism: "Living Space for the German People" in the east. In this way, as also by means of the continuing nationalism of the nontotalitarian states, all good starts for a global understanding of peoples—the League of Nations—or at least for a European understanding between the former opponents in the war—Briand/Stresemann—were finally condemned to failure. The world economic crisis of 1930 led with its army of millions of unemployed to a complete disorganization of world commerce and to serious social upheavals in the industrial nations, which finally helped to smooth Hitler's route to power in Germany. The world economic crisis marks the end of the era of liberal economics and the beginning of a national state policy of control-

---

* Wilhelm Weber
[1] *AAS* 36–41 (1903–8); *AAS* (Rome 1909ff.); *Acta Pii X,* 5 vols. (Rome 1905–14).
[2] *AAS* 6–14 (1914–22); *Actes de Benoît* (Latin and French), 3 vols. (Paris 1924–26).
[3] Bolshevism: Class ideology on an economic basis; Fascism: "La Nazione" as ideological basis; National Socialism: "Blood-and-Soil" ideology, emotional racism.

ling and standardizing. The hectic fever with which the individual nations reacted to the severe depression by ever new restrictive measures consolidated the crisis. "The cyclical crisis produced a structural crisis of the world economy. The crisis *in* the system became a crisis *of* the system."[4] The crisis led to the injury especially of the small and middle independent livelihoods, to a further concentration in the economy—financial capitalism—and thereby to a serious derangement of the world political and inner social equilibrium.

After the Second World War (1939–45) thinking in terms of political blocs (NATO, the Warsaw Pact), problems of conventional and nuclear rearmament, of the Cold War, and locally restricted warlike confrontations were increasingly prominent, partly in connection with the West-East conflict (Korea and Vietnam), partly in connection with the elimination of the former European colonial rule (Algeria and Angola), partly from very dissimilar motives (Hungarian revolt, suppression of the reform socialism of Prague, the Middle East conflict). Alongside the West-East conflict the North-South problem emerged more clearly, namely, the tensions from the imbalance between the developed industrial nations of the northern hemisphere—"First" and "Second World"—and the populous but economically undeveloped and hence poor and partly hungry countries of the so-called "Third World."

However, the picture would be incorrect if note were not taken also of positive starts and developments, even if not all or only few were actually developed. To be named here would be the above-mentioned idea of Europe,[5] the activity of the International Worker's Organization (ILO) at Geneva, which was founded in 1919 and since then has displayed a comprehensive and beneficial activity,[6] the development of labor and social law, especially in Germany in the period between the wars, the beginnings of a new international order of law and peace, such as the establishing of the

---

[4] Cf. on this A. Predöhl, *Das Ende der Weltwirtschaftskrise: Eine Einführung in die Probleme der Weltwirtschaft,* rde vol. 161 (Hamburg 1962), here 9.

[5] On 4 September 1929 A. Briand submitted the plan, then rejected by England, of the "United States of Europe" (customs and economic union). Count Coudenhove-Kalergi had prepared the way, as regards propaganda, with his Pan-European movement.

[6] Pius XII had called attention, with praise, to the activity of the ILO in an address to the members of the Executive Council of the International Labor Exchange on 19 November 1954 (*AAS* 46 [1954], 714–18; *UG*, 6040–48. In his encyclical *Mater et Magistra* John XXIII expressed his high esteem (103), and Paul VI paid a visit to the organization on the occasion of his visit to the World Council of Churches at Geneva in 1969 and delivered a much noted address (cf. *HK* 23 [1969], 7, 301f.).

United Nations with its subsidiary and/or successor organizations— UNESCO, FAO, UNICEF, etc.—toward and after the end of the Second World War, the "Declaration of the Rights of Man" by the United Nations of 10 December 1948, and the founding of the European Community, to name only a few of the most important happenings.

The newer Catholic social doctrine, called into being since Leo XIII (1878–1903),[7] experienced in the period after the two world wars, especially since the encyclical *Quadragesimo anno* of 1931, a vast further development and acquired the contour of a "system," if one understands by a social doctrinal system logically arranged and coherent propositions on the structural principles underlying society. Simultaneously there grew also reflexively the Church's self-consciousness of possessing its own social teaching and of having to present it as obligatory. In his encyclical *Mater et Magistra* of 1961, John XXIII thus expressed this self-awareness: "We especially point to the fact that the social teaching of the Catholic Church is an integrating component of the Christian doctrine of mankind."[8] "For this reason it is especially important that Our children not only know the principles of the social doctrine but also be formed according to them."[9]

The most important questions and problems with which the social message of the Church had to do were proposed to it through the development indicated earlier in outline. They constitute the "life-centered problems" of the most recent phase in the development of Catholic social teaching.

Thus Pius XI (1922–39)[10] had to deal with the totalitarian ideologies and dictatorship movements of Socialism/Communism, of Fascism, and of National Socialism. To each of the three he devoted a special encyclical.[11] In the world economic crisis, which announced the breakdown and end of the era of liberal economics with the social ills appearing in its wake, appeared the second great social encyclical in the strict sense, *Quadragesimo Anno,* which, as a follow-up of the encyclical *Rerum novarum* of 1891, which dealt almost exclusively with the classic social question of the nineteenth century, namely, with the labor

---

[7] *AAS* 11–35 (1878–1903); *Leonis XIII. Pont. Max. Acta,* 23 vols. with index (Rome 1881–1905; reprint, Graz 1971).

[8] John XXIII, encyclical *Mater et Magistra,* of 15 May 1961, 222.

[9] Ibid., 227.

[10] *AAS,* 14–31 (1922–39).

[11] Encyclical *Non abbiamo bisogno* (against Italian Fascism) of 29 June 1931: *AAS* 23 (1931), 285–312; encyclical *Divini Redemptoris* (against atheistic Communism) of 19 March 1937: *AAS* 29 (1937), 65–106; encyclical *Mit brennender Sorge* (against National Socialism) of 14 March 1937: *AAS* 29 (1937), 145–67.

problem, had as its subject the disorganization of society.[12] The experiences with the totalitarian dictatorships, especially with National Socialism, made Pius XII (1939–58)[13] the herald of the rights of the human person. Under him there emerged in a stupendous abundance of proclamations of the most varied sort (although he did not compose a social encyclical of his own in the strict sense), the ever clearer outlines of what can be termed Christian "personalism" and "solidarity." Thus is explained his almost obstinate insistence on the principle of subsidiarity. To Pius XII we owe remarkable and penetrating ideas on the problem of democracy, of toleration, and of public opinion. In his range of ideas, that of the underdeveloped countries appears early on. The universal or world common welfare led him to make the notion of a family of mankind again and again the subject of doctrinal expressions and proclaim the vision of a "world state" on the basis of federation. The era of John XXIII (1958–63)[14] was marked by two important social encyclicals which in their statements on the one hand continued the tradition of the Church's social teaching and on the other hand gave important impulses to the following council. *Mater et Magistra* has already been mentioned. The encyclical *Pacem in terris* of 1963[15] was experienced in both the West and East as a sensation. It constituted, as has rightly been said, the Pope's last will. In both encyclicals he extensively synchronized the social thought of the Church with the exigencies or, as John XXIII especially liked to express it, with the "signs of the time," or, as the same Pope demanded in his opening address to the Second Vatican Council on 11 October 1962, brought the Church an essential step nearer to *aggiornamento*. He sought to secure for the striving of mankind for justice and peace, by employing its own manner of speaking, the most profound and ultimate impulses from the Christian view of mankind and of society.

The Social Claim to Educate and Its Bases: Natural Law and Revelation ("Question of Competence")

In *Rerum novarum* Leo XIII had already laid claim to the social doctrine to teach. "With full confidence We approach this task and in the

---

[12] The heading of the encyclical of 15 May 1931 reads: "On the social order, its restoration, and its perfection according to the plan of salvation of the Gospel."

[13] *AAS* 31–50 (1939–58).

[14] *AAS* 50–55 (1958–63).

[15] The encyclical appeared under the date of 11 April 1963, Maundy Thursday, and bears the heading: "On peace among all peoples in truth, justice, love, and freedom."

awareness that the word belongs to Us" (13). Pius XI energetically repeated this claim in *Quadragesimo anno* and at the same time made it more precise against possible misinterpretations. "The deposit of truth entrusted to Us by God and the holy duty committed to Us by God to proclaim the moral law in its entire compass, to declare, and, whether or not he desires it, to press for its observance subject on this side both the social and the economic sphere without reservation to Our supreme judgment" (41).

Three considerations simultaneously justify and limit the Church's claim: (1) Society and economics cannot be considered apart from the moral law; (2) under this exclusive respect—"not in questions of a technical sort for which [the Church] neither disposes of the suitable means nor has received a mission, but in everything which is related to the moral law" (41)—a sovereign authority belongs to the Church or, respectively, the ecclesiastical teaching office; (3) this has nothing to do with unjust claims to power, as they are often imputed to the Church.[16]

Pius XII not only frequently confirmed this claim of his predecessors,[17] but regarded as a legitimation of the Church's claim the ontological fact of the "intrinsic involvement," as G. Gundlach calls it, of the Church with society and expressed this state of affairs in the controversial formula of the Church as the "vital principle of human society."[18] John XXIII unmistakably made the same claim when he had his first social encyclical begin, almost as with a roll of drums, with the words: "Mother and teacher of peoples is the Catholic Church" (*Mater et Magistra,* 1).

Pius XII, with appeal to Leo XIII, characterized as the "undeniable sphere of the Church" the judgement on those principles "of the eternally valid order . . . which God, the Creator and Redeemer, has

[16] Already in his first encyclical, *Ubi arcano* of 23 December 1922 (*AAS* 14 [1922], 673–700) the Pope had solemnly asserted: "The Church would regard it as an encroachment for it to intervene without cause in earthly matters." Quoting himself, the Pope resumed this central statement in 41 of *Quadragesimo anno.* Literature on the Church's claim to a social doctrine: O. von Nell-Breuning, S. J., *Die soziale Enzyklika* (Cologne 1932, reprint 1950), 59f.; G. Gundlach, S. J., *Die Kirche zur heutigen Wirtschafts- und Gesellschaftsnot. Erläuterung des Rundschreibens Papst Pius' XI. "Quadragesimo Anno"* (2d ed., Berlin, 1949), 17f.

[17] Especially clearly in his radio message on Pentecost, 1 June 1941: *AAS* 33(1941), 195–205; *UG,* 493–522. The address occurred on the Golden Jubilee celebration of *Rerum novarum.*

[18] Pius XII made his own this word, coined by G. Gundlach, S. J., first in his address of 20 February 1946 to the College of Cardinals (*UG,* 4106), later twice more, both times in radio messages to German *Katholikentage* (Bochum, 4 September 1949: *UG,* 611; Berlin, 17 August 1958: *UG,* 4520).

made known through natural law and revelation." His essential statement in this question is: "Rightly: for the principles of natural law and the truths of revelation both have, as two in no way opposite but parallel water courses, their common source in God" (*UG*, 498).

The idea of natural law, undoubtedly dominant in the newer Catholic social doctrine since Leo XIII, experienced under Pius XII an important further development. The "authenticity of natural law," still always a problem in a developed dynamic society, was appealed to by Pius XI in connection with the right of property, which, as "history shows," "is not immutable" (*Quadragesimo anno*, 49). But while in tradition an authenticity or "mutability" of natural law was derived rather *ab extra,* that is, from the changes of external circumstances or conditions (*circumstantiae*), for Pius XII there ensues from the study of the history of the development of law the fact that, under special conditions, specific rights can change *ab intra,* from their content. Of course, there is an unchangeable nucleus in natural law.

Pius XII developed this idea in greater detail in one of his most noted addresses, which he gave on 13 October 1955 to the *Centro Italiano per la Riconciliazione Internazionale.*[19] Because the matter is sufficiently important, the decisive sentences are repeated here verbatim: "The study of history and of legal development from remote times teaches that, on the one hand, a change in economic and social (and often also in political) situations demands new forms of those postulates of natural law to which the systems hitherto prevailing can no longer do justice; but, on the other hand, that in connection with these changes the fundamental demands of nature always recur and pass themselves on, with greater or less urgency, from one generation to the others."[20]

In his address of 7 September 1955 to the participants of the Tenth International Congress of Historians[21] Pius XII had already formulated for the Church the claim, as "historical power," as "living organism," regularly to intervene in the sphere of public life "in order to assure the correct balance between duties and obligations on the one side and rights and freedoms on the other."[22]

Also with Pius XII we still find the problem, drawn along from tradition, especially by Leo XIII, of defining the relations of natural law,

[19] *AAS* 47 (1955), 764–75; *UG*, 6275–99. The address was concerned with the problem of "coexistence and common life of peoples in truth and love."
[20] *UG*, 6286.
[21] *AAS* 47 (1955), 672–82; *UG*, 5893–5914. The close succession in time of this and the address mentioned in n. 19 shows how Pius XII moved the problem of the historicity of law precisely to that moment.
[22] *UG*, 5901.

truth, and the discovery of truth. True, there is expounded by him in connection with the discussion of democracy the essential function of public opinion for a democratic commonwealth. In the complete absence of public opinion must be seen "a lack, a weakness, a sickness of social life."[23] But the truth, also the true perception of the norms of natural law as possessed "objective" truth, is claimed for the Church and the teaching office in such a manner that all other tribunals, even public opinion, must stand almost rather as hearers, as receivers of the second rank.

In this context one can now—in contrast to almost all other statements in which there is incorrectly mention of a "turn" in thought—ascertain in John XXIII a genuine breakthrough to new shores. If he speaks of truth or of the rights bestowed by God on mankind in its very nature, then he presupposes the entire traditional theology of these rights, in regard to which, however, Leo XIII, Pius XI, and also to a great extent even Pius XII had basically come to a standstill. But this did not satisfy John XXIII. To him it was not a question, in an encyclical, moreover, that was oriented to the whole pluralistic world, only of the absolute, eternal, changeless truth, which, furthermore, is not capable of being imposed by the teaching office in an ideologically dismembered world. For him the truth was concretized, knowledge of truth grows in the "veracity" of mutual human relationships. Supported on the hope of rational understanding and love among people,[24] the optimistic Pope believed in the realization of veracity in human relationships as the basis of the feasibility of every knowledge of truth. Truth is no longer a merely possessed, guarded, and authoritatively interpreted objective *Depositum;* truth occurs rather in the freedom of mankind as a social process of truth finding. Here is present a gifted understanding of the so powerfully fatigued formula of the identity of "theory and practice."

Because of the importance of the matter, the central statements of the Pope will again be presented here verbatim: The "happening of truth" lives by this, "that people mutually exchange their perceptions in the bright light of truth, that they are put in the position of making use of their rights and fulfilling their duties, that they are incited to strive for spiritual goods, that from every honorable thing they . . . gain an occasion for common honest joy, that they seek in tireless desire to share among themselves and receive from one another the best they

[23] Address to the participants in the International Catholic Press Congress of 17 February 1950 in *AAS* 42 (1950), 251–57; *UG,* 2132–53; here, 2134.
[24] Corresponding to the axiom frequently quoted by Thomas Aquinas: "Homo homini naturaliter amicus"; cf. *Contra Gentiles,* 3, 117; 4, 54, and elsewhere.

have. These values affect and control everything that is related to scholarship, economics, social institutions, development and organization of the state, legislation, and finally to all other things that constitute externally human coexistence and develop in constant progress."[25] In order that truth "may function" in this way, the right to free expression of opinion and to information in conformity with truth must be respected: "From nature people have . . . the right . . . to seek the truth freely and to express their opinion while respecting the moral order and the common good, to disseminate it, and to exercise any profession; finally, to be informed of public events in accord with the truth."[26] "The truth further commands that a person let himself be guided in the use of the manifold possibilities which were created by the progress of modern means of publication and by which the mutual understanding of peoples is promoted by the highest objectivity."[27]

In these sentences can rightly be seen the fundamental ethical justification of democracy and at the same time of an ethics of public communication in accord with the times. In the climate of the encyclical *Pacem in terris,* Paul VI was then able during the council in his own first encyclical *Ecclesiam suam* of 6 August 1964 to proclaim the dialogue with the world in keeping with the new model of ecclesiastical communications,[28] and the Second Vatican Council was able to acknowledge what in the understanding of the truth the Church owes to the world and its striving for truth. "The experience of the historical past, the progress of scholarship, the riches which lie in the various forms of human culture, through which human nature comes ever more clearly to manifestation and new ways to the truth are opened redound also to the Church's good."[29]

Social Principles: Personality, Subsidiarity, Solidarity, Common Good, Universal Common Good

At the beginning of his encyclical on peace John XXIII puts the central principle of all human social organization: "At the basis of any human coexistence that should be well ordered and fruitful must lie the

[25] Encyclical *Pacem in terris,* 38.
[26] Ibid., 12.
[27] Ibid., 90; cf. on this especially G. Deussen, *Ethik der Massenkommunikation bei Papst Paul VI. (Abhandlungen. zur Sozialethik* 5), ed. by W. Weber and A. Rauscher (Paderborn 1973), 66f. and passim; cf. on the whole matter also E. W. Böckenförde, *Kirchlicher Auftrag und politische Entscheidung* (Rombach Academy paperback 55) (Freiburg i. Br. 1973), especially 81ff.
[28] Encyclical *Ecclesiam suam,* AAS 56 (1964), 609–59.
[29] Pastoral constitution *Gaudium et Spes,* 44, 2.

principle that every human being is by essence a person" (*Pacem in terris*, 9). "If we consider the dignity of the human person according to revealed truths, we must value it even much more highly" (*Pacem in terris*, 10).

1. Pius XI and especially Pius XII had already established the social doctrine of the Church definitively and unmistakably as "personalism." Everything social is related to the person and must promote its perfection. In other words, society has no end in itself, it is no domineering superego but has a ministerial character. The state has to promote the security of the person by guaranteeing the rights of the person as rights implanted in its nature by God. However, at times other social conditions require other emphases. Thus Leo XIII had primarily to defend the existing social order in its basic structure—state, state authority, private property—against anarchist and Marxist strivings, while the experiences with totalitarian states or movements—persecution of Catholics in Russia, Mexico, Spain, Fascism, National Socialism—caused Pius XI to speak again and again for the protection of human freedom and dignity and for the defense of the rights of the Church. But then Pius XII became especially the herald of human liberty and of the dignity of the human person.

To avert from the start any charge of individualism, Pius XII stressed that human rights are not by chance proclaimed as inviolable and inalienable against the state, but that they belong precisely to the "most precious in the common good" (*UG*, 213),[30] for which the state has to stand up. And so "they can never be sacrificed to the common good, precisely because they are essential ingredients of it" (*UG*, 213).[31] This truth is so central for Pius XII that he emphatically exclaimed: "This is the Catholic world view!" (*UG*, 213).

To become politically effective, the rights of the person need a foundation in postive law, a demand which Pius XII had made and which was taken over verbatim by John XXIII from his predecessor.[32] "To the human person also belongs the legal protection of its rights, which must be effective and impartial in harmony with the true norms of justice, as Our predecessor of happy memory, Pius XII, admonishes: 'From the divinely established legal order results the inalienable right of

---

[30] Address to the participants of the International Congress for Humanistic Studies of 25 September 1949 in *AAS* 41 (1949), 555–56; *UG*, 356–61. Here the Pope expressed himself on the natural law as the basis of the Church's social doctrine.

[31] Message to the *Katholikentag* in Berlin of 10 August 1952 in *AAS* 44 (1952), 723–27; *UG*, 203–18.

[32] On the list of basic or human rights, which John XXIII, in comparison with his predecessor, greatly expanded, cf. *Pacem in terris*, 11–27.

the human being to legal security and with it to a tangible legal sphere, which is protected against every attack of caprice' " (*Pacem in terris,* 27).[33]

2. All other principles of Catholic social doctrine, especially the principle of "Catholic" subsidiarity that has entered into general linguistic use, follow from the principle of the person with logical cogency. Already long evident in accord with its esential content in its beginnings,[34] in Leo XIII especially established in connection with the preeminence of the family over the state—cf. *Rerum novarum,* 10: "Since domestic common life, according to both the notion and the reality, is earlier than the civic community, so too its rights and duties have precedence, because they are closer to nature"; cf. also *Rerum novarum,* 38, in relation to free social unions and their relation to the state—it finds its classic definition in *Quadragesimo anno:* "Just as whatever the individual man can accomplish on his own initiative and with his own abilities must not be taken from him and allotted to the activity of society, so it is contrary to justice to claim for the wider and higher community whatever the smaller and subordinate communities can achieve and lead to a good end; at the same time it is entirely injurious and confuses the entire social order. *Every activity of society is subsidiary in conformity to its nature and concept;* it should support the members of the body social but must never destroy or absorb them . . . . The better the hierarchical order of the various socializations is maintained through strict observance of the principle of subsidiarity, the more social authority and social effectiveness stand out and the better and more fortunately is the state administered" (*Quadragesimo anno,* 79–80).

The principle of subsidiarity finds its justification as much in the liberty of the person as also in the structure of the smaller life groups, whose rights to life must not be curtailed by encroachments of more extensive social organizations ("statism"). On the one hand it protects the identity and privacy of the person and of the intermediate groups and institutions between the individual and the state—"defensive" function—and on the other hand it demands, according to the original meaning of the word, "help (*subsidium*) from above to below," if the individual or the smaller life groups, for example, the family, fail in their task of educating, with or without guilt—"responsible" function. It goes without saying that Pius XII as a determined defender of the rights of mankind especially stressed the "defensive" function of the principle

[33] The quotation from Pius XII is taken from the Christmas message of 24 December 1942 in *AAS* 35 (1943), 9–24; *UG,* 219–71; here, 261.
[34] Cf. J. Höffner, *Christliche Gesellschaftslehre* (5th ed., Kevelaer 1968), 50.

of subsidiarity. Other situations demand other accentuations of the principle.

Pius XI characterized the principle as "gravissimum illud principium" (*Quadragesimo anno,* 79), which, with regard to the importance of the principles of solidarity and of the common good, must probably not be translated as "sovereign principle" but rather as "extremely significant principle." Pius XII calls the principle a "principle constantly defended by the social doctrine of the Church,"[35] and emphasized its validity "even for the life of the Church, without prejudice to its hierarchical structure."[36]

With John XXIII we find the principle of subsidiarity frequently referred to in *Mater et Magistra* directly (53) and indirectly (for example, 165), less in its defensive function than in its positive function of the support of society in regard to the weaker. In *Pacem in terris* the Pope also directly considers the principle (140). Here he especially stresses the right of the smaller life groups, of the *corps intermédiaires* within the political community (cf. *Pacem in terris,* 24).

3. In the human person identity—singularity, individuality—and being part of society—socialization, mutual dependence, and need for society as a reference point—are intertwined. Person is "identity in the rational subject." From this state of being flows the principle of solidarity, by which all individualism and all collectivism is rejected. On the basis of these considerations the personalism of Catholic social doctrine is presented under the aspect of "solidarism."[37] This name not only aims to express an ethical attitude of solidarity but to express a state of being, namely, the fact that all people in their respective social relations—individuals among themselves, in the union of the family, in the intermediate groups, in the state, in the community of nations—stand in an ontological union and reciprocal obligation to one another. This union demands social and legal organization in the sense of the principle of subsidiarity, by which the uniting of the two principles takes place. The Popes have not employed the concept of solidarism, but have argued, especially Pius XII, essentially in the sense of solidarism. More frequently, on the contrary, is the "principle of

[35] Letter to the directors of the Twenty-Fourth Social Week of France of 18 July 1947 on basic questions of the economic order in *UG,* 3250–57; here 3255.
[36] Address to the College of Cardinals of 20 February 1946 in *AAS* 38 (1946), 141–51; *UG,* 4086–4111; here 4094.
[37] The principle of solidarity was scientifically justified and presented especially by H. Pesch (d. 1926), G. Gundlach (d. 1963), and O. von Nell-Breuning, who also gave its social-science system the name of "Solidarism," which, however, was unable to impose itself.

fraternal solidarity" affirmed, both as an ontological as well as an ethical principle of action.[38]

4. The service function of society and of the state lies in promoting the common good. This does not consist, as corresponding to the individualistic concept, in the sum total of individual goods but has its own quality. It also does not oppose the just claims and expectations of individuals, but, as Pius XII said, the rights of the person pertain to the "most precious in the common good" (*UG*, 359).[39] But it is the task of the state to reduce the often egoistic claims to one measure to be expected of and tolerable to all. To this extent the idea and realization of the common good stand against the pure standpoint of interest and power.

There have been controversies as to whether the common good is to be defined in the sense of *bona communia,* hence primarily in regard to content, or whether rather it aims at the making possible of *bene vivere in communitate,* that is, at the organizational side of society. The question is not only of academic interest, since in a pluralistic society a consensus as to the content of the common good, apart perhaps from the *minima moralia,* may be difficult to reach and besides in an ideologically colored dictatorship the content of the common good can be decreed in a totalitarian fashion—common good=good of the German people= good of the Aryan race. Both Pius XII and John XXIII stressed the primarily organizational function of the common good. This appears clearly from the descriptive definition which John XXIII gives in *Mater et Magistra.* According to the "correct notion of the common good," this embraces "the aggregate of those social presuppositions which make possible or easier to people the full development of their values" (*Mater et Magistra,* 65). From this definition it follows that the content or "values" do not belong primarily to the common good, that this rather presupposes them and should make possible and promote their development. Exactly in this sense had G. Gundlach, the adviser of Pius XII of long standing, already interpreted the common good in his commentary on Pius XII's Christmas address of 24 December 1942,[40] when, characterizing the common good as "organizing element," he declared it to be impossible "that the organizing element as such

[38] As regards the matter, the principle of solidarity occupies much space in the first encyclical of Pius XII, *Summi Pontificatus* of 20 October 1939 (*AAS* 31 [1939], 413–53; *UG,* 1–92; here, especially 25–37; cf. also *UG,* 3293–94 from the Christmas message of 24 December 1952 in *AAS* 45 [1953], 33–46; see also *Pacem in terris,* 114, 117ff.).

[39] See n. 30.

[40] In *Periodica* 32 (1943), 79–96 and 216–24. Here according to G. Gundlach, S. J. *Die Ordnung der menschlichen Gesellschaft* I (Cologne 1964) 108–27.

determines that which is to be organized, which ideally presupposes it, namely, the inner structure of social life with the objective 'common goods' (the person with the cultural and religious values)."[41]

Thus the circle again ends with the individual, whose development ultimately serves the common good. Thus the common good is the correct organizing principle—in the sense of becoming—or, respectively, as the correct organization—in the sense of being—of society, a view which is possible only with regard to society's subsidiary and solidarist character. Thereby all principles of the Catholic social doctrine culminate in the common good.

5. There is no encyclical in which the common good is so often and in such diverse connections appreciated and stipulated for a wholesome common life as in *Mater et Magistra*.[42] However, after it had been regarded in the past predominantly under the aspect of the national state—the state as primary guarantor of the common good—after the early peace efforts of Benedict XV and Pius XI, under the growing impression of the "unification of the world," the threat of a nuclear catastrophe, and the problem of underdeveloped countries, the idea of a world common good more and more gained ground. Pius XII saw in the relations to the other states an integrating part of the internal common good. "Serve," he said to journalists, "it [your people and state], however, in the conviction that its good relations to other nations, the understanding of their peculiarity, and the respect for their rights belong equally to the *bonum commune* of your own people and more effectively prepare for and consolidate peace as many another means."[43] Finally, John XXIII speaks clearly of the "universal common good" (*Pacem in terris,* 132ff.), from which he deduces the necessity of a world state with "universal political power" (*Pacem in terris,* 137). But even on this high plane the human person must remain the ultimate goal of all social life. "Just as the common good of individual states cannot be defined without regard to the human person, so also not the universal common good of all nations together" (*Pacem in terris,* 139). Thereby, once again the personalist character of Catholic social doctrine is proclaimed in unmistakable clarity.

[41] Ibid., 114.
[42] Cf. E. Welty, *Die Sozialenzyklika Papst Johannes' XXIII. "Mater et Magistra,"* mit einem ausführlichen Kommentar sowie einer Einführung in die Soziallehre der Päpste (Herderbücherei 110) (Freiburg i. Br. 1961), 74f., especially also the index: keywords "Gemeinwohl" and "Gemeinwohlgerechtigkeit," 215.
[43] Address to the members of the Union of the Foreign Press in Rome of 12 May 1953 in *AAS* 45 (1953), 399–402; *UG,* 2119–31; here, 2129.

State and State Power—Democracy

The most important theological principles concerning state, state power, and common good as the goal of the state had been elaborated in a long tradition to the end of the pontificate of Leo XIII in their basic features. To these belong especially the tracing back of state and state power to God as the Creator of socially oriented humanity and the binding of state power in regard to the maintenance of the common good to the natural law as expression of the *Lex aeterna*. Questions about the best form of state and government could play a subordinate role in a simple theoretical structural grid that confined itself more to principle.

The Popes since Benedict XV could assume all this as known in essentials and as the certain doctrine of the Church. A brief recapitulation in the appropriate context was sufficient. But meanwhile the new and pressing questions had to do with a detailed specialization of the tasks of the state in view of the totalitarian developments since the First World War, a nuanced justification of state power under the presuppositions of a modern democracy, the question of the functional conditions of democracy in general, and finally the problem of moral norms in a pluralistic democratic society. Thus were the essential themes of the Church's political doctrine designated in the first half of the twentieth century.

1. As regards the end of the state, it was defined by all Popes since Pius XI unambiguously in the light of the social principles further developed above. Especially in connection with the totalitarian movements Pius XI underlined the instrumental character of the state as well as of society in general in relation to the human person. This is nothing else than "a natural means which one can and should use to achieve his goal; for human society exists for people and not vice versa."[44] Pius XII more precisely stated the task of the state in enjoining on it the protection of the rights of the human person (*UG*, 3455).[45] In this sense the state is primarily a state of law for the guaranteeing of the areas of personal freedom of the citizens. It is at the same time a welfare state, without, however, having to be a state affording total relief; for law and justice oblige it to undertake all political and socio-political measures only with consideration of private initiative, that is, in accord with the principle of subsidiarity. Pius XII warned against the relief state ("Etat-Providence"), "which should grant to each of its citizens for

---

[44] Thus Pius XI in his encyclical *Divini Redemptoris* of 19 March 1937 against atheistic Communism.

[45] Address to the public administration scholars on the meaning and limits of state interference of 5 August 1950 in *UG*, 3450–57.

all the vicissitudes of life claims to achievements that are ultimately unrealizable" (*UG*, 3270).[46] Pius XII also regarded the state only as a means—it is "subordinate to the person and has the sense of a means" (*UG*, 3763)—and rejected all state planning (*UG*, 6120).[47] But these considerations in no way exclude the acknowledgment of the necessity of a state authority capable of functioning and equipped with power. In an address to a group of the Youth Union of the Christian Democratic Union of West Berlin on 28 May 1957 Pius XII characterized this acknowledgment precisely as an expression of a "Christian" concept of politics. "The state is not an ultimate, and there is no state omnipotence, but only a state power, and 'Christian politics' has a strong feeling for it. For without power the state cannot accomplish its goal of assuring and promoting the common good by means of a legal and social order adhered to by all" (*UG*, 6250).[48]

John XXIII, who, as noted earlier, stressed the principle of subsidiarity more from its "positive" side—"help from above to below"—expressly says that the state must intervene in the economy "today to a more comprehensive degree than before" (*Mater et Magistra*, 103), that it "more and more penetrates areas which pertain to the most personal concerns of mankind and" are "therefore of the greatest importance" (*Mater et Magistra*, 60). But at the same time the limits of its competence are imposed on the state. They lie, to give a few examples, in the common good (*Mater et Magistra*, 65, 147, 151), in the fundamental rights of the person and the autonomy of the free social groups (*Mater et Magistra*, 52, 65), in the principle of subsidiarity—or, respectively, in its "defensive" function (*Mater et Magistra*, 53, 117, 152)—in the God-given arrangement and obligation of values (*Mater et Magistra*, 205ff.). In order that the state may remain a state of law under modern conditions, which is expressly to be emphasized, John XXIII regards the separation of powers—"that threefold classification of offices"—as "appropriate to human nature" (*Pacem in terris*, 68). This is the first time that the separation of powers was expressly mentioned in papal social teaching.

2. As regards the legitimization of the concrete agents of state power at a given time, over and above the theological and natural law derivation of the state's authority in general, Leo XIII in his encyclical *Diuturnum illud*[49] strongly repudiated the liberal thesis that "all power

---

[46] Address to the participants in the International Congress for Social Science of 2 June 1950 in *AAS* 42 (1950), 485–88; *UG*, 3258–72.

[47] Address to the Italian Society for Water Supply on the superiority and tasks of private initiative in the life of society of 13 April 1956 in *UG*, 6118–24.

[48] *AAS* 49 (1957), 287f.; *UG*, 6249–52.

[49] Of 29 June 1881 in *ASS* 14 (1881f.), 3–14.

proceeds from the people." What Leo intended to strike at is clear, namely, the "Contract Thesis," according to which—without any reference to God as the Creator of mankind and its society—the autonomous individuals creatively produce the state, as though in a quasi-contract (Rousseau's *contrat social*), and hence naturally possess also the absolute right in relation to the appointment of the holder of state power.

Since the republican problem was now in hand because of his *Ralliément* policy, Leo XIII sought to aid himself with the construction in order that the people of the state might indeed have the possibility of "designating"—the "Designation Theory"—the actual holders of state power but not of appointing and commissioning them—the "Delegation Theory"—in order that the real investiture might follow, as it were, rather from God as Creator of the state. In this way the possibility of a compromise between the republican type of state on the one hand and the connection of state power to its divine origin on the other hand seemed to be maintained. Despite this compromise, whose difficult theological background considerations could not, of course, be comprehended by the theologically less trained wider public, there remained until today a strong mistrust of Leo XIII's attitude to the republic and to democracy. In this context the old Scholastic doctrine, of Thomas Aquinas in its beginnings and fully developed by Francisco Suárez, of the sovereignty of the people unified in the state would have offered itself spontaneously. Pius XII mentions the doctrine, though only *en passant,* when he speaks of the "thesis which outstanding Christian thinkers at all times have championed," the "principal thesis of democracy," that "the original agent of the political power coming from God [is] the people, not the 'mass' " (*UG,* 2715).[50]

3. This raises the question of democracy in the Church's social doctrine. As late as the time of John XXIII the basic principle was repeated that it cannot "be decided once and for all which type of state is the more suitable or which is the most appropriate manner in which the state power fulfills its task" (*Pacem in terris,* 67); for the "necessities of life of any sound community" "are fulfilled or at least can be fulfilled under the same conditions as in other [than democratic] types of government conformable to law" (*UG,* 2713).[51] Apart from this traditional principle,[52] Pius XII testified to a clear sympathy for peoples

[50] Address to the Sacred Roman Rota of 2 October 1945 on the difference between the ecclesiastical and the civil jurisdiction in *AAS* 37 (1945), 256–62; *UG,* 2702–24.
[51] Ibid.
[52] That tradition in general can also become a fetter was expressed by the Anglican D. L. Munby in an article on *Gaudium et Spes,* in which he sees in it a "restriction" of the

who require "a system of government that is more in harmony with the dignity and liberty of the citizens" (*UG*, 3469).[53]

For Pius XII it especially mattered to ask which assumptions must be realized for the functioning of democracy. He saw before him the empty appearance of a purely formal democracy, which "serves only as a disguise for something wholly undemocratic" (*UG*, 3482). It must be noted that Pius XII stressed this in the radio address for the last Christmas of the war in 1944, hence on the eve of the foreseeable end of two dictatorships—Fascism and National Socialism—and of the possibility thereby being sketched of a democratic state constitution for the nations concerned after the war's end. The state, including the democratic, "does not mechanically contain and unite in itself a formless aggregation of individuals in a defined territory, it is and must be an organized and organizing unity of an actual people" (*UG*, 3475). This was said against the individualistic notion of democracy, according to which faceless abstract individuals join together politically. Pius calls it more often "mass" in contrast to "people." For him the state citizen as a person is always *personne située,* that is, a person to be seen in different social contexts.

Pius XII thereby recalls the fact especially annoying today that people are unequal for the most diverse reasons. But this in no way injures "the civic equality of rights"; it gives to each, "vis-à-vis the state,

---

Church's social doctrine "that continuity must be maintained, and hence new insights must be expressed in terms of old ideas. Some of them make themselves all too painfully noticeable in the text [of *Gaudium et Spes*]" ("Das Wirtschaftsleben im Urteil des Konzils und des Weltkirchenrates," *Oeconomia Humana. Wirtschaft und Gesellschaft auf dem II. Vatikanischen Konzil* [Cologne 1968], 461).

[53] Christmas message of 24 December 1944 in *AAS,* 37 (1945), 10–23; *UG*, 3467–3510. Here there is question of the most important address of Pius XII and probably in general of the Popes of modern times on the problem of "true democracy." The concept "democracy" was not always unambiguous in the Church's terminology. In the nineteenth century by "Christian democracy" was meant especially the rising social reform movement among Catholics of Western and Central European countries, which, however, was understood primarily as a "social" movement and did not necessarily coincide with the striving for "political democracy." After Leo XIII this linguistic use ceased and at the latest since Pius XII there has been understood by it, when there is talk of democracy, a political idea in the strict sense and not a general social concept. The demand for "democratization of all spheres of life," the slogan "democracy as life-style," often used as political war cries, have found no entry into the language of the Church and of Catholic social teaching. Catholic social doctrine sees the justified concern which is concealed behind these formulas, without conforming to their exaggerations, in the better application of its social principles—the principle of subsidiarity—and, more recent in terminology, in the realization of more "participation," "taking part" by all people in the process of the political, social, economic, and even ecclesiastical life, adequately, better, and objectively considered.

the right . . . to lead his own personal life in honor" (*UG,* 3478). In other words, the freedom of the person gives him the right to be "different" while maintaining intact the civic political equality of rights. That the continuation of such tension between the poles of freedom and equality needs, of course, the "genuine spirit of community and fraternity" (ibid) Pius knows and he thereby makes known that he does not overlook one of the three ideals of democracy which has meanwhile fallen into oblivion, namely the "principle of fraternity." The Christmas address of 1944 is thus a real comprehensive hermeneutic interpretation of the ideals of "Liberty, Equality, and Fraternity" (cf. especially *UG,* 3478).

4. Leo XIII and Pius XI had already deduced, arguing from the fact that people are by nature unequal, that the state must be an organic functional structure in which a large plurality of various groups and institutions in their own right seek to realize the common good by means of the enclosing function of the state. Neither an antagonistic class society nor a faceless, classless society corresponds to this "organic" concept. In this context must be viewed the Pope's insistence on family and private property as areas of freedom of the person within the state, and also on the much abused "corporate order," which is better designated as "meritocracy." Pius XI contrasted the idea of the meritocracy to the economic social chaos into which liberalism had plunged society.[54] Since G. Gundlach had evidently already decisively assisted in preparing the idea for *Quadragesimo anno*[55] and strongly favored it until his death in 1963, it becomes clear why Pius XII also came back to it so frequently, while in *Mater et Magistra* John XXIII no longer spoke of it directly. However, he considered the plural diversity of social life and political compromise among groups as very necessary. But his allusion to the "present day" (*Mater et Magistra,* 66) should probably mean that there can be no permanently obligatory ideal solution. John thereby abandons the concrete model but not the fundamental idea of the "corporate order" when he demands that the social systems lead their own life and be able "really to develop by virtue of their own right" (*Mater et Magistra,* 65).

5. Only in outline can still other important presuppositions for the progress of democracy from the view of papal social teaching be

[54] Pius XI developed the idea in *Quadragesimo anno,* 81–87, immediately after the classic definition of the principle of subsidiarity (79–80), which, moreover, in this formulation goes back to G. Gundlach, S.J., since he saw in it an especially important case of applying the principle. Later he came back to it once more in *Divini Redemptoris.*

[55] Cf. also O. von Nell-Breuning, S.J., "Der Königswinterer Kreis und sein Anteil an *Quadragesimo anno,*" J. Broermann, P. Herder-Dorneich eds., *Soziale Verantwortung. Festschrift für Goetz Briefs zum 80. Geburtstag* (Berlin 1968), 571–85, especially 579ff.

mentioned: Democracy cannot rely exclusively on legal assurances, otherwise it is condemned to fall. It depends "on the moral character of the citizens" (*UG*, 4393).[56] From this it also follows—Pius XII thus addresses the problem of an élite for democracy—that precisely in a democracy high moral demands must be made on the holders of state power. Of course, those people "whose spiritual and moral predisposition is sufficiently sound and fruitful [will find] in themselves the spokesmen and overseers of democracy . . . men who personally live from those predispositions and understand how to transform themselves in fact" (*UG*, 3486).[57] Also important is the political education of the citizens, not only the instruction on the manner of operation of democratic institutions but especially the introduction "to the protection of their true interests and especially of their conscience" (*UG*, 1779).[58] Pius XII very urgently admonishes Christians to exercise the right to vote and elect, the neglect of which means a danger for democracy (*UG*, 4305).[59] Not least is it required that the Christian in a democracy make himself available for the construction of an enduring order of law and peace both within and without (*UG*, 180).[60]

6. As regards the relations of Church and state, Benedict XV in his address on the occasion of the secret consistory of 21 November 1921[61] had proclaimed the inalienable right of the Church to freedom from all state interference. Pius XI demanded, vis-à-vis the totalitarian states, the right of the citizens to free exercise of their faith[62] and the right of the Church to proclaim its message and to form consciences.[63] Pius XII spoke of a "legitimate laicism of the state" (*UG*, 4555),[64] which was always a principle of the Church. Nevertheless between Church and state there must not prevail a cool and separating atmosphere. A "complete" separation of the two cannot be approved (*UG*, 3985).[65] In other respects Pius XII does not tire of presenting the

[56] Christmas address of 23 December 1956 on the Christian image of mankind in *AAS* 49 (1957), 5–22; *UG*, 4377–4420.

[57] See n. 53.

[58] Address to the teachers and students of the Italian public normal schools of 19 March 1953 in *AAS* 45 (1953), 230–38; *UG*, 1771–91.

[59] Letter to the chairmen of the Forty-First Social Week of France of 14 July 1954 in *Osservatore Romano* of 21 July 1954; *UG*, 4296–4312.

[60] Letter to the Catholic Youth of Germany of 23 May 1952 in *AAS* 44 (1952), 527–31; *UG*, 168–82.

[61] Allocution *In hac quidem* of 21 November 1921 in *AAS* 13 (1921), 421–524.

[62] Encyclical *Mit brennender Sorge; M,* 311.

[63] Encyclical *Ubi Arcano; M,* 1130.

[64] Address to the Picene (=the Marches) People's Group of 23 March 1958 in *AAS* 50 (1958), 216–20; UG, 4545–55.

[65] Address to the Sacred Roman Rota of 29 October 1947 in *AAS* 39 (1947), 493–98; *UG*, 2744–58.

fortunate impact of the Church on the state (for example, *UG,* 4103f, 3450f.).[66]

The Church and the Social Errors of the Age

SOCIALISM–COMMUNISM

In the nineteenth century socialism became the chief adversary of the Church and of social Catholicism in the social sphere. While Leo XIII had had to deal essentially with a complete Marxist ideology,[67] which moreover had not yet acquired any political relevance of great importance, Pius XI could attest for socialism a development which he concisely sketched as follows: "If in Leo's time socialism was chiefly at least a homogeneous structure with a definitely complete doctrinal system, today it has developed in two sharply opposed and violently contending main trends, without, of course, having forsaken the anti-Christian basis common to all socialism."[68] Pius XI spoke of "socialism become Communism" and of the "more moderate direction which today the designation 'socialism' still retains."[69]

---

[66] Address to the College of Cardinals of 20 February 1946 in *AAS* 38 (1946), 141–51; *UG,* 4086–4111. Address to the public administration scholars of 5 August 1950 in *UG,* 3450–457.

[67] Cf. the encyclical *Quod Apostolici muneris* of 28 December 1878 in *AAS* 11 (1878), 369–76; *M,* 139–67; also the encyclical *Rerum novarum* of 15 May 1891 in *AAS* 23 (1890 seqq.), 641–70; *M,* 510–71, especially 514–17.

[68] *Quadragesimo anno,* 111.

[69] Ibid., 112f. "Socialism" (Communism) appears from the nineteenth century both as an idea and also in the form of political movements. The developments and increasing differentiations in the ideological sphere make it extraordinarily and in a growing degree difficult for the teaching authority of the Church to take a position on the "socialism" syndrome. While even under Pius XI the pretty thick category: Communism—"moderate" socialism (=revisionism, liberal-democratic socialism) could to a degree uncover the ideological and political reality, this is no longer sufficient for the period after the Second World War and especially since the 1960s, after Soviet Communism and Maoism became the great antagonists in world politics and Neo-Marxist currents spread into the public discussion and especially into the academic sphere. Precisely these latter obtained through the elaboration of the "Paris Manuscripts" of the young Marx from 1844—only rediscovered in 1932, in connection with the resistance to the Fascist and Nazi dictatorships that were then being established, indirectly by way of the United States since the 1960s—the greatest importance also in Europe. On this to the present there is no precise stand taken by the Church's teaching office, at most the warnings issued by Pope Paul VI because of the invasion of Neo-Marxism into various modern theologies—"Theology of Liberation," "Theology of Revolution," "Christians for Socialism," and the like—in his apostolic letter *Octogesima adveniens* of 14 May 1971 to Cardinal Maurice Roy against an all too thoughtless adoption "of Socialist tendencies and their various developments" by Christians (*Octogesima adveniens,* 31; cf. also the following numbers of the letter).

In *Quadragesimo anno* the Pope did not employ many words in the criticism of Communism, probably because among Christians and Catholics doubts in regard to it are scarcely possible. What especially characterizes Communism in the Pope's view is, first, the open and ruthless force with which it seeks its goal, then its hostility to God and Church. However, what concerned the Pope was the warning against the heedlessness of those "who, regardless of the danger threatening from this side, look on calmly as the exertions of a violent and bloody revolution are borne into the whole world" (*Quadragesimo anno,* 112). Just as he did to the two other totalitarian ideologies of his day, Fascism and National Socialism, Pius XI also devoted to "atheistic Communism" a special encyclical, which appeared on 19 March 1937 and began with the words *Divini Redemptoris.*[70] In it the Pope provided evidence that the Marxist doctrine at the basis of Communism experienced an expressly atheistic interpretation in dialectical materialism. In this way mankind was robbed of its freedom, the spiritual foundation of its human way of life and its dignity.

Pius XII also adhered clearly and unambiguously to his predecessor's express condemnation of the social system and the ideology of Communism. By means of decrees of the Holy Office of 1 July 1949 and 28 July 1950 not only membership in the Communist Party but even its promotion was threatened with excommunication.[71] The Pope could not conceive of the hope of "peaceful coexistence" with the Communist systems as a compromise but only as "coexistence in truth."[72] Blows against the rights of the Church, for the most part connected with persecution and imprisonment of leading bishops, were answered by the Pope with the excommunication of those responsible, as in the cases of the Yugoslav Archbishop Stepinac on 14 October 1946, the Hungarian Cardinal Mindszenty on 28 December 1948 and on 12 February 1949, of the Czech Cardinal Beran on 17 March 1951, and of the Polish Cardinal Wyszyński on 30 September 1953.

John XXIII put the accents differently. Not only that in the spring of 1963 he received in audience the son-in-law of the then first secretary of the Central Committee of the Communist party, Nikita Khruschev, and that he sent Cardinal König of Vienna and an official of the Secretariat of State to Budapest and thereby took the first steps in the direction of a new Vatican "Eastern Policy"; in doctrinal evaluation he

---

[70] *AAS* 29 (1937), 65–105; *M, 168–247.*
[71] Decree of the Holy Office on membership in the Communist Party of 1 July 1949 in *AAS* 41 (1949), 334; Decree of the Holy Office on membership in Communist Youth Organizations of 28 July 1950 in *AAS* 42 (1950), 533; cf. other pertinent documents in *HK* 13 (1958 seqq.), 2, 69.
[72] Christmas message of 24 December 1954 in *AAS* 47 (1955), 15–28; *UG,* 6307–39.

also sought cautious nuances. In his encyclical *Pacem in terris* he believed he could distinguish between the ideology of Marxism-socialism on the one hand and certain humane concerns on the other. He wrote: [It is] "entirely appropriate to distinguish specific movements which deal with economic, social, cultural questions or policy from false philosophical doctrinal views on the nature, origin, and end of the world and of mankind, even if these movements originated in such doctrinal views and are stirred up by them.[73]

The years of the "Dialogue between Christianity and Marxism" starting after John XXIII, the breaches in the dike, which occurred in various parts of the world in the form of a "Theology of Revolution," "Liberation Theology" on a Marxist basis, led Paul VI, in order to round out the picture, to warn of a confusion of Christianity and Marxism. And so he wrote in his apostolic letter *Octogesima adveniens* of 17 May 1971—the eightieth anniversary of *Rerum novarum*—: "If in Marxism as it is concretely lived these different facets and questions can be distinguished which present themselves positively for the reflection and action of Christians, it would be foolish and dangerous to reach the point where one forgets the inner bond which basically joins them together, that one adopts the elements of the Marxist analysis without recognizing its relations with the ideology and participates in the class struggle and appropriates its Marxist interpretation while neglecting to perceive the type of totalitarian and brutal society to which this method of proceeding leads."[74]

Quite different and more difficult for the discussion within the Church was the prolonged confrontation with what Pius XI in *Quadragesimo anno* had termed the "moderate trend" in socialism. Again and again the discussion was enkindled by two central statements of the Pope: "Socialism, no matter whether as doctrine, as historical phenomenon, or as movement, . . . is always irreconcilable with the doctrine of the Catholic Church—for then it would have to cease to be socialism: the opposition between Socialist and Christian notions of society is irreconcilable."[75] "If socialism, like any error, also contains something right, which the Popes have never denied, still at its foundation lies a concept of society which is proper to it but stands in opposition to the authentic Christian concept. Religious socialism and Christian socialism

[73] *Pacem in terris,* 159; especially this passage was at that time applauded by Communist states. The Polish Communists had a larger than life-size statue erected to the "Pope of the peace encyclical" on the Oder at Wroclaw near the church of "Mary of the Sand," which can still be seen there.

[74] Apostolic letter *Octogesima adveniens* of 14 May 1971; *AAS* 63 (1971), 401–41.

[75] *Quadragesimo anno,* 117.

are contradictions in themselves; it is impossible to be simultaneously a good Catholic and a real Socialist."[76]

That the discussion, especially in Germany, did not get more strongly under way until after 1945 and then especially since the "Godesberg Program" of the Social Democratic Party of Germany is explained, first, by the fact that during the period of National Socialism public discussion was not possible, and, second, by the fact that the Social Democratic Party, in its effort to change from a class party to a popular party with its program of 1959, especially had to assure the Catholic part of the population that the socialism which Pius XI had meant in *Quadragesimo anno* had nothing in common with the Social Democratic Party after the Second World War.

The just quoted verdict of Pius XI against socialism appeared with the claim of being able to say with certainty what socialism really is. According to Pius XI the special ideological nucleus of socialism, which makes it what it is, is not Marxism or class conflict, but, as it is put tersely in the just quoted passage from *Quadragesimo anno,* "a concept of society . . . which is proper to it but stands in opposition to the authentic Christian concept." The unmistakably proper basic axioms as regards the Christian notion of society are according to *Quadragesimo anno,* 118f.: the human being was created by God as a person with his social nature, in his own image; also the necessary social authority is based ultimately in God, the Creator of mankind and final end of all things. Also, the commentary of the encyclical: "Of all this, socialism knows nothing; completely unfamiliar and indifferent to it is this exalted definition of both mankind and society; it sees in society solely a useful institution."[77]

The claim to know what socialism is and to repudiate it as such was accordingly based by Pius XI on the incontestable fact that socialism was indebted to an ideological liberalism which withdrew mankind and its sociability from its origin and reference to God and thereby drove it to a road which the Christian could no longer accept. O. von Nell-Breuning expressed it thus: "With good reason socialism is called 'the natural child of liberalism'" or, respectively, "proletarian liberalism."[78]

Pius XII said nothing on the theme of "moderate" or "liberal" socialism which went beyond Pius XI. In regard to him it can be admitted that from his viewpoint he had to add nothing essential to the verdict of *Quadragesimo anno.*

In the years around the death of Pius XII (1958–59) falls a period of heightened discussions of the relations of Christianity and socialism,

[76] Ibid., 120.
[77] Ibid., 118.
[78] Cf. K. Forster, ed., *Christentum und demokratischer Sozialismus* (Munich 1958).

especially of the Catholic Church and liberal socialism. The meeting of the Catholic Academy in Bavaria on "Christianity and Democratic Socialism" in January 1958 became a much noticed event in the political life of the Federal Republic of Germany: at it for the first time representatives of the Social Democratic Party and of German social Catholicism met to undertake the effort to demolish the traditional oppositions which were not for the last time still determined by the verdict of *Quadragesimo anno*. The leader on the Catholic side at this meeting was the adviser of Pius XII, the German Jesuit Gustav Gundlach, lecturer at the Gregoriana in Rome. He obtained such great attention because, to the general amazement, he came to terms in much greater detail with the rationalism in socialism, and even in liberal socialism, than with Marxism, so that, as the *Süddeutsche Zeitung* then reported dumbfoundedly, he "scarcely mentioned Marx's name, but instead all the more took offense at the liberal element in social democracy."[79]

But in this way the chief item of criticism was identical with what *Quadragesimo Anno* had also criticized, and the burden of proof that this criticism was wrong lay with the Social Democrats and those Catholics who exerted themselves to build bridges.

In two documents addressed to the German Catholics[80] an attempt was made to effect for the socialism of the Godesberg Program a Catholic approval and a revision of the harsh "no" of the encyclical *Quadragesimo anno*. Naturally, the manner of argumentation was criticized. All unsuitable passages were omitted as clearly disturbing, especially the central text in 118 on the picture of mankind, on the *humanum* as the normative force of all politics.

The leading Catholic social theologians of the day, G. Gundlach and O. von Nell-Breuning, were in agreement in their estimation of the Godesberg Program. The latter stressed the fundamental differentiation from the Christian beginning when in 1960 he unmistakably declared in the first of the two above mentioned brochures of the Social Democratic Party:[81] "Much, it may be said, very much is common, but still not everything. . . . It is especially to be asked—and here our 'but' is inserted. . . . May one, while reading the encyclical, end with

---

[79] *Süddeutsche Zeitung* of 13 January 1958. On the meeting of the Catholic Academy in Bavaria and its background, cf. for details J. Schwarte, *Gustav Gundlach, S.J. (1892–1963). Massgeblicher Repräsentant der katholischen Soziallehre während der Pontifikate Pius' XI. und Pius' XII* (Diss. Münster 1974; abbreviated printed ed. Münster 1975).
[80] *Der Katholik und die SPD* (Bonn 1959); *Katholik und Godesberger Programm. Zur Situation nach Mater et Magistra* (Bonn 1962).
[81] O. von Nell-Breuning, S.J., "Der Katholik und die SPD," *Echo der Zeit*, no. 7 of 14 February 1960, 1f.

Number 120 and pass over the subsequent paragraphs as not present?" (Numbers 118 and 119 on the Christian view of mankind had also been disregarded.) "Nevertheless," continues von Nell-Breuning, "the title to Numbers 121–22, 'Cultural Socialism,' should catch the eye . . . and the concluding words of 122: 'At the beginning of this cultural socialism stands cultural liberalism; at its end stands cultural Bolshevism.' " Accordingly the answer to the quest for a Catholic approval can logically only fail: "But in the cultural area—and ultimately society and economy are cultural affairs—liberal democratic socialism must first rid itself of its liberal [liberalistic] legacy." A "new edition will then be able to bring that decisively important element which not by chance is apparently lacking in the present one, but in accord with the situation of affairs must unfortunately be lacking." However, the document of 1962 did not bring, in this regard, the "decisively important element," namely, the renunciation of the "liberalistic legacy," and so up to the present for many it is not clear that the "no" of *Quadragesimo anno* to ideological socialism could be overcome in the form of cultural socialism.

Also the encyclical *Mater et Magistra* of 1961 brought no essentially new aspects for the further discussion and hence no alleviation for the discussion. At first John XXIII adopted the repudiating attitude of *Quadragesimo anno* to the "more moderate," revisionist socialism (*Mater et Magistra*, 34). Later he spoke of "ideologies" which aim to eliminate inner social and international tensions with inadequate means and on false routes, because they possess no correct picture of mankind.[82] And so the discussion of the Church and liberal socialism remained for the future on the agenda beyond John XXIII and the council.

FASCISM–NATIONAL SOCIALISM

Whereas Communism and socialism not only still exist but have experienced a powerful expansion in the whole world and have penetrated with their ideology even into theology and partly into the Church, Italian Fascism and National Socialism, with which Pius XI had to deal, did not survive the end of the Second World War.

Italian Fascism[83] under the leadership of the "Duce" Mussolini never

---

[82] Cf. on this: *Die Sozialenzyklika Papst Johannes' XXIII. Mater et Magistra*, ed. by E. Welty, 144 (*Komm. zu MM*, 110) and 190f. (*Komm. zu MM*, 213).

[83] Cf. E. Nolte, *Die faschistischen Bewegungen* (*dtv-Weltgeschichte des 20. Jahrhunderts*) (Munich 1973). In contrast to National Socialism, "Fascism" in the period after the Second World War, especially in the socialist camp, had moved beyond its concrete historical form of Italian Fascism to become a generic and systematic concept with a glittering content. It corresponded, according to Karl D. Bracher, to the need to find a counter-idea to Communism, socialism, and democracy. However, an even

assumed so rigid and ideologically monistic a position as did its counterpart in Germany and its opponent in Russia. Nevertheless, one can designate as its ideological nucleus, under the influence of Hegel and of his Fascist interpreter, Giovanni Gentile (d. 1944), who was minister of education from 1922 to 1925 and in 1923 was responsible for the Fascist reform of education, the Hegelian doctrine of the total state. "La nazione" became the key idea. This involved internally a strong, antiliberal, collectivist policy, and externally imperial claims around the Mediterranean—"Mare nostro": annexation of Libya and Ethiopia and occupation of Albania and Greece during the Second World War. The "Dottrina del Fascismo" culminated in the profession of a national imperialism.[84]

The preindividualistic, preliberal, and pre-Fascist values of the family, the people, and the Church, or religion, respectively, worked to consolidate the national idea in the interior sphere. And so Fascism's attitude toward the Church was at first entirely friendly, and Mussolini esteemed it as especially a national cultural agent. And so, following two and one-half years of discussions there occurred the solution of the so-called "Roman Question" and a concordat in the Lateran Treaties of 11 February 1929. The Catholic religion was confirmed as the religion of the Italian state. Nevertheless, there ensued strong tensions, because the total "ethical state" claimed for itself exclusively all rights in the area of education and of youth work and hence curtailed the Church's influence. Only a few months after the conclusion of the Lateran Treaties Pius XI, in a letter of 30 May 1929 to Cardinal Secretary of State Gasparri, attacked the totalitarian interpretation of the treaties by the Fascist state. In the winter of 1930 began Fascism's struggle against "Catholic Action" and in March 1931 open war broke out over the

---

more important role is played by "the growing rejection of the Western liberal theory of totalitarianism in so far as this is based on the comparability of the dictatorships of the right and the left, especially of Fascism, National Socialism, Stalinism, and recently also Maoism; its scheme of the confrontation of democracy and dictatorship is, really simplifying it, suspect as an invention of the Cold War and should be supplanted by the of course no less pithy opposition of Socialism-Fascism" (Karl D. Bracher, "Der Faschismus," *Meyers Enzyklopädisches Lexikon* 8 [Bibliographisches Institut Mannheim, Vienna and Zürich 1973], 547–51; cf. also Dieter Albrecht, "Zum Begriff des Totalitarismus," *Geschichte in Wissenschaft und Unterricht* 26 [Stuttgart 1975], 135–41). On this idea of Fascism, constructed for propaganda purposes especially by the East, there is no direct position of the teaching authority. Indirect criticism is contained in the critical position on the violations of human rights or totalitarian social forms.

[84] Cf. "Faschismus," *Staatslexikon*, 3, 6th ed. (1959), 223–31; also, "Faschismus," *LThK* 4, 2d ed. (1960), 29–31.

autonomy of the Catholic youth organizations. This produced the encyclical *Non abbiamo bisogno* of 29 June 1931,[85] in which the Pope spelled out his fiery protest against the limiting of ecclesiastical activities in public life and against the unilateral interpretation of the Lateran Treaties. The reaction on the part of Fascism was marked by deep emotions against the Church.[86] After the dust which had been raised by the encyclical had settled, there came about on 2 September 1931 an agreement whereby the Catholic youth organizations were restricted to religious and educational tasks.

In *Quadragesimo anno*[87] Pius XI attacked Fascist corporatism, the politically monopolistic compulsory organization of employers and employees.

A still more dangerous opponent of the Church sprang up in Germany with the seizure of power by National Socialism in 1933.[88] In contradistinction to Italian Fascism, which essentially disavowed a political theology of its own, National Socialism understood itself as a doctrine of salvation of racist and nationalist style, which raised a total claim to the soul of the German person.

Although in the effort soon to realize a first very important foreign policy success Hitler was able to reach a concordat with the Holy See on 20 July 1933, confrontations were not slow in coming. In addition to the malicious struggle against the Christian faith with all the means of propaganda and of administration, there was especially the "neo-pagan" doctrine, there were the scientifically totally unqualified expositions of revealed religion and its origins in the Old Testament—Cardinal Faulhaber of Munich-Freising: *Judentum-Christentum-Germanentum*—

---

[85] *AAS* 23 (1931), 285–312; *M*, 248–98.

[86] In the *Gazzetta*, the official organ of the Fascist Party of Calabria and Sicily, one could read on 12 July 1931 the sentence: "Se il Duce ci ordinasse di fucilare tutti i vescovi non esisteremmo un istante." On the entire matter, cf. also the introduction to *Non abbiamo bisogno* in I. Giordani, ed., *Le encicliche sociali dei Pape da Pio XI a Pio XII,* 3d ed. (1948), 421–24.

[87] The Pope sees the essential difference from the "corporate order" favored by him in the statism of the Fascist solution (cf. *Quadragesimo anno,* 91–95). The Pope shares the "apprehension" of those who think that "the state puts itself in the place of free self-activity," the new corporative constitution has "an extremely bureaucratic and political emphasis" (ibid., 95).

[88] B. Stasiewski, *Akten deutscher Bischöfe über die Lage der Kirche 1933–1945* 1: *1933–1934* (Mainz 1968), 2: *1934–1935* (Mainz 1976), 3: *1935–1936* (Mainz 1978); H. Boberach, *Berichte des SD und der Gestapo über Kirchen und Kirchenvolk in Deutschland 1934–1944* (Mainz 1971); "Nationalsozialismus," *Staatslexikon* 5, 6th ed. (1960), 905–23; "Nationalsozialismus," *LThK* 7, 2d ed. (1962), 802–5; "Katholische Kirche und Nationalsozialismus," *Staatslexikon* 10, 6th ed. (1970): cf. especially the collaborative volume, D. Albrecht, ed., *Katholische Kirche im Dritten Reich* (Mainz 1976), with bibliography and a voluminous report on the research.

which provoked the Church to resistance. On 14 March 1937, five days before the encyclical *Divini Redemptoris* against atheistic Communism— a timely coincidence in which can be seen a clever, tactical move—the Pope published in German the encyclical *Mit brennender Sorge,*[89] in whose first, ecclesio-political part he protested against the "treaty reinterpretation, treaty evasion, treaty undermining, and treaty violation" in relation to the concordat, while in the second, religious part he expressly took to task the teachings of National Socialism: racial delusion, myth of "blood and soil," the principle that "that is right which benefits the [German] people," the effort to create a German national Church not bound to Rome. A quite mild protest by the German ambassador at the Holy See, Diego von Bergen, was rejected by the cardinal secretary of state.

With the encyclical *Mit brennender Sorge,* Pius XI thought he had taken only a first step in the confrontation with racism. Racism appeared to him as an especially virulent ideology against the religiously based unity of the human species. Thus it was made known through a sensational publication from the pen of Thomas Breslin in *The National Catholic Reporter* of 15 December 1972 and 19 January 1973 to a wide public that Pius XI had on 22 June 1938 commissioned an encyclical, the outline of which was supplied by the American Jesuit John LaFarge and by Gustav Gundlach under the title "Societatis Unio."[90] Because of the change in the See of Peter in March 1939 this encyclical was never published.

In his address to the College of Cardinals of 2 June 1945[91] Pius XII dealt in detail with National Socialism and its consequences for the future. His repeatedly presented appeals toward the end of the war not to impose the war released by Fascism and National Socialism and the crimes perpetrated by them as a moral burden on entire peoples—the "collective guilt thesis"—[92] attracted notice. He thereby already led across to the theme of the understanding of peoples after the war.

[89] *AAS* 29 (1937), 145–67; M, 299–315.
[90] On the background which induced Pius XI to publish a special encyclical against racism and on the preliminaries to a draft, cf. the detailed presentation in J. Schwarte, op. cit., 72–100; there see also a detailed indication of the content of the draft of the encyclical from the pen of G. Gundlach. S.J., 88–94.
[91] *AAS* 37 (1945), 159–68; *UG,* 3531–48.
[92] Thus in the address to the College of Cardinals on the Pope's nameday, 2 June 1944 in *AAS* 36 (1944), 166–75; *UG,* 4236–65; here, 4258; also in the Christmas message of 24 December 1944 in *AAS* 37 (1945), 10–23; *UG,* 3467–3510, here 3500.

Understanding of Peoples: "World State"

In his exertions for peace after the outbreak of the First World War, Benedict XV had again and again referred to the moral force of law vis-à-vis the power of weapons. He was especially concerned further to develop international law on the basis of moral norms and also to inculcate international institutional provisions for a lasting order of peace.[93]

Although the pontificate of Pius XI was not troubled by a world war, still the Pope suffered severely from the consequences of the First World War and the preparedness for war, by no means eliminated from the world but on the contrary renewing itself, with the prospect of an even more terrible war. For this reason he based both his election motto "Pax Christi in Regno Christi" and his first encyclical *Ubi arcano* of 23 December 1922[94] entirely on the idea of peace and of the understanding of nations. The Pope complained that there was "no human tribunal which could oblige all nations to an international law code in accord with the time."[95] The Pope discreetly offered the aid of the Church, which could be understood entirely in the sense of an arbitration function.[96]

After all the efforts to arrive at an understanding by means of the League of Nations and the Pan-European movement had foundered, after a catastrophic Second World War had afflicted humanity in extensive parts of the world, the Popes of the war and postwar periods saw one of their chief tasks in taking a stand with their means and possibilities for the understanding of peoples. Pius XII considered it as the "special mission" of his pontificate "to contribute in patient and almost grinding activity to leading humanity back to the paths of peace."[97] The Pope demanded an organization of the community of nations with the character of a federation. Into this community must be inserted the sovereign rights of the individual nations "in the framework of international law."[98] Hence, to be repudiated is a principle of the national state which "consists [in] the confusing of national life with nationalistic policy"; for "the national life [is] something nonpolitical,

---

[93] Cf. his admonition to peace "Dès le début" of 1 August 1917 in *AAS* 9 (1917), 417–20; *M*, 1083–93.

[94] *AAS* 14 (1922), 673–700; *M*, 1094–1160.

[95] *M*, 1132.

[96] *M*, 1133. It is noteworthy that Pius XI had no relations with the League of Nations, which had met at Geneva since 1920 at the suggestion of President Wilson.

[97] Christmas message of 24 December 1955 in *AAS* 48 (1956), 26–41; *UG*, 6340–74.

[98] Address to the Association of Catholic Jurists of Italy of 6 December 1953 in *AAS* 45 (1953), 794–802; *UG*, 3963–86, here 3967.

. . . which only then [became] the principle of the dissolution of the community of nations when people began to exploit it as a means to political ends."[99]

The community of nations presupposes another concept of sovereignty than that of nationalism. The individual state is no longer "sovereign" in the sense of absolute absence of restraints.[100] It is subordinate to international law but not to the extent that it thereby completely loses its independence. Pius XII emphasized that even international law is subject to natural law. Corresponding to his ontological, natural law beginning, questions of national statehood, of sovereignty and its limits, of international association, are not left to the good pleasure of peoples but are determined by the "nature of the thing" in the historical context of the moment. Hence, agreements among states, though belonging formally to positive law, oblige by virtue of natural law if "they contain nothing which would be contrary to sound morality."[101] Pius XII regarded the present organization of nations, the United Nations, in its early stage as not yet ideal, since it had come into being on a "war solidarity" rather than on a true solidarity.[102] However, he said it was an expression of the wish of peoples for a more jointly responsible cooperation, it is a possibility "of speaking to the world conscience from an elevated spot."[103]

Pius XII followed with special sympathy the efforts for unification in Europe, in fact he saw in the unification of Europe "one of the concrete demands of the hour, one of the means of assuring peace to the entire world."[104] He spoke of the "risk" of Europe and stressed that it "is a question of a necessary risk, of a risk, however, which is in accord with current possibilities, of a reasonable risk."[105] As early as 1940 the Pope had seen in a new, united Europe a model for the unity of the family of nations, the possible "start of a new world epoch."[106]

[99] Christmas message of 24 December 1954 in *AAS* 47 (1955), 15–28; *UG*, 6307–39, here 6326.
[100] As in n. 98 in *UG*, 3967.
[101] Address to the "Centro Italiano di Studi per la Riconciliazione Internazionale" of 13 October 1955 in *AAS* 47 (1955), 764–75; *UG*, 6275–99, here 6287.
[102] Christmas address to the College of Cardinals of 24 December 1948 in *AAS* 41 (1949), 5–15; *UG*, 4133–57, here 4150.
[103] Address of 28 October 1947 to the ambassador of El Salvador in *AAS* 39 (1947), 491–93.
[104] Christmas message of 23 December 1956 in *AAS* 49 (1957), 5–22; *UG*, 4377–4420, here 4411.
[105] Christmas message of 23 December 1953 in *AAS* 46 (1954), 5–16; *UG*, 654–78, here 674.
[106] Christmas address to the College of Cardinals of 24 December 1940 in *AAS* 33 (1941), 5–14; *UG*, 3567–93, here 3582.

If Pius XII had already again and again implored solidarity for a beneficial international order of peace, John XXIII energetically carried this idea further, especially in his encyclical *Pacem in terris.* "Since the reciprocal relations of states should be regulated in conformity with truth and justice, they must be especially promoted by energetic solidarity. . . . With reference to this, we must keep before our eyes that the state's power was instituted, by its very nature, not to force people into the limits of the existing political community, but especially to look out for the common welfare of the state, which can certainly not be separated from that of the entire human family" (*Pacem in terris,* 98).

The Pope was convinced that "considering the present state of human society, both the political organization as also the influence of which the individual state power disposes in relation to all other nations of the world [are] to be regarded as inadequate to foster the common good of all peoples" (*Pacem in terris,* 135). From this "there follows conclusively for the sake of the moral order that a universal political power must be instituted" (*Pacem in terris,* 137), in other words, that mankind must come to a sort of world state. But the Pope knew that such a general political power, which should lead to a "universal common good" must "be based on the agreement of all peoples and not be imposed by force" (*Pacem in terris,* 138). And for such a "world state" the principle of subsidiarity must hold good, by which "those relationships are regulated which exist between the authority of the universal political power and the state power of individual nations" (*Pacem in terris,* 140).

The Pope regarded as important steps, even if not without criticism, the founding of the United Nations and the Universal Declaration of Human Rights of 10 December 1948 (*Pacem in terris,* 142f.). In an effort to manifest the Holy See's active interest in an international order of peace, even on the institutional side, he maintained representatives, usually through so-called permanent observers, at many international organizations, including the United Nations and UNESCO, to which, during his time as nuncio at Paris, John XXIII had been assigned as the first permanent observer.

The problem of the underdeveloped countries, which came more clearly in view under Pius XII, experienced under John XXIII a special attention in his two social encyclicals, *Mater et Magistra* and *Pacem in terris.* Finally, Paul VI expressed the thorny problem in the concise formula: "Development, the new name for peace."[107]

[107] Encyclical *Populorum progressio* of 26 March 1967. Heading to 76ff.

CHAPTER 8

*Main Lines of the Development of Theology between the
First World War and the Second Vatican Council**

The Departure from Neo-Scholasticism in Systematic Theology
TEMPORAL AND INTELLECTUAL PRESUPPOSITIONS

The end of the First World War did not produce for Catholic theology
that epochal radical change that occurred on the Protestant side,
especially in Germany, and became visible as a radical turning from
liberal to dialectical theology,[1] from cultural Protestantism to neoortho-
doxy.[2] In accord with the stronger forces of continuity in Catholicism,
which had grown further through the defense against Modernism,
here the further development took place not in dialectical leaps but in a
continuous development and in positive progress. Hence at the beginning of this period the effects of the First Vatican Council and the not
always positive result of the Modernist controversy became still more
clearly discernible. As regards the negative consequences of the
suppression of Modernism for Catholic theology, the verdict of R.
Aubert must be noted, that "the total balance . . . was less negative
than has often been claimed." This applies especially to German
theology, which around the turn of the century, it is true, discussed
problems raised with the so-called Reform Catholicism,[3] but was not
seized by the highest waves of this crisis. The position and the general
assessment of this theology, represented especially by the university
faculties, in the awareness of the age can be characterized by the fact,
episodic to be sure, but still not entirely untypical, that in connection
with an inquiry internally organized at some universities in regard to the
elimination or retention of the theological faculties the overwhelming
majority of professors of the profane disciplines expressed themselves
for retention.[4]

---

* Leo Scheffczyk

[1] Technically and biographically this change can be especially clearly grasped in the
correspondence of K. Barth and A. von Harnack: "Karl Barth. Ein Briefwechsel mit
Adolf von Harnack," *Theologische Fragen und Antworten,* 3 vols. (Zollikon 1957).

[2] On this cf. the instructive presentation of W. Trillhaas, "Die evangelische Theologie
im 20. Jahrhundert," *Bilanz der Theologie* II, 88–123, especially 101ff.

[3] On the evaluation of this movement, the title of which is not entirely precise, cf.,
among other works, Y. Congar, *Vraie et fausse réforme dans l'église* (Paris 1950); A.
Hagen, *Der Reformkatholizismus in der Diözese Rottenburg* (Stuttgart 1962); A. Kolping,
Katholische Theologie, 46f.

[4] Transmitted in K. Eschweiler, *Die zwei Wege der neueren Theologie* (Augsburg 1926), 9.

Of course, this vote was and is not actually to be evaluated as a judgment on the distinguished state of Catholic theology, especially not in respect to *all* its disciplines. For Germany the cheerful promise of J. I. Döllinger (d. 1890) at the Munich Assembly of Scholars in 1863, according to which the homeland of Catholic theology would lie here for the future,[5] was not fulfilled, especially not for systematic theology (dogmatic theology), which advanced further in the paths of a not excessive but still moderate Neo-Scholasticism. On this road it at first admitted neither the stimulation coming from M. J. Scheeben, the "most precious flower of Neo-Scholasticism," according to K. Eschweiler, for the intellectual deepening and organized grasping of the rational Neo-Scholastic system nor even the fruitful knowledge, coming from France, of Neo-Thomism, which, with P. Rousselot (d. 1915) and J. Maréchal (d. 1944), tried to establish a synthesis between genuine Thomism and modern philosophy. In this it was followed by systematic theology in the Romance countries, which, in keeping with its self-evaluation of a didactically moderate "school theology," assumed a superiority only in individual cases over the traditional Neo-Scholastic statement of problems and its answers.[6]

The melting down of this hardness and a revival occurred through forces and impulses which lay outside the narrow bounds of systematic theological specialists and was rooted in the area of the general awareness of the age like a new philosophical thought. The temper of Catholic life and the consciousness of the faith in the period after the First World War made it possible to admit these tendencies and to integrate them in a manner which gave to Catholicism not only inner drive but also a certain radiation to the surrounding world. While a not unimportant basic tendency drew from the political and cultural crisis situation on the basis of a biologically determinist thought the conclusion concerning the "Decline of the West,"[7] in the Catholic sphere, especially in Germany, there was awake the conviction of the capability of regeneration on the part of the Church and the culture from the forces of the spirit, which of course was the spirit of traditional Christian humanist culture and of the Catholic faith. At that time there

---

[5] Cf. also L. Scheffczyk, *Theologie im Aufbruch und Widerstreit. Die deutsche katholische Theologie im 19. Jahrhundert* (Bremen 1965), 276; G. Denzler, "Ignaz von Döllingers Vermächtnis an seine Hörer," *MThZ* 21 (1970), 93–101.

[6] As such prominent particular achievements which Neo-Scholastic systematic theology deepened in individual problems with a return to patristics and in intellectual independence may be mentioned, among others: M. de la Taille, S. J., *Mysterium Fidei* (1921); E. Masure, *Le sacrifice du chef* (1932); A. Vonier, *A Key to the Doctrine of the Eucharist* (1925).

[7] O. Spengler, *Der Untergang des Abendlandes*, 2 vols., 30th ed. (Munich 1922).

appeared simultaneously the programmatic formulations of *The Awakening of the Church in Souls* by Romano Guardini in 1921 and of the establishing of a "New West," the title of a periodical of Catholic intellectuals that appeared between 1926 and 1930. The concerns expressed in them were further accentuated in the generally prevalent notions of the "living," the "organic" and "authentic," the "emotional," and of "history," of "personality," and of "appreciation of value." Acting as catalyst was the "German Rembrandt," Julius Langbehn (d. 1907), rediscovered by the converted painter and writer, B. Momme Nissen, O.P. (d. 1943). Langbehn grasped Catholicism as "spirit of the whole" and taught this understanding, but on the other hand he abetted nationalistic thought also.

These ideas proceeding from a new temper of life were taken up by corresponding "life movements" and reflected in diverse ways, such as the youth movement, going back to the period before the First World War, the rising liturgical movement, and also the Bible movement, which, of course, because of its being restricted to smaller groups cannot be equated with the first two movements mentioned. The idealistic ardor which belonged to these movements, supported especially by lay persons, and which of course became only to a degree useful to the "hierarchical apostolate of the Church" in the Catholic Action of Pius XI, was certainly not free from restorative tendencies, and therefore today occasionally the pejorative designation of "Neo-Romantic" is given to it. But the label is correct neither in its historical parallelism nor in relation to the objective content, because, despite certain common traits in style and content, for example, in the rediscovery of the Middle Ages,[8] what is distinctive dominates, especially in the rejection of subjectivism and irrationalism.

This can clarify a view of the philosophical undercurrents on which these movements were based and which, indirectly by way of a prescientific discussion,[9] also influenced the new starts in Catholic theology. It was a partly surprising, but partly obvious turn on account of the paradoxes of Kantianism as well as of Neo-Kantianism, which occurred after the First World War and was denoted by the catchword or slogan of the "resurrection of metaphysics."[10] In accord with its

---

[8] A work characteristic of this "rediscovery" from the non-Catholic area, which, however, found a loud echo in the likewise very vital Catholic academic movement, was P. L. Landsberg, *Die Welt des Mittelalters und wir,* 3d ed. (Bonn 1925).

[9] For these motives from the "prescientific" sphere, which finally communicated themselves also to theology, the works of the universally oriented R. Guardini (d. 1968) were representative.

[10] Cf. also P. Wust (Leipzig 1920). Also influential was H. Heimsoeth, *Die sechs grossen Themen der abendländischen Metaphysik* (Berlin 1922).

objective content, however, it was a question here, not of a mechanical renewal of Aristotelianism or of Wolffianism as of the less vital Neo-Thomism in Germany, in contrast to the France of A. G. Sertillanges, É. Gilson, and J. Maritain, and despite Pius XI's encyclical *Studiorum ducem* of 1923 on the sixth centenary of the canonization of Thomas Aquinas, but of an investigation of being that had become more critical, which was influenced both by the new unspeculative ontology of N. Hartmann (d. 1950) and by the doctrine of reality of H. Driesch (d. 1943), but especially received stimulation from the "view of reality" of the phenomenology of E. Husserl and M. Scheler and its philosophy of value, represented by J. Hessen and D. von Hildebrand. Thereby attention was also powerfully directed to the other basic current of Western Christian intellectualism, namely, to the Augustinian-Franciscan thought in philosophy and theology. This new doctrine of knowledge and being, which did not understand metaphysics as a search for an abstract posterior world and ventured upon the new draft of a "Christian philosophy"[11] as embodiment of a *philosophia perennis,* itself remained open to the philosophy of life of W. Dilthey (d. 1911),[12] even if it repudiated the elements of historicist relativism present in it.

However, the most persistent influence in the 1920s and 1930s on the consciousness of the faith that was rearticulating itself was exercised by the philosophy of life and phenomenology, the latter not without the mediating role of the gifted M. Scheler (d. 1928), whose lot in life, of course, reflected the imbalances, tensions, and situation of the groping attempts in the Catholic intellectual life of the time. Only in regard to the rising existentialism of M. Heidegger and the Philosophy of Existence of K. Jaspers was the reaction generally negative,[13] despite the mediating efforts from France of Gabriel Marcel, but this was partly based on the obscurity and individuality of this thought and its language, with which, as P. Wust attests,[14] even the professional philosophers had their difficulties.

[11] As a work characteristic of this aim may be mentioned A. Dempf, *Christliche Philosophie. Der Mensch zwischen Gott und der Welt* (Bonn 1938).

[12] Cf. for the acceptance of W. Dilthey: J. Höfer, *Vom Leben zur Wahrheit. Katholische Besinnung am Lebenswerk W. Diltheys* (Freiburg 1936).

[13] Cf., for example, the view, characteristic of the time, of M. Pfliegler, *Vor der Entscheidung. Überlegungen zur seelischen Bedrohtheit der heutigen Menschen* (Salzburg and Leipzig 1937); *Heilige Bildung. Gedanken über Wesen und Weg christlicher Vollendung* (Salzburg 1933); *Die pädagogische Situation. Gedanken zur gegenwärtigen Lage religiöser Erziehung* (Innsbruck 1932).

[14] Cf. also the extract from a letter of 1929 in F. Heinemann, *Existenzphilosophie lebendig oder tot?* (Stuttgart 1954), 88.

THE TURNING OF DOGMA FROM "REASON" TO "LIVING"

The turning of the dogmatic method of reflection to the "living" and to "religious value," also partly inspired by the suggestions of the philosophy of religion, for example, by *Das Heilige* (1917) of R. Otto, at first made its appearance only sparingly. But the formulations, appearing in various forms, of the theme "Dogma and Life,"[15] the efforts to disclose the life value of dogma—and even if at first it was only in corollaries at the end of the positive presentation[16]—the connection between theology and spirituality in the works of Columba Marmion (d. 1923)[17] and A. Gardeil, O.P.,[18] created an atmosphere which could not entirely refuse to have anything to do with Scholastic dogma for long, although the texts and manuals that had meanwhile become standardized were still kept in Neo-Scholastic strictness. Of course, this experienced a pleasing relaxation through the admission of newer problems in Pohle-Gierens (9th ed. [1936], 10th ed. by J. Gummersbach, S.J.) and through the regard for the history of dogma in F. Diekamp (7th ed. [1934], 11th ed. by K. Jüssen).

It was only consistent and a proof of the accuracy of the systematic work when thereupon the question of method and the problem of the way of systematic theology was again taken up by it. The most basic and stimulating effort in this regard, that of K. Eschweiler (d. 1936) in the German area, determined the point of departure of theological thought, following M. J. Scheeben and against G. Hermes, not from a neutral reason but from faith and the reasonableness inherent in it,[19] which was to be developed by theology in accord with the method of intellectual scientific knowledge. In this way theology was, on the one hand, anchored in the supernatural basic faith essential to it, but, on the other hand, it was confirmed as a theoretical science. Hence a special significance belonged to the last named factor, because at about the

---

[15] Thus the representative book of E. Krebs, *Dogma und Leben,* 2 vols. (Paderborn 1921–25 and later); A. Rademacher, *Religion und Leben. Ein Beitrag zur Lösung des christlichen Kulturproblems,* 2d ed (Freiburg 1929); after the Second World War, among others: J. Ranft, *Vom Dogma und vom lebendigen Geist* (Würzburg 1949); B. Poschmann, *Die katholische Frömmigkeit* (Würzburg 1949).

[16] Thus in the dogmatic theology, already determined by biblical and historical thought, of B. Bartmann, *Grundriss der Dogmatik,* 2 vols., 2d ed. (Freiburg 1931).

[17] Cf., among other works, *Christ in His Mysteries* (Maredsous 1919; English: St. Louis 1939).

[18] Here must be mentioned especially the work significant also for the question of theological method: *La structure de l'âme et l'expérience mystique,* 2 vols. (Paris 1927).

[19] K. Eschweiler, op. cit., 24 and passim. K. Adam, *Glaube und Glaubenswissenschaft im Katholizismus,* 3d ed. (Rottenburg 1920 1923), points in a similar direction. For a critical evaluation cf. A. Kolping, op. cit., 102f.

same time other theological basic concepts came under discussion: the affective-charismatic concept of T. Soiron, O.F.M., based on the Franciscan tradition,[20] the mystical devotional type of A. Stolz, O.S.B. (d. 1942), derived from patristics,[21] which was inspired by the studies on the spiritual life, cultivated especially in France by H. Bremond, R. Garrigou-Lagrange, and the periodical *La vie spirituelle,* and a "kerygmatic" type which appeared under the name of "Proclamation Theology."

The theology of a living proclamation, intended especially by the Innsbruck theologians, J. A. Jungmann,[22] F. Dander, F. Lakner, H. Rahner, and others, was supposed to present its own way and field of work in addition to the theoretical essential dogma and direct revealed truths directly to the listener in the language of kerygma. Although this attempt cannot simply be designated as "stillborn"[23] because of the further operation of its intention, yet it could not be realized in method and would also have been a disadvantage for the still sought unity of theology.

Previously the aim of approximating dogmatic theology to the modern temper of life and of making it fruitful for the living faith had been realized in a more convincing way by Karl Adam (d. 1966) in his *Das Wesen des Katholizismus* (1924; 12th ed. [1949]), which, taking as a basis the phenomenological view of essence, the psychology of religion, and the scriptural concept of the Body of Christ, revealed a mystical understanding of the essence of Catholic Christianity and of the Church. Here the theme of the Church, especially questioned in those years, which had hitherto had a place only in apologetics, was made a subject of dogma and thereafter more richly developed from the dogmatic viewpoint.

This occurred emphatically in the *Dogmatik* of M. Schmaus (1938, 6th ed. [1964]), in which the religious and existential, as well as the scientific motives of the period before the beginning of the Second World War, received an authentic summary. Taking up the affirmative of the kerygmatic concern of an easing of the tension between scientific faith and living faith, but without sacrificing the scientific way of knowledge, the attempt was here undertaken to derive dogma from the sources of Scripture and genuine patristic tradition,

[20] Cf. T. Soiron, *Heilige Theologie* (Regensburg 1935).
[21] A. Stolz, *Manuale theologiae dogmaticae,* 6 fasc. (Freiburg 1939–43).
[22] Of initial efficacy was especially J. A. Jungmann, *Frohbotschaft und unsere Glaubensverkündigung* (Regensburg 1936). For the criticism, cf., among others, E. Kappler, *Die Verkündigungstheologie* (Fribourg 1949), and A. Kolping, op cit., 163ff.
[23] Thus R. Aubert, "Katholische Theologie im 20. Jahrhundert," *Bilanz der Theologie* II, 37.

both of which came up for detailed discussion and were no longer presented only in *dicta probantia,* and to disclose it to the understanding of an age which was influenced by Nietzsche's philosophy of life and by Heidegger's and Jasper's philosophy of existence that was gaining influence.[24]

To be sure, the unique character and importance of this work, which was also the first to make use, for scriptural argumentation, of Kittel's *Wörterbuch zum Neuen Testament,* otherwise still held in suspicion in Catholic theology, can only be fully understood if the developments that had in the meantime taken place in historical as well as biblical theology are assessed and the fact of the opening up of dogma with respect to the influences from both areas. For historical theology this influencing goes without saying, since the representatives of the system almost without exception had gone through the school of historical theological investigation, which was then concentrated especially on the Middle Ages, with C. Bäumker, M. Grabmann, A. Landgraf, É. Gilson, M. de Wulf, J. de Ghellinck, J. Koch, B. Geyer (d. 1974), and others. Retrospectively it may also be established that these entirely solid investigations really required the chief energies of the theologians active in systematic theology, so that, apart from the exceptions mentioned, a stronger actualization of the Catholic world of faith and of dogma lying in the sphere of the possible did not occur. In this regard it was due to a preference for detailed research and to the deemphasis on summary presentations of theology and of the history of dogma that the knowledge from history was not used to its full extent for the historical understanding of dogma. A really historical understanding of dogma, as developed, of course with a one-sided aim, on the Protestant side by the triple constellation Harnack-Loofs-Seeberg, had not yet started in the Catholic theology of the 1930s. Nevertheless, the beginnings in this direction, which were made as early as the First World War with J. Tixeron[25] and were carried further in a continuing succession, must not be overlooked.

---

[24] Supported by similar aims was the work of the Dutchman, A. Janssens, *Leerboeken der dogmatica en der apologetica* (Antwerp 1925ff.); but also D. Feuling, *Katholische Glaubenslehre* (Salzburg 1937), and the "dogma for the laity" newly appearing in this day, as in the works of J. P. Junglas (1936) and L. von Rudloff, O.S.B. (1934, 5th ed. 1949).

[25] *Histoire des Dogmes* (Paris 1912-14, 11th ed. 1930). On the rise and development of the Catholic history of dogma cf. J. Beumer, "Theologie und Dogmengeschichte," *Bilanz der Theologie* III, 471–503; likewise the introduction of M. Schmaus to the new complete sketch undertaken after World War II: *Handbuch der Dogmengeschichte,* ed. by M. Schmaus, J. R. Geiselmann, H. Rahner, IV, 3: B. Poschmann, *Busse und Letzte Ölung* (Freiburg 1950), V–XI.

Historical awareness, becoming stronger, and interest in the development of dogma are especially attested by the then notable effort of the Spaniard, F. Marín-Sola, O.P. (d. 1932), concerning the homogeneous development of dogma,[26] in which, to be sure, it was not the history of dogma as such that was pursued but instead a fully worthwhile theory of the development of dogma was demonstrated with the aid of historical facts that were not always interpreted in a manner free of doubt.[27] Questions in the history of dogma were to experience a further stimulus on the eve of the definition of Mary's Assumption in 1950, when it was shown that the problem of the relation of revelation and history still needed some intellectual work within Catholic theology.[28]

On one point the fecundity of the encounter of historical research and interest in systematic theology appeared clearly in the period before the First World War, and also afterwards, namely, in the *mysterium* theory conceived by Odo Casel, O.S.B. (d. 1948), which pushed the theme of sacramental theology, then as highly regarded as the theme of the Church, into the foreground in an original way and gave occasion to a discussion of considerable intensity. The Maria Laach Benedictine, proceeding from the history of religion and literature, who felt obliged to the liturgical movement and its progress toward the originality and authenticity of liturgical life, interpreted the sacramental acts of the Church, especially the Eucharist, no longer in the sense of the Scholastic theory of *effectus,* according to which the believer received only effects from the saving deeds.[29] Instead, the saving act should make itself present, according to the new interpretation, which, however, sought support in Greek patristics, as such and in its being, of course *in mysterio,* that is, under the veil of symbols. Although this theory did not establish itself in its entirety because of the historical as well as the objective problems inherent in it, nevertheless it certainly contributed to the deepening of the Catholic understanding of the sacraments.[30] This contribution, still critically evaluated by Pius XII,[31]

[26] *L'évolution homogène du Dogma catholique,* 2 vols., 2d ed. (Fribourg 1924).

[27] Critical evaluation in H. Hammans, *Die neueren Erklärungen der Dogmenentwicklung* (Essen 1965), 147ff.

[28] On the development of Mariology cf. H. M. Köster, "Die Mariologie im 20. Jahrhundert," *Bilanz der Theologie* III, 126–47.

[29] Cf. the pertinent publications on the theme: "Die Messe als heilige Mysterienhandlung," *Bened. Monatsschrift* 5 (1923), 20–28, 97–104, 155–61; *Zur Idee der liturgischen Mysterienfeier* (Freiburg 1923).

[30] T. Filthaut, *Die Kontroverse über die Mysterienlehre* (Warendorf 1947) tells about the controversy down to 1947; cf. also B. Neunheuser, "Eucharistie in Mittelalter und Neuzeit," *Handbuch der Dogmengeschichte* IV/4b (Freiburg 1963), 64(literature), and A. Kolping, o. cit., 138f.

[31] Encyclical *Mediator Dei* of 1947 (*DS,* 3855).

but, on the contrary, regarded benevolently in its main features by the Second Vatican Council,[32] also offered certain points of departure for the ecumenical dialogue, which was at that time accepted only with hesitation by systematic Catholic theology.[33]

In spite of this not lifeless or even stagnating condition of dogmatic theology before and immediately after the First World War, in contrast to modern pluralism it still supplied the image of inner compactness, which results not least from its unquestioned anchoring in the faith and from its positively understood ecclesiastical essence. In comparison, the new starts may be regarded as less radical and relatively trivial, and the connection with tradition may be found fault with. Nevertheless, it must be considered that especially the German theology and Church could oppose the dangers of Nazism in this basic outlook, which was also true of the especially threatened faculties of the Catholic universities. The picture supplied by the Protestant faculties was, with a few exceptions, much less favorable in this matter.

Many of these positive developments toward a more vital grasp of dogma and its interpretation in regard to salvation were, especially in Germany, interrupted or ended by the catastrophe of the Second World War. A new beginning took place especially in France, where the characteristic spirituality and the speculative strength had already been concerned with questions of the basic position of systematic theology and in this connection had come to a criticism of the scientific deductive theology of the past.[34] These tendencies took shape in the works of a group of theologians, to which belonged, among others, H. Bouillard, H. de Lubac, J. Daniélou, and Y. Congar, all lumped together under the pretty colorless designation of the "Nouvelle Théologie." What was characteristic of these efforts did not appear prominently under this label, namely, the attempt to orient theology again more definitely to the biblical-patristic tradition, but in the horizon of modern thought and its *desiderata*. Thus the origin of this trend of theological interest was connected not coincidentally with the appearance of a new edition of the Church Fathers, *Sources chrétiennes*, which intended to make fruitful for modern thought the ancient wealth of the tradition of the faith and thereby, contrary to the narrowly

---

[32] *Sacrosanctum Concilium*, no. 104.

[33] Ecumenical theology also developed in this period, at first only in particular initiatives—A. Rademacher, P. Simon, R. Grosche, O. Karrer, H. Urs von Balthasar—and outside systematic theology—M. Laros, M. J. Metzger.

[34] Thus already in M. D. Chenu, *Une école de théologie* (Le Saulchoir 1937), and L. Charlier, *Essai sur le problème théologique* (Thuilles 1938). Both works were put on the Index on 6 February 1942.

oriented Scholastic theology, to emphasize again Augustinian theology and the Greek universalism of salvation of Origen, using the paradigmatic guiding principle of H. Bouillard: "A theology which would not be timely would be a false theology." The means employed in this regard of a spiritual exegesis, a personalist concept of the truth of faith and its "historical" interpretation, and an option for a certain diversity in theology must have seemed dangerous to the representatives of a strictly oriented Thomistic theology of essence.[35] In their not always entirely objective criticism they dealt more with the ever present possibilities for false conclusions, for example, a making of grace immanent, a raising of dogma to evolution, a relativism of the knowledge of truth, than with really present failings and distortions. Hence the suspicion of a resurgence of Modernism was unjustified. Nevertheless, Pius XII was induced in the encyclical *Humani generis* of 1950, without mentioning this theological trend,[36] to point to the mistaken tendencies which were found not so much in the original initiators of this movement as in some of its one-sided interpreters. The encyclical neither intended nor produced a limiting of theological research or a stagnation of theological development. But it exposed a process of theological ferment, which, because of the concentration of dogmatic theology on Mariology in the years before and after the definition of Mary's Assumption in 1950,[37] had not yet entered the general awareness. This process was marked by a deeper reflection of systematic theology on the authenticity of mankind, the Church, and theology,[38] on the related problems of hermeneutics,[39] on the doctrine of evolution[40] just brought to light by Teilhard de Chardin (d. 1955) and his writings, hitherto known only fragmentarily, as well as on the urgency

[35] Then came sharp objections from Thomistic thinkers, such as R. Garrigou-Lagrange, "La nouvelle théologie où va-t-elle?" *Angelicum* 23 (1946), 126–45, 24 (1947), 5–19, and M. Labourdelle, "La théologie et ses sources," *RThom* 46 (1946), 353–371, 47 (1947), 5–19.

[36] The Pope used the very expression in an address to the General Congregation of the Jesuits of September 1946.

[37] For this development cf. the explanations of H. M. Köster, "Die Mariologie im 20. Jahrhundert," *Bilanz der Theologie* III, 132.

[38] Dutch theologians now took part in this discussion to a greater extent, including E. Schillebeeckx in *Theologisch Woordenbock* I (1952); cf. also *Gesammelte Schriften* I (Mainz 1965); P. Schoonenberg, "Theologie in Selbstbesinnung," *Annalen van het Thiymgenootschapp* 44 (1956), 225ff.

[39] Cf. also the cooperative volume, *Fragen der Theologie,* ed. by J. Feiner, J. Trütsch, F. Böckle (Zurich and Cologne 1957).

[40] One of the first opinions in the German area is in T. Deman, "Französische Bemühungen um eine Erneuerung der Theologie," *ThRev* 46 (1950), 61ff.

of ecumenical efforts[41] and the problems of the concern with a secularized world at the "end of the new age."[42] The results of the posing of these critical questions were entirely positive in the material as well as in the formal: historical thought dared to draw near to outlines of salvation history and history of theology;[43] the long treated theme of the Church, which had been discussed in the encyclical *Mystici Corporis* especially under the mystical-organological and hierarchical aspect, was expanded into the dimension of the communitarian, in which also the lay element played a stronger role;[44] in Christology, which was stimulated and enriched by the confrontation with Déodat de Basly's (d. 1937) doctrine oriented in Scotism, the interest in the manhood and the humanity, the *psychologia,* of Christ was prominent.[45] A special significance, which until the present has experienced no diminution, was gained by the theme of the relations of "nature and grace,"[46] again brought into discussion by H. de Lubac; in its solution the concept of the unity of creation and redemption, of the worldly and the Christian, of the immanence and the transcendence of the divine, must be distinguished.

All these profound problems of systematic theology were discussed with a sharpened consciousness and answered throughout in the sense less of "supranaturalistic" and "extrinsic" ideas and models. Hence it probably did not entirely do the situation justice when, around the mid-1950s, it was said that "the dogma of today [is] very orthodox but not

---

[41] H. Urs von Balthasar, *K. Barth* (Cologne 1950); H. Fries, *Bultmann, Barth und die katholische Theologie* (Stuttgart 1950); O. Karrer, *Um die Einheit der Christen. Die Petrusfrage* (Frankfurt 1953).

[42] Thus the stimulating book of R. Guardini (Basel 1950).

[43] Important contributions to this were made by, among others, J. Pieper, *Über das Ende der Zeit* (Munich 1950); H. Urs von Balthasar, *Theologie der Geschichte,* 3d ed. (Einsiedeln 1959); H. Rahner, "Grundzüge katholischer Geschichtstheologie," *StdZ* 140 (1947), 408–27; H. de Lubac, *Histoire et Esprit. L'Intelligence de l'écriture d'après Origène* (Paris 1950); J. Daniélou, *Das Geheimnis vom Kommen des Herrn* (Frankfurt 1951).

[44] Among others, by H. de Lubac, *Katholizismus als Gemeinschaft* (Einsiedeln and Cologne 1943); *Betrachtung über die Kirche* (Graz 1954). Previously, in Germany M. D. Koster, *Ekklesiologie im Werden* (Paderborn 1940), had indicated the necessarily appearing anterior placement of the "People of God," of the salvation collectivity, before the individualistic salvation personalism.

[45] This appears clearly in the cooperative work of A. Grillmeier and H. Bacht, eds., *Das Konzil von Chalkedon,* 3 vols. (Würzburg 1951–54); cf. here especially J. Ternus, "Das Seelen- und Bewusstseinsleben Jesu. Problemgeschichtlich-systematische Untersuchung," III, 81–237.

[46] H. de Lubac, *Surnatural. Études historiques* (Paris 1946), and "Le mystère du surnatural," *RSR* 37 (1949), 80–121.

very alive."[47] But perhaps at the basis of this verdict lay the right instinct that a thorough basic concept and a comprehensive systematic overview were missing from the deepened posing of questions and intellectual efforts. And so K. Rahner outlined at this time the new program of a dogmatic theology of salvation history,[48] the implementation of which, of course, was taken up only later.[49] But as regards this theology's claim to orthodoxy, it hit upon a positive state of affairs in so far as theology after the Second World War, despite the totally different kinds of beginnings and trends of interest, still worked from a strongly developed awareness of the obligation to the common tradition and its inalienable content. This appeared especially clearly in connection with the confrontation and adaptation of the program of demythologizing developed by R. Bultmann, which especially affected Christology. The reply, given to this program, for example, by J. R. Geiselmann in his book on Christ,[50] was established by a profoundly biblical as well as by a hermeneutically acute historical thought, which, however, was not subject to a philosophical option of "authenticity," in which the objective salvation history was condensed with its alleged meaning to the *punctum mathematicum* of the existential faith decision and of the subjectivistic *pro me*. Here "authenticity" was understood not without the reality of real history and its transmission in the tradition of the Church. Characteristically, in theology on the eve of the Second Vatican Council the theme "Scripture and Tradition"[51] was again taken up and, with the abandonment of the unorganic "Two-Sources Theory," led towards a unified concept, which was thus adopted by the council.[52] Only in this state of affairs can it be considered that the council was determined by the spirit and content of the theology preceding it. Therefore, in relation to the dogmatic motive, the question "Who determined the theology of the council?" can be answered by a competent representative of the theology following the First World War: "An intensive work . . . for a good thirty years."[53] But it may also be added that in dogma the council neither would nor could go beyond the results of this work.

[47] K. Rahner, *Über den Versuch eines Aufrisses der Dogmatik: Schriften zur Theologie* I (Einsiedeln 1954), 22.
[48] Ibid., 29–47.
[49] *Mysterium Salutis. Die Grundlagen heilsgeschichtlicher Dogmatik,* ed. by J. Feiner and M. Löhrer, I (Einsiedeln, Zurich and Cologne 1965).
[50] *Jesus der Christus* (Stuttgart 1951).
[51] Cf. the cooperative work with the report of the first meeting of the working community of Catholic dogmatic and fundamental theologians in 1956 at Königstein: *Die mündliche Überlieferung,* ed. by M. Schmaus (Munich 1957).
[52] *Dei Verbum,* no. 9.
[53] Y. Congar, *Situation und Aufgabe der Theologie heute* (Paderborn 1971), 31.

The "Theological" Deepening of Moral Theology

The intellectual movements appearing after the First World War changed also the figure of moral theology, even if the development here proceeded only slowly, which had its reason in the fact that the appearing Catholic moral teaching, especially exposed to modern philosophical ethics and to pugnacious cultural Protestantism, had more strongly to guard against attacks which were forcing it to tenacity and determined it to a certain integralist attitude.[54] Characteristic of the situation at the beginning of the century were the attacks of the Marburg Protestant systematizer, W. Herrmann (d. 1922), R. Bultmann's teacher, against the inflexible Catholic precept morality, which allegedly stifled the moral sentiment, and the Catholic reply from the pen of the Lucerne theologian A. Meyenberg (d. 1934), entitled *Die katholische Moral als Angeklagte* ("Catholic Morality as the Accused").[55] Thus it goes without saying that the presentations of moral theology partly assumed an apologetic character and in spite of their solidity and intellectual clarity—as seen for example in J. Mausbach's repeatedly published *Die katholische Moraltheologie und ihre Gegner* ("Catholic Morality and Its Opponents")[56]—were unable to achieve a positive adjustment to the spirit of the age. Still, at this time individual representatives of this field took the podium to promote a new orientation of their science with a disregard for its legalistic and casuistic traits. In favor of the still present awareness of the unity of ethical and dogmatic theology was especially the proposal of A. Müller, who, followed M. J. Scheeben's idea of grace, pleaded for a "theological morality" which should be based on the mystery of the faith and on the reality of grace.[57] J. Mausbach, in an opinion significant for the history of the time, sought to reduce,[58] around the turn of the century, the tensions arising in regard to the reform of moral theology: in it was even sounded the demand that "the moral norm must accommodate [itself] in accord with nature to the essential changes which the development of humanity and of nature brings." Of course, this should

---

[54] Cf. J. Ziegler, "Moraltheologie im 20. Jahrhundert," *Bilanz der Theologie* III, 316–60, especially 319ff.; E. Hirschbach, *Die Entwicklung der Moraltheologie im deutschen Sprachgebiet seit der Jahrhundertwende* (Klosterneuburg 1959); P. Hadrossek, *Die Bedeutung des Systemgedankens für die Moraltheologie in Deutschland seit der Thomasrenaissance* (Munich 1950).

[55] Lucerne 1901.

[56] Cologne 1901, 5th ed. 1921.

[57] A. Müller, "Ist die katholische Moral reformbedürftig? *Katholik* (1901), II, 346ff., 402ff.

[58] The most recent suggestions for reform of moral theology and criticism of them in *ThRev* 1 (1902), 1–8, 41–46.

take place only with the means supplied by Thomistic philosophy and the *philosophia perennis*. Nevertheless, the *Catholic Moral Theology*[59] conceived by him was a progressive step in the sense that it did not develop a pure teaching of precepts but a doctrine of virtue which was directed to the loftiest principle of the honor of God and to the principle of the perfection of being. True, the speculative orientation and penetration also sought stronger support in biblical doctrine, without, however, more deeply fathoming this, in accord with the contemporary situation of the use of the Bible in systematic theology.

There also came to light in O. Schilling, professor at Tübingen, and his *Moraltheologie,*[60] not without influence from the Tübingen tradition, the endeavor to develop moral theology from a supernatural beginning, which he found in the principle of *caritas*. However, in regard to content he remained extensively indebted to Thomas Aquinas and Alphonsus Liguori. On the other hand, the strong regard for the socioethical aspect presented something relatively new.

The fact is that these new starts from the German sphere, in which as early as the nineteenth century a relatively unique "German type" of presenting moral theology had been developed by J. M. Sailer and J. B. Hirscher, were at first not further elaborated, and dominance lay in the still existing preponderance of the "Roman type" of moral theology, which in the manuals and texts of H. Noldin,[61] B. Merkelbach,[62] D. M. Prümmer,[63] and others asserted its influence in the direction of a doctrine of duties, often oriented to the Decalogue, with a strongly juridical and casuistic element. Since these works were widespread in the French area, despite the different method of Saint-Sulpice,[64] directed more to practical use in pastoral care, and in the Anglo-Saxon linguistic sphere, the renewal trends could be established only with difficulty. The additional pragmatic viewpoint in this sphere was especially extremely prominent in the moral manual of T. Slater (d. 1928), who declared in the introduction: "Manuals of moral theology are technical works . . . just as the texts of the lawyer and the physician . . . . They deal with what is duty under penalty of sin. They are books of moral pathology."[65]

---

[59] Münster 1915–1918, 3 vols., and later.
[60] Münster 1922, 2d ed. 1949.
[61] *Summa theologiae moralis,* 3 vols. (Innsbruck 1901–02, 30th ed. 1952).
[62] *Summa theologiae moralis ad mentem D. Thomae et ad normam iuris novi,* 3 vols. (Paris 1930–33, 10th ed. 1959).
[63] *Manuale Theologiae moralis secundum principia S. Thomae,* 3 vols. (Freiburg 1915, 15th ed. 1961).
[64] Cf. J. Ziegler, op. cit., 325.
[65] Ibid., 325.

In view of such lack of appreciation, of course not too generalizing, of the deeper concern of moral theology, it goes without saying that in the 1930s the call for a new basis of the "theological character" of moral theology became ever stronger. The affirmative answer which now soon came to it was inspired by the spirit of the newly appearing biblical thought, which at that time created in moral theology an even more vigorous expression than in contemporary dogmatic theology. This changed attitude underwent an imposing formation in the five-volume *Handbuch der Katholischen Sittenlehre* of F. Tillman, which had its center in the "idea of the imitation of Christ" (Vol. III)[66] and its "realization" (Vol. IV).[67] By means of an extensive abandonment of casuistic and practical applications, which Tillmann assigned as legitimate functions to the texts of casuistic moral theology, there succeeded here a new type of supernatural foundation of Christian morality on the ethos of love and its being made concrete in the Sermon on the Mount. Not an excessive natural-material morality, but a supernatural motivation of Christian life on the person and work of Jesus stood here in the center of ethics, which thus advanced from the position of a morality of commands and prohibitions to one of a direction inspiring and forming life. Even if Tillmann did not succeed, in a more flat view and estimation of the evidence of Scripture, in taking soundings of the full depths and problems of the testimony of Scripture, still the theological fecundity of this effort cannot be doubted. Despite occasional criticism, such as that of O. Schilling, this draft was considerably acknowledged as a directional work, which, "as no other . . . contributed to extricating Catholic moral theology as a science from a centuries-old rigidity."[68] The basing of moral theology on a biblical-theological foundation was also decisive for other efforts around this time, such as for F. Jürgensmeier[69] and E. Mersch,[70] who oriented the Christian ethos on the concept of the "Mystical Body." The theological deepening and intensification of the Christian ethos, which was achieved here through the tying of moral theology to exegesis, to ascetical,[71] and to dogmatic theology,[72] and which continued long after in the striving for a rightly

---

[66] Düsseldorf 1934, 4th ed. 1953.
[67] Düsseldorf 1935f., 4th ed. 1950–53.
[68] Thus the verdict in *Hochland* (1934); cf. also A. Kolping, op. cit., 175.
[69] *Der mystische Leib Christi als Grundprinzip der Aszetik,* 2d ed. (Paderborn 1933).
[70] *Morale et corps mystique* (Paris 1937).
[71] Cf. on this theme R. Egenter, "Über das Verhältnis von Moraltheologie und Aszetik," *Theologie in Geschichte und Gegenwart, Festschrift für M. Schmaus,* ed. by J. Auer and H. Volk (Munich 1957), 21–42.
[72] Among others, P. Delhaye reflected on this in "Dogme et morale. Autonomie et assistance mutuelle," *AnGr* 68 (1954), 27–40.

understood "dogmatic moral theology," to use a phrase of R. Egenter, was characteristically no hindrance to a widening of moral theology and its extension into the areas of the humanities. Tillmann's work had also laid the ground for this extension corresponding to the relation of moral theology to life and had supplied further stimulation; for here not only "the philosophical foundation of Catholic moral teaching"[73] was offered, but the "psychological bases"[74] were reflected and the "sociological bases" were considered.[75] In T. Müncker's moral-psychological contribution the results of psychoanalysis, hitherto still suspect in Catholic circles, were also included. The stronger relationship thereby reached with the "bordering questions," as W. Schöllgen puts it, and with the humanities was further developed after the Second World War by French, Dutch, and German theologians—M. Oraison, A. Snoeck, W. Heinen, R. Egenter—and promoted in newly appearing periodicals (*Arzt und Christ* [1954]).[76] In addition, the orientation, always to be made more profound, to revelation was not forgotten and, among other things, was fostered by the original attempt of J. Stelzenberger (d. 1972) to develop moral theology, with reference to J. B. Hirscher, as "the moral doctrine of the Kingship of God."[77] Noteworthy, however, was the continuing impact of Mausbach's more speculatively interested sketch, which G. Ermecke completed in a new edition as a "Christological synthesis."[78] A certain definitive bringing together of the various basic concepts was accomplished by B. Häring in his work, *Das Gesetz Christi,*[79] which succeeded in uniting the three normative principles—imitation of Christ, *caritas,* rule of God—in an excellent manner. Meanwhile, interest in the working out of the history of moral theology and its problems was reawakened and documented in publications rich in content.[80]

In view of the thoroughly positive state which moral theology achieved, by overcoming considerable resistance and a still thoroughly

---

[73] T. Steinbüchel, Vol. I (1938, 4th ed. 1951).

[74] T. Müncker, Vol. II (1934, 4th ed. 1953). Earlier L. Ruland, *Handbuch der praktischen Seelsorge,* 5 vols. (Münster 1930–40), had considered the practical importance of psychology and medicine in a new sort of intensity.

[75] W. Schöllgen, Vol. V (1953).

[76] Cf. also A. Niedermeyer, *Pastoralmedizinische Propädeutik. Einführung in die geistigen Grundlagen der Pastoral-Medizin und Pastoral-Hygiene* (Salzburg and Leipzig 1935).

[77] Paderborn 1953, 2d ed. 1965.

[78] Münster, 9th ed. 1953.

[79] Freiburg 1954.

[80] As examples may be mentioned O. Lottin, *Problèmes de Psychologie et de Moral au XIIe et XIIIe siècles* I–V (Louvain and Gembloux 1942–59), and the series edited by M. Müller, *Studien zur Geschichte der katholischen Moraltheologie* (Regensburg 1954–61).

disunited situation in the 1930s, it may seem astonishing that in the 1950s there also was heard talk of the "crisis of moral theology," which threatened to jeopardize again the firm position that had been obtained. J. Leclerc especially reproached the current moral doctrine and instruction with a lack of dynamism and enthusiastic force, too little regard for philosophy, failure to consider the world situation of Christianity, and no understanding of progress.[81] Here was evident something of that artificially nourished disquiet which, with the demand for a "complete transformation" of moral theology and a new beginning at zero, served an organic progress less. It thus happened that moral theology in the years before the Second Vatican Council became more eager for discussion and more stimulated by the resumption of the question of the principle of morality, by the questionable experiments of an existential and situation ethics,[82] against which the teaching authority had taken a stand in 1952 and 1956, but not unconditionally more fruitful. The council itself had not accepted such experimenting considerations, but had regard for the fundamental results of modern moral theology, as, for example, in relation to religious freedom, the relative autonomy of secular matters, the importance of service to the world, the organic articulation of the ends of marriage and a personal notion of marriage, which, however, partly in the question of methods of birth regulation did not disavow tradition and gave no room to subjectivism.[83]

In the total view of the process of development of moral theology in the period after the First World War the fact of the dissociation and autonomy of two new partial disciplines from the whole body must not remain unnoticed: the science of *caritas*, which of course grew out of practical theology, and that of Christian social doctrine and sociology. Above all, in the wake of the pioneering social encyclicals since Leo XIII, Christian social doctrine has won an increasing importance, which is borne by a work of research now lasting more than one generation.[84] Of course, considering the youthful status of this science and also the involvement of natural and supernatural rules in it, it cannot cause surprise that the questions of the proper subject and the function of Christian social teaching are still under discussion. The ideas are still confronted by a preeminently philosophical discipline, which makes use

---

[81] J. Leclercq, *Christliche Moral in der Krise der Zeit* (Einsiedeln 1954).
[82] The critical confrontation was made by, among others, D. von Hildebrand, *Wahre Sittlichkeit und Situationsethik* (Düsseldorf 1957).
[83] Cf. the pastoral constitution *Gaudium et spes*, especially no. 50.
[84] Information on the state of the research in R. Henning, "Christliche Gesellschaftslehre," *Bilanz der Theologie* III, 361–70.

of faith only as a clarifying auxiliary function, and a properly theological discipline, which proceeds from faith. And so "the dialogue on how the dignity of mankind, social justice, and ecclesiastical ministry *sub luce Evangelii* maintain and receive their claim, is certainly not at an end."[85]

FROM "APOLOGETICS" TO "FUNDAMENTAL THEOLOGY"

The modern striving for a deeper accessibility of the living, organic, and personal in the faith as well as in the understanding of the Church led also in the traditional apologetics to new accentuations, which ensued especially from the discussion of the different ways and methods of this relatively young theological discipline. A. Gardeil (d. 1931) declared that it was a "badly defined doctrine [whose] subject and method [presented] a problem for theologians."[86]

The development of this branch of theology in the twentieth century may best be understood if it is seen under the aspect of the religio-existential as well as of the theoretical scientific search for the more exact definition of the specific subject of this discipline and its total presentation.

While the impulses for the founding of Fundamental Theology came especially from Germany in the nineteenth century, with J. S. von Drey in 1853, the new orientation in the twentieth century was first suggested by French theologians, who sought to put the "proof of the credibility of Christianity" proper to this field on a new basis with reference to the increasingly more comprehensive modern experience of life. The traditional, purely objective, and "externally" arguing *demonstratio christiana* and *catholica* could no longer satisfy a foundation of faith that took into account the totality of the modern social, moral, and philosophical question.

Already at the end of the nineteenth century attempts were made to establish the so-called "Apologetics of Immanence" by F. Brunetière, L. Ollé-Laprune, and G. P. Fonsegrive, but M. Blondel (d. 1949) first enabled it to achieve a real breakthrough. Without wishing to deny the merits and importance of classical apologetics, Blondel aimed to deepen the inadequacy of a purely rational and positivist argumentation by attending to the subjectivity and transcendentality of human fulfillment (*L'action* [1893]).[87] This incentive to an "inner" apologetic involving subjective factors led, despite a first considerably disavowing attitude, to a spread of the scope of apologetics, to which A. Gardeil

[85] Ibid., 369.
[86] Cf. for what follows J. Schmitz, "Die Fundamentaltheologie im 20. Jahrhundert," *Bilanz der Theologie* II, 197–245, especially 200.
[87] A thorough assessment of Blondel's concern and its relevance to fundamental theology is offered by A. Kolping, *Fundamentaltheologie* I (Münster 1967), 60ff.

attributed, in addition to the strongly scientific proof of the credibility of the faith, a subjective practical foundation of faith. In addition, Gardeil called for an "apologetic theology," which should be developed as a self-reflection of supernatural theology on its epistemological bases. If the concept, which was again discussed also in Germany in a somewhat modified form in the 1950s, ultimately did not establish itself, still it consolidated the rising tendencies to the integration of "external" and "internal" apologetics and promoted the unity of rational credibility and the awaking of the inner willingness to believe. Later in Germany A. Lang especially followed this aim.[88] With the last mentioned element the importance of the supernatural, grace-filled motivation of faith moved to the foreground, as, parallel to the total concept of theology recommended in Germany by K. Eschweiler, the effort became noticeable to develop fundamental theology, or apologetics, also from a standpoint inside the faith, which of course brought it close to dogma and to a degree threatened to jeopardize its autonomy. Even authors coming from the older rational objectivating school concept, such as R. Garrigou-Lagrange[89] and J. Brinktrine,[90] felt an obligation to this tendency. But in them the separation between the supernatural motive of faith and natural credibility was so sharply marked that the strict demonstrability of natural credibility, and thereby of the rational scientific character of apologetics, was maintained, but an underground dualism continued.

M. Masure, building on the thought of R. Rousselot (d. 1915), opposed to this option, somewhat objectivistic and inclined to disintegration, an "inductive procedure," in which the external signs of credibility were to be opened up as a result of their invisible importance and their supernatural value.[91] In this regard the moral disposition of the subject and the influence of grace are appraised with full importance for the origin of the assent to faith, which in this "Apologetics of the Sign" was also made powerfully dependent on the community of faith, as well as of believers, that is, on a social character.

These "stimuli" to the development of an "integral apologetics" and its orientation to the personal reality of mankind by B. Welte enjoyed in Germany general assent and only occasionally encountered criticism.[92] Nevertheless in the textbook literature of T. Specht, H. Dieckmann, J.

[88] *Fundamentaltheologie,* 2 vols. (Munich 1954).
[89] *De revelatione ab Ecclesia proposita* (Rome 1918, 5th ed. 1950).
[90] *Fundamentaltheologie. Offenbarung und Kirche,* 2 vols. (Paderborn 1938, 2d ed. 1947–49).
[91] *La grande route apologétique* (Paris 1939).
[92] Thus in E. Seiterich, *Wege der Glaubensbegründung nach der sogenannten Immanenzapologetik* (Freiburg 1938).

Brunsmann, and H. Straubinger the old outlines retained the upper hand; they were more obliged to the "Romance form" of apologetics, as opposed to the "German form," which also had regard for the philosophy of religion. Thus at first the new impulses made an impact rather in individual presentations, which appealed, among other things, to the act of faith and the miracle, both of which were more strictly involved in the sphere of influence of the grace of faith.[93] This tendency, as already indicated, approached the apologetics of dogma and its method, but also evoked new attempts to define the place and proper justification of this discipline.

These exertions became even more prominent in Germany after the Second World War. They were, first, conditioned by the crisis of faith, coming more sharply into awareness, and the "new profile of the unbeliever,"[94] on which especially fundamental theology had to take a stand; but were also caused by a deeper scientific theoretical awareness of the problem, which was likewise made keener by the situation of the time.[95] Here they first led to a sharper theoretical differentiation within this discipline, which was expressed in the distinction between "apologetics" and "fundamental theology." The term "fundamental theology," ever more establishing itself in place of the defensive-appearing term "apologetics," was to be understood as a self-reflection, immanent in the faith, on the motive of one's own faith, according to H. Lais, and separated from the "apologetics" directed to the unbelievers and proving the "credibility of faith." But at the same time the idea of "fundamental" experienced a new orientation in the progress of modern reliance on science, while it was brought to the meaning of an investigation of foundations, a theological methodology or epistemology. Thus "fundamental theology" was conceived as "theological basic science" after a sort of theological doctrine of principles, which should elaborate and reflect the material as well as the formal principles of theology.[96] A still greater expansion was experienced by the concept of "fundamental," and hence the assigning of the functions of fundamental theology, in K. Rahner, who joined "fundamental theology" with a previous "formal" theology and sought to develop the former as the phenomenology of religions and of Christianity with its

---

[93] Cf. also, among others, H. Lang. *Die Lehre des heiligen Thomas von Aquin von der Gewissheit des übernatürlichen Glaubens* (Augsburg 1929); K. Adam, "Vom angeblichen Zirkel im katholischen Lehrsystem und von dem einen Weg der Theologie," *WiWei* 6(1939), 1–25.

[94] Cf. also A. Kolping, *Katholische Theologie gestern und heute,* 221ff.

[95] On this more thoroughly C. Geffré, "Die neuere Geschichte der Fundamentaltheologie," *Concilium* 5(1969), 418–29.

[96] Thus especially G. Söhngen, "Fundamentaltheologie," *LThK* IV, 452.

culmination in a theory on the "approach of the single to the true religion."[97] But in such an expansion the unity of the subject threatened to be lost again, for such a fundamental theology had the theological scientific theoretical concern common to all theological disciplines, whereas in content it had to be in conflict, as "philosophy of faith," with the philosophy of religion. Therefore these efforts were subject to a not unjustified criticism with regard to the distinction which existed between the foundation of faith and that of theology as a science, and which could be overlooked only to the injury of the clarity and stringency of this discipline.[98] Thus, basically the idea could not be refuted that the task of fundamental theology lay first in the foundation of the act of faith and in the motive of credibility.

This basic discussion, which was related also to the recently defined relationship of fundamental theology and apologetics,[99] would then as today, where the discussion has still not ended, have been able to awaken the impression that this discipline is in a crisis which affects its existence. As a matter of fact, this claim is still brought forward. However, it must not be overlooked that fundamental theology, despite this uncertainty, did not actually avoid the function of laying the foundation of faith and in this regard involved an abundance of new questions, which were proposed to it by the modern intellectual development. To these belonged, among others, the problems of hermeneutics, of the authenticity of revelation, of existential and transcendental philosophy, but also questions of ecumenism. The Second Vatican Council especially took up what remained of these exertions and sanctioned them in its historical concept of revelation and of its relation to mankind,[100] without thereby legitimizing the excessive tendencies of the "anthropocentric."

The Evolution of Historical Theology with the Aid of the Historicocritical Method

THE PROGRESS OF CHURCH HISTORY

Catholic church history, as research and teaching, achieved a high status already in the course of the nineteenth century and did not fall behind it in the twentieth. As early as the beginning of this century it became clear that the historicocritical method would be maintained still freer

---

[97] "Aufriss einer Dogmatik," *Schriften zur Theologie* I, 29–34.
[98] Thus, among others, A. Lang, I, 30. A. Kolping, *Fundamentaltheologie* I, 75ff., gives instructive information on the problem and its complications.
[99] Cf. also H. Lais, "Apologetik," *LThK* I, 723–28.
[100] For this proof is offered especially by the dogmatic constitution *Dei Verbum* and the pastoral constitution *Gaudium et spes*.

and more decisively than before. In this it was inevitable that the judgments on the ecclesiastical past were more strictly adapted to the assumptions of natural history and that they thereby became also more sober and severe. Symptomatic of this new beginning in the twentieth century can be considered L. Duchesne's (d. 1922) *Histoire ancienne de l'Église,*[101] which, because of his method and presentation, strictly in keeping with the history of religion, of the history of the origin of Christianity was put on the Index in 1912. The extremely positive verdict of A. von Harnack on this work proves[102] that Catholic Church historical investigation was no longer inferior to the Protestant in form but probably permitted the conclusion that in this case it had not yet surely taken the "theological" direction. The attitude of the thoroughly critical S. Merkle (d. 1945) is to be characterized here as more appropriate; it appeared, for example, in its different evaluation of the Enlightenment philosophy,[103] although at that time this did not find general acceptance in the Catholic world. Such expressions of a critical awareness were as little to be attributed to Modernism as the initiatives of A. Ehrhard (d. 1940), working in all areas of church history, who gave to this discipline some stimulation toward its actual and cultural-determinant interpretation. Thus it happened not by chance that out of this historical thought flowed also impulses for the new shape of the Church in modern times, which appeared, among other places, in the much discussed *Catholicism and the Twentieth Century in the Light of the Church's Development in the New Age* (1901). The perspectives offered here for a meeting of Church and secular world could still be termed modern today, but of course they also display the limits set for all concepts and prognoses gathered from history; for, of the two conditions there named for a meeting between Church and world—turning of *modern thought* away from anti-Christian prejudices, turning of *the Church* from an absolutizing of the Middle Ages—the second has indeed been fulfilled in a not always easy development, but not the first, as the appearance of the great movements of apostasy in the first third of the twentieth century shows.

The élan and the interest in intellectual and cultural history which a church history thus oriented showed at the beginning of the century in its representatives, was, it is true, slowed but not entirely suppressed by the Modernist controversy and the catastrophe of the First World War, which brought disillusionment to optimistic cultural thought. It was

---

[101] Three vols. (Paris 1906–10 and later); cf. *Mons. Duchesne et son temps* (Rome 1975).
[102] Cf. also G. Denzler, "Kirchengeschichte als theologische Wissenschaft," *Bilanz der Theologie* III, 458.
[103] *Die katholische Beurteilung des Aufklärungszeitalters* (Berlin 1909); to the contrary, A. Rösch, *Ein neuer Historiker der Aufklärung* (Essen 1909).

only natural that after the end of the war the perspectives in ideas should be de-emphasized and a calm research should appear predominant, with historians of all nations participating. It included and expanded all areas of church historiography: archeology, with J. Wilpert (d. 1940) and J. P. Kirsch (d. 1941); ancient church history and patrology, with F. J. Dölger (d. 1940) and B. Altaner (d. 1958); the Middle Ages, modern times, and hagiography, with H. Delehaye (d. 1941) and P. Peeters (d. 1950); the new history of the missions, with J. Schmidlin (d. 1944); and the especially assiduously cultivated history of the Popes, which, with L. von Pastor (d. 1928), J. Schmidlin, and F. X. Seppelt (d. 1956), posed an equivalent counterweight in this field to Protestant research. A special significance because of its affinity to a deeply felt concern of the age was acquired by the investigations of A. Baumstark (d. 1948) and C. Mohlberg (d. 1963) in the history of liturgy, the results of which indicated the way to the liturgical movement.

The intensification of the work of research could not remain without an impact on the exterior organization of the research profession. And so in the course of this widespread activity there came about a recent specialization and separation of individual fields, such as iconography and folklore. On university faculties there resulted, for the same reasons, a dichotomy of the spheres of work and the professorial chairs—ancient church history/patrology, history of the Middle Ages and of modern times—which after the Second World War was followed in some places by still further divisions, such as the church history of a nation.

The works mentioned extended not only to the fundamental investigation of the sources and their editing, in regard to which Catholic researchers in a masterful fashion made their own the precision of the historical method, as, for example, H. Denifle (d. 1905), F. Ehrle (d. 1934), and F. Stegmüller; they proceeded likewise to a comprehensive opening up of new auxiliary means through encyclopedias, lexica, and publication agencies, such as T. Klauser's *Reallexikon für Antike und Christentum* and Hefele-Leclercq's *Dictionnaire d'archéologie chrétienne et de liturgie* (1924–53); but they also produced new total presentations of church history and likewise more detailed particular presentations elaborated with a new type of hermeneutical understanding. This is true especially of the research in the German sphere, which was still in touch with the roots of historical thought in the nineteenth century. Hence its interests went also to the working out of the historical details, of the specific and organic, while the work in the Latin countries sphere was still interested chiefly in emphasizing the general and the universal. Thus are explained, among other things, the origin of works which revealed the deeper understanding of original Christianity in its specific peculiarity by F. J. Dölger (d. 1940), a new view of the history of the Reformation by J. Lortz, a deeper penetration of the history of the councils by G. Dumeige, H. Bacht, and H. Jedin, and the attempt at a presentation of church history according to the history of ideas.[104] These and like achievements, which had to have an impact on the teaching profession, produced for church history in the German university faculties a leading position which for a time seemed to surpass dogmatic theology, especially when this was taught according to the Neo-Scholastic textbooks. Thus in retrospect it can be ascertained that Catholic church history not only exploited the favor of the spirit of the age, which was unlocked for historical thought, but, conversely, promoted and positively determined this inclination. In this connection, this discipline, which at the beginning of the century had still awakened the suspicions of the ecclesiasitcal *magisterium,* proved itself, in its solidity and objectivity, more and more to be the support of Catholic thought. It was surely no accident that the most striking and effective replies to the Nazi ideology in Germany were given by historians, such as W. Neuss's *Antimythos,* in 1934.

On the whole, even after the Second World War church history retained this positive upward development. The tensions which appeared in the course of the preparation for the dogma of Mary's Assumption between positively oriented history and the different procedure of the justification of the faith resulted from the nature of the matter and were overcome without false dramatizing. In the course of the methodical self-reflection of theology the discussion of the theological character of church history was again taken up and understood by an emphatically theological idea in a salvation-history sense, as, to quote O. Köhler, "mediator between world history and salvation history." Nevertheless, it was to be perceived since the 1950s in the stage when "history" dissolved into "authenticity" and the intellectual orientation was preeminently to the present and future, that historical thought was pushed to the defensive,[105] which may be a reason for the current phenomena of disintegration in Christianity and Church.

OVERCOMING RESISTANCE TO THE HISTORICAL METHOD IN BIBLICAL SCHOLARSHIP

While in church history the historicocritical method ever more established itself from the beginning of the century and could be managed

---

[104] J. Lortz, *Geschichte der Kirche in ideengeschichtlicher Betrachtung,* 20th ed. (Münster 1932, 1959).

[105] Thus G. Denzler establishes: "The interest in church history, in fact in history in general, is slight today," in *Bilanz der Theologie* III, 464.

without hindrance in this field, clear limitations ensued for exegesis. In this regard the points of departure for a rise of this discipline were not the worst at the end of the nineteenth century, a situation to which especially the founding of the École biblique in Jerusalem by M. J. Lagrange in 1890 and the works published in the *Revue biblique* since 1892 and in *Études bibliques* since 1900 contributed decisively. The establishment of Catholic biblical criticism undertaken by Lagrange[106] was taken note of even in Germany, where it led, among other things, to the conception by F. von Hummelauer, S. J. (d. 1914), of the idea of an organic notion of inspiration ("economy of salvation") and to the generic historical classification of biblical primitive history, the "vision hypothesis."[107] The *Biblische Zeitschrift,* edited by J. Goettsberger and J. Sickenberger since 1903, worked also in the direction of this thoroughly moderate criticism. But a strongly conservative faction represented by L. Méchineau and L. Fonck opposed this *école large;* this group sought especially to emphasize the principle of fidelity to tradition in scriptural work. A mediation between the opposing forces was hindered by the condemnation of Modernism and of the liberalizing tendencies in the decrees against these emanating from the Biblical Commission in 1903. Although this ecclesiastical agency, like the Biblical Institute, also founded by Pius X in 1909, were intended per se for the positive advancement of scientific scriptural studies, at first they displayed a retarding influence on exegetical research within the Church, which thereupon turned partly to safe peripheral areas, such as textual criticism.

Thus it was not possible for Catholic exegesis to adopt without restriction the results of Protestant scriptural scholarship and the methods of literary criticism, of the comparative science of religion, of the history of tradition and form which lay at its basis. To be sure, it was in this way also spared the mistakes, appearing ever more clearly today, which pertained to the employment of this method, especially in the beginning, and its extreme use.[108] Much as one may occasionally complain that A. Loisy's (d. 1940) suggestions for the use of the historicocritical method were too seldom applied to Holy Scripture, still M. Blondel, here amazingly farsighted, recognized in his confrontation with Loisy that the historical absolutizing of this method could not do justice to Christianity, especially in the form of Catholic dogma,

---

[106] Of epoch-making impact here was especially *La méthode historique* (Paris 1903).

[107] F. von Hummelauer, *Exegetisches zur Inspirationsfrage* (Freiburg 1904).

[108] Cf. also, of course projected out of today's retrospect, the research of G. Maier, *Das Ende der historisch-kritischen Methode* (Munich 1974).

because it threatened finally to lead to a reduction of the whole natural-supernatural reality to the plane of naturalism and positivism.[109]

The tension here showing itself between history and dogmatic faith and the task implicit in it of mediating between exegesis and dogma, which would thereafter prove to be an essential motive force of Catholic theology in the first half of the twentieth century, could not yet be absorbed after the First World War by Catholic exegesis for the reasons given. Nevertheless, it by no means refused to have anything to do with the knowledge coming from Protestant scriptural scholarship, although the biblical encyclical *Spiritus Paraclitus* of Benedict XV in 1920 warned against "the novel methods of profane science." True, this opening of exegesis occurred in a cautious way, which especially bore fruit in the preferred fields of work of research into the history of the text and literary criticism. But the results found expression also in the respectable works of "introduction" to both the Old and the New Testament, which appeared, among other places, in the prudent adoption of the results of the criticism of the Pentateuch, of the clarification of the sources by J. Wellhausen (d. 1918) as well as in the genre research of H. Gunkel (d. 1932), but also in the Two-Sources Theory relating to the synoptic question.[110] Also the understanding of the history of the form of the Gospels, brought to light by K. L. Schmidt, M. Dibelius, and R. Bultmann around the turn from the second to the third decade, was recognized by Catholic exegesis—H. J. Vogels, M. Meinertz, J. Sickenberger, P. Benoit—in its positive aims and critically adopted.

If no real originality belonged to Catholic exegesis between the two world wars, in comparison to the Protestant, and its strength lay rather in historical-philological precision than in total theological plan, it in no way remained preoccupied in literary-critical and philological explanation. The exertion for a deepened and total view of Holy Scripture led also to first sketches of the genre, long cultivated in Protestantism, of "biblical theology," by F. Ceuppens, P. Heinisch, A. Lemonyer, F. Maier, O. Kuss, and F. Prat, even if these outlines at first, as a consequence of their attachment to the dogmatic tradition, preferred the systematic collective view to historical analysis and its problems.

---

[109] M. Blondel, *Histoire et dogma* (Paris 1904).

[110] As paradigmatic of this new type of introduction can be regarded: J. Nikel, *Grundriss der Einleitung in das Alte Testament* (Münster 1924); J. Goettsberger, *Einleitung in das Alte Testament* (Freiburg 1928): F. Vigouroux et al., *Manuel Biblique,* 14th ed. (Paris 1917, put on the Index); A. Wikenhauser, *Einleitung in das Neue Testament,* 5th ed. (Freiburg 1953, 1962); A. Robert and A. Tricot, *Initiation Biblique,* 3d ed. (Paris 1954); A. Robert and A. Feuillet, *Einleitung in die Heilige Schrift,* 2 vols., 2d ed. (Freiburg 1966).

Teaching on the university faculties and also work on the newly appearing biblical commentaries profited from this deeper theological penetration into the spirit and content of Holy Scripture. In addition to the strictly scientific and detailed commentaries, whose prototype was in France the commentary founded by M. J. Lagrange in *Études bibliques* from 1903 and in Germany the never completed *Handbuch zum Alten Testament,* edited by J. Nikel and A. Schulz from 1911 to 1933, there arose a relatively new genre of exegetical work in the form of the biblical explanations extending beyond the world of specialists, which were directed to a broader circle of readers and to the religiously educated laity.[111] These efforts were pushed further and made available even for practical preaching through biblical homiletic works—"Keppler School," F. Tillmann—to which, of course, the corresponding understanding was not offered among the parish clergy.

Still, these efforts remained precisely a proof of the interest in the Bible newly awakened by exegesis, as did also the Bible movement, which, recommended also by the Popes since Pius X, gained influence in various forms in all European countries—in Germany and elsewhere through the founding of the "Catholic Bible Work" in 1933, in Austria in close connection with the "Popular Liturgical Apostolate" of Pius Parsch.

It was probably a fruit of this positive development of the understanding of Scripture in Catholicism and of the method cultivated in the Pontifical Biblical Institute by Augustine Bea that the *magisterium* through Pius XII in the biblical encyclical *Divino afflante Spiritu* of 1943 proposed caution in regard to modern scriptural scientific methods and recommended to the exegetes to use "prudently" the auxiliary means offered by the modern sciences and to define precisely the literary genres. This official doctrinal pronouncement of the "Liberating Encyclical," often regarded as a breakthrough, was followed by similarly directed official pronouncements in the letter of the Biblical Commission to Cardinal Suhard in 1948[112] down to the instruction of the Papal Biblical Commission on "the historical truth of the Gospels" of 1964,[113] which on the one hand insisted on the "historical truth" of the Gospels, but on the other hand warned against the influx of philosophical and ideological prejudices in the operation of the historical method. At the same time it gave reason to think that

---

[111] To this belonged, among others, in Germany the *Bonner Bibel* (1912ff., 4th ed. 1931ff.); in Holland the commentary on the New Testament by J. Keuler (1935ff.).
[112] Cf. A. Kolping, op. cit., 260.
[113] R. Marlé, "Historische Methoden und theologische Probleme," *Bilanz der Theologie* II, 260.

the exegete must pursue his work not only as a responsible investigator but also as a believing theologian of the Church.

Exegesis used this freedom just granted to it with great élan, which found expression in newly conceived commentaries, such as the *Herder-Kommentar,* in fundamental investigations in biblical theology, as also in the "biblical dictionaries" indispensable for the deeper, comprehensive grasp of the deep layers—*Bibellexikon* of 1951, *Bibeltheologisches Wörterbuch* of 1950. Even if here and in general the breadth and originality of Protestant biblical scholarship, with its richer tradition, naturally could not be equalled, still a closing of the gap and an approximation to its format became evident. Thereby biblical scholarship also within Catholic theology advanced to a similar position, as befitted it in the sphere of Protestant theology. This resulted, for obvious reasons, in a stronger influence on the systematic disciplines, in relation to which exegesis gained a certain superiority after the Second World War.

For the relations of this discipline to dogma, as in general for its ecclesiastical and faith status, some problems had to ensue, which in the 1950s had not yet made an appearance. Thus it is noteworthy that Catholic biblical scholarship at this time exercised, it is true, caution, for example, in the effort to justify the new Marian dogma, but also did not deny the ecclesiastical position (consult, for example, the problem of the *ultimum fundamentum* of this doctrine in Scripture).[114] Even more attempted at this time was the building of a bridge to dogmatic theology and to the dogma proceeding from Scripture, as when, for example, the route from the New Testament to the doctrine of Chalcedon was shown to be legitimate,[115] a point of departure for the later dogma of original sin was acknowledged in Romans 5:12–19,[116] and in the New Testament precursors of ecclesiastical dogma were found in the presymbols.[117]

From this basic attitude must probably also be explained the fact that Catholic exegesis in the debate, advancing like an avalanche, over R. Bultmann's thesis on demythologization, did not abandon itself to the fashionable trend, but exercised a sensible and firmly

[114] This theme is taken up, among others, by A. Bea, "La sacra scritura 'ultimo fundamento' del domma dell'Assunzione," *CivCatt* 101 (1950), 547–61.
[115] Thus R. Schnackenburg, "Der Abstand der christologischen Aussagen des Neuen Testamentes vom chalkedonischen Bekenntnis nach der Deutung R. Bultmanns," *Chalkedon* III (1954), 675–93, especially 687.
[116] O. Kuss, *Der Römerbrief* I (Regensburg 1957), 273.
[117] H. Schlier, "Kerygma und Sophia. Zur neutestamentlichen Grundlegung des Dogmas," *Die Zeit der Kirche* (Freiburg 1956). The essay first appeared in 1950–51 in *Evangelische Theologie.*

fundamental criticism, which still did not underestimate what was positive in Bultmann's concern.[118] The Second Vatican Council recognized intact the results of the epochal upward development of Catholic exegesis since the Second World War and confirmed to this discipline its leading role within theological scholarship in a series of significant statements, as when it approved the application of literary criticism and the rules of modern hermeneutics,[119] when it placed the ecclesiastical *magisterium* as a ministerial function below the Word of God in Scripture,[120] and evaluated all of Scripture and its study as "soul of all theology."[121] Of course, the council also expressed the obligation of ecclesiastical scholarship to cling to the theological bases of exegesis according to faith, in the doctrine of inspiration,[122] in the identification of Scripture and God's Word,[123] and in the emphasis on tradition and Church as the ultimately binding courts of interpretation.[124] Of course these positive statements of the council could not completely develop and clarify the problem involved in them for the self-understanding of exegesis. The ever more clearly appearing effort of exegesis in the succeeding years, in connection with the nonobservance of the principles mentioned, to understand itself as the really basic theological science could not be of use to it for long, chiefly as the opposition, which came to light in the strongly divergent events, made itself noticed as a hindrance.

The Rise of Pastoral Theology to a Scientific Theological Discipline

THE INCREASED SIGNIFICANCE OF GENERAL (FUNDAMENTAL) PASTORAL THEOLOGY

The initiatives, which proceeded from the theology oriented to preaching and from the Bible and liturgical movements, could not remain without effect in the "pastoral care science," especially since these had come into prominence as early as the end of the nineteenth century through a certain flexibility and capacity for accommodation. As a visible sign of this may be regarded the differentiation, beginning

---

[118] Evaluation of the position of the exegesis in this controversy in K. Hollmann, *Existenz und Glaube. Entwicklung und Ergebnisse der Bultmann-Diskussion in der Katholischen Theologie* (Paderborn 1972), 40–79.

[119] *Dei Verbum*, 12.

[120] Ibid., 9.

[121] *Optatam Totius*, 16.

[122] *Dei Verbum*, 11.

[123] Ibid., 9.

[124] Ibid., 9, 10.

around the turn of the century, of pastoral theology into homiletics, catechetics, and liturgy, oriented to the Three Offices Doctrine.[125] Of course, this specialization was purchased with the disadvantage that now there was left for general pastoral theology only a relatively meagre space, which, provided with the colorless designation of "hodegetics," was filled out as regards content with a professional instruction for the pastor which engaged especially in practical directions for its official exercise. Such a "clerical" formal object not only excluded the relation to the entire community but even formally hindered a really scientific elaboration of this subject. And so it was actually taught more in the manner of a technique which should be practiced by the individual pastor on the individual believer than in the manner of a theological reflection. It required a long way until this "remnant" of a pastoral theology again developed to full stature, gained scholarly features, and also again displayed its integrating function relative to the separated partial disciplines.

In fact, the rise of pastoral theology from a practical instruction for the pastor for the individual care of his charges to a scientific theological discipline is one of the most positive advances of the history of theology in the first half of the twentieth century. It is self-evident that this progress was completed not uninfluenced by external factors—negative: pastoral and social distress of proletarianization, departure of the masses from the Church; positive: youth, Bible, and liturgical movements—but it still had its own origin in an inner theological area, namely, in the understanding of the significance of Church and community for the self-realization of the Christian in a world which was ever more alienated from the Christian faith.

The actions initiated in the non-scientific area—Pius XI's Catholic Action in 1925; Workers' Movement of J. Cardijn in 1912 and H. Godin in 1943; Young Christian Workers, and so forth—were first expressed only sparingly in scholarly work, as, for example, V. Lithard's *Précis de Théologie Pastorale*[126] with its emphasis on Catholic Action, in G. Stocchiero's *Pratica Pastorale*[127] with its summons to the Church to turn to the world, and in C. Noppel's *Aedificatio Corporis Christi*[128] with the tendency to the inclusion of the laity into the hierarchical apostolate of the Church and to the notion of a care of souls supported by the community.

[125] Cf. also V. Schurr, "Pastoraltheologie im 20. Jahrhundert," *Bilanz der Theologie* III, 371.
[126] Paris 1929, 3d ed. 1941.
[127] Vicenza 1912, 5th ed. 1936.
[128] Freiburg 1937, 2d ed. 1949.

These impulses were increasingly accepted and scientifically investigated by L. Bopp in his *Zwischen Pastoraltheologie und Seelsorgewissenschaft,*[129] which also included the still suspect results of psychoanalysis in the circle of its reflections on pastoral theology. To a greater degree the knowledge of the human sciences, especially psychology and medicine, was included in this phase of development of the research into pastoral theology,[130] just as in moral theology.

But a really theological basic concept only established itself since the 1940s, when, not least on the basis of the utilization of historical knowledge rather than the previous route of pastoral scholarship since the Enlightenment, the proper goal of this science was recognized by F. X. Arnold as "the theological understanding of the pastorally operating Church and its types of activity." The basic theological idea, which C. Noppel had found in the then quite attractive concept of the Body of Christ, was here concretized into the "God-Man Principle." The deeper-lying intention went, on the one hand, to a departure from the anthropocentric narrowness of the pastoral theology of the Enlightenment, on the other hand to the pushing back of the guiding idea, felt as illegitimate, of the salvation-mediating Church, in contrast to which, with the "God-Man Principle" the "Divine Incommunicability" and direct relationship of all the work of salvation moved into the foreground, while only the character of a tool, of course of a personal sort, was acknowledged for the Church itself. In this definition of aim was really found a very fortunate synthesis of the contemporary concerns and movements in dogma, scriptural theology, liturgy, and history. The "unity of theology" here found once again a clear expression that could hardly be better achieved later.

In favor of the religious theology content of this basic pastoral start there speaks, among other things, the then appearing demand for a "care of souls from the altar," as J. Pascher calls it, which indeed set up a high ideal, but nevertheless was not perceived as a slogan and became quite effective in union with the liturgical incentives of the epoch.

Immediately before the beginning of the Second Vatican Council the scientific elaboration of fundamental pastoral theology achieved new progress with the publication of the *Handbuch der Pastoraltheologie.*[131] In it this discipline was emphatically developed out of the nature of the Church and the "theological analytics of the situation of the Church," to

[129] Munich 1937.
[130] As examples the periodical *Arzt und Seelsorger* (since 1925) and the works of A. Niedermeyer on pastoral medicine may serve.
[131] Edited by F. X. Arnold, K. Rahner, V. Schurr, L. M. Weber, and F. Klostermann, 4 vols. (Freiburg 1964–69).

quote K. Rahner, was defined as its basis. This ecclesiological concept appeared more comprehensive than the previously prevailing "God-Man" or personological foundation. It anticipated in much the results of the "Pastoral Council,"[132] as the Second Vatican understood itself, as, on the other hand, the council also sanctioned these results. Hence it is comprehensible if thereafter pastoral theology, borrowing an idea from Schleiermacher, understood itself as the "crown"[133] of theological scholarship. However, the postconciliar development seems to show also the dangers of this claim to exclusiveness, which are contained in it, namely, that theology as a whole is subject to practical ends.

THE CATECHETICAL RENEWAL

The new *theological* orientation with the utilization of general scholarly knowledge made itself especially noticeable positively also in the partial discipline of catechetics, which naturally had to find special attention in the age of a general awakening of youth and its own psychological assessment.[134] To be sure, in catechetics the textual analytical, deductive method of the improved Deharbe Catechism and its preference for the abstract rational presentation as well as its basically apologetic outlook still remained predominant. As an example the *Catechismus Catholicus* published by Cardinal Gasparri in 1930 can serve: in its narrow, theoretically doctrinally conceived manner it did not correspond to the new pedagogical, didactic, and religious psychological demands. Only in the 1930s, especially in Germany and France, did there begin a turning to the kerygmatic direction of presentation, which, following models of a period before Neo-Scholasticism—J.B. Hirscher and his "salvation history" orientation—after a not unproductive "controversy on method," sought a renewal on the bases of the newer theology, the Bible, preaching, and pedagogical understanding.

Here also the inspiring principle consisted in the synthesis of "religion and life,"[135] which could counteract the previous separation of teaching and life and the intellectualistic orientation of instruction. The "Munich Catechetical Method" of textual development in three formal

---

[132] For this the pastoral constitution *Gaudium et spes* must especially be regarded as fundamental.

[133] Thus V. Schurr, "Pastoraltheologie im 20. Jahrhundert," *Bilanz der Theologie* III, 375.

[134] These tendencies found expression in the work by E. Spranger, *Psychologie des Jugendalters* (Leipzig 1924, Heidelberg, 27th ed. 1963), which is esteemed and much read even in Catholic circles.

[135] Thus the title of the collection organized by G. Götzel of the Munich Catechetical Union (Munich 1922).

stages—presentation, explanation, stimulation—defined by H. Stieglitz (d. 1920), following O. Willmann, found, after initial resistance, acceptance in Germany as in most other European countries. But it was also fostered by stimulation from other areas, as by the Work School Principle, according to G. Kerschensteiner (d. 1932), which activated in a new way the peculiar activity of students and group instruction. By means of psychology and the philosophy of value the "principle of experience" also more strongly found admission into catechetical instruction, whereupon the formal stages were modified to the triad of value experience, value exposition, and value realization.

Also very significant were the initiatives which proceeded from Austria, specially interested in practical theology since the Josephinist reform. The *Religionsbüchlein* published by J. Pichler as early as 1913, with its wide extension into more than fifty languages, intended the turning away from the theoretical doctrine following in the wake of Neo-Scholasticism to personal proclamation of salvation and address. These efforts did not accomplish a formal breakthrough until the 1930s, when, following general pastoral theology, the establishing of a proper material kerygmatic and of a material-kerygmatic method occurred with M. Pfliegler and J. A. Jungmann. Here Christocentrism and the biblical foundation were elaborated in a new way to structural elements of religious instruction and of a "thematic didactic play method," which also facilitated a more intimate union between catechesis and biblical instruction. On the whole, in the course of this development catechetics reached the status of a special form of preaching, which not only proved the theological depth of this movement, but also gave evidence of the unbroken strength of the awareness of faith to introduce the aim of kerygmatics among school-pedagogical conditions.

Of course, this development would not have been thinkable without the stimulus coming from France, where since the separation of Church and state the necessity of the external as well as of the internal reform of religious instruction was especially pressing. But the realization of these aims did not occur until after the First World War—pastoral letter of Bishop A. Landrieux of Dijon in 1922—when the "Munich Method" was also accepted there, and the historicobiblical and salvation history orientation was then definitely set in motion. The *Catéchisme a l'usage des Diocèses de France* (1940, 2d ed. 1947), constructed on these foundations, first developed the types of a specific didactic play catechism with clear founding in Holy Scripture, with inclusion of the church year, with consideration of elements of a work of instruction, and with the purposeful orientation to the inner participation in prayer and in religious practice. The model work supplied decisive stimuli to the

Katholischer Katechismus der Bistümer Deutschlands, which after seventeen years of preparation was published in 1955 and by being translated into some thirty languages had a worldwide effect. Of course, soon after the Second Vatican Council it was regarded as no longer suited to the times, which could be less a judgment of its absent qualities than a sign of the quickly changing situation of the age, which catechetics was hardly able to follow with its outlines.

And so, after the Second Vatican Council there again broke out the controversy over method, ignited at the beginning of the century, in the wake of the manifold strivings for adaptation, but also with the rise of the principle of pluralism, which put the unity of catechetics as a science to the test. The move to existential anthropology, becoming effective thereafter, brought about not only a certain turning away from the kerygmatic and biblical orientation, considered as fundamentalist and biblicist, but also produced the danger of leveling catechetics as a kerygmatic communication of the truth of faith in favor of a purely school history of religious information and of a religious and moral offering. True, the Second Vatican Council acknowledged[136] catechetical instruction as the first means of help in the Church's task of educating, but it also clearly placed it in the "service of the Word,"[137] and did not inaugurate its narrowly existential or informative direction.

THE TURNING OF HOMILETICS TO KERYGMATICS

Following the rise of catechetics and in a certain parallelism to it, there also took place in homiletics an upward movement, which benefited from the stimulation of historical, biblical, and liturgical theology. The difficulties and problems of this ecclesiastical service to people of the mass-epoch and modern industrial society could not but be especially dramatically prominent in the Church's preaching ministry. The disparity between the expenditure of work here occurring and the visible success spread the impression of a "collapse" of preaching, which Benedict XV's encyclical on preaching, *Humani generis* (1917), appearing during the First World War, complained of without being able to oppose anything substantial to it. This lay not only in the unfavorable state of the times, which prevented a stronger echo of the papal doctrinal letter, but even more in the missing theological foundation of homiletics, which was more and more strongly dependent on the idea of a "theory of spiritual eloquence."[138] In this connection interest in preaching and the effort for its greater efficacy were not slight, as the

---

[136] *Gravissimum educationis,* 4.
[137] *Dei Verbum,* 25.
[138] Thus the title of a work, not unimportant in its day, by J. Jungmann, 2 vols. (Freiburg 1877, 4th ed. 1908).

growth of special periodicals,[139] of systematic instruction,[140] of practical means of assistance,[141] but also of more profound theological and spiritual guides[142] prove. The putting of these exertions into practice was done by a series of impressive preaching figures, such as Bishop P. W. Keppler (d. 1926), A. Donders (d. 1944), Cardinal Faulhaber (d. 1952), R. Guardini (d. 1968),[143] and others, whose activity, especially in the Germany of the Nazi era, did not remain without echo. If it also appears somewhat exaggerated to speak of this epoch beginning after the First World War as of an "age of homiletics,"[144] still on the whole a suitable estimation of the effort of this period is thereby given.

The novelty and central point of this effort is only appreciated, however, if one points to the biblical-theological foundation. Compared with the previous exertions of homiletics in regard to preaching, which were of a predominantly formal-rhetorical sort, though not without regard for the religious subject, there occurred at the end of the first third of this century in the framework of the development of fundamental pastoral theology also an application of the kerygmatic to preaching as its material and formal principle. From this principle was derived the joining of the content of preaching to Scripture, which led in practice to the rediscovery of the homily as the form directly modeled on the reading and interpretation of Scripture, but from it also derived in the formal realm the personal character of address, the authority of Christ lying in the Word, and the conviction of the quasi-sacramental efficacy of this Word in the believing hearer. In the theoretical elaboration of these theological bases the works of J. A. Jungmann[145] and others showed the way. In the practical application of these principles the explanations of preaching by F. Tillmann,[146] which were on a high level, accomplished much that was significant.

After the Second World War the theological basis of kerygmatics experienced also from the side of dogma a broad support and deepen-

---

[139] Cf., among others, *Kirche und Kanzel* (Paderborn 1918–43); *Chrysologus* (Paderborn 1860–1939).

[140] Thus, among others, F. Schubert, *Grundzüge der Homiletik,* 3d ed. (Graz 1934).

[141] To it belonged especially A. Koch, *Homiletisches Handbuch,* 12 vols. (Freiburg 1937ff.).

[142] Cf., among others, A. D. Sertillanges, *Verkünder des Wortes* (Salzburg 1936).

[143] Guardini's importance in this field was recently assessed by F. Wechsler, *Romano Guardini als Kerygmatiker* (Paderborn 1973).

[144] Thus V. Schurr, op. cit., 385.

[145] *Die Frohbotschaft und unsre Glaubensverkündigung* (Regensburg 1936).

[146] *Erklärung der sonntäglichen Evangelien* (Düsseldorf 1918, 8th ed. 1950); *Erklärungen zu den sonntäglichen Episteln* followed in 1921 and the 5th ed. in 1950, and *zu den festtäglichen Episteln und Evangelien* (1940, 2d ed. 1950).

ing in the development of a "Theology of the Word," which was conceived not without stimulation by the Protestant theology of the Word.[147] Also this meeting of homiletics and dogma may be regarded as an example for the awareness of unity of the theological disciplines, which was significant for the state of all of contemporary theology.

Of course, after the Second World War the inadequacies of this kerygmatic were felt, with the emergence of the notion of "radical authenticity" into theological thought—demythologizing—with the turn to philosophical-theological existentialism, and with the appearance of reflection on the phenomenon of secularization. They concerned not only the precritical, somewhat unhistorical previous exegetical justification—thus, for example, especially discernible in R. Guardini's interpretation of the life of Jesus in his attractive book *Der Herr*[148]—but also the authoritative address of this "kerygmatic" and its defective adaptation of the message to the one "addressed," who was no longer to be seen only as "object" of the address and also rather to be "met" in his secularized environment. But contrary to these critical objections, which became still stronger after the Second Vatican Council, although the council accepted and gathered together all these impulses in its sober attitude, it must be considered that the problems touched on in them were articulated but not solved. It even seems that the radical solutions—preaching as "information"; preaching as a form of a "political" theology—on the whole approximated rather a step back and a withdrawal from the center. All together, a glance backward to the homiletic and pastoral theological efforts of the period before the council could establish what generally holds good for the development of theology: the building of a bridge to the contemporary believer. Overall the mediation to the spirit of the age succeeded not badly and perhaps better than that of modern theology in its too pronounced and intentional striving for modernity and accommodation to the spirit of the time. As historical experience can teach, theological scholarship must not merely "straggle behind," it must also, to a certain extent, lead.

THE REESTABLISHMENT OF LITURGY AS "THEOLOGY OF WORSHIP"

Unquestionably the liturgy had the most extraordinary and for the outside observer the most visible rise in the first half of this century. It developed in this period from a peripheral theological science, which was still included by the constitution *Deus scientiarum Dominus* of 1931

---

[147] Cf., among others, O. Semmelroth, *Wirkendes Wort. Zur Theologie der Verkündigung* (Frankfurt 1962).

[148] *Betrachtungen über die Person und das Leben Jesu Christi* (Würzburg 1937, 13th ed. 1964).

among the auxiliary disciplines of theology,[149] to that of a necessary and important "principal subject," a position attributed to it by the Second Vatican Council.[150] In this connection the original incentives and impulses for this development characterizing modern Catholicism lay at first not in the purely scholarly sphere, even if scholarship after a certain starting time opened itself to the new awakened forces, regulated them, and influenced them in turn (see Chapter 9).

Stimulated by the liturgical movement, liturgical scholarship also displayed an activity of a new type, which now had as its subject no longer only historical work on the sources, which had been intensively under way since the turn of the century in the course of the growing interest in history.[151] Now ensued the widening and deepening of the work to a sort of "theology of worship," which was accomplished with the acceptance of the equally vigorous ecclesiological and sacramental thought in this period by the theological foundation of the pastoral-practical movement. Its aim was directed to raising the theological stock of ideas from the liturgical sources to the goal of their more profound exploration, but also to the fructification of the entire life of faith. Pius XII later gave to this aim the motto taken from tradition of the *lex supplicandi,* which is to determine the *lex credendi.*[152] In the course of this orientation there occurred considerations, pressing to the essential, on the "spirit of the liturgy,"[153] on the connection between "liturgy and the Kingdom of God,"[154] on the meaning of the Eucharist,[155] as well of the sacraments,[156] all of which contributed to the enrichment of dogmatic theology. Again the greatest significance for this intellectual foundation-laying was gained by the *mysterium* theory of

---

[149] This corresponded somewhat to its classification by the Code of Canon Law, Canon 1365, par. 2.

[150] *Sacrosanctum Concilium* 16.

[151] In the nature of examples for this matter are the works and editions, partly quoted in the church history survey, of A. Franz (d. 1916), *Die Messe im Deutschen Mittelalter* (Freiburg 1962); M. Férotin, *Liber Mozarabicus Sacramentorum* (Paris 1912); C. Mohlberg (d. 1963), *Liber Sacramentorum Romanae Ecclesiae Ordinis Anni Circuli* (Rome 1960); *Missale Gallicanum Vetus* (Rome 1958).

[152] Encyclical *Mediator Dei* (1947).

[153] R. Guardini, *Vom Geist der Liturgie* (Freiburg 1918, 19th ed. 1957); *Liturgische Bildung* (Rothenfels 1923).

[154] Cf. also J. Kramp, *Messliturgie und Gottesreich. Darlegung und Erklärung der kirchlichen Messformulare,* 3 vols (Freiburg 1921, 5th ed. 1922).

[155] The following may serve as examples for this liturgical-theological orientation: J. A. Jungmann, *Die liturgische Feier. Grundsätzliches über Formgesetze der Liturgie* (Regensburg 1939); J. Pascher, *Eucharistia. Gestalt und Vollzug* (Münster 1947).

[156] J. Pinsk, *Die sakramentale Welt* (Freiburg 1938).

O. Casel (d. 1948),[157] in the discussion of which the work was altogether motivated to the theological clarification of the Sacrifice of the Mass and of sacramental reality.[158] It was not least of all the process of theological deepening which obstructed an externalization of the aims, lying within the area of the possible, and which finally also paralyzed the fears and resistances to this movement, that occasionally increased enormously.[159] A clarification to be understood in the affirmative sense was finally produced by Pius XII's encyclical on the liturgy, *Mediator Dei* (1947), which by way of suggestion already made known the desire for reforms in liturgy, whereas the hitherto practical efforts in regard, for example, to Gregorian chant[160] and church music,[161] had operated rather in the sense of a restoration. The Pope introduced some significant reforms, including the approval of numerous rituals with vernacular texts and songs, the introduction of a new translation of the psalms, the *Psalterium Pianum,* but especially the renewal of the Holy Week and Easter Vigil Liturgies. The fact that these reforms were either prepared or accompanied by research,[162] ever more intensified after the Second World War, as well as by the work of the newly founded Liturgical Institute[163] and the liturgical congresses[164] produced for liturgical scholarship a theological importance which was highly esteemed by the Second Vatican Council. The council itself had multiplied the tasks of this discipline with its reforms, carried out or announced. But it could not be foreseen that it would be necessary for the liturgy in the era beginning after the council, when the liturgical

---

[157] In addition to the works cited in n. 30, special notice should be given to the parts of his literary remains that have been published of his planned "special life work": *Das christliche Opfermysterium. Zur Morphologie und Theologie des eucharistischen Hochgebetes,* ed. by V. Warnach (Graz, Vienna, and Cologne 1968).

[158] On the results to the end of World War II information is supplied by T. Filthaut, *Die Kontroverse über die Mysterienlehre* (Warendorf 1947).

[159] An expression of these fears and tensions is presented by the brochure of J. Kassiepe, *Irrwege und Umwege im Frömmigkeitsleben der Gegenwart* (Würzburg 1940).

[160] The reform of the chant obtained from Pius a new impetus through the motu proprio of 1904 and the decree of 29 April 1911.

[161] Cf. also the motu proprio on church music, *Tra le sollecitudini* of 22 November 1903.

[162] As examples the following may be referred to: J. A. Jungmann, *Missarum Sollemnia* (Vienna 1948, 5th ed. 1962); *Liturgisches Jahrbuch* (1950ff.); *La Maison-Dieu* (1945ff.); M. A. P. Schmidt, *Introductio in Liturgiam Occidentalem* (Rome, Freiburg, and Barcelona 1960); C. Vagaggini, *Il senso teologico della Liturgia* (Rome 1957); C. Floristan, *El año litúrgico,* 2d ed. (Barcelona 1966).

[163] In Germany: the Liturgisches Institut at Trier (since 1947); in France: the Centre de Pastorale Liturgique at Paris (since 1947); in Italy: the Centro di Azione Liturgica at Genoa (since 1947).

[164] Here may be named selectively: Frankfurt 1950; Munich 1955; Assisi 1956; Nijmegen 1959.

movement branched out and an at times excessive wave of experimenting and adapting followed it, to look back again rather at the "spirit
of the liturgy," as R. Guardini expressed it, and the theological bases of
its work as *Opus Dei*.

The formation and growth of liturgical scholarship, which was
intentionally placed here at the end of the first phase of the history
of theology in the first half of the twentieth century, can, it is true
not be taken as the supreme value for reaching a verdict on the
total development of the theology of this period, because naturally
a development does not proceed in all departments of knowledge
in the same way. Hence the entire verdict on this theological period
must also be more cautious. Nevertheless, it cannot be expressed
negatively: Measured by the standard of scholarship, the accomplishments of the historicocritical work of theology stand on no low
stage; in the systematic sphere the effort for a more vital grasping
and stating of the truths of faith was not to be underestimated,
even if great syntheses remained rare. As regards the claim of this
theology on the Church, it felt itself on the whole to be rather the
serving agent of the body of teachers and believers than as a critical
tribunal. And so its calls for reform were moderate and restrained,
although it was precisely in this moderation that they had their
effect in the Church and did not leave the faithful uninfluenced. As
regards this theology's ecumenical and world relations, the total attitude may often seem to the modern observer to be strongly intro-
verted, too self-centered, and too little open. True, the "bringing
back of the world"[165] was also its concern, which it intended to
realize not by means of external activities and proclamations but by
the interior way of penetration into the *mysterium* of salvation,
which remained the real object of its work. Surely there resulted
from this the danger of an imbalance of the "sapiential," "contemplative" factor to the detriment of direct and world-related action,
the limits of which it recognized in a certain sobriety. Here it was
more realistic than the enthusiastic optimism of an A. Ehrhard at
the beginning of the century, and under the impression of the
powers of wickedness that burst forth in two world wars it could
rightly be convinced that the modern world would never abandon
its aversion to Christianity. Nevertheless, this theology, with all its
limitations and boundaries, prepared the council of the "Church's
opening up to the world" and paved the way for it.

[165] Thus the title of a book by O. Bauhofer (Freiburg 193⁻), highly regarded in its day.

CHAPTER 9

Movements within the Church and Their Spirituality[*]

In the years following the First World War there ensued a series of new starts, indeed an extensive and profound renewal of religious and ecclesiastical life in Central Europe. The reasons for this are many-layered: first of all, the concentration and consolidation of church life in the nineteeth century under the guidance of Popes such as Pius IX, Leo XIII, and Pius X produced their fruit. Very different in character, style of leadership, and determination of goals, these Popes made their contribution each in his own way. What had long been regarded as dead proved to be alive. The experience of the war and of the collapse of a liberal, individualistic culture that believed in progress created a new openness to transcendence and the predetermined truths of revelation, as well as to the form of religious life in the ecclesial community. The philosopher Peter Wust (1884–1940) indicated the keyword, applicable also to other fields, with titles such as "resurrection of metaphysics" (1920) and "the return of German Catholicism from exile" (1924). The call of the age for the "spirit of the whole," as expressed by Julius Langbehn, the demand for the organically grown, for life as the genuinely real and creative against intellectualism and materialism, against isolation and uprooting, the turning to the original, to the sources, away from the manufactured, derived, and merely imagined were united with the new self-consciousness of awakened religious forces. These were expressed especially in the liturgical movement, the Bible movement, and the lay movement supported by a new awareness of the Church. But these were not currents moving parallel and to be separated from one another; rather, they influenced one another and supported one another. At first they affected smaller circles of academicians and youth in the associations of the Catholic youth movement, whereas the broad strata of the communities were further supported in their religious life by the forms of devotion characteristic of the nineteenth century: devotion to the Blessed Sacrament, to the Sacred Heart of Jesus, and to the Virgin-Mother Mary. But the development of the decades from 1920 to 1950 was noted for the fact that these more traditional forms of devotion were also affected by reflection on Holy Scripture, the theology of the Fathers, and the liturgy of the Church and the Christocentrism contained in it.

[*] Erwin Iserloh

The Liturgical Movement

The beginnings of the liturgical movement extend into the nineteenth century; they are related to the renewal of Benedictine monasticism. The Belgian abbey of Maredsous, founded in 1872 from Beuron, which had been established in 1863, in 1882 published a people's missal, the *Missel des Fidèles*. Anselm Schott (1845–96), who had lived at Maredsous during the temporary suppression of Beuron in the *Kulturkampf,* followed this example in 1884. By means of his *Mass Book* he aimed, as he said in the foreword, "to contribute a little so that the Church's rich treasure of prayer, which is set down in its sacred liturgy, may become more and more accessible and familiar to the faithful."

The impetus to the liturgical movement as a breakthrough of the laity to active participation in the Church's liturgy proceeded from Belgium. It had been preceded by the decrees of Pius X of 1903 and 1904 on the chant and of 1905 on frequent and early Communion. In keeping with his motto, "To unite all things in Christ," the Pope aspired to the renewal and consolidation of the Christian spirit of the faithful. "The first and indispensable source from which this spirit is drawn," so Pius X stressed in the motu proprio of 1903, "is the active participation of the faithful in the sacred mysteries and the public and solemn prayer of the Church."[1] A Benedictine of Mont César, Lambert Beauduin (d. 1960), was deeply affected by these ideas of the Pope. Before his entry into the monastery—he was professed in 1907—he had been a diocesan priest at Liége and had belonged to the "Labor Chaplains," a community of worker-priests. Accordingly, also as a monk he strove to work among the people by means of the liturgy, that is, to move out of the narrow framework of academic circles into the congregations. At the National Congress of Catholic Works, inaugurated by Cardinal Mercier, he demanded at Mechelen in 1909 that the missal itself should be disseminated as the prayerbook but at least that the complete text of the Mass and of Sunday vespers should be made available to the people in a vernacular translation. This congress became the "Mechelen Happening"[2] through the enthusiastic talk of a layman, the history professor Godefroid Kurth (d. 1916). In it he traced religious ignorance back to the still greater ignorance of the liturgy. He concluded thus: "Give to the faithful an understanding and, as a consequence, a love for the mysteries which they celebrate, give them the missal to use, and with it

---

[1] *ASS* 36 (1903–04), 388.
[2] B. Fischer, "Das 'Mechelner Ereignis' vom 23.9.1909," *LJ* 9 (1959), 203–19; E. Iserloh, "Die Geschichte der Liturgischen Bewegung," *Hirschberg* 12, (1959), 113–22, 115.

replace the many mediocre prayerbooks." An enthusiastic assent of the congress was given. A few weeks later there appeared in a large printing for Advent the first fascicle of *La vie liturgique,* a small booklet which provided the liturgical texts with the corresponding explanations.

In Germany the liturgical movement at first remained confined to academic circles. The spiritual leadership belonged to the abbey of Maria Laach under Abbot Ildefons Herwegen (1874–1946). In 1913 he celebrated Holy Week with a group of academicians—among them men such as the future Chancellor Heinrich Brüning and French Foreign Minister Robert Schuman[3]—and revealed to them the liturgy as source of piety. At Maria Laach in 1918 the first "community Mass" was celebrated as *Missa recitata* or, preferably, *dialogata.*

The Catholic youth, affected by the general German youth movement, first the Fountain of Youth under Romano Guardini, then the student movement New Germany, and finally the Association of Young Men and the Storm Band under Ludwig Wolker (1871–1955), enthusiastically adopted the new manner of celebrating the liturgy. In the liturgy these youth found a realization of their longing for community, for essential and authentic form, and for the embodiment of religion in "sacred signs." For their part they promoted the liturgical movement with their untroubled enthusiasm to victory against resistance and abuses as well as against theological hesitations. The spontaneously growing new liturgical practice was from the start accompanied and clarified by a theology which united strictly scientific, even historicoarchaeological investigation with proclamation and piety. Especially effective in the area of liturgical formation was Romano Guardini (1885–1968) with his *Vom Geist der Liturgie* (1918), *Liturgische Bildung* (1923), *Von heiligen Zeichen* (1927), and his scriptural-theological introduction, *Der Herr* (1937). He led to reading and reflection on Holy Scripture, but also encouraged that the world should be taken seriously and interpreted with the eyes of faith. From 1923 professor in Berlin of Philosophy of Religion and Catholic Worldview, he understood these as "the unity of that view which embraces the living reality of the world by faith."

The texts of the Ordinary of the Mass, published by the three communities mentioned for common prayer in the "Community Mass," give a picture of the growing liturgical and religious and pedagogical experience: The *Gemeinschaftliche Andacht zur Feier der heiligen Messe,* published by Guardini in 1920, provided the text of the Mass only with paraphrasing interpretive additions. The *Missa* composed in 1924 by Father Joseph Kramp (1886–1940) for the "Union of New Germany"

---

[3] R. Schuman, "Ein Blatt dankbarer Erinnerung," *LJ* 9 (1959), 194.

led to the praying aloud of the entire Mass from the prayers at the foot of the altar to the Last Gospel except for the canon, without making any distinction between the public prayers of the priest and the congregation and the private prayers of the priest. This booklet was an expression of the first excess of zeal in which people felt that the community nature of the Mass was expressed by the fact that all prayed everything, which threatened to lead to an empty, loud operation and supplied welcome material to critics. The *Kirchengebet* published in 1928 by Ludwig Wolker made the newer knowledge its own, especially in the later issues, and, in accord with the "High Mass Rule," asked which prayers belonged to the priest, the reader, and the congregation respectively, and which were to be prayed quietly. The translations of the *Kirchengebet,* which had a circulation of several million, were transformed into new editions of diocesan prayerbooks.

This route of the liturgical movement into the congregations was first taken in the German language area by the "Popular Liturgical Apostolate" of Klosterneuburg near Vienna under Pius Parsch (1884–1954). In his own publishing establishment he published the texts of the Sunday liturgy—25 million down to 1930—in order to "bring the Church's worship to the simple folk." He revealed the meaning of the liturgy for a new biblical piety in books such as *The Church's Year of Grace* (1923, 14th ed. 1952–58) in three volumes, *Lernt die Messe verstehen* (1931), and in the periodicals *Bibel und Liturgie* (1926ff.) and *Lebe mit der Kirche* (1928ff.).

"Popular liturgy and pastoral care" were also the supporting elements of the parish work of city pastors such as Georg Heinrich Hörle (1889–1942) at Frankfurt, Konrad Jacobs (1874–1931) at Mühlheim in the Ruhr, Joseph Könn (1876–1960) at Cologne, and of the Oratory of Saint Philip Neri, founded at Leipzig in 1930. Starting with the axiom that all participation has to take place in accord with the capabilities of the participant, there was sought a celebration of Mass and of the Liturgy of the Hours that would do justice to both the liturgy and the congregation. Thus there came about the "Prayed Sung Mass" and the "German High Mass," in which the texts were sung in melodies adapted to the German language, and priest, servers, choir, and congregation performed the parts of the liturgy proper to them.

With such a distribution of roles the danger of an activist industry was banned; in the liturgical happening there were periods when the individual, priest or member of the congregation listened quietly or silently sought union with the common action or assented to the effecting word of the priest. If liturgical piety meant extension of often narrow and egoistic prayer to the concerns of the Church, immersion in the movement through Christ in the Holy Spirit to the Father, it is still not a substitute for prayer in the "private room," that is, for the intimate encounter of the individual with God. Community prayer demanded that reflective "personal" prayer should not become a soulless idling. This integration of the public congregational prayer and the prayer of the individual has still not been fully achieved. This shows the difficulty of terminology. For the latter must not be "private," and the former must not be impersonal. It is not enough that one praying liturgically should lend only his lips to the Church for the praise of God. In the 1930s there were violent confrontations over this.

Exaggerations, narrow-mindedness, and wilfullness of overzealous circles from the liturgical movement led to anxious and passionate criticism, among other places, in the lively book of the popular missionary M. Kassiepe, *Irrwege und Umwege im Frömmigkeitsleben der Gegenwart* (1939), and in A. Doerner's *Sentire cum Ecclesia* (1941). But there was no "official short circuit," against which R. Guardini had warned in 1940 in his "Word on the Liturgical Question," a letter to Bishop Stohr. Instead, the conflicts led to the German bishops' taking up the liturgical efforts, and so the liturgical movement became the liturgical renewal directed by the Church's authority. In 1940 the Episcopal Conference formed the Liturgical Section under Bishops Albert Stohr and Simon Konrad Landersdorfer and a Liturgical Commission of experts in theory and practice. Their work led to the 1942 "Guidelines for the liturgical structure of the parochial liturgy."

A memorandum of Archbishop Konrad Gröber of Freiburg, which he submitted on 18 January 1943 to the Curia and his fellow-bishops,[4] threatened to lead to a new crisis. The seventeen points "giving occasion for uneasiness" were, among others: the imminent schism in the clergy, an "alarmingly flourishing mysticism of Christ" as a consequence of an exaggerated interpretation of the doctrine of the *Corpus Christi Mysticum,* the overstressing of the doctrine of the general priesthood, the "thesis of Meal-Sacrifice and Sacrificial Meal," the "overemphasis of the liturgical," the effort to make the congregational Mass obligatory, and the use of German in the Mass. "Can we German bishops," thus concluded Conrad Gröber, "and can Rome still keep silent?" This memorandum crossed a letter of Cardinal Secretary of State Maglione, which the chairman of the Episcopal Conference, Cardinal Bertram, received on 11 January 1943. In it there was complaint against

---

[4] T. Mass-Ewerd, *Die Krise der Liturgischen Bewegung in Deutschland. Studien zu den Auseinandersetzungen um die "Liturgische Frage" während des Zweiten Weltkriegs auf Grund bisher unveröffentlichter Dokumente* (Regensburg 1977); F. Kolbe, *Die Liturgische Bewegung* (Aschaffenburg 1964), 72–75.

encroachments by radical representatives of the liturgical movement, a report on them was demanded, and a series of proposals was made as to how the good in it could be fostered.

In the opinion of the West German bishops of 8 April 1943 to the Roman inquiry there was expressed how very much the celebration of the liturgy had become a source of strength in the age of National Socialism and of the war. "German Catholicism has been for ten years in abnormal circumstances. An activist young clergy and an equally activist Catholic youth that is enthusiastic for the faith see themselves more and more abruptly repressed on all sides. . . . Add to this, that it is of great importance to zealous young priests to give at least to the youth in the Church an awareness and experience of community, to bind them to the Church, and thereby to deepen and consolidate them in the faith."[5]

On 10 April 1943 Cardinal Bertram gave to Rome a comprehensive report on the origin of the liturgical movement, on the forms of congregational participation in Mass, including the German High Mass as a "sung Mass, joined with popular singing in German," and on the "defects and mistakes of the liturgical movement." An indirect position on the controverted questions was indicated as early as Pius XII's encyclical *Mystici corporis,* because in it the Pope acknowledged the understanding of the Church by the liturgical movement and termed the new understanding of the sacred liturgy the cause of a deeper consideration of the riches of Christ in the Church.

On 24 December 1943 Maglione made known the Roman decision to Cardinal Bertram. In it the religious and pastoral fruits of the liturgical movement were praised but a warning was lodged against arbitrary innovations, the desires made known by Bertram relative to the forms of Mass were granted, and work on a German ritual was encouraged. Finally, it was suggested to the bishops to take the leadership in hand. The final point of the Roman examination and the point of departure for the liturgical reform pursued by the Curia came in the encyclical on the sacred liturgy, *Mediator Dei,* of 20 November 1947. In it Pius XII made use of the keyword of "active and personal participation." The liturgy is "the public worship which our Redeemer, the Head of the Church, gives to the heavenly Father and which the community of believers offers to its Founder and through him to the eternal Father. . . . It displays the total public worship of the Mystical Body of Jesus Christ, namely, the Head and his members."[6]

A Roman commission was established in 1946–47 for the reform of the liturgical books. In the "Liturgical Institute" the German bishops

[5] T. Maas-Ewerd, loc. cit.
[6] *AAS* 39 (1947), 521–95, 528f.

created a work center at Trier. Corresponding institutions arose in other countries, such as the *Centre de pastorale liturgique* at Paris. In addition to liturgical congresses at Frankfurt in 1950, Munich in 1955, and Assisi in 1956, international study meetings took place. The Congregation of Rites approved the German ritual in 1950, in 1951 occurred the restoration of the Easter vigil, and in 1955 the renewal of all of Holy Week. The precept of the Eucharistic fast was greatly mitigated in 1953 and 1957 and thereby the way for the general permission for evening Mass was opened. Even after the announcement of the council and although the general reform of the liturgy was reserved to it, in 1960 a reform of the rubrics of breviary and Mass was decreed. It produced a simplification and served the real and meaningful performance of the rites and prayers. All these preliminary activities make it understandable that at the council the "Constitution on the Sacred Liturgy" (1963) was the first item ready for a decree and also that the postconciliar reorganization of the liturgy could proceed quickly. The council made the active participation of the congregation, called for by Popes Pius X, Pius XI, and Pius XII, possible in a way that no one could have expected and thereby took up the aims of the liturgical movement for the Universal Church (see Chapter 4). Meanwhile, it had spread to other European countries—for example, to the abbey of Silos in Spain—and to America—to Saint John's Abbey in Collegeville—where it obtained a social and ethical character.

New Awareness of the Church and the Scriptural Movement

The liturgical movement was an expression of a new awareness of the Church, just as, conversely, the celebration of the liturgy permitted an entirely new experience of the Church as community. As early as 1921 Romano Guardini had declared in lectures "on the Meaning of the Church": "A religious movement of incalculable import has begun: the Church is awaking in souls."[7] Against religious individualism and subjectivism Guardini showed: "The religious life no longer proceeds only from the I, but at the same time awakens in the opposite pole, in the objective, formed community" (p.13).

It could be expected that youth which, in the name of truthfulness and personal responsibility, stood up against convention and the claims to authority on the part of civil society would have rejected the Church with its foreign legality and its rigid institutions. On the contrary: In the Church's liturgy wide circles of youth found a vital expression and a corroboration of their longing for community and at the same time

[7] R. Guardini, *Vom Sinn der Kirche* (Mainz 1922), 1.

correction and support in their predetermined and established position. Church was experienced not so much as institution, as agent of salvation, but as fruit of salvation, of community of life and love, whose center and foundation is Christ himself. "Christ the Lord is the real I of the Church."[8] He is the head, and Christians have life and salvation as members of his body. Church was seen preeminently as *Corpus Christi mysticum*. If hitherto, especially in the nineteenth century, the Catholic had understood the Church as something like a collective person, to which he belonged, whose adherent or child he was, which he defended and loved, and in which he believed, so now there is question of a community, which he believes and whose member he is. The Christian does not stand facing the Church, but in it: "We are the Church," is said in many addresses and professions. Submission to the Church or, better, into the Church does not mean self-alienation but self-discovery: "To that extent I am a Christian personality, when I am a member of the Church and the Church is living in me. If I speak to it, then I say, in a fully profound understanding, not 'you' but 'I.'"[9]

Thus the Church could be understood, in fact experienced, as a principle of life, not so much as a legislator but as the source of strength and in the effort for the neighbor as the motive of moral and ascetical exertion. Books such as *Der mystische Leib Christi als Grundprinzip der Askese* (1936) by F. Jürgensmeier or *Morale et Corps mystique* (1937) by E. Mersch are characteristic of this. Altogether people wanted to move away from a casuistic and individualistic doctrine of sin to a doctrine of virtue as the message of the imitation of Christ. This was the direction taken by the *Handbuch der katholischen Sittenlehre* (1931–37) of the former exegete, Fritz Tillmann (1874–1935), with the volumes *Idee der Nachfolge Christi* and *Die Verwirklichung der Nachfolge Christi*.

The scriptural movement had made it possible to get to know this Christ, to meet him not in the rarefaction of Neo-Scholastic theology or of catechisms, but directly in Holy Scripture. Christocentric piety was awakened and deepened by means of the text of the New Testament itself in good vernacular translations and a series of scientifically based books on the life of Jesus, such as M. J. Lagrange, *L'Évangile de Jésus-Christ* (1928); L. de Grandmaison, *Jésus-Christ, sa personne, son message* (1928); J. Lebreton, *La vie et l'enseignement de Jésus-Christ, notre Seigneur* (1931); F. M. Willam, *Das Leben Jesu im Lande und Volke Israel* (1933); K. Adam, *Christus unser Bruder* (1926) and *Jesus Christus* (1933); R. Guardini, *Der Herr* (1937); and others. The program of Catholic youth

---

[8] Karl Adam in *Das Wesen des Katholizismus*, which appeared in its first edition in 1924, in its thirteenth in 1957.

[9] Ibid., 33.

read: "Life formation in Christ." Jesus, undiminished Man in his divinity, became the model, and the "Christus totus," Christ continuing to live as the Church, was seen as the basis of one's own life and of love of neighbor. Untroubled by an opposition between the historical Jesus and the Christ of faith, people directly took up the text of the Gospels in private reading of Scripture or in "Bible Groups," sought to make present, in the style of the *Spiritual Exercises* of Saint Ignatius Loyola, the scenes, situations, and figures described there, and to find the "application" to their personal life. Characteristic of this sort of biblical work is the book by Martin Manuwald, S. J., *Christuskreis. Der Jugend und ihren Führern.*"[10]

Catholic Action

Corresponding to the new awareness of the Church in broad circles of the laity and their understanding that a person could be a living member in the body of Christ only if the life stream is passed on, was the summons by the Popes to the lay apostolate, to Catholic Action. At the beginning of his pontificate, which was put under the motto "The Peace of Christ in the Kingdom of Christ," Pius XI, alluding to the general priesthood of all believers, summoned to "active work for the spread and renewal of the Kingdom of Christ."[11] In a letter of 13 November 1928 to Cardinal Bertram and elsewhere, the Pope several times defined *Actio catholica* as the "participation of the laity in the apostolate of the hierarchy."[12] It is a "social movement" with the aim "of advancing the Kingdom of our Lord Jesus Christ and thereby communicating to human society the highest of all goods." Catholics, in their sharing in the hierarchy's apostolate, should be put in the position "of spreading everywhere the principles of the Christian faith and of Christian doctrine, defending them energetically, and giving effect to them in private and in public life."[13] The Pope saw the Church preeminently as the Kingdom of God on earth. In conformity with this was the institution of the solemnity of Christ the King in the jubilee year 1925. Christ's royal dominion was based on the innate right of his divine and human natures as well as on the acquired right of his work of redemption. Only in the recognition of his Kingship in private and public life can a world without peace and help find peace. "The plague of our age," stressed the Pope in the encyclical *Quas primas* on the institution of the solemnity of Christ the King, "is the so-called laicism,

[10] Nuremberg 1930.
[11] *AAS* 14 (1922), 695.
[12] Ibid. 20 (1928), 385.
[13] Ibid.

with its errors and godless aims." Catholics have "neither that social position nor that influence . . . which those really should have who hold high the torch of truth." The Pope attributes this deplorable state of affairs "to the indifference and timidity of the good, who withdraw from the fight or make only a weak resistance. . . . But if only all the faithful understand that they must fight under the standard of Christ the King with courage and perseverance, then they will strive with apostolic zeal to lead the alienated and ignorant souls back to the Lord, and they will exert themselves to maintain his rights inviolate."[14]

The organization of Catholic Action under strict guidance of the hierarchy was strongly determined by the situation of the Church in Italy under the Fascist regime, which wanted to assure the Church only a meagre freedom of movement for its impact in the world and which especially claimed for itself the education of the young. A crisis arose even after the Lateran Treaties as a consequence of the totalitarian claims of Fascism. In the sharp encyclical *Non abbiamo bisogno* on 29 June 1931[15] Pius XI warded off the attacks on Catholic Action, whose nonpolitical character had been established in ARTICLE 43 of the concordat and himself attacked the absolutizing of the state. On 2 September 1931 an agreement was reached whereby the Catholic Youth Associations were incorporated into the state organization, Balilla, in which their own chaplains should provide religious instruction. Catholic Action, on the contrary, was to be able to work freely and independently. Its purely religious character and its direct dependence on the hierarchy were to be assured by its organization according to parishes and dioceses and a rearrangement according to "natural states" and not according to professions.

This model could not be realized or encountered opposition in countries like Germany, where for decades in the free sphere of the Church a series of associations related to various professions had been established, which, indeed, saw in the apostolate an essential element of their work, but in relative independence of the bishops were able to undertake functions and make decisions which did not pertain to the direct mandate of the bishops. They incorporated the idea of *Actio catholica* and of the apostolate as work for the Kingdom of Christ the King into their program and their work, without making essential changes in the structure of these societies.

In Belgium and France Catholic Action gained a special position as a "specialized" organization, that is, oriented to defined professions, such as working youth, rural youth, and students. In Belgium there was

[14] Ibid. 17 (1925), 606.
[15] Ibid. 23 (1931), 285–312.

established in 1924–25, as a continuation of the existing *Jeunesse syndicaliste* founded by the priest Joseph Cardijn (1882–1967, a cardinal in 1965),[16] the *Jeunesse Oeuvrière Chrétienne* (JOC), which was approved by Pius XI in 1925, adopted in France on the Belgian model in 1926, and then, especially after 1945, spread throughout the world. In West Germany after the Second World War there was at first no agreement as to whether the workers' unions—as was compulsory in the Nazi period—should be further established on the basis of parishes according to states of life and nature—male and female youth, men and women—or be again distinct according to profession—workers' unions, journeymen's unions, rural people, New Germany, academic associations, and so forth. The decision was again overwhelming for the latter form. The Young Christian Workers (CAJ) was basically the only new foundation as regards organization and method of work. It was called into being in 1947[17] and operated like the JOC, separated into male and female youth. The training took place according to the principle "see, judge, act." The young worker was to be led to see the concrete reality of his life, to evaluate and form it in the light of the Catholic faith. It especially mattered to the CAJ to fill a firm nucleus of "protagonists" with a missionary spirit by retreats and social and political study meetings. Correspondingly there arose for student youth the *Jeunesse étudiante chrétienne* (JEC) and for rural youth the *Jeunesse agricole chrétienne* (JAC).

In view of the numerous forms of the lay apostolate, differing in directness, intensity, and the structure required by the situation, Pius XII was moved to expand the concept of Catholic Action and to distinguish various forms of the organization and gradations of dependence on the hierarchy. Concerning the Marian congregations he declared in the apostolic constitution *Bis saeculari* of 27 September 1948 that they could be termed "with full right Catholic Action under the guidance and support of the Blessed Virgin Mary."[18] If Pius XI spoke of the participation of the laity in the hierarchical apostolate, Pius XII preferred to speak of collaboration or help.[19] According to the encyclical *Mystici corporis* of 29 June 1943, Christ requires the help of his members. "A really awesome mystery . . . that the salvation of

[16] J. Cardijn, *Was ist die CAJ?*, 3d ed. (Essen 1955); idem, *Die Schicksalsstunde der Arbeiterschaft* (Essen 1955).

[17] J. Angerhausen, "Die Christliche Arbeiter-Jugend, die deutsche CAJ," *TThZ* 63 (1954), 280–88; J. Angerhausen, M. Meert, *CAJ, Weg der Umkehr* (Essen 1957).

[18] *AAS* 40 (1948), 393–402.

[19] Address of Pius XII to the Catholic Action of Italy on 4 September 1940, *AAS* 32 (1940), 362.

many is dependent . . . on the cooperation which the shepherds and the faithful . . . have to provide."[20]

In his address to the First World Congress of the Catholic Lay Apostolate on 14 October 1951, the Pope stressed that dependence of the lay apostolate on the hierarchy admitted gradations; the narrowest was that for Catholic Action: "It is a tool in the hand of the hierarchy and should be, as it were, the extension of its arm. Hence, by its nature it is subordinate to the chief shepherds of the Church. Other organized or unorganized works of the lay apostolate can relinquish their free initiative to a greater degree, each as its aims require."[21] As the Pope emphasized at the Second Congress for the Lay Apostolate in 1957, Catholic Action can—understood as an organization—claim no monopoly for itself. It bears well the character of an official lay apostolate. The apostolate of prayer, of vocation, and of life witness can be termed lay apostolate in the broader sense. Further there is the "free apostolate" of individuals and groups that put themselves at the disposal of the hierarchy and let themselves be assigned tasks by it for a limited or indefinite time. There remained the danger that the lay apostolate would be restricted to the tasks which take place in the Church itself or which are worked out by the laity as the "elongated arm of the hierarchy" and came from the field of vision of the strictly lay functions of interpretation of the world, guidance of the world, and sanctification of the world. The conciliar decree "On the Apostolate of the Laity" seeks to meet this danger by stressing, among other things, that the laity "exercise their apostolate in the Church as in the world, in the spiritual as in the secular order" (ART. 5). According to the "pastoral constitution on the Church in the world of today" there must be made a "clear distinction between what Christians as individuals or as a group do in their own name as citizens who are directed by their Christian conscience and what they do in the name of the Church together with the shepherds."[22]

The Spiritual Exercises Movement

If in the mind of Pius XI the first goal of Catholic Action is to form the conscience of Christians in so powerfully Christian a way that at any time and in any situation of private and public life they are in a position to find the Christian solution of the many problems that arise,[23] then the

[20] *AAS* 35 (1943), 213.
[21] Ibid. 43 (1951), 789.
[22] ARTICLE 76; cf. *Lumen gentium*, ART. 36.
[23] So also the decree "On the Apostolate of the Laity" of the Second Vatican Council, ART. 20.

Ignatian *Spiritual Exercises* were a valuable help in this. It was their aim to lead to the personal sanctification required as the basis of apostolic spirit and life as a preliminary to the sanctification of others. The number of participants in the Exercises grew by leaps and bounds in the 1920s. If into the nineteenth century they were conducted almost exclusively by Jesuits, now other orders also took part, to a degree in a form corresponding to their special spirituality. Since the Exercises Convention at Innsbruck in 1922 and Pius XI's constitution *Summorum Pontificum*[24] of 25 July 1922 and his encyclical on the promoting of the *Spiritual Exercises*[25] of 20 December 1929, it is possible to speak of an Exercise Movement. Pius XI named as the worst sickness of the day the "continuous passionate devotion to the external world" and the "insatiable greed for wealth and pleasure," which no longer let people think of eternal truths and of God, the first cause and last end. The Exercises should provide place, time, and quiet for this. The sharing by groups of Catholic Action in the Exercises especially gladdened the Pope. "Many take part in them, the better to equip themselves and to keep themselves ready for the Lord's battles. Thus they find not only prop and support perfectly to develop in themselves the ideal of the Christian life; not rarely they also find in their heart a mysterious call from God, who invites them to the holy service and the fostering of the good of the neighbor's soul and this incites them to the exercise of a full apostolate."[26] In 1936 the Jesuits alone gave 16,043 courses with 680,788 taking part. Add to this in the missionary areas 631 courses with 24,225 participants.[27] In Germany 109,000 men, women, and youths made the Exercises in 1955.[28] After the Second World War they became part of the extraordinary care of souls, systematically promoted and attended by pastoral officials.

If the Exercises, in accord with their origin, aimed rather at conversion of life, the "great decision" of the adult, as H. Rahner expresses it, then the pastoral care of the young developed in religious days of recollection ("retreat days," "free times") forms of training in the spiritual life and of a deepening of faith suited to the mentality and situation of the young and students. According to Ludwig Esch, S. J. (1883–1956), who in the years 1919 to 1951 gave the Exercises for 54,884 pupils, students, and priests, these provided "a new setting on the right road, a growth in the setting of goals, a clarifying in

---

[24] *AAS* 14 (1922), 420–22.
[25] *Mens nostra*, *AAS* 21 (1929), 689–706.
[26] *AAS* 21 (1929), 689–706, 691, 701.
[27] H. Becher, *Die Jesuiten. Gestalt und Geschichte des Ordens* (Munich 1951), 400.
[28] *HK* 11 (1956–57), 73f.

regard to self and the entire world of the faith, but thereby also a profound joy."[29]

Eucharistic Piety in Transition

The liturgical movement and the reflection on the Bible were at first matters for circles of youth and academicians. Parish congregations were first affected by them after 1930. The broad mass of the Catholic people was still supported by the great currents of the traditional piety of the nineteenth century, which lived and found expression in the worship of the Eucharist, devotion to the Sacred Heart of Jesus, and the veneration of Mary and the saints. But it is characteristic of the situation that the old was gradually permeated by the new and thereby experienced a deepening and return to essence and center. This becomes especially clear in the Eucharistic piety, which until the end of the nineteenth century was almost exclusively a worship of adoration, then as the Eucharistic movement led to frequent Communion, and only after uniting with the liturgical movement again understood the Eucharist as a sacrifice of thanksgiving, which the Lord celebrates with his Church and into which the Christian enters fully by sharing in the sacrificial meal.

Dogmatic theology used to treat the Sacrament of the Altar in three sections, which were isolated from one another: (1) the Real Presence of Christ in the Eucharist, which had as a consequence the merit of adoration; (2) the Eucharist as sacrament, that is, as Communion; (3) the Eucharist as sacrifice.[30] For devotion the deciding factor was the presence of Christ in the tabernacle or in the monstrance. The Mass was seen predominantly as the means for "confecting" the sacramental presence, and therefore attention was focused on the moment of transubstantiation. But even this happening was covered over, because the Mass was often celebrated, for the sake of special solemnity, before the Blessed Sacrament exposed on the altar, and from the start this presence had to be venerated by, among other things, kneeling, before the Lord offering himself became present under the appearances of bread and wine and the congregation could go through him and with him and in him before the Father.

Although Pius X had demanded in 1903 that the faithful should draw the Christian spirit "from the first and real source, namely, from active participation in the holy mysteries and the public and official prayer of

---

[29] L. Esch, *Neue Lebensgetaltung in Christus,* 7th ed. (Würzburg 1952), 296; E. Holzapfel, L. Esch, *Ein Leben für die Jugend* (Würzburg 1963).
[30] Thus still L. Ott, *Grundriss der Dogmatik,* 3d ed. (Freiburg 1957), XVf.

the Church,"[31] whereby he gave the keyword for the later liturgical movement, he did not himself, in the decree *Sacra Tridentina synodus* on daily Communion of 1905[32] and in the First Communion decree *Quam singulari* of 1910, go into the connection of Mass and Communion and treated the value and the significance of frequent and early Communion by itself in isolation. The "Eucharistic movement" inaugurated by him thus became the "Communion movement"[33] in its own development, independent of the liturgical movement, in fact in some respects retarding it. It did not produce the breakthrough to a common view of Mass and Communion. The fostering of frequent, even daily Communion brought about that—in accord with the Pope's desire[34]—the worship of adoration no longer occupied the first place within Eucharistic piety and relaxed that only too close connection of confession and Communion. However, from now on Communion was seen in isolation: isolated from what happened at Mass, but also isolated in so far as the understanding of Communion saw only the union of the individual soul with Christ but not the community of those communicating; characteristically in the decree *Sacra Tridentina synodus* there was no reference to *Communio* as community in the body of Christ.

It was in keeping with this isolated understanding of Communion that the real happening at Mass was· completely overlapped and concealed by the preparation for the reception of Communion and by the thanksgiving and that one prayed one's own Communion devotions. To obtain time for the thanksgiving, Communion was often distributed before Mass or after Mass in order not to detain long those not communicating. The Eucharist was especially at the service of the religious and moral character formation of the individual, it was regarded as "countermeans for the freeing from daily sins and preservation from mortal sins."[35]

Even after the First World War the situation seemed not essentially different, and as late as 1928 it could be said in a lecture at the Second Catechetical Congress at Munich: "Holy Communion . . . in spite of Pius X's decrees on Communion still has not always in the awareness of the people the significance proper to it in the liturgy."[36] Only the

---

[31] Motu proprio *Tra le sollecitudini* of 22 November 1903, *ASS* 36 (1903–4), 331.

[32] *ASS* 38 (1905–6), 400–409; *Quam singulari, AAS* 2 (1910), 577–83.

[33] Cf. H. Fischer, *Eucharistiekatechese und Liturgische Erneuerung* (Düsseldorf 1959), 11–24.

[34] According to *Sacra Tridentina synodus* the meaning of Communion is not "chiefly . . . to render God honor and adoration," *ASS* 38 (1905–6), 401; Rohrbasser no. 193.

[35] *Sacra Tridentina synodus, ASS,* ibid.; Rohrbasser no. 193.

[36] Quoted from H. Fischer, *Eucharistiekatechese,* 45.

encounter and connection with the liturgical movement at the beginning of the 1930s assisted the Eucharistic movement to the correct theological self-understanding and to an effective breakthrough in the following period. With its efforts for as active a participation as possible by all in the celebration of Mass, the liturgical movement led to Communion as a sacrificial meal being organically added to conscious and active participation in the action of sacrifice and forming a whole with it. In the course of this development to an "organic" understanding of the Mass the preparation for Communion was increasingly seen in the celebrating of the Sacrifice of the Mass itself and no longer relegated to the Communion devotion that ignored what happened at Mass. Assiduous ascetical exertions, characterized by concern for the worthiest possible Communion, gradually gave way to a more uncomplicated and more joyful Communion and Mass piety, by which were increasingly created more favorable presuppositions for the early and frequent reception of Communion.

No longer the consummated sacrament, that is, the sacramental presence of the Lord under the species of bread and the adoration of his divinity, stood in the foreground, but the process, the celebration in which with thanksgiving the surrender of the Lord to the Father, his sacrifice, becomes present and he, as Mediator, leads us to the Father. The only too static notion of the Eucharist was overcome, and the Eucharist as an action was more strongly stressed, for example, the abolition of exposition during Mass, which was in any event contrary to the Church's decrees, and the custom, twice recommended by Pius XII in *Mediator Dei* (1947), of giving Holy Communion with Hosts consecrated during the same Mass.[37]

The new understanding of Communion and Mass only slowly acquired influence on the organization of Eucharistic congresses. Before and after, here the worship of adoration was in the foreground, joined to a powerful demonstration of faith, so that the procession, arranged with great display, appeared as the climax of each congress. The growing internationalizing of the congresses, at whose head stood a papal legate from 1906 on, gave these meetings the character of a "World Corpus Christi."

After the First World War the series of congresses began again at Rome in 1922. The world's disunion experienced in the war evoked for this and the succeeding congresses a new accentuation: the Host was honored as the symbol of the unity among peoples and asserted as the sole means of leading people together to lasting union. At Rome's desire

---

[37] *AAS* 39 (1947), 564f.; Rohrbasser nos. 305 and 307.

there followed congresses at intervals of two years: in 1926 at Chicago, in 1928 at Sydney, in 1930 at Carthage, in 1932 at Dublin. Latin America was first added in 1933 at Buenos Aires. There followed those at Madrid in 1936 and Budapest in 1938. Once again war interrupted the series of congresses, which was not continued until 1952 at Barcelona. In the organization of this congress the growing together of the liturgical and the Eucharistic movements found clear expression: the closing procession no longer constituted the climax, beside which, more or less without visible connection, Masses and the distribution of Communion took place, but the common celebration of the Eucharist was moved directly into the center.

The complete elaboration of this new accentuation took place at the Munich Congress in 1960, for which Josef Andreas Jungmann had awakened to new life the idea of the *statio*. As early as 1930, on the occasion of the Eucharistic Congress at Carthage, Jungmann had called attention to the custom, frequently attested in the ancient Church but acquiring a special form in the Roman Church of the Middle Ages, whereby the bishop on specific Sundays and feasts of the year, but especially in Lent, celebrated a migratory Mass in the most important churches in order to make visible the notion of the unity of bishop, clergy, and people.

This *Statio Urbis,* as Jungmann said, could serve as model for a *Statio Orbis,* the experience of the community of the Church in the common Eucharistic celebration as the climax of the Eucharistic Congress. Jungmann's suggestion, hardly noticed in 1930, was adopted in the episcopal pastoral letter for the Munich Congress of 1960. Thus the community Eucharistic celebration, in which the Universal Church became experienced and visible as the Mystical Body of Christ, gave to this congress a special character and emphasized with incomparable clarity the preeminence of the sacrificial event in union with the sacrificial meal as contrasted with the adoring gaze. The notion of the *Statio Orbis* deprived this congress of the character of a triumphalist stressed self-celebration; the stress lay not on demonstration but on the daily accomplishment of the sacrifice.

The organization of the Munich World Congress in accord with the concept of the *Statio Orbis* allowed the spirit of the liturgical renewal to acquire a quite visible form and thereby facilitated the preparation of new liturgical arrangements by the Council.

Devotion to the Sacred Heart of Jesus

Devotion to the Sacred Heart of Jesus, which achieved a high rank in the nineteenth century because of papal encouragement, occupied also in the twentieth century a broad area in popular piety; very widespread was the observance of the first Friday of the month as Sacred Heart Friday, joined with Communion and prayer for an intention determined each month by the Pope. The effort for a solid theological foundation of this devotion by recourse especially to biblical statements, but also to patristic theology, marked both the work of theologians and expressions of the *magisterium;* this work was all the more urgent, as trashy, sentimental distortions were a great danger in this devotion that appealed to the affective-emotional classes.

In the encyclical *Miserentissimus Redemptor* of 1928 Pius XI gave the feast of the Sacred Heart the highest liturgical rank, with a new Mass formulary and office. In view of the needs of the day, the encyclical called for penance and expiation, which occupy "always the first and foremost position in the honoring of the most Sacred Heart of Jesus" (no. 135). Through the papal regulations the devotion to the Heart of Jesus and its incorporation into the liturgy achieved a first goal; the theological foundation also here reached an important stage as the attempt was made to join the Heart of Jesus mysticism with the theology of the Fathers and to consolidate the devotion to the Sacred Heart in the central mysteries of salvation.

The world crisis of the 1930s again afforded the Pope the occasion to recommend the devotion to the Sacred Heart as a means of salvation in the encyclical *Caritate Christi compulsi* of 3 May 1932. Considering the misery of the period, the godlessness, and the hatred of every religion, joined in socialism with the struggle for one's daily bread, the Pope commanded the holding of public Masses of atonement on the solemnity of the Sacred Heart.

Under Pius XII, who in his first encyclical had referred to the consecration of the human race to the Sacred Heart, exertions in regard to the devotion to the Heart of Jesus reached a climax, especially in regard to theology. True, at this time doubts and objections were also heard, for example, that the devotion to the Sacred Heart fostered a purely individualistic piety, which in view of the growing awareness of community in the sphere of the Church could not but evoke grave hesitations. To others some vivid presentations and devotional forms seemed rather repulsive; others again attributed to the devotion to the Sacred Heart a historical right, it is true, as a reaction to the sentiment-destroying and rigoristic Jansenism and as a Christianization of subjectivism in the nineteenth century, but they were inclined to deny the importance of this cult for the twentieth century and the tasks allotted to it. And some raised the reproach of particularism: one element, the heart, would be dissociated from the person of the Redeemer and hence a total view would be made more difficult.

An intensive theological work, especially in the 1950s, sought to take into account the doubts that were becoming loud and the difficulties by undertaking to clarify the heart in its total character, the physical as well as the spiritual included, from biblical expressions of the Old and New Testaments.

"Heart is," as Guardini writes, following Blaise Pascal, "the spirit in so far as it is in contact with blood . . . . Heart is the spirit made hot and sensitive by blood, but at the same time spirit elevated by the clarity of contemplation, by the distinctness of character, by the precision of judgment. Heart is the organ of love. . . . It is that which is experienced in the heart."[38] Thus the Heart of Jesus is the symbol of the love of the Redeemer, as love of the Father and of mankind. Devotion to the Heart of Jesus means to let oneself be embraced by this love of Jesus. It must be expressed in a serving apostolic life.

The fruit as well as the point of departure of such exertions for a theological justification of devotion to the Sacred Heart in accord with the time were the statements of Pius XII in his encyclical *Haurietis aquas* of 15 May 1956. This document took issue with the most varied misunderstandings and errors and sought—contrary to the minimizing of this cult as based on a private revelation—to make clear that the devotion to the Sacred Heart "can look back to an advanced age in the Church and has in the Gospels themselves a solid foundation, so that tradition and liturgy clearly favor it." The reason for this cult, which is distinguished as the "most effective school of the love of God," is twofold: the first consists in this, that Christ's heart, "the noblest part of human nature, is hypostatically united with the person of the divine Word; hence to it must be paid the same worship of adoration by which the Church honors the person of the incarnate Son of God . . . . The second reason results from this, that his heart, more than all other members of his body, is a natural indication or symbol of his unending love for the human race."[39]

The Pope's explanations, which apply in detail especially to biblical statements, end in the admonition that in the devotion to the Sacred Heart there is "no question about just any traditional form of piety, which may, according to the preference of each, be treated lightly or underestimated in relation to other forms, but of a practice of divine adoration, which, like no other, is able to lead to Christian perfection. . . . Everyone who then has a slight estimation of this great gift of Jesus Christ to the Church is pursuing a dangerous and unholy matter and is offending God himself."[40]

[38] R. Guardini, *Christliches Bewusstsein. Versuche über Pascal* (Leipzig 1935), 177.
[39] *AAS* 48 (1956), 316.
[40] Ibid., 346.

Despite the encouragement of and propaganda for the devotion to the Sacred Heart by the official *magisterium,* it seems to be fading more and more from the awareness and life of piety of the members of the Church. This probably has less theological than spiritual-historical reasons. An age like ours, which sees so strongly in Jesus the "Man for us," would have to have in it understanding for love that is self-sacrificing and consumed for the neighbor; but to see and honor this represented in the bleeding Heart of Jesus—for this there is lacking today the sense of the symbol.

Devotion to Mary and Mariology

The growth of the Marian movement from the second third of the nineteenth century continued on into the twentieth. Pius XI and Pius XII continued the line of their predecessors in the promoting of devotion to Mary. Among believers it received impetus from appearances of Mary, especially from that at Fátima in Portugal, which was made to three Portuguese children in 1917. It and also the appearances in the Belgian localities of Beauraing in 1932–33 and Banneux in 1933 obtained ecclesiastical approbation.[41] They led to a brisk pilgrimage. At Fátima Mary demanded especially the praying of the rosary for the peace of the world, the consecration of Russia to her immaculate heart, and Communion of reparation on the first Saturday of each month. Pope Pius XII, whose episcopal ordination occurred at Rome on 13 May 1917, the day of the first appearance of Mary at Fátima, regarded himself throughout his life as bound to the aims of Fátima in a special way. On 8 December 1942 he performed the consecration of the entire human race to the Immaculate Heart of Mary.[42] On 7 July 1952 he finally addressed to all the people of Russia an encyclical in which they were dedicated to the Immaculate Heart of Mary. To spread the aims of Fátima there was established, at the urging of the Canadian Bishop Dignan, a "Rosary Crusade," which had a worldwide expan-

[41] Cf. *LThK,* 2d ed., VII, 64: "Ecclesiastical approbation does not mean an infallible assurance of the supernatural origin of the appearances. It means: (1.) The alleged event contains nothing against faith and morals; (2.) it can be made public and become the object of cult; (3.) it offers, like other historical events, sufficient arguments that the fact of its supernatural cause can be reasonably accepted by human faith." The ecclesiastical officials are very cautious in regard to recognition. As opposed to the three appearances of Mary approved since 1930, thirty have been expressly repudiated.
[42] Cf. the consecrating prayer, "Regina del Santissimo Rosario," *AAS* 34 (1942), 345f.; Rohrbasser nos. 546–49.

sion. In 1947 there arose in Vienna, under Franciscan leadership, the Rosary Atonement Crusade.

Marian piety and the lay apostolate were now in close connection. Thus in the lay organization, the "Legion of Mary," which was founded by Frank Duff in Dublin in 1921 and spread rapidly on all the continents, especially in mission countries. With an aggressive tone like that of the Legion of Mary, there appeared also the Militia of the Immaculate Conception, founded in 1917 by Father Maximilian Kolbe (1894–1941), who later died in a concentration camp, and also the Blue Army of Mary, called into being in 1947 by Harold von Colgan. The last named sees its task principally as the spreading of the message of Fátima.

The lay apostolate of the Marian congregations, which are called "Marian" not only "because they take their title from the Mother of God, but especially because the individual members promise an especially interior veneration of the Mother of God and give themselves to her through a complete surrender of consecration,"[43] received encouragement and impetus from Pius XII's apostolic constitution *Bis saeculari* of 1948. In 1953 was founded the World Association of Marian Congregations, which since 1956 is a member of the Conference of International Catholic Organizations. From the spirit of the Marian congregations proceeded, at first depending on the Pallottines, the Schönstatt Movement, building on the educational work of Father Josef Kentenich (1885–1968); Marian sisters, Marian brothers, and Schönstatt priests are the agents of the work.

In encyclicals Pius XI and Pius XII several times expressed their views on problems of Mariology and devotion to Mary and gave new impulses or took up such. Thus in 1937 Pius XI in the encyclical *Ingravescentibus malis*[44] recommended the rosary, with clear allusion to Fascism and Communism, in view of the threatening world situation. A series of new Marian feasts was introduced: in 1931, on the occasion of the fifteenth centenary of the Council of Ephesus, of the feast of the Maternity of the Blessed Virgin Mary on 11 October, in 1944 the feast of the Immaculate Heart of the Blessed Virgin Mary on 22 August, and finally in 1954 the feast of Mary our Queen on 31 May. The climax of the papal initiatives came with the proclamation of the dogma of the bodily Assumption of Mary into heaven on 1 November 1950. The proclamation was preceded by a survey of the episcopate of the world. This confirmed that the bodily Assumption of Mary was a firm

---

[43] *Bis saeculari*, no. 189, *AAS* 40 (1948), 401; Rohrbasser no. 1631.
[44] *AAS* 29 (1937), 373–80.

conviction of faith of the members of the Church and almost unanimously agreed to the opportuneness of the definition. According to the dogmatic bull *Munificentissimus Deus,* Mary, who was already a sharer in the full redemption, is a sign for mankind, threatened in a secularistic world of materialism; mankind should recognize in Mary that human fulfillment is to be found only in God: it is to be hoped, said the Pope, "that through the contemplation of the glorious example of Mary there may grow ever stronger the insight into what high value human life has, when it is used to carry out the will of the heavenly Father and to act for the welfare of the fellow man. And it can also be . . . expected that the truth of Mary's Assumption may show to all clearly to what noble end we are destined in body and soul. Finally, faith in the bodily Assumption of Mary into heaven will strengthen faith also in our resurrection and lead to energetic activity."[45]

Marian literature, powerfully increased in the twentieth century, reached its climax in the 1950s in regard to mere number of publications: thus, between 1948 and 1957 about one thousand titles per year appeared. Not rarely these works contained exaggerations which went far beyond the measure found in the dogma and liturgy of the Church. All the more, theologians such as Otto Semmelroth, Hugo and Karl Rahner, Michael Schmaus, and others, sought to open up the biblical and patristic sources of Mariology and to consider the ecumenical problem. Inspired by the works of early Christian tradition, which had treated Mary not for her own sake but in the framework of the divine economy of salvation, theologians of the 1940s and 1950s dealt with Mary and her privileges no longer as isolated, but with a view to the entire doctrine of salvation: thus Mariology was seen in its relations to Christology, ecclesiology, and eschatology. Mary was no longer the object of a merely individual cult—just as also the individualistic understanding of the Church in these years yielded to a more community-related view—but she was seen in the framework of the theology of salvation, hence in connection with redemption, humanity, Church, and perfection: Mary, prototype or type of the Church.

Also concerned for a new basis for devotion to Mary were the Marian congresses, which took place on regional, national, and international levels. Further, there were formed societies for Marian studies, and in 1950 an international Marian Academy was founded. In Germany must be mentioned the Mariological Workers Community of German theologians; in France the Institut Catholique at Paris received a special Mariological chair; and at Rome the Mariological Academy was made a papal academy by a motu proprio of John XXIII of 8 December 1959.

---

[45] *Munificentissimus Deus,* no. 201, *AAS* 42 (1950), 553–771.

Institutes, academies, societies, and working communities published the results of their individual investigations and meetings in numerous periodicals and cooperative works. With the end of the pontificate of Pius XII, as whose Marian climaxes must be given the years 1950, 1954 (the Marian Year), and 1958 (centenary of Mary's appearance at Lourdes), there began a slackening of enthusiasm in devotion to Mary and Mariology, a tendency which even the suggestions of the Second Vatican Council could not stop and which lasts till today. The council composed no Marian schema of its own, but dealt with Mary within the schema on the Church. Here Mary appears expressly as "type of the Church with respect to faith, love, and perfect unity with Christ."[46] For the rest, the Second Vatican Council imposed on itself with regard to Mariology an intentional caution; it had "no intention of proposing a complete doctrine of Mary or to decide questions which were not yet fully clarified by the work of theologians."[47] The constitution presented Mary's position in Christ's salvific work but avoided the term "Coredemptrix," which since the beginning of the twentieth century quite often stood in the center of the discussion and had even been used by the Popes, but had given occasion to misunderstandings.

In regard to the fear that, because of the devotion to Mary and the emphasis on the cooperation of the Mother of God in the work of redemption, the image of Christ would be obscured, the council made it clear that "in the honoring of the Mother, the Son, on account of whom everything is . . . is correctly known, loved, and glorified, and his commandments are observed."[48] But in the veneration of Mary the correct measure must be maintained. Thus the council admonishes "to promote generously the veneration, especially the liturgical, of the Blessed Virgin" and thereby "also to hold carefully aloof from every false exaggeration as well as from too summary an attitude in contemplating the unique dignity of the Mother of God."[49]

The Spiritual Development of the Orders

The continuing growth since the second half of the nineteenth century of the number of members of the orders and congregations as well as of the number of their foundations was at first maintained in the twentieth century. More or less clear variations within the development can be

[46] Dogmatic Constitution on the Church, *Lumen gentium*, ART. 63.
[47] Ibid., ART. 54.
[48] Ibid., ART. 66.
[49] Ibid., ART. 67.

explained by a parallel reflection on the history of the period and to a great extent referred to external factors.[50]

Whereas, following the recovery from the losses of the First World War, a "monastic spring" was clearly to be recorded in Germany, there appeared toward the end of the 1920s a noticeable slackening of the growth, which found expression in 1936 in the orders of sisters in a slight decline in the number of recruits; this was in part the effect of the low birthrate of the years between 1914 and 1920 but must also especially be regarded for the following period under the aspect of the propaganda of the National Socialist regime. Its measures hostile to the orders reached their climax in the decree by Rudolf Hess of 19 November 1940 whereby entrance into monasteries was stopped. After the end of the Second World War, it is true, the number of members of the orders was stabilized in a thereafter slight growth, but the number of novices reached only little more than half of the prewar recruits. Also to be coped with were the severe damages done to the religious life because of members killed in the war, a considerable migration movement, and the loss of houses and schools of the orders. If after the war the orders could again attend to their tasks in the schools, then this meant additional deficiencies in the charitable work, in which meanwhile the sisters had found a field of activity. In part, the losses were compensated by the religious expelled from Eastern countries.

If the development of the religious clergy is compared with that of the diocesan clergy, it must be stated, at least for Germany and its Western neighbor nations, that during the postwar years the religious clergy could record a relatively larger growth than the diocesan clergy; for example, whereas between 1948 and 1958 in France the number of diocesan priests decreased about sixty percent, the number of religious priests in the same period rose about 1,417, that is, 28.7 per cent.[51] The reasons for this were the readiness for radical response after the experiences of the war and the collapse and the demand for stability and security, which were promised by the *vita communis* of the religious community. In mission lands the stronger increase in native religious priests must also be attributed to the fact that missionary work was almost exclusively in the hands of the orders and the model of the diocesan priest was absent.

As regards the distribution of the recruits among the various orders, a "change of tendency" must be noted: While from the beginning of the

---

[50] Cf. Becker, "Der Schwesternnachwuchs seit dem Ende des Ersten Weltkrieges bis zur Gegenwart, zusammengefasst wiedergegeben," *HK* 4(1949–50), 233f.

[51] Cf. J. Kerkhofs, "Aspects sociologiques du sacerdoce," *NRTh* 82(1960), 289–99, 291; see also Chapter 11.

century the recruits applied chiefly to the "active" communities and among these the more recent congregations and those more adapted to the needs of the time had on an average a larger growth than the ancient types of orders,[52] from the 1950s especially the number and spread of the contemplative communities increased. At the Mainz *Katholikentag* of 1948 Friedrich Wulf tried to explain the change that was becoming apparent thus: "In many newer communities it was the purpose, it was specific tasks, which created a community . . . . True, even in the establishing of the modern religious rules an effort was made to follow great models, for example, the Franciscan or Augustinian rule was made the basis, but people still were unable to grasp the living spirit of these models. And so they made almost all alike down to the most trivial details, but there was usually lacking the profound uniform basic structure, which gives to all expressions of piety a definite form and a definite character. This could not but have an especially clear impact in a period of crisis, as we experienced it, and especially in large communities the spiritual formation of the younger members of the order left much to be desired. . . ."[53]

Raymond Hostie[54] proceeded from similar observations when, alongside numerical growth as a mark of all religious communities in the twentieth century, he specified "stability of the organizational structure" and a certain "immobility."[55] The latter appeared in a certain rigidity in the interpretation of the rule and a concealing of the basic uniformity of communities by emphasizing originality in unessential externals and in an isolation of the monasteries from the general cultural development. It was no accident that, in the renewal movement within the Church of our century, monasteries such as Solesmes, Subiaco, Beuron, Maria Laach, and others took part: by recourse to monastic origins they gained a clear ideal and hence were in a position to supply new impulses. Against this background must be understood the efforts of the Popes to bring the orders back to the essential by reflection on the spirit of the respective founders and law which inspired them and thereby to free them for the tasks of the day.

After Pius XI (1922–39) had worked successfully for an adjustment between the liturgical reform movement of the Benedictines and the

---

[52] Cf. *HK* 8 (1953–54), 311; statistics on the recruits for the orders (1940–52): growth of the orders on the average 19.13 percent, of the congregations on the average 33.54 percent.

[53] A. Scheuermann, "Um die Zeitnähe des Ordensstandes," *GuL* 24 (1951), 274–84, 280.

[54] R. Hostie, *Vie et mort des ordres religieux* (Paris 1972), cf. 253–73.

[55] Op. cit., 253.

tradition of the exercises and of devotion to the Sacred Heart of the Jesuits, the exertions for a reform of the orders achieved its climax in many pronouncements of Pius XII (1939–58). The prelude to the accommodation of the orders to the time and its needs, as desired by the Pope, was given in an article, inspired by his ideas, by the Jesuit Riccardo Lombardi in *Civiltà Cattolica*.[56] Although religious were admonished in it not to be "adventurers" in order that "the conservative viewpoint may always retain its validity alongside the mood for innovation,"[57] still they should as "the highly motivated avant-garde in an anxious hour give to reform the example of the greatest preparedness in relation to the new positions demanded by the welfare of humanity."[58] "Avoid," Lombardi called upon the religious, "a stagnating rigidity which would remove you from the course of life; on the other hand, be unchanging, as a river is unchanging, which is fed from an everlasting source but constantly renews itself in the stream!"[59]

This impulse found its continuation at the First International Congress of Religious at Rome in 1950, which was under the slogan determined by the Sacred Congregation for Religious: "The renewal of the states of perfection adapted to the present day and its circumstances." In his address[60] to some five hundred representatives of the orders and secular institutes the Pope called upon the religious: Motivated by the conviction that the Catholic faith is able to form every age, "pay attention to the opinion, judgment, and morals of your environment and accept what you find good and just in it as valuable indications; otherwise you cannot be advisers, help, support, and light to your fellow human beings. . . . There are areas, indeed very many, in which you may, in fact must, adapt yourselves to the style and needs of the time and the people. . . ."[61]

Especially for the contemplative orders of women the Pope derived from this the duty to "reasonable modernization,"[62] which should find its expression not least in a "moderate participation in the apostolate."[63] The apostolic constitution *Sponsa Christi*[64] of 21 November 1950, decisive in this context, accordingly supplemented, among other things,

[56] *Civiltà Cattolica*, 19 March 1949, no. 6.
[57] Op. cit., 84.
[58] Op. cit., 82.
[59] Op. cit., 89.
[60] *L'Osservatore Romano*, no. 289, of 9–10 December 1950.
[61] *AAS* 43(1951), 34.
[62] Ibid., 10.
[63] Op. cit., 11.
[64] Op. cit., 5–24.

the strict prescriptions of inclosure for monasteries of nuns with the modified form of the so-called "little papal inclosure." In ARTICLE 8 of the constitution, with reference to the economic security of the orders, there was imposed on the nuns the obligation to a suitable work, which was consistent "not only with the law of nature but equally with a duty of penance and expiation."[65] In a glance at the lack of recruits the Pope in 1952 repeated his plea to the superiors of orders: "Pay attention, especially in this age of a vocation crisis, to this, that the behavior, manner of life, and asceticism in your religious families not become hindrances or reasons for refusal. . . . Adapt yourselves in all things which are not essential, so far as reason and regulated charity permit."[66] Pius XII's special concern was for the formation of the recruits. He demanded a uniform formation of the young religious by "proved and selected personalities."[67]

A further effort to lead the monasteries out of their isolation went in the direction of a greater cooperation, both through "coordinating of the diocesan clergy and the religious clergy"[68] and through stronger contact of the individual religious communities with the competent bishops as with Rome, and finally through cooperation or, respectively, even merger of monasteries. Results appeared in the form of unions, chiefly of monasteries of women, and in an improved organization and coordination of the efforts of the orders from Rome as the center. In spite of some very promising new starts, however, the reform efforts led on the whole—as also hints of the Pope in his talk at the Second International Congress of Religious at Rome in 1957 confirmed[69]—to further difficulties, among others in the interpretation of the vow of obedience, rather than to fruitful renewal. The chief problems seemed to be the form and exercise of authority, the common life with experiments of small communities, uncertainty in regard to function, the age structure, and so forth.

It was damaging for religious that they were scarcely supported by the believing awareness of the community, let alone that of the broader public. Their services were expected, there were protests when communities closed houses because of lack of recruits, but there was no effort to offer a solution in prayer, meditation, and concern to the problems of the life and recruitment of the orders.

In this situation there occurred new types of attempts at a uniting of

[65] Op. cit., 13.
[66] J. Zürcher, *Päpstliche Dokumente zur Ordensreform* (Einsiedeln 1954), 122ff.
[67] Apostolic constitution *Sedes Sapientiae* of 31 May 1956, *AAS* 48 (1956), 354–65, 358.
[68] *GuL* 24(1951), 92; cf. no. 7.
[69] Cf. *AAS* 25(1958), 34ff.

the monastic ideal with the demands of the apostolate through an extensive breaking away from the framework of the old orders and congregations. As an example may be mentioned the Little Brothers of Jesus, which, as a continuation of the work of Charles de Foucauld (1858–1916), realized a new type of apostolate "in the midst of the world." With complete abandonment of inclosure, they live together in communities of about four members and separately pursue a secular calling. As their founder tried, by an exemplary life, to bring the Gospel to the tribes in the Sahara, so his brotherhoods pursued the same goal in the non-Christian and, for evangelization, very accessible "desert" of our modern secularized civilization. Out of the strength of the love and imitation of Christ, they seek through the simplicity of their life-style and hospitality to be open to the encounter with the Lord in people. And so the Eucharist and Holy Scripture constitute the support of their community. "Work for the sanctification of the world," Charles de Foucauld has the Lord say and thereby expresses the essential element of his vocation, "work for it as my Mother, wordless, silent, build your retreats in the midst of those who do not know me, carry me into their midst by erecting there an altar, a tabernacle, and bring there the Gospel, not by mouth but by example, not by preaching it but by living it."[70] By 1960 the number of brotherhoods grew to forty-five in twenty countries with a total of 216 brothers. Since 1939 there has been a female branch of the Little Sisters of Jesus with like aims.

The Secular Institutes

Whereas the new impulses for a reform and adaptation of the orders and congregations to the needs of the time proceeded essentially from the Holy See, there was active around the middle of the twentieth century in the "secular institutes" a form of striving for Christian perfection which had developed without the cooperation and to a degree under the skeptical observation and repudiating reactions of the official ecclesiastical offices. The members of these new communities, whose beginning extend back to the early nineteenth century, strove to realize the life of the evangelical counsels as individuals or in small groups in the midst of the world; without public vows and without being bound to a strictly organized community life, they felt themselves entirely bound to the apostolate in the milieu of the moment, especially of a secular calling.

---

[70] Quoted from H. Urs von Balthasar, "Kirchenerfahrung dieser Zeit," *Sentire Ecclesiam,* ed. by J. Daniélou and H. Vorgrimler (Freiburg 1961), 743–68, 754.

Soon these communities turned out to be as necessary as suited to the apostolic permeation of the secularized world. The number of *Instituta saecularia* grew. The initial opposition on the part of theologians and the Curia was to a great extent based on the traditional teaching of the inseparability of the state of perfection and solemn profession. But the then ensuing papal approval, at first only in individual cases, was all the more possible when Leo XIII in the constitution *Conditae a Christo* of 8 December 1900[71] had recognized the congregations that had already reached flowering as communities of religious and as a state of perfection.

Protracted preliminary work by ecclesiastical commissions and consultations by the Congregation of the Council in union with the Holy Office and the Congregation of Religious paved the way for the recognition of secular institutes as a "third state of perfection" by Pius XII's apostolic constitution *Provida Mater Ecclesia* of 2 February 1947.[72] The norms of this constitution applied to "communities, both of clerics and of lay persons, whose members observe the evangelical counsels in the world for reaching Christian perfection for the complete fulfillment of their apostolate."[73] The Church recognizes the dedication of life of the members of secular institutes and their vows or promises but does not grant either the public nature of these vows in the form of a solemn profession or make obligatory their "common life or living under the same roof";[74] "one or several common houses"[75] are, however, desired as centers of formation and meeting, as dwelling places of the leaders of the union, and for the reception of individual members for reasons of health or other considerations. The connection between the institute and its members is a "perpetual or temporary" one,[76] as well as a "mutual and perfect" one.[77] The right to found "secular institutes" pertains to the bishop, with the obligation of consulting the Congregation of Religious and reporting to it.

A year after *Provida Mater Ecclesia*, Pius XII on 13 February 1948 issued the motu proprio *Primo feliciter anno*,[78] in which the "secular institutes" were expressly praised and confirmed. In it the Pope thanked for the "help which brought to the Catholic apostolate in extremely great providential wisdom consolation in our evil age that

[71] *ASS* 23(1900–1901), 341–47.
[72] *AAS* 39(1947), 114–24.
[73] Ibid., 120.
[74] Op. cit., ART. II, par. 1, p. 120.
[75] Op. cit., ART. III, par. 4, p. 122.
[76] Op. cit., ART. III, pars. 3, 1, p. 121.
[77] Op. cit., ART. III, pars. 3, 2, p. 121.
[78] *AAS* 40(1948), 283–86.

has fallen to pieces."[79] The stressing of the striving for perfection, which should "be adapted to life in the world in all things and brought into harmony with them,"[80] as well as the emphasis on the apostolic activity of the "secular institutes," which should be carried out "not only in the midst of the world, but, so to speak, out of the world,"[81] make clear the change which the notion of "secular institutes" has gone through since their origin: Whereas it originally was meant in the sense of a purely negative limitation in relation to the religious state, and in the preparations for *Provida Mater Ecclesia* there was still consideration of including the new societies in the concept of "religious state," now with the stressing of the "worldly" character of the secular institutes the qualitative distinction to the orders appeared in a manner which assisted the notion of "secular institutes" to an independent development and a positively filled autonomy. The new departure, which was rather hindered than encouraged by tendencies to "claustration," through the making aware of the general vocation released forces for sanctification which opposed the increasing clericalization of the orders and in general the tension between clergy and laity. Areas not yet reached or attainable—especially in the missions—could be opened up for apostolic penetration.

The number of secular institutes grew by 1962 to fifteen communities of papal right, about sixty of diocesan right, and a still greater number of unions which were just seeking ecclesiastical approbation. In the great majority these were communities of women, and strikingly enough many of them in Latin countries.

Because of the considerable number of existing "secular institutes" and the great diversity of their tasks, here only a few of the most important can be mentioned as representative: As "the authentic model of the secular institute"[82] the *Opus Dei* is designated in the papal charter of approbation. It is one of the most widespread, numerically strongest, and, on account of the professional excellence of its members, most influential "secular institutes." The community was founded at Madrid. for lay persons and priests by the young priest José María Escrivá de Balaguer (1902–75) under the name of *Sociedad Sacerdotal de la Santa Cruz y Opus Dei* and, as the first of the "secular institutes," obtained papal approval on 24 February 1947. At the beginning of the 1960s it already comprised around fifty thousand members from sixty-five

---

[79] Ibid., 283.
[80] Op. cit., 284f.
[81] Op. cit., 285: "non tantum in saeculo, sed veluti ex saeculo."
[82] Quoted from O. B. Roegele, "'Opus Dei': Legende und Wirklichkeit einer umstrittenen Gemeinschaft," *Opus Dei—Für und Wider* (Osnabrück 1967), 148–80, 152.

nations and virtually all classes and professions, including some 2 percent priests.

An essential center of gravity of the activities of the institute lies in the field of the religioideological and scholarly formation and training of the academic recruits. This was seen in the founding in 1952 of its own university, recognized by the Holy See in 1960, in the Basque provincial capital, Pamplona, as a first step to other foundations of schools in many countries. But the stressing of the profession as the chief means of personal sanctification and of the apostolate became the occasion for the forming of centers of *Opus Dei* in the worker's quarters of large cities, whereby the chief stress lay on the erecting of places of formation and of pastoral care in the milieu of the workers' calling. Members of *Opus Dei* also put themselves at the disposal of the missions, and thereby they joined apostolic activity with professionally qualified work of development. In Peru *Opus Dei* undertook one of the most difficult missionary areas of Latin America. Finally, a series of literary and publicity activities in periodicals and publishing must be mentioned.

Likewise of papal right is the institute of the *Prêtres du Prado,* which is restricted to French members but is typical of many communities of a like orientation. It was founded in the nineteenth century as purely a community of priests by Father Chevrier (1826–79), who was closely linked to the Curé d' Ars, Saint Jean Baptiste Marie Vianney. In accord with the aim fixed at that time, the members aspire, even today, to make the Gospel credible to the poor through personal poverty. While the work threatened to fail in Chevrier's lifetime, the number of members increased in the present century from thirty-two in 1922 to 610 priests in 1960, as well as 202 sisters, whose sphere of activity extends far beyond France to Africa, Japan, Chile, and elsewhere. The members see the sphere of their apostolate especially in parochial care of souls, but also work as catechists and pastors among the workers and the working youth.

The most important German contribution to the development of the secular institutes is the multibranched Schönstatt Work with its international expansion. It was called into being in 1914 by Father Josef Kentenich (1885–1968). To this work belonged a group of Marian apostolate lay communities as well as several secular institutes, of which first the "Schönstatt Marian Sisters" obtained in 1948 the papal *Prodecretum laudis,* a step toward definitive recognition, which came on 8 December 1976. The long-range goal consists in the "Marian formation of the world to Christ." In conformity with the spirituality of "working-day sanctity," a "dynamic relation to the world" should make it possible for the institute, in the most suitable form of the moment,

THE DIVERSITY OF THE INNER LIFE

whether as individuals or in the group, to carry out the tasks in Church and world. The male branch includes, besides the institute of the "Schönstatt Fathers," who are chiefly professionally active for the Schönstatt Work, the "Schönstatt Priests" as a community of diocesan priests and the less strong "Schönstatt Marian Brothers." The members of the community of the "Ladies of Schönstatt" remained in their lay calling and frequently devoted themselves secondarily to various apostolic tasks in the Church's pastoral care and *caritas*. A two-year novitiate and two tertiarates should consolidate and deepen the religious life of the members by means of further religious formation and introduction to study. Due to the unobtrusiveness of their dress and life-style many of the women were able to continue their apostolic work to an astonishing degree even during the Nazi period. Around 1976 the "Schönstatt Marian Sisters," with more than twenty-eight hundred members from almost thirty nations, were the largest female secular community in Germany. Since 1933 they have expanded outside, among other places to South Africa, Brazil, Argentina, Uruguay, Chile, the United States, Australia, and Switzerland. During the period of the war and persecution the institute undertook tasks in some Slavic countries. The centers of gravity of its efforts lie in the fields of education and *caritas*. Community experiences in this branch of the Schönstatt Work a very intensive emphasis: One who desires to enter leaves his former group in life and places himself entirely at the disposal of the institute. The members are prepared for the tasks of their calling by an intensive schooling of eight and one-half years. After the completion of their training they are divided into intern members, who live with uniform dress in the home community, and extern members at individual posts in religious or secular dress, as well as the Sisters of Adoration.

Through its many-faceted apostolic commitment, the new form of life of the "secular institutes" had a favorable impact on the pastoral attitude of the old orders and on making aware the close connection of the contemplative ideal with the apostolate. Hans Urs von Balthasar also points to the importance of the "secular institutes" for the choice of a state of life by the unmarried woman.[83] If she sees herself not called to the religious state, then, since admittance to the priesthood is denied her, she can easily incur the tension of an unclear intermediate stage between the simple "unmarried life" and virginity undertaken from religious motives. Here membership in a "secular institute" can offer a function in life and support.

[83] Cf. H. Urs von Balthasar, *Der Laie und der Ordensstand.* (Freiburg 1949), 93–97.

While the "secular institutes" in their adaptation to the needs of the time also supplement the old orders and congregations in many ways with the élan of a new departure, for their part they are supported by the spirituality living in these orders, so that, in the continuity of the Christian striving for perfection, no break but an enrichment pointing to the future may occur.

Worker-Priests

The ecclesiastical authority also directed to secular institutes the groups of dedicated pastoral workers who, searching for new ways to regain for the faith the workers alienated from the Church, were willing to share their daily work, their manner of life, and their environment. A highly motivated experiment became in its beginnings the "scandal of the twentieth century and the drama of the worker-priests."[84] In 1943 Fathers Henri Godin (1906–44) and Yvan Daniel had issued a report on the Christian conquest of the proletarian classes under the title *Is France a Mission Land?*[85] The work, which courageously expressed what had long been known but not admitted, proceeded from the observation that, for the proletariat alienated from the Church, the traditional parish was entirely inaccessible, because it required of it the changing of its mentality and way of life, and conversely the parochial care of souls scarcely penetrated into the modern pagan world. Loyal to the model of Gregory the Great in regard to the Anglo-Saxons and to the efforts of the mission in remote lands for native priests and a preaching adapted to the manner of thinking and intelligence of the natives, one should bring to the workers' world a pure religion purged of human additions which enclose a civilization. Was not Saint Paul a pagan with the pagans and a Jew with the Jews? A year previously, on 5 October 1942, on the initiative of the Assembly of the Cardinals and Archbishops of France at Lisieux, the priestly seminary of the *Mission de France* had been opened. It was supposed to attract to the de-Christianized areas suffering from a lack of priests those who were capable of entering into the mentality of the outsiders. Cardinal Suhard (1874–1949) of Paris, who had approved Godin's report before its appearance, formed in 1944, under the name of *Mission de Paris,* a group of priests who, freed from ordinary parochial ministry, were to seek and go new ways of the apostolate. They proposed to "hold up the Catholic priesthood as a model in a missionary manner, beginning with the dependent, deprived, collective life of the poor of this day, through the same living conditions, . . .

---

[84] A. Collonge, *Le scandale du XXᵉ siècle et le dràme des Prêtres-ouvriers* (Paris 1957).
[85] *La France, Pays de Mission?* (Paris 1943).

through the clear intention of belonging to a given social class and of living on the level of the best of its members."

The designation "worker-priest," *prêtre-ouvrier,* for a priest who worked a full day at a job, was not distinguishable externally from a worker, and was not at first known as a priest in his closest environment, came into use through the *Diary of a Worker-Priest* by Henri Perrin, S. J.[86] The book told of the activity of French priests among their countrymen who were prisoners of war or those bound to work in Germany. The access into the life-style of the working world here offered by the situation was experienced as an effective apostolic possibility and after the war was continued by priests, including members of the Mission de Paris, Lyon, and other industrial towns. It was less concerned, after the example of Saint Paul (1 Cor. 9:15–18), to earn one's livelihood by one's own work; rather, according to Cardinal Suhard, the work of these priests was "the act of naturalization of the priests among people to whom he was hitherto only a foreigner; suffering and ready for penance, he shares in human existence."[87] In his 1947 pastoral letter "Growth or Decline of the Church,"[88] which obtained worldwide attention, the cardinal had demanded an apostolate of incarnation in the overcoming of Modernism and integralism. "Adaptation means not compromises, not systematic substitution of the old by the new, a fortiori not mutilation of the Gospel but only integral and intelligent incorporation of this Gospel into that which is to be converted. . . . To be an Apostle means to undertake in so far as it can be properly undertaken all of the human and of the world which man had fashioned for himself, to permeate all. All, which means, apart from sin, all values, even those hitherto foreign to the Christian, in so far as it is not simply a question of mankind's own mad ideas."[89]

The boundaries indicated by the cardinal between the required adaptation to the world and becoming uniform with the world (Rom. 12:2), the falling victim to the world, cannot easily be carried through in daily life and demands great religious strength and a considerable gift of discernment. This and a basic philosophical and theological formation for the confrontation with the ideology of Marxism have not rarely been lacking. Solidarity with the workers and this included sharing in struggles over wages and strikes in a front with the Communists brought the worker-priests into the twilight. And at the Curia there was

[86] *Journal d'un prêtre-ouvrier* (Paris 1945).
[87] Cardinal Suhard, *Le prêtre dans la Cité* (Paris 1949).
[88] *Essor ou déclin de l'Église* (Paris 1947).
[89] Ibid., 63–67.

concern for their spiritual life and the preeminence of the priesthood proper and pastoral care. On 23 September 1953 there was issued through Nuncio Marella to twenty-six bishops and religious superiors the request to break off the experiment.

Meanwhile, public opinion had been attracted in a sensational way to the worker-priests through the press and Gilbert Cesbron's novel that appeared in 1952, *The Saints Go to Hell,* which obtained a circulation of more than two hundred thousand copies and many translations. Secrecy about the measures of the Curia, as was demanded, was impossible. Millions of Frenchmen had gained a great sympathy for the worker-priests and were indignant. In difficult discussions among Rome, the bishops, and the worker-priests possibilities were sought for continuing the apostolate under other conditions—only three hours work per day, life in a community of priests. Not all the approximately one hundred priests followed the directions of the bishops. Others, in an understanding with the bishops, quietly made new efforts. In March 1957 the Assembly of the Cardinals and Archbishops of France founded the Mission Ouvrière in an effort to make possible in modified form the presence of the priest in the workers' milieu. On the occasion of his first visit, in June 1959, to John XXIII, from whom as the former nuncio at Paris a special understanding was anticipated, Cardinal Feltin, archbishop of Paris, made a report on the matter. To his request that in special cases worker-priests might again be appointed as full-time workers, there was made known to him on 3 July the decision of the Holy Office that for the future every sort of factory work should be forbidden to priests. "The Holy See," said the decision of the Holy Office, "is of the opinion that for the apostolate in workers' environments it is not essential to send priests into the workers' milieu and that it is not possible to sacrifice to this end the traditional notion of the priesthood, even if the Church sees in this apostolate one of its dearest tasks. . . . It is true that the priest, like the Apostles, is a witness (cf. Acts 1:8) but a witness of the resurrection of Christ (cf. Acts 1:22), as of his divine and redeeming mission. He gives this witness especially by the word and not by manual labor among factory workers, as if he were one of them." Factory work makes it impossible to pursue the priestly duty of prayer. Even if some accomplish this, they should devote their time better to their priestly office than to manual work. "Did not the Apostles institute the diaconate precisely in order to free themselves from temporal affairs . . .? (Cf. Acts 6:2, 4)."[90] The bishops should reflect whether it is not the time to

[90] *HK* 14 (1959–60), 77.

establish for the apostolate in workers' environments secular institutes whose members could be taken from priests and lay persons, of whom the latter could pursue the apostolate of work without temporal limits. The priests give their lay brothers a basic instruction and spiritual formation adapted to the workers' life, advise them in their problems, and support them in their difficulties. Father Loew, O.P., followed this route at Marseille with the secular institute "Saint Peter and Saint Paul," in which lay persons and priests devoted themselves together to the worker mission on the parish basis. The "Little Brothers of Jesus," a brotherhood in the spirit of Charles de Foucauld, also traveled a similar road.

The community called "of the Prado" after one of the former amusement sites purchased by the founder in a slum quarter of Lyon, worked with mission teams, three to five strong, of priests and lay brothers, who settled in the midst of workers' areas and earned their own livelihood. Auxiliary Bishop Alfred Arcel pursued a cobbler's trade in Lyon-Gerland as head of a team in homework until 1959. He had to give up this activity but remained superior of the "Prado" and, as auxiliary bishop, collaborator with Cardinal Gerlier.

The basic feature common to the religious movements here discussed, the spirituality from which they arose or by which they were stamped in their course, is difficult to pinpoint. The spirituality of these decades seems most clearly characterized by a Christocentrism that is oriented to the apostolate. The historical Jesus, "Christ our Brother," came alive again: Jesus assumed our concrete life and fulfilled it in his death and resurrection. In his passage, *Pascha,* through death to glory he expanded his existence—limited to him as an individual during his earthly life—to the "mystical Christ," who has us participate by baptism in his destiny and his divine life. This is accomplished in the Church, which is the body of Christ mysteriously united to it in a living unity. The new life of the child of God, Christ in us and we in Christ, is a task for the Christian. He should form his life and the world in Christ to the honor of God the Father. But Christocentrism means not a spiritualistic reversion to individualistic interiority or flight from the world, but, on the contrary, the stressing of the fully human and of the world, which is included in the spiritual life.

If in Jesus Christ divinity and humanity have become a personal unity, without admixture or separation, then the "yes" to Christ means also a "yes" to people and to his earthly creation. The human is not annihilated in him but confirmed and surrendered. "If the human and earthly, nature and culture, are to be accepted, then this happens on the highest and purest level in Christ's human nature." "The miracle, the shocking, does not lie in a man's becoming God but in the incarnation of God. This makes the Christian exult."[91]

Like theology, so also spirituality stands under the sign of a turning to the world: the taking seriously of one's own worth and one's own destiny in the light of the mystery of the incarnation of God. Creation and incarnation are seen in intimate connection. The Logos, in whom everything was created, became Man in order to lead everything back to God. The incarnation is not intended first with reference to redemption from sin; it is the goal and crown of creation and would have happened even without the fall into sin. "Through him and by him everything was created" (Col. 1:16). God's "yes" to the world in creation finds its confirmation and fulfillment in the incarnation. From here on one strives to refute by word and deed Nietzsche's charge and that of the Marxists, that Christ misued the world for a beyond, that Christianity is far from people and their problems.

This is promoted by works such as V. Poucel, *Against the Opponents of the Body* (1937); G. Thils, *Theology of Earthly Realities* (1947); M. D. Chenu, *Theology of Work* (1955); Y. Congar, *The Layman: Outline of a Theology of the Laity* (1953); G. Philips, *The Layman in the Church: A Theology of the Lay State* (1952); Alfons Auer, *The Christian Open to the World: Principles and History of Lay Piety* (1960). The salvation history line—creation, incarnation, Parousia—makes one think of Jean Daniélou's *Secret of History* (1953), and of Hans Urs von Balthasar's *Theology of History* (1950), but again makes one aware of the eschatological feature of Christianity in contrast to an often too optimistic incarnational theology.

In asceticism the active virtues were more strongly stressed. It was explained that the Christian can only assure his own salvation if he is concerned for the salvation of the others. The diversity of Christian manifestation in a rapidly changing political, economic, and social environment became clear and with it the necessity of again preparing for it. This required a greater measure of personal responsibility and gave to the spiritual and moral life an unequally greater dynamism. It penetrated more strongly into the awareness that not only the human acts directly related to God—prayer, meditation, and liturgy—are religious, but everything that is done for the honor of God, in accord with Paul's statement: "Whether you eat or drink or whatever else you do, do all for the glory of God" (1 Cor. 10:31). Thus it is significant that on the four-hundredth anniversary of the death of Saint Ignatius (d. 1556) "in actione contemplativus" or the "to find God in all things" was

---

[91] K. Adam, *Christus unser Bruder* (Regensburg 1926, 3d ed. 1935).

stressed as the message of the saint for our day.[92] It corresponds to this, that "working-day sanctity" became the characteristic slogan for the spirituality of religious movements, and the "little way" of Thérèse of Lisieux obtained new luster.[93] In contrast to the disillusioned and self-centered Christocentrism of the *Devotio moderna,* for the "little" Thérèse it meant to love Jesus above all, to save souls for him, in order that he might be loved more.

[92] E. Coreth, "In actione contemplativus," *ZKTh* 76 (1954), 55–82; E. Iserloh, "'Gott finden in allen Dingen,' Die Botschaft des heiligen Ignatius von Loyola an unsere Zeit," *TThZ* 66 (1957), 65–79, reprinted in E. Iserloh, *Verwirklichung des Christlichen im Wandel der Geschichte* (Würzburg 1975), 99–113; J. Stierli, "Das Ignatianische Gebet: 'Gott suchen in allen Dingen,'" *Ignatius von Loyola,* ed. by F. Wulf (Würzburg 1956), 151–82.

[93] I. F. Görres, *Das verborgene Antlitz. Eine Studie über Therese von Lisieux* (Freiburg 1944); new edition: *Das Senfkorn von Lisieux,* 9th ed. (Freiburg 1964); H. Urs von Balthasar, *Therese von Lisieux. Geschichte einer Sendung* (Cologne 1950); *Therese vom Kinde Jesu. Selbstbiographische Schriften. Authentischer Text* (Einsiedeln 1958); A. Combes, *Die Heilandsliebe der heiligen Teresia von Lisieux* (Freiburg 1951).

CHAPTER 10

Developments in the Clergy since 1914*

The Swiss theologian Hans Urs von Balthasar, on the occasion of the Third Synod of Bishops at Rome in 1971, expressed the conviction that the clergy is today "the clear trouble spot of the Church."[1] In this connection he had in mind the role of priests within the postconciliar development, especially within the reform of the liturgy just as much as the alarming tendencies in the clergy itself and its relations to the episcopate.

The most recent "priestly crisis" cannot be understood and properly explained against the background of the immediately preceding decades. Its roots go deeper. At the beginning of our century individual priests and groups of priests had taken an interest in bridging the chasm between Church and theology on the one side and the modern world and its temper on the other side, and hence had demanded reforms within the Church.[2] Even then there was question of the language of the

* Norbert Trippen
[1] J. Höffner, H. Urs von Balthasar, eds., *Bischofssynode 1971. Das Priesteramt* (Einsiedeln 1972), 6.
[2] From the abundance of contemporary reform writings let the following be named as quality examples: H. Schell, *Der Katholizismus als Prinzip des Fortschritts* (Würzburg 1898: on the Index!); A. Ehrhard, *Der Katholizismus und das zwanzigste Jahrhundert* (Stuttgart and Vienna 1901). Less balanced reform efforts are described by A. Hagen,

liturgy, of church discipline, of the Church's stance in the social question, as well as of problems of the clerical state, for example, the obligation to celibacy, the relations between priests and bishops, and the form of clerical education. As widespread as the aims of such priestly groups were their motivation and character. They extended from Romolo Murri's *Democrazia Cristiana* in Italy and Marc Sangier's *Sillon* in France to the Swabian cranks who wanted to found a union of priests for protection of the interests of the clerical state against Bishop Keppler of Rottenburg.[3] In 1901 there took place in Vienna a quite well attended Austrian clergy meeting, which aimed to improve the feeling of solidarity among the priests as well as their social position and material situation. However, the Austrian episcopate forbade the repetition of this meeting.[4]

All these initiatives in the clergy, effected independently of the episcopate and directed to inner church reform goals, fell under Pius X's suspicion of Modernism and were suppressed in this Pope's struggle against the heresy assumed by him to be everywhere. The encyclical on Modernism, *Pascendi*, of 8 September 1907, again forbade priests to take the editorship of newspapers and periodicals without the previous permission of the bishops, who were moreover obliged to supervise the activity of priests as reporters or collaborators on such publications. The bishops should permit congresses of priests only in very rare cases.[5] At the same time the Scholastic orientation of theological studies and strict rules for the education of priests in seminaries were decreed, so that the suppression of these reform groups in the clergy succeeded, especially since the First World War and the subsequent upheavals left no room for a further confrontation with Modernism that was not desired by Benedict XV.

Between the two world wars there appeared or developed a few associations of priests, which pursued, however, purely religious and ascetical or legal and economic aims.[6] There were no tensions worthy of

---

Der Reformkatholizismus in der Diözese Rottenburg (1902–1920) (Stuttgart 1962); cf. also N. Trippen, *Theologie und Lehramt im Konflikt. Die kirchlichen Massnahmen gegen den Modernismus im Jahre 1907 und ihre Auswirkungen in Deutschland* (Freiburg, Basel, and Vienna 1977), passim.

[3] Hagen, op. cit., 51–61.

[4] F. Funder, *Vom Gestern ins Heute. Aus dem Kaiserreich in die Republik* (Vienna 1952), 342ff. A similar congress had already taken place at Bourges in 1900 (Hagen, op. cit., 51).

[5] In question are paragraphs 34 and 35 of the encyclical *Pascendi:* A. Michelitsch, *Der biblisch-dogmatische "Syllabus" Pius' X. samt der Enzyklika gegen den Modernismus und dem Motu proprio vom 18. November 1907*, 2d ed. (Graz and Vienna 1908), 346ff; cf. Trippen, op. cit., 29.

[6] Konrad Algermissen provides a survey of these class unions in *LThK* 8 (1936), 471ff.

mention between episcopate and clergy. The system of the strictly secluded seminary training functioned, even if it was already regarded as antiquated and occasionally smiled at by more far-sighted academic teachers and numerous students. However, there was no thought of a fundamental reform but of assisting in a mild practical application of the existing order. Exegetes, dogmaticians, and church historians, especially in the state academic chairs in Germany, were able to distinguish between research hypotheses and results and what might have been publicly represented and published.

A limited field of activity for autonomous reform tendencies of the younger clergy that were not always familiar to and approved by the episcopate was supplied especially in Germany by the youth movement and, in connection with it, the liturgical movement in the 1920s and 1930s.[7] On the travels of youth, priestly dress must first be laid aside. Corresponding decrees in diocesan synods, as, for example, in the Cologne diocesan synods of 1922 and 1937,[8] then spoke clearly. The introduction of the "community Mass" with the recitation of the vernacular translation parallel to the Latin Mass texts occurred not without tensions between liturgically active circles of youthful priests and the older pastors or the episcopate. Also the beginnings of the ecumenical movement, pursued by individual priests and lay groups, were in no way under the encouraging benevolence of all bishops. Nevertheless there prevailed among the diocesan clergy a relationship of serene loyalty between priests and bishops. There was in the clergy no basic criticism of the Church, its doctrine, and its discipline. The *Hymns to the Church* of Gertrud von Le Fort reflect a widespread outlook even in the clergy of those decades.

The worker-priests in France[9] can be regarded as a first movement in the clergy in which postconciliar points of discussion on the priestly state and priestly life seemed to be anticipated. It is characteristic of its starting situation in the early 1940s that this movement was begun by the French episcopate: When during the war several thousand French seminarians and members of Catholic Action were forced to work in German factories, the bishops of France founded a secret pastoral work to take care of them. Twenty-five priests put themselves at their disposal. The experience of this enterprise with an entirely different

---

[7] On the Youth Movement see the general bibliography for this chapter.

[8] *Die Diözesan-Synode des Erzbistums Köln 1922 am 10.11 und 12. Oktober* (Cologne 1922), 31: "It is especially prescribed that clerical garb is obligatory even for travel and especially for travel. If a cleric is forced to make journeys on which he probably cannot wear clerical dress, he should previously inform the vicar general." Corresponding decree of the synod of 1937, ibid. (1937), nos. 28, 51.

[9] See the general bibliography for the chapter.

priestly activity and life-style constituted the basis for the *Mission de Paris* after 1946. Renouncing the middle-class manner of life, priests sought to live as workers among the workers. However, it soon appeared that, because of the solidarity with the working class and its social and political goals, conflicts with the ecclesiastical authorities could not be avoided. The relations of the worker-priests to the parish priests were increasingly strained, because the latter lived in a bourgeois mentality and had no understanding of the demands of the workers and their priests. The bishops of France were partly concerned for the social position of the worker-priests, the Roman Curia rather for their spiritual life. In 1953–54 the experiment was interrupted at Rome's direction. The majority of worker-priests finally submitted to the pertinent decrees and returned to their diocese or order. The attempt and its failure occupied French and European public opinion until the eve of the council.

The Second Vatican Council expressed itself in two decrees on the formation and on the ministry and life of priests, but the question of priests did not supply any of the council's central subjects. For the succeeding unrest among priests quite other statements of the council were of indirect but all the more persistent effectiveness, above all the dogmatic constitution *Lumen gentium,* with its new self-understanding of the Church as the pilgrim "People of God," but also the higher valuation of the general priesthood of the faithful and the opening to the world in the pastoral constitution *Gaudium et spes.* The reconsideration and the change which the council produced, most clearly visible in the liturgy, led to an interior insecurity in many priests, to public discussions on the priestly office and the priestly form of life, to the rapid increase of resignations of their office by priests, finally to the forming of groups of priests with partly sociopolitical, partly anti-hierarchical, partly class-solidarity goals. Within a short time there was a strong mobilization of public interest for the question of priests within and outside the Church, which of course again quickly evaporated.

In the effort to trace this development that erupted and peaked between 1968 and 1971, one must not lose sight of the fact that countries and continents were affected differently by it. Neither in Poland and other Eastern bloc states nor in Vietnam or the missionary Churches of Africa was there a disturbance comparable to that in Western Europe and North and South America. The inner uncertainty and external solidarity of many priests developed in part out of the theological and reform impulses of the Second Vatican Council, but in part also out of the ideological pluralism and the lack of spiritual orientation of the Western democracies. Hardly accidental must have been the temporary connection of this group of priests with the unrest at the Western universities and in the younger generation in general. Had not the council, more unambiguously than earlier ecclesiastical pronouncements, referred pastoral care to the service of the world and the recognition of its proper values? Thus the repercussions of developments outside the Church on the clergy of the Western world could not be absent.

With the end of the council there began in Europe and America a theological discussion on the raison d'être of a priesthood based on a sacramental ordination and undertaken for life. Do the beginnings in the New Testament offer a dogmatically satisfactory justification? it was asked. The lack of priests, the permanent diaconate restored by the council, and the higher valuation of the general priesthood of the faithful as well as their being entrusted with pastoral services hitherto reserved to priests made unavoidable the question in what did the *differentia specifica* of the ordained priest consist in contrast to other believers active in the pastoral ministry.[10] If the priesthood as a special state, in contrast to the rest of the faithful, came under discussion in relation to theology and the inner structure of the Church, the decline of authority during those years in the Western democracies went out of the way to make acute the question of the self-understanding and role of the priest in Church and society. Just as in the secular sphere only authority based on objective competence and transmitted for a limited time would be tolerated, so too priests and their "solidarity groups" that were being established demanded that the official priestly ministry be justified, no longer sacramentally (vertically) but functionally, that is, by service to the congregation (horizontally); it had to be bestowed for a time and, depending on the circumstances, could be exercised in a secondary occupation. The priest had to become involved in the world and its problems and legitimize himself to his fellow citizens by a civil profession.

Younger priests especially were affected by these considerations. At first, these considerations led to their demanding the abandonment of priestly dress and class privileges. Here there was probably more at stake than an external approximation of life-styles and customs to the environment. For many there lay here the profession that sacramental ordination did not essentially distinguish the priest from the other members of the People of God.

Parallel to the discussion over the office and function of the priest and

---

[10] For the "uncertainty of role" of many priests, cf. the contributions of Glatzel in the *Jahrbuch für christliche Sozialwissenschaften* and in the *Stimmen der Zeit* (cf. the bibliography for the chapter). For the discussion on the office: Küng, *Wozu Priester? Reform und Anerkennung kirchlicher Ämter;* Schuh, *Amt im Widerstreit.*

in inner dependence on it was a confrontation over the obligation of priests to celibacy. At the council there had been widely opposed standpoints and motions on the extension of this obligation and its theological justification within the Decree on the Ministry and Life of Priests.[11] Pope Paul VI had finally rendered the discussion harmless when on 10 October 1965 he sent a letter to the president of the Conciliar Praesidium, Cardinal Tisserant, in which he requested that the question of celibacy not be discussed in full council and announced a statement to the clergy on priestly celibacy. This letter to Cardinal Tisserant was read in the *aula* on the next day and determined the further decisions of the council fathers. In number 16 of the Decree on the Ministry and Life of Priests it was recognized that celibacy is "not demanded by the very essence of the priesthood, as the practice of the Ancient Church and the tradition of the Eastern Churches show. . . . But celibacy is in many respects proper to the priesthood." As justification were cited the identification of the priest with Christ and the greater availability for the priestly ministry. "This holy Synod approves and reconfirms the law for those who are chosen for the priesthood, in regard to which the Spirit gives it the confidence that the Father will generously give the calling to the celibate life . . . if only those who participate in the priesthood of Christ through the Sacrament of Orders humbly and insistently pray for it, together with the whole Church."

Precisely this last expectation seemed in the succeeding years not to be realized. If it is hardly possible to obtain exact figures on the number of those who abandoned the official priesthood, still the research of the Swiss Pastoral Sociological Institute must have come close to reality when it reckoned between 1963 and 1970 from twenty-two to twenty-five thousand resignations in the diocesan clergy, corresponding to 5 percent of the clergy.[12] Especially alarming is the preponderance of younger priests among those leaving. This trend converged with the shockingly declining number of candidates for the priesthood and especially of priestly ordinations.[13] These last dropped, for example, in the German Federal Republic from 506 in 1965 to 213 in 1972; it is precisely here that the contrast to Poland and some mission countries is crystal clear: there is no lack of recruits there at this time.

This distressing development may have induced Paul VI very soon to redeem the promise to the council fathers of a statement on priestly

---

[11] Cf. also F. Wulf, S.J., "Kommentar zu Art. 16 des Dekrets 'Presbyterorum Ordinis,'" *Das Zweite Vatikanische Konzil* 3, 214–21, especially 217.
[12] Reproduced in Siefer, *Sterben die Priester aus?* 76f.
[13] Ibid., 77–89.

celibacy. The encyclical *Sacerdotalis caelibatus* of 24 June 1967 did not, however, contribute to relaxing the tensions over the celibacy discussion but rather made them more acute. As was stressed in the later survey of priests, a great number of priests, especially those positively decided in the celibacy question, had not even read the encyclical,[14] whereas the troubled younger clerics regarded its content as disillusioning. The Pope adopted the essential statements of the conciliar decree on the celibacy of priests, but continued in the justification of celibacy, in the retaining of the union of the priestly vocation and the obligation of celibacy as well as in the estimation of those who abandoned the priesthood as "pitiable deserters" in the traditional ideas and arguments.

The temporarily violent discussion of celibacy took place in the mass media, in journalism, and a rapidly growing literature of brochures, but also in lectures and organized discussions.[15] In this connection it became clear that the obligation of celibacy of priests was no longer understood, not only by a large portion of the younger clergy, but also in broad levels of the Catholic people and was no longer approved without more ado.

The dissatisfaction with the celibacy encyclical must have been one of the determining events for the founding, still in preparation, of the solidarity groups of priests in various European countries. Thus the meetings and publication organs of these groups were then also the forum in which the demands and expectations in regard to the celibacy question were articulated not as representing the entire clergy—the groups included only a very small percentage of priests—but still for an active stratum of younger priests in the Western hemisphere. It was again and again stressed that it was not a question of suppressing celibacy as a freely accepted charism but of ending the legal obligation of celibacy for all priests of the Latin Church. Even more strongly was it demanded that tried men in the married state, *viri probati,* be admitted to priestly ordination—a demand that had already been rejected by the council!—and married priests allowed to exercise their office further.

In close connection with the obligation of celibacy there was discussed in groups of priests the question whether the "official priesthood" and the "clerical state" were even replaceable, to what extent priests were included with the powers supporting society and

---

[14] This is given, for example, by the interpretation of the Italian survey of priests (*Il Sacerdozio ministeriale, Problemi del Clero in Italia,* Editrice Studium [1970]); Simmel, *Priester zwischen Anpassung und Unterscheidung,* 147: "The encyclical *Sacerdotalis Caelibatus* was virtually not read; what happened was that it was criticized rather than studied."

[15] Cf. also the general bibliography for the chapter.

had lost touch with the day-to-day world.[16] There was heard the demand for a professional activity of priests, for closer solidarity with the working class and the peripheral social groups. Finally, the meeting of priests at Chur in 1969 demanded also a political commitment of priests against capitalistic and totalitarian systems in favor of a more just and humane society. If such demands were powerfully inspired by the political situation of some European states and especially of Latin America, the demand for inner democratization of the Church, for collaboration of priests and lay persons in the making of ecclesiastical decisions, was based on conciliar statements, which seemed to point in this direction, but which were often enough excessively interpreted. People pressed for transparency in the decision-making process and exercise of authority in the Church, especially for the sharing by clergy and people in the selection of bishops and the filling of other ecclesiastical positions of leadership.

The effort to represent such demands, especially the specifically professional, more effectively, to find solidarity for episcopally disapproved experiments in liturgy and pastoral care, or even to effect changes of awareness in favor of ecclesiastical or political reforms, was the basis on which, from the beginning of 1968, priest groups appeared in various European countries. To be sure, in ARTICLE 7 of the decree on priests the council had obliged the bishops to establish a Priests' Senate,[17] representing the *presbyterium* of the diocese, and in many countries this directive of the council had already been complied with. But the Priests' Senates found their place and field of activity only slowly among the existing and canonically firmly established advisory bodies of the dioceses. In any event, they proved to be unsuited to parry and overcome the unrest in the clergy. The priest groups appearing at the same time proceeded partly from older informal discussion groups and communities of priests or were founded on the basis of concrete opportunities, such as the encyclical *Humanae vitae* in the summer of 1968. With surprising rapidity there arose organized associations and principle papers on the diocesan level, but also

---

[16] There was a broad discussion on these subjects at the conference of delegates of European priest groups from 5 to 10 July 1969 at Chur: Holenstein, *Churer Dokumente.*

[17] "They [the bishops] should be glad to listen to them [the priests], should even ask their advice and discuss with them what the care of souls demands and what promotes the welfare of the see. But in order to do this, a circle or council of priests should be created in a manner suited to today's circumstances and requirements, who would represent the *presbyterium,* whose form and norms must still be canonically determined. This council can effectively support the bishop in the government of the diocese with its advice" (*Das Zweite Vatikanische Konzil* 3, 175ff.).

supranational contacts.[18] Various "solidarity groups" from West German dioceses amalgamated into a federation at Königstein on 26–27 May 1969 into the "Working Community of Priests' Groups in the German Federal Republic."

The priest groups in the various European nations had a different orientation conditioned by the political and inner-ecclesiastical situation.[19] The German SOG groups developed an overwhelmingly professionally specified goal, which was critical of the hierarchy. The Netherlands group *Septuagint* occupied an influential position in the contemporary development process of the Dutch Church. It was supported by broad strata of the clergy and faithful and had continuous contact with the Dutch bishops. The French groups, *Concertation* and especially *Échanges et Dialogue,* stood in an extraordinarily tense relation with the hierarchy. Still without prospects was the position of the Spanish and Portuguese groups in view of the contemporary political and inner-ecclesiastical circumstances in both nations.

The very differently structured and oriented European priest groups reached the apogee of their importance in 1969 when they met, so to speak, as a contrasting program to the contemporary episcopal symposium, at Chur[20] from 5 to 10 July, and, parallel to the Second Synod of Bishops, from 10 to 16 October at Rome,[21] for a "Conference of Delegates of European Priest Groups." On these occasions, the groups, their aims, and their style of procedure in regard to the bishops, going beyond all the usual amenities, became familiar to the public. At Chur the delegates demanded admittance to the episcopal symposium, which had chosen as its theme "The function of the priest today." But the bishops refused to admit the priests' representatives; there were indeed contacts on the periphery, some informal talks between individual bishops and delegates of the priests. And it may be said that the consultations of the bishops took place under the impression of the appearance and demands of the priest groups.

The Conference of Delegates of Priest Groups at Chur passed several resolutions, which were put together by the sharply antihierarchical French group, *Échanges et Dialogue:* the "Resolution on Work," "Reso-

[18] Development and activity of the priest groups are reflected in their publications, in Germany especially in *Imprimatur* (Trier) and *SOG-Papiere* (Bochum) (cf. the bibliography for the chapter).

[19] On the different orientation of the European priest groups: Werners, *Jahrbuch für christliche Sozialwissenschaften* 12 (1971), 187f.

[20] On the conference of delegates at Chur and its proclamations: Holenstein, ed., *Churer Dokumente;* idem, *Der Protest der Priester;* Raske-Schäfer-Wetzel, *Eine freie Kirche für eine freie Welt,* 55–72.

[21] On the conference of delegates at Rome: Raske-Schäfer-Wetzel, op. cit., 83–177.

lution on Celibacy," "Resolution on the Commitment of Priests." In addition there were a text on "The Permanent and the Changing in the Episcopal Office in the Church," which presented a reply to the talk of Cardinal Döpfner on the same subject to the episcopal symposium, and a letter "To our Brother in Peter's Office, Paul VI."

Three months later in Rome the next conference of delegates, on the occasion of the Synod of Bishops, wanted to be received by Paul VI, but the Pope refused. The conference, in the rooms of the Waldensian faculty, worked for a theological elaboration of the priests' insecurity as to role but was under stronger internal tensions than the meeting at Chur. There appeared only "study documents" of which it was said[22]: "The texts are not accepted in all individual formulations, they are not regarded as definitive statements but as the point of departure for new reflections." The themes were: "On the Local Church," "On the Bishop," "On the Petrine Ministry," "A Church for the World," "Ministry of the Priest."[23]

It seems that with these two large conferences of 1969 the Priest-Group Movement had already exceeded its high point. The European groups were themselves aware that they had got themselves too much entangled in a—partly only due to prevailing circumstances—class problem. The radical attempts at a public overcoming of these problems aroused only in passing the interest of the ecclesiastical and noneccle-siastical public, did not further assist those immediately concerned, and at times gave the impression of a new "left" clericalism. And so the organizers of the "Congress of Priestly Solidarity" at Amsterdam from 28 September to 3 October 1970 sought for ways to a new contact with the people and the world.[24] The meeting had as its theme "Church in Society," and non-European, especially South American, priest groups were also invited. But the course of the congress revealed an internal discord and a considerable difference of opinion between the European groups, hitherto predominantly concerned with questions of class, and the Latin Americans, arguing from a political revolutionary standpoint. And there was disappointment over the slight public interest. Where, at the congresses in Chur and Rome, throngs full of expectation had prevailed, now sizeable holes gaped: on the press benches. Not only for the press but also for the organizers themselves there was missing in Amsterdam the program of contrast to a meeting of bishops.

[22] SOG-Papiere 1969, no. 5 (25 November 1969), 29.
[23] The report in the SOG-Papiere 1969, no. 5, 24–43, and Raske-Schäfer-Wetzel, Eine Freie Kirche für eine freie Welt, from p. 83, give no ultimate clarity as to exactly what the titles of the texts are and by how many delegates the individual texts were accepted.
[24] The SOG-Papiere 1970, 342–57, reports in detail on the congress at Amsterdam, with facsimile printing of press articles.

If in 1971 it was still written concerning the priest groups that they were "a reality no longer to be imagined as nonexistent," which made up 10 to 15 percent of the diocesan clergy,[25] that was already outdated at that time. The priest groups and their publication organs either disbanded expressly on their own or they quietly discontinued their work. Some still vegetated for a while without attracting attention. More enduring than these progressive groups were the traditionalist priest groups that arose or revived as a reaction, for example, the "Movement for Pope and Church," which found its adherents predominantly in the middle and older generations of the clergy.

If one asks about the reasons for this rapid end of an awakening that was so energetically pursued, there must be named, apart from the too wide spectrum in views and goals, which became apparent in the large gatherings, an inadequate theological basis and argumentation, an appearance unbalanced by inner insecurity and marked by the sociological orientation of those years. For the too highly set reform aims and the growing flood of proposals and contributions to discussions the organization and the material basis of the groups proved to be inadequate.[26] The leading forces in these groups were not rarely priests who were themselves unsure in their role or were even stuck in an acute vocation crisis. Because of apostasies, numerous groups lost their initiators and leading minds.

The bishops met the inner insecurity and external solidarity in the clergy, at times under antihierarchical signs, totally unexpectedly and unprepared. How did the papacy and the territorial episcopates react? The gamut extended, at first, from surprised nervousness by way of helplessly watching patience to the attempt at open dialogue with the priests on the edges of the conferences at Chur and Rome. A cautious reserve in regard to the priest groups was forced on the bishops by the fact that, for example, the "SOG papers" of the German and Austrian priest groups published numerous cases of conflict of individual priests with their bishops, dramatically arranged as "documentation," and in so doing gave publicity to personal letters of the bishops to individual priests.

The German bishops made a very early theological contribution of high quality to the overcoming of the priests' crisis by the doctrinal letter on the priestly office[27] issued at their plenary meeting on 11 November 1969. In a biblical and dogmatic consideration the bishops

---

[25] Thus Werners, *Priestergruppen*, 202.

[26] In almost every fascicle of the *SOG-Papiere* occurs the complaint of being unable to master the organizational problems, especially the flood of paper.

[27] *Schreiben der deutschen Bischöfe über das priesterliche Amt. Eine biblisch-dogmatische Handreichung* (Trier 1969).

sought to clarify what had become unsure: the understanding of the office of priest based on the New Testament and developed in the history of the Church. This document of the German bishops was of importance for the choice of themes and the course of the Third Synod of Bishops at Rome in 1971. "The Priestly Ministry" was one of its chief themes. The document issued by this Synod, "The Office of Priest," was decisively stamped by Cardinal Höffner and Hans Urs von Balthasar. It led beyond the biblical-dogmatic consideration to a statement on the basic questions of priestly ministry and priestly life.[28]

Parallel to these exertions for a theological and spiritual mastering of the crisis of the priesthood proceeded the attempt at an inventory carried out by sociological methods. Even if the priest groups with their radical programs represented only a minority, in the years after the close of the Second Vatican Council it became in general ever clearer that the clergy no longer constituted a closed unity among themselves and with the bishops. The uncertainty in regard to this phenomenon offered to some territorial episcopates the occasion to permit or even to commission surveys or inquiries among their priests by scholarly institutes employing the methods of the public-opinion poll.[29] From 1969 to 1972 such inquiries, more or less simultaneously but independent of one another, took place in the Netherlands, the German Federal Republic, Italy, Austria, Switzerland, Spain, and the United States. Not counting the Netherlands, about 43 percent of the Catholic priests of the world were affected by this wave of interrogation.[30] Since these inquiries were variously accented and carried out by different methods, did not take place at exactly the same time, and were colored by the ecclesiastical and political context in the different countries, a comprehensive comparison of them is not without problems. Nevertheless definite common tendencies and also regional differences are clearly visible.

The questions which were submitted to the priests referred first to the background, development, and living conditions of priests. Precisely in this area considerable differences appeared among the individual countries. A second series of questions dealt with the functions of the priest and the difficulties connected with them. Understanding of function and calling, spiritual life, and celibacy constituted a third complex, with which finally was closely associated the relationship of the priests to the Church and the authorities. The outcome of the interrogations operated on the one hand in a sobering and at the same

[28] J. Höffner, H. Urs von Balthasar, eds., *Bischofssynode 1971. Das Priesteramt* (Einsiedeln 1972).

[29] Report of research and literature in the bibliography for the chapter.

[30] Simmel reaches this evaluation in Forster, ed., *Priester zwischen Anpassung und Unterscheidung*, 127.

time calming manner after the shocking rise of the priest groups. Seventy-nine percent of the German priests declared, for example, that they were content, or even very content, with their activity of the moment; 12 percent answered "pretty well," and only 5 percent were not especially, or not at all, satisfied.[31] To be sure, 51 percent of the German priests declared it necessary or worthy of consideration that obligation to celibacy be abolished in the future, but 59 percent had no hesitation, despite the celibacy obligation, in advising young men to the priestly calling.[32] On the other hand, there could no longer be overlooked what people had long not been ready to admit: "The priesthood is not monolithic, a broad spectrum of pastoral and theological positions is recognizable, and hence an inner-ecclesiastical tension, which appears to some as fatal, to others as a sign of hope. There is hardly a question of fundamental importance any more on which priests would be of one opinion and on which they would not express themselves very clearly in one sense or another."[33] Despite a certain difference, which stands out in Europe somewhat between the upset situation in the Netherlands via Germany and Austria to the still more stable ecclesiastical situation in Switzerland, the inquiries made clear uniform trends: An increasing stratum of younger priests in Europe and the United States is critical of the "vertical" understanding of the priestly office and bases the priestly ministry not so much in relation to sacramental priestly ordination as a result of preaching and the administration of the sacraments, as rather "horizontal-functional" in the sense of a service to mankind and to the unity of the congregation. With this understanding of the office is united the rejection of a special priestly state, clerical dress, and the joining of the priestly office and obligatory celibacy, which is found to be not adequately based theologically and burdensome. Even more definitely than the demand for the "uncoupling" of priesthood and obligatory celibacy was the demand for the admission of proved married men to the priesthood—not only by the younger priests but, for example, in Germany by 79 percent of all priests.[34] With this notion of the office and of the appropriate manner of life of the priest there was joined in the younger clergy a critical attitude toward ecclesiastical authority and its carrying out of its office, the demand that priests and lay persons take part in the calling of the holders of office, just as an extensive collaboration in pastoral work and the leading of the community be intended for the laity in general.

[31] Schmidtchen, *Priester in Deutschland,* 76–81.
[32] Ibid., 66–76.
[33] Ibid., XII.
[34] Ibid., 69. Similar or even stronger desires resulted from the surveys in other countries.

Other results of the surveys were conditioned by regional peculiarities: In Austria and Switzerland 60 to 70 percent of the priests obtained their education in ecclesiastical boarding schools, in Italy and Spain the percentage must have been still higher. In Germany, on the other hand, 65 percent of the priests spent their school years at home and attended public schools. But it is striking that just in the first named countries their formation was felt by the priests as insufficient and the demand for a more qualified improvement was clearly raised. Generally widespread was the demand for specialization in priestly activity and supplementary secondary studies. The special political situation of Spain in the late Franco epoch was reflected in statements of the Spanish priests on Church-state relations.[35]

The temporary keystone in the great chain of inquiry was constituted by the inquiry among the German priesthood candidates in 1974.[36] The results make known how even in a brief period of time not unessential nuances can occur: "One can neither speak of a return to conservatism nor of a continuation of a generally critical trend. Instead, something new, perhaps unexpected, happens. In their open, partly critical attitude the priesthood candidates are much like the young priests—in general, they entirely resemble them rather than the older ones. But then the new must be noticed: a different, perhaps strengthened drive toward spirituality. Among the authenticating ideas of the candidates there are clearly prominent the concepts of being borne by Christ's commission and of the personal relation to God. This is expressed not only in this question about the authenticating of the office but also in numerous other connections."[37]

With this a last and decisive effect of the crisis of the priesthood is touched: the insecurity and decimation of the recruits for the priesthood. Parallel to the forming of solidarity groups of younger priests there occurred in European and American countries a convulsion of the previous system of seminary education and theological studies.[38] Every-

---

[35] Especially Simmel tries to trace common trends and differences in the results of the inquiries (Forster, ed., *Priester zwischen Anpassung und Unterscheidung*, 127–48).

[36] G. Schmidtchen, *Umfrage unter Priesteramtskandidaten* (Freiburg, Basel, and Vienna 1974).

[37] Ibid., 1.

[38] A first inventory on the question of priestly formation occurred at the beginning of 1966 on the occasion of a broadcast series of West German radio: L. Waltermann, *Klerus zwischen Wissenschaft und Seelsorge* (Essen 1966). The discussion of the reform proposals for the formation of priests and the study of theology which has since taken place is hardly comprehensible. The efforts for the reform of the study of theology in Germany were expressed in the previous five fascicles *SKT =Studium Katholische Theologie, Berichte-Analysen-Vorschläge*, edited by the commission "Curricula in Theologie" of

where the number of priesthood candidates dropped strongly, so that not a few diocesan seminaries and religious houses of studies had to close. In particular, the externally strictly isolated manner of life of the seminaries could not be maintained. Seminarians demanded the possibility of being permitted to live individually or in groups in the midst of the other students in their places of study. The previous curriculum of theological studies, the narrow Neo-Scholastic dogmatic theology, the unconnected juxtaposition of theological disciplines in the program of studies, the unsatisfactory inclusion of didactic-pedagogical and pastoral-practical disciplines, were perceived as inadequate for the preparation for priestly and other pastoral ministries, especially as soon the number of students, even of females, increased, who began a study of theology without the intention of becoming priests. The education of such students, for example, in Germany, for a chiefly professional career as teachers of religion, demanded the development of corresponding programs of study and organization of examinations, which were included in the framework of the formation of other teachers.

The concern for a reorganization of the seminary education of priests and of theological studies had already occupied the Second Vatican Council. The decree *Optatam totius* on the formation of priests, of 28 October 1965, was characterized by some, chiefly the Protestant observers at the council,[39] as one of the most productive and important conciliar texts. In balanced instructions the way was pointed to a reform of priestly formation and, for the first time with this clarity, the value of human maturity and the properties of character esteemed by people in prospective priests was stressed. In the discussions it became clear that the demands for a reform of priestly education were very different in the several continents and countries. And so the council decided on an incisive shifting of competencies in the area of priestly formation: no longer the curial Congregation of Studies and Seminaries, but the episcopal conferences should in the future have the legislative competence for this sphere. "Hence for individual peoples and rites a proper 'order of priestly formation' should be introduced. It is to be set up by the episcopal conference, reviewed from time to time, and approved by the Apostolic See. In it the general laws should be so adapted to the special local and temporal circumstances that the formation of priests

---

the West German Faculty Meeting by E. Feifel (Zurich, Einsiedeln, and Cologne 1973–75).

[39] Thus by O. Cullmann and J. C. Hampe in A. Arens, *Priesterausbildung und Theologiestudium* (=*Nachkonz. Dokumentation* 25), 5.

may always correspond to the pastoral demands of the countries in which the priests have to exercise their ministry."[40]

In 1966–67 Cardinal Garrone, prefect of the Congregation of Studies and Seminaries, in four circulars admonished the chairmen of the episcopal conferences to carry out this mandate quickly.[41] However, many episcopal conferences were taken unawares by the reorganization in the training of priests and were in no position to achieve a required reorganization in the brief time, so that it was possible only to attempt national educational organizations.[42] Hence on the occasion of the First Synod of Bishops in 1967 Cardinal Garrone arranged for a *Ratio Fundamentalis*, a framework for the education of priests throughout the world. In it lay the danger that the Congregation of Studies and Seminaries would again take over the competence which the council had just granted to the episcopal conferences. However, the *Ratio Fundamentalis Institutionis Sacerdotalis* of 6 January 1970,[43] essentially elaborated by the Italian Jesuit Paolo Dezza, the Spanish diocesan priest Germano Martil, and the German Benedictine Abbot Augustinus Meyer, avoided this danger. It produced an orientation framework for the legislation of the episcopal conferences with a proposal in examples and preformulations, which took none of their competence from the bishops. When the reform of priestly formation was perceived as urgent under the pressure of contemporary circumstances, the determination showed that the episcopal conferences within a year should draw up a *Ratio Nationalis* and submit it to the congregation for approval.

With all the imperfections and the marks of haste which adhere to the *Ratio Fundamentalis*, it must as a whole be regarded as a positive framework for priestly education outlined against the background of the situation existing in many countries. In content it follows the *schema* of the decree *Optatam totius* and is concerned with the pastoral theology of the clerical vocation, seminaries and their direction, the candidates for the priesthood, their human, spiritual, scholarly, and pastoral formation, as well as with the continuing education of the priests after their seminary days. The necessity of some continuing professional training was at this time definitely demanded in the survey of

---

[40] *Optatam totius*, no. 1 in *Das Zweite Vatikanische Konzil* 2, 315ff.

[41] A. Arens, op. cit., 5–66 describes the efforts for a reform of the formation of priests down to the *Ratio Fundamentalis* of 6 January 1970.

[42] Very noteworthy attempts of this sort by the German bishops' conference are given in "Neuordnung der theologischen Studien für Priesteramtskandidaten" (1968) and "Leitlinien für die Priesterausbildung" (1970), *Priesterausbildung und Theologiestudium*, 541–63, and 265–77.

[43] *AAS* 62(1970), 321–84; *Priesterausbildung und Theologiestudium*, 68–263.

priests by priests of Latin countries, formed in a narrow Neo-Scholasticism and exclusively educated in isolated seminaries, and it constituted one of the central points of the program of the priest groups of Europe and South America. The delay of a year, determined in the *Ratio Fundamentalis,* for the setting up of regional or territorial organizations of priestly formation was not to be observed for the reason that not only the territorial episcopates but also others who were to take part—regents, directors of boarding schools, professors—had to prepare for a cooperation and finally for an agreement. The work on the *Rationes Nationales* was not finished in a moment. The consolidation made clear in the survey of the candidates in the German Federal Republic in 1974 allowed like tendencies to be assumed in the younger clergy. The acute crisis seemed to be followed by a phase of sober seeking. It would be a fallacy to assume that the development would quickly lead back to the interior and exterior uniformity characteristic of the clergy in the first half of this century.

This insight must have been the occasion for the traditionalist groups in the clergy, especially for the movement around the former missionary Bishop Marcel Lefebvre, to forcibly bring about this uniformity in the education, theology, spirituality, and discipline of priests by a return to old forms and with radical means. In this connection Lefebvre appeals, not without reason, to Pius X and the struggle of this Pope against the dangers of Modernism and its reform efforts. As the investigation of this anti-Modernist struggle, intensively pursued in the last years, shows, it indeed suppressed Modernism but did not master the problem inherent in it. To an even stronger degree can the anti-Modernism of today's traditionalist groups prove itself to be a way of error.

CHAPTER 11

*Religious Communities and Secular Institutes**

The Orders between Persistence and Change

The history of religious institutes of the nineteenth century was characterized by the unanticipated resurgence of the old orders and the founding of many new congregations. When the First World War broke out, this period drew to a close. Most religious institutes had been consolidated and found their manner of life and field of action, and there began for them a period of unforeseen growth. In the years 1920–

* Viktor Dammertz, O.S.B.

352

60 almost all religious communities experienced a hitherto unprecedented influx of novices. This extraordinarily strong accumulation was certainly conditioned also by external factors—the world economic crisis with massive unemployment; inadequate possibilities for education and professional goals outside the monastery, especially for women. This explains also the relatively high number of departures during the time of probation. Nevertheless, in the case of most of the young people who decided for the religious life, this choice was based on religious motives. Readiness for commitment to the Church and for service to people, as well as concern for the salvation of one's soul, were an effective motive in the decision for the religious vocation.

The end of the First World War presented the communities with a new situation: the peace treaties altered the map of Europe. Because of this, the institutes were compelled to adapt their own structures to the new boundaries; in particular, the national states just established were not pleased that their religious should be directly subject to foreign tribunals. On the other hand, the events of the war contributed to a destruction of the state-Church system and of some laws hostile to the Church, so that now also for the orders previously existing legal restrictions and state regulations disappeared. The great misery which the First World War left and which was intensified by the subsequent economic crisis meant a challenge for the institutes, especially in the social and charitable sphere. Not least due to the influx to the novitiates were the communities able to provide effective aid.

Within the Church the new Code of Canon Law meant some significant changes for the religious institutes.[1] They not only aimed at a generally welcomed simplification, at greater clarity and legal security, but they bore especially an emphatically pastoral, spiritual accent. The legislator had obviously striven to create a legal order which should facilitate an authentic religious life. Of course, this all-inclusive codification of the canons for religious also involved negative consequences. The prescriptions of the canons for religious, partly going into great detail, attempted, it is true, through repeated references to the particular law of the individual institutes, to take account of the variety of religious life, but nevertheless promoted a considerable thrust toward uniformity and the leveling of the religious life.[2] Since Canon

---

[1] A. Scharnagl, *Das neue kirchliche Gesetzbuch,* 2d ed. (Munich and Regensburg 1918), 61–70.

[2] This leveling had already become standard in the restoration of the nineteenth century; the individual institutes often differed more in the form of their habit and other externals than in their spirituality (R. Hostie, *Vie et mort des ordres religieux* [Paris 1972], 249–51, 264–73).

THE DIVERSITY OF THE INNER LIFE

489 annulled all regulations of rules and statutes which were contrary to the norms of the code, the institutes were asked to adapt their constitutions to the new code, and, in making the necessary changes, to employ where possible the words of the code itself.[3] On 6 March 1921 the Congregation of Religious published norms for the formulation of the statutes of the new congregations, which also obtained great importance for the existing communities in the course of the revision of the constitutions.[4]

All these prescriptions confirmed the tendency already discernible under Leo XIII to centralize the structure of the religious life; in particular, the institutes of papal right should be united more closely to Rome.[5] The prescription proved to be especially harmful in the long run which required that the constitutions must contain neither historical references nor quotations from Scripture, the councils, the Fathers, or the works of other authors, and *a fortiori* no rather long ascetical directions, detailed spiritual admonitions, or mystical reflections. They should be confined instead to the canonical decisions on the special character of the respective institute, its aims and functions, on the essential content of the vows, on the acquiring and loss of membership, on the life-style of the religious, as well as on the government of the institute.[6] If brief spiritual texts were tolerated (and it must be admitted that these directions excluded really excessive and often very subjective and transient ascetical and edifying statements from the constitutions), this narrowing of the fundamental document of each institute favored a lasting codification of the institute's life, especially as it was no longer clear that the canonical decrees on the structure of religious life were derived from spiritual foundations. Also it could not fail to happen that the new statutes of many institutes in their structure and content looked very much alike and so the character of the individual institutes threatened more and more to disappear. This was true especially of the many congregations founded in the nineteenth and twentieth centuries, which could not have recourse to one of the old religious rules. Their statutes were often enough not much more than a reproduction, only poorly accommodated to the current situation, of the model statutes provided by the Holy See as guidance.

---

[3] *AAS* 10(1918), 290, 13(1921), 538f.

[4] Ibid., 13(1921), 312–9; these norms extended back to a similar document of 1901, to which were appended even detailed model statements. In 1937 the Propaganda issued similar norms for the religious institutes subject to it (L.R. Ravasi, *De Regulis et Constitutionibus Religiosorum* [Rome, Tournai, and Paris 1958], 187–257).

[5] U. Stutz, *Der Geist des Codex Iuris Canonici* (Stuttgart 1918), 246–50.

[6] Normae, cap. IV–V in *AAS* 13(1921), 317f.

Still, many of the young people who entered the monastery found spiritual and religious security in the existing strict organization. Incorporation was facilitated for them by the patterns of religious life which were given to them. In the instructions of the novitiate more was said about constancy and submission, sacrifice and renunciation, obedience and confidence in the superiors than about innovation, self-development, and personal initiative, just as the Church itself proved to be very much an unshakable institution and guarantor of order and security in the breakdown of the period between the wars.

But developments in Church and society were not without their effects on monasteries. The liturgical movement and the striving for a piety nourished on Holy Scripture evoked disgust among religious with the prayer formulas and devotional exercises of some communities, as well as with the often very petty directives of a moral and ascetical character which governed the everyday life, especially of female religious, even in details, and left little room for personal responsibility. More and more the lack of a religious life directly oriented to the Bible was felt. Besides, religious in many countries saw themselves challenged by a growing secularization of public life and the alienation of many from the Church. Measures hostile to the Church, suppressions of monasteries, and open persecution presented existentially to the religious affected by them the question of their vocation. Religious often found themselves inadequately equipped for an intellectual confrontation with an environment which faced the Christian faith with indifference, rejection, or even hostility.

The Second World War and its consequences tore many institutes of men and women from their traditional organization and transplanted them to situations in which they had to come to independent decisions and prove themselves in their spiritual vocation without being able to count on leadership and guidance "from above."

The Rise of New Types of Communities

Against this background must be viewed the origin of new kinds of communities. As early as the turn of the century Charles de Foucauld (1858–1916) planned to establish a community of Little Brothers of Jesus that departed from the traditional structures. In the following years he sketched several rules but at his violent death he left behind no disciples. The seed he had scattered sprang up only later. In 1933 René Voillaume and some followers founded at El-Abiodh-Sidi-Cheikh on the edge of the Sahara the community of the Little Brothers of Jesus, which was recognized as a congregation of episcopal right in 1936 and in 1968 obtained a papal decree of approbation. The Little Brothers of

Jesus live in brotherhoods of usually three to five members, preferably in environments which are not accessible to the Christian message or are entirely alienated from it. They want to attest the love of God less through preaching than through solidarity with the people among whom they live. Their model is Jesus, the worker of Nazareth. Their effort is to shun all division. And so they make themselves with their work a part of the occupational world of their neighborhood, live in small dwellings which are in keeping with the milieu, and extensively adjust themselves to their environment in the externals of life. Their spirituality is characterized by a piety which is nourished especially on the cult of the Eucharist and reflection on Scripture. Every brotherhood is directed by a "responsible person," and the entire congregation is subject to the superior general. According to the latest figures, the institute numbers sixty-eight fraternities, in which live 232 members, including sixty-four priests.[7] In the same spirit there arose in 1939 at Touggourt in the Sahara the community of the Little Sisters of Jesus, which was erected as a congregation of episcopal right in 1947 and in 1964 obtained a papal decree of commendation. To it belong 990 sisters in 212 communities.[8] These religious communities inspired by Foucauld's spirit differ from the traditional institutes especially through a strong emphasis on brotherhood, which should be experienced in the small community, the team, through a new interpretation and realization of poverty, which is understood as wholehearted common destiny with the strata of population oppressed by poverty with all their insecurity and lack of protection, and through their unobtrusive presence "in the heart of the masses" "in the midst of the world," where they intend to influence through nothing other than their exemplary Christian life. Later arose other communities, which likewise were oriented to Charles de Foucauld, as in 1956 the fraternity of the Brothers of the Virgin of the Poor, to whom the model for their contemplative life is Jesus, praying and doing penance in the desert, and the community of Little Brothers of the Gospel, erected as a congregation of episcopal right in 1968, who also wish to live among the poorest, not only to share their poverty in solidarity, but to preach the gospel to these poor.[9]

To live in the midst of the world is also the motto of the secular institutes, which in part already existed for a long time as "pious unions"

[7] R. Voillaume, *Mitten in der Welt* (Freiburg 1960); *LThK*, 2d ed., VI, 329f.; *Annuario Pontificio 1975*, 1199.
[8] *LThK*, 2d ed., VI, 330; *Annuario Pontificio 1975*, 1252.
[9] "Une nouvelle forme de vie monastique. La Fraternité de la Vièrge des Pauvres," *Rythmes du monde* 10(1962), 207–15. Lecture of R. Voillaume before the *Unio Superiorum generalium* in November 1975 (unpublished).

or without any ecclesiastical approval, but only found their recognition as a canonical state of perfection through the apostolic constitution *Provida Mater* of Pius XII of 2 February 1947 and obtained their basic organization in the motu proprio *Primo feliciter* of 12 March 1948 and in the instruction of the Congregation of Religious of 19 March 1948.[10] It is proper to the secular institutes that their members live on principle in the midst of the world. By the *character saecularis* they are essentially distinguished from the religious state, the *status religiosus,* with which, however, the striving for perfection unites them in a form approved by the Church. The wearing of a religious habit, common life in community after the manner of the orders, and in general any approximation to the life-style of the religious communities, are not in accord with the essence of a secular institute. True, the members bind themselves to a life according to the evangelical counsels, not through official vows but through private promise, oath, or something similar. Even if in many of them there is often present the inclination to adapt themselves to the traditional communities in this or that form, and some institutes are still grappling with their profile,[11] they are clearly and consciously distinct from "religious" in their manner of life.[12]

Meanwhile, there are many secular institutes which were established by the bishops with Rome's *Nihil obstat;* six institutes of men and twenty-one of women have so far become of papal right.[13] The best known and most influential of them is the *Opus Dei.* Its male branch was founded in Spain in 1928 by the priest J.M. Escrivá de Balaguer (1902–75); on 24 February 1947, a few weeks after the appearance of *Provida Mater,* it was the first secular institute to obtain the papal decree of approval, and in 1950 it obtained definitive confirmation. This branch includes priests, who are united within the institute in the *Societas Sacerdotalis Sanctae Crucis,* and laymen, who, in accord with the statutes, must constitute the majority. The ordinary members, who must have

---

[10] *AAS* 39(1947), 114–24: 40(1948), 283–86, 293–97; cf. L. Beyer, *De Institutis saecularibus documenta* (Rome 1962).

[11] F. Wulf, *Die Säkularinstitute nach dem Zweiten Vatikanischen Konzil* (Meitingen and Freising 1968), 28f.

[12] But since they, like religious, are subject to the same Roman Congregation, the latter on the occasion of the reform of the Curia of 1967 was renamed and now is *Sacra Congregatio pro Religiosis et Institutis saecularibus* (SCRIS) (apostolic constitution *Regimini Ecclesiae universae,* ART. 71, *AAS* 59[1967], 912).

[13] H. A. Timmermann, *Die Weltgemeinschaften im deutschen Sprechraum* (Einsiedeln 1963); A. Wienand, ed., *Das Wirken der Orden und Klöster in Deutschland* II (Cologne 1964), 636–68; *Annuario Pontificio 1975,* 1200, 1325f. On 20 September 1970 there were twenty-one secular institutes of papal and seventy-nine of diocesan right, to which belonged 30,000 women, 3,000 priests, and 400 lay brothers as members. *Opus Dei* is not included in these statistics (*Vita consecrata* 7[1971], 151, n. 1).

had a complete theological program, if possible with a doctoral degree, and a broader, likewise complete training in another academic profession, as well as the "Oblates," in regard to whose education not such high claims are made, bind themselves by vows to a life according to the evangelical counsels. Even married men can be admitted as extraordinary members, who seek to realize the spirit of the evangelical counsels in a manner of life corresponding to their situation. For the rest, the members pursue their professions and exert themselves for the Christian permeation of the families, the working world, and public life. In general they are not to be known as members of the Opus Dei; usually they appear not as a group, but each works in his place in the sense of the institute, in regard to which a characteristic élite-awareness unites them. However, the institute also appears as performer of common tasks. Thus, it is responsible for the Catholic University of Navarre at Pamplona, founded in 1952 and erected by the Holy See in 1960; with its thirteen faculties and scholarly institutes it ranks as one of the best universities in Spain; a majority of professors belong to Opus Dei. Further, the institute supports centers of study and student homes in many university cities. Outside Spain, Opus Dei has spread to about fifty other countries, especially Italy, France, and Latin America. The prelature *nullius* of Yauyos in Peru is entrusted to the community of Priests of the Holy Cross. In admitting members, the institute makes no distinctions of class, but it appeals especially to intellectuals, and it is well known that members of Opus Dei occupy many important posts of the political, economic, and cultural life of Spain. The ensuing involvement in the affairs of daily politics, joined to a certain secretiveness, has led to serious attacks on the institute. In addition to the male branch, in 1930 a female branch, marked by the same spirit, was founded, which meanwhile has also obtained papal confirmation. It forms a special secular institute with independent organs of government, but is, however, subject to the president general. After the founder's death in 1975 the professor of canon law Alvaro del Portillo was elected second president general of Opus Dei.[14]

The Acclimatization of the Orders in Mission Lands

New routes were also traveled in mission lands. In his encyclical *Rerum Ecclesiae* of 28 February 1926, Pope Pius XI appealed to missionaries to

[14] O.B. Roegele, "Das 'Opus Dei.' Legende und Wirklichkeit einer umstrittenen Gemeinschaft," *Hochland* 54(1961–62), 430–39; *HK* 22(1968), 353f., 29(1975), 536. In the *Annuario Pontificio 1975*, 1200, *Opus Dei* is given as a secular institute, although

devote themselves more strongly to the Church's intimate relationship with these countries. He pushed not only for the training of native priests and catechists but also for the establishing of communities of male and female religious. True, he regarded it as legitimate for missionaries to admit candidates from mission lands into their own communities, but admonished the mission superiors: "Reflect without bias and conscientiously whether it would not be better to establish new religious communities which were more in accord with the concerns and interests of the natives as well as the local situation and special circumstances." He especially urged the founding of contemplative monasteries, from which he expected a fruitful influence on evangelization.[15] The missionary decree of the Second Vatican Council again underscored this instruction and pointed to the necessity of making the religious life indigenous in a form suited to the respective culture and circumstances of individual peoples (ARTICLE 18).

Even if there were previously, especially in Asia, several congregations of native sisters, their number increased quickly after the appearance of the mission encyclical. It grew in Africa between 1920 and 1960 from nine to seventy-nine, although here at first great obstacles rooted in the tribal idea had to be overcome. For the ideal of the celibate life was at first totally foreign to the African mentality: a woman and her dowry were regarded as part of the wealth of her tribe, and the tribe to which she was turned over on the occasion of the marriage treasured her especially as mother of the children which she bore for the tribe. Only slowly did an understanding of the ideal of the religious life for the woman grow. The low educational status of many girls, due to the nonexistent school system, meant further impediment, especially in view of the independence of these African communities. In Asia, however, the presuppositions were much more favorable. In regard to the native applicants for the priesthood the missionaries in Asia generally preferred an integration into their own community. The cultural level of these countries facilitated such a common life. Even in Africa some of the missionary religious institutes chose this route, for example, the Holy Ghost Fathers, the Oblates of the Immaculate Virgin, the Franciscans; on the other hand, the efforts of the institutes founded exclusively for the mission, such as the White Fathers and Mill Hill Missionaries, were chiefly concentrated on the training of an

---

it allegedly no longer regards itself as such, in any case it obviously no longer collaborates with the other secular institutes (*Vita consecrata* 7[1971], 32, n. 5).
[15] *AAS* 18(1926), 77–79.

African diocesan clergy, an attitude which was for a long time intentionally fostered by the Congregation for the Propagation of the Faith.[16]

The appeal of Pius XI for the founding of contemplative monasteries at first found no very loud echo. The mission superiors were especially concerned to gain native collaborators in the pastoral, social and charitable, and educational sphere. Only after the Second World War and especially after the Second Vatican Council did the number of contemplative foundations greatly increase. Up to 1968 their number in Africa alone rose to twenty-seven monasteries of men and sixty-two of women. Whereas these houses of men all follow the Benedictine Rule—Benedictines, Cistercians, Trappists—among the houses of women, besides twenty modeled on the Benedictine type, ten convents of Poor Clares and seventeen of Carmelites are counted. In addition there are various other monasteries of women, seven fraternities of the Little Brothers and forty-four of the Little Sisters of Jesus, as well as one fraternity each of the Little Brothers of the Virgin of the Poor and of the Little Sisters of the Most Sacred Heart.[17] For the support and promotion of the Benedictine foundations in the Third World there arose at Vanves near Paris the *Secrétariat de l'aide à l'implantation monastique* (A.I.M.), which in 1973 took care of a total of sixty African, fifty-three Asian, ninety-one Latin American, and ten Oceanian monasteries of monks and nuns.[18] For a comprehensive exchange of views and experiences on the problems of the monastic life in the Third World, the superiors and superioresses of Africa met at Bouaké, Gold Coast, in 1964 and at Rome in 1966, those of Asia at Bangkok in 1968, and those of Latin America at Rio de Janeiro in 1972 and at Bogotá in 1975.[19]

The strivings to make the religious life indigeneous in these lands and to accommodate it to the local situations proved to be difficult. The first experiments in this area were planned and implemented by Europeans. Only the native religious succeeded by patient work in discovering an organic and enduring adaptation in fidelity both to the essential

[16] Cf. W. Henkel, "Congregazioni autoctone," *DIP* II, 1588–93; J. Casier, "Africa," *DIP* I, 130–40; P. Tchao Yun-Koen, "Cina," *DIP* II, 1026–8.

[17] *DIP* I, 137; on Carmel in the mission cf. *DIP* II, 451f.

[18] *Secrétariat de l'aide à l'implantation monastique,* "Monastic Growth," 1973 supplement to 1970 handbook.

[19] Detailed report in *Rythmes du monde* 13(1965), no. 1/2; 14(1966), no. 4; 16(1968), no. 4; 17(1969), no. 1/2; *Bulletin de l'A.I.M.* no. 9(1969), 7–27, no. 15(1973), 7–22, no. 19(1975), 7–21.

elements of the Christian religious life as well as to the cultural heritage of their own people.[20]

Religious Reform under Pius XII

In the congregations of the new type and the secular institutes it was believed that the goal sought could not be realized in the traditional structures of religious life. New routes were sought for shaping the life in accord with the evangelical counsels in a contemporary form. Meanwhile, however, there was no lack of reform plans and desires in the existing orders. However, it was in accord with reality that these were discussed in small groups of members of the orders and were not given wide publicity. It was Pope Pius XII, who as early as the first months of his pontificate, but especially from the end of the Second World War, made the *accommodata renovatio,* the renewal in accord with the times, of religious life an essential point of the program of his pontificate. This renewal should likewise be marked by fidelity to the traditional heritage as well as by courage for wise adaptation. In his talks and letters to individual religious communities he returned again and again to this great concern.[21] The papal directives make clear that they aimed to regulate a process of fermentation which was meanwhile under way in many religious communities and was especially spelled out in some general chapters. The Pope strongly emphasized the obligation not to attack the essentials of religious life and of the particular institute[22] and not to be unduly influenced by the current views and opinions.[23]

The Roman Congregation of Religious took up the aim of renewal of religious life in accord with the time when, for the first time in history,

---

[20] "Einheimische Schwestern und Brüder in Afrika," *Pro mundi vita, Centrum informationis,* Heft 15 (Brussels 1966); D. Plum, "Sind Mönche in Afrika ein Fremdkörper?" *HK* 28(1974), 494–97.

[21] The earlier documents are collected in extracts in *Acta et documenta Congressus generalis de statibus perfectionis* I (Rome 1952), 3–49; J. Zürcher, *Päpstliche Dokumente zur Ordensreform* (Einsiedeln 1954); cf. D.M. Huot, "Summus Pontifex Pius XII et accommodata renovatio in statibus perfectionis," *Apollinaris* 32(1959), 360–68; A. Scheuermann, "Die Ordensleute in den Dokumenten des Zweiten Vatikanischen Konzils," *AkathKR* 134(1965), 337–40.

[22] Thus, for example, in his talk to the Jesuits on 17 September 1946: "Ante omnia oportet Constitutionibus vestris et universis earundem praescriptis firme fideles sitis. Instituta Ordinis vestri possunt, si id congruens esse videatur, ad nova temporis adiuncta hic illic immutando accommodari; attamen quod praecipuum in iis est, nequaquam tangatur perpetuumque consistat" (*AAS* 38[1946], 383).

[23] Cf. Address to the superiors general of 11 February 1958 in *AAS* 50(1958), 153–61.

in the Holy Year 1950 it convened at Rome an International Congress for (male) Religious, which dealt in many lectures and reports with the *accommodata renovatio statuum perfectionis*. This general theme was discussed in three subdivisions in regard to the life and claustral discipline of religious, their formation and instruction, and their apostolic work.[24] Two years later a Congress of Superioresses General took place at Rome,[25] which also treated of the question of reform of the institutes, as did the "Second General Congress on the Timely Renewal of the States of Perfection," which the Congregation of Religious summoned to Rome in 1957 and planned under the energetic guidance of the then secretary, A. Larraona (1887–1973).[26]

From these large congresses proceeded the stimulus for a closer collaboration of the orders, whether on the national or the international plane. In many countries appeared conferences of superiors of the male and the female institutes, which were officially recognized by the Holy See and erected as institutions of papal right.[27] On the international level were held the *Unio Superiorum generalium* (USG) for male religious in 1957 and the *Unio internationalis Superiorissarum generalium* (UISG) for female religious in 1965, both of which took place at Rome. In addition there appeared in 1959 the *Confoederatio Latino-Americana Religiosorum* (CLAR) with headquarters in Bogotá, which as the umbrella association of all orders on that continent acquired great significance subsequently, especially as partner of the Latin American Episcopal Conference (CELAM).[28]

Even before the first international congress met, the Pope undertook a partial reform. On 21 November 1950 he published the apostolic constitution *Sponsa Christi* on nuns, which was followed two days later by directives for its implementation from the Congregation of Reli-

---

[24] *Acta et documenta Congressus generalis de statibus perfectionis* I–IV (Rome 1952f.). The theme of the congress was: "Statuum perfectionis praesentibus temporibus atque adiunctis accommodata renovatio" (ibid. I, 59).

[25] *Acta et documenta Congressus Internationalis Superiorissarum generalium* (Rome 1953).

[26] Cf. G. Ruiz, "Congressus generalis alter de accommodata statuum perfectionis renovatione a S. C. de Religiosie indictus," *Com Rel* 36(1957), 387–84.

[27] Cf. *Annuario Pontificio 1975*, 1477, 1327–49; R. Soullard, "Les unions de superieurs majeurs," *L'année canonique* 18(1974), 221–30; *DIP* II, 1423–31. These mergers could, of course, look back to a long history in some countries. Thus the modern *Vereinigung Deutscher Ordensobern* (VDO) goes back to the Conference of Superiors which was formed when, on the occasion of the Katholikentag at Krefeld in 1898, the superiors of the seven mission houses then existing in Germany met and decreed regular meetings for the future (K. Siepen, "Die Vereinigung Deutscher Ordensobern nach Akten und Berichten des Generalsekretariats der VDO," *Ordenskorrespondenz* 5[1964], 104–25).

[28] *Annuario Pontificio 1975*, 1327; on the CLAR see also *DIP* II, 1418f.

gious.[29] Entirely in the spirit of the papal reform program, these documents first underscored the unalterability of the contemplative life, the propriety of solemn vows, and the unrenounceable papal enclosure for all nuns. However, in adaptation to new requirements the rules on enclosure were modified, namely, by the creation of the so-called little papal enclosure, which permitted a meeting of nuns and outsiders in an area of the enclosure that was intended for work directed to the outside. The obligation to a proper, productive work was stressed. True, a high apostolic value was acknowledged in the very life of nuns; nevertheless, in so far as the constitutions provided, definite works of the apostolate were approved. Finally, these documents vigorously recommended the uniting of autonomous monasteries of nuns into federations so that they could give effective help to one another in this work of renewal. However, convents of nuns often only hesitatingly complied with this recommendation.[30] A broader area which stood in need of reform was that of the formation and instruction of candidates for the priesthood in religious communities. As early as 1924 in an apostolic letter to the superiors of orders Pope Pius XI had indicated the necessity of a solid education of religious clerics, oriented to the heritage of Saint Thomas. The same concern was the object of the instruction of the Congregation of Religious of 1 December 1931, which at the same time, in the period of the great flood of novices, urged a careful selection of candidates.[31] Pope Pius XII also, throughout his pontificate, was concerned for a good formation of religious, especially of the priests, through which they should be equipped for the manifold tasks which were imposed on them in the period of the upheaval that was becoming ever more clearly outlined.[32] Finally, on 31 May 1956 appeared the apostolic constitution *Sedes Sapientiae,* followed on 7 July by general statutes of the Congregation of Religious in the form of directives for implementation.[33] These documents treated not only the forming of candidates for orders of males and for the priesthood, but attributed great importance to their education in

---

[29] *AAS* 43(1951), 5–24, 37–44. On 25 March 1956 there was issued a further instruction of the Congregation of Religious, which, on the basis of previous experiences with the new legislation, reorganized the matter of enclosure in monasteries of nuns (*AAS* 48[1956], 512–26).

[30] On the entire matter cf. A. Larraona, *La nuova disciplina canonica sulle monache* (Rome 1952). The "little inclosure" was again abolished after the council (motu proprio *Ecclesiae Sanctae,* II, 32 in *AAS* 58[1966], 780f.).

[31] *AAS* 16(1924), 133–48, 24(1932), 74–81.

[32] In 1944 the Pope set up in the Congregation of Religious a special commission to direct and supervise this formation (*AAS* 36[1944], 213f.).

[33] *AAS* 48(1956), 354–65; X. Ochoa, *Leges Ecclesiae* II (Rome 1969), 3516–38.

pastoral theology as good shepherds of souls. As something new, they prescribed by common law after the completion of the study of philosophy and theology, oriented to the care of souls but more theoretically presented, and the reception of ordination, one additional year devoted to pastoral introduction and practice. And it was urged on all religious institutes to oblige the young fathers, after several years of work, to a year of probation, a sort of second novitiate. In accord with the papal pronouncements of 1931 and 1956, all clerical religious institutes were occupied with the revision of their *Ratio studiorum.*

However, Rome's concern was not only for the education of religious priests. In an effort to equip orders of women for their tasks that were becoming more difficult, the Congregation of Religious on 31 May 1955 erected the papal institute Regina Mundi at Rome, which was associated with the theological faculty of the papal Gregorian University. In it women religious were to be prepared in a three-year theological course both for the tasks of directing the members of their institute and for pastoral charges, especially in the area of schooling and education.[34] Rome thereby took up a burning concern of the Congress of Superioresses General of 1952.

The Second Vatican Council and Its Effects

At this stage of the process of a prudent, even timid "timely renewal" came the announcement of the Second Vatican Council, which, with its program of *aggiornamento,* aroused in wide circles of the Church, even among religious, great and partly also utopian hopes for a comprehensive reform and a profound renovation. The first schema on religious, which had been worked out by the preparatory commission, hardly went beyond what had been planned in reforms under Pius XII and had been in part introduced or implemented. It was understood as a rectilinear continuation of the Pian reform of the institutes.[35] Hence it did not correspond to the expectations which had been placed in this conciliar document on many sides. After tenacious work in the conciliar commissions and lively debate on the place and mandate of the institutes in the Church, at the close of the council there were on hand two important texts, which were expressly concerned with the religious state. Chapter 6 of the Dogmatic Constitution on the Church (AR-TICLES 43–47) aimed to define the theological place of the orders in the

---

[34] X. Ochoa, op. cit. II, 3394f.; cf. the statutes of the institute, issued on 11 February 1956 in ibid., 3457–60.

[35] Cf. F. Wulf, "Einführung zum Ordensdekret," *LThK,* 2d ed., *Zweites Vatikanisches Konzil* II (Freiburg, Basel, and Vienna 1967), 250f.

Church. Advisedly, the chapter on the general vocation to sanctity in the Church preceded it. The Decree on the Appropriate Renewal of the Religious Life presupposes these statements and is concerned more in detail with the principles and with particular points of the reform of religious. It is the only one of the documents issued by the council that adopted the program of *aggiornamento* in the heading, in connection with which, of course, it could refer to the formula of *accommodata renovatio* coined under Pius XII.[36] The desired timely renewal is defined in the key statement of this decree; it mentions "constant return to the sources of every Christian life and to the spirit of the origin of the individual institutes, but at the same time their adaptation to the changed conditions of the time" (ART. 2).[37]

The reform program which is presented in the decree on the religious life and in the directives issued for its implementation[38] differs essentially in its presuppositions from all preceding efforts in this direction. The reform of the orders under Pius XII was effected by the Holy See and centrally directed. Little latitude was given to the individual institutes for independent decisions. The directives for implementation of the decree on religious now declares: "The religious communities have themselves above all to implement a suitable renewal of the religious life and indeed mainly by means of general chapters" (no. 1). To a special general chapter to be convoked in from two to three years was given full authority to modify particular prescriptions of the constitutions by way of experiment in so far as neither the essence nor the character of the institute was affected; they were promised that experiments contrary to the current general canon law would gladly be permitted by the Holy See, but of course it was required that they must be implemented wisely. The stage of experimentation could be extended, in accord with these guidelines, to as long as fifteen years (no. 6). In the preparation for this reform chapter all members should be involved in a suitable manner through a comprehensive and open survey (no. 4). Together with this decentralization of the reform there occurred a further revision: each institute should strive to

---

[36] Over and above this a special section is devoted to religious in the Decree on the Pastoral Office of Bishops, which treats of their inclusion in the total pastoral work of the individual dioceses (ARTS. 33–35). In the foreword of the Decree on Education for the Priesthood it is said that the prescriptions of this document affect chiefly diocesan priests but are to be applied with the corresponding adaptations to the religious clergy.

[37] Of the commentaries on the decree on religious the following are outstanding: F. Wulf, *LThK*, 2d ed., *Das Zweite Vatikanische Konzil* II (Freiburg, Basel, and Vienna 1967), 249–307; J.M.R. Tillard, Y. Congar eds., *L'adaptation et la rénovation de la vie religieuse* (Paris 1967).

[38] Motu proprio *Ecclesiae Sanctae* of 6 August 1966, Part II in *AAS* 58 (1966), 775–82.

preserve or recover its own image, because in this diversity of religious life lay a genuine advantage for the Church. The institutes should investigate the spirit and the original intentions of the founders and the proper healthy traditions and loyally maintain this special legacy in each institute.[39] Finally, again in contrast to the prescriptions issued after the appearance of the Code of Canon Law, it was ordered that the constitutions must consist not only of canonical directives on the nature, goals, and organs of the institute, but must also contain the scriptural and theological principles of the religious life and statements on its relation to the Church and the heritage proper to the particular institutes. The spiritual and the juridical elements must constitute a unity in the constitutions.[40] Clearly these regulations wanted to eliminate the defects which, five decades earlier, after the appearance of the Code of Canon Law, had shown up because of an excessive centralization, leveling, and legalization.

Three guiding principles were given to the reform chapters as a standard for their decrees: renewal had to take place in fidelity to the spirit of the founder and the sound traditions of the institute, in obedience to the directions of the council, and in receptiveness to the signs of the time. Now the proposed renewal of religious life is primarily a spiritual event; hence it is difficult to grasp and to measure. However, in general it can be said that the religious institutes worked in the preparation of their reform chapter and in the discussions and decrees of this chapter in the light of the documents of the Second Vatican Council for a deepened view of the religious life and an up-to-date organization, and rethought the position and mission of their institute in the Church and the world of today.[41] Of course, the lack of clear statements of aim, approved by all, often led to tensions even within individual communities,[42] and made difficult the discovery of jointly decided solutions. In a partly irksome learning process most reform chapters adopted a middle way. Hotheaded champions of a radically new organization of the religious life were, on the whole, as disappointed as were the religious who had hoped that everything would continue in the customary old way. In connection with these reform efforts of the chapters there developed a very lively discussion on the meaning and spirituality of the orders in today's world, which offered some help but occasionally went so far that the basic values of

---

[39] Decree on religious *Perfectae Caritatis,* ART. 2b.

[40] *Ecclesiae Sanctae,* II, 12–14.

[41] Cf. J. Beyer, "Premier bilan des chapitres de renouveau," NRTh 95(1973), 60–86.

[42] Cf. "Pluralismus und Multiformität im Ordensleben heute. Eine Situations studie," *Pro mundi vita, Centrum informationis,* no. 47(Brussels 1973).

the religious life were questioned. The chief subjects of this discussion were first the religious vows and their concrete realization, in connection with which was especially included the knowledge of the humanities. Then questions of life in community found great interest. Here too much attention was given to psychological and sociological viewpoints, for example, the rules of group dynamics. From this resulted an often one-sided preference for small communities to the disadvantage of the large ones. Finally, the relation to the world stood in the focus of the discussion. At stake was the answer of the institutes to secularization, their openness to the world, their responsibility for the world.[43] Discussion was accompanied by experiment. The general chapters for the most part made vigorous use of the possibilities granted to them. Usually the desires for adaptation regarded as necessary did not break up the framework of the institute's traditional life. However, some experiments exceeded the lines laid down[44] or slipped out of the hands of the orders' superiors. Especially the small communities, which sprouted up in some places, in particular in Holland and the United States, were and are a favorable field of experimentation for more or less radical innovations.[45] These "communes" are obviously inspired by the life-style of the Little Brothers and Little Sisters of Jesus. If many of them proved not to be viable and soon again fell apart, this lay not least in the fact that they lacked the spiritual depth of the communities of Father de Foucauld. The discussions and experiments produced useful starts and impulses. On the other hand, there were undoubtedly also uncontrolled growth and signs of decay.[46] To ward off these errors and debasements was the Pope's aim when on 29 June 1971 he sent to religious the apostolic doctrinal letter *Evangelica testificatio* on the renewal of the religious life in accord with the Second Vatican Council.[47]

[43] Cf. P. Lippert, "Zwischen Umbruch und Selbstbesinnung. Die Orden im gegenwärtigen Wandel von Kirche und Gesellschaft," *HK* 29(1975), 346–53. A glance into the present state of the discussion is provided by *Concilium* 10(1974), 461–540.

[44] Thus the dared and failed attempt to subject a whole monastery to psychoanalysis (*HK* 20[1966], 127–29; 21[1967], 356–58), or the attempt to have a monastery work together with its group of friends on a common basis (ibid. 23[1969], 551–53).

[45] In Holland there were in 1969 no less than 215 such "life groups" (J. Kerkhofs, *Das Schicksal der Orden. Ende oder Neubeginn.* [Freiburg, Basel, and Vienna 1971], 15; cf. F. Wulf, "Die Zukunft des Ordenslebens," *GuL* 43[1970], 227).

[46] Cf. the different evaluation in the interview of Cardinal Daniélou in *GuL* 45(1972), 458–63, and in the article of the abbot primate of the Benedictine Confederation, Rembert Weakland, "Krise und Erneuerung des Mönchtums heute. Eine Bilanz nach zehn Jahren," *GuL* 47(1974), 299–313.

[47] *AAS* 63(1971), 497–526; cf. also the commentary of A. Schneider, *Erneuerung des Ordenslebens* (Trier 1973).

For the rest, in this phase of the search for new ways the Holy See maintained a rather waiting, even if carefully observing attitude. All the more surprising was the Pope's exerting of a direct influence on the discussions of the General Congregation of the Jesuits. The Thirty-First General Congregation of this society in 1965–66[48] had already issued reform decrees, but the decision on an up-to-date rule of poverty in the society and on the elimination of the canonical distinction between the "professed," who alone had all the qualifications of full membership with the fourth vow of special obedience to the Pope, and the "coadjutors," who were either *coadiutores spirituales* (priests) or *coadiutores temporales* (lay brothers), was postponed. The Thirty-Second General Congregation, from December 1974 to March 1975, was again concerned with these problems. A large majority of the 236 delegates expressed themselves in a test vote for the abolition of "rank" and wished to admit all Jesuits to the four vows. Whereas the General Congregation in no sense saw the priestly and apostolic character of the society jeopardized in this decision, the Pope saw in it a serious deviation from the original intention of the founder. Hence in several comments before and after the test vote he rejected such a change.[49]

The most critical and lamentable phenomenon of the recent period is the many departures from religious communities, which, together with the lack of recruits, have led to a strong rise in the ratio of the old to the total population of the houses and forced the institutes to a drastic reduction of their work in Church and society. Unfortunately, because of the absence of reliable evidence,[50] no exact picture can be gained for the entire Church. However, spot-checks can make the trend clear. Thus in Germany the number of religious priests doubled between 1915 and 1932 from 2,015 to 4,024 and up to 1941 increased further to 5,282. This upward development continued in the postwar years and reached its climax in 1971 with 6,825 religious priests. Thereafter an at first still slow drop-off began, which however soon accelerated because of the age structure. With 6,589 in 1974 the number of religious priests was of course still considerably above the figures of the period before the First World War. On the other hand, in regard to religious brothers

[48] The convocation of this General Congregation in the spring of 1965 was made necessary by the fact that, after the death of the General J.B. Janssens (1889–1964, general since 1946), a successor had to be elected. The election fell on the Basque, Father Arrupe (b. 1907). This General Congregation was interrupted to await the close of the council and came to an end in the fall of 1966 (*HK* 19[1964–65], 563–67, 21[1967], 33–37).
[49] F. Wulf, "Wohin steuern die Jesuiten? Ein Bericht," *GuL* 48(1975), 137–47; E. Coreth, "Die Jesuiten, der Papst und die Gesamtkirche," *HK* 29(1975), 472–77.
[50] Cf. A. Faller, "De statistica Religiosorum," *ComRel* 35(1956), 72–84.

in Germany the maximum figure of the prewar period—7,990 in 1937—could never again be equaled, in fact, their number is today, with 3,513, less than in 1915, when there were 3,799 brothers. After the Second World War the apogee, following the severe war losses among religious brothers, came in 1955 with 4,789 brothers. The number of novices in the German novitiates of male institutes, which in the 1950s was about 900, fell rapidly after 1961 and in 1973 reached its nadir with 129. In 1974 it again rose slightly to 152.[51] In the female institutes in Germany also the maximum figure of members in the prewar period was exceeded. Their number grew from 64,249 in 1915 by about half to 97,516 in 1941. The first enumeration after the Second World War yielded 88,934 female religious, and from then on until 1957 their number climbed to 93,260. Thereafter the tendency was retrogressive, in the most recent years very rapidly: in only the five years between 1969 and 1974 their number dropped by about 10,000, from 86,340 to 76,924. The number of female novices in the German religious houses in the period before the Nazi seizure of power fluctuated relatively constantly between 5,500 and 7,000. The year 1935 brought a maximum of 7,488 candidates, then the number dropped quickly to 1,865 in 1941. The decade 1950–60 shows a weak downward curve from 3,996 to 3,264 novices, two years later there were only 2,793, in 1966 less than 2,000, and in 1970 not even 1,000. With 405 novices, the year 1974 brought the lowest point thus far.[52] Apart from the reverses during the period of National Socialism and the Second World War, these numbers may be typical of many countries of Western Europe and North America, whereas the religious institutes in some places of the Third World indicate a strong growth at this time.[53]

A similar picture is sketched in the statistics published by individual religious institutes. The Society of Jesus in 1914 counted altogether 16,894 members. This number grew continually to 1965, when the maximum was reached with 36,038 members; in 1974 there were only 29,436. In the published statistics the number of 4,032 scholastics for

---

[51] F. Groner, *Kirchliches Handbuch. Amtliches statistisches Jahrbuch der katholischen Kirche Deutschlands* 25(1957–61), 524, 536, 26(1962-1968), 533, 27(1969–74), 41.
[52] Ibid. 25(1957–61), 538, 26(1962–68), 533, 27(1969–74), 41.
[53] Cf. G. Moorhouse, *Bastionen Gottes. Orden und Klöster in dieser Zeit* (Hamburg 1969), 90–94. In *Informationes*, edited by the Congregation for Religious (SCRIS), a statistic is offered which classifies for the end of 1974 the percentage proportion of novices and temporarily professed in the total number of religious and even arranges it by continents (1[1975], 95–98). Of course, in this summary only institutes of papal right are included to the extent that they are subject to the Congregation of Religious. Besides, it must be noted that in mission lands usually the time of probation of the novitiate and of temporary profession lasts longer, often twice as long as in Europe.

1974 means the lowest figure for this century; in 1965 there were still 9,865 of them. Also the number of novices dropped in this decade almost by half, from 1,555 to 804. In the same period 1,530 fathers left the Society of Jesus with a dispensation.[54] In religious institutes of papal right alone, 1,615 religious priests abandoned the priestly ministry in 1972. 1,355 brothers and 3,507 sisters in perpetual profession were dispensed from their vows.[55]

The reasons for this falling-off of religious vocations in the last fifteen years are many-layered. As especially the look at the novitiate shows, the council did not cause the crisis of recruits—it was already present— it could not, however, eliminate it but rather accelerated it. Especially to be mentioned as reasons are the general insecurity, especially of young people, following the upheaval in society and Church, the uncertainty of role, conditioned by this, of many religious, the polarization of opinions becoming evident in religious communities, also a narrow presentation of marriage and sex and their significance for the autonomous development of persons, an at times unrestrained criticism of every form of authority, and the influence of the welfare and consumer society on the thought and attitude of youth in the industrialized countries. But on the other hand another circumstance must not be overlooked. An inquiry among male religious in the German Federal Republic showed that, according to the situation of 1 January 1965, 78 percent of religious priests and even 86.5 percent of religious brothers came from families with four and more children. More than 42 percent of the fathers and almost 58 percent of the brothers were born in rural communities of less than five thousand inhabitants.[56] But the family of many children has become a rarity today, especially in the country, and so this source for religious vocations is to a great extent exhausted. Besides, today in the industralized nations educational opportunities and professions are available to all girls, whereas earlier they were accessible almost exclusively to religious women.

A slight upward development that can be ascertained on the level of the entire Church in the last two years gives the Congregation of Religious occasion for cautious optimism.[57]

The enhanced collaboration of male and female religious superiors on the national and international level since the council became of great

---

[54] *DIP* II, 1280, 1284; cf. also *HK* 19(1964–65), 563, and *Jesuiten. Wohin steuert der Orden?*, 2d ed. (Freiburg, Basel, and Vienna 1976), 13–18.
[55] *Annuarium statisticum Ecclesiae 1972*, 213, 217, 219; cf. ibid., 70–84.
[56] W. Menges, *Die Ordensmänner in der Bundesrepublik Deutschland* (Cologne 1969), 63, 130; 51, 129.
[57] *SCRIS, Informationes* 1(1975), 96.

importance. The conferences of superiors, urged as early as the Congress of Orders in 1950, were now set up in almost all countries, to the extent that they did not exist before the council.[58] The Roman unions of superiors general and of superioresses general acquired a new importance because in a much greater degree they were invited by the congregations of the Curia for consultations and exchange of experiences. Several times a year sixteen elected representatives of these unions—eight male and eight female superiors general—meet with the cardinal prefect, secretary, undersecretary, and other leading officials of the Congregation for Religious and Secular Institutes.[59] In the last years the congregation has issued no important document affecting all religious institutes which was not suggested by the unions or about which they had not previously heard.[60] Similarly the contact of the superiors and superioresses general of missionary institutes was established with the Congregation for the Evangelization of Peoples. The "Council of Eighteen" meets several times a year with the authoritative officials of that congregation. Also outside this organizational framework the efforts of the congregations of the Curia for increased contact with the religious communities are unmistakable. Visits of the cardinal prefect, the secretary, or one of the undersecretaries to general chapters, meetings of national conferences of superiors, and other formal or informal gatherings, not only at Rome but also in other cities and countries of Europe and overseas have belonged for several years to the normal program of these curial offices.[61] The exchange of experience, which is thereby facilitated, has a very positive impact.

The Orders in the Field of Tension between Church and State

The religious institutes were especially exposed in the field of tension between Church and state. They were for the most part extraordinarily severely affected by the anti-Church measures of a government. The laws of the *Kulturkampf* had an aftereffect on the orders, partly even far into this century. In Germany the "Jesuit Law" of 1872 was not entirely repealed until 1917. Norway abolished the prohibition of Jesuits, which was incorporated into the constitution, in 1956, and in Switzerland the article on denominational exceptions in the constitution of the federa-

---

[58] *Annuario Pontificio 1975*, 1327–49; *DIP* II, 1423–31.
[59] Cf. "Attività del Consiglio dei 16," *SCRIS, Informationes* 1(1975), 89–94. This body is called the "Council of Sixteen" because of the sixteen religious who belong to it.
[60] Cf., for example, A. Schneider, *Instruktion über die zeitgemässe Erneuerung der Ausbildung zum Ordensleben* (Trier 1970), 16–18.
[61] "Les rencontres des Responsables de la SCRIS avec les Religieux chez eux." *SCRIS, Informationes* 1(1975), 83–89.

tion, which forbade the Society of Jesus and the "societies affiliated" with it and prohibited new foundations of all institutes, did not come to an end until after a majority of only some 55 percent of the citizens had expressed themselves in favor of its abolition in a referendum in 1973.[62]

Hence it goes without saying that the Church, wherever there was question of negotiations for a concordat with a government, exerted itself to secure by treaty the legal situation of the institutes, their right to erect new houses, and the free exercise of the activities proper to them. In countries with a sufficient number of native religious the Church was usually prepared for the compromise that the higher superiors of the institute must have corresponding citizenship in the nation.[63] Of course, this protection by concordats was to prove to be of little effect in many nations in the succeeding decades.

In Mexico the conflict between Church and state, going far back into the nineteenth century, reached a climax in the first decades of this century. In 1917 the country obtained a new constitution, which, among other things, forbade celibacy, religious vows, and the religious state. Religious were expelled from their houses, their schools and other institutions were closed. After two years these regulations were somewhat modified, but in 1926 they were again put into effect in full severity. Their transgression was strictly punished. Among the best known victims of this persecution, which did not ebb until the end of the 1930s, was Father Augustinus Pro, S.J. (1891–1927), who with great skill and presence of mind worked as a pastor in Mexico City underground and after his imprisonment was falsely charged with sharing in an assassination attempt on former President Obregón and for this reason was shot without any legal proceedings. His process of beatification was introduced in 1952.[64]

A republic was proclaimed in Spain in 1931 and a constitution put into force which had as its aim a radical separation of Church and state and hit hard at the religious institutes, since it not only subjected them to state supervision but also supplied the legal basis for the expropriation of all property of religious. The Society of Jesus was dissolved and its property was confiscated by the state. If the riots of 1931 against the

[62] H. Liermann, *Kirchen und Staat* I (Munich 1954), 14f.; *HK* 11(1956–57), 167, 27(1973), 322–24.
[63] Concordat with Bavaria (1924), ARTS. 2 and 13, par. 2; Poland (1925), ART. X; Rumania (1927), ART. XVII; Lithuania (1927), ART. X; Italy (1929), ART. 29b; Baden (1932), ART. V with concluding protocol; Austria (1933), ART. X; German Reich (1933), ART. 15; Portugal (1940), ARTS. III and IX; Spain (1953), ART. IV; and the Dominican Republic (1954), ARTS. IV and X.
[64] *LThK* VII, 2d ed. (1962), 151–55; *LThK* VIII, 2d ed. (1963), 776; J. Echeverria, *Der Kampf gegen die katholische Kirche in Mexiko* (München-Gladbach 1926).

Church were still locally restricted, the storm broke out furiously against the monasteries during the three-year civil war, which followed General Franco's coup d'état of 1936. The cruel balance of the age of terror: in addition to 4,184 diocesan priests and seminarians, 2,365 male and 283 female religious were murdered, as well as many lay persons.[65]

In Germany at first National Socialism found sympathizers among a certain segment of the Catholics as well as among some of the religious. An especially unfortunate role was played by an outsider, Abbot Alban Schachleiter (1861–1937), who had been expelled from his abbey, Sankt Emaus at Prague, in 1918 and had lived in Bavaria since 1921; he expected from Hitler the realization of his own German national ideas, and so from 1922 he recruited for him and his movement in talks and appeals and let himself be misused as a pretense. Energetic rebukes and even penal measures of the archepiscopal ordinariate of Munich and of the superiors of the order could not make the aging abbot change his tune.[66] After the seizure of power the Nazi government in ARTICLE 15 of the concordat guaranteed the freedom of religious communities and the unimpeded exercise of their activities both in the pastoral and in the educational and social and charitable sphere; the private schools of the orders were even dealt with in a special article (ART. 25). But the orders were soon able to experience the true aims of the new holders of power.[67] This began with annoying searches of the houses and interrogations. In 1935–36 a series of show-trials was conducted, chiefly against religious because of transgressions against rules on foreign exchange; heavy sentences of imprisonment were decreed against the accused.[68] While the trials on foreign exchange were still in progress,

---

[65] A. Montero Moreno, *Historia de la persecución religiosa en España 1936–1939* (Madrid 1961), 762, 765–67.

[66] G. Engelhard, *Abt Schachleiter, der deutsche Kämpfer* (Munich 1941); H. Witetschek, *Die kirchliche Lage in Bayern nach den Regierungspräsidentenberichten 1933–1943* I: *Regierungsbezirk Oberbayern* (Mainz 1966), 1, n. 1; now cf. also L. Volk, *Akten Kardinal Michael von Faulhabers 1917–1945* I: *1917–1934*(Mainz 1975), passim.

[67] On what follows cf. J. Neuhäusler, *Kreuz und Hakenkreuz* (Munich 1946), I, 122–64; II, 250–92.

[68] After the war several of those then condemned—many had meanwhile died—applied for the juridical annulment of these verdicts and obtained their rehabilitation. The courts came to understand that these "verdicts issued in 1935–36 had come primarily from political reasons and followed the aim of bringing the Catholic orders and, with them, the Catholic Church into discredit with the German people" (E. Hoffmann, H. Janssen, *Die Wahrheit über die Ordensdevisenprozesse 1935/36* [Bielefeld 1967], 265).Cf. the justification of the verdict of the State Court of Berlin-Moabit of 27 February 1951 (ibid., 270). A Bonn dissertation on the foreign exchange trials is being prepared by Petra Rapp.

preparations were being made for a second series of trials against religious and priests. From the end of 1935, but especially in 1936 and 1937, the Gestapo searched in monasteries and in boarding schools and nursing homes conducted by monasteries for evidence of moral failings in order to be able to denounce the monasteries as hotbeds of immorality. The intensity of the searches, the methods employed in the inquiries, the fixing of the dates of the proceedings, ordered by the executive, as well as the carefully prepared and centrally directed evaluation for propaganda purposes make clear that the authorities were not mainly concerned for the punishment and elimination of evil situations. Instead, here the orders were to be affected in their entirety. Not by accident did the chief trials reach their climax in the months following publication of the encyclical *Mit brennender Sorge* of 14 March 1937.[69] But above all these trials were steps toward a still more comprehensive goal that was thus formulated in a secret instruction of the Ministry for Security of 15 February 1938: "The orders are the militant arm of the Catholic Church. Hence they must be forced out of their spheres of influence, curtailed, and finally annihilated."[70] To this end the government, following the successful military campaigns in the West at the high point of its power, made ready for a new blow. On the most varied pretexts, but often without any justification, many religious houses were confiscated between the fall of 1940 and the spring of 1941 and the religious expelled from the monasteries or even from the very districts of their former residences, as long as they were not required for the continuance of farm work or made liable to service.[71] These measures were stopped at the beginning of the Russian campaign, and the total annihilation of the orders was put off until the postwar period in order not to evoke further unrest among the Catholic population. Of course, these measures extended also to the countries and territories incorporated into the Reich and to the occupied areas. There they were carried out more severely and ruthlessly because no concordatal restrictions existed. Thus a thirteen-points program of 1940 for occupied Poland, the "Warthegau," provided under number 12: "All communities and monasteries are abolished, since these are not in accord with the German policy of morality and population."[72] Many religious were thrown into prisons and concentration camps, several were executed. Among these last was the

---

[69] J. Neuhäusler, op.cit. I, 133–44; H.G. Hockerts, *Die Sittlichkeitsprozesse gegen katholische Ordensangehörige und Priester 1936/37* (Mainz 1971).
[70] Quoted in J. Neuhäusler, op.cit. I, 123.
[71] Ibid., 148–64.
[72] Quoted in B. Stasiewski, "Die Kirchenpolitik der Nationalsozialisten im Warthegau 1939–1945," *Vierteljahrshefte für Zeitgeschichte* 7 (1959), 55.

Polish Franciscan, Father Maximilian Kolbe (1894–1941), who, taking the place of another prisoner, died in the starvation barracks of the Auschwitz concentration camp and was beatified in 1971, the Jewish philosopher and Carmelite nun Edith Stein (1891–1942), who was dragged from the Carmel at Echt in Holland, to which she had fled, in order to share the fate of the other Jews, and the Jesuit Alfred Delp (1907–1945), who was executed in Berlin-Plötzensee for alleged high treason against the nation.[73]

The persecution of the Church which broke out in Russia after the Bolshevik October Revolution affected chiefly the Orthodox monasteries; however, the few Catholic religious houses were not spared.[74] Only after the victory over Poland and when, after the Second World War, the Baltic countries and eastern Poland were definitively annexed to the Soviet Union did Catholic religious houses in large numbers fall into the Communist power sphere. In Latvia and the formerly Polish part of the Ukraine religious men and women were expelled from their houses and forced to return to civilian life; their houses fell to the state.[75] In Lithuania, where about 80 percent of the population professed the Roman Catholic faith, such severe measures were at first not feasible. At first the government was content with a strict supervision and spying on the monasteries, but after 1944 all religious houses here were suppressed.[76]

In the countries in which the Communists seized power after the Second World War, regard for the denominational situation likewise obviously played an important role in the proceedings. The harshest measures occurred everywhere in the years before 1956. In Albania the orders were entirely extirpated. The foreign religious were expelled, the Albanians were forced to put aside their habit and become part of the economic process.[77] Something similar was true of Bulgaria.[78] In Czechoslovakia all religious houses were occupied by the militia in April 1950 after a highly publicized show-trial of ten religious had taken place in Prague on the allegation of high treason.[79] Religious of various communities were crowded into "concentration monasteries," the male and female religious still capable of work were requisitioned for places in farming and in factories. Some sisters were allowed to

[73] B.M. Kempner, *Priester vor Hitlers Tribunalen* (Munich 1966), documented the verdicts against many other religious.
[74] Cf. J.S. Curtiss, *Die Kirche in der Sowjetunion* (Munich 1957), 80–83.
[75] A. Galter, *Rotbuch der verfolgten Kirche* (Recklinghausen 1957), 66, 91.
[76] Ibid., 81; *HK* 19(1964–65), 261.
[77] A. Galter, op.cit., 239f.; *HK* 22(1968), 195.
[78] A. Galter, op.cit., 252f.
[79] *HK* 4(1949–50), 411.

continue caring for the aged, the sick, and the invalids because of the lack of other personnel. "At the end of 1951 there was in all Czechoslovakia not a single religious house apart from the concentration convents,' which were in reality compulsory labor camps."[80] The mitigations and relaxations of the Dubček era[81] were again annulled, step by step.[82] Of the 160 religious houses which there were in Rumania in 1945, only twenty-five still existed in 1953.[83] The Hungarian minister for popular education, József Révai, explained in a speech delivered at the beginning of June 1950: "In the people's democracy religious are no longer needed because they no longer correspond to their vocation, indeed they sabotage the tasks of democracy. Hence it is necessary that as soon as possible it be made impossible for them further to harm the interests of democracy."[84] Shortly thereafter began a wave of deportations of religious. The Hungarian episcopate tried to avert the worst and on 30 August 1950 signed a treaty, which, among other things, provided that eight Catholic schools—six for boys, two for girls—might again be opened and the religious needed for the administration of their schools continue in this function. A *numerus clausus* was imposed on these communities in regard to the acceptance of new members.[85] All other religious communities were suppressed in September 1950 against the protest of the episcopate, and the approximately ten thousand male and female religious were ordered to leave their houses within three months, to discard the habit, and to take up a secular occupation.[86] In 1968 the eight approved monasteries counted, according to the figures of government offices, 232 fathers, twenty-seven novices and students, and fifty-nine sisters.[87]

In Yugoslavia the situation of the orders in the first ten years of Communist rule was no less miserable. In Bosnia-Herzegovina and Slovenia all religious houses were suppressed and many religious were arrested and killed. One hundred thirty-nine Franciscans alone fell victim to the persecution. In the mid-1950s there occurred a relaxation of tension, which had as a consequence an amazing revival of the orders,

---

[80] A. Galter, op.cit., 202–6, quotation 205; *HK* 15(1960f.), 561.
[81] *HK* 22(1968), 211, 412.
[82] *HK* 24(1970), 304f., 571f., 25(1971), 186, 27(1973), 609.
[83] A. Galter, op.cit., 301.
[84] Quoted in A. Galter, op.cit., 346, n. 79.
[85] There was question of two schools each of the Benedictines, Franciscans, Piarists, and the School Sisters of Szeged (A. Galter, op.cit., 352, n. 90).
[86] A. Galter, op.cit., 345–53; *HK* 5(1950f.), 33f.
[87] *Pro mundi vita, centrum informationis,* Heft 19(1967), 10–12.

especially in the republics of Slovenia and Croatia, where the number of members of the orders rose considerably since 1958.[88]

A similar picture results for Poland. Here at first there were years of misery and distress. Religious were removed from schools, hospitals, and other institutions. Up to 1953 54 religious had been killed, 200 deported, 170 thrown into prison.[89] On 14 April 1950 an agreement was reached between the government and the Polish episcopate, which in ARTICLE 19 contains the guarantee: "Orders and congregations of religious will have full freedom of action in the framework of their calling and the laws in force."[90] Nevertheless, at first there occurred further imprisonments. Not until the mid-1950s did the situation calm down, and the number of religious has since then grown significantly, both in the male and the female institutes.[91] Poland may be the only Socialist country which today can dispose of a considerable number of religious for use in mission lands.

In China and North Korea there are no more religious houses. The foreign missionaries were expelled, the not inconsiderable number of native religious were sent home in so far as they did not perish. The fate of the orders in Indochina, especially in Vietnam, is unknown at the moment.

The glance at the last six decades of church history shows how very much the orders live in and with the Church. Periods in which ecclesiastical life flourished were for the orders times of interior and exterior growth and vitality; in ages of crisis, on the contrary, they proved to be especially vulnerable. This dependence on the total ecclesiastical climate, however, must not cause the orders to forget that in all generations healing influences and impulses are expected from them. Precisely in this consist the heritage and task which religious communities in their totality have received from the great founders, who in the Church's periods of need created cells of inner renewal in order through them to permeate the Church with fresh energy.

[88] A. Galter, op.cit., 403f.; *LThK* V, 2d ed. (1960), 1193; *Pro mundi vita, Centrum informationis,* no. 19(1967), 10, 13.
[89] A. Galter, op.cit., 157.
[90] *HK* 4(1949f.), 413.
[91] *Pro mundi vita, Centrum informationis,* No. 19(1967), 10–12; *HK* 26 (1972), 205.

CHAPTER 12

*Educational System, Education, and Instruction**

Church and Society in Their Relation to the Educational System

The influence which the Church can exert on the educational system of our time is dependent on its position in the social and political system of the moment,[1] the legal, moral, and material conditions prevailing in it, the relations of the Church's educational mission to the expectations of the population or, respectively, the aims of the government—and all this is often dependent on the history in which and out of which the Church's educational efforts have acquired their national character.[2] The influence thus depends also on the Church itself: from its understanding of its function and from the ideas and energies which it proclaims in favor of its educational mission and which can apply to the apostolic mission in the stricter sense and to the service of the world in the broader sense.

In Europe the educational system, earlier established by the Church and for a long time determined by it, lost much ground after the introduction of the general obligation of going to school, the taking over of schools and universities by the state, the emphasizing of science and of the secular in instruction, and the rapid increase of voluntary school attendance—*explosion scholaire.* Educational systems with overwhelmingly Catholic—for example, in Belgium—or at least nonstate educational institutions—for example, the Netherlands—are the exception. In the United States the Catholic educational system has powerfully gained in substance in the course of this century and has reached a point where further increases scarcely seem any longer possible, and the distinction in regard to the education and formation imparted in non-Catholic institutions is beginning to decrease. In the Latin American nations there is, it is true, a stability in Catholic educational institutions,

---

* Paul-Ludwig Weinacht
[1] Cf. UNESCO, ed., *World Survey of Education* V (Paris 1971), 27f.
[2] On the extensive and intensive interpretation, extending back to par. 13, II, 12 of the common law, of the idea of school supervision in Germany, cf. T. Oppermann, *Kulturverwaltungsrecht* (Tübingen 1969), 252f. For the historical situation of schools under free auspices, especially of the Catholic schools in Europe, cf. W. Schultze, ed., *Schulen in Europa*, 3 vols. (Weinheim and Berlin 1968), the relevant chapters. On the colonial stamp of the African educational system, cf. T. Hanf, "Erziehung und politischer Wandel in Schwarzafrika," D. Oberndörfer, ed., *Systemtheorie, Systemanalyse und Entwicklungsländerforschung* (=*Ordo Politicus* 14) (Berlin 1971), 536.

but the great task of mass education which cannot be accomplished by them reduces their earlier importance. In the missions of the nations of the Third World the situation is determined by the form of decolonization, "nation building," and socioeconomic development; socialist regimes which are modeled on the protecting powers of the Communist camp, whether dominated by Moscow or Peking, are hostile to the Church's educational mission; the same is true where a non-Christian religion, such as Islam, is the state religion. More favorable are the circumstances in countries supported by Western powers. In the Communist states of Europe and Asia the Church was radically excluded from the educational system.

On the whole few generalizations can be made on the present state of the educational system established or determined by the Church or oriented to it. The generalization according to which the impact of the religious factor[3] in instruction and education slackens and the Church is either excluded from the educational system or withdraws from it is surely too sweeping. For it mistakes the new type of exchange relations between Church and society as they were expressed and urged in the pastoral constitution *Gaudium et spes* and introduced a turning in Catholic school policy.

While before the Second Vatican Council the Catholic Church understood education as an integrating element of an educational process of the faithful to be religiously founded and forming part of the Church's responsibility, and accordingly placed the greatest value on the institutionalization of the "Catholic school," the Protestant Church, at least in Germany, had given up such ideas since the 1950s. In its 1958 declaration of the school question the Protestant Church in Germany made known that it understood itself not first of all as an educational power struggling for influence but as the custodian of liberty. In this was expressed the Lutheran conviction, preserved in Protestantism, of the necessity of a "strictly secular government." Here school no longer meant—a few years before the pastoral constitution *Gaudium et spes*—an innate function of the Church but an objective task which could be provided for in a wordly and sensible way, even in collaboration with non-Christians.[4]

The educational system is not only the means and addressee of

[3] Cf. also F. Schneider, *Vergleichende Erziehungswissenschaft* (Heidelberg 1961), 154ff.
[4] On the so-called Protestant School Doctrine cf. A. von Campenhausen, *Erziehungsauftrag und staatliche Schulträgerschaft. Die rechtliche Verantwortung für die Schule* (Göttingen 1967), 129ff. On the problem of community relations between the Protestant and the Catholic school doctrine, cf. E.M. Heufelder, O.S.B., "Gibt es ein gemeinsames Leitbild für katholische und evangelische Erziehung?" *Una Sancta* (private printing, 1966), 229ff.

ecclesiastical influence; it also has an impact of its own on the Church. Such repercussions occur over the conditions of formation of the ecclesiastical recruits—state reforms of education, in Germany: the altered status of humanistic programs, and so forth—over changes in the curriculum[5] and of the conditions of scholarship in which theology is expressed, over the type of teaching in religious instruction—the didactics of religious instruction—and not least over the expansion of the hitherto charitably restricted services in the field of school and nursing through the professionalization of the teaching personnel. These changes got under way on a broad front without its being already discernible which formula—rationalization of the *mysterium,* adaptation to the world, loss of the *philosophia perennis,* dissolution of unity or viable diversity, dialogue, new catholicity, and so forth—is suited conclusively to describe the direction of the process.

Catholic Educational and School Doctrine

The doctrinal expressions of the Popes on the educational system must be understood as concretizations, relevant to the occasion and the time, of the apostolic task of the Church to proclaim and attest the message of Jesus Christ, to assure the conditions for the realization of this apostolate against encroachments and decay and constantly to improve it and in this regard to express ever more strongly the personal importance of education and solidarity with those who, like UNESCO since 1946, have also set as their goal the education and training of all peoples.[6]

In the first half of the twentieth century the Church was interested in retaining Christian education intact as an integral element of formation in and spreading of the faith. The Holy See exerted itself in the reorganization of the educational system in Europe after the First World War to assure the Church's interests by diplomatic means—the concordat policy—by the encouraging of ecclesiastical educational institutions, for example, the recognition of universities as "papal universities," by establishing a Christian educational system independent of the state, and by support of the missions, especially under Pius XI, to promote the spread of the faith through educational institutions.

[5] The central themes, which are discussed under the term "curriculum," are educational aims, teaching content, and organization of learning (cf. also K. Frey in L. Roth, ed., *Handlexikon zur Erziehungswissenschaft* [Munich 1976], with citation of further literature [p. 85]). For the discussion of the reform of theological study cf. "Kommission 'Curricula in Theologie' des Westdeutschen Fakultätentages," by E. Feifel, ed., *Studium Katholischer Theologie, Berichte, Analysen, Vorschläge* 1–5 (Zurich 1973–75).
[6] H. Fries, ed., *Handbuch theologischer Grundbegriffe* I (Munich 1962), 319ff.

At the same time, that is, from the end of the First World War, the Popes, beginning with Benedict XV's letter of 19 April 1919, *Communes litteras,* formulated a relatively complete "Catholic educational and school doctrine," which on the basis of biblical and theological statements, of traditional ecclesiastical ideas on education, *paedagogia perennis,* as well as of pertinent articles from the Code of Canon Law (Canons 1372–83), contained doctrinal propositions on education and school under compulsory aspects and determined the epoch down to the Second Vatican Council. In addition to the already mentioned letter *Communes litteras,* its standard document is Pius XI's encyclical *Divini illius Magistri* of 31 December 1929;[7] also to be mentioned are the messages of Pius XII—address to the Youth of the A.C.I., to the Fathers of Families of France of September 1951—the message of John XXIII of 30 December 1959 on the thirtieth anniversary of the appearance of Pius XI's encyclical on education as well as passages of the encyclical *Mater et Magistra* of 15 May 1961.

All the expressions were based on the twofold right of the Church, which, first, by virtue of its teaching function, has to educate its members for full citizenship in the Kingdom of God, and, second, by virtue of its supernatural motherhood, brings forth, nourishes, and trains souls for the divine life of grace, according to the encyclical *Divini illius Magistri,* nos. 16 and 17.[8] Against the background of a really centennial loss of the Church's power to regulate education and in view of the threat to Christian cultural values from liberalism and Modernism in Europe and North America, the Popes raised the demand for the material catholicity of the educational world of its members, that is, either educational institutions must stand under Catholic auspices and responsibility or state and other educational institutions must be permeated by the Catholic spirit. These demands were pinpointed from two sides: Catholic Christians were obliged in conscience to send their children to Catholic schools; non-Church, mixed, or neutral schools were forbidden to them in Canon 1374 and the encyclical *Divini illius Magistri,* no. 79; the Church itself claimed an

---

[7] *Die christliche Erziehung der Jugend, Enzyklika "Divini illius magistri" von Pius XI., Lateinisch-deutsche Ausgabe, eingeleitet und mit textkritischen Anmerkungen versehen von R. Pfeil* (Freiburg, Basel, and Vienna 1959).

[8] Pius XI's encyclical on education appeared three decades after the beginning of radical school reform. It quite critically opposes pedagogical naturalism, which, while seeking to draw "out of the child," had slight regard for the claim of objective organizations and confused education with development (cf. also F. Pöggeler in *Dokumente des II. Vatikanischen Konzils* V: *Declaratio de educatione christiana/Über christliche Erziehung* [Trier 1966], 10).

all-embracing right of supervision of the schools, guaranteed only fragmentarily by concordat.

Within the papal teaching the role of the state was defined to the effect that it has a right to educate and must exercise it, not immoderately by a school monopoly but according to the principle of subsidiarity, with regard for the parents' right. Its tasks lay especially in the spheres of training state officials and education in citizenship. In the papal teaching the parents always ranked as the innate and professional educators of their children. However, their right of education was not "autonomous" but one participating in the mandate of salvation and the Church's *magisterium* and pastoral office. The vigorous defense of this denominational right of parents by the Church was marked characteristically by the obligation of the parents to exercise their right in accord with their duties as Catholic parents—baptism, Catholic training of the children. In the concrete this could mean that they had to vote for Catholic denominational schools, if possibilities of voting were available and corresponding ecclesiastical directives were at hand.

The Catholic educational and school doctrine assumed as a condition of its effectiveness that traditional ecclesiastical authority, the structure of social institutions, and a certain "Catholic milieu" were intact. On such a basis it was possible that a few simple so-called "Catholic educational principles" were respected: the right of parents, family and school instruction in accord with the denomination, rejection of coeducation, and care for an instruction proper to each sex. They could easily be integrated into the system of Church doctrine and canon law and possessed the character of commandments. The great success, at least in Germany, of the Church's school policy was attributed by a person in the Protestant camp even to the "binding of the consciences of Catholics" by Church directives.[9]

The Second Vatican Council and the Postconciliar Period

After the Second World War there appeared throughout the world new situations in the sphere of education which could not but convulse the Catholic educational and school doctrine. Education was assigned social functions and became, especially in the countries of the Third World, but also in the industrialized nations, a strategic point of social development. Even in the field of personality education a social desire for adaptation and ascent claimed recognition, which demolished overnight waves of respect once encompassing Catholic schools. The road of separate and particular cultures to a

[9] A. von Campenhausen, op. cit. (above, n. 4), 119f.

modern, Western, secular, and dynamic educational society, concerned with economic growth and the growth of information, seemed to indicate the direction of general progress.

From the viewpoint of the Catholic educational system there were various problems: the problem of the quality and of the comparable standards relative to the developed non-Catholic educational institutions; the problem of quantity in view of newly appearing needs in accord with the degrees of education—basic education, eradication of illiteracy; the problem of subsistence in view of rising building and maintenance costs; the problem of spirituality in view of the reduced number of clerical teachers or political exactions on the part of the governments of the moment—thus in Pakistan and Egypt religious instruction in Islam must be given; finally, the problem of self-understanding: as agent of the spreading of the faith or as a regular school for children of Catholic families or as an offer by Catholics to all, that is, as an instrument of Christian service to the world.

In its "Declaration on Christian Education" the council confirmed the basic features of the traditional Catholic school doctrine in the question of the function of education, of those qualified to educate—"first and preferably" the parents, subsidiarily the state, in a specific way the Church—of the natural law character of the parents' right and its confirmation in the question of the "choice of school" for the child; it also affirmed the assumption of the rights of education by means of the "child's right," which is not applied without distinction but must be seen by means of the child's natural abilities and his supernatural goal lying in the coresponsibility of the Church.

Traditionally the means suited to this goal and hence obligatory were seen in institutions of material catholicity. In this point the council proved to be more realistic and open: Since it happens that an ever larger area of education is fact-oriented, which neither positively nor negatively touches upon the meaning of Christian existence, it all amounts to the *formatio christiana* keeping in step with the *formatio profana*. And since it likewise happens that Catholic Christians are ever more frequently educated in mixed or neutral schools, where the Christian development of the school is institutionally not possible, the religious instruction remains possible, and—in the event that it does not take place in the school—at least the moral and character formation is guaranteed by the Christian spirit. Here the council puts great hope on the personal model of Christian teachers and fellow students, and it refers to the necessity of spiritual help even when this cannot result from within the school district.

With these adaptations to current conditions of Christian existence in the world, a giving up of institution and program bound to the *schola catholica* is not necessary, even if precisely here in the postconciliar period differences of opinion emerge. In the declaration itself the "Catholic school" is claimed for the educational mandate of the Church against all monopolizing tendencies of the state. Catholic school—this is principally the nonstate school under ecclesiastical or free auspices of a Catholic spirit. In the mission lands it is the first source of divine life and bearer of human culture with a strong apostolic content. As a program it means the exhibition of the "presence of the Church in the modern world," as demanded in the pastoral constitution *Gaudium et spes;* its function is the apostolate, that is, education and formation must serve the spread of God's Kingdom and, along with that, the welfare of the earthly community and its eternal salvation. The character of the educational apostolate defines also the function and position of the teacher in Catholic schools: it depends on him to what extent the aims and initiatives of Catholic schools are realized. Hence he needs a fundamental and constantly renewed formation in the profane and the religious areas and in teaching methods. He should be in a dialogue with his pupils,—inspired by the Christian spirit and extending beyond the school-day, and work intimately with the parents. In this place, hence in part of the program referring to the teacher in the Declaration on Christian Education, occurs the traditional reminder that Catholic parents have the duty "of entrusting their children, when and where this is possible, to Catholic schools, to support these in accord with their means, and to cooperate with them for the good of their children" (ARTICLE 9).

The program of the *schola catholica* extends over the total grade structure of the educational system, beginning with schools of the elementary and secondary grades, which "lay the foundation of education," for the professional schools, the institutes for adult education and for social professions, special schools, and institutions for the education of teachers and catechists.

On the universities the declaration expresses itself in a triple aim; it expects from them the training of the national leaders, scholarly contributions to the discovery of truth and to the problems of the modern world—undernourishment, sickness, unjust distribution, and so forth—and finally it expects the institutionalizing of religious and scientific faculties or at least institutes and, from these, contributions to the dialogue between faith and reason, which, if they conscientiously observe one another's conformity with law and competence, can come together in the one truth. These expectations set the framework for "Catholic universities": they deserve encouragement, but so that they stand out, not by their number, but by their scholarly achievement (ART. 10). The statements of the council on the university system remain throughout in the framework of the papal pronouncements of Pius XII, John XXIII, and Paul VI.

The postconciliar period is determined by a partly violent difference of opinion on the existence and range of a Catholic theory of education. Between conservative and progressive theoreticians various passages from conciliar documents were offered as proof of the ecclesiastical nature of their respective ideas. According to the selected theological or ideological relationship in each case there stood out in the Catholic school doctrine long familiar[10] or entirely new features. The newer ones appealed to the Pastoral Constitution as "Magna Carta of the Christian World Understanding and World Mission" and sought to "rethink" the Catholic educational and school doctrine in its light. What is Catholic is understood, not as the culture-determining, religious content, but as form of solidarity, world responsibility, and condition of cooperation with all persons of good will: What must be done concretely is not different for the Catholic from what everyone can aspire to and understand. The Christian faith provides, as regards content, no new insights for the organization of the world and of humans living together; in fact, Catholics would not even have the right to a culture of their own. Since the Church makes its own general human demands and stands up for them, "Catholic schools" must not be understood as special institutions of Catholics for Catholics, but as integrating elements in the "front of all of goodwill" under the idea "of creating in common with them a world in humanity, justice, and freedom."[11]

Similar results are reached by whoever takes as a guiding principle the new nonmetaphysical anthropology of the pastoral constitution, according to which the human being is "defined by his responsibility toward his fellows and toward history." Responsibility toward history is then understood as the obligation to participate in scholarly progress in all varieties and as the abandonment of that older Augustinian outlook, whereby education has meaning for the Christian only where it ceases to be empty curiosity (curiositas) and assumes a relation to eternal salvation. The council simply makes progress and knowledge a duty

---

[10] Cf., for example, the memorandum composed by Dr. F. Heckenbach, *Heilstheologische Begründung der katholischen Schule* (*Études et Documents* no. 4, OIEC) (Brussels 1967). The essential proposition of the memorandum, formulated in evident opposition to the idea of autonomous fields of reality, reads: "Every pedagogical autonomy is destroyed by revelation and the incarnation and is only meaningful as salvation pedagogy" (p. 4).

[11] W. Seibel, "Bildung und Kultur in den Konzilsdokumenten," *Christliche Erziehung nach dem Konzil* (=*Berichte und Dokumente,* edited by Kulturbeirat beim Zentralkomitee der deutschen Katholiken) (Cologne 1967), 29f.

because in the anthropological view, which corresponds to the situation of today's world, work in it must be understood as a form of fraternity, of humanity, of responsibility, hence in the last analysis as an overflow of the Christian commandment of love. In such a context it is the conscientious duty of Christian parents, in choosing the school for their children, to give the preference to the "Catholic school," seen and justified as the criterion of social liberty. The pluralism of society, hence not a metaphysical but a political principle, justifies the institution "Catholic school." But then may it, as such, be made a conscientious duty for Catholics? Three restrictive considerations are named: (1) the Declaration on Religious Freedom intends that only one who believes of his own accord can be bound in conscience; (2) the pastoral constitution binds the secular discipline to its respective subject matter, hence also the Catholic school to the modern demands on "school"; (3) the Declaration on Christian Education demands that a Catholic school must be Catholic not only formally but materially.

Only if all three factors are present can there exist an obligation in conscience for the parents to exercise their right to the free choice of a school in favor of the Catholic school.[12]

In the postconciliar period further decisions were added to the Catholic educational and school doctrine by the Holy See as well as by regional episcopal conferences and other bodies, such as synods. They begin with the commentary of Bishop Doctor Pohlschneider on the German translation of the Declaration on Christian Education, which especially emphasizes the principle of the "apostolate" and attaches it to many conciliar texts.[13] The notion of the Church's mission of salvation in the educational system—not only its solidarity with "all people of good will"—is the "dominant guiding idea of the declaration."

If one surveys the messages of the Holy See published since then, the impression can arise that the reference to the Declaration served rather the inner Church dialogue, since in it the interests of institutions under Catholic or ecclesiastical auspices are especially well expressed and justified;[14] on the other hand, the pastoral constitution or the encyclical *Populorum progressio* are readily quoted when solidarity with extraecclesiastical organizations should be expressed, whether on

[12] Cf. J. Ratzinger, "Das Menschenbild des Konzils in seiner Bedeutung für die Bildung," *Christliche Erziehung* (preceding note), 62f.

[13] For example, the dogmatic constitution *Lumen gentium,* no. 17, the Decree on the Church's Missionary Activity *Ad gentes,* nos. 35–41, the Decree on the Apostolate of the Laity, nos. 28–32.

[14] Cf. the message on the centenary celebration of the founding of the Catholic universities in France in *AAS* 67 (1975), 695, and finally the document of the Congregation for Catholic Education by Means of the Catholic School of 5 July 1977.

the occasion of the anniversary of the eradication of illiteracy campaign of UNESCO[15] or of the twenty-fifth anniversary of the founding of UNESCO.[16]

The Latin American Church placed its resolutions on education entirely under the idea, urged by *Gaudium et spes,* of the coresponsibility for the process of transformation of the Latin American peoples and their liberation. Clear postponing of accent *vis-à-vis* Western European and North American philosophy and theology were discernible.[17] Starting with the Catholic University of Santiago de Chile, capitalism and liberalism were blamed for the postcolonial servitude of Latin America and it was believed that in this spirit the real identity could never be found. The promise for the problems of Latin America lies not in the industrialized countries of the First World, but in Latin America itself. The task for education consists in enabling the Latin American illiterates "to develop a cultural world themselves, as creators of their own progress, in a creative and original way."[18]

The line which the Holy See pursues in the assuring and promoting of ecclesiastical interests in the educational system of the European states is not different from the preconciliar line: by means of treaties between the respective nations and the Holy See prescriptions of concordats in force are extrapolated or supplemented.[19] More powerfully than in the preconciliar phase, the pronouncements of the council and of the Popes are placed in close contact with declarations of other sovereign political bodies, and the unity of all peoples of good will in the one goal is stressed, thus formulated by Paul VI on the occasion of the twenty-fifth anniversary of the founding of UNESCO: "construire un monde fraternel," "promouvoir une civilisation de l'universel."[20] The Declaration on Christian Education in ART. 12 had already pointed

---

[15] *AAS* 61 (1969), 665.

[16] *AAS* 63(1971), 837f. Furthermore, the Declaration on Christian Education, ART. 1, is relevant to the *droit à l'éducation.*

[17] Cf. J. Ratzinger, "Der Weltdienst der Kirche. Auswirkungen von 'Gaudium et Spes' im letzten Jahrzehnt," *Internationale Katholische Zeitschrift,* 4th year (1975), no. 5, 439ff. (444f.).

[18] *Die Kirche in der gegenwärtigen Umwandlung Lateinamerikas im Lichte des Konzils. Beschlüsse der II. Generalversammlung des Lateinamerikanischen Episkopates, Medellin v. 24. 8. bis 6.9.1968* (Essen [ADVENIAT] 1970), 49f.

[19] Appendix to the treaty with Austria of 9 July 1962 on 25 April 1972 in regard to subsidies for salaries in Catholic schools of public law, in *AAS* 64 (1972), 478ff.; also the modification of the concordat with Lower Saxony of 26 February 1965 on 21 May 1973, in *AAS* 65(1973), 643ff.; also the treaties with Rhineland-Palatinate on 15 May 1973, in *AAS* 65(1973), 631ff., and with the Saarland on 21 February 1975, in *AAS* 67(1975), 248ff.

[20] Cf. n. 16.

in this direction, that people must strive with all their means that "an appropriate coordination may come into being among Catholic schools, and between them and the other schools that cooperation may be fostered which the welfare of all human society demands." Coordination and cooperation were realized in the inner Catholic sphere by a liaison office for the national school bureaus and societies in Brussels, the *Office International de l'Enseignement Catholique* (OIEC); active in relation to UNESCO in Paris is the *Centre Catholique International de Coordination auprès de l'UNESCO* (CCIC)[21] The first permanent observer of the Holy See at the General Secretariat of UNESCO was, by the way, Monsignore Roncalli, the future Pope John XXIII.[22]

Catholic Education in the European and North American Educational Systems

Catholic exertions in regard to education were realized within the pertinent historical and regional circumstances which on the one hand determined the character of the Church and on the other hand the character of its relations to the social and political milieu. The following types are of use for a comparative presentation of the Catholic educational system: In the twentieth century there are native and mission Churches, intimate with and distant from the state, rich and poor, persistent and reformist Churches, national and foreign educational traditions, complete and, in looking at functions and the structure of grades from the elementary to the tertiary sphere, incomplete educational offerings.

The European countries are, like the United States, conspicuous in that they received their national cultures from a common Christian European history, differed from one another in it, and more or less strongly emancipated themselves from it. Where the system of separation between state and Church was realized on the model of the Weimar Constitution, there was no occasion to support a complete educational offering under church auspices; it sufficed if Catholic interests could be assured within the state educational system.[23] In this case talk of the state-school monopoly made no real sense. If the constitutional situation was, as in France, hostile to the Church—*laïcité*—its educational power can still be taken into account indirectly.[24]

In the United States matters were different from the start. Here, in

---

[21] *LThK*, second supplementary volume (Freiburg 1967), 401f.

[22] This circumstance was called to the attention of the director general of UNESCO by Pope Paul VI (cf. *AAS* 63[1971], 837f.).

[23] Cf. A. von Campenhausen, op. cit., and T. Oppermann, op. cit., 35ff.

[24] Cf. W. Schultze, ed., *Schulen in Europa* II A, 574, 583f.

order to allow the Catholic immigrants in a society at first unfriendly to Catholics a church education, a Catholic educational system free of the state had to be constructed. From the basis of the local ecclesiastical primary schools there arose from the second half of the nineteenth century an educational system which, supported by a native Church, was stamped in the national American educational system, and provided a functional and, in regard to grades, complete educational offering. Up to the 1960s it showed itself equal to the financial demands. The great majority of North American Catholics in this century received, partly or entirely, their education in Catholic institutions.[25]

In what follows, these institutions in European countries and North America are described on the respective grades of the national educational system. A defining first section, which, for reasons of uniform understanding of the total educational plan, is oriented to the German Federal Republic,[26] is then followed by a historically treated second section.

PRESCHOOL AREA

In the elementary area the teaching methods of early childhood lie outside the family, that is, the institutions supplementary to family training after the completing of the third year of life to the beginning of school. Here the children should obtain the training necessary for their internal and external growth. In this regard two viewpoints are in the foreground: in one of them there is an attempt to foster the process of child development beyond the possibilities available at home—"compensatory education"; in the other, to achieve a gradual transition to learning in school—"preschool."

The legal rules to which the institutions of the elementary area of the various nations are subject are quite different: While countries such as Belgium, France, and England have incorporated preschool into the educational system—France considers it an integrating component of the primary school system—the Netherlands and Italy regulate the preschool system separately in law. The responsibility for the elementary area lies partly with the officials of the educational system, partly, especially in the Scandinavian countries, with the social offices.

In the industrialized states education in the elementary area is, to be sure, systematically organized, but, apart from preschool classes, it is not obligatory and also not altogether under the auspices of the state and locality. Especially in Belgium, Denmark, the Netherlands, Italy, Switzerland, the German Federal Republic, and the United States,

---

[25] *New Catholic Encyclopedia* 5, 141ff. ("United States: 20th Century").
[26] *Bund-Länder-Kommission für Bildungsplanung, Bildungsgesamtplan* I, 2d ed. (Stuttgart 1974), 18ff.

institutions of the elementary area are overwhelmingly under free auspices.

The proportion of children who attend a preschool institution varies from country to country. The highest numbers of attendance for children from age three to age five are recorded by Belgium (over 90 percent), the Netherlands and France (over 70 percent). Among the five-year-olds the numbers for Belgium and the Netherlands are more than 90 percent.[27]

The Church's organization for the poor and the school has traditionally cared for children in need of aid and without parents, in the area of formation and looking after little children; the kindergarten movement established by Fröbel in the middle of the nineteenth century then favored pedagogic initiatives in the ecclesiastical sphere also. Religious institutes, parishes, and welfare societies became operators of kindergartens, and, where there were no contrary legal regulations, as above all in France after 1886, the most important operators of preschool institutions. Since the Second World War these institutions have come ever more under state supervision—regulations on minimal demands in size and in the qualification of personnel—and were subsidized by public means; nevertheless, they were able to preserve a considerable freedom of movement in their pedagogical organization.

If the older kindergarten pedagogy paid attention especially to the care of the children by games and common activities to relieve the mothers and described its theory on the basis of the natural process of maturation in the course of life, it recently regarded more carefully the learning possibilities of the earliest years of life and tried purposefully and systematically to use it for the development of youthful strengths. In the Catholic sphere Maria Montessori had preceded this trend, but she had less impact in Germany than she had in Italy, Switzerland, and the United States; modern early pedagogy continues the beginnings made by Montessori and extends them from the cognitive and emotional to the total social development of the children. The education practice of church kindergartens stands today in the field of tension of various claims and far-reaching but often inadequate criticism: on the one hand it should admit the results of early pedagogy, especially of the psychology of learning without the pressure of school achievement, and on the other it should take into account the aims of

---

[27] B. Trouillet, *Die Vorschulerziehung in neun europäischen Ländern* (=*Dokumentationen zum in- und ausländischen Schulwesen* 8), ed. by DIPF, 2d ed. (Weinheim and Berlin 1968), 208ff.

antiauthoritarian education, and finally find a way where religious education is practicable when, as in the German Federal Republic, children from homes of the most varied denominations are accepted.[28]

PRIMARY AND SECONDARY SPHERES

The primary sphere includes the first organized and obligatory instruction suited to a school. It can last between three years—lower grades of the ten-class general educational polytechnical secondary school of the German Democratic Republic—and six years, in England and Sweden. Apart from the special schools of the Communist states, the rule prevails that in the primary sphere all children in the first grade are taught in common; in Germany the unitary elementary school, regularly of four years, has been maintained since 1920 on constitutional grounds. The idea is to provide pupils with a common body of knowledge before they continue their education. The early pedagogy, intent on individualization, required a proper continuation in the primary sphere; but no way has yet been found to satisfactorily unite the principle of grouping and individualization with the principle of year-classes over several years.

The secondary sphere I includes methods of education which are subject to the full-time school obligation and in general embraces the fifth to tenth school year. At the end of the secondary sphere I lies a school-qualifying conclusion with a partly selective, partly distributive function.

Thus the tension-filled aims such as orientation, individualization of educational offerings, and avoidance of premature fastening to a definite educational program in the secondary sphere II rank as the common pedagogical task of the educational methods here summarized.

Considerable educational-political explosive power has adhered in the years since the Second World War in Western European countries to the question whether secondary sphere I should be organized in one grade ("integrated") or in columns of an "articulated" school system. Behind this are concealed controversial sociopolitical, pedagogical, education-economic, and political-structural issues, which became decisively effective in various countries in varying combinations.

Secondary sphere II embraces in increased variety and diversity

---

[28] Cf. G. Hundertmarck in L. Roth, ed., *Handlexikon zur Erziehungswissenschaft* (Munich 1976), 111ff.

educational courses which are based on secondary sphere I and usually follow it immediately. They are either vocational and full-time; part-time with practical instruction; concerned with purely academic preparation; or they have a double function. In the last case, they either allow a student to graduate and to proceed to the tertiary sphere, or they certify attendance and permit the student to earn a living.

If in secondary sphere I organizational integration and multiple linking are posed as alternatives, then the multilayered problems in secondary sphere II require a different treatment. In connection with the inclusion of vocational practice in education there is the question of the duration, but especially of the harmonizing and co-ordinating; the question of the relations of basic and special education (often confused with the question of the proportion of "general education" to vocational education) leads into institutional as well as into curricular problems (education by grades); the question of the equality of vocational and general education is today aspired to partly through the elimination of the separation between the two systems and through facilitation of the transition, partly through special encouragement of the proper character of the vocational sphere of education as an autonomous and justified system in secondary sphere II. The question of equality also plays a role in the admission to the university curriculum, which possesses a strategic function not only for the total educational and business system of a country but also for the life chances of a person leaving secondary sphere II. To the extent that the completion of secondary sphere II not only ends an extended basic education and not only qualifies for entry into the earning world, but also opens up access to study in the tertiary sphere, its function is by no means clearly defined. On the one hand it represents only one of several conditions which must be present if one wishes to continue to study. In the Soviet Union, for example, only the qualification for competition for a study position is connected with the completion of the ten-year school, whose concluding ninth and tenth classes are regarded as "complete middle school," that is, secondary grade II, but the distribution of the study position depends on further conditions, including the annual numbers in the state education and labor force plan, the results of the examination for entrance into the university, and so forth. The former German regulation which required both the school-leaving examination as well as the general qualification for the university constituted the other extreme. The older rule on the school-leaving examination had to be modified from the mid-1960s for the study courses or the university positions for which more applications were available than could be accommodated. This is being done with the aid of a central admission office.[29]

The Church's exertions and interests in education had lost their institutional basis in most European states because of the complete devastation produced by the Enlightenment and secularization. Where other means did not succeed, the Church had to substitute for what had been lost in popular breadth (ecclesiastical inspection of the school system) and pedagogical concepts (Jesuit schools) by means of specific education and *caritas*. Hence there appeared under the auspices of clerical orders educational institutions in the area, traditionally reserved to the control of the home, of the education of girls as well as the care and instruction of the handicapped. Concern for ecclesiastical recruits was expressed in the promotion of boarding schools of humanistic style and in the founding of regionally important boarding schools at state humanistic high schools.

In the Netherlands there developed an unusually strong denominational educational system: it had been desired by both the Calvinist and the Catholic side and was not only formally assured in 1917—"the imparting of instruction is free"—but also with regard to the claim to state support. A law of 1920 made basic schools of a public and a private character financially equal. In 1960 a secondary school law followed this. Similarly favorable conditions exist in Belgium, where more than half of all students receive instruction in Catholic schools. Spain also, since the Franco era, offers the Catholic Church a wide influence: it is socially acknowledged as an educational power, consults with state tribunals on educational problems, imparts religious instruction in all schools, possesses a number of its own teaching institutes, and has control of not a few others. In France, of course, as a consequence of the laicism doctrine of the state, the Church is excluded from the public educational system, but privately it is not only tolerated but, since the Fifth Republic, it is also strongly supported. The basis of the favorable relationship between the state and the private school system was the "Rapport Lappie," which in 1959 saw to the passage of a law which permitted the state to conclude support agreements with private schools. In 1965 at least every fourth secondary pupil attended a private institution, most of them a Catholic one.[30]

---

[29] Cf. H. Scheuerl, *Gliederung des deutschen Schulwesens* (=*Deutscher Bildungsrat, Gutachten und Studien der Bildungskommission, 2*) (Stuttgart 1968); S.B. Robinsohn, ed., *Schulreform im gesellschaftlichen Prozess. Ein interkultureller Vergleich* I (*Bundesrepublik Deutschland* by C. Kuhlmann, *DDR* by K.D. Mende, *Soviet Union* by D. Glowka) (Stuttgart 1970).

[30] W. Schultze, *Schulen in Europa* I (Germany), II (France, Netherlands, Belgium), III (Spain, Italy).

The special German type of denominational school in the public school area, that is, the primary and secondary school conducted under state auspices but denominationally defined in personnel and program, has, since the second half of the 1960s, been merged into Christian community schools, which could better do justice to the pedagogical and educational-economic demands. The compatibility of these community schools with the constitution was declared by the Supreme Court in the spring of 1976. The compatibility with the principles of Catholic school policy is no longer challenged by the bishops.[31]

In the United States legal and social obstacles to a Catholic education in the framework of the public schools were experienced by the Catholic minority, differently than in Germany. On the other hand, the Catholic parochial school movement that took place led since the second half of the nineteenth century to the construction of an institutional pedagogical substructure for a Catholic educational system, which in 1920 included more than 6,500 primary schools with over 40,000 teachers and 1.7 million pupils.

In 1960 there were already 4.5 million pupils in these schools. Besides the parochial schools, which constituted the greatest number of Catholic primary schools, there were also, chiefly in connection with secondary schools, primary schools under the sponsorship of religious institutes and, in lesser number, also under the sponsorship of lay Catholics—the Montessori schools.

Still greater than in the primary sphere was the growth of Catholic schools in the secondary sphere. If in 1920 there were still little more than 1,500 schools with just about 130,000 pupils, their number had grown in 1960 to almost 2,400 schools with more than 800,000 pupils. The size of schools measured against the number of pupils per school tripled or quadrupled in this period so that more and more secondary schools outgrew the financial and administrative capacities of the parishes and, often under the responsibility of religious institutes, became diocesan schools. (The first central high school arose in Philadelphia, Pennsylvania, in the 1890s.) Today about 40 percent of all Catholic youth of school age attend a Catholic high school, and this even though their attendance is subject to tuition. In view of the

---

[31] For the development of the relations of educational science and school to the Catholic Church see now K. Erlinghagen, "Katholische Kirche und Erziehung und Bildung," G. Gorschenek, ed., *Katholiken und ihre Kirche* (=G 200–202) (Munich and Vienna 1976), 240ff. (246). Numbers for Catholic school statistics in *Kirchliches Handbuch. Amtliches statistiches Jahrbuch der katholischen Kirche Deutschlands,* ed. by F. Groner, 23(1944–51), pt. 5. Between 1944 and 1951 the proportion in denominational popular schools in Germany was 86 percent; 58 percent were Catholic.

mounting costs of building and maintaining schools, conditioned among other things by the increase of lay teachers, it of course is to be expected that the Catholic school system in the United States can for the present experience no further expansion.

The educational aims and methods in the Catholic schools developed in close connection with those of the public and non-Catholic schools. They, like these latter, were fixed in the vicissitudes of the national history—World War I, New Deal, World War II, sputnik shock, and the like—and dependent on the intellectual impulses, such as J. Dewey's pragmatism, and social movements like coeducation, the civil rights movement, and so forth.[32] Nevertheless, they gained powerful help from the papal educational teaching, especially the encyclical *Divini illius Magistri* of Pius XI. The seven goals to which Catholic schools in the United States are directed are a pragmatic combination of general and specific Catholic principles in the educational sphere. Students should be: (1) intelligent Catholics, (2) spiritually vigorous Catholics, (3) cultured Catholics, (4) healthy Catholics, (5) vocational Catholics, (6) social-minded Catholics, (7) American Catholics.[33]

TERTIARY SPHERE

In the tertiary sphere a distinction must be made between universities and instructional places with other professionally qualifying courses—trade schools or higher technical schools, which require as condition of admittance a completion of the secondary sphere II.

The universities have the function of preparing for professional activities which require the employment of scientific knowledge and methods or the capacity for artistic creation. They can but do not have to be places of "research"; where they unite teaching with research, as, for example, the German universities, their rank is higher than if they are specialized technical universities. Modern research in the social and natural sciences is, however, organized more and more outside the tertiary sphere.

In countries with predominant or exclusive auspices of the state the differences of achievement of the universities are indeed less strong than in countries with predominantly free auspices, such as the United States, but the extension of the university sphere set in motion around institutions which were previously to be counted in the secondary sphere II a hitherto unknown process of distinction of level. This

---

[32] *New Catholic Encyclopedia* 5, 142–46.
[33] *Ibid.* Vols. 13, 21.

process can be employed by state planning and managing for inner classification of "all universities": then new structural classification marks of a uniform university system take the place of the university structure: distinction and classification of courses according to content, duration, completion in more application-oriented and more research-oriented courses with simultaneous coordination of related courses and reciprocal recognition of courses taken and completions. But the distinction of level can also be made institutionally visible and lead to a differentiation of grades within the tertiary sphere.[34]

With the expansion of the tertiary sphere not only is account taken of the change of professional educators and their increasingly greater scientific and technical specialization but also a quantitative problem is answered. It is hoped that the problem of the mounting inquiry about the place of studies on the basis of increasing opportunities of study—free instruction, subsidizing of living costs out of the public means—can be solved by a large number of brief profession-qualifying studies being offered, which can rank partly as "basic studies" for continuing courses, and by establishing more difficult criteria, such as special qualifications for completion of secondary sphere II, brief studies, entrance examinations, and so forth.

Still, education in the tertiary sphere is not confined to the traditional institutions or those recently added in this sphere; it is also imparted by correspondence courses, which in principle enable the participant to qualify from his place of work at the moment. This type of study is most powerfully cultivated in the Communist countries; during the Khrushchev era there were in the Soviet Union more students (54.8 percent) in evening and correspondence courses than in day and direct study (45.2 percent).[35]

In the so-called tertiary sphere there were from time immemorial ecclesiastical functions and interests. Through the stormy development of the post-Enlightenment sciences at the universities the older faculty organization, in which theology occupied the first place, was basically upset: in part it fell into a peripheral situation, in part it had to leave the universities altogether, as at the Université de France. But other goals of the older universities in Catholic countries also changed: first and most important, the cultivation of ecclesiastical and secular sciences on the basis of the Catholic world view, then the integrating, oriented to it, of the special branches of science through the scholarly exertion of the academicians, and finally also the representation of the

[34] *Council of Europe, Diversification of Tertiary Education* (Strasbourg 1974).
[35] O. Anweiler et al., *Europäische Bildungssysteme zwischen Tradition und Fortschritt* (Mülheim 1971), 137.

sciences in the undecided question about an ethically and religiously acceptable meaning of life. The situation at the universities worsened so powerfully here and there that certain universities, according to N. A. Luyten, had to rank as "antireligious fortresses."

For from the second half of the nineteenth century there had begun, as a reaction to the Enlightenment, secularization, and liberal or laicizing state-Church policies, a movement for the "Catholic University," which was active everywhere but especially where an adequate concordat or corresponding other regulation of the domains of research and education of state and Church, standing side by side or mixed together, was lacking. Since in Germany the on the whole positive development of the nineteenth century was continued beyond the era of the Weimar Republic and, apart from the retarding tendencies during the Nazi period, kept up also after the Second World War, in this country there occurred no founding of "Catholic Universities." Since the 1960s the legal position of the civil and ecclesiastical philosophical and theological universities, for example, in Bavaria, has been regulated on the model of the Catholic faculties at the universities.

In the rest of Europe the situation of the Catholic universities is quite different: in France, where there are such universities at Paris, Lille, Angers, Lyon, and Toulouse—the Université de l'Ouest at Angers was founded as early as 1875, originally to cover the need for teachers for the numerous private Catholic schools of western France—there are statutory restrictions through the circumstance that academic degrees— apart from those in theology—may be granted only by the state Université de France, so that the nontheological faculties of the Catholic universities have established themselves as preparatory institutions for the state examinations.

The rank of a national university for Belgium belongs to the ancient and at the same time Catholic University of Louvain, which by virtue of its Philosophical Institute, associated with Cardinal Mercier, was a leader in Neo-Thomistic research and teaching and which through the breadth of its faculties educated about 50 percent of all students in Belgium—in 1970 about 27,000. However, it was not spared the linguistic strife between the Flemings and Walloons and in 1966 had to be divided into two—Louvain and Ottignies.

The most important Catholic university for Spain, that of Navarre at Pamplona, was only founded in 1960 by *Opus Dei.* Support and direction of this university follow the concordat of 1953, as is true also of the older Catholic universities, for example, Salamanca (1940).

Of special significance for the movement for Catholic universities, appearing in the nineteenth century, is the United States, where today, in addition to a large number of colleges, there are more than thirty-two

Catholic universities; the first of them was founded in 1887 as the Catholic University of America at Washington under the laws of the District of Columbia and two years later was endowed by Leo XIII with papal status by the letter *Magni Nobis Gaudii* of 7 March 1889.

The first function lay in the extension of theological studies, that is, graduate studies, for priests, who obtained their basic training at one of the 125 so-called colleges or ten seminaries. Ten years later there followed a faculty of philosophical and social sciences, in which even black students were enrolled, and women acquired admission in 1928. The Catholic University was supported by the American episcopal conference and all parishes through annual collections; it retained its center of gravity in the area of graduate studies and in the 1960s had about 5,000 students, including 1,300 priests and 400 religious women, but its capacity was considerably greater.

In 1924 there was an attempt at founding an International Federation of Catholic Universities (IFCU) by the newly established Catholic Universities of Milan (1920) and Nijmegen (1923) and the venerable University of Louvain; through this federation the exchange of experience should be institutionalized across national boundaries and the organizational phases of new foundations facilitated. After an interval produced by the war, cooperation was again resumed from Rome in 1949 and the union itself given a canonical status.[36] Today universities of forty countries in Europe, America, Asia, and Africa are united, each of which must, in order to become a member, have at least three faculties, including one for nontheological studies. In Latin American nations there are more than thirty Catholic universities of the most heterogeneous rank—four alone were founded between 1960 and 1964; the most important is probably the Universidad Católica of Chile, with more than 5,000 students. In Canada there are six Catholic universities; the most important is that of Montreal, with over 20,000 students. For Africa the Catholic University Lovanium, founded by Louvain, could gain importance.[37]

In the course of the twentieth century Asia acquired several Catholic universities through missionary institutes from Europe but especially from North America. The University of Aurora was founded in 1903 by French Jesuits at Zikawei, China, and in 1909 transferred to Shanghai. It included faculties for law, natural sciences, the humanities, and medicine. In 1937 the Religious of the Sacred Heart opened there a division for the higher education of women. At Tientsin in 1922 French Jesuits founded an Institut des Hautes Études, which was

---

[36] Apostolic letter *Apostolicas Studiorum Universitates*, AAS 42(1949), 385.
[37] *LThK*, second supplementary volume, 395f.

officially recognized in 1948 as a university under the name Tsinku. But the greatest national and international importance belonged to the Catholic University of Peking, which, founded in 1924 by American Benedictines at the request of Pius XI, was recognized as a state university under the name Fu Jen as early as 1927, and in 1933 was entrusted to the Society of the Divine Word. The three Chinese universities, which enjoyed great repute through their education and scholarship—*Monumenta Serica* of Fu Jen and *Bulletin de l'Université Aurore*—were closed after the Communist seizure of power, and the religious who were not Chinese were expelled. Thus was broken a development to which Teilhard de Chardin had given powerful incentives through his works in the 1920s—discovery of Sinanthropus in 1924. Two Catholic universities—Sophia University at Tokyo in 1913 and Nagoya in 1949—appeared in Japan.[38] At the beginning of the 1960s there were in Asian countries fifteen Catholic universities, whose existence and work were, of course, greatly conditioned by contemporary political circumstances.

Nevertheless, more important in the long view must have been the function in the contemporary national and regional context— "educational planning"—and the quality of the research as well as its international radiation. In this sense the Second Vatican Council declared in regard to Christian education at universities: Catholic universities must be disseminated and fostered in a suitable manner to the various parts of the world, however, so that "they should be noteworthy not so much for their numbers as for their high standards. Entry to them should be made easy for students of great promise but of modest resources, and especially for those from newly developed countries" (Declaration on Christian Education, ART. 10).

CONTINUING EDUCATION (EDUCATION OF ADULTS)

In addition to and following the three or four educational areas a broad field is opening for the resumption of learning, which has an abundance of goals, forms, institutions, and organizational conditions. In recent years this field of learning is considered an autonomous and equivalent educational area—*éducation permanente,* life-long learning, recurrent education. Here not only interests beside and beyond the professional should be cultivated, but also social desires of advancement satisfied and, more and more, possibilities be offered for reviving professional knowledge and preparedness. Since rapid social change, the progress of

---

[38] A. Mulders, *Missionsgeschichte. Die Ausbreitung des katholischen Glaubens* (Regensburg 1960), 472, and S. Delacroix, ed., *Histoire Universelle des Missions Catholiques* 3 (Paris 1958), 273.

science, and technical progress let professional knowledge become outdated and bring enduring changes in the professional sphere, it has become necessary to carry the phase of the "school year" far beyond the entire professional life. Today one sees in constant further improvement the continuation, completion, and renewal of the educational process in the elementary, primary, secondary, and tertiary spheres, and also an alternative to these.[39]

The area of constant further improvement can be brought, in accord with its multifunctionality, only with difficulty under uniform institutional rules. In countries where various social groups, groups of the economy, the Churches, the communities, and so forth, participate in the educational function of this sphere, it is necessary to produce an indispensable minimum in community through local and supralocal collaboration of the agents of the institutions of further development or through the bringing together of previously separately pursued educational aims, especially of the professional and the general political, cultural, and other areas. Recently the attempt has been made, in the framework of uniform curricula and on the basis of a legal "educational leave," to grant to the professionally related education a certain preference and to orient the structure of the further improvement sphere to professional requirements—accumulation of course credits, certificates, demands on the educational personnel, and so forth.

Catholic adult education in Europe was a reply to the challenge of the first Enlightenment, which varied according to respective historical conditions. Its history is still scarcely investigated, although more so in Germany and Austria (I. Zangerle). In Germany Catholic adult education was set up as a popular enlightenment with an apologetic purpose and from the middle of the nineteenth century entered the circle of popular educational movements, where it sought to impart in "schools for adults" a "general Christian instruction," as in the *Katholische Verein Deutschlands* of 1848. After the first aim—the gathering of the Catholic parts of the population into unions and associations—had been accomplished and its ideological and political consolidation against liberalism had succeeded, the second aim became prominent in view of the *Kulturkampf*, namely, to contribute to the formation of consciousness and to defend the status achieved. With the relaxing of the danger, this aim decayed and gave way to cultivation of popular education until, under the direction of A. Heinen and the influence of the Hohenrodt League, new impulses flowed into the Popular Union for Catholic Germany—

---

[39] E. King et al., *Post-Compulsory Education, A New Analysis in Western Europe* (London and Beverly Hills 1974), 44.

400

"intensive" or "formative" popular education. The period between the First and the Second World Wars is characterized by exertions for new organizational forms of cooperation between the Catholic associations and societies—Central Educational Committee of All Catholic Societies of Germany (ZBA)—and new concepts of education—in 1925 the first Catholic Congress of Popular Education at Paderborn; to be sure, the Catholic work of education remained within the bounds of its tradition and its sociophilosophical, historically scarcely specified principles and opened itself up not at all or only weakly to the historical reality of the political society of its time. Thus, facing Nazi domination, it remained politically isolated and was abolished together with the rest of social Catholicism—in 1933 dissolution of the ZBA. After 1945 Catholic adult education first joined the surviving institutional remains of the prewar period—independent evening studies at home, and so forth—after 1950, stimulated by the example of the Protestant academies, in Catholic academies, which understood themselves as places for "the dialogue of the Church with the world," in the words of B. Hanssler. The former orientation to the education of workers, farmers, and artisans was not thereby abandoned, but perhaps changed in favor of a strengthened inclusion of groups related to the intellectual.[40] Finally there occurred the construction of local educational works, which competed with the popular universities and other institutions and often played an important role within the local or regional educational offerings. From the juxtaposition of various Catholic educational institutions ensued not only a need for organizational agreement in the inner-ecclesiastical field, for example, in 1957 the Federated Workers' Community for Catholic Adult Education (BAG); there resulted also the necessity of reaching agreement with the competing institutions of continuing education. A powerful impulse to this came, on the part of the state, from new regulations of the public subsidies, a second from the pedagogical and adult education discussion conducted under the catchword "emancipation" since the mid-1960s, and a third impulse, still hardly to be evaluated in its consequences, from the Second Vatican Council. The pastoral constitution on the Church in the Modern World accelerated the end of the older integrally conceived Catholic adult education in Germany and caused a revolutionary consideration of new ways of adult education under Catholic auspices.

[40] F. Messerschmid, "Geschichte der Katholischen Akademien," F. Pöggeler, ed., *Handbuch der Erwachsenenbildung* 4 (Stuttgart 1975), 208ff.

In Austria this development was already indicated since the "radical new beginning" of 1945 on the basis of other historical assumptions and especially of the line of conflict moving in Catholicism itself between social status and class-oriented thought.[41] The Federated Workers' Community for Catholic Adult Education in Austria (BAKEB), founded in 1963, belongs, like its German sister union (BAG), to the European Federation for Adult Education (FEECA), founded in 1963, in which cooperation among the German-speaking members is especially close.

In the United States the Church's adult education was up to the Second World War little more than a part of the traditional social and mission work. The new era of the adult education movement began in the 1950s and reached certain high points in the 1960s. They were connected with the consolidation of the Church's outside and assistance services, the spread of the ideas of adult education, and the initiatives of the Second Vatican Council. Three currents now determined the Churches' adult education: the ecumenical movement, the involvement of the Churches with the national problems of the United States—poverty, racism—appearances of secularization in the formerly Puritan-oriented public. The model of the Churches' adult education, which was also adopted by Catholic adult education, was the Indiana Plan, developed in 1954 by P. Bergevin and McKinley and published in 1970, which tested new principles of the education of mature students in a scientifically accompanied series of seminars. With the adaptation of the plan proceeded a consolidation of the organization; in 1958 the National Catholic Education Association was founded, which in 1959 published the *Handbook of Catholic Adult Education.* The social extent of the Church's adult education in the United States is considerable; 12 percent of the participants in adult education took part in 1962 in the courses offered by churches and synagogues; a total of 3.2 million.[42]

Catholic adult education in Europe and the United States will be powerfully affected in the future by the trends which appeared at the Third International UNESCO Conference; there a worldwide development for an integrated, publicly responsible, internationally solidified, functional, scientifically based, and professionalized adult education was noted. Whether and in what form such peculiarly Catholic adult education will maintain itself in such trends will de-

[41] Cf. I. Zangerle, "Geschichte der katholischen Erwachsenenbildung," F. Pöggler, ed., op. cit. (n. 40), 208ff.
[42] F. Laack, *Die amerikanische Bildungswirklichkeit. Idee, Stand und Probleme der Adult Education in den USA* (Cologne 1976), 88, 150, 154ff.

402

pend on many circumstances, such as: whether the upsetting impact of the Second Vatican Council will be followed by a phase of critical and believing reconstruction, whether the next generation of educators of adults recognizes this task as its own and possesses the necessary prerequisites for it, and finally, whether the political and social circumstances for an at least partly self-determined activity of free agents will be maintained or will have to be secured anew.

Conditions for Catholic Education in Other Areas of the World

In contradistinction to Europe and North America, where the ecclesiastical educational system was active within the national educational traditions and was operated or controlled by native Churches, in the other regions of the world other and often very complicated circumstances exist. On the basis of the statistical situation only a survey of the schools and universities of the primary to the tertiary sphere is here given; again among them the part current in ecclesiastical sponsorship stands in the center of interest. It acts as representative of the "Catholic educational system."[43]

Latin America differs in a specific way from the only recently decolonized states of Africa and Asia. On the one hand the instruction remains oriented to the leading families at the schools of the countries of their origin;[44] on the other hand, cultural fusions and admixtures of races have occurred which have permitted the rise of a special Latin American society and proper national cultures, whose development perspective seems in no sense about to come to terms with the Western or Communist industrial nations.[45] Seen as a whole, the efficacy of the institutionalized educational system was slight: every other inhabitant of the Latin American continent is illiterate, the shares of the gross national product destined for the educational system are less than those of the industrialized nations. To be sure, the portions have gradually increased since the 1950s. For example, Mexico in 1958 invested 1.5

---

[43] The statistics in this part refer, unless otherwise noted, always to the Catholic educational system under private or "free" auspices; cf. also CIEO, *Études et Documents* no. 5: *The Situation of Catholic Education in the Various Continents* (Brussels 1969).

[44] For the Catholic universities see the section "Tertiary Sphere," above.

[45] Cf. E. L. Stehle, *Indio-Latein Amerika* (Düsseldorf and Oberhaussen 1971); A. García, "Die lateinamerikanische Theologie der Befreiung, I" *Internationale Katholische Zeitschrift*, 2d year (1973), no. 2, 400ff.; R. Vekemans, "Die lateinamerikanische Theologie der Befreiung II. Ein Literaturbericht," ibid., D., 434ff.

percent of the national product in education, in 1963 it was 2.7 percent and in 1966 3.1 percent.[46]

The Church's historical role in the educational system is seen in the strong share of church institutions in the school and university area. Of course, for the longest time they were not attuned to the developmental needs of the country and in function and organization they were both incomplete and unbalanced. The defects of the public educational system were uninterruptedly expressed in the ecclesiastical educational system: there was a lack of institutions for mass education—"eradication of illiteracy"—for professional education, for the training of middle-level administrative personnel, and so forth. Thirteen percent of the pupils attended Catholic institutions. The highest percentage, over 25 percent, was reached in Bolivia and Chile, followed by Brazil, Colombia, Ecuador, and Guatemala, with from 20 to 15 percent, then by Argentina, Mexico, Nicaragua, Panama, Peru, and Venezuela, with 15 to 10 percent, and, finally, with less than 10 percent in Costa Rica, Honduras, and Paraguay. The religious instruction of the mass of those of school age is not assured and can only partly be accomplished by extra-school institutions. The connection of the school system with the state means only in a few cases regular subsidies for building and maintenance costs, as especially in Argentina, Chile, and Surinam; in other countries there is no established financial help, for example, in Colombia, except for the Catholic universities, Ecuador, Paraguay, and Peru. Since the increased social tensions of the 1950s and the revolutionary disturbances of the 1960s, the Latin American Church has powerfully exerted itself for the expanding and renewing of its educational commitments.[47] In 1963 the Permanent Secretariat of the Latin American Episcopal Conference at Bogotá (CELAM) was reorganized. It has prepared the realization of the conciliar documents *Gaudium et spes* and the Declaration on Christian Education on the Latin American continent. The outcome of its work was the resolution "Human Development," issued in 1968 by the Second General Assembly of the Latin American Bishops at Medellín, in which is said: "Latin America seems to be still living under the tragic sign of underdevelopment, which separates our

[46] P. Latapí, *Diagnostico Educativo Nacional, Centro de Estudios Educativos* (Mexico City 1964). The relatively high state of illiteracy must be seen in relation to the increase of population and the contemporary decrease of the proportion (cf. also UNESCO, *World Survey* (n. 1), Vol. 5, 66f. Between 1960 and 1966 the proportion of the school population in the total population rose from 14 to 18 percent.

[47] Cf. J. R. Vaccaro, "Latin America," in CIEO, *Études de Documents* no. 5 (n. 43 above), Doc. 3.3.

brethren not only from the enjoyment of material goods but also from their own human realization." Education, hence the achieving of Catholic schools, is defined in this situation as the "decisive factor in the development of the continent." The direction in which the development should go—the "total development of the person and of all persons"—must be made possible and encouraged by education; in view of the magnitude of the task, systematic education by means of schools or colleges is not enough; so far as Catholic schools take part in education, they must admit all social classes without discrimination—"democratization." The Catholic school should be open to its local and Latin American environment, pursue its adaptation and reorganization, be open to ecumenical dialogue, and become the cultural, social, and intellectual center within society. In an effort to achieve the goal of an open-minded and democratic Catholic school, the Episcopal Conference of Medellín supported the right to free choice of school and suitable financial contribution.[48] The Christian educational impulses are no longer communicated only through canon law or theology but through sociology and educational planning.

The significance of this document is great: It places the national organizations of the Latin American Church under a common reform, even, in each case according to the situation, revolutionary program, brings it, again according to the circumstances, into conflict with state offices, and sets up for broad circles of the population not only a sign of hope but also a standard by which the actions of the ecclesiastical agents of education can be measured.

The educational system supported by the Churches of Africa is due, as in Asia, to Christianity, which in wide areas accompanied European colonialism and imperialism. The European missionary institutes represented a European program of education, which reflected the proper character and interest of the colonial power of the time, "displaced education."[49] The European face of educational policy is still especially visible in Africa.[50]

France's *mission civilisatrice* demanded a centralized and laicized school system also in the colonies. British colonial power aimed at an African society by means of the principle of "indirect rule," employed

[48] *Die Kirche in der gegenwärtigen Umwandlung Lateinamerikas* (see n. 18).
[49] See, besides the titles given in n. 38, especially H. Jedin, "Weltmission und Kolonialismus," *Saeculum,* 1958, 393ff.; M. Merle, *Les Églises Chrétiennes et la Décolonisation* (Paris 1967); S. Neill, *Colonialism and Christian Missions* (London 1966).
[50] Also from the sociological viewpoint: T. Hanf, *Erziehung und politischer Wandel in Schwarzafrika* (n. 2).

vernacular languages, and encouraged in its sphere private educators, especially mission societies. The Belgians promoted Catholic mission schools in the Congo for the aims of a controlled social life and of an economy that would supplement the home economy. The training of administrative personnel, which meant little to the total Belgian colonial policy, did not take place; an exception was the training of clergy. For the rest it was typical of most African areas that only a basic schooling was allowed to the blacks. In South Africa, South West Africa, and Rhodesia must be added the special circumstances of a white Africanism, which sought to maintain itself ethnically, socially, and politically against a native and partly united black majority and subordinated the educational policy also to this end.

The situation of the Catholic educational system changed[51] when, after the Second World War, the epoch of the decolonization of Asia and Africa began, and new leading powers with new methods and aims appeared. In addition to the United States there were the Soviet Union and from the 1960s the People's Republic of China, as well as a few smaller Communist states, such as Cuba and the People's Republic of Vietnam. Arab nationalism in the Near and Middle East consolidated the position of Islam, and the political and cultural influence of Europe declined. In this age of total change there appeared in the former colonial territories two currents, both equally unfavorable to the Catholic educational system: the first, more cultural and political, was awaking nationalism; the second, more economic and sociopolitical, was the policy of development. "Nation building" and socioeconomic development became the goals of official policy; the educational system should also contribute to its realization. More than once nation building was based on precolonial—and this usually means non-Christian—traditions; also the ideologies with which the policy of development, especially that of a Marxist orientation, were supposed to be supported proved to be hostile to the Christian. Instruction in European languages, especially in the primary sphere, was restricted, special proofs of training were made obligatory on the teaching personnel, the legal position of the Catholic school system became insecure. If "nation building" and development are understood as the entire political function in the hand or under the control of the state, then it appears inevitable that the freedom to found and maintain schools, on the basis of which the missionary system had developed, had to be curtailed.

The African states rising to sovereignty were not inclined to let the

---

[51] Cf. M. Ekwa, "Africa," CIEO, *Études et Documents* no. 5, Doc. 3.2, and the report based on Ekwa: *Catholic Education in the Service of Africa, Report of the Panafrican Catholic Education Conference* (August 1965).

status quo of the colonial educational system continue. As soon as they saw the means and ways to liquidate it they did so. Still, it did not yet succeed everywhere. Some nations took the school into the state's monopoly and gave to the Catholic private schools, in addition to the state schools, a legal status of their own—Zaire, Tanzania, Burundi, Ruanda—others decreed, as a sign of the state's school monopoly, the suppression or assumption of control of private Catholic schools by the state—Republic of Congo, Guinea, the Central African Empire, Sudan, Malawi, Ghana before 1967, and most recently the revolutionary socialist states of Ethiopia, Mozambique, and Somalia.

The situation of the Catholic school system at the beginning of the 1960s, for which there are statistics, was as follows in Africa: The Catholic proportion in the total African population then amounted to ca. 10 percent—25 out of 270 million. Of African pupils, every third went to a Catholic school. In the individual states these averages differed greatly: Of fifty-six states nine had a Catholic proportion in their population of more than 40 percent, thirty of less than 10 percent. Hence there was in only a few states a developed and capable school system, especially in the former Belgian Congo, but Catholic schools, wherever they existed, performed as much as two-thirds of their services for non-Catholics and were an important site of the encounter of non-Christians with Christians of various denominations, especially with Catholics. As special problems, finally, the following presented themselves: number and quality of teachers, their missionary motivation, their situation in regard to payment—only a few states, such as Zaire, have the means and the intention to pay salary supplements to the regular teacher salaries in Catholic schools—and the conscious share of Catholic schools in nation building and development.

Such questions were treated at regional conferences since the spring of 1967 and placed under the express command to base Catholic education on the principles stated in the conciliar texts, as well as concretize these principles in the light of the special African problems.

The strengthening of the racial unrest and of the nationalist movement in the white-dominated Apartheid states of the south and southwest has since 1976 led the Catholic schools, despite all repressive measures, to depart from the state policy of racial separation and to open their doors to pupils of all races.

In the Near and Middle East, as regards the religious situation, Catholics are an express minority and face an uncommonly complicated situation.[52] The countries of this part of the world be-

---

[52] Cf. also I. Maroun, "Near and Middle East," CIEO, _Études et Documents_ no. 5., Doc. 3.1.

long mostly to Islam—the states of the Arab League—partly to Orthodoxy—Greece and Cyprus—or to Judaism—Israel; only one state has a considerable Catholic proportion in the total population—Lebanon. In this area in the mid-1960s a half-million pupils attended Catholic schools, a number which, meanwhile, especially after the destruction of Beirut and many Christian localities, has probably declined considerably. Christianity in this part of the world contains two elements—a missionary and a native—Maronites, Copts, Chaldeans, Orthodox. Both were or are, each in its own way, active in the educational sphere. The native and mostly rural worshipping communities have for centuries given instruction in language and literature in order to maintain their cultic-religious integrity in the midst of a foreign-speaking and foreign-believing environment—instruction under the mulberry tree on a stone. Mission communities aspired to European educational standards and soon became the urban center of attraction for non-Catholic pupils. In Lebanon the complete and well attended Catholic schools were recognized and subsidized by the state.

The problems of the Catholic school system of today agree in much with those which occur in Africa and have to do with the historical burden of the former colonially useful institutions, with the orientation to European educational standards, not least with the claim to partial independence vis-à-vis the state school system. The stresses of the colonial period are seen in Algeria, Morocco, Tunisia, and Libya, and will, if at all, only then be eliminated when the native population again asks about the good services of mission schools and is allowed to ask. In this way the political aspect is indicated: In socialist Arabic countries Catholic schools were in many places abolished. In the other nations of the Islamic world they are at least subject to pressure, not least through the coordination practice of the Arab UNESCO, the regional branch of UNESCO formed by the Arab League, which strives for the regional uniformity of teaching and learning to the disadvantage of the Catholic school system. It is self-evident that under such conditions the principles of the council can only with difficulty be employed and developed in the Catholic educational sphere and all depends on whether the Universal Declaration of Human Rights, rules of the United Nations, the Charter of UNESCO on non-discrimination in questions of educa-tion and teaching are observed by the states which once agreed to them.

Most difficult of all is the situation of the Catholic educational system under the conditions in Asia. Of the seventeen countries evaluated in the 1968 report of the CIEO,[53] only the Philippines may be regarded as a Catholic country—the Catholic proportion is more than 80 percent—

---

[53] Cf. W. Perfecto, "Asia," CIEO, *Études et Documents* no. 5., Doc. 3.4.

Macao and Vietnam just reach 10 percent, all the others are far less. India, for example, in 1966 estimated 60 million pupils and students, of whom 1.8 million attended Catholic educational institutions—860,000 were themselves Catholic, hence less than half of those who were in these schools. The figure of 50,000 pupils and students in Catholic institutions given for Cambodia, out of a total of 650,000, is surely out of date since the seizure of power by the Communists.

The political changes on the map of Asia since the late 1940s have worsened the situation for the Catholics more and more.[54] Even where the Communists did not come to power, the Catholic educational system can develop only a small part of the impact to which it is destined. Often the non-Catholic environment demands that the missionary and pastoral character of the Catholic schools be suppressed; in Islamic lands, like Egypt and Pakistan, or Buddhist countries "ethics" or even a non-Catholic religion must be taught. If, as in the Philippines, thirty of one hundred pupils in the primary and secondary sphere take part in Catholic religious instruction, this is an extremely favorable condition for the Asian area. In some countries maintenance costs for Catholic schools are subsidized by the government, since institutions do not yet exist; in this context strict controls are ordinarily exercised. In Malaysia and Singapore the government even appoints the teaching personnel in agreement with the ecclesiastical authorities.

The range of Catholic schools is of importance regionally rather than socially; true, they partly penetrate deeply into areas not reached by the government, but they affect only the upper strata. Since the Second World War not a few of today's leading personalities attended Catholic schools. The future of these schools is seen less in quantitative expansion than in an enhancement of quality.

Among the aims is the substitution of European by qualified native teachers and the adaptation of native cultural traditions, then the recognizable tying of the educational work of Catholic schools into the development program of the respective governments. At the same time this means recognition of differentiated services for the Church: from the religious education of Catholic children to collaboration in a formation, worthy of human beings, of the social circumstances in the particular country.[55]

---

[54] Cf. for the China mission: A. Mulders, *Missionsgeschichte* (n. 38), 472f.
[55] The discussion on the services of the Church, by which the question of educational offerings is also affected, today finds a loud echo in the framework of missiology (cf. also J. M. Van Engelen, "Tendenzen in der Missiologie der Gegenwart," *Internationale katholische Zeitschrift*, 3d year (1974), no. 3, 230ff.

CHAPTER 13

Information and the Mass Media*

Among those social changes which affected the Church's activity in
essential points in the twentieth century were the developments in the
field of mass communication. True, the Church and journalism always
stood in certain reciprocal relations, and the critical confrontation with
the press as it was becoming free had already started in the first decades
of the nineteenth century, for example, under Gregory XVI.[1] However, the twentieth century first produced that full development of
those "instruments of social communication"—the Vatican linguistic
usage since 1963—which are summarized under the notion of mass
media or means of mass communication: to the modern press in its
forms as informing and opinion making daily and weekly with a large
circulation, recreational press, and specialist press have been added the
cinema, radio, and television. Their technical development, as in
general the industrialization of publicity production, evoked also the
development of new agents of public communications offerings which
caused new markets to appear: phonograph records, recording tape,
eight-millimeter film, video disk, and, not to be forgotten, the paperback, which is changing the book market.

Since the turn of the century the Church saw or sees itself facing
essentially five important phenomena and developments in mass communication with which it must come to terms; for changes in the mass
communication system of particular nations, of entire cultural groups,
and in individual cases even of "world society" affect the activity of the
Church, especially in its mandate to preach and in its pastoral commission. These five points are: (1) the decline, in some countries the
disappearance, of the "opinion press"; (2) the new, so-called audio-
visual media—cinema, radio, television; (3) the grasping of totalitarian

---

* Michael Schmolke
[1] Cf., for example, even though outdated, L. Bethleem, *La Presse* (Paris 1928); also, for
the sake of the contemporary sources, R. Pesch, *Die kirchlich-politische Presse der
Katholiken in der Rheinprovinz vor 1848* (Mainz 1966); M. Schmolke, *Die schlechte Presse.
Katholiken und Publizistik zwischen "Katholik" und "Publik" 1821–1968* (Münster
1971), and for the Protestant side, despite the misleading title, K. W. Bühler, *Presse und
Protestantismus in der Weimarer Republik* (Witten 1970).
[2] "Journalism" is used as a generic term for any public and actual social communication,
hence also for its pretechnical forms; it is then only feasible to speak of mass
communication if social communication is effected by means of the modern, technically
conditioned media—press, film, radio, and television.

410

political systems for the publicity institutions in various countries; (4) the completely new tasks and opportunities which result for the use of communications means in the underdeveloped countries; and (5) the disintegration of the "Catholic public" in countries or cultural groups where this concept of practical journalism,[2] but also of pastoral work, had been used for decades with some justification. As a sixth point, which however arose not against the Church but from the Church as a reaction to the journalistic opposition, the organizational and, recently, theoretical confrontation of the Church with mass communication deserves special notice.

As useful as these categories are for the analysis of our theme, still they are not all, on the basis of their differing time dimensions, suited for the historical classification of the subject; they will appear in various sections as aspects of new problems.

The Catholic Claim and the "Colorless Press"

If the Catholic discussion of journalism in the nineteenth century was predominantly determined by the struggle against the "bad press"—*mauvaise presse, stampa perversa, stampa negativa*—the early twentieth century brought a new enemy: more correctly, the knowledge that, in addition to the "bad," that is, the liberal, socialist, and occasionally even Protestant press, a new form of newspaper had appeared—the "color-less press." The Catholic press, as the only "good press," was, to be sure, respected by many Catholic critics only as the lesser evil,[3] but it still had gained some noteworthy initial successes in the last third of the century that was ending. Proud of enterprises such as *De Tijd* (1845), *Kölnische Blätter* (1860; from 1869 *Kölnische Volkszeitung*), *Germania* (1871), or *La Croix* (from 1883 as a daily), for some time it was overlooked that meanwhile a new type of newspaper had appeared— the informative newspaper, *presse d'information,* which, differing from the classical type of the nineteenth century, the "opinion newspaper," abandoned partisanship or clear ideological lines. The Catholic press, on the contrary, was conceivable only as an "opinion press"; also the many small papers, which the statistics of founding of Catholic newspa-pers show to have increased during the *Kulturkampf*[4] or a little later as foundations of local or regional "press associations," especially in

---

[3] J. Lukas, *Die Presse, ein Stück moderner Versimpelung* (Regensburg 1867), 116: "The press as it has sprouted up today, is a great evil; our Catholic press is something good because it is the lesser evil."

[4] Cf. M. Schmolke, "Zur Gliederung der katholischen Pressegeschichte Deutschlands," *Communicatio Socialis* (=CS) 3(1970), 311–27.

Bavaria and Austria,[5] took care of further growth, were, despite their character as local papers, opinion newspapers. In the United States (*The Sun*, 1833; *The New York Herald*, 1835), in France (*La Presse* and *Le Siècle*, 1836), and in England (*Daily Telegraph and Courier*, 1855), newspapers "for all," which in order to achieve the widest possible circulation not only lowered their price but also renounced partisanship, had existed the longest.[6] In Germany the first newspapers of this sort occasionally appeared from 1871, using the title, or element in the title, of "general advertiser." The idea soon had an unpleasant connotation. The general advertising press lacked staunchness, and this is what constituted its "colorlessness." The fact that the "colorless press" was a publishing success, that, in regard to the issues, only with it did the age of the mass press begin, only made it more suspect.

The general advertisers were the "bad press" of a new sort, which were regularly condemned in Germany from 1889 at the general Catholic meetings: "Away with these wolves in sheep's clothing from all Catholic houses, from all Catholic families, from all Catholic communities!" said Ernst Lieber in 1895. Authors such as Joseph Eberle, Viktor Kolb, later Felix Hardt, and a legion of pamphlets struggled against undermining tendencies. Especially typical of this phase of the "press apostles" are the books of Joseph Eberle (*Grossmacht Presse*[7]) and Giuseppe Chiaudano (*Il Giornalismo Cattolico*[8]). While Eberle chiefly denounced the general non-Catholic press, Chiaudano made clear all that the Catholic press must not do, but which north of the Alps it had long presumed to do, for example, in the discussion of *dubia* or the criticism of ecclesiastical decisions, in opposition to the Jesuit father's statements on the "necessità dello spirito di disciplina e di obbedienza." And the Code of Canon Law summarizes in Title XXIII the rules of censorship and prohibition, which, in consequence of a strict observance, had made almost impossible to Catholics a normal participation in the journalism of the time, active and passive. Where they took part in social communication as publishers, journalists, and readers, they could never entirely do this, if they were conscientious, without a bad conscience. The broken relationship of the Church to journalism had by no means been overcome when the age of the "new media" began.

---

[5] Cf. K. Nüssler, *Geschichte des Katholischen Pressvereins* (Diss. Munich 1954); R. Kohlbach, *Kreuz und Feder* (Graz 1933); K.M. Stepan, *Stückwerk im Spiegel* (Graz and Vienna 1949).

[6] W. B. Lerg, "Die Anfänge der Zeitung für alle," W. B. Lerg, M. Schmolke, eds., *Massenpresse und Volkszeitung* (Assen 1968), 1–46.

[7] J. Eberle, *Grossmacht Presse. Enthüllungen für Zeitungsgläubige, Forderungen für Männer* (Mergentheim 1910), 3d ed. (Regensburg and Vienna 1920).

[8] G. Chiaudano, *Il giornalismo cattolico* (Turin 1910).

Film and Radio in the Early Phase

Shortly before the turn of the century film presentations, at first as *varieté* attractions, and since 1920 the radio were ready for the use of the public. The early history of the Church's confrontation with these new media has as yet hardly been investigated. It can be taken as certain that at first it was not recognized as a publicity medium of general social and political relevance. Popular education and art were the spheres to which the cinema—the first term used for the movies—and the radio were assigned. With the catchword "educational functions" people noticed them quite early, at least in Central Europe, while in the United States, which quickly developed into the motherland of the great film industry, ecclesiastical attention was focused more strongly on the excesses of the content of the moving picture. For example, at the general assemblies of the Catholics of Germany there was criticism of the "poisoned abuses of the cinema," but at Aachen in 1912 in *Kino-Reform-Anträgen* there was adherence to the goal of the "positive reform work." Today it is almost forgotten that as early as 1910, in the framework of the Popular Association for Catholic Germany at Mönchen-Gladbach, there was founded the "Photographic Society with Limited Liability," which provided, loaned, or supplied together with the necessary equipment slide series and soon didactic films. A series of writings, *Lichtbühnen-Bibliothek* and the technical periodical *Bild und Film* (from 1912), supplemented the offering until the First World War ended these constructive efforts.[9] After the war the film work and the Catholic radio work, at first pursued by free initiative, settled in special workers' groups in the Central Educational Committee of the Catholic Associations of Germany (ZBA), founded in 1919.

Of course, both the ZBA and the Fulda Episcopal Conference at first hesitated when, after the official beginning of public radio broadcasting in Germany in October 1923, possibilities resulted for ecclesiastical collaboration in the organizing of broadcasting. The broadcasting of liturgical actions, a problem which has not been thoroughly discussed even today, caused anxiety, while access under the titles of art and popular education was less problematic.[10] More eagerness for risks was present in the movie: with its own production firms—Leo-Film of Munich in 1927, Eidophon of Berlin—a Catholic share in moving

---

[9] Cf. also E. Ritter, *Die katholisch-soziale Bewegung Deutschlands im neunzehnten Jahrhundert und der Volksverein* (Cologne 1954), 277. A survey of Catholic efforts in regard to the film after World War I are given in a "Kino-Nummer" of the *Augustinus-Blatt* 26(1922), no. 5/6. In preparation: H. Schmitt, *Die kirchliche Filmarbeit in Deutschland von ihren Anfängen bis 1945* (Diss. Bonn).

[10] On this thematic area, G. Bauer, *Kirchliche Rundfunkarbeit 1924–1939* (Frankfurt am Main 1966).

picture offerings could be financed. But the enterprise was a failure, and in 1933 Leo-Film dragged the Munich Leohaus, the chief office of the Catholic social associations, into bankruptcy. Film work as an educational function and increasingly as a function of a protecting pastoral theology was, however, able to consolidate itself. The American example of the Legion of Decency, founded in 1933, and its growing influence on American film production made a powerful impression. Also the collaboration in radio was permanently established. True, there was no success, as there was in the Netherlands, Spain, or Portugal, in setting up its own radio system or companies to produce programs. But the intensive cooperation, which was especially pushed by the radio prelate, Bernhard Marschall—"the Catholics have cooperated in radio from the start"[11]—assured the place for the Church's collaboration despite the control over radio quickly instituted by the Nazis.

This first phase of the Church's concern with film and radio found a certain conclusion in the establishing of international organizations: In April 1928 the *Office Catholique International du Cinéma* (OCIC) was founded at The Hague, and also in 1928 there appeared, following the Cologne international press exhibition *Pressa*, the *Bureau International de la Radiophonie Catholique*—after World War II, UNDA. The first director of the bureau was Bernhard Marschall, just as earlier the Leo-Film director, Georg Ernst, had assumed the presidency of OCIC.[12] However, in the succeeding years the American model of the Legion of Decency acted as a standard, that is, the practice based on "moral codes," rather amounting to a censorship-like pastoral care of protection, established itself. It found the respect of the American film producers[13] and the approval of the Pope: Pius XI was moved by the work of the legion to issue the film encyclical *Vigilanti cura* in 1936:[14] for the future moral evaluation listings of films were to be issued in all countries and made known to the faithful.

[11] Report of the Essen Katholikentag 1932, 241.
[12] Contemporary source: G. Ernst and B. Marschall, eds., *Film und Rundfunk. Zweiter Internationaler Katholischer Filmkongress, Erster Internationaler Katholischer Rundfunkkongress. Gesamtbericht* (Munich 1929).
[13] A Jesuit, Father Daniel Lord, was requisitioned for the elaboration of a "Production Code" as a norm, also the "Hays Moral Code" of 1929–31, renewed in 1939 (V. Engelhardt, *Kirche und Film* [Düsseldorf 1958], 42ff.; U. Gregor, E. Patalas, *Geschichte des Films* [Munich 1973], 205f.).
[14] Cf. C. Ford, *Le Cinéma au service de la foi* (Paris 1953).

The Development of the Catholic Press in the International Survey

When there is mention of "Catholic press," there ordinarily result difficulties in defining it. These arise, on the one hand, from the fact that Catholic press does not have to be an unconditionally ecclesiastical press, and, on the other hand, from the question of the criteria by which a nonecclesiastical but still Catholic press should be determined to be Catholic. In our context "Catholic press" will then be understood if at least one of the following four features is encountered: (1) name, for example, in the title or subtitle: "Catholic Newspaper for . . ." "Diocesan Paper . . ."; (2) connection, with ecclesiastical officials and/or institutions, or Catholic associations, movements, parties; (3) active denominational adherence of the person or group of the editorial board or editor; and (4) clearly recognizable determination of the center of gravity of the content.[15]

The origin of a distinctively Catholic press seems to be promoted by definite social structures but impeded by others: Extreme diaspora situations permit Catholic periodicals to appear only marginally, as the examples of England or of the Scandinavian countries show; but even traditionally purely Catholic societies, wherever possible still with the state-Church character of the Catholic denomination, are not unconditionally favorable to the distinction, for example, Spain and Italy. This changes the moment when strong laicizing or anti-Church movements appear, for example, in France and recently in Poland. Also operating favorably are the existence of approximately equally strong and large denominational groups, the polarization in fashion-setting Christian or socialist-liberal political parties, or also the denominational underpinning of a pluralistic society; to this extent Germany, Austria, Switzerland, and the Netherlands are classic Catholic press countries, and even the United States has produced a varied Catholic press system. Growing prosperity and comprehensive, varied, and politically unhindered assistance with communications offerings seem to weaken the denominational press, as also the party press, whereas political communications pressure—control of the press, bringing the press into line—to the extent that it does not completely eliminate denominational publication, consolidates the remaining agencies. The conditions mentioned here have determined the history of the Catholic press in the twentieth century—naturally, different in the various social and political organizations. For the German-speaking countries of Europe and the Netherlands a similar development has resulted in this connection in so far as the Catholic press usually moves closer to the Catholic parties or

[15] M. Schmolke, *Die schlechte Presse,* 28f.

supports these parties without its thereby becoming, apart from some exceptions, a strictly regulated party organ, as is the case, for example, with the Communist and Social Democratic Parties as well as the NSDAP. The party relationship developed before the First World War, whereas since the end of the Second World War a growing aloofness becomes discernible.

In Germany until 1933 Catholic press and Center press were de facto identified, despite numerous discussions of differences. Resulting from the *Kulturkampf,* this press reached the quantitative climax of its development shortly before the First World War. Statistics of the "St. Augustinusverein zur Pflege der katholischen Presse," founded in 1878, name 446 "Catholic newspapers" for 1912 and a total number of subscribers of 2.625 million.[16] The number of titles dropped, it is true, after the war, but not greatly—there were 434 in 1931—but of course concentration procedures had taken place, so that for a long time one could no longer speak of 434 independent newspapers; the circulation was then estimated at 2.5 million.[17] (There is no reliable and, as regards categories, uniform statistic of the Catholic press in Germany or elsewhere in the world.[18])

The general customary relation to the Center Party caused the Catholic daily press, after the Nazi seizure of power in 1933 or at the latest after the self-dissolution of the Center, to fall into the category of the "civic" press controlled by the Nazi press. This meant merely that it was not at once eliminated, as was the press of the KPD and SPD by means of the decree for the "Protection of People and State" of 28 February 1933. Goebbels' statement of 4 October 1933—"Absolutely no obstacle stands in the way of the multiformity of the public opinion press"[19]—did not assure the "civic" newspapers any sort of free room. The formerly Catholic among them were, even if at first direct prohibitions were rare, exposed to all the measures of conformity of the

[16] W. Kisky, ed., *Der Augustinus-Verein zur Pflege der katholischen Presse von 1878 bis 1928* (Düsseldorf 1928), 227 and 229.

[17] H. Kapfinger, "Die Struktur der katholischen Presse," J. W. Naumann, ed., *Die Presse und der Katholik* (Augsburg 1932), 211–28.

[18] A survey is attempted by O. Groth, *Die Zeitung* II (Mannheim, Berlin, and Leipzig 1929), 436–38. Leads to the statistical sources may be found in M. Schmolke, *Die schlechte Presse,* pp. 395–416; among others, the following indications of literature: K. Bringmann, J. Frizenschaff 1888, M. Grünbeck, F. Hülskamp 1875, H. Keiter 1895 and 1913, W. Kisky, K. Löffler 1924; also the press statistics of L. Woerl, which are given in the bibliography in M. Schmolke, op. cit., 372, n. 147.

[19] "Rede des Reichsministers Dr. Goebbels vor der deutschen Presse bei Verkündung des Schriftleitergesetzes am 4. Oktober 1933," quoted from the copy in H. Schmidt-Leonhardt and P. Gast, *Das Schriftleitergesetz vom 4. Oktober 1933,* 3d ed. (Berlin 1944), 9–22, here 14.

Nazi press policy. In 1934–35 occurred the spectacular throttling of the *Rhein-Mainische Volkszeitung,* which in the last years of the Weimar Republic had, alongside *Germania* and the *Kölnische Volkszeitung,* acquired a supraregional stamp of a progressive Catholic type. Some papers, such as the *Deutsches Volksblatt* or the *Badischer Beobachter* of Karlsruhe, founded in 1848, found no way to escape the restrictions of an ever increasing number of new directives on press policy, and in 1935 they gave up.[20] Others, such as the *Kölnische Volkszeitung,* which in 1932 had just fallen into an economic crisis affecting its existence, or the *Germania,* were able to survive, but the Catholic legal line of the *Germania* (close to Hitler's first vice chancellor, Franz von Papen) did not always meet with the approval of its public: not suppressed literally but deserted by its own readers, it suspended publication on 31 December 1938.[21] The remaining, mostly smaller, daily press was exposed to various concentration procedures, which were for the most part assisted by Nazi measures. Their aim was to bring as many as possible of former Catholic papers into one of the Nazi collective publishing companies; in Catholic matters the Vera-Verlagsanstalt GmbH and the Phönix-GmbH were specialists. It was obligatory to sell to them if, for example, a publisher could no longer publish because of exclusion from the compulsory professional organization of the Reich press office.[22]

In the same Reich press office, on the other hand, the Catholic newspaper press, as a "professional organization Catholic Church press," could create for itself something almost like a reservation; until 1936 it was granted, among other things, by utilization of the idea, unclear in the concordat, of the "official diocesan papers," as the only kind of press brought under the protection of the 1933 concordat, relatively extensive and, after 1936, still some protection. Under political pressure, until 1936 the number of titles and the total circulation rose from 9.6 to 11.4 million between 1933 and 1936. Not until 1936 did those measures begin which, before the general shutting down of papers in 1941, caused almost three-fourths of the 416 titles of 1936 to disappear, but which also gained by force the kind of "diocesan paper" that thereafter determined the structure of the Catholic press in

[20] S. Kessemeier, *Katholische Publizistik im NS-Staat 1933–1938* (Münster 1973), 18f.
[21] For the *Kölnische Volkszeitung* and *Germania* cf. the pertinent articles by R. Kramer and K. M. Stiegler in H. D. Fischer, ed., *Deutsche Zeitungen des 17. bis 20. Jahrhunderts* (Pullach 1972). The historiography of the Catholic press in the Third Reich has been recently supplemented by the dissertation of M. Hüsgen, *Die Bistumsblätter in Niedersachsen während der nationalsozialistischen Zeit* (Hildesheim 1975) and on the whole placed on a more solid basis.
[22] Cf. Kessemeier, op. cit., 20ff.

Germany and Austria: in each diocese there was now to be only one diocesan paper, to be decided and authorized by the bishop.[23]

The Second World War also meant a clear determining boundary line for the Catholic press in many other countries of Europe. For Germany and a little later for Austria it appeared earlier than for the Netherlands, Belgium, Poland, or France. In all these nations in the two decades of 1920–40 the Catholic press displayed a certain stability, although tending rather to concentration than to expansion. An overview, already in the shadow of the approaching catastrophe, was supplied by the "World Exposition of the Catholic Press," which was held at Vatican City from 12 May 1936 to 31 May 1937 with strong international participation—sixty-three exhibitors, mostly of countries or groups of countries from all the continents. The volume of reports[24] is not only one of the few comprehensive sources for the status of the Catholic press in the 1930s, it also makes known the European situation: Germany was represented by a total of two and one-half printed pages—France by thirty-four; from the information on Germany one learns a few historical titles, the circulation of *Germania* (7,500), but also data on the *Völkischer Beobachter,* the *SA-Mann,* and the *Schulungsbrief,* while Italy and Austria were tersely represented with lists of their still voluminous stocks, although the volume of reports did not appear until 1939.

In Austria the Christian Social *Reichspost,* founded in 1894, had as early as 1912 driven the conservative Catholic *Vaterland* (1860–1911) from the field. After the First World War it remained the leading Catholic voice, approving the corporate state, anti-Marxist, but also critical of the plans for *Anschluss,* whose forcible realization in 1938 meant the end of the paper, directed since 1902 by Friedrich Funder.[25] The Catholic press of the Austrian lands was supported by the "Catholic Press Associations," founded everywhere toward the end of the nineteenth century. Their tradition proved to be so strong even after the end of the Second World War that the publishing enterprises proceeding from them, mostly medium-sized, could provide the foundation of the new diocesan papers as well as of those newspapers which were Christian-oriented and supported the Austrian People's Party.

---

[23] For statistics cf. K. A. Altmeyer, *Katholische Presse unter NS-Diktatur* (Berlin 1962), 79 and 94–98. On the actual situation as regards the "diocesan papers"—one or several per diocese?—cf. M. Hüsgen, op. cit., 120–23.

[24] Istituto Cattolico per la Stampa, ed., *La Stampa Cattolica nel Mondo* (Milan 1939).

[25] F. Funder, *Vom Gestern ins Heute* (Vienna 1952); cf. also R. Barta, "Katholische Pressearbeit in Österreich," K. Richter, ed., *Katholische Presse in Europa* (Osnabrück 1969), 43–62.

In Vienna there was after 1945 no recourse to the tradition of the Catholic daily of the *Reichspost;* the weekly *Die Furche* understood itself as the agent of tradition. In addition to the Innsbruck *Volksboten* (since 1973 *Präsent*), it represents the type of weekly newspaper for the intellectual Catholic reading public. The leading cultural newspaper, *Wort und Wahrheit,* founded in 1946, was discontinued in 1973.

The Catholic press in Switzerland goes back, with some important organs, to the same period when in Germany the *Kulturkampf* brought about the rise of Catholic papers: *La Liberté* of Fribourg and *Vaterland* of Lucerne were founded in 1871, the *Basler Volksblatt* in 1872, and the *Ostschweiz* of Sankt Gallen in 1874. "The Catholic population seems to have felt the need for their own local papers, with which they could identify politically and religiously, as with the associations, which indeed contributed essentially to the defining of their identity in Swiss society."[26] The most recently founded, the *Neue Zürcher Nachrichten* (1896 as an association paper, 1904 as a daily), developed not only in competition with the *Neue Zürcher Zeitung* but became the best known Catholic paper of a large Swiss city, while the *Vaterland,* as the "conservative central organ for German Switzerland," still functions not only to form opinion but also to effect economic stability. For the Swiss press also attempts to assure its existence by concentration measures, which have recently led to intensive cooperation with the calming poles *Vaterland* and *Ostschweiz* and have brought about some changes in the news press.

The activity of the English Catholics found journalistic expression in the founding of only a few important newspapers: *The Tablet* (1840), *The Universe* (1860), *The Catholic Herald* (1884), and *The Month,* founded by Jesuits in 1864, look back to noteworthy traditions. France, on the other hand, now as earlier is counted among the important countries for the Catholic press. The publicity activities of the nineteenth century, rich in number and in conflict, found a concluding climax in the establishing of the Maison de la Bonne Presse by the Assumptionists, especially Vincent de Paul Bailly. That Catholic publicity center in the Rue Bayard at Paris, which adopted the "good press" as a program into the title of the firm, proceeded from the founding of two periodicals, which were then for decades essential voices of the Catholic publicity of France: in 1872–73 Bailly began with *Le Pèlerin,* founded originally as a monthly organ of the *Conseil Généréal des Pèlerinages,* but in 1877

---

[26] F. P. Schaller, *Notstand im christlichen Pressewesen* (Einsiedeln and Zurich 1974), 154f. For the situation in Switzerland cf. also. C. Holenstein, "Katholische Presse in der Schweiz," in K. Richter, op. cit., 63–70; also E. Fehr, "Schweiz: Katholische Presse in der Krise," *CS* 8(1975), 150–52.

transformed into a popular illustrated periodical, which a little later had a circulation of over 100,000. In 1880 a monthly periodical, *La Croix*, was added; in 1883, changed into a daily paper, *La Croix* developed into the "Quotidien catholique par excellence."[27] In its founding period comparable to the *Germania* or the Lucerne *Vaterland*, *La Croix* nevertheless proved to be also a quantitatively successful newspaper; popular in its first decades, it still surpassed the 100,000 circulation in the decade of its founding, reached 185,000 even before the First World War (1912), and is said to have had its record year in 1937 with a circulation (unverified) of 300,000. These are numbers which remained out of reach of the Catholic daily in Germany. In the Second World War *La Croix* first withdrew to Bordeaux, then to Limoges. There on 21 June 1944 it interrupted its publication for the first time, and after the liberation of France it had to endure a process of gaining permission again, which spoiled the starting conditions. The postwar circulation was around 100,000 and did not increase again until the annexation in 1959 of *La Croix du Nord* of Lille, founded in 1889. The Second Vatican Council caused interest to grow again, and the circulation reached about 140,000, but the gains of the paper, which in accord with its own self-awareness aimed to correspond to the standards of a *journal d'opinion* as well as of a *journal d'information*, could not be maintained. *La Croix du Nord* was in 1968 reduced to a weekly. The Catholic daily press of France shrank between 1958 and 1964 from nine to four independent papers, among which only *La Croix* was of importance, but the periodical press lived on the rich diversity to which it had developed in the nineteenth century and the first third of the twentieth century. In the mid-1960s it was believed that, after the disappearance of the parish papers, one could still speak of about one thousand titles.[28] Besides the Bonne Presse, the most important publishers are the Union des Oeuvres Catholiques de France, founded in 1871, and, since 1945, the publisher of the illustrated *La Vie [Catholique Illustrée]*, which, alongside *Le Pèlerin [du 20ᵉ Siècle]*, reached a half-million in the mid-1960s. The Sunday press is powerfully represented in the chain of the various *Croix-Dimanche* editions (in 1964 in fifteen *départements*), begun in 1889 under the title of *La Croix du Dimanche*, the political appendix to the *Pèlerin*. The Catholic publishers of France early devoted

[27] J. and P. Godfrin, *Une Centrale de la Presse Catholique, La Maison de la Bonne Presse et ses Publications* (Paris 1965), 134.
[28] C. Ehlinger, "Katholische Presse in Frankreich," in K. Richter, op. cit., 95–115; cf. also G. Hourdin, *La Presse Catholique* (Paris 1957).

special attention to the children's and youth press. Some titles, like *Nade* (1914) or *Reccord* (precursor of *L'Echo du Noël*, 1906) go back to the time before the First World War. A fairly large number of titles long persisted with rather small circulations. The supraregional weekly press with intellectual pretensions exhibited for a long time a wing-formation, like comparable media in Germany: *La France Catholique*, founded in 1925, was classified as conservative, *Témoinage-Chrétien*, founded in 1941, as progressive; both circulations dropped to about 50,000 by 1968.

The development of the Catholic press of France took place on the whole independently of the official Church. The "in structural view . . . independent Catholic press," to quote Ehlinger, was united in two associations in 1951 and 1952, the *Association Nationale des Périodiques Catholiques de Provence* (ANPCP) and the *Centre National Catholique de Presse* (CNPC). "The registration of a periodical or newspaper in one of these associations amounted to a clear indication of the membership of these publications in the Catholic press."[29]

In Spain "it would not be false to maintain that all daily newspapers which . . . appear today regard themselves as in some sense Catholic. However, not all rightly deserve this designation."[30] The problem of the Catholic press after the end of the civil war was to so adapt itself under a government that was officially friendly to the Church in a nonliberal democratic system that a specifically Catholic profile could again be discernible. The press law of 22 April 1938 left little latitude for this, and the new, more generous press law of 18 May 1966 was altered by restrictions in 1968. A Catholic profile was sought in three ways: (1) as regards the daily press, through collaboration in groups, of which the *Editorial Católica* and the newspaper chain of *Opus Dei* could each be found, in second or third place behind the Cadena del Movimiento (In the *Editorial Católica* there appeared with *Ya* of Madrid, founded in 1935 and having a circulation of 140,000 in 1968, one of the three great dailies of the country.); (2) as regards the periodicals, through a more or less clear attitude of opposition, which, as in the case of *Signo* in 1967, could run the risk of their existence; (3) in the training of journalists, to which special attention was paid by the Catholic side. Internationally noteworthy and in Spain not only recognized by the state but meanwhile standard-setting, is the journalism curriculum founded as the institute for journalism in 1958 on the

[29] Ehlinger, op. cit., 111.
[30] A. Montero, "Kirche, Katholiken und Presse in Spanien," in K. Richter, op. cit., 116–42, here 122.

Facultad de Ciencias de la Información of the *Opus Dei* University of Navarre at Pamplona.[31]

The growth of the Catholic press of Italy was determined into the twentieth century by the conflict between the Italian state and the Papal state. For decades the nationally minded press could be sure to conform to the official view. The Catholic press of the entirely Catholic country was, on the other hand, from the beginning politically in a defensive posture. *L'Osservatore Romano* began to appear on 1 July 1861 as "giornale politico-morale"; while it was under the control and encouragement of the Interior Ministry of the Papal State (but in the beginning, outside of it) and appeared, together with the official *Giornale di Roma* of 1849–70, as a quasi-private political newspaper, the expression used by Montini did not yet apply to it: "Non per nulla, come si dice, è 'il giornale del Papa.'" The purpose of the new paper was defense: "'to unmask calumnies' and, as was later added, 'to refute what was hurled against Rome and the Roman papacy.'"[32] In the period between 1870 and 1929 *L'Osservatore Romano* appeared as a political daily, alongside other Roman newspapers, but in a special development, as is said in a contribution of the first number of 4–5 November 1929, indicating as place of publication the Città del Vaticano: "Under the Pontificate of Leo XIII the *L'Osservatore Romano* ever more assumed the character of an organ of the Holy See. . . ."[33]

The succeeding fifteen years saw *L'Osservatore Romano,* like the rest of Italy's Catholic press, in a difficult position. However, there were direct encroachments only after Italy's entry into the Second World War. Besides occasional prohibitions of its sale in Italy—"now [at the beginning of 1940] the Catholic paper of Vatican City has too many readers, who must be carefully supervised!"[34]—on 13 June 1940 was suppressed *L'Osservatore Romano*'s custom of printing the armed-forces reports of the warring powers. Still, the circulation in the war years is said to have risen to more than 300,000 copies.

After the Second World War *L'Osservatore Romano* so developed "officially, as regards the announcements coming from the Vatican and semiofficially as regards the rest,"[35] that it evoked conflicting evalua-

[31] Cf. J. Liminski, "Journalistenausbildung an der katholischen Universität von Navarra in Pamplona," *CS* 8(1975), 153–64.

[32] D. Hansche, "Zur Geschichte des *L'Osservatore Romano, CS* 3(1970), 13–23 and 99–109, here 13f.—in Hansche also the pertinent literature on the history of *L'Osservatore Romano.*

[33] Cf. Hansche, op. cit., 100.

[34] Quoted ibid., 101.

[35] I. Weiss, *Il potere di carta. Il giornalismo ieri ed oggi* (Turin 1965), 107, quoted from Hansche, op. cit., 103.

tions: on the one hand, for example, addressed by *The Times* as belonging to the "world press,"[36] on the other hand, it was criticized even by Catholic journalists because of the various dependencies of its editorship and its hardly justified journalistic work. In view of the poor working conditions, however, the intentional international expansion was noteworthy, despite the modest circulation, about 70,000, of the branch editions. In addition to the illustrated sister paper, *L'Osservatore della Domenica,* a weekly since 1934, in 1951 a Latin American weekly edition came into existence in Buenos Aires. Since 1948 there has been an Italian weekly edition, since 1949 a French, since 1968 an English, since 1969 a Spanish, since 1970 a Portuguese, and since 1971 the "Weekly Edition in German."[37]

For the rest, the Catholic press of Italy, like that in other countries of Western Europe, was subject to increasing concentration pressure after the Second World War.[38] Of its not very numerous daily newspapers[39] *L'Avvenire d'Italia* of Bologna, founded in 1896 and rich in tradition, had to combine, for economic reasons but also for the sake of a progressive outlook, with *L'Italia* of Milan, founded in 1912; their new title is *Avvenire.* At first hardly noticed on the outside, from 1931 a Catholic recreational periodical in Italy developed into presumably the Catholic periodical with the highest circulation in the world, the *Famiglia Cristiana.* Founder, owner, and publisher is the religious community *Pia Società San Paolo,* internationally active in the sphere of Catholic publicity. Through a skillfully organized sales system in parishes it caused the former Sunday sheet to grow into a modern family illustrated journal, which printed its jubilee edition for its fortieth year of existence in an issue of 2 million.[40] In comparison to this, the diocesan weekly press, despite the large number of more than one hundred titles, is underdeveloped. Within the *Unione Cattolica Stampa Italiana* (UCSI), it has combined in a special group, the *Federazione Italiana Settimanali Cattolici* (FISC).

Dissolution of Catholic journalistic unions seems, on the other hand, to mark a decisive turn in that country which can be described as the

---

[36] Cf. H. D. Fischer, *Die grossen Zeitungen* (Munich 1966), 294.

[37] E. Bordfeld, "Der *Osservatore Romano*—Wochenausgabe in deutscher Sprache," *CS* 7(1974), 155–59; also G. Deussen, "Der deutschsprachige *Osservatore Romano*— überflüssig?" *CS* 5(1972), 343–45.

[38] Cf. D. Hansche, "Krise und Ende des *L'Avvenire d'Italia, CS* 3(1970), 348–51.

[39] Cf. the *Annuario 1970* of the Unione Cattolica Stampa Italiana (UCSI) (Rome 1970), P. VI: "La stampa cattolica in Italia," 491–556. The most recent information on the Catholic press of Italy is given by the announcement no. 2094 in the *KNA-Informationsdienst,* no. 40/1976, of 30 September 1976, p. 4: "Italiens Kirchenpresse: eine aufschlussreiche Statistik."

[40] E. Bordfeld, "40 Jahre *Famiglia Cristiana,*" *CS* 4(1971), 126–28.

sociologically and sociohistorically most productive field of historical investigation of the Catholic press: the Netherlands. The union *Katholieke Nederlandse Dagbladpers* and the *Katholieke Nederlandse Journalisten-Kring,* both reestablished at the wish of the episcopate in 1945 and 1946 respectively, suspended their activity in 1968–69. Catholic journalists and also their public were bored, at the latest since the Second Vatican Council, with "columnization" *(verzuiling)* as the special form for expressing pluralism in the Netherlands.[41] Of the continually relatively strong Catholic daily press since the apologetically struggling nineteenth century—in 1937 there were thirty-two Catholic daily newspapers out of a total of seventy-nine—that paper proved to be the most vital which displayed itself after the Second World War as a *journal d'information* with a political Catholic policy of socially oriented progressivism without especially hiding its Catholicity: *De Volkskrant* of Amsterdam could raise its circulation from 150,000 in 1947 to 206,000 in 1974, and also a Catholic-oriented local press acquired a considerable share of circulation. On the other hand, other organs, which had marked the "column" or "pillar" Dutch Catholicism of the 1920s and 1930s, such as *De Maasbode* (1868–1959) or *Het Centrum* (1884–1960), merged or entirely disappeared, and the traditional agent of the Catholic press, *De Tijd* (1845–1974), pined away to an end after the Second World War, even as it had consciously made a decision for the function of a forum between the Catholic fronts.[42] All together, the share of at least the Netherlands press that followed Catholic traditions remained quite high. Something similar is true also for neighboring Belgium, whose Catholics achieved a stable political and journalistic position still earlier. The split into a conservative and a Christian-Democratic faction shortly before the turn of the century resembles Austrian precedents. Among the great papers of Belgium Catholic titles in French—*La Libre Belgique* since 1883—as well as in Flemish—*De Standaard* since 1914—were able to maintain good positions—in 1968 their respective circulations were 170,000 and 290,000.[43] Unique, at best only comparable to *L'Osservatore Romano,* is the role played by the *Luxemburger Wort* in the little Benelux nation: the largest newspaper

[41] G. W. Marsman, *De Katholieke Dagbladpers in sociologisch perspectief* (Assen 1967); idem, "Katholische Presse in den Niederlanden," in K. Richter, op. cit., 71–81.
[42] J. Hemels, "Katholische Presse in den Niederlanden," *CS* 8(1975), Pt. I: pp. 1–22; Teil II: pp. 123–46. For Scandinavia cf. J. Berg, "Skandinavien: Die katholische Presse," *UCIP Informations* no. 4 (Geneva 1976), 8f.
[43] L. Boone, "Situation und Zukunftstendenzen der katholischen Presse in Belgien," in K. Richter, op. cit., 95–115.

of the country with an uninterrupted tradition since 1848 and a stable circulation of 73,000.[44]

Hence while in most countries of Europe worthy of mention in connection with the Catholic press Catholic duties were able to continue to a certain degree beyond the Second World War, this turning-point meant, *cum grano salis,* for Germany and those nations which were thereafter reckoned as socialist, including Catholic Poland, the end of the Catholic daily press. The licensing policy of the Allied occupying powers and the founding of the Christian-Democratic Union that intentionally went beyond denominations prevented the reestablishing or establishing of dailies.[45] Only one newspaper was authorized as a bearer of the tradition of the Weimar period, Johann Wilhelm Naumann's *Augsburger Tagespost* on 28 August 1948, from which emerged the supraregional *Deutsche Tagespost* of a strictly conservative Catholic outlook but weak in circulation—less than 30,000. When, after the abolition of the compulsory licensing in September 1949, the "Old Publishers" tried to reestablish the traditional titles or their continuations, some Catholic publishing companies also took part. However, most of these foundations again disappeared from the market, among them the *Deutsches Volksblatt,* founded at Stuttgart in 1848, interrupted under the Nazis, then resumed until 1965, the *Badische Volkszeitung* of Karlsruhe, discontinued also in 1969, and the *Trierer Landeszeitung/Saarbrücker Landeszeitung,* suspended in 1972.

Quickly and stably twenty-two diocesan newspapers were reestablished and in part newly founded in the Western Zone and two—*St. Hedwigsblatt* in East Berlin and *Tag des Herrn* in Leipzig—in the Soviet Zone. Besides them there appeared in the West a richly developed press for associations, youth, and religious institutes. (In 1949 publishers and editors united in the Arbeitsgemeinschaft Katholische Presse e. V. [previously Arbeitsgemeinschaft Kirchliche Press; AKP], and Catholic publicists of all the media in 1948 in the Gesellschaft katholischer Publizisten Deutschlands). Recreational periodicals could develop only modestly; cultural periodicals suffered, except for the *Stimmen der Zeit,* from deconfessionalization (*Werkhefte, Frankfurter Hefte,* [*Neues*] *Hochland*); finally political weeklies confronted a quantitatively not adequate target group and could not go beyond the circulation minimum that assured existence. Even the circulation, stable for years and oscillating from 50,000 to 60,000, of the

[44] J. Gelamur, "Luxemburger Wort," *Journalistes Catholiques* 21 (Geneva 1973), special double number, 33–35.

[45] Cf. also M. Schmolke, *Die schlechte Presse,* 268.

Rheinischer Merkur of Cologne and Koblenz, founded in 1946, regarded as Catholic and close to the Christian Democratic Union but politically and as a publishing enterprise independent, could not, in view of increasing production costs, retain its economic independence; in 1974 the paper passed into ecclesiastical majority ownership. The politically ambitious but not successful *Echo der Zeit* of Recklinghausen, proceeding in 1952 from the Cologne *Katholischer Beobachter,* was suspended in 1968 in favor of the promising experiment which the Catholic Church in the German Federal Republic had assumed after the Second World War: in 1968 after almost three years of preparatory work the weekly *Publik* of Frankfurt am Main was founded. According to its differently elaborated program, it was supposed to be the leading voice of German Catholicism and at the same time the forum for the expression of diametrically opposed opinions in the postconciliar period. Because with this idea no sufficiently large and stable body of subscribers could be acquired, *Publik* was ended in the autumn of 1971 after it had cost a total of at least 30 million German marks.[46] At that time the Catholic press had long left behind the climax of its postwar development—in 1963 there was talk, without a reliable basis, of 400 titles and a total subscription of 16 million. The twenty-two diocesan papers—in 1963 they had a total circulation of 2.45 million—had lost, apart from some exceptions, portions of their readership year by year—in 1974 they had less than 2 million readers.[47] The Catholic youth press died out.[48] While the first postconciliar phase in Germany generally gave the impression of an intellectually strengthened Church, the decline of the publicity potential began to cause anxiety.[49]

[46] M. Schmolke, ed., *"Publik"—Episode oder Lehrstück?* (Paderborn 1974). On the economic aspect of publishing see U. Nussberger, *"Publik* als Testfall verlagswirtschaftlicher Planung," *CS* 9(1976), 126–42.

[47] F. Oertel, *Dialogform Kirchenpresse* (Limburg 1972).

[48] J. Hoeren, *Die katholische Jugendpresse 1945–1970* (Munich 1974) Deutsches Institut für wissenschaftliche Pädagogik, D.I.P.—Information no. 8. On the development of the Catholic youth press in Austria, see H. Pürer, "Kirchliche Jugendpublizistik in Österreich," *CS* 7(1974), 137–52.

[49] A similar negative trend is apparent in the Catholic press of the United States and Canada, whose history has not been investigated well enough to permit a comprehensive comparison with the European viewpoint. The completely multisided, to a great extent diocesan-oriented periodical system represents altogether the largest circulation block with the world's Catholic press. However, it declined from 27.7 million in 1968 to 22.7 million in 1973. Among the more than 400 titles are ca. 120 diocesan papers. The Jesuit periodical *America* of New York, founded in 1909, must be the best known paper, nationally and internationally. The association of Catholic journalism in the

Information about the Catholic Press in the German Democratic Republic and in the neighboring states to the east moves scantily in the entire postwar period. In the German Democratic Republic persons are restricted to the two ecclesiastical papers mentioned above and the nonperiodic publications of the Leipzig St.-Benno-Verlag. The Czechoslovak paper, *Katolicke Noviny,* appearing in a Czech and a Slovak edition, was always regarded as close to the priests' movement, "Pacem in terris," that was friendly to the government, while in Poland the weekly *Tygodnik Powszechny* of Cracow, founded in 1945, in the framework of the Znak group, and with it some diocesan papers as well as the Warsaw monthly *Więź,* were able to maintain relative independence, competing with the Pax group and its organ, *Slowo Powszechne.* In Socialist Yugoslavia the periodical *Glas Concila,* founded in 1962 in connection with the Second Vatican Council, established itself unexpectedly rapidly; but the circulation, rising to 180,000, produced an especially attentive political supervision, which had numerous prohibitions and confiscations as its consequence.

Catholic News Agencies

A need to provide the Catholic press with special information material, by means of press or news agencies, was understood before the turn of the century. From this there occurred in Germany the founding in 1879 of the *Centrums-Parlaments-Correspondenz* (CPC) to serve Catholic political ends, an initiative not of the Center Party but of the *Augustinusverein zur Pflege der katholischen Presse.* It and its succeeding institutions—CPC-GmbH, ZPK-GmbH—supplied Catholic newspapers more poorly than correctly with information from the parliamentary activities of the Center—down to the dissolution of the ZPK in 1922.[50] Catholic press agencies in the strict sense only appeared in the First World War: in 1917 at Fribourg in Switzerland the KIPA (Catholic International Press Agency); the American National Catholic News Service of Washington also goes back to 1917. It grew out of the press department of the National Catholic War Council, founded in 1917, and later renamed the National Catholic Welfare Conference, and today the United States Catholic Conference.[51] The third, for Catholic

United States, the Catholic Press Association (CPA), cooperates internationally with the German AKP. References to the crisis in P. Jordan, "NC News Service in der Krise der katholischen USA-Presse," *CS* 3(1970), 257–62.

[50] M. Bornefeld-Ettmann, "Die Centrums-Parlaments-Correspondenz (CPC)," *CS* 1(1968), 318–25.

[51] P. Jordan, op. cit., *CS* 3(1970), 257–62.

concerns, "great" agency is the KNA (Catholic News Agency of Bonn and Munich),[52] emerging in 1952 from its precursors, the KND and CND. Besides its current service, it has developed a whole division of special services, has at its disposal a European and overseas net of correspondents, and was one of the driving forces in the collaboration of Catholic news agencies beginning at Rome with the Second Vatican Council: in 1971 it found a definite form in an international union of Catholic news agencies, in which KNA, KIPA, Kathpress of Austria, CIP of Belgium, and KNP of the Netherlands[53] maintain joint editorship under the designation CIC (*Centrum Informationis Catholicum*). For a long time there was regarded as a really semiofficial Roman agency the International Fides Service,[54] founded in 1927 in connection with the Congregation for the Propagation of the Faith, which, however, declined ever more in importance when, since the Second Vatican Council, the Vatican's press work was concentrated in the Sala Stampa and intensified.

In 1936 there were Catholic agencies or similar institutions in sixteen countries, in 1971 in twenty-one.[55] Of course, their efficacy is not unquestioned in relation to the expense—cf. the case of KNP—and especially in countries of the Third World—for example, DIA, Zaire; CNI, India—their existence is jeopardized.

Radio and Television under the Restrictions of Commercial or of Public Control

Since the radio became a public medium in 1922, three forms of organization have developed: radio as a state industry, radio as a public law institution, and radio as a private economic undertaking, which sells its broadcast time partly to a third party and from the net proceeds draws not only subsistence but a profit. The first two types are predominantly based on financing by the fees of participants and are characterized by the mark of public control, in part directly by the state, in part by special social control bodies, for example, in Germany the *Rundfunkräte,* in Austria the *Kuratorium* of the ORF.

In accord with the respective "radio constitution" of each nation the

---

[52] Katholische Nachrichten-Agentur, ed., *De instrumentis informationis,* 2d ed. (Bonn 1972).
[53] The KNP had to suspend activity in 1973 (cf. E. Oudejans, "Geschichte und Ende des 'Katholiek Nederlands Persbureau' [KNP]," *CS* 6[1973], 144–51).
[54] J.J. Considine, "Die Gründung des internationalen Fides-Dienstes," *CS* 5(1972), 53–56.
[55] For 1936: "La Stampa Cattolica nel Mondo," op. cit., 36. For 1971: *Journalistes Catholiques* 19(Paris 1971), no. 56/57, p. 9.

Church has various favorable opportunities of participating in or at least of influencing radio and television. Only state radio systems in countries fundamentally hostile to the Church completely exclude its cooperation.

To give a comparative international description of the entire development is impossible because of lack of space. In general it can be said that the Church makes use of all types of possibilities available, but often has by no means exhausted them. The private economic pattern provides two opportunities in those countries where it is followed, hence especially in the United States and in the countries of Latin America and Asia that are influenced by the United States: a) the sale of broadcast time for church broadcasting, practiced, for example, in the United States and Japan, and b) the establishing of private broadcasting facilities, for the countries here mentioned are rather liberal in the granting of radio concessions. The second method was followed successfully especially by international Protestant agencies. Thus arose, among others, the Voice of the Andes at Quito as early as 1931; the Radio Voice of the Gospel of Addis Ababa, in 1963; the Far East Broadcasting Company, founded in 1945 with headquarters in Whittier, California, and principal Asian headquarters since 1948 at Manila; and Trans World Radio of Monte Carlo, founded in 1954 as Voice of Tangiers, which since 1959, as Radio of the Gospel, supports a German branch at Wetzlar.[56] Comparable on the Catholic side would be the enterprise Radio Veritas, established with German aid at Manila/Quezon City, which started its operation in 1968 and had to struggle with many difficulties presented by the state, and the Federation of Catholic Broadcasters, also active in the Philippines, with headquarters at Manila. In countries with public law or similar broadcasting systems, the Church shares in the social control of broadcasting institutions, for example, through radio councils, in the framework of the legal possibilities on the one hand, while on the other hand, it employs the possibilities of forming its own preaching broadcasts, for example, conveying the Mass, and of cooperating in the broadcasting of sections appropriate for Church and religion, by constituting them or advising. These distributions of competition are clearly marked, especially in the German Federal Republic, where in the first year after the Second

---

[56] K. H. Hochwald, "Trans World Radio und Evangeliums-Rundfunk," CS 2(1969), 56–58; C. Jahn, Frequenzen der guten Nachricht. Rundfunksender "Stimme des Evangeliums" Addis Abeba (Erlangen 1973); G. H. Ledyard, Sky Waves. The Incredible Far East Broadcasting Company (Chicago 1963). Summary: J. Schmidt, Massenmedien als Instrumente der Mission. Missionsrundfunk als Beispiel (Diss. Heidelberg 1974). New is the attempt for a Catholic diocesan television in Chicago; cf. F. J. Eilers, "ctn-Diözesan-Fernsehen in Chicago," CS 9(1976), 39–41.

World War the project of a special Christian "Bamberg Broadcast" failed,[57] and in Austria. In the course of the ideological "columnization," the broadcast system of the Netherlands developed fully. While the Nederlandse Omroep Stichting is the sponsor of the entire broadcasting system, the program is produced by several, mostly ideologically oriented operating enterprises, the position of which depends on the number of participants acknowledging them. Since 1925 the Katholieke Radio Omroep (KRO, Hilversum) handles the Catholic role.[58] While foreign observers not rarely regard the Dutch system as the ideal realization of pluralistic broadcasting work, there are in the Netherlands also many critical voices.

In 1931 the Vatican established its own radio station under the name Radio Vatican; at first its broadcasting techniques operated with very modest means. Since the construction in 1952–57 of Santa Maria in Galeria on a tract outside Vatican City, twenty-five kilometers north of Rome, Radio Vatican beams broadcasts on medium wave, shortwave, and ultra shortwave to the whole world in some thirty languages.[59]

Church Journalism in the Third World

In many countries of the Third World the ecclesiastical journalism of the present is based on foundations laid in the colonial period by missionary work. In this regard, two different centers of gravity can be determined: In some countries of Asia, but especially in Africa, it began early with Christian press work; in Latin America, on the contrary, there developed from modest beginnings a fruitful field of Catholic radio work, especially in the area of educational radio. Catholic "radio schools" and comparable institutions or program offerings appeared after the Second World War in, among other places, Bolivia, Brazil, Chile, the Dominican Republic, Ecuador, Colombia, and Peru. Catholic broadcasters were, in this connection, not oriented only to the aim of teaching, but especially developed systems of social communication that served the rural population, to move up in these occasionally newspaperlike information sheets to radio programs and school courses, as in the internationally well known radio school project, Radio Sutatenza in Colombia, the weekly newspaper *El Campesino* with a circulation of 70,000. The enterprise supported since 1949 by the

[57] Cf. M. Schmolke, *Die schlechte Presse,* 272f.

[58] J. Hemels, "Der katholische Rundfunk im niederländischen Rundfunksystem," *CS* 8(1975), 213–29.

[59] E. Schmitz, "Sender des Friedens," K. Becker, K. A. Siegel eds., *Rundfunk und Fernsehen im Blick der Kirche* (Frankfurt 1957), 32–40; A. Kochs, "Radio Vatikan," *Funk-Korrespondenz* 23(1975), no. 4, pp. 1–4, and no. 5, pp. 5–8.

Acción Cultural Popular (ACPO), founded in 1947 by the chaplain José Joaquín Salcedo, was able to lower considerably the number of Colombia's illiterates and make important contributions to village development.[60]

In general church journalism in the Third World in the decade after 1960 came ever more under the idea of the promotion of development.[61] This is a new emphasis in contrast to the missionary and pastoral motivation which for decades long determined Catholic press activity in many African and some Asiatic countries, such as India. The more African states became independent, the more frequently Catholic newspapers and periodicals fell into difficult situations: On the one hand, they were the politically less burdened representatives of a journalistic expertise which was lacking in many of the young states, on the other hand they came into conflict with politically prejudiced systems but also into economic difficulties, which caused the Union Catholique Internationale de la Presse to ask anxiously: "La presse catholique d'Afrique est-elle condamnée?"[62] Many Catholic papers, rich in tradition—including the Catholic daily *Munno,* founded at Kampala, Uganda, in 1911 but forbidden in 1976; the weekly *Afrique Chrétienne* of Kinshasa, Zaire (1961); *Afrique Nouvelle* of Dakar, Senegal, founded in 1947, suspended in 1972, revived in 1974, forbidden in 1976; *L'Effort Camerounais* of Yaoundé, Cameroon (1955); *La Croix du Dahomey* of Cotonou, Dahomey (1946); or *The Standard* of Cape Coast, Ghana (1939), with persistent difficulties—had to stop publication for a time or permanently; others, such as *Kiongozi* of Dar es Salaam, Tanzania (1950), remained alive. Political prohibitions or hindrances came from totally different directions: in Zaire the entire Catholic press was suspended in 1973, in "white" Rhodesia the critical attention of the government was concentrated on the products of the Catholic publisher, Mambo Press (Gwelo).

Despite manifold dangers and economic straits there exists in Africa and Asia a Catholic press of modest dimensions but of astonishing diversity.[63] In this regard the founders and editors, mostly members of

---

[60] S. A. Musto, *Massenmedien als Instrumente der ländlichen Entwicklungsförderung* (Berlin 1969).

[61] Cf. the bibliography, "Church and Communication in Developing Countries," compiled by W. Herzog (Paderborn 1973), and the Sodepax-Konferenz-Bericht, "Church, Communication, Development" (Geneva, n.d. [1971]).

[62] Africa issues no. 62/63 and no. 64/65 of the periodical *Journalistes Catholiques* (Paris 1972).

[63] Cf. F. J. Eilers and W. Herzog, *Catholic Press Directory Africa/Asia* (Paderborn 1975); F. J. Eilers, *Christliche Publizistik in Afrika* (St. Augustin 1964); C.H.M. Verhaak, *Aspecten van de pers in Oost-Afrika* (Grave 1974); J. Hosse "Die katholische Presse im

missionary orders or companies, attempted early to publish in the national vernaculars. This is true also of the journalistic opening up of very remote areas, for example, Oceania, and obviously in general for broadcasting work in all missionary lands.[64]

To promote an understanding of the problems of the missions and today of the underdeveloped countries—such is the goal set for itself by the quite strongly developed mission press[65] in the United States and many countries of Europe. Its beginnings, marked in Germany by the founding of the periodical *Die katholischen Missionen* in 1873, extend back into the nineteenth century. For a long time the popular periodicals were welcome reading material as recompense for sacrifice for the sake of the mission. The changed relationship to the Third World—aid for development, encouraging of structure, the new auxiliary works *Misereor, Adveniat,* and so forth—caused interest to go back to the classical mission journalism; the circulations of many papers declined, and there appeared, proceeding from the first freely initiated concentration procedures in the Catholic press market, a new type of mission magazine, which was at times published in common by several religious communities active in the mission: in Germany *Kontinente,* since 1966, at first twelve, later twenty-five representatives; in the Netherlands *Bijeen* (1968), with seventeen representatives; in Spain *Tercer Mundo* (1970), with six representatives; in France, less successful, *Peuples du Monde* (1965).[66] In addition, a few individual titles, some of them of strong circulation, could continue, whose steadfastness rests on the combination of family entertainment and mission aims.

Church and Mass Communication in Theory and Organization

The rather negative relation of the Church to the journalistic media since the Reformation evoked as early as the nineteenth but especially in the twentieth century a large number of papal and episcopal

französischsprachigen West- und Zentralafrika," *CS* 5(1972), 156–62; T. Luiz, *Indian Catholic Press* (Bombay 1971); J. Barret, "Katholische Presse in Indien," *CS* 1(1968), 43–45.

[64] F. J. Eilers, *Zur Rolle der Publizistik in der Missionsarbeit des Fernen Ostens und Ozeaniens* (Münster, 1965); idem, "Presse und Funk im Territorium von Papua und Neuguinea," *CS* 1(1968), 197–208, 295–307.

[65] L. Janek, "Katholische Missionszeitschriften in den USA," *CS* 4(1971), 226–32; J. Simmers, "Missionspublizistik in den Niederlanden," *CS* 1(1968), 40–43; M. Eigenmann and F. H. Fleck, "Schweizer Missionsjournalistik," *CS* 3(1970), 339–43; F. J. Eilers, "Arnold Janssen als Publizist. Ein Beitrag zur Geschichte der deutschsprachigen Missionspublizistik," *CS* 8(1975), 301–23.

[66] J. Hosse, "Missionspresse im Wandel der Zeit," *CS* 5(1972), 348–51.

decisions, whose basic tone was condemning to rejecting, only occasionally encouraging the "good" (Catholic) press. Meanwhile, they fill their own professionally specialized source collections.[67] A change began with the first really mass-media encyclical, the film encyclical *Vigilanti cura* of Pius XI in 1936.[68] As regards content, this encyclical introduced binding control institutions: On the model of the American Legion of Decency there arose in many countries Catholic offices for evaluating films, as after the Second World War in Germany, Austria, and Switzerland Catholic film commissions, whose activity was very beneficent in their informative ingredient but meanwhile was out-of-date in their aim of moral guidance.[69] The pacemaker function of *Vigilanti cura* was the fact that there was now a media encyclical at all. It was followed in 1957 by *Miranda prorsus,* a second encyclical, which treated of the audio-visual media,[70] and in 1963 by the decree *Inter mirifica* of the Second Vatican Council.[71] Actual progress in the—in the real sense—theoretical confrontation of the Church with the mass media was produced by an address of Pius XII in 1950 to the Third International Congress of the Catholic Press at Rome,[72] and the pastoral instruction *Communio et Progressio,*[73] brought about by the just mentioned conciliar decree but only prepared in 1971. Pius XII recognized and described mass communication as a social function in presenting public opinion—"natural echo," "common response"—as unalterable by natural law for the functioning of society. Unfortunately, then the decree *Inter mirifica,* which especially stressed the Church's right to possess and use the mass media as well as the morally "right employment of these instruments," remained "considerably behind the doctrine developed by Pius XII."[74] On the other hand, *Communio et Progressio* produced not only important results of modern journalistic and communications science, but presented generally relevant social principles: the function of the media as communications institutions,

[67] E. Baragli, ed., *Cinema Cattolico,* 2d ed. (Rome 1965); Radio Vaticana, ed., (1) *Documenti Pontifici sulla Radio e sulla Televisione 1929–1962* (Vatican City 1962), (2) *Documenti Pontifici sulla Stampa 1878–1963* (ibid. 1963), (3) *Documenti Pontifici sul Teatro 341–1966* (ibid. 1966); also, G. Deussen, *Ethik der Massenkommunikation bei Papst Paul VI.* (Paderborn 1973).

[68] *AAS* 28(1936), 249–63.

[69] A. Paffenholz, "Katholische Filmbewertung in der Diskussion," *CS* 2(1969), 5–12.

[70] *AAS* 49(1957), 765, 805.

[71] *LThK* 1 (supplementary volume) (Freiburg 1966), 116–35.

[72] *AAS* 42(1950), 251–57.

[73] *Communio et Progressio. Pastoralinstruktion über die Instrumente der sozialen Kommunikation, Nachkonziliare Dokumentation* 11 (Trier 1971).

[74] O. B. Roegele, "Das Konzilsdekret 'Über die Werkzeuge der Sozialen Kommunikation,'" *Publiziskik* 9(1964), 305–47, here 319.

which gather "contemporaries around a round table, as it were," the right to information and free choice of information, freedom of communications, necessity of media pedagogy (instead of censorship and Index), acknowledgment of the untrammeled individuality of journalistic work, the claim of Catholic journalists, communications institutions, and the Catholic public to the helping partnership of the Church. Without abandoning standards—common welfare, human dignity, objectivity—the withdrawal from the "defense principle"[75] and from the moralizing discrimination between "good" and "bad" press becomes pleasantly clear.

The instruction also points, by suggestions, to the absence of a journalistic organization, as it can be established in the Churches of many countries. Comprehensive tasks are attributed to the already existing international journalistic associations, while in reality these organizations, despite historical and nation unifying merits, today can do justice to their very narrow determining of functions often only with difficulty. In this connection there is question of the *Union Catholique Internationale de la Presse* (UCIP), founded in 1927—its precursor in 1923—UNDA (*Association Catholique Internationale pour la Radiodiffusion et la Télévision*) proceeding from the *Bureau International de la Radiophonie Catholique,* founded in 1928, and the *Office Catholique International du Cinéma* (OCIC).[76] The UCIP, divided professionally into five federations—newspaper and periodical publishers, news agencies, journalists, journalist science, and ecclesiastical press—and regionally into several continental subassociations, acting as international representative in appearance with world congresses of the Catholic press, sees its general aim in the fostering, organizing, and representing of the work of Catholic journalists and press associations on an international plane, especially in the spheres of activity of professional ethics and theology of mass communication, promotion of Catholic journalism in underdeveloped countries, and representation in international organizations (United Nations, UNESCO). UNDA, which owes

---

[75] M. Schmolke, "Zehn ideengeschichtliche Beobachtungen zur Pastoralinstruktion *Communio et Progressio*," F. J. Eilers et al., eds., *Kirche und Publizistik. Dreizehn Kommentare zur Pastoralinstruktion . . .* (Paderborn 1972).

[76] J. Iribarren, "L'Union Catholique Internationale de la Presse (UCIP)," *CS* 3(1970), 49–55; also, on the obscurity concerning the real foundation year of the UCIP, references in *UCIP Informations,* no. 4/1976, p. 2, and no. 1/1977, pp. 1f. (If the UCIP celebrated its fiftieth anniversary in 1977, then it referred to the founding at Brussels in 1927 of the Bureau International des Journalistes Catholiques.) J. Schneuwly, "UNDA-Katholische Internationale Vereinigung für Hörfunk und Fernsehen," *CS* 3(1970), 144–51; E. Flippo, "Office Catholique International du Cinéma (OCIC)," ibid. 4(1971), 28–34.

essential impulses to the first and second International Catholic Radio Congress at Munich in 1929 and Prague in 1936, has likewise built continental subgroups in South America, Asia, and Africa, and takes care of the international cooperation as well as the interdenominational with the World Association for Christian Communication (WACC). UNDA and OCIC give international radio and film prizes respectively. The chief tasks of OCIC lie in the collaboration of about fifty national Catholic film bureaus, in the study of film art and economics in accord with Christian categories of values, in the initiating of new Catholic film movements, and in the effort for artistically and educationally worthwhile films.

For new international functions, namely the advisory promotion of Catholic journalism in underdeveloped countries, the Catholic Media Council was founded on the basis of the cooperation of UCIP, UNDA, and OCIC at Aachen in 1969. Its tasks are the international exchange of experience, the coordinating and advising of planning, the utilization of scholarly results, and not least the professional preexamination of concrete promotional projects. The journalistic projects of supporting Catholic auxiliary and mission works are represented on the Board of Trustees.[77] The CMC elaborates and advises projects, which are encouraged by the auxiliary works of Belgium, the Netherlands, Austria, Switzerland, England, Ireland, the United States, and Germany.

Concluding remark: The considerable theological, organizational, economic, and journalistic expense with which Catholic journalism, now as earlier, is carried out and also the (relatively late beginning) positive official teaching and pastoral attention to problems of mass communication cannot obscure the fact that at the latest since the Second Vatican Council a striking withering of integration[78] is to be observed on the part of the "Catholic public," and especially in the "strongly" Catholic journalistic countries, in which Catholic media were not able to remain traditionally conservative, but had to constantly stand out with respect to non-Catholic groups of the population, hence especially clearly in the United States, the Netherlands, Switzerland, the German Federal Republic, but also in Austria. The fact that a growing part of the potential Catholic public avoids the specifically

---

[77] K. R. Höller, "Publizistische Medienplanung für Entwicklungsländer 'Catholic Media Council,'" *CS* 5(1972), 57–63.

[78] On the idea cf. F. Groner, "Integrationsschwund in der katholischen Kirche Deutschlands," *Jahrbuch für christliche Sozialwissenschaften* 12(1971), 215–39; cf. also the contributions of H. Fleckenstein and R. Bleistein in K. Forster, ed., *Befragte Katholiken-Zur Zukunft von Glaube und Kirche* (Freiburg i. Breisgau 1973).

Catholic journalism, and the assured observation that this process is quantitatively similar to the decline of the numbers that attend Mass, will possibly be the characteristically basic feature of the history of Catholic journalism of the second half of the twentieth century. Documents of some postconciliar synods have sought to take this development into account, at least as a start.[79]

[79] References to literature in M. Schmolke, "Kirche und gesellschaftliche Kommunikation," D. Emeis and B. Sauermost, eds., *Synode—Ende oder Anfang* (Düsseldorf 1976), 303–15, as well as P. Pawlowsky, "Kirche und Massenmedien nach den österreichischen Synoden," *CS* 9(1976), 233–54.

CHAPTER 14

*Charity and Ecclesiastical Works of Assistance**

Laying the Foundations in the Nineteenth Century

Caritas, as a turning to fellow believers and other persons who are in need, ranks alongside the proclaiming of the Good News as a basic function of the Church.[1] Hence the intensity of charitable activity is always an indicator of its spiritual vitality. However, its present social-charitable activity differs in many respects from that of previous centuries. It proceeded entirely out of the charity movement of the nineteenth century, for then were developed those ideas and working methods which, spreading from Europe, have in timely fashion influenced almost all countries. And so a look at the nineteenth century is indispensable for the understanding of the present.

The numerous secularizations became a powerful and mostly overlooked precondition of the new surge of charity in the nineteenth century—not only in the France of the Revolution, with the nationalization of the Church's property in 1790, the suppression of the orders in 1792, the nationalization of hospitals in 1793, and in the German Reich with the Imperial Delegates Final Recess in 1803, but in most countries of the North Atlantic and Iberian world they withdrew the old social institutions from the Church's control. In this way the Church lost the traditional means of support of its care of the poor, but at the same time it was relieved of the often antiquated obligations of the foundations. Accordingly, the secularizations compelled new initiatives and they

* Erwin Gatz
[1] Basic is R. Völkl, *Dienende Kirche—Kirche der Liebe* (Freiburg 1969); idem in *HPTh,* 2d ed. I, 415–48.

facilitated the appearance of that mobility and of that large-scale concept, which, in view of the increase of population and of all those miseries accompanying industrialization, were urgently necessary. And the Church had to devote its attention to the new social problems, if it would continue to be credible. European Catholicism, particularly in France and Germany, but also in Italy, thus undertook enormous social-charitable exertions in the course of the century. They are partly explained by the conviction, generally represented until far beyond the middle of the century, that the social question could be solved only by free welfare work. Only slowly did the idea establish itself that here only state intervention with the cooperation of free personnel could help. This was introduced in the German Empire by Bismarck's social legislation of 1883–89, while other states partly followed suit much later. From these originally modest beginnings there gradually developed comprehensive social security systems and large organizations that introduced a "fundamental change of the care for existence."[2] They culminated in the concept of the "social state," which intervened in the social sphere by directing without degenerating into a total welfare state.[3] It represented the reply to the Industrial Revolution and the restratifications in the wake of the great wars and economic crises. The aims of the state were expanded in the social state to social justice and the creating and maintaining of institutions for the protection of the individual in the various situations of life. The fact that state budgets in the industrialized countries today designate up to one-third of their total for social works is eloquent testimony.

This development deeply affected ecclesiastical charity,[4] for in this way its center of gravity in the industrialized states increasingly shifted from economic to spiritual and personal help, without excluding the economic.[5] For the rest the social-charitable personnel of the Church and the social agencies of the state cooperated to a considerable extent in almost all countries, even in those where Church and state were formally separated. The Church particularly brought to this teamwork its religiously motivated collaborators, while the state offices set aside partly considerable financial means for social institutions under the Church's auspices. The Church's financial contribution for this work was based, after the loss of the old foundations, partly on Church means of taxation but chiefly on gifts.

[2] *HPTh* II/2, 396–402.
[3] H. Peters in *StL*, 6th ed., 7(1962), 394f.
[4] On the sociopolitical development in Germany, France, England, and the United States, see B. Seidel in *Handwörterbuch der Sozialwissenschaften* 9 (Göttingen 1956), 532–72.
[5] On the specifics of *caritas*, R. Völkl in *HPTh* II/2, 403–23.

Concern for the whole person is characteristic of charity on the basis of its fitting into the care of souls. But since the Enlightenment growing secularization and alienation from the Church have incessantly and increasingly questioned its denominational method. The Church's personnel, who had long devoted themselves almost without competition to the charitable tasks of a homogeneous society, could no longer entirely measure up to the growing functions. Since the nineteenth century, therefore, other agents of free welfare work have pushed themselves beside the Church's charity; among them decided Christians collaborated, and they were partly inspired by Christian motives.[6] To the secularization of society corresponded, with a certain reluctance, the secularization or laicization of social work. Today the Church is only one—even though of the utmost importance—of those social forces which are devoted to these tasks. For the rest, in opposition to an all-embracing state social and assistance policy there have not been lacking voices since the nineteenth century which claimed charity even under the changed circumstances as an unchangeable basic function of the Church, even if needing to be kept up-to-date. The demand for the unimpeded growth of the Church in the social sector also was derived from religious freedom. For this was taken from it only in totalitarian states, whereas, for example, in the German Federal Republic in 1961 precedence was accorded to the free representatives of social and youth assistance in accord with the principle of subsidiarity;[7] recently, on the other hand, tendencies making for state management are again appearing.

During the nineteenth century synods and individual bishops repeat-

[6] In the chiefly professionally exercised areas of social work religious, working virtually without compensation, dominated into the twentieth century. Lay personnel took a place beside these to a greater extent only since the financial assurance of social work. German Empire in 1883: law on the health insurance of workers; Prussia in 1885: rules for schools for nurses. In other countries also since then a stronger founding of nursing schools is to be observed (F. Bauer, *Geschichte der Krankenpflege* [Kulmbach 1965], 257ff.).

[7] Federal law on social aid and law on youth welfare (1961). According to these not only aid for maintaining life is assured, but "in special life conditions." A corresponding judgment of the Federal Constitutional Court at Karlsruhe on 16 October 1968: "To the self-understanding of the Christian Churches and the exercise of religion belongs not only the area of faith and worship but also freedom of development and effectiveness in the world, as this corresponds to its religious and ministerial function. Active love of neighbor is, according to the New Testament, an essential task for the Christian and is understood by the Catholic and Evangelical Churches as a basic church function" (Quoted in *Caritas-Korrespondenz,* Freiburg 1969-1/2, R.4).

edly recommended the traditional care of the poor,[8] but in reality official ecclesiastical initiatives in this area were isolated and locally restricted. The charity movement arose rather from its basis in the communities where it had always rested. Only in our century have an extensive and finally global view and corresponding organization established themselves.

From the nineteenth century charity was administered essentially by two groups. On the one hand, these were the various local charity groups, which at times operated without the cooperation of the clergy and often renounced any publicity. They found their classical form in the Conference of Saint Vincent de Paul, founded by Frédéric Ozanam at Paris in 1833, which became the model for similar establishments in many countries.[9] Particularly in Germany, where the ecclesiastical association system was more strongly pronounced than elsewhere, there was formed, alongside the Saint Vincent Conferences and their female counterpart, the Saint Elizabeth Conferences, a large number of groups with social-charitable and often very specialized tasks.[10] On the other hand, in recent times the parish first appeared as an institution qualified for charity,[11] but of course the activity of the traditional societies was not supposed to be affected adversely by this.

In addition to these small groups, often merged into working communities and predominantly established on the local level, from the nineteenth century the many newly founded congregations assumed the chief burden of charitable work. The Daughters of Charity were, it is true, already represented before the Revolution in some European countries but began their global expansion only in the nineteenth century. For the rest, there then appeared those occasionally wildly growing large numbers of male and female congregations, which provided for social work a mainly professional personnel, thoroughly qualified by a professional code of ethics.[12] In the territory of the

---

[8] The various provincial synods of the nineteenth century proceeded just as little beyond this as did two projected decrees of the First Vatican Council (E. Gatz in *AHC* 3[1971], 156–73).

[9] A. Foucault, *Histoire de la Société de S. Vincent de Paul* (Paris 1933). On early charity groups in Germany, see Gatz, op. cit., 351–71. On the development in the United States, see D. T. McColgan, *A Century of Charity. The First One Hundred Years of the Society of St. Vincent de Paul in the United States*, 2 vols. (Milwaukee 1951).

[10] Details in *KH*, 1907ff.

[11] J. Kessels in *JbCarWiss*, 1962, 9–42; *Werkbuch der Caritas* (Freiburg 1968); *Pastorale. Caritas und Diakonie* (Mainz 1974).

[12] O. Braunsberger, *Rückblick auf das katholische Ordenswesen im 19. Jahrhundert* (Freiburg 1901); more comprehensive: Heimbucher.

German Reich, for example, there were scarcely several hundred at the beginning of the nineteenth century, but before the First World War 47,545 female religious and 1,963 male religious in 5,036 and 101 houses, respectively, were at work.[13] In the other Catholic countries the growth was similar.[14] The founding and expansion of these communities took place to a great extent without the directing intervention of church authorities. At that time there was coordination among them only in isolated cases.

Ecclesiastical charity, like its secular counterpart, was divided since the nineteenth century into an "open" and a "closed" sphere, a distinction which the legislation of the French Revolution made. To the open sphere belong those works of assistance that can scarcely be grasped statistically, particularly as they were performed in the communities. Beside them the institutions rapidly appearing from the mid-century, and with them the "closed" work, acquired growing importance. But the most fundamental change in ecclesiastical social work since the nineteenth century lies in the elimination of the traditional care of the poor, which was concentrated on the elementary livelihood of its protégés, by a differentiated and specialized care of people in their various needs.[15] The professional formation of collaborators and the classification of the institutions in professional spheres were a self-

---

[13] Liese, *Wohlfahrtspflege und Caritas,* 280.

[14] There have been statistical surveys for the entire Church for only a few years. A. Battandier, *Annuaire Pontifical Catholique,* 41 vols. (Paris 1898–1948), gives some material on the status of the orders. Rich in material also for the social-charitable activity: *Bilan du Monde, Encyclopédie Catholique du Monde Chrétien,* 2 vols. (1st ed. 1958–60, 2d ed. 1964). On the number of religious, see *Annuario Statistico della Chiesa* (Rome 1968ff.). Reliable statistical material for charitable achievements from the period before the First World War is available only for particular countries. The numbers of members of congregations of women supply a starting point because these devoted themselves to charitable tasks, of course in varying intensity from country to country. Baumgarten gives, among other things, the following numbers: Europe (180 million Catholics): 329,811 female religious in 25,043 houses; France (39.1): 183,901; Italy (32.9): 31,342; Spain (18.7): 25,545; Germany (19.2): 32,831; Austria-Hungary (37.6): 23,146; Netherlands (1.7): 8,110; England (1.38): 10,118; Latin America (56): 6,909; United States (10.7): 53,987, 885 welfare institutions, 249 orphanages.

[15] This change in meaning found expression in the nomenclature of theological lexica. Wetzer and Welte (2d ed. [1883]) does not yet contain the keyword *caritas,* but (1st ed. [1882]), 1354–75, makes a detailed contribution to the care of the poor. Similarly: *RE* 2, 3d ed. (1897), 92–103: care of the poor, for which, as it occurs in the Church, the principle of free will is urged (rejection of recourse to taxation). M. Buchberger, *Kirchliches Handlexikon* 1(1907), then gives (885f.) a brief contribution "Charitas," which in the stricter sense is described as "the totality of the systematically organized freewill assistance activity springing from religious Christian motives." The care of the poor (I, 340–44) is granted considerably more space. This changes only with *LThK,* 2d ed.

evident consequence of this development. For the rest, educational and health assistance were not definitely separated.[16] The religious and the ecclesiastical institutions not only accepted this development but supported it to a decisive degree in the industrialized nations.[17] They not only supplied their personnel for it, but by opening up private sources of financing often first made possible the creating of such institutions. While the financing of institutions in countries with progressive social legislation is today to a great extent cared for by social security institutions or by the public, church personnel as well as other agents of free welfare in the countries of the Third World more and more finance this work largely out of their own means. The new types of social-charitable work outlined here grew in the traditionally Christian countries of Europe. In addition, an autonomous charity was able to develop also in the United States and Canada.[18] Over and above this, the European methods of work were carried by the missionary institutes into all parts of the world, since the works of love have from time immemorial been counted as an integrating part of the missionary method.[19]

National Organizations

The just mentioned, almost incalculable diversity of charitable efforts illustrates that there was at work not a planned procedure but a spontaneous movement. True, there was no lack of bishops interested in charitable and later also in social-political activities, but the Church leadership, despite its good will, stood aside and made scarcely any gestures to canalize the new breakthrough. In an age of increasing entanglements and of a more spacious thought, however, this fragmentation constituted a serious danger. Individual societies, as, for example, the Conferences of Saint Vincent de Paul, quite early combined, but a coordination involving all fields of charity was only attempted from the turn of the century. In this field Germany took the lead, although the Catholics themselves here lagged behind corresponding exertions of other welfare associations.[20] Those who prepared for the founding of a

[16] In the older hospitals of the nineteenth century, on the other hand, aged charges, patients, and orphans lived together.

[17] For the German development, see Gatz, op. cit., 464–573.

[18] Religious communities expelled from European countries in the course of the nineteenth and twentieth centuries, for example, contributed to this.

[19] Cf. L. Berg, *Die katholische Mission als Kulturträger,* 2d ed., III (Aachen 1927), 3–200.

[20] As early as 1848 the gifted organizer Heinrich Wichern had urged the merger of the Evangelical welfare works into a "Central Committee for the Domestic Mission of the German Evangelical Church."

German charity society were the Capuchin Cyprian Fröhlich (1853–1931) and the cofounder of the *Volksverein für das katholische Deutschland* in 1890, the district councilor Max Brandts (1854–1905). But the project was first realized by the brilliant organizer, Lorenz Werthmann (1858–1921).[21] The Limburg priest went to Freiburg im Breisgau in 1886 as court chaplain of Archbishop Christian Roos (1886–98) and there became acquainted with the Church's social work. Important preliminary stages of the later organization were constituted by the founding of the periodical *Caritas* in 1895 as the first professional organ of this type in German[22] and of a "Charity Committee" as the circle of promoters of the periodical. Werthmann edited the periodical personally until his death. From 1896 the "Committee," in which Werthmann set the tone, conducted annual study meetings—*Caritastage*—which likewise served the spread of the idea of charity. In February 1897 it called for the founding of a *Caritas Verband für das katholische Deutschland*. After initial hesitations on the part of the episcopal leadership of Cologne and Freiburg because of Werthmann's independence of action, there occurred on 9 November 1897 the planned founding, with headquarters at Freiburg,[23] on the occasion of the second *Caritastag* at Cologne. Its aim was to be study and publication, the education of coworkers, professional charitable work, and coordination. While the organization made progress only with difficulty for two decades, despite the intensive efforts of the first president, Werthmann, the association achieved great successes in other fields.[24] This was true also of the charity science developed at Freiburg, which in 1925 acquired a scholarly institute and a chair at the university—since 1964 it has been called *Institut für Caritaswissenschaft und Christliche Sozialarbeit*. In addition, before the founding of the *Karitasverband,* Werthmann organized a special library, which gradually grew into a study center unique in its kind.[25] In the midst of the First World War the episcopal conference at Freiburg in 1915 and that at Fulda in 1916 recognized the Freiburg central office as a "legitimate gathering of the diocesan societies into one uniform organization." Thereby the early history of the association ended and its organizational rise was introduced.

The German example acted as a stimulus beyond the national

[21] Liese, *Werthmann;* K. Borgmann, ed., *Lorenz Werthmann, Reden und Schriften* (Freiburg 1958).

[22] In 1896 there appeared in German thirty-four relevant periodicals. *Caritas* was quickly consolidated: in 1897, 2,000; in 1917–18, 10,000; in 1974, 25,000.

[23] Since 1909: *Caritasverband . . .;* 1919: *Deutscher Caritasverband* (DCV). First article: Liese, "Werthmann," 142–46.

[24] Survey: H. Wollasch in *75 Jahre DCV,* 33–87.

[25] H. J. Wollasch in *Caritas '71,* 191f. 1971: 110,000 volumes.

boundaries. Thus in 1903 the Austrian welfare societies joined in one national merger.[26] But the charitable organization became more important in the United States[27] because of its order of magnitude. The initiative proceeded from the New York religious Barnabas of the Brothers of the Christian Schools. In youth work over the years he had felt the isolation of the individual charitable groups as a serious flaw, and in 1908 he proposed to Bishop Thomas J. Shahan, rector of the Catholic University, the convoking of a charity conference. An organizational committee then decided the establishing of a national conference, at which 400 delegates met on 25–28 September 1910 at the Catholic University. Shahan became the first president (until 1925) and William J. Kerby the secretary of the newly established National Catholic Charities Conference (NCCC). Its functions, like those of the DCV, were to be the educating and informing of the members. This was effected by working-meetings, the establishing of places of formation, and the publication of the *Catholic Charities Review* in 1916.[28] During the first years the horizontal connection with the charitable religious institutes was inadequate, although these then carried out 75 percent of the total work. Hence, as secretary (1920–61), John O'Grady in 1920 inaugurated the founding of the National Conference of Religious on Catholic Charities as the organ representing the congregations with the NCCC.[29]

The establishment of other national charity associations took place between the two world wars, especially in Europe—in Switzerland (1920), Hungary (1931), Luxemburg (1932), Belgium (1938), Ireland (1941), and Spain (1942), then in Poland and Yugoslavia and also in Syria, whereas France still held itself aloof.[30]

International Cooperation

An international charity assistance, or at least one that extended beyond the frontiers of nations, was already included in the mission to the pagans and then with the care of emigrants of the late nineteenth century.[31] Then it became a pressing need because of the misery

[26] L. Krebs, *Das caritative Wirken der katholischen Kirche im zwanzigsten Jahrhundert* (1927), 2; a good survey of the diversity of charitable exertions in F. Anhell, *Caritas und Sozialhilfen im Wiener Erzbistum* (1802–1918), 1971.
[27] D. P. Gavin in *NCE* 10(1967), 229f. (biblio.).
[28] First survey of charitable activity: *Directory of Catholic Charities* (Washington 1922).
[29] B. M. Faivre in *NCE* 10(1967), 230f.
[30] Date of founding in *Caritas Internationalis,* 1970–72.
[31] At the Mainz Katholikentag of 1871 there was founded, at the urging of the Limburg merchant, Peter Cahensly (1838–1923), the *St. Raphaelsverein zum Schutz deutscher*

attending wide circles of population in the countries affected by war. Alongside the national charity institutions, the Holy See, from the beginning of the war, also developed a vigorous war welfare care.[32] This concentrated on the prisoners of war and the civilian population in the occupied countries. In addition, the Holy See helped many individuals through consultation and donations. Besides this, it directed requests for help to the Catholics of the countries not greatly affected by the war. Particularly in the United States considerable donations were there- upon made; the German-Americans' awareness of solidarity with their homeland was still great and was influential as a motive for making donations.

The foreign aid during and after the First World War had made the international cooperation of charitable works of assistance an urgent necessity. It is significant that the impetus for a permanent merger proceeded from Germany, where charity was as strictly and effectively organized as in no other country. As early as 1918 Werthmann had pointed out that an international union was necessary,[33] and in February 1920 the Catholic delegates at the congress of the Union Internationale des Secours aux Enfants at Geneva urged this desire.[34] In this way the insight was put across that a "World Charity Society" should be founded.[35] The Holy See approved the project. And so, on the occasion of the World Eucharistic Congress at Amsterdam in July 1924, at the invitation of the Preparatory International Charity Com- mittee sixty delegates from twenty-two nations met for a four-day conference.[36] Here the establishment of a permanent "Charity Confer- ence" with headquarters at Lucerne at the Swiss Central Office of Charity was decided.[37] The preeminent tasks were to be the uniting of all charitable organizations as well as reciprocal information, while an international aid fund could not yet be realized. Then in 1926 the second conference at Lucerne stated as its aim the promotion of all charitable efforts, the exchange of information, the beginnings of

---

katholischer Auswanderer, which was later involved in the conflicts over "Americanism." It was among the initiators of the Commission Internationale Catholique pour les Migrations of Geneva, founded in 1951.

[32] Schmidlin III, 218–26; J. Kreyenpoth, Die Auslandshilfe für das Deutsche Reich (Stuttgart 1932), 56–59, 87f; see also Chapter 2.

[33] L. Werthmann in Caritas 24(1918–19), 1–6. On the beginnings of international cooperation, see J. Hafenbradl, Caritas Catholica. Internationale Caritasorganisation 1924 bis 1950 (Freiburg 1968), here 17.

[34] Protocol in Hafenbradl, appendix, 1–4.

[35] Thus, Caritas 25(1920–21), 90.

[36] K. Joerger in Caritas 29(1924), 183–88.

[37] This had been instituted in 1920.

cooperation, and finally the representation of charity in international welfare societies.[38] It also decreed the founding of the sections *Iuventus, Migratio, Infirmitas, Paupertas, Sobrietas,* and *Literae.* In 1928 the conference constituted itself as a permanent organization with the name *Caritas Catholica,* as Pius XI had desired, in order to emphasize the religious motivation of the work here accomplished. The director of the *Caritas* of Strasbourg, Paul Müller-Simonis, became the first president, and in 1938 he was succeeded by Josef Tongelen, director of the *Caritas* of Vienna.

That collaboration beyond national boundaries even in the inner Catholic area was not without problems appeared when a congress of charity, planned for Strasbourg in 1927, had to be canceled at the last moment because of strained German-French relations.[39] Subsequently the delegates met repeatedly in Switzerland, but international cooperation was considerably impeded after 1933 under Nazi pressure and in 1937 it was stopped.[40] Despite these setbacks, the first union of national charity associations had powerfully strengthened their solidarity. Above all, the effects of the exchange of experiences must not be lightly underestimated. Furthermore, *Caritas Catholica* caused the founding of new national charity associations.

Consolidation of Charity between the World Wars

After the First World War the charitable institutions in many countries were intensively consolidated. In this connection must be noted not only the improved organization but also the multiplication and the differentiation. In 1930 charity in all countries included:[41]

Closed Relief	Number of Institutions	Number of Beds	Number of Personnel
Health Care	15,700	752,000	135,000
Educational Care	13,400	668,600	70,600
Total	29,100	1,420,600	205,600

Half-Open Relief
Number of Institutions 96,300
Average Number of Daily Visitors 2,390,000

Open Relief
Number of Institutions 140,000

[38] K. Joerger in *Caritas* 5(1926), 317.
[39] Hafenbradl, 32–36.
[40] Op. cit., 45–48. The sources on this period are extraordinarily meagre.
[41] H. Auer in *KH* 17(1930–31), 108–201, here 118.

Personnel Active in Charitable Work

Mother-House Sisters Active in Charity	350,000
Religious Brothers Active in Charity	32,000
Other Personnel Officially Active Chiefly in Charity . . .	120,000
Total of Personnel Officially Active Chiefly in Charity . . .	502,000
Catholics Active in Charity in an Honorary Capacity . . .	6,650,000

These activities varied according to country, from the differentiated institutions in industralized states to the weakly developed structures in the Churches with Iberian backgrounds.[42] In the missions also during this epoch European models were still the pattern.[43] According to the summaries provided by L. Berg,[44] in the territories subject to the Congregation for the Propagation of the Faith there were the following institutions and personnel in the service of charity in 1930:

Asia (7 million Catholics):
165 physicians and 787 nurses; 293 hospitals with 18,109 beds; 1,325 pharmacies with 11,773,021 consultations; 33 leprosaria with 5,722 patients; 1,073 orphanages with 66,995 orphans; 253 homes for the elderly with 10,645 charges.

Africa (4.9 million Catholics):
30 physicians and 281 nurses; 267 hospitals with 9,470 beds; 1,074 pharmacies with 11,662,898 consultations; 59 leprosaria with 5,548 patients; 617 orphanages with 30,675 orphans; 132 homes for the elderly with 4,664 charges.

America (2.9 million Catholics):
4 physicians and 36 nurses; 53 hospitals with 1,759 beds; 130 pharmacies with 147,104 consultations; 4 leprosaria with 331 patients; 92 orphanages with 3,920 orphans; 14 homes for the elderly with 520 charges.

[42] *KH* gives information on the charitable accomplishments of Germany. For other countries the national directories give references.
[43] Rich material for the charitable activity in mission territories in: *Annales de la Propagation de la Foi* (Paris and Lyon 1822ff.); *Missions Catholiques* (Lyon and Paris 1868–1964); *Die katholischen Missionen* (Freiburg 1873ff.); *ZMR* (Münster 1911ff.).
[44] L. Berg, *Christliche Liebestätigkeit in den Missionsländern* (Freiburg 1935), here 19ff. He relies on *Guida delle Missioni Cattoliche* (Rome 1934). Detailed information on charity in mission countries (1929), which also extends beyond the areas subject to the Congregation for the Propagation of the Faith in B. Arens, *État actuel des Missions Catholiques* (Louvain 1932), 151–92.

Australia, Oceania, New Zealand (2.15 million Catholics):
7 physicians and 51 nurses; 107 hospitals with 3,668 beds; 278 pharmacies with 958,570 consultations; 12 leprosaria with 1,178 patients; 126 orphanages with 9,545 orphans; 18 homes for the elderly with 1,601 charges.

European Mission Countries (.9 million Catholics):
5 physicians and 8 nurses; 51 hospitals with 3,295 beds; 7 pharmacies with 43,285 consultations; 67 orphanages with 1,855 orphans; 11 homes for the elderly with 238 charges.

Charity in the Totalitarian State

Charity in the German Reich first came into conflict with a totalitarian state after 1933. Thereby the DCV suffered severe losses, but it still was able, under its capable tactician-president, Benedikt Kreutz (1921–49), to retain the greatest part of its substance and especially its ability to function.[45] On the other hand, other free welfare associations were dissolved—in 1933 Welfare Work and Christian Workers' Aid—or incorporated into the National Socialist People's Welfare (NSV), founded in 1933, or brought into line—in 1933 the Equal Welfare Society, later actually also the German Red Cross. The concordat assured the continuation of the Church's social institutions (ARTICLE 31), and the bishops energetically exerted themselves for this. Nevertheless, after 1934, 1,200 kindergartens had to be closed or turned over to the NSV. The same fate befell 300 stations of the mobile care of the sick, 156 Travelers' Aid Societies, 136 employment exchange offices for the protection of girls, 35 seminaries for kindergarten teachers and female youth leaders, and 2 social schools for women. And in 1938 the Institute for Charity-Science at the University of Freiburg was suppressed. The Nazi state tried to limit charity as far as possible to the care of the physically or mentally handicapped. Another serious restriction was the limiting of charitable gatherings, which were of decisive significance for the funding of the work.[46] Severe losses

[45] R. A. Ihorst, *Zur Situation der katholischen Kirche und ihrer caritativen Tätigkeit in den ersten Jahren des Dritten Reiches* (Dipl.-Arbeit Freiburg 1971); K. Borgmann, "Der Deutsche Caritasverband im 'Dritten Reich,'" *75 Jahre DCV* (1972), 92–99.

[46] While the DCV collected and distributed from 27 to 30 million RM in checks and cash for the winter assistance work (WHW) in 1932–33, it obtained in 1939 from the huge yields of collections of the Nazi WHW, in which it had had to participate, a donation of only 131,000 RM (F. Klein, *Christ und Kirche in der sozialen Welt* [Freiburg 1956], 241).

were also experienced by the charitable orders and congregations, which before the Second World War had more than 70,000 nursing personnel in Germany.[47] In spite of the enormous need for the care of the wounded, entry into charitable communities was no longer granted after 1940, although a formal prohibition did not occur. Thereafter the number of members of institutes sharply declined in Germany.[48] After the war's end this development was stopped for only a few years. During the Nazi epoch religious also had to leave many public institutions, where they were replaced by the rival establishments of the Nazi Sisters. *Caritas* President Kreutz for his part had in 1937 called into existence the *Caritas* sisterhood for sisters not bound by enclosure—in 1939 they had 5,000 members. Finally, the war offered opportunity for the confiscation of 1,871 institutions (the total was 3,971), and 1,358 were destroyed or severely damaged by war measures.[49] Nevertheless, the DCV was able to save essential areas before the Nazi grasp and even to create new institutions for aid. Of 4,000 kindergartens, 70 percent remained under Church auspices, and the hospitals could also continue their activity. The DCV brought effective help to many persecuted by the Nazi regime.[50] On the other hand, the risk for those handicapped threatened with murder was very difficult and often useless.

While charity was curtailed in so many ways, the difficult situation also compelled positive new starts. Among these were the activation of parish charity and personal acts of charity not measurable by statistics.[51] And reflection on the founding and responsibilities (tasks) of the Church's social work was intensified in these years.[52]

Assistance in Emergency and Catastrophe since the Second World War

The miserable condition of millions at the end of the war and the vast displacements of populations—30 million refugees in Europe—evoked,

[47] On the Nazi tactics, see H. G. Hockerts, *Die Sittlichkeitsprozesse gegen katholische Ordensanhörige und Priester 1936/37* (Mainz 1971).
[48] 1935: 7,500 novices; after 1940 ca. 4,000 persons could still evade the prohibition to receive novices; 1950: 3,600 novices, thereafter a strong decline.
[49] K. Borgmann in *75 Jahre DCV*, 97.
[50] In 1934 Kreutz founded the *Caritas-Notwerk* for the thousands of discharged officials and employees. The dispossessed *St. Raphaelsverein* was a help to many persecuted in the emigration; L. E. Reutter, *Katholische Kirche als Fluchthelfer im Dritten Reich. Die Betreuung von Auswanderern durch den St. Raphaels-Verein* (Recklingshausen 1971). In 1939 there appeared in Berlin the *Caritas-Reichsstelle für nichtarische Katholiken*.
[51] Cf. J. Kessels in *JbCarWiss* (1962), 18f., 23.
[52] K. Borgmann in *JbCarWiss* (1957), 108.

as in 1919, a worldwide readiness to assist. The discrimination against Germans and the long period of strictly closed state boundaries of course created conditions other than after the First World War. On the other hand, the great aid organizations had meanwhile been more strictly organized and thereby made more capable of achievements.[53] The great misery also compelled charity to extraordinary exertions. Thus in 1944 Italy obtained a national charity organization in the Pontificia Opera di Assistenza. France followed in 1946 with the founding of the "Secours Catholique" by the Conference of Cardinals and Archbishops.[54] At its head stood, as secretary general, Jean Rodhain, who during the war had organized pastoral care for French prisoners of war and slave laborers in Germany. The French merger was oriented on the American and German model. In many countries appeared similar organizations, which originally were intended to alleviate actual misery but soon grew into permanent central offices.[55] All other aid institutions were surpassed by those of the American Catholics.[56] The War Relief Services (WRS), founded by the bishops in 1943, were incorporated into the National Catholic Welfare Conference (NCWC), and united the hitherto fragmented particular initiatives. They concentrated on direct help for refugees, prisoners of war, and all other victims of war. The assistance measures first beginning in Europe were soon extended to almost all countries devastated by the war. WRS worked in 1945 in sixty-two countries and throughout supported some missions, but it also claimed the cooperation of local institutions. Then when it was apparent that the organization produced by the war continued to be necessary for the future, the episcopate in 1955 renamed the WRS the Catholic Relief Services (CRS). Up to 1963 the assistance work distributed relief material (food, medicine, clothing) to a total amount of $1.25 billion overseas. The entire Catholic emergency help of the postwar period would not have been thinkable without the immense achievements of the 30 million American Catholics. These financed their activities exclusively by donations. In addition, since 1950 the American government put superfluous food at its disposal.

Even before the American aid, the help of the Vatican and of Switzerland began in Germany. When later the war misery disappeared in European countries, the activity of the existing assistance works was

---

[53] Cf. M. Vorgrimler in *JbCarWiss* (1958), 86–101.

[54] As early as 1936 the episcopate had attempted a merger of the French charitable institutions; N. Bayon, *Le grand Q[uartier] G[eneral] de la Charité; le Secours Catholique* (Paris 1955).

[55] Survey in *75 Jahre DCV,* 61ff.

[56] E. E. Swanstromm in *NCE* 3(1967), 328f.

concentrated on help in catastrophes, which had never before occurred to such a degree, as well as on measures for other countries hurt by the war and on the always smouldering problem of refugees.

On the other hand, the Church's social work could not but endure considerable damage in Communist-ruled countries. In all the "People's Democracies" outside the German Democratic Republic[57] the Church's social works and institutions were nationalized or withdrawn from the influence of Church direction—Poland, U.S.S.R. in 1949,[58] China in 1950.[59] The personnel of religious institutes were partly taken into the service of the state but had to renounce any pastoral activity. Besides, various waves of refugees from countries under Communist domination repeatedly made assistance measures necessary—in 1956, for example, 200,000 refugees from Hungary. Let Hong Kong be cited as an especially striking example. The population of the Crown Colony rose through the stream of Chinese refugees from 1.5 million in 1946 to 4 million in 1966. The Catholic Church grew incomparably stronger from 30,000 in 1946 to 233,000 members in 1967. These produced wonderful accomplishments in the social sphere.[60]

Caritas Internationalis

After the war the revival of *Caritas Catholica* was variously stimulated,[61] but at the same time there appeared a tendency toward a dissolution of the Swiss central office and the creation of an independent bureau, perhaps also situated in Switzerland, which should cultivate contact with the non-Catholic welfare societies. Then in 1947 occurred, due to French initiative, the founding of an *Auxilium Catholicum Internationale,* with headquarters in Paris, for extraordinary assistance measures, which was regarded at Lucerne as an undesirable competition. The director of the Swiss *Caritas,* G. Crivelli, who was working for the continuation of *Caritas Catholica,* founded in 1924 and never dissolved,

[57] *Caritasarbeit. Jahresbericht '70* (Berlin 1971) names the following Catholic social institutions: 234 institutions with 12,567 beds; 165 half-open institutions with 8,190 places; 191 nursing stations; 550 other social assistance institutions; thirty-nine places for education and continuing formation.
[58] In China in 1948 there were, among other things, 254 Catholic orphanages and 196 hospitals with 81,628 beds (*HK* 5[1950], 201).
[59] The *Caritas* of the U.S.S.R., entirely under state control and state-financed, in 1955 ran 115 institutions with 9,300 beds. Its name is the only thing it has in common with the ecclesiastical organizations (*HK* 10[1955–56], 109).
[60] Details in *Caritas Hong Kong. Annual Report 1971–1972.* According to this, church representatives here support, among other things, four hospitals, four homes for girls, two centers for professional education, seven kindergartens, and seven social centers.
[61] Cf. W. Wiesen in *StdZ* 72(1946), 42f.; also, Hafenbradl, 53ff., and appendix, 33–44.

stressed on the contrary that other national societies would have to be established before an international merger.[62] At the suggestion of the Holy See there then followed in 1950 the founding of an "International Charity Conference."[63] On the occasion of the Holy Year, the president of the *Pontificia Commissione di Assistenza,* Ferdinando Baldelli, after consultation with the Papal Secretariat of State, had invited the national societies to a study meeting at Rome from 12 to 15 September 1950. At this appeared sixty delegates from twenty-two nations, including the directors of twelve national charity associations.[64] The desire of the Secretariat of State was a stronger and more systematic organization on the international level. A central office should serve for coordination, information, and representation, but the delegates expressed concerns in regard to the future autonomy of the national associations. Nevertheless, on the last day of the conference they united for the establishing of an "International Charity Conference" with headquarters at Rome. This should take care of the tasks mentioned but not attack the individuality and autonomy of its member organizations. The statutes, which the Holy See approved in 1951 *ad experimentum,* envisaged as organs the general assembly, an executive committee, a general secretariat, and delegations at international organizations.[65] The national episcopates, informed by the Secretariat of State, approved the new foundation, except for the United States, where at first there were reservations. At the founding meeting on 12 and 13 September 1951, of the twelve delegations only two non-European, those from the United States and Canada, were represented. The meeting took the positions envisaged by the statutes, according to which it sought the greatest possible international distribution. In the executive committee the chief Catholic countries were represented—the United States, France, and Germany, also Italy and, as representatives of the smaller nations, the Netherlands, Canada, and Spain. The delegation at the United Nations was given to Switzerland. Baldelli of Italy became president, and O'Grady of the United States vice-president. Karl Bayer, a German hitherto active on the *Pontificia Commissione di Assistenza,* was elected secretary general. The meeting confirmed Rome as headquarters of the

---

[62] Thus at the Central European Charity Conference of 1948 at Lucerne. Protocol in Hafenbradl, appendix, 57–69.

[63] Also the unpublished work of G. Wopperer, "Caritas Internationalis, Entwicklung, Organisation und Tätigkeit," Ms. 1957; C. Bayer, K. Joerger in *An der Aufgabe gewachsen,* 194f.

[64] Hafenbradl, 70f. The non-European countries were represented only by the chairmen of the NCCC of the United States.

[65] The statutes have since then been often modified, most recently in 1972, and published as a special printing.

conference, but expressly desired that the secretariat be accommodated outside Vatican City. Preeminent tasks were to be the gaining of other national societies, the making of contact with the United Nations, and the creating of an agency in New York. The budget for the first fiscal year, which was proportioned among the participating associations—United States 28 percent, Luxemburg 2 percent—was a quite modest twelve thousand United States dollars.

In spite of this restricted framework, the general secretariat displayed a vigorous activity. It established the connection with the national member organizations and divided, as had the earlier *Caritas Internationalis,* into particular professional groups. It placed special importance on information[66] and the compiling of archives. The delegations in New York and Geneva promoted collaboration with international delegations and with agencies of the United Nations. The organization renamed in 1954 *Caritas Internationalis* quite early gained consultative status in the Economic and Social Council (ECOSOC), in the International Assistance Work for Children (UNICEF), and in the Food and Agricultural Organization (FAO) of the United Nations. *Caritas Internationalis* had considerable success also in the promoting of charity in those countries which hitherto had no corresponding organizations. Following a journey by Bayer through Latin America to gain information and recruits, many national associations appeared there in 1955–56.[67] Corresponding foundations also occurred in Africa and Asia, and, while only twelve countries were represented at the first meeting in 1950, the number of members grew to eighty in 1972. Correspondingly the central service offices were completed.[68] Over and above this, there took place in 1954 the coordination with the *Société de Saint-Vincent-de-Paul* at Paris and the *Association Internationale des Charités de Saint-Vincent-de-Paul* at Paris, and in 1958 that with the *Confédération Internationale Catholique des Institutions Hospitalières* of Nijmegen, which participated as permanent observers in the general assemblies and on the executive committee. To the earlier existing delegations was added in 1968 another at UNESCO in Paris. Further, *Caritas Internationalis* displayed a vigorous assistance in catastrophes, for example, in floods—in the Netherlands and Belgium in 1953—earthquakes, and political complications, for example, in 1954 the care of refugees from Vietnam, in 1956 the care of refugees from Hungary, and in 1970 aid to Biafra.

---

[66] Since 1955 there appears regularly the service for news and information, *Intercaritas,* in German, and at somewhat longer intervals also in English, French, and Spanish.
[67] Best survey: *Caritas Internationalis 1970–1972.*
[68] Ibid.

Catholic Works of Assistance

From the middle of this century there appeared a completely new understanding of charity that was actually revolutionary because of the separation from preaching. This resulted from the insight, more and more penetrating into awareness, that the Church also must make a contribution to the development of the Third World.[69] Ecclesiastical social work in its manifold specializations was from time immemorial bound up with the mission, and as late as 1962 T. Ohm emphatically demanded the inclusion of charity in evangelization. "A mission which disregards the really religious for the 'social gospel' is no mission."[70] The population explosion and the spread of the industrial types of society led, however, in the Third World to a pauperism whose dimensions far exceeded the problems of the industrial society coming into being in the nineteenth century. The missionaries now had to show very impressive achievements in the social sector; education oriented to economic and technical progress, hence to self-development, had been, on the other hand, disregarded by them.[71] Basically they did not question the colonial foundation. Even before most former colonies had obtained political independence, a new awareness of responsibility and a reorientation of social work for the countries of the Third World established themselves. Classical charity was not suspended by this fact but it was supplemented by "help for self-help," hence the encouragement of self-development. In motivation this is identical with its older sister but it must be clearly separated from preaching and no longer understands itself, as the former did, as an indirect mission. On the other hand there are also assistance works which accomplish decidedly pastoral works of development.

This new type of charitable activity has not been able to establish itself equally in all countries.[72] The largest of the Catholic assistance organizations, CRS, began, for example, in 1960 with its own projects of help in development, but, then as earlier, stressed direct help. The new idea made itself most strikingly felt in the German Federal Republic. At the suggestion of Vicar General Josef Teusch of Cologne, who thereby took up the initiatives of various Catholic groups and societies, Cardinal Frings proposed to the German Episcopal Conference in 1958 the founding of the activity *Misereor* against hunger and sickness in the world.[73] The business office was erected at Aachen, and

[69] On the principles, see J. Schmauch in *HPTh* IV, 618–23.
[70] T. Ohm, *Machet zu Jüngern alle Völker* (Freiburg 1962), 639–658, here 657.
[71] Cf. C. Erb in *HPTh* IV, 624–45.
[72] Ibid., 629–39.
[73] U. Koch, F. Merz in *KH* 26(1969), 435–42.

in this way the intimate relationship with the German branch of the papal work of spreading the faith, *missio,* then located there, was expressed. Nevertheless, *Misereor* was supposed to be run not as a mission but as an enterprise for assisting development. The first collection on Palm Sunday 1959, with a yield of 33.4 million German marks, surpassed all expectations and contributed to the rapid consolidation of the new foundation. The donations of those attending Mass—up to 1973 they amounted to 786.7 million German marks—constitute the decisive source of revenue of the bishops' assistance work. The choice of project, which a professional committee decides, is concentrated not on direct aid for the signs of misery but tries to deal with the causes and to foster personal initiative. On the other hand, the aid of the German Catholics for catastrophes is directed by the DCV. The "Workers' Community for Development Aid," founded in 1959 by *Misereor* and other Catholic societies, serves also the enlisting, preparing, and informing of helpers in development—by 1974 there were some seventeen hundred.

In addition, the German bishops in 1961 established the activity *Adveniat* to support the pastoral tasks of the Church in Latin America.[74] The activity, first conceived as a single collection for the education of priests, was finally continued as all-embracing aid for the carrying out of pastoral care in Latin America. Up to 1972 the German Catholics spent 621.1 million German marks for this end—the Christmas collection. That clear distinction and organizational separation of development and pastoral assistance which is practiced in the German Federal Republic, has not been imitated everywhere, for the aid works of other nations, which appeared partly at the same time or a little later, often unite other functions with development aid.[75] This is true, for example, of the "Lenten Sacrifice of the Swiss Catholics." Its means are divided, since the founding in 1962, by thirds among development aid, the foreign missions, and domestic Swiss projects. Naturally, the desire to give development aid directly or indirectly to the foreign missions, especially in lands with an old mission tradition, is lively. Moreover, the implementation of many projects is referred to the missionary substructure and is carried out in a certain personal connection with the mission work. There were precursors of the later aid works in various countries—in England the Miss-A-Meal Movement, in Austria in 1958 family fast day—but the real wave of foundations began only with the Second Vatican Council, which confronted bishops and Catholicism with worldwide problems. During the council occurred the founding of

[74] H. Lüning in *KH* 26(1969), 422–52.
[75] Survey: CIDSE, Brussels 1974.

episcopal aid works in Belgium (in 1961 *Carême de Partage*, later *Entraide et Fraternité/Broederlijk Delen*), the Netherlands (in 1961 *Bisschoppelijke Vastenaktie*), in France (in 1961 *Comité Catholique contre la Faim et pour le Développement*), in England and Wales (in 1963 Catholic Fund for Overseas Development), in Austria (in 1964 *Koordinierungsstelle für internationale Entwicklungsförderung*), and in Australia (in 1964 Committee for Overseas Relief). Individual new foundations first concentrated on strictly defined projects, in which the former colonial ties played a role—Belgium in Zaire, France in its former African colonies. Since then the notion has increasingly expanded to become global.

The first stimuli for the cooperation of the national assistance works were expressed even before the council. In 1960 a small group of experts urged this concern on the occasion of the Eucharistic Congress at Munich. But the formal initiative for a foundation came only four years later, when on 5 November 1964, during the third session of the council, Cardinal Frings appealed to the episcopal conferences of all countries for the establishing of aid works against hunger, poverty, sickness, and illiteracy. Beyond this he suggested the international merger of already existing organizations. This impulse found a very positive echo among the council fathers. Other discussions of this question as well as the temporary founding of a workers' community with a view to the instituting of a center of information and coordination on 8 May 1965 went back to Frings's suggestion. The episcopal conferences represented in it—Belgium, German Federal Republic, France, Netherlands, Austria, Switzerland, United States—decreed on 18 November 1965, with the consent of the Holy See, the founding of a permanent workers' community and of a secretariat, which in 1966 took up its activity in Brussels. The national character and autonomy of the members of this *Coopération Internationale pour le Développement Socio-Economique* (CIDSE) were thereby not touched. Its directing agency is the general assembly, which meets about every three years. It decides the principles and functions of the CIDSE. In addition there are an administrative committee ("Commission"), which determines the activity of the secretariat, and a managing board of directors. The secretary general is at the same time secretary of the general assembly, of the commission, and of the management committee and directs the secretariat. The first chairman of CIDSE was Cardinal Frings. His successors were Cardinal Bernhard Alfrink of Utrecht, Cardinal Leo Josef Suenens of Brussels, Hans Peter Merz of *Misereor* of Aachen, and Meinrad Hengartner, a Swiss. Since 1967 the secretary general has been August Vanistendael.

The goal of CIDSE consisted from the first neither in the giving of their means by its members nor in the imparting of instructions, but in coordination, information, and consultation. Hence, among other things, all projects were registered at Brussels and a comprehensive card file of experts was compiled. In addition, CIDSE stimulated the instituting of other assistance works, which meanwhile are no longer restricted to the industrialized nations, but have found admittance to the Third World. Such assistance works appeared in Malawi—in 1968 the Christian Service Committee of the Churches in Malawi—where the work overlaps the denominations, also in Canada (in 1969 the Canadian Catholic Organization for Development and Peace), Thailand (in 1968 the Catholic Council of Thailand for Development), Indonesia (in 1971 *Lembaga Penelitian Dan Pembangunam Sosial*), Rhodesia (in 1972 the Commission on Social Service and Development), and finally Ireland (in 1973 Trocaire), the Caribbean (in 1973 Christian Action for Development in the Caribbean—ecumenical), and Nordic countries (in 1969 Nordisk Katolsk Utvecklingshjaelp), and Spain (in 1974 Secretariado de Cooperación al Desarrollo). The Australian assistance work, on the contrary, disappeared because it cooperated more powerfully with *Caritas Internationalis.*

The working methods of the assistance works are varied and are not impaired in their respective characteristics. In this regard aid for the Third World is often united with measures inside the donor country. Naturally, this applies especially to the assistance works of the underdeveloped countries. While large assistance works, such as *Misereor,* can take into consideration extensive programs and greater projects, the smaller assistance works are restricted to partial programs or small projects.

The financing of aid activity is based primarily on donations (collections) of the faithful. In their differing amounts is without doubt expressed something of the vitality of Catholicism in the various countries. On the other hand, the statistics of CIDSE comprise, it is estimated, only a fourth of the aid-means for development produced by Catholics, for the accomplishments made by religious communities and particular groups or individuals appear in no list. The donation yield of assistance works related to CIDSE amounted in 1973 to 50.1 million United States dollars,[76] not counting Spain, Ireland, and the United

[76] *CIDSE News Bulletin* of April 1974 gives the following individual sums: German Federal Republic 35,924,181 in American dollars, Canada 2,928,888; Austria 2,479,334; Belgium 3,134,292; Scandinavian countries 49,431; France 1,339,358; England and Wales 664,437; Netherlands 2,347,499; Switzerland 2,049,941. Very informative is the per capita yield of donations in the individual countries. This amounted in the German Federal Republic to 1.32 American dollars; Canada .34; Austria .37; Great Britain 1.15; Belgium .35; France .03; Netherlands .46; Switzerland

States. In the Netherlands, the German Federal Republic, Switzerland, and Canada the Church's aid projects for development were financed also out of state means.[77] Despite initial hesitations this cooperation has not operated to the detriment of the Church's independence, since the donation occurred exclusively in accord with objective aspects. If regard is had, in addition, for the very large sums for aid from CRS, which of course to a great extent are made possible by the government because of the presence of superfluous food, which must not be regarded as real development help,[78] as well as of the donation yield of *Adveniat,* which like *Caritas Internationalis,* is equally a consultative member of CIDSE, then the total value of help provided in 1973 by these organizations amounted to 248,342,155 United States dollars.

The functions of the papal commission *Iustitia et Pax,* founded in 1966, lie in the area of study and promotion, not of social action. And the council *Cor unum,* founded by Paul VI in 1971, is intended to further the more intensive cooperation of charity and development aid as well as agents in any way occupied with them.[79]

There has never been any dearth of official church recommendations of the traditional care of the poor. But only the Second Vatican Council found, on the basis of experiences endured for a century, a new view and expressly approved and recommended the social-charitable activity as well as the ecclesiastical development aid meanwhile developed. True, there is no special conciliar document which is devoted to charity or development aid, but expressions on them are found in various contexts.[80] According to these, charity is acknowledged as the Church's basic function and activity. This is true not only for the ethos of the turning to those suffering need but also for organized charitable activity, which is expressly, even in its branches extending beyond denominations, approved and recommended. Unambiguous also is the profession of development aid, for which clear norms are given in

---

.82 (per Catholic). These donations were used for, among other purposes, the following fields: education 22.55 percent, health care 18.48 percent, agriculture 16.05 percent.

[77] CEBEMO (Netherlands): 7,531,797 American dollars; Central Office for Development Aid (German Federal Republic); 22,183,599; CIDA (Canada): 1,761,882.

[78] In 1973: 138,947,516 American dollars. The surplus means herein contained came from state donations.

[79] On 15 July 1971 Paul VI outlined this distribution of functions in a letter to Cardinal Secretary of State Villot.

[80] In detail in Völkl, *Dienende Kirche,* 260–338; cf. particularly the decree on the apostolate of the laity, ART. 8, and the pastoral constitution, ART. 86; R. Völkl, *Diakonie und Caritas in den Dokumenten der deutschsprachigen Synoden* (Freiburg 1977).

ARTICLE 86 of the pastoral constitution. Their aim is full human development—"plena perfectio humana"—which indeed refers to the aid of the industrial nations, but primarily challenges the capabilities and traditions of the Third World—"non solis opibus alienis, sed propriis plene explicandis necnon ingenio et traditione propria colendis." Thus were the principles originally formulated and practiced in the North Atlantic world accepted for the Universal Church.

CHAPTER 15

*History of the Ecumenical Movement**

The Development of the World Council of Churches
and Its Route from Amsterdam (1948) to Nairobi (1976)

The beginnings of the ecumenical movement go back to the nineteenth century. Neither theology nor church leaders supplied the impetus to it, but rather the free groups of religious renewal, which were partly in conscious opposition both to the theology of the Enlightenment and to organized ecclesiastical systems. In addition to the Oxford Movement in the area of Anglicanism, there were above all associations of youth and of the Christian Student Movement. The Young Men's Christian Association (YMCA) and the Young Women's Christian Association (YWCA), founded in England in 1844 and 1854 respectively, soon spread to Europe and North America. Supranational and supradenominational and also organized in an emphatically evangelical and missionary context, they were referred from their own center to the *ecumene.* In contrast to the liberal theology of the time, persons were convinced that the unity of the Church could be found only on the basis of a clear creed. This was expressed in the Paris basic formula of the YMCA of 1855, which begins thus: "The Young Men's Christian Association has the aim of joining such young men together who acknowledge Jesus Christ, in accord with Scripture, as their God and Saviour." Here was unmistakably prepared the later basic formula of the World Council of Churches. At first the YMCA acquired importance for the founding of the Christian Students' World Union, which was joined at Vadstena in Sweden in 1895 by the student movements of many countries in the Protestant sphere. From it or the YMCA respectively proceeded the leaders of the ecumenical movement of the twentieth century, such as John R. Mott (1865–1955), Nathan Söderblom (1866–1931), and Willem A. Visser 't Hooft (b. 1900).

* Erwin Iserloh

Mott had played a decisive role in the preparing and implementing of the World Mission Conference of Edinburgh in 1910, which was intended to bring the various mission societies to collaboration. This was first institutionally assured in a continuing committee (1910–20) and then in the International Mission Council, which from 1921 to 1942 was under Mott's chairmanship. From the World Mission Conference at Edinburgh proceeded the decisive impetus to the ecumenical movement. If, according to John 17:23, the credibility of the Christian message depends on the unity of Christians, then the disunion in the mission, with its numerous mission societies working alongside and in opposition to one another, could only be experienced with the greatest pain.

At Edinburgh questions of faith and of ecclesiastical organization were excluded, but no agreement on them was to be expected. On the basis of this procedure it was possible to gain the cooperation of the High Church branch of the Anglican Church. Catholics and Orthodox were not invited.

The practical experience expressed by the American missionary bishop from the Philippines, Charles Brent (1862–1929), that one could not stop at practical collaboration but must ask questions precisely about doctrinal differences for the sake of unity, gave the stimulus to the movement Faith and Order. At a preparatory conference in Geneva in 1920 the Protestant Churches of Germany and France were not represented. Those of Switzerland declined to participate officially because among them there was no assumption that faith in the divinity of Christ must be acknowledged as an essential dogmatic basis. A continuing committee took over the rest of the preparation until finally on 3 August 1927 the first World Conference for Faith and Order could meet at Lausanne. There were 385 men and nine women representing 108 ecclesial communities. The reports of the work groups on the themes unity of the Church, its message, its nature, its creed, its function, its sacraments, and on the unity of Christianity and the separated Churches were not adopted, but only received for transmission to the Churches. The experience of the great difficulties which opposed unification produced a salutary sobriety. There was a willingness not to conceal contradictions but honestly to expose them. Above all, the Orthodox were concerned with stating their viewpoint clearly. With them and the Anglicans the Protestants came into contact with a strongly ecclesiological-sacramental mentality; on the other hand, the Lutherans' fear of everything institutional and hence of a concrete Church became obvious.

From the experience "Doctrine separates—service unites" the movement Life and Work movement sought to prepare on another route, namely, through practical work for peace and social work, on the international level of the *ecumene*. At the meeting of the World Union for the Work of the Friendship of the Churches in 1919 at Oud Wassenaer near The Hague and following its activity and the exertions of the International Conciliation Union, Bishop Nathan Söderblom (1866–1931) of Uppsala urged a world conference on questions of social ethics. Dogmatic questions were to be excluded. Progress resulted more quickly than in the case of Faith and Order. As early as 1925 the World Conference for Life and Work was able to meet at Stockholm. It was the first expressly ecumenical conference. Representatives of all the great ecclesial communities, except the Roman Catholic Church, were present. The importance of the conference lay, of course, more in the fact that it took place at all than in its content and outcome. Brilliant festive gatherings and worship services could not conceal the deep dissents. If some, chiefly the Anglo-Saxons, intended to bring about the Kingdom of God by a constituting of social conditions in accord with God's world plan, others believed, especially the German Lutherans, that they must stress the transcendence of God's Kingdom and its eschatological character. The conference was carried further in a continuing committee with various working groups, which from 1930 on was active in Geneva as the World Conference for Life and Work.

The relationship of German Protestantism to the ecumenical movement was considerably disturbed between the two world wars. If after 1918 "ecumenical cooperation was immensely impeded"[1] by the thesis of the sole guilt of Germany for the outbreak of the world war in the Treaty of Versailles, the question of attitude toward the Nazi state was posed for ecumenical groups from 1933. This problem was especially delicate when two German groups, the "German Evangelical Church" and the "Confessing Church" exerted themselves for recognition and collaboration. The World Council for Life and Work expressed itself in support of the Confessing Church and in 1934 decided to discuss at the next world conference the theme "Church, State, and People." For, because of the rise of totalitarian states, this old theme had caught fire in a new, even more acute form. The continuing committee of Faith and Order declared, on the other hand, for the admission of representatives of the official German Evangelical Church. The difficulty was removed when the Nazi state made participation in the world conference impossible for both groups—as for German delegations in general.

The suggestion of the World Conference for Life and Work at

---

[1] A. Deissmann, *Die Stockholmer Weltkirchenkonferenz* (Berlin 1926), 749; M. Pribilla, *Um kirchliche Einheit* (Freiburg 1929), 97–100.

Oxford in July 1937 to combine the two movements into a corporation and establish a World Council obtained also the assent of the Conference for Faith and Order at Edinburgh in August 1937. A committee discussed the constituting of the World Council at Utrecht in 1938. But because of the outbreak of war a plenary meeting could no longer be convoked. Not until 1948 did there occur at Amsterdam the establishing of the World Council of Churches; Faith and Order was to continue as a committee of the council and deal with questions of doctrine.

The first plenary meeting of the World Council of Churches at Amsterdam from 22 August to 4 September 1948 stood under the theme: "The Confusion of the World and God's Plan of Salvation." The basic formula adopted at the start reads: "The World Council of Churches is a community of Churches which acknowledge our Lord Jesus Christ as God and Saviour." According to the constitution, not individuals or associations but only Churches can be members. For at stake is a community of autonomous Churches, not a "superchurch." The World Council may be a help to the member Churches in their efforts for unity and in matters which can be done in common. "But it is alien to the council to wish to seize upon any functions which belong to the member Churches or to control them or wish to enact laws for them."[2]

At Amsterdam 147 Churches were represented by 351 delegates from forty-seven countries. Fundamentalist Protestant groups, for example, the Lutherans of the Missouri Synod of North America, had refused to join, because they missed a clear and solid dogmatic position and, a few days before the meeting of the plenary assembly, had founded the International Council of Christian Churches.

The Orthodox were represented chiefly through envoys of the ecumenical patriarch of Constantinople and of the Greek Church. A gathering of the heads of the autocephalous Churches under the direction of the Patriarch of Moscow had declined participation in the World Conference. The Roman Catholic Church also was not represented; only individual theologians had obtained permission from the Curia for private participation.

The plenary meeting at Amsterdam had the task of giving the World Council a constitution and, in view of the world torn apart and bled to death by the war, to gain clarity on the mandate of Christianity in and for the world. In Section 1, under the direction of Bishop Hanns Lilje and with the cooperation of Karl Barth, the unity of the Church and inner renewal were stressed under the theme "The Church in God's

[2] Constitution of the World Council of Churches of 30 August 1948 in *Die Unordnung der Welt und Gottes Heilsplan* V (Tübingen 1948), 168.

Plan of Salvation." In this connection it became obvious that the ideas of the unity of the Church differed very deeply.

There were serious conflicts in the "political" Sections 3—"the Church and the dissolution of the social order"—and 4—"the Church and international disorder." Here the world political and ideological struggle between East and West entered. It was bluntly stated in the talks of the American John Foster Dulles (1888–1959) and of the Prague theology professor Joseph L. Hromadka (1889–1969). In opposition to the harsh rejection of atheistic and materialistic Communism by Dulles, Hromadka offered an emotional criticism of the capitalistic West. The conference saw itself facing the task of upholding the Christian community despite all "Iron Curtains" and at the same time of standing up for human liberty and social justice. It was stressed that "Christianity must not be identified with any particular system" and there was a warning against a bringing of the Church into line with a totalitarian system. In Section 3 it was emphasized as a supplement that the preserving of their independence in the face of the conformity and conflicts of the world must not mean any world-alienating neutrality of the Churches.

Amsterdam was only a beginning. It aimed to clarify, deepen, and expand the theological range of the very generally held basic formula and to find the right working method of the World Council. If there was great caution in the programmatic claim, it was hoped all the more, thanks to the importance of the institution and the sharing in dialogue and in work, to create ecumenical facts, which would in time permit it to proceed more energetically to the question of truth. In the declaration of the Central Committee at Toronto in 1950, "The Church, the Churches, and the World Council," it was again emphasized: "The World Council of Churches is not and must never become a super church. It is not the 'World Church.' It is also not the 'Una Sancta,' of which there is mention in the creed. . . . Each Church reserves to itself, in accord with its constitution, the right to ratify or reject the statements or actions of the council. . . . Within the World Council there is room for the ecclesiology of every Church which is ready to share in the ecumenical dialogue. . . . From the membership it does not follow that every Church must see the other member Churches as Churches in the true and full meaning of the word."[3]

This declaration was intended to make easy the admission of the Orthodox Churches into the World Council. In addition to individual small national Churches and the Russian Church-in-exile, only the ecumenical patriarch of Constantinople and the Church of Greece had

[3] Quoted from *Kirchliches Jahrbuch der EKD,* 1951, 78 (Gütersloh 1952), 225–29.

become members of the World Council at Amsterdam in 1948. The patriarchs of Alexandria, Antioch, and Jerusalem had soon followed. Favored by the change of Moscow's foreign policy after the death of Stalin (1879–1953), efforts were made, especially by the Evangelical Church of Germany, for contacts with Russia. In August 1956 the Central Committee of the World Council met in Hungary. At the same time the patriarch of Constantinople, Athenagoras I (1886–1972), worked for a collaboration of all Orthodox Churches, including that of Russia. This led to the Pan-Orthodox conferences on Rhodes since 1961 and to the entry of the Churches of Russia, Bulgaria, Rumania, and Poland into the World Council at New Delhi. Here on 19 November 1961 met the third plenary assembly of the World Council of Churches under the slogan: "Jesus Christ—Light of the World." The second plenary assembly had taken place at Evanston on Lake Michigan in 1954. At New Delhi the International Council of the Mission was integrated into the World Council as an autonomous section, the Commission for World Mission and Evangelization.

The Orthodox stood up for giving the status of an autonomous section to Faith and Order, hitherto only a report of the division of studies, and thereby to give greater weight to the question of truth. Their demands and questions facilitated also the acceptance of the Trinitarian expansion of the Christological basic formula. It now reads: "The World Council of Churches is a community of Churches which confess the Lord Jesus Christ in accord with Holy Scripture as God and Saviour, and therefore try in common to fulfill that to which they are called, to the honor of God, the Father, Son, and Holy Spirit." Especially the "young Churches," whose importance the selection of the meeting place within the Asiatic world intended to stress, urged the early realization of visible unity of the Churches and intercommunion. The detailed report of Section 3, "Unity," took this into account; it was approved "whole and entire" by the plenary assembly and recommended to the churches for study. In emphasizing the necessity of *visible* unity it meant, according to Edmund Schlink, "a real progress on the way to overcoming an ecclesiological Docetism."

Meanwhile, 198 member Churches belonged to the World Council. At New Delhi for the first time an official Roman Catholic delegation was present at the plenary meeting of the World Council, with five representatives of the Secretariat for the Unity of Christians at Rome and two representatives of Cardinal Gracias of Bombay. The "World Responsibility of the Churches," since Amsterdam in 1948 the prevailing theme of the conferences of the World Council, came strongly to the foreground since 1966, the year of the change in the general secretariat from W.A. Vissert 't Hooft to Eugene Carson Blake. The

World Conference for Church and Society at Geneva in 1966, the third following Stockholm in 1925 and Oxford in 1937, which was predominantly occupied with social ethical questions, was supposed to give "the Christian reply to the technical and social revolution of our age." It was marked by a top-heaviness of laity and by an almost equally strong representation of the Churches of Africa, Asia, and Latin America as of those of Western Europe and North America. Experts and the disconcerted were supposed to speak to the Churches and there were discussions of their answer to the challenges of the revolutionary changes of the day.

Out of the conviction that the social responsibility of Christians must not be limited to the personal relations of the individual Christian to his neighbor, "Love through Structures" became a chief slogan of the conference and revolution theology a heated topic of discussion. In the message of the conference it was said: "As Christians we must stand up for change. . . . Today many of those who devote themselves to the service of Christ and their neighbor take a more radical and revolutionary position. They in no way deny the value of tradition and social order but they are in search of a new strategy, by the aid of which basic changes can be carried out in society without too great a loss of time. . . . At the present time it is important that we recognize the deeper mooring of this radical position in Christian tradition and give it a rightful place in the life of the Church. . . ."[4]

The conference demanded active participation of the Christian Church in the struggle for racial equality. The World Council of Churches was supposed to establish, among other things, a secretariat for the elimination of racism. This change to social and political commitment determined the theme of the fourth plenary assembly, which met at Uppsala from 4 to 20 July 1968, under the scriptural text, "See, I make all things new," and saw as signs of the time "sensational steps into a new scientific land, the protest of rebel students, the alarm over political murder and hostile clashes." In view of the reports, emotionally delivered before 704 delegates, many guests, and journalists, on "Rich and Poor Nations," "Racism or World Community," "Christianity and Human Rights," "Work of the Church in a Revolutionary World," it became difficult to bring the "gospel of conversion" to accommodation with the "gospel of social responsibility."[5] This tension, further sharpened since 1969 by the development of an

---

[4] H. Kruger, ed., *Ökumenische Bewegung 1965–1968, Beiheft z. Ök. Rundschau* no. 12/13 (Stuttgart 1970), 334.

[5] Message of the fourth plenary assembly, from *Ökumenische Bewegung 1965–1968*, 446f.

ecumenical program for the fighting of racism and a call to the member Churches for donations for the support of liberation organizations, drove the World Council into the shattering test of a polarization. According to the resolution of the Central Committee at Addis Ababa in 1971 the money must not be used for military purposes. Further, a study on violent and nonviolent methods for causing social change was to be undertaken.

In 1972 with the choice of Philip Potter, a Methodist from Jamaica, a Christian of the Third World became secretary general of the World Council of Churches. At the conference of the Commission for World Mission and Evangelization of the World Council at Bangkok from 29 December 1972 to 8 January 1973, with the theme "Salvation of the World—Today," the delegates from Africa, Asia, and blacks from the United States were in a majority. "Salvation" was understood with the strong stress on "liberation," the work of salvation seen as a fight against exploitation, political suppression, and alienation. The aloofness from the Western Churches because of their "membership in colonial power structures" went as far as the demand for a "moratorium": at least temporarily the Churches of the Western world should stop sending out persons and money.

The geographical proximity to the great Asiatic religions suggested dialogue with them as a particular section theme. Thereby was posed the question of the right of mission, and the danger of a syncretism became acute in connection with the demand for "contextualizing" of the Christian message or the making of Christianity indigenous in the cultures of the Third World.

To judge from the preparations, the accent at the fifth plenary meeting, which took place from 23 November to 10 December 1975 at Nairobi, Kenya, with the theme "Christ liberates and unites," should have been placed on internal world problems, such as racism, sexism, and education. The great majority of the 757 delegates from 271 member Churches (with observers, advisers, and journalists there were ca. 2,300 participants) decided, however, for the theological themes of Sections 1 ("confession of Jesus Christ") and 2 ("unity of the Church"), and rising opposition, especially from the delegates of Orthodoxy, thwarted a slipping into the horizontal. The One Church was understood as a conciliar community of congregations which profess the same faith, celebrate the same baptism and the same Lord's Supper, and recognize the spiritual officers of the others. It was obvious that the World Council of Churches is not this conciliar community but is to prepare it. Worship, scriptural work, and spirituality occupy a broad space. Thus Nairobi became a "spiritual happening." In a "spirituality for combat," or, better, a "spirituality of commitment" the effort was made to recover the positive uniting of the proclamation of Christ and of social responsibility. It was attempted to surround anti-racism with a large program for the realization of human rights. Thus there was compulsion also to deal with the situation in the Soviet Union. The denial there of religious liberty led to the harshest debates; as generally at Nairobi, however, the course in this question also stood for integration and compromise. But the World Council of Churches will not fulfill its task with a passage from a "conflict *ecumene*" to a "community *ecumene*," if, as Lortz says, this is an "*ecumene* without truth."

The Share of the Roman Catholic Church
in the Ecumenical Movement

With the participation of Catholic delegates in the plenary assembly in New Delhi a deeply rooted hesitation of the Roman Curia vis-à-vis ecumenical meetings was overcome. Convinced that it, and in the full sense only it, visibly represented the one, holy, catholic, and apostolic Church founded by Jesus Christ, the Roman Catholic Church was concerned that this claim could be made relative if it sat down with other ecclesial communities at the conference table.

To the invitation from the Scandinavian Lutheran archbishops to Pope Benedict XV to send representatives to Uppsala for an ecumenical conference on 8 September 1918, Cardinal Secretary of State Gasparri asserted that everything would be agreeable to the Pope which operated for peace and Christian brotherhood, because it "smooths the path for what the Gospel expresses in the words: 'that there may be one flock and one shepherd.'"[6] But there was no mention of a representation of the Pope at the proposed conference. Instead, on 4 July 1919 a decree of the Holy Office forbade any participation in congresses for the promotion of unity without the permission of the Holy See. As early as 16 May 1919 Benedict XV had given the decision to a delegation which brought him the invitation to the conference of Faith and Order: "The teaching and practice of the Roman Catholic Church in regard to the unity of the visible Church of Christ are well known to everyone, and so it is not possible for the Catholic Church to participate in a congress like the one proposed. However, His Holiness wishes under no circumstances to disapprove the congress in question for those who are not united with the See of Peter."[7]

[6] Letter of 19 June 1918; text in M. Pribilla, *Um kirchliche Einheit,* 319.
[7] R. Rouse, S. C. Neill, *Geschichte der Ökumenischen Bewegung 1517–1948* II (Göttingen 1958), 16.

The lively interest of Pius XI in movements for unity applied especially to Orthodoxy. As a scholar, an apostolate of the spirit was in first place in his eyes. For this he in 1922 established the Oriental Institute at Rome and required also an intensive study of the theology and liturgy of the Eastern Churches. Here he saw a special task for the Benedictines. In addition to the abbey of Niederaltaich on the Danube, this call was heard by the priory founded at Amay-sur-Meuse in 1925 and transferred to Chevetogne, Belgium, in 1939. It celebrated the liturgy in Eastern rites, cultivated the theology and spirituality of the East, and published the periodical *Irénicon*. In the Pope's view it is . . ."necessary for reunion especially that people know and love one another. . . . The separated parts of a gold-bearing rock are likewise gold-bearing."[8]

This could have been used of relations with Protestants. Accordingly, in an address in the consistory of 24 March 1924, Pius XI asked for ecumenical efforts in regard to all separated Christians: "We will be obliged to all Catholics who strive, under the impulse of divine grace, to facilitate admittance to the true faith for their separated brothers, whoever these may be, by dispelling their prejudices, keeping in view unadulterated Catholic teaching, and especially making evident in themselves the feature of disciples of Christ, for there is love."[9] In practice, however, the Pope occupied a rather reserved attitude in regard to Protestant ecumenism: in his view, that of historian and scholar, everything remained too much on the surface, that is, he missed the basic study of the sources, especially of the Church Fathers; as a churchman, he saw the danger of relativism and indifferentism. For some Catholics and many Protestants, especially for the participants in the conferences of Stockholm and Lausanne, it was a keen disappointment that the Catholic Church was absent. Archbishop Söderblom and with him others went so far as to conclude from this conduct that Rome thereby showed to the whole world its sectarian spirit and placed itself outside the totality of Christianity.

After Lausanne, Pius XI in the encyclical *Mortalium animos* of 6 January 1928 subjected the ecumenical movement, as it had thus far developed, to a sharp criticism: "Can we endure . . . that the truth, in fact the truth revealed by God, be made the object of negotiations?"[10] In the Pope's view the Catholic Church took an interest in the ecumenical movement only so far as this meant a return to the sources of faith, to the Gospel and tradition.

[8] G. H. Tavard, *Geschichte der Ökumenischen Bewegung* (Mainz 1948), 120.
[9] *AAS* 16(1924), 123f.
[10] *Ökumenische Dokumente,* ed. by H. L. Althaus (Göttingen 1962), 168f.

Despite the official refusal, private observers were present, with papal and episcopal approval, at the World Conference for Life and Work in Stockholm in 1925 and at that for Faith and Order in Lausanne in 1927: from Germany Max Joseph Metzger (1887–1944) and Hermann Hoffmann (1878–1973). It can be said that in Germany the situation was in some respects favorable for the meeting of the denominations: Here the number of "denominations" was not so large as, for example, in the United States, and in the great Churches of the nation one had to deal with partners in dialogue who were to some extent committed to a creed. At the universities were Catholic and Protestant theological faculties which with the aid of the historicocritical method demolished some prejudices and exposed common foundations. The history of the Reformation and the life and work of Martin Luther were, especially after the appearance in 1939 of the *Reformation in Deutschland* by Joseph Lortz (1887–1975), presented more objectively and with more understanding of its religious motives, and the Catholic share in the guilt for the schism was candidly admitted. The threat to the Churches and to Christianity from National Socialism contributed substantially to the rapprochement of the denominations. Now what was important, beyond all differences, was to save the Christian substance. It worked in favor of the cooperation of the denominations that Protestantism, as "Confessing Church," thought better of its being as Church.

Among the pioneers of Catholic ecumenism in Germany were Arnold Rademacher (1873–1939), Max Pribilla (1874–1956), Robert Grosche (1888–1967), the founder of the periodical *Catholica* (1932), Matthias Laros (1882–1962), Joseph Lortz, Karl Adam (1876–1966), and Max Joseph Metzger. In 1938 the last named founded the brotherhood *Una Sancta,* with the aim of working for unity through prayer and fraternal meetings. Due to his initiative there took place larger meetings at Meitingen near Augsburg in 1939–40. Suspected by Nazi officials as an apostle of peace, spied on and often imprisoned, Metzger was executed on 17 April 1944.

In France ecumenical thought was roused by Paul Couturier (1881–1953), who spread and spiritually deepened the World Octave of Prayer for the Unity of Christians from 18 to 25 January, which had been suggested by Anglicans, and by M. Yves Congar, O.P. (born 1904). There was to be prayer for "the unity of all Christians, as Christ desired."

After the Second World War there arose in many places *Una Sancta* circles of lay persons and theologians as sites of productive encounter of Catholics and Protestants in prayer and discussion. Their spontaneity naturally declined, the clearer it became how long and difficult was the road to unity. The monitum *Cum compertum* of the Holy Office at Rome, issued on 5 June 1948 before the first plenary assembly of the World Council at Amsterdam, seemed to produce a setback. In it was inculcated, with reference to the regulations of canon law (Canon 1325, par. 3), that participation in discussions of faith with non-Catholics was allowed only with the previous permission of the Holy See. More positive in tone were the directives for its implementation in the instruction *De motione oecumenica* of 20 December 1949. In it the bishops were requested not only to bestow their attention on strivings for unity but to foster and direct them. Meetings and discussions with non-Catholics were regarded as a desired opportunity to make known to non-Catholics a knowledge of Catholic teaching. To the bishops was given for three years the faculty of granting the necessary permission of the Holy See for participation in ecumenical dialogues. "The very important work of reuniting all Christians in the one true faith and in the one true Church," so the instruction concluded, "must more and more become one of the preferred functions of all pastoral care and a chief concern of the urgent prayer of all believers to God."[11]

After the Second World War the discussions of theologians received a strong stimulus. At the initiative of the archbishop of Paderborn, Lorenz Jaeger (1892–1975), and of the Lutheran bishop of Oldenburg, Wilhelm Stählin (1883–1975), theologians of both denominations met annually in Germany since 1946 to discuss common and separating doctrines. With the decisive participation of the Dutch professor of theology, Jan Willebrands (b. 1909), there was formed in 1952 the International Conference for Ecumenical Questions, whose work was incorporated into the Secretariat for Promoting Christian Unity established in 1960 by Pope John XXIII and directed by Cardinal Augustin Bea (1881–1968). In 1962 it obtained the official status of a conciliar commission and as such was able authoritatively to prepare the Decree on Ecumenism of the Second Vatican Council (see above, Chapter 4).

The council was to introduce a new epoch of the Ecumenical Movement within the Catholic Church. It professed ecumenism as a movement produced by the spirit, which is the task "of the whole Church, of the faithful as well as of the shepherds" (ARTICLE 5). It must be supported by the spirit of penance and inner renewal. The Catholic Church knows that it shares in the guilt for the split and it is aware that it has not always properly preached the truths of faith entrusted to it, so that it became difficult for people to find the truth. Thus it sees itself summoned to a "lasting reformation" (ART. 6). But if one can have access "only through the Catholic Church of Christ, which is the

[11] *AAS* 42(1950), 146f.

common means of salvation, to the entire fullness of the means of salvation," (ART. 3), there are still "many important elements or goods by all of which the Church is built up and acquires its life, even outside the visible limits of the Catholic Church" (ART. 3). The Holy Spirit uses the separated Churches and communities as "means of salvation." Catholics are asked "joyfully to acknowledge and highly to esteem the really Christian goods from the common heritage which are found among the separated brethren" (ART. 4).

Of course, the differences still existing despite all that was common could not be concealed. "Nothing is so alien to the ecumenical spirit as false irenicism." Doctrinal differences that cause separation had to deal especially with the nature of the Church and with its power, its office. Because of the absence of the sacrament of orders, Protestants have "not preserved the original and complete reality of the Eucharistic mystery" (ART. 22). Hence "the doctrine of the Lord's Supper . . . and of the ministerial offices of the Church [are especially] necessarily the subject of the dialogue" (ART. 22). This discussion is carried on in the field of tension of the common and the separating. But one must not rest content with dialogue. The council called to common prayer. In it the grace of unity must be asked for, but the community persisting despite the split must be attested. Further, the separated brothers must work together in service to the world. This practical work is possible, even if persons are of different views in the questions of principles of morals and of the relationship of Church and society. Without prejudice to some criticism—it was especially objected that in the decree the Catholic Church saw itself as the center around which the other Churches stood more or less close, like concentric circles—the decree was generally praised; it "opened new doors for ecumenical contacts."[12]

To implement the conciliar decree the Secretariat for Promoting Christian Unity at Rome published guidelines for practical collaboration and dialogue with the non-Catholic Churches in 1967 and 1970 in the *Ecumenical Directory.* If ecumenism is an affair not only of church leadership but of all Christians, then it is important to activate "ecumenism on the spot," that is, to bring Christians together on the level of the congregations for dialogue, prayer, and common ministry to the world. This will be aided by the Roman document on "Ecumenical Cooperation on the regional, national, and local level" of 7 July 1975. In 1973 the union of dioceses of the German Federal Republic joined the Working Community of the Christian Churches in Germany,

---

[12] W.A. Visser 't Hooft, "Die allgemeine ökumenische Entwicklung seit 1948," *Geschichte der ökumenischen Bewegung 1948–1968,* ed. by H. E. Frey (Göttingen 1974), 32.

founded in 1948 and similar to the Councils of Christians in other countries. Likewise the Catholic dioceses became members of the Working Community founded on the level of the German federal states.

Membership of the Catholic Church in the World Council of Churches is still subject, of course, to various kinds of difficulties. On the basis of the existing charter the weight of the Catholic Church, preponderant in members, would be too heavy. A "common working group" consisting of eight representatives of the World Council and of six of the Catholic Church was set up and undertook its work at Bossey near Geneva in June 1965. This was related to all questions for which the World Council itself was competent; in the first place, it was to gain information on the possibilities of dialogue and cooperation and eliminate sources of tension. The Ecumenical Work Community for Justice, Peace, and Development (Sodepax), set up at first on a trial basis by the papal commission for development assistance, *Iustitia et Pax,* and by the World Council in 1968, aims to help all races, peoples, and religions in the struggle against misery and war. Since the fourth plenary assembly of the World Council at Uppsala in 1968 nine Roman Catholic theologians belong as full members to the Faith and Order commission, embracing 150 persons.

The doctrinal dialogue was and is conducted in various groups on the national and international level. Except for the dialogue in 1971 between the Roman Catholic Church, the Lutheran, and the Reformed World Union on "the theology of marriage and the problem of mixed marriages," these discussions are bilateral, that is, they are conducted by the Catholic Church with one denominational Church at a time on the international, regional, and national level. Contact talks with the Lutheran World Union (LWB) led to the establishing of the study commission "The Gospel and the Church," which held five sessions in 1967–71 and collected its "working results" in 1971 in the so-called *Malta Paper.*[13] No complete agreement could be reached on function and intercommunion. The dialogue was continued by the Common Lutheran-Catholic Commission, newly constituted in 1975. A document on "The Lord's Supper" is in preparation.

"The Eucharist" (1967) and "Eucharist and Office" (1970) have also been the chief themes of the Catholic-Lutheran dialogue in the United

---

[13] *Evangelium—Welt—Kirche. Schlussbericht und Referate der römisch-katholisch/ evangelisch-lutherischen Studienkommission 'Das Evangelium und die Kirche' 1967–1971. Auf Veranlassung des lutherischen Weltbundes und des Sekretariats für die Einheit der Christen,* ed. by Harding Meyer (Frankfurt 1975); cf. H. Meyer, *Luthertum und Katholizismus im Gespräch* (Frankfurt 1973).

States since 1965.[14] It became clear that the way to intercommunion lay only by way of harmony in the understanding of the Eucharist and a mutual recognition of ecclesiastical offices. On the basis of the talks the participants thought they could invite their respective Churches to acknowledge the validity of the offices of the other Church and the real presence of Jesus Christ in its Eucharistic celebrations.[15] Then the commission in the United States turned to the question of the papal primacy.[16] The inner consistency of this further step was perceived: "Our earlier discussions had concentrated on the ministry of office in the local communities. Now we concentrate on the unifying and organizing function of this office for the Universal Church—on the question of how a definite form of this office, that is, the papacy, has served the unity of the Universal Church in the past and how it can serve it in the future."[17] There was a striving for a certain agreement on the necessity of a special office for the entire Church. Of course, the structure and exercise of the office had to be discussed in still more detail. The talks, which are still in progress, produced in 1974 the report "Office and Universal Church," which dealt with the primacy and not yet with the problem of infallibility.

The International Anglican-Roman Catholic Commission summoned in 1970 by the Pope and the archbishop of Canterbury, came in the so-called Windsor Statement of 1971 to an "essential agreement on the doctrine of the Eucharist" and in 1973 to a basic consensus on "Office and Ordination" in the "Canterbury Statement." In these, to be sure, the question of the Petrine office and of the recognition of Anglican orders was excluded and reserved for a later discussion.[18] This was taken up in 1974. In 1976 it led in Venice to the acceptance of a declaration on "Authority in the Church."[19] In connection with authority in questions of faith for the *koinonia* of local Churches there were also taken up the primacy of the Bishop of Rome and his special responsibility for faith and doctrine of the Universal Church. There was demanded an appropriate balance between the primatial, collegial, and synodal exercise of authority, but recognition of a special position of

---

[14] G. Gassmann, M. Lienhard, M. Meyer, H. V. Herntrich, eds., *Um Amt und Herrenmahl. Dokumente zum evangelisch/römisch-katholischen Gespräch. Ök. Dokumentation* I (Frankfurt 1974), 55–102.

[15] Ibid., 88 and 99f.

[16] Report and working papers in H. Stirnimann, L. Vischer et al., *Papsttum und Petrusdienst (Ök. Perspektiven* 7) (Frankfurt 1975).

[17] Ibid., 93f.

[18] G. Gassmann, M. Lienhard, H. Meyer eds., *Vom Dialog zur Gemeinschaft. Dokumente zum anglikanisch-lutherischen und anglikanisch-katholischen Gespräch. Ök. Dokumentation* II (Frankfurt 1975), 129–48; *HK* 28(1974), 93–97.

[19] Text in *HK* 31(1977), 191–95.

the Bishop of Rome in a reunited Church as a service to its unity and catholicity was underscored. "The only episcopal see which claims a universal primacy, which has also exercised and still exercises such an *episcope,* is the episcopal see of Rome, the city where Peter and Paul died. It seems fit that in any coming unity a universal primacy, such as we have described it, be exercised by this episcopal see."[20]

Discussions with the Methodist World Union have shown remarkable agreement in the sphere of spirituality and piety. As a result, the Dialogue Commission of the United Methodist Churches and of the Roman Catholic Church in the United States published in January 1976 a statement "Holiness and Spirituality of Ecclesiastical Office."

The positive development of the relations of the Roman Catholic Church and the World Council of Churches found expression in the visit of Paul VI to the central office of the World Council at Geneva on 10 June 1969. But at the same time it became clear that the expectations expressed at Uppsala in 1968 of an imminent membership of Rome in the World Council prejudiced the development. "With all fraternal candor it is said: We are not of the opinion that the question of membership of the Catholic Church in the World Council is ready to the extent that one can or must give a positive answer to it"[21] (Paul VI).

[20] Ibid., 194.
[21] H. Krüger, ed., *Ökumenische Bewegung 1969–1972, Beiheft z. Ök. Rundschau* no. 28(Stuttgart 1975), 140.

CHAPTER 16

*The Dissident Eastern Churches**

By "Eastern Churches"[1] are designated those Christian communities which were established within and outside the eastern half of the Roman Empire or, respectively, sprang from these as daughter Churches. Intellectual-historical and political influences contributed to a multiform development, which produced many foreign Churches in the twentieth century. The emigration of well-known theologians and philosophers of religion from Russia in 1917, the erecting of Orthodox theological educational institutions in the West,[2] the admittance of

* Bernhard Stasiewski
[1] J. Chrysostomus, *Ostkirche,* 256f.
[2] For example, at Paris (Saint Sergius Institute for Orthodox Theology), Jordanville (Holy Trinity Monastery and Seminary of the Russian Orthodox Foreign Church), and Chambésy, cf. D. Papandreou, "Das Orthodoxe Zentrum des Ökumenischen Patriarchates in Chambésy bei Genf. Entstehung, Aktivitäten, Perspektiven," *Internationale Katholische Zeitschrift* 4(1975), 323–30.

almost all Eastern Churches into the World Council of Churches, and their participation in its meetings and committee sessions have substantially contributed to a mutual understanding of Eastern and Western Christianity. The sympathy of the free world during persecutions of Christians in the Communist power sphere, the Sovietizing of eastern Central Europe, the atheistic religious policy of the socialist states of the Eastern bloc, which controlled all religious statements through state ecclesiastical officials and restricted them to the liturgical field, and discussions of human rights have kept alive the interest in the fate of the Eastern Churches. The tensions between Islam and Christianity, power-political confrontations in the Middle East, and restrictions on ecclesiastical life in Arabic-speaking states have caused the ecclesiastical history of the time to focus attention on the Eastern Churches.

Here the diversity of Eastern Christianity can be presented, not in the form of reports by countries, which would have to extend to all five continents,[3] but only in survey: it includes in the order of their origin the Orthodox Churches with the four ancient patriarchates, the Church of Georgia, the patriarchates appearing in medieval and modern times, and the remaining autocephalous or autonomous Orthodox Churches,[4] as well as the Eastern, pre-Chalcedonian, and National Churches of the Nestorians and the Monophysites.

The Orthodox Churches

From the Byzantine Imperial Church proceeded the Slavonic missions which gained Bulgarians, Serbs, Rumanians, and Russians for Orthodox Christianity. In addition to the patriarch of Constantinople, the patriarchs of Alexandria, Antioch, Jerusalem, and Georgia consolidated Orthodoxy in Egypt and the Middle East and spread it into inner Asia. The daughter Churches of the ecumenical patriarchate preserved the heritage in the area of the Eastern Slavs, the Balkan Slavs, Rumania, and Greece. After the collapse of Turkish domination in southeastern Europe several Orthodox peoples obtained political independence and ecclesiastical autonomy, so that new autocephalous territorial Churches developed.

THE FOUR ANCIENT PATRIARCHATES

While the ecumenical patriarchate of Constantinople lost its eparchies in Asia Minor as a result of the Turkish-Greek war of 1922–23 and had

[3] Cf. the survey in *Oriente Cattolico,* op. cit., 466–88.
[4] For the autocephalous (independent) and autonomous (half-independent) Churches which are generally recognized within Orthodoxy, and the Orthodox communities whose canonicity is partly disputed, cf. J. Madey, *Die Kirchen des Osten,* 18f.

to struggle with Turkey for its existence, it still gained authority by the voluntary subordination of Churches[5] that developed between the two world wars and afterwards. Within the totality of Orthodoxy and beyond, it was increasingly recognized as the spiritual center.

It owed this strengthening above all to the personality of Patriarch Athenagoras (1948–72).[6] After his election he paid special importance to the bringing together of all the Orthodox and he had as his long-range goal the unity of all Christian Churches. His initiatives for the implementation of the first three Pan-Orthodox conferences on Rhodes,[7] which were followed by a Pan-Orthodox Council, his meeting with Pope Paul VI in Jerusalem in 1964, his sharing in the common declaration,[8] proclaimed simultaneously on 7 December 1965 at Saint Peter's in Rome during the ninth public assembly of the Second Vatican Council and at Saint George's Church in the Phanar, the patriarch's residence, whereby the mutual excommunications of the Western and Byzantine heads of the Churches in 1054 were to be erased from the memory of the Churches, his visit to Pope Paul VI in Rome at the end of October 1967, to the World Council of Churches in Geneva at the beginning of November 1967, and to Western and Eastern church leaders, make clear the extent of his ecumenical efforts. He constantly stood for the improvement of pastoral care and the formation of the clergy. When the Greek Orthodox Theological University at Chalkis on the Isle of Princes, Heybeli, near Istanbul, at which also students from the patriarchates of Antioch and Alexandria and the Monophysite Church of Ethiopia studied, was closed in 1971 by the Turkish educational officials in the course of the secularization of private universities—only the "Little Seminary for Priests" could continue its teaching activities for students from Turkish territory—he exerted himself for a genuine ascetical, spiritual, and scholarly education at other places, for example, on the island of Crete. He was able to acquire a worldwide esteem once again for the ecumenical patriarchate.

His successor, Demetrios I, elected by the twelve metropolitans of the Permanent Synod, after 1972 continued the dialogue on the love of

[5] For example, the Orthodox Churches in Finland and Estonia, parts of Czechoslovak Orthodoxy, and the Paris metropolitanate of the Russian Foreign Church.
[6] B. Ohse, *Der Patriarch Athenagoras I., ein ökumenischer Visionär* (Göttingen and Regensburg 1968); V. Gheorghiu, *La vie du patriarche Athénagoras* (Paris 1969); R. Stupperich, "Athenagoras I. Ökumenischer Patriarch von Konstantinopel. Ein Nachruf," *Kirche im Osten* 6(1973), 11–19.
[7] 24 September to 1 October 1961, 26–28 September 1963, 1–5 November 1964.
[8] C. Patock, H. Tretter, "Zur Aufhebung des Bannes vom Jahre 1054," *OstkSt* 15(1966), 196–209; *Tomos agapis. Vatican-Phanar 1958–1970* (Rome and Istanbul 1971), 278–97; J. Ratzinger, "Das Ende der Bannflüche von 1054. Folgen für Rom und die Ostkirchen," *Internationale Katholische Zeitschrift* 3(1974), 289–303.

neighbor with the Christian Churches in an effort to move closer to Pan-Orthodox unity and through it the unity of all Christianity. Even if the extent of the direct jurisdiction of the patriarchate of Constantinople was further curtailed by schisms in the twentieth century and the tensions with the archbishop of Greece over a group of eparchies were not relieved, still it embraced ca. 1.5 to 2 million faithful[9] in Turkey, on the Greek islands, on Mount Athos, and in many foreign eparchies. In 1903 there were 7,432 monks in the monasteries on Athos.[10] Despite the measures of support from the patriarchs of Constantinople and other Orthodox Churches, their number had meanwhile declined to ca. 1,100.[11] The struggle over the acceptance of new monks from the Churches in the Communist sphere of power, the closing of the Athonias university, which had existed from 1749 to 1940 and from 1953 to 1971, injured the community of the twenty monasteries of the monastic republic, which, as an outstanding center of Orthodoxy, could in 1963 look back on a millennium of spiritual radiation.

In rank the patriarchate of Alexandria stands in second place within Orthodoxy. In comparison to the Monophysite Coptic Church with ca. 3 million faithful, its 100,000 members in Egypt have no easy position. The number of Greeks dropped because of emigration in the course of the twentieth century. Patriarch Nicholas V (1936–39) sought by means of a new law on the election of the patriarch to consolidate the predominance of the Greek clergy. His successor, Christopher II (1939–66), conceded to the synod of his Church only limited functions, and despite its opposition he ordained several bishops to care for the Orthodox in Africa and strengthened the mission to the pagans of Kenya, Tanganyika, and Uganda. This made substantial progress since 1968 under Patriarch Nicholas VI. His accommodating of Arabic-

---

[9] In these and the following statistics on individual Eastern Churches there is question of estimates, since the data in handbooks and special investigations differ greatly from one another. Cf., among others, M. Lehmann, op. cit., 24–26; M. Lacko, "Die nicht-chalkedonischen orientalischen Kirchen," *Atlas zur Kirchengeschichte* (Freiburg, Basel, and Vienna 1970), 78; M. Lacko, J. Martin, "Die orthodoxen Kirchen," ibid., 80; P. Wiertz, I. Doens, "Übersicht über die Kirchen des Ostens," E.v. Ivánka, J. Tyciak, P. Wiertz, op. cit., 723–50; *Oriente Cattolico*, op. cit., 842f.; W. Krohl, "Verzeichnis der Autonomen Katholischen Kirchen in der Welt," *Kirchliches Jahrbuch für die Alt-Katholiken in Deutschland* 75 (Bonn 1976), 62–68; *Jahrbuch der Orthodoxie*, op. cit.

[10] *Le millénaire du Mont Athos 963–1963, études et mélanges*, 2 vols. (Chevetogne 1964); P. Huber, *Athos. Leben, Glaube, Kunst* (Zurich and Freiburg 1969); E.A. de Mendieta, *Mount Athos. The Garden of the Panaghia*, trans. from French by M.R. Bruce (Berlin 1972); P.M. Mylonas, "Der heilige Berg Athos," *Alte Kirchen und Klöster Griechenlands. Ein Begleiter zu den byzantinischen Stätten*, ed. and trans. by E. Melas (Cologne 1972), 91–119.

[11] 1928: 4,848; 1959: 1,641; 1972: 1,146.

speaking faithful, his ecumenical contacts, which led in 1970 to the founding of a common Council of Churches of the Copts, Ethiopians, Syrians, Malabar Christians, and the Greek Orthodox patriarchates of Alexandria, Antioch, and Jerusalem, his encouraging of its own printery for the church press, theological periodicals, and publications, and the memorial celebrations of the sixteenth centenary of the death of Saint Athanasius at Alexandria and Cairo testify to the vitality of this patriarchate.

The direction of the patriarchate of Antioch passed in 1931 with Alexander III (to 1958) from Greek to Arab hands, after the constitution of 1929 had placed at the patriarch's side a National Council constituted by four metropolitans and eight delegated laymen. The two factions struggling for predominance, one of which aimed to maintain the Greek tradition while the other was of a Syrian national orientation, counterbalanced each other. Alexander III intensified the internal and external consolidation and joined the American communities firmly to his patriarchal association, and in this Exarch Anton Baschir was of assistance. Under Theodosius VI (1958–70) a schism of a few Syrian eparchies threatened to wreck the unity of the patriarchate, which took care of approximately 350,000 faithful, but it could be eliminated by the accommodating influence of Elias IV (from 1970), elected by the Greek eparchs. He restored the dioceses in eastern Turkey, vacant since the First World War, named bishops for Saudi Arabia and Australia-New Zealand, completed the restoration of the priests' seminary Belement, and reformed the valid canon law, in which, among other things, definite requirements for candidates for the episcopacy and an extensive representation of the laity on the diocesan and the parochial levels were established.

The patriarchate of Jerusalem, with ca. 70,000 faithful, is "today no more than a noble relic."[12] Patriarch Damianos (1897–1931) settled the difficulties between the Greek minority and the Arabic majority in his Church. Under Patriarch Timotheos (1935–55) the number of Greeks declined through emigration. In consequence of the political tensions in the Holy Land, the end of the British mandate in 1948, the partition of Palestine, and the proclamation of the State of Israel, the Patriarchal Church was split between Israel and Jordan. During the celebration of the fifteenth centenary of the Council of Chalcedon in 1951 the schism between the Arabs, who constituted almost 99 percent of the faithful, and the Greeks could be healed to a degree. Patriarch Benedict I (from 1957) controlled the difficulties by skillful negotiations with Jordan and Saudi Arabia, by a new constitution for the members of the Brother-

[12] K. Onasch, op. cit., 76.

hood of the Holy Sepulchre and the founding of a school for its recruits, with a Greek and an Arab section. He undertook foreign journeys to Orthodox Church leaders and asked aid for his Church, compressed in Jordan and Israel, which suffered from the consequences of Israel's two wars of 1956 and 1967. He made ecumenical contacts, for example, with Pope Paul VI in 1964, and opened an ecumenical institute for higher theological studies on the Tantur Hill between Jerusalem and Bethlehem.

The autonomous Monastery of Saint Catherine on Mount Sinai[13] celebrated the fourteenth centenary of its existence in 1966. Since, because of Israel's June War of 1967, it was cut off from connection with its archbishop residing in Cairo, it subjected itself in 1968 to the jurisdiction of the patriarchate of Jerusalem, with which it had been united for centuries.

THE ORTHODOX CHURCH IN GEORGIA

The Georgian Orthodox ecclesiastical community in the Caucasus, issuing from the Patriarchal Church of Antioch, had been subjected to a Russian exarch in 1817, but in 1917 it declared its independence and restored its Catholicate. After the incorporation of Georgia as the Transcaucasian Soviet Socialist Republic (1922–37, since 1937 the Soviet Socialist Republic of Georgia) into the Union of Soviet Socialist Republics, the faithful suffered under the pressure of antireligious propaganda. Their Catholicos Ambrose (1921–22) complained in a letter to the World Economic Conference of Genoa in 1922 of the atrocities of the Bolsheviks; with all the higher dignitaries of the Church, he was arrested and died in prison in 1927. Under Catholicos Kallistratos (1932–52) ecclesiastical communion was in 1943 again restored with the patriarchate of Moscow and a certain freedom of movement was made possible to the Georgian Church. It was preserved because of the collaboration of Catholicos Melchisedek III (1952–60) and especially of his successor, Ephraem II (1960–72), with the Patriarchal Church of Moscow, and their declarations of loyalty to the regime. Catholicos David V tried to fill his fifteen eparchies, of which several were vacant when he took office, with suitable persons and to consolidate the Georgian Church, with its from 750,000 to 1 million faithful and four monasteries. Disagreements between the patriarchal leadership and the priesthood, internal repression of the Church by

[13] H.L. Rabino, *Le monastère de Sainte-Cathérine du Mont Sinai* (Cairo 1938); H. Skrobucha, *Sinai* (Olten and Lausanne 1959); G. Gerster, *Sinai, Land der Offenbarung* (Berlin 1961); M.B. Schlink, *Sinai Heute. Stätten der Gottesoffenbarung zwischen Nil und Moseberg,* 3d ed. (Darmstadt and Eberstadt 1975).

Communist officials, and police actions against the youth impaired ecclesiastical life.

THE PATRIARCHATES ORIGINATING IN THE MIDDLE AGES AND IN MODERN TIMES

The Bulgarian Orthodox Church[14] already had its own patriarchate in the Middle Ages, but lost it in the period of Turkish domination. When in 1870 it established an autonomous exarchate, the result was schism between Sofia and Constantinople. After the death of the exarch Joseph (1877–1915) the state did not permit a new election, and until 1945 the Church was administered by the Holy Synod. A synod convoked by the government in 1921 outlined a reform program, but it could not be realized. An assembly of the bishops, which in 1927 dealt with, among other things, problems of religious instruction and education, saw to the completing of the academy founded at Sofia in 1923, the formation of the clergy, and the ecclesiastical cooperative system. After Bulgaria had been declared a people's republic in 1946, religious instruction in the public schools was abolished, the greatest part of the Church's landed property was confiscated, ecclesiastical social work and ecclesiastical cooperative life were impeded. The protests of Exarch Stojan (1945–48) to the government, his efforts for the imparting of religious instruction in Sunday schools, and his defense of the Christian faith in newspapers and pamphlets led to his removal by the Holy Synod, which was prepared to cooperate with the regime. The new constitution of 1947, with appendixes in 1961 and 1965, and the law on creeds of 1949 completed the separation of Church and state and placed the Churches under strict state supervision. The Holy Synod and the administrators of the exarchate, especially Cyril (1951–53), urged the reestablishment of the Orthodox patriarchate of Bulgaria. A recognized church historian, preacher, and organizer, who had proved his loyalty to the regime by taking part in state organizations and national party and anniversary celebrations, he was elected patriarch in 1953 and held the office until 1970. Most Eastern Churches assented to the elevation in rank, the ecumenical patriarch only in 1961. Cyril tried to parry the state's totalitarian claim by his often scholarly publications, cooperation in the "peace movement," participation in the state celebration in honor of Cyril and Methodius in 1963, completion of the theological academy at Sofia and of the two priests' seminaries still left to the Church,

---

[14] The first Bulgarian patriarchate with its seat at Achrida existed from 927 to 1018, the second at Trnovo from 1235 to 1393. In 1870 the sultan granted the constituting of an independent exarchate, which was not recognized by the patriarchate of Constantinople until 1945.

THE DIVERSITY OF THE INNER LIFE

continuation of an official paper and of ecclesiastical periodicals, and by his foreign journeys, on which he proved to be a promoter of ecumenism. In 1967 he succeeded in obtaining that a few monks might return to the Rila monastery, a Bulgarian national sanctuary and Marian pilgrimage place for a thousand years, which had been closed in 1961 on orders of the government, and had been declared a national memorial spot and been transformed into a tourist attraction. His successor, Maximos (since 1971), heads 6 million faithful, about two-thirds of the total population, with 1,500 priests, who are paid by the state, in 11 metropolitanates in Bulgaria and 2 foreign dioceses. The Church retains 120 monasteries, with ca. 400 monks and nuns, rural farming areas with twenty industries of its own; to it was granted a monopoly of the production and sale of candles, crosses, and devotional objects. But external security is jeopardized by the constant atheistic propaganda, which regards religion as a hindrance to social development and directs the process of overcoming religion.

The Serbian Orthodox[15] strove after the erecting of the Kingdom of the Serbs, Croats, and Slovenes in 1918—renamed the Kingdom of Yugoslavia in 1929—for the restoration of their patriarchate. In 1920 the metropolitanate of Belgrade, patriarchate-in-exile of Karlowitz, the Bosnian, Dalmatian, Macedonian, and the Montenegrin hierarchy united into a uniform Serbian Church, at whose head the metropolitan of Belgrade, Demetrios (1920–30), appeared as patriarch. It lasted almost ten years until the organization and legislation of the Orthodox patriarchate of Serbia were terminated. The tensions between the Orthodox—in 1931 48.7 percent—and the Catholics—in 1931 37.4 percent—led in 1935 to a conflict. The government wanted a concordat with the Holy See but Patriarch Barnabas (1930–37) rejected it. The occupation of Yugoslavia by Germans, Italians, and Bulgarians in 1941, the creation of an independent Croat state with a Catholic majority in the population, in which in 1942 a Croatian Orthodox Church with 1.8 million faithful was established, nationalistic conflicts and partisan struggles impeded the pastoral activity of Patriarch Gabriel V (1938–50), who was imprisoned in 1941, and of his representative, Joseph (1941–46).

Tito's seizure of power in 1944, the founding of the federated People's Republic of Yugoslavia in 1945, which expressed separation of Church and state in the constitution of 31 January 1946, and the policy of the government, which aimed to exclude the Church from public life, produced a struggle against the Church. Patriarch Gabriel V was able to

---

[15] The Serbs had had their own patriarchate in 1351–1459 and 1557–1766, and in 1789 had maintained the autocephaly of their Church.

prevent the union of the Serbian Church with that of Moscow, sought by the patriarchate of Moscow in 1947, and to restrain the association of Orthodox priests, called into existence the same year, which demanded the extension of the rights of the lesser clergy. Under his successor, Vikentij (1950–58), the strained relations with the government improved after the liberation of church leaders condemned in the first postwar years and the filling of vacant sees and parishes by means of the law on the legal status of ecclesiastical communities of 27 May 1953, but the seizure of church property and land, the payment of ecclesiastics and of retired persons by the state, the restrictions on the teaching activity and the number of students of the theological faculty of the University of Belgrade, which in 1952 was transformed into an academy, the support given by Tito to the efforts for independence of the Macedonian Church[16] made clear that the Patriarchal Church was only tolerated. Patriarch German, in office from 1958, tried, relying on the loyalty of broad strata of the population, to make the most of the possibilities left to him. He established theological schools, for example, in the monastery of Krka in Dalmatia in 1965, to provide for the threatening lack of priests, took care for the improvement of professional theological periodicals, and protested against the impeding of religious instruction and the restrictions on the care of souls, in which connection he appealed to the regulations of the constitution of 7 April 1963. After the abrogation of the law on religion of 1953, the individual republics issued laws for their area, which allowed more authority to the local administrative officials than hitherto. The attacks by the Communists against the ecclesiastical press, stepped up since 1972, tightening of censorship, imprisonment of priests, prohibition for youth to take part in the feast of Saint Sava (d. 1235), patron of Serbia, indicate a deterioration of the climate. The approximately reckoned 8 million faithful were cared for at the time by 26 hierarchs—1 patriarch, 2 metropolitans, 22 bishops, and 1 episcopal vicar. In addition to the 21 spheres of jurisdiction at home, there are 5 abroad. The well constructed church organization, with more than 4,000 churches, the 75 monasteries of men and 75 of women, with 350 monks and 800 nuns, and the appearance of periodicals, however, cannot conceal the fact that the Patriarchal Church suffers under the pressure of the regime.

After the abdication of the last tsar, Nicholas II, the Orthodox Church in Russia, which after the abolition of the patriarchate of Moscow (1589–1721) experienced an epoch of state Church regime under the Holy Synod with supervision by a procurator, succeeded in restoring the Moscow patriarchate at its council in the fall of 1917. On 5

---

[16] See below, p. 491.

November 1917 the metropolitan of Moscow, Tikhon,[17] was elected patriarch. The October Revolution of 1917 and the establishing of the Russian Soviet Federated Socialist Republic in 1918—since 1922 the Union of Soviet Socialist Republics—under the dictatorship of the Bolsheviks completely changed the situation in Russia.

The decree of 19 January 1918 completed the separation of Church and state, it declared the possessions of ecclesiastical and religious communities to be the people's property. ARTICLE 13 of the constitution of 10 July 1918 firmly established this principle of separation and granted to all citizens, in addition to liberty of conscience, also the right of antireligious propaganda. The fundamental rejection of religion and the fully conscious attacks on it excluded the Patriarchal Church from public life, restricted it to the ecclesiastical sphere, and exposed hierarchs and clergy to administrative chicanery and calumnies. During the civil war between the Whites and the Reds in September 1919 Patriarch Tikhon forbade ecclesiastics to take part in the political confrontations. But his protest against the confiscation decreed by the government in February 1922 of objects of value and of worship in the churches, from the proceeds of which allegedly the growing famine was to be alleviated, was the occasion for his imprisonment from May 1922 to June 1923. The regime demanded the dissolution of the hierarchy, it expected to split and destroy the Patriarchal Church by means of the "Living Church"[18] that it supported. Because of the news of the execution and imprisoning of many bishops and priests, Tikhon decided to sign a declaration submitted to him, "that from now on I am no longer an enemy of the Soviet Union."[19] Many of the faithful withdrew again from the "Living Church," which existed until 1946. The patriarch's declaration of loyalty and his appeal to the faithful to follow him in this attitude saved the existence of the Patriarchal Church, it is true, but they changed nothing in the intentions of the regime. The three candidates designated by Tikhon (d. 1925) in his last will to take charge of the administration as his representatives after his death were imprisoned or banished. The leadership of the Church was without a patriarch for eighteen years.

[17] Cf. J. Chrysostomus, *Kirchengeschichte Russlands der neuesten Zeit* I; R. Rössler, *Kirche und Revolution in Russland. Patriarch Tichon und der Sowjetstaat* (Cologne 1969); J. Chrysostomus, "Gedanken zum 50. Todestag des Patriarchen Tichon von Moskau und Ganz Russland, 25. März/7. April 1925," *OstkSt* 24(1975), 318–32.

[18] M. B. B., "Der misslungene Versuch zur Vernichtung der Russisch-Orthodoxen Kirche in den Jahren 1922–1923 und die Niederlage des linken Kommunismus," *OstkSt* 22 (1973), 105–49; J. Chrysostomus, "Eine lehrreiche Episode aus der neueren Kirchengeschichte Russlands. Gedanken über den Artikel von A. Krasnov-Levitin über den 'Untergang der Erneuerungsbewegung,'" ibid., 302–15.

[19] J. Chrysostomus, *Kirchengeschichte Russlands der neuesten Zeit* I, 373.

Metropolitan Sergius—deputy patriarchal administrator from 1925 to 1937, patriarchal administrator from 1937 to 1941, and patriarch from 1943 to 1944—was also imprisoned. Because of the intensified persecution of the Church, the appearance of the League of the Militant Atheists, which in 1932 had more than 5 million members, and the threat of further anti-Church measures, Sergius, after his release in March 1927, accommodated the government by a declaration of loyalty, to which he also bound all the faithful. Several bishops did not consent, and there developed the Church of the Catacombs, which has maintained itself until the present. Despite Sergius's subservience, the Church was without rights. The religious law of 8 April 1929 extraordinarily curtailed the possibility of effectiveness of the Churches. A law of 18 May 1929 changed ART. 13 of the constitution in the sense that only freedom of the practice of acts of worship and antireligious propaganda were guaranteed. The closing of churches and monasteries, the imprisoning and deporting of ecclesiastics, the dissolution of congregations in 1928–30 and 1935–37 pointed out the threatened status of the Patriarchal Church,[20] even if in 1937 50 million of the population—27 percent of the total—belonged to it. The occupation of the Baltic states, Bessarabia, and eastern Poland by the Soviet Union improved its situation, because the number of its priests, monasteries, and institutions was increased, but of course they were soon caught in the wake of the persecution. The outbreak of the German-Soviet war on 22 June 1941 produced an unanticipated turn: Sergius called for prayer services, and church collections yielded more than 300 million rubles for armaments. The administration of the patriarchate published a cooperative volume,[21] in which the persecutions of Christians were denied and punishments were traced to political crimes. Stalin honored Sergius's procedure, received him on 4 September 1943, and let him be elected patriarch by nineteen hierarchs on 8 September. On 23 September a sort of concordat came into existence, according to which the Church could establish two ecclesiastical academies and eight seminaries for priests. The state Department of Churches for the Affairs of the Orthodox Church,[22] which took up its activity on 10 October 1943, was supposed to foster further normalization and supervise the exact observance of the pertinent governmental directives.

[20] While the Orthodox Church in Russia on the eve of the First World War counted over 54,174 churches, 51,105 priests, 350 monasteries of men, and 473 monasteries of women, there were in the Patriarchal Church of Moscow in 1939 only 5,225 churches, 5,665 priests, and 37 monasteries.

[21] *Die Wahrheit in Russland* (Moscow 1942).

[22] In 1943–60 it was directed by C. G. Karpov; his successor is W. A. Kurojedev. They continued the supervisory office of the Procurator of the Holy Synod in tsarist Russia.

The metropolitan of Leningrad, Alexis,[23] became Sergius's successor. As three-time bearer of the Order of the Red Workers' Banner and recipient of the medal for the defense of Leningrad, he cooperated intimately with the government. He was elected patriarch (1945–70) in February 1945 at a council in Moscow in which forty-six bishops took part. The church statute adopted even before his election by this assembly strengthened the centralization of ecclesiastical administration. The accommodating attitude of the regime must be referred to the support which Alexis gave it in foreign and domestic policy, for example, in the dissolution of the Uniate Church in the Ukraine and Podcarpathia in 1946–50, the entering into relations with other Orthodox Churches, and his championing of the Soviet peace ideology. Until the death in 1953 of Stalin, to whom the patriarch dedicated a pious work of condolence, and in the years of de-Stalinization the Orthodox Church was able to develop within the limits set for it by the state. Through the releasing of ecclesiastics from concentration camps, the restoration of confiscated churches, the reconstruction of the hierarchy, the formation of clerics in seminaries and by correspondence courses, several propaganda journeys of the patriarch outside the country, and the strengthening of the activity of the ecclesiastical foreign office, which strove for influence on Orthodox emigrant Churches, the position of the Patriarchal Church was stabilized within and outside the Soviet Union. The *Žurnal Moskovskoj Patriarchii*,[24] appearing since the end of the Second World War, supplied the clergy with valuable information and stimulation through its contributions on church history and dogmatic and pastoral theology and its comprehensive news on the life of Orthodoxy and of the ecumenical movement. At the Ecclesiastical Academy in the Monastery of the Holy Trinity at Sagorsk near Moscow and in Leningrad there was given a qualified theological education. But this inner consolidation was endangered by the Pan Union Society founded in 1947 for the dissemination of political and scientific knowledge, which renewed militant atheism through publications and meetings, and the decree of the Central Committee of the Communist Party of the Soviet Union on 10 November 1954 on the failures in the implementation of scientific-atheistic propaganda among the population. Under Khruschev, who was secretary general of the Central Committee from 1953, and minister president from 1958 to

---

[23] J. Müller, *Patriarch Alexius* (Berlin 1967); G. Seide, "In Memoriam. Zum Tod des Hochheiligen Patriarchen von Moskau und ganz Russland am 17. April 1970," *Kyrios,* n.s., 10 (1970), 130–48.

[24] R. Rössler, "Das Journal des Moskauer Patriarchats als Spiegel kirchlicher Entwicklung in der Sowjetunion (seit dem Zweiten Weltkrieg)," *Jahrbücher für Geschichte Osteuropas,* n.s., 4 (1956), 26–63.

1964, and who died in 1971, there began a new persecution of the Churches. From 1959 to 1964, in addition to systematic campaigns of defamation, there were trials of higher and lower clerics, who were burdened with fines for crimes, the closing of ca. 10,000 churches out of 20,000, 50 monasteries out of 68, and 5 seminaries out of 8. The protests of the patriarch and the remonstrances of the ecclesiastical opposition against administrative measures of local officials, which was written down underground in the *Samizdat* literature,[25] had as a consequence that the state Department of Churches under Kurojedev sharpened the restrictions against the Church, Metropolitan Nikoly, who had directed the Church's foreign office since 1944 and was among the closest co-workers of Alexis, was replaced by Bishop Nikodim, and the Council of Ministers of the Union of Socialist Soviet Republics in 1961 forced the changing of ART. 4 of the status of the Church approved in 1945, whereby the administration of the congregations was withdrawn from the parish priests. Nikodim, since 1963 metropolitan of Leningrad and Novgorod, quickly gained influence in the Holy Synod and tried to preserve the interests of Russian Orthodoxy by elastic negotiations with the state Department of Churches and his positive relationship to the World Council of Churches[26] and to the Roman Catholic Church.[27] When in 1970 Patriarch Alexis died at the age of ninety-three, he was regarded as one of those with the best prospects of succeeding him.

At the council in Moscow in 1971 the patriarchal representative Pimen was elected patriarch by acclamation. He continued the policy of his predecessor in order not to endanger the minimum of existence assured to the Church by the state. His support of the Communist World Peace Movement, his many journeys to foreign countries, on

[25] *Die hektographierten "Selbstveröffentlichungen": Samizdat, Cronaca di una vita nuova nell'URSS* (Milan 1974); R. Medwedjew, ed., *Aufzeichnungen aus dem sowjetischen Untergrund. Texte aus der Moskauer Samisdat-Zeitschrift "Das XX. Jahrhundert"* (Hamburg 1977).

[26] In 1961 the Moscow patriarchate was admitted to the World Council of Churches, which it had earlier opposed in polemics.

[27] Nikodim, by his exertions for the ending of the conflict between the Patriarchal Church and the Old Believers separated from it (Raskolniki), brought about at the Moscow National Council in 1971 the annulment of the excommunication pronounced on them in 1666. In 1971 he gave up the direction of the Office for Foreign Affairs, which Metropolitan Juvenalij assumed. Nikodim became chairman of the office for relations among the Orthodox sister Churches and other Christian Churches and communities. In the same year he became secretary general of the Christian Peace Movement. In 1974 he obtained the exarchate for Western Europe. In July 1975 Pope Paul VI received him with the delegation headed by him from the Moscow patriarchate. In December 1975 the fifth plenary assembly of the World Council elected him as its president.

which he tried to unite the Orthodox Churches in the People's republics, the Middle East, and the free world closer to himself, his emphasized concern for Orthodox tradition and liturgy, his assurance that normal relations existed between Church and state in the Soviet Union, were unable to mask the danger to the Orthodox faith. The defamation of religious feasts, which were said to be based on imagined events and myths and which were replaced by Socialist celebrations, the intensifying of the antireligious propaganda, which was seen in the tightening of ideological instruction in adult education programs, at universities, in the army, and in the efforts of 10,000 functionaries of atheism, the government's methods of suppression, which, among other things, represented the religious education of children as assault, the sending of believers to psychiatric clinics, and protests of citizens' rights groups, which stood up for human rights and religious liberty, made clear that the Patriarchal Church could not freely develop. The religious law enacted in June 1975[28] codified the guidelines, long expressed in secret instructions, of the Soviet state-Church, further blocked off the living space of the Churches, manipulated the life of congregations, and intensified the competition of the state's offices of supervision. About 30 million faithful—12 percent of the total population—are aware of their difficult situation and endure the restrictions imposed on them. The possibility of action of bishops and priests is curtailed, but the overwhelming majority of the clergy[29] strive as far as possible to proclaim the Gospel and celebrate the liturgy and demonstrate the unbroken will to live of the Patriarchal Church. In addition to 45 dioceses—10 metropolitans, 12 archbishops, and 25 bishops—in the Soviet Union, there belong to it the Ukrainian exarchate with 14 dioceses—2 metropolitans, 8 archbishops, and 4 bishops—the exarchates in Western Europe—in addition to Exarch Nikodim, 1 metropolitan, 1 archbishop, and 2 bishops—Central Europe—1 metropolitan and 2 archbishops—and Central and South America—5 bishops.

The Rumanian patriarchate arose after the First World War through the merger of the Rumanian national Church with the Churches of

[28] G. Simon, "Verhärtung durch Festschreibung. Zum neuen Religionsgesetz in der Sowjetunion," HK 30 (1976), 263–301; idem, Das sowjetische Religionsgesetz vom Juni 1975 (Cologne 1976).

[29] But cf. J. Chrysostomus, Die Problematik der heutigen russischen Kirche, 213: "There is still another difficulty: it is quite possible, even likely, that the government will infiltrate its people, that is, those who serve the state rather than the Church, into the ranks of the clergy. The faithful are annoyed and made insecure by these facts, hence they occasionally condemn the entire hierarchy which tolerates this. But what can the hierarchy of an imprisoned Church undertake against this if it does not want to lose the last supports of church life in Russia? Therein really lies today the balance in the question of the problem of the Moscow patriarchate and its entire tragedy."

Karlowitz, Sibin, and Czernowitz.[30] The difficulties which ensued in the Kingdom, almost doubled in size by the union of various territories, were noticeable also in the ecclesiastical sphere. The constitution of 1923 declared Orthodoxy the prevailing Church and decreed a uniform organization with five metropolitanates. It was realized by a law and the statute of the Rumanian Orthodox Church of 1925. Its synod proposed the elevation of the metropolitan see of Bucharest to the rank of a patriarchate, and the establishment took place on 27 February 1925. On 27 September Miron, metropolitan of Bucharest, was solemnly enthroned as first patriarch (1925–39) with the assent of the ecumenical patriarch of Constantinople. From 1927 to 1930 he belonged to the government's Council of Three and in the last years of his life he took over the post of minister president. Through his participation in the forming of a uniform canon law, the assimilation of the varied structures of the metropolitanates subordinate to him, his championship of a basic study of theology and his openness to the ecumenical movement, he deserved well of his country. He was succeeded by the metropolitan of Moldavia, Nikodim (1939–48), who as abbot and bishop had worked for the renewal of Rumanian monasticism. The Second World War, in which Rumania had to cede frontier areas, recovered parts, in 1944 was occupied by Soviet troops, the Communist regime since 1945, and the proclamation of the People's Republic of Rumania in 1947 impeded the carrying out of planned reforms. Nikodim urged the faithful to cooperate in the reconstruction of the state.

As his successor was elected Justinian (1948–77), metropolitan of Moldavia. As a versatile diplomat, a purposeful ecclesiastical politician, and man of confidence of the regime,[31] he approved the coexistence between the Orthodox Church and the Communist state leadership. In the church statute of 1948 he was able to extend his competence, even if the synod came under state supervision. In 1948 he played a decisive role in the forcible union of 1.5 million Uniate Rumanians with the Orthodox Church. He strengthened the patriarchate by directives to the clergy on a social apostolate suited to the changed circumstances, reform of monasticism, rules for preaching, building of the ecclesiastical press, and deepening of theological formation. Of course, he had also to submit to serious interventions in church life. The suppression of the Ministry of Worship in 1957 and the subordination of the Church to the Department of Worship introduced, with a continuous bombard-ment of atheistic propaganda and the spread of calumnies, a persecution

---

[30] Cf. E. C. Suttner, 50 *Jahre rumänisches Patriarchat* (1975), 136–60.

[31] Justinian had personal relations with the Communist party leader, Gheorgiu Dej (1952–55) minister president, from 1955 first Secretary of the party, from 1961 chairman of the Council of State, d. 1965).

of the Church, in which many monasteries were closed and many monks and nuns were arrested.[32] Temporarily, the patriarch was under house arrest. Nevertheless, he held to his reform program. In 1966 the Department of Worship approved a new regulation for theological studies, and in 1967 a modification of the church statute, which made possible the completion of the hierarchy. If from 1970 on the state's influencing of the synod was extended, and in 1974 a law decreed the secularization of all articles of art still in the possession of the churches and in private ownership, the patriarch's self-assurance remained unbroken. Justinian's cooperation in the Communist Peace Movement, in Pan-Orthodox conferences, and in the World Council of Churches, and his visits to foreign Orthodox and Catholic Church leaders consolidated his general esteem. On the occasion of its fiftieth jubilee celebration in 1975 more than 14 million faithful belonged to the Patriarchal Church. Its hierarchy consisted of 4 metropolitanates in Rumania, with 2 archbishops, 6 bishops, and 8 episcopal vicars and of 3 foreign areas of jurisdiction,[33] with 1 archbishop, 1 bishop, and 1 episcopal vicar. Two theological institutes and 7 seminaries care for the recruits of the clergy, numbering ca. 9,000. Several periodicals are published by the patriarchal administration and individual dioceses. Justinian's loyalty contributed to this, that the Orthodox Church in Rumania, in comparison to the other countries under Communist rule, has to some extent preserved its previous situation. In June 1977 Justin, former metropolitan of Moldavia, took up his legacy as fourth Rumanian patriarch.

OTHER ORTHODOX CHURCHES

In the course of the centuries, especially in the last decades, a series of Churches have separated from the historically developed and already described structure of Orthodoxy and become autonomous.

In the Mediterranean Area

The Orthodox Church of Cyprus has been autocephalous since the Council of Ephesus in 431.[34] Archbishop Cyril III (1916–33) was recognized by the British occupation authorities, who in 1925 declared the island a crown colony, as ethnarch, but came into conflict with him,

[32] Between 1959 and 1971 the number of monasteries and sketes (monastic settlements) dropped from 1,657 to 575, the number of nuns from 4,000 to 1,493, the number of priests from 10,153 to 8,564.

[33] There is question of the Rumanian Orthodox missionary diocese in the United States, the Rumanian Orthodox archdiocese of Western Europe, and the Orthodox Catholic diocese of France, which was established in 1937 and in 1972 made the motion for admission to the Rumanian patriarchate.

[34] Cf. Hippolytos, "Die Autokephale Apostolische Orthodoxe Kirche Cyperns," *Ekklesia* X (1941), 177–229.

because he supported the national Greek unity movement, *Enosis,* which sought a union with Greece. An uprising that broke out in 1931 was suppressed, and two bishops and various clerics had to leave the country. From 1933 to 1947 the archbishopric was administered by the chairman of the Holy Synod, Bishop Leontios of Paphos, as administrator, who could not be elected as archbishop until 1947. Under his successors, Makarios II (1947–50) and Makarios III (1950–77),[35] the Greeks—80 percent of the total population—fought for their independence. In the disturbances of 1955–56 Makarios III and other ecclesiastics were banished. After the election of the archbishop, who had returned from exile in 1959, as president of the republic and the proclamation of Cyprus as an independent state in 1960, a certain calm ensued. In the next years Makarios III tried to revise the constitution of Cyprus of 16 August 1960, which had granted certain rights to the Turkish minority—20 percent of the total population—in favor of the Greek Cypriots. The countermeasures of the Turkish inhabitants produced struggles in 1963, which could only be ended in 1965 by the use of United Nations troops. Makarios III recognized that the union of Cyprus with Greece could not be accomplished. Murders and attempted uprisings, behind which stood the Greek military government, caused a crisis which led to war between Greece and Turkey. In the course of it, the Turks conquered the northeastern part—40 percent—of the island. Makarios had deposed three bishops at a synod in March 1973 because of the abandonment of *Enosis,* but in July he was confirmed at a large synod as archbishop and president of the state. The ecclesiastical organization carried out by him in 1973 for 450,000 faithful, with 1 archbishopric, 6 metropolitanates, and 650 clergy, his efforts for the building of new churches, his care for the better paying and pensioning of ecclesiastics, the transformation of the minor seminary in Nicosia into a theological faculty, his care of 11 monasteries with 89 monks and 75 nuns, and his receptiveness to the ecumenical movement characterized his concept of his pastoral office.

As regards the number of the faithful—ca. 7 million—the Orthodox Church in Greece belonged, after the patriarchates of Moscow, Rumania, and Serbia, to the four largest Orthodox communities of the present. Only gradually were the Holy Synod and the archbishops[36] of the day able to loosen their dependence on the state's ecclesiastical domination, beginning with the church constitution of 1923, which expanded the ecclesiastical self-administration under Archbishop Chry-

---

[35] K. Kerber, *Makarios Kirchenfürst oder?* (Diessen/Ammersee 1964); P. N. Vanezis, *Makarios. Faith and Power,* 2d ed. (London, New York, and Toronto 1972).
[36] Differing from the situation among the Slavic Orthodox Churches, the archbishop of Greece is above the metropolitan.

sostom I (1923–38), through protracted confrontations because of the method of election of the archbishop and bishops and the competence of the Holy Synod, down to the church statute decreed in 1969 by the military government, but it was annulled in 1974. Archbishops Chrysanthius (1938–41) and Damaskinos (1941–49) eliminated the internal church damages which the Second World War and the civil war planned by the Communist partisans had caused. During the negotiations between state and Church on the reduction of the number of episcopal sees there occurred in 1965 a conflict in which Archbishop Chrysostom II (1962–67) was supplanted by the Archimandrite Jerome. As a university professor of canon law and practical theology, he had favored a separation of Church and state, as archbishop he authoritatively took up reform measures which his predecessors had already advised, but the opposition to his procedure and his dependence on the military regime caused his retirement in 1973. His successor, Archbishop Seraphim (from 1974), tried to bridge the gulf between his electors and Jerome's adherents and to realize the already started raising of the educational level and living standard of the clergy and the renewal of the monastic life.[37] He confronted the problems which the industrialization of Greece, the de-Christianization and the migration of the population presented to the Church. Orthodoxy is still deeply rooted among the people. The archbishopric is divided into 76 metropolitanates. Two faculties at Athens and Saloniki and 12 theological schools care for the training of the clerical recruitment, for which, however, not enough candidates apply. The brotherhood ZOË, social and charitable communities, and numerous periodicals promote church life.

In contrast to the Greek Church, which has the ability to develop freely, the Orthodox Church is completely suppressed in Albania. It had proclaimed its autocephaly in 1922, and in 1937 this was recognized by the ecumenical patriarch; in 1938 it numbered ca. 200,000 faithful—10 percent of the population—with 1 metropolitan, 4 bishops, 200 priests, 29 monasteries, and 2 seminaries. But after the Communist seizure of power in 1946 it, like all other religions in the People's Republic of Albania, fell into complete dependence on the regime. Archbishop Christopher (1937–49) was deposed; his two successors, Paisios (1949–66) and Damian (1966–73)—the latter died after six years in prison—could do nothing against the tight control exercised over the Church. Hoxha, secretary general of the Albanian Communist Party, in 1967 declared Albania to be the first atheistic state in the world, had all laws annulled which regulated relations between

[37] 1973: 174 monasteries of men with 798 monks, 209 monasteries of women with 2,552 nuns. Their number is retrograde.

state and Church, and intensified the struggle against religious traditions. All churches were closed and turned into clubhouses, markets, and factories, the bishops[38] were imprisoned, and the ecclesiastical organization was shattered. A few priests still work underground.

After the Balkan wars of 1913–14 the Orthodox Macedonians were under Serb, Bulgarian, and Greek ecclesiastical authority; most of them lived in Yugoslavia. Since 1944 they have worked for the autonomy of the archbishopric of Achrida, incorporated in 1767 into the patriarchate of Constantinople. In 1958–59 Serbian Patriarch German had to assent to the declaration of autonomy of a Macedonian ecclesiastical assembly and the election of his auxiliary bishop, Dositej, as archbishop of Achrida and Macedonia. When the Orthodox Church in Macedonia, in an understanding with the state authorities, proclaimed its autocephaly, there were tensions with the Serbian mother Church. Archbishop Dositej completed the church organization with 6 metropolitanates and 1 abroad, 600,000 faithful, 300 clerics, and 1 seminary, introduced the Macedonian language into the liturgy, and made ecumenical contacts. In 1975 the Church adopted a constitution, but the development of its life was impeded by Yugoslav legislation, which intensified antireligious decrees in the Republic of Macedonia in 1976.

In connection with the self-administration of Crete at the end of the nineteenth century, the see of Gostyna became an autonomous Orthodox metropolitanate with its seat at Heraklion in 1900. From the political annexation of Crete by Greece in 1913, the Orthodox have had to observe not only the guidelines of the patriarchate of Constantinople but also those of the Greek national Church. In 1967 the Orthodox Church in Crete[39] was elevated by act of the patriarch to an archbishopric with seven metropolitanates and was granted partial autonomy, which it might develop into autocephaly. Archbishop Eugenios is responsible for 450,000 faithful, 335 priests, 34 monasteries with 187 monks and 74 nuns. The Orthodox academy on Crete developed into a center for adult education. After the closing of the patriarchal school at Chalkis,[40] the university at Heraklion, administered in common by the Greek state and the Church, assumed its functions in 1973.

[38] Two Albanian bishops still work in North America but only among the emigrants: Bishop Stefan subordinated the Albanian Orthodox Diocese in America directed by him with his seat in South Boston to the Orthodox Church in America in 1971. Bishop Mark, with his seat at Jamaica Plain, Massachusetts, is in union with the Greek Orthodox archdiocese of North America, which belongs to the ecumenical patriarchate.
[39] A. Alevisopoulos, "Die orthodoxe Kirche von Kreta," *Wegzeichen. Festgabe zum 60. Geburtstag von Hermenegild M. Biedermann OSA,* ed. by E. C. Suttner and C. Patock (Würzburg 1971), 233–44.
[40] See above, p. 475.

In East Central Europe and the Far East

The Orthodox Church in Finland[41] was until 1917–18 a component of the Russian Church; in the Finnish republic established after the First World War it was granted rights alongside the Lutheran state Church. After the patriarch of Moscow, Tikhon, had recognized its autonomy in 1918, the church leadership subjected itself to the ecumenical patriarchate, which in 1923 confirmed its autonomy. In 1939–44 the diocese of Karelia, in which were a majority of the Orthodox congregations, was incorporated into the Soviet Union. After 1945 the exertions of the patriarchate of Moscow to extend its supremacy over the Finnish Church collapsed. Archbishop Paavali, in office since 1960, with two dioceses and two monasteries subject to him, is trying to restore the ecclesiastical life of the 60,000 faithful—1.3 percent of the population—and to reduce the growing number of mixed marriages between Orthodox and Lutherans.

Between the two world wars there lived in Poland almost 4 million Orthodox—12 percent of the population—who in 1923 merged into the Orthodox Church in Poland; in 1924–25 the ecumenical patriarch assented to its declaration of autocephaly. The ecclesiastical policy of the Polish government opposed the national Ukrainian and White Russian tendencies toward the autonomy of the Orthodox population. In 1938–39, 130 churches and two monasteries were destroyed. The partition of Poland in 1939 and the German occupation of the Ukraine in 1941–44 split Polish Orthodoxy into the Church in the *Gouvernement General* and two Churches in the Ukraine.[42] In the areas occupied by the Soviets, the Orthodox were incorporated into the patriarchate of Moscow. Under Metropolitan Dionisij (1923–48, d. 1961), who was removed from office by the government of the People's Republic of Poland because of his collaboration with the Germans, the numbers of the Orthodox decreased to 350,000 after the cession of East Poland to the Soviet Union, but in 1948 it increased by the coming over of 100,000 Uniate Ukrainians after the forcible annulment of the Union of Brest of 1595–96. In 1948 Patriarch Alexis of Moscow possessed supreme jurisdiction over Polish Orthodoxy and in 1951 he consented to its autocephaly. Metropolitan Makarij (1951–61) created a new church organization for the Orthodox scattered through resettlement throughout Poland with the archbishopric of Warsaw-Bielsk and the three bishoprics of Bialystok-Gdansk, Lodz-Pomerania, and Wroclaw-

---

[41] T. Rohner, "Die orthodoxe Kirche Finnlands," *OstkSt* 12 (1963), 314–25.
[42] F. Heyer, *Die orthodoxe Kirche in der Ukraine 1917 bis 1945* (Cologne-Braunsfeld 1953).

Szczecin, which was completed, with the aid of the Holy Synod, by his successors, Timoteusz (1961–62), Jerzy (1962–64), and Stefan (1964–69). Since 1970 Metropolitan Vassilij has been its head, with ca. 400,000 faithful, 225 congregations, and one monastery each for monks and nuns. The process of integration of the Russian, Ukrainian, and White Russian congregations is accelerated by two theological educational centers in Warsaw and Chylice and by publications in Polish, Russian, and Ukrainian.

The uniting of the Hungarian, Russian, and Serbian Orthodox remaining in Hungary after the First World War caused great difficulties, since the patriarchates of Constantinople, Serbia, and Rumania claimed rights of jurisdiction. In 1947 the Orthodox Church in Hungary—40,000 faithful, 50 congregations, 37 ecclesiastics—was taken over by the patriarchate of Moscow, which entrusted the church administration to an archimandrite and in 1949 granted it autonomy. In 1959 it acquired a Hungarian ritual.

The Orthodox in Czechoslovakia united, after the First World War, two smaller groups in Bohemia-Moravia (ca. 20,000 faithful) and in Slovakia (9,000) and a larger group of 112,000 in Carpatho-Ukraine. Most congregations belonged to the Serbian, a few to the ecumenical patriarchate. In the German protectorate of Bohemia-Moravia and in Slovakia they were forbidden during the Second World War. In the Czechoslovak People's Republic they revived and in 1947 they experienced a considerable growth through the repatriation of 30,000 Volhynia Czechs and in 1949–50 through the incorporation of almost 350,000 Uniate Catholics from the forcibly suppressed dioceses of Mukačevo and Prešov. In 1946 the Orthodox Church in Czechoslovakia was incorporated into the patriarchate of Moscow, which sent to Prague as its exarch Jelevferij, who in 1948 became archbishop. In 1951 Patriarch Alexej released him from his obedience and declared the Church's autocephaly. The metropolitans Jelevferij (1951–55), Joann (1956–64), and Dorotej (since 1964) unified the church organization (4 dioceses) and expanded the Orthodox theological faculty in Prešov and the ecclesiastical press. When the Communist Party leadership under Dubček in 1968 allowed the reconstitution of the Uniate Catholic Church, more than 200 congregations of Orthodoxy were dissolved and the number of its faithful—Czechs, Slovaks, Ukrainians, Russians—dropped to 100,000. In addition, from 1969 the Orthodox fell under strict control of the officials of the State Church Department and, like all other Churches, were subjected to the influence of increasing antireligious propaganda.

Out of the Russian Orthodox missionary work in the Far East grew two independent Churches in China and Japan. After the outbreak of the revolution in 1917 many Orthodox Russians remained in China[43] and Manchuria; their centers in Charbin, Peking, and Shanghai exercised a certain power of attraction even on the native population. In 1920 Tikhon, patriarch of Moscow, entrusted the direction of the Church to Archbishop Innokentij (1902–31). Through the influx of refugees from Lithuania, White Russia, and other parts of the Soviet Union, who subordinated themselves to the Russian Foreign Church, the church organization was expanded for 200,000 faithful. The juxtaposition of various jurisdictions, political confusion, civil wars, and the proclamation of the People's Republic of China in 1949 induced a large part of the Russian faithful to emigrate to North and South America and Australia. The Russian Foreign Church lost all its property in China and Manchuria. The patriarchate of Moscow appointed Archbishop Victor of Peking as exarch (1950–56), gave the see of Shanghai to the Chinese Bishop Simeon, who had been ordained in Moscow by Patriarch Alexej, and 1957 granted autonomy to the Orthodox Church in China, with five bishops and 20,000 faithful. Its head, the Chinese Bishop Basileios (1957–62), resided in Peking. In his time there began, after the expulsion of all Russian clerics, the closing of churches. During the Cultural Revolution of 1966–69 all churches were destroyed or deprived of their purpose, and the church organization was shattered. It cannot be ascertained whether the Chinese clergy survived the persecution of Christians and how they operate underground.

The beginnings of the Orthodox Church in Japan go back to the Russian clergy working in Tokyo at the embassy after 1861. In the period between the wars it was incorporated into the Russian Foreign Church and in 1939 produced its own constitution. From 1945 the patriarchate of Moscow strove to attach the congregations again to itself. In 1961, on the occasion of the centennial celebration, it sent a delegation to Tokyo and in 1967 appointed Bishop Nikoly as metropolitan. In 1970 it granted autonomy to the Church in Japan, with 1 archbishop, 2 bishops, 38 priests, and ca. 40,000 faithful.

FOREIGN CHURCHES

The number of Orthodox Christians outside the original lands of the Eastern Churches is estimated as 4 million. About one-half belong to the jurisdictions already described, especially in North and South America, Australia, and various Western European nations. In addition, emigrant Russians, Ukrainians, and White Russians have set up autonomous Churches, especially in America.

[43] G. Seide, "Die Russisch-Orthodoxe Kirche in China und in der Mandschurei seit dem Jahre 1918," *OstkSt* 25 (1976), 166–92.

The Russian Orthodox Church outside Russia, which, founded in Constantinople, designated itself as autocephalous in 1920, in 1921 transferred its seat to Karlowitz,[44] in 1944 to Munich, and in 1955 to Jordanville, New York, in the United States. It includes many congregations which reject the atheistic government of their homeland and, despite several splinterings, still maintains itself. In 1963 and 1972 respectively the Bulgarian Orthodox Foreign Church in America and the Rumanian Orthodox Missionary Diocese in the Western Hemisphere joined it. Since 1964 the Metropolitan Filaret in New York is the head of the Russian Orthodox Foreign Church, with 7 dioceses in North America, 3 in South America, 3 in Europe, and 1 in Australia-New Zealand, 22 monasteries, and 1 theological educational center at Jordanville, its intellectual center, which also publishes two periodicals. In addition, individual congregations in Africa, Asia, Europe, and the United States have subjected themselves to it. Its hierarchy—2 metropolitans, 11 archbishops, 5 bishops, and 1 episcopal vicar—and 150,000 faithful are unanimous in their rejection of antireligious Communism, but their notion of the Church, their claim to represent all Russian emigrants in their synods, and their isolated position in the totality of Orthodoxy jeopardize their future.

The Orthodox Church in America, whose beginnings lie in the Russian mission to Alaska at the end of the eighteenth century, in 1919 made the first moves to its autonomy, declared its autonomy in 1924 and its autocephaly in 1970. The patriarchate of Moscow, which in 1931 and later wished in vain to restore union with it, consented, whereas the ecumenical patriarchate refused. Metropolitan Irenej, since 1965 archbishop of New York, since 1970 first hierarch of the autocephalous Church, and the Holy Synod direct 11 dioceses[45]—6 metropolitans, 7 bishops, 800,000 faithful—3 theological seminaries, 4 monasteries, and a comprehensive ecclesiastical press organization. In the liturgy, besides Church Slavonic and English, Albanian, Greek, Rumanian, Spanish, and the native tongue of Alaska are used.

Emigrant White Russians, with reference to the autocephaly proclaimed by Metropolitan Melchisedek at Minsk in 1922, established the White Russian Orthodox Church in Exile in 1948. At its council in May 1972, 39 delegates of congregations in the United States, Canada, Belgium, and England elected Archbishop Andrei of Cleveland as metropolitan, assisted by an episcopal vicar for the pastoral care of 5,000 faithful, and decided on a constitution.

The Ukrainian Orthodox Foreign Church in 1973 united three

[44] It called itself the Synodal Church of Karlowitz.
[45] Under it is also the Albanian archdiocese of America.

Ukrainian church groups in an independent unity: The Ukrainian-Greek Orthodox Church in Canada, which had originated in 1918 and had declared itself autocephalous in 1951 with its first metropolitan Hilarion, is administered since 1975 by Metropolitan Mstyslav, in office since 1969, of the autocephalous Ukrainian Orthodox Church in Exile—3 dioceses in Australia, England, and Western Europe, and 20,000 faithful—since 1971 also metropolitan of the Ukrainian Orthodox Church in the United States and South America—1 archbishop, 2 bishops, and 130,000 faithful.

In the last years all Orthodox emigrant Churches tended to a comprehensive church organization, with the aim of creating a patriarchate for America. The membership of many congregations in their mother Church, the persistence of national peculiarities, and the consolidating of the independent Churches in America that had grown in the twentieth century allowed at the time no prospect for realizing this plan.

The Orthodox are aware of the fact of their fragmentation. From an all Orthodox Council,[46] which the patriarch Athenagoras had urged in 1961, they expected a clarification of basic theological questions and problems of pastoral care, of the canon law organization of the diaspora, of their relations to one another and to the ecumenical patriarchate, and of their honorary rank and attitude to the *ecumene*. The prosynodal conference at Chambésy in 1971 drew up a catalogue of more than one-hundred themes, which was restricted and made more precise at the Orthodox Academy on Crete in 1974 and at the first preconciliar conference at Chambésy in 1976.

The Eastern Pre-Chalcedonian National Churches

To this group belong two Nestorian Churches and several Monophysite Churches: the West Syrian Jacobite, the Syrian Orthodox in India with its branches, the Coptic, the Ethiopian, and the Armenian.

THE NESTORIAN CHURCHES

The Apostolic Catholic Church of the East, as the self-designation of the Nestorian or Assyrian Orthodox Church officially reads, has never recovered from the crisis into which the First World War threw it. After the death of Patriarch Simon XX Paul (1918–20) he was succeeded by

---

[46] F. W. Fernau, "Die Ostkirche im Vorfeld ihres Konzils. Konstitutionelle Gegenwartsprobleme der Orthodoxie," *Ökumenische Rundschau* 20 (1971), 140–57; D. Papandreou, "Zur Vorbereitung der Panorthodoxen Synode," *Una Sancta* 29 (1974), 161–165; R. Stupperich, "Die Heilige oder Grosse Orthodoxe Synode," *Kirche im Osten* 17 (1974), 180f.; H. J. Härtel, "Die erste vorkonziliare panorthodoxe Konferenz in Chambésy," *Der christliche Osten* 32 (1977), 83–89 and 92.

his twelve-year-old brother, Simon XXI Jesse (1920–73), who was first sent to England for his theological formation. The Assyrians, who had settled in northern Iraq and along the Syrian frontier, were exposed to new persecutions in Iraq in 1933–36, and many emigrated to the United States. From 1940 the patriarch resided at Chicago, from 1954 at San Francisco. In 1961–62 he visited his congregations in southern India, where in 1907 Uniate Thomas Christians, as descendants of adherents of Bishop Mellos, had joined the Nestorian Church as Mellusians, and in Lebanon and Iran, whereas entry into Iraq and Syria was denied him. He did not succeed in recovering his authority, shaken by his decades-long absence. When in 1964, without a synodal decision, from San Francisco he decreed liturgical innovations by curtailing the length of Lent and introducing the Gregorian Calendar, the result was a schism. In 1968 the Mellusian Bishop Thomas Darmo of Trichur was elected patriarch by his opponents, but he died a year later. In 1970 there occurred an understanding between the Iraqi government and the Nestorians, who in 1933 and 1961 had taken part in the Kurds' struggle for freedom. All churches expropriated or destroyed in the last five decades were to be given back or rebuilt. The esteem of Simon XXI Jesse seemed to become consolidated after his visit in Iraq, but criticism of his stay abroad did not end. The desire for his return became stronger when the dissatisfaction of many Nestorians became noticeable in their passing over to the Jacobite Church and the Uniate Chaldeans. In 1973 the patriarch gave up his office and married the same year. A synod in Lebanon deposed him, laicized him, and deprived him of the power to dispose of all church property.

Thereby the Nestorian Old Church of the East gained the prospect of uniting all Nestorian groups in Iraq, Iran, Lebanon, India, Syria, Turkey, the Soviet Union, the United States, and on Cyprus—ca. 100,000 faithful. Since 1969 Catholicos-Patriarch Addai II has worked for this end from Baghdad.

THE MONOPHYSITE CHURCHES

The West Syrian Jacobite Church is subject to the patriarch of Antioch and the entire East. The title recalls the flowering of the Syrian Orthodox Church in the early Middle Ages. The patriarchs, who after the First World War stabilized ecclesiastical matters in the Middle East and had to struggle with the movement for autonomy of the Indian daughter Church, removed their residence from Diarbekr to Homs in 1932 and to Damascus in 1959. Ignatius XXXVIII Ephraem (1933–57) acquired merit as a church historian, founder of a seminary, and through the building of schools and the printing of liturgical books. In 1953 he erected a special eparchy for Jacobites who had emigrated to the United States. His successor, Ignatius XXXIX Jacob III Severus (from 1957), united more closely by means of repeated visitation journeys his congregations in Iraq, Jordan, Lebanon, North and South America, southern India, and in the hills of Tur 'Abdin in southeastern Turkey—ca. 120,000 faithful. He took an interest in the Turkish foreign workers scattered in the diaspora—in the German Federal Republic, the Netherlands, and Switzerland. Since 1964 he has been assisted by a lay council of twelve members, which takes care of financial, technical administrative, and educational questions. Furthermore, he championed a union of all Monophysite Churches and made contacts with representatives of Orthodox and other Christian Churches. The erecting of churches, monasteries, and schools are signs of a certain revival of this Patriarchal Church.

The Syrian Christians in South India, for whom the collective name of Thomas Christians is often employed, are today split into fifteen different communities.[47] Conflicts between the Jacobite Thomas Christians and the West Syrian patriarchate of Antioch led in 1911 to the independence of the Syrian Orthodox Malabar (Malankara) Church.[48] The Indian metropolitan Dionysius VI (1908–34), from 1912 catholicos of the East, accorded to the patriarch of Antioch only a primacy of honor. Efforts for reconciliation of the two Churches failed. The ecclesiastical constitution issued under Catholicos Mar Basileios III George II (1929–62, d. 1964) deprived the patriarch of any administrative function in India. Difficulties and litigation, prolonged for decades, over church property between the majority of the faithful in the Malabar Church and the minority, which clung to union with the patriarch, produced a tense atmosphere. In 1950 there ensued a certain understanding, which was confirmed by the preparations for the nineteenth centennial Thomas Celebration celebrated in 1952 by all Christian denominations.[49] The two struggling groups in 1955 recognized the patriarch of Antioch as the highest spiritual authority and agreed on the subordination of the faithful in South India to the catholicos residing at Kottayam. In 1958 Patriarch Ignatius XXXIX Jacob III Severus assented to their autonomy under Catholicos Basileios III George II. Basileios IV Eugene I (1964–75), appointed administrator at his desire in 1962, was enthroned by him. He devoted himself to the completing of ecclesiastical institutions. On the revision

---

[47] F. Verghese, *Die Syrischen Kirchen*, 11–14; cf. also P. J. Podipara, op. cit., 178–89.

[48] "Malankara" is in the Majalajam language the term for "Malabar," the southwest Indian coastal plain, in which live most Syrian Orthodox faithful. "Malankara" is the short form of "Malankara Orthodox Syrian Church."

[49] The Apostle Thomas is said to have landed at Mailapur near Madras in A.D. 52 and begun his mission.

of the church constitution[50] the Malabar Church was in 1967 designated as part of the Syrian Orthodox Church. But the agreement arrived at by way of discussion in no sense ended the internal difficulties between the adherents of the functioning catholicos and the patriarch of Antioch; in several cities two rival bishops confronted each other. Of the ca. 1.25 million faithful, since 1975 three-fourths adhere to Mar Basileios V Matthew I and one-fourth to Mar Basileios Paul II, both of whom bear the title of catholicos of the East and metropolitan of Malankara.

Besides the small Monophysite Church of Thozhijur (Andschur) in North Cerala (4,000 faithful), which ca. 1772 separated from the Syrian Orthodox mother Church as an independent Jacobite Church, the Syrian Mar Thomas Church must be mentioned. At the time of its origin in the nineteenth century, in addition to the question of autonomy, the alleged recourse to the Old Christian Church of Saint Thomas, the adoption of reform ideas, Anglican influences, and changes in the liturgy played a role. From these reformed Jacobites, also called Anglo-Syrians, whose 250,000 faithful are directed by Metropolitan Yuhana Mar Thomas at Tiruvalla, there split away in 1961 the Evangelical Saint Thomas Church in India, to which ca. 2,500 adherents in ten congregations belong.

The Coptic Church, under the "Pope and Coptic Patriarch of Alexandria and all Africa," gained in internal stability in the last decades, despite the political changes in Egypt, Arab nationalism, and the strengthening of Islam. Under Patriarch Cyril V (1874–1927) the Copts obtained in the constitution of 1923 civil equality with Muslims; the constitution proclaimed in 1956 guaranteed the equality of all citizens without regard for religion, but actually Islam remained Egypt's state religion. His successors had to contend with the lay representation in the National Council (Maglis Milli), which strove to extend its right to share in church administration. Patriarch John XIX (1928–42) increased the church schools and the printing of publications in church history and dogmatic theology. With Macarius III (1944–45) a proved practical shepherd of souls was elected, who showed himself open to efforts for church reform. Joasaph II (1946–56) protested against the growing Muslim fanaticism, which aimed to drive all non-Muslims from public offices, and in 1948 regulated the relations with the Ethiopian Church. When, after a vacancy of three years, an agreement had been achieved between the National Council and the Holy Synod on the election of the new patriarch, Cyril VI (1959–71) occupied the Coptic patriarchal throne. He reorganized the ecclesiastical administration by a series of committees for instruction, press, and monasteries. In 1960 he

---

[50] P. Verghese, *Die Syrischen Kirchen*, 169–80.

opened the new Coptic theological academy at Cairo. In spite of the confiscation of the greatest part of church property by the government, he succeeded in maintaining good relations with President Nasser (1956–1970), who financially supported the establishing of a patriarchal center and the rebuilding of Saint Mark's Cathedral at Cairo and took part in the laying of the cornerstone. His cooperation in the movement of liturgical renewal, in which the Arabic language established itself, in the formation of priests and monks, in the lessening of tension with the Ethiopian Church, in the holding of conferences with Monophysite and Orthodox Churches, especially in the Monophysite Synod at Addis Ababa from 7 to 21 January 1965,[51] in the dedication celebration of Saint Mark's Cathedral from 24 to 26 June 1968, and in the pastoral care of emigrant Copts attest to the diversity of his successful activity. He was succeeded by Bishop Amba Schenucha, responsible since 1962 for religious education, who as patriarch since 1971 is called Schenucha III. He reorganized the education of priests and monks and completed the theological academy. Like his predecessor, he stood for a rapprochement of the Monophysite Churches and a reunion of Eastern and Western Christianity.[52] The Coptic Church with ca. 4 million faithful suffers from Muslim intolerance, but its consolidation, the spiritual power of its monasteries, the receptiveness to modern problems, and its missionary work among Muslims deserve notice.

The Ethiopian Church, one of the oldest Christian national Churches, daughter Church of the Coptic patriarchate, acquired its autocephaly in 1959 through the determined exertions of Haile Selassie, Negus from 1928 to 1930 and Emperor from 1930 to 1974 (d. 1975). For decades he strove to make the forces of the religious tradition of his country fruitful for the present by tightening the external organization and reforms of the Church. He saw to the printing of liturgical books with texts in the ecclesiastical language, Geez, and their translation into the Amharic language of conversation, the founding of a theological seminary at Addis Ababa in 1944, which in 1961 was integrated into the university as the theological faculty, and theological schools in the individual eparchies, raised the level of cantors, deacons, and monks, and insisted on preaching.

While the Coptic patriarchs appointed an Egyptian monk as metropolitan and abuna ("our Father") of the entire Ethiopian Church, five

[51] The Synod met under the chairman Cyril VI (cf. *The Oriental-Orthodox Churches Addis Ababa Conference, January 1965* [Addis Ababa 1965]; E. Hammerschmidt, "Die Kirchenkonferenz von Addis Ababa," *Kirche im Osten* 9 [1966], 13–21.)

[52] After the visit of Schenucha III to Pope Paul VI in May 1973 a mixed commission of Catholics and Copts was set up, which held its first general meeting in March 1974.

Ethiopian monks were assigned to Abuna Cyril (1926–50) as bishops. The freeing of the Ethiopian Church from the Coptic was hastened by the Italian occupation of the country (1935–36), which entrusted native dignitaries with ecclesiastical administration, and the centralizing imperial administration of the Emperor after his return from exile in 1941. In 1946 Cyril returned to Egypt; in 1948 he turned over the administration of the Church to the native Etschegen Basileios, the superior general of all monasteries, monks, and nuns. Under Abuna Basileios (1951–59) the number of Ethiopian bishops was increased, the educational and charitable systems completed. At the insistence of Emperor Haile Selassie, Coptic Patriarch Cyril VI elevated him to patriarch and catholicos of Ethiopia (1959–70). To the Coptic patriarch remained only the supreme direction of the jurisdictional sphere of Saint Mark, which embraced also Ethiopia, and the right to ordain the Ethiopian patriarch. In addition to intensifying the formation of priests, teachers of religion, and missionaries, Patriarch Basileios cultivated relations with all Monophysite Churches.[53] He succeeded in obtaining in the radio station "Voice of the Gospel," established in the capital in 1963 by the Lutheran World Association, and in the state radio system, broadcasting time for the Patriarchal Church. In broadcasting work conservative and progressive ideas clashed. Theophilos I (Tewoflos, 1971–76) became his successor. His effort to continue church reform was hampered by the revolution of 1974–75, which deposed and interned Emperor Haile Selassie in 1974, annulled the privileges of the state Church, and expropriated its landed property. The patriarch protested against the draft of a new constitution, which envisaged equal religious rights for all Ethiopians—40 percent Monophysites, 35 percent Muslims, 20 percent pagans—but promised support of the regime. A heavy tax imposed on the episcopate was welcomed by the lower clergy; it had hopes from the political and social upheavals for an improvement of the living conditions of the Church, which had been burdened by the connection with the toppled dynasty. These "People's Priests" partly adopted directions which the first two patriarchs had already begun, including improvement of instruction and preaching, acceptance of connections with the sister Churches, but had encountered the hidden resistance of many clerics and monks, and partly they aligned themselves with radical reform demands. True, Theophilos I was able, by his personality, to bridge over the opposition that broke

---

[53] At the Synod of Addis Ababa in 1965 (above, n. 1) there was discussion of ways and means of gaining more young intellectuals for service in the Church and of missionary groups for the proclamation of the Gospel and instruction of the newly baptized.

out among his ca. 12 million faithful, but he was supplanted by Patriarch Malaku Walda Michael.

The Armenian Apostolic Church, or Gregorian Church,[54] is at present split among the catholicates of Echmiadzin and Cilicia, the patriarchates of Constantinople and Jerusalem, and a widespread diaspora. When the Armenians in the Ottoman Empire defended themselves against their increasing oppression, they were cruelly subjugated by the Turks in six waves of pogroms from 1894 to 1922, but especially in 1915–16.[55] Because of bloody massacres, deportations to Syria and Mesopotamia, forced conversions to Islam, and emigration, the patriarchate of Constantinople lost two-thirds of its faithful; some 2,050 churches and 203 monasteries were burned. By the Peace Treaty of Sèvres in 1920, Armenia again became a separate nation, but it was able to maintain its independence only one month before it was divided between Turkey and the Soviet Union.

The catholicate of Echmiadzin, which had been subject to the control of the Russian state Church since 1836, recovered its independence for a brief period (1917–20) after the Russian Revolution. In the Transcaucasian Republic of the Soviet Union (1922) the Church fell into the wake of Communist domination. Catholicos Kevork V (George, 1912–30) successfully opposed the Armenian Reformed Church propagated by the regime from 1924–25, a parallel to the "Living Church,"[56] which was joined only by a few bishops. Among the people it found no echo. And so the government tried to put pressure on the catholicos, "the supreme patriarch of all Armenians," for gaining the Armenians in foreign countries. Catholicos Choren (1932–38), who as administrator had already made extensive declarations of loyalty, obtained the reopening of some churches and the restoration of church property for the maintenance of the cathedral and the monastic establishments of Echmiadzin. Although in his pastoral letters he greeted the achievements for the economic and cultural uplifting of Soviet Armenia, he became a victim of the increasing persecution of the Church. Deputy Catholicos Kevork, in office since 1938, was powerless against further closings of churches and imprisoning of priests. In the Second World War he summoned the Armenians to join together for armed unity. Stalin permitted his election as Catholicos Kevork VI (1945–54), the

[54] The Church takes its name from Gregory the Illuminator (d. ca. 325), first bishop of all Armenia (cf. A. S. Atiya, op. cit., 317–22).

[55] J. Bryce, *The Treatment of Armenians in the Ottoman Empire 1915–16* (London 1916); F. Nansen, *Betrogenes Volk. Eine Studienreise durch Georgien und Armenien als Oberkommissar des Völkerbundes* (Leipzig 1928); J. Lepsius, *Der Todesgang des armenischen Volkes,* 4th ed. (Potsdam 1930); B. Brentjes, op. cit., 9–15.

[56] See above, p. 482.

recovery of the seminary at Erivan—all ecclesiastical educational centers had been closed in 1928—and the publication of a periodical. The appeal of the catholicos to the Armenians abroad to return to Soviet Armenia, his styling himself "patriarch of all Armenia" instead of the previous "of all Armenians," his claim to leadership of all Armenian jurisdictional areas, and his collaboration with the Patriarchal Church of Moscow facilitated for him the ordination of ten bishops and a certain stabilizing of church life, but he could not make up for the severe damage[57] the Church had suffered between the two world wars. At the Church assembly of 1955–56, in which ninety-seven delegates from the Soviet Union and forty from abroad took part, Vasgen, the Armenian supreme shepherd of the Bulgarian-Rumanian diocese, was elected catholicos. As a leading member of the peace movement in Rumania and because of his positive statements on the support of the Armenian national character by the Soviet Union, he was agreeable to the regime. Through his foreign journeys (1956–61), through the national synod convoked by him to Echmiadzin in 1962—of 137 delegates eighty-seven were from abroad—and the "All-Armenian Synod" at Echmiadzin in 1969, which was to prepare for an Armenian Orthodox council, he bound the patriarchates of Constantinople and Jerusalem closer to his catholicate, even if he did not succeed in realizing the desired rapprochement with the catholicate of Cilicia. The versatile catholicos undertook other foreign journeys, on which he consolidated the relations to the diaspora eparchies subject to him, made contacts with Eastern and Western church leaders, and helped his Church acquire international repute. His reports on the revival of religious sentiment in Soviet Armenia cannot conceal the fact that his Church of ca. 2 to 3 million faithful has only slight possibilities of development. To the catholicate belong another 500,000 Armenians in Iraq, Western Europe, and North, Central, and South America.[58]

The Armenian Apostolic Church of the catholicate of Cilicia, which is responsible for Armenians in Lebanon, North America, Syria, Iran, and on Cyprus—600,000 faithful—has maintained its independence. Its catholicoi resided from 1293 to 1921 at Sis, the capital of the medieval Little Armenian Kingdom of Cilicia. Persecuted by the Turks, the Armenians fled to Syria and Lebanon, where they created a new center at Antelias, north of Beirut. The successive catholicoi Garegin (1945–

[57] The number of churches dropped between 1915 and 1954 in European Russia from 1,446 to 89, in the Armenian Soviet Republic from 491 to 38, in Georgia from 287 to 14, in Azerbaijan from 473 to 30. In the Georgian capital of Tiflis, of the 28 Armenian churches before the First World War, only 2 are left (W. Kolarz, op. cit., 166f.).
[58] The Armenians in the United States are under an archbishop in New York in only a loose dependence on the catholicate of Echmiadzin.

52) and Sarech I (1956–63) struggled with the Catholicate of Echmiadzin over the security and the extension of their jurisdiction until Catholicos Choren, in office from 1963, succeeded in consolidating his Church internally and externally, and made contacts with the other Monophysite communities and with Orthodox and Western Churches.

The Armenian Gregorian patriarchate of Constantinople now cares for 50,000 Armenians in Turkey.[59] To the Armenian patriarchate of Jerusalem belong 6,000 faithful in Israel and Jordan. Both patriarchates are pretty intimately united to that of Echmiadzin.

The Eastern national Churches have in their venerable liturgies preserved the primitive Christian stock of ideas to the present. Conditioned by political circumstances, they lived considerably isolated for centuries. Not until the twentieth century did they meet one another, loosen the hardened fronts among them and Orthodoxy, and begin dialogues with the Roman Catholic Church. In 1971, 1973, and 1976 Monophysite and Catholic theologians met at Vienna[60] to prepare the way for a reunion of the separated Churches. In the center of their discussion stood the Christological definition of the Council of Chalcedon, on whose formulation a unanimous interpretation was sought, and the value and evaluation of ecumenical councils and of the "Petrine Office." The beginnings of mutual understanding of Eastern and Orthodox Churches, of Eastern and Western Christianity, are becoming clear. When and how the diversity of Eastern Churches will flow into the unity asked by Christ in his high-priestly prayer (John 17:20–21) lies on another plane.

---

[59] Before 1914 there were in Turkey 1,700 parishes and 1,600 churches, in the mid-twentieth century 42 parishes and 38 churches (W. Kolarz, op. cit., 150).

[60] The consultations took place in the framework of the foundation *Pro Oriente,* called into existence by Franz Cardinal König in 1964.

The Church in the Individual Countries

CHAPTER 17

The Church in Northern, Eastern, and Southern Europe*

The end of the First World War produced fundamental upheavals in northern, eastern, and southern Europe. On the ruins of the destroyed Habsburg and Romanov empires arose new or very different national states, which in their reorganization and the building of their new structure made use of the help of religious groups. In the overwhelmingly Catholic countries, such as Lithuania, Poland, and Hungary, therefore, Catholicism flourished, whereas in countries with a majority of Orthodox population, like Rumania, Yugoslavia, and Bulgaria, the independent Eastern Churches[1] obtained a leading position. However, in these states, as also in Czechoslovakia, which represented a sort of special case, and in the Scandinavian and Baltic countries with a Protestant majority, the Catholic Church was able to develop freely, due to the middle-class democracies. Only the Soviet Union constituted an exception. For its Communist, strictly antireligious ideology led to an unprecedented anti-Church struggle, which, after the Second World War, in consequence of the Soviet seizure of power in eleven nations in all of eastern and southern Europe, it was extended to almost 70 million Catholics. Only from the early 1960s did the situation begin to relax gradually in the course of international politics. The long-range method of the interior withering of the Church replaced the open struggle against it. But the changed international situation also made it possible for the Holy See, through a reoriented policy, to hasten to the aid of the oppressed Church in the East.

The Scandinavian Countries

In Denmark Catholicism could continue after the First World War its upsurge that had begun at the turn of the century. As a result of numerous and important conversions the number of the faithful grew within eighteen years from 3,000 to 15,000, and in 1938 to 22,000 in a

---

* Gabriel Adriányi
[1] Cf. the explanation in Chapter 16.

Protestant population of 4.2 million. Due to the circumstances of domestic policy, the Church displayed a vigorous activity in pastoral care, charity, the press, and the care of youth. Thirty new churches, chapels, seven schools, and nine hospitals were built. The number of Catholics rose also on the Danish islands. In 1923 the Holy See established a prefecture apostolic in Iceland, which was raised to a vicariate apostolic in 1929. Great ecclesiastical celebrations and meetings[2] made clear the strength and importance obtained by Danish Catholicism. The German occupaticn of Denmark from 1940 to 1945 brought trouble for the Church especially in economic respects. However, the Catholic renewal could not only maintain itself but continue its development. During and after the Second World War Denmark admitted for the time being some 250,000 refugees, including 24,000 Catholics, and this especially gave an impetus to charity. In keeping with the favorable development of the postwar years, Pius XII in 1953 made Copenhagen a diocese and placed it immediately under the Holy See. Since then Danish Catholicism has displayed a vigorous activity, especially in the care of souls, education, and social work.

Because of the powerful Lutheran state-Church system, the unfamiliarity of Catholicism, and the large diaspora, the Catholic mission in Sweden was able to develop less favorably. Through tireless missionary work, but especially through the immigration of ca. 20,000 Catholic refugees during and after the Second World War, especially from Eastern Europe, the situation of the Church could gradually improve. In the process of the erecting of the autonomous Scandinavian hierarchy, Pius XII in 1953 also elevated the vicariate apostolic of Stockholm to a bishopric. True, in the most recent period the Church obtained a greater importance, numbering in 1974 already 63,063 faithful, with 26 parishes, 115 diocesan priests, 77 male religious, and 230 female religious; but, now as earlier, the old difficulties[3] hampered a more comprehensive evangelization.

As in Sweden, the Catholic mission in Norway could acquire greater importance only in the most recent period because of immigration and conversions. Here the number of Catholics in a population of 3.6 million grew in 1974 to 9,127, who were cared for in 17 parishes by 20 priests, 34 male religious, and 382 sisters. Here too in 1953 Pius XII founded its own ecclesiastical organization: out of the vicariate apostolic erected in 1931 came the see of Oslo and two other vicariates apostolic.

[2] In 1923, visit of Cardinal Willem van Rossum; and 1926 Saint Anschar's Year; in 1932 Eucharistic Congress at Copenhagen; in 1935 Saint Knut's Year; cf. also W. van Rossum, *Die religiöse Lage der Katholiken in den nordischen Lädern* (Munich 1924).

[3] For example, lack of financial means, great distances, Protestant milieu.

Of course, in Norway Catholics represent a very small minority in the diaspora, but their religious life is exemplary.

Like Sweden and Norway, the Catholic Church in Finland has only a small number of faithful—2,959 in 1974—who live dispersed among 4.6 million Protestants. Here in 1955 Pius XII organized its own hierarchy, the see of Helsinki, after the Finnish Catholics had in 1920 been separated from the archbishopric of Mogilev and obtained a vicariate of their own. In spite of some restrictions,[4] the Church in Finland enjoys free activity.[5]

The Baltic Countries

The Republic of Estonia, proclaimed on 2 April 1918 but only recognized in international law on 26 January 1921, embraced at its independence 47,549 square kilometers with a population of ca. 1.1 million, of whom 77.6 percent belonged to the Lutheran and only 2,327—.2 percent—to the Catholic Church. In 1940 the latter were cared for in six parishes by eleven priests and about twenty religious of both sexes. Since the faithful had previously been subject to the Russian archbishopric of Mogilev, a special apostolic administration, under a titular archbishop, was erected for them in 1925. The first Soviet occupation in 1940, then the incorporation of Estonia after the end of the German occupation into the Soviet Union in 1945, and the implementation of the Soviet religious policy completely destroyed the organization and life of the Church in Estonia.

Like Estonia, the Republic of Latvia appeared on 18 November 1918 as a result of the collapse of the Russian Empire, and, also like Estonia, it did not receive recognition in international law until 26 January 1921. The new nation had a total area of 65,791 square kilometers with a population of 1.8 million. The majority of the population was Lutheran—58 percent—but here the number of Catholics amounted to 450,210 souls—23.69 percent—in 1930. For them the Holy See restored the old see of Riga as early as 1918 and removed it from the earlier diocesan union of Mogilev and Kaunas. Because of religious liberty and the accommodating policy of the state, the Church was able quickly to develop. There appeared religious institutions, societies, seminaries, a Catholic theological faculty and a considerable Catholic press. In order further to complete the ecclesiastical organization and to

---

[4] For example, the founding of monasteries is forbidden.

[5] For the Scandinavian missions cf. the *Jahrbücher des St.-Ansgarius-Werkes, St. Ansgar*, published by the directors of the *St.-Ansgarius-Werk* of Cologne and of the *St.-Ansgar-Werk* of Munich.

clarify the relations of state and Church, Latvia conducted discussions with the Holy See in 1920, which ended on 30 May 1922 with the concluding of a concordat.[6] The concordat guaranteed the Church full possibility of development and called into existence the archbishopric of Riga and the suffragan bishopric of Kurland-Semgallen, with its seat at Liepaja. The outbreak of the Second World War, the events of the war, the forcible annexation of the country to the Soviet Union on 21 June 1940, and Soviet domination also made a quick end of the flourishing life of the Church here too. All church organizations were forbidden, and bishops were imprisoned. The number of priests dropped from 207 in 1944 to 143 in 1967. After 1963 the situation relaxed a bit. Thus the one vicar general for the two sees of Riga and Liepaja could take part in the Second Vatican Council and in 1964 receive episcopal ordination at Rome.

Lithuania declared its political sovereignty on 16 February 1918, but, after Poland had occupied Lithuanian Vilna, and Lithuania the district of Memel that was under Polish rule, it was recognized in international law only on 8 May 1924. The republic covered 58,810 square kilometers with a population of 2.3 million, of whom 1.7 million were Catholics. They lived in two dioceses and in 1929 had 388 parishes and 1,072 priests.[7] Although the overwhelming majority of the population was Catholic, and the Church had fostered the independence of Lithuania with all its power in the most recent past, there occurred repeated conflicts between Lithuania and the Holy See because of the question of Vilna. When the Polish concordat of 1925 left the see of Vilna with Poland, the diplomatic relations assumed in 1920 between Lithuania and the Vatican were broken. On 4 April 1926 Pius XI created a Lithuanian ecclesiastical province by the bull *Lituanorum gente*.[8] He elevated Kaunas to an archbishopric and subjected to it four new dioceses and a prelacy *nullius*. But since this took place without previous consultation with the Lithuanian government, the government did not recognize the papal bull. Long and difficult negotiations between the Holy See and Lithuania led on 10 December 1927 to the concluding of a concordat.[9] It restored diplomatic relations between the Vatican and the republic, guaranteed the complete freedom of the Church, and confirmed the new Lithuanian ecclesiastical organization. Church life flourished. In 1939 there were already 800 parishes, more than 1,500 priests, and 600 candidates for the priesthood in 4 semi-

[6] *AAS* 14(1922), 577–81
[7] Of whom 38 were religious priests.
[8] *AAS* 18(1926), 121–23.
[9] Ibid. 19(1927), 425–31.

naries and a Catholic theological faculty. Also the Catholic press and religious institutes renewed themselves energetically. But the political conflicts from 1938 on, the Second World War, the invasion of the Soviet army after a three-year occupation by the Germans (1941–44), and the incorporation of Lithuania into the Soviet Union on 3 August 1940 made a quick end of this development. The new rulers denounced the concordat in 1940 and introduced the same measures as in the two other Baltic nations. Also there occurred a mass deportation, which annihilated not only the entire hierarchy and a great part of the clergy but also a third of the Catholic population of Lithuania. In 1955 there were only one bishop, impeded from carrying out his office, and 75 seminarians. The number of priests dropped in 1969 to 834, of whom 300 had passed the age of sixty years.

After 1963 the situation became a bit easier. In 1965 a Lithuanian vicar capitular could be ordained a bishop at Rome, in 1968 a Lithuanian priest in his own country, and in 1969 two other priests. In 1967 two bishops could journey to Rome. However, just how unfree the Church is in the Soviet Socialist Republic of Lithuania was shown by the most recent letters of protest and complaint of Lithuanian Catholics and priests, which have in part become known in the West.[10]

The Soviet Union

When, on the collapse of the Empire of the Tsars, the Bolshevik Russian Socialist Federated Soviet Republic arose in 1918, then in 1922 the Union of Soviet Socialist Republics, there was in the new state only a shrinking Catholic minority. For the number of Roman and Uniate Catholics decreased as a consequence of the independence of Poland and of the Baltic nations from 15 to 1.6 million, who now lived among 78 million of other faiths, of whom 71 percent were Orthodox. The Catholics of the Roman Rite, mostly foreigners or non-Russians, were in Russia itself subject to the archbishopric of Mogilev and its four suffragan sees and were all cared for by ca. 4,600 priests in 4,234 churches and 1,978 chapels. But the new frontiers of the state left only the archbishopric[11] and two other dioceses and the vicariate apostolic for the Crimea, the Caucasus, and Siberia, the apostolic administration of the Armenian Rite, and the exarchate of the Slavonic Byzantine Rite in their former extent.

On 23 January 1918 the new rulers proclaimed separation of Church and state and began at once with the dissolving of the

[10] Cf. *HK* 26(1972), 339–45.
[11] In 1918 two old dioceses, Minsk and Kamenec, were again attached to the archbishopric.

organization of the Catholic Church. By 1923 all bishops were imprisoned, expelled, or shot. The normal church administration came to an end with the hierarchy. The number of priests dropped rapidly also through natural and violent deaths, deportations, imprisonment, and the preventing of reception of the priesthood by candidates. All seminaries and the important ecclesiastical academy at Petrograd[12] were dissolved. Most churches and chapels were closed or profaned. Within a few years the external religious life of the Church had been completely destroyed.

In view of this situation, the Holy See left nothing untried to stop the destruction of the Church. But repeated diplomatic interventions achieved only the freeing and expelling of Archbishops Eduard von Ropp in 1920 and John Cieplak in 1923. The papal assistance mission in the Soviet Union, visited by famine, which was carried out with the cooperation of the Divine Word Missionaries and a donation of ca. 2 million dollars in 1922–24,[13] did not realize the missionary expectations connected with the giving of aid. Now as earlier, the authorities kept any church activity away from works of charity.

Because of the serious ecclesiopolitical situation and the great upheavals in Eastern Europe, as early as 1917 Benedict XV established the Congregation for the Eastern Churches and in the same year the Institute of Oriental Studies. In the former a special "Commission for Russia" was formed, which worked as an independent office from 1925 to 1934. Since it was of interest to the new Soviet state to obtain recognition in international law, it had been ready to have a nuncio sent to Moscow, despite the retaining of its church policy. The negotiations foundered when Pius XI made the resumption of full diplomatic relations dependent on the attitude of the Soviet government to the Church.

Meanwhile diplomatic "feelers" were not ended. Thus Pius XI could in 1925 and 1926 authorize a member of the papal "Commission for Russia," the Jesuit Michel d'Herbigny, who was ordained a bishop, to arrange a new organization of church administration in the Soviet Union and send him to Moscow. There in 1926 he erected nine apostolic administrations[14] and secretly ordained four bishops. However, this was soon discovered by the state. Monsignor d'Herbigny had

[12] Cf. A. Petrani, *Kolegium Duhowne W Petersburgu* (The Ecclesiastical Academy at Petersburg) (*Towarzystwo Naukowe* 12) (Lublin 1950).
[13] Cf. M. D'Herbigny, "L'aide pontificale aux enfants affamé de Russie," *Orientalia Christiana* 4(1925), 1–80; J. Kraus, *Im Auftrage des Papstes in Russland* (Veröffentlichungen des Missionspriesterseminars St. Augustin, Siegburg, no. 21) (Steyl 1970).
[14] Moscow, Mogilev-Minsk, Leningrad, Kharkow, Kazan-Samara(Kuibyshev)-Simbirsk(Ulyanovsk), Odessa, Saratow, Caucasus, and Georgia.

to leave the country, and the new bishops were imprisoned. The reorganization of the Church collapsed thereby. Now the whole of ecclesiastical life was paralyzed. Only some fifty to sixty priests escaped the measures of terror, and their activity was strictly supervised. From 1933 a priest in the American Embassy at Moscow could function for the personnel and celebrate Mass in the church of Saint Louis.

After his predecessor had already in 1920 rejected the Communist ideology in the motu proprio *Bonum sana,*[15] Pius XI condemned Bolshevism and its violence in numerous declarations,[16] especially in the encyclicals *Miserantissimus Redemptor,*[17] *Caritate Christi compulsi,*[18] and *Divini Redemptoris.*[19] And on 2 February 1930 he summoned all Christianity to prayer services against Communism.[20]

The events at the beginning of and during the Second World War, especially the annexation of eastern Poland, the Baltic nations, Bessarabia, and the Carpatho-Ukraine by the Soviet Union, and the Soviet military occupation of Eastern Europe, as well as the decision of the three-power conference at Yalta from 4 to 11 February 1945 to leave all of Eastern Europe under Soviet influence, had as a result a cruel way of the cross for some 70 million Catholics in eleven countries. The harshest blow, of course, fell on Catholics in the areas incorporated by the Soviet Union.

As early as 1939 the state had moved with all its means against the Uniate Armenians and Ukrainians (the Ruthenians) who lived in the archdiocese of Lvov and its suffragan sees. Church property was confiscated, seminaries were closed, monasteries and churches were plundered. After the end of the German occupation and the second Soviet invasion, the persecution of the Church was resumed and the forcible reincorporation of the Uniates was carried through. The annexation to the Patriarchal Church of Moscow was enforced by an illegal synod on 8 March 1946 after the imprisonment of ten bishops and apostolic administrators. In this way the Catholic Church in the Ukraine was liquidated.[21] In a similar fashion there occurred the return of the Uniates in Carpatho-Ukraine. After the bishop of Užhorod had

---

[15] *AAS,* 12(1920), 313–317.
[16] Enumerated in ibid. 29(1937), 67.
[17] Ibid. 20(1928), 165–78.
[18] Ibid. 24(1932), 177–94.
[19] Ibid. 29(1937), 65–106.
[20] Ibid. 22(1930), 89–93.
[21] Cf. the talk of Pius XII on 14 November 1952 in *AAS* 44(1952), 876–78; also, W. de Vries, "Soppressione della Chiesa greco-cattolica nella Subcarpazia," *CivCatt* 102, 2(1950), 391–99, and M. Lacko, "The Forced Liquidation of the Union of Užhorod," *Slovak Studies* 1(1961), 145–85.

been eliminated by a fatal automobile accident in 1949, the state's arbitrary measures climaxed on 15 August 1949 in the proclaiming of reunion with the Orthodoxy of Moscow. Meanwhile, 67 churches had been expropriated and 18 priests imprisoned.

In 1963 the Vatican's Eastern policy was able to effect the release from prison of the Ukrainian metropolitan of Lvov, Josyf Slipyi. However, the sad situation of the Church in the entire Soviet Union is unchanged.[22]

Poland

Proclaimed by the Central Powers on 5 November 1916, the sovereign Polish state was restored in the Peace Treaty of Versailles on 28 June 1919 after more than a century of total partition. About the same political boundaries were reinstituted as after the second partition in 1793. In 1927 the Republic of Poland included, after some correcting of the frontiers, 385,030 square kilometers; in 1921 it had 27.1 million inhabitants, of whom 20.3 million—75 percent—were Catholics, including 3.5 million Uniates, 2.8 million—10.5 percent—Orthodox, 2.8 million—10.5 percent—Jews, and 1 million—3.8 percent—Protestants. In addition the new nation comprised a variety of national minorities, for the Poles constituted only ca. 78 percent of the population.

If Polish Catholicism was in modern times, especially however during the difficult period of the partition of the state, the unselfish bearer of national interests and the strongest promoter of the reestablishment of state sovereignty, it is not to be wondered at that, thanks to its unbounded popularity, it played a key role in the reconstruction of the state and in public life. Since the boundaries of the ecclesiastical provinces were often at variance with those of the state, the reorganization of the Church's structure took precedence for the episcopate in the reconstruction and standardization of church life. There began discussions between the papal nuncio, Achille Ratti (1919–21), the future Pope Pius XI, the episcopate and the government. They proved to be difficult, but were successful. After nine episcopal sees had been filled in 1919 and in 1920 the diocese of Lodz and in 1922 two apostolic administrations[23] had been erected, there ensued on 10 February 1925 the signing of a concordat[24] between Poland and the Holy See. On the one hand, the concordat guaranteed the complete liberty of the Church and granted the Curia influence on the organization of the Church in

[22] Cf. also R. Urban, *Die tschechoslowakische hussitische Kirche* (*Marburger Ostforschungen* 34) (Marburg 1973), 111–17.
[23] Danzig, Katowice.
[24] *AAS* 17(1925), 273–87.

Poland, but on the other hand it took into account the national political wishes of the government.[25] The new diocesan arrangement of Poland was agreed upon in ARTICLE 9; it resulted on 28 October 1925 in the bull *Vixdum Poloniae*,[26] which in addition to the three existing archbishoprics—Gniezno, Lvov, Warsaw—established two new metropolitanates—Cracow and Vilna—and five more bishoprics. This new ecclesiastical organization was a compromise solution. For the Holy See was seeking to keep the historical dioceses in existence, while the government aspired, by the ecclesiastical reorganization, to obliterate the frontiers of the period of partition.

Although, because of the stern state direction and some state encroachments,[27] sometimes serious tensions existed between Church and government, ecclesiastical life was able to develop fully. The Church's greatest efficacy appeared especially in public life. Poland presented itself as an expressly Catholic country. But the inner life of the Church also flourished. From 1918 to 1939 the number of bishops increased from 23 to 51, the number of priests to 12,940 (43 percent), the number of religious priests to 16,663 (62 percent), that of lay brothers to 4,567, that of female religious to 16,820, that of religious houses to 2,027. Ecclesiastical congresses,[28] great pilgrimages, Catholic associations and organizations,[29] intensive parochial care of souls,[30] new synodal laws, a greatly improved Catholic press, basic theological instruction in seminaries and on Catholic theological faculties,[31] general Catholic education and the Catholic University of Lublin,[32] founded in 1918, deepened the faith decisively. But this did not prevent the Polish episcopate from energetically Latinizing[33] the strong Uniate Ukrainian Church.[34]

[25] Cf. K. Blaszczyński, *Concordatum cum Republica Polonia* (Warsaw 1925); A. Systerhenn, *Das polnische Konkordat vom 10. Februar 1925* (Cologne 1925); F. Grübel, *Die Rechtslage der römisch-katholischen Kirche in Polen nach dem Konkordat vom 10. Februar 1925* (Leipzig 1930).

[26] *AAS* 17(1925), 521–28.

[27] In 1935 the so-called Wawel Conflict; in 1938 actions of expropriation and destruction against Orthodox in Lublin; cf. B. Spuler, "Die orthodoxe Kirche in Polen," *Osteuropa-Handbuch, Polen,* ed. by W. Markert (Cologne and Graz 1959), 114–18.

[28] In 1927 the Eucharistic Congress in Poznan; in 1937 the Congress of Christ the King in Poznan.

[29] Among them, Catholic Action with 621,820 members.

[30] There were 1,172 new parishes.

[31] Warsaw, Cracow, Lvov, Vilna.

[32] Cf. *Kniega jubileuszowa 50-lecia Katolickiego Uniwersytetu Lubelskiego, praca zbiorowa* (Lublin 1969); A. Petrani, op. cit.

[33] Cf. H. Koch, "Die unierte Kirche in Polen," *Osteuropa-Handbuch,* ed. by W. Markert (Cologne and Graz 1959), 109–13.

[34] It had in 1932 2,371 parishes, 2,654 priests, and 192 male religious.

On 1 September 1939 Poland was attacked by Germany and, seventeen days later, by the Soviet Union. Poland soon succumbed to superior strength and was again partitioned. Its western areas were for the most part allotted to Germany with 16.9 million Catholics—80.8 percent of all the Catholics. The southern part and the remainder of Poland was made a sort of German colony as the *Gouvernement General,* while the Soviet Union incorporated the eastern areas of Poland, which in the course of the Second World War also came under German occupation from 1941 to 1944–45. The inclusion of the eastern parts of Poland in the Soviet Union (1939–41) produced a brutal persecution of the Church. But also in the areas occupied by Germany the fate of the Polish Catholics was unbearable. Nazi directives deprived the Church of its liberty and almost outlawed it, the clergy was decimated, a great part of the bishops and priests were arrested and taken to concentration camps, all associations and organizations were forbidden, and worship was restricted to a minimum. At the end of the war the Church in Poland had to lament the death of 4 bishops, 1,996 priests, including the Blessed Maximilian Kolbe, 113 clerics, and 238 female religious. A total of 3,647 priests, 389 clerics, 341 lay brothers, and 1,117 sisters were confined in concentration camps. The Holy See, which had very sharply condemned the partition of Poland and the oppression of the Polish Catholics, could not help the afflicted Church.

The restoration of the Polish state on 5 July 1945, in which Poland had been compensated for its eastern areas that had been annexed by the Soviet Union with the eastern areas of Germany as far as the Oder-Neisse line, brought the Church only a temporary relief. For soon there began also in Poland, with the aid of the Soviet occupation, the setting up of a Communist political system. On 16 September 1945 the new Polish government denounced the concordat. But first the Church had to tackle the rapid restoration of church administration and of religious life because of the vast losses in the war and the great territorial changes. This was facilitated by the fact that in 1945 Poland was reduced in size by about one-fifth, but the proportion of the Catholic population—especially through the replacing of the expelled Germans, who were partly Protestants, by Catholic Poles from the eastern areas—grew to 97.8 percent. On 15 August 1945 Cardinal Primate August Hlond erected five apostolic administrations in the formerly German eastern areas. Religious life could again develop. However, the original religious toleration of the state was supplanted by a latent attitude of hostility to the Church. Between 1946 and 1948 the government tried to drive the Church's activity out of public life into the area of the sacred. Severe measures of curtailment affected especially Catholic education, the pastoral care of youth, and the

Catholic cultural and educational system. Also an effort was undertaken to split the clergy[35] by the creation of a national Church. The struggle against the Church erupted openly in 1951. An abundance of administrative measures affected the Church, such as the dissolution of all ecclesiastical organizations, except that of charity, the secularization of church schools, hospitals, and orphanages, and the expropriation of church property. The episcopate was forced to conclude an agreement[36] with the government on 14 April 1950. While the Church renounced its land and promised its help in the integrating of the new western areas, the state guaranteed a minimum of church activity.

The state did not observe the agreement. The government placed men of its confidence as vicars capitular in the apostolic administrations, displayed a propaganda campaign, and further persecuted the Church. Many bishops, including Primate Stefan Wyszyński, and hundreds of priests were imprisoned, while the collaborating "patriotic priests" obtained key positions. The number of male religious houses dropped ca. 40 percent, that of female houses ca. 45 percent. The number of diocesan priests sank from 8,624 in 1945 to 2,247 in 1953. A decisive ecclesiopolitical change did not occur until October 1956, when the Polish Communist party abandoned the former Stalinist course and entrusted the direction of the state to the moderate Wladyslaw Gomulka. He ended the imprisonment of Wyszyński and the priests and on 7 December 1956 concluded a new agreement[37] with the Church, which essentially guaranteed the Church activity agreed to in the previous treaty, even if still more curtailed. This time the government kept its word. New vicars general could be installed in the administrations, and church life could again develop, even if modestly. Renewed tensions between state and Church appeared only in isolation, as on the occasion of the message of reconciliation of the Polish episcopate to the German Catholics on 18 November 1965[38] and of the millennium celebration of the conversion of Poland in 1966.

Paul VI, who would have liked to visit Poland, accommodated Polish desires in the context of his Eastern policy. In 1971 he beatified Maximilian Kolbe, and, after the German Federal Republic had signed the Treaty of Warsaw on 7 December 1970, he took up the reorganization of Poland's western territories on 28 June 1972. The previous apostolic administrators became diocesan bishops, three new sees were

---

[35] "Pax" or "Patriot Priests' Group."

[36] Text in *Ostprobleme* 2(1950), 469ff.

[37] Text ibid., 9(1957), 237.

[38] Cf. *Versöhnung oder Hass? Der Briefwechsel der Bischöfe Polens und Deutschlands und seine Folgen. Eine Dokumentation mit einer Einführung von O. B. Roegele* (Osnabrück 1966).

erected, and German ecclesiastical jurisdictions, that is, dioceses, were separated from the Polish western territories.[39] Thereby the Polish western lands became autonomous in canon law.

The contacts and negotiations between the Vatican and the Polish government were not thereafter interrupted. This all the more, because Polish Catholicism with its uncrushed vitality has remained an unmistakable element of the Polish people. In 1965 the Church in Poland had more than 27.1 million mostly very zealous and practicing faithful, more than 6,699 parishes, 14,420 diocesan and 3,408 religious priests, 4,994 religious brothers, 25,472 sisters, and 3,027 religious houses. In 1974 the number of bishops was 77, the number of candidates for the priesthood 4,200. Nonetheless, the possibility of development of the Church in Poland, as Cardinal Primate Wyszyński assured the Roman Synod of Bishops in 1974, remains restricted, as earlier.[40]

Czechoslovakia

When on 28 October 1918 the Republic of Czechoslovakia, with 140,546 square kilometers and 13.6 million inhabitants, of whom 95 percent were Catholics, was constituted out of territories of the crumbled Austro-Hungarian Monarchy, the situation of the Church in the new state began to appear quite complicated and difficult. A nationalistic and anticlerical Czech ruling class acquired power. The anti-Roman, nationalistic tendencies which for decades had grown in the Czech clergy under the direction of the Jednota society and now peaked in the powerful and, especially among Czech intellectuals, very popular Away-from-Rome movement,[41] first led to serious conflicts within the Church, and then on 8 January 1920 the proclaiming of the Czech National Church.[42] This and other Protestant religious communities, as well as Orthodoxy in the Carpatho-Ukraine that belonged to the republic, soon experienced the widest spread through massive state support.[43]

---

[39] Cf. H. Stehle, "Der Vatikan und die Oder-Neisse Linie," *Europa-Archiv* 27(1972), 559–66.

[40] Cf. S. Lammich, "Die Rechtsstellung der römisch-katholischen Kirche in der Volksrepublik Polen," *Österreichisches Archiv für Kirchenrecht* 23(1972), 3–15.

[41] Cf. P. Mai, "Die Tschechische Nation und die Los-von-Rom-Bewegung," *Beiträge zur ostdeutschen und osteuropäischen Kirchengeschichte. Festschrift Bernhard Stasiewski* (Cologne and Vienna 1975), 171–85.

[42] *Cirkev Československá*, since 1971 *Cirkev Československá husitska*.

[43] The census of 1930 gave, in a population of 14.7 million, besides 10.8 million Catholics, 585,041 Uniates, and 356,838 Jews, 1.1 million Protestants, 145,598 Orthodox, 854,638 of no denomination, and 739,385 members of the Czechoslovak National Church.

In addition, the government prepared to adapt the church organization, which now consisted of two archdioceses and ten bishoprics, to national interests and to approximate the diocesan boundaries to the national frontiers. In November 1918 Archbishop Count Paul Huyn had to leave Prague, and in 1919 four bishops in Slovakia had also to resign or were deported to Hungary. In order to put pressure on the Church, the state on 11 August 1919 sequestered 251,925 cadastral yokes (ca. 126,000 hectares) of church property in Slovakia. Various church schools were secularized, and especially by means of the Sokol Unions a massive nationalistic anticlerical propaganda was promoted.

The Holy See, which had taken up diplomatic relations with Czechoslovakia as early as October 1919, tried by all means to stop the exodus from the Church and to normalize the situation. In accord with the desires of both sides, there soon began diplomatic negotiations, which proved to be difficult. As a mark of his willingness to accommodate, on 16 December 1920 Benedict XV appointed three Slovaks to the local sees under the assumption that two of their predecessors, who had had to emigrate to Hungary, would be provided for by Czechoslovakia. Although the Czechoslovak ambassador to the Holy See, Kamill Krofta, guaranteed this in writing in the name of his government, the promise was not kept. This was the reason why the Vatican later, in the carrying out of the so-called *Modus vivendi,* made its concessions dependent on the previous settlement of the material questions.

After long negotiations the apostolic administration of Trnava in Slovakia was erected and a titular bishop placed at its head. However, the see of Rožnava remained vacant from 1920, for the Czechoslovak government intended to dissolve it because of is Hungarian majority and integrate it into a new Slovak metropolitanate that was to be established. Relations between state and Church noticeably deteriorated. When, before the approaching parliamentary elections, the Slovak bishops on 26 November 1924 in a common pastoral letter, with which the Czech bishops declared their solidarity, urged the faithful to hold themselves aloof from all parties that were hostile to the Church and religion and refused Communion to the members of radical parties, the state pressure increased. Trials were instituted against priests, church feasts were abolished, new anticlerical laws were enacted, and on the occasion of the celebration to honor Hus in 1925 the nuncio was forced to leave. But the government soon had to yield because of the domestic and foreign policy conditions. In the summer of 1927 the government promised to permit the Catholic Popular party, to restore Catholic schools, and to regularize the sequestered church property. The negotiations led on 17 December 1927 to a *Modus*

THE CHURCH IN THE INDIVIDUAL COUNTRIES

vivendi.[44] In this were agreed: the imminent assimilation of diocesan boundaries with the political frontiers of the nation, the restitution and the administration of the sequestered church property by an episcopal commission, the autonomy of the religious orders, and the free nomination of bishops by the Holy See, subject to the state's right of veto. And the interrupted diplomatic relations between the Vatican and Czechoslovakia were restored.

But the implementation of the *Modus vivendi* foundered on the objections of Czechoslovakia to undertaking the restoration of church property before the rearrangement of diocesan boundaries. Thereupon the Hungarian government sequestered the property of the Slovak dioceses that lay in Hungary, and Cardinal Primate Jusztinián Serédi introduced a suit at the International Court at The Hague. This led again to further tensions in the relations between the Vatican and Prague, which were made worse by the forced resignation of Archbishop František Kordač.[45] The nuncio Pietro Ciriaci was attacked, excluded from the discussions, and hence recalled in November 1933. But the government yielded again before the parliamentary elections of 1935. This time the negotiations led to the restitution of the sequestered church property, whereupon Pius XI issued the bull *Ad ecclesiastici regiminis* of 2 September 1937.[46] The boundaries of the Slovak sees were assimilated to the national frontiers, the dioceses and the two administrations—Trnava of 1922 and Satu Mare of 1930—were separated from the Hungarian diocesan organization and placed directly under the Holy See. Furthermore, the Pope promised the erecting of two new metropolitanates, one in Slovakia and one in Carpatho-Ukraine.[47]

Meanwhile, the expansion of the Third Reich not only caused the destruction of Czechoslovakia,[48] but led in the areas occupied by

---

[44] *AAS* 20(1928), 65f.

[45] A. K. Huber, "Franz Kordačs Briefe ins Germanikum (1879–1916)," *Archiv für Kirchengeschichte von Böhmen, Mähren, Schlesien* 1(1967), 62–184; F. Lorenz, "Ein Presse-Fall in der katholischen Kirche im Jahre 1931. Erkenntnisse aus der Affaire Kordač-Ciriaci," *Kirche, Recht und Land. Festschrift zum 70. Lebenjahr von Weihbischof Prof. Dr. A. Kindermann* (Königstein and Munich 1969), 194–210.

[46] *AAS* 29(1937), 366–69.

[47] When after the Vienna Award of 2 November 1938 important parts of Slovakia again became Hungarian, and Hungary also occupied the Carpatho-Ukraine, the bull *Dioecesium fines* of 19 July 1939 (not in the *AAS*) again subordinated the dioceses in these territories to the previous Hungarian metropolitan sees; the earlier situation persisted until 1945.

[48] On 6 October 1938 the republic first became a federation, then on 4 March 1939 Slovakia became an independent republic, but on 16 March 1939 Bohemia-Moravia became a *Reichsprotektorat*.

Germany to a real struggle against the Church. Ecclesiastical administration, press, and organizations were restricted, and hundreds of priests were imprisoned. Most sees remained vacant. The situation of the Church was normal only in the Slovak Republic, at whose head was the Catholic priest Josef Tiso. Here there were difficulties only with the Uniates of the dioceses of Prešov and Mukačevo, since, because of massive state pressure, their number greatly declined by 60,000 in favor of the Orthodox.

In spite of the political and economic difficulties, the lack of priests, and an antiecclesiastical propaganda, the Church was able to revive in Czechoslovakia in the postwar years, in many areas even develop anew. A vigorous renewal took place especially in the school system and the press and among the religious orders and associations. Great meetings, congresses,[49] and celebrations strengthened Catholic self-consciousness.

On 9 May 1945, after the Second World War, there emerged with the support of the Soviet occupation the Czechoslovak People's Democratic Republic. The former political boundaries could be restored, apart from the Transcarpathian district, which was ceded to the Soviet Union. The country now included 127,869 square kilometers, with ca. 13 million inhabitants. On 25 February 1948 by means of a coup d'état the Communist party obtained power, which began at once with the establishing of a Communist state system. The hierarchy,[50] just established, and the reviving religious life, which had at first, however, suffered a harsh setback through the expulsion of hundreds of thousands of Catholics of German and Hungarian nationality, were paralyzed. The apostolic internuncio, Xaver Ritter, was expelled from the country. A series of administrative measures deprived the Church of its rights and its possibilities in the apostolate. Catholic schools, all seminaries and religious orders, organizations and societies, and the Catholic press were suppressed, religious instruction in the schools was ever more curtailed, the clergy was split by a pro-Communist Priests' Peace Movement, headed by Josef Plojhar, and the leading ecclesiastical personalities, bishops, including Josef Beran, were condemned in show trials to long prison terms. On 14 October 1949 the state Department of Churches assumed full control of the Church. On 28 April 1950 the Uniate see of Prešov was transferred to the obedience of the Orthodoxy of Moscow.[51] However, neither the clergy nor the

[49] In 1929 the Eastern Congress in Prague; in 1936 the Catholic Congress in Prague.
[50] Josef Beran became archbishop of Prague in 1946, Josef Matocha, archbishop of Olmütz.
[51] Cf. R. Urban, op. cit., 111–17.

faithful complied with this return, but as soon as circumstances allowed the Uniate diocese was reestablished. It is again permitted (since 13 June 1968) and numbers ca. 120,000 faithful.[52]

Negotiations between the Vatican and Czechoslovakia, which began in the course of the Church's new Eastern policy because of the changed political situation, led in the early 1960s to a slight relaxing of tension. In 1962–63 four bishops were able to take part in the Second Vatican Council, in 1965 Cardinal Beran was exiled, two seminaries could be opened, and, fostered by the political change of climate,[53] several bishops and priests were reinstated. After the military occupation of Czechoslovakia by the Soviet Union and the states of the Eastern bloc on 21 August 1968, however, the situation of the Church significantly worsened. Neither new discussions nor new appointments of bishops in 1973 could stop this. The Church suffers, among other things, also from a lack of priests. For the number of priests fell from 7,330 in 1948 to 3,100 in 1967.

Hungary

The military defeat of the Central Powers and the collapse of the Austro-Hungarian Monarchy let loose an internal political chaos in Hungary at the end of October 1918, which climaxed on 16 November 1918 in the proclamation of the republic and on 21 March 1919 in the constituting of a Communist Soviet Republic. It opened a new chapter in the history of Hungary and its Church. On the basis of a new constitution, issued on the model of that of Soviet Russia, the state was separated from the Church. This meant the secularization of all Church property—114,700,000 crowns in cash and 639,000 cadastral yokes, that is, ca. 320,000 hectares—and of the Catholic school system— almost 3,000 schools of every sort. A ruthless dictatorship pursued the openly proclaimed goal: the total annihilation of the Churches. Religious instruction was everywhere forbidden, most church institutions, monasteries, and episcopal residences were confiscated and plundered, and seventeen of the faithful, including nine priests and one sister, were executed for their loyalty to the Church. When on 1 August 1919, after a reign of terror of 133 days, the Soviet Republic collapsed because of the invasion of Rumanian troops, bleeding Hungary, occupied by Serbs, Rumanians, and Czechs, except for a small remnant, could think only of a "Christian course" in its reconstruction.[54]

[52] Ibid., 115–16.
[53] So-called Dubček Era or Prague Spring of 1968.
[54] Cf. S. Jankovics, "Az egyház a tanácsköztársaság idején" (The Church in the Period of the Soviet Republic), *Katholikus Szemle* 21, 1–4 (Rome 1969), 15–24, 121–31, 234–42, 346–56.

The kingdom was restored, and all laws of the Soviet republic were annulled. The new Hungarian government was under the administration of the royal representative, Miklós Horthy (1920–44), on the basis of a constructive cooperation with the Christian religious communities, especially of the Catholic Church. A decree of the Council of Ministers renounced the exercise of the royal right of patronage, but later the government secured for itself the customary political right of veto. There existed between Church and state a very good relationship, which helped the Church to develop fully its efforts for renewal. The governments saw in the Church a dependable ally, and they were concerned for the Church's restoration and even for its growth. And in 1920 diplomatic relations were established between the Holy See and Hungary.

By the Treaty of Trianon of 4 June 1920, Hungary lost two-thirds of its earlier national territory and one-third of its own population. To the new state were left 92,963 square kilometers, with 7.6 million inhabitants, of whom 5.2 million (66.1 percent) were Catholics, 1.6 million (21 percent) Calvinists, 497,000 (6.2 percent) Lutherans, and 473,000 (5.9 percent) Jews. The new frontiers corresponded neither to the ethnographic nor the previous ecclesiastical boundaries. Of the twenty-six dioceses, not counting Croatia-Slovenia, only four remained entirely unimpaired. Six bishoprics retained their sees in Hungary, but lost a great part of their territories. Now the episcopal sees of seven bishoprics belonged to neighboring states, but still retained areas in Hungary. Nine dioceses were completely separated from Hungary. Because of the new territorial frontiers, the Hungarian Church lost almost half of all its property—ca. 336,100 hectares.

Because of the loss of church property, which had especially hurt the archbishopric of Esztergom, because of the impeding of the jurisdiction of Hungarian bishops in the parts detached from their dioceses, because of the removal of Hungarian bishops from their local offices, on account of the organizational ecclesiastical independence of the detached areas, and on account of the nationalistic policy of the successor states, there arose several controversies between the Hungarian episcopate and the neighboring states, which were settled in the diplomatic manner by means of the Vatican and the governments. The complicated ecclesiopolitical situation was still further complicated by the first and second Vienna awards of 2 November 1938 and 30 August 1940 as well as by the occupation of the Carpatho-Ukraine and northern Yugoslavia by Hungary, since areas earlier detached, with some 4.5 million Catholics, returned to Hungary. Hungary lost them again in 1944–1945.

In spite of its doubtful economic situation, the Church was able energetically to renew itself. Of course, politically this was conditioned by the preceding tragic years of war and revolution and the impact of the Treaty of Trianon, which produced the consolidation of the conservative forces and an alliance with the Church. Besides, in Hungary there was no Catholic answer to the Enlightenment, Josephinism, and liberalism. Thus the Catholic renewal came, long delayed, only after the turn of the century, but then, accelerated by external events, it was all the more stormy in appearance. Under the leadership of Cardinals-Primate János Csernoch (1912–27) and Jusztinián Serédi (1927–45) there appeared apostolic bishops—Gusztáv Majláth, Gyula Glattfelder, Tihamér Tóth, and others—among them the most outstanding personality of Hungarian Catholicism since Cardinal-Primate Péter Pázmány (d. 1637), Ottokár Prohászka (1858–1927).[55] The imposing Catholic renaissance was connected with the revival of the religious orders, the origin of a notable Catholic press, the complete renewal of the Catholic intellectual life and of the Catholic school system, and the establishing of many important societies and organizations.[56] The Hungarian Catholic Days, the anniversary celebration of Saint Emeric in 1930, and the Thirty-Fourth International Eucharistic Congress at Budapest in 1938 gave eloquent testimony to the inner renewal of Hungarian Catholicism.

However, the close relationship of the Church with the state proved to be detrimental when Hungary, in keeping with its revisionist policy, got caught in the wake of German National Socialism. It was hard for the Church to separate itself from the state. Hence it could only slowly display the struggle against National Socialism. However, with Nuncio Angelo Rotta and Primate Serédi in the lead, it subsequently did so decisively. It was due to the Hungarian episcopate and the Church that 10,000 Hungarian Jews could escape death during the German occupation (1944–45).[57]

The military occupation of Hungary by the Red Army on 4 April 1945 also produced substantial changes in the relations of state and Church. Hungary gradually became a Socialist People's Republic in 1949, in which the Communist Party acquired absolute power. The employment of the ecclesiopolitical principles of the Communist Party also came to full flower in Hungary. As early as April 1945 Nuncio Rotta had to leave the country. By means of an abundance of administrative measures from 1945 to 1950 the Church was deprived of

[55] Cf. A. Schütz, "Ottokar Prohaśzka. Ein grosser Bischof der Gegenwart," *Hochland* 28, 1(1930–31), 322–39.

[56] In 1937 there were 157 societies with more than one million members.

[57] Cf. also A. Meszlényi, *A magyar katholikus egyház az emberi jogok védelmében* (Achievements of the Hungarian Catholic Church for Human Rights) (Budapest 1947).

all its property, its societies, its schools—3,344 of every sort—its institutions, the press—only twenty printeries—all religious orders— 2,582 male and 8,956 female religious in 705 houses—and its freedom of movement. In an effort to divide the clergy, there arose in 1950 the so-called Priests' Peace Movement, a clerical collaboration with the state authorities. Cardinal Primate József Mindszenty (1945–74) and the episcopate, with the help of religious institutions and inner renewal, unsuccessfully led a defensive struggle. The power of the Church was broken, and its leading personalities were condemned in show trials to long imprisonment: Mindszenty[58] in 1949, Archbishop József Grösz in 1951. The Church was completely excluded from public life.

In 1950 an agreement[59] between state and Church was forced on the episcopate; it completely surrendered the Church to the system in return for trivial concessions by the state. Even the popular uprising of 1956 was unable to halt this process. Meanwhile, the Vatican's Eastern policy, introduced under the auspices of the international policy of a relaxation of tensions, made possible in 1964 the concluding of a partial accord between Hungary and the Holy See. Since then, on four occasions (1969, 1972, 1974, 1975) appointments to the Hungarian episcopate could take place. However, neither the exiling of Mindszenty in 1971 nor his removal from office in 1974 nor the appointments of bishops and other efforts of the Holy See were able to impede or suspend the further consistent implementation of the Communist religious policy in Hungary.

Rumania

At the end of the First World War the Kingdom of Rumania doubled its territory by means of the incorporation of Bessarabia, Transylvania, great parts of the Banat, eastern Hungary, and Bukovina. Hence in 1919 it grew to 295,049 square kilometers and had 14.6 million inhabitants, the majority of whom—more than 70 percent—belonged to Orthodoxy. The previously religiously (Orthodox) and nationally (Rumanian) homogeneous Danube state became a heterogeneous kingdom with a diversity of national minorities and religious groups.

---

[58] Cf. G. Péterffy, *Il cardinale Mindszenty. La vita e l'anima d'un martire* (Rome 1949); N. Boer, *Cardinal Mindszenty and the Implacable War of Communism against Religion and Spirit* (London 1949); S. Mihalovics, *Mindszenty, Ungarn, Europa. Ein Zeugenbericht* (Karlsruhe 1949); N. Shuster, *In Silence I Speak. The Story of Cardinal Mindszenty Today and of Hungary's "New Order,"* (New York 1956); J. Vecsey, ed., *Kardinal Mindszenty. Beiträge zu seinem siebzigsten Geburtstag* (Würzburg 1972).
[59] Text in E. András, J. Morel, *Bilanz des ungarischen Katholizismus* (Munich 1969), 83– 85.

For, among other things, 1.6 million Hungarians and 2.5 million Catholics, including ca. 1.4 million Uniates, were awarded to Rumania by the Treaty of Trianon of 4 June 1920. With the new political frontiers, five entire dioceses and parts of three others came under Rumanian rule. In view of the fact that the union of all Rumanians in a great national state had been advocated by Orthodoxy for decades, and also that Rumanian Orthodoxy regarded the Roman Catholic Church as foreign, since its faithful were predominantly German or Hungarian, and, on the other hand, the Rumanian Uniates as traitors, there fell to Orthodoxy in the state leadership, as in Yugoslavia, a dominating role and an intransigent attitude. Hence, Rumanian ecclesiastical policy, striving for national and religious unity, was directed against the national minorities and against Catholics. This was clearly expressed also in the constitution of 28 March 1923, since paragraph 22, in opposition to the Treaty of Paris in regard to protection of national minorities, which had been signed on 9 December 1919, declared Rumanian Orthodoxy the "dominant religion," granted precedence to the Rumanian Uniates over other religious groups, and designated both as "Rumanian Churches."[60]

The Catholic Church in Transylvania, where the change of sovereignty often degenerated into acts of violence against the Church, soon lost its property—277,645 cadastral yokes, ca. 140,000 hectares—through the unilateral land reform and a great number of its schools and boarding schools through new school laws. Conversions to Orthodoxy were encouraged by state means. Their number grew in the former Hungarian territories from 1,803,257 in 1910 to 2,086,097 in 1927. When in 1923 Bishop Gyula Glattfelder of Timisoara protested against the church policy measures, he had to leave Rumania and transfer his episcopal see to Szeged in Hungary. In vain Bishop Gusztáv Majláth of Transylvania also protested in the Senate at Bucharest in 1923 and in 1925 before the League of Nations at Geneva.

The Holy See, which had established diplomatic relations with Rumania in 1920, soon recognized that the continued existence of the Uniate Church and the assuring of the minimal rights of Roman Catholics were possible only with the support of the Rumanian Uniates and was ready, in order to achieve this goal, to abandon the interests of Roman Catholics of Hungarian and German nationality. The negotiations among Bucharest, the Vatican, and Budapest lasted for seven years and were very difficult, since at stake was the rearrangement of the Church's organization and of church property. In the framework of the rearrangement Bishop Raimund Netzhammer had to resign the see

---

[60] Cf. N. Brinzeu, *Cultele in Romania* (Church Politics in Rumania) (Lugoj 1925).

of Bucharest. The negotiations were concluded on 10 May 1927 with the signing of a concordat.[61] It was ratified on 7 July 1929 and implemented by the apostolic constitution *Solemni Conventione*[62] on 5 June 1930. It established a new Latin metropolitan see with four bishoprics, guaranteed to the bishops the free exercise of their office, recognized ecclesiastical institutions and religious orders as juridical persons; church schools could be founded, and a so-called *patrimonium sacrum* was to arise from the church property, enumerated by name. The Church conceded the usual right of veto in the appointing of bishops and accommodated the national desires of the government.

Scarcely had the treaty been signed when the Rumanian Orthodox nationalists demanded the immediate dissolution and expropriation of the Transylvanian so-called *status catholicus,* the organ of the autonomous administration of the Transylvanian Catholics, since this still rich *status* was not enumerated in the property list. The negotiations, resumed between the Vatican and the Rumanian government, ended on 30 May 1932 with an *accordo.* The *status* and its rules were recognized under the proviso of state control. Meanwhile, the extremists continued their attacks and questioned the agreement because of its coming into being outside conformity with the constitution. Not until 2 March 1940 did a royal rescript ratify the *accordo,* after the property of the *status,* in the amount of 610 million *lei,* had been turned over to administration by the state.[63]

Between the two world wars Catholicism, despite all the difficulties, was able not only to maintain but also to renew itself. Inner religious life was especially deepened, but the Catholic press and social life could be vigorously improved. In 1932 the Roman Catholic Church counted 1.2 million faithful, 513 parishes, 898 priests, 200 male religious in 56 monasteries, and 1,432 sisters in 66 convents, while the Uniates had in 1,593 parishes 1,579 priests, in 8 monasteries 24 male religious, and in 11 convents 185 sisters.

After the Vienna Award of 30 August 1940 important parts of Transylvania were restored to Hungary, which reestablished there the earlier condition of the Church. Between the two peoples there occurred excesses, even in the ecclesiastical sphere. The end of the Second World War permitted Rumania to revive in its old frontiers, except for Bessarabia, which was incorporated into the Soviet Union.

[61] *AAS* 21(1929), 441–56.

[62] Ibid. 22(1930), 381–86.

[63] Cf. J. Scheffler, "A katholikus egyház jogi helyzete Romániában" (The Legal Status of the Catholic Church in Rumania), *Notter-Emlékkönyv* (Budapest 1941), 965–84; idem, "Az erdélyi Katholikus Státus küzdelmes husz éve" (Twenty Hard Years of the Catholic State in Transylvania), *Magyar Szemle* 40(1941), 299–310.

On 6 March 1945 a Communist government was imposed on the state; on 12 March 1948 it abolished the monarchy and proclaimed the People's Republic. It issued a Communist constitution on 24 September 1952. The concordat was repudiated on 17 July 1948, and on 4 August 1948 a so-called Law on Worship went into effect. In this the government recognized only two bishoprics—Alba Julia and Jassy—and considered the others as nonexistent. The dissolution of the Uniate Church was decreed on 2 December 1948, after a group of Uniate priests had decided to return to the Orthodox on 1 October 1948. The six Uniate bishops and all other bishops, including those who had been secretly ordained bishops by the nuncio before his expulsion, were arrested and condemned to long prison terms. The church administration was paralyzed, the religious orders were dissolved except for five houses, all Catholic schools and institutions were abolished, the Catholic press was forbidden. And the effort to establish a Rumanian National Church was undertaken.

Only gradually there occurred a relaxing of tensions. In 1955 the bishop of Alba Julia was released from prison but he remained under house arrest until 1967. In 1970 and 1971 he was allowed to travel to Rome and in 1971 he obtained a coadjutor with the right of succession. But neither the exertions of the Holy See in the course of its Eastern policy nor the visits of Rumanian Minister President Gheorge Maurer in 1968 and of the chairman of the Council of State Nicolae Ceausescu in 1973 to Paul VI could ease the harsh fate of the Catholics in Rumania.

Yugoslavia

The Kingdom of the Serbs, Croats, and Slovenes, called Yugoslavia since 3 October 1929, originated on 1 December 1918 through the union of the southern Slavic territories of the Austro-Hungarian Monarchy with Serbia and Montenegro. The formation of the state took place, because of the military occupation of southern Hungary, not without acts of violence against the Catholic Church, and Cardinal Secretary of State Pietro Gasparri protested to Belgrade against them. The new state included 248,987 square kilometers, with a population of 12 million, a variety of nations and religious communities, including 5.5 million Orthodox, 4.7 million Catholics, and 1.3 million Muslims. The predominance of the Orthodox Serbs, who were establishing their own state, in comparison to the Catholic Croats and the unclarified legal status of the church organization[64] required a reorganization of the Church and the prompt clarification of relations of state and Church, all

[64] Only two of the ecclesiastical provinces remained in the old boundaries.

the more since the previous concordats with individual countries[65] had been annulled by the founding of the new kingdom.

The preference for Orthodox Serbs in the administration of the state and the military, on the occasion of land reform and colonization, and in the distributing of state finances for religious communities, even though according to the constitution of 28 June 1921 all recognized religious communities were made equal, led to serious tensions between Church and state. On 23 July 1919 the Serbian school law of 1904, which recognized no church schools, was extended to all areas of the state. In this way the Church lost all its elementary and secondary schools. And twenty monasteries and 920 cadastral yokes (ca. 460 hectares) of church property were transferred to the state. Various religious societies, such as the Marian Congregations, were dissolved, and the youth in school were compelled to join the antireligious youth organization, *Jugoslovenski Sokol*. The bishops protested in vain against these measures in a common pastoral letter in 1923 and 1933. They accomplished only the opposite—the sharpening of the suppression. Hence the episcopal conferences in 1924 and 1925 proposed the concluding of a concordat.

As early as 1920 the Holy See sent a nuncio to Belgrade and was ready to conduct discussions on the diplomatic level. As a token of its good will, it erected the apostolic administrations of Banat in 1922 and Bačka in 1923, established the archbishopric of Belgrade in 1924, and made Skopje an exempt see in 1924. Thereby the Church had in Yugoslavia 4 archdioceses, 14 bishoprics, 2 apostolic administrations, 1,839 parishes, 3,109 priests, 1,409 male religious, of whom 941 were priests, and 3,754 sisters. The negotiations for the concordat were difficult. It was only on 25 July 1935 that an agreement was signed, after the state had already regulated its relations with the Orthodox in 1929, the Muslims in 1931, and the Protestants and Jews in 1933.

The concordat[66] guaranteed the reestablishing of the church organization, the free nomination of bishops by the Holy See, the free activity of the Church, church property, state subsidies, ecclesiastical celebration of marriages without a previous civil marriage, church associations and organizations, schools, and religious orders, in brief, the complete religious freedom of Catholics. For its part, the Holy See promised to elevate the apostolic administrations to bishoprics. Hence the concordat envisaged the equality of Catholics with the Orthodox.[67] Precisely for this reason, however, Orthodoxy under the leadership of Patriarch

[65] Latest on 24 July 1914 with Serbia.
[66] Not published in *AAS* because of nonratification; text in Mercati, vol. 2, 202–16; biblio. in Schöppe, 558.
[67] Cf. M. Lanović, *Konkordat Jugoslavije e Vaticanom* (Yugoslavia's Concordat with the Vatican) (Belgrade 1935).

Varnava led a relentless fight against the agreement. When the *Skupština* (House of Delegates) accepted the concordat on 23 July 1937, the Holy Synod of Yugoslavia excommunicated all Orthodox members of the government and of parliament who had voted for the acceptance. Hence Minister President Milan Stojadinović did not submit the concordat to the Senate at all, but removed it from the agenda and informed the Synod that in new negotiations with the Vatican the patriarchate would first be consulted. In this way a concordat in Yugoslavia was made dependent on Orthodoxy, that is, forever excluded. However, as a consequence of the domestic and foreign policy situation, the spirit of the concordat could be realized. Church life flowered. Especially in the press, education, the societies, the care of souls, and the religious orders a rise was noticeable.

The Second World War was an especially severe blow to the Church. From 27 March 1941 Yugoslavia was occupied by German and Italian troops. Croatia declared itself an independent kingdom (1941–45), but in reality it was a satellite state dependent on the Axis Powers. There the government was very accommodating to the Catholic Church, but it often compelled it to collaborate and involved it in the bloody conflicts of the Croatian *Ustaza* and the Serbian partisan bands. These circumstances led at the war's end, on the occasion of the expulsion of the German population, to cruel acts of violence also against the Catholic Church. A pastoral letter of the bishops in 1945 bemoaned the murder of 243 priests and the plundering and destruction of many churches.[68]

After the Second World War, Yugoslavia became a federated Peoples' Republic on 29 November 1945, with the old political and diocesan boundaries.[69] Although the constitution of 31 January 1946, while separating state and Church, guaranteed liberty of conscience and religion, there soon occurred, as in the other neighboring socialist states, a massive persecution of the Church. Up to 1946 ca. 13 percent of the clergy were executed, ca. 50 percent were imprisoned, including Archbishop Aloysius Stepinač[70] of Zagreb. The Franciscan order alone had 139 victims. Catholic schools and organizations were liquidated, monasteries were for the most part dissolved, religious instruction and ecclesiastical activity were almost completely stopped, and a union of

---

[68] Cf. V. Novak, *Magnum Crimen. Pola vijeka klerikalizma u Hrvatskoj* (Magnum Crimen. A Half-Century of Clericalism in Croatia) (Zagreb 1948).
[69] The state's area was expanded with 8,851 square kilometers in Istria and Dalmatia.
[70] Cf. H. O'Brien, *Archbishop Stepinač, the Man and His Case* (Westminister 1947); R. Pattee, *The Case of Cardinal Aloysius Stepinač* (Milwaukee 1953); cf. also the official presentation of Yugoslavia: *The Case of Archbishop Stepinač* (Washington 1947); also S. Simič, *Vatikan protiv Jugoslavije* (The Vatican against Yugoslavia) (Titograd 1958).

collaborating priests was founded to split the clergy. After a temporary relaxation following the break of President Josip Broz Tito with the Cominform in 1950 and after a new intensification of the situation by the elevation of Stepinač to the College of Cardinals in 1953, the papal nuncio was expelled. But the Church did not give in. On 23 September 1952 the bishops sent a letter of energetic protest to Tito and repeatedly told him that they were not empowered to conclude an agreement with the government.[71]

After the death of Cardinal Stepinač in 1960, the situation gradually relaxed. On 26 June 1964 the Holy See made direct contact with Yugoslavia. The discussions led on 26 June 1966 to an agreement,[72] which guaranteed the liberty of the Church but also affirmed the loyalty of the Church to Yugoslavia. Diplomatic relations were also restored between the Holy See and Yugoslavia. On 14 August 1970 an internuncio was sent to Belgrade. Indications of further relaxation were the raising of the apostolic administration of Bačka to a bishopric in 1968, the more extensive autonomy of the apostolic administration of Banat by the naming of a titular bishop in 1971, and in the same year Tito's visit to the Vatican. Despite some difficulties, the Church in Yugoslavia now enjoys a relative freedom of religion. This appears especially in the interior life of the Church. In 1961 the Church, despite serious losses, could again count 2,514 parishes, 2,462 diocesan and 1,145 religious priests, 1,491 brothers, 5,380 sisters, and 5,725,000 faithful. This favorable development continued in the following years. In 1974 there were in Yugoslavia 764 candidates for the priesthood, 2,817 male religious, of whom 1,728 were priests, 8,622 sisters, and 3,001 diocesan priests.[73]

Bulgaria

The Kingdom of Bulgaria came out of the Second Balkan War in 1913 and the First World War of 1914–18 diminished in size. It now had a total of only 103,146 square kilometers in area; 8,900 square kilometers of valuable territories, like access to the Aegean Sea, had been lost. The country counted in 1926 5.4 million inhabitants, of whom, however, only 45,491—.83 percent—were Catholics, among them 5,598 Uniates, who lived in one bishopric and one vicariate apostolic.

[71] Cf. W. de Vries, "Kirchenverfolgung in Jugoslawien," StdZ 146 (1949f.), 362–68; idem, "Die neue Welle der Religionsverfolgung in Jugoslawien," ibid. 151(1952f.), 442–51; K. S. Draganovič, "La Chiesa nella Repubblica Jugoslava," CivCatt 97/III (1946), 3–13, 318–24; 105/I (1954), 716–30; 105/II (1954), 105–20.
[72] Cf. HK 20(1966), 410f.
[73] Cf. the latest statistics and a summary in HK 31(1977), 318–24.

Eighty-four percent of the population belonged to Orthodoxy, 13 percent to Islam. The economically ruined country sought the revision of the unfavorable Treaty of Neuilly of 27 November 1919, but was visited by domestic and foreign policy difficulties. Despite this unhappy situation, the Church was still able to display a vigorous activity. Up to 1944 the number of faithful grew to 57,000. An apostolic exarchate for the Uniates could be established in 1926, and the Church ran more than 18 institutes, including 10 schools, 2 hospitals, and 6 orphanages. There resided at Sofia a representative of the Holy See as apostolic delegate without diplomatic character. From 1925 to 1934 he was Giuseppe Angelo Roncalli, later Pope John XXIII.

The Soviet occupation of Bulgaria on 9 September 1944 led on 15 September 1945 to the proclamation of the republic and on 15 October 1946 to the constituting of a People's Republic. A new constitution of 4 December 1947 and a law on worship of 17 February 1949 began the curtailing of religious freedom. Soon a ruthless persecution of the Church erupted. The Church lost all its organizations, institutes, bishops, and most of its priests and religious.

In the course of the gradual relaxation of tensions John XXIII was able in 1962 to welcome two Bulgarian bishops at the Second Vatican Council, and in 1968 Paul VI could receive a Bulgarian pilgrimage and in 1969 a delegation of the Bulgarian government at the Vatican. Mutual contacts have not been broken since then, but the situation of the Church in Bulgaria is unchanged.

Albania

Albania was able to reestablish its political sovereignty after the First World War, and it covered 27,538 square kilometers with 833,000 inhabitants. Of these, in 1929, 563,000 were Muslims, 181,051 Orthodox, and 88,739—10.6 percent—Catholics. The church organization was divided into 2 archdioceses, 3 dioceses, and 1 abbey *nullius*. There were 120 parishes, 143 diocesan and religious priests, 84 brothers, and 66 sisters. The country, which had to contend with backwardness and misery, acquired in the Catholic Church a special support, especially in charity and education. The Catholic mission, supported for decades by Italy, received an exceptional stimulus. Up to 1944 the number of religious grew to 321, of whom 116 were natives. The Italian missionary work was especially intensified from 1939, after Italian troops had occupied Albania on 7 April 1939 and had subordinated it to the Kingdom of Italy. In southern Albania there arose an apostolic administration, which was administered by the envoy of the Holy See residing in Albania from 1920, an apostolic delegate.

The Albanian war of resistance (1941–44) and the end of the German and Italian occupation gave the Albanian Communists the opportunity to erect a Communist political system[74] and completely to suppress the allegedly "colonizing" Catholic Church. All foreign missionaries, sisters, and the apostolic delegate were expelled, all ecclesiastical administrations and organizations were dissolved, all bishops, priests, and religious were shot, imprisoned, or scattered. An attempt was made in 1951 to found a national Church. Since Albania separated from the rest of the Eastern bloc states led by Moscow and, under the guidance of China, put itself in complete isolation, the Vatican was unable to make any contacts at all with it. In 1973 Albania proudly declared that it was the first socialist country to have closed the last church and extirpated religion.

[74] On 11 February 1946 Albania became a People's Republic.

CHAPTER 18

*The Church in The German-Speaking Countries**

Germany

In the frenzy of national solidarity to which the peoples of Europe gave themselves as they moved against one another at the beginning of the First World War, the German Catholics were as much caught up as were other ideological groups. Just the forces which had stood sharply opposed, at least for a while, to the Empire's domestic policy overwhelmingly experienced the urge to show an undoubted profession to the German national state by the evidence of patriotic acceptance of sacrifices. This was true of the social democratic electorate no less than of the Catholic part of the population. And so there was a great attempt in the war effort to grasp at the opportunity to refute, once and for all, the accusation of a lack of loyalty to the Empire, hurled during the *Kulturkampf.* It was all the easier for the individual to accept the consequences of entering the war when the decision on war and peace was, according to Catholic political theory, so completely the responsibility of the rulers that its necessity or avoidability was not a subject of discussion for the simple citizen with his limited viewpoint. And while guiding principles of Catholic social doctrine in domestic policy caused distance and alternatives to political reality, the few general principles of the Church's ethics of war did not suffice in the field of foreign policy

* Ludwig Volk, S. J.

to give a critical judgment in the concrete case on the *ultima ratio* of the use of weapons. Thus there originated also the self-assurance with which Bishop Faulhaber of Speyer in 1915 declared the European conflict for the German side as the "academic example of a just war,"[1] more the inclination to premature identification than an exhaustive recognition of the facts.

Compared with the lines of communication, which led from all episcopal sees of the *orbis catholicus* to the Vatican central office, the interrelationships among the national Catholicisms of Europe were only meagerly developed. This explains why a committee composed of prominent French laymen and prelates perceived so few restraints in supporting the antagonism of the warring parties in the ecclesiastical sphere also. Especially venomous was the impact of the attempt, undertaken in a polemical work,[2] to throw suspicion on the German Catholics of a diffused and global lack of loyalty to the faith. Naturally, those attacked defended themselves with a counterpublication.[3]

By means of a questionable attack a little later, the Belgian Cardinal Mercier threatened to involve the hierarchy in the dispute over the war. Concentrating entirely on the miseries of Belgium, which, without any provocation, had become the first victim of hostilities through the German invasion, the archbishop of Mechelen appeared to his German brothers in office to cooperate in setting up an episcopal tribunal.[4] He intended to free the Belgian civil population from the accusation of sniper warfare, hence from that accusation by which the German army command had sought to justify bloody reprisals in the first weeks of the war. Since Mercier at once publicized his project without any internal close contact, he caused the most serious embarrassment for those addressed. Only with difficulty was Cardinal Hartmann (1851–1919), since 1914 chairman of the Prussian episcopate, restrained from an equally public retort. Absolutely loyal to the Empire, even if without the political ambition of his predecessor Kopp, Hartmann hesitated between overcaution and inflexibility. In 1917–18 he displayed little foresightedness and sense of reality in his opposition to the elimination of the undemocratic three-class franchise in Prussia.[5] The fact that the spokesman of the Prussian bishops, in contrast to the other bishops, opposed an overdue constitutional reform weakened the power of

[1] M. Faulhaber, *Waffen des Lichts* (Freiburg 1918), 132.
[2] Cf. A. Baudrillart, ed., *La Guerre Allemande et le Catholicisme* (Paris 1915).
[3] Cf. G. Pfeilschifter, ed., *Deutsche Kultur, Katholizismus und Weltkrieg* (Freiburg 1915).
[4] Cf. L. Volk, "Kardinal Mercier, der deutsche Episkopat und die Neutralitätspolitik Benedikts XV. 1914–1916." *StdZ* 192(1974), 611–30.
[5] Cf. R. Patemann, "Der deutsche Episkopat und das preussische Wahlrechtsproblem 1917/18," *Vierteljahrshefte für Zeitgeschichte* 13(1965), 345–71.

conviction of a common pastoral letter of All Saints Day 1917, which sought to exorcise the revolutionary unrest in the underground.

Presented with a fait accompli in November 1918 through the military defeat and the proclamation of the republic, the Center party concentrated on giving full effect to its political weight in the national constituent assembly.[6] What the party accomplished in the discussions on the constitution, both constructively and as preventive measures, considerably surpassed what could be expected from its numerical strength.[7] If nevertheless the Fulda episcopal conference in November 1919 registered doubts, from the viewpoint of the Church's self-awareness, against individual items of the constitutional work, this concern for rights[8] was a precaution for possible future controversies, but not a criticism of what had been achieved at Weimar by the delegates of the Center.

In May 1917 Benedict XV had entrusted the Munich nunciature to Eugenio Pacelli, one of the most capable curial diplomats. He came as precursor of the Pope's work for peace, directed to all the warring leaders, but a personal visit of the nuncio to the imperial headquarters was unable to secure from the Germans the concessions which a further discussion of the project that had prospects of success would have required.[9] After the constitutions of the *Reich* and of the states had built political life on a republican plan, the nuncio faced a field of activity of vast extent. In the establishing of a nunciature for the *Reich* at Berlin, which Pacelli administered from Munich in a personal union from 1920 to 1925, and in the accreditation of the hitherto Prussian envoy, von Bergen, as ambassador of the *Reich* at the Holy See, there was reflected the importance which in Berlin was attributed to diplomatic relations with the Vatican.

The Foreign Office worked especially to have this developed in a concordat with the *Reich* in international law in the critical convulsions of the first postwar years, because it assured itself[10] of a consolidation, with the moral power of the Church, of the German frontiers in dispute in the east (Upper Silesia) and west (the Saarland). But the desire for a concordat that would apply to all German dioceses flagged when at the end of 1923 the period of political weakness had been overcome. For his part, Pacelli did not lose sight of the long-range goal of a concordat

---

[6] Cf. R. Morsey, *Die deutsche Zentrumspartei 1917–1923* (Düsseldorf 1966), 163–245.
[7] For the content of the ecclesiastical articles of the Weimar Constitution cf. Bihlmeyer-Tüchle, 500.
[8] Printing of the announcement: L. Volk, ed., *Akten Kardinal Michael von Faulhabers 1917–1945* Vol. I: *1917–1934* (Mainz 1975), 111f.
[9] On the Holy See's peace policy during World War I, cf. above, Chapter 3.
[10] Cf. L. Volk, *Das Reichskonkordat vom 20. Juli 1933* (Mainz 1972), 1–24.

with the *Reich,* but at first he had to make certain of the state concordat with Bavaria,[11] planned as early as 1919. Well disposed to the Vatican's ideas of state and Church, but by no means uncritically opposing them, the cabinet posts held by the Bavarian Popular Party offered, from Pacelli's view, more favorable presuppositions for the creating of a "model concordat" than other state governments, in which the Catholic parties had a less strong position. If the nuncio hoped to gain from the Bavarian precedent a sort of norm, by which the readiness for concessions of future treaty partners would be measured, the agreeableness displayed by Bavaria in no sense acted as a stimulus, but rather consolidated the inclination against a concordat of the socialist, liberal, and Protestant groups. Only after protracted preliminary discussions was the treaty signed at Munich on 29 March 1924 and approved by the *Landtag* at the beginning of 1925.

The collaboration of the bishops could not long evade the centralizing tendencies of the new state organization. The distinctly tribal consciousness of the Bavarian bishops opposed a merging of the conferences of Fulda and Freising, which had operated side by side, following an all-German prelude from 1867 to 1872, since the beginning of the *Kulturkampf.* Also, the autocratic rule which Cardinal Kopp had exercised over the Prussian episcopate was still vivid in memory. Thus in 1920 there first occurred a personal bridging of the episcopal main line, while each of the two conference chairmen was invited to the meetings of the sister conference. Without regard for regional preferences, the bishops in north and south were finally united in a single consultative community in 1933 by the Nazi totalitarianism that sought uniformity; within its framework, of course, the Freising conference continued to exist, and the West German episcopal conference was reorganized from 1934 in special meetings, mostly at Kevelaer.

The chairmen of the Bavarian episcopate, Michael von Faulhaber (1869–1952), since 1917 archbishop of Munich and Freising, had already acquired from Speyer, where he had worked as bishop from 1911, a reputation as a preacher of the faith and critic of the age of great stature. Of a princely appearance and from 1921 a cardinal, Faulhaber seemed destined by providence to step into the vacuum which the forced departure of the Wittelsbachs had created in the sensitivities of broad strata of the population.

From the baroque element in the appearance of the archbishop of Munich no connecting line led to the figure of Cardinal Adolf Bertram (1859–1945) of Breslau, a sober Lower Saxon. Bishop of Hildesheim

---

[11] For the course of the negotiations cf. G. Franz-Willing, *Die bayerische Vatikangesandtschaft 1803–1934* (Munich 1965), 181–227.

in 1906, of Breslau in 1914, and cardinal in 1916, in 1920 he assumed the chairmanship of the Fulda episcopal conference. Conversant with law, worldy-wise, zealous, and extremely diligent, he proved to be the master of written memoranda to governmental officials on every level.

The Catholics in the south and west of the *Reich* expressed their assent to the Weimar state neither unanimously nor with equal decisiveness.[12] How strongly their views diverged came to light in 1922 at the Munich *Katholikentag* in the sensational controversy between Cardinal Faulhaber and the president of the meeting, Adenauer.[13] Neither spoke for himself alone but for a considerable following, the one as spokesman of a royal Bavarian, the other as representative of a Rhenish democratic Catholicism. True, Faulhaber's harsh judgment was directed first at the revolution as such, but all later interpretations did not soften the thrust at the present reality of the republic.

One of the most significant gains, which the Catholic Church, along with all religious bodies, owed to the republican constitution was the exclusion of state influences in the bestowal of ecclesiastical offices. To regard this as progress was denied to the bishops so long as the constitutional law remained a dead letter, because the ministerial officials of individual German state governments opposed a stubborn resistance to the transforming of this constitutional norm into administrative practice. Cardinal Bertram and Nuncio Pacelli reacted in notably different ways to the ever clearer obstructionist tactics of Prussia, by far the single most powerful state, with 60 percent of the population of the *Reich*. While the chairman of the Fulda episcopal conference first aimed to see the constitutional point of departure restored before the granting by treaty of possibilities of hearing agencies in the appointment to church offices could be discussed, the nuncio was bound to the prospect of being able to move on to talk of a concordat even before the overdue liquidation of the *Kulturkampf* laws.

Prussia's willingness for a treaty, however, only made itself felt after the Bavarian model had stirred in Berlin the desire likewise to move up to the "concordat state." In regard to content, the Prussian concordat of 14 June 1929 could only lag behind the Bavarian model because of differently arranged parliamentary circumstances,[14] and with the renunciation of school regulations it became almost a torso, because it even lacked what from the Vatican's viewpoint only made a treaty with the Church really a concordat. Nevertheless, the positive yield was significant: the erecting of the see of Berlin, the elevation of Breslau

---

[12] On the route of the German Catholics from the Empire to the republic, cf. H. Lutz, *Demokratie im Zwielicht* (Munich 1963).

[13] Cf. *Akten Kardinal Michael von Faulhabers* (above, note 8) nos. 127–33.

[14] Cf. D. Golombek, *Die politische Vorgeschichte des Preussenkonkordats* (Mainz 1970).

and Paderborn to archepiscopal status with a new distribution of the suffragan sees, the participation of the Prussian cathedral chapter in the election of the bishop. The state of Baden followed with the concordat of 12 October 1932.

In regard to cultural policy the 1920s were under the auspices of the conflicts over the *Reich's* school law demanded by the Weimar Constitution.[15] There had already been bitter struggles over the school article in the discussions of the constitution. They had the character of a compromise, and, despite several attempts, the Center Party did not succeed in putting through the equality of rank, prescribed by canon law for the denominational school, with the public school favored by the cultural and political Left.

The ideological oppositions broke out again over three drafts of laws submitted in the course of the years. Although the Catholic school organization sought to gather the advocates of the denominational school without regard for party boundaries, and in a campaign for signatures in 1922–23 some 75 percent of all Catholics qualified to vote opted for this type of school, this changed nothing in the majority situation in the *Reichstag*. Since the prospects for a *Reich* school law that would have partly corresponded to Catholic ideas thereby disappeared, the defenders of the denominational school finally turned entirely to the defensive under the slogan "Rather no *Reich* school law than a bad one."

In its beginnings an offshoot of the Popular Union for Catholic Germany, the Catholic school organization had experienced a steep ascent since 1913, while the Mönchen-Gladbach branch-enterprise fell into a crisis of existence.[16] After a maximum membership of more than 800,000 in 1914, the social, economic, and political upheavals of the war and postwar periods had so obstructed the Popular Union that in 1928 it counted only 400,000 members. After the Catholic association system in Germany had displayed, up to the beginning of the war, an amazing breadth, dynamism, and diversity, now the dark sides of the differentiation became perceptible. For the most part liable to subscription in several societies, the members first economized in times of need in what was unnecessary. Moreover, the superorganization favored a certain weariness of association. In the Mönchen-Gladbach case a lack of economic decisions and the struggle against a crippling mountain of debts did more than was needed to cause the glorious "Union of Unions" to become one of the first victims of Hitler's liquidation policy

---

[15] Cf. G. Grünthal, *Reichsschulgesetz und Zentrumspartei in der Weimarer Republik* (Düsseldorf 1968).
[16] Cf. E. Ritter, *Die katholisch-soziale Bewegung Deutschlands im 19. Jahrhundert und der Volksverein* (Cologne 1954), 355–495.

in mid-1933. Once on its way down current, the Popular Union foundered on the inability of its leaders to shape it beyond the socioethical goals of the time of foundation to the general Catholic union, a plan which, in view of the distribution of functions in the association sector that had meanwhile occurred, apparently had little chance in any case.

The exemplar of "Catholic Action" was based on a quite similar idea, as it was preached by Pius XI cocksurely and emphatically. In 1928 Nuncio Pacelli was supposed to supply the initial kindling in an address at the *Katholikentag* in Magdeburg. If the response, despite the good will of the laity who were called to share in the hierarchical apostolate of the Church, as the official definition said, was not really satisfying, the principal reason was that the papal appeal outlined a program which was not only realized in a diversity of ways in the Catholic association life of Germany, but looked back to a long tradition and did not, as in most of the Latin countries, encounter an association-organizational vacuum. A stricter reference of the independent lay societies to the hierarchy would rightly be felt by these as a vexation and retrogression. Conversely the prospect was not unwelcome to some bishops of breaking the concentration of power of the superdiocesan central association by appeal to "Catholic Action." In fact, Catholic Action was never really able to get a foothold in Germany, and what was so called despite all failures did not go beyond a minimal exertion owed to the papal initiator.

Without ignoring the representation of legitimate church claims and interests among the *Reich* officials, and stressing the primacy of the pastoral in his understanding of his episcopal office, Cardinal Bertram respected the existing institutional distribution of competencies between the entire episcopate and the Catholic Center Party and Bavarian People's Party. He was thoroughly opposed to a competitive juxtaposition on the field of Church politics, before which his predecessor Kopp showed no dread at all. In any event, Bertram, by commission of his fellow bishops, internally occupied a position toward individual projects of laws to the extent that inner church interests were concerned, but for the rest the freedom of decision of the Catholic delegates was left intact, however much current ideas aspired to see in them mere agents of the executive power of the Church's leadership.[17]

On the outside the Church's closeness to the Catholic parties was manifested in a number of clerical bearers of mandates, the not entirely uncritically so-called Center prelates, who mostly belonged to the

---

[17] Cf. also R. Morsey, "Kirche und politische Parteien 1848/49," A. Rauscher ed., *Kirche, Politik, Parteien* (Cologne 1974), 19–56.

distinctive, even if not leading, minds of their parties but had to thank not their clerical status but their professional achievements. Pope Pius XI had fundamental reservations about the conflict-laden double commitment of pastoral care and party politics without abruptly cutting off the connections that had grown historically. In Germany the problem of interfering professional fields in the life of the nuncio's adviser and leader of the Center, Ludwig Kaas, became as evident as in Austria in the activity of the prelate Ignaz Seipel, who had risen to be chancellor.

That the Weimar Constitution of 1919 was serious about the demand for equality, without distinction, of all citizens and thereby realized the points of the program to whose implementation the founders of the Center had earlier joined together, could not be without repercussions on the inner unity of the electoral body.[18] For with the demolition of the last vestiges of the *Kulturkampf* the previously attractive long-range goals had become pointless. As the conviction among Catholics loyal to the Church, formerly self-evident, of the indispensability of the Center constantly waned, it could be gathered from election statistics in consequence of which the proportion going over to the Center and the BVP in the votes cast between 1919 and 1933 dropped from 18 percent to 14 percent.[19] Between the loss in external recruiting power and the disappearance in inner cohesion existed a clear connection. Symptomatic of the strengthening of the centrifugal forces was the inability at the end of 1928 of the Center representatives to agree on a successor to Wilhelm Marx, who had resigned, as party chairman. For the first time in the history of the Center an ecclesiastic, the Trier prelate Ludwig Kaas (1881–1952), had to take the chairmanship in order to bridge the gulf between the wings.

Just as before, the Catholic parties could count on the indirect support of the episcopate in the form of electoral pastoral letters before critical votes. Not made use of sparingly enough, such episcopal appeals to Catholic cohesion concealed the danger of weakening the force of episcopal authority in case it needed to pronounce on ultimate ideological questions. The bishops felt themselves obliged to just this after the sudden increase of Hitler's National Socialist party to a mass movement of millions in 1930. One after another they underlined the incompatibility of Christianity and National Socialism

---

[18] Cf. J. Becker, "Das Ende der Zentrumspartei und die Problematik des politischen Katholizismus in Deutschland," G. Jasper, *Von Weimar zu Hitler 1930–1933* (Cologne 1968), 344–76.

[19] Cf. J. Schauff, *Das Walhverhalten der deutschen Katholiken im Kaiserreich und in der Weimarer Republik* (Mainz 1975).

in the spring of 1931.[20] The prohibition to join the Hitler movement was based on the racism and nationalism of his party, on the extravagance and malice of its agitation, on its violence against those who thought differently. In the daily papers the warnings of the German episcopate against National Socialism provoked an unusually more violent reaction than the directives[21] issued in 1921 in regard to atheistic socialism and based on the same principles.

With their authoritative refusal the bishops could influence Catholics who might be thinking of changing their vote, and this was proved when on 5 March 1933 Hitler "clearly obtained the least votes in the parts of the *Reich* that had a Catholic majority,"[22] but they could not prevent other strata of the population from turning to the Nazi movement. Not by accident did there occur with the agony of the Weimar state the outbreak of an intellectual current within German Catholicism, which under the collective term *Reichsideologie* produced an immense number of publications between 1929 and 1934, but remained almost exclusively confined to intellectual circles in its influence.[23] In the quest for a counterimage to the depressing political reality, authors of the most varied provenance came together in the attempt to revive the medieval notion of the Empire. In fact historically concealed illusionism, the concept was nonetheless in the process of exercising a considerable fascination on some contemporaries. It received religious impulses from the *consecratio mundi,* demanded at the same time by the liturgical movement. With the mutual institutional interpenetration of the original powers of state and Church the representatives of the *Reichsideologie* painted an image, the actualization of which had failed more than once in the history of Europe. This alone was not enough to destroy the counterfeit brilliance of the utopia, but the trend was too academic and elitist to influence the electoral process. This was the true measure of the actual political relevance of this movement and not the deluge of writings on the *Reichsideologie.* This applies to the period before as well as after Hitler's accession to power on 30 January 1933.

[20] Printing of the episcopal stand: B. Stasiewski, ed., *Akten deutscher Bischöfe über die Lage der Kirche 1933–1945* Vol. I: *1933–1934* (Mainz 1968), Appendix nos. 5–7 and 11–13.

[21] For the suggestion relevant to the tasks of pastoral care in regard to antifaith unions, see W. Corsten, *Sammlung kirchlicher Erlasse, Verordnungen und Bekanntmachungen für die Erzdiözese Köln* (Cologne 1929), 619–24.

[22] R. Morsey (above n. 17), 31.

[23] Cf. K. Breuning, *Die Vision des Reiches* (Munich 1969), but with overemphasis on the political relevance.

Two decisions settled matters for the attitude of Catholics attached to the Church toward this event: the agreement of the Center to the Enabling Law on 23 March and the proclamation of the German episcopate, indirectly dependent on it, five days later.[24] Appealing to the assurances in Hitler's governmental declaration, the bishops conditionally withdrew their general prohibitions and warnings against the National Socialist Party. They took this step, not in an opportunist adaptation but with the purpose of sparing their flocks a worrisome test that was daily showing itself more sharply. This was done first in the conflict between loyalty to the Church and the obedience of the citizen, which became acute the moment when in Adolf Hitler a politician began to personify the authority of the government, who was at the same time leader of a party with an ideological appeal. In this dilemma the cautiously formulated position of the episcopate freed to that part of the German Catholics who wanted cooperation the way to collaboration, without however intending thereby to recommend Hitler's party.

In league with Vice-Chancellor von Papen (1879–1969), Hitler surprised the Vatican at the beginning of April 1933 with the offer of a concordat with the *Reich*. To the Church he promised the guarantee by treaty of the denominational schools, for his part he demanded, on the model of the Italian concordat, a prohibition on the clergy taking part in party politics. For a short time he was fascinated by the idea of dealing the Catholic parties a mortal blow by forcing the Church to withdraw all clerical office-holders; in the long view the advantages of a comprehensive regulation of the relations of state and Church seemed to be in his grasp. Franz von Papen's motives were more multifaceted. As a Catholic he wanted for the Church what he regarded as best. As a politician he speculated on his reputation as a successful protector of the Church's interests in order thereby to underpin the claim to represent the Catholic part of the population in Hitler's cabinet.

Around the vice-chancellor gathered the alliance "Cross and Eagle," a group inspired by the *Reichsideologie,* which had as its goal to build a bridge between the Catholic Church and the Nazi state. Taken with as little seriousness by the Nazi side as by the Catholic people, within a short time the Papen establishment was as isolated as was its protector in the cabinet. After the change of name to "Workers' Community of Catholic Germans," it was taken in tow even in its organization by the

---

[24] On the redirection released by the *Reichstag* election of 5 March 1933, cf. L. Volk (above n. 10), 59–89. For some aspects of the much treated relations of Church and National Socialism, cf. D. Albrecht, ed., *Katholische Kirche im Dritten Reich* (Mainz 1976), with citations of the literature.

Nazi party in the fall of 1933. Numerically a tiny group, it disappeared from the scene a year later, after it had served its time as a pretense. In contrast to the Evangelical Church, in which the church organization broke into pieces over the opposition between Nazi "German Christians" and the denominational movement, the German Catholics avoided a self-destructive polarization, which enabled them to preserve their inner cohesion during the years of totalitarian oppression between 1933 and 1945.

In the summer of 1933 the revolutionary process of controlling everything in Germany outstripped the Roman negotiations for a concordat. When on 20 July the treaty[25] was signed at the Vatican, there were no longer any Catholic parties which the article on depoliticization, demanded by Hitler, could have injured. They had not fallen victim to any rule of the concordat but had been liquidated as had been the entire parliamentary system.

All the greater exertions were made by the Vatican negotiators to create by the concordat protection for the no less threatened Catholic associations. Accordingly, in addition to the assurance of existence for the denominational school, the guaranteeing of the Church's association system gained urgent present significance. As can be gathered from the layers of the article on the protection of the associations (ARTICLE 31), the offensive to bring everything under the control of the Nazi organization was stopped by these regulations of the concordat at an extremely critical time for the afflicted Catholic societies. What was thought of as a peace treaty changed unexpectedly into an instrument of defense. After the defeat of the frontal attack, the war against the denominational societies was continued with more subtle methods—despite the concordat. Not to belong to the pertinent Nazi organizations meant for the future a severe handicap for professional promotion and in some places also for social repute. By the prohibition of double membership Nazi organizations excluded members of Catholic associations from admission and hence from their special rights in order thereby to move them to abandon the ecclesiastical associations. Not all societies showed the same spirit of resistance. While the Catholic Teachers' Association capitulated as early as August 1933,[26] the association of Catholic German women teachers maintained itself in spite of all pressures until it was forcibly dissolved by the Gestapo in the autumn of 1937. From the summer of the same year on, the

[25] For the content of the concordat, cf. Bihlmeyer-Tüchle III, 517–19; Schmidlin, PG IV, 164–66.
[26] Cf. H. Küppers, Der Katholische Lehrerverband in der Übergangszeit von der Weimarer Republik zur Hitler-Diktatur (Mainz 1975).

Catholic association of young men, especially annoying to the Nazi regime, was suppressed by the state police in one diocese after another.[27]

After the crushing of domestic political (parliamentary opposition) and inner party counterforces (the "Röhmputsch") and the death of President von Hindenburg on 2 August 1934, Hitler saw in the Christian churches the chief obstacle for a Nazi permeation of the entire population. With the help of a network of seemingly unconnected regulations the Nazi regime thus sought to drive every ecclesiastical influence out of public life. This became especially obvious in the gradual repression of Catholic journalism.[28] The first victim was the Church-oriented daily press. After 1933 Catholic papers could no longer be designated as such in the title, and in 1935 they were transformed into mere acclamation agents by a legally concealed decree of the propaganda ministry. To muzzle the Church's periodical system Propaganda Minister Goebbels made use of different methods. They extended from warnings through temporary prohibitions to the complete suppression of a periodical.[29] To this were added trivial prescriptions on the organization of the content in order to deprive the church publications of any attraction to readers and bring them into the odor of a musty religiosity. From 1936 pastoral letters could no longer be printed even in the diocesan newspapers protected in the concordat.

Especially malicious, because it aimed purposely to mislead, was the invention of the *Auflagenachricht*. Made obligatory by the propaganda ministry, it had to be accepted by Catholic papers without regard to its content and without its compulsory character being indicated or its being criticized. While all freedom was permitted to anticlerical agitation, gestures toward a counter-defense were answered with prompt sanctions. However, excess of power did not necessarily mean power of conviction. When in the summer of 1937 Goebbels made use of the morals trials of individual religious to mobilize his complete media potential for a week-long campaign against the Church, at the end it was not so much the credibility of the Catholic orders as that of the Nazi press that was in doubt.[30] Economic difficulties because of the war finally supplied the pretext in mid-1941 completely to silence the Church press, still strong in circulation, except for a handful of theological professional journals.

[27] Cf. B. Schellenberger, *Katholische Jugend und Drittes Reich* (Mainz 1975).
[28] Cf. K. A. Altmeyer, *Katholische Presse unter NS-Diktatur* (Berlin 1962).
[29] K. Gotto, *Die Wochenzeitung Junge Front/Michael* (Mainz 1970), describes an individual case as an example.
[30] Cf. H. G. Hockerts, *Die Sittlichkeitsprozesse gegen katholische Ordensangehörige und Priester 1936/37* (Mainz 1971).

The Nazi authorities laid greater value on camouflage in their school policy[31] that directly contradicted the statements of the concordat of 1933. Decisive ministerial edicts were "not intended for publication." The certainly to be anticipated resistance of Catholic parents to the forcible introduction of the public school was neutralized by periodically staggered regional procedures, pseudovoting was interpreted for the result desired. Religious instruction had previously become an object of reform, its imparting was often removed from clerics and turned over to teaching personnel not authorized by the Church, who then reduced the number of hours provided for it. Schools of orders were compelled to close and entrusted to state or communal management.

On the government's part even the *Reich* Church Ministry, created in 1935, was unable to bring order into the chaos of competencies characteristic of the Hitler state. The reason was not because the church minister, Hanns Kerrl (1887–1941), was not powerful enough within the party to impose his will against more powerful rivals with ambitions in church policy. His office lacked a directly subordinate executive agent, whereas the lesser ranking Police Chief Himmler possessed in the Gestapo an instrument which he used in its proper perfection of power, without much concern for the church minister. Consequently it was not Kerrl who determined the course of the struggle for suppression of the Church, but his rivals, Himmler, Heydrich, Bormann, and Schirach, who for their part emulated one another in radical activity.

For the bishops the ideology, claims to power, and claims to domination of a totalitarian ideological state were as strange phenomena as for most contemporaries, so that they first had to find their way in the new reality. Against every encroachment of this political system in the Church's sphere Cardinal Bertram, as chairman of the entire episcopate, protested in writing with appeal to the legal situation, as he was accustomed to do and without letting himself be misled by the lack of results of his ideas. A chain of diplomatic notes[32] from the Holy See aimed in the same direction. The Vatican's protest against the disregard of the concordat left nothing to be desired in clarity and sharpness. Since it was in vain, in fact for the most part remained even without a reply, Pius XI finally broke his silence by denouncing the hostility of the Nazi regime before the whole world in the encyclical *Mit brennender Sorge* of March 1937.[33]

[31] Cf. R. Eilers, *Die nationalsozialistische Schulpolitik* (Cologne 1963) esp. 22–28 and 85–98.
[32] Cf. D. Albrecht, ed., *Der Notenwechsel zwischen dem Heiligen Stuhl und der Deutschen Reichsregierung* Vol. I: *1933–1937* (Mainz 1965), Vol. II: *1937–1945* (Mainz 1969).
[33] Cf. the definitive text in contrast to the preliminary draft of Cardinal Faulhaber in D. Albrecht, op. cit. Vol. I, 404–43.

Differing from the Pope, Cardinal Bertram could not then decide upon a departure from his policy of memoranda, when despite the best intentions its ineffectiveness could no longer be doubted. The bishop of Berlin, Preysing, demanded a revision of this defensive tactic as early as autumn 1937 but he could not put this over at Breslau.[34] After Hitler's passing to an expansionist foreign policy, introduced with the annexation of Austria in March 1938, the agitating pressure in domestic politics lessened temporarily, it is true, but the goal of gradually confining and finally destroying the Church was unchanged. It was carried further, with still more brutal harshness, after the outbreak of war in the fall of 1939 under the pretense of alleged war requirements.

With the elimination of the Catholic kindergartens, unilaterally decreed by the state's edict, the last hindrance to the total grasp of the rising generation fell. Unpopular priests were reprimanded by the Party or were sent without trial to the concentration camp at Dachau, where many succumbed to hardships or mistreatment.[35] Because he had not appeared to vote in the *Reichstag* elections in April 1938, Bishop Sproll of Rottenburg was expelled from his official headquarters by organized riots, removed from his diocese by the Gestapo, and only freed from exile by the collapse of the Nazi state.[36]

In 1940–41 the Gestapo undertook a raid in the grand manner when it arbitrarily confiscated by turns abbeys, religious houses, and seminaries and threw the occupants into the streets. At the same time the Nazi dictatorship, in the elimination of the emotionally ill, euphemistically called euthanasia, and in the deportation and murder of the European Jews pushed the perversion of the *Reich* to dimensions beyond the human power of conception. Nevertheless, Cardinal Bertram could not be moved from the policy of internal protest, which he unerringly continued. In his understanding of his office, determined by the experience of the *Kulturkampf,* the maintaining of the administration of the sacraments and of the parochial care of souls held absolute precedence over other episcopal duties, in the concrete case to publicly standing up for basic personal rights. The spokesmen of an energetic progressive defense did not intend the total break feared by

---

[34] Cf. W. Adolph, *Hirtenamt und Hitlerdiktatur* (Berlin 1965).

[35] Cf. also R. Schnabel, *Die Frommen in der Hölle* (Frankfurt 1966); E. Weier, *Die Geistlichen in Dachau sowie in anderen Konzentrationslagern und Gefängnissen* (Mödling 1972). The statistics of the various authors are not uniform. According to the hitherto most comprehensive and basic listing in E. Weiler, pp. 75 and 82, 67 out of 304 German priest prisoners died at Dachau, and 18 out of 83 Austrian.

[36] Cf. P. Kopf, M. Miller, eds., *Die Vertreibung von Bischof Joannes Baptista Sproll von Rottenburg 1938–1945* (Mainz 1971).

the cardinal of Breslau with its devastating consequences. However, this was not the alternative to the policy of memoranda, disavowed by its total ineffectiveness. For the holders of power were by no means insensitive to the pressure of opinion of a great part of the population, which the exposure of the crimes of the regime would have had to produce. What they feared and the Church's members hoped from its bishops, the unique echo, appeared in the summer of 1941, which the three great sermons of Bishop Galen (1878–1946) of Münster against the violent domination of the Gestapo and the murdering of the emotionally ill elevated to an event of European rank.

Differently from the action on euthanasia, which could not be hidden despite all efforts at camouflage, there came into view for the observer inside Germany only the last but one act of the "final solution of the Jewish question," forcible deportation, and even this only in a local sector. As early as 1935 the Fulda Episcopal Conference had united the assistance efforts of the *Sankt Raphaelsverein* and the German Charity Association in the "Assistance Committee for Catholic non-Aryans," but the boundaries of its success were very narrowly drawn through the restriction on the admittance of people from overseas.[37] A local center of gravity was constituted by the "Assistance Work in the Episcopal Ordinariate of Berlin," which Bishop Preysing had called into being. In the last common proclamation of the episcopate during the Nazi epoch, the Decalogue Pastoral Letter[38] of August 1943, which stressed the indivisibility of the right to life in all clarity, there was also unmistakable thought of "men of foreign races and descent." Of course, matters did not proceed as far as a public protest of the bishops against the annihilation of the Jews.

What fate was destined for the Church in the event of a victorious outcome of the war was demonstrated by Hitler's representatives in the territories annexed to the *Reich* in the West and East. After the *Anschluss* in March 1938 Austria was declared a territory freed from its concordat and in its ecclesiastical institutions abandoned to the forcible rule of the party functionaries. Austria, Lorraine, and in extremely radical fashion the Warthegau[39] supplied the negative proof for the protective influence which the concordat with the *Reich,* despite highly defective respect, produced to the end in the dioceses of the old *Reich.*

[37] Cf. L. E. Reutter, *Katholische Kirche als Fluchthelfer im Dritten Reich* (Recklinghausen 1971).

[38] Text in K. Hofmann, ed., *Zeugnis und Kampf des deutschen Episkopats* (Freiburg 1946), 75–84.

[39] Cf. B. Stasiewski, "Die Kirchenpolitik der Nationalsozialisten im Warthegau," *Vierteljahrshefte für Zeitgeschichte* 7(1959), 46–74.

After the unconditional surrender on 8 May 1945, the victorious powers liquidated, with the rest of Hitler's rule, also the inner constitution of the German political system. In many places the Church was the single institution which was able to keep its personal identity beyond the zero hour. Its generally known spiritual opposition to National Socialism gave it, at least among the Western Allies and in the initial phase of the communal reorganization, a certain authority, but soon other influences gained the upper hand in the military governments of the four occupation zones.

In view of the unmistakable material misery the Church's efforts in the first postwar period were especially directed to charitable help.[40] The wretchedness moved to its climax with the stream of millions of refugees from the East, who, robbed of all they had, were driven from their ancestral homes. Arbitrarily drawn zone frontiers disrupted dioceses and carried the German partition into the ecclesiastical sphere. After Cardinal Bertram's death on 6 July 1945, a German vicar capitular, Ferdinand Piontek, functioned in Breslau, but a month later he was induced to resign by the determined Cardinal Hlond. As primate of Poland, the latter himself assumed the diocesan administration, so that, provided by the Holy See with the title of apostolic administrator, he could immediately send auxiliary bishops to the eastern areas of Germany now placed under Polish administration.

Under the chairmanship of the archbishop of Cologne, Josef Frings (b. 1887, archbishop in 1942, cardinal in 1946), the German bishops met at Fulda in August 1945 for their first postwar meeting. As previously against the violations of rights by the Nazi regime, they now protested for a nation without a voice at the Allied Control Council, against anarchy and arbitrariness, against the automatic interning of merely nominal party members, against the expulsion of millions of East Germans from house and farm. During the war years Pope Pius XII had maintained an intensive correspondence with many German bishops.[41] The Pope's voice was also the first which appealed on a world level for discretion and justice toward the defeated,[42] while the wave of hatred released by Hitler turned back in full fury on the Germans in their totality.

After the closing of all diplomatic representations in Berlin by the victorious powers, not excepting the apostolic nunciature, Pius XII left

[40] H. J. Wollasch, ed., *Humanitäre Auslandshilfe für Deutschland nach dem Zweiten Weltkrieg* (Freiburg 1976).
[41] Cf. B. Schneider, ed., *Die Briefe Pius' XII. an die deutschen Bischöfe 1939–1945* (Mainz 1966).
[42] Thus in the address to the College of Cardinals on 2 June 1945. Text in B. Wuestenberg, J. Zabkar, eds., *Der Papst an die Deutschen* (Frankfurt 1956), 103–10.

nothing untried to remain present, advising and helping, through an informal representation at least. Thus there originated the Vatican Mission at Kronberg near Frankfurt in late autumn 1945. From 1946 it was splendidly occupied by Aloysius Muench (1889–1962), an American bishop of German ancestry,[43] and became the germ cell of a revived representation of the Holy See in Germany, which was transferred to Bad Godesberg after the establishing of the Federal Republic in 1951 and was elevated to a nunciature.

Population displacements of unprecedented size, introduced by Nazi resettlements and flight before bombs, climaxed in the influx of over 11 million expelled from their homeland, who, apart from the humanitarian needs, also created completely new problems of pastoral care. In some regions confessional boundaries, which had been more or less fixed since the Reformation, were shifted without plan and order or became entirely outmoded by a fundamental mixing of Catholics and Protestants. That thereby a diaspora situation arose virtually everywhere was first made painfully known to many participants at the Mainz *Katholikentag* of 1948 in the brief formula "Germany—Mission Country."

As in all areas, also in the religious the reconstruction proceeded from the bottom up. There struck the great hour of the parish principle. Hence the bishops in no sense made a virtue of necessity when they sought to organize the care of souls according to the so-called natural states and energetically resisted the formation of superdiocesan central associations in the old style. Nevertheless, although these rose again from the ruins and the worn-out parish principle lost in brilliance, no renaissance of any length was allowed to the Catholic associations. The great period of the denominational mass organizations with their members amounting to the hundreds of thousands was apparently over. To the change of climate of a dread of every organizational connection there contributed not a little in the early postwar period the rigorism with which especially the American occupation power subjected the last member of the Nazi Party to the process of de-Nazification. But the definitive change was first introduced with the arrival of television in the 1950s, whereby a competitor entered the scene which damaged every form of sociability outside the home.

The war of annihilation of National Socialism against Christianity had simply forced churchmen and politicians of both denominations without question into one defensive front. From the start this removed all reservations which might have made it difficult for the Catholic bishops, after the founding of the Christian Social Union (CSU) in Bavaria and

---

[43] Cf. C. J. Barry, *American Nuncio, Cardinal Aloisius Muench* (Collegeville 1969).

the Christian Democratic Union (CDU) in the rest of Germany, to agree to an integrated party of a basic Christian direction. Hence not without skepticism they saw how staunch adherents of the Center called it again into being on a purely denominational basis, as in North Rhine-Westphalia, and thereby split the Catholic electorate. The outcome was that the notion of union became fully productive in some regions only with a certain delay. The electoral pastoral letters of the postwar period became more blurred after the resumption of this tradition in the 1960s; they especially stressed the duty of voting and the necessity of voting for candidates of proved Christian outlook. Only in a very few individual cases was there an ecclesiastical representative. The postconciliar inclination of the younger theology professors to be active for so-called election initiatives was countered by the German episcopal conference in the fall of 1973 with the prohibition "for a priest to take a stand publicly within a party, for a party, and for the election of a party."[44]

During the preliminaries for a constitution of the Federal Republic, which was established in 1949 in the territory of the three Western occupation zones,[45] the episcopate exerted itself energetically for an anchoring of the rights of parents in the Bonn basic law, but the proponents could not carry the day in the parliamentary council. Also heavily fought was the continued validity of the concordat of 1933. What on this point was established in a more general way in ARTICLE 123 of the Federal Constitution was differently interpreted according to the viewpoint of each party. For obligatory clarification the second Adenauer cabinet appealed to the Federal Supreme Court at Karlsruhe, complaining in 1955 against the state of Lower Saxony because of its nonobservance of the school regulations of the concordat. The verdict of 26 March 1957 agreed on the one hand to the continued validity of the treaty, but denied to the Federation the power to enforce provisions of the treaty where these touched the cultural supremacy of the states.[46] Unsatisfactory as the Karlsruhe verdict, seen as a whole, turned out to be for the ecclesiastical partner to the treaty, nevertheless it became the impetus for a bilateral agreement between the state of Lower Saxony and the Holy See, the concordat of 26 February 1965. The concordat concluded with Rhineland-Westphalia on 15 May 1973 took care of regulating the school question.

According to the norms established by the Second Vatican Council,

---

[44] HK 27(1973), 549.
[45] For the time period after the founding of the Federal Republic and on the correction of F. Spott's presentation, cf. K. Forster, "Deutscher Katholizismus in der Adenauer-Ära," Konrad Adenauer und seine Zeit II (Stuttgart 1976), 488–20.
[46] Cf. F. Giese, F. A. v. d. Heydte, Der Konkordatsprozess (Munich 1957–59).

the German Episcopal Conference, actually in existence for decades, gave itself its proper statute in 1967 and a legal structure in the union of the dioceses of Germany. At the end of 1965 its leadership had passed from Cardinal Frings, who remained archbishop of Cologne until 1969, to the Munich Cardinal Julius Döpfner (1913–76, bishop of Würzburg in 1948, bishop of Berlin in 1957, cardinal in 1958, and archbishop of Munich in 1961). Whether the auxiliary bishops, called by the council to participate in the conference and in some places increased rapidly, would be conducive to the function of the bishops' assemblies remains to be seen. In addition to the complete conference there also existed on the regional level the Bavarian and the West German Episcopal Conference and the East German conference of ordinaries, but participation by these last in the plenary meetings at Fulda has been forbidden since the erecting of the Berlin Wall in 1961 through the policy of demarcation.

In the tracks of the Eastern policy pursued by the SPD-FDP government coalition since 1969 and yielding to the stubborn pressure of Poland's episcopate and government, the Holy See at the end of June 1972 for its part recognized the Oder-Neisse Line as Poland's frontier and in the territories annexed to Poland created a new diocesan arrangement. The German Democratic Republic strove for an analogous concession from the Vatican in order to maintain through the merger of West German enclaves and its own jurisdictional areas a diocesan division whose circumscription would coincide with the state frontiers.

Austria

In Austria, where the proclamation of the republic in 1918 deprived the Catholic Church of its imperial protector, tension-filled cultural-political times dawned after the First World War. If in Germany social democracy suspiciously rejected the Church, so too the ideologically incomparably virulent Austrian Marxism fought it with an aggressive hostility.[47] In Austria, 90 percent Catholic, the oppositions were polarized as regards party politics into the two great blocks of the Christian Socialists and the Socialists.

The latter went far beyond the atheistic or nonreligious basic attitude of the Socialist International in the sense that they imprinted on the ideological ingredients of the party program the stamp of exclusiveness. Socialism was called a counterreligion, and whoever wanted to profess it had to break with the Church. Only against this background can the at times fanatical agitation be understood with which the freethinking

[47] Cf. P. M. Zulehner, *Kirche und Austromarxismus* (Vienna 1967).

electors and members of the Socialist party, standing on the left, sought to separate from the Church. Occurring in two waves, the departures from the Church between 1918 and 1928 amounted in a total population of 6.1 million Catholics to 135,000, an alarming process for the Church. The fact that the leadership of the Christian Socialists and of the federal government rested for years in the hands of a priest produced an additional ingredient of tension in domestic politics. Monsignor Ignaz Seipel (1876–1932), chairman of the Christian Social party from 1921 to 1930, acquired as federal chancellor from 1922 to 1924 and from 1926 to 1929 influence and esteem beyond Austria.[48] The caliber of a statesman was attested to him even by his political opponents, but he also had to struggle with the vocation problem of the priest-politician. He was able to feel its specific vulnerability when he was denounced as a "prelate without leniency" because of his use of the police after the burning of the Palace of Justice at Vienna in 1927. In any event, from the episcopate's viewpoint the disadvantages of a commitment of clerics to party politics so clearly prevailed that the Austrian episcopal conference at the end of 1933, hence a year after Seipel's death and the elimination of parliament by Dollfuss, called upon all priests to give up the mandates exercised by them.

In so far as the archbishop of Vienna resided in the capital of Austria, he was affected much more strongly by governmental events as chairman of the episcopate than was Cardinal Bertram at Breslau. In 1918, during the period of transition from monarchy to republic, Gustav Piffl (1864–1932, archbishop in 1913, cardinal in 1914) maintained a soberly shrewd attitude. His successor, Theodor Innitzer (1875–1955, archbishop in 1932, cardinal in 1933), was a man of charity, who, for example, stood up for the Jews in the period of persecution.[49]

The bishops viewed, not without reservation, the experiment of a Christian corporate state, introduced by the Christian Socialist Federal Chancellor Dollfuss (1932–34) and continued by Schuschnigg (1934–38), but they did not intend, for their part, to create difficulties for the Catholics of the government, hard pressed by Hitler and his Austrian followers. For this reason it was also not unproblematic to withdraw from the government's course, because the planners of the corporate state appealed to a papal encyclical. Now, of course, the derivation of this project from *Quadragesimo anno* was controvertible, but this did not

---

[48] Cf. K. v. Klemperer, *Ignaz Seipel, Staatsmann einer Krisenzeit* (Graz, Vienna, and Cologne 1976).

[49] Cf. V. Reimann, *Innitzer, Kardinal zwischen Hitler und Rom* (Vienna 1967).

hinder critics from charging the Church with coresponsibility for the Austrian effort to implement it. In 1930 negotiations for a concordat were conducted with the Curia, in order especially to do away with the confusion over marriage which socialist state officials had brought up when they sought to overcome the strictness of the state-Church marriage legislation of the monarchy by dubious acts of self-help. Only the government of Dollfuss brought the treaty[50] to a conclusion on 5 June 1933, not without the expectation of thereby substantially consolidating its "position in domestic and foreign policy.[51]

In the days of the *Anschluss* euphoria in March 1938, Cardinal Innitzer temporarily succumbed to the deceptive maneuvers of the Nazi agents, but as early as October he was the butt of violent demonstrations of displeasure on the part of the Nazis.[52] Meanwhile, the brutally instituted oppression of the Church had done away with all illusions. In order to create a free field of operations the Austrian concordat was declared not binding, while the validity of the concordat with Germany was restricted to the old *Reich*. This permitted the state and party officials more drastically to curtail the Church's sphere of influence in Austria within five months than they had been able to do in Germany in five years. By means of unilateral decrees, associations were dissolved, Catholic schools and theological faculties— Innsbruck, Salzburg, Graz—were closed, religious property was confiscated, religious instruction in accord with the school plan was abolished.

In a new wave of departures from the Church there was some displeasure in 1938–39 over the attitude of the bishops in the atmosphere of the Dollfuss era. While the state subsidies for the payment of the clergy had been paid up to then out of the religious fund established by Joseph II from church property, and deficits had been met through annual appropriations of parliament, the new rulers struck out the state payments and replaced them by a system of church contributions. Devised from clear motives for the economic weakening of the Church, the new rule had a thoroughly reverse effect, since the donation from the people was regarded not as a burdensome obligation but as a profession of the faith and of the Church.

In contrast to Germany, which was not "freed," as was Austria, but was "conquered," an Austrian political government could be set up at Vienna in April 1945 before the end of the war, although for a decade it

---

[50] For the content cf. Schmidlin, *PG* IV, 126–28.
[51] Cf. E. Weinzierl, *Die österreichischen Konkordate von 1855 und 1933* (Munich 1960).
[52] Cf. J. Fried, *Nationalsozialismus und Katholische Kirche in Österreich* (Vienna 1947); E. Weinzierl, "Österreichs Katholiken und der Nationalsozialismus," *Wort und Wahrheit* 18(1963), 417–39 and 493–526, 20(1965), 774–804.

had to share its authority and competence with the four occupation powers. During the years of the rule of force under the Nazis, the destruction of external points of support led to a deepened consciousness of the current pastoral tasks and stirred impulses which displayed themselves productively in the postwar age.

After 1945 the Austrian People's Party, as successor of the Christian Social Party, and the Socialist Party of Austria worked together for more than two decades in coalition cabinets, both overcoming the hostile attitude displayed during the first republic.

Between the government parties the legal obligatory force of the concordat of 1933 was long disputed. Finally a compromise was reached in regard to Rome to agree in principle to the continuing validity but at the same time to attach to it the wish for a new treaty. However, Pius XII would have nothing to do with a sacrifice of the content of the concordat. Only under his successor were discussions resumed which led to a series of individual agreements.

These especially put the diocesan organization on a definitive basis by eliminating the provisional arrangements which had prevailed after 1919 as transitional solutions. Thus the diocese of Eisenstadt was erected on 23 June 1960 in Burgenland, annexed to Austria after the First World War, and the dioceses of Innsbruck on 7 July 1964 and Feldkirch on 7 October 1968 out of North Tyrol and Vorarlberg parts of the see of Brixen. The regulation of problems of property law in the treaty of 23 June 1960 also contributed to the relaxation of tension in state-Church relations. In return for an annual adjusting payment, thereafter the religious fund was transferred, up to 90 percent, to the possession of the state. As early as 1945 the bishops had spoken out for the maintenance of the system of church contributions. Likewise in the treaty of 9 July 1962 a satisfactory compromise was worked out for the financing of Catholic private schools.

The ground had first to be prepared for an understanding of the coalition partners over partly highly controversial material in a gradual demolition of cultural-political oppositions. Contributing not unsubstantially to this was the fact that the last champions of anticlerical Austrian Marxism of the period between the wars had moved increasingly into the background in the course of the generation change since the mid-1950s.

Switzerland

Four linguistic communities, still partly separated from one another by transverse denominational boundaries, make Switzerland not only in territorial politics a common system of complex diversity. With five bishoprics directly subject to the Holy See, which exist side by side without any connection and without constituting an ecclesiastical province, it constitutes also a special case in church organization. From this again the Swiss Episcopal Conference developed an enclosing function for supradiocesan unity, as belongs to the episcopal communities of no other countries to the same degree.

Initial steps for a resumption of relations with the Holy See, broken off in the nineteenth century, developed during the First World War when a papal agent made a permanent stay in Switzerland with the assent of the Federal Council in order to promote the humanitarian assistance work of Benedict XV. It was then only a step to the accrediting of a nuncio in Berne in 1920. Because it was quite certain that there would be rejection from some Protestant groups, no Swiss diplomat was sent to the Vatican.

Although in their concrete coexistence the traditional denominational contrasts gradually lost their sharpness, there was not for decades a thought of eliminating from the Swiss constitution the anti-Catholic article forbidding monasteries and Jesuits. The actually liberal administration of the disputed stipulation was able to lessen its weight in practice, but it was ultimately neither in conformity with the constitution nor appropriate to remove the thorn of the legal inequality. A turn was first produced by the revision of the constitution on the basis of the popular vote of 20 May 1973. Of course, on reflection it is correct that only 55 percent of those voting were in favor of the removal, and no less than 44 percent for the retaining, of the undemocratic burden. To this extent the event was instructive for the severity with which a part of the Protestant Swiss themselves clung to deeply rooted denominational prejudices against the advice of their political and ecclesiastical leadership.

Politically, the greatest number of Swiss Catholics feel themselves bound to the Christian Democratic People's party, which was founded in 1912 as the Swiss Conservative People's party. In the parliamentary elections of 1975 it obtained 21 percent of the votes cast, because of which, beside the Social Democrats with ca. 25 percent and the Liberals with more than 22 percent, it ranks as an almost equally strong political force.[53]

The Situation in the German-Speaking Area after the Second Vatican Council

After the close of the Second Vatican Council the Catholic Church in the German-speaking area was confronted to a considerable degree

[53] On the present situation cf. R. Weibel-Spirig, "Katholizismus in der Schweiz," *HK* 30(1976), 211–17.

with equally constituted developments and problems. Since the programmatic conciliar decrees coincided with a worldwide "culture
revolution," their realization, beginning after 1965, was only parti-
ally identical with the intentions of the council fathers. As a consequence one must distinguish between what is expressed in the conciliar decrees and what came from them under the diverting
influence of catalysts outside the Church. In the wake of partly
radical movements of emancipation, which blindly identified the
change with progress and despised objective justifications, the content of the decrees issued became secondary and had to yield to
the appeal to an imaginary "spirit of the council." Wherever it was
called up, those inspired by it understood it mostly as sanction for
any sort of change. In place of a quiet, organic, and well planned
translation of the conciliar ideas into the reality of the Church
stepped the capricious impetus of the revolutionary spirit of the
age; in place of a reliable organization, arbitrary experiment. More
than other areas of church life, the liturgy was affected by this.
That the annoying high-handedness of priests remained uncorrected,
unauthorized special developments were at first accepted and then
even made into norms, was no way to strengthen the irresolute
leadership authority. The territorial episcopates displayed more continuity and decisiveness in the defense of basic ethical values, as, for
example, in confrontations concerning the freedom from punishment of abortion, in connection with which their calls for protest
demonstrations in the Federal Republic and the impetus to a collecting of signatures in Austria produced a noteworthy echo.

On the other hand, through the freeing of theological investigation from worn-out and discredited control mechanisms a situation
was created which exposed the average believer to unaccustomed
burdens. That a powerfully pursued questioning did not spare even
the essential ingredient of the Catholic faith but raised it pluralisti-
cally to the same level as peripheral concerns made the question of
what is characteristically Catholic ever more unanswerable. In view
of the confusing talk of the theologians and the extraordinary reserve of the *magisterium,* insecurity and confusion spread among the
faithful. So long as the lower point of intervention remained concealed from the simple believer, doubts oppressed him as to
whether he should interpret the reserve of those responsible as
justifiable tolerance or opportunistic permissiveness. To await calmly
the resolution of theological differences of opinion became problematic for the holders of the teaching office not least because the mass
media, interested in controversies within the Church because of
their sensational value and essential imponderableness, as self-ap-

pointed advocates taking the part of the "weaker" as determined by them, carried into the last village what should have matured only in the private discussions of experts.

After the superabundantly distributed advance laurels for the post-conciliar epoch, the disillusionment over the actual course of the development was inevitable. However, it explained only to a small degree why the union between the mass of the faithful and the institutional Church was so strikingly loosened. Even when the turning away did not go to a formal break, although the departures from the Church grew to an alarming degree, where faith activity is statistically capable of being determined, incontrovertible data indicate loss of authority and disappearance of trust. In the falling curve of regular Mass attendance and reception of the sacraments, especially in baptisms and weddings, can be read how the most deeply non-Catholic concept of the dispensability of the Church's ministry of salvation draws ever wider circles. An impetus to such ideas of relativeness was first given by the ecumenically conceived evaluation of the other Christian denominations, still more of course the crude propagating of a churchless "anonymous Christianity," by which the meaning of being a Catholic becomes entirely questionable to the average believer.

Even the liturgical reform, introduced with high expectations, made the churches not fuller but more empty. The universally accepted prelude, the permitting of the vernacular, was followed by a period of uncontrolled experimentation, which stood under the auspices of a subjectivism completely foreign to the Catholic notion of worship. The new Mass formularies, meanwhile definitively prescribed, have tried to check this, it is true, but in no sense to stop it. Thus in the place of a form of Mass of monolithic compactness there appeared a variable schema, whose subjectively filled vacuum continues to keep even the faithful who love the Church away from Sunday Mass. There was no lack of voices to oppose to the allegedly outdated concept of the Church of the people the new ecclesiological pattern of a "congregational church," which wanted to be, no longer for all, but only for the "decided." From such a viewpoint the distancing movement no longer appears as a weakening of the Church's wholeness but as a process of selection, which it aims to foster.

The priest's idea of his office and self-awareness were hardest hit by the general crisis of the Church. This was expressed externally in an abrupt numerical decline, so that ever fewer parochial offices could be filled by a priest, an emergency which will nevertheless be worked out completely only in the future. This overturning of the age pyramid was caused by a drop in the number of recruits and by the turning of many active priests to other professions.

Offshoots of antiauthoritarian and antiinstitutional currents produced in some dioceses loose unions of priests of the middle and younger generations, which understood themselves as a critical pendant to the bishop's authority. Although there was no lack of journalistic support and echo to the various priests' solidarity groups during the foundation period, 1969–70, these disappeared again a little later from public discussion. That they were formed at all was an indication of the limiting of the episcopal freedom of decision.

The Church's official authority can withstand attacks from within and without as long as it is based on firm principles and does not wreck itself by inner contradiction. Faith in the conformity of principle of episcopal activity has now been shattered precisely in those groups of the people who hitherto have stood, not against, but for the maintenance of the bishop's authority. Their criticism was let loose by the differing use of the executive power through the prohibition of celebrating Mass in the Tridentine Rite. This stands in striking contrast to the indulgence with which the bishops for years overlooked liturgical aberrations and arbitrariness. The passive leaving alone in the one and the resolute postponement in the other case have inevitably aroused suspicion that not primarily objective requirements but the measure of anticipated readiness to obey could determine the decisions of the pastoral office. If the use of the episcopal authority should only too often be guided by pragmatic considerations, which lie in the attempt to deal liberally with the progressives and authoritatively with the conservatives, or, to say it pointedly, to meet the one as powerless Church of love, the other as loveless Church of power, then the outcome could only be a growing alienation.

After some preliminary deliberations and fumbling efforts to bring the impulses of the council into a practicable program on the parish level in diocesan synods at Hildesheim and Vienna, the trend toward synods on the national level established itself at the end of the 1960s. As the first, there was constituted in Würzburg at the beginning of January 1971 the Common Synod of the Dioceses of the German Federal Republic. This was followed, though with a partly differently constituted order of procedure, by the Austrian Synodal Process and the Swiss Synod '72. By way of the start to "Germanize" the council, the Würzburg meeting, with its catalogue of themes at first embracing more than fifty points, went considerably beyond the framework of the council. However, then in fact only eighteen proposals were enacted, many with impressive majorities, others, like the draft "Church and Workers," only after sharp controversy. To the Catholics of central Germany the road to Würzburg was closed by the restrictive policy of the German Democratic Republic. As in all areas of Communist domination, the Church of the German Democratic Republic is under strict state supervision and enjoys only that freedom of movement which is officially allowed it, in the German Democratic Republic since 1957 by the Office for Church Questions. Left to themselves the Central German Catholics established their own church assembly, the "Pastoral Synod of the Jurisdictions in the German Democratic Republic," which held its meetings in the Dresden court church.

Ten years after the Second Vatican Council the Church as a whole has obviously not crossed the postconciliar valley of reform in all its breadth. In what form and with what authority it will come out of this process of change only the future can show. Thus in the German-speaking area also the forerunners of a new cohesion and stability, without which a regaining of lost terrain is unthinkable, are not yet in sight.

CHAPTER 19

The Church in the Benelux Countries*

Belgium

After the war of 1914–18, in which the patriotic bearing of Cardinal Mercier increased its reputation, the Church of Belgium found itself facing a new reality. The introduction of the general right to vote ended the dominance of the Catholic Party that had been in power since 1884. In order to maintain the religious influence on the still Christian parts of the population and to restore it in the areas where it had been lost, the bishops, under the sure leadership of Cardinal Van Roey (1925–61), exerted themselves to increase those institutions and organizations whose legal status the law of 1921 on nonprofit associations had finally regulated. Further, the bishops worked for the political unity of the Catholics, which seemed to be very necessary in order to defend these organizations and to promote a specific notion of society.

The Catholic educational system expanded further and was progressively organized until the founding in 1957 of the National Secretariat for Catholic Education. Thanks to the reconciliation of the parties, the law of 1914 on subsidies was applied after the war to elementary schools. From 1921 to 1969 the proportion of pupils who attended Catholic schools grew from ca. 46 to 51 percent. The long neglected professional training now became the preferred object of the clergy. The financial problems of the Catholic school system, already long

* Belgium and Luxemburg: Andre Tihon; The Netherlands: Johannes Bots, S.J.

present, led from 1950 to 1958 to a new school conflict. This was settled by a "school treaty," which the three great parties signed and the parliament ratified in 1959. In the same manner the state little by little assumed almost all the costs of university education. Except for the university area, religious instruction was imparted to a growing degree in almost all educational systems publicly operated.

The social organizations took root powerfully. The Christian unions which in 1925 included only one-fourth of the membership of socialist unions, outstripped these in the 1950s and displayed a growing pugnacity. The professional groups were rich and numerous and variously organized. The assurances of reciprocity and the institutions of the health system and of the social sphere constituted a dense and ever more active network.

Among the apostolic works, Catholic Action experienced an upsurge especially among the youth. The *Action catholique de la jeunesse belge* was in principle intended for all groups, but the *Jeunesse ouvrière chrétienne* (JOC), established by Abbé Cardijn right after the war, finally brought it about that it was accepted as a specialized movement of Catholic Action. Its dynamism had as a consequence the transformation of the general Catholic Action into specialized movements, which at a given moment were aimed at students, middle class, and farmers. From 1926 on the influence of the JOC moved beyond Belgium and finally reached the other continents. Alongside the traditional youth groups a Catholic branch of the Boy Scouts was also formed.

In order to take account of and accomodate the growth of the population from 7,423,784 inhabitants in 1910 to 9,650,944 by 1970— 30 percent—the rhythm of which of course slowed down, the bishops created new parishes, especially in the developed areas of high population density and in the thickly inhabited regions. This permitted the retaining of the average number of 2,126 to 2,374 inhabitants per parish from 1919 to 1972, which had increased between 1850 and 1910 from 1,444 to 2,126. The number of dioceses grew, through the founding of the sees of Antwerp in 1961 and Hasselt in 1967, from six to eight.

This extraordinary growth of the ecclesiastical administrative organization was compensated by the fact that the diocesan clergy grew relatively faster up to 1960 than the population. The number of priests rose between 1910 and 1960 from 7,857 to 10,386, but then dropped to 9,113 by 1972. Among the female religious the growth was much less: in 1910 there were 47,975, in 1947 their number reached a climax with 49,624, among whom the female religious of Belgian origin increased from 32,393 to 42,275. After a period of slow decline to 46,675 until 1960, a clear falling off can be seen: in 1972 there were only 35,331 nuns. The institutes of men experienced a greater growth, from 5,747 in 1910 to 10,056 in 1947. They stayed at this level until 1960—10,414—but then until 1972 experienced a very strong decline to 6,044.

In an effort to assure the Catholics a maximum in organizational strength, the bishops stood for the retention of a strong and united Catholic party. For the sake of this goal, of course, the tensions which threatened to split the Catholics in two had to be relaxed: on the one hand, the conflict between the various social classes, on the other hand that between the Flemish and the Walloon factions. In order to limit the first problem, in 1921 the Catholic party was transformed into a *Union catholique belge*. This included the former conservative and Walloon *Féderation de Cercles* and the *Ligue nationale des travailleurs chrétiens*, which in 1919 took the place of the *Ligue démocratique*, then the *Boerenbond*, which represented the agricultural interest, and finally the *Féderation des classes moyennes*, founded in 1919. In order to preserve unity, the episcopate in 1935, but especially from 1937 on, condemned "Rexism," a movement with a Fascist tendency founded by L. Degrelle. Vis-à-vis the Flemish movements, the bishops sought to moderate their exertions and to fight the nationalist parties. The effort was made to bring the Catholic forces together again with the aid of the Congress of Mechelen in 1936 and in 1937 to reform the party by creating a Catholic bloc, which embraced a Flemish and a Walloon wing.

After the Second World War, in which the episcopate played a very much more cautious role than in 1914–18, the attempt to overcome the split between Catholics and anticlericals by means of a *Union démocratique belge* soon collapsed. During the following decades the *Parti social chrétien*, which tended a little farther to the left than the former Catholic party and was easily de-confessionalized, gathered, especially in Flanders, the greatest part of the faithful around it. This party maintained its role as support for the Catholic organizations and especially for the Catholic instructional system. But as soon as the school treaty had been concluded, the linguistic tensions split the Catholics more and more and finally led to the separation of Louvain from the francophone university in 1966–68. Thereafter the party experienced a considerable decline in favor of the regional parties.

Attendance at Sunday Mass remained during the entire period on a low level: in 1950 ca. 50 percent of the population to whom the command applied were present at Sunday Mass. In 1964 the proportion had dropped to 45 percent, and from then on it went down quickly: in 1972 it was only 34 percent. A difference between particular regions is clearly discernible: Flanders with 48 percent, the Walloon areas with 31 percent—in regard to which, of course, there are enormous differences between the industrial areas and the Ardennes—and Brussels with 23 percent in 1967. In contrast to this, people maintained the essential practices, such as baptism, church weddings and ecclesiastical burial. In 1972 there were still 90 percent of baptisms, 82 percent of weddings, and 84 percent of church burials. Even in regions like Seraing and perhaps also Charleroi, which ca. 1900 were strongly influenced by anticlericalism, these religious practices again increased in the period 1914–20. In the period between the two world wars, Antoinism, a religious movement of adherents of a miracle-healing sect, whose founder died in 1906, acquired a certain expansion in specific regions with a Walloon population. Some even turned to Protestantism.

But these internal difficulties could not impair very powerful missionary efforts. These included the activity of Father Lebbe, the initiatives of Father Charles for teaching the faith, and the founding of societies for promoting new forms of missionary presence, for which, for example, the AUCAM (1925) and the AFI (1937) were of special significance. The number of missionaries, monks and nuns, rose from 4,759 in 1940 to 10,070 in 1960. In the same way concern was manifested for the Universal Church by the founding of the college for Latin America in 1954. In a country in which the non-Catholic minorities have little importance, the ecumenical movement developed on a higher level. This is attested by the Malines Conversations with the Anglicans from 1921 to 1925 and the foundation in 1926 of the Priory of Amay by Dom Lambert Beauduin, which is dedicated to the work for reunion and in 1939 was transferred to Chevetogne.

In internal life several movements among a minority led to a deepening of faith. These were, as early as the period between the two World Wars, but especially after 1945, the liturgical movement and the biblical renewal movement, stimulated by the group of the Louvain teacher, L. Cerfaux, also the "Residential District Groups," and finally apostolic works like the Legion of Mary. Furthermore, a foreign office for the pastoral care of immigrant workers was organized.

Side by side with the pastoral activity, the Catholic University of Louvain constituted an important center of Christian self-realization: some of its professors played an important role at the Second Vatican Council. Soon the new currents stirred in the conciliar atmosphere caused confusion which, however, operated less spectacularly and less toward renewal than in the Netherlands.

Luxemburg

The Grand Duchy of Luxemburg, occupied by Germany from 1914 to 1918, had to turn to Belgium after the war. After the abdication of

Marie Adélaïde, whom Grand Duchess Charlotte succeeded, and after the introduction of the universal right to vote in 1919, the Catholic party founded in 1914 came to power; it was able to keep in first place up to the present. In this party, the clergy played a powerful role. With the appointment of Monsignor Nommesch to the episcopal see in 1920, this political change made possible the reintroduction of religious instruction in the state elementary schools.

In contrast to the other Benelux countries, the Church has almost no schools of its own. On the other hand, the Church dominates the most important daily paper in the country, and pastoral care can rely firmly on the traditions of a region which up to ca. 1950 preserved a rural mentality, although heavy industry had settled in the country even before 1914. Religious practice remained in a good state: in 1957 at Clerfaux 99 percent made their Easter Communion; of course, this number declined in Luxemburg to 55 percent or in an industrial deanery such as Esch-sur-Alzette to 51 percent.

The Netherlands

PERIOD OF FLOWERING (1919–60)

The development of the Catholic Church in the Netherlands after the First World War ran in broad outline parallel to that in other European countries: thus, as elsewhere, the Dutch Catholics—ca. 30 percent in 1850, then increasing to ca. 40 percent by 1950—came to the conviction that their faith would be jeopardized in living together with those thinking otherwise. The ideology whereby the others preserved their cultural, social, and political interests was to such a degree anti-Christian among liberals and socialists and anti-Catholic among Protestants that the Catholics saw themselves forced to subordinate a series of life spheres, even those not of a strictly religious nature, to their own management.[1] As regards the construction of entirely defined denominational associations for a community life and for cooperation, the Dutch Catholics went much farther than the Catholics in any other country. In this regard they also went much farther than the other ideologically marked groupings in their own country, namely the Protestants (ca. 40 percent) the socialists, and the liberals, the so-called "pillars," who likewise had their own "pillar" organizations. There thus arose the absolutely singular situation that the Dutch Catholics, although they lived together in a modern pluralist society with Protestants, humanists, socialists, and so forth, nevertheless associated almost

---

[1] J. Bots, "Aggiornamento," *Grote Spectrum Encyclopedie* (1975), 210–12.

exclusively with other Catholics.[2] In turn there were organized on a Catholic basis: the charitable institutions, the care of the sick and of the emotionally disturbed, the press—the supraregional dailies De Tijd and De Maasbode, both founded ca. 1850—the educational system—from kindergartens to the Roman Catholic University of Nijmegen, founded in 1923, and the Catholic School of Economics in Tilburg, founded in 1927—politics—Roman Catholic political party of 1898, since 1946 Catholic Popular Party (KVP)—social life in corporate organizations for the religious and moral interests of employees and economic life through unions, which more and more served economic interests— 1903, later under the name Dutch Catholic Union Alliance (NKV). And finally the entire field of entertainment—sports associations, and so forth. In 1926 a special Catholic broadcasting system, KRO, was founded.

This self-sufficient system, whereby the Catholics took secular activities into their own hands, developed further to about 1960. In this regard the Second World War was not much more than an interlude. The Catholics of the Netherlands remained at this time in a patient and unprovoking, consistently unselfish manner imperturbable under the courageous leadership of the archbishop of Utrecht, Monsignor Johannes de Jong, a cardinal in 1946. Many, even non-Catholics, saw in him a sort of personification of the spiritual resistance against National Socialism. In regard to the German occupation the bishops had recourse to the scorched-earth policy: as soon as the Germans extended their hand for one of the Catholic organizations, they gave the officers and members instructions to withdraw from all offices and to renounce their membership.[3] The fact that the bishops were ready to destroy the monuments of the emancipation with their own hand is a proof of the deepest religious justification of the Catholic commitment in these secular fields. At the moment when the Catholic faith saw no more possibility of continuing to work in them, in their opinion these institutions had no more meaning. After the war the bishops passed a resolution to reestablish the earlier social and cultural organizations on a Catholic basis. Decisive for this was the pastoral argument: together with the great majority of Catholics they believed it was no longer possible to be responsible for withholding from the faithful the molding strength of their institutions, in any event not at this time in the moral disorder at the end of the war.

Around 1953 the Netherlands had overcome the consequences of

[2] A. Lijphart, The Politics of Accommodation: Pluralism and Democracy in the Netherlands (Berkeley 1968).
[3] L. J. Rogier, In vrijheid herboren (The Hague 1953), 741.

the war and the loss of the colonies. In 1953 the Dutch Catholics celebrated in complete unity the centenary of the restoration of the hierarchy. Considered from without, it seemed that only a little changed in the situation of the Church in the Netherlands to 1960. External activity was astounding in all areas. The organization of the ecclesiastical province was further improved. Bishoprics were erected at Rotterdam and Groningen in 1955. Thereby the number of dioceses increased from five to seven. Catholic secondary schools were spread over the country: eight out of ten Catholics of higher schools attended a Catholic secondary school. In contrast to almost all other countries, Catholic parents needed to make no financial sacrifice for this, for the entire denominational school system was 100 percent supported by the state. Catholics had leading positions in all areas of Catholic life. As the largest party—ca. 30 percent—in the government they were firm partners in the coalition with socialists or with Protestants and liberals. Ninety percent of the Catholic electorate voted for the KVP, 79 percent were subscribers to a Catholic daily, 90 percent were subscribers to the KRO.[4]

Also in the social and socioecclesiastical respect, Dutch Catholicism had special results: the workers did not leave the Church en masse. On the contrary: together with the middle class they formed precisely the supporting force of the Dutch believing community. From the social idealism of Catholics—H. Poels, 1868–1948; A. Ariens, 1860–1928—proceeded a transforming and adjusting strength to the whole Dutch society; it induced Pope Pius XI in 1931 on the occasion of an audience for a delegation of Dutch Catholic workers at Rome to declare that "there is no country in the world in which the doctrine of *Rerum novarum* is so well understood and is realized in fact."[5] In this respect the Netherlands stood alone at the top.[6]

The spiritual and ecclesiastical life in the stricter sense flowered here with "tropical" vitality. While in the century between 1855 and 1952 the number of Catholics trebled, the number of priests had become six times as large: from 624 to 3,695 per decade.[7] In 1967 there were in the Netherlands ca. 13,500 priests (4,000 diocesan priests in 7 dioceses and 9,400 religious priests in 34 orders and congregations), ca. 7,000

[4] J. M. G. Thurlings, *De wankele zuil. Nederlandse katholieken tussen assimilatie en pluralisme* (Nijmegen 1971), 127.
[5] P. H. Winkelman, "Nederland," *150 jaar katholieke arbeidersbeweging in West-Europa 1789–1939* (Hilversum 1961), 350.
[6] J. B. Sloot, "Van kerkelijk spreken naar sprekende kerk. Een sociologische analyse van de officiële verklaringen van het Nederlands episcopaat 1945–1974" (ms., Nijmegen 1974), 79.
[7] J. J. Dellepoort, *De priesterroepingen in Nederland* (The Hague 1955), 51.

brothers and almost 32,000 sisters in 111 orders and congregations (89 active and 22 contemplative).[8] This means that for every 100 Dutch Catholics there was one priest, brother, or sister—in France .45; Belgium, .79; Spain, .42; England, .69; Germany, East and West, .47; Switzerland, .77; Austria, .39.[9]

The expansion of its evangelizing activity was always the most eloquent sign of the vitality of Dutch Catholicism. In this regard the Netherlands was favored by the consequences of the anti-clerical developments in Germany and France. Many missionary congregations fled to the Netherlands. While the Dutch Catholics did not even constitute 2 percent of the total of Catholics in the world, in 1939 they accounted for 11 percent of all priest missionaries. In 1954 7,000 missionaries—priests, brothers, sisters—were active in the overseas missions, that is, one missionary for 600 Dutch Catholics—1 for 1,500 Belgians, 1 for 2,600 French, 1 for 1,200 Italians and Spaniards.[10]

DISINTEGRATION (1960–70)

The 1960s were marked by a sudden increase of prosperity. The Netherlands moved into the circle of the ten richest countries in the world. The coalition cabinets of the postwar period, of Catholics with partners of the left and right, let this wealth benefit the weaker members of society with the aid of a broadly constructed system of social legislation. In 1967 expenses for social welfare amounted to 26.3 percent of the gross national product as contrasted with 22.1 percent in West Germany and 19.4 percent in Belgium.

More than other ideological groups, the Catholics profited from this increase in prosperity. Their persistent struggle for emancipation began to bear its choicest fruits at this time. Within the circle of Catholics the academically educated especially benefited from the good times. And precisely this group of people began to become very numerous in the 1960s.[11] Young university-trained Catholics from the middle class rose in great numbers with their functions of leadership into the so-called upper middle-class. As often happens with the nouveaux riches, their rise went parallel with an assimilation to the hierarchy of values of this upper middle-class on the one hand and a loss of the feeling of union with the class and traditions in

[8] *Katholiek sociaal kerkelijk instituut, Broeders- en zusters-religieuzen in Nederland per 1.1.1967* (The Hague 1967), 19.
[9] W. Kusters, "Situatieschets van het Nederlands katholicisme 1968. Crisis en riskerend vertrouwen," *Riskante kerk, vijf jaar Pastoraal Instituut van de Nederlandse Kerkprovincie* (The Hague 1968), 148.
[10] F. van Heek, *Het geboorteniveau der Nederlandse Rooms-Katholieken* (Leiden 1954), 170.
[11] J. M. G. Thurlings, op. cit., 31.

which they had grown up on the other hand. This social break-through acquired in them an ideological stamp and a corresponding justification in the so-called "breakthrough idea," which had already gained ground since the war, especially in the effort "to break out" of the special closed Catholic organizations to collaboration with others in neutral, supradenominational organizations. This break-through idea was at first restricted to a pretty small circle, but in the course of the postwar years exercised a growing power of attraction on the Catholics who were in process of emancipation, especially on the intellectuals, for whom this period was especially favorable in the social and economic respect. When the bishops determined that the process of alienation from the Church (between 1930 and 1947 an average of 10,000 Catholics annually left the Church) always won influence on those Catholics who did not belong to the "pillar" organizations, which acted as replacement for the traditional integrat-ing factors that were becoming looser—village, neighborhood, fam-ily—in a pastoral letter of 1 May 1954 they came out against the breakthrough idea. In it they pleaded for "unity in an association of their own and from there for cooperation with others while reserving their independence" (no. 15). True, the Dutch Catholics received this pastoral letter[12]—with threats of ecclesiastical penalties for listen-ing to the socialist radio, VARA, and for reading socialist writings—in general without special comment; resistance was confined to a small group of intellectuals. In the 1960s these last obtained support from a large group of young academicians, priests, and laity, who together formed the advance guard of the Dutch movement of re-newal.

Sociological investigations confirm that in the hierarchy of values of these nouveaux riches the free development of the personality and the "being able to be oneself" stood in high esteem. Authenticity, freedom, majority, pluralism, openness, rationality were the ideals favored by them. These obviously positive values were burdened with ideology by them so that they were appropriated with a certain exclusiveness, which the nouveaux rich cultivated. There was an allergic reaction to comple-mentary values, such as the meaning of sacrifice and renunciation, rights of the community and the validity of authority, the transcendence of God, which were expressed, among other ways, in the creeds which were beyond reason, in mystic symbols and rites.[13]

Of course, this hierarchy of values, accepted in all welfare states by

---

[12] Ibid., 121.
[13] O. Schreuder, "Die deprivierte Mitte," W. Weymann-Weyhe, *Die offene Kirche* (Düsseldorf 1974), 234–64.

the so-called social center and with the help of instruction, of the mass media, and of the entertainment industry, which were dominated by the new intellectual elite, was forced on the other classes.[14] What was special, however, in the Dutch situation was that this new class knew how to force its power to a greater degree than elsewhere also on the average people of the Church. It could impose its image of people on all "ordinary" believers and on ecclesiastical developments. In its exercise of power the new elite obtained support from the same factors which originally constituted the power of the Dutch communities of believers: the strong and varied organizations and the high density of communication, now entirely especially strengthened by television with its power of suggestion and its leveling presentation.[15] As on the occasion of a dam bursting, through these channels a constant stream of criticism and doubts poured over the Dutch Catholics, who were much less prepared for it than the faithful elsewhere. This intensive, never diminished publicity set a process of fermentation in motion which made clear the magnitude and breadth of the Dutch movement of renewal. Mass expressions of it were, among others, the "Teilhard mode," the "Robinson mania" (40,000 copies of *Honest to God* were bought in four months), the unrest over the *New Catechism* (a half-million copies), the 15,000 dialogue groups after the council, the sudden, almost complete end of auricular confession, and the massive drop in the number of priests, brothers, and sisters. On the one hand there began in 1965 a massive departure of priests and religious: 1,732 priests (549 diocesan and 1,183 religious between 1965 and 1975, almost three times as many as the world average)[16] and between 1961 and 1970 4,300 lay religious (1,600 brothers and 2,700 sisters with perpetual vows).[17] On the other hand, the number of priestly ordinations dropped from 318 in 1960 (91 diocesan and 227 religious priests) to 20 in 1976 (4 diocesan and 16 religious priests). In neighboring countries, such as Germany and Belgium, the number of ordinations dropped to 50 and 40 percent respectively, in the Netherlands to less than 10 percent. And the faithful also remained apart from the Church in large numbers: attendance at Sunday Mass dropped from 70.75 percent in 1961 to 34 percent in 1976. The number of mixed marriages almost doubled between 1955 and 1972.[18]

[14] H. Schelsky, *Die Arbeit tun die anderen. Klassenkampf und Priesterherrschaft der Intellektuellen,* 2d ed. (Opladen 1975).
[15] W. Kusters, op. cit., 164.
[16] L. J. Rogier, P. Brachim, *Histoire du catholicisme hollandais depuis le XVIe siècle* (Paris 1974), 227.
[17] Jan Roes, *R. K. Nederland 1958–1973* (Nijmegen 1974), 26.
[18] *Kaski over gemengde huwelijken in Nederland* (March 1974).

In the transition from one phase to the other it seemed as though the Dutch Catholics had found support in Monsignor W. Bekkers, bishop of the largest Dutch diocese, Den Bosch (1960–66), and a famed television speaker. A few months after Bekkers's sudden death in May 1966 appeared *The New Catechism: Proclamation of the Faith for Adults,* a book with many merits but also with weaknesses of Dutch welfare Catholicism. These weaknesses were in connection with the one-sided incarnational theology, which focused on the downward-moving love of God for humans in Jesus Christ but less on the upward movement of the person to God in Jesus's sacrificial death and in the self-sacrifice of the person, in fact the latter was considered almost as a contradiction of the former.[19] Corrections from Rome in 1968 in regard to original sin, the virginal birth, the sacrificial character of the Eucharist, and so forth were not accepted by the authors. Then the bishops let these corrections be published only in a special brochure.

Most extensive were the changes in connection with the education of priests. Within a few years all fifty minor seminaries had disappeared from the scene. Between 1963 and 1969 all thirty-two philosophical and thirty theological institutions were concentrated in five larger cities. Typical of the Dutch movement of renewal is the extent and compactness in this movement of concentration. The new project contained some positive points—openness, the corresponding instruments for work, selection of professors, better payment since the complete financing on the level of the university. But opposing these were negative points—the halving of the number of students—1,000 instead of 2,000—of whom only a small number sought a celibate priesthood.[20] The episcopate had no great influence on the course of events relating to these institutions.

The Dutch Pastoral Council, which held six meetings at Noordwijkerhout from 1966 to 1970, seemed to be a sort of crowning of the work of the Dutch renewal movement. As "council" it understood itself in the sense of a "Total Council of all the Faithful of the Ecclesiastical Province." But the documents so strongly breathed the spirit of the newly established upper middle-class that the council has been qualified as a typical "middle-class enterprise," whose representatives undertook to try to create a renewed Church on "its model and likeness." The references to the Second Vatican Council must be regarded as an ideologically stamped selection of the renewal needs of middle-class

---

[19] J. Ratzinger, "Theologie und Verkündigung im holländischen Katechismus," *Dogma und Verkündigung* (Munich and Freiburg i. Br. 1973), 77.
[20] *Katholiek Archief* 30(1975), 158.

Catholics.[21] The meeting interpreted the enormous fluctuation of the last years entirely positively and irreversibly.[22] The dramatic climax was the discussions on the abolition of obligatory celibacy. Despite the urging of the Pope not to treat this point, the meeting wanted by this very point to demonstrate its coming of age and freedom. The Pope made his protest clear by ordering the pronuncio, A. Felici, to stay away from the gathering. By an overwhelming majority the Council expressed itself for the so-called decoupling and for the reintroduction of married priests in the priestly ministry.

Since then the Dutch ecclesiastical province has given a clear example of the destiny which befalls a Church when it exchanges the direction of the legitimate holders of office for the power of persons who dominate opinion. Catholic faithful, who expressed the desire for the usual Catholic liturgy within the possibilities of the renewed official missal, parents who wanted to have their children given Catholic religious instruction, were characterized as "conservative," "unworldly," "intolerant," and the like, by the group which had power over the means of communication. Nowhere was the inner laceration of the Dutch believing community more visible than in the liturgy. In 1976 there was still no prospect that in the foreseeable future an official Dutch edition of the renewed missal would appear. People feared the normative impact of such an edition.

The desire for activity in the area of liturgy—734 liturgical worker groups in 1975—and the struggle against celibacy have burdened Dutch welfare Catholicism with the odium of being especially an inner church movement. "Critical communities"—ca. one hundred in 1976—had the desire to correct the onesidedness fostered by them. But by opposing the Church just as critically as they did society, they isolated themselves from the Church and furthered the process of disintegration, as Cardinal Alfrink said.[23]

In summary it can be said that, in comparison to the other ecclesiastical provinces, the crisis in the Netherlands began earlier and that the spirit of the enlightened bourgeoisie institutionalized itself in new church structures, so that at first glance it is not to be expected that a movement more directed to the Universal Church could quickly make its influence prevail on minds. Unless, of course, Rome would let the suppressed voices of the "ordinary" Catholics have more support, as

[21] O. Schreuder, op. cit., 254.
[22] M. Schmaus, L. Scheffczyk, J. Giers, *Exempel Holland. Theologische Analyse und Kritik des niederländischen Pastoralkonzils,* 2d ed. (Berlin), 49.
[23] "Kardinaal Alfrink in Kruispunt KRO-radio op 13.1.1974." *Analecta aartsbisdom Utrecht,* Feb. 1974, 136.

happened in the naming of Monsignor Doctor A. Simonis as bishop of Rotterdam on 30 December 1970.

The cadres of the dioceses—deaneries, administrative groups, councils, theology professors, and so forth—staged in newspapers, radio, and television a week-long campaign against this papal appointment.[24] From this it became obvious how Dutch Catholicism was dominated by a small group of powerful persons, who exercised their domination through the mass media; the majority of the people of the diocese expressed themselves for the bishop.[25]

At the naming of the bishop of Roermond, Doctor J. M. Gijsen, in February 1972 the same scene was repeated: protests in the press, on radio, and on television on the part of the cadres, agreement with this new bishop on the part of the great majority of his flock, who, however, could not assert themselves in the general communications happening.[26] Throughout the entire country there appeared a growing movement of opposition, the "Open Church." A sociological analysis[27] of this movement proves that the leaders and members belong to those categories which in our Western society exercise "a new priestly domination": the intellectuals and half-intellectuals from the "Third Sector" of the Relief State.[28] Its considerable influence is the mightiest factor for the explanation of the crisis in the postconciliar Church in many Western countries. What is special about the Dutch church province seems to be only that this stratum has a firm grip on all key positions within the Church.

[24] *Archief der kerken,* 26 (1971), nos. 6–7.
[25] T. Steltenpool, *Orthodoxie verboden?* (n.d.), 26.
[26] "Opinie-onderzoek in verband met de benoeming van de bisschop van Roermond, t.b.v. Redaktie 'Kenmerk' door Intomart," *Noordse Bosje* 15(Hilversum).
[27] O. Schreuder, op. cit., 250f.
[28] H. Schelsky, op. cit., passim.

CHAPTER 20

*Catholicism in Italy**

In 1914 one could hardly speak of an Italian Church as of a homogeneous structure. The differences among the various regions were very great, and because there was no episcopal conference coordination was absent. The 279 dioceses were, also through the weight of tradition, not arranged in a rational way. Besides very large dioceses, such as Milan and Novara, there were, especially in the south, many very small

* Luigi Mezzardi

dioceses. In 1885 there were 76, 381 diocesan priests in the service of 20,707 parishes, while the number of seminaries amounted to 11,569. In 1911 there were 67,147 diocesan priests; the number of religious priests in that year amounted to 6,644, that of nuns to 38,609.[1]

The education of the clergy was in general defective, and for this there were chiefly two reasons: the consequences of the Modernist crisis and the backwardness of the greatest part of the seminaries, to which a productive dialogue with secular culture was foreign. After the dissolution of the theological faculties at the state universities in 1872, academic degrees were earned either in the local faculties or at the Roman universities with mainly foreign teaching personnel and hence at a great distance from the problems of Italian reality. For its part the anti-Modernist repression had removed qualified professors from the seminaries and at that time deprived the students of outstanding texts, as, for example, the church history books of F. X. Funk and F. X. Kraus and the patrology of G. Rauschen.[2]

The fact that the clergy came predominantly from the country had, however, permitted the priests to keep in contact with social reality. While the students to some degree held themselves aloof, the tradition of the pastors close to the people proved to be very fruitful. For this, especially in the north, the parishes were the place where one could encounter the Christian experience: it was the place of religious instruction, of social and charitable education, and also of political orientation. In the south, on the other hand, the clergy was faced with a situation in which the emotional elements and the weight of folklore were much greater.[3]

[1] G. Bertolotti, *Statistica ecclesiastica d'Italia* (Savona 1885); also, *Sommario di statistiche storiche d'Italia 1865–1965; Annuario statistico italiano;* L. Cavalli, *Sociologia della storia italiana* (Bologna 1974); S. S. Acquaviva, *L'eclissi del sacro nella civiltà industriale* (Milan 1967); S. S. Acquaviva, G. Guizzardi, *Religione e irreligione nell'età postindustriale* (Rome 1971); for the Protestants: F. Manzotti, "I Valdesi a Guastalla e nella bassa padana," *Nuova rivista storica* 41 (1957), 418–55; A. Moscato, M. N. Pierini, *Rivolta religiosa nelle campagne* (Rome 1965); G. Spini, "Movimenti evangelici nell'Italia contemporanea," *Rivista Storica Italiana* 80 (1968), 463–98; F. Barra, "Millenarismo predicazione evangelica ed agitazioni contadine in Irpina dall'età giolittiana al fascismo," *Ricerche di storia sociale e religiosa* 3 (1974), 161–88.

[2] M. Guasco, *Fermenti nei seminari del primo' 900* (Bologna 1971); idem, "L'organizzazione delle scuole e dei seminari tra Leone XIII e Pio X," in the collection *Modernismo, fascismo e communismo,* a cura di G. Rossini (Bologna 1972), 192–204. Characteristic is the Lanzoni case: L. Bedeschi, *Lineamenti dell'antimodernismo. Il caso Lanzoni* (Parma 1970).

[3] Useful: AA. VV., *Chiesa e religiosità dopo l'unità,* 4 vols. (Milan 1973); AA. VV., *Chiesa e spiritualità dell'ottocento italiano* (Padua 1970); M. Mariotti, *Forme di collabora-*

The religious life had a visible upsurge, and appeared especially in the sphere of charity with Don Orione, of aid for immigrants with Scalabrini and Cabrini, and of the press with Don Alberione. Eleven orders of men were founded after 1900, among them the Consolata Missionary Fathers in 1901, the Sons of Divine Providence in 1903, and the Paolini in 1914. The number of orders of women founded after 1900 amounted to 120, of which fifty-four were in the north, twenty-six in the center, and forty in the south and on the islands. Typical are the multiple foundations: Don Giuseppe Alberione (d. 1971) founded the nine communities of the Paolini family, and Don Luigi Orione (d. 1940) four communities. Within this impetus in the religious life, the flowering of the missionary system is especially interesting. In the wake of Daniele Comboni (d. 1881) and Angelo Ramazzotti (d. 1861), the founders of the Comboniani and of the Pontifical Institute for Foreign Missions (PIME), Giuseppe Allamano (d. 1926) and Guido Maria Conforti (d. 1931) not only founded the institutes of the Consolata and the Xaverians, but they contributed also to the awakening of a mission awareness among people and clergy, especially through the work of Father Paolo Manna (d. 1952).

In 1911 Italy had 35,845,000 inhabitants—in 1872 there were 27,303,000. Over 37 percent of this population was still illiterate—in 1871 illiterates had constituted 70 percent of the total. Catholics made up 95.1 percent of the population, Protestants .36 percent. At that time there were 874,523 persons—2.5 percent—who declared they belonged to no religion, while 653,404 did not answer this question. The areas with the strongest religious indifference were at Leghorn (18.4 percent) and Reggio Emilia (14.1 percent). Emilia-Romagna was the region with the highest percentage of those leaving the Church (9.63 percent). But this phenomenon of de-Christianization was not restricted to the upper social classes; it appeared also in the strata of the simple folk, as, for example, in Emilia and Tuscany. In the country social distress favored the external retention of religion. Anticlericalism[4] and religious igno-

---

zione tra vescovi e laici in Calabria negli ultimi cento anni (Padua 1969); A. Gambasin, Gerarchia e laicato in Italia nel secondo ottocento (Padua 1969); C. Bellò, Società ed evangelizzazione nell'Italia contemporanea. Linee di una storia e di una pastorale (Brescia 1974).

[4] On anticlericalism in the Risorgimento, see S. Jacini, "La tradizione anticlericale del Risorgimento italiano," Studium 32 (1936), 348–56, 406–16; G. Pepe, M. Themelly, L'anticlericalismo nel Risorgimento (Manduria 1966); G. Verucci, "Anticlericalismo, libero pensiero e ateismo nel movimento operaio e socialista italiano (1861–1878)," in AA. VV., Chiesa e religiosità dopo l'unità II (Milan 1973), 176–224; P. Scoppola, "Laicismo e anticlericalismo," ibid., 225–74. G. Spadolini, Per una storia dell'anticlericalismo: I repubbulicani dopo l'unità (Florence 1963); M. Sylvers,

rance were very widespread. Also, the theological instruction of the laity was inadequate because of the powerful overemphasis on the Roman Question, which directed the best energies predominantly to the political and social sphere. Important figures of this period were: Bartolo Longo (d. 1926), promoter of the pilgrimage to Pompeii, the Blessed Giuseppe Moscati (d. 1927), the sociologist Giuseppe Toniolo (d. 1918), Pier Giorgio Frascati (d. 1925), Giulio Salvadori (d. 1928), and Vico Necchi (d. 1930). There was not, however, the typical French phenomenon of a return of the intellectuals to the faith.

The First World War affected Italian Catholicism in a phase of transition after the dissolution of the *Opera dei Congressi* (1904), which the anti-Modernist repression followed with the encyclical *Pascendi* of 1907. In the social sphere Pius X in July 1904 had dissolved the *Opera dei Congressi,* that organization of intransigence, which for thirty years had coordinated in its five sections almost all Catholic societies of the peninsula and had served as polemical mouthpiece for the protest of the Pope against the Italian government because of its "guilt" in the occupation of the Papal State and in an antiecclesiastical legislation which displayed little feeling of social needs.[5] As soon as it had become clear that the opposition between the Old Guard represented by Ettore Paganuzzi and the new generation embodied by Romolo Murri was unbridgeable and that the democratically minded young people were at the helm, the Pope, by means of the letter of Cardinal Merry del Val, had declared the great central organization, whose president had been named by the Pope, to be dissolved and replaced it by three unions, one for the people, one for the economic-social area, and one for the electoral campaigns, which were now directly subject to the bishops. With this drastic measure, which Monsignore Radini Tedeschi regarded as a catastrophe, the Holy See was pursuing several purposes. It especially disapproved of Murri and his democracy of a Christian stamp, which was based on the autonomy of Catholics in the political sphere. Further, there was an accommodation to the efforts of individual church dignitaries, who wanted to exercise a decisive influence in the Catholic movement. Finally, the suppression of the *Opera dei Congressi* fitted into the plans of Pius X for a restoration of disciplinary unity and strict

---

"L'anticlericalismo nel socialismo italiano (dalle origini al 1914)," *Movimento operaio e socialista* 16 (1970), 175–89; A. Azzaroni, *Socialisti anticlericali* (Florence 1961); G. Verucci, "Valori religiosi e valori laici," *Quaderni storici* 6 (1972), 543–64; A. M. Mojetta, *Cento anni di satira anticlericale nei giornali dal 1860 al 1955* (Milan 1975).
[5] On the *Opera dei Congressi,* see A. Gambasin, *L'attività sociale nell' opera dei Congressi (1874–1904)* (Rome 1958); G. De Rosa, *Storia del Movimento cattolico in Italia,* 2 vols. (Bari 1968); F. Candeloro, *Il movimento cattolico in Italia,* 3d ed. (Rome 1974) (Marxist).

obedience, which not only the theological Modernism of a Buonaiuti had jeopardized, but also the political Modernism of a Murri with his demand for independence from the hierarchy.[6]

In the area of the electoral campaigns the *non expedit* was weakened. The fear of a strong advance of the Socialists induced Pius X to undertake a dialogue with Giolitti and the moderate liberals, which led to the "Gentiloni Pact" of 1913. Gentiloni, president of the electoral union, promised the votes of the Catholics to those liberal candidates who obliged themselves in writing to respect a few conditions—rejection of divorce, defense of religious instruction in the schools, and so forth. In this way the moderate clerical influence, *clerico-moderatismo,* was strengthened. Italian Catholicism lived with this divided attitude—disciplinary rigidity on the one side, political opening to the moderate liberals on the other—until it was drawn into the First World War, which also for the Church marked a change in the peninsula.

The bishops at first stood for neutrality, except for a few prelates who subscribed to a nationalistic tendency.[7] However, when on 24 May 1915 the Italian government began hostilities against the Central Powers, obedience to the secular authority caused bishops and people to uphold the war. Only a few isolated personalities, such as the Barnabite Alessandro Chignoni, remained loyal to the pacifist attitude.[8] But there were also only a few of the bishops who succumbed to the temptation to violent reaction and chauvinistic rhetoric.[9]

The war evoked no substantial renewal of faith. The psychologist Father Agostino Gemelli proved that, after a momentary revival of an external piety as a consequence of the anguish at death, a return to

[6] The basic work on Italian Modernism is P. Scoppola, *Crisi modernista e rinnovamente cattolico in Italia* (Bologna 1975); the documents of the modernists are published in the annual *Fonti e documenti* of the University of Urbino, edited by the Centro Studi per la storia del modernismo, first issue in 1972.
[7] P. Scoppola, "Cattolici neutralisti e interventisti alle vigilia del conflitto"; A. Prandi, "La guerra e le sue consequenze nel mondo cattolico italiano"; A. Monticone, "I vescovi italiani e la guerra 1915–1918" (these three essays are in *Benedetto XV, I cattolici e la prima guerra mondiale,* 95–152, 153–205, 627–59).
[8] A. Chignoni, "Il cristianesimo e la guerra," *Coenobium,* June–July 1915, October–December 1915; Monsignore Volpi, bishop of Arezzo, remained opposed to the war, apparently not so much because of pacific convictions as out of sympathy for Catholic Austria; cf. Monticone, op. cit., 641.
[9] The nationalist terminology speaks of the "secular decisions of Italy's destiny," calls independence to mind with rhetorical phrases, and designates the Mother of God as "protector of Italy"; if the nationalist bishops constituted only an unimportant minority, they still had a much greater echo, because the press and the official propaganda emphasized them; cf. Monticone, op. cit., 635–37.

indifference can be ascertained.[10] Much more radical was *Coenobium,* the periodical of the Christian opposition, which branded it a scandal that the "theology of the sword" all too easily justified the war.[11]

The reliable support of the Italian Church for the government and the active participation in the fatherland's war was for the Catholics the signal for the ending of the opposition to the state and their entry into politics. In an effort to sanction this new line, Don Luigi Sturzo (d. 1959) in 1919 created the *Partito Popolare Italiano,* and the Holy See abolished its *non expedit.* This new political formation, which had been preceded by the founding of the *Confederazione Italiana dei Lavoratori,* with a Christian outlook, warred against the liberal state; it denounced its excessive centralization and its slight respect for the freedom of teaching and for local autonomy.

Because its registered members were recruited especially from the rural classes, Sturzo's union took up the agrarian question, for which it advocated a bold reform program—partition of the *latifundia* with extensive cultivation, promoting of small ownership. It cultivated good-neighbor relations with the moderate trade unions, which were against indiscriminate strikes, especially the political, and occupation of factories. In coordination with the Socialists and at the same time with them it led a decisive fight for the eight-hour day and realized some social demands—ownership of stock and share in profits by workers, legal recognition and equality of rights for all union organizations. Although the Popular Party had originated in an openly declared social orientation, it fought the anarchist violence of the Socialist extremists, but could also not realize collaboration with Socialists in the government: attempts at this in 1921 failed not on social questions, but on the school problem and in 1924 because of the veto of the Holy See. In connection with Sturzo's initiative the political autonomy of Catholics vis-à-vis the hierarchy constituted the most important innovation. Although the Popular Party wanted to be the voice for the democratic appeal of the Catholics, it developed nondenominationally. Cardinal Gasparri repeatedly declared that the new union arose "without the intervention of the Holy See" from the consistent effort of the Catholic movement for adaptation to democratic society, in which each interest was promoted by the activity of the interest groups of the moment. Benedict XV had facilitated such a process, which surpassed the political-religious exaggeration of the *Opera dei Congressi* and its succes-

[10] A. Gemelli, *Il nostro soldato* (Milan 1917), 132f.; cf. also his article "Il nostro programma e la nostra vita," *Vita e Pensiero* 1 (1916), no. 1.
[11] A. Prandi, op. cit., 174; cf. also the article by A. M., "I cleri di tutte le nazioni di fronte alla guerra mondiale," *Coenobium* 1, July 1918.

sor societies, by separating the field of politics from that of religion. While the new party organism did not present itself as the absolute final stage for the realization of political unity among Catholics, in reality, because of the special circumstances, it embraced almost the entire majority of Catholicism; the unanimous uniting of the Catholics on the political level had been caused by the necessity of reacting against the antipapal and anticlerical spirit of the other parties. Decidedly and incessantly Don Sturzo championed the autonomous role of the Catholic layman, who should act in the secular sphere freely and courageously with personal responsibility and not as the standing army of the hierarchy.

Although socialists and liberals fought it, the Popular Party gained sympathy in the elections of 1919 and acquired 100 delegates' seats, whose number grew two years later to 107, when the threatening spectre of Fascism had already appeared in the country. Don Sturzo was among the first to understand the incompatibility of the Gospel with the Fascist regime, that regime which embodied the pagan idolatry of the state, the antievangelical principle of power, and the Machiavellian spirit.[12] In November 1922 the Popular Party sought cooperation with the Fascists in the government in an effort to guide it into a normal liberal channel. However, it was at once expelled by Mussolini when in April 1923 he had set foot on the crooked path of despotism, and, like all democratic formations, was suppressed. Together with other like-minded persons, such as Ferrari, Donati, and others, Don Sturzo had to leave the country. De Gasperi was jailed. Only a very few former adherents of the Popular Party, so-called clerical Fascists, joined the dictatorship. The mass of Catholics was divided into two groups. Some participated actively, even though they remained in Italy, in the secret struggle of antifascism, especially in the group of the Guelfs, led by Malvestiti at Milan and in several other cities, under Alcide De Gasperi and Igino Giordani in Rome, and under Guido Gonella and other leaders of the resistance. The majority belonged to Catholic Action, which, with considerable difficulty, was able to survive as the place for exclusively religious instruction and as a nursery for the future. It would have been almost impossible that the Catholic world of Italy should have adapted itself to Fascism, which was based on a party program hostile to the Church and had a large number of rabid anticlericals in its ranks.

---

[12] L. Sturzo, *Pensiero antifascista* (Turin 1925); Sturzo's hostility to Mussolini showed even in the single meeting which he had with him in 1921; cf. S. Tramontin, "Mussolini la questione romana e i rapporti con i popolari in un documento inedito," *Humanitas* 24 (1970), 469–75.

The founder of Fascism came from the Romagna and in 1919 had appeared on an election list together with Podrecca, the head of the most powerfully anticlerical-oriented newspaper, *Asino*. Perhaps he was favored by the fact that he was originally guided by no precisely defined doctrine. Fascism originated in 1919 under the auspices of change and demand for action. After Mussolini had in 1914 abandoned socialism, which represented neutrality, and was converted to interventionism, he more and more moved toward the right, where he found the assistance of the nationalists, of the middle class, and finally also of the upper middle-class strata and of the landed proprietors. He did not have the sympathy of the Catholics, who even energetically fought him with the aid of the Popular Party. Mussolini's tactical skill was, like his political sagacity and his ability to enthuse the masses, equal to the most sophisticated Machiavellianism. He understood that he could not consolidate the power seized on 28 October 1922 by an extraparliamentary route without coming to an accommodation with the Church. At once, in 1923, although he at the same time expelled the Popular Party from his cabinet, he gained the hierarchy by some concessions in favor of denominational schools and other concessions. Many Catholics gradually put aside their mistrust and drew closer to the new regime, to which they attributed the merit of restoring order and the forcible suppression of socialist violence. And the struggle against the Freemasons and liberalism was a good deed in the eyes of the Catholic public. True, the Fascist shocktroops were guilty of crimes by invading Socialist party headquarters and clubs of Catholic Action, murdering the Socialist deputy Giacomo Matteotti in June 1924, and beating Don Minzoni, pastor of Argenta in the Romagna, to death.[13] But the middle-class circles made small gangs of thieves responsible for such criminal deeds, and these were not identified with Mussolini's movement. Thus is to be explained why the Holy See abandoned the Popular Party completely and undertook direct discussions with Mussolini for the solution of the Roman Question. The Duce made use of the opportunity and was happy to show himself very generous with privileges in order to end the strife between Church and state, which neither Cavour in 1860 nor Crispi in 1887 nor Orlando in 1919 had been able to settle.[14]

Almost all bishops welcomed the concluding of the Lateran Treaties on 11 February 1929 as an important event; Cardinal Ascalesi of Naples characterized Mussolini as the renewer of Italy. But not all Catholics

---

[13] L. Bedeschi, *Don Minzoni il prete ucciso dai fascisti* (Milan 1973); AA. VV., *Antifascisti cattolici* (Vicenza 1968) (contains writings of Bishop Rodolfi and of Don Mazzolari and Ferrari).

[14] F. Margiotta-Broglio, *Italia e S. Sede dalla grande guerra alla Conciliazione* (Bari 1966).

agreed with this. Father Giulio Bevilacqua, who lived at Rome in the house of Monsignore G. B. Montini, did not conceal his dismay over the unexpected and regrettable news that the Church had implicitly gone security for a despotism. The priest complained especially of the Fascist violence to which he had himself fallen victim at Brescia and which was opposed to Christian gentleness. He surely could approve neither the dealing with the human person as a mere instrument nor the state's monopoly of the education of youth.[15] De Gasperi, on the other hand, who had only recently emerged from Fascist prison, expressly distinguished between the treaty, which he evaluated positively because it put an end to any claims of the secular power, and the concordat, which he regarded as dangerous because of the possibility of a secret understanding between Church and dictatorship.[16]

But the scruples of this élite did not prevent the Italian people in the plebiscite of March 1929 from sanctioning Fascism with 9 million votes in contrast to only 135,000 "no" votes. A further occasion for enthusiasm offered itself in 1936 when Italy occupied Ethiopia. A year earlier, on 28 October, Cardinal Schuster in a sermon in the Milan cathedral had sung a paean of praise to what seemed to him as a campaign of evangelization and a work of Christian civilization for the good of Ethiopian barbarians—the same cardinal who, three years later, attacked the regime because of the racial laws which crushed Christian universalism. It was not difficult for Mussolini to represent the enterprise in Spain as a holy crusade against atheistic Bolshevism.

There can be no question that Catholicism and Fascism existed side by side in the best understanding; it must rather be established that the Catholic consensus was of a passive rather than an active nature and was again and again interrupted by many acts of opposition. Catholic Action and especially Youth Action can be seen as controverted points. In ARTICLE 43 the concordat recognized the organizations belonging to Catholic Action insofar as their activities took place outside political parties and under direct dependence on the church hierarchy and for the realization of Catholic principles. What was then the real attitude of the Catholic movement in regard to the dictatorship? The evaluation of contemporaries is varied. Giuseppe della Torre, chief editor of *Osservatore Romano,* wrote that the meeting between Fascism and Catholic Action was a collision. On the other hand, De Gasperi spoke of the "pitiful spectacle" which some top leaders offered to their associations by their too broad compromises. In reality, the movement with its

[15] G. Bevilacqua, *Scritti tra le due guerre,* E. Gianmancheri, ed., (Brescia 1968); A. Fappani, *P. Giulio Bevilacqua prete e cardinale sugli avamposti* (Verona 1975).

[16] A. De Gasperi, *Lettere sul Concordato* (Brescia 1970).

organizations in four divisions—male youth, female youth, men, women—with its registered members presented a power factor in regard to numbers which could not but arouse the suspicion of the regime. Open battle broke out in the spring of 1931. Mussolini was suspicious that Catholic Action wanted to take the place of the Popular Party and therefore dissolved 5,000 groups of male and 10,000 groups of female youth with a total of 800,000 members.[17]

He had thereby severely hit those whom Pius XI had designated as his most loyal adherents. The attitude of the Italian episcopate hardened for several months. Pius XI let Mussolini know through Father Tacchi-Venturi that after long reflection and hesitation he was now convinced that he must censure Fascism, which he then branded in the encyclical *Non abbiamo bisogno* of 29 June 1931 as a pagan idolatry of the state. After a first phase of open opposition the desire not to destroy peaceful coexistence prevailed. On 2 September an agreement was signed which confirmed the right to life of Catholic Action in keeping with ART. 43 of the concordat, but at the same time laid down some restrictive measures: The organization had to limit its field of activity to the purely religious sphere; all associations on the diocesan level were placed under the bishop's responsibility, whereby they were cut off from the central direction.

After the crisis of 1931 Italian Catholicism experienced no further shocks. The majority of the episcopate had a benevolent attitude toward the regime, except for some basically antifascist-minded bishops—Gaggia at Brescia, Elia della Costa at Padua and then at Florence, Endrici at Trent. But sympathy never passed to complete reconciliation. No Italian bishop made the Fascist ideology his own. If the bishops were accommodating to Mussolini in words, they could never be designated as "Fascist" in the sense that they had made compromises with the main ideological theses of Fascism; rather, one could speak of an a-Facist episcopate.[18]

The episcopate was oriented extensively in the spirit of the concordat, which recognized the validity in civil law of religious weddings, introduced Catholic religious instruction in all schools, except the universities, and accepted some typical aspects of the Christian state.[19] On this foundation there developed a pastoral practice which made

[17] A. Martini, *Studi sulla questione romana e la Conciliazione* (Rome 1963), illustrates also the history of the origin of the Lateran Treaties and the conflict of 1931 and the final battle of Pius XI in 1938 on the occasion of the race laws.
[18] S. Tramontin, *Cattolici popolari fascisti nel Veneto* (Rome 1975); R. Moro, "Afascismo e antifascismo nei movimenti intellectuali di Azione Cattolica dopo il '31," *Storia Contemporanea* 6 (1975), 733–801.
[19] G. Martina, "I cattolici di fronte al fascismo," *Rassegna di Teologia* 17 (1976), 170–94.

harmony between civil and canon law its pivotal point—religion of the state, defense of morality, families of many children. The coexistence of the Church with Fascism had, however, only externally the appearance of an agreement; in reality, the basic dissent continued, and each tried to gain the greatest advantage in regard to the other side.[20] In fact, no convinced Catholic occupied a leading position in the regime, just as no Fascist of the first hour was permitted greater responsibility in Catholic Action.

After years of a doubtful modus vivendi there occurred in 1938 the definitive break, when Mussolini, even though in moderate form, imitated Hitler in the persecution of Jews. Bishops such as Schuster or Nasalli-Rocca, who had sympathized with the activity of the dictatorial Italian regime, heartily concurred with Pius XI when on Christmas Eve he thanked the "most noble ruler" and his "incomparable" prime minister for the religious peace in Italy, but then immediately in his address complained of the bad handling of Catholic Action and the violation of the marriage regulations of the concordat by the racial laws.

Italy's participation in the war on Hitler's side contributed likewise to the cooling of relations between the Church and Fascism. The clergy became still more hostile to and distrustful of the Social Republic of Italy, which, under the protection of Hitler's arms, Mussolini established on 8 September 1943 and which the Holy See never recognized.[21] When in the last phase of the Second World War the mass of Catholics held themselves aloof from Fascism, the active minority of anti-Fascist Catholics, which hitherto had fought in secrecy, rose in armed resistance[22] and then established the *Democrazia Cristiana.*

At the end of the Second World War there occurred in Italy a first phase of religious revival, which took place on the three levels of politics, organization, and piety. These levels were closely united and resulted from different factors: from a defensive attitude supported by concern in regard to the Communist Party and the laicized culture; from the idea that Italy must be defended as an officially Catholic country; finally, from an understanding of the Church with a hierarchical structure in the shape of a pyramid instead of a *communio.*[23]

---

[20] Don Primo Mazzolari, who was an irreconcilable opponent of Fascism; cf. P. Mazzolari, *Diario e lettere (1905–1972),* A. Bergamaschi, ed., (Bologna 1974).

[21] *Riservato a Mussolini, Notiziari giornalieri della Guarda Nazionale repubblicana novembre 1943–giugno 1944* (Milan 1974).

[22] M. Bendiscioli, *Antifascismo e Resistenza,* 2d ed. (Rome 1974); R. A. Webster, *La croce e i fasci* (Milan 1964), is informed in the historical area, but shows only incomplete knowledge of Catholic doctrine.

[23] The most effective synthesis comes from G. Martina, *La chiesa in Italia negli ultimi trent'anni* (Rome 1977).

With the collapse of Fascism on 25 April 1945 there was presented the problem of the succession to the regime. De Gasperi united in himself the hope of the liberal and also of the social Catholics and wanted to avoid a return to the "historical railing," *storico steccato,* hence the frontal opposition between Catholics and laicists. And so he sought to direct the political experience of Italy in the democratic sense to a party which could be the guarantee of the value of freedom and of political pluralism. But the parties of the left—Giuseppe Dossetti, Giorgio La Pira—objected to De Gasperi's line and complained that the *Democrazia Cristiana* had actually become a party of order and was not sufficiently committed in the social sphere.

The "Christian Democratic hegemony" served to defend civil and religious freedoms. The political unity of the Catholics was partly destroyed by the "Communist Catholics," namely, Felice Balbo, Franco Rodano, and Gabriele de Rosa,[24] a tiny minority, which opposed the fact that many Catholic workers opted for the extreme left. From the viewpoint of organization and numbers, Catholic Action represented an imposing power in the first postwar years. The number of registered members increased in the unions of men from 150,866 in 1946 (with 6,140 groups) to 285,455 in 1954 (with 12,224 groups). The unions of women, divided in 1946 among 10,389 and in 1954 among 16,389 groups, grew from 369,015 members in the period after the war to 597,394 in 1954. The male youths embraced 9,951 groups—5,504 urban and 4,447 rural—while their total number in 1954 had jumped to 15,709—6,472 urban and 9,237 rural groups; the number of members rose from 367,392 to 556,752 in 1954. The female youth constituted the imposing branch: in 1946 there were 13,898 groups among them, in 1954 there were 19,026; the number of members in the respective years rose from 884,992 to 1,215,977.[25]

The religious upsurge was conditioned by the political struggle. Catholic Action seemed to become a reservoir of the leadership cadres for the *Democrazia Cristiana.* Besides initiatives of a social sort, in connection with which one thinks especially of Carlo Gnocchi (d. 1952), those with a more political character appeared, as, for example, the civic committees, *comitati civici.*[26] The decisive points of spirituality in the parishes were the cult of the Eucharist and of the Mother of

---

[24] S. Tramontin, *Sinistra cattolica di ieri e di oggi* (Turin 1974); N. Antonetti, *L'ideologia della sinistra cristiana. I cattolici tra chiesa e comunismo (1937–45),* (Milan 1976); G. Campanini, *Fede e politica 1943–1951. La vicenda ideologica della sinistra D.C.* (Brescia 1976).

[25] *Annuario dell'Azione Cattolica Italiana* (Rome 1954).

[26] G. Baget-Bozzo, *Il partito cristiano al potere. La DC di De Gasperi e di Dossetti,* 2 vols. (Florence 1974).

God—especially typical in the postwar period were Marian pilgrimages—and marks of honor for the Pope. The traditional pilgrimages, whose centers had been at Loreto and Pompeii, were increased by new centers, as, for example, to San Giovanni Rotondo by Father Pio of Pietralcina (d. 1968) and to Syracuse. The apostolate of Father Riccardo Lombardi also found many collaborators; its goal was to proclaim Christianity in the "Crusade of Goodwill" and "Center of the Better World" as the sole alternative to the modern world.[27]

But the cultural impetus was almost totally absent. There was a lack of centers for investigation and for general cultural initiatives. The book market itself preferred the production of edifying literature and the translating of foreign works.[28] Italy encountered great difficulties with theological renewal. The series of biblical works directed by Salvatore Garofalo was begun in 1947 with outdated programs. Also typical was the aversion to Jacques Maritain's integral humanism. Nevertheless there occurred, even if only with severe efforts, a freeing of Italian theological culture from provincialism in the years after 1960, thanks to foreign influence. To be mentioned as especially vital centers are: Turin with Michele Pellegrino, Milan with Carlo Colombo, Brescia with the publishing house Morcelliana, Father Giulio Bevilacqua (d. 1965), Mario Bendiscioli at Milan, Bologna with the Centro di Documentazione di Scienze Religiose founded by Giuseppe Dossetti, and Rome with Giuseppe De Luca. Two "obedient prophets" especially played the most important roles in the process of fermentation in Italian Catholicism: Primo Mazzolari and Lorenzo Milani.[29]

In the first years after 1900 persons were of the opinion that a specially important role had to be attributed to a university for Italian Catholics. The long-desired institution became a reality in 1921 and was the work of the converted Franciscan, Agostino Gemelli (d. 1959), assisted by Armida Barelli (d. 1952) and Vico Necchi. The Catholic University of the Sacred Heart aimed in the sphere of higher culture to emphasize the ideal of a free school and a Christian culture.

---

[27] P. Lombarde, *Per un mondo nuovo* (Rome 1951); idem, *Esercitazioni per un mondo migliore* (Rome 1958).

[28] As late as 1974 there were 231 translations of 593 works of a theological character (cf. *Annuario delle statistiche culturali* 15 [1974], 31).

[29] P. Mazzolari, *La chiesa, il fascismo, la guerra* (Florence 1966); A. Bergamaschi, *Un contestatore di tutte le stagioni* (Bologna 1968); idem, *P. Mazzolari nello scandalo di "Adesso"* (Turin 1968); L. Bedeschi, *Obbedientissimo in Cristo. Lettere di don Primo Mazzolari al suo vescovo 1917–1959* (Milan 1974). Characteristic for Milani is the changing fate of his book, *Esperienze pastorali* (Florence 1957). Concerning him, cf. N. Fallaci, *Dalla parte dell'ultimo, vita del prete Lorenzo Milani,* 3d ed. (Milan 1974); F. Tognaccini, "Don Milano nell'evoluzione dell'opinione pubblica," *Testimonianze* 18 (1975), 97–108.

The purpose of this institution was the founding of a center for the creating of an organic culture, in a sense of a new *Summa* of knowledge, the educating of the leading classes of the country, and the freeing of the new generation from the influence of the laicized and unbelieving state school. Gemelli saw himself faced with the choice between the French model of a university completely free from the state's sphere of influence and the model of Louvain. Thanks to support by Benedetto Croce and Giovanni Gentile, he obtained state approval in 1924, which, it is true, meant a partial diminution of autonomy, but also a valuable official recognition. Later, other decisions had to be made, such as were determined by the chronic economic difficulties, and a choice had to be made between a university for the masses or for an elite. Around 1931 the ideological pluralism was restricted. But altogether the balance for the first half-century of existence was positive in regard to the level of scholarly production, while the ideal of an all-embracing education and not only one limited to the professions was only partly achieved. The reasons for this were: the lack of a faculty of theological sciences—a department for religious sciences was only established in 1969—the excessive number of students, the effects of the struggle against modernists, the absence of qualified Catholics in critical fields of scholarship.[30]

Around 1960 Italian society underwent radical changes: a rapid industrialization, a doubling of the per capita income between 1950 and 1970, a decline of those occupied in agriculture—from 42.2 percent in 1951 to 17.3 in 1971—a powerful and chaotic displacement of great masses of people from the south to the north and from country to city. Now arose the mass university. The number of students increased from 210,228 in 1955 to 886,894 in 1974–75. The considerable increase of votes for parties of the left proceeded along with a noticeable loss to the *Democrazia Christiana*—from a majority in 1948 to 38.3 percent in 1963—and so the "Opening to the left" had to take place, that is, an alliance of the Catholic Party with the Socialists. At the time the political power of the unions also grew.

The religious situation, of which one could have made a snapshot for the period before 1962 at the traditionalist Roman Synod held by John XXIII, changed fundamentally. Of course, this was not true of the institutional sphere, which remained for the most part unchanged. In 1974 there were 284 dioceses, 41,700 diocesan priests, 21,069 religious priests, 5,843 lay brothers, and 150,179 nuns. The vocation crisis

---

[30] G. Rumi, "Padre Gemelli e l'Università Cattolica," AA. VV., *Modernismo, fascismo, comunismo . . .* , G. Rossini, ed. (Bologna 1972), 204–33; M. Sticco, *Appunti per una biografia di un uomo difficile* (Milan 1974).

caused the number of priestly ordinations to drop from 955 in 1964 to 759 in 1969. The number of inhabitants per parish rose between 1964 and 1969 from 1,965 to 2,179. In the rise the presence of the Church was felt in the various sections of welfare—in 1964 there were 4,181 institutes, in 1969 there were 4,565—and of the educational system— 3,825 institutions in 1964 and 7,001 in 1969.[31] Meanwhile, the Italian episcopate succeeded, with the founding of the Italian Episcopal Conference in 1969, in working out uniform pastoral guidelines.

The crisis of the postconciliar period had significant effects in Italy also. The Catholic association system suffered an obvious setback at the end of the 1960s. The crisis had already advertised itself when Carlo Caretto in 1952 and then Mario Rossi (d. 1976) in 1954 withdrew because they were not in agreement with the conservative political line followed by President General Luigi Gedda.[32] After 1968 pressure to spontaneous actions reduced the maneuverability of the movement in the extreme.

The critical situation of the Catholic world was revealed also in the political sphere by the increase of votes for the Communist Party and by the turning of declared Catholic representatives such as Paolo Brezzi and Raniero La Valle to this party, which made questionable the very existence of a Catholic Party. The present situation was also made more difficult by the seething of ecclesiastical cases of conflict, such as the Isolotto Congregation and Abbot Franzoni. The referendum for the abolition of divorce ended with a victory of 59.26 percent for the advocates of divorce as opposed to 40.74 percent for its opponents, and placed before the Catholic world the much greater problem of how in a pluralistic society Christian ideals can be assured.[33]

[31] *Segretaria di Stato, Raccolta di tavole statistiche* (Vatican City 1971ff.).

[32] M. Rossi, *I giorni dell'onnipotenza. Memoria di un'esperienza cattolica* (Rome 1975).

[33] The following can be established as positive: the development of the secular institutes, new movements such as the Focolari and Communione e Liberazione, and the new Catholic Action and the central groups of the new Pentecostal and Catechumen Movements. Cardinal Giacomo Lercaro (d. 1976), one of the promoters of the reform of the liturgy, deserves a special place among the most important figures of the latest history.

CHAPTER 21

*The Catholic Church of France**

The denunciation of the concordat in 1905 produced between Rome and the Church of France a more intimate relationship than ever before.

* Pierre Blet, S. J.

In addition, the accessions of Benedict XV and Pius XII roughly coincided with the outbreak of the two world wars, which had an impact on the interior life of the French Church. And so it is admissible to divide this latest sector in the life of French Catholicism according to the three pontificates of Benedict XV, Pius XI, and Pius XII.

Under Benedict XV

The state of war in which France was placed by the declaration of war of 3 August 1914 hastened considerably a development already begun in the ecclesiastical situation of France. The Dreyfus Affair had shown that the Catholics, whom patriotic republicans had long charged with placing the interests of the Church above those of the nation, stood in the front line of patriots, that is, of nationalists.[1] At that time the radical left represented pacifist tendencies, and the relations of the Catholics with the government were thereby not better. The voting on the law for the introduction of a three-year period of military service in August 1913 had made it clear: this very republican government had understood that it had to do something better than devote itself to the excluding of clerical influence. The declaration of war strengthened this tendency: in view of the threat to the country's frontiers, clericalism ceased to be the chief enemy. This change was expressed on both sides in concrete actions: priests and seminarians submitted with enthusiasm to the general obligation to military service, and the expelled religious returned in order to comply with the mobilization order, pastors prevented by age preached from the pulpit the duty to obey the induction order and make the financial sacrifices caused by the war. For his part, Minister of the Interior Malvy suspended the implementation of the laws of 1905 against the property of religious communities that had not yet been liquidated.

Influential Catholics, including prelates such as Monsignore Baudrillart, established a Catholic committee for the support of French foreign propaganda with the aid of brochures and lectures. These were especially intended for Catholic countries such as Spain and Latin America, where the anticlerical policy of the government had greatly reduced French influence. Of course, anticlericalism did not entirely disappear. It continued during the war in connection with the diplomatic exertions of Benedict XV for ending the "unnecessary shedding of blood"; the Vatican was presented as a power which absolutely favored the Central Powers. The French Catholics now aimed to demonstrate that they kept themselves aloof from the papal policy.

[1] R. Rémond, *La droite et les droites en France.*

Thus the Dominican Father Sertillanges proclaimed in a sermon, whose text the cardinal archbishop of Paris had censured, from the pulpit of Notre-Dame in Paris: "Most Holy Father, we cannot comply with your words of peace to the present. We are sons who say "no, no. . . ."[2] But still more than through such sensational rhetoric, the Catholics and their clergy were freed from any doubt as to their patriotic devotion by the spectacle which 25,000 priests, religious, and seminarians called to military service offered, half of whom accepted misery in the trenches, and 4,608 of whom never returned.[3]

The comradeship which had united pastor and teacher in the slime of the trenches and under the bombardment of cannon left lasting impressions. On the day of demobilization many participants in the war returned with the determination to preserve "the sanctified union." Clemenceau could still conduct the negotiations at Versailles in a spirit which was as hostile to the Holy See as to the Habsburg Monarchy. But the elections of 1919 produced a majority of moderates in the Chamber of Deputies, who were opponents of the sectarian laws from the beginning of the century. Of course, these laws could not be revised, for the Senate remained under the influence of the radical party; but when Clemenceau became a candidate for president of the republic in the elections, the nationalists made him atone for his obdurate anticlericalism: they preferred Deschanel, and Clemenceau left politics.

It was known that Clemenceau was against restoration of diplomatic relations with the Holy See; but the experience of the war had taught that it was a disadvantage for France to have no such connection as an embassy at the Vatican represented. Besides, the reversion to France of the provinces of Alsace and Lorraine, to which in 1871 Bismarck had allowed the status of the Napoleonic concordat, raised questions which demanded dialogue with the Holy See; for the generals and the first high commissioners had promised to the Alsatians and Lorrainers the maintenance of their religious status. In order to keep their word, people had to renounce the principles of centralizing Jacobinism and laicism and grant that the two provinces retain their regime in accord with the concordat, that priests there be paid by the state, and that the school remain denominational. The government of the Republic had to begin conversations with Rome and resume from the break of 1905. The representative of the law of separation, Aristide Briand, was one of the first to express himself for the reestablishing of a French embassy at the Holy See, and many members of the former government shared his opinion. The Catholics worked for the realization of this project, and

[2] A. Dansette, *Histoire religieuse de la France, contemporaine sous la IIIe république*, 490f.
[3] R. Rémond, *Histoire du Catholicisme en France. La période contemporaine*, 558f.

585

the Holy See showed itself to be very accommodating. However, the idea encountered the resistance of anticlerical opponents and also did not find the good will of the extreme right, who saw in it a sort of recognition of the hateful regime by the Holy See. Nevertheless, the project, which included the reestablishing of an embassy at the Holy See and the installing of a nuncio at Paris, was approved by the Chamber of Deputies, but rejected by the Senate. When Aristide Briand became president of the council, he nevertheless on 17 May 1921 named Jonnart as French ambassador to the Holy See, and the new president of the Republic, Deschanel, in July accepted the credentials of Nuncio Ceretti.[4]

The resumption of diplomatic relations with the Vatican neither allowed the restoration of the concordat nor improved the material situation which the expropriations since 1905 had created. Nevertheless, Benedict XV conceded to the French government a right in regard to the naming of bishops: the Holy See would communicate to the Quai d'Orsay at the proper time the name of the newly chosen before publication in order to accommodate, if necessary, objections of a political sort that might occur.[5] Only in the dioceses of Strasbourg and Metz did the concordat remain in force, whereby the French government had the right of nominating.

After these first agreements, discussions were resumed in order to create a basic juridical situation for the value of church property in France. The Church societies rejected by Pius X could be taken into consideration in so far as they were founded on the basis of the agreements which had been worked out between the Church and the state, and with the presupposition that the authority of the hierarchy was assured. Nevertheless, with all respect the French bishops opposed an agreement which seemed to contradict the rejection which Pius X had imposed on them little more than ten years earlier. The acceptance of new societies, named diocesan societies, was the act of Pius XI, the new Pope. In 1924 he declared that he agreed that in each diocese a society should be founded under the presidency of the bishop to administer church property and to accept foundations and legacies.[6]

Under Pius XI

This regulation contained no compensation for the expropriations of 1905, it even left religious buildings in the ownership of political

[4] A. Dansette, op. cit., 502–5.
[5] R. Rémond, *Histoire du Catholicisme*, 565.
[6] A. Dansette, op. cit., 505–10.

communities and contained assurance neither for the Christian school nor the religious orders. Hence it was unable to arouse any enthusiasm among the faithful, who declared "war against laicism and its principles even to the annulment of the unjust laws which proceeded from them."

People were already on the eve of an election in which an anticlerical left and a right allied with the Church opposed each other. The vote of May 1924 was in favor of the alliance concluded between the radicals and the socialists and elevated Édouard Herriot to the position of president of the Council. For a moment people believed that the age of Combes had returned: the head of the government announced that he intended to abolish the embassy at the Holy See and would invoke the expulsion laws against religious, who had returned to France as a result of the mobilization; Herriot also promised that he would enforce the laicization laws in the provinces of Alsace and Lorraine. But he ran into an opposition which he had not foreseen. The *Fédération Nationale Catholique,* whose president was General de Castelnau, organized protest meetings, and the Freemasons were accused of having conspired at the same time against the Church and against French unity. The Alsatians and Lorrainers publicly expressed the desire that the promises in regard to worship and school should be kept. The religious threatened with explusion loudly pointed out their character as war veterans and through the pen of Father Doncoeur cried out the eventually famous: "We will not go!" The succeeding financial crisis put an end to the left coalition and made it understood that in 1925 anticlericalism had lost its impetus in the election struggles.

Of course, this did not absolutely prove that France had again become Christian: in wide areas of the population indifference took the place of hostility to religion. True, religious events such as the pilgrimage to Lourdes, the celebrations at the canonization of Joan of Arc,[7] and a little later the pilgrimages to Lisieux brought together passionately committed believers, as was also true of the rallies of the *Fédération Nationale Catholique.* Religious practice made progress in the middle class and especially among students and at the big schools. As forerunner of the *Jeunesse Étudiante Catholique* (JEC) in 1929 the *Fédération Française des Étudiants Catholiques* from 1922 on founded local groups. But apart from this elite there were, as is well known, large groups in the population that had been educated outside the Church in the laicized schools. The *Association Catholique de la Jeunesse Française* continued its work in order to prepare its members for civic activity in the future. The *Semaines Sociales* carried their educational work further

[7] Ibid., 503.

in order to inform the Catholics on the social doctrine of the Church and its effects. For the same end the *Action Populaire,* which had moved from Rheims to Paris in 1919, improved its publications. *The Confédération Française des Travailleurs Chrétiens* worked to unite all unions to which all wage earners in commerce and industry belonged, and in 1920 it already had 140,000 members.[8]

Nevertheless, many Catholics saw in the removal of the Freemasonic and anticlerical Republic the basic assumption for the return of France to the faith of the Fathers. The alliance between nationalism and Catholicism, consolidated by the war, found embodiment in the movement of the *Action Française,* whose changing fate had serious consequences. There was a unique alliance between the leader of *Action Française,* Charles Maurras, who was a pupil of Auguste Comte, and the conservative Catholics who joined his movement. But Maurras declared all agents of de-Christianization, rationalists, Freemasons, and Protestants to be enemies of the French nation and extolled Roman Catholicism as the necessary foundation for the reconstruction of the monarchy. *Action Française* found in the Catholic area, in youth, in universities and seminaries, in the religious orders, and even in the body of bishops an assent which to a degree inclined to enthusiasm.

This influence of a movement which glorified nationalism, which made no secret of its aim to unite the Catholics against the Republic, met the resistance of democratic Catholics. It was also unable to obtain the assent of Pius XI, who was seeking a reconciliation with the Republic. Moreover, the personal attitude of Maurras and his slogan "Politics in First Place" urged caution. The first warning, which came from France at Rome's demand, was a letter of the archbishop of Bordeaux, Cardinal Andrieux, of 25 August 1926. The letter contained gross distortions, it is true, but nevertheless Pius XI gave it his general assent.[9] But at the same time it became known that several books by Maurras had been put on the Index, a decision which was under way as early as 1911 but which had again and again been postponed by Pius X and Benedict XV. Immediate violent counterattacks of *Action Française* were answered by Rome with sanctions: On 29 December 1926 the reading of the newspaper of *Action Française* and membership in this union were entirely forbidden. The consequence of disobedience was refusal of the sacraments, and priests who absolved those not repentant became reserved cases *ratione sui.* The leaders of *Action Française* characterized these measures as the result of a plot which had been contrived for the advantage of democracy and Ger-

[8] R. Rémond, *Histoire du Catholicisme,* 583.
[9] A. Dansette, op. cit., 583f.

many, and with their anticlericalism they competed with the radicals, who were otherwise attacked by them. Some Catholics appealed to the freedom of political opinion to disregard the Roman prohibitions. The directive for the refusal of the sacraments was often ignored but also often applied with a severity which exceeded the intentions of the instructing office. In the clergy and the religious orders the condemnation of *Action Française* not only involved the retirement of Cardinal Billot but also the withdrawal of a whole class of leaders and the election of new men,[10] who were not prepared for the functions they had to assume.

In 1927 Father Lhande published his book, *Le Christ dans le Banlieu.* In it he revealed to the faithful and even to the clergy of the capital that in the immediate geographical neighborhood, namely, in the midst of their own parishes, existed masses of people to whom the Church was not only foreign but entirely unknown. The construction association, founded by the new archbishop, Cardinal Verdier, for the building of churches in the suburbs was not sufficient to alter the situation. At the same time Abbé Guérin, vicar in a workers' parish, obtained knowledge of the *Manuel du Jociste Belge* of Abbé Cardijn. He believed that he could find there the solution for the problem of the education of young workers, for that problem to which the *Action Catholique de la Jeunesse Française,* in his opinion, gave only an insufficient answer. The ACJF, which celebrated the fiftieth anniversary of its founding in 1936, invited young workers and young bourgeois to common meetings; but because it aimed chiefly at the formation of a leadership elite, it reached the young workers only with difficulty. Entirely in the meaning of Abbé Cardijn, who had in mind a movement restricted to the working class, young French workers held their first meeting at Clichy in October 1926. The newspaper edited by them, *Jeunesse Ouvrière,* appeared in January 1927 in its first issue. The movement (JOC) quickly stirred enthusiasm and spread to Lille, Lyon, and Marseille. The hierarchy, with Cardinal Dubois at Paris, assisted by Canon Gerlier as director of the associations, and with Cardinal Liénart at Lille supported the movement. When the "Popular Front" came to power in 1936 and began a movement of strikes and occupation of factories, great hopes were centered on the picked troops of militant adherents of the Christian Young Workers' Movement, *Jocists,* who defended their rights and those of their worker colleagues, but still always maintained loyalty to the faith and its moral demands. From this moment on, the union of Christian workers acquired a new upsurge;

[10] Ibid., 603.

by 1938, 2,400 unions with 500,000 members existed.[11] The celebration of the tenth anniversary of JOC from 16 to 21 July 1937 brought together at Paris ca. 80,000 *Jocists* and took on the features of a triumph.

Long before this success began to be clear, persons began to apply the rules of the workers' movement also to other fields. In 1929 the *Jeunesse Agricole Catholique* (JAC) joined the ACJF, and now there appeared also the *Jeunesse Étudiante Catholique* (JEC). The *Jeunesse Maritime Catholique* (JMC) was founded in 1932, and in 1936 the *Jeunesse Indépendante Catholique* (JIC). These movements also had female branches and all joined the ACJF, which from then on appeared as a union of autonomous movements under the control of the hierarchy.

Likewise, as the JOC had closely joined the CFTC, the JAC expanded to the *Ligue Agricole Chrétienne* and soon after to the Farmers' Family Movement, while on the other hand the *Action Catholique Indépendante* and the *Action Catholique Indépendante Feminine* and the *Mouvement des Ingenieurs et Chefs d'Industrie Catholique* formed their counterparts in the middle-class sphere.

The special character of all these movements consisted in their apostolic orientation. The Scout Movement, on the other hand, basically had in view the training of youth, and so its pedagogical method was based on physical activity and a life in the group. In 1938 it had in France and overseas 78,000 young followers and became the nursery for vocations to the priesthood and the religious life.[12] Many scout groups were recruited from the pupils of Catholic high schools, in which vocations found a favorable environment.

While in this period the élan of movements of Catholic Action was well known, still the goal of all zealous exertions of the hierarchy and of all financial sacrifices of the faithful remained the more traditional form of the education of young men in the Christian schools. The laws of 1905 had severely hurt the congregations active in schools but had not changed the legal bases which proclaimed the principle of free instruction, namely the Falloux Law of 15 March 1850 for high school instruction, the law of 12 July 1875 for university instruction, the law of 30 October 1886 for elementary school instruction, and the law of 25 July 1919 for the training of technical experts. But apart from this last-named law, which expressly envisaged the granting of financial aid, this legislation refused any assistance to private education. Hence the faithful united in several associations to defend the existence of Christian schools and demand for them the granting of public assis-

[11] *Annuaire général catholique,* 1938, LX.
[12] Ibid. LXXIII.

tance. Thus the *Alliance des maisons d'education chrétienne,* founded in 1872, from which came in 1925 the syndicate of *Directeurs et Directrices des maisons d'éducation chrétienne,* was involved in the publication of texts for instruction and published its own periodical, *L'Enseignement chrétienne;* in 1938 1,061 houses belonged to the association.[13] The *Association de Chefs de Familles de France* aimed to stress the rights of Christian families, loudly proclaimed war against a standardized elementary school, and demanded of candidates in election to the legislative bodies assurances of the intact freedom of instruction.[14] Together with other unions it represented the viewpoint that freedom also presupposed school proportion, that is, the proportional dividing of the sums of money expended for education between the state and the private schools corresponding to the number of pupils.

A first demand in this sense, a projected law with the stipulation that pupils in possession of a scholarship could choose between the two kinds of school, was rejected by the Senate in 1920. The Catholics, encouraged to this by the FNC, insisted on their demand and were, in expectation of this regulation, ready to make considerable financial sacrifices for their schools. The growth of the high school stage between the two world wars achieved a degree that upset the radical left: in 1931 this area included 1,011 high schools with 150,000 pupils in contrast to 560 state high schools or lyceums with 225,000 pupils. In the period from 1930 to 1938 these figures were still higher: 1,271 high schools with 209,460 pupils in 1934–35 and 1,400 high schools with 230,607 pupils in 1937–38.[15]

Despite the retaining of the laicist laws and official neutrality, the feeling of the threat from without, evoked by the remilitarizing of the Rhineland, the *Anschluss* of Austria to the German *Reich,* and the expectation of the annexation of Czechoslovakia by Hitler, produced a new rapprochement between the government of the Third Republic and of the Church. A journey of Pope Pius XI to France for the dedication of the basilica of Saint Thérèse de Lisieux was planned. Cardinal Secretary of State Pacelli was received as the Pope's representative[16] in 1937 at Paris and Lisieux with the same honors as were customary for a head of state. Without repudiating its official laicism, the Third Republic came closer to the Church on the brink of its collapse.

[13] Ibid. LXVI.
[14] Ibid. LIX.
[15] P. Gerbod, "Les catholiques et l'enseignement secondaire," *RHMC* XVIII, 391, n. 2.
[16] F. Charles-Roux, *Huit ans au Vatican* (Paris 1947), 212–37.

Under Pius XII

Two years later, when the diplomatic missions of Cardinal Pacelli to both secular and Catholic France were still remembered, Pacelli was elected as successor of Pius XI on 2 March 1939. This election was greeted in France with enduring satisfaction; for it was known that he would undertake all efforts to save the peace which daily became more fragile. It is true that his offers of mediation in May 1939 with a view to a peace conference (see above, Chapter 3) were without prospects, but he was able to establish another peace through reconciliation with *Action Française.* In the course of years the leaders of *Action Française* had understood that they were making a mistake with the precipitate break in relations. On the other side were the penalties which had been imposed on the adherents of *Action Française,* in clear opposition to the concluding of concordats with the Fascist and Nazi governments, which could be charged with more than mere verbal violence. Pius XI had accepted with kindness the attempts at a rapprochement by Maurras, which the Carmel of Lisieux had suggested, and on 20 October 1938 the committee director of *Action Française* wrote a letter which was submitted to the Holy Office. The accession of Pius XII was accompanied by no hesitation. George Bonnet, minister for foreign affairs, replied to the nuncio as a result of his inquiry, that this question should be treated exclusively in the religious sphere. Although some bishops expressed hesitations, on 10 July 1939 the *Osservatore Romano* published the decree of the Holy Office which lifted the excommunication imposed on *Action Française* at the same moment in which a letter of the periodical disavowed all theories that were contrary to the teachings of the Church. The Second World War was near and created new problems for the Church of France.[17]

The declaration of war of 3 September 1939 proceeded this time from France and England and was the result of the German invasion of Poland, which for its part was a consequence of the Soviet-German nonagression pact. The Catholics were in agreement with the government, and the declaration of war let them see in the war a new crusade against the powers of evil, which Pius XI had unmasked in his two encyclicals against National Socialism and Communism. But the great mass of the population had for a long time lulled itself in the hope that the war of 1914 had been the last of all wars. And so it did not feel again the patriotic élan of August 1914. Priests, religious, and seminarians joined in the mobilization with members of all social strata and there encountered religious indifference and ignorance rather than hostility.

---

[17] A. Dansette, op. cit., 607–11; P. Lesourd, *Dossier secret de l'Église de France* II, 444–46.

The collapse of June 1940 could not be charged to the Church, which had lost all influence on political and even on public life. Rather it was the Catholics and the military leaders who were inclined to make the laicized school responsible because it had educated the new generations. The collapse again evoked feelings which had temporarily fallen into oblivion because of the harmony between the two powers. Thus preachers pointed out that the defect was God's punishment for the nation's official atheism. But on the other hand they strove to revive hope by indicating that Providence had always had pity on France. Once it had sent the country the eighteen-year-old Joan of Arc, and now it sent Pétain, the eighty-year-old venerable man. The hierarchy, in general very hesitant with its expressions, declared with a certain vigor in regard to the new regime the obligatory loyalty for the government, in which were many Catholics, also through the appeal which the regime directed to the spiritual values, and finally through measures such as the abolition of Freemasonry and especially through a new legislation which corrected the laws of the Third Republic in two essential points, namely, education and religious institutes. A law of April 1942 lifted the prohibition of the orders and provided for a legal recognition of religious communities. The new school laws reintroduced religious instruction in state lyceums and high schools and granted certain financial subsidies to the Christian schools.[18]

Of course the devotion of the clergy to the Vichy regime was not unconditional. Tensions soon arose, and first of all in the education of youth. In a letter to the head of state the bishops protested that the state laid its hand on youth: "A uniform youth—no!" The anti-Semitic policy followed by the occupying power likewise met resistance, which found its formal expression in declarations or letters of the archbishops of Lyon and Toulouse, Gerlier and Saliège, and of Bishop Théas of Montauban. Thus encouraged, many priests, religious, and religious institutions could preserve Jews, especially their children, from deportation. The *Service du Travail Obligatoire* (STO), that is, the drafting of young French workers for German war industry, created new problems of conscience, for which the church authorities found various solutions.[19] Meanwhile, the religious sentiment awakened by the defeat and

---

[18] P. Lesourd, op. cit. II, 491f. A law of 1940 annulled that law which forbade religious to give instruction, and which, incidentally, had not been applied since World War I. On 10 March 1941 a law introduced religious instruction on a voluntary basis in state educational institutions. A law of 6 January 1941 conceded to the congregations a contribution to the costs for light, heat, furniture, and mess in private schools. In 1942 and 1943 Catholic and Protestant faculties obtained extraordinary donations.

[19] R. Rémond, *Histoire du Catholicisme,* 611–23. Some religious superiors made the journey to Germany an obligation of conscience for their seminarians. Also the JOC

the disadvantages of the war called forth mass movements such as that of the *Grand Retour:* countless faithful from 1943 to 1946 carried a statue of Mary from Boulogne through the whole of France. Millions of pictures and rosaries were distributed, and millions of signatures were collected under the text of the consecration to the Immaculate Heart of Mary.[20]

When in 1944 the provisional government of General de Gaulle abolished the government of Marshal Pétain, the new power in the state aspired to purge the episcopate, which it accused of compliancy toward the Vichy regime. Together with the demand for the recall of Nuncio Valerio Valeri it demanded the resignation of some bishops. Pius XII agreed to replace his nuncio, because there was question of a measure which affected all envoys accredited to the Vichy regime, but he absolutely refused a purge of the episcopate. The new nuncio Angelo Roncalli brought it about that this decision was accepted and resignations were limited to three.[21] From this time on, the French episcopate created for itself a common organization. Since 1919 the cardinals and archbishops had customarily met and on occasion published common statements. Immediately after the Second World War the permanent Secretariat of the Episcopate was established, and finally in 1951 there took place the first plenary meeting of all French bishops.

In public life it was a new phenomenon that declared Catholics participated in the provisional government of General de Gaulle and then in the government of the Fourth Republic, which succeeded it in 1946. Again and again people who came from the ACJF were to be found in ministerial offices in ever quicker succession. Only the Ministry for National Education remained closed to them. The constitution adopted by a bare majority of votes on 13 October 1946 decided anew that the republic was a laicized state and freedom of teaching was excluded from the consitutionally legal freedoms. Nevertheless, the hierarchy, unperturbed, continued the struggle for the free school. As early as 13 March 1946 a declaration of the French cardinals and archbishops affirmed: "The entire French episcopate is determined to maintain the freedom of instruction by all the means at its disposal."[22]

---

expressed itself for the journey out of solidarity with those who had no possibility of avoiding it. Cardinal Liénart declared that it was up to each individual whether to obey the summons, and the ACJF supported resistance, whereby it oriented itself to the numerous "maquis" Catholics. A former member of ACJF later became president of the National Council of the Resistance Movement.

[20] R. Rémond, *Histoire du Catholicisme,* 621.
[21] Ibid., 620.
[22] A. Deroo, *L'épiscopat français dans la mêlée de son temps 1930–1954* (Paris 1955), 126f.

In the autumn of 1947 a public demonstration of the French Catholic educational system supplied the opportunity to recall "the complementary service which free instruction does for the country" and it was again emphasized that "justice, freedom, and equality" demand that the Christian school system receive its share in the financial expenditures which the state dispenses for the education of French youth. In the same year the treasury brought suits against the organizers of charity bazaars, which were held to cover school costs. In some cases this brought even bishops to court and thereby gave them the opportunity to call to mind the principles of justice. The politicians could not be entirely deaf to such appeals. In 1948 two decrees empowered state and local commissions to consult on a form of support for free schools. This again called forth the opposition of the entire left, and in some parts of the press were again heard the tones of the old anticlericalism. Despite this, the bishops in 1949 again insisted that "the Christian school is the concern of everyone who is called a Christian," and they admonished parents of their duty to care for a Christian education of their children.[23] Finally a law of 28 September 1951, called *Loi Bérangé,* granted to free elementary schools a subsidy of thirty-nine francs per year and per pupil as a contribution to the teachers' salary. This law quite obviously did not claim to have solved the school question, but it aimed only to make a beginning.

The new development introduced by this law was the work of the new government, which General de Gaulle had formed on his return to power. A law of 31 December 1959 gave the free schools the choice among four solutions: full integration into the state school, full freedom of the status quo, a social treaty whereby the state would appoint the teachers and lay down the general plans of instruction while undertaking all the costs of instruction, and finally individual treaties according to which the teachers chosen by the school would be subject to the conditions of state examinations and controls and would be paid by the state. In 1966 there were 11,700 institutions with individual treaties and 54,000 high school teachers paid by the state.[24]

These regulations did not silence all discussion of the free school. This type of school met objections from Catholics themselves, not only among those who advocated the state school system, from which they knew that it could give a testimony of great apostolic importance, but also in the clergy itself, where some asked what was to happen with the traditional institutions. These attitudes can be all the better understood when one considers that Catholics not only knew how to succeed in the

[23] Ibid.
[24] *Panorama de la France,* 896f.

cultural sphere but even also in the leadership strata of the state universities, which for a long time had with good reason been regarded as an instrument of de-Christianization. The intellectual and scholarly renewal of French Catholicism has since gone beyond the ecclesiastical frontiers. Such large-scale works as the *Histoire littéraire du sentiment religieux en France* by the abbé and member of the Academy Bremond achieved a great success. The *Dictionnaire de Théologie catholique* continued the efforts from the first years of this century. In 1937 was begun the scriptural series *Unam Sanctam,* in which soon appeared the epoch-making *Catholicisme* by Father de Lubac, and which not long after included the works of Father Congar. The *Histoire de l'Église* of Fliche and Martin had already begun, and Gilson was publishing his works on the history of Scholasticism, by which even Jacques Maritain was inspired and on which he relied in the investigation of the relations between Christians and modern society, in a perspective moreover that really stood close to that of the periodical *Esprit,* founded in 1932 by E. Mounier. During the war Fathers de Lubac and Daniélou founded the collection *Sources chrétiennes* for textual editions and translations of patristic texts, in which soon researchers from the ranks of the diocesan priests and of the orders collaborated with members of the state universities. Only a little later began the collection *Théologie.*

Obviously, however, these works reached only a restricted elite. Only a few publications with a wider circulation, such as *Les Etudes* and *La Vie Intellectuelle,* could obtain a larger public for their investigations, but they caused difficulties and precautions which influenced the encyclical *Humani generis* of 1950. Other works, on the other hand, served direct practice. Thus in 1930 Gabriel Le Bras had founded in France the sociology of religion in attaching practicing Catholics to various categories according to their belonging to the environment of their native country, their social class, and their professional status. On this line lay also the book *Problèmes missionaires de la France rurale,* written in 1945 by Abbé Boulart. A less scholarly work in its methods, *France pays de mission?* had been written by Abbé Godin, and in 1950 it produced as many as 100,000 copies. The presentation of a world which had been formed outside the Church and the problems which this world raised for the Church made a deep impression on Cardinal Suhard, archbishop of Paris from 1940 to 1959. He decided on the founding of a Mission de France together with his interdiocesan seminary at Lisieux. This mission included a program and a special regulation of the phases of education for work in the workers' world. In May 1949 the Mission de France was granted a temporary statute by Rome. Finally an apostolic constitution of 15 August 1954 gave it a clearly defined status: as a prelacy *nullius,* whose territory was the ancient Cistercian Abbey of Pontigny. In 1955 the mission counted 181 priests.[25]

Cardinal Suhard had also undertaken by way of experiment to allow "worker priests." This initiative was based on various experiences, especially the setbacks in the apostolate in the proletariate environment, the positive experiences of the Dominican Father Loew, who had been a dockworker at Marseille, and of the priests and seminarians who had been drafted for compulsory work during the war. To become workers in order to understand the worker, to make oneself understandable to the worker and to bring him the message of Christ: this was the basic idea which led Cardinal Suhard to permit some priests to take up work in the factories. In 1946 there were six worker priests in Paris and a few others in Provence; in 1947 a group was established at Limoges, and others followed these. There were about ninety worker priests when in 1951 the Holy See ordered the suspension of recruiting. This undertaking had begun with obviously very high-minded priests, but without previously giving them the corresponding preparation, and so it incurred the most serious difficulties. The worker priests saw themselves confronted with a harshness of life they had not imagined; they frequently committed themselves to trade-union actions and in many cases let themselves be gained for the theory of class conflict, while others among them did not know how to maintain their priestly life and celibacy intact. In September 1953 the nuncio Marella informed the bishops that they must recall the priests subject to them, and religious superiors received a corresponding instruction from the Congregation of Religious. At the end of 1956 all religious had obeyed the command to leave, and about forty diocesan priests had likewise submitted, while a somewhat larger number proved by their resistance how urgently necessary Rome's intervention had been.[26]

This was not the end of all efforts of the hierarchy in regard to the apostolate in the workers' world. As early as 1943 Cardinal Suhard had established the *Mission de Paris,* and in the following October Father Epagneul founded the community of *Frères missionaires des campagnes* for the rural proletariat.[27] The *Fils de la Charité,* founded by Father Anizan in 1913, likewise continued their work in this environment. One of them, Abbé Michoneau, in 1946 published the experiences he

[25] A Dansette, *Destin du catholicisme français,* 145–49, 247–61, 300–305.

[26] Ibid., 292. P. Montlucard and his movement Jeunesse de l'Église formed for a while the intellectual center of the worker priests and declared that the reform of society was the essential presupposition for the evangelization of the proletariat. Whether they played a decisive role in this development of the experiences among the worker priests is an open question.

[27] Ibid., 342–47.

had had in the five years of his pastoral activity in the parish of Colombes in a book with the programmatic title *Paroisse communauté missionaire.*[28] At Lyon the *Prêtres du Prado,* under the direction of Monsignor Ancel, united physical labor with the priestly and apostolic life in a parish association and a priestly community—in 1955 there were 514 priests. "Right in the heart of the masses," according to the rule of Father Voillaume, the *Petits Frères de Jésus* sought to unite existence in the world through manual labor and contemplation in the religious community.[29]

These exertions of various types showed that the hopes placed in the specially oriented movements had not been fulfilled. These movements, as, for example, the JOC, had been able to train an elite of persons who had been loyal to their function to the point of heroism but who did not succeed in dealing with the difficulties of the milieu of the moment and the class-struggle mentality. In 1956 a crisis became visible between the ACJF, which claimed the entire religious schooling of all five movements (JOC, JEC, JAC, JIC, and JMC), and the JOC, which sought autonomy in this area.[30] The resignation of its president led in practice to the dissolution of the old ACJF. The JAC, on the contrary, was less dependent on its social milieu. Hence it did not suffer as much as the JOC during the crisis of 1956 and was able to maintain its membership and strength of personality in agriculture (Rémond, 655f.).

One can regard these movements which caused shocks in the French Church as signs of its vitality. The numbers of vocations to the priesthood and the religious life also testify to vitality in the postwar period. Of course, some other numbers could at first glance produce the impression of a catastrophe: Of 35,000 parishes, in which in 1880 one priest took care of the Church's ministry, in 1930 10,000 no longer had a resident priest. But these bare figures are deceptive, for they contain parishes with 300 and fewer inhabitants, who lost the priest who had been assigned to them in the nineteenth century. In reality, the number of diocesan priests, which amounted to 54,800 in 1913, had dropped to 46,980 in 1929 and to 42,486 in 1948.[31] If these figures are compared with those of the French population, then one arrives at the ratio of one active diocesan priest to 832 inhabitants in 1913, to 960 in 1929, and to 1,029 in 1950.[32] Perhaps characteristic of the religious

[28] Ibid., 311–13.
[29] Ibid., 214–17.
[30] Ibid., 399f.; F. Boulard, *Essor ou déclin du clergé français?* 132 and 164.
[31] R. Rémond, *Histoire du Catholicisme,* 655f.
[32] A. Dansette, *Histoire religieuse,* 632.

condition of the nation is what Boulart terms the ordinations quota, that is, the number of young priests ordained for every 10,000 young men twenty-five to twenty-nine years old. This quota, which for 1902 amounted to fifty-two, fell to thirty between 1909 and 1913. It rose only very slowly on the eve of the war of 1914 and only experienced a noticeable diminution between 1934 and 1938, when it dropped to somewhat above forty. The interruption because of war and imprisonment caused this figure to rise to fifty for 1946–47, but from 1947 to 1949 it fell again to forty. If ordinations are compared on an average of every ten years, then there were 1,535 for the decade 1899–1908, 800 for 1919–28, and 1,088 for 1929–38.[33]

Apostolic activity is dependent on the occupation of young priests together with older priests, many of whom have passed the age of sixty. In 1946 an inquiry yielded 41,573 diocesan and religious priests in the active care of souls, of whom 28,777 were active in parishes and 7,166 in education.[34]

Neither in this present period nor in earlier times can the depth and quality of the Christianity of people be estimated by seeking to penetrate to its innermost being. One can at most, with the aid of the methods of investigation which Gabriel Le Bras so highly praised, provide a sort of chartlike survey of religious practice. Such a chart distributes the French population in almost equal parts into regions with Christian parishes, in which 45 percent take part in Sunday Mass and receive Easter Communion, and into such regions in which the number of practicing Catholics falls below 45 percent and which can be designated as "areas indifferent to Christian traditions." Outside these two larger groups there are still zones not to be overlooked in size, which belong to several sections, and those which are to be reckoned among the great urban masses of the population, in regard to which they constitute zones for mission work.[35]

---

[33] F. Boulard, "Les vocations sacerdotales en France. Le bilan d'un demi-siècle," NRTh 72 (1950), 486.

[34] F. Boulard, Essor ou déclin, 109. For the last decade the following figures result:

1965	646	1969	345	1973	219
1966	566	1970	285	1974	170
1967	489	1971	237	1975	161
1968	461	1972	193		

[35] G. Le Bras, "Description de la France catholique," NRTh 70 (1948), 835, 845; map, pp. 840f. The author distinguishes three zones of Christian parishes: In the west the province of Brittany, the départements of Manche, Mayenne, parts of Maine-et-Loire, also Deux-Sèvres, and the forest area of La Vendée form a broad sector; a still wider sector is formed by Alsace, Lorraine, and Franche-Comté; a third block in the center

Even if France was not a Christian country in its entirety on the eve of the Second World War, still it presented the picture of a nation in which the Catholic Church possessed solid positions: a very thick network of rural parishes, a network of urban parishes and religious institutions at least in accord with the demands of the hour, an educational group active especially in the field of elementary schooling, and finally a prudent intellectual elite. The contrasts, like the gains from the beginning of the century, to some degree compensate, so that the Church of France seemed to be in a favorable starting position to regain the terrain lost in a century. It will be the task of the historians in the next centuries to investigate the reasons which led to the development in the most recent period and to the postconciliar crisis.

---

includes three *départements* and parts of three others. Add three regions of lesser extent, which show a high population density: in the *départements* of Nord and Pas-de-Calais, in some Alpine cantons, and a third nodal point at the foot of the Pyrenees. Another group is formed by the so-called "indifferent to Christian traditions" group. Here the author distinguishes a broad strip which runs through all of France from the north to the southeast and to which belong twenty entire *départements,* nine others almost in their entirety, and ten more in great part; next to this group must be placed a bloc which in the south of the Massif Central embraces two whole *départements,* seven others almost entirely, and two more in great part. In these two last-named blocs are found about twenty cantons with regularly practicing Catholics; but they are interspersed with missionary areas, in Yonne to two-thirds, in Aube to one-half, on the east edge of Loiret and in Creuse, Haute-Vienne, and Corréze. These third zones of mission territory are covered with districts of the great urban mass population, in which the proportion of nonbaptized children reaches 20 percent.

CHAPTER 22

*The Church in Spain and Portugal**

Spain

In 1914 there were sixty-one dioceses, including the two now independent vicariates of Fernando Póo and Morocco, and nine archiepiscopal sees, which have today increased to eleven. In contrast to the 34,000 priests at that time, in 1972 there were 24,000. The male religious amounted to ca. 11,000 in 1925, to ca. 31,000 in 1972. In 1925 there were 35,000 sisters, in 1965 91,000.

* Spain: Quintín Aldea Vaquero; Portugal: Antonio da Silva.

The history of the Spanish Church in the last decades is divided into three parts: the Monarchy of Alphonso XIII (1914–31), the Second Spanish Republic and the Spanish Civil War (1931–39), and the postwar period after 1939.

THE MONARCHY OF ALPHONSO XIII (1914–31)

The year 1914 did not play as decisive a role in the history of Spain as it did in the other European countries. But it produced a great shock, which operated like an avalanche in the course of the disquieting years of the twentieth century. The concern of contemporary Catholics was concentrated on a series of neuralgic points: the hotly discussed problem of the two Spains—the traditional and Catholic Spain and the liberal and reforming Spain—the tensions between religion and politics as concomitant symptoms of the liberalism of the nineteenth century, the question of education, the social problem, and so forth. All of them crossed the path of the Spanish Church. There is no intention of dwelling unduly on this matter and treating the problems thoroughly, but something must be said on a few points in order to sketch the features of Spanish Catholicism.

The Problem of the Two Spains

This theme represents the background of all other problems, and contains a concept of the national life by means of definite guidelines and principles. What is the historical background of Spain? What is its destiny as a nation? On the answer to these questions depends the idea of the present history of Spain and with it the function which the Church must exercise in it. The basic answers which have been given to solve the historical riddle of Spain and which constitute the origin of the problem of the so-called two Spains[1] goes thus: "Progressivism and traditionalism are the true and decisive comrades-in-arms of our twentieth century from the Cortes of Cádiz to the Restauración de Sagunto," so says, quite rightly, Laín Entralgo.[2] After the restoration of 1874 the two opposed tendencies basically remained, with the natural change of reforms and renewals the two chief representatives of the Spanish drama. This situation prevailed with more or less serious incidents until 1936. On both sides were logically outstanding representatives. In the first third of the twentieth century there prevailed the prototype of the Catholic wing, Marcelino Menéndez Pelayo (1856–1912), even after his death, like El Cid in the saga, an incomparable master, who united in his person and in his gigantic work all works of Spanish culture. As no other, he raised a song of praise to the Catholic

[1] C. Sánchez Albornoz, *Espāna, un enigma histórico* II (Buenos Aires 1971), 670.
[2] P. Laín Entralgo, *Espāna como problema* (Madrid 1949), 14f.

601

unity of Spain in the epilogue of his *Historia de los Heterodoxos Españoles:*
" . . . Spain, preacher of the gospel in half the world; Spain, terror of
heretics, light of Trent, sword of Rome, cradle of Saint Ignatius . . . ;
this is our greatness and unity: we have no other."[3]

On this line lay the declarations of the Popes and of the Spanish
episcopate in their encyclicals, briefs, speeches, or pastoral letters
respecting the glorious traditions of the nation. This tradition was
constantly the background and determined the manner of speaking of
the Church's officials; national greatness and Catholic tradition were
one.

Facing this traditionalist position of Catholic Spain stood the other
Spain, which we find incarnate in one of the greatest representatives of
modern Spanish thought: José Ortega y Gasset (1883–1955). On 23
March 1914 he said on the occasion of a lecture delivered by him in the
Teatro de la Comedia at Madrid: "We are sure that a great number of
Spaniards agree with us that the destiny of Spain is intimately connected
with the progress of liberalism."[4] In this connection he explained what
he understood by liberalism: "that radical stimulation, always vital in
history, which tries to exclude from the state every influence of
extrahuman nature and which always expects from the new social
measures a better result than from the old and traditional."[5] Hence, an
end to the influence of the Church, because it is subject to human
influence, and an end to the old traditions. In still more definite words
he confronted tradition and consolidated his ideas in his work on
tradition, *Meditaciones del Quijote,* which appeared in 1914: "The
traditional reality in Spain has consisted precisely in this, permanently
to destroy the opportunities of Spain. No, we cannot follow tradition
. . . just the opposite is commanded: We must proceed against
tradition, beyond tradition."[6] For Ortega y Gasset the Church was a
permeating leaven. "Without doubt the Church is antisocial, religion is
exclusive."[7] In the same way he thought of religious education: "The
denominational school is, in comparison with the nondenominational,
the beginning of anarchy, because it represents a singular pedagogy."[8]
For him regeneration, that is, renewal, would bring Spain real political
health, synonymous with Europeanization. "Spain was the problem,

[3] M. Menéndez Pelayo, *Historia de los heterodoxos españoles* VI (Santander 1948),
508.
[4] J. Ortega y Gasset, *Obras completas* I (Madrid 1957), 303.
[5] Ibid.
[6] Ibid., 362f.
[7] Ibid., 519.
[8] Ibid.

and Europe the solution."[9] In this way European Spain should lift itself above the traditional, that is, the unholy, unchurchly Spain. Around these two Spains were assembled and organized the Spaniards, intellectuals, workers, and peasants. The life of the Church unfolded by constraint within this sociological environment which influenced all its national and international activities.

Christian Syndicalism

In his lecture at the Teatro de la Comedia in 1914 Ortega y Gasset declared that the two current modern tendencies in Spanish public life were the Socialist Party and the trade-union movements.[10] Without intending to oppose this thesis, it is clear that the union movement and with it the so-called Social Question had won powerful importance in national events. What measures did the Spanish Church take, once it was faced with this serious problem?

Some historians and sociologists have sought, from the viewpoint of the second half of the twentieth century, to play down the countless initiatives which proceeded from the Church to render this problem harmless. The Church could be charged with neither passivity nor ignorance. Despite great difficulties, which had to be mastered, it laid for itself a road through the shaken social world. After the death of the Jesuit Antonio Vicent (1837–1912), "the patriarch of Spanish social Catholicism," as his famous pupil Severino Aznar called him, the Christian union movement began to gain in strength and extent. The ideal solution would have been at this moment the formation of workers' or peasants' unions without group ideologies. But considering the fact that the union acted in an antireligious manner and firmly attacked the Church, there was nothing else left except to organize the Christian union; in regard to this there occurred within the Catholic ranks a strong polemic, which partly absorbed the energies of the Catholic union. Nevertheless, successes could be attained among the peasant unions, since the rural population adhered to the Church more than did the industrial workers. Hence it is incorrect to speak of a failure of Christian unions[11]

The Church unions, regardless of whether they were denominationally oriented or not, had to follow the Church's guidelines; hence they could not offer the worker the revolutionary stimulus of the *Unión General de Trabajadores* (UGT) or of the *Confederación Nacional del*

[9] Ibid., 521.
[10] Ibid., 277.
[11] J. N. García Nieto, *El sindicalismo cristiano en España* (Bilbao 1960); D. Benavides, *El fracaso social del catolicismo español o Arboleya Martínez, 1870–1951* (Barcelona 1973).

Trabajo (CNT), otherwise they would stand outside the Church's social doctrine and would not have been ecclesiastical unions. Gil Robles, one of the best politicians of that time, testified to a great momentum in the *Confederación Nacional Católica Agraria*. It was one of the organizations with which people would have to reckon.

SECOND SPANISH REPUBLIC AND CIVIL WAR (1931–39)

In an effort to end the social-political confusion which externally impaired Spanish life in the first third of the twentieth century, three political solutions were tried in succession: a concrete application of parliamentary government by Antonio Maura; the dictatorship of General Primo de Rivera, established on 13 September 1923; the Second Republic of 1931.[12]

The first two efforts were unsuccessful. The result of the communal elections of 12 April 1931, which had favored the monarchy numerically, produced the abdication of Alphonso XIII and the proclamation of the republic on 14 April. Seen from the religious standpoint, this meant the official establishment of anticlericalism in Spain, which within six years drove the Spanish Church into a frightful catastrophe without comparison in the history of the Church. The burning of monasteries and churches on 11 May 1931 and the expulsion of the bishop of Vitoria and of the primate of Toledo from Spain were clear indications of the religious attitude of the most powerful agents of the new Spanish policy. The spirit of the constitution of the republic was stamped by *sectarismo* to such a degree that even the president of the republic, Niceto Alcalá Zamora, conceded that those measures were an invitation to civil war.[13] Concerning ARTICLE 26 of the constitution, which dealt with the religious orders, Jóse Mariá Gil Robles, minister of that republic, says in his *Memorias:* "The enacting of ARTICLE 26 of the basic law was not only a remarkable injustice but represented a mistake with incalculable consequences. The religious problem was changed into a state of war with the danger of conflict between the two Spains."[14] Nevertheless, the ecclesiastical dignitaries recommended to the Spanish Catholics "respect and obedience to the lawful authorities and cooperation in all those matters whose aim was the general welfare and social peace."[15]

---

[12] J. Vicens Vives, *Aproximación a la historia de España* (Barcelona 1960), 215–18.
[13] A. Montero, *Historia de la persecución religiosa en España 1936–1939* (Madrid 1961), 29.
[14] V. Palacio Atard, "Iglesia y Estado. La Segunda República Española (1931–1939)," *Diccionario de Historia Eclesiástica de España* II (Madrid 1972), 1181.
[15] "Exposición del Cardenal Primado al Presidente del Gobierno provisional, el 3 de junio 1931," A. Montero, op. cit., 29.

Even the members of the cabinet were surprised by the respect shown by the Church toward the republic. But they still did not feel induced to change their damaging attitude; on the contrary, the antireligious legislation went further. On 24 January 1932 a law was passed whose content was the abolition of the Society of Jesus; it had to seek its salvation in exile. The justification of the law was that the Jesuits paid obedience to a foreign power, the Pope. Some days later the divorce law was enacted; immediately thereafter there appeared in the *Gaceta* a decree on the secularization of cemeteries. Another decree prescribed that the cross be removed from the schools. All these measures injured in the keenest way the sensitivities of the overwhelmingly Christian families. In the face of this more or less open persecution nothing else was left to the Church than to issue a sharp protest. At first, on 25 May 1933, the Spanish episcopate published a "Declaración sobre la ley de Confesiones religiosas."[16] A few days later, on 3 June, appeared Pius XI's encyclical *Dilectissima nobis,* in which he lamented the situation in Spain.[17]

A clear example of the anticlerical extremism of the left was the uprising in Asturias in October 1934, in which an effort was made to set up a dictatorship of the proletariat. Fortunately, the revolt lasted only a few days. But this was long enough cruelly to murder thirty-four clerics, including minor seminarians, and to burn or desecrate fifty-eight churches. This was the program of action envisaged by the Marxist revolution for all of Spain. If this side had gained the victory, then this frightful martyrdom would have extended throughout Spain. In this situation the question of Antonio Montero was justified: "Is it necessary to point out that on the edge of the actual civil war and before it erupted, the program of the persecution of the Church was prepared to the last detail?"[18]

THE CIVIL WAR (1936–39)

Out of the elections of 16 February 1936 there emerged as victor, with the aid of the prevailing election system, which provided a bonus for the majority, the Popular Front, that is, a union of all the leftist parties. This victory was fostered by the votes of the members of the CNT and the split of the right parties. The new government tried unsuccessfully to satisfy its electors. Then political disintegration overtook the broad public. The leader of the national bloc, José Calvo Sotelo, drew in the parliament a sad balance of the events within the Popular Front government of six weeks from 16 February to 2 April 1936: there

[16] A. Montero, op. cit., Apéndice Documental, 655.
[17] Ibid., 675.
[18] Ibid., 52.

occurred 199 attacks and burglaries, 36 of them on churches; 178 fires were counted, including 106 churches burned down and 56 destroyed; 74 dead and 345 wounded were to be lamented. A few months later Calvo Sotelo himself was murdered in the night of 13 July 1936 by Popular Front police. This deed was declared an expressly political crime and sharply condemned by the sensible population of the country. It occasioned the *Movimiento;* the only way out was civil war. The army and the right joined in the struggle against the Marxist revolution. The *Movimiento Nacional* rose on 18 July; the two Spains were divided into two battlefields: the Red and the National Zones.

The Red Zone

The Church did not take part in the *Alzamiento.* But through the bishop of Gerona, Dr. Castañá, it proclaimed "the gratitude that an innocent victim feels for its generous defender."[19] One year after the outbreak of war the Spanish bishops on 1 July 1937 addressed all the Catholic bishops of the world. In their letter they expressed in their concern for religion, home, and humanity not an empty thesis but "the events which characterize our war and give it its special features." Spain was divided in two: on the one side the Communist revolution with its barbaric, antireligious, and anti-Spanish licentiousness, on the other side the National Movement with its respect for the religious and national order. In this situation the Church, always remaining within its pastoral sphere and without pawning its spiritual freedom, had no other way out than to place itself on that side which "took the field for the defense of order, social peace, traditional civilization and homeland, and not least the defense of religion."[20] The tone of the episcopal letter was moderate, of emotional balance and realistic attitude. Only two bishops did not sign it: the archbishop of Tarragona, Francisco Cardinal Vidal y Barraquer, and the bishop of Vitoria, Mateo Múgica. The former, because he believed secret written information to the bishops of the various nations would be more effective and joined with less danger of reprisal against those who still lived in the Red Zone than a public common letter; the latter, because he was outside his diocese. The rest of the episcopate, forty-three bishops and five vicars general, signed it.

[19] A. Pérez Balaguer, *Enciclopedia Universal Ilustrada. Suplemento anual 1936–1939* (Madrid 1944), 1551. Monsignor José Cartañá was a Catalan; his nomination as bishop occurred during the republic (29 December 1933) and hence did not depend on the right of presentation.

[20] A. Granados, *El Cardenal Gomá, Primado de España* (Madrid 1969), 348; L. Aguirre, *La Iglesia y la Guerra española* (Madrid 1964) (all on the common letter); C. Bayle, *El mundo católica y la "Carta colectiva del episcopado español"* (Burgos 1938).

The echo of the common letter was loud. "All members of the episcopate [ca. 900 bishops] replied by recognizing the legitimacy of the war on the part of national Spain and its character as a crusade for the Christian religion and civilization," said the future Cardinal Pla y Deniel.[21]

Meanwhile the real confrontation was carried out on the battlefield and beyond the fronts. It demanded of the Spanish Church a heavy tribute of blood and glorious martyrdoms. Twelve bishops of the dioceses of Sigüenza, Lérida, Cuenca, Barbastro, Segorbe, Jaén, Ciudad Real, Almería, Guadix, Barcelona, Teruel, and the auxiliary bishop of Tarragona died as martyrs. True to their evangelical task and with full knowledge of the danger to which they were exposed on the outbreak of war, they still remained at their posts. "I cannot leave out of fear; here is my duty, cost what it may," said the bishop of Cuenca to those who recommended flight. And for this reason the other shepherds remained with their flocks. All fell, sooner or later, with bodies riddled by bullets.

Because of their office, 4,184 priests had to die; they were hunted like game. Some dioceses suffered very heavy losses, as, for example, that of Barbastro; there 123 of the 140 pastors died, at Lérida 270 out of 410, and at Toledo 286 out of 600. Of the religious 2,365 died, some of them between seventeen and eighteen years old. Worst hit were the following institutes: Claretians with 259 dead, Franciscans with 226 dead, Piarists with 204 dead, Marists with 176 dead, Brothers of the Christian Schools with 165 dead, Augustinians with 155 dead, Dominicans with 132 dead, and Jesuits with 114 dead. The number of murdered sisters amounted to 283; even as women they were not spared persecution and torment. Altogether 6,832 priests, sisters, and brothers sacrificed their lives for the faith: an unmistakable proof of the vitality of the Spanish Church. As regards the type of martyrdom, no method known in history was overlooked: mutilation, death by fire, or even crucifixion.

The National Zone

At the outbreak of the *Movimiento* a religious movement was to be noted among the Spanish people and the warriors. There was a genuine rebirth of the religious life in the entire country. Victories at the front were celebrated with Masses, Te Deums, and *Salve Reginas*. The new government began to draw up new laws with a Christian meaning. The cross was again hung in the schools, and religious instruction was again introduced. Important laws, such as the *Carta Magna del Fuero del*

[21] A. Granados, op. cit., 178.

Trabajo of 1936 for the support of families, were oriented to the Church's social teaching. Great amounts of money were made available for the reconstruction of more than 20,000 destroyed churches. The corps of chaplains was reintroduced. All churches and chapels, the residences of bishops and priests with their grounds, and seminaries and monasteries were exempted from the land tax. In May 1938 the Society of Jesus was again permitted, with restoration of all rights and goods it had enjoyed before its dissolution. On 2 February 1939 the juridical status of all religious orders was restored. The republican legislation on divorce and civil marriage, the secularizaton of cemeteries, and the limitations on Catholic burials were repealed. In short, all those rights were again recognized in the Church which were contained in canon law. Respect for the Church and its institutions was again holy and removed from any discussion.

The chaplains at the front wrote a glorious chapter for the history of the Spanish Church. Among those who perished must especially be named the Jesuit Fernando Huidobro, favorite pupil of Martin Heidegger; the process for his beatification has begun.

SPAIN IN THE POSTWAR PERIOD (SINCE 1939)

The thirty years between 1939 and 1970 can be divided into two parts, of fifteen years each, which were marked by two different sorts of generation: a traditional generation (1939–55) and a critical generation (after 1955). The two groups are the same in exterior structure but different in dynamism.

The Twofold Trend

TRADITIONAL GENERATION. The religious organization in the Spain of the postwar epoch had its origin in the glorious Catholic tradition that was the ideal of the Spain which had once gained victory on the fields of battle. Hence one can speak of an amazing revival of the content of this tradition. Of this there were the following signs: strengthening of Church authority and respect for Church offices; increase of ecclesiastical vocations; improvement of ecclesiastical institutions and refounding of institutions; the wide extension of charitable activities, as, for example, the missions; spiritual exercises and religious courses; jubilee years with pilgrimages to Santiago de Compostela and Holy Week processions; attendance at Sunday Mass and reception of Easter Communion; the strong movement of the lay apostolate with Catholic Action, the Marian congregations, and other institutions. Religious books obtained a dominant position on the national book market. Religious publishers, such as El Mensajero, Sal Terrae, El Apostolado de la Prensa, la Biblioteca de Autores Cristianos, spread the works of the great authors throughout the world. The climax of this period was the concordat of 1953 as the embodiment of the classical principles of the canon law then in force and of the traditional spirit of Catholic Spain.[22] It would take us too far afield to evaluate all phenomena. The influence of the Spanish Church on Spanish society was enormous. Probably until then the Spanish Church never had so many possibilities of forming a society by means of Christian ideals. In 1940 the Church had charge of 60 percent of all high schools and hence could exercise its influence on youth in so critical a period of life; in 1955 it was still 42 percent.[23] Furthermore, the Church gave religious instruction in public schools and universities and was able to exercise influence in this way also. As regards the piety of the population, there can be noted, as an example only, that the missionary group of the Jesuit province of León alone could organize 2,118 missions in Spain betwen 1940 and 1965, among them some in large cities with up to 60,000 participating in one mission.[24]

CRITICAL GENERATION. In the course of the years the number of members of a small group of Catholics with an outlook directed to Europe and the world grew. This movement let itself be guided by the political philosophy of Jacques Maritain in questions of relations between Church and state. It also caused the introduction of liturgical forms from beyond the Pyrenees and the dissemination of foreign points of view and unfamiliar morals in Spain. The more these trends gained in importance, the certainty was strengthened that the block of classical Spanish thought began to crumble and that the traditional concept of Spanish life incurred the danger of losing its vigor. The polemic on the theme, carried out on the national and international level, had reached its highest intensity when the Second Vatican Council began. Some of the most important, hitherto disputed points of the notion of Christian life were raised by it to postulates. This fact produced a deep crisis on several levels of Spanish Catholicism, which to this day has not been removed.

Institutions

As outstanding representatives of the institutions within Spanish Catholicism must be mentioned: the episcopal conference, some

---

[22] A. Martín Artajo, "El Concordato de 1953," *Diccionario de Historia Eclesiástica de España* I (Madrid 1972), 595–99. The author of this article was foreign minister at the time of the ratification of the concordat.

[23] *La educación en España, Survey S.I.* (private archives).

[24] *Archivo de la Prefectura de Misiones Populares de la Provincia de León, S.I.*

institutes, Catholic Action, and the National Catholic Association of Propagandists.

EPISCOPAL CONFERENCE. Since its establishment after the Second Vatican Council, the episcopal conference took over the control and administration which were previously cared for by the conferences of metropolitans. The decisions of the conference theoretically have no binding force for each diocese, but they are observed as if they were obligatory. In general, today the Spanish Church reacts on the collegial plane in all common questions. What is there discussed and decided is therefore of great general importance. The guidelines issued by the episcopal conference are in practice observed in the entire country. One of the most important stands of the episcopal conference was the declaration of January 1973 on "The Church and the political community," which was passed by a vote of fifty-nine for and twenty against, a situation in which is reflected the sociological structure of the episcopal conference. In this declaration the most important themes were treated which concerned the relations of Church and society, of Church and public order, the relations between Church and state with regard for the Catholic religion as the state religion, the revision of the concordat of 1953, and the renunciation of privileges and of the paying of ecclesiastics.

RELIGIOUS COMMUNITIES. The improvement of the traditional institutes already in existence and the founding of new institutes are consequences of the religious revival of the postwar period. Altogether there are, according to the 1973 statistics, ca. 80 institutes of men with 24,281 members, apart from the 6,700 members who work outside Spain, especially in Latin America. As regards membership they are divided as follows: Jesuits 3,431; Salesians 2,535; Franciscans 2,174; Brothers of the Christian Schools 2,012; Dominicans 1,636; Piarists 1,303. These institutes displayed a great activity in schools and the press. Outstanding among the lay institutes is the Sociedad Sacerdotal de la Santa Cruz, or, for short, Opus Dei, founded at Madrid in 1928 by Monsignor José María Escrivá and recognized as an institute in 1947. According to statistics there were in 1966 in Spain 242 active institutes of women with 72,301 sisters, and 29 contemplative institutes with 19,211 sisters. The apostolic activity of these sisters is directed chiefly to schools: in 1967 56.12 percent were active in schools, while 20.28 percent performed their ministry in the health fields.

CATHOLIC ACTION. In 1926 Spanish Catholic Action was subjected to a profound restructuring. Previously it had been rather a loose union of the personnel present as a central organization; all Catholic personnel retained their own autonomy. After 1939 a strict centralization of all activities of the lay apostolate was introduced; it led to confrontations among the current personnel and partly impaired their work. From 1945 special institutions appeared with the founding of *Juventud Obrera Católica* (JOC) and *Hermandad Obrera de Acción Católica* (HOAC). On 5 December 1959 the conference of the Spanish metropolitans issued the new "Statute of Catholic Action," which consolidated the already existing central unity. This statute was replaced by a new statute issued on 1 February 1968 by the episcopal conference.

Asociación Católica Nacional de Propagandistas. Among the Catholic lay groups that exercise great influence on Spanish public opinion must be mentioned the *Asociación Católica Nacional de Propagandistas*. Founded at Madrid in 1908 by the Jesuit Ángel Ayala with the aim of preparing a group of the Catholic Men's Union of Saint Louis for Catholic propaganda, it had as president the future Cardinal Ángel Herrera Oria, who possessed an extraordinary gift for organizing. In 1911 it bought the Madrid newspaper *El Debate* and a year later Herrera founded *El Editorial Católica* as economic and ideological support of the paper. The union was concerned with all problems which preoccupied the Spanish Church in this century. After the war *El Debate* was stopped and in its place appeared *Ya,* which together with *ABC* are the two most important daily newspapers of the country. After the war *La Editorial Católica* began the publication of the series *Biblioteco de Autores Cristianos,* which today consists of more than three hundred volumes. The great activity of Catholic propaganda, without precedent in the history of the Spanish Church, achieved its climax in 1947 with the founding of the Centro de Estudios Universitarios (CEU); a division of the Centro is today the Colegio Universitario de San Pablo at Madrid with 5,000 students and eight faculties.[25]

Portugal

The development of Portuguese history in this century went through three phases: the anticlerical revolution of the bourgeoisie of 1910 (1910–26); the new regime (1926–60); and the era of the Second Vatican Council from 1960.

THE ANTICLERICAL REVOLUTION (1910–26)

After the overthrow of the monarchy by the republican forces, the latter proceeded against the Church. The bishops were sharply attacked

[25] J. L. Gutiérrez, "Asociación Católica Nacional de Propagandistas," *Diccionario de Historia Eclesiástica de España* I, 144–47.

because of their rejection of the divorce law of 20 April 1911 and in the course of 1912 driven from their dioceses, with one exception—the archbishop of Évora. Diplomatic relations with the Holy See were broken until 1918, and clerics were deprived of their property. The wearing of the cassock and the exercise of their activity as directors of committees named by the state in the sphere of the administration of the Church were forbidden to the clergy. Minor seminaries were closed by law, and of the major seminaries only five were spared from this measure, those of Braga, Pôrto, Coimbra, Lisbon, and Évora. A law of 22 February 1918 permitted the existence of two seminaries, but the confiscated buildings were not given back. Still, the seminaries at Angra in the Azores (1914), Viseu and Braga in the former Jesuit house (1915), Pôrto and Pôrto Alegre (1919), Guarda (1920), Lamego (1921), and Lisbon (1931) resumed their activity.

By recourse to the laws of Pombal and those of the liberal regime of 1834 the members of 164 houses of thirty-one orders were expelled. But from 1917 on some congregations were reorganized. The revolution also forbade religious instruction in elementary and high schools and closed the theological and ecclesiastical faculty of Coimbra. Nevertheless, in the First World War there were again field chaplains.

The lay apostolate awoke as a reaction to these measures. Thus in 1913 occurred the reactivation of the *Centro Académico de Democracia Cristã* (CADC), founded at Coimbra in 1903. At the same time was founded the *Centro Católica,* which from 1915 sent its representatives to the Chamber of Deputies and the Senate, even though only a small number.

THE NEW REGIME (1926–60)

With the movement of General Gomes da Costa and the presidency of General Carmona begins a new order of authoritarian character, whose most important representative became Oliveira Salazar. This movement led in the area of the relations between Church and state to the concordat of 1940. The position of the Church improved; it included seventeen dioceses and three archdioceses.

The statistics of 1947 give a total of 4,500 priests, one priest for every 2,000 inhabitants. Seminaries were restored or newly built with occasional state aid.

The number of religious sisters and brothers grew considerably. The communities obtained a little financial help from the state in proportion to the number of active missionaries and students. Around 1947 there were in the country some 400 religious priests and in 1952 ca. 4,400 sisters.

Religious instruction was reintroduced in the elementary and high schools. The number of schools with religious direction, especially schools for girls, increased, although they were attended mostly by the rich segment of the population and although there was no state aid. The education in these schools was primarily humanistically oriented and scarcely scientifically. Around 1930 a university institute for social assistance was founded at Lisbon. Jesuits taught in the philosophical university institute, run exclusively by them, which in 1947 was recognized as an ecclesiastical faculty.

In the field of journalism the following deserve mention: *Estudos* of the CADC of Coimbra (since 1922), *Brotéria* (since 1925), *Lumen* (for the clergy since 1930), *Portugal em África* (since 1944), *Revista Portuguesa de Filosofia* and *Itinerarium* (both since 1945). Among the most important institutions for social communication are the newspaper *Novidades* and the Catholic Broadcasting Radio Renascença, which was silenced by the revolutionary forces in 1975 and was later given back by the government.

The number of traditions in worship was increased by the great crowds on pilgrimage to the national shrine of Fatima since 1931. In addition, catechesis and liturgy again grew in importance, especially due to the exertions of the Lisbon seminary and the Benedictines. The lay apostolate began to take new routes. After the prohibition of political parties it withdrew from political life, to which so far the *Centro Católico* had devoted itself, and strengthened its collaboration with the church authorities. In 1932 the bishops founded the official *Acção Católica,* which in November 1933 obtained a juridical statute confirmed by Pope Pius XI. Portugal's missionary work produced in Angola up to 1940 as many as 500,000 Catholics with 174 missionaries, in Mozambique as many as 60,000 Catholics with 126 priests; but up to 1970 as many as 2.5 million in Angola and 1.25 million in Mozambique.

UNDER THE INFLUENCE OF THE
SECOND VATICAN COUNCIL (FROM 1960)

The Portuguese Church appeared at the council with only its bishops, hence without *periti.* In other words, it was a preponderantly traditional and authoritarian Church. In 1968 it numbered 4,500 diocesan and 900 religious priests; hence there was a slight increase in comparison to 1947, but this was also caused by the growth of the population, everything else being equal. These relations also remained constant in regard to the rural or urban origin of vocations.

At this time there were 18 major seminaries and 22 minor seminaries; the latter had 2,800 pupils in 1952 and 900 in 1968. The major seminaries had 4,049 students in 1952; by 1968 they decreased to 3,977. The general crisis in the seminaries extended also to the orders.

By 1960 the *Acção Católica* achieved its zenith. In this regard the national meetings of the *Juventude Católica Universitária* from 1953 to 1963 represented the climax. Among the ranks of the lay apostolate movements were to be observed which tended to achieve a greater independence in regard to the episcopate. By 1960 the statistics list the number of 95,000 members of *Acção Católica,* that is, 1.2 percent of the population. In the field of the university apostolate the founding of the Catholic University at Lisbon and of two other universities must not be forgotten. Still, the realities did not correspond to the structures. In the confrontation of the Church with the revolution of 1974 it was revealed that the former was poor, apolitical, without organized youth, with seminaries overtaken by crisis, and without adequate personnel. The present difficulties in the country have produced a concentration of Catholic forces, which allow one to hope for new initiatives.

CHAPTER 23

*The Countries of the English-Speaking Area**

Europe
GREAT BRITAIN

Population

The Catholic population of England and Wales in 1914 was estimated as 2,100,446, including 3,872 priests; in contrast there was a total population of 36,204,679 in 1911. There were 1,837 Catholic churches, chapels, and missions, of which 1,307 were authorized by civil law for marriages. At the same time there were 518,969 Catholics in Scotland, including 577 priests; they had 427 churches and chapels. When in 1966 the total population of England and Wales amounted to 48,075,000, the Catholic population had grown to 4,000,695, including 5,096 diocesan priests and 2,791 religious priests, with 3,446 public churches and chapels and 1,196 private devotional sites. In the intermediate time the Catholics had spread equally in the large cities and suburbs, but not in the rural areas; Catholicism remained an urban phenomenon. At the same time the

* Robert Trisco

number of Catholics in Scotland rose to 809,680 in a total population of 5,191,000.

This growth was based partly on the natural increase of the population, on conversions, and on the immigration of refugees from the continent, especially Poles and Ukrainians, but chiefly on immigration from Ireland. In fact, about three-fourths of the Catholics in Great Britain were of Irish descent, insofar as they were not themselves born in Ireland. The heterogeneity proceeding from this was gradually broken down by the integration of the immigrants into British Catholicism. The annual number of adult converts—between 12,000 and 10,000—remained almost unchanged from 1925 to the Second World War, in spite of the growth of the total population. Many converts were the future or present husbands or wives of Catholics. Of the rest, more Catholics came from the middle class, who were better able to cope with the claims of the Church than the lower class, and in proportion there were more converts among the Nonconformists, whose organized religious life quickly dissolved, than among the Anglicans. Meanwhile, however, the Church suffered a constant "loss"; even a great part of the children who came from Catholic schools soon gave up their practice of religion. These factors prevented the percentage of Catholics in England from increasing notably. Partly as a consequence of the prejudices of their fellow citizens and partly because of their own cultural inferiority, the influence of the English Catholics in public life did not correspond to their numerical strength.

Organization

From 1911 there were in England and Wales three metropolitan sees—Westminster, Liverpool, Birmingham—and thirteen dioceses. In 1916 the archdiocese of Cardiff emerged from the diocese of Newport in Wales, with Menevia as its only suffragan see. New episcopal sees were erected in 1917 at Brentwood and in 1924 at Lancaster. In 1965 the diocese of Southwark was raised to metropolitan status, and at the same time its suffragan see of Arundel and Brighton was erected. There were then in England and Wales five provinces with five archdioceses and fourteen dioceses. In addition, in 1957 the archbishop of Westminster was named apostolic exarch for the Ukrainians of the Byzantine Rite, which numbered more than 20,000 adherents; in 1961 Augustine Eugene Hornyak, O.S.B.M., a Ukrainian priest, was made his auxiliary bishop, and six years later he himself became apostolic exarch for Great Britain.

In Scotland from 1878 the archdiocese of Saint Andrews and Edinburgh had existed as metropolitan see with four suffragans, and the archdiocese of Glasgow had belonged to no ecclesiastical province; in 1947 the last named became a metropolitan see with two suffragan sees, which were newly erected at Motherwell and Paisley.

Furthermore, the archbishop of Westminster represented the episcopate in discussions with the government. The following occupied this post: 1903–35, Francis Bourne, a cardinal in 1910; 1935–43 Arthur Hinsley, cardinal in 1937; 1943–56 Bernard Griffin, cardinal in 1946; 1956–63 William Godfrey, cardinal in 1958; 1963–75 John Heenan, cardinal in 1965; and since 1976 Basil Hume, O.S.B., cardinal in the same year.

From the reign of Elizabeth I Great Britain had no diplomatic relations with the Holy See, but after the outbreak of the First World War the government sent Sir Henry Howard to convey the congratulations of the King to the newly elected Pope Benedict XV and to explain to him the reason for the entry into the war. The British representative stayed in Rome as extraordinary ambassador and minister plenipotentiary "on special mission." In 1920 the legation was made a regular and permanent institution. But the relations were never brought to reciprocity. No nunciature was established in London; in fact not until 1938 was an apostolic delegation opened in the British capital. The first apostolic delegate was an Englishman, William Godfrey, who took care of this post until he became archbishop of Liverpool in 1953.

Educational System

In 1914 343,472 pupils were educated in 1,169 Catholic primary schools and 24,129 in 387 Catholic secondary schools. In conformity with the Education Act of 1902 denominational schools had to be erected and repaired by voluntary offerings, although the expenses of maintenance and the salaries of teachers were paid out of public funds. They were endangered by the inability of the faithful in an age of rising costs to care for adequate premises and equipment. Discussions conducted in a friendly atmosphere between representatives of the state and the Church produced the "Scottish solution." In accord with the Scotland Education Act of 1918, the directors of the already existing Church schools or those to be established in the future were authorized to sell their schools to the education authorities, to lease them, or to transfer them in other ways. But the education authorities could themselves also erect new denominational schools. The officials were from then on to exercise complete control over the schools, including the appointment and dismissal of teachers, but in this connection the teachers on hand were to retain their positions. In the future no teacher could be appointed before he or she had been accepted by the relevant denominational corporation, "in regard to religious faith and character."

An unpaid supervisor, who had likewise to be accepted by the denomination, was to be appointed for every school. The supervisor had the right of access to all classes which were specified for religious instruction and worship, and he had to report to the Church authorities on the effectiveness of the religious instruction that was given. (In Catholic schools this supervisor was normally the parish priest, and diocesan inspectors had permission to give examinations in religion.) Thus was ended the administrative dualism, as the local authorities desired it, but the religious dualism was retained, because the bishops insisted on it in order to preserve the Catholic character of their schools. In spite of their security precautions and the fact that this agreement was to a great extent the work of William Francis Brown, whom the Pope had named as apostolic visitor for Scotland the previous year, the Scottish bishops and the Catholics in general were frightened by it. Finally, the Holy See with its only intervention in educational questions directed them to accept the agreement. This regulation functioned smoothly from the beginning and in the course of time was regarded from the Catholic standpoint as one of the best arrangements in the entire world. The Scottish Catholics opened many free schools for the primary and secondary grades and several colleges operated by religious orders, and all were supported by local and national public financing. (A few private Catholic schools which raised instructional fees likewise continued in existence.)

The situation of the Catholics in England and Wales differed from that of the Scots in many respects and in 1918 the bishops could not agree to give up the rights of ownership of their schools. Between 1914 and 1930 the Catholics built ninety-six schools with 60,000 places at a capital expenditure of £1,700,000. Meanwhile, construction costs steadily mounted and many of the older schools had to be replaced or expanded, and, especially in the cities, new schools had to be erected. The burden became intolerable. In order to draw public attention to the injustice of their situation, the Catholics organized great protest gatherings and called upon the members of parliament to give assistance. After the founding of the Irish Free State in 1921, English Catholics no longer had many friends in parliament, and the Labour Party had many members who by tradition were hostile to Catholicism, although it depended, especially in certain areas, also on the votes of the Catholic English workers. In 1931 the Catholic Educational Council decided to carry out a campaign for the adoption of the Scottish system in England and Wales, but the prospects of achieving this goal became less as each year passed, partly because the National Teachers' Association did not want to accept any system that would have meant the introduction of denominational instruction in a much larger number of schools under state ownership and religious examinations for specific teachers.

In 1936 the Catholics were forced to accept aid under conditions that were quite other than favorable. The Education Law of this year authorized the local authorities to contribute 50 to 75 percent of the costs for the erecting of voluntary schools. These schools had become necessary by the express intention of the state to raise the age of leaving school to fifteen years on 1 September 1939 and to "reorganize" the educational system. In order to correspond to the demands of the Free Churches and of the National Association of Teachers, this regulation had to be severely limited in time: applications had to be filed within three years; only the furnishing of the high schools was provided, although there was a greater need for the reorganization of the elementary schools; the teachers in those schools which obtained building subsidies had to be appointed by the local school officials, if even a small part of them—on which the directors of the schools and the officials had to agree—had to be "reserved" teachers, that is, such as were chosen in discussion with the school administration and were qualified to impart the relevant denominational instruction. In all voluntary schools there had to be given, in the event the parents wished it, a nondenominational religious instruction in keeping with the teaching plan prescribed for the local public schools. Finally, the aid was only permitted, but not prescribed as an obligation. Because the Catholics, under the leadership of the new archbishop of Westminster, Arthur Hinsley, feared that the Catholic high schools would lose their students to the better equipped public schools if they were not reorganized, they decided to make use of the offer and at the same time to work to retain their elementary schools.

The effects of these legal measures were not entirely satisfactory, although because of them a good by-product resulted: the setting up of diocesan school commissions in places where previously there had been none. The reorganization in rural areas, which included the erection of central schools, was delayed by the difficulties growing out of the great distances and the need of means of transportation, and it threatened to divide the life of the parish congregations. In the cities the development proceeded faster. Many offices, including London, were ready to grant the full financial subsidy, 75 percent, conceded by the law; others gave 50 percent. The single ill-famed case as a contrary example was Liverpool. There the constant immigration of Irish had caused an acute overcrowding of the Catholic schools in the areas of the dockyards. Under the influence of the local conservatives, allied with the militant Protestants, the city council had refused to grant the aid for the erection of denominational schools. When the Catholics did not succeed in the local elections in getting revenge for this provocation, the state education office intervened and held back a part of the sum which the state treasury assigned annually to the Liverpool office. Finally a compromise was reached in 1939, when parliament adopted a special law for Liverpool, whereby the city council was empowered to build high schools and then lease them to the denominational corporations at rents between 25 and 50 percent of the costs of the loan.

When the Second World War broke out, only 44.8 percent of the Catholic school districts had been reorganized. Even in 1942 there were still no less than 399 dilapidated Catholic school buildings on the "Black List" of the education office—this list included schools with defective equipment. The continuation of the reorganization was prevented by the war, and the age of leaving school could not be raised at the intended time. Of the 289 Catholic applications, which were submitted in accord with the law of 1936, only the nine approved were implemented. Although there was only one English community without a Catholic school—Morley near Leeds—almost 20 percent of the Catholic children in the country were not in Catholic schools. Nevertheless, the 1,200 Catholic schools made up 12 percent of the voluntary schools and instructed 8 percent of the total population of obligatory school age.

When the government began with the planning of a coherent system in the sphere of the primary grades, the secondary grades, and the higher school system, the Catholics began an active campaign of organized opposition to this project—the *Green Book* of 1941—and emphatically demanded that in their schools the denominational character remain intact. The Catholic Parents' Associations, the first of which was founded in 1940 at Ilford in the diocese of Brentwood, were increased on the parish level and coordinated by diocesan councils, which for their part were represented in an interdiocesan Council of the Catholic Parents' and Electors' Association. Its chief concern consisted for several years in assuring and promoting Catholic interests in the educational system.

Before a law was introduced in parliament there were long discussions with the president of the Board of Education, R. A. Butler, and representatives of the Anglicans, the Catholics, the Free Churches, and the teachers. However, the Catholic speakers were isolated, for the Anglicans had acquiesced, and the Free Churches and the professional associations had the upper hand. Because the Catholics failed to obtain even the slightest concessions, they opposed the law until parliament had passed it. The result showed that people in England and Wales, who, differently from Scotland, were already strongly de-Christianized, could not appeal to an influential public opinion which was convinced that religion formed the heart of education; one could claim only "equality of opportunity," the right of parents to have their children educated in their own faith and at no greater cost than what their non-Catholic neighbor had to pay.

The Education Law of 1944, the "Butler Act," provided financial aid for three categories of denominational primary and secondary schools. In all these schools all costs for secular and religious education were to be defrayed from public sources, but the state retained the right to assure itself that the schools were needed and that new schools were erected only to the extent that the national finances permitted: (a) The "voluntary aided schools" should remain totally denominational. But the state was now ready to pay to the school administrators 50 percent for approved necessary repairs and improvements and up to 50 percent of the expenses for specific reconstructions. Normally the school administrators were helped by loans with favorable conditions, and auxiliary services—medical examinations, school meals—were paid for by the state. (b) The "special arrangement schools" were supported in accord with the provisions of the law of 1936; the applications filed within the prescribed time, which had not been approved or implemented, could now be revived with the necessary alterations in the previously determined conditions in regard to a limiting of the number of those teachers who were recognized because of their qualifications for imparting denominational instruction. Other regulations should be the same as for the first category. (c) "Controlled schools" were to be financed and supported exactly as if they were public schools, with the exception of some concessions, which were made as an accommodation for the cession of the buildings, for example, the right of the denominational officials to name one-third, instead of two-thirds, of the school administrators.

The Catholics completely rejected the "controlled" status. As a result, they faced the most difficult task of raising the funds needed for their "voluntary aided schools"—half the costs of modernizing, reconstruction in new places, and accommodation of "transferred" students—and also the means for their "special arrangement schools"—from one-fourth to one-half—and for new schools—the total costs of building sites and the buildings. The heaviest burden was for the Catholics, especially for male and female religious institutes, the secondary school system because of the higher age for obligatory schooling and because of the abolition of all fees in the state schools. The existing Catholic secondary schools for the most part accepted the status of elementary schools, and, except for those which were especially instituted for the higher classes, strove to be recognized by the education authorities as "effective" in their various categories. By 1948 the number of "recognized" schools had risen to 109, and the number of those which obtained state money to 73.

Two supplementary laws of 1946 and 1948 eased somewhat the burden laid on the Catholics, but the expenses mounted further. A pupil's place, which had cost ca. £60 in 1939, in 1949 required between £191 and £400, with variations from diocese to diocese. Meanwhile, the number of Catholic children who did not go to Catholic schools rose from one to four. In 1950 the hierarchy proposed some redress and set up an "Action Committee" to guide local deputations drawn from the parishes and lay organizations; they were to inculcate these proposals in the candidates for parliament during the general election of that year. Although the Catholic electors were informed of the positions of the candidates, this campaign did not succeed in obtaining noteworthy support from them, especially because no political party showed an inclination to take up this controversial matter.

Because the Catholics were not in a position to erect sufficient secondary schools, from 1956 they again made demands for state aid, but this time they did not have recourse to public agitation. Some 30 percent of the Catholic children of school age were at this time not in Catholic schools, although the Church had, between 1945 and 1959, raised the number of its schools by almost 25 percent, that is, by more than 300 schools, created 100,000 new school places, and projected a further 150,000. The education law of 1959 was accepted in part as answer to the demands of the Catholics and Anglicans. This law raised the aid due previously from 50 to 75 percent and granted subsidies of 75 percent for the erecting of new voluntary secondary schools, which were totally or very greatly necessary to take those children from the primary schools of the same denomination which had existed on 15 June 1959 or who came from such primary schools as had been erected to replace the schools existing at this same time. For the Catholics the limitation imposed by the date and the exclusion of aid for the building of primary schools was, of course, a disappointment.

In 1966 there were among the Catholic voluntary schools in England and Wales 1,801 primary schools and schools for all ages, with 441,358 pupils, 388 modern secondary schools, with 142,670 students, 62 classical secondary schools, with 29,520 students, and 39 secondary schools of other sorts, with 24,347 students; in addition, there were 56 schools with direct aid and 36,146 pupils, 557 independent schools with 114,964 pupils, and 42 special and approved schools with 3,404 pupils, hence altogether 2,945 Catholic schools with 792,389 students.

In view of these numbers the Catholics again presented their requests and demanded 85 percent of all building costs. Finally they were satisfied with the provisions of the education law of 1967, which was introduced by the Labour Government and accepted by parliament almost without opposition. The state raised not only the existing subsidies for all voluntary schools or those supported by special arrangement, so far as they were paid for approved repairs and improvements, to 80 percent, but it now also counted what was still more important, 80 percent for the erecting of entirely new schools or for the expansion of existing schools, even if such aid had previously not been granted to these. The government was able to concede these increased subsidies in part because the churches had established more harmony among themselves.

In order to be able to supply these schools with personnel, the existing teachers' training schools were improved and new ones were established. The erection of five new institutions for teacher training in the years after 1960 was the result of long discussions with the Ministry of Education and the Council of Catholic Education. In 1968 there were fourteen Catholic institutions for teacher training in England and Wales.

The attempt to found a Catholic university was not made in these years. However, in 1922 the University Catholic Federation of Great Britain had been founded to unite the Catholic associations at the English universities; it was attached to the *Pax Romana,* from which it had obtained the stimulus for its founding. It was reorganized in 1942, when the nongraduates founded the Union of Catholic Students and the graduates the Newman Association; the two organizations cooperated closely. The Union began with the publishing of a periodical and of an annual, in which in detail were presented the various methods by which it aspired to stress the Catholic influence in the life and works of the universities. The Newman Association attracted graduates from various professions and states of life; it set up a center in London and some active local branches. It also began the publishing of a monthly bulletin, *Unitas,* and displayed useful activities such as vacation courses, lecture series, and public university courses, some of which obtained recognition fom the University of London Extension Board.

Social Movement

The chief impulse for the social movement was the Catholic Social Guild. A group of priests and lay persons from the middle-class intellectuals had founded it in 1909 for the following ends: (1) to facilitate dialogue between Catholic students and workers; (2) for assistance in the achieving of applications of Catholic principles to actual social conditions; (3) to awaken in Catholic circles a greater interest in social questions and to assure their cooperation in the promotion of social reforms according to Catholic guidelines. With the encouragement of the hierarchy, this guild pursued these goals predominantly through study clubs or groups; in 1914 there were ninety-five such groups, with about one thousand members, which were concentrated in the north of England, and, in opposition to the expectations of the founders, consisted almost entirely of workers. Although adequately trained leaders were missing, the number of study clubs rose to 379 by 1938; during the war this number dropped, again rose to 337 in 1950, and decreased after that. Within the educational program for adults the guild introduced a correspondence course, for which it granted certificates and diplomas. In addition, it produced and disseminated literature which treated social questions; it planned and promoted instructional programs, some textbooks, and examinations for the various groups. From the middle of 1911 to 1920 the guild published a *Quarterly Bulletin,* from 1921 on the monthly *The Christian Democrat* and the *Catholic Social Year Book;* it published many timely penny brochures and the series of books, *Catholic Studies in Social Reform,* which were used by the study clubs as manuals. Especially influential were its publications on international law after World War I and on the union system and employee-employer relations. Under the guidance of the guild days of recollection for workers were held; in the first fifteen years after World War I more than 9,000 persons at Birmingham and elsewhere took part in these days of recollection. Finally, the guild trained lecturers and instituted lectures. In 1919 the headquarters of the administration was moved from London to Oxford. The number of members rose to 3,910 up to 1939, and, following a decline during the war, to 4,166 in 1948.

In 1920 the guild arranged the first summer vacation course lasting one week. Its aim was to bring different classes together, to awaken understanding between employers and employees, and to make Catholic social doctrine known in broader circles. The number of participants rose from year to year and peaked in 1948 with 230; after that it declined, and at the end of the 1950s the vacation courses were stopped.

In 1921 the guild founded the Catholic Workers' College at Oxford in order to educate men, and from 1923 women also, as leaders for their worker colleagues. This was a "monument" to Charles Plater (1875–1921), one of the founders of the guild. The first principal of the college was Father Leo O'Hea, S.J., who in 1924 became also the editor of the periodical *The Christian Democrat* and manager-secretary of the guild. The college instituted courses on political and economic theory and history, likewise on social ethics and moral philosophy, but also on special themes, such as unions, community administration, and international relations. In 1925 it was recognized by the Education Office because of its provisions for adult education and empowered by the university to grant diplomas. All students received stipends from the financial means which came from varied sources, and from 1926 they could also receive a stipend of the Education Office. Most students came from England, Scotland, and Wales, but in later years there were also a few from abroad. In the first twenty-six years of its existence the college trained only 146 students. Nevertheless, some of its graduates were active in community politics and in the union movement.

When interest in the study groups slackened, obviously because study was regarded as an end in itself instead of a means to an end, action groups were founded. Likewise in 1954 the guild called the action group service into being, which from week to week supplied a system and a plan for study. This change could not entirely transform the trend to inflexibility. A new "Program for Social Action," drafted chiefly by Michael P. Fogarty, was published in 1957 in the *Catholic Social Year Book,* but in consequence of differences of opinion which led the guild into a crisis in the late 1950s, it was not realized. Finally, lay persons obtained the leading position, after the offices of the manager-secretary in 1958 and of the principal of the College of Workers in 1962 had been filled by them; they were merely advised by a priest, whom the bishops had named as moderator.

In the course of the years the guild took a stand for definite concerns. After World War I it supported a guaranteed minimum wage and the family money plan. In 1926 it supported the general strike, until Cardinal Bourne condemned it. In the disturbed years after 1920 and 1930 the guild stood up for the unions and their rights. In its publications it explained the "corporate order" which Pius XI had recommended in *Quadragesimo Anno.* In the years after 1940 the guild found fault with the welfare state, but most Catholics gradually came to consider it with limited approval.

True, the Catholic Social Guild avoided detailed plans or programs and thereby was satisfied to promote a knowledge of general principles, which the individual Catholic could then apply to special situations; but some of its members from the very start favored a clearly articulated, concrete program that was based on a policy of social reform. Some of them, especially among the younger, devoted themselves to the doctrine of Distributism, which was represented by Hilaire Belloc, Gilbert Keith Chesterton, Eric Gill, and Father Vincent McNabb, O.P. The "Distributists" abhorred both industrial capitalism and socialism and recommended instead a wide distribution of property to private ownership. They presented their theory in numerous articles, which they published in *The New Witness* (1912–23), *G.K.'s Weekly* (1925–36), *The*

Weekly Review (1936–47), *The Defendant* (1947–56), and finally *The Distributist.* The literary basis of the movement was strengthened by a social structure when in 1926 the Distributist League was founded in London. Within three months there arose affiliates in the large cities of England and Wales. At regular intervals the league organized public lectures and discussions on timely affairs; these events were attended by a relatively large number of auditors. But all their exertions led only to unimportant results, partly because of differences of opinion among the Distributists themselves. While a few called for action, Chesterton and his adherents were satisfied with propaganda—although, Chesterton and Belloc submitted proposals and recommended their implementation to the government. The members of the league were also not in agreement on the right to property and the use of machines; Father McNabb, an extremist, condemned them together with industrialism as a whole as an evil. Controversies of this sort left in the broad public the impression that they were utopian theoreticians and uncritical admirers of medieval civilization. The Birmingham Plan, proposed in 1928 by the affiliate in that city and later revised from time to time, was the most practicable, and *The Distributist Program,* which was published by the league in 1934, outlined the practical measures by which the ideal situation could be realized. But there were only a few persons willing to make the required renunciation of all those comforts and amenities which industrialization had contributed and again lead a simple handicraft life. Besides, other Catholics, especially members of the Catholic Social Guild, reviled the Distributists as unrealistic. From ca. 1939 every effective activity of the league ended, but individual Distributists continued in the years after 1950 their publications and proposals on their theory.

The recommendation of the Distributists for the gaining of the necessary livelihood by agriculture as a form of practical action was realized in the Back-to-the-Land Movement. In 1929 The Scottish Catholic Land Association was founded, and in 1931 and 1932 five regional Catholic agricultural societies were established in England. The six associations were represented by a standing joint committee, and *Land for the People,* begun by the Scots in 1930, was the common organ until 1934; in this year it returned to control by the Scots. At the same time the associations in England and Wales were reorganized as the Catholic Land Federation, which established a new official organ, *The Cross and the Plough.* Each local society had as its protector the local bishop or bishops, a priest as chairman, and a layman as secretary. According to Monsignor James Dey, chairman of the federation, the chief function of the associations consisted of establishing communities of small farmers with the secondary occupations united with them. In this way the natural right of man to private ownership would again be confirmed; unemployment would be mitigated, and Catholic life on the land would be renewed. Because the urbanized proletariat had first to be educated in agricultural methods, the societies instituted teaching farms, in which unmarried men should obtain a three-year teaching program in theory and practical instruction and also spiritual direction. However, these farms had only a brief life because of lack of money. For the same reason the societies could not set aside any land for settlement by independent farmers. The hierarchy entirely refused to approve and support a collection and thereby to give this movement official recognition, because it feared that this money would be diverted from the budget for the building of schools and churches in new localities, and because it doubted the financial practicability of the entire plan. Also the general indifference of the Catholics, doubts that the small holdings were a means against unemployment, and their distrust of the leading theoreticians in the movement, and also the lack of any support at all by the government—all this contributed to the dissolving of the associations and of the federation. However, The North of England Catholic Land Association, with corresponding subsidies from the government, until 1942 trained young men as farm workers—first for three months in a youth hostel or a home, then with a farmer—and *The Cross and the Plough* continued its issues until mid-1949.

During the great economic crisis, other Catholics, such as Father Paul Crane, S.J., John Fitzsimons, and other members of the Catholic Social Guild, saw in the work of Peter Maurin and Dorothy Day in the United States a model for action. In June 1935 they founded a new periodical, *The Catholic Worker,* whose first editor was John Ford. This newspaper was sold in all large cities on the streets, and the sellers formed discussion and action groups. In imitation of the American model they established Friendship Houses in some places. Among clergy and laity not everyone approved the aims of this movement, but *The Catholic Worker* continued until 1959. In that year its last editor, Robert P. Walsh, became organizational secretary of the Catholic Social Guild and editor of its monthly, *The Christian Democrat.*

Around 1935 *The Christian Democrat* had directed attention to the *Jeunesse Ouvrière Chrétienne* in Belgium and France, and, when the Young Christian Workers were officially founded in England in 1937, their directors were selected from a study group of the Catholic Social Guild, which consisted of sellers of the newspaper *The Catholic Worker.* Father Gerard Rimmer founded the first group, and one of its members was Patrick Keegan, the future president of the World Union of Christian Worker Movements. The movement of the Young Christian Workers spread quickly and reached a part of the population which the Catholic social movement had previously not affected, but before the outbreak of World War II their organization had still not acquired a solid basis. The YCW also began with the preparation of boys and girls, before they left school, and from this work emerged the Pre-YCW, which Keegan founded in 1949. Also in the postwar years former members of the YCW developed the Family Social Apostolate to put its religious principles into practice in married life.

The Catholic Social Guild, the Catholic Women's League, the Catholic Education Council, and other organizations appointed delegates to the Catholic Council for International Relations, which had been founded in 1924 as a sort of uniting committee. Its function was to establish unity of action among the Catholics of all nations in all matters which affected their faith and to foster the business of international peace. Its work was chiefly of the educational type and was carried out by public announcements and international conferences.

Between the two world wars there appeared still other organizations. A lay group, which had regularly visited the ships in the harbor of Glasgow, established the Apostleship of the Sea in 1920. In the following year the administrator of the archdiocese approved the temporary guidelines and statutes. In 1922 Archbishop Donald A. Mackintosh communicated the blessing and a letter of recognition from Pius XI and became the first president of the society. Its task was the spiritual care of seamen. The work soon spread in Great Britain and to other countries; in 1927 200 churches in numerous harbors of the world were designated as sailors' centers. The administrative headquarters was first transferred from Glasgow to London, and in 1952 Pius XII established the general secretariat at Rome.

While the beginnings of an organization of Catholic contractors had only slight success, the British Catholic workers belonged to the general unions and never tried to establish unions of their own. But they held an annual National Conference of Catholic Trade Unionists and later founded diocesan associations of Catholic unionists. Two former students of the Catholic Workers' College founded the first of these associations with the consent of the bishop of Hexham and Newcastle in 1942, after the Congress of Unions at Blackpool had declared its opposition to state aid for denominational schools. After the war the local associations were united in a national corporation. It aimed at the organization of the opposition to Communist intrigues in the unions and worked to make its members better Catholics and better unionists. In both respects it achieved remarkable successes, but in the years after 1950 the energy and influence of the Catholic unionists slackened.

The apparently most impressive movement which was started by

Catholics during these years was the Sword of the Spirit, founded in 1940 by Cardinal Hinsley, an ardent patriot, who made a deep impression on the English people especially by his moving radio talks in the first years of World War II. It was the goal of this movement to assert the principles of Christianity and of the natural law against National Socialism and other totalitarian doctrines, for this end to support the national interest in the war, to seek for the postwar period a regulation and reorientation of Europe on the basis of such principles, and to unite all citizens for these goals. The activities of this movement were under the keywords "Prayer"—including sermons, retreats, days of recollection, and spiritual reading—"Study"—including lectures and discussion groups, for whose leadership plans were handed down—and "Action," which should be undertaken not in the name of the movement itself but through individuals and groups, who acted according to its principles. The original stimulus to this movement came from Christopher Dawson, who was first named lay leader and later was vice-president. Also many other prominent lay persons, men and women, were active in it, and groups were established among the French, Belgians, Poles, and Czechs who had fled to Great Britain and were living there in exile. But the totality of Catholics in the nation was not prepared for this movement. And because the other bishops had not previously been consulted, many of them gave no effective support. Nevertheless, it was at first enthusiastically welcomed by the Protestants. One of its first results was in December 1940 a declaration, signed by Cardinal Hinsley, by the archbishops of Canterbury and York, and by the moderator of the Free Church Federal Council. In it all accepted the five points of Pius XII for peace and added to them five criteria of their own, according to which economic situations and proposals could be examined. Such a cooperation with Protestants caused some Catholics to conjure up the danger of a dogmatic compromise or of indifferentism. Therefore the movement of the Sword of the Spirit soon decided, although it had invited to membership all men of good will who were willing to recognize the Catholic leadership, that non-Catholics could be only associate members without voting right. In spite of the disappointment thereupon expressed in some Protestant publications, Christian charity could be preserved thanks to the good offices of the Anglican bishop of Chichester, G. K. Bell, and others. The high point of this movement was reached in June 1942, when representatives of the Sword of the Spirit and those of Religion and Life, a similar movement among Protestants, composed a declaration on their collaboration, in which they appealed to the total Christian population of the country to act together in order to assure a noticeable influence of Christian teaching and of Christian witness in the solving of social, economic, and civil law problems at this time and in the postwar period. Accordingly, community weeks and meetings were held in all England, and local Christian councils were set up, not only to plan these events and realize them, but to put pressure on all parties who had to do with religious problems common to all denominations. This sort of interdenominational cooperation ceased when, with the end of the war, its chief propelling power was eliminated. The death of Cardinal Hinsley in March 1943 had deprived the Sword of the Spirit of his dynamic leadership, and in the first postwar years its activity generally slackened. Because of double work and overlapping, a coordination of its goals and actions with those of other Catholic societies could not be completely achieved. Under the new archbishop of Westminster, Cardinal Griffin, the center of gravity moved to the international area, to the social and political actions of Catholics on the continent, to the work of the United Nations and the special organizations affiliated to it, and to aid for refugees in Great Britain. In this way the "Sword" movement corresponded to a need which no other Catholic organization fulfilled. By 1954 it had lost its character as a mass movement and had become a center for the spread of information on all concerns of the Church in the whole world; furthermore, it was supposed, when necessary, to summon Catholic public opinion to action.

Catholics had always been free to support any of the greater political parties. Cardinals Bourne, Hinsley, and Griffin and other bishops frequently gave this answer when questions arose in regard to the Labour Party and its alleged championing of socialism. Most Catholics belonging to the working class actually preferred the Labour Party by an overwhelming majority; such membership for its party helped to prevent the party from developing into socialism.

Catechetical and Apologetic Work

The organized catechetical and apologetic work of the Catholic Church in Great Britain was promoted in various ways. The Catholic Truth Society, founded in 1884, circulated small and inexpensive writings, including some with a devotional and pedagogical content for Catholics and others for the information of Protestants. The founder of the society, James Britten, worked zealously up to his death in 1924. When in 1921–22 the headquarters of the society was moved and enlarged in order to accommodate a circulating library, an expansion of the program was due to the leadership talent and professional knowledge of an American, William Reed-Lewis. The publications of the society and its lectures were often concerned with particular themes of current interest, such as social and political ideologies in the years after 1920 and 1930, and later with birth control; but such controversial writings were never so important to the society as those which were aimed at the instruction of Catholics. Branch offices were set up throughout England and also in Scotland, Australia, India, Hong Kong, and the United States.

Another method for the instruction of non-Catholics was street-preaching, which was directed to all who wished to stop and listen. This was the function of the Catholic Evidence Guild, which Vernon Redwood, a New Zealander, had founded in London, with the permission of Cardinal Bourne, in 1918 shortly after the end of the war. The first guild worked only in the archdiocese of West-minster, but eventually independent guilds were also founded in other English dioceses and in the United States and Australia. In the springtime of the first guild there was elaborated a training program which took care of teaching courses in theology, philoso-phy, and Scripture; it was brought to the candidates, as meetings were held in the open; they were examined by study directors and other chaplains whom the local bishop had appointed, and there was also present a lay person, who as *advocatus diaboli* represented the crowd of listeners. The Marble Arch in Hyde Park became the most popular spot for speaker platforms in London. This sort of presentation to the outside was limited to Catholic doctrine; contro-versial questions of a social and economic nature and all political questions were strictly excluded. The text of the guild, *Catholic Evidence Training Outline,* which first appeared in 1925 and thereaf-ter in revision, had been composed by Frank Sheed and Maisie Ward, two of the best known lay members. Of course, the work of the guild was impaired by the war, but after that it was intensified. In 1949 there were eighteen guilds with a total of 638 members and 302 speakers ready to act in England.

Liturgical Movement

In Great Britain the liturgical movement had a slow start and achieved no very great success before the Second Vatican Council. The Society of Saint Gregory was founded in 1929. It published the periodical *Music and Liturgy* and conducted summer vacation courses. After World War II it expanded its area of work by giving up its earlier preference for music and shortened the name of its periodical to *Liturgy.* But the movement only obtained real esteem after the encyclical *Mediator Dei* and some decrees had been issued from Rome.

Samuel Gosling, an English priest, came to the conviction that the retention of Latin as the only liturgical language of the Roman Rite was a serious impediment to pastoral work. In 1943 he founded the English Liturgy Society for clerics and lay persons, who "want to promote the use of the vernacular in public Mass in so far as this is in harmony with the teachings and traditions of the Church." In the next year he started a small periodical, *The English Liturgist,* which he published until his death in 1950. The society obtained only modest support and encountered bitter opposition, but it exercised a direct influence even in the United States, where the American Vernacular Society was established in 1946.

Journalism

After 1914 only a few new newspapers and periodicals of importance were begun, but many of the old ones were continued. In 1915 Wilfrid Ward resigned as editor of the *Dublin Review,* but his successors continued the tradition on the same high level and with the same broad view, especially Shane Leslie, Denis Gwynn, and Christopher Dawson, who also composed numerous books, especially historical and biographical works. The periodical remained in the possession of the archbishop of Westminster. In 1961 its name was changed to *Wiseman Review*—shortly before, Norman St. John-Stevas became editor—and four years later again back to the *Dublin Review.* In the winter of 1968–69 it stopped appearing. Among the periodicals published by religious orders, the *Month,* the organ of the Jesuits, was continued in its original intellectual style until 1949. From then on its editor, Philip Caraman, S.J., began a new series, which devoted as much attention to literature and the arts as to theology and philosophy; this policy, for its part, was again changed in 1964. The *Downside Review* reflected the scholarship of the Benedictines in that abbey. In 1920 Bede Jarrett, O.P. founded *Blackfriars* as the organ of the Oxford Dominicans.

The weekly *Tablet* was continued by John George Snead-Cox until 1920 according to conservative guidelines, with little sympathy for the political ambitions of the Irish; it was essentially the mouthpiece of the old Catholic families. Its defensive and hostile attitude toward Anglicans was retained by Ernest Oldmeadow, a converted Methodist minister, whom Cardinal Bourne had chosen as editor in 1923 chiefly for his polemical skill. As religious controversies lost ever more in power of attraction, the circulation of the paper dropped to less than 3,000, and in 1936 Cardinal Bourne's successor sold the *Tablet* to a group of laymen, among them Douglas Woodruff, who then replaced Oldmeadow as editor; by expanding the areas of interest for the paper he succeeded in again stabilizing its existence. Woodruff made it an outstanding source of news, especially on foreign affairs, and he employed a number of competent journalists.

Among the other old weekly papers the London *Universe* prospered because it used the techniques of modern journalism. After it had acquired the *Catholic Times* in 1962, it increased its circulation to more than 300,000 and in this way became the most widespread religious newspaper in the entire country. Although the *Catholic Times* had likewise been modernized, it had retained more of its original character and for the future remained the preferred paper of many Catholics of Irish birth or ancestry. The *Catholic Herald* addressed a growing number of Catholic students at the provincial universities. When in 1934 a group of lay persons had acquired it, they completely transformed it. From then on Count Michael de la Bédoyère, who occupied a middle position between the *Tablet* and the *Universe,* edited it until 1962 in a very capable manner. After his retirement Desmond Fisher became editor and directed the paper as a journal of opinion, which treated world news of all sorts from the Catholic standpoint. The *Glasgow Observer* remained the only Catholic weekly published in Scotland; it appeared in the eastern and northern areas of the country under the title of *Scottish Catholic Herald;* it became in reality an affiliated enterprise of the London *Catholic Herald.* Some other English and Irish Catholic weekly papers also published Scottish editions. The *Catholic Times* ran for forty years as an appendage of the *Welsh Catholic Times,* which appeared at Cardiff and was stopped in 1962.

IRELAND

Population

In the twenty-six counties of the Republic of Ireland the number of Catholics in 1926 was altogether 2,751,269 in a total population of 2,971,992, and in 1961 it was 2,673,473 in a total of 2,818,341. After the acquiring of independence, the percentage of Catholics grew with each census, whereas the total population declined, because emigration was stronger than the natural growth. Thereby the republic became, in regard to religion, constantly more homogeneous. In addition, the great majority of these Catholics practiced their faith, and so Catholicism was more visible in Ireland than in any other English-speaking country. In the six counties of Northern Ireland, on the other hand, the total population grew from 1,256,561 in 1926 to 1,425,462 in 1961, while the number of Catholics increased from 420,428 to 498,031.

In 1916 there were in all thirty-two counties 3,022 diocesan priests and 715 religious priests. The religious institutes had 97 houses of priests, 131 convents of nuns, and 43 monasteries of monks. Fifty years later there were 3,964 diocesan priests and 2,072 religious priests. The religious institutes had 160 houses for priests, 201 for brothers, and

648 for nuns. Meanwhile many priests and religious had left Ireland to work in other English-speaking countries or in the missions.

Political Development

At the outbreak of World War I there was still violent debate on the already long spiritedly discussed question of Home Rule for Ireland. The chief difficulty resulted from the refusal of the Protestants in Ulster to accept an arrangement whereby Catholics would constitute the majority and so be in the position to bring clericalism to power or introduce a theocratic state. The Catholics, for their part, feared that in a partition of the island the Catholics in Ulster would be oppressed by a Protestant majority and that in the granting of autonomy to these northern parts of the country the principle of denominational education would be replaced by that of mixed education.

In the first years of the war the episcopate and clergy generally supported the participation of the Irish in the mobilization and recruiting. But at the end of 1915 this original enthusiasm for the war exertions changed to apathy. Edward Thomas O'Dwyer, bishop of Limerick, declared that it was England's and not Ireland's war. Although the hierarchy had several times condemned the Irish Republican Brotherhood, which organized the uprising in 1916, it did not unanimously disavow the rising. The rebel leaders, who took part in the Easter rebellion were at least nominally Catholics, and of those who were jailed and condemned to death all except one received the sacraments before their execution by the British. However, public opinion as a whole condemned the immoral means they had used to assert the claim of the Irish people to independence. Of course, then the cruel treatment by the British government brought the rebels the sympathy of the people. Bishop O'Dwyer expressed the general indignation at the harshness of the British suppression.

When the Irish Parliamentary Party had lost the confidence of the public, the bishops and especially the younger priests gradually gave preference to the Sinn Fein Movement and at the same time helped to keep it from recourse to physical force. In fact, between May 1916 and the beginning of 1919 no noteworthy acts of violence occurred in Ireland. In this period the participation of those who claimed the title Sinn Fein conferred on the usual operations of a political party of the new movement the aura of trustworthiness which it needed in order to find the approval of the clergy on a broader basis. The primate of All Ireland and archbishop of Armagh, Cardinal Michael Logue, however, expressed in a pastoral letter of November 1917 his opposition to the Sinn Fein, because he regarded its dream of establishing an Irish Republic as a utopia, which would likely end in disaster.

When the military service law was submitted to parliament, in order to give the government authority to apply the conscription of troops also to Ireland, which had hitherto been exempted from it, the permanent committee of the bishops and individual bishops warned the British government in the spring of 1918 against the effort to force through such a law. Later the entire hierarchy condemned compulsory conscription as an inhuman law of suppression. The Irish people, they said, had the right to resist this law by every means that was in accord with the law of God. The bishops instructed the clergy to use certain practical measures to avert this wrong. By the fact that they placed themselves at the head of the campaign against the draft, the bishops maintained their influence on the people and fostered in fact, especially in the west, a better cooperation between the clergy and the Sinn Fein.

After the *Dáil Éireann* had proclaimed the Irish Republic in 1919, the Anglo-Irish war erupted. The British government tried to induce the bishops to condemn the rebels, but they refused. Some bishops openly supported the loan of the *Dáil*. When in 1919 the *Dáil* instituted courts of arbitration, it took care that priests were *ex officio* judges in these courts for lesser legal cases. Thus through the lower clergy the Church acquired a voice in the national movement without the risks of a direct commitment of the bishops. The participation of the clergy in the courts also gave the republic at least a certain degree of legitimacy. When the Irish Republican Army (IRA) led its pitiless attacks on the British troops, and the latter exercised brutal retaliation, many bishops declared that the attacks of the IRA were deplorable but understandable in view of the suppression by the authorities. In October 1920 the hierarchy censured the furious reprisals of the government as cruelties and excesses. Because many volunteers maintained with the assent of a few clerics that the killing of a policeman or of a British soldier was not murder but a war action, the bishop of Galway, Thomas O'Dea, made clear the Church's view that no legal authority in Ireland had declared or authorized war against the police. Nevertheless, many priests approved membership in the IRA. With the approval of the *Dáil,* its president, Eamon De Valera, proclaimed in March 1921 the formal acknowledgment of a state of war with England and responsibility for the actions of the IRA. But when in June De Valera personally asked the hierarchy for a formal recognition of the republic, the bishops merely emphasized the right of Ireland to choose its own form of government. The agreement of December 1921 between the British government and the Irish plenipotentiaries on the establishing of the Irish Free State was welcomed by the Church with a feeling of relief and joy. The hierarchy as such did not approve this agreement, but several bishops did so as individuals.

After the treaty had been ratified by the *Dáil Éireann* in 1922, De Valera and the IRA rejected it and the government created by it. At first the bishops hoped for a constitutional solution of the crisis; only when the obdurate Republicans led by De Valera began the civil war against the new government led by William T. Cosgrave as president did the hierarchy announce a general excommunication of all those against the treaty. In a common pastoral letter of 10 October 1922 the hierarchy declared that the government of the Free State possessed the legitimate authority, that it was a serious wrong to resist it by armed force, and that the guerrilla war continued by the Republicans was to be condemned. The Republicans, on the other hand, disdained this condemnation and continued the war until De Valera summoned his adherents the following spring to stop hostilities. Although some few among the Republicans were still resentful toward the Church for decades, De Valera did not become the rallying point for an anticlerical party.

Ecclesiastical Organization

When Ireland was politically divided, this did not affect the territorial integrity of the Church. From then on the ecclesiastical and the political spheres of jurisdiction no longer coincided. The four provinces with twenty-eight dioceses retained their previous boundaries, and the hierarchy continued to act as a single body. Generally, the bishops met twice a year, and a permanent committee, consisting of the four archbishops, two bishops as secretaries, and one member elected from each province, met quarterly. National councils in which representatives of the lower clergy and the religious institutes took part were held at Maynooth in 1927 and 1956.

Relations with the State

In 1929 the Irish Free State established full diplomatic relations with the Holy See. Thereafter, an apostolic nuncio resided at Dublin, and an Irish ambassador at Rome. The first nuncio was Paschal Robinson, who occupied this post until his death in 1948; he was born in Ireland and grew up in the United States. A concordat was never discussed.

In the absence of the Republican delegates, who declined to recognize the *Dáil* elected in 1922, a constitution for the Free State was decided by this body in the same year. In it the Catholic Church was not even mentioned; freedom of religion was merely guaranteed to every citizen, and all laws were declared null and void which would subsidize any religion or give preference to anyone because of his religious faith or his position. Nevertheless, from the start the Cosgrave governments, which consisted predominantly of

Catholic ministers, and the *Dáil* dominated by him showed their readiness to employ the power of the state for the protection of Catholic moral values. Thus in 1923 they approved the law for film censorship, in 1924 and 1927 the laws against strong alcoholic drink, and in 1929 the law for the censorship of publications, provided by a censorship committee consisting of one Catholic priest as chairman, three Catholic laymen, and one Protestant.

In 1927 De Valera and a majority of the Republicans decided to enter the *Dáil* as the Fianna Fail Party. A minority of unreconciled Republicans, under the name of the Irish Republican Army, rejected the status quo for the future and strove for the forcible union of Northern Ireland with the twenty-six counties. The hierarchy formally condemned the IRA in a common pastoral letter of 1931. At the same time it also condemned as Communist the Saor Eire organization allied with it. The Saor Eire gradually disappeared, but the IRA remained active, and the Communist influence in it was furthermore strong. By 1935 the bishops in their Lenten pastoral letter frequently warned the faithful against Communism. In January 1956 the hierarchy again condemned the IRA and declared it was a "mortal sin for a Catholic to become or to remain a member of an organization or society which claims the right to bear arms or to use them against its own or another state," and "likewise sinful for a Catholic to cooperate with such an organization or society, to applaud it, or to support it in other ways." Nevertheless, many pious Catholics still supported the IRA. These Irish accepted the authority of the Church in the sphere of religion but rejected it in the area of politics.

When De Valera became Prime Minister in 1932, he continued the policy of his predecessors with the upholding of Catholic values and even identified "Irish" with "Catholic." Thus the supplementary decree of 1935 to the penal law forbade the sale and the import of contraceptive means (Section 17), and the law against public dance establishments of the same year eliminated an evil against which bishops and priests had long taken the field.

The constitution of 1937 respected Catholic teaching in regard to the family, marriage, education, and private ownership. With special reference to religion it declared: "The state recognizes the special position of the Holy Roman Catholic and Apostolic Church as the custodian of the faith which the great majority of citizens profess" (ARTICLE 44). It also recognized the Protestant, the Jewish, and other religions existing in the nation. This article had been introduced on De Valera's personal initiative; the bishops had not asked such recognition. Afterwards the authorities never agreed whether the "special position" could have any juridical effect. Although this constitution championed Catholic values to a greater degree than that of 1922, the state still did not always concede to the Church the status of a person in public law and also no financial means or subsidies at all. The Church itself was not empowered to possess property or to undertake public-law activities; it always had to employ the trustee system and obtain its entire income from the voluntary gifts of the people. On the other hand, the state claimed no influence on the naming of bishops or on other internal affairs of the Church. The Supreme Court of the Irish Free State had declared in 1926 that the canon law of the Catholic Church was a foreign law in civil law and in civil courts, whose validity had to be proved by expert witnesses. The constitution of 1937 did not change the status of canon law and thereby did not exclude the difficulties which occurred in marriage-law cases from the differences between canon law and civil law, although the constitution also forbade divorce.

In the south no large political party ever assumed an anticlerical attitude. Even the Labour Party supported the upholding of Catholic value concepts.

Educational System

Nevertheless, the Irish Free State was helpful to the Church in the area of education and allowed it to exercise over the schools in the twenty-six counties more control than in any other country in the world. In the constitution of 1937 the state recognized the family as the proper and natural teacher of the child; it guaranteed respect for the unalterable right and duty of the parents to care, in accord with their means, for the religious and moral, intellectual, physical, and social education of their children. For primary education, up to the age of fourteen, the state also granted for the future subsidies to all school boards which complied with its instructions; these subsidies were to cover the salaries of teachers, specified maintenance expenses, and two-thirds of the construction costs for new schools—more than two-thirds in areas of poverty. The state did not establish a competing system of its own. The primary schools were in private ownership, and almost all were allied with one or another denomination. Each school was controlled by a school director, who appointed the teachers; in the case of the Catholic schools the pastor was usually also the school director. On the other hand the state prescribed the curriculum, inspected the schools, and gave the examinations. Some of the Catholic secondary schools were the property of lay persons, but most were in the possession of dioceses or religious institutes. On this basis, by a law of 1924 the Irish Free State introduced a system of per capita subsidies under the condition that definite rules were observed. These subsidies proved to be ever less adequate, but they were not raised until 1954. In June 1964 the Catholic Church managed 4,848 primary schools with 489,448 pupils, out of a total of 502,201 pupils in the republic. There were altogether 573 Catholic secondary schools in the academic year 1964–65, and they educated 92,989 pupils.

Irish politicians were satisfied with the school system, which left control in the hands of clerics. The bishops reacted promptly to every proposal to reduce their influence. But from 1963 several important reforms in the educational system were prescribed by law with the consent or at least the approval of the hierarchy.

In the field of higher education the hierarchy had, long before the achieving of independence, asked for the erecting of a university which was acceptable to Catholics. In 1908 the British government agreed to this request with the founding of the National University of Ireland, with colleges at Dublin, Cork, and Galway. Although formally nondenominational, it was intended to assure a considerable influence to the Catholic hierarchy in its governing bodies. Nevertheless, the archbishop of Dublin, John Charles McQuaid, considered it necessary in 1944 to forbid Catholics "to enter the Protestant university of Trinity College without the previous permission of the diocesan bishop," and he declared that disobedience to this prescription was a mortal sin, and perseverance in disobedience made one unworthy to receive the sacraments. The National Council of 1956 likewise forbade Catholic youth, under threat of mortal sin, to attend Trinity College and Catholic parents or guardians to send young men there. Only the archbishop of Dublin should be competent to decide under what circumstances and with what guarantees against the danger of apostasy attendance at this institution could be tolerated. In practice, however, dispensations were frequently granted.

Social Movement

In the first three decades of the twentieth century the social movement was relatively weak among Irish Catholics because they had to devote their energies chiefly to the political struggle and the work of church building and the religious organization. The social movement was delayed also by the intellectual backwardness of the Catholic population. Progress was speeded after the publication of the encyclical *Quadragesimo Anno* by Pius XI in 1931. In the same year Father John Hayes founded *Muintir na Tire* (People of the Land), a production association, which later held agricultural weekends and weeks and study congresses. It developed into a movement for the improvement of social life in the rural areas of Ireland, which was threatened with annihilation by the irresistible march of industrialization. Local societies were formed, which represented each sector of the community, and particular interests were subsumed under a higher group on the level of the parish, which represented the organizational unity. This movement was not formally Catholic, but Catholic priests and laity actively supported it. Prominent Protestants were also members of these local societies and took part in the meetings. The underlying ideology can be termed "occupational." *Muintir na Tire* became one of the most important intermediaries for the spread of Catholic social doctrine in Ireland.

Among the newspapers, the weekly *The Standard,* founded in 1928, was from 1938 on the most effective organ for propagating Catholic social teaching; its preference was the association system. Its editor-in-chief, Doctor Alfred O'Rahilly, professor and later president of the University College at Cork, wrote on economic and religious themes.

In the late 1930s the bishops proclaimed social doctrine ever more loudly in their pastoral letters. Three bishops were especially known for their interest in the social question: John Dignan of Clonfert, who in 1936 accepted from the government the chairmanship of the new national social security for the sick; Michael Brown of Galway, who stubbornly opposed every inappropriate spread of state power; Archbishop McQuaid, who devoted his special attention to social welfare. In 1941 McQuaid created the Catholic Social Service Conference for the coordination and spread of charitable work in view of the deficient situation, because of the war, in nourishment, clothing, and especially heating material as well as in the areas of dwellings, occupation, and care of mothers. The conference used voluntary cooperation and obtained aid from the state and local officials. In Dublin it changed the type and manner of social work.

The founding of the Christus Rex Society announced new progress of the social movement; it was approved by the Irish hierarchy in 1945 and held its first congress the next year. Its membership was restricted to diocesan priests, but members of religious institutes and lay persons often gave talks at the annual congresses. Its goals were: "to clarify public opinion on social questions and help in the forming of a public awareness that is sensitive to social grievances . . . ; to promote the study of Catholic social doctrine among the clergy and through them among the laity; to encourage Irish priests to common exertions with a view to abolishing social evils and realizing the principles of the social encyclicals in public life." In 1947 the society began the publication of the quarterly *Christus Rex,* which became the leading periodical for the discussion of social questions in Ireland.

One of the best known publicists and speakers on social questions in the postwar period was Cornelius Lucey, professor of ethics at Maynooth from 1921 to 1951, coadjutor bishop of Cork from 1951 to 1952, and from 1952 bishop of Cork. Bishop Brown also gave expression to his views on public affairs. Both bishops represented conservative ideas.

When the government proposed a law for the "Care for Mother and Child," the hierarchy unanimously decided in April 1951 that this plan was opposed to Catholic social doctrine. Then when the minister of health, Doctor Noel Browne, resigned for various reasons, there began in the press a controversy on the role of the hierarchy. The bishops were concerned about the dangers which resulted from the growth of the state's power and the possibility of an un-Christian sexual teaching. When in 1952 the government proposed a new health law, the hierarchy likewise intervened in order to put through a few supplements, as, for example, one which assured the free choice of a hospital for each individual. The chief reason for the efforts of the Irish hierarchy to exert influence on the precise prescriptions for social services in the country was that it was against the centralizing tendencies of the government and its bureaucratic forms. But still, on the whole relations between the hierarchy and the government were friendly from 1923 to 1970; there were only a few cases of open conflict.

In contrast to other European countries with a large Catholic proportion in the population, in Ireland no workers' union was created which was fostered by or united with the Church. The political exertions and actions of the workers' movement were aimed at avoiding church objections, and the danger of Marxist infiltration declined after 1921. The example and the influence of the British unions and the desire to maintain unity with the numerous Protestant workers in the north constituted further factors, which saw to it that the workers' movement in Ireland remained totally secular.

Lay Apostolate

In 1921 there was founded at Dublin that organization which was to become one of the largest organized movements of the lay apostolate in the whole world: the Legion of Mary. A group of lay persons, motivated by awareness of their Christian vocation to be witnesses and inspired by the teachings of the Popes, met in the church of Saint Nicholas of Myra in Francis Street with the curate, Father Michael Toher, to seek suitable methods with which they could transform their discussions on the mystical body of Christ and the writings of Saint Louis Marie Grignion de Montfort into concrete action for the service of their fellow men. The form of their organization was influenced also by the Saint Vincent De Paul Society, with which they were all connected. Their lay leader was Frank Duff, a young state official. Originally the new society was called Association of Our Lady of Mercy; in 1925 the name was changed to the Legion of Mary, and the titles which were given to all parts of its organization were taken from the usage of the old Roman army. The work began with visiting the sick in the South Dublin Union Hospital. Soon the legion directed its attention to organized prostitution and opened at Dublin its first home for prostitutes. In 1927 it founded the Morning Star Home for destitute men and the Regina Coeli Home for women.

The legion decided that its membership should be open to men and women from all educational strata, so long as they were practicing Catholics and at least eighteen years old. It was expected of the members that they lead an exemplary life and possess the "spirit of the Legion" or desire to possess it. They had to take part in the weekly meeting of their group, in which they were formed and spiritually stimulated by legion prayers, spiritual reading, and guidance from the spiritual leader; also they had to devote a considerable part of their free time each week to an apostolic work allotted to them, at least two hours. It was required of each member as his personal responsibility to recruit new members, both active and auxiliary. Auxiliary members performed only a service of prayer. The leadership of the legion lies in a *concilium,* the headquarters of which has always remained at Dublin. It was to consist of representatives of all legionary societies which were in immediate relations with it, and of the members of the Dublin *curia* and of the spiritual director appointed by the Irish bishops. This strict supervision of the lesser units by the superior councils assured, together with the manual of guidelines, which was later translated into twenty-five languages and 125 dialects, the uniformity of the legion throughout the world. The legion declared its readiness to carry out any type of social service and Catholic Action, which the local ordinary or parish priest asked or approved. At the weekly meeting of the *praesidia,* the smallest units, an oral report had to be made on the work done and then the work for the coming week was assigned. Gradually the house visits of legionaries, who went in pairs, became their characteristic activity. Also, the legion took care of homes, clubs, and study groups, distributed pamphlets and Lenten books, and gave catechetical instruction. All these activities had to be directed to individuals, but the giving of material help was forbidden. In the forty years since the founding, more than 60,000 active groups were founded, which worked in more than 1,500 dioceses, vicariates, and prefectures on five continents. In 1964 there were more than 1 million active and more than 9 million auxiliary members. A legion was first established in the United States in 1931.

North America

THE UNITED STATES

Population

In 1914 it was assumed that the Catholic population of the United States amounted to 16,067,985 with 18,568 priests in a total population of 99,117,567. In 1964 the Catholic population had increased to 44,874,371 in a total population of 183,783,493. Although it continued to grow after that, the rate of growth had already declined, in that year it amounted to 1.7 percent in comparison to 2.4 percent in 1963. The downward trend in the number of baptisms began in 1962 and was doubtless an indication that the practice of artificial birth control had spread further and that the national birthrate was reflected in it. In the same decade other high points were also reached, which were then followed by a decline: 59,892 priests in 1967, 181,421 sisters in 1966, and 12,539 brothers in 1967. The degree of "shrinkage" in the Catholic population has not been ascertained exactly, but it must have been considerable.

The immigration from Europe, through which the Catholic population had grown so rapidly until 1914, first dropped because of World War I and thereafter because of restrictive laws. These laws were motivated in part by the fear on the part of Protestants that the country could be inundated by Catholics and Jews. The Emergency Quota Law of 1921 limited the number of immigrants from each country per year to 3 percent of the respective national group living in the United States in 1910. The Immigration Law of 1924 reduced this number to 2 percent and set the population figure of 1890 in place of that of 1910 until the newly prescribed system took effect in 1929; from then on, a quota of immigrants was granted for each European country which was based on the proportion which the members of a specific nationality who had lived in the United States in 1920 had possessed in the same year in regard to the total number of the population; the key figure was 150,000. These measures greatly lessened the entrance of Catholics from eastern, central, and southern Europe, and in 1931 President Hoover lowered the quotas so strongly because of unemployment that the immigration of European Catholics almost stopped entirely for the rest of this decade. However, hundreds of thousands of Mexicans and French Canadians, who were exempted from the quota restrictions, moved across the southern and northern frontiers. There also came Catholics from American possessions, especially Puerto Ricans, who settled in New York and some other cities, and Filipinos, who went to California. After World War II Spanish-speaking Catholics poured into the northern cities, and many European Catholics came into the country in accord with the stipulations of the Displaced Persons Act of 1948. The principle of national origin, which favored the Nordic peoples, was again confirmed in the McCarran-Walter Law of 1952, despite the protests of Catholics and others.

The Church gradually lost its immigrant status and its opposition attitude and thereby gained more and more esteem among non-Catholics. Besides, after World War II more Americans than previously acknowledged their membership in a denomination. Many of them felt attracted to the Catholic Church, which constituted the largest individual body in the country and conducted respected institutions on the local and national level. By the fact that the Church exposed itself more to the glare of publicity, it brought the blind zealots to silence and gained more open ears for its demands. The apostolate for converts gained in esteem through the holding of hours of consultation in the parishes, through the free distribution of literature, for which advertisements in the secular newspapers solicited, and through individual talks with entirely individual instruction. In this way 146,212 converts were received into the Church in 1960; this was the highest number which was ever ascertained for a single year. In the following period the annual figures dropped again.

A constantly increasing percentage of Catholics lived in cities. Even in 1967 there were of the altogether 3,080 rural districts in the United States still 671 without a permanent priest. The fact that almost 40 million Americans did not live within reach of a priest was characteristic of the predominantly urban character of American Catholicism.

Of the approximately 20,300,000 blacks in the United States, only 747,598 were Catholics in 1964.

Organization

In 1914 there were in the United States fourteen ecclesiastical provinces and eighty-four dioceses; in addition, there was still one vicariate apostolic and one Ruthenian Greek diocese. At this time there were 9,740 churches with resident priests and 4,911 missions with churches. Fifty years later there were 27 archdioceses, 114 dioceses, one Ukrainian Catholic archeparchy, two Ukrainian Catholic eparchies, and two eparchies of the Byzantine Rite. In these jurisdictional areas there were 17,455 parishes, 515 missions, and 4,594 stations. The archdiocese with the largest number of Catholics was Chicago.

Although the archbishops took care to hold annual meetings, the entire hierarchy was not organized until September 1919 when 92 of the existing 101 ordinaries took part in the first general meeting at the Catholic University of America in Washington, D.C. They decided by an overwhelming majority to establish the National Catholic Welfare

Council, as the organization was originally called. It was a logical further development of the National Catholic War Council, which had been founded in August 1917 by the delegates of sixty-eight dioceses and twenty-seven national Catholic associations to coordinate the efforts of the popular Catholic groups in the contemporary emergency by six committees of priests and lay persons, which in turn were active under a controlling committee of bishops. The effectiveness of the war council in its various efforts made it seem desirable to have a permanent organization on the national level for the coordination and stimulation of actions in the period of peace. Pope Benedict XV had in a general way agreed that commissions for the handling of school and social problems should be set up and that they should hold annual general meetings. But because some bishops feared that the organization would interfere in the jurisdiction of the ordinary in their own dioceses, they transmitted their objections to the Holy See. Cardinal Gaetano De Lai, secretary of the Consistorial Congregation, and some other officials of the Roman Curia for their part were afraid that the NCWC would promote the beginnings of a "national" Church in the United States. They persuaded Benedict XV to revoke the approval granted by him provisionally and by way of experiment. He had already drafted a decree for the dissolution of the organization but was prevented by death from signing it. His successor, Pius XI, thereupon signed this decree and had it published. The administrative committee of the NCWC protested against this decision and delegated from its ranks the bishop of Cleveland, Joseph Schrembs, to explain the arguments of the NCWC at Rome. In protracted discussions he convinced De Lai and other cardinals. On 2 July 1922 a new decree was issued which approved the organization according to the original plan; only the name was easily changed by substituting the word "Conference" for "Council"; in this way the organization, which was erected on a voluntary basis and had only an advisory function, could not be misunderstood as a legislative body. However, it became the highest authority in the decisions of the Catholic Church on public affairs and on the implementing of commonly agreed-upon guidelines. In addition to the administrative council there were created right from the start five departments: for education, lay activity, press, social action, and the missions; three more, for immigration, legal questions, and youth, were later added. The first business manager or secretary general was John Burke, C.S.P., the former editor of the *Catholic World* and chairman of the meeting at which the war council had been founded and also chairman of the Committee for Special Actions in the period of the war. He served in this position until his death in 1936. The NCWC continued its function until it was reorganized in 1967 and thereafter, as the United States Catholic Conference, constituted a corporation in civil law. At the same time the National Conference of Catholic Bishops came into existence as a canon law corporation.

In these years the founding of parishes continued on the territorial and national level. When the world economic crisis began, the Poles alone had approximately one thousand parishes in the United States. When after World War II many Catholics began to move from the large cities to the suburbs, the number of national parishes declined.

Educational System

In 1914 there were 230 Catholic colleges or high schools for young men and 680 academies or high schools for girls; in addition, there were 5,403 parochial schools, attended by 1,429,859 children. In 1964 there were 1,557 high schools of the dioceses and parishes with 677,169 students and 901 private high schools, for the most part conducted by religious men and women, with 391,255 students. At the same time 4,471,415 pupils were registered in 10,452 elementary schools of the parishes and institutes, and 85,201 in 450 private elementary schools. After 1964 began a downward trend in proportion to the previous numbers of registrations, not only in the Catholic but also in the public schools.

During this period Catholic schools were affected by several state laws on which, one after the other, decisions were rendered by the Supreme Court of the United States. In 1922 the voters of Oregon approved a petition in which it was required that, with a few expressly named exceptions, all children from age 8 to age 16 had to attend public schools from September 1926, in connection with which parents or guardians who disobeyed this law were to be condemned to a fine or prison or—in each case according to the seriousness—to both. Two societies of Freemasons claimed the authorship of this law, and the Ku Klux Klan, along with other secret societies, supported it with the assertion that only in public schools could children be taught to respect and maintain the free institutions of the nation. Religious prejudice, patriotic zeal, and nationalistic mistrust were the chief motives for the advocates of this law. Both the already existing and the recently founded Catholic organizations resisted, and even several Protestant groups issued declarations in which the law was condemned. The Sisters of the Holy Names of Jesus and Mary, who operated several schools in Oregon, and the Mill Hill Academy filed motions for the issuance of a temporary injunction by which the state should be forbidden to put the law into effect. After the District Court of the United States had issued the injunction in 1924, the state attorney general of Oregon appealed to the Supreme Court. But in the meantime the legislature of Michigan had agreed that constitutional amendments on voting should be submitted to the voters whereby the parochial schools in this state should be abolished. But in 1924 these proposals were rejected by considerable majorities, after similar proposals there had already been rejected four years earlier. In 1925 the Supreme Court of the United States declared the Oregon law unconstitutional, confirmed the rights of parents, and set limits to state authority. This decision annulled all other attempts to do away with Catholic schools by way of legislation.

In the following period other states sought to assist in various ways children who attended nonpublic schools, but these were attacked in the courts. In 1930 the Supreme Court confirmed as constitutional a law of Louisiana which allowed the state to supply textbooks to children in all schools. This decision was based on the theory that not the schools themselves or their administrators, the churches, were the beneficiaries of such state grants, but the children. This theory of "child benefit" became the justification for the asking of state aid for children in private schools. In the celebrated case *Everson* vs. *Board of Education* the Supreme Court in 1947 recognized as constitutional a law of New Jersey, which approved the use of public funds to reimburse parents for expenses incurred by transporting their children to all schools, public or private. Nevertheless, only less than half of all states put buses at the disposal of children who attended private schools. In 1968 the Supreme Court of the United States decided that neither the individual state constitution nor the Constitution of the United States was violated by a law of the state of New York which demanded that the public schools lend nonreligious schoolbooks to pupils in private schools, including the parochial, in grades seven through twelve. In the same year the state of Pennsylvania granted direct payment of public money to private schools for services in nonreligious school subjects. But the Supreme Court of the United States later declared this law invalid because the concept of the "purchase of services" was incompatible with the First Amendment to the U.S. Constitution. The constitutions of thirty-three states forbade any use of public funds for the support of denominational schools.

Some bishops and other Catholics had, besides, not wanted any state aid for their schools, because they feared an interference, joined with it, of the state into the Church's control of the schools. In 1961 the administrative committee NCWC stated that the federal government, if it generally supported the school system, must also give to Catholic children the right to claim support, because they were otherwise victims of a discriminatory legislation. Nevertheless, Congress excluded nonpublic schools from the aid which it granted to the schools in specific districts, in which special burdens were laid on the local taxpayers by a federal institution. The 1965 Elementary and Secondary Education Act, also called the Johnson Education Act, included also the children of private schools by granting them a share in specific special programs, which were undertaken by a local educational office and implemented by a public school; thus, for example, courses for the physically handicapped or socially ill-adapted children, supplementary classes in reading and mathematics, library services, health and food services, books, and even clothing—of course, only for children from low income families. The constitutionality of this law was doubted by various groups, as by Protestants and other Americans United for the Separation of Church and State, by the American Jewish Congress, and by the American Civil Liberties Union, all of which constantly strove to prevent any public aid, even indirect, for Catholic schools.

The regulations for the imparting of religious instruction to Catholic children who attended public schools varied according to the laws of the particular states. There arose controversies over other stipulations according to which pupils were granted absence from the public schools for a specified time to enable them to take part in religious instruction. When in 1948 an objection was raised before the Supreme Court of the United States to a plan approved by the legislature of the state of Illinois, the Supreme Court forbade the imparting of religious instruction on the premises of public schools during school hours and declared such a practice a violation of the First Amendment. However, four years later the same court declared that "released time" programs were constitutional if the pupils left the public school during regular school hours in order to receive denominational religious instruction. In 1964 there were 1,119,800 students in public high schools on released time and 3,067,794 pupils in elementary schools on leave of absence who received Catholic religious instruction.

Responsibility for the assuring of religious instruction for these children in public schools was entrusted to the Confraternity of Christian Doctrine. Although the confraternity had been introduced in the United States as early as 1902, it had grown only slowly until Pius XI issued his motu proprio *Orbem Catholicum* in 1923. The best-known promoter of the Confraternity in the United States was Edwin V. O'Hara, first bishop of Great Falls, Montana (1930–39), then of Kansas City, Missouri (1939–56); he was also chairman of the Bishops' Commission from its founding in 1934 until his death in 1956. Under his leadership a Catholic center was erected in Washington, D.C., in 1933 to provide information and advice to the diocesan organizations. Besides the instruction of children who attended public schools, the confraternity organized in many places programs for religious vacation courses, discussion clubs for parents, teachers, and adults, special religious courses for handicapped children, correspondence courses in religion, training centers for lay teachers of religion, university retreats, religious radio programs, and an apostolate of goodwill which was aimed at those outside the Church. In 1935 the first national Catechetical Congress was held in Rochester, New York, and this was then followed by yearly congresses until 1941, when a five-year cycle was introduced. The publications department of the national center published an information service, which was intended especially for diocesan directors, and also textbooks and other practical literature. In the early 1940s the confraternity subsidized revisions of the several editions of the Baltimore Catechism and a new translation of the Bible. It introduced the new catechetical methods and techniques developed in Europe and adapted them to American needs.

In the area of higher education there were in 1964 295 Catholic colleges and universities, in which 366,172 students were registered. The Catholic colleges had increased in this period; between 1914 and 1956 thirty colleges for men were opened, but in the last-mentioned year nine of them were again closed. Thirty-seven colleges for women were founded between 1915 and 1925, and nineteen between 1925 and 1930; in 1950 there were 116 colleges for women and in 1970 there were 137. Some Catholic colleges were too small to be able to maintain an academic level; some were so close to one another geographically that they competed for potential students, and none of them was adequately equipped. But the Catholic institutions of the higher educational system received, in contrast to the Catholic elementary and secondary schools, some state aid directly. Thus, for example, the veterans of World War II and of the Korean War obtained federal funds for instruction and livelihood, regardless of what educational institution they decided on, and the National Defense Education Act of 1958, which was intended to improve instruction in mathematics, natural science, engineering, and modern languages and in 1964 was extended also to English, geography, and other fields, made no distinction in regard to Catholic colleges and universities; it even granted loans for schools of the middle level which belonged to the Church. Federal officials made agreements with such schools for research projects or granted them subsidies for this purpose, and there were also federal funds at their disposal for the construction of buildings.

In the late 1950s 9 Catholic universities had graduate schools, which could grant doctoral degrees, but half of them restricted their doctoral program to a few fields. The Catholic universities and colleges also instituted many professional school faculties. In 1955 23 of them had professional schools for management or commerce and finance, 6 for medicine, 21 for law, 12 for engineering and architecture, 14 for nursing, 10 for education, 8 for dentistry, 5 for pharmacy, 4 for music, 6 for social service, 2 for industrial relations, 1 for diplomacy, 1 for physical education, 1 for journalism, and 1 for oratory. Many other Catholic colleges and universities had programs for some of these professional areas but they had not organized them as separate professional schools. In 1936, furthermore, 42 Catholic teachers' seminars were conducted; but when colleges and universities began to offer programs in pedagogy the number of teachers' seminars declined. In 1955 there were 3 diocesan teachers' colleges and 21 normal teachers' seminars which were under Catholic direction; of the latter a few were only for the members of religious institutes, while others also admitted lay persons as students.

The Newman Movement was organized for the religious instruction and pastoral care of the ever growing number of Catholic students who attended secular universities and colleges. By 1925 a few bishops and priests, especially Jesuits, attacked the concept of such Catholic foundations as that which had begun in 1920 at the University of Illinois to offer religious courses recognized at the university; the opponents feared that a positive program of religious instruction would attract students to the secular universities who would otherwise have gone to Catholic colleges. The educational importance of the Newman apostolate was not officially recognized until 1962, when the College and University Division of the National Catholic Educational Association completed its regulations to the effect that it gave membership to Newman educational centers, even if not full membership.

The Federation of Catholic College Clubs was established in New York City in 1915; although it consisted officially only of student clubs, it was in reality directed by the faculties, alumni, and chaplains. In 1938 it became the Newman Club Federation. Due to the efforts of its chaplain general, John W. Keough, who watched over its growth from 1917 to 1935, it successfully resisted the persistent opposition. In fact, for many years it was merely tolerated by the church authorities. But in 1941 it obtained full membership in the College and University Division of the National Council of Catholic Youth, which had been instituted by the American hierarchy. Then it acquired a permanent headquarters with a managing secretary in the Youth Division of the NCWC. After World War II the number of full-time chaplains rapidly grew, and in 1950 the National Newman Chaplains Association was established as an organization. In addition to the meetings and institutes which it offered, in 1962 it opened an institution for the training of new chaplains. In order to gain Catholic teachers and administrators from secular institutions for these unions, the National

Newman Association of Faculty and Staff was called into being in 1959. In 1962 the various national organizations were united and formally approved as constituents of the National Newman Apostolate, which for its part became a fully qualified section in the Youth Division of the NCWC. In the meantime religious sisters and brothers and educated laymen in ever greater numbers had been appointed to the staffs of the Catholic centers and parishes that were reproducing themselves at secular universities in order to support the chaplains with their teaching and pastoral tasks. In 1965 there were 250 full-time chaplains and 1,022 part-time chaplains who worked in 203 Newman Centers and in other quarters determined by chance at more than 900 secular institutions and there cared for more than 800,000 Catholic students.

American Catholics were also concerned with creating special possibilities of education for blacks. The Sisters of the Blessed Sacrament for Indians and Colored People, established by Mother Katharine Drexel, erected many elementary and high schools for blacks in the South. With the financial support of the foundress, the sisters opened Xavier University of Louisiana, for which the arrangements were concluded in 1918; colleges for the humanities and natural sciences, for teachers and for pharmacy were opened at the beginning of the 1920s, and in 1937 a graduate school which offered the master's degree. This was the first and only Catholic university for blacks in the United States. After World War II blacks, including the Catholics, left the rural areas of the South in ever greater numbers for the large cities in the North and the far West, where they were closer to the Church's ministry. Most of the black beneficiaries of Catholic educational work were non-Catholics. The same was true also of the social services performed by Catholics, as, for example, of the Friendship Houses of Catherine De Hueck, of which the first was founded in 1938 in Harlem, the black quarter of New York, and also of Fides House, erected in 1940 at Washington, D.C.

Social Movement

From the end of World War I the Catholic Church in the United States became actively involved in social justice. In 1919 the administrative committee of the National Catholic War Council published an announcement which in the future was called the "Bishops' Program for Social Reconstruction." Its author was Father John A. Ryan, professor of moral theology at the Catholic University of America, who especially by means of his writings on the ethical and economic aspects of the wage system had become the best known and most productive American representative of the social doctrine of Leo XIII. The Bishops' Program was to a great extent intended to counteract the socialist influence on the program for social reconstruction of the British Labour Party; it aimed at improving the conditions of the workers partly by voluntary collaboration in industry and partly by legal measures on the level of the individual states. It was a progressive document, evoking opposition; it proposed concrete reforms, like minimum wages, insurance against unemployment, sickness, and age. Some Catholics and others regarded such reforms as too radical and they were not established in law until the 1930s. In November 1919 the plenary meeting of the bishops published a comprehensive pastoral letter, which contained a section on industrial relations. With reference to Leo XIII they stressed the moral and intellectual aspect of the social question and its solution; they deplored unnecessary strikes, in regard to which only the claims of the mutually struggling parties were considered and the rights of the public were disregarded, and they recommended that a quarrel which could not be settled by discussions between the parties concerned should be submitted to arbitration. They stated that unions of workers or professionals were necessary, but "must be supplemented by societies or meetings which are composed of employers and employees," because they would maintain the common interests rather than the differing strivings of the two parties.

From 1920 the NCWC Department of Social Action was the chief agent for propagating the Church's social doctrine. It published some books and many praiseworthy brochures, it financed lectures in Catholic colleges and universities. In 1922 it founded the Catholic Conference on Industrial Problems, which up to 1940 held almost one hundred national and regional meetings in various places; for it had been proved that this was the most effective method to acquaint both non-Catholics and Catholics with the Church's position. The divisional director, Father Ryan, with his assistant, Father Raymond A. McGowan, developed a general program for industrial democracy, whereby the worker would be made an integrating element of this system. Pius XI's encyclical on the reconstruction of the social order, *Quadragesimo anno,* confirmed many of Ryan's proposals, especially the principle of the living wage, which should include the support of the worker's family.

With different stress, the American Catholics sought to apply the papal social teachings to the sufferings of their country during the Great Depression. Because Ryan based his economic analysis chiefly on the underconsumption theory of John A. Hobson, he was extremely critical of President Hoover's caution and cordially welcomed the policy of his successor. President Franklin D. Roosevelt invited Ryan to serve as policy adviser for the New Deal, and in 1934 he became a member of the industrial professional committee of the National Recovery Administration. He regarded as the climax of his life's work the Fair Labor Standards Act of 1938, the first law that prescribed a minimum wage and maximum weekly hours for the employees of firms which were involved in interstate commerce. But because Ryan trusted in the state as the only institution which could provide social justice, he was opposed by other Catholics, who feared that the centralizing of power in the federal government was dangerous for a religious minority and who were more uneasy than appeared to him to be justified by the threats from secularism, Communism, war, and the welfare state.

Finally, Ryan came into open conflict with the so-called Radio Priest, Charles E. Coughlin, pastor of the Shrine of the Little Flower at Royal Oak, Michigan. The latter had achieved national fame because at the beginning of the depression he had boldly attacked the abuses in the American economic system and offered remedies inspired by *Rerum novarum* and later by *Quadragesimo anno.* His ordinary, Bishop Michael James Gallagher of Detroit, encouraged him to propagate the social teachings of the papal encyclicals and remained his confidant, adviser, supporter, and defender until his death in 1937. Although Coughlin always stressed the right to private property, he found fault with the old industrial capitalism or plutocracy; he blamed the "international bankers," questioned the possibility of democracy because of the corrupt and self-seeking nature of politicians, supported extensive measures of the government for the economy, protection of the small business people and farmers, and a just wage for workers. In 1936 he founded the weekly newspaper, *Social Justice,* which within one year achieved a circulation of 1 million copies. Cardinal William O'Connell, archbishop of Boston, then publicly criticized Coughlin, even though never using his name, as a hysterical demagogue, and finally other Catholic bishops and priests, newspapers and periodicals, even *Osservatore Romano,* reprimanded him for intolerance of differences of opinion and for mixing in politics. His opponents accused him of seeking the creation of a Fascist dictatorship and mocked his financial proposals. In his extremely popular radio talks on Sunday afternoons he showed a growing disillusionment with American political institutions at the end of the 1930s and championed the establishing of a corporate state for bringing about social justice. In 1938 his newspaper proclaimed and demanded the organization of the Christian Front as a general alliance of Catholics and Protestants against Communism. He openly expressed his antipathy for Jews and suspected them of being Communists who had conspired for the destruction of Christian culture, but he rejected the inevitable reproach of anti-Semitism brought against him. Many Catholics were as ready as were Protestants likewise to regard Jewish "money changers" as responsible for the economic misery of the nation and the world. Cardinal George Mundelein, archbishop of Chicago, and other prominent Catholics from clergy and laity sought to keep the Church aloof from any incitement to racial prejudice and race hatred. Coughlin's newspaper appeared as the advocate of the Fascist regimes in Germany and Italy, because they opposed Communism, but he himself professed to be anti-Nazi. He preached nationalism, isolationism, and hatred of England when international tensions were deteriorating into armed conflict. At the end of 1940 he was put off the radio because both the national networks and the local stations declined to renew his contracts for broadcasting. In 1942 the government obtained the suspension of the newspaper *Social Justice* by the threat of a suit because of the crime of insurrection, allegedly begun with its opposition to the war. The new archbishop of Detroit, Edward Mooney, commanded Coughlin to discontinue all public statements. Nonpartisan judgments admitted that this priest was sincerely disturbed by the misery of the poor and the Communist danger and denied that he was a Fascist, but they conceded that he understood nothing about the economy and that the eclectic solutions which he proposed were ineffectual because of his all too simplistic, unsystematic, and confused analysis of the situation.

Many of the better educated and wealthy Catholics who took no pleasure from Coughlin's proposals founded the league of Social Justice on the national level in 1932 in order to study and apply the economic teachings of Pius XI. The director of this movement was Michael O'Shaughnessy, an oil manager and industrial publicist, who also published the *Social Justice Bulletin* as a monthly for timely events in this area. Although the league never counted more than 10,000 members, it seems to have exercised a widespread influence through the press and various Catholic organizations. It promoted a reform of the capitalist social order through control of the seeking of profit and by industry being forced to consider also the interests of the workers and the public as a whole.

Another search for a solution of the contemporary problems was undertaken by a group which aspired to alleviate the misery of individuals by direct contact and was not prepared to await clerical leadership or trust guidance by the hierarchy. Well known in this group was Dorothy Day, a recently converted journalist, who had previously been a radical activist and Communist. In 1932 she started the Catholic Worker Movement. She took up the idea of a Christian synthesis, as Peter Maurin, an itinerant social thinker from France, proclaimed it; he longed to repair, with the aid of an integral Catholicism, the unity of modern society shattered by secularism. The program advocated by him contained three points: (1) Round-table discussion by workers and intellectuals; (2) Friendship houses, in which Catholics could do justice to their personal responsibility toward the poor by doing works of mercy; (3) Farm communes, in which Catholic workers and students could learn to take care of themselves and build cells for a future Christian social order. Miss Day opened in Manhattan a House of Hospitality, which united the functions of a soup kitchen, a discussion club, and a reform center. Up to 1940 thirty such houses were erected in various cities. On 1 May 1933 she began the publication of the monthly *Catholic Worker,* which presented social doctrine in concrete guiding principles and in a brief time achieved a circulation of over 100,000. In order to supply an example for a really Catholic community and a model for the solution of the problem of unemployment, the Catholic Workers in 1936 established a farm commune in the neighborhood of Easton, Pennsylvania. It received great publicity but also harsh criticism as an example of romantic and utopian agrarianism. In addition to their assistance to the poor by their own voluntary poverty, by manual and intellectual work, and by the bestowing of personal attention, the Catholic Workers took part in strikes and demanded the forming of unions, although, according to their theory, they put little trust in unions or other centralized institutions. They sought by these practical methods to oppose Communist influences, to demonstrate Christian love, to inculcate spiritual values as a counterpole to materialism, and to promote personal sanctification. In addition, they fought anti-Semitism and discrimination against blacks. During the Spanish Civil War they came out for neutrality, and when the danger of America's involvement in World War II grew, many of them became pacifists and refused military service for reasons of conscience. These controversial positions caused internal decline and external repudiations. The strong emphasis on personalism prevented the Catholic Workers from solving the problems of society by an intelligent concept of the relation of the individual to the state and of his confidence in the capability of the government.

In 1937 a group of Catholic Workers, under the direction of John Cort, founded the Association of Catholic Trade Unionists in New York with the aim of making known to their members a knowledge of Catholic social teaching in order that these could then apply its principles in their own unions. Hence it advocated also the spread of the union system and supported justified strikes. It opened an evening school for workers, held training sessions, and published a newspaper, the *Labor Leader.* Other workers' schools, in which the students were instructed in practical subjects, such as public speaking, parliamentary procedure, and Communist tactics, were under the direction of diocesan officials, Jesuits, fraternities, and colleges. In this way more than

7,000 persons were annually prepared to reform and democratize their unions. The Catholics, who were represented in great numbers in the unions and in some even had an overwhelming majority, contributed to the ending of the Communist influence which had threatened the independence of the whole worker movement. When this aim was achieved in the postwar years, the workers' schools and the ACTU turned their efforts to removing other abuses in the unions, as, for example, gangster methods and the exploitation of members by unscrupulous bosses.

Not only the urban industrial workers and craftsmen but also the farmers constituted objects of special concern for the Church in the period between the two world wars. Edwin V. O'Hara had studied the problems of the rural population while he was still a priest of the archdiocese of Portland, Oregon; in 1920 he was invited to set up a bureau for agriculture in the NCWC Department of Social Action. He successfully proved the value of vacation schools for children, of religious correspondence courses for children and adults, and of associations. In 1923 he convened a meeting of Catholic agricultural leaders, at which the National Catholic Rural Life Conference was founded, and he was made its managing secretary. This society later counted thousands of laymen in its ranks, who were organized under diocesan directors and agricultural chairmen in some Catholic societies. In cooperation with the religious and secular organizations in the locality, they promoted committees for the development of communities, cooperative sales societies, credit unions, and educational institutions.

A further aspect of social justice which became consciously clearer to American Catholics in these years was the just treatment of members of the black race. Doctor Thomas W. Turner, a black Catholic teacher at the Hampton Institute in Virginia, in 1917 organized the Committee against the Extension of Race Prejudice in the Church, which made personal appeals to the bishops to do away with prejudice in churches, societies, schools, and seminaries. In order to enlarge the scope of this work there was founded in 1925 a militant organization called Federated Colored Catholics of the United States. In the first five years its leaders were exclusively black. The number of members claimed by them, more than 100,000, probably came from the affiliation of Catholic parishes and parish organizations. Interest in it grew among white clerics and lay persons, and in 1932 this change was reflected in the new title, then adopted, of National Catholic Federation for the Promotion of Better Race Relations.

However, the conscience of white Catholics was only gradually sharpened for the unhappy situation of blacks, and for a long time people were concerned only about local conditions. In 1927 Father John La Farge, S.J., founded the Catholic Laymen's Union, a group of blacks who were active in professional and business life. Seven years later the union convoked a mass meeting at New York, at which, with the approval of the archbishop, Cardinal Patrick Hayes, the first Catholic Interracial Council in the United States came into existence. In the succeeding thirty years more than sixty such associations were created in various places in the nation. Until 1962 Father La Farge was chaplain of the New York society and until 1960 his headquarters was a center of the movement for justice in race relations; he published the monthly *Interracial Review,* formed an exchange office for information, distributed educational materials, and performed advisory services for other societies. However, each society was autonomous, responsible only to the local ordinary, and each decided independently how to bring the influence of Catholic doctrine to bear in its special situation. The chief activity of the societies was of an educational sort. In second place was its aim of eliminating racial discrimination in Catholic churches, schools, hospitals, and other institutions and societies. Finally their efforts should be united with those of other organizations for racial equality and social actions and cooperate with these for the welfare of the community as a whole. In 1960 the Catholic Interracial Councils and similar organizations founded the National Catholic Conference for Interracial Justice, with the aim of assisting the local societies and other Catholic institutions in the development of full-time professional staffs and in their programs; besides, they were to represent the societies on the national level. Their central office in Chicago became the office of exchange of information and a source for publications and technical capabilities. It held national meetings which were attended by their members in great numbers.

After World War II some bishops in the country caused a stir by their decisions in regard to the racial question in their respective dioceses. In 1947 Archbishop Joseph E. Ritter instructed his priests to end racial segregation in the schools of the archdiocese of Saint Louis with the beginning of the school year, and when irritated parents threatened to obtain a temporary court injunction against his orders, he warned them against this, because in accord with Catholic law they would automatically incur excommunication for impeding a bishop in the exercise of his pastoral duties. In 1948 the archbishop of Washington, Patrick A. O'Boyle, began the integration of white and black pupils in the Catholic schools of this archdiocese. In June 1953 Bishop Vincent J. Waters of Raleigh opened all Catholic churches, schools, hospitals, and other institutions in North Carolina to all, regardless of their color, and he did not yield before the severe opposition of some Catholics and non-

Catholics. All these courageous steps had been taken before the Supreme Court of the United States ended racial segregation in the public schools with its famed decision of 17 May 1954. Likewise in 1953 Archbishop Joseph F. Rummel excluded racial segregation also from the churches of the archdiocese of New Orleans after he had first achieved this in Catholic societies and associations. But not until 1962 did he venture to order the end of racial segregation also in the Catholic schools of his archdiocese, and even then he still encountered violent opposition from some lay persons.

Liturgical Movement

The Liturgical Movement was introduced into the United States chiefly by persons who were also interested in social action. The reformers of the liturgy sought to overcome individualism, which both in the Church and in secular society isolated people from one another, and so they aspired to make Catholics more keenly conscious of their membership and solidarity in the mystical body of Christ. The leading representative of this movement, Virgil Michel, a Benedictine monk of Saint John's Abbey, Collegeville, Minnesota, was also a prominent interpreter of the social encyclicals. He had undertaken extensive study journeys to Europe and there consulted the leaders and experts, especially Lambert Beauduin. Michel brought the ideas of liturgical renewal back to the United States and spread them in the monthly *Orate Fratres,* which first appeared in Advent 1926; in 1951 the title was changed to *Worship.* He also founded the Liturgical Press, which publishes texts, books, and brochures. The first liturgical "meeting" was held at Saint John's Abbey in 1929, and since 1940 a national Liturgical Week is held annually with the support of the Benedictine abbeys of the United States. The Benedictine Liturgical Conference, which formed the organ for implementing the annual "weeks," decided to reorganize on a broader basis, and in 1944 it was transformed into an association as the Liturgical Conference. In the 1950s its membership increased, because the liturgical reforms proceeding from Rome drew attention to its activity; this activity was widened to satisfy the requirements of dioceses and parishes. In addition to Michel, who died in 1938, Gerald Ellard, S.J., professor at Saint Mary's College in Kansas, was likewise a pioneer; with his books and periodical articles, in conection with his teaching and lecturing, he promoted the movement in the United States. For a while it encountered the opposition of some conservative prelates, but it gradually put itself across. Lay persons procured hand missals in English in ever larger numbers, and the Dialogue Mass spread more and more. Gregorian chant became better known, after the Pius X School of Liturgical Music, founded at Manhattanville College in 1916, had fostered it. Nonliturgical forms of devotion, like novenas, accordingly lost some of their popularity. Nevertheless, American Catholics were hardly prepared for the fundamental reforms which resulted from the Second Vatican Council.

The Situation in American Society

At least into the 1960s many fellow citizens regarded Catholics with secret distrust and open hostility. Anti-Catholicism was furthered, especially in the South, by periodicals such as *Tom Watson's Magazine,* published by the fanatical United States senator from Georgia, and *The Menace,* whose circulation reached its peak with 1.5 million in 1915. Even after Catholics had in World War I proved their undisputed loyalty, which was maliciously disputed by their enemies, they experienced in the early 1920s a new wave of attacks by the revived Ku Klux Klan, which also denounced and threatened Jews and blacks. The Klan expanded from the South to the Midwest and the far West, and at its peak counted 5 million members; but after 1925 it lost its reputation when the crimes and scandals of its leaders were exposed. When in 1928, for the first time in American history, the Democratic Party nominated a Catholic, Alfred E. Smith, governor of New York, as its presidential candidate, the anti-Catholic forces again stirred up religious hatred by attacking the candidate's Church and contributing to his defeat in the election. Catholics were not only effectively excluded from the highest office in the country, but between 1789 and 1933 only four Catholics held posts in the cabinets of the presidents.

For Catholics the election of Franklin D. Roosevelt signaled the beginning of a new era in American society. Al Smith had roused his fellow Catholics, especially in the big cities, to support the Democratic Party; Roosevelt obtained their devotion by the recognition which he gave them and the skillful treatment which he allotted to them. Many of the American bishops, including first of all Cardinal Mundelein, publicly proclaimed their approval of Roosevelt's policies, especially in the first terms of his administration. And the Catholic press took a generally positive attitude toward the New Deal. However, many Catholic leaders and newspapers deplored the president's decision to recognize the Soviet Union and to institute diplomatic relations with it, although they appreciated the efforts he made in the negotiations to secure guarantees of religious freedom. The Knights of Columbus and others also strongly criticized his silence and inaction in regard to the persecution of Catholics by the Mexican government. When Father Coughlin, who had supported Roosevelt at the beginning of his presidency, later attacked him both because of his economic policy, especially in regard to currency, credit, and banks, and also because of his alleged favoring of Communism, Monsignor John A. Ryan defended the president in 1936 in a national radio address. In the previous year Coughlin had founded the National Union for Social Justice, which was intended to act as a lobby of the people or as a civic-minded non-partisan force, to give emphasis to the demand for legal mooring of those reform principles which he extracted from the papal encyclicals and in keeping with this to work for the nomination and election of like-minded candidates to Congress in each party; it attained a membership of perhaps 5 million, especially among the workers of Irish and German descent in the East and Midwest, and it also achieved some of its goals. Later the radio priest created the Union Party and chose as its presidential candidate William Lemke, for whom he then conducted in 1936 an energetic but, as it finally turned out, useless election campaign.

Because of the well-known opposition of the Church to Communism, anti-Catholic propaganda declined during the Cold War. Nevertheless, some loud opponents continued to find public attention. The most notorious among them was Paul Blanshard, who directed his diatribes against the Church's authoritarian and antiliberal principles and accused the hierarchy of undermining American values and the ideals of freedom and democracy. He was the chief spokesman for an organization which had been founded in 1947 and called itself Protestants and Other Americans United for the Separation of Church and State, later Americans United for the Separation of Church and State. It worked with a great display of votes to prevent any public aid to parochial schools, which it designated as divisive and un-American; it also denied to any Catholic the ability to hold a public office. The nomination of another Catholic by the Democratic Party in 1960, John F. Kennedy, evoked a new outburst of antireligious feeling, and the candidate deemed it necessary to deny beforehand that the Church could exercise any influence at all on his official decisions. Political scientists have stated that many people who normally belonged to the Democratic Party voted against Kennedy because of his religion. After he had been elected by a very slender majority, he consistently resisted all proposals to support at least those parents who had to bear extra expenses so that they could send their children to Catholic schools. His electoral victory, his nonpartisan administration of his office, and his unusual popularity among all classes of the population lessened anti-Catholicism as a force in American society, and two years after his tragic death the declaration of the Second Vatican Council on religious liberty confirmed this effect still more; the American bishops had especially insisted on it.

When on 23 December 1939 President Roosevelt named Myron C.

Taylor, an Episcopalian, as his personal representative to Pope Pius XII with the rank of ambassador, an anti-Catholic outcry was raised. Taylor's job was to establish a connection between the two leading personalities in the promotion of peace and to coordinate the assistance of the Vatican and of the United States during and after the war. When Protestants protested strongly against the sending of an ambassador as a violation of the principle of the separation of state and Church, and demanded the ambassador's recall, Roosevelt insisted that this temporary mission did not involve the establishment of diplomatic relations. Although the opponents declared their opposition again at the end of the war, Taylor exercised his office until his recall in 1950. In October 1951 President Harry Truman nominated General Mark Clark as ambassador at the Vatican, but the Protestants raised such a storm of indignation that the president later withdrew the nomination at the general's request, before it was discussed in the Senate.

The Position of the Church in International Affairs

The unfriendly attitude of many of their fellow citizens did not deter the American Catholics from giving their opinion on international affairs. At the outbreak of World War I most writers in Catholic newspapers and periodicals advocated neutrality, and many, especially in the Midwest, even took the side of the Central Powers. Catholics of Irish birth or descent were of course against the British, and the German Catholic *Centralverein* pledged its total sympathy to Germany in 1914. Although a few bishops, such as Cardinal James Gibbons of Baltimore, praised President Woodrow Wilson for not intervening in the conflict in Europe, the majority of American Catholics opposed the foreign policy of the government, which favored the Allies, and, as it seems, the majority voted in the presidential election of 1916 for the Republican candidate. Some of the leading Catholics, however, admonished their coreligionists not to tread upon the sensitivities of other Americans by participating in German-American efforts for union or entering into partisan politics. But as soon as the United States had entered the war, a wave of patriotism drowned all pro-German inclinations.

After the war American Catholics generally opposed Wilson's peace policy, partly because he refused to work for the independence of Ireland. They brought forward many reasons against the anticipated entry of the United States into the League of Nations and, together with the majority of their fellow citizens, took refuge in isolationism. However, a few leaders, such as Father John A. Ryan, Judge Martin T. Manton, and Professor Carlton J. H. Hayes founded in 1927 the Catholic Association for International Peace for the instruction "of all men of good will on their obligation" to bring about world peace by justice and charity. The association championed many measures which were later realized, as, for example, for technical support and foreign aid. From Wilson's first administration to Roosevelt's second, American Catholics urged the government incessantly but vainly to intervene in Mexico in favor of the persecuted Catholics.

Even before World War II the American bishops at the request of the German hierarchy had supported all who had to flee from persecution by the Nazis by means of the Catholic Committee for Refugees and Refugee Children, founded by them. In 1940 they founded the Bishops' War Emergency and Relief Committee and took up a special collection in all churches for its support. The next year began the annual collections on *Laetare* Sunday for support of victims of war among the people of fifteen nations and among those who had sought refuge in various places in Europe and the Middle East. In 1942 the bishops established the War Relief Services, and in the next year this obtained the certificate for admission to the National War Fund, from which they obtained financial support until 1947. Meanwhile, the bishops continued the *Laetare* Sunday collections to obtain money for purely religious tasks, to which belonged special applications for aid from the Holy See and from numerous bishops and Catholic organizations abroad. In 1947, they expanded their annual appeal for donations in order to support the comprehensive program for help overseas, for rehabilitation, and for resettlement, which the War Relief Services had carried out. Even before the ending of hostilities the War Relief Services began their operations in the countries freed from the Axis Powers in Europe, Africa, and Asia. Shortly after the war's end there began also comprehensive aid programs in the hitherto hostile countries: Germany, Austria, Hungary, and Japan. But the assistance actions which were under way in Poland, Hungary, Czechoslovakia, Rumania, and Yugoslavia were forbidden by the Communist governments of these countries. Although the War Relief Services originally were to be only an institution for a limited time, it was later understood that they were permanently needed; and so in 1955 their name was changed to Catholic Relief Services of the NCWC. Because of their connections with local agencies and their expanding network of aid programs, the Catholic Relief Services were in the position of making full use of the surplus food which the American government in the 1950s destined for overseas assistance. In addition, they distributed clothing which Catholics had donated in the yearly collection at Thanksgiving. At the end of 1963 the Catholic Relief Services had shipped overseas food, clothing, medicines, and other means of help with a total weight of 5.6 million tons and a total value of $1.25 billion and had distributed these to needy persons and institutions. They helped more than 400,000 refugees settle in the United States or in other havens. They extended their field of activity to more than seventy countries, especially to the newly arising nations of Africa and the underdeveloped countries of Latin America, in which connection they promoted with greater emphasis than before technical aid, such as projects of self-help, which was intended to end social injustices, economic situations of dearth, sickness, and ignorance. In this way from the Catholic Relief Services came the greatest voluntary private organization for providing aid of the United States overseas.

American Catholics displayed their feeling of responsibility for other countries also by encouraging the foreign missions with personnel and money. Before World War I only a few Americans had gone abroad to proclaim the message of faith. Although the first religious congregation which was established in the United States for this purpose, namely, the Catholic Foreign Mission Society of America, usually called Maryknoll Missioners, founded by James A. Walsh and Thomas F. Price, had been approved by the American bishops and allowed, as an experiment, by Pius X as early as 1911, the first group of missioners under Price's leadership and with South China as goal, did not leave until 1918. In the postwar years many other religious institutes, especially the Society of Jesus, also sent men and women to the foreign missions. In 1958 Cardinal Richard Cushing, archbishop of Boston, founded the Missionary Society of Saint James the Apostle for the restoring and preserving of the faith in Latin America; it was to consist of diocesan priests, who voluntarily obliged themselves for five years, and they were to develop among the poor a life in the parish community. Within five years there were ninety-three members from nineteen different dioceses in English-speaking countries. Earlier, in 1950, the Grail, an international lay movement of Catholic women, had begun a regular course of training for the missionary apostolate of the laity. A lay organization for men and women was approved under the title of Papal Volunteers for Latin America. Within three years 245 papal volunteers served without pay, usually for a period of three years, in twelve countries; they were invited by the local bishops and were active predominantly in the area of education, medicine, and social work.

In 1966 9,303 American priests, brothers, sisters, and men and women from the lay state worked in many countries of America, Asia, and Latin America. American Catholics supplied donations to the missionary institutes and the papal work for the propagation of the faith; in 1919 the total sum for this already amounted to more than $1 million per year, and in 1966 alone the sum for the papal work was approximately $16 million.

Lay Movements

In the decades following World War I laymen began to display a greater activity in the Church. The National Council of Catholic Men and the National Council of Catholic Women were established under the National Catholic Welfare Conference in 1920 as a merger of parochial, supraparochial, diocesan, individual state, and national organizations. By 1965 about 10,000 organizations with a total membership of about 9 million joined the National Council of Catholic Men, and 14,000 organizations with almost 10 million members the National Council of Catholic Women. Both parent organizations created a broadly conceived program for spirituality, information, civic and social action, family life, youth, and international affairs. They provided aid to the affiliated organizations in the planning and implementation of local programs. Of course, in most places they operated by means of diocesan societies of Catholic men and women. The national associations represented the Catholic laity in other national and international organizations and at meetings of both a religious and a secular sort, and also in committees of Congress. To the men's council was given the responsibility for all Catholic radio and television programs, which were regularly broadcast on the national networks. The best known program was the "Catholic Hour," which was broadcast from 1930 by the National Broadcasting Company. In 1971 the two associations united as the National Council of Catholic Laity.

Two specialized lay movements acquired national importance. The Cana Conference began as a series of retreats which Father John P. Delaney, S.J., conducted in Saint Louis in 1944. Such meetings, which were more unstructured and relaxed than spiritual exercises in the strict sense, were intended to apply religious principles to the secular aspects of married life in a manner which was sensible to twentieth-century Americans. These meetings instilled community sense and led to the forming of Cana Clubs for regular study and prayer in the homes of participants together with a chaplain. A further result was participation in the social apostolate to a greater extent. In most dioceses directors of family life were appointed, and thousands of priests and lay persons were gained for the implementing and spreading of this movement. In addition, numerous Pre-Cana Conferences for engaged couples spread, and for widowed persons Naim Conferences, also called Post-Cana Clubs, were formed. The Bethany Conference was a further extension for single persons.

A similar function was performed by the Christian Family Movement, which had begun in Chicago as a Catholic Action group for men and in 1947 was transformed into an organization for married couples by Mr.

and Mrs. Patrick Crowley. The basic units consisted of from five to six couples, usually from the same parish, who met in their homes and carried out a program for discussions and actions in the area of the lay apostolate. These units rapidly increased; by 1963 more than 40,000 couples actively took part in the group meetings that occurred every two weeks in the United States and Canada; in other countries there was probably an equally large number. In 1949 a national coordinating committee with headquarters in Chicago was set up to exchange ideas and reports of experiences with the help of some publications and annual programs. The members of every group were to examine from time to time a special aspect of family, cultural, political, economic, or international life, come to a judgment on whether it was entirely humane and Christian, and then decide possible actions, which were to be undertaken by the couples, either individually or collectively. Most participants, however, were chiefly interested in family problems, as, for example, the rapidly increasing national divorce rate.

Other organizations of Catholic Action which had begun in the United States after World War II were the Young Christian Workers and the Young Christian Students, which had been founded on the European model. In the same period the Exercises Movement led to a deepening of the spiritual life of the laity in the midst of secular professional activity. Catholic professional societies likewise prospered.

Journalism

After World War I the Catholic press underwent a noteworthy development. The ownership of most newspapers was transferred by lay persons to the dioceses. But even then, when a diocesan weekly newspaper was designated as "official organ" or "the voice" of the local authorities, a distinction was made between authoritative views of the Church and the opinions of the publisher. There now also appeared Catholic newspaper chains. In 1929 the newspaper *Catholic Register,* which had begun five years earlier with the publication of a national edition, published at Denver under the direction of Monsignor Matthew J. W. Smith its first edition for another diocese, and within nine years this system increased to nineteen editions, with a circulation of 400,000; in 1964 it had thirty-three editions with a total circulation of 778,196. The paper *Our Sunday Visitor,* which had been founded in 1912 by Father, later Bishop, John Francis Noll of Fort Wayne, Indiana, chiefly for apologetic purposes as a reaction to anti-Catholic and pro-Socialist newspapers, began in 1937 the publication of an edition for another diocese; in 1964 it produced eleven diocesan editions, a Canadian national edition, and a national news edition, with a total circulation of 892,148. Other chains of smaller size were formed in Ohio and Wisconsin. In 1969 there were eighty-nine locally published diocesan papers with a total circulation of 4,229,065.

The first larger Catholic daily newspaper in English in the United States was the *Tribune,* founded in 1920 at Dubuque, Iowa, by Nicholas E. Gonner, and two years later moved to Milwaukee, Wisconsin. It was strongly apologetic in tone. After Gonner's death the book publisher William George Bruce bought it along with others and continued it until 1942. Another Catholic daily, the *Sun Herald,* was started in 1950 at Kansas City, Missouri, by a group of Catholic laymen under the leadership of Robert Hoyt, but the next year it was stopped because of insufficient subscriptions. A few of this lay group in 1964 began the *National Catholic Reporter.* This weekly became very familiar among liberal Catholics, because it gave religious news without restrictions and critically interpreted it; it even incurred censure from the bishop of Kansas City, but this was ineffective.

In order to supply Catholic newspapers with news on national and international affairs the NCWC News Service was established in 1920; it took over the work of a smaller agency which had previously been operated by the Catholic Press Association of the United States and Canada. It erected an overseas service, hired correspondents in almost every part of the world, obtained subscriptions in sixty-five countries, and finally supplied services for leading articles, pictures, radio, and eventually also for television and some other services. The Catholic Press Association, founded in 1911, also held annual meetings, published a monthly and a historical "annual," and promoted the increase of circulation and the advertising business; it likewise especially supported the Catholic press in Latin America and the mission press in general.

Catholic newspapers in foreign languages appeared and again disappeared during this period. Among German publications some continued even after World War I, such as the important daily *Amerika* at Saint Louis, which ended in 1924. In 1936 there still were twenty-three German-language Catholic papers, but in World War II they all stopped or changed over to English, as did *The Wanderer* of Saint Paul. Of the ten papers in Polish which existed in 1940, all suspended appearance in the succeeding years except for the *Dziennik Chicagoski (Polish Daily News),* which the Resurrectionists had founded in 1890 and which also supplied local, national, and international news. Also two Italian weeklies, *La Voce del Popolo,* founded at Detroit in 1910 and *Il Crociato,* founded in 1933 by the diocese of Brooklyn, continued to appear after World War II. Newspapers in Spanish and in a few Slavonic languages in addition to Polish were also published under Catholic patronage. In 1964 there were altogether thirteen foreign-language papers with a total circulation of 195,434.

Among Catholic magazines those prospered which were concerned with the home and foreign missions. *Extension,* the organ of the Catholic Church Extension Society (founded in 1906), in 1963 provided 400,000 readers every month not only with news on the mission work fostered by the society in the United States, but also articles of general interest. The first magazine which promoted the foreign missions exclusively was published by the Maryknoll Missioners, first under the title *Field Afar* and later *Maryknoll.* In the 1960s it increased its circulation to more than 300,000.

Magazines which had been founded before World War I continued to exist side by side. The organ of the Third Order of Saint Francis, *St. Anthony Messenger,* had begun in 1893 and became a popular family magazine, which in 1960 had a circulation of 330,000. The oldest Catholic newspapers which appeared at this time were the *Catholic World* of the Paulists, in which the effort was made to bring the faith into relation with American society, and *Ave Maria* of the Congregation of the Holy Cross, which aspired to form family life in a Christian way. Other magazines published by religious institutes with a broad circulation were: the *Messenger of the Sacred Heart* (1886, by Jesuits), the *Liguorian* (1913, by Redemptorists), the *Sign* (1921, by Passionists), and the *Voice of St. Jude* (1913), later called the *U.S. Catholic* (by Claretians). The two most important opinion-forming weeklies were *America,* begun in 1909 and published by Jesuits, and *Commonweal,* begun in 1924 and published by lay persons, both of which sought to treat contemporary problems and cultural themes from a Catholic standpoint. The *Catholic Digest* had a circulation of 650,000 in 1964. In the same year there were published fifty-nine consumer magazines with a total circulation of 7,042,996, fifty business and professional magazines with a circulation of 455,931, 241 magazines which accepted no advertisements with a total circulation of 12,934,017, and twenty-four foreign-language magazines with a total circulation of 228,988, under Catholic patronage. In the next five years these numbers quickly dropped. Nevertheless, the total circulation of the Catholic press in the United States in 1969 amounted to 25,599,766.

By 1964 journalism was offered as an academic course in one form or another in about half the Catholic universities and colleges in the United States. The only College of Journalism was founded in 1915 at Marquette University in Milwaukee, but graduate study in the mass media was later likewise instituted in other Catholic institutions. In recent years ever more courses in radio and television were offered. In the academic programs both technical courses in theory and practice of the various communications media were contained, as well as theoretical courses on their role in society and their professional ethics.

Statistics prove that the connection of Catholics with their Church dropped considerably before 1968, when Pope Paul VI issued the encyclical *Humanae Vitae.* A famous sociologist of religion refers the decline of traditional forms of church practice, for example, attendance at Sunday Mass, to the strong repudiation on the part of many of the faithful to the teaching contained in this papal document on birth control. Other analysts are of the view that rather a whole complex of various factors played a role: the growing secularism, an exaggrated personalism, thorough permissiveness, libertinism, and antinomianism, an anti-"Establishment" attitude and religious indifferentism, as has been characteristic of the manner of thought in the United States and in many other countries of the free world since the beginning of the 1960s. The loss of respect for Pope and bishops is due to the fact that certain theologians publicly and at times loudly held themselves aloof from declarations of the *magisterium.* The most important Protestant Churches in the United States experienced a similar downward trend; only the smaller fundamentalist and Pentecostal sects, which appealed to special revelations or made lofty demands on their adherents, have grown disproportionately. Although the teachings and reforms of the Second Vatican Council were generally greeted by American Catholics, the hope and expectation of a new flowering of the Church in the United States have not been realized in the postconciliar period.

CANADA

Population

Between 1911 and 1961 Canada's total population rose from 7,206,643 to 18,238,247 inhabitants. In this period the number of Catholics increased from 2,841,881—39.4 percent—to 8,342,826—45.7 percent. However, Catholics were not uniformly distributed: 56 percent lived in the province of Quebec. When in 1951 Catholics constituted 44.7 percent of the Canadian total population, they were divided among the individual provinces according to the following percentages: 88.0 in Quebec, 50.6 in New Brunswick, 45.5 in Prince Edward Island, 40.6 in the Northwest Territory, 34.0 in Nova Scotia, 33.6 in Newfoundland, 28.5 in Saskatchewan, 28.3 in Manitoba, 25.7 in Ontario, 23.8 in Alberta, 20.9 in the Yukon, and 15.0 in British Columbia. In the same year the Catholic population, according to nationalities, was distributed thus: 66.7 percent French, 7.9 Irish, 5.9 English, 3.5 Ukrainian, 2.9 Scottish, 2.6 Polish, 2.5 German, 2.2 Italian, 1.4 native

Indian, and 4.4 other. The percentage of Catholics within each individual nationality amounted to 96.7 of the French, 34.5 of the Irish, 10.2 of the English, 56 of the Ukrainians, 11.8 of the Scots, 74.8 of the Poles, 24.7 of the Germans, 89.6 of the Italians, and 53.5 of the native Indians.

Organization

In 1914 there were ten archdioceses, twenty-five dioceses, five vicariates apostolic, one Ruthenian bishop, and one prefecture apostolic. Fifty years later there were fifteen archdioceses of the Latin Rite—fourteen provinces plus Winnipeg—one province of the Ukrainian Byzantine Rite, forty dioceses, one abbey *nullius,* three eparchies, and eight vicariates apostolic.

Educational System

In each province the Catholic elementary and secondary schools stood in one or another relationship to the secular authorities. In the province of Quebec the schools were regarded as public institutions and were supported by general taxes, but supervised by Catholic and Protestant committees of the Council of Public Instruction. Hence the two systems developed pretty much in independence of each other: The Catholic system followed the French tradition in education, and the Protestant followed the English. Private or independent schools played a more important role in Quebec than in other provinces. The most important were the classical colleges; they offered an eight-year course which one entered upon completing elementary school and which led in two stages of four years each to the bachelor's degree. In 1965 there were thirty-two classical colleges for men and nine for women, which were affiliated to Laval University, and twenty-seven colleges for men and six for women, which were associated with Montreal University.

Newfoundland also had a system of provincial denominational schools. Here the five large denominations operated their own schools under the supervision of a school superintendent, who was responsible to the deputy minister of education of the province. All schools followed the same curriculum.

In Ontario, Saskatchewan, and Alberta the first school which was erected with the support of taxes in one community had always to be a provincial school, open to all children. But the school law allowed Catholic or Protestant minorities to withdraw from the provincial school system and establish their own school-sponsoring bodies and schools, which were termed "separate" schools. The local inhabitants could choose which system they wanted to support with their taxes, and usually they made their choice according to their religion. Both the provincial and the separate schools were subject to the jurisdiction of the provincial Department of Education and both obtained provincial aid. In Saskatchewan and Alberta separate Catholic schools could be erected only in the large cities where Catholics were represented in sufficient number. In Ontario separate schools could offer only the eight elementary and two lower secondary grades; hence Catholics had to erect private schools for the three higher secondary grades.

The provinces on the Atlantic coast—New Brunswick, Nova Scotia, and Prince Edward Island—and Manitoba in accord with the law maintained only provincial schools, but on the basis of a "Gentlemen's Agreement" there were, within the provincial school system in areas where there were many English and French Catholics, also English-language and French-language Catholic schools. Outside the French-language areas of Manitoba, for example, Saint Boniface, the Catholics had also to finance at their own expense their private or parochial schools, in addition to the taxes which they had to pay for the support of the provincial schools.

British Columbia likewise provided only a provincial system, and such schools could under no circumstances be denominational; hence Catholics were forced to support their own schools in addition to the provincial schools. In the Yukon and Northwest, thanks to the collaboration of dominion and local authorities with the denominational bodies, systems had been developed in which Catholic elementary schools for the sparse population of Indians, Eskimos, and whites obtained full support through taxes from the government and the local authorities.

In 1962 nineteen Catholic colleges and universities were authorized to grant academic degrees. They had almost 25,000 students, and another 10,000 attended the colleges affiliated to them, predominantly in Quebec. The total number of 35,000 made up about 30 percent of all the students who were registered in Canadian colleges and universities.

All these institutions were in the east, but they differed considerably in size and capacity. In the coastal provinces there were nine, the largest of which was Saint Francis Xavier University in Antigonish, Nova Scotia, which was under the patronage of the diocese and acquired an international reputation for its research on cooperatives and its adult education. In the province of Quebec, Montreal University, which had been attached for forty years to Laval University in Quebec City, became an independent institution by a document of the provincial government in 1920. In 1954 the University of Sherbrooke obtained a similar charter. In Ontario the University of Ottawa, the first bilingual Canadian university, was run by the Oblates of Mary Immaculate. Saint Michael's College, directed by the Basilian Fathers, was united with the

University of Toronto; it was the first Catholic college of the humanities which agreed to an arrangement whereby it maintained a certain degree of independence but granted its degrees through the university. Assumption University at Windsor, also conducted by the Basilians, likewise became independent in 1953, but ten years later decided to stop granting academic degrees, except in theology, so that it could merge with the new nondenominational University of Windsor. The Laurentian University of Sudbury, which was founded as such in 1960, had been earlier, since 1913, a college run by the Jesuits, and was formally united with Huntington University, an institution of the United Church of Christ.

In western Canada there were no independent Catholic colleges or universities, because the legislators refused to grant to each province more than one academic degree-granting institution. But the Basilians and Jesuits founded colleges, which were united with the provincial universities in various ways or were affiliated to them. Thus, in the sphere of higher education these two orders experimented with new forms of merger with non-Catholic universities for the sake of the academic and economic advantages which they sought thereby.

Social Movement

Various sources gave the theoretical impulse for the Canadian Catholic social movement. In addition to the papal encyclicals, the pastoral letters of the bishops also treated social questions, in which connection they passed from the problems predominantly connected with agriculture and rural life at the beginning of the twentieth century to problems of industrialization and the working class in the later decades. In 1950 the archbishops and bishops of the civil province of Quebec issued a common pastoral letter entitled "The Workers' Problem in the Light of the Church's Social Doctrine," in which they took a bold stand on some points, as, for example, in regard to the codetermination of the worker in the direction of an industry. Two private institutions provided further theoretical fuel: the École Sociale Populaire, founded in 1911, promoted social studies, issued publications, and from 1920 supported the annual *Semaines Sociales du Canada,* which brought together leading personalities of social doctrine and of social action in order to consult together on common concerns. And the École des Sciences Sociales of Laval University, founded in 1932, made noteworthy contributions.

The workers' union (local syndicates), organized on a formally Catholic basis by priests and laymen in various parts of the province of Quebec, merged in 1921 with the *Confédération des Travailleurs Catholiques du Canada.* At first non-Catholics could be members but not hold office. This restriction was gradually ended. Likewise, every union had a chaplain, a Catholic priest, who at first was authorized to inform the bishops of every decision which, in his opinion, was contrary to Catholic social doctrine; in practice, the chaplains rarely exercised this right and finally became merely moral advisers, who attended all meetings and could present their views but had no vote. In its original constitution the *confédération* expressly declared its loyalty to the social doctrine of the Catholic Church, but in 1960 the denominational ties were broken; the expression "Christian principles" was put in their place, and the name was changed to *Confédération des Syndicats Nationaux.* From the late 1930s the Catholic syndicates had about one-third of all members of unions of the province of Quebec in their ranks; the others belonged mainly to international (American) unions. However, the *confédération* exercised on the worker movement as a whole and on worker legislation an influence which was in no proportion to its size and persumably was based on its social and ideological concerns.

An expressly Catholic movement was also started for workers in agriculture. In 1924 2,400 farmers meeting in Quebec city founded the *Union Catholique des Cultivateurs.* This organization defended and fostered the general interests of the rural population, especially in regard to the educational system. In the 1950s it also established rural syndicates in order to deal collectively with the buyers of farm products. In 1965 there were almost 700 local syndicates with more than 50,000 members as opposed to a possible membership of 65,000 to 70,000. As in the workers' syndicates, the role of the chaplain developed from that of a participant exercising power to that of a moral adviser or attorney, but the word "Catholic" was not removed from the organization's name.

For Catholic manufacturers and employers there was no permanent organization until the *Association Professionnelle des Industriels* was founded in 1943. It was intended to protect the interests of management and promote a Christian social order. In 1965 it numbered ca. 500 members, who for the most part belonged to small or medium firms. Despite its limitation it played a leading role and, it is true, by cooperation with other groups, in which regard it directed the attention of management to the working class and to the human problems in business life. It was also an active member of the *Union Internationale Chrétienne des Dirigeants d'Entreprise.*

CHAPTER 24

The Church in Latin America*

In Latin America lives about one-third of the world's Catholic population, but its internal strength does not correspond to its statistical strength. The causes go back partly to the colonial period, others were added from the time of emancipation at the beginning of the nineteenth century and have grown still stronger. The structure of the population was decided by the political-economic domination of the former colonial masters, the Spaniards and Portuguese, who did not, it is true, like the white immigrants to North America, decimate the original inhabitants—the Indians—or force them into reservations; however, the Christian mission did not succeed in overcoming pagan magic and the corresponding morality among them. The immigration from Europe, especially to Argentina and Brazil, strengthened the white element, whose interbreeding with Indians and the black slaves brought from Africa produced a third unstable element of mestizos and mulattoes respectively.

The biggest problem confronting the Church was the unequal distribution of landed property. The white upper class in large-scale operations cultivated the greatest part of the productive acreage available and kept the peasants in extreme poverty. Similar social tensions existed in the mines, for example, in Bolivia, and in the industrial areas of rapidly growing vast cities, such as São Paulo and Buenos Aires, with high unemployment and slums. The market difficulties of the raw materials countries as a consequence of the world economic crisis promoted the pauperization of the masses.

The Church's proclamation in preaching and catechetics was in many places insufficient, the native clergy was partly inactive and strongly authoritarian. In this way is explained the fact that in almost all countries of Latin America groups of priests were formed who aspired to alter the social structures by nationalization of the means of production and the establishment of Marxism, if necessary by force; in this way the Church would fulfill its true mandate. The episcopate, whom the progressive priest groups more or less correctly charged with supporting the "exploiters," warned against revolution with changing success, but did not from the outset repudiate the socialist experiment of Allende in Chile, though on the other hand it held itself aloof from autocratic regimes, as in Paraguay.

* Félix Zubillaga, S.J.

An indication of the internal weakness of the Latin American Church, and at the same time a contributing cause of the crisis in which it exists, is the lack of native priests and religious, which could be lessened, but not eliminated, by immigration from abroad, especially from Europe—for example, in Bolivia, where there is one priest for 17,000 faithful. Also important, though not yet more important, would be the improvement of the theological and spiritual formation of future priests, for which the *Adveniat* program of the German Catholics hopes to offer help.

The situation of the Church of Latin America was a constant concern of the Popes. Benedict XV strengthened the position of the nuncios, who up to then had been partly *Delegati Apostolici ed Inviati straordinari,* by the decree of 8 May 1916, which stated that these should rank as permanent representatives of the Holy See—*Internuntii Apostolici.* Pius XI improved the diocesan division in almost all countries of Latin America: in Venezuela in 1922–23, in Bolivia in 1924, in Paraguay in 1929, in Colombia and Argentina in 1934, but especially in Brazil, so that "no country in the world, except China, even only approximately experienced so great an increase of its ecclesiastical circumscriptions," as Schmidlin says.

The Latin American episcopate met in connection with the Thirty-Sixth International Eucharistic Congress at Rio de Janeiro from 25 July to 4 August 1955 and established the Latin American Episcopal Conference—*Consejo Episcopal Latino-Americano* (CELAM), which was confirmed by Pius XII on 2 November 1955. The first annual meeting at Bogotá in 1956 enacted its statutes. CELAM supports a permanent secretariat and publishes a monthly *Boletín Informativo.*

The Conference of Medellín from 26 August to 7 September 1968, organized following the Eucharistic Congress of Bogotá and opened by Pope Paul VI, in which 155 bishops and 137 representatives of the priests, sisters, and laity took part, strove for a change in the pastoral and social work of the Church and its uniformity. Cardinal Samorè and the archbishops of Lima and Teresina held the chairmanship as representatives of the Pope. The consultations were based on a "Basic Document" composed by CELAM. The conference stated that in Latin America there existed a "situation of institutionalized power," which justifies a legitimate defense but not a revolutionary uprising. The Church wants to be a "ferment" in the structural changes that are to be quickly sought. Economic, social, and agrarian reform, an *educación liberadora,* are indispensable. Pastoral care must take an interest in the intellectual leadership classes, promote a Christian family policy—up to 40 percent of men over fifteen years old live in *uniones libres*—catechesis must be oriented to social change, and for this purpose the establishment of a catechetical periodical *Catequesis Latinoamericana* with headquarters at Asunción was decreed. It was impressed on the diocesan and religious clergy that, in view of the deep poverty of wide strata, it must itself "live poverty." Following the Conference of Medellín the national episcopates in many pastoral letters set up guidelines for pastoral work and undertook organizational measures.

The ecclesiastical situation in the individual countries of Latin America has developed in such diversity, not least as a consequence of frequent changes of the forms of government and of the governments, that our presentation must be arranged according to countries.

BRAZIL

Brazil has a total area of 8,511,965 square kilometers and in 1976 had 104 million inhabitants; in 1971 89.3 percent were Catholics. About 60 percent are whites, the rest blacks, mulattoes, and other half-castes, only ca. 2 percent are Indians.

Ecclesiastical Organization

In 1957 there were: twenty archdioceses, seventy-seven dioceses, thirty-one prelacies, and one abbey *nullius,* and 3,722 parishes, two-thirds of which were staffed by diocesan priests, one-third by religious, and in which some 30,000 sisters worked.

In 1939 the bishops held a plenary council; since 26 October 1945 there has been an Episcopal Conference (CNBB), which was approved by Pius XII. To it belong the residential bishops of all rites, the coadjutors, auxiliaries, and bishops charged with a special function, and all bishops who have their ecclesiastical residence in Brazil. The functions of the Episcopal Conference include the fostering of cooperation with other episcopal conferences and of contact with the state in concert with the nunciature. Since 1891 there has been separation of church and state; it was abolished in 1934 but reintroduced in 1946.

Lack of Priests

In his letter of 18 December 1910 Pope Pius X wrote: "We are convinced that, in accord with the desires of the Holy See, you will constitute a clergy which will be redemption and light of the world; the laity trained for this will participate in its tasks."[1] Even then the lack of priests was the most serious problem of the Church in Brazil. Pius X wrote to the Brazilian bishops on 6 June 1911: "You must undertake all efforts so that sufficient priests will be at the disposal of the faithful."[2]

---

[1] *BIB,* 106.
[2] Ibid., 106f.

Nevertheless, Pius XI, after the visit of three apostolic delegates, had to state in his letter of 20 January 1927: "Everywhere too few priests, in some areas none at all, hence restricted in their services to the faithful, although religious brothers and sisters from Europe offer great support. It is to be deplored that so few vocations come from the young, and even then these cannot realize their desires because no means are available and the seminaries are insufficient."[3]

Catholic Action

A great help for the promotion of Catholic Action in Brazil was the letter of Pope Pius XI of 12 October 1935 to Cardinal Sebastião Leme and the bishops, in which he presents Catholic Action as a work of divine Providence for the faithful who are ready to work still more closely with the shepherds; the bishops and priests for their part can, with this assistance, exercise their functions on a still broader basis, which is of great importance considering the small number of priests in Brazil.[4] In a letter of 21 January 1942 to Cardinal Leme Pius XII expressed his thanks and his joy that the Brazilian Marianists "are capable coworkers in the spreading of the Kingdom of Jesus Christ and that they are accomplishing a vast apostolate by many works"; he also desired "that these groups might grow and become stronger from day to day and furthermore work with their usual obedience for the spreading of God's Kingdom, preach in the families and in society, always in harmony with traditional truths and Catholic principles, which do not change but remain constant for all times."[5] In accord with the wishes of Pius XI the Brazilian episcopate on 9 June 1935 published a document, accompanied by announcements for every diocese, on the statutes of Brazilian Catholic Action, examined and provided with the Pope's blessing.[6]

Piety

The Brazilian level of piety was, apart from particular variations, relatively high in 1965. Inquiries which were conducted in the archdiocese of Ribeirão Prêto, a traditional area with a slow growth of the urban population, for example, in Patrocínio Paulista, a place of ca. 3,000 inhabitants, which in the last years listed an increase of 1,200 inhabitants, yielded a result of 52 percent Sunday churchgoers. Other areas with a more rapid increase of the urban population, such as Sertãozinho, Jardinópolis, and Ribeirão Prêto, yielded only 22 percent,

[3] Ibid., 108.
[4] Ibid., 108f.
[5] Ibid., 109f.
[6] Ibid., 90.

24 percent, and 18 percent. This piety, which is present in the interior of Brazil and especially in the underdeveloped areas in the north and northwest, and even in cities such as Salvador, Rio de Janeiro, São Paulo, Belo Horizonte, and Recife, attests to a Christian vitality, although in some points it needs examination; it must still grow into the renewal of the Second Vatican Council.[7]

Too Few Priestly Vocations

The Brazilian Church has too few priestly vocations for its pastoral tasks. Without intending to go into the deeper reasons for this fact, the following statistics show it: in 1962 there were 922 diocesan seminarians and 1,772 seminarians for religious institutes; in 1968 there were only 870 and 1,665. This loss in vocations has a still greater significance, if it is considered that in 1962 Brazil had 79.096 million inhabitants and in 1968 89.37 million. If these numbers are compared it can be seen that in 1962 there was one seminarian for every 27,504 inhabitants, in 1968 one for every 35,257. The assistance of foreign clergy has decreased in recent years. In 1967 98 diocesan priests and 265 religious priests came to the country, a year later there were only 64 and 184 respectively.[8]

Without a doubt this lack of priests has effects on piety. Thus a census of 1962 and 1963 shows that 50 million Catholics, or 70 percent, do not attend Sunday Mass. At São Paulo it was 3.5 million. In other cities the proportions were similar. On the other hand, according to a study of the Brazilian Institute for Public Opinion and Statistics (IBOPE) at São Paulo, the inclination to secularization is powerful: at São Paulo alone in 1962–63 a half million television sets were installed; the broadcasts reached 3 million viewers. In the capital of the state of São Paulo there are today seventeen radio stations, five television stations, and two more programs will soon begin their operation; also, eighteen daily newspapers, some of them with a circulation of ca. 200,000 copies; almost 250 movie houses; and dozens of periodicals. Other cities and states of Brazil offer the same picture; in this way public opinion is formed, canalized, and dominated by financially powerful press concerns. The Brazilian Church tried to construct a front against this powerful propaganda, although many state broadcasting stations beam programs of a religious character. In 1972 the Church had 199 radio transmitters, including A Aparecida, a station with considerable range; 152 periodicals with a large circulation; three

---

[7] Cf. A. Rolim, O.P., "Em tôrno da Religiosidade no Brasil," *REB* 25 (1965), 11–27.
[8] Cf. A. Gregory, "Anteprojecto de pesquisa sôbre as causas do Excasseamento de Vocações Sacerdotais," *REB* 31 (1971), 389–93.

television stations—in Rio de Janeiro, Brasilia, and Pôrto Alegre—which since March 1972 have broadcast programs in color.

Brazil has need of 60,000 priests—this number is determined by the national Secretariat of Priestly Vocations; but only ca. 350 priests are educated in a year. With this quota the desired number would be achieved in 200 years, but by then Brazil would have ca. 400 million inhabitants.[9]

Care of Souls

The fifth plenary meeting of the Episcopal Conference published after its discussions of 2 to 5 April 1962 the following declaration: The 135 participants are aware of the desires and hopes of the 166 ecclesiastical spheres of jurisdiction, the 12,000 priests of the nation, and all members of religious institutes, seminarians, collaborators in the lay apostolate, and the faithful in the 4,500 Brazilian parishes. They state that the Episcopal Conference achieved its goals and that the pastoral activity of the bishops produces better results in the nation. The regular meetings, the exchange of experiences, the common planning and cooperation bring it about that ever broader areas of the country profit from the methods employed. Thus there are, for example, today greater possibilities of solving the problems of priestly vocations, training catechists, and making preparations for programs and projects. The impact of *caritas* grows in importance, and also the solving of the social tasks of the Church, especially in the field of education and of agricultural associations. Likewise the enlightenment of public opinion on important questions of the family, education, and the Church's social doctrine; special organizations with the goal of strengthening the presence of the Church; exchange of opinion and cooperation with other episcopates; aid from priests from other countries or money donations from foreign Catholics for Brazilian works; the organization of the lay apostolate.[10]

The result of the common pastoral care was, for example, the mobilization of the diocese of Bajé for catechesis in 1962. Similar initiatives were begun in many other dioceses under the motto "Without catechism, no religion." This action extended to all public schools which hitherto had had to get along without religious instruction. A central team of religious brothers, sisters, and professors undertook to develop an educational plan for teachers of religion and to organize religious instruction. The program was submitted at a meeting of the clergy; also the method was explained according to which religious

[9] Cf. Fr. P. A. de Assis, O.F.M., in *REB* 23 (1963), 433–35.
[10] *REB* 20 (1960), 485–90.

instruction should be given, and many suggestions for modifications were incorporated. The program was sent to all teachers. The committee sessions yielded the following guidelines: elaboration of a general plan for instruction in the public schools; training of catechists in every diocese; forming of a department for religious education; a list of consultants for state and communal schools; catechetical centers in the parishes; intensive courses; provision of aid for high schools; encyclicals to the parishes.[11]

A comprehensive and systematic program worked out for pastoral care went into effect within the Brazilian Church for the years 1966–70.[12] The thirty-two ecclesiastical provinces of Brazil have been since 1970 under four cardinals and 272 archbishops and bishops. Their work is divided among the following regions: *North Region I:* states of Amazonas, Acre, Mato Grosso, and parts of the territories of Roraima and Rondônia; total area 2,215,099 square kilometers, 1,299,829 inhabitants (.58 inhabitant per square kilometer), 86 parishes (15,114 inhabitants per parish), 237 priests (3,484 inhabitants per priest). *North Region II:* state of Pará and territory of Amapá; total area 1,366,598 square kilometers, 2,222,142 inhabitants (1.63 inhabitants per square kilometer), 119 parishes (18,673 inhabitants per parish), 290 priests (7,662 inhabitants per priest). *Northeast Region I:* states of Maranhão, Piauí, and Ceará; total area 722,917 square kilometers, 8,923,154 inhabitants (12.35 inhabitants per square kilometer), 362 parishes (24,649 inhabitants per parish), 759 priests (11,756 inhabitants per priest). *Northeast Region II:* states of Rio Grande to Norte, Paraíba, Pernambuco, and Alagoas; total area 236,801 square kilometers, 10,668,794 inhabitants (45.05 inhabitants per square kilometer), 458 parishes (23,398 inhabitants per parish), 856 priests (12,463 inhabitants per priest). *Northeast Region III:* states of Sergipe and Bahia; total area 581,915 square kilometers, 8,408,787 inhabitants (14.45 inhabitants per square kilometer), 538 parishes (23,572 inhabitants per parish), 569 priests (14,778 inhabitants per priest). *East Region I:* states of Guanabara and Rio de Janeiro; total area 43,334 square kilometers, 9,006,292 inhabitants (207.83 inhabitants per square kilometer), 425 parishes (21,191 inhabitants per parish), 1,245 priests (7,233 inhabitants per priest). *East Region II:* states of Minas Gerais and Espírito Santo; total area 573,796 square kilometers, 12,876,902 inhabitants (2.24 inhabitants per square kilometer), 1,019 parishes (12,636 inhabitants per parish), 1,948 priests (6,610 inhabitants per priest). *Central Region:* Federal District and parts of the states of Minas Gerais and

[11] Ibid. 22 (1962), 758.
[12] Ibid. 26 (1966), 377–79.

Goiás; total area 156,023 square kilometers, 1,079,836 inhabitants (6.92 inhabitants per square kilometer), 57 parishes (18,944 inhabitants per parish), 127 priests (8,502 inhabitants per priest). *West Central Region:* state of Goiás; total area 526,664 square kilometers, 2,566,703 inhabitants (4.87 inhabitants per square mile), 158 parishes (16,244 inhabitants per parish), 313 priests (8,200 inhabitants per priest). *Far West Region:* state of Mato Grosso and part of the territory of Rondônia; total area 1,228,903 square kilometers, 1,724,601 inhabitants (1.4 inhabitants per square mile), 95 parishes (18,153 inhabitants per parish), 521 priests (6,870 inhabitants per priest). *South Region I:* state of São Paulo, total area 244,906 square kilometers, 18,150,239 inhabitants (73.51 inhabitants per square kilometer), 1,194 parishes (15,201 inhabitants per parish), 2,911 priests (6,235 inhabitants per priest). *South Region II:* state of Paraná; total area 196,541 square kilometers, 6,958,420 inhabitants (35.4 inhabitants per square mile), 990 priests (7,028 inhabitants per priest). *South Region III:* state of Rio Grande do Sul; total area 267,528 square kilometers, 6,715,198 inhabitants (25.1 inhabitants per square kilometer), 563 parishes (11,927 inhabitants per parish), 1,523 priests (4,409 inhabitants per priest). *South Region IV:* state of Santa Catalina; total area 95,483 square kilometers, 2,922,449 inhabitants (30.6 inhabitants per square kilometer), 242 parishes (12,070 inhabitants per parish), 626 priests (4,668 inhabitants per priest).

The comprehensive pastoral perspective in an increasingly industrialized society, with all the accompanying symptoms, lays bare the inadequacy of the parishes for an effective work. This work must include a geographical area which we call the human zone, and it requires an integrated pastoral care. The plan of the Episcopal Conference refers to the conformity between the human zone and the pastoral zone. Because of the rapid industrial growth of Brazil the Church cannot allow itself to be taken in tow by history, it must foresee the development and adjust its work to this.[13]

Goals of the Church: The eleventh meeting of the Episcopal Conference from 16 to 27 May 1970, in which thirty lay persons of both sexes took part, proposed guidelines for a new orientation of the Church in Brazil. In the Church of Christ, it emphasizes, we are all equal because of the faith, baptism, and the common destiny. In this community lay persons and shepherds have a common responsibility for the building of the Church as a sign of the unity of people among themselves and of society with God.[14]

[13] *ACB* (1970–71), 2179–2208.
[14] *REB* 30 (1970), 415–25.

Catholic Universities and Schools

Four universities in Brazil have the status of papal universities: Rio de Janeiro since 22 January 1947, São Paulo since 25 January 1947, Pôrto Alegre since 1 November 1950, and Campinas since 8 September 1956. In Rome there has been since 1943 the Pontifício Colégio Pio Brasileiro, whose students, Brazilian citizens, attend lectures at the Gregoriana. The following Catholic universities must also be mentioned: Minas Gerais in Belo Horizonte, Campinas, Paraná in Curitiba, Goiás in Goiâna, Pernambuco (archdiocese of Olinda and Recife) with a theological institute, Pelotas and Petrópolis with institutes for theology, philosophy, and the humanities, São Leopoldo (archdiocese of Pôrto Alegre) with the university Do Rio dos Sinos (UNISINOS) and with a theological faculty and a university, Catholic law faculty at Santos, Catholic University of Salvador (archdiocese of Salvador); Manaus has a theological faculty, Taubaté a theological institute and a theological program for the laity.[15] In Curitiba the Claretians have operated since 7 May 1962 a *Studium Theologicum* in connection with the papal Lateran University at Rome, with theological programs for priests and lay persons.[16] The Conference of Brazilian Religious Superiors (CRB) inaugurated on 25 January 1965 the Theological Institute of São Paulo with four divisions— philosophy, theology, pastoral care, and catechetics.[17] The Theological Institute of Pôrto Alegre (1968) and similar institutions run by Franciscans, Jesuits, and other orders also have scholarly reputations.

The bishops of South Region I, with headquarters at São Paulo, met in 1969 with the religious superiors, male and female, of the region, in view of the defective schooling. The 130 persons present, including twenty bishops, decided to organize and support, within the range of the possible, centers, school clubs, and curricula for workers, in cooperation with the government and the religious institutes. They recommended the appointment of a bishop for the pastoral workers. They also recommended the use of educational television and a better employment of the means of social communication. They ascertained in the area of catechesis the faulty planning, lack of instructional means, and insufficient time for instruction. The São Paulo bishops were encouraged to send teachers of religion to every high school, although this measure would mean a considerable financial expense.[18]

---

[15] These cultural institutes are listed in *Annuario Pontificio 1975* and in *ACB* (1970–71).
[16] *REB* 22 (1962), 757.
[17] *REB* 25 (1965), 349f.
[18] Ibid., 30 (1970), 178f.

Newspapers, Periodicals, Means of Social Communication

Since 1949 the Franciscans at Petrópolis have published the quarterly *Eclesiástica Brasileira,* with voluminous information, articles, studies, and reviews of works on the Brazilian Church. Also from the Franciscans of Petrópolis there has appeared since 1968 the monthly *SEDOC—Serviço de documentação*—with an international ecclesiastical documentation and commentaries and especially orientation to Latin America and Brazil. Since 1969 there have appeared two new theological periodicals: *Atualização* and *Perspectiva theológica. Atualização* offers theological information for lay persons; its coworkers are the professors of the Central Institute for Philosophy and Theology of the Catholic University of Minas Gerais. Its aim is to supply theological truth. *Perspectiva theológica* appeared on the occasion of the twentieth anniversary of the founding of the Theological Faculty of Cristo Rey at São Leopoldo, whose professors are the editors. As a means of investigation and information it set for itself as its special function the fostering of the presence of theological thought in the university world.[19] Since 30 November 1969 there has appeared weekly a Brazilian edition of *Osservatore Romano.*[20] On 12 December 1969 the information center *Ecclesia* (CIEC) was opened at São Paulo, whose purpose is to manage contact offices in all São Paulo cities, in the largest cities of the country, in America and Europe, and a Catholic news agency. *Ecclesia* has, for example, twenty-five radio stations and some 400 teachers and 5,000 assistants, who move across the country to make possible an education for Brazilians in the most remote areas.[21] A creative step of the Brazilian Church was to cut a series of records which reproduced the catechism in stories, told by means of actual happenings. The editors are priests, who are supported in their work by radio and television technicians. Each record has from three to four stories.[22]

Ecclesiastical Shortcomings

One feature of the Brazilian Church in the last ten years is its insecurity. In this period the adherents of Afro-Brazilian cults have increased about tenfold. In Salvador these centers have grown from 59 to over 900; in Recife there are almost 1,000; there are thousands in Rio de Janeiro and São Paulo. Spiritism has spread especially in the cities of the south; the Protestant Church of Brazil has the highest growth rate in the world. In this growth the Pentecostalists are ahead, followed by

[19] Ibid., 182.
[20] Ibid., 180.
[21] Ibid., 180f.
[22] Ibid., 22 (1962), 757.

Lutherans, Methodists, Presbyterians, and Baptists. Thirty percent of the Brazilian population maintain relations with spiritism. In the small state of Guanabara there are, for example, more than 10,000 centers, *postos terrenos,* approved by the government, where spiritism is engaged in. The same thing happens at São Paulo, Rio Grande do Sul, Minas Gerais, Bahia; 162 periodicals and newspapers recruit for it. The majority of visitors continue to call themselves Catholics. In 1953 the Brazilian Episcopal Conference declared that of all deviations spiritism was the worst.[23]

Communist infiltration, promoted among Brazilian students by the *União Nacional de Estudiantes* (UNE), was condemned on 1 June 1962 by Cardinal Jaime Barros Câmara, after consultation with the twenty-eight archbishops of the nation. He indicated the necessity of establishing a national student union with Christian principles.[24] A tireless but strongly demagogic proponent of the social activity of the Church is Helder Pessoa Câmara, born in 1909, second general assistant of the Catholic Action of Brazil, in 1952 auxiliary bishop of Rio de Janeiro, since 1964 archbishop of Olinda and Recife.

Religious Orders, Pastoral Cooperation

A positive element for pastoral cooperation with the Episcopal Conference is the Conference of the Brazilian Orders (CRB), founded on 11 February 1954 as the permanent union of all religious brothers and sisters. In 1972 there were in Brazil 11,279 brothers and 41,893 sisters; with the episcopate they constitute one of the most active groups within the Brazilian Church. They also made a significant contribution within Brazil's Catholic Action, founded in 1935. In the "Movement for a Better World," called into being by Father Lombardi in 1960, the goal of which is to supply help to the bishops, priests, religious, and lay persons in their work, priests, brothers, and sisters cooperate decisively. They move across Brazil and up to 1964 had presented 750 educational courses for bishops, priests, and seminarians, which were attended by 46,907 persons in twenty-two states and fifty-one dioceses. On the recommendation of John XXIII, the first effort for a common pastoral care was undertaken in 1962. The most important aim was the renewal of parishes, of the clergy, of the Catholic schools, and the integration of the workers. District secretariats were erected, and they were directed by a bishop, two priests, usually male religious, and

[23] Cf. *REB* 31 (1971), 402–7; B. Kloppenburg, "O Fantástico Crescimento das Igrejas Pentecostais no Brasil," *REB* 26 (1966), 653–56; "O Espiritismo no Brasil," *REB* 19 (1959), 842–71; *AICA* 16, 792 (2 March 1972), 17f.; *AICA* 17, 874 (20 September 1973), 25f.
[24] *REB* 22 (1962), 497f.

several sisters. The sisters obeyed the appeal on a broad basis: they began new models of apostolic work: they assumed responsibility for parishes without pastors and worked in the district secretariats and in national institutions.

The Postconciliar Period

The Second Vatican Council produced an intensive participation of religious in the care of souls, both on the level of the diocese and on that of the state and nation. This cooperation in pastoral care is expressed in statistics thus: 1,803 brothers from clerical institutes; 1,602 brothers from secular institutes; 41,581 sisters, of whom 1,295 are cloistered; out of 13,135 priests, 8,105 are religious. Of the 4,500 Brazilian parishes, 2,000 are cared for by religious brothers and 32 by sisters. Of the 225 bishops, 97 are religious. Altogether 53,117 brothers and sisters work in the Brazilian Church. If one can speak of a genuine pastoral care in the north and far west of Brazil, in the states of Mato Grosso, Acre, Amazonas, and Pará, this is due to the thousands of religious who have renounced the comforts of Europe, the United States, or southern Brazil.[25]

Other church movements: There is no dearth of other ecclesiastical movements in Brazil. Thus, for example, there is the *Asociação de Educação Catolica* (AEC), founded in 1945, whose slogan is "Service." Its goals consist in uniting all Catholic educators—religious and lay; it is dedicated to the spread of Christian pedagogy and of the social doctrine of the Church, collaboration and presence in state bodies and similar organizations.[26] Another effective movement are the *Cursillos de Cristianadad,* which in the opinion of the Brazilian bishops "have brought about a profound change of general morality in society." In the archdiocese of São Paulo alone five priests devote themselves exclusively to the *Cursillos;* eight such *Cursillos* take place monthly. In all of Brazil sixty *Cursillos* are held in one month.[27] Of further great importance is the cooperation of the Legion of Mary in pastoral care. After its founding in 1951 it had the following structure in 1961: two senates (national council and district council), 166 curias (inferior councils), and 2,701 *praesidia* (local councils) with 24,914 active members, 158,580 assistants, and 79,155 helpers. The successes achieved speak for themselves: 1,814 adult baptisms, 7,429 rectified marriages, 15,560 persons brought back to the sacraments, 34,696 confessions and

---

[25] C. Nogara, "Vida religiosa no Brasil," *SEDOC* 4 (January 1972), 845–58.
[26] Cf. M. da Cruz, *1945. Vinte anos a serviço da educação* (1965).
[27] *AICA* 17, 847 (15 March 1973), 23, 26f.; detailed information on the history of the "Cursillos de Cristiandad" in Brazil in *SEDOC* 6 (July 1973), 75–100.

communions of the sick, 1,504 conversions. Further, the institution cares for 2,419 catechists' schools, with 175,531 hours of instruction for 39,769 children and 24,783 adults. The legion also employs groups for special tasks, as, for example, the care of recidivists (three groups) and of non-Catholics (one group). From its midst have come 357 vocations, 1,877 priests and 136 sisters. A further 1,877 members of the legion obliged themselves to attend Mass daily and communicate.[28] At the suggestion of Father Peyton, the apostle of the family rosary, and after an intensive recruitment, a mass rally of ca. 1.5 million persons took place on 16 December 1962 at Rio de Janeiro; 400 of them signed the promise to pray the rosary in the family.[29]

Formation of New Priests

From 23 to 26 October 1972 seminary professors met at Petrópolis to define the criteria and guidelines for the education of new priests.[30]

Catholic Missions among the Indians of Brazil

The Brazilian Church strove to continue its tradition among the Indians. The Catholic missionaries, united in *Consejo Indigenista Mis-ionero* (CIMI), work according to the following guidelines: (1) slow education without haste or pressure, without breaking with the past; in this connection interference in the life and faith of the natives must be avoided; (2) knowledge of their cultures—and hence mastery of their languages—respect for them; this means that the native may freely select models offered to him. This does not mean: all or nothing. The work of the missionary must be slow but effective and enduring.[31]

Fraternal Associations

In his letter of 24 January 1974 to its chairmen, Pope Paul VI encouraged the Episcopal Conference to supply the light of faith to every Brazilian by the fraternal associations campaign. The campaign was proclaimed under the motto "Where is your brother?" This question contains an examination of conscience for all, what is done for the defense of our brothers' life, independently of their origin and of the conditions in which they live.[32]

---

[28] *REB* 23 (1963),220f.
[29] Ibid., 218; cf. ibid. 25 (1965), 311–13.
[30] *SEDOC* 5 (December 1972), 712–17.
[31] Ibid. 6 (June 1974), 1398f.
[32] Ibid. 6 (May 1974), 1232–38.

ARGENTINA

Argentina has an area of 2,987,000 square kilometers and in 1976 ca. 25 million inhabitants, of whom 94.9 percent were Catholics in 1971. Since World War I, industrialization; since 1930, an autarchist and planning phase, with growth of the proletariat.[33]

In 1974 the Church was organized in twelve archdioceses, forty dioceses, two prelacies, and one ordinary each for the Uniate Greek Orthodox and the Ukrainians. As an example of the internal structure, the archdiocese of Buenos Aires in 1969 was served by 353 diocesan priests, 84 priests from outside the diocese, 539 religious priests, a total of 976; 137 parishes, 52 other churches; 95 houses of male religious; and 246 houses of sisters, with 3,720 sisters.[34]

Outstanding among the Catholic organizations are: *Junta Coordinadora de Superiores de Religiosos, Comisión Católica Argentina de Inmigración, Obra de Vocaciones Sacerdotales, Acción Católica* with many subdivisions, *Consejo Superior de Educación Católica, Movimiento Familiar Cristiano, Asociación Católica de Dirigentes de Empresa, Servicio Católico de Ayuda.*[35]

Since 1960 Buenos Aires has had a papal Catholic University, and in addition a theological faculty and several other institutes on the university level. Catholic universities or university institutes are also to be found in Córdoba, Santa Fe, La Plata, Mar del Plata, San Juan, Tucumán, Bahía Blanca, Villa María; seminaries for priests in Buenos Aires, Azul, Catamarca (regional seminary), Córdoba, La Plata, Paraná, Rió Cuarto, Rosario, Salta, and Santa Fe.[36]

The politically most decisive event was the intervention in 1943 under the direction of General Rawson, which brought the liberal phase to an end. Juan Domingo Perón, vice-president of the republic and minister of defense in the government of the *Oficiales Unidos* (G.O.U.), labor minister under Pedro P. Ramírez, developed a policy of social reform and in 1946 emerged as victor in the election.[37]

With the support of the workers and by means of his new doctrine, *Justicialismo,* he exercised his dictatorship until 1955. The foundation of his policy soon faltered, so that the country was faced with a new crisis. Perón, who in the beginning had practiced a policy of friendly

---

[33] Cf. V. Vives, *Historia social y económica de España y América* IV/2, 655–70.

[34] *República Argentina. Anuario eclesiástico* (1961), 131.

[35] Ibid., 117.

[36] Ibid., 1137–39.

[37] Cf. G. Furlong, *The Church in the 20th Century,* 783f.; R.E., Argentina (*Época independiente*), 347f.

coexistence with the Church, strengthened his totalitarian aims from 1952 without sparing the Church. The official press began to make fun of Catholics, Catholic meetings and the university *athenea* of Santa Fe and Córdoba were forbidden; the cross was removed from official areas; religious instruction was forbidden in the schools; a divorce law was enacted, and houses of prostitution were again approved.

Nevertheless, the Church remained unflinching, and the episcopate clung to its position with the support of the faithful. Lay persons and priests were arrested and abused. The persecution reached its climax on 11 June 1955; a large crowd gathered in Buenos Aires around the cathedral and on the neighboring plaza in order to hear Mass; then they moved in deep silence to the Congress buildings. A few days later, on 16 June, an attempt at revolt that miscarried was used by the government to mobilize its adherents. On the first day several churches were burned—San Francisco, San Roque, Santo Domingo, San Miguel, San Nicolás, and so forth. Also the episcopal palace, with the entire structure and the historical archives, became a victim of the flames. These events, without precedent in Argentina, produced a sharp reaction within as well as outside the country.[38]

In the period after Perón (from 1955) the revolutionary junta began to restore justice and peace. Although the divorce law, enacted in Perón's time, was deprived of force, the anti-Catholic cabinet members succeeded in maintaining the prohibition of religious instruction. During the government of Frondizi (1958–62) the law on freedom of education was passed, a law which has consistently been boycotted by liberals and Freemasons since 1952. Its establishment was the basis for the creation of Catholic universities.[39]

The Argentine Church after the Council

After the council the Catholic Church of Argentina, over and above the problems contingent on the political and socioeconomic situation, experienced other crises of an internal character. The twentieth International Congress for Sociology, held at Rió Tercero, Córdoba, from 5 to 11 September 1963, describes the period after 1930 as follows: "A time which was dominated by tensions and confrontations, conditioned by the existence of two opposed tendencies: the dynamic and the traditional,"[40] and which extended to theological, ascetical, pastoral, and psycho-sociological dimensions.

---

[38] Cf. G. Furlong, op.cit., 784; R.E., op.cit., 348.
[39] *XX Congreso internacional de Sociologiá. Estudios* (Buenos Aires 1963), 597–99.
[40] *SEDOC* 2 (Sept. 1969), 351–58; ibid. 2 (Oct. 1969), 491–506.

The declaration of the Argentine episcopate to the nation in 1969 can be regarded as a complete program. In it the bishops declare the Church to be the Sacrament of Christ and the possession of the poor, and they desire that the Argentine Church not only preach spiritual poverty but that it also live the poverty of Christ, helping the poor, while the Christian community makes itself responsible for its poor, and that justice rule social life so that each may keep what is his and all may be agents of the peace of Christ.

The decrees issued at Medellín, say the bishops, compel us to coordinate the common action; a beginning of this is made in the national pastoral plan with direct application to the basis of strengthening the parishes, and as a means of evangelization and of the physical presence of the Church in economically and geographically removed areas. To this end the bishops desire to set up in each diocese a commission for the means of social communication or at least to name a responsible person who maintains permanent contact with the Episcopal Conference and its departments of press, radio, cinema, and television in all those questions which concern exchange of information, curricula, moral orientation, and evaluation of behavior, prices, and so forth. The bishops have as their first duty to live according to the principles of pastoral co-responsibility.[41]

Difficulties within the Argentine Church

The tense situation which prevailed for some time in Argentina, accompanied by acts of violence, kidnappings, and murders, which caused a wave of protests, induced the Episcopal Conference on 12 August 1970 "as true shepherds of the Church" to communicate to all their message with the truth and love of Christ and his Church. The bishops recalled that the task entrusted by Christ to the Church is of neither a political nor economic nor social but of a religious nature, but from it proceed advantages, light, and strength, which represent an aid for the organizing and strengthening of human society. It does not authorize priests, by virtue either of their office or of the Church's social doctrine, to join any revolutionary movement whatsoever which seeks a Latin American socialism with the aim of socializing the means of production, the economy, and cultural policy; this also not with the justification that a social revolution allows a direct employment of force as a means of relieving the oppressed. In concord with Pope Paul VI the bishops condemned terrorist methods as means of struggle and declared openly: A movement of priests is Christian and has justification

[41] Ibid. 4 (Aug. 1971), 191–97.

in the Catholic Church only in so far as it accepts the definition of the Second Vatican Council in the decree *Lumen Gentium* (no. 8).[42]

The priests replied to the bishops' declaration on behalf of the Third World during a meeting at Córdoba on 3 and 4 October 1970 in seven chapters and seventy paragraphs. In it they said they could not accept errors and guilt which others, especially the government and press, wanted to shift to them. Although they are ready to do penance, they are, however, of the opinion that others are the guilty ones. To the chief charge of the episcopal document to the priests of the Third World— deciding for socialism—they answered as follows: "It is familiar to everyone—and hence to our bishops—that, if the political collectivist solution also represents a danger, the actual situation which puts our people under pressure is of a capitalist nature: the Latin American entrepreneur system; for this reason the present economy corresponds to a false notion of the right of private ownership of the means of production and of the goals of the economy." The Congress of Medellín (*Justicia* 10) was called to mind, and in this connection was supplemented: "No one can fail to recognize that the most urgent task in Latin America consists in achieving a complete renewal of the evaluation and measures of the entrepreneurs in regard to their goals, organization, and management.

"This situation," continued the priests, "induces us to demand the search for a new social system in which man is not exploited by man; in order to bring about such a solution, we see no other way than the socializing of the means of production, power, and culture."[43]

The Determining of the Functions of Priests

On 3 June 1972 the priests published at Buenos Aires for the Third World a common answer to the questionnaire on the preparation for the Synod, which was to take place at Rome with the theme of the function of priests. This questionnaire, sent by Monsignor Juan Carlos Arámburu, auxiliary bishop of Buenos Aires, to the priests of the archdiocese, contained the following sections: the function of the priest; temporal activity of the priest; the priest as "sign of unity"; "universality" of the priest; the new priesthood; prayer; celibacy. In this regard it was expressed that the priest is in the service of the redemption of mankind, and hence his activity must be in harmony with the activities of people and of society, otherwise not only are guidelines

[42] Ibid. 197–234.
[43] Ibid. 234–38.

abandoned but also forces and realities are denied which contain evangelical values such as justice and brotherhood.[44]

The "Emergency Housing Districts" of Buenos Aires

In his letter of 22 September 1969 Arámburu referred to the "Emergency Housing Districts" of Buenos Aires, a "sad and painful reality," which needed the service of the Church and are open "to the poor." He encouraged priests, religious brothers, and laity to cooperate further in this apostolic task.[45] Only a profound revolutionary action can bring a solution and transform these slums into workers' quarters.[46]

The "Priests for the Third World" United with the People

On the occasion of their fifth meeting in August-September 1972 the "Priests for the Third World" declared that, in view of the political and socioeconomic situation, they were united with the people. They stressed this pastoral position in a progammatic document,[47] in a letter to the Argentine episcopate,[48] and in another document in which they declared their intention not to leave their oppressed people in the lurch.[49]

The voices of the bishops: In this climate of political and economic confusion the Episcopal Conference met at San Miguel from 19 to 21 October 1972. Its announcement contains the following points: historical reality (I); the negative aspects of the Argentine situation (II); positive aspects and human values (III); liberalism and Marxism: political, economic, and social order (IV); socialism (V); possible decisions (VI); preparations (VII); urgent problems (VIII); summary (IX); specific contributions (X). The position of the bishops is clear: the economy must serve people and not vice versa; private ownership, even in the means of production, must accommodate itself to the general welfare; neither liberalism nor Marxism; nationalization limited to the needs of society or in questions of the defense of private property or of national sovereignty; a broad sharing of workers and employees in enterprises guarantees identification with the goals set; having a voice in the great political questions; providing of help for the coordinating organs; truth and loyalty in the quest of the general welfare of the

[44] Ibid. 3 (Sept. 1970), 341–43.
[45] Ibid., 343–46.
[46] Ibid., 346–48; ibid. 5 (Feb. 1973), 1011f.
[47] Ibid. 6 (Oct. 1973), 501–12.
[48] Ibid. 5 (Feb. 1973), 1011–16.
[49] Ibid., 1016.

nation.[50] The Argentine Church thereby testified to its balance and efficacy within its pastoral task, the aim of which is the redemption of people.

The Church's Functions

Cardinal Raúl Francisco Primatesta, archbishop of Córdoba, explained during the Roman Synod of 1974 the evangelizing and liberalizing aspect of the Argentine Church. In this connection he remarked that the individual is considered as the object of evangelization in his individuality, in his transcendence, in his dynamism, and in his development. This evangelizing work devotes its special attention to the nonpracticing.

Further, the object of evangelization is the Universal Church in all its elements, society as such, and the individual in all vocations. "It is important to avoid the clericalization of the laity and the secularization of the priests." The cardinal dealt also with the accusation that the Church enters into no secular compromises; with the mistakes of some members of the clergy, who use the Word of God for their political aims; with the cooperation of women in evangelization and the evaluation of the work of religious brothers and sisters.

The cardinal called attention to the fact that the object of evangelization is the totality of revelation under the guidance of the Church. The content of revelation must be entirely presented: the transcendence of evangelization, its dimension and spread to worship; the problem of faith, culture, and religious sentiment; the points of contact between the Gospel and liberation as one of the most important questions of Latin America.[51]

PARAGUAY

Paraguay has a total area of 406,752 square kilometers and 2.57 million inhabitants, of whom more than 90 percent are mestizos; in 1971 96.2 percent were Catholics (United Nations statistics of 1976). The history of Paraguay shows disturbed years in the most recent past. Under the presidency of José Guaggiari (1930–32) the country was unable to avoid a frontier quarrel with Bolivia. The outcome was the Chaco War of 1932–35, which ruined the country and caused great losses among the male youth. After the war Paraguay began industrialization. In recent years relations with the United States and Bolivia have been strengthened. The methodical development of the airways is expressed in a flourishing economy;

[50] Ibid., 1017–24.
[51] *Osservatore Romano*, 3 Oct. 1974.

Asunción grows in importance as a commercial junction. According to the latest computations of the CEPAL 1,552 large landowners and foreign firms possess 31.5 million hectares of the land, while 250,000 families with about 1 million persons control only 500,000 hectares.[52]

Ecclesiastical Organization

The archdiocese of Asunción has as suffragans the dioceses of Caacupé, Concepción, Coronel Oviedo, San Juan Bautista de las Misiones, and Villarrica, the prelacies of Alto Paraná and Encarnación, the vicariates apostolic of Chaco Paraguayo and Pilcomayo.[53] The most important Catholic associations are: Catholic Association of Paraguay, Christian Family Movement, Legion of Mary, Christian Curricula, Third Order of Saint Francis, and Salesian Societies. There are 181 parishes and 21 which can be classified as such; 202 priests and 181 religious brothers; 18 religious houses of men and 39 of women.[54]

Educational Institutions

Since 2 February 1965 the republic has had the Catholic university Nuestra Señora de la Asunción at Asunción with faculties of philosophy, pedagogy, law, political science, and political economy. Also in Asunción are faculties of law, politics, and social science, founded in 1960, and a university institute for family education, founded in 1963; a university of theology and religious science, founded in 1971; a university of international law. In Villarrica there are faculties of philosophy and education, founded in 1961, and a juridicopolitical and social science faculty. Concepción has a faculty of philosophy and education; Encarnación, an educational and philosophical faculty. Religious institutes run numerous schools and institutes.[55]

Protests of the Bishops

In a letter of 29 January 1969 the archbishop of Asunción, Juan José Anibal Mena Porta, asked the president of the Republic, Alfredo Stroessner, "with consideration of Christian demands for justice, to examine the situation of those who, by order of Your Excellency and without trial, are under police custody, either because of their ideology

[52] *Christus,* 410 (July–December 1970), 778f.; SC, Paraguay (Época independiente), 172–75.
[53] *Annuario Pontificio* (1977) 957.
[54] *Annuario eclesiástico del Paraguay* (1972), 21–27.
[55] *Annuario Pontificio* (1974) 1371; *Annuario eclesiástico del Paraguay* (1972), 27–29.

or because of alleged crimes of antidemocratic subversion."[56] On the occasion of the consultations on a draft of a new law, "The Defense of Democracy and of the Political and Social Order of the State" (1969), the bishops, as shepherds and citizens, sent a letter to the Congress and expressed their concern in view of the danger which the new law could represent for the country's awareness. According to the bishops' opinion it was a question here of a glorification of absolutism, which had often been condemned by the Popes.[57]

On 22 October 1969 the Jesuit Father Francisco de Paula Oliva, professor at the Catholic university of Asunción, was expelled from the country. As a protest, on the very same day teachers and students organized a *Via Crucis,* at the end of which the police dispersed the participants. In a declaration of 26 October 1969, the episcopate informed all the faithful of these events and threatened with excommunication all who mistreated priests and sisters. As a sign of its protest and pain, the Church of Paraguay gave up the celebration of Masses on this day.[58] Father Bartolomé Vanrell, the Jesuit provincial, also protested in a letter to the minister of the interior against the expulsion of Father Vicente Barreto,[59] and Monseñor Bogarín Argaña, bishop of San Juan Bautista de Las Misiones, in a letter to Father Barreto condemned the conduct of the authorities.[60] The kidnapping of the priest Uberfil Monzón, collaborator of the Lay Secretariat of CELAM, by police officers on a public street near the Uruguay Plaza became the occasion for a series of complaints by church authorities.[61]

In its meeting of 18 December 1970 the Episcopal Conference declared its solidarity with the desires and hopes of the population and stated that the strivings for peace and justice were in a blind alley. The bishops indicated the injustices in the country and expected from those responsible that they would listen without emotion to the voice of the Church's representatives.[62]

Two Worlds Developing

On 15 May 1972, following a meeting of 8–10 May, the archbishop of Asunción, Ismael Blas Rolón Silvero, S.D.B., together with priests and many lay persons, issued a document in which they expressed them-

---

[56]*Christus* 410 (July–December 1970), 780–83.
[57]*SEDOC* 2 (Jan. 1970), 921–24.
[58] Ibid., 924–26.
[59] Ibid. 5 (Oct. 1972), 491f.
[60] Ibid., 492–94.
[61] Ibid. 4 (Aug. 1971), 240–50.
[62] Ibid., 239f.

selves on the kidnapping and expulsion of Father José Caravias, active at Piribebuy in the Diocese of Caacupé. The analysis of the situation, they said, places the nation before two worlds: a sociopolitical authoritarian system, which existed with the aid of propaganda only for the advantage of a few; on the other hand, we experience the slow growth of a Church reforming itself, which takes a stand for more justice. The participants in the meeting pointed out the injustices perpetrated against the Church.[63]

When on 14 May Paraguay celebrates the anniversary of its independence, the archbishop of Asunción wrote to the chief of protocol of the government on 10 May 1972, it would be logical to believe that this memorial day would be in tune with the right of all citizens to liberty. In all churches of the archdiocese there would be prayers on 14 and 15 May that the freedom achieved by our ancestors would also become full reality.[64] In an open letter of 18 May 1972 the Episcopal Conference justified the nonparticipation of the religious schools in the festivities at the desire of the students themselves without their having been in any way influenced.[65]

The Function of Priests

To do away with misunderstandings and doubts, the competent committee of the Episcopal Conference on 16 May 1972 published a statement on the function of priests, especially since more and more priests were accused of playing a totally subversive role in politics. In it the judgments of the Second Vatican Council were taken into consideration. Priests who live together with the peasants, said the document, tried to expose the harshness of life with the light of the Gospel, always within the guidelines recognized and issued by the bishops. Bishops, priests, and laity know very well that a continuing renewal is indispensable. To this task they devoted all their energy. The rights of the authorities and the national constitution are respected, and the faithful are urged to respect them also.[66] In an open letter to all the faithful on the occasion of the regular meeting of 1972 the bishops stated: If persons are oppressed, whether by unjust economic structures or abuses of power, the Church embodies the prophetic complaint and acts as a moral force in favor of liberation and human rights. The Church must not be seen as a political party, especially as its function surpasses every secular function and every political schema. Its goal is of

[63] Ibid. 5 (Oct. 1972), 495–500.
[64] Ibid., 500f.
[65] Ibid., 505–7.
[66] Ibid., 501–3.

an eschatological nature, and the liberation of people sought by it can only be fully achieved in the next world.[67]

Church-State Relations

The advisory organ for the relations of Church and state, established in 1973 by the Episcopal Conference, should be oriented to maintaining the freedom and independence of the Church according to the teaching of the Second Vatican Council and the directions of the Medellín Congress in harmony with the position occupied by the Church of Paraguay. Affairs of interest to both sides should be discussed, especially if they have a national impact; further, studies should be undertaken on the relations of Church and state. The present constitution of Paraguay officially recognizes the Catholic religion, and the archbishop of Asunción is a member of the Council of State. In addition, subsidies and other advantages in favor of church institutions are maintained.[68]

URUGUAY

Uruguay has a total area of 186,926 square kilometers and in 1972 had 2,972,871 inhabitants; 90.6 percent are Catholics. Since 1911 dictatorships and democratic systems have alternated in the Uruguayan government. In 1951 Andrés Martínez Trueba reformed the constitution: a council of nine replaced the president; the council of ministers and both chambers were retained; new social legislation established the welfare state; the public service industries and many other enterprises were nationalized. The elections of 1958 for the first time gave victory to the "white majority," whereas the "colored" party emerged as victor of the elections of 27 November 1966. The National Executive Council was abolished, and there was a return to the presidential system; Oscar Gestido was elected president in 1967. The events of the last years have produced no internal calm in the country. Uruguay records an unsteady growth in the number of inhabitants. The population consists almost entirely of whites, together with a very small number of mestizos; the Indians have died out. The country's economy is restricted almost exclusively to cattle raising. Ninety percent of the rural enterprises engage in cattle breeding, only 10 percent in agriculture; but the metal, textile, and chemical industries have developed.[69]

[67] *AICA* 17, 817 (August 1972), 31f.
[68] Ibid. 874 (September 1973), 27f.
[69] R. E., Uruguay (Época independiente), 870; Vicens Vives, op. cit. IV/2, 653f.

Ecclesiastical Structure

Uruguay has one metropolitan see, Montevideo, with the suffragan dioceses of Canelones, Florida, Maldonado-Punta del Este, Melo, Mercedes, Minas, Salto, and San José de Mayo y Tacuarembó.[70] There are 215 parishes in the nation, 92 other pastoral stations, 698 priests, 230 male religious, and 1,981 sisters.[71] The new constitution, ratified in 1935 by a referendum of the people with 280,000 affirmative, 10,000 negative, and 70,000 abstentions, permits freedom of abortion and euthanasia. Immorality is spread by means of the so-called biographical movie; about 80 percent of the cinema productions at Montevideo were of a pornographic nature. The government was content to issue a law on biographical films for minors.

The republic had no official religion. In the effort to obtain a greater liberty in regard to its public announcements and to support its schools, the Church makes progress. The great Eucharistic Congress of 1934 gave Catholicism a powerful impetus. The Church's educational institutions increased because of the freedom recognized in the constitution. Ca. 20,000 children were instructed in schools of religious institutes, many others in parochial schools. Catholic Action received new impulses through the instruction of 31 January 1955 of the bishop of Salto to his priests to support it. The Church's pastoral work was impaired by the immorality, the pornography, the influence of the Freemasons, Protestantism, especially at Montevideo by the Salvation Army and the Y.M.C.A.[72] On the occasion of its meeting in October 1968 the episcopate of Uruguay accepted the decrees of Medellín and bound itself to translate these into practice, with special attention to the problems of the poor and the oppressed. The bishops referred the current situation to a growing moral crisis, which originated in a materialistic concept of life and had effects on the public, economic, social, cultural, and family order. It is the task of the Church to strengthen awareness, to inspire and promote, to stimulate and to support all initiatives which contribute to the formation of the person, and to condemn all that is directed against justice and peace. True liberation must have as its basis inner change. The Christian message stresses rather the change in the person than the necessity of structural change.[73]

[70] *Annuario Pontificio 1977*, 957.
[71] *Guiá de la Iglesia católica en el Uruguay* (1973).
[72] *Revista Javeriana* 4, 355–63.
[73] *SEDOC* 1, 1439–41.

Celibacy

In the note of 14 April 1970 on priestly celibacy the episcopate of Uruguay expressed the desire to orient in harmony with their pastoral function priests, religious, and Catholic laity, to avoid misunderstandings which cause only harm. In agreement with the Pope and the bishops of the entire world they explain the true idea of the Church in regard to priestly celibacy and identify themselves with the relevant statements of the *magisterium*. Celibacy is suited to bring home to many young people, who rebel against the bourgeoisie and seek a new world, the value and power of attraction of a vocation which obliges them to total sacrifice to God and mankind. The bishops desire and hope that those who follow God's call will receive an answer of faith and love from the People of God.[74]

Renewal in the Light of the Second Vatican Council and of the Congress of Medellín

In a pastoral letter of 22 November 1970 the bishops proclaimed their wish to push forward the renewal desired by the Second Vatican Council and the second meeting of the Latin American episcopate at Medellín. The Church of Uruguay, like the Church in general, is in a critical stage full of fears, expectations, and hopes. The bishops understand the complaint of many Catholics who see the inner unity of the Church in jeopardy. The Church, whose function consists in continuing to the end of time the presence, task, and redeeming work of Jesus Christ, must renew itself in accord with the ideals of the Second Vatican Council, without identifying this function with that of the Christian lay person in the social, economic, and political liberation of people. The lay person must be supported by his Christian vocation, but he cannot appeal to an official representation of the Church, for this does not belong to his sphere of duty; this would mean a retrogression into a new kind of clericalism. Dialogue in the Church is always constructive, clarifies prejudices and doubts, strengthens faith, demands mutual understanding, accepts legitimate pluralism, and gives it a new value. Finally, it brings about that all are of one mind (1 Cor. 10). To those who hope for an elimination of injustice by the employment of force the bishops retort that force is neither Christian nor evangelical and that one evil cannot be fought with a greater evil. Instead of seeking the guilty, people must ascertain what deeds or omissions led to this situation.[75]

In a letter of 12 June 1972 the permanent Commission of the

[74] Ibid. 3, 779–81.
[75] Ibid. 4, 995–1005.

Episcopal Conference repeated, "in view of the difficult situation in the country," that the bishops also desire profound changes in the country in order to create a fraternal solidarity among all; hence the radical demands of the subversive groups must be regarded as a new mistake among many others. Further, the letter condemned the inhuman treatment of prisoners, independently of whether they were subversively active or not. Tortures cannot produce peace, not to mention that confessions extracted under terror are valueless and cause injuries that cannot be repaired.[76]

CHILE

Chile has a total area of 741,767 square kilometers and in 1968 had a population of 8,262,556 inhabitants and in 1976 of 10.4 million. In 1969 the Church of Chile included five archdioceses, fourteen dioceses, two prelacies, and two vicariates apostolic. At the same time there were 971 diocesan priests and 1,553 religious priests active in 734 parishes. There were 281 houses of male religious and 647 of female, and 342 educational institutes with 294,534 pupils, 14 hospitals, and 159 other relief institutions.[77]

The Chilean economy had developed by leaps and bounds during World War I; but the new wealth was for the benefit of only a thin upper class, so that in 1920 Alessandri was elected president as representative of the disadvantaged masses. Since he could not keep his promises, not least because of the boundary strife with Peru and Bolivia over the port of Arica and the Saltpeter Coast, he was toppled by the military under General Ibáñez, who became president of the republic, first in 1927, then again in 1952, and who continued the process of industrialization that had already begun. The Falangist Party, which had separated from the Conservative Party in the years after 1940, joined with the Communists in the election. Their commitment in the social sphere evoked strong tensions between the church leadership and the youth, which led to the dissolution of the *Asociación Nacional de Estudiantes Católicos* (ANEC) and other societies of Catholic Action. Nevertheless, progress in the social field is the most conspicuous phenomenon of the Chilean Church of that period. The farmhands organized unions, agrarian reform was discussed—things not permitted previously. The official Church gradually turned away from the great proprietors and thereby took its place in this new development.

In the course of the years after 1950 the fact of economic underde-

---

[76] Ibid. 5, 603–6.
[77] Cf. Vivens Vives, op. cit. IV/2, 636–41; *Guiá parroquial y guiá eclesiástica de Chile* (Santiago de Chile 1969).

velopment became ever more obvious. The nation regarded itself as poor. It did not escape the young Catholics that, despite a technical progress, the poverty of the broad masses became greater; they concluded that the social question could not be solved independently of the economic and political problems.

In Search of a Uniform Ecclesiastical Activity

The general situation demanded uniform action: lay persons and priests joined in a common action with the aim of transforming the old *Falange* into *Democracia Christiana.* Influence on this development was also exercised by the *Centro Bellarmino* (1959), the *Alianza para el Progreso* (1961), the pastoral letters of the Chilean episcopate on the situation in agriculture and the political and social duty of Catholics (1962), and finally the stimuli of the Second Vatican Council. The underdeveloped state of the nation was regarded on one side as a consequence of the development of the rich countries, especially of the United States; on the other side the models of Cuba and Vietnam—names such as Fidel Castro, Camilo Torres, Ché Guevara—and the guerrilla wars in various countries of South America contributed to the growth in many of the revolutionary idea and the hope for a new human being on a new continent by means of a radical modification of the system.

The Conference of the Latin American Episcopate at Medellín in 1968 condemned with full publicity the dependence of the continent and announced a program of church reform, which stirred a loud echo in Chile. At Allende's election in 1970 the Catholics supported all candidates. In a spoken and written word—newspapers and periodicals—it was expressed that the Church was not basically against this government of a Marxist stamp.[78] Catholics on the right regarded the faith as an exclusively religious attitude, oriented to God alone. In relation to politics they persisted in the, in their view, only valid Catholic viewpoint and regarded themselves as guardians of morality and religion. They refused a change of their old morals and any novelty. On the left they were for the most part young priests, who had committed themselves in workers' and students' environments, and lay persons with an ideology of the left. For these a political confrontation and a revolution were unrenounceable, since only it meant the total redemption of mankind; they were an affair of the individual Christians and of the Church itself. The majority of the Chilean Church, bishops, priests, and faithful, were oriented to the center. Without having expressly decided for the *Democracia Cristiana,* they preferred it to all

[78] A. Fontaine, S.S.C.C., "La Iglesia católica chilena en los últimos 20 años," *Mensaje* 202–3 (Sept.–Oct. 1971), 422–52.

other parties. They desired a nonpolitical Church, devoted only to conciliar reform and renewal. Nevertheless, they regarded the opening to the world as an ingredient of theology and spirituality, but proceeding from the principle of autonomy. In this group, of course, various opinions were combined.

The majority of Catholics is today anticapitalist and represents a certain non-Marxian socialism. Starting from the renewing spirit of the Second Vatican Council, the Chilean Church has reformed its liturgy, accepted priests who represent new ideas, allowed changes in the religious life, and begun a broad dialogue with the political organs and other denominations.

Attempt at a Balance

The bishops, by means of their varied activities in the dioceses claimed, but did not have sufficient time, to adapt themselves to the problems of the entire country and to devote themselves to them. Also, their contacts with the secularized world suffered from the same shortcoming, so that a dialogue with lay persons and priests who were prepared to help and a total plan could come into existence only with great difficulty. As positive elements of the life of the Chilean Church can be listed progress in the reform of the religious life with many new perceptions, especially in the practical care of souls. The classical youth movements, of great efficacy in previous years, are in a serious crisis. The disintegration within the priestly vocation is regrettable; many priests abandon their vocation, and in general it lacks vitality.[79]

Christians for Socialism

Eighty priests met in Santiago de Chile from 14 to 16 April 1971 to speak on the topic "Participation of Christians in the Building of Socialism in Chile." "The Eighty," as they were called, affirmed their membership in the clergy and at the same time their sympathy with socialism: they then formed a "Priests' Secretariat of Christians for Socialism." Eight months later the word "Priests'" was dropped, since they began to accept lay persons also into their ranks. At the end of their first meeting they composed a "Declaration of the Eighty," in which they expressed their wish to work together with the Marxists for the construction of socialism in Chile. Marxism, they said, is a means for the analyzing and changing of society; the Christian faith must be freed of everything that prevents the faithful from cooperating with the Marxists. A week later, on 23 April 1971, twelve professors of theology of the University of Santiago de Chile in an open letter declared their

[79] A. Fontaine, S.S.C.C., "Situación actual de la Iglesia chilena," *Mensaje* 201, 367–72.

agreement with the declaration of "The Eighty." From this moment on, expressions of sympathy for this movement increased in and outside Chile. Three months later, from 16 to 18 July, about 200 priests participated in a meeting which was organized by the "Priests' Secretariat of Christians for Socialism." Thus originated the "Group of 200." From these two cells, constituted exclusively by priests, arose the movement "Christians for Socialism," which spread from America to Europe.

The movement obtained a strong stimulus through the meeting of the groups with Fidel Castro, on the occasion of his visit to Chile. 140 priests attended the meeting. They adopted the theses represented by Castro that Christians should regard themselves as "strategic," and not only tactical, "allies" of the Marxists in the liberation of Latin America, and that the Christian can accept Marxism as a method with a quiet conscience without coming into conflict with his faith. Castro invited twelve Chilean priests to Cuba, to work there voluntarily for some weeks. Following this, they published in the Cuban newspaper *Gramma* a declaration on 6 March 1972: condemnation of capitalism as source of all evil in Latin America, historical necessity of socialism, moral obligation of all Christians to fight together with the Marxists for liberation from institutionalized force. At the Episcopal Conference in Punta de Tralca from 7 to 11 April 1973, the bishops, after a comprehensive theological and pastoral assessment of the orientation of the clergy, came to the following conclusion: No priest and no religious can join the movement "Christians for Socialism."[80]

Situation of the Chilean Church

On the occasion of the Roman Synod of Bishops of 1974 Monseñor Valdés Subercaseaux, bishop of Osorno, explained the situation of the Chilean Church: Since the beginning of the century the Chilean people have been under the influence of the errors of economic liberalism and of Marxian materialism. Among the 85 percent of Catholics it is difficult to ascertain how many of them take an active part in the Church's life. The Church is aware of the social problem, and many priests and lay persons are working for its solution. But first it is neccessary to change the mentality of persons in order then to alter the unjust social

---

[80] B. Sorge, *Le scelte e le tesi dei "Cristiani per il socialismo" alla luce dell'insegnamento della Chiesa* (Turin 1974); "Evangelio, política y socialismo. Documento de trabajo de la Conferencia episcopal de Chile," *Christus* 438(Mexico, 1 May 1972), 32–42; "Primer encuentro. Cristianos por el socialismo (documento final)," *Christus* 440(Mexico, 1 July 1972), 53–58; "Jerarquías chilena y mexicana ante el primer encuentro latinoamericano de 'cristianos por el socialismo,'" *Christus* 442 (1 Sept. 1972), 41–59; *AICA* 16, 793 (2 March 1972), 15f.; *AICA* 16, 807 (8 June 1972), 28f.; *SEDOC* 4(Nov. 1972), 614–32.

structures. Today the young rarely devote themselves to the religious and priestly vocation or to the lay apostolate. They prefer to dedicate themselves to social and political action. The intellectuals—priests and lay—represent another problem, because they often question ecclesiastical life, the Pope, the priestly identity, and the importance of the religious life. "Liberation Theology" leads to a purely secular-oriented social activity and pushes spiritual values into oblivion. The Chilean Church, said the bishop, does not remain inactive and is seeking new forms of evangelization.[81]

BOLIVIA

Bolivia has a total area of 1,126,240 square kilometers and is, then, the fifth largest nation in South America. In 1960 it had 3,371,791 inhabitants,[82] of whom 63 percent were Indians;[83] in 1976, according to the UN statistics, 5,470,000 inhabitants, of whom more than 50 percent were Indians and 28 to 30 percent mestizos.

Ecclesiastical Structure

Bolivia has four metropolitan sees: La Paz with the prelacies of Corocoro and Coroico, Sucre with the suffragan sees of Potosí and Tarija, Cochabamba with Oruro and the prelacy of Aiquile, and Santa Cruz de la Sierra; six vicariates apostolic: Chiquitos, Cuevo, El Beni, Ñuflo de Chávez, Pando, and Reyes.[84] In 1960 there were 189 diocesan priests, 763 religious brothers, 1,733 sisters, and 354 parishes. The formalism of the Bolivian Church of 1970 produced the following organizational commissions: doctrine and catechesis, means of social communication, seminaries and vocations, lay apostolate, liturgy, music and art, education, social actions, missions, economic planning. In addition, the following secretariates were set up: missions, means of social communication, education, doctrine and catechesis, social studies, Bolivian *Caritas*. In 1974 there were in Bolivia 913 priests—355 diocesan and 558 religious—and 1,637 sisters; of these last, 931 were foreigners. Lay movements with effective activity are: *Legión de María, Movimiento familiar cristiano,* and *Cursillos de cristianidad.* Over and above these are numerous institutes, the Catholic University of La Paz under the direction of the Jesuits, schools, high schools, homes for the aged, hospitals, which are administered by religious, male and

---

[81] *Osservatore Romano,* 4 Oct. 1974.
[82] *Anuario eclesiástico de Bolivia para el año del Señor 1960; Guía de la Iglesia de Bolivia* (1970), 5–9.
[83] *Christus* 410 (Mexico, July–Dec. 1970), 740.
[84] *Annuario Pontificio 1977,* 954.

female.[85] At Sucre the Jesuits operate the broadcasting company "Radio Loyola."

The Bolivian people have the lowest standard of living of the American continents. Mine workers suffer severely from the change from the high temperatures underground to the cold of the mountains, where their dwellings do not provide adequate protection. A great part of the miners therefore are tubercular: their life expectancy is about thirty-five years. At the moment the Corporación minera boliviana (COMIBOL) is the largest mining enterprise with 25,000 employees and is responsible for 60 percent of the total gross national product. Politically, Bolivia is a turbulent country. Since independence it has had more than 180 changes of government.[86]

Human Solidarity

At the meeting of the bishops, priests, and laity in Cochabamba in February 1968, in which they sought to bring their understanding of their roles into harmony with the Second Vatican Council, they published a declaration: the schools are not accessible to all social classes, especially the poor; the support of the priests is particularly not realistically taken care of; the youth, hope of the Church, and social justice are neglected; means available are used for the building of houses and churches and in this the Christian community is forgotten; ecclesiastical office is often exercised more as a right than as a ministry. For the future the Church will do everything to measure up to its duty and responsibility; in this regard it relies on all Bolivians and on all countries and undertakings which share in the development of Bolivia.[87]

Defense of the Miners

Jorge Manrique, archbishop of La Paz, several bishops, forty-five miner-priests, and some lay persons met at Oruro in July 1968 and analyzed the situation of the miners and the treaty concluded in March 1968 between state and Church on the mining problem. In a letter from La Paz of 20 July 1968 the miners' union (ASIB) presented its demands to the group. The Church should end its connection with the regime; they, the Christian union members, are revolutionaries.[88]

[85] *Anuario eclesiástico de Bolivia para el año del Señor 1960; Guía de la Iglesia de Bolivia* (1970), 5–9.
[86] *Christus* 410 (Mexico, July–Dec. 1970), 740f.
[87] Ibid. 386 (Mexico, Jan.–July 1968), 362–67.
[88] *SEDOC* 1 (Dec. 1969), 887–94.

The most important social and religious problems of the country were taken up by the bishops in a document of 15 August 1968: The Church is in the service of truth, justice, and fraternal charity; it must especially promote the realization of social justice in a dynamic of development to freedom on the regional, national, and international plane. It must renew itself by a social pastoral work: "We are aware," it was said, "that worldly work is a redeeming work, because the function of Christ is of a universal nature. Through the impetus of fraternal charity we are ready to cooperate with all men of goodwill, because every man is redeemed by Christ, is a child of God, who claims our cooperation and our services.[89]

Miner Priests

The fourth Congress of Miner Priests published the decrees of Oruro of 31 July 1969: Capitalism is condemned, "aware of the redeeming message of Christ and of our task in the world, we oblige ourselves to intensify our exertions in the service of Bolivia's miners in their struggle for freedom."[90] On the basis of information on the collaboration of priests in the mass rallies and on political sermons, members of the Episcopal Conference declared on 10 September 1969: "We are of the opinion that the function of priests is incompatible with membership in a political party, if it demands compliance with peculiar objectives of party doctrine which close the door to other groupings; thereby their universality in the service of all is placed in question." They support their attitude with the teaching of the Second Vatican Council and the declarations of the Congress of Medellín of 1968.[91]

The opposition between the Bolivian Episcopal Conference and the Secretariat for Social Action caused the chairman of the Commission for Social Action, Jesús Agustín López de Lama, bishop of Corocoro, to resign his office. The secretariat was temporarily closed; the decision affected the relations of the conference to *Iglesia y Sociedad para América Latina* (ISAL), a movement which cooperated very closely in Bolivia with the Secretariat for Social Action.[92]

New Initiatives

At the time forty-five Aymará Indians were preparing for the diaconate. These natives—ca. 3.3 million of them live in the mountains of

---

[89] Ibid. 1 (April 1969), 1365–88.
[90] *Christus* 410 (Mexico, July–Dec. 1970), 742–44.
[91] Ibid., 744–46.
[92] *SEDOC* 4 (Feb. 1972), 1005–10.

Bolivia and Peru—are catechists, who after training are ordained deacons in order to care for their fellows.[93]

In this declaration Cardinal José Clemente Maurer, C.S.S.R., archbishop of Sucre, proposed to sell all the property collected by the Church of Bolivia in the course of four hundred years in order to expedite the construction of social institutions. Following this proposal the Oblates donated all their goods for the building of schools and public hospitals in Bolivia.[94]

Within its social program, the Church of Bolivia built houses for poor families and persons of moderate means.[95] Every residential district provided a church, school, outpatient department, and other services. The land for construction was donated by the Franciscans of Sucre. The construction itself was financed by donations which Cardinal Maurer collected in Trévesis, his diocese of origin.[96] Furthermore, ca. 200 hospitals were built in the country by the Church, and almost all savings groups came out of the parishes. Several programs for systematic education were taken up by the Church. In the entire country there was a network of centers which originated in the Church's initiative. More than 2,000 volunteers worked in the programs of several broadcasting companies which were heard in hundreds of centers. This entire work was realized by the Church by means of institutions of various kinds.[97]

Increase of Priestly Vocations

Although the number of priestly ordinations is still too small in comparison with the priests needed, said Cardinal Maurer of Sucre, vocations are increasing in Bolivia. Some eighty seminarians will shortly be ordained, and married deacons will soon help the overburdened priests. The latest statistics establish that, of 913 priests who are active in the sixteen dioceses, only ca. 200 were born in the country.[98] North American missionaries support five catechetical centers among the Aymará Indians and in recent years have trained some one thousand catechists. Of these, 100 were chosen for the diaconate. The positive experience among the Aymarás has led to this beginning among the Quechuas, whose number is estimated at 1.2 million. In Bolivia there are 293 North American missionaries, including two laymen, forty-two diocesan priests, 11 religious priests from five congregations, and 138 sisters from four congregations. The Maryknoll Congregation supplies

[93] *AICA* 15, 758f. (17 June 1971), 31.
[94] Ibid. 16, 803 (11 May 1972), 23.
[95] Ibid. 17, 810 (29 June 1972), 17f.
[96] Ibid. 18, 8, 893 (31 Jan. 1974), 19.
[97] Ibid. 17, 873 (13 Sept. 1973), 17f.
[98] Ibid. 17, 817 (17 Aug. 1972), 30.

the largest number, with 62 priests and 43 sisters.[99] Cardinal Maurer and the minister of religion found words of praise for the Maryknoll Brothers because of their helpful efforts for so many Bolivians in the struggle against illiteracy with the aid of the radio. The Bolivian broadcasting companies form a society which has constructed nine transmitters and is under the direction of these missionaries.[100]

Authentic Justice and Humanization

The Bolivian Commission *Justicia y Paz,* founded at the beginning of 1973, in view of the situation in the nation condemned in a statement the restriction on freedom of the press and the persecution of the political opponents of the regime. The Bolivian Workers' Central Office is ignored and the unions are manipulated from above. All liberal activities are suppressed, and intrusions are increasing in regard to both democratic institutions and private persons. Injustices are perpetrated against those of different political views, political prisoners live in miserable conditions in the prisons, and deaths by torture take place. Despite many promises, the regime has not thus far stopped these methods.[101]

PERU

Peru has a total of 1,285,215 square kilometers, and according to the 1974 census 13,672,052 inhabitants,[102] of whom two-fifths are Indians and an equal number mestizos. Ca. 75 percent of the population is Catholic.

The Peruvian episcopate consists of fifty-three members, of whom seven are archbishops, twelve residential bishops, four bishops with superdiocesan functions, eight auxiliary bishops, eight vicars apostolic, and fourteen prelacies. The Church provinces are Lima, Huancayo, Piura, Trujillo, Arequipa, Ayacucho, and Cuzco. With the bishops, the retired priests, and the priests outside Peru, Peru numbers 967 diocesan and 1,492 religious priests, altogether then 2,459. In addition, the statistics show 597 religious brothers, 4,395 sisters of contemplative orders, 810 parishes with pastors, and 284 parishes without pastors.

Since 1973 the republic has been divided into eight pastoral regions: the northern mountain chain in the area of Cafamarca; the northern coast in the territory of Trujillo; the central mountain chain in the area of Huancayo; the area of Lima; the central coast in the territory of Ica;

[99] Ibid. 17, 831 (23 Nov. 1972), 26f.
[100] Ibid. 18, 833 (22 Nov. 1973), 29f.
[101] *SEDOC* 6 (Dec. 1973), 741–45.
[102] Basadre, *Chile, Perú y Bolivia independientes,* 6f.; *Anuario eclesiástico del Perú* (1974).

southern Peru in the area of Arequipa; the southern Andes in the area of Cuzco; primitive forest in the territory of Pucalipa.[103]

Educational Institutions

Since 1917 Lima has had a Catholic university, which on 30 September 1942 was given the title "papal" by the Holy See and which was recognized by the state as a national university in 1949. The University of San Cristóbal, founded in 1668, continued its work in the twentieth century as an official institute for higher ecclesiastical studies, associated with the papal university. However, only 8 percent of the students in the entire republic attend the Catholic university. More than one hundred schools are run by diocesan or religious priests, more than one hundred fifty by sisters.[104]

The religious-philosophical positivism, which achieved its greatest importance at the Universidad Nacional de San Marcos in the years after 1920, fell for a while under the influence of Bergson. Finally it was supplanted by Marxism when representatives such as José Carlos Mariategui (1895–1930), a figure of great repute in all of Latin America, and the Marxist Victor Raúl Haya de la Torre occupied chairs there. An investigation of opinion in the university sphere—2,101 questioned—revealed that some 20 percent professed themselves to be atheists or "not believers in the Church." In fact, atheism was on the march.[105] As early as 15 June 1939 the Episcopal Conference had complained in an encyclical that "humanitarian" societies were pursuing Communist goals, "socialization" was making progress, as were pornography and divorce; with the aid of the school monopoly "a school without God" was being sought.[106]

The Social Sphere

On 3 October 1968 the troops overthrew President Belaúnde in a coup d'état. Juan Velasco Alvarado formed the new government, which proclaimed land reform in May 1969, an organic law of the Peruvian university in February 1969, and an industrial law in July 1970. This comprehensive revolution forced the Peruvian Church to revise its position. After the publication of the encyclical *Populorum progressio,* there was formed in March 1968 a group of priests to realize the social apostolates. The so-called group ONIS—*Oficina Nacional Información*

---

[103] *Anuario eclesiástico del Perú* (1974).
[104] G. Lohmann Villena, "Perú," *New Catholic Encyclopedia* XI, 184–92; M. B. Murphy, *Pontifical Catholic University of Peru,* 193.
[105] Cf. F. Interdonato, S.J., *El ateísmo en el mundo actual. Estudio aplicado al Perú,* 29, 33, 74–89, 373–76.
[106] *Revista de la Universidad católica del Perú* VI, 206–19.

Social—often supported the measures taken by the government in favor of a higher social justice.[107] In the decrees of the second meeting in October 1969 it was said: In the planned separation of Church and state no deceptions should be practiced in an effort to retain the existing situation; the agricultural property of dioceses and congregations must not be excluded from the land reform; mentality, attitude, and manner of life must be changed in order to break with the conditions of privilege.[108]

On 2 July 1970 the Permanent Commission of the Peruvian Episcopal Conference published a letter in which the collaboration of the Church in the construction of a better world was made concrete. The bishops admitted that, by their defective loyalty to the Gospel, Christians have contributed to the origin of the present situation, and regarded it as a duty of the Peruvian Church to carry through a revision of all ownership in immovable property and goods of every sort of the dioceses, congregations, and ecclesiastical institutions. The meeting reminded teachers of their great responsibility in education and admonished them to intensify their pastoral action in public and private schools and to cooperate with the state educational authorities.[109]

From 30 April to 2 May 1971 a workers' parish in Lima brought together more than thirteen hundred persons; the invitation proceeded from the laity. Among those invited were representatives of the *Movimiento de Trabajadores Cristianos,* of *Juventud Obrera Católica,* of the *Unión Nacional de Estudiantes Cathólicos y Movimiento Sacerdotal* (ONIS). Seventy study groups worked out several resolutions, including this one: There prevails in the nation an injustice, which especially burdens the lower classes. This situation cannot be accepted by any Christian. The new society must be classless, with community possession of the means of production. The Church must give up its privileged property position, its involvement with the state, and repressive pastoral methods. Therefore, the religious institutes must give up their schools which are reserved to the rich. They desire a Church which supports the oppressed, not the oppressors. They propose to form contemplative and active groups with a coordination committee, to promote works of documentation to prove the oppression of the majority of Peruvians, and finally they claim to form themselves as representatives of the formation of opinion and organs of information in and outside the Church.[110]

[107] *Christus* 410 (July–Dec. 1970), 762; *SEDOC* 2 (Nov. 1969), 657–60.
[108] *SEDOC* 2 (May 1970), 1437–40.
[109] *Christus* 410 (July–Dec. 1970), 762–77.
[110] R. Antoncich, S.J., "Lima: 'Cristianos en un mundo de injusticia.' Primer encuentro por una Iglesia solidaria," *Mensaje* 200, 307f.

At the conclusion of their forty-second conference at Lima, 19–27 January 1972, the Peruvian bishops published a letter on evangelization and explained the guidelines and aims for the propagation of the faith, even to its introduction in school.[111] At the Roman Synod of Bishops of 1974 Monseñor Durand Flores called attention to the successful work of the pastoral Priests' Councils, in which for five years also religious priests, sisters, and lay persons, as well as representatives of the eight regions, had participated. The chief concern was for the 6 million Indians, whose piety was still mixed with pagan elements. They had to be shown that the external activity, processions, sacraments, and even the Mass, are means of experiencing the state of being God's children.[112] At the Roman Synod the auxiliary bishop of Lima, Schmitz Sauerborn, likewise referred to the Christian tradition of the country; it is important to preserve it by having the Church take an interest in persons and in human rights.[113]

ECUADOR

Ecuador has an area of 283,561 square kilometers and in 1968 had 4,509,768 inhabitants; the Vatican statistics for 1971 give 6,297,000 inhabitants and 5,359,000 Catholics. The country is divided into three ecclesiastical provinces: Cuenca, Guayaquil, and Quito. Cuenca has three suffragans: Azogues, Loja, and Machala. Guayaquil embraces the diocese of Puertoviejo and the prelacy of Los Ríos. To Quito belong the sees of Ambato, Guaranda, Ibarra, Latacunga, Riobamba, and Tulcán. There are five vicariates apostolic: Esmeraldas, Méndez, Napo, Puyo, and Zamora, and three prefectures apostolic: Aguarico, Galápagos, and San Miguel de Sucumbios.[114]

Of the 762 diocesan priests in 1968, 65 percent (432) do pastoral work in the parishes, 11.2 percent (86) are in administration, 4 percent (31) are in superparochial pastoral care, 3.9 percent (31) are active as teachers in seminaries.[115] In the country there are 898 religious priests, who belong to eighteen different institutes. The diocese with the most religious priests is Quito with 287, followed by Guayaquil with 141, Puertoviejo with 41, and Cuenca with 60. Twenty-two percent of the religious priests devote themselves to teaching—37 percent, if one considers those active in seminaries; 22 percent are in parish work, 18

[111]*SEDOC* 5 (Dec. 1973), 751–68.
[112]*Osservatore Romano,* 3 Oct. 1974.
[113]Ibid., 10 Oct. 1974.
[114]*La Iglesia en el Ecuador. Estudio del personal de 1968* II/1, Análisis, 1, 12; *Annuario Pontificio* (1977), 957.
[115]*La Iglesia en el Ecuador,* ibid., 4, 13.

percent are entrusted with other pastoral duties, 17 percent are occupied in administration. The total number of male religious is 1,576, of sisters 3,622. A great many of them are active in schools, headed by the Christian Brothers, the Salesians, and the Jesuits.[116]

School System

Eighty percent of Ecuador's schools are public. According to Paragraph 16 of the 1906 constitution the school system is public, free, and lay. In accord with Paragraph 151, 21 (1929), private schools remain under state control. The situation worsened further after the proclamation of totalitarianism (Paragraph 142, 3, [1945]) in education; a year later, in 1946, Marxian totalitarianism was annulled and the right of their own type of education for their children was transferred to the parents. A subsidy of 20 percent of the costs incurred was approved for the lay school which was neither for nor against religion, presupposing that it did not charge fees. From the start, the Church fought laicism and put personnel and financial means at the disposal of the building of its own schools. The pupils of the lay schools, who often came from Christian families, were not regarded in a friendly manner and remained isolated; the teachers often had the feeling of being regarded as traitors. Later the Church organized a pastoral action also outside the school: youth centers, Catholic Action, and so forth, in order to better care for youth living apart from the Church. In recent times the opposition has broken down, and the desire for rapprochement and cooperation has become apparent. The Church makes its contribution through *Caritas,* social concern, libraries, and direct contact with teachers.[117]

Political and Socioeconomic Position of the Church

The episcopate of Ecuador treated the political and socioeconomic problems of the country through its Permanent Commission in two documents. The point of departure of the first, that of 31 December 1967, was the elections of 2 June 1968. The second document, published at Easter of 1968, produced some guiding principles for the building of a "creative peace." The bishops indicated that in a Church which wants to retain its internal autonomy, the members of the clergy and of religious institutes must renounce political rights and duties which pertain to them as members of the political community in order thereby to hold themselves aloof from party conflicts. They recall the "programmatic statement" of the Ecuadorian episcopate: The Church

[116] Ibid., 15–44; *Estudio de la viceprovincia del Ecuador* III/1: *Estudio del personal. Estudio de las residencias y parroquias,* 4.
[117] *La Iglesia en el Ecuador,* ibid., 49.

of Ecuador can in the sense of its permanent function neither identify itself with a political group nor bind itself to a system; no political grouping can claim the quality of a Catholic institution or ecclesiastical authority.[118] In the second document it is stressed that peace demands the unity of all citizens, for the development of all social strata, especially of those of modest means and those standing apart; this is the necessary presupposition for a creative peace.[119] On 20 June 1969 the Episcopal Conference at Baños outlined the function of the priest in the world and gave guidelines for dialogue and coresponsibility with economic life, work, and for celibacy.[120]

First National Assembly of Ecuadorian Priests

As the outcome of the first meeting with the participation of ninety-nine priests from almost all dioceses of the country, three bishops, and two foreign priests—from Peru and Bolivia—seven seminarians, and twelve young lay persons, there was published a detailed statement with the following content: crisis of the clergy; collegiality; authority and obedience in the Church; autonomy of the Ecuadorian Church; economic position of the clergy; priestly celibacy; priests and freedom; priests and politics; formation of priests; the priest as a man and the priestly vocation. Obedience means coresponsibility, coparticipation, and dialogue; evangelization represents a liberating message, which interprets in the world the historical process proclaimed by the Holy Spirit. The priest has within the Christian community the right to occupy political positions in harmony with his conscience. An ever more secularized society, which denies a vocation devoted to sanctification, demands that the priest live by a professional work and not by his spiritual ministry, which should be gratis, but this does not prevent priests who exercise only the latter from obtaining the necessities of life from their communities.[121] The bishop of Riobamba, Monseñor Leónidas Proaño Villalba, proposed in a letter of 1969 an ideal program of poverty for the basic renewal of his diocese.[122]

In Search of an Integral Development

The Permanent Committee of the Commission *Justicia y Paz* of Ecuador complained at the conclusion of the meeting at El Inca of 18–19 December 1970 that the slight economic growth of the preceding

[118] *SEDOC* 2 (Aug. 1968), 233–38.
[119] Ibid.
[120] Ibid. 2 (Nov. 1969), 669–72.
[121] "Primera convención nacional de presbíteros del Ecuador," *Christus* 410 (Mexico, July–Dec. 1970), 318–55.
[122] *SEDOC* 2 (June 1970), 1587–90.

years was obtained at the expense of the lower classes of city and country and for the benefit of the upper and middle classes and a certain higher developed working class, and proposed to coordinate all initiatives and private or public programs in order to achieve the desired progress.[123] A meeting of more than one hundred priests in April 1971 accepted the decrees of Medellín and condemned the civil and religious persecution of persons who were engaged in the liberation and renewal of the Church. The priests declared that the Church as a community of faith adheres to the destiny of the human being and sees itself justified in criticizing, in condemning injustice, oppression, and abuse of power, and finally in keeping alive hope as the motivating power of a permanent renewal. Hunger, illiteracy, unemployment, exploitation of workers and peasants, concentration of power in a few hands are the consequences of the capitalism dominant in the country. They concede their cosharing in the capitalistic system if they defend, in the name of God, private ownership of the means of production.[124] Thereupon the Episcopal Conference from 2 to 4 March 1972 elaborated a comprehensive pastoral plan: reevaluation of the person, evangelization and deepening of the faith, role of the visible Church.[125] The government was requested, in regard to the politically suspect, to respect the basic rights of citizens in investigations, and they point out the right of prisoners to come before a nonpartisan court. This attitude results not from political or partisan motives but as a contribution to the welfare of the country.[126]

The Church Facing the New Agrarian Law

The bishop of Riobamba, Monseñor Leónidas Proaño Villalba, in a letter of 1974 to the president of the republic analyzed the situation of the peasants in the province of Chimborazo: Of the 400,000 inhabitants of this province, 300,000 are *campesinos* and 52 percent illiterate. The impoverished areas do not offer the small owner even the most elementary living conditions, and in other areas the *latifundia* stifle every effort for survival. Monseñor Proaño examines the deficiencies of the new law and offers the cooperation of the Church in applying it.[127]

The Church in the Present

At the 1974 Roman Synod of Bishops the archbishop of Guayaquil, Echevarría Ruíz, made known that a text had been worked out which

[123] Ibid 4 (Sept. 1971), 361–65.
[124] Ibid., 365–69.
[125] Ibid. 5 (Dec. 1972), 747–60.
[126] *AICA* 17, 842 (18 Feb. 1973), 40f.
[127] Ibid., 18, 900 (21 March 1974), 23f.

contained the guidelines of the history of salvation and the method of administering the sacraments. The text was distributed among priests, religious, and catechists in order to assure unity of arguments and of manner of presentation. It was thereby attempted to actualize the theological formation of the clergy. The successes of these initiatives have become visible in small communities, parishes, and at the Eucharistic Congress.[128]

COLOMBIA

Colombia covers 1,130,000 square kilometers and has about 24 million inhabitants,[129] of whom 97.5 percent are Catholics.[130] The people of the mountains differ in their religious outlook from those of the lowland, due to geographical and climatic conditions. About 98 percent of the Colombian population inhabits the mountain area, with a higher and more uniform culture. In the country parishes piety is mixed with superstitious concomitants and numerous errors as a consequence of earlier struggles and of the lack of priests.

In 1948 the republic had 1,074 parishes, 2,263 churches and chapels, and 1,642 priests. At that time the seminaries were attended by 560 candidates for the priesthood; in the minor seminaries there were 1,780 pupils. Altogether there were 10,488,669 Catholics. In 1966 4,214 priests were active, of whom 2,632 were diocesan and 1,852 religious; there were 2,221 brothers and 15,086 sisters.[131] In 1971 the Vatican statistics counted 56 ecclesiastical jurisdictions and 1,851 parishes.

Since 1944 Catholic Social Action has been established in urban and rural professional associations. The urban associations are organized in regional societies, such as the *Unión de Trabajadores de Antioqua* (UTRAN), with seventy unions and more than 30,000 members. The rural professional associations constitute the *Federación Agraria Nacional* (FANAL), with 400 unions and more than 100,000 members; it publishes an organ for the leading members, the weekly *Justicia Social,* with a circulation of 300,000, in addition to newspapers and prospectuses. All these urban and rural associations gradually joined the *Unión de Trabajadores Colombianos* (UTC), which counts more than 300 unions and over 150,000 members. The national *Junta* for social actions consists of the archbishops of Bogotá, Medellín, Cartagena, and Popayán; they have collaborators on the national and local level.

---

[128] *Osservatore Romano,* 2 Oct. 1974.
[129] Cf. V. Vives, op. cit. IV/2, 594f.
[130] *AICA* 17, 852 (19 April 1973), 21f.
[131] *Revista Javeriana* 57 (Bogotá 1962), 110.

School System

In Antioquia alone—apart from the Pontificia Universidad Bolivariana with 104 professors—there were eleven colleges with 1,537 students, which are run by priests. Altogether 3,932 students in the republic attended institutions of higher learning, which were likewise under priestly management. The statistical handbook of 1948 counts 413 modern secondary schools with 90,787 students and 1,040 public schools with 74,942 pupils, a total of 1,453 schools and 165,724 pupils. It is to be noted that the high schools run by priests and religious institutes are attended by 80 percent of the students in the country. As coordinating element of the private schools there functions the *Confederación de Colegios Católicos,* which for several years has published an educational periodical.

Colombia has two papal universities: the Pontificia Universidad Javeriana at Bogotá, since 31 July 1939 with faculties of theology, canon law, philosophy, literature, education, law, economic and social sciences, medicine and dentistry, engineering and architecture; the Pontificia Universidad Católica Bolivariana (Medellín), since 10 August 1945 with faculties of law, political and social sciences, economics and business, philosophy and education, literature, engineering, electricity and chemistry, architecture, city-planning and fine arts.[132] Important cultural centers are also the San Bartolomé and Rosario schools in Bogotá, from which have come the most outstanding representatives of the so-called generation of the "Centennial Anniversary." New seminaries arose at Bogotá, Medellín, Manizales, Ibagué, Popayán, Garzón, Barranquilla, and San Gil, which are conducted by priests and religious brothers, especially by Lazarists and Eudists, and accomplish an immense teaching function.

Missions and Missionaries

The Colombian missions embrace extensive areas; geographically considered, more than half the nation is occupied by foreign missionaries; they are mostly Augustinians, Carmelites, Jesuits, and especially Capuchins.

Catholic Initiatives

One of Colombia's most original institutions and at the same time the one with the greatest response in the country is the Workers' Circle and Savings Bank of Father José María Campoamor, who died in 1949; it supports agencies in many cities of the republic. A like importance

---

[132] *Annuario Pontificio* (1974), 1371, 1374.

belongs to the activity of Monseñor Agustín Gutiérrez in the model parish of Fómeque or the Eucharistic Schools of Medellín, founded by the pastor of the San José parish, which on the occasion of the Catechetical Congress at Boston received special honor.

There are three leper stations: Aguas de Dios, Contratación, and Caño de Loro, which are cared for by the Salesians. And the Society of Saint Vincent de Paul is heavily involved in this sphere. According to statistics of 1938, the Church supports 107 social welfare institutions at its own expense. Forty homes for the aged are cared for by religious, but only twenty-eight of them receive state support. Of the eighty orphanages, only nine obtain state help. Nevertheless, the number of welfare institutions increases.[133]

The Voice of the Bishops

Since 1948 we have known the most important problems of the Colombian Church through the episcopal documents. From 20 June to 3 July of that year the Episcopal Conference examined the most pressing problems of the Church and the solutions suited to them in an effort to preserve religion and nation from great dangers. In this connection they elaborated three topics: Communism, "which was, alas, already very deeply rooted," the Church's social teaching, the sole means of loosening the social tensions between capital and labor in the order of mercy and justice, and finally "the most important errors of doctrinaire liberalism" in questions which affect religion.[134] The pastoral letter of 30 November 1951 developed the following themes: the dignity of Christian life; the necessity of religious education; deplorable vices for lack of Christian life; drunkenness; loss of self-esteem by women because of the lack of Christian awareness; Christian life of society, Christian mercy, effects of violence in Colombia.[135] At the beginning of Lent, on 11 February 1955, the bishops explained the position of the Church in regard to unions and condemned the *Confederación Nacional de Trabajadores* (CNT), whose leaders had from the start repudiated the Church's authority, because it was influenced by socialist tendencies and radiated a Peronist character in the broadest sense. A further topic was Peronist justicialism, condemned by the Church because of its totalitarian claims, and the dangers of socialism.

---

[133] Cf. J. Álvarez Mejiá, S.J., "La Iglesia católica en Colombia," *Revista Javeriana* 28 (Bogotá 1947), 102–10; E. Ospina, S.J., "Diez años de vida católica en Colombia," *Revista Javeriana* 30 (Bogotá 1948), 251–61.

[134] F. Velázquez, S.J., "Las direcciones de la conferencia episcopal," *Revista Javeriana* 30 (Bogotá 1948), 65–68.

[135] "Pastoral colectiva del episcopado colombiano," *Revista Javeriana* 37 (Bogotá 1952), 3–9.

The bishops were likewise concerned with Colombian socialism and its doctrine: that the goals of society are directed only to material welfare, that the economy should be collectivist. In this connection the bishops again explained the Church's social doctrine.[136] Also the pastoral letter on the occasion of Lent 1958 dealt with the social problems and their solution, based on the papal teachings.[137]

The nineteenth Episcopal Conference at Bogotá in mid-September 1958 in an appeal called upon all Colombian Catholics to practice Christian charity. In the last part and under the title "Practical Applications" they recommended the sincere unity of all Colombians without exception, effective punishment of crimes, moderation in the criticism of political opponents, in both the printed and the spoken word, and true interest in the solution of social problems and the reduction of prices for basic foods as an expression of goodwill by producers and merchants. In addition, they suggested a social reform in regard to the equal distribution of the profit sought, the implementation of savings measures and capital investments in management in order to guarantee full employment and assure cooperation in common projects. The conference published two more instructions: one on a general cultural campaign, the other on the rights of the Church, the state, and the family in education.[138]

Agricultural Reform

The National Congress of Agriculture at Bogotá 24–27 November 1959 treated in two working groups the difficult topic of land reform from the Church's viewpoint: In one there took part representatives of the bishops, clergy, universities, agricultural authorities, and employers; in the other sat representatives of the farmers, small landholders, and tenants, who belonged to various agricultural organizations. There was agreement as to the necessity of assisting the agricultural worker to grow into his role as landowner, just as into the role of father of a family, citizen, or Christian, and to awaken in him the readiness to accept outside help. Two-thirds of the population earn their living from agriculture. According to the statistics of CEPAC there are in Colombia 32 *latifundia* with a total of more than 480,000 hectares, 120,000 *minifundia* with only 54,000 hectares, and so on the average hardly two and a half hectares per farm, and a further 268,000 small farms with less than two hectares each. Previously this situation was a good

---

[136] "El episcopado colombiano condena la CNT. Pastoral colectiva," *Revista Javeriana* 43 (Bogotá 1955), 129–238.
[137] *Revista Javeriana* 49 (Bogotá 1958), 37.
[138] Ibid. 50 (Bogotá 1958), 43f.

soil for Communist propaganda. The Colombian Church, on the other hand, was always bound by means of its pastors to the rural population. For the farmer the pastor represented the leader, who was followed without hesitation, not only in spiritual but in material affairs. From colonial times, priests were the pioneers in the construction of streets, aqueducts, schools, and hospitals.[139]

Communist Infiltration in the University

The twentieth Episcopal Conference at Bogotá in a document examined the national crisis which impaired social life, analyzed its bases, and offered guidelines for a suitable solution. The Church seeks reform of the social structures, but declares at the same time: A true Catholic cannot reconcile the religious attitude with injustice and violence in the social field. Only an integrated Catholic concept, so the announcement says, will overcome the Communist threat. It is not a crust of bread that the Colombian people demand but complete respect for the dignity of the person, integrated by Christ into the unity of the Church.[140] The Episcopal Conference indicated the danger of Communist infiltration into education, especially in the nation's universities.[141]

The Postconciliar Church

In April 1965 the archbishops of the eight most important dioceses of Colombia expressed themselves on the present situation of the nation and the problems which jeopardize the stability of institutions and could lead to anarchy and chaos. The most important causes: the violence prevailing for many years, with many deaths; unemployment and crowding of people in poor lodgings, conditioned by the move of large masses of persons from the countryside to the cities; exaggerated quest for profits; speculation with all goods; attacks on and kidnappings of persons; destroyed families, left in the lurch by the father; obscene films and those that glorify violence and crime; the progress of Communism—supreme danger for religion and country. Peace, say the bishops, is the result of truth, justice, love, and liberty, for which they pray.[142]

---

[139] V. Andrade, S.J., "Es necesario conocer el planteamiento católico de la reforma agraria en Colombia. Primer congreso nacional católico de vida rural (Bogotá 24–27 Nov. 1959). Congreso nacional compesino, 25–28 Nov. 1959," *Revista Javeriana* 53 (Bogotá 1960), 3–6.

[140] J. Martínez Cárdenas, S.J., "Declaración de la jerarquía," *Revista Javeriana* 54(Bogotá 1960), 683–86.

[141] "Comunismo en la Universidad de Colombia?" *Revista Javeriana* 54(Bogotá 1960), 683–86.

[142] "Orientación de la jerarquía," *Revista Javeriana* 63 (Bogotá 1965), 412–16.

The National Plan for Pastoral Care

Presented in 1966 to the twenty-second Episcopal Conference, it followed the recommendations for pastoral reform of the Second Vatican Council and was approved by the Church of Colombia.[143] Pastoral action had to be extraordinary, thanks to the sacrifice with which it was pushed; uniform, that is, the same solutions for the same problems; planned, that is, with exactly established aims and priorities.[144]

Pastoral Letter to the International Eucharistic Congress

The Colombian bishops issued a pastoral letter to the International Eucharistic Congress at Bogotá of 18–25 August 1968, with the following topical content: In the sense of the congress, which in the light of faith represents an echo of life in the Church renewing itself, and in the spirit of the Second Vatican Council, one must try to construct the genuine Christian community. It will stand at the focal point of all nations and be a way to the unity of men.[145] Shortly before, on 4 May 1968, the twenty-second Episcopal Conference had directed a message to priests.[146]

The Priestly Group of Golconda

The group first met in July 1968 to go more deeply into the encyclical *Populorum progressio,* and for the second time in December of the same year to discuss the social problems of Colombia. The final document explained its ideological guidelines. The priests regarded their participation in the political life of the nation as a duty of conscience and an exercise of charity in its deepest sense. In the orientations for their activities they rejected the idea of restricting themselves to limiting work which would lose sight of national and international perspectives. Futhermore, they asserted their strict rejection of neocolonial capitalism, which is incapable of solving the problems of their country. A form of society of a socialist stamp is necessary. It should extirpate all types of exploitation of men by men and be in harmony with the historical tendencies of this period and the characteristics of Colombians.[147]

Implementation of the Medellín Decrees

The Episcopal Conference met at the beginning of July 1969 to discuss the application of the decrees of Medellín. Despite the justified desire

[143] "El plan pastoral del episcopado colombiano," *Revista Javeriana* 67 (1967), 321f.
[144] Cf. ibid., 351f.
[145] Cf. *SEDOC* 2 (Aug. 1968), 225–30.
[146] Ibid. 1 (Oct. 1968), 571–85.
[147] Ibid. 1 (May 1969), 1453–60.

for change, three positions could be maintained. The first is indifference, in regard to which only one's own interests matter and one acts as though the problems of change do not concern one; this attitude is comfortable, but very dangerous. As a second attitude there is that of the integralists; they desire to preserve everything because everything has a value, the loss of which can be painful; this attitude makes change difficult and intensifies the tensions with the champions of change. Finally, there are the radicals: they are in the front line and irreconcilable; they regard the past as a mere failure and steadfastly proclaim the new order. Amazingly, the conservatives and the radicals often join hands and thus one dogma replaces the other. The Church, on the other hand, which now unconditionally needs a renewal, must live in a permanent process of conversion from the Gospel, and this especially demands an interior reform by each and every member of the Church. The Church is there to serve people. Thus is manifested its desire for change, from immobility to dynamism, the effect of which will be the renewal of the whole person.[148]

Birth Control

In view of the government's birth control campaign, the Colombian episcopate published a statement on 2 October 1969. In it the problem of family planning is examined. The Church claims the right to interpret natural law and to defend the personal rights of people. The problem of birth control, like every other related to human life, must be considered in the mirror of the human being and his natural and supernatural vocation.[149]

Land Reform and Limitation of Property

The Permanent Commission of the Episcopal Conference in 1971 proposed a land reform and a limitation of the landed property which could belong to one person or one group, including the Church and the state. The declaration was published the day preceding a twenty-four-hour general strike which was proclaimed by the unions to achieve urban and agricultural reforms. Colombia can no longer wait for land reform.[150]

Catholic-Anglican Dialogue

From 9 to 14 February 1971 there took place at Bogotá a meeting between Catholic and Anglican bishops which had been prepared by

---

[148] Ibid. 2 (Nov. 1969), 649–54.
[149] Ibid. 2 (May 1970), 1461–63; cf. *Revista Javeriana* 68 (Bogotá 1967), 197–209.
[150] *AICA* 15, 754f. (20 May 1971), 26f.

the ecumenical division of CELAM and the *Conferencia Anglicana Latinoamericana* (CALA). Ten bishops from each side took part; their aim was an exchange of ideas as well as a better acquaintance. Four themes were to be discussed: Holy Scripture; relations between Catholics and Anglicans in Latin America; authority, office, and sacraments; cooperation in the missions.[151]

Social Security for the Clergy

In its last plenary meeting in 1971, the Episcopal Conference unanimously decided to establish social security for the priests. This guarantees almost 3,000 priests against the risks of old age, sickness, and in the case of death.[152]

VENEZUELA

Venezuela is a federal republic with 912,050 square kilometers and 11 million inhabitants, of whom ca. 100,000 are Indians; 94 percent are Catholics. The great natural resources, gold and petroleum, cause an imbalance in the economic structure of the nation, for to the degree that the production of petroleum increases, workmen abandon agriculture; at the same time the cost of living has so grown that as early as 1942 Venezuela was one of the most expensive countries in the world.[153]

Ecclesiastical Organization

From the beginning of the twentieth century the Church of Venezuela has had a considerable lack of priests, caused especially by the suppression of the monasteries in the nineteenth century. The archdiocese of Caracas had capable archbishops: Juan Bautista Castro (1904–15), Felipe Rincón González (1916–46), Lucas Guillermo Castillo (1946–55), Rafael Arías Blanco (1955–56). Castro in particular fostered a better formation of the clergy, spread of devotion to the Eucharist, retreats for men, founding of colleges by religious, systematic spread of catechesis, rearrangement of dioceses by a better common pastoral care, founding of seminaries and new parishes, and improvement of Indian pastoral care. In 1962 the republic had three archdioceses, twelve dioceses, one prelacy *nullius,* and four vicariates apostolic.[154] In 1975 there were six archdioceses: Caracas, Mérida, Ciudad

---

[151] Ibid. 15, 758f. (17 June 1971), 33–35.
[152] Ibid. 17, 813 (20 July 1972), 31f.
[153] Cf. V. Vives, op. cit. IV/2, 609–12; Maldonado, *Anuario católico de Venezuela* (1962), 55–65.
[154] V. Iriarte, *La arquidiócesis de Caracas de 1900–1966,* 365–69; Maldonado, op. cit.

Bolívar, Barquisimeto, Maracaibo, and Valencia; seventeen dioceses and four vicariates apostolic: Caroní, Puerto Ayacucho, Machiques, and Tucupita.[155]

In 1971 there were 798 parishes. Lay organizations consist of, among others, Catholic Action, Catholic Young Workers, the Legion of Mary, The Christian Family Movement, a union of Catholic teachers, a center for film culture; the *Opus Dei* and the Venezuelan Society of Saint Vincent de Paul are active.[156]

The Catholic university Andrés Bello, founded 25 September 1953, was elevated to a papal university on 29 September 1963. The seminary of Santa Rosa, interdiocesan since 1927, was entrusted to the Jesuits in 1916, but since 19 August 1956 to the Eudists. In the 175 Church schools and 312 colleges 104,414 students were instructed.[157]

In keeping with the motu proprio *Ecclesiae Sanctae,* a Priests' Council with eighteen members and a Pastoral Council were established on 6 August 1966. Several commissions were incorporated in the Secretariat for Social Action, Education, and Vocations: for liturgy, sacred art, church music, and travel movements, which exercised their activity in sixteen different places; a Secretariat for Church Information with a research center for social and socioreligious questions was added.[158] To make up for the lack of priests, the meeting for the promotion of pastoral vocations, held at Caracas from 14 to 19 April 1967, proposed to the bishops the founding of appropriate centers.[159]

Situation of the Church

The common pastoral letter on the occasion of the nineteenth centenary of the martyrdom of the Apostles Peter and Paul, issued from Caracas on 22 March 1967, describes the real situation of the Church of Venezuela: "Although only a few deny the existence of God, a 'practical' atheism has spread, which consists in forgetting God and every spiritual order, indifference toward the Church, adoration of prosperity as the *ultima ratio* of life and of the creation of mankind. For not a small number sin is already a meaningless word, for they know no fundamental difference between good and evil." In the effort to adapt oneself to modern thought and with disregard for the Church's *magisterium,* Christianity is given an arbitrary and fruitless interpreta-

[155] *Directorio de la Iglesia católica en Venezuela* (1975), 400f.
[156] Ibid., 300–356.
[157] Ibid., 341; Maldonado, op. cit.; *Annuario Pontificio 1977,* 1404.
[158] V. Iriarte, op. cit. 369.
[159] L.C.; *Conclusiones de la I asamblea arquidiocesana de pastoral vocacional. Sic* 30, 254–56.

tion and thereby uncertainty of faith is created.[160] In a memorandum of the Bureau for Social and Economic Studies of 1967 attention is called to the fact that in 1963 46.3 percent of the newly born were illegitimate, 20 percent of the total population had had no education, the teachers of all grades were uninterested in religion. Pastoral care must conclude especially that Christian social doctrine must be introduced into the seminaries and Catholic universities as an obligatory course.[161]

Social Works

The Work for the Protection of the Child (OPAN) was founded in 1948 by Alfonso J. Alfonzo Vaz. There children from ages six to eight were accepted so that they could grow up in a family environment in various units; in 1962 six houses with 120 places were already in operation.[162] The work *Fe y Alegría* takes care of abandoned children. Established at Caracas in 1955 by a group of university students under the direction of Father José María Vélez, it first worked in the poorest quarters of Caracas, but then spread out to the entire city and its neighborhood, and supports preschools, public and vocational schools, an institute for apprentices with attached schools for secretaries and printers. In the urban quarter Unión de Petare a model center was erected with the following departments: public school with 2,000 pupils, public evening school for adults and youth, children's outpatient department, recreational centers for children and youth, cutting and sewing courses, mess. Similar institutions were established in the interior of the country, at Maracay, Valencia, Barquisimeto, and Maracaibo, and outside the republic in El Salvador, Nicaragua, Panama, Ecuador, Peru, and Bolivia.[163]

Care of Souls

A special importance pertains to the Episcopal Conference of 27 August to 5 September 1970. One priest from each diocese and representatives of religious institutes took part in the discussions. Important themes were: mixed marriages; definitive rejection of drugs; education of priests in seminaries with special attention to a formation of future priests that is close to reality, which should be assured by practical activity in various professions. A sign of the changed times was

[160] *XIX centenario del martirio de los apóstoles Pedro y Pablo. Carta pastoral colectiva. Sic* 30, 261–63.
[161] *Síntesis sociales elaboradas por el CIAS. Informe sobre la realidad de Venezuela, Sic* 30, 371–80.
[162] Maldonado, op. cit., 101.
[163] Ibid., 100f.; *AICA* 17(1972), 817, 25–27, 29.

the participation of sixty priests from other dioceses, who arrived without invitation in order to express their partly different opinion on important questions. Thus the Church must take a greater stand for the liberation of the people and declericalize itself, that is, understand the episcopal and priestly office as a service and grant the laity a cooperation in the direction of the Church. They proposed to the episcopate a permanent dialogue, because they felt themselves to be the Church and coresponsible for its mission.[164] Previously, on 19 July 1969, the Venezuelan episcopate had sent a letter to the priests on the model of the priest. The bishops asserted that hitherto in Venezuela there had been no internal confrontations as elsewhere. On the question of celibacy they noted: The general priesthood of the baptized differs not only in degree but essentially from the priesthood of orders, whose sacramental character unites it with the High Priest Christ, the Head. It is a baseless supposition that the ecclesiastical law of celibacy will be changed or abolished.[165] Seventy-five priests replied to this letter that in fact hitherto there have been no open confrontations in the clergy on the function of the Church, but this does not mean that the situation in Venezuela does not contradict the spirit of the Gospel. The clergy must be desacralized and cease to feel themselves a privileged class. In regard to celibacy it is primarily a question why and how the priest can act theocentrically and at the same time anthropocentrically. With appeal to the words of Pope Paul VI and of the Congress of Medellín, these priests stated: "If we do not henceforth share in the process of social liberation, all else is of no use." The Church of Venezuela carries out no evangelization of the poor, because it is closely connected with power and wealth, it does not evangelize the rich in order not to explain to them the demands of the Gospel. Even more: It supplies no proof that it is a Church in the service, first, of the poor and then of all others.[166] The pastoral plan provides for the evangelization of ca. 100,000 Indians, who for the most part live in the prelacy of San Fernando de Apure and in the vicariates of El Caroní, Machiques, Puerto Ayacucho, and Tucupita. The mission of the Spanish Capuchins at Santa Teresita de Cavanayen possesses a model character.[167]

As the archbishop of Maracaibo, Roa Pérez, reported at the 1974 Roman Synod of Bishops, small charismatic groups, consisting mostly of young people, make themselves noted in Venezuela, who stand in

---

[164] J. I. Arrieta, *La conferencia episcopal nacional* I: *Ambiente de la conferencia,* II: *Tematica de la conferencia, Sic* 33, 348–51.
[165] *SEDOC* 2 (May 1970), 1448–52; *Christus* 410, 794f.
[166] *SEDOC* 2, 1453–60; *Christus* 410, 795–808; cf. also *SEDOC* 4, 1013–18.
[167] Maldonado, op. cit., 490; *AICA* 17, 809, 12f.

opposition to the ecclesiastical authority, and in the clergy there is also Marxist influence. Catechetical instruction is unsatisfactory. The state school allows religious instruction, but not in the schools which teach higher levels than the minimum requirements of compulsory school attendance.[168]

CUBA

Cuba has a total area of 114,500 square kilometers and in 1968 had a population of 4,315,000 urban inhabitants and 3,759,100 rural dwellers. According to the 1970 statistics, the population reached 8,553,385, of whom 70 percent are white, 12.4 percent black, and 17.3 percent mulattoes; 3,819,000 were Catholics in 1977.

From 1940 to 1944 Fulgencio Batista was president of the republic; he pursued a policy that favored the workers. In 1944 he was succeeded by Ramón Grau San Martín. After several uprisings Batista became president again in 1952, until he was overthrown by the revolution of Fidel Castro. On 1 January 1959 Oswaldo Dorticós Torrado was sworn in as president, but in reality Fidel Castro decided policy. The agricultural reform and the economic quarrel with the United States brought about the rapprochement of Castro with the Soviet Union, sealed with the defense pact of September 1962. The economic blockade imposed by the United States would almost have led to a military confrontation, had not the Soviet Union withdrawn from the island. The Cuban opposition and the danger of international measures of boycott forced Castro to tone down his policy. On 1 January 1961 Cuba was declared a socialist republic.[169]

Ecclesiastical Structure

Cuba has two archdioceses: San Cristóbal de la Habana, with the suffragan sees of Matanzas and Pinar del Río, and Santiago de Cuba, with the suffragans of Camagvey and Cienfuegos-Santa Clara.[170] In 1971 there were on the island 228 parishes, but only 208 priests, which means more than 41,000 inhabitants per priest. Of the 208 priests 112 were from orders or congregations, and of these there are 21 Jesuits, 18 members of Foreign Mission Society of the Province of Quebec, 15 Franciscans, 20 Capuchins, besides Carmelites, Passionists, Dominicans, Salesians, Christian Brothers, and Claretians. These 112 religious priests care for a total of 577 parishes, churches of religious and

[168] *Osservatore Romano*, 2 Oct. 1974.
[169] Cf. G. Bleiberg, ed., *Diccionario de Historia de España. Cuba en el siglo XX* I, 2d ed. (Madrid 1968), 1049f.
[170] *Annuario Pontificio* (1977), 952.

chapels, and 285 pastoral stations. They also work in the diocesan curias, on episcopal commissions, and in other institutions; 58 of them are active in the archdiocese of Habana and the capital city. In addition, there are 236 sisters from fifteen congregations; most strongly represented among them are the Sisters of Mercy with 76 members.[171]

Pastoral Letter of the Bishops

In view of the problematic situation in Cuba the episcopate on 7 August 1960 published a common pastoral letter with the following content: The Church has always joyfully taken note of all those measures which make a contribution to the improvement of the level of life. In this connection it has noted with satisfaction for a year that a land reform is planned, which provides compensation for the owners and enables many workers to take into their own possession the acres worked by them. There is word of great industrial plans, which would not disturb private industry, with the intention of creating many new places for work for the struggle against unemployment. It was stated that the authorities were working to lower the cost of living and to raise the income of families. New hospitals, schools, and social lodgings were to be built, and not least of all it was desired to take up the fight to restore the public finances. The social reforms, to the extent that they aimed, with respect for human rights, to improve the economic, cultural, and social situation of those of moderate means, would have the support of the Church. A reason for anxiety for the bishops was, however, the continued progress of Communism, the acceptance of intimate economic, cultural, and diplomatic relations with the most important Communist countries, and the fact that journalists, politicians, union leaders, and even personalities of the government had often sung the praise of the social order of these countries. If one proceeds from the fact that Communism and Catholicism are mortal enemies, one must definitely condemn Communism, which in one way or another destroys human rights.[172]

The Economic Situation of the Cuban Church

In an open letter of 4 December 1960 to Fidel Castro the bishops explained the economic situation of the Church in Cuba: publication of revolutionary texts with clearly Marxist tendency; arrest of several priests who had read the bishops' letter of 7 August 1960 in the churches; antireligious campaign on the national level with increasing

[171] "Almanaque de Caridad. Directorio eclesiástico de Cuba 1971," *AICA,* 16, 788 (27 Jan. 1972), 33–35.
[172] *Revista Javeriana* 55 (Bogotá 1961), 99–102.

THE CHURCH IN LATIN AMERICA

use of force; mass rallies with the approval of the authorities, at which priests were reviled; insulting of the bishops and of Catholic institutions by representatives of quasi-Catholic associations, who try to fight the Church's leadership. The letter enumerates various events of this campaign against the Church; the bishops hope that the government will take the necessary measures to stop the constant attacks against Catholics.[173]

The archbishop of Santiago de Cuba gave to his pastoral letter of February 1961 the heading: "With Christ or Against Christ." In all openness he said: "For us at this moment the hour of fear is past—in case it ever existed at all. We are fighting Communism—we still say it—not for counterrevolutionary, partisan political, economic, or social reasons. We are fighting it because we know that we thereby display a positive service as we fulfill a holy duty. It is a fight for life or death, between Christ and Antichrist. And so each must choose his leader. As regards Catholics, they must know that the hour to prove our power of resistance and our readiness to fight has come. If God is for us, says Saint Paul, who can overcome us? Your will be done, O Lord! May he give us the peace that is based on truth and justice." Thus ended the letter and with it also a section of history.[174] The Church of Cuba will for the future be a Church of silence.

The Persecuted Church

Only the most important events will be mentioned. The date 1 May 1961 was abundant in expressions and deeds of the government against the Church. In his speech Fidel Castro accused the "Falangist" clergy of having taken part in the frustrated invasion of the island at the Bay of Pigs and made known that as a countermeasure the Spanish and other foreign priests would be expelled from the country, their property confiscated, and religious instruction approved only in churches. The press later reported that this order had as its consequence the emigration of hundreds of priests, brothers, and sisters to other countries. Of the then 730 priests on the island, only the approximately eighty Cubans could remain to care for 6.5 million persons. The bishops, who called for a land reform, saw their demands partly fulfilled by the reform of 1959. For the implementation of a reform of education they organized a mass demonstration in Havana at the end of 1959. Toward the end of 1961 Father Germán Lence, born a Cuban and leader of a Catholic society, caused a great stir in the capital when in sermons and lectures he violently attacked the Cuban bishops and praised the Cuban

[173] Ibid., 103–6.
[174] Ibid., 107–11.

725

revolution. It is not surprising that Fidel Castro publicly praised him in a speech of 27 November 1960 before the University of Havana. Lence was later suspended *a divinis.* In March 1961 a bombing attempt occurred at the Nobel Academy in La Víbora, the Old City quarter of Havana, in which a few professors and students were injured. The explosive charge was probably set by collaborators of the government in order to be able to develop a press campaign against the priests, which then actually took place. This affair entered history under the title "Revolution of 2 March." The daily *Combate* designated it on 8 May 1960 as an internationally planned campaign, that more than 2,000 priests and religious had applied for permission to emigrate; in this regard it was ignored that in a speech of 1 May 1960 Fidel Castro had announced their expulsion from the island. Spokesmen of the government stated that an anti-Communist was also a counterrevolutionary. Thus in Cuba the Church lives in a permanent state of persecution.[175]

The Standpoint of the Bishops

In March 1969 the Cuban bishops had translated into practical guidelines of renewal the results of the second plenary assembly of the Latin American episcopate. At their meeting in April of the same year they chose as the topic of discussion Pope Paul VI's opening address at the Congress of Medellín of 1968; they were aware of being the conduit of the papal pronouncements. On 10 April 1969 they published the papal speech in Havana. They adhered to the recommendation of the Pope, who in his talk described as follows the attitude of the Christian in a suffering world struggling for its further development: "We must advance the deep, foreseeable transformation which is necessary in many areas of our present society, as we love more and learn to love; we must do this with judicious energy, with perseverance and confidence in people, and with the assurance of the faith in the help of God and the power of the good."[176]

At the close of their meeting of September 1969 the Cuban bishops issued a statement with the following themes: problem of faith; analysis of faith; present-day atheism; deficient expressions of faith; growth of faith; liturgy; bible; catechesis; ways to faith. "This is the hour in which we must discover the presence of God among us; it is a question of proving our maturity and not of a death struggle. Maturity and growth mean to let something die in order to gain new knowledge. Hence an hour in which, surrounded by snobbery or extreme deviation and human sin, the desire for justice and authenticity of human

[175] "Cuba: La Iglesia católica y Fidel Castro," *Revista Javeriana* 55, 278–92.
[176] *SEDOC* 2 (Sept. 1969), 347–52.

relations grows on the personal level among the various social groups and in the sphere of international relations." As sheperds in the service of the Cuban Church, the bishops encouraged their faithful to keep alive their love of Christ in this national situation, unprecedented in Latin America. They expressed their hope that they may find in this situation the means which are suited to show their brothers the way to God.[177]

Decrease of the Cuban Clergy

In the last years the number of Cuban priests has dropped by more than 10 percent. In 1969 there were ca. 215, in 1970 202, in 1971 only 193, although 15 priests were ordained in this year. This decrease must be referred to cases of death—the average age is sixty-seven—and emigration. Those priests who leave the country are foreigners—60 percent of the priests in the country are of foreign ancestry. The reasons for leaving are age, sickness, or the ending of their obligation in Cuba. The losses through return to the lay state are minimal in Cuba. Almost the only activity still allowed to the Cuban priest is the care of the churches. The government has formally promised to admit a few Cuban priests who have studied abroad and foreign priests who want to work in Cuba. But, as of 1974, hence, in practical terms, today, this promise has not yet been kept. In 1972 there were 58 Cuban seminarians and some candidates for the priesthood; but this number is inadequate in the long run to make up for the losses of the last years.[178]

THE DOMINICAN REPUBLIC

The Dominican Republic on the island of Santo Domingo has an area of 48,442 square kilometers and ca. 4.4 million inhabitants. It includes the archdiocese of Santo Domingo and the dioceses of Barahona, La Vega, Nuestra Señora de la Altagracia de Higüey, San Juan de la Maguana, and Santiago de los Caballeros. In the coordination of the national pastoral care there is collaboration among the commissions for liturgy, means of communication, religious education, charity, social action (Iustitia et pax), lay apostolate, vocations, seminaries, religious institutes and missions, legal and concordat affairs, the national secretariat for community pastoral care, the Dominican Conference for Religious, the Dominican Caritas, and the National Association of Catholic Schools.[179]

[177] Ibid. 2 (June 1970), 1581–88.
[178] AICA, 16, 803 (11 May 1972), 23f.
[179] Annuario Pontificio (1977), 953; Directorio de la Iglesia católica en República Dominicana (1972), 8–12.

The archdiocese of Santo Domingo had in the census of 1970 in an area of 8,007.72 square kilometers 1,374,939 inhabitants, with 100 parishes, which were attended to by 40 priests and 181 religious. Eighteen institutes of men and 34 of women worked in the field of pastoral care in parishes, schools, high schools, academies, and other institutions. The archdiocese has 3 universities, 56 elementary schools, and 13 high schools. Health institutions number 17 hospitals and 1 leprosarium. To the archdiocese belong 215 priests and 65 assistants.

The other dioceses display a similar structure. Santiago de los Caballeros has, with 11,003.41 square kilometers and 1,047,683 inhabitants, 38 parishes, 35 priests, 66 religious priests, 32 brothers, and 257 sisters. In addition, there are in the diocese 10 institutes of men and 15 of women. The diocese has the Catholic university Madre y Maestra, the school for the humanities Arzobispo Merino, and the minor seminary San Pio X, and 23 schools. The diocese of Vega has, with 8,142.73 square kilometers and 751,620 inhabitants, 36 parishes, 24 priests, and 58 religious priests, 7 institutes of men and 11 of women, and 20 schools. The diocese of San Juan de la Maguana has, with 15,165.25 square kilometers and 560,086 inhabitants, 19 parishes, 3 priests, and 31 religious priests, 6 institutes of men and 12 of women, and 10 schools. The diocese of Nuestra Señora de la Altragracia has, with 6,614.37 square kilometers and 276,930 inhabitants, 13 parishes, 11 priests, and 7 religious priests.[180]

The Concordat between the Holy See and the Dominican Republic

The concordat was signed in Vatican City on 16 June 1954. The essential agreements are as follows, in the words of the text: Paragraph 1: "The Catholic, apostolic, and Roman religion remains the religion of the Dominican nation." Paragraph 3: "The Holy See is empowered to proclaim and publish all directives affecting the Church; furthermore, to be in contact with prelates, clergy, and faithful of the nation, and vice versa." Paragraph 9: "The erection, modification, or suppression of parishes, benefices, and ecclesiastical offices . . . are subject to the ecclesiastical authority, in accord with the canon law." Paragraph 11: "Ecclesiastical persons cannot be interrogated by judges or other officials in regard to deeds and facts which have been made known to them under the seal of Confession." Paragraph 15: "The Dominican Republic recognizes full civil rights of those marriages which are contracted in accord with the canon law." Paragraph 19: "The Church may establish seminaries or other educational institutions without restriction; their internal structure is not and cannot be infringed upon by the state. The

[180] *Directorio de la Iglesia católica en República Dominicana,* 13–170.

titles granted in them have the same validity as those granted in state institutions." Paragraph 21: "The Dominican state guarantees to the Catholic Church full liberty to found and maintain under its direction schools of every type. Because of the social gain for the nation the state will support them materially. Religious instruction in these schools is organized and imparted by the Church. The instruction provided by the state in the public schools will be oriented to the principles of Catholic doctrine and morality."[181]

The Church in Public Life

Monseñor Juan Félix Pepén y Solimán, bishop of Higüey, in 1968 published a pastoral letter with an appeal to the consciousness of all that the situation of the propertyless farmer be investigated and a reform in accord with the pastoral constitution *Gaudium et spes* be set in motion. Against the strong criticism that at once appeared, the clergy took its place at the bishop's side.[182]

In July 1969 the Dominican government refused to grant a visa to Fathers Sergio Figueredo, S.J., and Graciano Varona, O.S.B. In spite of the intervention of the nuncio and the bishops, the government persisted in its attitude; this caused the Jesuits to make known their attitude to the case. They testified to Father Figueredo's loyalty to the norms and spirit of the Church in his activity. "Our attitude," said the Jesuits, "is that of service; it is based on the Gospel and on the teaching of the Church, has no partisan political relationship, and is free from the exercise of any sort of pressure in the area of civilian life; it will challenge only the personal and common consciousness. We are ready to carry out this renewal entirely as proof of our service to the People of God in the Dominican Republic."[183]

Cardinal Octavio Antonio Beras Rojas, archbishop of Santo Domingo, thus presented the ecclesiastical situation in the republic at the 1974 Roman Synod of Bishops: The courses for the preparation for baptism and marriage have experienced a great upsurge. Since great importance pertains to the problem of "Liberation" as expression of the Christian purpose, two types of pastoral activity have been started: by the first the sense of human brotherhood and the state of being children of God is awakened, by the second "Liberation" is recommended which makes the Church more credible and the presence of God in society more clearly evident. In order to intensify the participation of the laity in evangelization and thereby to alleviate the lack of priests, the "assemblies of presidents" have been called into being. The bishop

---

[181] *Estudios* 469, 40–44.
[182] *Sic* 32, 188–94.
[183] *SEDOC* 3, 361–64.

expressly entrusts prepared lay persons with the function "of organizing an assembly and presiding over it." In this connection they should explain the Word of God, administer Communion, and, if they are qualified, take care of the spiritual and material welfare of the congregations and bring the Eucharist to the sick. The president, who is supported by a council, can be single or married, but he must display a definite maturity, be a practicing Catholic, have adequate financial means, obtain the consent of the congregation, and prepare himself in catechetical programs of a total of 280 hours. This new institution has produced better results than the diaconate of married persons. The meeting of families, taking place twice a month, has also had good results; they are under the direction of a well-prepared moderator. A national institute annually decides the program and gives directions and guidelines for implementation.[184]

PANAMA

Panama has a total area of 75,650 square kilometers and ca. 1.5 million inhabitants, of whom 18 percent are Creoles, 10 percent Indians, 52 percent mestizos, 15 percent blacks, and 5 percent mulattos; in 1971 85.5 percent were Catholics.

The Situation of the Church

The nation embraces the archdiocese of Panama, the dioceses of Chitré, David, Santiago de Veraguas, the prelacy of Bocas del Toro, and the vicariate apostolic of Darién.[185] In 1971 there were 102 parishes. The recruitment for the priesthood has inadequate results: from 1940 to 1950 seven priests were ordained, from 1951 to 1960 eleven, and from 1961 to 1964 three. Religious vocations are also rare. Of the 148 religious priests on hand in 1967, the majority were foreigners; the same is true of the 53 assistants and of the 364 sisters. Private educational institutions are usually in the hands of religious.[186]

The following are active on the national level: Catholic Action; the Association of Catholic Women with houses throughout the country; the Christian Family Movement; the Catechetical School, which takes care of the formation of teachers in religious instruction; the Marian Congregation *Stella Maris;* the Secretariat for Social Courses. The Catholic Center of Education is the focal point of all apostolic en-

---

[184] *Osservatore Romano,* 2 Oct. 1974.

[185] *Annuario Pontificio* (1977), 953; *Anuario eclesiástico de Panamá* (1965), 18–36, 129–70.

[186] The statistics on the clergy of the individual areas of jurisdiction in *Anuario eclesiástico de Panamá* (1965), 23–62.

deavors. Also to be named are: the papal missionary works; the Secretariat for the Christian Faith with 62 centers in Chiriqui, 62 in Santiago, and 64 in Panama; the Catholic Work for Emigrants; and Radio Hogar.[187]

Social Revaluation

Following its meeting of 19 to 21 February 1968 at Colón, the episcopate proclaimed the decrees enacted, which dealt with the social situation in the nation, and announced a national synod with participation of the laity at the end of the year. The bishops designated as incompatible with the Church's social doctrine the fact of the concentration of landed property in a few hands, while the majority of the rural population lives in poverty. Christians who are economically well-off are reminded that the faith must express itself in deeds. Workers and peasants are encouraged to use their scanty means for the education of their children and to give up unnecessary expenses. With a reference to the impending election fight, the bishops indicated the danger that, because of accusations made by the one side or the other, families could be torn apart. Those responsible for the means of communication—press, radio, television—were reminded by the bishops of their responsibility, which demanded that they maintain objectivity in their presentation of events, despite personal views. They also called attention to the fact that Christian festivals are not suitable occasions for political activities.[188]

Religious Life in Central America and Panama

The bishops of Central America and Panama organized the first meeting for reflection at Panama from 16 to 20 March 1970. At it the following topics were treated: lack of priestly vocations; renewal and adaptation of the religious life; lack of superiors in the mostly native congregations; tensions between native and foreign priests; demands of sisters for more autonomy in the solving of their problems; apathy in regard to the National Conference of the Orders, especially on the part of the men.[189]

Arrest and Expulsion of Father Luis Medrano, S.J.

On the occasion of the arrest and expulsion of Father Luis Medrano, S.J., director of Radio Hogar in Panama City, Monseñor Marcos Gregorio McGrath, C.S.C., archbishop of Panama, in the course of a

[187] Ibid., 56–62.
[188] SEDOC 2 (Aug. 1968), 237–40.
[189] Ibid. 3 (Sept. 1970), 347–54.

Mass carried on television, delivered a talk which dealt with this occurrence. He presented the expulsion of Medrano as a sign of the abolition of free speech in Panama and claimed for the Church the freedom which its function required. The hard truth was, he said, that often in a democracy the rights of all become the privileges of the few; these few prevent necessary reforms by exercising their political and economic power. The Church openly expresses itself for a development favoring all persons and claims for every person a minimum of freedom of opinion, the inviolability of his home, and "a fair trial in case of arrest."[190]

The Church and Reform of the National Constitution

In view of the announced reform of the constitution, the bishops on 27 June 1972 issued a decision in behalf of the human values anchored in the constitution. They pointed out that the majority of the population—natives, peasants, and recipients of social support—must be taken into consideration. They constituted the majority, and this majority demanded priority. They must obtain the possibility of participating in political life, use the institutions of health care and education, and acquire jobs. Paragraph 36 of the now valid constitution recognizes the Catholic religion as the religion of the majority of the population; the Catholic religion is taught in the schools. The participation of the pupils in acts of worship is not a duty if such is so desired by the parents or their representatives. This regulation is regarded by the bishops as a recognition of the Church within the national structure.[191]

After nine months of silence Archbishop Marcos Gregorio McGrath delivered an address on 23 August 1972 on the occasion of a protest Mass which had been organized by a lay group to proclaim their sympathy with the Archbishop, who had become the target of a defamatory press campaign. He had been charged with being too intellectual, too indecisive, not a Panamanian, a friend of politicians and the wealthy, and an enemy of the regime; he was a bishop for councils and for conferences at Medellín. The archbishop took a position on all these points as follows: "I ask all my priestly brothers, the cooperating laity, and all others to have understanding and pardon for my mistakes; for my part, I try to understand and forgive those of the others, although I do not always succeed. They are my real brothers."[192]

[190] Ibid., 361–64.
[191] Ibid. 5 (Jan. 1973), 875–80.
[192] Ibid., 880–88.

NICARAGUA

The Republic of Nicaragua has a total area of 139,000 square kilometers and 1.8 million inhabitants, that is, about twelve inhabitants per square kilometer; 17 percent are Creoles, 5 percent Indians, 9 percent blacks, and 70 percent mestizos. Other sources list 7 percent Creoles, 50 percent mestizos, and about 33 percent Indians. The most important products are coffee, cotton, and bananas. The country depends on agriculture.[193] By the bull *Quam iuxta* of 2 December 1913, Pius X detached Nicaragua from the archdiocese of Guatemala and established the new ecclesiastical province of Nicaragua. At present the archdiocese of Managua has as suffragans Estelí, Granada, León, and Matagalpa, the prelacy of Juigalpa, and the vicariate apostolic of Bluefields.[194]

Apostolic Activities

Several institutions take part in national pastoral care: the Episcopal Conference, the national seminary, the work for ecclesiastical vocations, the friends of the seminary, the papal missionary works, the Conference of the Religious of Nicaragua (CONFER), the Christian Family Movement, the means of social communication, including the Catholic Radio of Nicaragua and the broadcasting schools.

The most important cultural institutions are the Central American University, founded in 1961 and run by the Jesuits, with faculties of law, humanities, education, engineering, economics, veterinary science and zoological technique, and with the institute Mater Ecclesiae for religious culture.

According to the statistical handbook of 1967 there were in the republic 13 institutes of male religious and the Christian Brothers, 20 of female religious, who display their activity in parishes, chapels, schools, social works, outpatient departments, and hospitals. The other six jurisdictional areas have between 9 and 21 parishes and a corresponding school system.[195]

National Constitution

Since the Constituent Assembly was dominated by a radical group, there went into effect on 14 April 1939 a new constitution in which the name of God did not appear. The state has no official religion; the laicized school is institutionalized in the educational institutions oper-

---

[193] Cf. *Diccionario de historia de Espana. Nicaragua* (Época independiente) III, 2d ed. (ed. by G. Bleiberg) (Madrid 1969), 38–41.
[194] *Annuario Pontificio* (1977), 953: *Anuario eclesiástico de Nicaragua* (1967), 15.
[195] *Anuario eclesiástico de Nicaragua* (1967), 19–25.

ated by the state and the communes. The avowedly Catholic country expressed itself in favor of the private schools of religious, in which the number of pupils grew rapidly; even the opponents sent their children to these schools. The best known schools in the country are the Colegio Centroamericano del Sagrado Corazón de Jesús, run by the Jesuits, and the Instituto Pedagógico de Varones under the direction of the Christian Brothers; both are in Managua.[196]

Activity of the Church

In a pastoral letter of 19 February 1972 to priests, faithful, and fellow citizens, the bishops note that the Church itself has a message to deliver on the political stage, for the subject of politics is the person with all his rights and duties, which must be protected. The bishops want the political field of activity of the Church and the function of the bishops and priesthood "to work for the aim of peace and justice with all means which are in harmony with the Gospel," to be understood as a contribution to the establishing of a just order, especially where the human problems are the most difficult. The Church, say the bishops, proposes principles which proceed from the faith, advocates a change of structures and ideas, and expresses itself for bold innovations and a more just order. The bishops demand for every citizen the possibility of free decision, without fear of reprisal and a guaranteed legal protection for everyone. They further support the forming of associations, unions, and so forth, and free political elections in canton and community. These demands are unconditional, if a better world is to be built.[197]

HONDURAS

The Republic of Honduras has, according to the situation in 1972, a total area of 116,160 square kilometers and 2,975,985 inhabitants, of whom 2,440,000 were Catholics in 1971. Ecclesiastical Division: the archdiocese of Tegucigalpa with the diocese of Comayagua, San Pedro Sula, Santa Rosa de Copán, and the prelacies of Choluteca and Inmaculada Concepción de la B.V.M. in Olancho. The archdiocese of Tegucigalpa has 3 districts and 37 parishes with 17 native and 25 foreign priests and 52 religious brothers; the diocese of Santa Rosa de Copán has 25 parishes, 4 vicariates, and 4 chapels, cared for by a small number of priests; the diocese of San Pedro Sula has 16 parishes with attached chapels and about 40 priests; the diocese of Comayagua has 10 parishes with 15 priests. The prelacy of Choluteca counts 16 parishes

---

[196] *Revista Javeriana* 13 (1940), 301f.
[197] *Christus* 446 (Jan. 1973), 46–50; *SEDOC* 5 (Nov. 1972), 606–14; *SEDOC* 6 (Oct. 1973), 493–500.

with about 40 priests, the diocese of Olancho has 7 parishes with 22 priests. The religious brothers in charge of parishes, chapels, and schools, and the sisters for schools and the welfare institutions are distributed throughout the nation.[198]

The *Caritas* of Honduras devotes itself to several tasks: to awaken the self-consciousness of the poor person, to investigate his real situation and the causes impeding the development of his personality; to give impetus and be concerned with community tasks by the inclusion of new forms of cooperation. Social care is an ingredient of pastoral care: direct help for the lower classes; resocialization and incorporation into the community; support in local and national concerns, in the event of natural catastrophes or similar emergencies.[199]

The broadcasting station at Suyapa is a national institution of private character with the goal of awakening among the rural population and later among the urban people the consciousness of the person in society. Every individual should understand his role as a member in the family and in society at all levels. The aims of this cultural communication do not consist in learning to read, write, and reckon and to acquire basic knowledge of religion or hygiene, but to bring the peasants to an awareness of their own possibilities and to take an active part in the development process of society, Church, and nation. The solution of this educational task is of decisive importance. The courses on Christian doctrine attract collaborators for pastoral work. The Coordinating Council supervises the methodical activity, organizes technical studies, and exerts itself for the financing. The catechetical center, which deals with the formation of catechists, provides the necessary didactic and informative material. The Christian Family Movement seeks to bring families together in order to emphasize the human and Christian values of the family. Lay persons are trained to promote a knowledge of the Bible in the basic communities with reference to the current situation of the Church. To support the maturing of youth, the Church encourages scout movements. The Legion of Mary supports pastoral tasks.[200]

The Voice of the Bishops

In a message of 4 September 1969 to the people, the bishops expressed themselves in regard to the national situation: "The painful events in our homeland compel us to reflect on them and become active. No one is free of guilt in the social injustices, the lack of respect for human dignity and of personal liberty. It is the duty of all citizens to cooperate

---

[198] *Annuario Pontificio* (1977), 953; *Anuario de la Iglesia de Honduras* (1973), 3–6.
[199] *Anuario de la Iglesia de Honduras* (1971).
[200] Ibid.

in the rebuilding of the country in all fields and without hatred, for every time there is hatred self-destruction is caused." The bishops sent an appeal to journalists and radio announcers to adopt and disseminate these guidelines.[201]

Land Occupation

In October and November 1969 19,000 farmers occupied the great landed estates in southern Honduras. A group of owners demanded an opinion from the Church. The bishop of Choluteca recognized the difficult problem of the case and the far-reaching social impact; but he wanted neither to approve nor condemn the land occupation. "Acts of violence should not be the means of confrontation among people," the bishop quoted Pope Paul VI after the latter's visit to Africa, "but understanding and love; it must no longer be said: Man against man, but man for men and with men."[202]

On 8 January 1970 the Episcopal Conference reiterated that the Church, in addition to its most important task of being concerned with the redemption of souls, must at the same time care for the human interests of daily life. Very profoundly affected by the misery of some parts of the population because of war, floods, land occupation, violence, or poverty, the bishops explained their own ideas on the present social situation in the country.[203] In view of the situation in agriculture, made more acute by new land occupations, the episcopate in 1972 took a stand in regard to proclamations making the Church responsible for this situation. The Church recognizes, theoretically and practically, private property, but also the necessity that possession be distributed to all social classes. The Church can never approve force, for this is not a human or Christian solution. It supports no political party, not even the Christian Democrats, as some think, and allows no different treatment of native and foreign priests.[204]

EL SALVADOR

El Salvador has a total area of 21,146.08 square kilometers and, according to the census of October 1970, 3,480,281 inhabitants. The average number of inhabitants amounts to 58.8 inhabitants per square kilometer. About two-thirds of the population live in rural areas.

The republic includes the archdiocese of San Salvador and the dioceses of San Miguel, Santa Ana, Santiago de María, and San

---

[201] *SEDOC* 2 (Jan. 1972), 926–28.
[202] Ibid. 2 (June 1970, 1595–98.
[203] Ibid. 3 (Feb. 1971),1007–13.
[204] Ibid. 5 (Jan. 1973), 887f.

Vicente.[205] According to the statistics of 1969 there are in the nation 200 parishes with an average of 17,402 inhabitants per parish, 219 diocesan priests, and 218 religious priests. The archdiocese of San Salvador and the diocese of San Vicente are relatively better equipped with parishes and priests than the other dioceses. Of the 437 priests, 226 were born in El Salvador—189 diocesan and 37 religious—hence 52 percent. In 1970 only 31 seminarians were studying theology and 91 philosophy. Priestly vocations drop constantly. The nation has an annual population growth of ca. 120,000. In order to maintain the present ratio of ca. 8,000 inhabitants per priest, fifteen new priests would be necessary every year; but at the moment only eight entered upon their office.

Religious cooperate in pastoral work; so too do lay persons, who exercise such activity in educational institutions throughout the country. Altogether, 29 institutes of women with 641 sisters, 127 students, 31 novices, and 10 postulants are active; together with the male institutes they care for the majority of the private educational institutions and all types of welfare institutions. The fact that a large number of marriages were not contracted in church must be referred to the sociocultural situation or the lack of priests.[206]

Institutions on the national level are: the Association of Religious, founded on 27 August 1966 as a central office for religious institutes; the national seminary San José de la Montaña, with a philosophical and theological faculty under the direction of the Jesuits; the university José Simón Cañas; supradiocesan are, furthermore, the General Secretariat for Parish Schools, the public association *Fe y Alegría* for the founding of educational institutions; the student-lodging *Doble Vía,* directed by *Opus Dei;* and so forth.[207] The old associations of the laity, such as *Guardia del Santísimo, Hijas de María, Caballeros adoradores,* have been replaced by new ones, for example, the Legion of Mary, the Christian Family Movement, and others, in which the priest is no longer the director but an adviser. In all dioceses there exists at least one institution for the education of the laity.[208]

The Land Problem and the Position of the Priests

In mid-1970 forty priests took a stand on the situation in the nation. In this regard they relied on the following data: 89 percent of the arable land is in the hands of 22 percent of owners and export firms. This

[205] *Annuario Pontificio* (1977), 952.
[206] *III Anuario eclesiástico de El Salvador* (1970), VII–XVI.
[207] Ibid., 33–45.
[208] Ibid., 45–56.

property includes 50 percent of the coastal area, the richest and with the better commercial ties, while 700,000 hectares lie fallow. The remaining 11 percent of the arable land is held by 78 percent of the owners, who have no sufficient means. The farmers live in a patriarchal system, unable to assume responsibility on their own. They receive starvation wages, live in huts or in unhealthy lodgings, without enough food or access to information and without any contact with civilization. Many emigrate to other countries, conditioned by the concentration of the land in the hands of a few and the rapid growth of the population. In regard to these conditions the priests urge the following views: There is no unconditional legal claim to ownership; the farmer must fight for his own human development, and all personnel necessary for this—teachers, priests, land experts, and the like—must support him; the state must have consideration for him also in its legislation and create the legal presuppositions. The Church must urgently support those exertions which promote this function, as, for example, the Association of Christian Farmers, societies, and so forth. The priests are of the opinion that land reform involves a part of the restructuring of the nation.[209]

Against the Use of Violence

In view of the tortures, murders, kidnappings, and other acts of violence perpetrated against priests, civilians, and military personnel, the bishops published a letter on 28 February 1971: Recourse to violence can never be Christian, it contradicts the Christian message, which calls for peace and love.[210]

Seminary for Priestly Vocations

On 19 September 1972 the Franciscans dedicated in San Salvador the new seminary Fray Junípero Serra, as a reply to one of the most pressing problems of the episcopate for the promoting of priestly vocations.[211]

The Abortion Law

In a pastoral letter of 1973 the bishops condemned the legalization of abortion, after the criminal code had designated it "as not punishable." The bishops expressly reject abortion if it is performed under circumstances which Christian morality cannot accept.[212]

---

[209] *Christus* 423, 7f.
[210] *SEDOC* 4, 251–54.
[211] *AICA,* 17, 829, 19f.
[212] Ibid. 17, 864, 23f.

GUATEMALA

Guatemala has a total area of 108,889 square kilometers, with about 5 million inhabitants, of whom in 1974 4.347 million were Catholics. The ecclesiastical administration is divided thusly: the archdiocese of Guatemala, with the dioceses of Huehuetenango, Jalapa en Guatemala, Quezaltenango, San Marcos, Santa Cruz del Quiché, Solola, Vera Paz, and Zacapa, the prelacies of Escuintla and Santo Cristo de Esquipulas, and the apostolic administrations of El Petén and Izabal.[213] Ecclesiastical Organizations: National Catholic Secretariat; National Seminary in the capital; *Caritas;* papal missionary works; the Catholic university Rafael Landívar, conducted by the Jesuits; National Catechetical Center; Centers for the Protection of Youth and Common Pastoral Care. Among the movements of the lay apostolate, the most important are: Catholic Action, Christian Family Movement, National Secretariat for Christian Courses, Marian Congregations, and Apostolate of Prayer.[214]

The religious of Guatemala, organized in the *Conferencia de religiosos y religiosas de Guatemala* (Confregua), founded the higher institute for religious culture, *Regina Coeli,* with 24 institutes for brothers and 39 for sisters (statistical handbook for Guatemala of 1971). There are 387 priests, 51 assistants, and 91 brothers active in teaching.

In the republic there are 141 parishes, 96 chapels, 105 high schools, 73 schools, 4 orphanages, 402 centers for the illiterate, 1 school for agricultural social service, 1 institute for Catholic education, 3 radio schools, 602 catechist centers, 5 broadcasting stations. Two hours per week are reserved for Catholic television broadcasting.[215]

Tensions

Three priests and one sister had to leave Guatemala for cooperating with the guerrillas. Two of the priests were blood brothers and belonged to the same congregation: Thomas and Arthur Melville. In a letter of 20 January 1968 Thomas Melville expressed his opinion on his expulsion from the Maryknoll Congregation. In order to prepare to end the poverty and the sad situation of Latin America, in which, in Melville's opinion, the Church authorities are guilty, there is only the route of armed revolution. In agreement with his brother Arthur he said: "We began with this: to make it clear to the Indians that no one, apart from themselves, would defend their rights. If the government and the ruling class use arms in order to keep them, the Indians, in

---

[213] *Annuario Pontificio* (1977), 953.
[214] *Guía de la Iglesia de Guatemala* (n.d.), 29–38.
[215] Ibid., 43.

poverty, then they have the right to take up arms in order to defend their God-given right to be men. We and all our adherents were regarded as Communists and asked by our religious superiors and the American embassy to leave the country. We did so. But I say I am just as much a Communist as was Jesus. What I did, I did, and I will do again, following the teaching of Christ and not that of Marx or Lenin. And I say further that we are more than the hierarchy and the United States government think. If the war becomes open, the whole world will experience that we fight neither for Russia nor for China nor for any other nation, but for Guatemala." The superior general of Mary-knoll declared: "The activities of Fathers Thomas and Arthur Melville represent a personal interference by American citizens in the internal affairs of a host land. Since they have declined to return to the United States in order to discuss the work accomplished in Guatemala, and because they also refused to comply with the request of their superior in Guatemala, they were suspended from their priestly office."[216]

Monseñor Mario Casariego, archbishop of Guatemala, addressed to his faithful at Easter 1968 a pastoral letter with an invitation to penance, prayer, and works of mercy, in an effort to atone for their own and others' many sins. On 16 March he was arrested, presumably because of this letter.[217]

Pastoral Guidelines

In a difficult time for the Church of Guatemala the bishops on 6 January 1970 laid down their pastoral principles in three theses: evangelization and catechesis, human valuation, and apostolate. The Catechetical Department of the National Catholic Secretariat especially should serve for evangelization. For human valuation they demanded that priests, religious, and lay persons concern themselves with the simple popula-tion; the bishops are ready to support these exertions, especially in case of persecution by the legal system, assuming that they are in accord with the Gospel. In the apostolate they take a stand for the collaboration of all priests, religious, and lay persons, and remind them that the Church should never mix in political activities. Priests or members of apostolic movements which exploit their position for a political activity are failing their pastoral task and doing great harm to the Church.[218]

The Christian and Political Activity

Starting from the idea that participating in elections is a conscientious duty, the episcopate in a new message of 28 May 1970 reminded the

---

[216] SEDOC 4 (Oct. 1968), 585–95.
[217] Ibid., 595–600.
[218] Ibid. 2 (June 1970), 1589–96.

priests and coworkers of the Church that the Church as such should remain far from every partisan political activity, and so in Guatemala it has entered into no obligations whatsoever with political parties and that it had no interest in whether this or that candidate gained the electoral victory.[219] In the name of the ecclesiastical province of Guatemala, the chairman and the secretary of the Episcopal Conference declared on 5 February 1971: "For a homeland that we love more than ourselves and which is in a chaos of unrest and pain, we as Christians reject and condemn every form of violence."[220]

MEXICO

Mexico has a total area of 1.963 million square kilometers and in 1969 had 47.3 million inhabitants, of whom 97 percent were Catholics, but their relations to the Church are mostly limited to baptism or a minimal contact in the course of life.[221] The 2 or 3 million Indians, for the most part baptized, live in a deplorable separation, although in recent years the exertions of religious have somewhat mitigated this situation.[222] The fact that more than 70 percent of the population were peasants or workers gave stimulus to the revolution of 1910. At the same time a Marxist influence was to be discerned through the so-called *Casa del Obrero Mundial* and the anarchist-Communist indoctrination by Flores Magón; the same is true of the socialist tendencies through the writings of Kropotkin, Proudhon, or Marx. The constitution of 1917 became a reservoir of the people's wishes, which emptied into the "Social Guarantees," whereby the state supported peasants and workers, victims of orthodox liberalism.[223] According to the United Nations statistics of 1976, the number of inhabitants amounted to 58.12 million, of whom 9 percent were Indians, 75 percent mestizos, 10 to 15 percent whites.

In the first decades of the twentieth century Mexico experienced a persecution of the Church. With a few exceptions, the bishops were imprisoned or banished, the priests almost in their entirety were kept in prison in 1914–15, sisters were expelled from the convents, Mass was forbidden, Catholic schools were closed, and almost all church property was confiscated.[224]

---

[219] Ibid. 3 (Feb. 1971), 1015–20.
[220] Ibid. 4 (Aug. 1971), 249–52.
[221] *GIMC,* 17–22.
[222] Ibid., 23.
[223] V. Vives. op. cit. IV/2, 570–73; "Fe y situación socio-politica de México, Equipo del S.S.M.," *Christus* 462 (May 1974), 46f.
[224] *BMI,* 355–61.

Constitution of 1917

The constitution of Querétaro of 5 February 1917 legalized the assault on the Church: nondenominational schools; prohibition of teaching by priests and religious; denial of state recognition of seminary studies; calling into question of celibacy and religious vows; prohibition of religious events outside the church and control by the civil authorities; prohibition of ownership by the Church and its organizations; expropriation of all direct or indirect church property in favor of the state; deprivation of all political and civil rights of priests; prohibition of the Catholic press and of all parties related to the Church.[225]

New Persecution: Plutarco Elías Calles

The persecution continued from 1917 to 1923. Calles (1924–28) demanded the application of the constitution of 1917. The Catholics established the "National League for Defense of Religious Freedom," which acquired publicity for itself and organized legal protests and boycotts. This organized opposition caused the president to issue three new laws. The second, called *Ley Calles,* forced the episcopate to stop all ecclesiastical events with participation of priests in all churches of the republic after 31 July 1926, the date when the law became effective. Now the struggle was harsher on both sides: the government applied the *Ley Calles,* the Catholics passed from passive to active armed resistance. During these years, 1926–29, the Mexican Church had its catacombs and martyrs: seventy-eight priests, religious, and lay persons were killed. Nevertheless, with a few exceptions, it remained steadfast in its faith and formed a closed front. All social classes were subject to persecution.[226]

Economic Boycott, the "Cristeros War"

Many Catholic organizations which were cared for and directed by the League planned an economic boycott to force the government to abandon the enforcement of the *Ley Calles.* Means for this were the total renunciation of all articles of luxury and a restriction in the use of the means of trade. But after all legal measures had been exhausted, the Catholics took up arms "in legitimate defense against an unjust tyranny." The armed movement was everywhere spontaneous and grew in importance from the end of 1926. It was directed by the League and its adherents were called *Cristeros* because of their war cry, *Viva Cristo Rey* and because of the crosses which they wore around the neck. The League itself called them "Defenders" and their army the

[225] Ibid., 361–71.
[226] Ibid., 373–412.

"National Guard." The movement was popular in more than half the states of the republic and counted about 20,000 armed men. Excesses occurred, but in general the war was waged with idealism, magnanimity, and self-sacrificing devotion. Usually, the fighters were young; they were recruited from students, workers, and peasants. There were great losses; but this war had also a positive aspect, since it shook up the awareness of the Catholic Mexicans and led to a modus vivendi, which must not be evaluated as the outcome of the war but rather as an enforced settlement.[227] The war was hard on both sides. Emilio Portes Gil, president from 1928 to 1930, stated in the press that "there is no conflict which cannot be terminated by mutual goodwill." Representatives of state and Church reached an agreement, which was ratified by Pope Pius XI in 1929 as the lesser evil and to avoid greater harm, namely the prohibition of Mass. There were protests and dissatisfaction on both sides. Many Catholics thought that what was accomplished bore no relationship to the sacrifices made, whereas many adherents of the government and the Freemasons called it a weak yielding by the president. But the agreed compromises were ever less observed by the government. The majority of the *Cristeros* submitted, but despite the amnesty some were murdered or executed. Others continued the fight or took it up again. The Church, oppressed by the persecution, had to continue to look on helplessly.[228]

Papal Documents

Pius XI attentively followed the events in Mexico and in his Encyclical *Acerba animi anxietudo* of 29 September 1932 deplored the nonobservance by the Mexican government of the negotiated modus vivendi. He praised the clergy and people of Mexico and asked the Catholics of the nation "to defend the holy rights of the Church" by prayer and the exercise of Catholic Action. The papal document was not well received by the government and the National Party, and the final sentences were interpreted as incitement to rebellion. As a result of this, the apostolic delegate, Leopoldo Ruiz y Flores, was expelled for the third time. The confiscation of Church property was continued by President Lázaro Cárdenas (1934–40), who also ordered that in all schools instruction should be given on the doctrine of socialism, Marxism, and atheism, and in sex education. These measures evoked a wave of protests, and for a time a new version of the bloody Calles regime was feared. But it soon appeared that such unpopular decrees could be carried out only by force; the government had to give in, and there were important changes

---

[227] Ibid., 412–26.
[228] Ibid., 432f.; D. Olmedo, "Mexico, Modern," *New Catholic Encyclopedia* IX, 780.

in the cabinet. However, anticlericalism consistently continued its campaign; it culminated in the closing of the seminaries.

Pius XI continued to follow the development. In a letter of April 1937 to the Mexicans he recommended that they organize peacefully, expand Catholic Action, and maintain the faith. Although the Pope allowed the lawfulness of armed resistance under certain circumstances, the Church as such must never go this way. After almost all seminaries had been closed, Pius XI decided, as a consequence of an offer by the American bishops, to found in the United States a seminary that should be attended by Mexicans who had no opportunity for this in their own country. In September 1937 the Papal National Seminary at Montezuma, New Mexico, was opened; it was operated by the Jesuits and from it came many priests who would later put their stamp on the Church.[229]

Balance Sheet of the Persecution

The Church of Mexico remained unbroken in its faith, but, conditioned by the persecution, it could concentrate neither on the education of youth nor on the spread of the Gospel or of Catholic social doctrine; care of Indians and of farmers and industrial workers retreated into the background. Priests were constantly threatened and had to limit themselves to the most necessary things. Nevertheless, the persecution caused the Mexicans to renew and further develop the old Catholic works and try out other new ones, and brought the knowledge that Christian and evangelical principles must be firmly anchored for a living Church that is in a struggle.[230]

Church and State since 1940

General Manuel Ávila Camacho (1940–46) ended the persecution. Without changing the constitution—only the paragraph on education was rendered harmless—he began an era of fraternization. All official circles were convinced that, in order to accomplish national progress, the Christian faith of the people must be respected. The most important elements of church activity in its pastoral function were Catholic Action, founded in 1928 during the persecution, thousands of catechetical centers, many catechist schools, and a journalism school. In 1920 the *Confederación Católica del Trabajo* was founded, which counted as many as 85,000 members, the *Liga Católica Nacional Campesina* of the middle class, and other religious, social, and cultural institutions spread throughout the republic.[231]

---

[229] Cf. *BMI*, 433–37.
[230] Ibid., 434f., Olmedo, loc. cit., 780.
[231] *GIMC*, 41–45; Vives, op. cit., 570–72.

Organization of the Mexican Church

In the first quarter of the nineteenth century Mexico, because of the revolution, experienced a sociopolitical and sociocultural change. After 1919 there began a process of industrialization, which was favored by foreign capital investments. Today Mexico is the Latin American country with the highest production capacity. This social change has had an impact also on ecclesiastical institutions in so far as, within these institutions, there is to be recorded a movement which strives for an authentic Mexican structure, less oriented to the colonial model. By 1969 Mexico had eleven archdioceses, forty-seven dioceses, one vicariate apostolic, one prefecture apostolic, and four prelacies *nullius;* in 1974 there were forty-nine dioceses.[232]

To overcome the difficult problems of common pastoral care, the bishops of Mexico have joined the *Unión de Mutua Ayuda Episcopal* (UMAE), an unofficial institution, which makes use of socioreligious and socioeconomic investigation to learn the social and religious situation of the individual dioceses and to develop a realistic and effective pastoral plan. The aim is to renew pastoral care on the basis of the knowledge of the Second Vatican Council, to adapt action to change and the development of modern Mexico. This forces the offering of Mexican solutions for the needs of Mexican society.[233] To the UMAE belong twenty-five dioceses with their bishops. To the North Gulf Region belong the dioceses of Matamoros, Ciudad Victoria, Tampico, Ciudad Valles, Tuxpan, and Huajutla; to the Central Gulf Region, the dioceses of Papantla, Jalapa, Veracruz, and San Andrés Tuxtla; other, not precisely defined regions embrace the dioceses of Zacatecas, Tula, Autlán, Zamora, Apatzingań, Tacámbaro, Ciudad Altamirano, Chilapa, Acapulco, Oaxaca, Tehuantepec, Tuxtla Gutiérrez, San Cristóbal, Tapachula, and Campeche. The organization has its headquarters in Mexico City, and to it belong priests and brothers of various dioceses and institutes. The UMAE works according to a proved theoretical-practical plan; general work plan for evaluating the presence of the Church in each region; renewal and planning at meetings of bishops, pastoral commissions, pastoral groups of priests with an organization team, socioreligious investigation in each region.

The goals thus far achieved are: basic courses for pastoral care in many dioceses; pastoral inquiries in many others; special courses for sisters and qualified lay persons; days of recollection and retreats for the clergy. As its means of communication the UMAE has its own

---

[232] *GIMC,* 41–45; Vives, op. cit., 570–72.
[233] *GIMC,* 84.

quarterly, *Servir,* which gives current information on pastoral questions.[234]

Parishes and Mission, Organization of the Clergy

In 1968 there were 2,644 parishes for 47,300,000 inhabitants, that is, 17,890 inhabitants per parish. Most recently the parish structure has displayed modifications in view of modern and industrial change. The number of parishes has increased in the dioceses of Mexico City, Morelia, Puebla, and Guadalajara, while it has declined in the ecclesiastical provinces in the south, the north, and on the Gulf of Mexico.[235]

Three mission territories are cared for in Mexico: (1) the northern area of Baja California; there on 13 July 1963 were established the dioceses of Tijuana, with an area of 80,000 square kilometers and 625,000 inhabitants, all of them Catholics, and the diocese of Mexicali, with 620,000 inhabitants in 58,636 square kilometers; (2) the southern area, with the prefecture apostolic of La Paz, with an area of 73,000 square kilometers and 89,000 inhabitants, all of them Catholic, and fourteen parishes with twenty-eight priests; (3) the mission of Tarahumara, established as a vicariate apostolic, with an area of 40,000 square kilometers and 122,000 inhabitants, all Catholic.[236]

In 1968 there worked in the Mexican dioceses 6,348 diocesan priests and 2,103 religious priests, a total of 8,451; hence there were 5,400 inhabitants per priest. The archdioceses with the highest averages are Guadalajara, Morelia, Puebla, and Mexico City.[237] For the training of priests there were in 1966 54 minor seminaries, 5 purely philosophical seminaries, 24 seminaries of philosophy and theology, hence a total of 83, and also the Pio Latino-americano at Rome. Four dioceses still have no minor seminary, 35 no major seminary.[238] Institutes of male religious maintain 402 houses; in the archdiocese of Mexico City alone in 1973 41 orders and lay congregations were active.[239] In 1965 there were 121 congregations of sisters with 1,244 members, who were for the most part occupied in education and nursing.[240] Of course, 90 percent of the schools are public and laicized. The private colleges, most of them run by religious, can impart no religious instruction because of legal

[234] Ibid., 84–92; A. Castillo, S.J., "Desaparación de la UMAE. Tragedia en la Iglesia Mexicana," *Christus* 436 (1 March 1972), 8f.
[235] *GIMC,* 57–71.
[236] Ibid., 72f.
[237] Ibid., 92–122.
[238] Ibid., 123–41.
[239] Ibid., 142–70.
[240] Ibid., 171–200.

regulations. This lack is in part compensated by the work of catechist centers.

There are universities in almost all states of the republic; some of them were formerly Catholic, but today all are public and lay; religion is not a course of instruction. The Ibero-American University, founded in Mexico City by Jesuits in 1943, was originally called Centro Cultural Universitario; the academic degrees given there are recognized by the Universidad Nacional Autónoma of Mexico.

Philosophical positivism, which dominated the environment at the universities until 1867, the year of the education law, was at the beginning of the twentieth century supplanted by Bergson's antipositivism. Most recently the influence of Ortega y Gasset (1883–1955), with an existential orientation, has become noticeable. This philosophical movement is strengthened by the presence of Spanish intellectuals.[241]

Episcopal Documents

The internal change within the Mexican Church in recent years finds expression in the pastoral outlook of the bishops. Before the Second Vatican Council they signed fifty-five documents in common, which were concerned predominantly with questions of faith or the economy; the problems of social justice, Catholic Action, and the lay apostolate were only barely touched. In the years of the council, 1962–65, they did not publish even one document, but since 1968 they have been concerned with human, political, social, and religious problems, which are related to the evangelization and salvation of people. These are the most important publications: pastoral letter on the Scout Movement of 9 February 1968;[242] pastoral letter on the development and integration of the nation of 26 March 1968;[243] explanation of *Humanae vitae* of 9 August 1968;[244] pastoral letter on the student movement of 9 October 1968;[245] information from the episcopate to the Mexican people on school reform of 22 August 1969;[246] pastoral references to the actualization of the lay apostolate in Mexico of 16 January 1970;[247] Episcopal Commission for Social Pastoral Care. Amendments to the document "Justice in Mexico"; Synod of 1971;[248] declaration of the episcopate

---

[241] Cf. *BMI*, 458f.; Vives, op. cit., 572f.; Olmedo, loc. cit., 783.
[242] *Christus* 386 (Jan.–June 1968), 459–62.
[243] Ibid., 394–430.
[244] Ibid. 398 (Jan. 1969), 8–10.
[245] Ibid., 12–15.
[246] Ibid., 116–77.
[247] Ibid. 410 (Jan.–June 1970), 254–72.
[248] Ibid. 432 (Dec. 1971), 30–45.

relative to some educational questions of 15 May 1972;[249] pastoral letter to the Mexican people on responsible fatherhood of 12 December 1972;[250] the Christian responsibility in the face of the social and political option of 18 October 1973;[251] appeal on the occasion of the Olympic Games of 1968.[252]

Piety of the Mexican

The Mexican experiences his faith mixed with atavisms which tie him to definite cult forms and traditional rites. Especially in the cities these traditions are gradually being lost; in the states they are still maintained, so that the activity of the faith is reduced to a few occasions in the year which have little to do with authentic Catholicism. The sacraments are regarded as an ingredient of social life; thus a person is baptized and married only to save face. Nevertheless, faith in God is deeply moored, and many would sacrifice their life for it; however, there is no substructure, no adequate knowledge of that in which to believe; morality is formalistic. The Mexican is often content with a symbolic piety to the extent that this fulfills certain fundamental needs. However, there are also persons and groups which experience religion more intensively because of their education.[253] Observations and personal contacts with groups of the middle cultural level—high school pupils, students, teachers, study groups of teachers and the professions—indicate the following results: growing estrangement from the Church as an institution; fear of being treated as "underage"; depreciation of their power of judgment and tutelage without regard for their own opinion; no listening to justified criticism by the competent authorities, whereby tensions and dislike arise and a growing alienation from the Church of just those persons who would represent a vital force in it.[254]

National Plan for Common Pastoral Care

In order to deepen and consolidate the faith of the people, there take place in all dioceses numerous study meetings of persons from all classes of society. In this connection a start is made with the ideas "Church" and "World"; from the outset purely sociological or naturalistic as well as theoretical or utopian versions are avoided; instead there is

[249] Ibid. 440 (July 1972), 41–52.
[250] Ibid. 447 (Feb. 1973), 46–51.
[251] Ibid. 459 (Feb. 1974), 48–62.
[252] Ibid. 386 (Jan.–June 1968), 586–608; cf. *Christus* 423 (Feb. 1971), 32.
[253] Cf. "Perfil religioso del mexicano actual," *Christus* 426 (May 1971), 24; ibid., 30–34.
[254] Cf. E. Cid, "Reflexiones sobre la situación religiosa," *Christus* 398 (Jan.–June 1969), 572–74.

a search for a total overview by means of the faith and of the present reality. The goals set in this are: an effective coresponsibility on all levels of the People of God; abolition of individualism in persons and institutions in order to achieve a unity of criteria, methods of acting, and attitudes for the solution of common problems.[255] By means of the teachings of the Second Vatican Council and of the Congress of Medellín of 1968, the Mexican bishops have taken a clear positon toward the question of the development and integration of the nation and on the Christian obligation toward social necessities. In this connection must be seen the closing in 1971 of the Jesuit institute Patria. The basic notion is that an adaptation to the present social injustice and cooperation in a structure that favors social alienation is not in accord with Christ and the Gospel.[256]

The faith, understood in its vital reality, includes *metanoia,* the complete changing of a person, which should be expressed in his social behavior. From this consideration the episcopate took a stand on the problem of development and integration, for example in its letter of 26 March 1968: "We cannot overlook what differences exist between the regional development of our country and the sectors of economic life . . . we cannot hide that we arrive at a point where the citizens seek and must accept profound changes, if one does not want to watch passively how the power of the strong and the servitude of the weak constantly grow; thus the state of injustice is sharpened, which cries to heaven because of the violence which is done to human dignity."[257] The obstacles to progress are also named, and which efforts are necessary for an integral development.[258]

The reactions are numerous. Many bishops, the majority of priests and religious, lay organizations, and the faithful have felt this program as correct, if the doctrine of the Gospel is applied in an apostolic and priestly spirit, like the Samaritan, who, without hesitation and full of love, took the poor and suffering man and assigned effective aid to him.[259] The *Institution Rougier,* founded on 3 October 1966, gives assistance by the prayer, sacrifice, and good works of diocesan and religious priests, whose sphere of activity is always described, without mentioning names.[260] The Legion of Mary, founded in 1921, places its members in the service of evangelization. The "Pilgrimage for Christ," a method preferred by the legion, extends to two or three weeks; the

[255] Cf. *Christus* 40 (July–Dec. 1970), 546–56.
[256] E. Maza, "Los jesuítas cierran el instituto Patria," *Christus* 424 (March 1971), 7f.
[257] *Christus* 386 (Jan.–June 1968), 398.
[258] Cf. ibid., 18–28, 404–10.
[259] Cf. ibid., 462 (May 1974), 49f.
[260] Ibid. 386 (Jan.–June 1968), 726f.

legionaries sacrifice their annual vacation and pay out of their own pocket part of the expenses for lodging and board at those places where they exercise their mission activity.[261] At its national meeting in Mexico City in February 1974 Catholic Action adopted as its program of action for the period 1974–77 service to the Church and to all people. In the concrete it was a question of the following tasks: training of committed coworkers; evangelization of persons; promotion of exchanges of human experiences; development of criteria which make possible a better organization between national and regional plans of action. The intellectual and action-oriented basic theses for the next national plan form the continuation of the guidelines issued in the sixteenth national assembly: education, evangelization, and encouragement of people.[262]

"Priests for the Poor"

The group appearing in public in April 1972 aimed to strengthen the presence of the Church as helper of people, especially of the poor and oppressed, in the fight for the building of a new society. The Church should "be the community of people who are committed to the changing of society, for this sign of change is the sign of the Spirit of God and leads people and nations to their calling."[263] On the occasion of their first congress, 21–23 November 1972, they published a document in which they rejected alternatives such as state capitalism. mixed economy, or social Christianity, and expressed themselves for a "socialist project," which should produce a radical alteration of the economic structures through the socialization of the means of production and their administration by collectives. The "socialist project" offers the only possibility of freeing oneself from the imperialistic structure of international capitalism. However, this plan cannot be implemented so long as it is not supported by the people. The "Priests for the Poor" choose this socialist expedient "in the name of the most elementary rights . . . as human beings, Christians, priests, who have the desire to follow the Church loyally." They are convinced that the function of the Church in Mexico and Latin America does not consist in organizing new versions of the Inquisition or in blocking the rise of the new persons, but, on the contrary, in working for the liberty of the children of God."[264]

[261] J. M. Ganuza, S.J., "La legión de María obra del espíritu," *Christus* 410 (Jan.–June 1970), 582–602.
[262] *AICA* 18, 893 (31 Jan. 1974), 23f.
[263] A. Castillo, S.J., "Un paso adelante.Sacerdotes para el pueblo," *Christus* 439 (June 1972), 7f.
[264] "Documento del primer congreso del movimiento 'Sacerdotes para el pueblo,'" *Christus* 447 (Feb. 1973), 54–57.

CHAPTER 25

The Young Churches in Asia, Africa, and Oceania

Even only an approximately complete presentation of the development of the young Churches from the middle of the twentieth century to the present would require several volumes. The available source material in the missions archives of the Congregation for the Evangelization of Peoples, formerly the Congregation for the Propagation of the Faith, at Rome, in the archives of missionary orders and societies, and not least in those of the young Churches themselves is simply inexhaustible. Here we must restrict ourselves to the most striking events, but select those which appear to us as the characteristic criteria of the most recent missionary era: end of the colonial epoch, indigenization of the mission Churches, transfer of direction of the missions to native hands, erection of regular ecclesiastical hierarchies, new attitude of Rome to the question of native rites, establishment of apostolic delegations and nunciatures, new estimation of cultures and of the great world religions, new missionary spirituality and missionary awareness in the so-called Christian countries. However, in addition to these topics, many other important mission questions appear, which, on account of their actual importance and because they belong essentially to a complete mission history, need a detailed presentation, such as development aid, cultural and social work, translation of Scripture into the vernaculars, linguistic research, apostolate of the press, fostering of native art and music, the inner ecclesiastical life of the communities, and so forth. We ask indulgence for the topics not adequately discussed here because of the restricted space at our disposal and the remaining lacunae. Finally we ask you to bear in mind that the absence of historical distance from the most recent happenings demands brevity and imposes caution in judgment.[1]

The guidelines for the development of the young Churches were determined by the Popes in their mission encyclicals,[2] by the Congrega-

* Joseph Metzler

[1] The origin of the young Churches in the period 1922–72 was presented in more detail by us in Volume III/2 of *Sacre Congregationis de Propaganda Fide Memoria Rerum* (Freiburg 1976), 464–577. Supplements to this in the other contributions of this volume. For this history of the Congregation for the Propagation of the Faith Pope Paul VI gave the collaborators the express permission to use and evaluate the archival sources of the congregation's archives, not yet released for research (cf. *Memoria Rerum* III/1, XX–XXI). The present contribution also profited from this permission.

[2] Cf. the biblio. for this chapter, especially T. Scalzotto, *I Papi e la Sacra Congregazione* . . . The pertinent passages of the mission encyclicals down to Paul VI also in A.

tion for the Evangelization of Peoples in its most recent instructions,[3] and by the episcopal conferences of the young Churches. There can be no doubt that it was precisely the missionary dicastery of the Curia, which was often disdainfully evaluated as a purely administrative office, that in the last fifty years took praiseworthy initiatives and paved the way for the development of the young Churches. That is why the Second Vatican Council, at which at first a few of the council fathers had advocated the abolition of this congregation, because they erroneously regarded it as a colonial institution—the contrary is the case: it was from the start an anticolonial institution[4]—expressly reconfirmed this congregation for a suitable and necessary *aggiornamento* and extended its competence.[5]

Reuter, *Summa Pontificia* Vol. II. Other important papal and conciliar mission documents in Appendix III of Vol. III/2 of *Memoria Rerum.*

[3] Published in the "Supplementum" of the *Bibliografia Missionaria.* In addition, all important documents of a general nature of the mission dicastery since 1961 are here, and also the decrees published in the course of each year. All instructions and pertinent documents are also in the above-mentioned Appendix III of *Memoria Rerum.*

[4] Cf. our article in the *Rheinischer Merkur* of 26 November 1976.

[5] One of the most important directives was that for the future "selected representatives of all of those who cooperate in the missionary work have an active role with a decisive vote: bishops from the entire world after hearing the episcopal conferences, as well as directors of the institutes and of the papal mission works" (mission decree of the Second Vatican Council, *Ad Gentes,* no. 29). In the subsequent papal documents, *Ecclesiae Sanctae* of 6 August 1966 (*AAS* 58 [1966], 757–87), *Pro comperto sane* of 6 August 1967 (*AAS* 59 [1967], 881–84), and *Regimini Ecclesiae Universae* of 15 August 1967 (ibid., 885–928), the number of these *membra adiuncta* was fixed at twenty-four—sixteen bishops, twelve of whom had to be missionary bishops, four superiors general of missionary institutes, four national directors of the papal mission works—to which was then added the secretary of the Congregation for the Propagation of the Faith, and a seat and vote were given in the "coetibus plenariis" of the Congregation to those "tamquam Membra in quibus res maioris momenti et naturam principii generalis habentes sint pertractandae" (*Pro comperto sane*). Some, who have regarded the "Council of the Twenty-Four"—which never existed as such, and besides there were twenty-five!—as a sort of covering organization of the Roman mission authority, designated these postconciliar measures as a "watering down" of the conciliar decree (cf. *Le missioni cattoliche* 97 [Milan 1968], 65f.; *Herder-Korrespondenz* 22 [Freiburg 1968], 168f.). In reality hereby the position of the *membra adiuncta* should be reevaluated, and the same right and voice be given to them in the plenary sessions, in which the most important decisions in mission affairs are taken, as to the cardinals and the other members of the congregation. This clarification is not unimportant for the understanding of the following exposition.

The Young Churches in Asia

THE FAR EAST

China

The mission Church in China gave promise of the fairest hopes after the establishment of the apostolic delegation in 1922, the elimination of tensions between foreign and Chinese clergy, the transfer of the direction of the ecclesiastical territories to the Chinese clergy, the elimination of the French protectorate, and the happy overcoming of the painful struggle over rites.[6] The Chinese National Synod of Shanghai in 1924 stood at the beginning of the new development. It became, so to speak, the foundation of the young Church in China. But the construction was impeded and finally completely destroyed by political events.

The Chinese-Japanese conflict of 1937–41 frightfully injured the mission. By December 1941 one bishop, one prefect apostolic, fifty-five priests, seventeen brothers, and nine sisters were murdered. They fell victim to the Communists, the partisans, and an unbridled soldiery. But the number of the faithful still increased in those years and in 1941 reached 3,128,157. The outbreak of the Japanese-American war on 7 December 1941 produced a new turn. The foreign missionaries were to a great extent interned. Three-fifths of the missionaries who were active in China in 1940 came from abroad. Eighty-five percent of these belonged to one of the two warring sides. The chief burden of the mission Church was transferred to the shoulders of the Chinese clergy.

Despite the confusions of the war and other inconveniences connected with it and injuries to the Church, Rome began to prepare the setting-up of the regular ecclesiastical hierarchy in China. At the beginning of 1942 there were in China eighty-eight vicariates apostolic and thirty-nine prefectures apostolic. The latter were gradually to be raised to vicariates and preferably transferred to the Chinese clergy. In 1946 there were already twenty-eight Chinese ordinaries, of whom twenty-one were bishops. Five thousand five priests—of whom 2,008 were Chinese—1,262 brothers, and 6,138 sisters took part in the missionary work. There were 1,037 seminarians, 3,524 students in minor seminaries, and 1,590 pupils in preparatory schools. The missionary personnel also included 6,748 male and 4,659 female catechists, and 7,799 male and 5,604 female teachers. In the first postwar consistory of 18 February 1946 Pius XII admitted the vicar apostolic of

---

[6] Cf. on this especially *Memoria Rerum,* 472–76.

Tsingtao, Thomas Tien Ken-sin, S.V.D., to the College of Cardinals.[7] He was the first Chinese cardinal. At the Pope's suggestion on this occasion he wrote a memorandum on the situation and problems of the Church in China. He thereby gave the final impulse to the erection of the hierarchy. The formal decision on this matter was made by the cardinals of the Congregation for the Propagation of the Faith in their sitting of 8 April 1946,[8] and Pius XII gave his approval in an audience on 11 April.[9] Twenty ecclesiastical provinces were erected, the vicariates and prefectures were raised to dioceses, twenty of them to archdioceses, and the ordinaries were made bishops or archbishops respectively. A month later Cardinal Tien was transferred to the archiepiscopal see of Peking,[10] which had been vacated before the erecting of the hierarchy by the resignation submitted by Bishop Paul-Léon-Cornélie Montaigne, C.M. It was fitting that the first Chinese cardinal have his seat in the nation's capital. Of course, the transfer of the archdiocese of Peking from the French Vincentians to the Chinese clergy was connected with it. Rome made provision that no objections should arise from the side of France, neither political, liturgical,[11] nor economic.

Two other events of 1946 were of great significance for the Chinese mission Church: the establishment of the internunciature on 6 July, that is, the admittance of direct diplomatic relations between the Holy See and the government at Peking,[12] and the beatification of twenty-nine Chinese martyrs of 1900.[13] The first internuncio was the titular bishop Antonio Riberi.

The statistics of the Chinese mission Church of 1948 yield the following picture: 3,276,282 faithful, 3,015 foreign and 2,676 Chinese priests, 632 Chinese and 475 foreign brothers, 5,112 Chinese and 2,351 foreign sisters, 216 hospitals, 254 orphanages, and 4,446 schools of various grades.

In the succeeding years Rome continued in an increasing measure to entrust the ecclesiastical jurisdictions to Chinese ordinaries. But the Communist occupation of the country and the only too well known

[7] AAS 38 (1946), 104.
[8] Archives of the Congregation for the Propagation of the Faith (=AP): Acta Sacrae Congregationis 317 (1946), f. 131^r–142^r.
[9] AAS 38 (1946), 301–13.
[10] Session of 6 May, audience of 10 May: AP, Acta 317 (1946), f. 174^r–188^r, AAS 38 (1946), 238, 360.
[11] The diplomatic representative of France in Peking enjoyed certain privileges in the church of the Vincentians.
[12] AAS 38 (1946), 313f.
[13] Ibid. 39 (1947), 307–11 (the Pope's homily).

political events attending it made all further Roman decisions in favor of the Chinese mission Church illusory. The connection with the outside world was more and more broken. Only in roundabout ways did the frightful news of the incipient persecution of the Church reach the rest of the world. With the governmental decree of 23 June 1950 on the suppression of "counterrevolutionary activity" began the systematic struggle against the Church. The foreign missionaries were expelled, often after ignominious show trials, mistreatment, and imprisonment. The internuncio was tactlessly banished.

In the apostolic letter of 18 January 1952 to the ordinaries in China Pius XII expressed his pain at the persecution of Christians and tried to comfort the faithful. He spoke of his love for the Chinese people, of his admiration of its historical and cultural past, of the task and the wish of the Church to encourage whatever is good, true, and beautiful among all peoples. He encouraged the Chinese Catholics. The Church, he said, can be fought but never defeated.[14] In the encyclical *Ad Sinarum gentem* of 7 October 1954 he condemned the persecution of Christians even more severely.[15] But these writings, like the news of the beatification of another fifty-six Chinese martyrs in 1955,[16] may not have become known in China. However, in 1958 about thirty Chinese bishops, loyal to Rome, and many priests and faithful were in prison because of their faith.

In these years the Communist regime changed its persecuting tactics and tried to construct a National Chinese Church separated from Rome. From December 1957 to January 1962 a total of forty-five Chinese bishops appointed by the state were ordained without papal approval. In the letter *Ad Apostolorum Principes* of 29 June 1958 Pius XII condemned these uncanonical episcopal ordinations,[17] and John XXIII in his address in the consistory of 15 December 1958 even used the word "schism" for them.[18] Also in his letter to the episcopate on Taiwan of 29 June 1961 Pope John again referred to the situation of the Church in Mainland China.[19] Pope Paul VI even tried to talk with Communist China. In an address of 20 October 1963 he said how gladly he would have embraced *all* Chinese bishops on the occasion of the Second Vatican Council.[20] On 31 December 1965, three months after

[14] Ibid. 44 (1952), 153–58.
[15] Ibid. 47 (1955), 5–14.
[16] Ibid. 381–88.
[17] Ibid. 50 (1958), 601–14.
[18] Ibid. 985.
[19] Ibid. 53 (1961), 465–69.
[20] Speech on the afternoon of Mission Sunday in the Collegio Urbano: "How happy We would be, with the bishops who are taking part in the council, to embrace also all

the Pope had come out in his speech before the United Nations in New York for the admission of states which were not yet members of the world organization, hence China also, he sent a personal telegram to Mao Tse-tung. The occasion was the request to promote peace in Vietnam. He ended with the words: "Nous vous prions d'accueillir cet appel ainsi que les voeux fervents que Nous formons devant Dieu pour le peuple chinois au seuil de l'anneé nouvelle."[21] However, the raising of the internunciature on Taiwan to the nunciature on 24 December 1966 was interpreted by some observers as an unfriendly act in regard to Communist China. The Pope corrected this impression in his memorable talk on 6 January 1967, when, on the occasion of the fortieth anniversary of the establishment of the hierarchy in China, he celebrated a Solemn Mass in Saint Peter's for the Catholics of China. On this occasion he said quite openly that it was his desire to have contacts with Communist China and to enter into friendly relations with it.[22] (On 31 January 1973 the pronuncio on Taiwan, Edward Cassidy, was made pronuncio in Bangladesh, and the nunciature on Taiwan was thereafter directed by a chargé d'affaires.) In the next few years the Cultural Revolution in China made all further efforts at contact useless. In the course of this revolution there occurred a new, very severe persecution of Christians, directed not only against the last foreign sisters in the Peking diplomats' school of the Sacred Heart, but especially against the faithful themselves. Church buildings were plundered, partly burned, or secularized.

In May 1970 Catholic bishops of the United States advised their government to leave nothing untried to arrange talks with Communist China. Perhaps the release three months later of the American Bishop James Edward Walsh from the Chinese prison he had been in since 1960 may be regarded as Mao Tse-tung's reply. In Rome, too, fresh hope was gathered.

By the end of 1971 reports were reaching Europe from China, of course very contradictory ones. Chinese Catholics living in the West had been able, by various channels, to make connections with their homeland, journalists and athletes received permission to visit China. From the meager news people thought it could be inferred that there were still in China ca. 1,000 functioning Catholic priests and sixty-five bishops, though of the latter forty-five had been appointed by the government without consulting the Holy See, and that the Church was

---

bishops of this immensely wide area [China]" (*Herder-Korrespondenz* 18 [1963–64], 112).

[21] *AAS* 58 (1966), 164.

[22] Ibid. 59 (1967), 68–71.

still alive in China, even though the number of faithful seemed to have dropped sharply. The persecutions were unable to suppress the Christian faith. Quite the contrary: under the external pressure the intensity of the faith increased. So said Father Ladany, S.J., in Hong Kong, one of the best informed persons on events in Red China. The assertion that there were no more Christians in China, he wrote, is false.[23] Since November 1971 Mass could be celebrated in one church, Nantang, in Peking. However, the faithful are mostly, even if not exclusively, members of foreign embassies.[24]

Taiwan

The events in Mainland China, which had as a consequence the departure of many priests and faithful for the island of Taiwan, pushed this long overlooked and unproductive mission area into the foreground since the 1950s. In 1949 Rome erected the prefectures apostolic of Taipei (for the Chinese congregation of priests of the *Discipuli Domini*) and Kaoshung (for the Dominicans), in 1950 the prefecture of Taichung (for the Maryknoll Missionaries), and in 1952 the prefectures of Chiayi and Hwalien (for Chinese diocesan priests and those of the Paris Mission Seminary respectively). At the same time Taipei was raised to an archdiocese and given to the *Discipuli Domini*. From then on evangelization made greater progress. Even the evangelization of the original inhabitants, who were estimated at 150,000 with twenty different languages, could be taken up. After overcoming the initial difficulties, a real conversion movement began among them, which became the most striking characteristic of the Taiwan mission of the 1950s. But the mission was able also to record successes among the Chinese refugees from the mainland. The student youths especially showed sympathy for the Catholic Church. Chinese diocesan priests, Jesuits, and Benedictine nuns taught at both state universities. Less numerous were the conversions among the Buddhist Taiwanese. In the decade of 1949–59 the total number of Catholics rose from 12,326 to 163,814 and today is approximately 290,000. In 1961 a part of the archdiocese of Taipei was erected as the diocese of Shinchiku. In addition to the missionaries already mentioned, there were Jesuits, Vincentians, Scheut Fathers (Congregation of the Immaculate Heart of Mary), Camillians, Franciscans, and members of the S.A.M. Mission Helpers, and many congregations of sisters. The Catholic University of Taipei, founded in 1963 by Archbishop Yü Pin at the urging of Pope John XXIII, was regarded as the successor of the Peking Fu-jen

---

[23] *Die katholischen Missionen* (Freiburg 1971), 15.

[24] Ibid. (Freiburg 1972), 148–52; (1973), 153–56; (1978), 39f.

University, and was intended to continue the Catholic university system flourishing on the mainland before the persecution. It began with 400 students and in 1973 had around 9,000 students and 554 professors, five faculties recognized by the state—philosophy, natural science, economics, law, foreign languages—and a theological faculty not recognized by the state. Since 1969 the last mentioned has published the theological quarterly *Shen Hsiao Lün Chi* (*Collectanea Theologica*). It aims to teach "Chinese" theology. That the Church embody itself organically in Chinese culture and remove the appearance of its foreign character is also the aim of the hierarchy.

Japan

In Japan since 1932 necessity ever more emphatically urged putting the direction of the young Church in Japanese hands. The first Japanese bishop, Januarius Hayasaka of Nagasaki, was appointed in 1927 and on 30 October he was ordained at Rome by Pius XI.[25] The situation long remained confined to this first measure of Japanization, whereas the Protestant mission advanced much faster on this route and had already relinquished almost all the ecclesiastical jurisdictions to Japanese. The complaint was heard that the Catholic Church still depended entirely on foreigners. This all the more, when the new intellectual outlook of the Japanese was marked by a mistrust of the Western world and by the conviction of the superiority of their own culture. This was not without consequences for the missionary situation of the Catholic Church. Finally from 1936 Rome made greater progress toward the Japanization of the Church. In fact, from now on events pushed on one another. The settlement of the controversy over the Japanese rites, that is, the permission for the faithful to take part in the purely civil customs of social life, "which nowadays are generally regarded as mere marks of courtesy and of mutual good will, even if they originally had a superstitious character," was the most important step in this direction.[26] When on 25 May 1936 Pius XI approved the relevant instruction of the Congregation for the Propagation of the Faith, he said that the faithful had not only the permission to share in these patriotic and civil ceremonies but the duty.

---

[25] *AAS* 19 (1927), 379f. (The Pope's homily). As early as the beginning of 1933 the bishop was forced to resign for reasons of health and other causes. In 1937 Paulus Aijiro Yamaguchi became his successor.

[26] Instruction of the Congregation for the Propagation of the Faith of 26 May 1936 in *AAS* 28 (1936), 406–09; *Sylloge praecipuorum documentorum recentium Summorum Pontificum et S. Congregationis de Progaganda Fide . . .* (Vatican City 1939), 537–40, N. 201; *Collectanea Commissionis Synodalis* 9 (Peking 1936), 872–74; *Memoria Rerum* III/2, 483–87.

This new attitude of Rome in regard to Japanese morals and customs could not prevent the Catholic Church and, in general, all Christianity from being drawn, in the next years, into the powerfully flourishing antiforeign Japanese nationalistic movement. The slogan put it: Christianity is a foreign religion, hence not for the Japanese. The attitude was further accentuated with the forcible takeover by Fumimaro Konoye in July 1940 and the higher valuation of the worship of the Emperor. The antiforeign animosity had as a consequence even sharper attacks on the Catholic Church as this was still to a great extent governed by foreign prelates. Only in Tokyo and Nagasaki was there a Japanese bishop and in Kagoshima a Japanese prefect apostolic. The "Law on Religious Corporations" of 25 March 1939 left no doubt that the government was seeking complete control of ecclesial communities and no longer recognized foreigners as representatives of the communities. Rome now hastened to turn over all ecclesiastical territories to Japanese prelates. The foreign bishops voluntarily resigned. Now the Japanese ordinaries could take steps toward legal recognition of the Catholic church communities by the state, in accord with the law on corporations. They worked out the "constitutions" of the Japanese Church and thereby acquired state recognition in May 1941. A little later the Protestant Churches followed this step. In this way the mission Church in Japan was spared immensely injurious consequences. Rome, of course, subjected these constitutions to strong criticism. One of the cardinals who had to pronounce judgment on them compared them to the Civil Constitution of the Clergy in the French Revolution. The apostolic delegate since 1933, Paolo Marella, who had shared substantially in the drafting of the constitution, was accused of having acted without consultation with Rome. Cardinal Pietro Fumasoni-Biondi, prefect of the congregation for the Propagation of the Faith from 1933 to 1960, saved the situation and hence the constitution of the young Church in Japan by making it clear that Rome had not at all been asked for approval of the constitution. On this occasion he expressed his joy that the Japanese mission Church had made such good progress in recent times and thanked the foreign missionaries for having voluntarily relinquished their position to the Japanese clergy. He expressed the hope that this example might be imitated in other mission lands also.[27]

A completely new missionary situation occurred in Japan after World

---

[27] This Italian prefect of the Roman missionary authority had already shown his sound sense of the present-day questions. Thus he had given the "green light" for the reopening and solving of the question of the Chinese Rites, to discuss this question contrary to the earlier directive of the Holy Office. For the details of the life and evaluation of the prefectship of Fumasoni-Biondi, cf. *Memoria Rerum* III/2, 313–15.

War II. The Shinto state worship was abolished. On New Year's Day 1946 Emperor Hirohito declared that the previous religious doctrines of the state were myths. Shintoism became a purely private religion. The antiforeign outlook of the Japanese seemed to become quite the opposite in the first postwar years. The prospects for the missions increased. At Yokohama, for example, the number of catechumens tripled at one stroke. Sisters were able to set up a higher school for girls at the Buddhist center of Nagano. The port city of Yokosuka, a military port, hitherto inaccessible to foreigners, very quickly became a flourishing center of Catholic missionary activity. The Protestant American supreme commander offered the Catholics several buildings for the erection of schools and of a hospital. Rome multiplied the missionary personnel. In 1958 there were in Japan 1,220 foreign and 359 Japanese priests, 166 foreign and 250 native brothers, 1,063 foreign and 3,050 Japanese sisters. In the two seminaries at Tokyo and Fukuoka there were 260 seminarians. In 1975 there were in Japan twelve native Japanese congregations of sisters of diocesan right and one secular institute.[28]

However, it must be stated soberly that, after years of hope-filled creativity, the results of the mission, in regard to numbers, do not correspond to the exertions of the missionaries. In 1958 there were only 266,000 Catholics in the population of 92 million, and ten years later only 345,000, whereas the total population had increased to 100 million. In 1974 there were 363,000 Catholics among 109.5 million inhabitants, and in 1977 392,000 faithful among 113 million. Happier is the increase of native vocations. Of the 1,966 priests, 869 are Japanese. The number of Japanese sisters amounts to 6,052. About 800 foreign sisters help them. And today the number of Japanese brothers is greater than that of the foreign.

However, this is not the only aspect to be considered in evaluating the young Church in Japan. The moral reputation of the Catholic Church and its influence on the public must not be underestimated. The Church "shows itself Japanese, speaks Japanese, shares according to its means in Japanese life. Hence, on the whole the Church presents a Japanese image, thanks especially to its native leadership."[29] It has become more attractive to the Japanese. The Second Vatican Council contributed substantially to this. The religious institutions cultivate a dialogue with the non-Christian religions in Japan and exert themselves for a close collaboration with them in the service of humanity.

[28] "Supplementum" of the *Bibliografia Missionaria,* Anno XXXIX–1975, Quaderno no. 18 (Rome 1976), 27–30.
[29] H. Dumoulin, S.J., *Die Bedeutung des Christentums in Japan: Die katholischen Missionen* (1977), 118–122, here 118.

Korea

In the young Church in Korea the ordinaries had been preparing the Korean clergy since 1927, by a mandate from Rome, to assume the direction of the mission. But the political situation made the transfer difficult. The Koreanization of the Church encountered the opposition of the Japanese occupying power, which wanted to see Japanese ordinaries in charge of the ecclesiastical jurisdictions. Nevertheless, in 1942, after the resignation of the vicar apostolic of Seoul (Keijo in Japanese), Rome appointed the Korean priest Paul Ro (his Korean name) Okamoto (his Japanese name) as his successor, first as administrator and then on 10 November of the same year as vicar apostolic with episcopal ordination. But in the case of Taiku, whose ordinary had likewise resigned, the Roman mission officials had to yield to the occupying power. They appointed the Japanese priest Irenaeus Kyubei Hayasaka as administrator. On 10 November 1942 they promoted him also to bishop, without, however, naming him as vicar apostolic.

With the growing tensions between Japan and the United States, the situation of the American missionaries in Japan and the conquered territories became ever more critical. Until 1941 the vicar apostolic of Heijo, the name from 1939 for Hpyeng Yang, William O'Shea, M.M., and his Maryknoll Missionaries were able to act freely. But in December of that year all except him and his secretary were interned. In June 1942 all American missionaries returned to the United States within the framework of an exchange of internees. Earlier O'Shea had given the necessary spiritual faculties to the Korean priest Francis Hong (his Korean name) Takeoka (his Japanese name). Confirmed by Rome on 18 February 1943, he understood superlatively how to guide the destinies of the mission through the unpropitious times. He even maintained good contacts with the Japanese authorities. After the end of Japanese domination of Korea Rome had a free hand in the filling of the ecclesiastical posts with Korean ordinaries. On 7 June 1947 Pius XII appointed Patrick James Byrne, M.M., as apostolic visitor of the missions in Korea, with the faculties of an apostolic delegate.[30] A little later, on 7 April 1949, an apostolic delegation was established in Korea, with Byrne as the first occupant.[31]

Severe external trials were in store for the Korean mission Church. Here the political events may be assumed as familiar. Because of the Communist occupation of North Korea, 57,000 Catholics were virtually cut off from the rest of the Church. Abbot-Bishop Boniface Sauer, O.S.B., of the abbey *nullius* of Tŏgwŏn that had been erected in 1940,

---

[30] *AAS* 39 (1947), 463.
[31] Ibid. 42 (1950), 327.

died as a victim of the new rulers as a consequence of mistreatment in a concentration camp. The vicar apostolic of P'yŏngyang, Bishop Francis Hong, was missing. Many missionaries were killed or deported, including Apostolic Delegate Byrne, who died in a prison camp on 26 November 1960.

In South Korea, on the other hand, the number of the faithful quickly grew to over 215,000 and in 1956 reached 241,830, among whom were to be counted 27,332 catechumens. Still, vis-à-vis the 20 million inhabitants, the Catholics constituted only a small minority.

In the succeeding years there came to the foreground the plan of erecting the ecclesiastical hierarchy, which took place on 10 March 1962.[32] Three ecclesiastical provinces were established: Seoul, with the suffragan sees of P'yŏngyang, Hamhŭng, Chunchŏn, Taejŏn, and Inchon; Taegu, with the suffragan sees of Chŏngju and Pusan; and Kwangju, with that of Jeonju. In addition, the abbey *nullius* of Tŏgwŏn continued, directly subject to the Holy See. There were around this time in South Korea more than 488,000 Catholics, 282 Korean priests (with 236 foreign priests), and 1,039 Korean sisters (out of a total of 1,170). Foreign communities active in Korea included: the Paris Mission Seminary, the Missionary Benedictines of Sankt Ottilien, Franciscans, Conventuals, Jesuits, the Hospitallers of Saint John of God, the Missionaries of Saint Francis de Sales of Annecy, Marianists, Salesians, Maryknoll Missioners, and the Columban Missionaries of Ireland; also, the Korean Samists and the Brothers of the Holy Korean Martyrs. There were five communities of Korean Sisters.[33] Of the foreign sisters, those of Saint Paul of Chartres had the most numerous representation. They counted 295 Korean sisters in their ranks.[34]

On 11 December 1963 Paul VI erected the internunciature of Korea,[35] which was changed to a nunciature on 5 September 1966.[36] Two further important events for the Korean mission Church of the most recent past were the beatification of twenty-four Korean martyrs of 1866 on 6 October 1968 and the creation of the first Korean cardinal, Stephen Sou Hwan Kim, in the consistory of 28 April 1969.

In the 1970s the Christian churches in South Korea, even though

[32] Ibid. 54 (1962), 552–55.
[33] Today there are in Korea six native congregations of sisters of diocesan right: "Supplementum" of the *Bibliografia Missionaria*, Anno XXXIX–1975, Quaderno no. 18 (Rome 1976), 22f.
[34] Cf. J. Chang-mun Kim and J. Jae-sun Chung, *Catholic Korea Yesterday and Today* (Seoul 1964).
[35] *AAS* 56 (1964), 235.
[36] Ibid. 58 (1966), 875.

they included numerically only a small part of the population, became the center of the intellectual opposition to the dictatorship of the Park regime. The tensions between Church and state led in August 1974 to the imprisoning of Bishop Tji Hak Soun of Wonju, who was condemned as an "agitator" by a military court to fifteen years in prison. In February 1975 he, with 150 other political prisoners, was released.

Today the young Church of Korea counts about 990,000 faithful in a total population of 40.5 million, not counting P'yŏngyang and Tokwon, for which, according to the 1978 *Annuario Pontificio,* no statistics are available.

SOUTHEAST ASIA

India

In the mission Church of India important happenings in the two decades before World War II helped to prepare the future. There was, first, the progressive transfer of the ecclesiastical direction into native hands, which of course proceeded much too slowly for the Indian clergy. Opposition and obstacles arose chiefly from the Indian caste system which frustrated some Roman plans. The abolition of the oath concerning rites freed the route on a broader level for the better Indianization of the young Church. After the publication of the instruction of 8 December 1939 on the Chinese rites there appeared the question of whether the missionaries in India had to continue to take the so-called oath on rites which in 1739 Clement XII had prescribed for all missionaries in the kingdoms of Madura, Mysore, and Carnatic. Right from the start obscurities had existed as to the extent of this obligation, which could not be cleared up in the succeeding period.[37] In the course of time Rome had replied to the doubts that cropped up with the stereotyped but by no means clarifying formula "nihil esse innovandum."[38] Considering this and the decision issued a few months earlier in regard to the Chinese rites, the cardinals of the Roman Congregation for the Propagation of the Faith decided in their session of 8 April 1940 that the obligation to the oath "sopra i riti

---

[37] Cf. especially the letters of 13 October 1744 and 6 February 1745 of the Roman mission dicastery in *AP, Lettere* 161f., 146^r–148^r, 171^r–174^v; also, *Collectanea S. Congregationis de Propaganda Fide* I (Rome 1907), nos. 594 and 607.

[38] Cf. *AP, Lettere* 331f., 532^v (letter to the superior of the Paris Mission Seminary of 20 July 1844); 351f., 296^v–297^v (letter of 18 May 1860 to the vicar apostolic of Jaffna); *Registro delle Risoluzioni del S. Offizio* 2 (1853), 34, no. 2; 6 (1873), 5; *Collectanea S. Congregationis de Propaganda Fide* I (Rome 1907), no. 993; *Lettere* 362f., 1058^r–1059^r (letter of 27 October 1969 in regard to an inquiry of the vicar apostolic of Colombo).

malabarici" was to be abolished; the Pope confirmed this in audience the next day.[39]

A second happening was the conversion of two bishops of the Syro-Malankarese, Mar Ivanios (Givergis Thomas) Panikervirtis and Mar Theophilus (Jacob Abraham) Kalapurakal, to the Catholic Church in 1930. This was a first success of the strivings for union between the Syrian Orthodox and the Catholic Church. The movement for union stopped. On 28 August 1977 Archbishop Mar Felixnose of the Independent Syrian Orthodox Malabarese Church, together with his secretary, completed his union with Rome.

Finally, still a fourth, not unessential chapter on the way of the Indian Church into the future must be mentioned. Portugal gradually renounced its missionary patronate in India and thereby ended a century-long tug-of-war with the missionary authorities in Rome. On the occasion of filling the Church offices with Indian ordinaries, there was no consultation with Portugal. No protest came from Lisbon on the division of those dioceses for which the agreement of 1928 had granted to the patron one final but quite small remnant of the patronate.[40] Even in Bombay the transition took place smoothly. According to the agreement just mentioned, the archbishop had to be alternately Portuguese and English. This stipulation put the Holy See in an embarrassing position, for in Bombay there were hardly any English and no Portuguese missionaries at all. In 1937 Rome had difficulty in finding a candidate. More in order to remove these difficulties than out of necessity, Archbishop Thomas Roberts, on the occasion of a visit to Rome in 1945, proposed that an Indian priest be given him as auxiliary bishop. The choice fell on Valerian Gracias, later the first Indian cardinal. Because he was an auxiliary bishop and not a coadjutor with the right of succession, Portugal could make no objections. If, sooner or later, the auxiliary bishop should be appointed ordinary— this was now the clear intention of Rome, and Archbishop Roberts was ready to resign in this case and surrender his position to the Indian bishop—the Portuguese government would be asked to renounce its privilege and not resist the indigenization of the Church in India. However, this was not to be necessary. In the mission treaty of 18 July 1950 Portugal renounced its rights in the nomination of the ordinaries of Mangalore, Quilon, Trichinopoly, Cochin, Saint Thomé (Saõ Thomé, Mylapore), and Bombay,[41] and on 4 De-

---

[39] AAS 32 (1940), 379.
[40] Ibid. 20 (1928), 133.
[41] Ibid. 42 (1950), 811–15.

cember of the same year Gracias became archbishop. Pius XII created him a cardinal in the consistory of 12 January 1953.

The mission treaty of 1950 had still other consequences. The bishops of Cochin and Mylapore were transferred to titular sees. In this way Rome obtained a free hand for the naming of the ordinaries of these former dioceses of the patronate. Cochin was divided into two new dioceses, Cochin and Alleppey, in accord with the two ethnic groups that had warred there with each other for centuries, and a broader territory, 130 kilometers from the rest of the former patronate diocese was separated and given to the bishop of Trivandrum as administrator. Likewise, the two heterogeneous and territorially widely separated parts of the patronate see of Meliapur were reconstructed ecclesiastically. The new dioceses of Tanjore and Vellore were erected, and the rest of the territories united to the archdiocese of Madras and Mylapore.

World War II did not produce for the Indian Church damage as great as had World War I. In general, missionary activity proceeded quietly. Only in Assam were material losses to be recorded. In 1945 the younger German and Italian missionaries, that is, those who had come after 1931, were temporarily interned. On 15 August 1947 the two independent states of India and Pakistan were founded. The result was that ecclesiastical territories were torn apart. Rome synchronized the diocesan boundaries with the political.

Meanwhile, the Indian missionary bishops had called into existence in 1944 the Catholic Bishops' Conference of India (CBCI).[42] The first Indian plenary council met at Bangalore from 6 to 18 January 1950. All ordinaries of the then fifty-two ecclesiastical circumscriptions of India, including the Archbishop of Goa and the bishops of the Eastern Rite in Malabar, who together represented 4.5 million Catholics, were present. It was a demonstration of the unity and compactness of the Indian Church, which publicly declared its loyalty to the new independent state. In the letter to Cardinal Norman Gilroy, archbishop of Sydney, whom Pius XII had appointed legate for the plenary council, the Roman purposes for the council were named: closer and uniform cooperation of the clergy among themselves and with the laity in all

---

[42] The first common Episcopal Conference of India had taken place in 1921 under the chairmanship of Apostolic Delegate Pisani following the Marian Congress at Madras. At that time the idea of an Indian plenary council had arisen. However, various circumstances, including the frequent change of delegates, prevented the realization of the plan. When at last in 1937 everything was ready for the summoning, difficulties unexpectedly appeared because of the Portuguese patronate, so that the council had to be postponed. Pius XII later eliminated the latter difficulties by naming as legate for the council the cardinal of Sydney.

ecclesiastical and missionary questions; increase of the native clergy and improvement of its formation; building of Catholic Action; founding of a Catholic university; intensified care of charitable and educational institutions; promotion of the apostolate of the press. The conciliar decrees in keeping with these wishes were approved on 29 January 1952. They concerned not only regular pastoral care but also missionary radiation. In the latter relation the following means, in addition to the traditional ones, were recommended: appointment of a few priests who, equipped with a basic knowledge of the language, customs, philosophy, and religions of India, should assume apologetical and catechetical work among the educated; creation of a Catholic literature also for the Old Catholics which wholly and publicly represented Catholic doctrine and was also outstanding "in its literary and technical aspect"; proclaiming of Catholic teaching by means of radio broadcasts by priests and educated faithful; spread of the Church's social teaching, which was almost unknown in India; founding of a periodical for social questions, in connection with the Episcopal Conference; exercise of the apostolate also among Christians separated from the Church.[43] Further, at the plenary council the statutes of the Episcopal Conference were approved. The most striking sign and the greatest significance of this plenary council consists in the fact that the young Church of India began to adapt itself extensively to the traditional morals and customs of the country.

Other significant events for the mission Church of India were the following: In 1948 Pius XII established the internunciature of India.[44] On 26 January 1951 he declared the Mother of God patroness of the country.[45] At the close of the Marian Year there took place in Bombay a National Marian Congress from 4 to 8 December 1954 under the chairmanship of Cardinal Gracias; it was intended to express anew the vitality of the Catholic Church of India, and actually produced a great echo even in the non-Catholic public. Likewise at Bombay there was held in November 1964 the Thirty-Eighth Eucharistic Congress, which Pope Paul VI honored with his presence from 2 to 5 November.[46] The Pope's journey to India became an event of the greatest importance for both Church and secular history. Nine hundred eighty journalists and a television crew of seventy-seven gave every detail of the phenomenal reception and stay of the Pope in India worldwide publicity. Other

---

[43] According to M. Bierbaum, "Das erste Plenarkonzil von Indien," *ZMR* 36 (Munich 1952), 161–72.

[44] *AAS* 42 (1950), 235. In August 1967 it was elevated to a nunciature with a pronuncio as titular.

[45] Ibid. 46 (1954), 398f.

[46] Ibid. 57 (1965), 113–40 (all details of the Pope's journey).

landmarks of the new orientation of the young Church were the plenary assembly of the Indian hierarchy at New Delhi in 1966, an International Theological Conference at Nagpur in 1971, the celebration of the nineteenth centenary of the death of the Apostle Thomas at Madras in 1972, and the "All India Consultation on Evangelization" at Patna in 1973. From 14 to 25 May 1969 Bangalore was host of the "All India Seminar" for the renewal of the Church of India, which was equivalent to a "pastoral council." It was the climax of an exhaustive process of teaching and opinion formation. The great topics were: Indianization of the Church, self-support of the local Indian churches, and dialogue with the non-Christian religions.[47] A noteworthy contribution to the development of an Indian theology was promised by the new faculty of the study of religion, which was opened on 3 July 1976 at Dharmaram College in Bangalore.

Through these and other manifestations the Catholic Church of India made itself a subject of conversation. Meetings, conferences, and seminars with important declarations found an international echo and "made obvious the desire for a revival and reorientation of ecclesiastical work."[48] Although a small minority, the Catholic Church in India is today a spiritual power, the results and importance of which cannot be expressed in numbers. In 1970 it published six daily newspapers, twenty ecclesiastical weeklies, and the two general weeklies, *Sanjivan* and *Orbit.* Catholic journalists are collaborators on the great daily and weekly papers of the country. The Indian clergy is numerous and through its good formation has gained greatly in quality and esteem. One of its most outstanding representatives, Archbishop Simon Lourdusamy of Bangalore, was called to Rome by Paul VI to direct the Dicastery for the Missions. The Indian congregations of sisters experienced a striking development, something of great importance, not only for the Church but for the whole nation, in a country where traditionally woman was accorded no place of honor. There are today in India twenty-three diocesan congregations of sisters and one female secular institute.[49] With the establishment of the first ashram at Kurisumala in 1957 began the adaptation of the contemplative life to Indian mentality and forms.

[47] Cf. *Die katholischen Missionen* (Freiburg 1970), 8–11. On the topic "dialogue" it should be noted that not too long ago it was still forbidden to learn Sanskrit and read books on Hinduism in major seminaries. The contact with Hinduism was regarded as a danger to the Christian faith. This attitude has changed radically in recent years due to the influence of the Second Vatican Council. The Catholic Church seeks better to understand Hinduism and to have a dialogue with its adherents.

[48] *Herder-Korrespondenz* 28 (Freiburg 1974), 7.

[49] "Supplementum" to the *Bibliografia Missionaria,* Anno XXXIX–1975, Quaderno no. 18 (Rome 1976), 32–37.

For all that, there has still been no success in bridging the abyss between Christianity and Hinduism. In the tradition-conscious Hindu circles Christianity is still regarded as foreign to Indian culture. This led in recent times to some deplorable obstacles for foreign missioners in some states, such as Assam. The Church hierarchy and the lay organizations leave nothing untried to remove the still existing prejudices and to eliminate all the bases for them. Above all, great exertions have been undertaken in the way of liturgical adaptation, as prescribed by the Second Vatican Council.

In 1978 the young Church of India consisted of eighty-three dioceses and two prefectures apostolic of the Latin Rite, seventeen dioceses of the Syro-Malabarese and two dioceses of the Syro-Malankarese Rites. The number of bishops—ordinaries, coadjutors, and auxiliaries—is 125. Three of them are cardinals. All except seven of the bishops are Indians. The number of the faithful of all three rites amounts to 10 million.

Pakistan

Large parts of the future West Pakistan belonged in ecclesiastical administration to the archdiocese of Bombay until 1948. After the founding of the independent Islamic nation of Pakistan, the diocese of Karachi was erected in West Pakistan on 20 May 1948. In East Pakistan—now Bangladesh—there had existed the diocese of Dacca since 1886. On 15 July 1950 Rome completed the ecclesiastical organization by the establishment of the ecclesiastical province of Karachi, with the suffragan sees of Multan, Lahore, and Rawalpindi, to which were added in 1958 Hyderabad and in 1960 Lyallpur, called Faisalabad since 1977, and that of Dacca, with the suffragan sees of Dinajpur and Chittagong, to which in 1952 was added Jesore, called Khulna since 1956.[50] No boundaries were determined for Kashmir and Jammu, for possession of which India and Pakistan were still fighting. Here on 17 January 1952 Rome erected instead the prefecture apostolic of Kashmir and Jammu, since 1968 called Jammu and Kashmir, and entrusted it to the Mill Hill Missionaries.[51] On the establishment of diplomatic relations with Pakistan, the delegation earlier erected in Karachi was on 9 October 1951 elevated to an internunciature, which on 27 December 1965 became a nunciature.[52]

The Islamic state of Pakistan guaranteed religious liberty in the constitution and assured the free exercise of religion by the religious

[50] AAS 43 (1951), 66–69.
[51] Ibid. 44 (1952), 513f.
[52] Ibid. 42 (1950), 878f.; 44 (1952), 712f.; 58 (1966), 134.

minorities. Nevertheless, here as everywhere else in the Islamic world, the proclamation of the Christian faith encounters insurmountable difficulties. The episcopate always tried to solve emerging timely problems, such as the school question, by direct negotiations with the government. The foreseeable limitations on foreign missionaries were compensated by the opportune "Pakistanization" of the episcopate and the clergy. The elevation of the archbishop of Karachi, Joseph Cordeiro, to the College of Cardinals on 5 March 1973 was well received even by the non-Catholic population and the government. However, one cannot speak of an influence of the small Catholic minority on public life. All private colleges, including four Catholic, were nationalized in September 1972. In October of the same year the same fate overtook the Urdu schools in the Punjab and some English schools. There were in 1972 381,000 Catholics in a population of ca. 65 million.

Bangladesh

In Bangladesh, independent since 1971, the Catholic minority is very dynamic. It exercises its greatest influence in the sector of education. In 1976 it maintained 274 educational centers, a noteworthy achievement for a community of only 130,000 Catholics—today they number 142,000 in a population of 71.5 million. Among them were sixteen high schools. On 2 March 1973 Paul VI erected the nunciature of Bangladesh.[53]

Sri Lanka

Evangelization on Sri Lanka, the former Ceylon, which regards itself as the refuge of the original, unadulterated Buddhism, is chiefly in the hands of the Oblates of Mary Immaculate, the Silvestrine Benedictines, and the Jesuits. They succeeded, in spite of some difficulties, in building a relatively strong Church and educating a numerous native clergy. Still, the process of transferring the direction of the Church to native hands began late.[54] Not until the partition of the archdiocese of Colombo and the founding of the new diocese of Chilaw on 5 January 1939 did the first native Oblate obtain an episcopal see. But he died before his episcopal ordination. In 1940 another native Oblate became his successor.

After the end of World War II Rome hastened to appoint a native of Sri Lanka, in fact a Singhalese bishop, as coadjutor with the right of succession. The choice fell on forty-four-year-old Thomas Benjamin

---

[53] Ibid. 65 (1973), 236.
[54] The bishop of Kandy, Beda Beekmeyer, O.S.B. Silv., appointed in 1912, was, it is true, born in Sri Lanka, but he came from a Dutch family which had lived in Sri Lanka for a little over a century.

Cooray, O.M.I., who later became Sri Lanka's first cardinal.[55] He became archbishop on 26 July 1947.

With the attainment of political independence on 4 February 1948, there began a campaign of harassment by Buddhist groups against the Catholic Church, which some intended to make responsible for the island's long colonial past. At first, this had as a consequence an "inferiority complex" on the part of Catholics, but the Church soon recovered from this. Rome continued to entrust the direction of the Church to native hands. Just the same, the young Church found it difficult to extend its missionary endeavors further. It increased practically only through natural growth. In 1958, of the 9.3 million inhabitants, 7.69 percent were Catholics. A large part of the native clergy was occupied in education and hence kept from the functions of evangelization. It is gratifying that at the insistence of Rome the clergy of Sri Lanka have since the 1960s undertaken foreign missions, first in Malaysia, then in India, Pakistan, and Bangladesh.

The Church received a new stimulus when on 22 February 1965 Archbishop Cooray became a cardinal. Under his chairmanship, the National Synod of 1968 sought to implement the directives of the Second Vatican Council in the Church of Sri Lanka. It courageously considered all the burning problems: cooperation between clergy and ordinaries, lay movements, religious instruction, liturgy, adaptation, and so forth, and decided for the elimination of the ghetto mentality of the Catholic Church within the nation, for positive collaboration in the national and cultural life, and for preparedness for cooperation with non-Christians in the solution of national problems.[56]

Nevertheless, the Church was not spared severe trials. In 1960 all private schools on Sri Lanka were nationalized. In 1964 the sisters assigned to state hospitals were removed. In January 1966 the government abolished the Christian Sunday and introduced the Buddhist *Poya* Day as the day of rest; it is computed according to the moon's phases. But this decision was annulled for economic considerations on 9 July 1971. Since Cooray's creation as a cardinal, the relations with the government have improved somewhat. On 11 December 1967 Rome established the apostolic delegation and on 6 September 1975 the

---

[55] Session of the cardinals of the Congregation for the Propagation of the Faith of 10 December, audience of 13 (not 14) December 1945.

[56] Cf. *Die katholischen Missionen*, 23–25. An important contribution to the improvement of the climate between Catholics and Buddhists was made by Bishop Edmund Peiris, O.M.I., of Chilaw by means of his economic and historical researches and publications. He was regarded as the best informed on the culture and history of Sri Lanka and took part in a brisk exchange of scholarly ideas with learned Buddhists.

apostolic nunciature of Sri Lanka.[57] On 4 December 1970 Paul VI stayed for three hours at the airport in Colombo on his return flight from Oceania and Australia. He was welcomed by 600,000 persons. The government, the Buddhists, Hindus, and Muslims had sent delegations. This papal visit contributed much to the improvement of the climate among the religious groups. Today the Catholic Church on Sri Lanka counts 965,000 members in a total population of 13 million, a fairly strong minority for Asiatic conditions.

Vietnam

The plenary Council of Hanoi, 18 November to 6 December 1934, altered the course of the future of the young Churches of French Indochina—the states of Tonkin, Annam, Cochin China, Cambodia, Laos, and Siam. The most important subjects treated were: implementation of the new *Codex iuris canonici* and of the papal mission encyclicals, adaptation to the present time, guidelines for the mission to pagans, uniform missionary methods, relations of the foreign priests with the native clergy, learning of the national languages, study of the native religions and cultures, founding of native religious communities, use of the vernacular by the faithful at Mass, preparation of native priests for direction of the Church, wearing of Annamite dress by the clergy, and the lay apostolate.

The appointment of the native priest John Baptist Tong as coadjutor bishop of Phat-Diem and his ordination at Rome by Pius XI on 11 June 1933 was the first step on the way to a native Church, and others quickly followed. The French colonial power thwarted some of Rome's plans, but it was unable any longer to stop the development.[58]

The political occurrences during World War II and the succeeding wars for independence and above all the partition of Vietnam on 20 July 1954 inflicted atrocious injury on the mission Church. The political division altered at one stroke the religious and ecclesiastical picture of Vietnam. Ten vicariates apostolic lay in North Vietnam, six in South Vietnam. 875,000 inhabitants moved from the north to the south, 80 percent of whom, that is, 650,000, were Catholics. In South Vietnam the number of faithful tripled. The Church did everything it could to solve the burning social and religious problems of the refugees. Pastoral care among the now 1.4 million faithful had to be reorganized. This number grew powerfully in consequence of a movement of conversion that got under way in the next few years.

The Church undertook special exertions in the educational and social

---

[57] *AAS* 67 (1975), 649.
[58] Cf. *Memoria Rerum* III/2, 507f.

and charitable fields. In 1966 264,801 pupils were counted in the 1,158 elementary schools and 83,103 students in the 178 high schools. In 1959 the episcopate of South Vietnam founded the University of Da Lat, which was recognized by the state the same year. It was intended to make a new contribution to the intellectual construction of the country, especially in the educational and cultural sphere. Mathematics, chemistry, agriculture, technology, philosophy, literature, and education were the branches of knowledge here cultivated. In 1965 there followed the establishment of a theological faculty in the Papal Seminary of Pius X, also at Da Lat.

In North Vietnam, on the contrary, the Church had to suffer more and more under Communist rule. All foreign missionaries were expelled in 1960. The activity of the native bishops and of the 200 remaining native priests was very greatly curtailed. The apostolic delegate since 1951, John Dooley, had to leave Hanoi because of sickness and was brought to the hospital at Phnom Penh. His vicar, Terence O'Driscoll, was expelled on 17 August 1959.

In South Vietnam there took place from 16 to 18 February 1959 at Saigon in the presence of the papal legate, Cardinal Gregory Peter Agagianian, the National Marian Congress, which was intended at the same time to celebrate the tercentenary of the nomination of the first vicars apostolic. Another important happening of the Jubilee Year was the establishment of the ecclesiastical hierarchy on 24 November 1960. Three ecclesiastical provinces were erected: in North Vietnam, Hanoi, with the suffragan sees of Lang Son, Hai Phong, Bac Ninh, Hung Hoa, Thai Binh, Bui Chu, Phat Diem, Than Hoa, and Vinh; in South Vietnam, Hué, with the suffragan sees of Qui Nhon, Nha Trang, and Kon Tum, and Saigon, with those of Vinh Long, Can Tho, Da Lat, My Tho, and Long Xuen. Hanoi and all dioceses in North Vietnam obtained native ordinaries, as did Saigon and all its suffragans and Hué and Qui Nhon.[59] Only Nha Trang and Kon Tum for the moment retained a foreign bishop. On the occasion of the establishment of the hierarchy, John XXIII sent a letter of congratulations to the Church in Vietnam on 14 January 1961.[60]

Pope Paul VI lost no opportunity to employ his prestige and diplomatic skill for the restoration of peace in Vietnam. In 1966 he sent the then apostolic delegate in Canada, Titular Archbishop Sergio Pignedoli, with a special message to the bishops meeting in Saigon.[61]

---

[59] AAS 53 (1961), 346–50.
[60] Ibid., 84–88.
[61] Ibid. 58 (1966), 911–14.

On 27 November 1970, on his flight from Dacca to Manila, he sent personal greetings to the governments in North and South Vietnam.

After the end of the thirty-years civil war, there began also for the part of the young Church in what had been South Vietnam a difficult time. In September 1975 twenty missioners were expelled from Da Lat. Thereafter the expulsion of foreign missionaries proceeded systematically.[62] The Church became more and more the "silent" Church. On 18 March 1976 Bishop Nguyên van Thuân, who had been appointed coadjutor of Saigon[63] before the seizure of power by the Communists, was imprisoned. He was regarded as one of the most capable bishops in Vietnam. He again obtained his freedom in July 1978. The archbishop of Hanoi, Joseph Marie Trin-nhu-Khuê, was created a cardinal by Paul VI in the consistory of 24 May 1976.[64] He received from the government permission for the journey to Rome.

Today the young Church in Vietnam numbers 2.8 million faithful in a total population of 47 million.

Laos

In Laos evangelization was carried out by members of the Paris Mission Seminary and French and Italian Oblates of Mary Immaculate. Despite encouraging starts, the mission still had not advanced beyond the initial stage in the 1950s. But at that time people felt they could speak of a wave of conversions among the animistic mountain tribes of the Meo and the Lao Theung in the uplands north of Vientiane; however, the political happenings impeded the evangelization of these peoples. Still, there arose a rather large number of Christian congregations which grew rapidly. But it was precisely the habitat of these mountaineers that became the field of operation of the Communist Pathet Lao. The part of the country occupied by them became inaccessible to the missionaries.

After South Vietnam had fallen at the end of April 1975 and Cambodia fourteen days later, Laos passed almost silently into the hands of the Communists in May. In the same month thirty French missionaries went to Thailand. In September twenty-nine Italian Oblates had to leave the country within three days.[65] Three native bishops

---

[62] Except for two members of the community of the "Little Brothers" of Charles de Foucauld and one of the "Little Sisters," all foreign missionaries were expelled up to 1976. The Church lost all its apostolic works, such as schools, student residences, orphanages, and hospitals. An exception was the Saint Paul Clinic in Ho Chi Minh City (Saigon).

[63] In 1967 he was made bishop of Nha Trang and on 24 April 1975 was appointed coadjutor of Saigon.

[64] *AAS* 68 (1976), 379.

[65] They are today active in other missions, especially in Indonesia and Senegal.

and a dozen native priests remained behind under difficult conditions to care for some fifteen thousand faithful.

Cambodia

The most recent events had a still much more tragic impact on the little mission Church in Cambodia. The from time immemorial "little flock," which was for the most part composed of immigrant Vietnamese, was ever more decimated. The Catholics were branded as agents of a foreign religion. One who had himself baptized a Christian was called a traitor. This is related to the fact that there were scarcely 5,000 Catholics of Cambodian ancestry. Most of them were descendants of emancipated slaves of earlier times. Today Christianity has no more possibility of life in radical Cambodia. It has been effaced.

Thailand

The young Church in Buddhist Thailand, formerly Siam, had to suffer from various sorts of persecution in the 1930s and 1940s. Christianity was rejected as the religion of the colonial power. After World War II the situation improved somewhat. The repeated coups d'etat diverted people from church policy. In 1953 there were, among 18 million inhabitants, at most 85,000 Catholics, mostly Vietnamese and Chinese, seldom Thais. But missionary activity was tolerated. Today the young Church counts 174,000 faithful in a population of 41 million. On 18 December 1965 the ecclesiastical hierarchy was erected.[66]

Burma

The Second World War produced serious damage for the mission Church in Burma. On the occasion of the conquest of the country by the Japanese and of the reconquest, almost all mission works—churches, schools, mission stations—were destroyed. And there occurred local persecutions of Christians. The constitution of the nation, independent since 4 January 1948, guarantees religious liberty. This did not exclude certain restrictions, for example, in regard to the entry of foreign missioners. And the state claimed the sole right to educate the youth. In an effort to accommodate the strong national consciousness of the population and to remove prejudices against Catholics, Rome pushed from 1954 for the transfer of the direction of the Church to native bishops. The ecclesiastical hierarchy was established on 1 January

[66] AAS 58 (1966), 554–56. Two ecclesiastical provinces were erected: Bangkok and Thare Nonseng with three suffragans each. Meanwhile, two other dioceses were established.

1955.[67] There were at that time, among 16 million inhabitants, only about 150,000 Catholics. Among them, however, were scarcely any Burmese, who professed Buddhism exclusively. Only the animistic mountain tribes of the original population were accessible to evangelization, as were immigrant Indians and Chinese. From 1966 to 1970 no less than 262 Catholic missionaries were expelled in keeping with the general tendency of the government to eliminate antinational influences as far as possible. Schools and charitable institutions were for the most part expropriated and nationalized. Residence permits were withdrawn from all missionaries who had entered after 1948. Nevertheless, the young Church is growing. Today it numbers 331,000 faithful in a population of 28 million.

The Malay Peninsula

The political changes on the Malay Peninsula repeatedly demanded the transformation of the ecclesiastical organization from the middle of this century.[68] At the same time Rome desired by its measures to give a new stimulus to the Catholic mission, to take into account the ethnic circumstances, to introduce the transfer of church government to native hands, to remove the basis for the ever louder complaints that the Catholic Church is not supranational but bound to the Western colonial powers, and finally to show the people that the Holy See understands and fosters the struggle of colonial peoples for independence. Today there are on the peninsula two ecclesiastical provinces, with two archdioceses and two suffragans each and the archdiocese of Singapore, which is immediately subject to the Holy See. The number of the faithful in this area amounts to 436,000.

Indonesia

To follow the evangelization and ecclesiastical organization on the 3,000 islands of modern Indonesia in all details would go beyond the scope of this work. We must limit ourselves here to some points which appear important to us. After World War II, during which 120 missionaries had been killed in Indonesia, the missionary activity was at once resumed. The new regime put no obstacles in the way, although most of the missionaries were Dutch; on the contrary, it valued their work, especially in education.

---

[67] *AAS* 47 (1955), 263–66. Two ecclesiastical provinces were erected: Rangoon with two dioceses and a prefecture apostolic, and Mandalay with one diocese and one prefecture. Today there are in Burma two archdioceses and one prefecture.
[68] Cf. *AAS* 47 (1955), 433–35, and 65 (1973), 126–28.

On 7 July 1947 Rome erected an apostolic delegation for Indonesia. On 15 March 1950 it was elevated to an internunciature and on 7 December 1965 to a nunciature.[69]

In 1960 Rome felt the time had arrived to erect an ecclesiastical hierarchy in Indonesia. As reasons for this were named: recognition of the missionary successes of the last years, contribution to the gratification of the strong nationalist stirrings in Indonesia, greater prestige of the Catholic Church with the government and the people. It was hoped by this measure to supply a new stimulus to evangelization in the island nation. And so on 3 January 1961 John XXIII established six ecclesiastical provinces with a total of twenty-five archdioceses and dioceses.[70] The metropolitan sees of Jakarta and Semarang received native archbishops.

After the United Nations had on 1 May 1963 given the former Dutch New Guinea, now West Irian, to Indonesia for administration, Rome decided on 10 November 1966 to establish the ecclesiastical hierarchy here too. The province of Merauke with two suffragan sees was formed.[71] With the creation on 26 June 1967 of the archbishop of Semarang, Justin Darmojuwono (since 1963), as the first Indonesian cardinal, Paul VI honored the Indonesian mission Church and the entire island population.[72]

All these young Churches of Asia have their own episcopal conferences, which boldly keep an eye on the current tasks and problems of the formation of dynamic individual Churches and seek to solve them by the most far-reaching adaptation to the traditional national circumstances, morals, and customs. In addition, all these episcopal conferences have joined in the Federation of Asian Bishops' Conferences (F.A.B.C.), whose statutes were approved *ad experimentum* by Rome on 6 December 1972. It held its first plenary meeting at Taipei from 21 to 27 April 1974, and at this new stresses were placed on the great themes: local church, dialogue with other world religions, aid for the development of the Church, ecclesiastical renewal, liturgical adaptation.[73] The vitality of the young Churches in Asia and their desire for cultural accommodation are likewise attested to by the very numerous native

---

[69] Ibid. 39 (1947), 468, 618f.; 42 (1950), 434; 58 (1966), 132f.
[70] Ibid. 53 (1961), 244–48; cf. ibid., 296–99 (the Pope's message of greeting).
[71] Ibid. 59 (1967), 483f., date: 15 November.
[72] Ibid. 59 (1967), 714.
[73] Cf. *Die katholischen Missionen* (1974), 167f.

religious communities of diocesan right, which were founded everywhere in the last few years and decades.[74]

The Young Churches in Africa

Evangelization on the African continent in the second half of this century was at last able, free from the bonds of colonialism, to embrace all the African peoples and tribes and their cultures credibly and successfully and lead to the founding of native Churches, which offered to the struggling young nations now achieving independence their help for the achievement of intellectual and material progress and the furtherance of peace and justice. The 1950s became, from the missionary viewpoint, the "Decade of Africa." If in 1950 all of Africa, so to say, was still under colonial rule, at the end of 1960 two-thirds of the African population lived in independent states. If in 1950 there were only two African bishops, at the beginning of 1960 there were already twenty-two. In the consistory of 28 March 1960 John XXIII created the first African cardinal.

The missionary development not only made progress with the political and social, but in its own way contributed to prepare for and fostered the political and social development. This notion is expressed repeatedly in the documents of the Congregation for the Propagation of the Faith. By means of the most important measures, such as the erection of an ecclesiastical hierarchy, the naming of African bishops, the Africanization of the Church, rearrangement of apostolic delegations, and so forth, Rome intentionally sought to approve and promote the independence movement of the African peoples. In the social sphere there appeared most unambiguously the contribution of the mission to the emancipation of the African woman, which it had helped to prepare by admitting black girls to religious institutes and by founding native congregations of sisters. At the same time this was a necessary precondition for the implanting of Christianity, for the social and cultural depression of the African woman was the "chief impediment to a permanent Christianization of the people."[75]

The external missionary development of Africa in this period is expressed in the following statistics: In 1922 the African mission Church, in so far as it was subject to the jurisdiction of the Roman missionary officials, was divided into 50 vicariates apostolic, 28 prefec-

---

[74] "Supplementum" to the *Bibliografia Missionaria*, Anno XXXIX–1975, Quaderno no. 18 (Rome 1976), 20–52.

[75] L. Kilger, O.S.B., "Watawa-schwarze Schwestern," *NZM* 1 (Schöneck 1945), 113–17.

tures apostolic, and 4 missions. On 31 December 1972 there existed in the same area 43 archdioceses, 236 dioceses, 15 vicariates apostolic, 21 prefectures apostolic, 1 prelacy, 1 apostolic administration, hence a total of 317 ecclesiastical territories. In 1978 there were on the entire African continent and its islands 49 metropolitan sees, 269 dioceses, 13 vicariates apostolic, 14 prefectures apostolic, 2 apostolic administrations, 1 prelacy, and 17 jurisdictions immediately subject to the Holy See, that is, they belong to no ecclesiastical province; there are also 2 patriarchates and 6 dioceses of Churches of the Eastern Rites. Altogether, there are 373 ecclesiastical territories. Of the 335 "Latin" bishops, 237 are Africans. Twelve belong to the College of Cardinals, and, of these, one, Bernardin Gantin, is a curial cardinal at Rome, president of the papal commission *Iustitia et Pax.* To follow this grand-scale development in detail is not possible within the limits of this work. Here, even more than in the Asiatic mission area, we must confine ourselves to the striking events and measures pointing the way.[76]

For the gradual Africanization of the Church Rome referred extensively to the cooperation of the missionary orders, congregations, and societies. Only where these were intent on training a native clergy could native ordinaries be appointed and entrusted with the government of the Churches. As early as 1925 Rome thought it could take the first step in this direction. But the plans could not be implemented until 1938. Pius XI gave the stimulus to this. In an audience of 24 May he said to the secretary of the Congregation for the Propagation of the Faith, Celso Costantini: "Will Divine Providence grant me the joy of ordaining an African bishop at Saint Peter's in Rome? The missions in Africa list today the most productive harvest in conversions."[77] In June of the same year he told Costantini that it was his "lively desire" to ordain an African bishop; he wished thereby on the one hand to reward and crown the activity of the foreign missioners in Africa and on the other hand to give a new impetus to the missions there. The preparations began at once, but it was only allowed to Pius XII on 29 October 1939 to ordain at Rome the first two African bishops of modern times,[78] together with ten other missionary bishops, including one Chinese and one Indian.[79]

---

[76] For more details cf. *Memoria Rerum* III/2, 519–43.
[77] *Agenzia Fides* (1939), no. 704–NI 211/39.
[78] There had already been a native African bishop in 1518: Henrique, son of the King of the Congo (cf. *BM* XV, 283). There is a report of another African bishop in N. Kowalsky, O.M.I., "Tobia Ghebragzer. Ein 'schwarzer' Bischof im 18. Jahrhundert," *NZM* 15 (Schöneck 1959), 198–204.
[79] *AAS* 31 (1939), 595–98 (the Pope's homily).

Another Roman decision about this time speaks clearly for the desire to Africanize the Church. In the Congo there had emerged a "question of rites." It had to do with supplanting of pagan burial ceremonies by Christian. The missionaries had sought to eradicate the entire pagan burial rite, which was called *Matanga*. However, they ran into resistance from the population. The faithful regarded themselves as bound from social motives to take part in the burial of their pagan countrymen and hence in those rites. No one observed the prohibition of the missionaries. Now in fact the *Matanga* consisted partly of superstitions, but also partly of completely indifferent usages. The Roman missionary office was asked for information. Appealing to the instruction of 1659,[80] this approved the plan of a "Christian Matanga," as the apostolic delegate and the bishops of the Congo had proposed. However, Rome advised the ordinaries, in connection with the drawing up of Christian burial ceremonies, to have regard for the customs that differed from tribe to tribe. This first step was followed after the Second Vatican Council by many others in the same sense in the area of liturgical adaptation.

In the 1950s the Africanization of the Church consistently progressed in the area of the transfer of ecclesiastical government to native hands. Gradually native bishops were named everywhere: Tanganyika in 1950,[81] Ruanda in 1952, Basutoland (now Lesotho) in 1952, South Africa in 1954, Sudan in 1955, Cameroon in 1955, Upper Volta in 1956, Belgian Congo (now Zaire) in 1956, Kenya in 1956, Nigeria in 1957, Ghana in 1957, and Togo in 1962.

Hence at the close of the "African Decade" twelve African nations and Madagascar had the first native bishops, and the process of transferring the government of the Church was in full swing. Furthermore, the regular ecclesiastical hierarchy was introduced in these and other countries. The 1960s saw the rise of the first African prelates into the College of Cardinals: in 1960 Laurean Rugambwa, bishop of Rutabo; in 1965 Paul Zoungrana, archbishop of Ouagadougou, and Owen McCann, archbishop of Cape Town, a white South African, also Léon-Étienne Duval, archbishop of Algiers, and Stephanos I Sidarouss, Coptic patriarch of Alexandria; in 1969 Joseph Malula, archbishop of Kinshasa, and Jérôme Rakotomalala, archbishop of Tananarive. In the 1970s followed: in 1973 Émile Biayenda, archbishop

---

[80] The latest edition of this important instruction for the attitude of the Roman mission authorities in questions of conduct in regard to native cultures from the earliest times of the mission dicastery in *Memoria Rerum* III/2, 696–704.

[81] The year of the appointment of the first native bishop is given in each instance.

of Brazzaville, and Maurice Otunga, archbishop of Nairobi; in 1976 Hyacinthe Thiandoum, archbishop of Dakar, Victor Razafimahatratra, S.J., archbishop of Tananarive, Emmanuel Nsubuga, archbishop of Kampala, and Dominic Ignatius Ekandem, bishop of Ikot Ekpene; and in 1977 Bernardin Gantin.

The second feature which gave its stamp to the "Decade of Africa" and brought the Africanization of the Church a good bit further was the erection of the regular ecclesiastical hierarchy in the mission Churches of the continent. There were good reasons for the introduction of the new mission organization. There was a desire to return to the earlier practice of the Church. The structure based on prefectures and vicariates was determined by history and had only a temporary character, and the reasons on which it was supported had for a long time had no further foundation.[82] Further, account was to be taken of the rapid progress of the African mission Church in the most recent period; the missionaries should be compensated for their efforts, and greater authority should be given to the ordinaries. Since the Anglican Church and the Protestant denominations were appointing bishops and archbishops who stood in great repute among the African population, the Catholic Church must not hold back. A further important reason, cited again and again in the documents, was the regard for the striving for independence of the African peoples. This demand should be intentionally encouraged, and it should be shown to the African peoples as well as to the whole world that Rome considered these peoples as mature enough to rule themselves. It was also not unknown in Rome that the Africans attributed a colonial character to the missions—even if incorrectly, at least as regards the missions of the Roman Dicastery—or imagined in them a pseudo-colonial appearance, and these in fact awakened in many the impression of a "religious colonization," because they were still to a great extent in the hands of foreign personnel. Hence the "old missions" should be replaced by "new missions," which were directed by natives.

The first step in the new direction was taken in 1950 in British West Africa, that is, in Sierra Leone, the Gold Coast (now Ghana), Nigeria, British Togo, and British Cameroon. Gambia was excluded, since there was only a *missio sui iuris* with few Catholics. On 28 April 1950 three ecclesiastical provinces were erected in this area, together with twelve bishoprics.[83] In addition to the already mentioned general reasons, in this case the following were also decisive for the erection of the

---

[82] Cf. N. Kowalsky, O.M.I., "Zur Entwicklungsgeschichte der Apostolischen Vikare," *NZM* 13 (Schöneck 1957), 271–86; also, *Memoria Rerum* I/1, 353–438; II, 220–34.
[83] *AAS* 42 (1950), 615–19.

hierarchy: the favorable missionary situation, the good prospects for the future, the rapidly increasing number of native priests,[84] the planned pilgrimage of several missionary bishops from West Africa to Rome for the Holy Year in May 1950, which it was intended to publicize in connection with the erection of the hierarchy, the previous nomination of an Anglican archbishop, and finally the desire of the British colonial government to see archbishops at the head of the Catholic Church as partners in negotiations.

On 11 January 1951 there occurred the establishment of the regular ecclesiastical hierarchy in South Africa, in Basutoland (Lesotho), and Swaziland (Ngwane). Four ecclesiastical provinces with twenty-one jurisdictions were constituted.[85] The archbishops of Cape Town, Durban, and Pretoria and the bishops of Johannesburg and Keimoes were South Africans of white ancestry. The special national character of this country brought it about that as yet no native black bishops could be named. However, less than two years later Rome began in Basutoland the transfer of the government of the Church to native bishops. And even in the Union of South Africa, today the Republic of South Africa, the government of the Church could not continue exclusively in the hands of the white clergy. As in all Africa, there too the national and self-consciousness of the Bantu peoples was gaining strength. They felt it to be humiliating that there were so few black priests, and were inclined to assign the guilt for this to the white missioners, whom they suspected of not giving the blacks credit for being able to have their own priests and bishops. With the division of the diocese of Mariannhill, the erection of the Zulu diocese of Umzimkulu, and the naming of the Mariannhill priest Bonaventura Dlamini in 1954, Rome wanted to accommodate the justified aspirations. However, further steps in this direction have to wait a long time.

In the South African mission Church the government's apartheid policy became a serious problem. The racial problem had begun practically with the first settlement by whites on the Cape and had become ever more serious and inflammatory from generation to generation, until, after World War II, it was, so to speak, made into a system by the government under the pretense of "separate development." What most irritated the black population and the half-castes and produced world publicity were the social injustices and vexa-

---

[84] In eastern Nigeria there were then: 479,840 Catholics, 260,277 catechumens, 230 foreign and 15 native priests; in western Nigeria: 176,807 Catholics, 42,198 catechumens, 203 foreign and 16 native priests; in the third province were 293,646 Catholics, 50,603 catechumens, 173 foreign and 12 native priests.
[85] AAS 43 (1951), 257–63.

tions which made the entire apartheid policy of the government, including its not to be undervalued good aims, unworthy of credence. A compromise became more and more impossible. In official documents the bishops repeatedly took a stand against the injustices. The declaration issued by the Episcopal Conference in July 1957 deserves notice.[86] The archbishop of Durban, Denis Eugene Hurley, O.M.I., especially stood up fearlessly for the rights of the colored population. As a South African by birth, he could do more in this respect.

Another trial of strength between the mission Church and the government took place in the school question. Because of the withdrawal of state support and the bishops' "no" to the nationalization of the schools, these came into sad financial distress. The two vicars apostolic of Windhoek and Keetmanshoop in South-West Africa, or Namibia, found a happier solution.

On 25 March 1953 Rome also established the ecclesiastical hierarchy in the countries of Kenya, Uganda, and Tanganyika in British East Africa, about ten years before these states obtained their political independence.[87] Four new ecclesiastical provinces with twenty-three bishoprics were founded.[88] There followed the erection of the hierarchy in Southern Rhodesia on 1 January 1955—one province with five jurisdictions[89]—and in French colonial Africa and Madagascar on 14 September of the same year—eleven provinces with thirty-eight archdioceses and dioceses.[90] On the same date, 14 September 1955, the vicariate apostolic of Rabat in Morocco became an archdiocese,[91] the vicariate apostolic of Ghardaïa in Algeria became the diocese of Laghouat,[92] and the prefecture apostolic of Jibuti in the then

---

[86] "Christianisme et ségrégation raciale (Déclaration collective des Évêques d'Afrique du Sud)," *Église Vivante* IX (Louvain 1957), 339–44. *La Documentation Catholique,* 39 Anneé T. LIV (Paris 1957), col. 1321–26.

[87] Kenya then counted, in a population of 5.4 million, 365,021 Catholics, 59,164 catechumens, 256 foreign and 14 native priests; Uganda: 1,134,057 Catholics out of 5 million inhabitants, 115,706 catechumens, 360 foreign and 133 native priests; Tanganyika: 785,677 Catholics out of 7.4 million inhabitants, 92,591 catechumens, 626 foreign and 134 native priests.

[88] *AAS* 45 (1953), 705–10.

[89] Ibid. 47 (1955), 292f. (the Pope's greeting of 24 April 1955). The number of Catholics amounted to 100,000 Bantu and 13,500 whites. There were 168 priests, 17 native seminarians, and 50 pupils in the minor seminary. The future prospects of the mission could be regarded as good, as the number of 20,000 catechumens shows.

[90] *AAS* 48 (1956), 113–19.

[91] In 1956 the diocese of Tangiers was erected here and made directly subject to the Holy See.

[92] Algiers, Constantine, and Oran are not subject to the Congregation for the Evangelization of Peoples.

French Somaliland, now, since 27 June 1977, the independent Republic of Djibouti, was likewise raised to a diocese and immediately made subject to the Holy See.[93]

Now only three quite large parts of Africa were without the normal ecclesiastical hierarchy: the Delegation Area of the Congo, British Central Africa, and the Sudan. It was introduced in the first two in 1959, in the Sudan in 1974. On 25 April 1959 Rome formed the two ecclesiastical provinces of Lusaka and Blantyre with five and three suffragan sees respectively.[94] The Belgian Congo, Ruanda, and Burundi were on the threshold of their political independence. Rome aspired to prepare the historical turning point by a series of ecclesiastical measures. The first concern was the appointment of a native auxiliary bishop for the future capital of the country. It was high time. The Catholic Church appeared to many Congolese as a foreign, colonial institution and was rejected by them. Hence on 2 July 1959 John XXIII appointed Joseph Malula as auxiliary bishop of Léopoldville, now Kinshasa.[95] On the same day the newly established vicariate apostolic of Goma was turned over to the native clergy. But the most important and striking event, whereby Rome wanted to assure the Congolese people of their readiness for greater independence was the erection of the ecclesiastical hierarchy on 10 November 1959 in the Belgian Congo and Ruanda-Urundi, now Ruanda and Burundi.[96] Eight ecclesiastical provinces with as many archdioceses and twenty-nine dioceses were formed.[97] Finally there occurred in the Sudan the establishment of the Church hierarchy, after the calming of the political situation, on 18 November 1974 with the formation of two provinces and a total of seven sees.[98]

---

[93] *AAS* 48 (1956), 113–19.

[94] Ibid. 51 (1959), 793–96. In Northern Rhodesia there were in 1958 385,485 Catholics, 71,505 catechumens, 284 foreign and 29 native priests in a total population of 2.1 million. In Nyasaland (Malawi), with 2.5 million inhabitants, the statistics are similar: 429,150 Catholics, 51,696 catechumens, 224 foreign and 50 native missioners.

[95] On 7 July 1964 Malula became archbishop of the capital and in the consistory of 28 April 1969 he was created a cardinal.

[96] As early as 1952 this measure had been mentioned. The establishment of the hierarchy was to be included in the new mission agreement between the Holy See and Belgium. But the Belgian Senate refused assent when the treaty came into existence on 8 December 1953.

[97] *AAS* 52 (1960), 372–77. In the Congo there were in a population of 13 million 4.3 million Catholics and 700,000 catechumens, 2,272 foreign and 298 native priests. Remarkable was the increase in native priests, as regards both their number and their training. Ecclesiastical institutions—schools, hospitals, and so forth—were well organized. A still better picture emerges from the statistics of Ruanda-Urundi: 1.6 million Catholics out of 4.5 million inhabitants, more than 500,000 catechumens, 163 native and 329 foreign priests.

[98] *AAS* 67 (1975), 164f.

With the setting up of the ecclesiastical hierarchy on the African continent a long historical development had come to an end. A new epoch of history had begun. Out of the mission Churches had come "Young Churches," young particular Churches. True, their missionary status endured and still continues. But now, as equally competent member Churches, they stand beside those in Europe, America, and Asia. Furthermore, they depend on the personal and material support of other member Churches. The foreign missionaries accustomed themselves to work and evangelize under native bishops. This must be reckoned to their credit. Difficulties were not wanted in the period of transition. The point of departure for the future development of the Young Churches of Africa was laid.

We designated the 1950s as the "Decade of Africa" in regard to the Africanization of the Church, the transfer of church government to African bishops, and the establishment of the ecclesiastical hierarchy. The 1960s also set a special mark on the young African Churches: the establishment of diplomatic relations between the Holy See and most of the African states that had achieved independence, and the reorganization of the apostolic delegations. The missionary organization and development had to keep pace with the rapidly advancing political, social, cultural, and economic upheavals of the African peoples in these years, which in an increasing measure gained influence on world politics. Vestiges of the colonial past had to be definitively obliterated. And so in 1960 a reorganization of the apostolic delegations in Africa was undertaken. Out of the two previous delegations of Nairobi and Dakar were formed four delegations: Nairobi for East Africa, Dakar for West Africa, Lagos for west central Africa, and Tananarive for Madagascar.[99] John XXIII and to a greater degree Paul VI entered into direct diplomatic relations with the African states as they became autonomous.[100]

Not all African states have honored the loyal attitude of the Church, its aid in the conflict-filled transition from the colonial epoch to political independence, and its not insignificant contribution to the securing of domestic peace. Often the new states had received the constitution of a Western democracy, which did not sufficiently take into account the African circumstances and mentality. Hence almost all states had inner crises to overcome. The disturbances often passed into the relations of the government of the moment with the church authorities or with the Church as such. The African hierarchy worked to mediate and to give to the African peoples a new life-style based on respect for the natural

[99] Ibid 52 (1960), 1000–1003.
[100] For the individual countries and dates see *Memoria Rerum* III/2, 536f.

rights of persons and on social justice and love. Still, in the 1960s and 1970s there occurred in several independent states of Black Africa severe conflicts between the heads of governments and church dignitaries.

In 1964 all European missionaries were expelled from the southern provinces of the Sudan; 278 Catholic and 28 Protestant missioners were affected. Only 32 native priests remained to care for 400,000 faithful. This was the result of the conflict between the more than 10 percent Christian southern provinces and the Arab population of the northern provinces. Not until 1971 could the first white missionaries—6 Jesuits—return to this area. Somewhat later 11 white sisters followed. A visit by the secretary of the Congregation for the Propagation of the Faith, Archbishop Sergio Pignedoli, to Khartoum in July 1968 and his personal contacts had prepared the way for the new government to be reasonable.

In 1967 the president of Guinea expelled all foreign priests and sisters on the pretext that they were preventing the Africanization of the Church. In December 1970 he had the archbishop of Conakry put on trial because of participation in a coup d'etat allegedly staged by Portuguese Guinea and condemned to compulsory labor for life.[101] In 1974 Guinea gave occasion for guarded optimism. For the first time the president received a delegation of African missionaries.

Missioners were also expelled from Burundi, Gabon, Uganda, Rhodesia, and South Africa. In Somalia on 13 January 1963 missioners were forbidden by law to make any sort of direct "propaganda" for Christian religions. In his message for the third anniversary of the revolution on 21 October 1972 President Siad Barre announced the nationalization of all private schools and printing companies. This measure especially hurt the mission work of the Catholic Church. Now the Church can be active there only in the charitable and social fields.

In Lesotho the Church was involved against its will in the domestic political partisan strife. The loyal and skillful conduct of the archbishop of Maseru was able to keep undesirable consequences away from the missions. The common difficulties in this country led to a more intimate collaboration of all Christian Churches. Since then, ecumenical relations have been quite exemplary.

During the two-and-one-half-year civil war in Nigeria against secessionist Biafra, the Church was in a difficult position. It was accused of supporting the rebels. After the war's end foreign missionaries were imprisoned and banished. In 1971 Nigeria experienced a special

---

[101] Cf. *Die katholischen Missionen* (1970), 26–28.

success in the Africanization of the Church: seven native bishops were appointed.

In Equatorial Guinea, the former Spanish colony that became independent on 12 October 1968, there were very soon tensions between the new president and the Church. In April 1971 the Spanish bishop of Santa Isabel (Malabo since 1974) was driven from the country. The government gave no reasons for this. More even than the foreign Claretians, the native priests had to let caution prevail, since sinister political intentions were easily imputed to them. Finally, religious worship was totally forbidden, all churches were closed, the last foreign priests, except for an eighty-year-old one in Bata, were expelled in July 1978. There remained in the country only the twenty native priests. World public opinion veiled itself in silence over the tragedy which has been playing there since 1969.

Serious situations of conflict appeared also in Zaire. During student disturbances in June 1969 at the Catholic Lovanium University in Kinshasa, founded in 1954, several students were killed. A renewed protest by the students on the second anniversary of this occurrence was for the government the occasion to close the university and conscript all students, including religious sisters, into military service. In the next school year teaching was resumed with new students, but now it was called the University of Kinshasa. A little later a real struggle against the Church broke out. Freedom of meeting in churches was strictly curtailed by several harsh decrees. The entire institutional Church saw itself threatened in its potential for action. The cardinal archbishop of Kinshasa had to leave the country for a while. Christian baptismal names were forbidden, instruction in the Christian religion was proscribed in all schools. Finally, however, the conflict was settled.[102]

In Burundi the Church had to suffer much during the mass murder of more than 100,000 members of the Hutu tribe in 1972. On 13 April 1977 all eleven Verona Fathers active there and some Italian mission helpers were expelled, evidently because they had protected the Hutu in the bloody civil war. Also in Uganda there occurred tensions between government and Church. In December 1972 a papal delegation, under the leadership of the cosecretary of the Congregation for the Propagation of the Faith, Bernardin Gantin, went to Uganda to settle the conflict. It was received by the president on 19 December. Here, too, relations improved later. Still, again and again unpleasant events occurred. In Malawi the president had the major seminary in Kachebere closed temporarily in April 1973, because his picture, which

[102] Cf. ibid., (Freiburg 1972), 91–94, 126f.

786

had been hung there, had been defaced, and the perpetrator could not be ascertained. The seminary was, it is true, reopened for the Malawi candidates for the priesthood, but the seminarians from Zambia and Mozambique had to leave the country.

In December 1970 the Cameroonian Bishop Albert Ndongmo of N'Kongsamba was tried by a military court for an allegedly attempted coup d'etat and participation in a conspiracy to murder the president, and condemned to death. The verdict was reduced by the president to life imprisonment. The bishop was pardoned on 14 May 1975. Since then he has lived in Canada.

In Rhodesia the tension between Church and state was intensified by the government's discriminatory racial policy, about which the Church could not be silent. On Palm Sunday 1970 in a daring pastoral letter the bishops announced that they had decided to disregard certain aspects of the new constitution and that, because of their convictions of faith, they would not trouble themselves about those laws which clearly contradicted the gospel message. As early as June 1969 the five Catholic bishops of the nation had protested against the government's racial policy. On 1 October 1976 Bishop Donal Lamont of Umtali was sentenced to ten years' imprisonment at hard labor because of his open letter of 11 August to the government, in which he had censured the racial policy. On 23 March 1977 he was banished. The appointment of the new black archbishop of Salisbury on 31 May 1976 was greeted by world opinion as a courageous step by Rome. Terrorist acts of the independence movement brought great damage to the mission in the most recent period. In the twelve months from June 1977 to June 1978 thirty-six missioners were killed by terrorists.

The Portuguese possessions in Africa were, until their independence—Guinea-Bissau on 10 September 1974, Mozambique on 25 July 1975, Cape Verde Islands on 6 July 1975, São Tomé and Príncipe on 12 July 1975, and Angola on 11 November 1975—late relics of a long-past colonial age. Despite its involvement with the colonial power, the Church did not neglect the evangelization of these lands and islands. But its activity in the service of the spreading of the Gospel was overshadowed and seriously burdened by the fact that it supported a system which, appealing to the expansion of Portuguese Catholic civilization, denied the people freedom and independence. It there came under the fire of public opinion. In the mission agreement of 7 May 1940[103] between the Holy See and Portugal the interests of the Church were defined, but at the same time it was anchored in the

---

[103] *AAS* 32 (1940), 217–44; A. Mercati, *Raccolta di Concordati* II, 232–64; literature also in *BM* XXIII, no. 872.

colonial system. On 25 July 1953 the first native priest was ordained in Mozambique, Alexandre José Maria dos Santos, O.F.M., who in 1974 became bishop of Maputo, formerly Lourenço Marques. Thereafter the formation of the native clergy in the Portuguese overseas possessions was more encouraged. The independence movements, appearing everywhere, opened the eyes of prelates and clergy. Some of these came into opposition to the colonial government. Finally consideration was given to the construction of native local Churches. This development was further intensified after the Second Vatican Council. However, there remained the connection of the Church with the state, and the Roman Congregation for the Propagation of the Faith, which, according to the mission decree of the council, should alone be competent "for all missions and all missionary activity,"[104] was for the future excluded from evangelization in the Portuguese overseas territories. Only after independence did it take over the direction of the mission Churches there. The rightly differently evaluated departure of the White Fathers from Mozambique in May 1971[105]—a unique incident in mission history—took place on the grounds that the political situation did not guarantee an integral proclamation of the faith.

After political independence the Church was pulled into the whirlpool of events. On 25 July 1975, exactly one month after independence, following a speech by the president, there began the nationalization of all ecclesiastical institutions in Mozambique. As grounds for this were cited the earlier support of the Church by the state and the fact that all these institutions actually belonged to the people. The government made no secret of its struggle against the Church. Half of all foreign priests left the country. Rome at once began to put the government of the mission Churches in these countries into native hands. For example, in Mozambique seven of thirty-five native priests were appointed and ordained bishops. From 9 to 13 September 1977 a National Pastoral Assembly was held in Beira. It was, so to speak, an inventory after two years of political independence. Guidelines were set up for the future pastoral care of the faithful and further evangelization. In Angola the twelve bishops, in a common pastoral letter of 14 December 1977, appealed to the government to respect the rights of religion. They admonished the faithful to stand firm in the faith and to work in peace for the welfare of the nation.[106] A reply of the government to this was obviously the expropriation of the radio station, Radio Ecclesiae, on 25 January, which had earlier to suspend its

[104] *Ad Gentes* 29 in *AAS* 58 (1966), 980.
[105] Cf. *Die katholischen Missionen* (Freiburg 1971), 161–65.
[106] *Internationaler Fides-Dienst 18. Januar 1978*, 28–31.

broadcasts. From 4 to 8 April 1978 the bishops of Angola held a plenary meeting, the outcome of which was again a common pastoral letter.[107]

As regards organization, there are today three ecclesiastical provinces in Angola: Luanda with four, Huambo with three, and Lubango with two suffragan sees; in Mozambique, the ecclesiastical province of Maputo with eight suffragans; the dioceses of Bissau and São Tomé and Príncipe are immediately subject to the Holy See; and the diocese of Cape Verde is a suffragan of Lisbon. Two of the eleven bishops of Angola are foreigners. One hundred native and 223 foreign priests, 8 native and 22 foreign brothers, 250 native and 350 foreign sisters are active in Angola. They are supported by 20,000 native catechists.[108] The number of Catholics amounts to ca. 3 million, which is half the population of the country. In Mozambique there are 1.5 million Catholics, or 18 percent of the population.

On 7 December 1974 the Holy See erected an apostolic delegation in Mozambique,[109] on 30 December 1974 in Guinea-Bissau,[110] and on 25 February 1975 in Angola.[111]

And here too some highlights of other, hitherto not yet or hardly mentioned young Churches of Africa, though unfortunately completeness must be waived. The young Churches in Egypt and Ethiopia have a special status and must follow special laws. They stand in the same position as the Orthodox Eastern Churches. In so far as they have Eastern Rites, they are under the jurisdiction of the Roman Congregation for the Eastern Churches. Likewise subject to it are all the vicariates apostolic of the Latin Rite in Egypt and the vicariate of Asmara in Ethiopia. Only the vicariates of Gimma and Harrar and the prefectures of Awasa and Hosanna in Ethiopia depend on the Congregation for the Evangelization of Peoples. In 1938 Pius XI had clearly defined the jurisdiction of these two Roman dicasteries, which until then overlapped.[112] The conquest and occupation of Ethiopia by Italy in 1936 posed new problems and tasks for Rome and the young Church of this country. Their solution was made still harder by the fact that the Italian government, unasked, expressed desires which it wanted to see

---

[107] Ibid., 3. *Juni 1978*, 313.
[108] Statistics of April 1978 in ibid., *14. Juni 1978*, 344. Further information on the situation of the Church in Angola and Mozambique in *Herder-Korrespondenz* 32 (Freiburg 1978), 302–9.
[109] *AAS* 67 (1975), 89f.
[110] Ibid. 174f.
[111] Ibid., 177.
[112] Motu proprio *Sancta Dei Ecclesia* of 25 March 1938 in *AAS* 30 (1938), 154–59; *Sylloge*, 567–73.

observed in the reorganization of the ecclesiastical situation. World War II brought new and great damage to the Church in Ethiopia. On 28 November 1942 100 missionaries, 300 sisters, two vicars apostolic, and one prefect were expelled and repatriated to Italy. Others had already left the country or had been imprisoned as military chaplains. Rome sent an urgent appeal to the White Fathers to dispatch there sixty missionaries to save the orphaned missions, and they did so. In 1945 Canadian Jesuits were entrusted with the organization of the educational system in Ethiopia.

Catholic mission activity in Botswana, formerly Bechuanaland, is still young. The first mission station, still in existence, was founded in 1928. Since 1959 there has existed there the prefecture apostolic of Bechuanaland, which was entrusted to Irish Passionists. The diocese of Gaborone, founded in 1966, today includes all Botswana. The number of Catholics has grown in recent years from 10,000 to 26,390 in 1977. In Swaziland (Ngwane) Italian Servites do the missionary work. Bishop Casalini, O.S.M., of Manzini, the only diocese in the country, in 1976 placed his episcopal see at their disposal. Since then a native bishop has headed the diocese. In 1977 the number of Catholics amounted to 35,000 in a population of 520,000. At Manzini Salesians conduct a technical school, and Dominican Sisters a girls' high school.

The 25,000 Catholics in Liberia in 1977 are a "small flock," but their influence is incomparably greater. It is due to the educational and health systems of the Catholic Church. Here in the age of foundation not only did the climate occupy the Catholic missionaries, but also the intolerance and rejection on the part of the Protestant Christians. The Catholic Church did not really obtain civil rights until the 1930s. Today its schools surpass the other mission schools in number and quality, and, in contrast to these, are spread over the entire country. In the young Church of Senegal, where the philosopher, poet, and statesman Leopold Sédar Senghor (who attended the mission school of the Holy Ghost Fathers, in 1968 received the Peace Prize of the German Book Trade in the church of Saint Paul in Frankfurt, and since 1969 has been a member of the French Academy of Moral and Political Science as Adenauer's successor) rules the nation, the Church is not a stranger to questions of the young state. This is proved by the official positions of the bishops on social questions and the powerful effort of Christians for all questions of development aid. The chief problem remains the relationship to Islam. In Gabon the government of the young Church is entirely in native hands. Of course, the number of foreign missioners is still preponderant—in 1975 there were seventy of them, compared to thirty-four native priests. However, the number of native vocations is growing. As regards organization, the young Church consists of one archdiocese with three suffragans. It counts a total of 393,000 baptized in a population of 1.2 million.

Mali, a stronghold of socialism, assures religious freedom to the young Church of the state. In 1967, of the 4.75 million inhabitants about 39,000 were baptized Catholics and 170,000 catechumens. Today among 5.2 million inhabitants there are 47,000 Catholics, with one metropolitan see and five suffragans. In Upper Volta, with one metropolitan see, eight suffragans, and 336,000 Catholics in a population of 5.8 million, the Episcopal Conference in 1970 issued clear directions for the adaptation of the Catholic liturgy to African morals and customs and to African sensibilities. Gambia, the smallest African state, is a typical product of the colonial epoch and of colonial policy. The greatest problem of the young Church, which counts 11,500 faithful in one diocese among a half-million inhabitants, is the native clergy. Since March 1974 there is a common seminary for Liberia, Sierra Leone, and Gambia.

The Catholic Church in Chad is one of the youngest of the African Churches. It exists officially only since World War II, even if the neighboring mission in Cameroon had previously "encroached" on this territory. The chief problems of the Church—one metropolitan see, three suffragans, 211,000 faithful among 3.8 million inhabitants—are here, too, native vocations and relations with Islam. In the most recent past the signs of a starting *Kulturkampf* against the Christian Churches increased. The government wants to lead the nation back to "precolonial culture" and to "African authenticity."

In the Democratic Republic of the Congo, the elevation of Biayenda to the College of Cardinals was unanimously welcomed and celebrated. Likewise, Catholics and non-Catholics were infuriated by his murder on the evening of 22 March 1977. A few days earlier, on 18 March, President Ngouabi had also been murdered.

At Abidjan, Ivory Coast, a theological faculty was opened in 1976, which had grown out of the Higher Institute for Religious Culture, founded in 1968. The chief concern of the new faculty is to give to the students a better understanding of African religious traditions. The bishops of English-speaking Africa are considering the founding of a similar faculty in Nigeria or Kenya. Also in Abidjan the Jesuits in 1962 founded an *Institut Africain pour le Développement Économique et Social* (INADES), with branch offices in other African countries, which gives courses at the institute and television courses, organizes courses in villages and cities, and has built up an imposing documentation and information service. In Benin there was a brief untoward incident. On 8 August 1977 the government forbade Bernardin Gantin, the former archbishop of Cotonou, who on 12 June of that year had been made a cardinal and was now visiting his homeland, all further journeys and any public appearance. This prohibition was issued after Gantin had celebrated a Mass in the church of Saint John at Cotonou for the victims of the shootings in Benin in January. Several government representatives, including the minister of the interior, had attended the Mass.

In Tanzania, where 20 percent of the population is Catholic and about 10 percent Anglican and Lutheran, there are today districts and tribes not yet touched by missionary preaching. Here the young Church of the nation still has a big task to implement.

Madagascar is a model example of a mission country in which the Church is growing quickly and steadily. At the beginning of the century it counted scarcely 120,000 faithful, in 1950 there were 700,000, and today they number 1.4 million in a total population of 7.9 million. However, the number of native priests was left behind, in comparison. In 1968 a National Catechists' Institute was established in Tananarive for the training of catechetical leaders. In the same year the bishops began a comprehensive pastoral planning. Cardinal Rakotomalala died unexpectedly on 1 November 1975. The population of the Comoro Islands voted in December 1974 whether to become independent or remain under French rule. The inhabitants of the island of Mayotte were for union with France. The other islands became independent. The population is almost exclusively Muslim. Of the 244,000 inhabitants, only 2,500 are Catholics, and of these almost 1,000 are Europeans. The pastoral work is entrusted to French Capuchins. The Seychelles, an archipelago of ninety-two islands, have been independent since 29 June 1976. Swiss Capuchins have worked there since 1921. On 25 July 1975 the native priest Felix Paul was ordained bishop. Of the 58,000 islanders, 53,000 are Catholics. Réunion continues to be a French possession. In 1975 Bishop Georges Guibert, of the Holy Ghost Fathers, resigned in order to make way for native personnel. On 2 May 1976 the native priest Gilbert Aubry became bishop of La Réunion or Saint-Denis.

In conclusion, let three important events for all the young Churches of Africa be mentioned: the canonization of the martyrs of Uganda in 1964, the message of Paul VI to Africa in 1967, and the Pope's journey to Uganda in 1969. On World Mission Sunday, 18 October 1964, Paul VI canonized the twenty-two martyrs of Uganda, who had been beatified on 6 June 1920 by Benedict XV. In the years 1885–87 they, together with another eighty Catholics, Anglicans, and Protestants, had been put to death in a persecution of Christians. They were thus the first Bantu in the calendar of saints of the Catholic Church. Many African bishops, priests, religious, and faithful came to Rome for the celebration. For the first time African choral singing and African drums were heard in Saint Peter's. In his homily the Pope spoke of the "present hour of decision for Africa." "The martyrs call for help" for the African Church, he continued. "Africa needs missionaries, especially priests, physicians, teachers, sisters, nurses, magnanimous persons to help the young and flourishing congregations, which still need much support, to grow in number and quality in order to become a people, the African People of the Church of God."[113]

In the message to Africa of 31 October 1967 Paul VI took up the present problems of the African peoples. He intended thereby to carry further the mission encyclical *Fidei donum,* in which Pius XII had already revealed his anxieties about the future of the African continent.[114] Here as there, the values of African culture were displayed. Paul VI stated sadly that not all missioners of past epochs had acknowledged these values. But he did not condemn the missionaries, because they were children of their age and were not immune to its prejudices. He called to mind what these missionaries in the past had done for the intellectual and material development of the African peoples. As the principal tasks of the present that would determine the future, the Pope indicated the struggle against illiteracy and the development of agriculture. He proposed the creation of a world fund for development aid, from which all needy states should be helped without secondary political aims. At the end the Pope invited the bishops of the whole world and all the faithful not to be remiss in help for the Churches of Africa. "In spite of some shadows, which We have indicated," he concluded, "We trust that Africa . . . , filled with reverence for the rights of God and the dignity of the person, will continue on the way of progress."[115]

The third event which we intend to mention here was the journey of Paul VI to Uganda from 31 July to 2 August 1969. It had been immediately preceded by another likewise epoch-making occurrence for the future of the African Churches—the first All-Africa Episcopal Symposium from 28 to 31 July at Gaba near Kampala.[116] Paul VI wanted to preside in person at the final session of the symposium. The second occasion of the journey was the dedication of the shrine of the martyrs at Namugongo. On these occasions too the Pope again spoke of his esteem for the African person, land, and culture. "We know no

[113] *AAS* 57 (1965), 693–703; *Internationaler Fides-Dienst* (1964), 549–55. On 22 June 1934 Pius XI declared Blessed Charles Lwanga patron of African youth. (*AAS* 26 [1934], 582f.).

[114] Of 21 April 1957 in *AAS* 49 (1957), 225–48.

[115] *AAS* 59 (1967), 1073–97. *Internationaler Fides-Dienst* (1976), 575–91.

[116] Cf. *Herder-Korrespondenz* 23 (Freiburg 1969), 421–26.

other desire," he said, "than precisely to accept and to foster what you are: namely, Christians and Africans. We want that Our presence here with you should be regarded as a recognition of your maturity, as Our desire and Our intention to prove to you that the communion which joins us together will in no way suppress but, on the contrary, will promote the original nature of the personality in private, ecclesiastical, and civic life." The Church, he said, has "been really planted in this blessed earth." Now, after this foundation has been laid, the Pope concluded, it is the function of the African Christians to reconstruct their Church on this continent themselves: "You Africans are now your own missionaries."[117]

A proof that the young Churches of Africa wished to go their "African" way, and for years have done so ever more independently, is the almost 150 native religious communities of diocesan right, which were founded everywhere.[118] These and other fortunate initiatives justify the hope that the young Churches of Africa will successfully solve also the modern problems which they encounter. Among these problems are the explosionlike growth of the number of Catholics and the increase, not keeping pace with it, of native priestly vocations, the urbanization, the education of an elite, the nationalization of education. Especially the disproportionately rapid growth of the number of Catholics—anually ca. 6 percent—poses for the church leadership problems whose solution must immediately be tackled. First is the increase of priestly vocations. No less important are the religious instruction of children and adult education. Likewise in regard to material things there arise vital and urgent tasks, such as the increase of the number of churches.[119] Another danger threatens the Church from the sectarian system. On no other continent is Christianity so fragmented as in Africa. There are approximately 5,000 "Christian" splinter Churches and sects, with some 7 million adherents. Most of them have grown up on the soil of Protestantism. However, a few have come also from a Catholic background. The largest "Catholic" sect—the Maria-Legio Church—arose in 1963 among the Luo tribe on the east shore of Lake Victoria in Kenya.[120] It is consciously African, bound to African tradition, and in this consists its power of attraction.

As in Asia, the Episcopal Conferences of Africa and Madagascar also have merged in the *Symposium des Conférences Épiscopales d'Afrique et de Madagascar* (SCEAM) in order to solve in common their mutual

[117] AAS 61 (1969), 572–91 *Internationaler Fides-Dienst* (1969), 367–75.
[118] Cf. the "Supplementum" to the *Bibliografia Missionaria,* Anno XXXVIII, 1974, Quaderno no. 17 (Rome 1975), 23–49.
[119] Cf. *Die katholischen Missionen* (Freiburg 1971), 3.
[120] Cf. *Die katholischen Missionen* (Freiburg 1970), 12–15.

problems.[121] In addition there are still the three regional groupings: *Association des Conférences Épiscopales du Congo, de la République Centrafricaine, et du Tchad* (ACECCT), the *Conférence Épiscopale Régionale de l'Afrique de l'Ouest Francophone* (CARAO), and the Association of Member Episcopal Conferences in Eastern Africa (AMECEA). From 24 to 30 July 1978 the symposium held its fifth plenary meeting at Nairobi[122] in the presence of Cardinal Opilio Rossi, president of the Papal Council for the Laity, of Archbishop Simon D. Lourdusamy, the secretary of the Congregation for the Evangelization of Peoples, of representatives of the European and South American Episcopal Conferences and of religious. The participants—nine cardinals and about sixty archbishops and bishops and delegates of the laity—represented the more than 50 million African Catholics. The chief topic of the symposium was "Christian Family Life in Africa Today." In his address, Lourdusamy stressed the necessity of an authentic and judicious inculturation of the Church.[123]

The Young Churches in Oceania

AUSTRALIA AND NEW ZEALAND

The growth of the Catholic Church in Australia and New Zealand in the last century is amazing. The ecclesiastical organization was already essentially complete by 1920 and in the course of the past fifty years has undergone only slight changes. From 4 to 12 September 1937 the fourth Plenary Council of Australia and New Zealand met at Sydney under the chairmanship of the papal legate, Giovanni Panico.[124] The chief tasks of the council were the implementation of the new *Codex iuris canonici* and the consideration of more uniform pastoral and missionary methods.

Special attention was given to the evangelization of the primitive inhabitants of Australia. This task has belonged exclusively to the

[121] English Title: Symposium of Episcopal Conferences of Africa and Madagascar (SECAM).
[122] Originally the plenary meeting was to take place in Kinshasa. However, the domestic political disturbances that had broken out there caused the transfer to Nairobi.
[123] "Inculturation, which is the consequence of the incarnational economy of salvation, is part and parcel of the mission of the Church and of the work of Evangelization it carries on. It is inseparable from the mission of the Church and indispensable for its evangelizing activity, simultaneous and all-dimensional with it." (*International Fides Service,* 23 August 1978, 378).
[124] The first plenary council was held in 1885, the second in 1895, the third in 1905. The fourth was supposed to be summoned in 1918 but rumors of an imminent ecumenical council in Rome and then the Twenty–Ninth World Eucharistic Congress at Sydney in 1928 delayed the implementation.

Australian Episcopal Conference since 22 March 1976, when Australia was removed from the jurisdiction of the Congregation for the Evangelization of Peoples and transferred to the normal ecclesiastical administration. The Episcopal Conference is now competent for missionary work among the few remaining pagans in the (mixed and full-blooded) Australian aboriginal population of fifteen thousand. Hence a great responsibility was given to the young Church. Its function is so to integrate the aborigines that their traditions and culture may be taken into account. The community pastoral work must especially enter into and have regard for their needs. In a statement on the occasion of the "National Day of the Aborigines," the bishops took a position on all pastoral and ecclesiastical questions related to this problem and supported the demands of the aborigines on the state, the most important of which was the legal definition of the right to their possessions in northern Australia. In 1966 there were already sisters among the Australian aborigines, and in 1969 a convent of their own was erected for them at Darwin.

The Fortieth World Eucharistic Congress, which took place at Melbourne from 18 to 25 February 1973, for a brief time directed the interests of the Universal Church to the Church of Australia. The often bitter experiences which the Catholics especially had to endure in this originally overwhelmingly Anglican country now belong definitely to the past. The Catholic Church stands up together with the other Christian Churches for the rights of the underprivileged and hence has gained in esteem through this activity and this collaboration.[125] Of the 13.6 million inhabitants, 3.6 million, or 26.4 percent, are Catholics.

Also in New Zealand the ecclesiastical organization was complete by 1920. There were one archdiocese and three dioceses. The number of Catholics on 31 December 1976 amounted to 446,000, or 14.2 percent of the inhabitants. In the northern half of North Island the Mill Hill Missionaries take care of the evangelization of the Maori. The first priest of this tribe was ordained in 1945. The mission among the Maori even today still encounters difficulties. It is not easy to contact these people. In 1968 the first Maori sister made religious vows in Wanganui, a settlement of the Congregation of Sisters of Saint Joseph of Nazareth.

THE PACIFIC ISLANDS

In Oceania[126] the ecclesiastical organization of the incipient young Church from time to time had to adapt itself to the territorial, ethnic, and political circumstances. It was not always easy to keep sight

---

[125] Cf. *Herder-Korrespondenz* 27 (Freiburg 1973), 196–202.
[126] Cf. the article by A. Freitag, S.V.D., in *ZMR* 36 (Münster 1952), 144–52, 214–22; 37 (1953), 283–93; 38 (1954), 121–31.

of and follow events, especially when here too the independence movement of the island inhabitants and the transition from the colonial epoch to the present began. The mission Church on the Mariana Islands and the Carolines—to begin with these and continue our progress through the Pacific clockwise—had very much to suffer in the First as well as the Second World War. The entire vicariate once again remained for a rather long time without missionaries. After the war the islands became an American mandate. Rome united the Caroline and the Marshall Islands in a new vicariate apostolic and subordinated the Marianas to the vicariate apostolic of Guam, where Capuchins were active. In 1965 the vicariate became the Diocese of Agana as a suffragan see of San Francisco. The islanders are almost all Catholics.

The Sandwich Islands, usually called Hawaii after the largest island, experienced, from the time they belonged to the United States in 1898, a missionary upsurge in so far as now American missionaries and especially missionary sisters came to the aid of the Picpus Fathers. From 1926 to 1940 Bishop Estevão Alencastre, S.S.C.C., directed the vicariate. Under him the mission made such progress that on 25 January 1941 Rome elevated the vicariate to a diocese as suffragan of San Francisco. On the Marquesas, where the Picpus Fathers had great freedom of movement from 1924 on, the mission saved the population from dying out. The islanders had declined to 2,500 persons and threatened to become entirely extinct. The missionaries did all they could to improve the people's hygiene. Since then the number of inhabitants is again on the rise. In 1943 there were 3,200 islanders, in 1973 5,600. They are almost all Catholics. Also on the Society Islands (Tahiti), the Gambier Islands, the Tuamotu Islands, and the Leeward Islands the colonial government long impeded Catholic missionary activity. A further obstacle to successful evangelization was the rivalry of the Protestant denominations, which had often preceded the Catholic mission. The Catholic missionaries realized greater successes on the Society Islands, whose population today is one-third Catholic. Since 1947 Chinese immigrants have also been included in the mission. From time immemorial the missionaries have championed the improvement of popular hygiene in order to prevent the extinction of the islanders, as well as the educational system and other works of intellectual and material development aid.

On the Cook and Manahiki Islands the Catholic mission did not flourish until very late. In 1926 there were among the 9,500 islanders only 450 Catholics, as compared with 6,330 Protestants. In 1949 there were 1,410 Catholics and 13,000 Protestants, but in 1972 there were 3,056 Catholics in a population of 26,217. On Wallis and Futuna, the Tonga archipelago, and the Niue Islands of central Oceania the Marists of Father Colin have done mission work since 1836. Their activity included also every sort of development aid for the native islanders. The enormous distances required a large number of mission personnel The cooperation of native catechists and missionaries was therefore essential. In 1950 there were already in this vicariate 24 native priests, 32 native brothers, and 227 native sisters. There had been a major seminary on Wallis since 1874. The first four native priests had been ordained in 1886. In 1935 Rome detached the islands of Wallis, Futuna, and Alofi and there erected a new vicariate. In 1950 the 9,000 islanders were all Catholics. The rest of the vicariate was named in 1937 after the Tonga Islands and in 1957 after these and Niue Island. Here the Catholic mission always had a difficult time in relation to the Protestant, which had embraced all the islanders as early as 1875. Today about one-fifth of the people are Catholics.

The Navigator Islands or Samoa were likewise entrusted to the Marists for evangelization. Here too all the islanders were converted to Christianity. In 1948 there were 20,000 and in 1973 36,798 Catholics in a total population of 174,866. Here too the Marists began early to train a native mission personnel. To Samoa belongs the honor of having obtained the first native bishop of Oceania. On 11 January 1968 Paul VI appointed the Marist Father Pius Taofinu'u as bishop of the diocese of Apia and Western Samoa, created just eighteen months previously.[127] An even greater significance belonged to the naming of the first Polynesian bishop in that on 1 January 1962 Western Samoa had acquired its political independence as the first island nation of Oceania. In the consistory of 5 March 1973 Paul VI created the first bishop in Oceania the first cardinal in Oceania. The Fiji Islands had been a British colony since 1874 and obtained their independence on 10 October 1970. Only in the 1920s could the Marists here think of training Polynesian priests. In 1923 they established a minor seminary at Cawaci. Only four of the first seminarians reached the goal, but a beginning had been made. From the catechists' school, founded earlier, there emerged in 1924–34 ninety qualified catechists and teachers.

In the vicariate apostolic of New Caledonia the formation of a native mission personnel was also not taken up systematically until recent times. The first two native priests were ordained in 1946. In 1950 there were also nineteen native brothers and eighty-eight native sisters. Thereby the preconditions for an autonomous Church was created here also. New tasks came to the mission because of the immigration of

[127] He was born on 9 December 1923 at Falealupo on Savaii, had been ordained a priest in 1954, had entered the Marist Congregation in 1962, and on 29 May 1968 received episcopal ordination.

Tonkinese and Javanese. Today, out of 135,000 inhabitants, 88,000, or 65.2 percent, are Catholics. The rest are Protestants and Muslims and a small remnant of pagans. The Marist mission on the New Hebrides was long regarded as a "hard quarry," not least because of the deadly climate. As regards numbers, the Catholic mission was unable to make great progress. In 1948, of the 60,000 islanders only forty-eight hundred were Catholics. But since then the number has increased quickly to 16,000 in 1976, out of 97,000 inhabitants. At this time the education of native priests was taken up, while there were native catechists and teachers even before World War II.

The most difficult mission of the Marists in Oceania was the Solomon Islands. When at last the preconditions for the construction of a native Church had been created and the formation of the native mission personnel began to produce the first successes, World War II caused the mission the greatest harm. The Japanese occupied more than half the islands. Most of the missioners were taken to Australia. Two priests and two sisters of the South Solomons and thirteen priests, brothers, and sisters of the North Solomons met death. Immediately after the war the Marists began to rebuild and quickly led the mission to a new flowering. At the end of 1976, of the 200,000 islanders, 37,000, or 18.5 percent, were Catholics. On 7 July 1978 the island chain achieved political independence.

In the vicariate apostolic of the Gilbert Islands, to which belonged also the Ellice and Phoenix Islands, the Sporádhes, Nauru (since 1923), and other islands, the Missionaries of the Sacred Heart did the mission work. The number of faithful rose from 13,500 in 1922 to 25,500 in 1972, that is, about 50 percent of the population. World War II brought unspeakable suffering throughout the entire mission area. Personal and material damages were very great. The Missionaries of the Sacred Heart also evangelized the vicariate apostolic of Rabaul, Papua-New Guinea. In World War II fifty-seven priests and brothers and ten native sisters lost their lives there, twenty-three by violence. One-third of the native population was deported or killed. The number of Catholics—in 1939 there were 45,000—dropped to ca. 8,000. The mission lost all material institutions and property. But after the war reconstruction got under way at once. American, Australian, and Irish Missionaries of the Sacred Heart came to help. The Australian government granted considerable support. The statistics of 1973 report 118,000 Catholics in a population of 170,000.

On British New Guinea, where, in addition to the Missionaries of the Sacred Heart, the Society of the Divine Word, Franciscans, Capuchins, Montfortians, Passionists, and a large number of communities of sisters are active, World War II wiped out a mission work that had just flowered. The vicariates of eastern and central New Guinea especially had to suffer much. Many missionaries lost their lives, the rest were deported to Australia. After the war, everything had to start again from scratch.

Altogether 118 priests and brothers and seventy-eight sisters lost their lives in Oceania and New Guinea during World War II, while others became unfit for work. Twelve hundred mission buildings were totally destroyed, 120 partly.[128] After overcoming the war's damages, Catholic mission activity and development aid in all Oceania revived to a new flowering. Rome considered raising the furthest advanced vicariates to dioceses. But this idea was again dropped, because a still more comprehensive plan was taken under consideration: the erection of a regular ecclesiastical hierarchy and, with that, the canonical setting up of the young Churches. During the Second Vatican Council Rome was unable to have direct contact with the ordinaries of Oceania in regard to this question. The discussions came to a decision during the last period of the council. On 21 June 1966 the hierarchy was erected in Polynesia, Micronesia, and Melanesia. Three ecclesiastical provinces were formed: (1) Nouméa (New Caledonia), with the dioceses of Port Vila (New Hebrides) and Wallis-Futuna; (2) Suva (Fiji Islands), with Apia (Western Samoa) and Tarawa (Gilbert Islands); (3) Papeete (Tahiti), with Taiohae (Marquesas). Further, the dioceses of Rarotonga (Cook Islands) and Tonga were established; the former was assigned as suffragan to Wellington, the latter was immediately subject to the Holy See. The arrangement of the ecclesiastical provinces had its difficulties in consequence of the fluctuating political situation. There were independent islands such as the Kingdom of Tonga and the Principality of Western Samoa; other islands were under mandate status or under condominium, still others were under colonial rule. And ethnic viewpoints could not be used as a basis. Thus Rome turned, to some extent, to the still existing zones of influence of England, France, the United States, and New Zealand. Out of regard for the national pride of the population of Tonga, this island became a diocese placed directly under the Holy See.[129]

The ordinaries of Papua-New Guinea and the British Protectorate of the Solomon Islands also requested during the last period of the council the erection of an ecclesiastical hierarchy in their mission territory. They indicated the movements for political independence and the intention of the Anglican Church to reorganize itself there. Although the mission Church there was still relatively young, it was regarded as

[128] Cf. P. O'Reilly in *NZM* 3 (Schöneck 1947), 106f.
[129] *AAS* 59 (1967), 201–3.

sufficiently consolidated to introduce a general ecclesiastical organization. In this way the foreign and native mission societies should be compensated for their devoted activity, a new impetus would be given to the mission Church, and here also the organization of the Church in vicariates and prefectures, often regarded as a relic of the colonial epoch, would be eliminated. Hence on 15 November 1966 three new ecclesiastical provinces were erected: (1) Port Moresby, with the suffragan sees of Bereina (Yule Island), Daru, Mendi, and Sideia; (2) Madang, with Aitape, Goroka, Lae, Mount Hagen, Vanimo, and Wewak; (3) Rabaul, with Bougainville (North Solomons), Honiara (South Solomons), Kavieng, and Gizo (Western Solomons).[130] The first Papuan bishop, Ludwig Vangeke, M.S.C., who had been the first Papuan to be ordained a priest, was ordained by Paul VI at Sydney on 3 December 1970. On 16 September 1976 Papua-New Guinea received its political independence. On 7 March 1977 a nunciature was established there.[131]

Among the greatest cares of most of the new residential bishops is the education of a native clergy. According to a report of 6 February 1970[132] there was at the time not a single native priest in some dioceses, such as Taiohae and Rarotonga. In the other dioceses the native clergy was, compared with the foreign, a minority, except on Wallis and Futuna, where thirteen native and six foreign priests were active. On 2 March 1972, therefore, Wallis and Futuna obtained a native auxiliary bishop. Tonga also had a rather large number of native priests—nine, as compared with twelve foreign—and so there too a native coadjutor bishop was appointed on 15 October 1971. Altogether, according to the report just mentioned, of 309 diocesan and religious priests in this area, eighty-six were natives. There were three seminaries: one major seminary in Nouméa and two minor seminaries in Paita in the archdiocese of Nouméa and Lano in the diocese of Wallis-Futuna. There were many native vocations to the sisterhoods. There were 229 native sisters as opposed to 653 foreign. Several native congregations of sisters were established. Altogether, today there are nine native congregations of sisters in this area and four congregations of brothers of diocesan right.[133]

A new ecclesiastical problem resulted on the Fiji Islands because of the immigration of ca. 30,000 Indians. The archbishop of Suva exerted

[130] Ibid., 480–82.
[131] Ibid. 69 (1977), 256. For the Solomon Islands the apostolic delegation still exists (ibid., 256f.).
[132] Cf. *Memoria Rerum* III/2, 552.
[133] Cf. the "Supplementum" of the *Bibliografia Missionaria*, Anno XXXIX–1975, Quaderno no. 18 (Rome 1976), 55–58.

himself to obtain Indian priests for them. The emigrant Indians abroad lost their contact with Hinduism and hence were more easily accessible to the Christian message.

In 1968 the bishops of Oceania joined together as the Episcopal Conference of the Pacific (CEPAC). In March 1968 they had their first plenary meeting.

THE PHILIPPINES

The "young" Church on the Philippines is no more a young Church than those in the United States or Canada. But it has not a few problems in common with the mission Churches, and, above all, it lies in the Third World. As a Spanish patronate Church it had from the start a regular ecclesiastical hierarchy. The four vicariates apostolic were only erected in the 1930s and 1950s respectively, were subject to the Roman missionary authorities, but belonged to one of the thirteen ecclesiastical provinces with the same number of archdioceses and a total of thirty-one dioceses and twelve prelacies. With 80 percent Catholics out of 42 million inhabitants, the Philippines are a Catholic country, the only one in Southeast Asia. Only on the southern islands do some 3 million Muslims live, who feel themselves to be an oppressed minority.

The most recent past repeatedly produced, especially in the 1970s, tensions between Church and state and within the Church. Ecclesiastical circles reacted differently to the imposition of martial law by the president of the Philippines. In a common pastoral statement the Episcopal Conference first declared that it recognized the right and duty of the civil authorities to take proper steps to protect the sovereignty of the state and to guarantee the peace and well-being of the nation, but then the bishops appealed to the leaders and to every individual of the people to make a serious examination of conscience. However, in the last analysis the seventy-five bishops were not united in their attitude to the government.[134] Subsequently the government repeatedly tried to put pressure on the Church.

The episcopate sees a special task in the fostering of a Filipino clergy. Lack of priests long was and still is a central problem of the Church of the Philippines, and therefore the mission work in the vicariates apostolic is to a great extent in the hands of foreign personnel. Nevertheless in the last twenty years a rapid increase of native priestly vocations could be recorded. Thus, for example, the number of diocesan priests grew between 1956 and 1966 from 1,430 to 2,503 and that of religious priests from 147 to 394. A new great and responsible

---

[134] Cf. *Herder-Korrespondenz* 28 (Freiburg 1974), 121–23; 29 (1975), 100.

function devolves on the clergy and hence on the entire Philippine Church today: the evangelization of Southeast Asia, to which it is racially and culturally closer than are the Western Churches. Besides, Filipino missioners are not exposed to the suspicion that they are emissaries of Western "imperialism." The missionary spread has already begun. The Society of the Divine Word missionaries have employed several of their Filipino priests in Indonesia, and the Sisters of the Society of the Divine Word were the first congregation of women to send Filipino sisters to the mission in New Guinea. Since 1967 Filipino Oblates have been active in Hong Kong.

In the last few years the Church saw itself repeatedly induced to defend human rights. On 8 January 1967 the bishops published a "Pastoral Letter on Social Work and Agricultural Development," by which they aspired to give the government hints for eliminating existing abuses. In January 1977 they wrote a courageous pastoral on the problems and difficulties existing between state and Church.

The church was also drawn into the armed confrontation between the Muslims and the state. In 1974, on the occasion of a raid by Muslim rebels on the islands of Jolo, almost the entire capital was destroyed and the Catholic cathedral was burned down. Nevertheless the approximately 7,000 Christians of the island did not regard the Muslims as their enemies. The hundred-year old Catholic church on the Sulu Archipelago has in recent years made great efforts to establish peace and reconciliation. About 98 percent of the Sulu Archipelago is Islamic.[135]

The above-mentioned responsibility of the Philippine Church for the evangelization of the peoples of Southeast Asia is seen also in the establishment of the radio station Radio Veritas at Manila, which began operation on 11 April 1969 and beams broadcasts in twenty languages to the areas of Oceania and Southeast Asia. The decision to establish this radio station was made at the Conference of the Bishops of Southeast Asia in Manila in 1958. The Roman Congregation for the Evangelization of Peoples, the assistance work of the German Catholic Church's *Misereor* and *Missio,* and the German Federal Republic bore the heavy burden of the financial expenses.[136] Since 1975 the radio has been subject to the Philippine Episcopal Conference.

Paul VI's journey to the Far East from 26 November to 5 December 1970 was a religious happening for the young Churches in Oceania, Australia, and all other countries which the Pope touched upon in the

---

[135] Cf. *Die katholischen Missionen* (Freiburg 1976), 197–201; (1978), 51–55; *Herder-Korrespondenz* 31 (Freiburg 1977), 60–63.
[136] *Internationaler Fides-Dienst 1969,* 214f., 232–34.

journey. At Manila Paul VI took part in the closing sessions of the Symposium of the Asiatic Episcopal Conferences, whose chief topics were the Church's aid for development and the pastoral care of university students. Referring to the meager successes which the proclamation of the Christian faith had achieved thus far in Asia, apart from the Philippines, the Pope said to the bishops: "If in the past an inadequate knowledge of the riches which are concealed in the various cultures has been able to prevent the spread of the Gospel, and a false picture of the Church resulted, it is up to you to explain that the salvation brought by Jesus Christ is offered to all peoples, and without distinction of conditions of life, without attachment to a privileged race, a continent, or a culture, and that the Gospel, far from wishing to eliminate 'the germs of the good in the hearts and in the ideologies of people or in their own rites and their culture,' has the effect of refining all these values, elevating them, and perfecting them to the honor of God (*Lumen Gentium,* 17; *Ad Gentes,* 22). Following the model of Jesus Christ, who shared the living conditions of his environment, the Asian can be Catholic and remain fully Asian. If we declared in Africa a year ago that the Church must above all be Catholic, then a pluralism is still justified and even desirable, namely in the manner of expressing one common faith in the same Lord Jesus Christ."[137]

From Manila the Pope went on 29 November to Samoa. There he sent an urgent appeal to the Catholics of the entire world, the purpose of which was the renewal of the mission spirit.[138] The next stop on the journey was at Sydney, where seventy-two bishops of Australia, New Zealand, and Oceania had gathered for a symposium, at which were discussed timely problems of the Church in this area: proclamation of the faith, development aid, youth, the priesthood, ecumenism. The Pope took part in the closing session. As the theme of his talk he selected the unity of the Church. This may have been done in relation to the special ecumenical circumstances in Oceania, where the vast distances, the lack in shepherds of souls, and the related absence, often weeks or months long, of the priest have led to special arrangements with other Christian Churches. In general the Catholic mission Churches in Australia and Oceania are very receptive to ecumenism. By way of Jakarta, Hong Kong, and Colombo, Paul VI returned to Rome from his journey to the Far East.[139]

[137] *AAS* 63 (1971), 25–26.
[138] Ibid., 47–50.
[139] The Pope's addresses during the journey in *AAS* 63 (1971), 10–83.

BIBLIOGRAPHY

BIBLIOGRAPHY TO INDIVIDUAL CHAPTERS

SECTION ONE

The Institutional Unity of the Universal Church

1. *Statistics*

STATISTICS OF THE WORLD'S POPULATION—STATISTICS OF THE WORLD RELIGIONS—PROPORTION OF CATHOLICS

SOURCES: Pertinent sources for statistics of world population in *Population Index* (Office of Population Research, University of Princeton, N.Y.); *Population Studies* (London School of Economics, Houghton Street, Aldwych, London, W.C. 2); and *Population* (27, rue du Commandeur, Paris 14e). For information on individual countries there are monographs called *Country Profiles* (Population Council, 245 Park Avenue, New York). Comprehensive source in the *Demographic Yearbook of the United Nations* (Statistical Office of the United Nations, New York), 1948ff., and the survey *A Concise Summary of the World Population Situation in 1970* (United Nations, N.Y. 1971), also the UN *Statistical Yearbook* (New York), 1948ff.

Statistics of World Religions: *Demographic Yearbook of the United Nations; World Christian Handbook,* ed. by E. J. Bingle et al., London, from 1949 at yearly intervals; *Kirchliches Handbuch für das Katholische Deutschland* (Freiburg i. Brsg. 1970ff.); *Atlas Hierarchicus. Descriptio geographica et statistica ecclesiae catholicae tum occidentis tum orientis,* ed. by H. Emmerich, S.V.D., (Mödling, Austria 1968) (Supplement: *Eine geschichtliche Einführung und Erläuterungen zu den Karten*) (1913), 2d ed. (1929) by Karl Streit S.V.D., Mödling, Austria; *Atlas zur Kirchengeschichte. Die christlichen Kirchen in Geschichte und Gegenwart,* ed. by H. Jedin, K. S. Latourette, and J. Martin (Freiburg 1970). —For Mission lands: *Internationaler Fides-Dienst* (Catholic) (Rome 1962); *Oriente Cattolico* (Oriental Christians) (Rome 1962); K. B. Westman and H. v. Sicard, *Geschichte der christlichen Mission* (Protestant) (Munich 1962); *Jewish Statistical Bureau* (Jerusalem 1959).—World Confessional map. *LThk* 6 (1961).

THE ORGANIZATION OF THE ENTIRE CHURCH FROM 1914 TO 1970

SOURCES: *Acta Apostolicae Sedis* (*AAS*) (Vatican City 1909ff.); *Annuario Pontificio* (Vatican City 1912ff.); *Kirchliches Handbuch für das katholische Deutschland* (Freiburg i. Brsg. 1907ff.); *L'attività della Santa Sede* (Rome 1938–39ff.); *Annuario Statistico della Chiesa* (Rome 1971ff.).

LITERATURE: The Roman Curia: J. Ferrante, *Summa Juris Constitutionalis Ecclesiae* (Rome 1964); N. Del Re, *La Curia Romana. Lineamenti storico-giuridici* (Rome 1970);

LThK 6 (Freiburg 1961) cols. 692–94; L. Pasztor, *La Curia Romana. Problemi e ricerche per la sua storia nell'età moderna e contemporanea* (Rome 1971).—College of Cardinals: H. W. Klewitz, *Die Entstehung des Kardinalskollegiums. Reformpapsttum und Kardinalskollegium* (Darmstadt 1957); *LThK* 5 (Freiburg 1960) cols. 1342–44; P. C. van Lierde and A. Giraud, *Das Kardinalskollegium* (*Der Christ in der Welt* 12) (Aschaffenburg 1965). — Curial Congregations: F. M. Cappello, *De Curia Romana,* 2 vols. (Rome 1911–13); V. Martin, *Les Congrégations romaines* (Paris 1930); A large number of monographs, for the most part doctoral dissertations for the individual congregations; *LThK* 5 (Freiburg 1960) cols. 1344–49. —Papal Diplomacy: U. Stutz, *Die päpstliche Diplomatie unter Leo XIII. nach den Denkwürdigkeiten des Kardinals Domenico Ferrara, Abh. der Preuß. Akademie der Wissenschaften,* Phil.-Hist. KL. 1925, no. 3/4, Berlin 1926; G. de Marchi, *Le nunziature Apostoliche dal 1800 al 1957* (Rome 1959); with a list of secretaries of state and nuncios from 1800 to 1956). —G. Ferroglio, *Circoscrizioni ed enti territoriali della Chiesa* (Turin 1946); P. Negwer, *Die kuriale Zirkumskriptionspraxis in ihrer Bedeutung für den gegenwärtigen Rechtsstatus der ostdeutschen Diözesen* (diss., Basel 1963). In addition: See handbooks and commentaries on Canon law as well has histories of the Church and the papacy.

2. Popes Benedict XV, Pius XI, and Pius XII—
Biography and Activity within the Church

GENERAL: Official acts in the *AAS;* a continuing report in the *AKR* by N. Hilling; J. Schmidlin, *Papstgeschichte der neuesten Zeit* III (Munich 1936), 179–339 (Benedict XV); IV (Munich 1939) (Pius XI); H. Hermelink, *Die katholische Kirche unter den Piuspäpsten des 20 Jahrhunderts* (Zollikon and Zurich 1949); G. Schwaiger, *Geschichte der Päpste im 20. Jahrhundert* (Munich 1968); C. Falconi, *I papi del ventesimo secolo* (Milan 1967); F. Sugrue, *Popes in the Modern World* (New York 1961); A. Oddone, "Azione pacificatrice e caritatevole del Papato contemporaneo," *CivCatt* 101 (1950), 68–82.

BENEDICT XV

The BIOGRAPHIES published during the lifetime of Benedict XV offer biographical material but no real evaluation: A. De Waal, *Der neue Papst* (Hamm 1915); A. Pöllmann, *Benedikt XV aus der Familie Della Chiesa* (Dießen 1915); A. Baudrillart, *Benoît XV* (Paris 1920); more information are the obituaries by H. Sierp, in: *StdZ* 102 (1922), 401–8; Funk, in: *Hochland* 19 (1921/22), 651–59.—Later Biographies: F. Vistalli (Hildesheim 1932); F. Pichon (Paris 1940); F. Hayward, *Un pape méconnu: Benoît XV* (Tournai and Paris 1955); W. H. Peters, *The Life of Benedict XV* (Milwaukee 1959).—Historical perspectives in F. Ehrle, "Von Pius X. zu Benedikt XV," *StdZ* 88 (1915), 201–19; S. Merkle, "Benedikt XIV—Benedikt XV," *Hochland* 12 (1914/15), 340–47. —New Letters: F. Molinari, "Il carteggio di Benedetto XV con Mons. Ersilio Monzani," *RSTI* 20 (1966), 410–50.

INTERNAL ECCLESIASTICAL ACTIVITIES: N. Hilling, "Die gesetzgeberische Tätigkeit Benedikts XV. bis zur Promulgation des Codex iuris canonici," *AKR* 98 (1918), 223–39, 378–406, 561–74; For the years after 1917, ibid. 103 (1923), 5–36; J. Kleijntjens, "Activité charitable de Benoît XV," *RHE* 43 (1948), 536–45; R. Leiter, "Die päpstliche Kriegsfürsorge," *StdZ* 100 (1921), 197–208.

Pius XI

To the BIOGRAPHIES published during his pontificate, the same comment applies as to those of Benedict XV: M. Bierbaum (Cologne 1922); A. Novelli (Milan 1923); U. Togani, *Pio XI. La vita e le opere* (Milan 1937); G. Galbiati (Cologne 1937); L. Townsend (London 1930); B. Williamson (London 1931); P. Hughes (London 1937). —Obituaries: *StdZ* 136 (1939), 1–9; A. Novelli in *La Scuola cattolica* 67 (1939), 624ff.; G. Galbiati, *Papa Pio XI* (Milan 1939). —Important for an understanding of his personality are the memoirs of two of his collaborators: C. Confalonieri, *Pio XI visto da vicino* (Turin 1937); E. Pellegrinetti, *Pio XI. L'uomo nel Papa e il Papa nell'uomo* (Rome 1940). —A comprehensive description of the personality and the work of Pius XI in the collection by the archbishopric of Milan: *Pio XI nel trentesimo della morte 1939/69* (Milan 1969); pages 5–58 list a detailed bibliography prepared by A. Rimoldi.

SPECIAL STUDIES: G. Galbiati, "La produzione scientifica di Achille Ratti," *Aevum* 13 (1940), bibliographical supplement 301–12; N. Malvezzi, *Pio XI nei suoi scritti* (Milan 1923); A. Ratti, *Scritti storici* (Florence 1932); G. Bobba and F. Mauro, *Achille Ratti. Alpine Schriften* (Regensburg 1936); F. Kraft, "Papst Pius XI. als Bibliothekar," *Festschrift Eugen Stollreither* (Erlangen 1950), 105–16; concerning his private correspondence, see N. Vian in *Mélange E. Tisserant* VIII (Rome 1954), 373–439; D. Bertetto, ed., *Discorsi di Pio XI,* 3 vols. (Turin 1959–61).

Pius XII

BIBLIOGRAPHIES: A. Rimoldi in *La Scuola Cattolica* 77 (1949), 88–108; B. Schneider in *AHP.* —Until 1939: Reliable information on family and development in H. Hoberg, *Papst Pius XII.* (Lucerne 1949); concerning his brother, consult B. Schneider, "Das Tagebuch des Francesco Pacelli," *StdZ* 164 (1958/59), 81–97; Y. de la Brière, "Pie XII avant son Pontificat," *Études* 239 (1939), 87–101; L. Kaas, ed., *Eugenio Pacelli, Erster Apostolischer Nuntius beim Deutschen Reich. Gesammelte Reden* (Berlin 1930); Eugenio Pacelli, *Discorsi e Panegirici 1931–1938* (Vatican City 1939); B. Wüstenberg and I. Zabkar, eds., *Pius XII. Der Papst an die Deutschen* (Frankfurt 1965), contains the Pope's speeches and open letters in German from 1917 to 1956.

During the Pontificate: In addition to the documentation contained in Hoberg until 1948, see M. Bierbaum (Cologne 1939); O. Walter (Olten 1939); F. Loidl (Vienna 1947); P. Dahm (Mönchen-Gladbach 1952); Konstantin Prinz von Bayern (Bad Wörishofen 1952); W. Sandfuchs (Karlsruhe 1956); A. M. Rathgeber (Kempten 1958); I. O. Smit, *Pastor angelicus* (Roermond 1949); G. Goyau (Paris 1939); P. Lesourd (Paris 1940); E. Buonaiuti (Rome 1946); W. Padellaro (Rome 1949); L. Veneziani (Pisa 1942); C. H. Doyle (New York 1945); O. Halecki (London 1954); R. C. Pollock, *The Mind of Pius XII* (London 1955).

Obituaries and Biographies since 1958: R. Leiber in *StdZ* 163 (1958/59), 81–100; A. Martini in *CivCatt* 109, 4 (1958), 233–46; G. Crosignani, "Aspetti della personalità e dell'opera di Pio XII," *Divus Thomas* 62 (1959), 3–33; I. Coppens, "Pie XII. In memoriam," *EThL* 34 (1958), 873–83; D. Tardini, *Pio XII* (Vatican City 1960), the most revealing biography by his closest collaborator; I. Giordani, *Pio XII, Un grande papa* (Turin 1961); G. Andreotti, *Pio XII* (Rome 1965); F. Engel-Janosi, "Der Stellvertreter Christi Pius XII. Aspekte seiner Gestalt," *Wort und Wahrheit* 23 (1968), 546–59; B. Schneider, *Pius XII.* (Göttingen 1968); K. N. Burton, *Witness of the Light. The Life of Pope Pius XII* (New York 1958); L. Chaigne, *Portrait et vie de Pie XII* (Paris 1966).

THE WORK OF THE POPE: Compilation of the most important decrees and decisions in *AKR* 122 (1947) and 128 (1958). *Discorsi e radiomessaggi di S. Stà Pio XII,* 20 vols. (Vatican City 1941–59); *Discorsi agli intellettuali 1939–1954* (Vatican City 1955); *L'attività della Santa Sede,* in annual volumes since 1945, unofficial. For the publications of documents from the Vatican Archives, see Chap. 3. —"Papst Pius XII. 1939–1958. Eine Dokumentation seines Pontifikats," *HK* 13 (1958/59), 57–71; "Pius XII im Urteil der nichtkatholischen Welt," *HK* 13 (1958/59), 233–46; *La vie d'Église sous Pie XII* (Paris 1959); G. B. Montini, "Pio XII e l'ordine internazionale," *La Scuola Cattolica* 85 (1957), 3–24; R. Losada-Cosmes, "Magisterio de Pio XII. Esquema doctrinal y boletín bibliográfico," *Salmanticensis* 3 (1956), 509–687; S. Mayer, "Die Bedeutung Papst Pius' XII. für das Recht, besonders das Kirchenrecht," *AKR* 130 (1961), 436–71; S. Álvarez Menéndez, "Pio XII Canonista," *Revista española de derecho can.* 13 (1958), 721–35; G. Falconi, *Il Pentagono Vaticano* (Bari 1958); I. Giordani, *Vita contro morte. La Santa Sede per le vittime della seconda guerra mondiale* (Milan 1956); several contributions with illustrations in *Osservatore della Domenica,* 28 June 1964; A. J. Muench, "Bilanz einer Nuntiatur 1946–1959. Schlußbericht des ersten Nuntius in der Nachkriegszeit," ed. by L. Volk in *StdZ* 195 (1977), 147–58.

3. *Foreign Policy of the Popes in the Epoch of the World Wars*

SOURCES

GENERAL: *AAS* 6 (1914)–38 (1946); *L'Osservatore Romano; L'attività della Santa Sede nel 1939. Pubblicazione non uffiziale* (annually from 1939); E. Marmy, ed., *Mensch und Gemeinschaft in christlicher Schau. Dokumente* (from 1832 to 1944) (Fribourg 1945).

REFERENCES: G. de Marchi, *Le Nunziature Apostoliche dal 1800 al 1956* (Rome 1957); L. Schöppe, ed., *Konkordate seit 1800. Originaltext und deutsche Übersetzung der geltenden Konkordate* (Berlin 1964).

MEMOIRS: G. Spadolini, ed., *Il cardinale Gasparri e la Questione Romana, con brani delle memorie inedite* (Florence 1972); L. von Pastor, *Tagebücher, Briefe, Erinnerungen,* ed. by W. Wühr (Heidelberg 1950); Beyens, *Baron, Quatre ans à Rome 1921–1926. Fin du pontificat de Benoît XV, Pie XI, les débuts du fascisme* (Paris 1934); F. Charles-Roux, *Huit ans au Vatican 1932–1940* (Paris 1947); E. von Weizsäcker, *Erinnerungen* (Munich 1950); L. E. Hill, ed., *Die Weizsäcker-Papiere* (Frankfurt 1974).

DOCUMENTS: T. E. Hachey, ed., *Anglo-Vatican Relations, 1914–1939: Confidential Annual Reports of the British Ministers to the Holy See* (Boston 1972); F. Engel-Janosi, *Vom Chaos zur Katastrophe. Vatikanische Gespräche 1918 bis 1938, vornehmlich auf Grund der Berichte der österreichischen Gesandten beim Heiligen Stuhl* (Vienna 1971); W. Steglich, ed., *Der Friedensappell Papst Benedikts XV. vom 1. August 1917 und die Mittelmächte. Diplomatische Aktenstücke . . . aus den Jahren 1915–1922* (Wiesbaden 1970); W. Steglich, ed., *Die Verhandlungen des 2. Unterausschusses des parlamentarischen Untersuchungsausschusses über die päpstliche Friedensaktion von 1917. Aufzeichnungen und Vernehmungsprotokolle* (Wiesbaden 1974); A. Struker, ed., *Die Kundgebungen Benedikts XV. zum Weltfrieden. Urtext und Übertragung* (Freiburg 1917); P. Scoppola, *La Chiesa e il fascismo, Documenti e interpretazioni* (Bari 1971), best introduction; C. A. Biggini, *Storia inedita della Conciliazione* (Milan 1942); F. Pacelli, *Diario della Conciliazione,* M. Maccarone, ed. (Vatican City 1959); F. Margiotta Broglio, *Italia e Santa Sede dalla grande guerra alla conciliazione. Aspetti politici e giuridici* (Bari 1966); F. Fonzi, "Documenti per la storia dei Patti Lateranesi. Due relazione di Domenico Barone," *RSCI* 19 (1965), 403–35; A. de Gasperi, *Lettere sul Concordato, con saggi di M.R. de Gasperi e di G. Martina* (Brescia 1970); L. Volk, ed., *Kirchliche Akten über die Reichskonkordatsverhandlungen 1933* (Mainz 1969); A. Kupper, ed., *Staatliche Akten über die Reichskonkordatsverhandlungen 1933* (Mainz 1969); D. Albrecht, ed., *Der Notenwechsel zwischen dem Heiligen Stuhl und der Deutschen Reichsregierung* I: *Von der Ratifizierung des Reichskonkordats bis zur Enzyklika "Mit brennender Sorge"* (Mainz 1965); II: *1937–1945* (Mainz 1969); H. Hürten, ed., *Deutsche Briefe 1934–1938. Ein Blatt der katholischen Emigration* I: *1934–1935,* II: *1936–1938* (Mainz 1969); *Pio XII, Discorsi e Radiomessaggi di Sua Santità* I (1940)–VIII (1946) [according to the years of his pontificate, beginning 2 March]; A. F. Utz and J. F. Groner, *Aufbau und Entfaltung des gesellschaftlichen Lebens. Soziale Summe Pius' XII.,* 2 vols. (Fribourg 1954); P. Blet, R. A. Graham [beginning with Vol. 3], A. Martini, B. Schneider, eds., *Actes et documents du Saint Siège relatifs à la seconde guerre mondiale* (Vatican City 1965ff.) [Contains reports on peace and war and the ecclesiastical situation in Germany, Poland, and the Baltic states]; *Le Saint Siège et la guerre en Europe: Mars 1939–août 1940* (=*ADSS* 1 [1965]); *Juin 1940–juin 1941* (=*ADSS* 4 [1967]); *Juillet 1941–octobre 1942* (=*ADSS* 5 [1969]); *Novembre 1942–décembre 1943* (=*ADSS* 7 [1973]); the documents for 1944/45 were published in 1978; *Lettres de Pie XII aux Évêques allemands 1939–1944* (=*ADSS* 2 [1966]), reissued with minor corrections by B. Schneider, P. Blet and A. Martini, eds., *Die Briefe Pius' XII. an die deutschen Bischöfe 1939–1944* (Mainz 1966), cited as: B. Schneider, *Piusbriefe*; *Le Saint Siège et la situation religieuse en Pologne et dans les Pays Baltes 1939–1945* I: *1939–1941,* II: *1942–1945* (=*ADSS* 3, 2 vols.); *Le Saint Siège et les victimes de la guerre: Mars 1939–décembre 1940* (=*ADSS* 6 [1972]); *Janvier 1941–décembre 1942* (=*ADSS* 8 [1974]); *Janvier–décembre 1943* (=*ADSS* 9 [1975]); the documents for 1944/45 appeared in 1978; L. Volk, ed., *Akten Kardinal Michael von Faulhabers 1917–1945* I: *1917–1934* (Mainz 1975); II: *1934–1945* (Mainz 1978); B. Stasiewski, ed., *Akten deutscher Bischöfe über die Lage der Kirche* I: *1933–1934* (Mainz 1968); II: *1934–1935* (Mainz 1976); III: *1935–1936* (Mainz 1978); H. Boberach, ed., *Berichte des SD und der Gestapo über Kirchen und Kirchenvolk in Deutschland 1934–1944* (Mainz 1971); *Die kirchliche Lage in Bayern nach den Regierungspräsidentenberichten 1933–1943* I: *Regierungsbezirk Oberbayern,* ed. by H. Witetschek (Mainz 1966); II: *Regierungsbezirk Ober- und Mittelfranken,* ed. by H. Witetschek (Mainz 1967); III: *Regierungsbezirk Schwaben,* ed. by H. Witetschek (Mainz 1971), IV: *Regierungsbezirk Niederbayern und Oberpfalz 1933–1945,* ed. by W. Ziegler (Mainz 1973).

IMPORTANT OFFICIAL PUBLICATIONS FOR FOREIGN AFFAIRS: For the period to 1918, surveys in: W. Baumgart, ed., *Quellenkunde zur deutschen Geschichte der Neuzeit von 1500 bis zur Gegenwart* 5; W. Baumgart, *Das Zeitalter des Imperialismus und des Ersten Weltkrieges (1871–1918)* 1: *Akten und Urkunden* (Darmstadt 1977).

FOR THE PERIOD AFTER 1918 AND THE SECOND WORLD WAR: USA: *Foreign relations of the United States. Diplomatic Papers.* Important supplements: *The World War,* 9 vols. (1928–33); *1919. The Paris Peace Conference,* 13 vols. (1942–47); *The Lansing Papers 1914–1920,* 2 vols. (1939–40); M. C. Taylor, ed., *Wartime Correspondence between President Roosevelt and Pope Pius XII* (New York 1947).

Germany: *Akten zur deutschen auswärtigen Politik 1918–1945:* (Series A [1918–25] has not yet been published), Series B (for 1925–33): 1 (Göttingen 1966)–9 (Göttingen 1976), for 1925–28; Series C (for 1933–37): 1 (Göttingen 1971)–5 (Göttingen 1975), for 1933–36; Series D (for 1937–41): 1 (Baden-Baden 1950)–13

(Göttingen 1970); Series E (for 1941–45): 1 (Göttingen 1969)–4 (Göttingen 1975), for 1941–42.

Great Britain: *Documents on British Foreign Policy:* Series I (for 1919–25): 1 (1947)–20 (1976), for 1919–22; Series IA (for 1925–29): 1 (1966)–7 (1975), for 1925–30; Series II (for 1929–38): 1 (1947)–15 (1975), for 1929–36; Series III (for 1938–39): 1 (1949)–10 (1961).

Italy: *Documenti Diplomatici Italiani:* Series 5 (for 1914–18): 1 (1954), 4 (1973), for 1914, 1915; Series 6 (for 1918–22): 1 (1956), for 1918/19; Series 7 (for 1922–35): 1 (1953)–9 (1975), for 1922–30; Series 8 (for 1935–39): 12 (1952)–13 (1953), for 1939; Series 9 (for 1939–43): 1 (1954)–5 (1965).

France: *Documents Diplomatiques Français 1932–1939:* Series 1 (for 1932–35): 1 (1964)–6 (1972), for 1932–34; Series 2 (for 1936–39): 1 (1963)–11 (1977), for 1936–38.

LITERATURE

GENERAL ACCOUNTS OF THE ERA OF THE TWO WORLD WARS: W. J. Mommsen, *Das Zeitalter des Imperialismus [1885–1918]* (Frankfurt 1969); R. A. C. Parker, *Das Zwanzigste Jahrhundert* I: *1918–1945* (Frankfurt 1967); T. Schieder, ed., *Handbuch der europäischen Geschichte* 6: *Europa im Zeitalter der Nationalstaaten und der europäischen Weltpolitik bis zum Ersten Weltkrieg* (Stuttgart 1968); R. Elze and R. Repgen, eds., *Studienbuch Geschichte* (Stuttgart 1974); K. D. Bracher, *Die Krise Europas 1917–1975* (Frankfurt 1976); P. Renouvin, *La crise européenne et la première guerre mondiale 1904–1918* (Paris 1934, 1969); M. Baumont, *La faillite de la paix 1918–1939* I: *1918–1935* (Paris 1945, 1967); II: *1936–1939* (Paris 1945, 1968); H. Michel, *La seconde guerre mondiale* I: *1939–1943* (Paris 1968); II: *1943–1945* (Paris 1969); P. Renouvin, *Les crises du XXe siècle* I: *De 1914 à 1929* (Paris 1957, 1972); II: *De 1929 à 1945* (Paris 1958, 1972); P. Gerbod, *L'Europe culturelle et religieuse de 1815 à nos jours* (Paris 1977); J.-B. Duroselle, *Histoire diplomatique de 1919 à nos jours* (Paris 1953, 1962); G. M. Gathorne-Hardy, *A Short History of International Affairs 1920–1939* (London 1934, 1968); W. Knapp, *A History of War and Peace 1939–1965* (London 1967); C. L. Mowat, ed., *The Shifting Balance of World Forces 1898–1945* (London 1968); W. P. Potjomkin, ed., *Geschichte der Diplomatie* (Berlin 1948), II: *Die Diplomatie der Neuzeit* [1872–1919]; III: *Die Diplomatie in der Periode der Vorbereitung des Zweiten Weltkriegs* [1919–39] (Communist view).

PAPAL HISTORY: J. Schmidlin, *Papstgeschichte der Neuesten Zeit* III: *Pius X. und Benedikt XV., 1903–1922* (Munich 1936); IV: *Pius XI., 1922–1939* (Munich 1939); H. Hermelink, *Die katholische Kirche unter den Pius-Päpsten des 20. Jahrhunderts* (Zollikon, Zurich 1949); G. Schwaiger, *Geschichte der Päpste im 20. Jahrhundert* (Munich 1968); G. Maron, *Die römisch-katholische Kirche von 1870 bis 1970,* in: *Die Kirche in ihrer Geschichte* 4, Nr. N2 (Göttingen 1972); R. Aubert, *Vom Kirchenstaat zur Weltkirche. 1818 bis zum Zweiten Vaticanum* (=*Geschichte der Kirche,* V/1) (Zurich 1976).

SYSTEMATIC PROBLEMS OF PAPAL FOREIGN POLICY: W. Gurian and M. A. Fitzsimmons, *The Catholic Church in World Affairs* (Notre Dame 1954); R. A. Graham, *Vatican Diplomacy. A Study of Church and State on the International Plane* (Princeton 1959), basic; R. Bosc, *La Société Internationale et l'Église. Sociologie et Morale des Relations Internationales* (Paris 1961); C. Alix, *Le Saint-Siège et les nationalismes en Europe 1870–1960* (Paris 1962); J. Chevalier, *La politique du Vatican* [1939–69] (Paris 1969); I. Martín, "Die Präsenz des Hl. Stuhls bei den Staaten," *Concilium* 6 (1970), 571–75; P. Ciprotti,

BIBLIOGRAPHY

"Funktion, Stellung und Bedeutung des Heiligen Stuhls im internationalen Recht," *Concilium* 6 (1970), 556–60; H. de Riedmatten, "Die Präsenz des Heiligen Stuhles in den internationalen Organisationen," *Concilium* 6 (1970), 561–70; K. Gotto, "Die katholische Kirche," H.-P. Schwarz, *Handbuch der deutschen Außenpolitik* (Munich 1975), 229–33.

THE PONTIFICATES OF THE INDIVIDUAL POPES: G. Rossini, ed., *Benedetto XV, i Cattolici e la prima guerra mondiale. Atti del Convegno di Studi tenuto a Spoleto nei giorni 7-8-9 settembre 1962* (Rome 1963); R. Leiber, "Die päpstliche Kriegsfürsorge," *StdZ* 100 (1921), 197–208; G. Quirico, *Il Vaticano et la guerra* (Rome 1921); J. Kleijntjens, "Activité charitable de Benoît XV," *RHE* 43 (1948), 536–45; H. Johnson, *Vatican Diplomacy in World War I* (Oxford 1933); W. W. Gottlieb, *Studies in the Secret Diplomacy during the First World War* (London 1957); F. Engel-Janosi, *Österreich und der Vatikan 1846–1918* II: *Die Pontifikate Pius' X. und Benedikts XV., 1903–1918* (Graz 1960); A. Martini, "La preparazione dell'appello di Benedetto XV ai governi belligerenti (1° agosto 1917)," *CivCatt* 113, 4 (1962), 118–32; A. Martini, "La nota di Benedetto XV ai capi delle nazioni belligerenti (1° agosto 1917)," *CivCatt* 113, 4 (1962), 417–29; W. Steglich, *Die Friedenspolitik der Mittelmächte 1917/18* (Wiesbaden 1964); V. Conzemius, "L'offre du mediation de Benoît XV du 1ier août 1917. Essai d'un bilan provisoire," *Religion et Politiques. Les deux guerres mondiales. Histoire de Lyon et du Sud-Est. Mélanges offerts à André Latreille* (Lyon 1972), 303–26.

C. M. Cianfarra, *The Vatican and the Kremlin* (New York 1950); M. Mourin, *Le Vatican et l'U.R.S.S.* (Paris 1965); J. Kraus, *Im Auftrag des Papstes in Rußland. Der Steyler Anteil an der katholischen Hilfsmission 1922–1924* (Steyl 1970); D. J. Dunn, "Stalinism and the Catholic Church during the Era of World War II," *CHR* 59 (1973), 404–28; O. Simmel, "Die Ostpolitik des Vatikans," *Internationale katholische Zeitschrift "Communio"* 3 (1974), 555–67; H. Stehle, *Die Ostpolitik des Vatikans 1917–1975* (Munich 1975); U. A. Floridi, *Mosca e il Vaticano. I dissidenti sovietici di fronte al 'dialogo.' Introduzione di M. Agurskij* (Ponte Sesto di Rozzano 1976).

D. Albrecht, ed., *Katholische Kirche im Dritten Reich. Eine Aufsatzsammlung* (Mainz 1976), with biblio.; R. A. Graham, *Il Vaticano e il nazismo* (Rome 1975); L. Volk, *Das Reichskonkordat vom 20. Juli 1933. Von den Ansätzen in der Weimarer Republik bis zur Ratifizierung am 10. September 1933* (Mainz 1972); M. Maccarone, *Il nazionalsocialismo e la Santa Sede* (Rome 1947); G. O. Kent, "Pope Pius XII and Germany. Some Aspects of German-Vatican Relations 1933–1945," *AHR* 70 (1964/65), 59–78; W. Harrigan, "Nazi Germany and the Holy See, 1933–1936: the Historical Background of *Mit brennender Sorge*," *CHR* 51 (1965/66), 457–86; L. Volk, "Die Enzyklika *Mit brennender Sorge*," *StdZ* 183 (1969), 174–94; H.-A. Raem, *Entstehung, Inhalt und Auswirkungen der Enzyklika "Mit brennender Sorge" vom 14. März 1937 in ihrem historischen Kontext* (diss., Bonn 1977); P. Duclos, *Le Vatican et la seconde guerre mondiale* (Paris 1955); B. Martin, *Friedensinitiativen und Machtpolitik im Zweiten Weltkrieg 1939–1942* (Düsseldorf 1974); J. Becker, "Der Vatikan und der II. Weltkrieg," D. Albrecht, ed., *Katholische Kirche im Dritten Reich* (Mainz 1976).

SURVEY OF RESEARCH: R. Lill, "Die Kirchen und das Dritte Reich. Ein Forschungsbericht," W. P. Eckert, ed., *Judenhaß—Schuld der Christen?!* (Essen 1966), 47–94; V. Conzemius, "Églises chrétiennes et totalitarisme national-socialiste," *RHE* 63 (1968), 437–503, 868–948; D. Veneruso, "Pio XII e la seconda guerra mondiale," *RSCI* 22 (1968), 506–53; U. von Hehl, "Kirche, Katholizismus und das nationalsozialistische Deutschland. Ein Forschungsüberblick," D. Albrecht, ed., *Katholische Kirche im Dritten Reich* (Mainz 1976), 219–51.

4. The Second Vatican Council

SOURCES AND LITERATURE

Because of the great numbers of accounts we present only a selected few.

POPE JOHN XXIII: Writings: *Il Giornale dell'Anima* (Rome 1964); *In Memoria di Mons. Giacomo Maria Radini Tedeschi, vescovo di Bergamo* (Bergamo 1916, Rome 1963); *Gli inizi del Seminario di Bergamo. Note storiche, con una introduzione sul Concilio di Trento e la fondazione dei primi seminari* (Bergamo 1939); *Gli Atti della Visita Apostolica di S. Carlo Borromeo a Bergamo,* 2 vols. in 5 parts (Florence 1936–57); *Il Cardinale Cesare Baronio* (Rome 1961); "Souvenirs d'un Nonce," *Cahiers de France 1944/53* (Rome 1963); *Scritti e discorsi 1953–1958,* 4 vols. (Rome 1959–62); *Discorsi, messaggi, colloqui del Santo Padre Giovanni XXIII,* 6 vols. (Vatican City 1958–65); *Lettere ai familiari* (Rome 1968; 727 letters, 1901–62).

Official Documents: *AAS* 50 (1958)–55 (1963); "Dokumentation," *Herder-Korrespondenz* 17 (1963), 449–76; L. Capovilla, *Giovanni XXIII in alcuni scritti di Don Giuseppe De Luca* (Brescia 1963), with correspondence, 1945–62, and thoughts of the writer, a friend of the Pope, 133–41.

Biographies: Written during the pontificate and therefore to be used with caution are those by A. Lazzarini, G. Santoro, A. Giovanetti, R. Garret, H. Picker; E. Radius, *Giovanni XXIII* (Milan 1966); N. Fabretti, *Papa Giovanni* (Rome 1966); L. Elliott, *Johannes XXIII* (Freiburg, Basel and Vienna 1975); E. Balducci, *Papa Giovanni* (Florence 1964); E. E. Hales, *Die große Wende* (Graz and Cologne 1966); G. Bara and D. Donadoni, *Giorno per giorno con Papa Giovanni* (Turin 1966); A. L'Arco, *Il segreto di Papa Giovanni* (Turin 1967); D. Agasso, *Il Papa delle grandi speranze* (Milan 1967).

On the Beginnings: D. Cogini, *Papa Giovanni nei suoi primi passi a Sotto il Monte* (Bergamo 1965); S. Álvarez Menéndez, "Juan XXIII desde el punto de vista jurídico-canónico," *Rev. española de derecho canonico* 18 (1963), 843–77.

From Obituaries: B. Schneider, *StdZ* 88 (1962/63), 241–54; G. Schwaiger, *AKR* 132 (1963), 3–30, with biblio. R. Aubert, "Jean XXIII. Un 'pape de transition' qui marquera dans l'histoire," *Revue nouvelle* 38 (1963), 3–33; G. Caprile, "Ricchezza di un breve pontificato," *CivCatt* 1963 II, 523–39; Dahm, *Johannes XXIII.* (Offenburg, n.d.).

BIBLIOGRAPHIES OF THE COUNCIL: A collection by G. Caprile to 1967 in: *Herder TK* III, 727–31; C. Dollen, *Vatican II. A Bibliography* (Metuchen, N.J. 1969); R. Laurentin, *Bilan du Concile. Histoire, textes, commentaires* (Paris 1969), 313–60; G. Garofalo and J. Federici, *Dizionario del Concilio Vat. II* (Rome 1969).

Preparation: *Consultázione per la preparazione del Concilio Vat. II. Dati statistici,* ed. by Pontificia Commissione Centrale preparatoria (Vatican City 1961); *Acta et documenta Concilio Oecumenico Vaticano II apparando,* Series I: *Antepraeparatoria,* contains Vol. I (1960) *Acta Johannis XXIII;* Vol. II in 8 sections (1960–61) *Consilia et vota episcoporum et praelatorum:* Secs. 1–3: *Europe,* Sec. 4: *Asia,* Sec. 5: *Africa,* Sec. 6: *North and Central America,* Sec. 7: *South America and Oceania,* Sec. 8: *Superiors of Orders,* plus 2 vols. of appendices; Vol. III (1961) *Proposita et monita SS. Congregationum Curiae Romanae;* Vol. IV (1961) *Studia et vota universitatum et facultatum ecclesiasticarum et catholicarum,* Sec. 1: *Rome,* Sec. 2: *Extra Urbem.* —Series II: *Praeparatoria:* Vol. I (1964) *Acta S. P. Johannis XXIII;* Vol. II in 4 sections (1965–1968) sessions of the Central Commission. Survey of the schemata prepared by the Prepatory Commission in *Herder TK* III, 665–726.

PARTICIPANTS: *Padri presenti al Concilio Ecumenico Vat. II* (Vatican City 1967), published by the Secretariat General. On the Composition: *HK* 17 (1962/63), 59ff.;

L'Osservatore Romano, special edition, 6 March 1966; R. Caporale, *Les hommes du Concile. Étude sociologique sur Vat. II* (Paris 1965); M. Galli and B. Moosbrugger, *Das Konzil. Ein Text- und Bildbericht* (Olten 1965); F. Vallainc, *Immagini del Concilio* (Rome 1966).

Statistics on various groups: P. A. Ysermans, *American Participation in the Second Vatican Council* (New York 1967); G. Conus, "L'Église d'Afrique au Concile Vat. II," *NZMW* 30 (1974), 241–55; 31 (1975) 1–18, 124–42; J. Wnuk, *Vatican II. Episkopat Polski na Soborze Vatykanskym* (Czytelnik 1964); *L'Église Grecque Melkite au Concile. Discours et notes du Patriarche Maximos IV et des Prélats de son Église au Concile Oecumenique Vat. II* (Dar Al Kalima, Beirut 1967); W. Dushnyck, *The Ukrainian-Rite Catholic Church at the Ecumenical Council 1962/65. A Collection of Articles, Book Reviews, Editorials* (New York and Paris 1967), with biblio.; W. Seibel, *Zwischenbilanz zum Konzil. Berichte und Dokumente der deutschen Bischöfe* (Recklinghausen 1963).

DECREES: *Sacrosanctum Oecumenicum Concilium Vaticanum II. Constitutiones, Decreta, Declarationes, cura et studio Secretariae generalis* (Vatican City 1966); J. Deretz and A. Nocent, *Konkordanz der Konzilstexte* (Graz 1968). —Translations and Interpretations: *Das Zweite Vatikanische Konzil. Konstitutionen, Dekrete u. Erklärungen, lat. u. deutsch. Kommentare,* ed. by H. Vorgrimler et al., 3 vols. (Freiburg 1966–68); *Vaticanum secundum,* ed. by O. Müller, W. Becker and J. Gülden, 4 vols. (Leipzig 1963–66); A. Beckel, H. Reiring and O. B. Roegele, *Zweites Vat. Konzil. Dokumente, Texte, Kommentare,* 4 vols. (Osnabrück 1963–66); H. Reuter, *Das II. Vat. Konzil. Vorgeschichte, Verlauf, Ergebnisse dargestellt nach Dokumenten und Berichten* (Cologne 1966); J. C. Hampe, *Die Autorität der Freiheit. Gegenwart des Konzils u. Zukunft der Kirche im ökumenischen Disput,* 3 vols. (Munich 1967). —English-language editions: *The Documents of Vatican II,* ed. by Walter M. Abbott (New York, 1966); *Commentary on the Documents of Vatican II* I-V, ed. by H. Vorgrimler (New York, 1967–69).

INDIVIDUAL DECREES: Constitution on the Sacred Liturgy (*Sacrosanctum Concilium*): Compilation of translations and first commentaries, *EphLiturg* 78 (1964), 561–72; additional lit. in 79 (1965), 465f. The subsequent volumes of *EphLiturg* contain all the instructions and relevant decrees; E. J. Lengeling, *Die Konstitution des Zweiten Vat. Konzils über die hl. Liturgie* (Münster 1964); M. Nicolaw, *Constitución Litúrgica del Vat. II* (Madrid 1964); special issue of the journal *La Maison Dieu* 77 (1964); H. Volk, *Theologische Grundlagen der Liturgie* (Mainz 1964); *Miscellanea liturgica in onore di S. Em. il Card. Giacomo Lercara, Arcivescovo di Bologna, Presidente del Consilium per l'applicazione della Costituzione sulla S. Liturgia,* 2 vols. (Rome, Paris, Tournai and New York 1966–67); J. Pascher, "Das Wesen der tätigen Teilnahme," II, 11–26 in G. Garrone, *Le rôle de la Constitutio de S. Liturgia sur l'évolution du Concile et d'orientation de la pastorale. La Liturgie: Concile et Après Concile,* ed. by the abbey of Solesmes (Tournai 1968).

Dogmatic Constitution on the Church (*Lumen Gentium*): General: *Constitutionis Dogmaticae "Lumen gentium" Synopsis historica,* ed. by G. Alberigo and F. Magistretti (Bologna 1975); J. Ratzinger, *Konstitution über die Kirche* (Münster 1965); G. Philips, *L'Église et son mystère au IIe Concile du Vatican. Histoire, texte et commentaire de la Constitution Lumen gentium,* 2 vols. (Tournai and Paris 1967–68); *De Ecclesia. Beiträge zur Konstitution über die Kirche des II. Vat. Konzils,* ed. by G. Barauna, 2 vols. (Freiburg 1966); C. Butler, *The Theology of Vat. II* (London 1967); P. Parente, *Saggio di una Ecclesiologia alla luce del Vat. II* (Rome 1968); H. Holstein, *Hiérarchie et Peuple de Dieu d'apres Lumen gentium* (Paris 1970); W. Aymans, "Die Communio ecclesiarum als Gestaltgesetz der einen Kirche," *AKR* 139 (1970), 69–90; A. Acerbi, *Due ecclesiologie. Ecclesiologia giuridica ed ecclesiologia di communione nella "Lumen gentium"* (Bologna 1975); H. Schauf, "Zur Textgeschichte grundlegender Aussagen aus 'Lumen gentium' über das

Bischofskollegium," *AKR* 64 (1972), 5–147; K. Rahner and J. Ratzinger, *Episkopat und Primat* (Freiburg 1961); U. Betti, *La dottrina sull'Episcopato nel cap. III della Costituzione dommatica Lumen gentium* (Rome 1968); W. Bertrams, *Papst und Bischofskollegium als Träger der kirchlichen Hirtengewalt* (Munich 1965); W. Aymans, *AKR* 135 (1966), 136–47. —Miscellaneous: J. Neumann, "Weihe und Amt in der Lehre von der Kirchenverfassung des Zweiten Vat. Konzils," *AKR* 135 (1966), 3–18; G. Rambaldi, "Note sul sacerdozio e sul sacramento dell'Ordine nella Costituzione Lumen gentium," *Gregorianum* 47 (1966), 517–41; P. J. Cordes, *Sendung zum Dienst. Exegetisch-historische u. systematische Studien zum Konzildekret "Vom Dienst und Leben der Priester"* (Frankfurt 1972); J. Ratzinger, *Die kirchliche Lehre vom Sacramentum ordinis: Pluralisme et Oecumenisme en Recherches théologiques* (Paris 1976), 155–66. No. 5 (1976) of *La Scuola Catholica* is devoted to ordinations; P. Bläser, "Die Kirche u. die Kirchen," *Catholica* 18 (1964), 89–107; W. Kasper, "Der ekklesiologische Charakter der nichtkatholischen Kirchen," *ThQ* 145 (1965), 42–62; E. Lamirande, "La signification ecclésiologique des communités dissidentes et la doctrine des 'Vestigia ecclesiae," *Istina* 10 (1964), 25–58; R. Laurentin, *La Vierge au Concile* (Paris 1965).

Dogmatic Constitution on Divine Revelation (*Dei Verbum*): J. R. Geiselmann, *Die Hl. Schrift u. die Tradition* (Freiburg 1962), in opposition, H. Lennertz, *Gregorianum* 40 (1959), 38–53; Y. Congar, *La Tradition et les traditions,* 2 vols. (Paris 1960–63); K. Rahner and J. Ratzinger, *Offenbarung und Überlieferung* (Freiburg 1965); E. Stakemeier, *Die Konzilskonstitution über die göttliche Offenbarung. Werden, Inhalt und theologische Bedeutung* (Paderborn 1966); O. Semmelroth and M. Zerwick, *Vaticanum II über das Wort Gottes* (Stuttgart 1966); J. Beumer, *Die kath. Inspirationslehre zwischen Vaticanum I u. II* (Stuttgart 1966); N. Lohfink, *Katholische Bibelwissenschaft u. historisch-kritische Methode* (Kevelaer 1966); A. Vögtle, *Die Kirche u. das Wort Gottes* (Würzburg 1967); H. de Lubac, *L'Écriture dans la tradition* (Paris 1966); A. Bea, *Das Wort Gottes u. die Menschheit. Die Lehre des Konzils über die Offenbarung* (Stuttgart 1968); H. Waldenfels, *Offenbarung. Das II. Vat. Konzil auf dem Hintergrund der neueren Theologie* (Munich 1969).

Pastoral Constitution on the Church (*Gaudium et Spes*): Commentaries on the individual chaps. in Vorgrimler, *Commentary on the Documents of Vatican II* I, 105–305; R. Tucci, "Introduzione storico-dottrinale alla Costituzione pastorale 'Gaudium et spes,'" *La Chiesa e il mondo contemporaneo nel Vaticano II* (Turin 1966), 17–134; *L'Église dans le monde de ce temps* (Paris 1967) (=*Unam sanctam* 65) with contributions by K. Rahner, H. de Reidmatten, M.-D. Chenu, E. Schillebeeckx et al.; J. Oelinger, *Christliche Weltverantwortung. Die Kirche in der Welt von heute* (Cologne 1968); Commentaries on the Pastoral Constitution of the Second Vatican Council in this series as Vol. 8: A. Langner, *Die politische Gemeinschaft* (Cologne 1968); as Vol. 10: H. de Riedmatten, *Die Völkergemeinschaft* (Cologne 1969).

NEWS COVERAGE: Press and Radio: W. Kampe, *Das Konzil im Spiegel der Presse* (Würzburg 1963), deals only with the first session; E. L. Hestow, *The Press and Vatican II* (Notre Dame and London 1967). Many continuing press and radio reports were issued collectively: those for the *Frankfurter Allgemeine Zeitung* by J. Schmitz van Vorst in four booklets, one for each session; L. Waltermann, *Konzil als Prozeß. Berichte im Westdeutschen Rundfunk über das II. Vatikanum* (Cologne 1966); H. Helbling, *Das Zweite Vatikanische Konzil. Ein Bericht* (Basel 1966); A. Wenger (*La Croix*), *Vatican II,* 4 booklets (Paris 1963–68); R. Laurentin (*Le Figaro*), *L'enjeu du Concile,* 3 vols. (Paris 1963–65), in: *Bilan du Concile* (Paris 1966); H. Fesquet (*Le Monde*), *Le Journal du Concile* (Le Jas 1966); G. Caprile (*Civiltà Cattolica*), *Il concilio Vat. II Cronache edite da "Civiltà Cattolica,"* 5 vols. (Rome 1965–69), R. La Valle, *Coraggio del Concilio,* 3 booklets (Brescia 1964–66); B. Kloppenburg, *Concilio Vat. II,* 5 vols. (Petropolis 1962–66); J. L. Martin Descalzo, *Un periodista en el Concilio,* 4 vols. (Madrid 1963–66); X. Rynne (pseudonym), *From Vatican City. Vat. Council II, Background and Debates,* 4 vols. (London 1963–65); id., *La révolution des Jean XXIII* (Paris 1963); J. Ratzinger, *Vaticanum II. Ergebnisse und Probleme,* 4 booklets (Cologne 1963–66); Y. Congar, *Vatican II Le Concile au jour le jour,* 4 booklets (Paris 1963–66).

PROTESTANT OBSERVERS: O. Cullman and L. Vischer, *Zwischen zwei Konzilssessionen. Rückblick und Ausschau zweier protestantischer Beobachter* (Zurich 1963); J. C. Hampe, *Ende der Gegenreformation* (Stuttgart and Mainz 1964); M. Lackmann, *Mit evangelischen Augen. Beobachtungen eines Lutheraners auf dem II. Vat. Konzil* (Graz 1963–66); *Dialog unterwegs. Eine evangelische Bestandsaufnahme zum Konzil,* ed. by G. A. Lindseck (Göttingen 1965); *Was bedeutet das Zweite Vatikanische Konzil für uns,* ed. by W. Schaetz (Basel 1966); G. Richard Molard, *Un pasteur au Concile* (Paris 1964); D. Horton, *Vatican Diary 1963. A Protestant Observes the Second Session of Vat. Council II* (Philadelphia and Boston 1964); R. M. Brown, *Observer in Rome. A Protestant Report on the Vatican Council* (Garden City, New York 1964).

EVALUATION AND RETROSPECT: J. Höffner, *Selbstverständnis und Perspektiven des Zweiten Vaticanischen Konzils* (Cologne and Opladen 1965); E. H. Schillebeeckx, *Die Signatur des II. Vaticanums. Rückblick nach drei Sitzungsperioden* (Vienna, Freiburg and Basel 1965); M. Plate, *Weltereignis Konzil. Darstellung—Sinn—Ergebnis* (Freiburg 1966); O. Karrer, *Das Zweite Vatikanische Konzil. Reflexionen zu seiner geschichtlichen und geistlichen Wirklichkeit* (Munich 1966); D. A. Seeber, *Das Zweite Vaticanum. Konzil des Übergangs* (Freiburg 1966); K. Rahner, O. Cullman and H. Fries, *Sind die Erwartungen erfüllt? Überlegungen nach dem Konzil* (Munich 1966); M. v. Galli, *Das Konzil und seine Folgen* (Lucerne and Frankfurt 1967). M. Serafian (pseudonym), *La difficile scelta. Il Concilio e la Chiesa fra Giovanni XXIII e Paolo VI* (Milan 1964); P. Felici, *Il lungo camino del Concilio* (Milan 1967); G. Palazzini, *Il Concilio Ecumenico Vat. II. Tra cronaca e storia* (Rome 1966); L. M. Carli, *La Chiesa a Concilio* (Milan 1964); C. Reymondin and L. Richard, *Vatican II au Travail. Méthodes conciliaires et documents* (Tours 1965); G. Garrone, *Le Concile. Orientations* (Paris 1966); J. Leclercq, *Vatican II—un Concile pastorale* (Brussels 1966); R. Prévost, *Pierre ou le Chaos* (Paris 1965); M. Nicolau, *Laicado y Santidad ecclesial, Colegialidad y Libertad religiosa. Nuevos problemos del Concilio Vat.* (Madrid 1964); J. Elizalde, *Concilio, categoría y anecdota,* 2 vols. (Zaragoza 1965–66); *El Concilio visto por los peritos españoles* (Madrid 1965); G. Bull, *Vatican Politics at the Second Vatican Council 1962/65* (London 1966); L. M. Redmond, *The Council Reconsidered* (Dublin 1966); G. McCoin, *What Happened at Rome? The Council and Its Implications for the Modern World* (New York 1966); R. Wiltgen, *The Rhine Flows into the Tiber. The Unknown Council* (New York 1967); J. Moorman, *Vatican Observed. An Anglican Impression of Vat. II* (London 1967); *The Second Vat. Council, Studies by Eight Anglican Observers,* ed. by G. C. Pauley (London 1967); L. Vischer, *Überlegungen nach dem Vat. Konzil* (Zurich 1966); H. Schlink, *Nach dem Konzil* (Munich and Hamburg 1966); H. Helbling, *Die evangelischen Christen u. das Konzil* (Würzburg 1967); *Wir sind gefragt. Antworten evangelischer Konzilsbeobachter,* ed. by J. W. Kantzenbach and V. Vajta (Göttingen 1966).

5. The Code of Canon Law and the Development of Canon Law to 1974
SOURCES AND LITERATURE

FOR CIC: *Acta Apostolicae Sedis 1917–1974;* N. Hilling, "Die gesetzgeberische Tätigkeit Benedikts XV. bis zur Promulgation des Codex iuris canonici," *AfkKR* 98 (1918), 223–

39, 398–406, 561–74; J. Noval, *Codificationis juris canonici recensio historico-apologetica* (Rome 1918); N. Hilling, "Zur Promulgation des Codex iuris canonici," *AfkKR* 98 (1918), 71–86; A. Scharnagl, *Das neue kirchliche Gesetzbuch* (Munich and Regensburg 1918); U. Stutz, *Der Geist des CIC* (Stuttgart 1918); A. Ortscheid, *Essai concernant la nature de la codification et son influence sur la science juridique, d'après le concept du Code de Droit Canonique* (Paris 1922); P. Gasparri and I. Serédi, *Codicis Iuris Canonici Fontes,* 9 vols. (Rome 1923–39); M. Falco, *Introduzione allo studio del, "Codex iuris canonici,"* (Turin 1925); Y. de la Brière, "La carrière du Cardinal Gasparri. Codification canonique et pactes concordataires," *Études CCII* (1930), 595–606; K. Mörsdorf, *Die Rechtssprache des CIC* (Paderborn 1937); P. Gasparri, "Storia della Codificazione del diritto canonico per la Chiesa latina," *Acta Congressus Juridici Internationalis* IV (Rome 1937), 1–10; F. Cimetier, *Pour étudier le Code de Droit Canonique. Introduction générale. Bibliographie. Réponses et décisions. Documents complémentairs. 1917–1938* (Paris 1938); D. Staffa, "Imperfezioni e lacune del primo libro del Codice di diritto canonico," *Miscellanea in memoriam Card. Gasparri* (Rome 1960), 45–73; K. Mörsdorf, "Der CIC und die nichtkatholischen Christen," *AfkKR* 130 (1961), 31–58; H. Schmitz, *Die Gesetzessystematik des CIC Liber I-III,* 18 vols. (Munich 1963); S. Kuttner, "The Code of Canon Law in Historical Perspective," *The Jurist* 28 (1968), 129–48.

ON THE DEVELOPMENT FROM 1918 TO 1962: N. Hilling, ed., *CIC Supplementum,* 2 vols. (Freiburg i. Brsg. 1925–31); I. Bruno, *CIC Interpretationes Authenticae seu Responsa a PCI a. 1917–1935 data* (Vatican City 1935); Supplement for the years 1936–50 (Vatican City 1950); E. G. Regatillo, *Interpretatio et jurisprudentia CIC* (Santander 1949); S. Mayer, ed., *Neueste Kirchenrechts-Sammlung,* 4 vols. (Freiburg i. Brsg. 1953–62); X. Ochoa, ed. *Leges Ecclesiae post Codicem iuris canonici editae,* 4 vols. (Rome 1966–74); N. Hilling, "Die gesetzgeberische Tätigkeit Benedikts XV. seit der Promulgation des Codex iuris canonici," *AfkKR* 103 (1923), 5–36; id., "Zum zehnjährigen Jubiläum des Codex Juris Canonici," *AfkKR* 108 (1928), 385–408; id. Die Gesetzgebung des Hl. Stuhles seit der Kodifikation im Jahre 1917," *AfkKR* 112 (1932), 3–36; id., "Die Gesetzgebung des Papstes Pius XI," *AfkKR* 119 (1939), 309–51; 120 (1940), 4–32, 169–200; S. Mayer, "Bedeutung Papst Pius' XII. für das Recht, besonders das Kirchenrecht," *AfkKR* 130 (1961), 436–71.

ON THE DEVELOPMENT SINCE THE SECOND VATICAN COUNCIL: F. Romita, ed., *Normae exsequutivae Concilii Oecumenici Vaticani II* (1963–69) (Naples 1971); H. Barion, "Das Zweite Vatikanische Konzil. Kanonistischer Bericht (I), (II), (III)," *Der Staat* 3 (1964), 221–26; 4 (1965) 341–59; 5 (1966) 341–52; *Lois et institutions nouvelles de l'Eglise catholique* (Paris 1966); L. M. Ö-sy, "Quantity and Quality of Laws after Vatican II," *The Jurist* 27 (1967), 385–412; F. Romita, *Il Diritto Canonico dopo il Concilio Vaticano II* (=*Bibliotheca Monitor Ecclesiasticus* 20) (Naples 1970); W. Bertrams, "Die Bedeutung des Vatikanischen Konzils für das Kirchenrecht," *ÖAfKR* 23 (1972), 125–62; U. Mosiek, "Die neueste Rechtsprechung der S. R. Rota," *ÖAfKR* 24 (1973), 160–99.

ON THE REFORM OF CANON LAW: K. Mörsdorf, "Grundfragen einer Reform des kanonischen Rechtes," *MThZ* 15 (1964), 1–16; id., "Streiflichter zur Reform des kanonischen Rechts," *AfkKR* 135 (1966) 38–52; E. Veis, *Zur Reform des kanonischen Rechts. Das Gespräch vor dem Zweiten Vatikanischen Konzil.* (diss., Freiburg i. Brsg. 1966); R. Bidagor, "La revisión del Código de Derecho Canónico—sus problemas," *Gregorianum* 49 (1968), 253–64; P. Feleci, "Il Concilio Vaticano II e la nuova codificazione," *Apollinaris* 42 (1969), 7–19; O. Giacchi, "Innovazione e tradizione nella Chiesa dopo il Concilio," *Ephemerides Iuris Canonici* 26 (1970), 9–24; F. Romita, "Quo iure vivimus post Vaticanum II': dal Codice Piano-Benedettino al futuro Codice Conciliare," *Monitor Ecclesiasticus* 95 (1970), 229–41; G. Baldanza, *L'incidenza della teologia conciliare nella riforma del diritto canonico* (=*Bibliotheca Monitor Ecclesiasticus* 26) (Naples 1970); R. G. Cunningham, "The Principles Guiding the Revision of the Code of Canon Law," *The Jurist* 30 (1970), 447–55; P. Lombardia, "Principios y técnicas del nuevo Derecho Canónico," *Ius Canonicum* 11 (1971), 22–36; R. Bidagor, "La Commission pontificale pour la révision du Code de Droit canonique," *L'Annee Canonique* 15 (1971), 97–107; J. Maldonado, "Los juristas ante el momento actual del Derecho Canónico," *Ius Canonicum* 11 (1971), 37–67; F. Finocchiaro, "La codificazione del diritto canonico e l'ora presente," *Ephemerides Iuris Canonici* 27 (1971), 251–72; W. M. Plöchl, "Um ein neues katholisches Kirchenrecht," *ÖAfKR* 23 (1972), 273–89; R. Baccari, "La Carità, sorgente della nuova legislazione canonica," *Monitor Ecclesiasticus* 97 (1972), 427–38; P. Fedele, "A proposito delle innovazioni proposte dalla Commissione per la revisione del C.I.C. in tema di consenso matrimoniale," *L'Annee Canonique* 17 (1973), 365–412; P. Felici, "De Opere Codicis Iuris Canonici Recognoscendi," *ÖAfKR* 25 (1974), 117–28; A. Scheuermann, "Das Schema 1973 für das kommende kirchliche Strafrecht," *AfkKR* 143 (1974), 3–63; K. Mörsdorf, "Zum Problem der Exkommunikation, Bemerkungen zum Schema Documenti quo disciplina sanctionum seu poenarium in Ecclesia Latina denuo ordinatur," ibid., 64–68; H. Schmitz, "Revision des kirchlichen Hochschulrechts," ibid., 69–100.

ON THE *Lex Ecclesiae Fundamentalis: Schema Legis Ecclesiae Fundamentalis. Textus emendatus cum relatione de ipso schemate deque emendationibus receptis* (Vatican City 1971); "Relatio universas contrahens generales animadversiones ad Schema Legis Ecclesiae fundamentalis ab Episcopis propositas," *Communicationes* 4 (1972), 122–68; *El Proyecto de Ley Fundamental de la Iglesia. Texto y análisis crítico. Redacción Ius Canonicum* (=*Cuadernos de la Colección Canónica* 13) (Pamplona 1971); V. Marcolino, *A propósito da Lei Fundamental da Igreja* (Braga 1971); "Lex Ecclesiae Fundamentalis. Bericht über die Arbeitsergebnisse eines Kanonistischen Symposions in München 1971," *AfkKR* 140 (1971), 407–506; *L'Année Canonique* 15 (1971), 593–95; 16 (1972) 13f.; W. Bertrams, "De praemissis et principiis Legis Fundamentalis Ecclesiae," *Periodica* 60 (1971), 511–47; G. Thils, *Une "Loi Fondamentale de l'Église"?* (Louvain 1971); W. Bertrams, "Communio, communitas et societas in Lege Fundamentalis Ecclesiae," *Periodica* 61 (1972), 553–604; R. Sobański, "La 'Loi fondamentale' de l'Église. Quelques réflexions," *NRTh* 94 (1972), 251–68; J. Beyer, "De Legis Ecclesiae Fundamentalis redactione, natura et crisi," *Periodica* 61 (1972), 525–51; J. Manzanares, "De Schemate Legis Ecclesiae Fundamentalis in Colloquio Hispano-Germanico adnotationes," *Periodica* 61 (1972), 647–62; L. Michelini di San Martino, *Lo Schema Legis Ecclesiae Fundamentalis e gli Ordinamenti Laici,* (=*Bibliotheca Monitor Ecclesiasticus* 37) (Naples 1972); B. Gangoiti, "Possibilità, convenienza e contenuto di una legge fondamentale nella Chiesa," *Angelicum* 49 (1972), 315–47; L. Vela Sánchez, "Christifidelium officia et iura fundamentalia descripta in Legis Fundamentalis Schematis textu emendato," *Periodica* 61 (1972), 605–23.

6. *The Holy See's Policy of Concordats from 1918 to 1974*

SOURCES

Acta Apostolica Sedis 1908–74; A. Mercati, *Raccolta di Concordati su materie ecclesiastiche tra la Santa Sede e le autorità civili,* 2 vols. (Rome 1919–54); Z. Giacometti, *Quellen zur*

Geschichte der Trennung von Staat und Kirche (Tübingen 1926); A. Giannini, *I concordati postbellici,* 2 vols. (Milan 1929–36); J. M. Restrepo, *Concordats conclus durant le Pontificat de Sa Sainteté le Pape Pie XI traduits en Latin et en Français* (Rome 1934); M. Nasalli-Rocca de Corneliano, *Concordatorum Pii XI P.M. Concordantiae* (Rome 1940); *Patti Lateranensi, Convenzioni e Accordi successivi fra il Vaticano e l'Italia fino al 31 dicembre 1945* (Vatican City 1972); *Convenzioni ed accordi fra il Vaticano e l'Italia* II: *Dal 1° Gennaio 1946 al 31 Dicembre 1954* (Vatican City 1955); A. J. Peaslee, *Constitutions of Nations,* 3d ed., 4 vols., ed. by D. Peaslee Xydis (The Hague 1965–70); A. Perugini, *Concordata vigentia* (Rome 1950); H. Liermann, ed., *Kirchen und Staat,* 2 vols. (Munich 1954–55); W. Weber, *Die deutschen Konkordate und Kirchenverträge der Gegenwart. Textausgabe mit den amtlichen Begründungen sowie mit Ergänzungsbestimmungen, vergleichenden Übersichten, Schrifttumshinweisen und einem Sachverzeichnis,* 2 vols. (Göttingen 1962–71); J. Wenner, *Reichskonkordat und Länderkonkordate* (Paderborn 1964); L. Schöppe, *Konkordate seit 1800. Originaltext und deutsche Übersetzung der geltenden Konkordate* (Frankfurt am Main and Berlin 1964); L. Schöppe, *Neue Konkordate und konkordatäre Vereinbarungen, Abschlüsse in den Jahren 1964–1969. Nachtrag zu "Konkordate seit 1800"* (Hamburg 1970); E. R. Huber and W. Huber, eds., *Staat und Kirche im 19. und 20. Jahrhundert. Dokumente zur Geschichte des deutschen Staatskirchenrechts* I: *Staat und Kirche vom Ausgang des alten Reiches bis zum Vorabend der bürgerlichen Revolution* (Berlin 1973); A. Läpple, *Der Religionsunterricht 1945–1975. Dokumentation eines Weges* (Aschaffenburg 1975).

LITERATURE

F. von Lama, *Papst und Kurie in ihrer Politik nach dem Weltkrieg* (Illertissen, Bavaria 1925); E. R. Huber, *Verträge zwischen Staat und Kirche im Deutschen Reich* (Breslau 1930); G. J. Ebers, *Staat und Kirche im neuen Deutschland* (Munich 1930); N. Hilling, "Die Konkordatsfrage," *AfkKR* 110 (1930), 121–35; E. Schneider, *Die Umschreibung der Bistümer in den Nachkriegskonkordaten* (Paderborn 1930); U. Stutz, "Konkordat und Codex," *Sitzungsberichte der Preußischen Akademie der Wissenschaften, Phil.-hist. Klasse* XXXII (Berlin 1930), 688–706; A. M. Koeniger, *Die neuen deutschen Konkordate und Kirchenverträge mit der preußischen Zirkumskriptionsbulle* (Bonn and Cologne 1932); A. Bertola, "Attività concordataria e codificazione del diritto della chiesa," *Archivio Giuridico "Filippo Serafini"* 111 (1934), 137–77; G. Goetz, *Die schulrechtlichen Bestimmungen der neueren und neuesten europäischen Konkordate in ihrer Beziehung zur jeweiligen staatlichen Schulgesetzgebung* (diss., Lam, Bavaria 1936); L. Salvatorelli, *La politica della Santa Sede dopo la guerra* (Milan 1937); Y. de la Brière, "Le droit concordataire dans la Nouvelle Europe," *Recueil des Cours* 63 (1938), 367–468; H. Barion, "Die kirchliche Betreuung völkischer Minderheiten," *Jahrbuch der Akademie für deutsches Recht* 5 (1938), 25–36; id., "Konkordat und Codex," *Festschrift Ulrich Stutz* (= *Kirchenrechtliche Abhandlungen* 117 and 118) (Stuttgart 1938), 371–88; M. Bendiscioli, *La politica della Santa Sede. Direttive—organi—realizzazione. 1918–1938* (Florence 1939); W. Weber, *Die politische Klausel in den Konkordaten* (Hamburg 1939); H. Barion, "Über doppelsprachige Konkordate. Eine konkordatstechnische Studie," *Deutsche Rechtswissenschaft* 5 (1940), 226–49; L. Link, *Die Besetzung der kirchlichen Ämter in den Konkordaten Papst Pius' XI.* (= *Kanonistische Studien und Texte* 18/19) (diss., Bonn 1942); J. H. Kaiser, *Die Politische Klausel der Konkordate* (Berlin and Munich 1949); J. Salomon, "La politique concordataire des États depuis la fin de la deuxième guerre mondiale," *Revue générale de droit international public* 59 (1955), 578–623; H. H. Schrey, *Die Generation der Entscheidung. Staat und Kirche in Europa und im europäischen Rußland bis 1953* (Munich 1955); R. Metz, "Le choix des évêques dans les récents concordats (1918–1954),"

L'Année Canonique 3 (1956), 75–98; H. Schmieden, *Recht und Staat in den Verlautbarungen der katholischen Kirche* (Bonn 1961); H. Maier, "Kirche und Staat seit 1945. Ihr Verhältnis in den wichtigsten europäischen Ländern," *Geschichte in Wissenschaft und Unterricht* 14 (1963), 558–90, 694–716, 741–73; G. Catalano, *Problematica giuridica dei concordati* (Milan 1963); A. Albrecht, *Koordination von Staat und Kirche in der Demokratie* (Freiburg i. Brsg. 1965); *Das Verhältnis von Kirche und Staat. Erwägungen zur Vielfalt der geschichtlichen Entwicklung und gegenwärtigen Situation* (= *Studien und Berichte der Katholischen Academie in Bayern* Heft 30) (Würzburg 1965); A. Hollerbach, *Verträge zwischen Staat und Kirche in der Bundesrepublik Deutschland* (Frankfurt 1965); J. Lucien-Brun, "Une nouvelle étape dans le droit concordataire," *Annuaire français de droit international* 11 (1965/66), 113–21; R. Metz, "L'intervention du pouvoir civil dans la nomination des évêques, des vicaires apostoliques et des vicaires aux armées, d'après les conventions signées au cours des années 1955 à 1965," *Revue de droit canonique* 16 (1966), 219–50; C. M. Corral Salvador, "Libertad de la Iglesia y intervención de los Estados en los nombramientos episcopales," *Revista Española de Derecho Canónico* 21 (1966), 63–92; K. Rahner, H. Maier, U. Mann, M. Schmaus, *Religionsfreiheit. Ein Problem für Staat und Kirche* (Munich 1966); K. Obermayer, "Die Konkordate und Kirchenverträge im 19. und 20. Jahrhundert," W. P. Fuchs, ed., *Staat und Kirche im Wandel der Jahrhunderte* (Stuttgart 1966), 166–83; P. Zepp, "Die Religionsfreiheit in den Konkordaten," H. Lentze and I. Gampl, eds., *Speculum iuris et ecclesiarum. Festschrift für Willibald M. Plöchl* (Vienna 1967), 417–25; O. Dibelius, *Überstaatliche Verbindungen der Kirchen und Religionsfreiheit* (diss., Bonn 1967); H. Reis, "Konkordat und Kirchenvertrag in der Staatsverfassung," *Jahrbuch des öffentlichen Rechts der Gegenwart*, n.s. 17 (1968), 165–394; G. Lajolo, *I concordati moderni. La natura giuridica internazionale dei concordati alla luce di recente prassi diplomatica. Successione di Stati—Clausola "rebus sic stantibus"* (Brescia 1968); A. Hollerbach, "Die neuere Entwicklung des Konkordatsrechts," *Jahrbuch des öffentlichen Rechts der Gegenwart*, n.s. 17 (1968), 117–63; A. W. Ziegler, *Religion, Kirche und Staat in Geschichte und Gegenwart*, 3 vols. (Munich 1969–74); A. De La Hera, "Confesionalidad del Estado y libertad religiosa," *Ius Canonicum* 12 (1972), 86–104; R. Moya, "El concordato en las actuales relaciones entre la Iglesia y el Estado," *Angelicum* 49 (1972), 348–66; C. Corral, "De relatione inter Ecclesiam et Statum in Schemate Legis Ecclesiae Fundamentalis," *Periodica* 61 (1972), 625–45; P. Leisching, *Kirche und Staat in den Rechtsordnungen Europas. Ein Überblick* (Freiburg i. Brsg. 1973); J. Sartorius, *Staat und Kirchen im francophonen Schwarzafrika und auf Madagaskar. Die religionsgeschichtliche Entwicklung vom Beginn der Kolonialzeit bis heute* (Munich 1973).

The Diversity of the Inner Life of the Universal Church

7. *Society and State as a Problem for the Church*

SOURCES

E. Marmy, ed.; *Mensch und Gemeinschaft in christlicher Schau. Dokumente* (from Gregory XVI, 1832, to Pius XII, 1944) (Fribourg 1945) A. F. Utz, O.P., and J. F. Groner, O.P., eds.; *Aufbau und Entfaltung des gesellschaftlichen Lebens. Soziale Summe Pius' XII.*, 3 vols. (Fribourg 1954–61), Vols. 1 and 2 1963; *Discorsi e Radiomessaggi di Sua Santità Pio VII.*, 20 vols. (Vatican City 1941–59); John XXIII, *Scritti e discorsi* (Siena 1959 ff.); A. F. Utz, O.P., ed., *La Doctrine Sociale de l'Église à travers les Siècles*, 4 vols. (Paris 1970); H. Schnatz, ed., *Päpstliche Verlautbarungen zu Staat und Gesellschaft. Originaldokumente mit deutscher Übersetzung* (Darmstadt 1973); I. Giordani, ed., *Pensiero sociale della Chiesa oggi. Documenti di Giovanni XXIII, di Paolo VI e del Concilio Vaticano II* (Rome 1974).

LITERATURE

TRANSLATIONS AND COMMENTARIES OF ECCLESIASTICAL DOCUMENTS: G. Gundlach, S.J., *Die sozialen Rundschreiben Leos XIII. und Pius' XI. Text und deutsche Übersetzung samt systematischen Inhaltsübersichten und einheitlichem Sachregister* (Paderborn 1931); O. v. Nell-Breuning, S.J., *Die soziale Enzyklika. Erläuterungen zum Weltrundschreiben Papst Pius' XI. Über die gesellschaftliche Ordnung* (Cologne 1932, reprinted 1958/63); G. Gundlach, S.J., *Die Kirche zur heutigen Wirtschafts- und Gesellschaftsnot. Erläuterungen des Rundschreibens Papst Pius' XI. "Quadragesimo anno"* (Berlin 1949); P. Jostock, *Die sozialen Rundschreiben: Leo XIII., Über die Arbeiterfrage. Pius XI., Über die gesellschaftliche Ordnung* (Freiburg, Basel and Vienna 1963); E. Welty, OP *Die Sozialenzyklika Papst Johannes' XXIII. "Mater et Magistra." Mit ausführlichem Kommentar sowie einer Einführung in die Soziallehre der Päpste* (Freiburg i. Brsg. 1965); J. Hünermann, *Die soziale Gerechtigkeit. Erläuterungen zum Sozialrundschreiben Johannes' XXIII. "Mater et Magistra"* (Essen 1962); O. V. Nell-Breuning, S.J., *"Mater et Magistra,"* StdZ 169 (1961/62), 116–28; J. Bless, *Mater et Magistra und praktische Wirtschafts- und Sozialpolitik. Erläuterungen und Erwägungen zur Sozialbotschaft Johannes' XXIII.* (Lucerne and Stuttgart 1965); A. F. Utz, O.P., *Die Friedensenzyklika Papst Johannes' XXIII. "Pacem in terris." Mit einer Einführung in die Lehre der Päpste über die Grundlagen der Politik und einem Kommentar* (Freiburg i. Brsg. 1965); J. Hünermann, *Kommentar zur Friedensenzyklika "Pacem in terris"* (Essen 1963); A. F. Utz, O.P., "Der politische Realismus Johannes' XXIII. in der Enzyklika *Pacem in terris*," *Die neue Ordnung* 19 (1965), 241–49.

GENERAL AND INTRODUCTORY ACCOUNTS OF SOCIAL DOCTRINE: W. Schwer, *Katholische Gesellschaftslehre* (Paderborn 1928); J. B. Schuster, *Die Soziallehre der Kirche nach Leo XIII. und Pius XII.* (Freiburg 1935); O. v. Nell-Breuning, SJ, *Zur christlichen Gesellschaftslehre. Beiträge zu einem Wörterbuch der Politik* 1 (Freiburg i. Brsg. 1947); id., *Wirtschaft und Gesellschaft heute*, 3 vols. (Freiburg i. Brsg. 1955 ff.); E. Muhler, *Die Soziallehre der Päpste* (Munich 1958); N. Monzel, *Solidarität und Selbstverantwortung.*

BIBLIOGRAPHY

Beiträge zur christlichen Soziallehre (Munich 1959); F. Klüber, *Grundlagen der katholischen Gesellschaftslehre* (Osnabrück 1960); E. Welty, O.P., *Herders Sozialkatechismus. Ein Werkbuch der katholischen Sozialethik in Frage und Antwort* 1 (Freiburg i. Brsg. 1963); 2 (1965); 3 (1962); G. Gundlach, S.J., *Die Ordnung der menschlichen Gesellschaft*, 2 vols. (Cologne 1964); W. Weber, "Kirchliche Soziallehre," E. Neuhäusler and E. Gossman, eds., *Was ist Theologie?* (Munich 1966), 244–65; J. Höffner, *Christliche Gesellschaftslehre* (Kevalaer 1975); N. Monzel, *Katholische Soziallehre*, 2 vols. (Cologne 1965–67); J. Messner, *Das Naturrecht* (Innsbruck, Vienna and Munich 1966); J. Höffner, *Gesellschaftspolitik aus christlicher Verantwortung*, ed. by W. Schreiber and W. Dreier (Münster 1966); *Jahrbuch des Instituts für Christliche Sozialwissenschaften der Westf. Wilhelms-Universität Münster*, ed. by J. Höffner (Münster 1960 ff.) (since 1968: *Jahrbuch für Christliche Sozialwissenschaften*, ed. by W. Weber [Münster 1968 ff.]); *Civitas. Jahrbuch für christliche Gesellschaftsordnung*, ed. by Heinrich-Pesch-Haus (Mannheim 1962 ff.).

NATURAL LAW AND REVELATION: M. Manser, O.P., *Das Naturrecht in thomistischer Beleuchtung* (Fribourg 1944); H. Rommen, *Die ewige Wiederkehr des Naturrechts* (Munich 1947); J. Fuchs, *Lex Naturae. Zur Theologie des Naturrechts* (Düsseldorf 1955); R. Henning, *Der Maßstab des Rechts im Rechtsdenken der Gegenwart* (Münster 1961); E. Haag, *Die Entwicklung der neueren katholischen Naturrechtslehre* (Zurich 1962); F. Böckle, ed., *Das Naturrecht im Disput* (Düsseldorf 1966); K. Peschke, *Naturrecht in der Kontroverse. Kritik evangelischer Theologie an der katholischen Lehre von Naturrecht und natürlicher Sittlichkeit* (Salzburg 1967); H. D. Schelauske, *Naturrechtsdiskussion in Deutschland. Ein Überblick über zwei Jahrzehnte: 1945–1965* (Cologne 1968); J. David, *Das Naturrecht in Krise und Läuterung. Eine kritische Neubesinnung* (Cologne 1969); J. Gründel, "Naturrecht," *Sacramentum Mundi* III (1969), 707–19; Herr, *Zur Frage nach dem Naturrecht im deutschen Protestantismus der Gegenwart* ed. by W. Weber and A. Rauscher (Paderborn 1972); F. Böckle and E. W. Böckenforde, eds., *Naturrecht in der Kritik* (Mainz 1973).

SOCIAL PRINCIPLES: G. Gundlach, S.J., "Solidarismus, Einzelmensch, Gemeinschaft," *Gregorianum* 17 (1936), 265 ff.; O. v. Nell-Breuning, S.J., *Einzelmensch und Gesellschaft* (Heidelberg 1950); id. "Solidarismus," *Wörterbuch der Politik* 5/2 (Freiburg i. Brsg. 1951), 357–76; A. P. Verpaalen, *Der Begriff des Gemeinwohls bei Thomas von Aquin. Ein Beitrag zum Problem des Personalismus, Sammlung Politeia* IV (Heidelberg 1954); A. F. Utz, O.P., "Der Personalismus," *Die neue Ordnung* 8 (1954), 270 ff.; id. *Formen und Grenzen des Subsidiaritätsprinzips* (Heidelberg 1965); A. Rauscher, S.J., *Subsidiaritätsprinzip und Berufsständische Ordnung in "Quadragesimo anno"* (Münster 1958); G. Wildmann, *Personalismus, Solidarismus und Gesellschaft. Der ethische und ontologische Grundcharakter der Gesellschaftslehre der Kirche* (Vienna 1961); J. Höffner, A. Verdross, and F. Vito eds., *Naturordnung in Gesellschaft, Staat, Wirtschaft. Festschrift für J. Messner* (Vienna 1961); J. Messner, *Das Gemeinwohl. Idee, Wirklichkeit, Aufgaben* (Osnabrück 1962); G. Gundlach, S.J., "Solidaritätsprinzip," *Staatslexikon* 7 (1962), 119–22; id., *Die Ordnung der menschlichen Gesellschaft*, 2 vols. (Cologne 1964); J. Schwarte, *Gustav Gundlach S.J. (1892–1963). Maßgeblicher Repräsentant der katholischen Soziallehre während der Pontifikate Pius' XI. und Pius XII.* (Paderborn 1975).

STATE, AUTHORITY, AND DEMOCRACY: H. Rommen, *Der Staat in der katholischen Gedankenwelt* (Paderborn 1935); O. v. Nell-Breuning, S.J., *Zur christlichen Staatslehre, Beiträge zu einem Wörterbuch der Politik* 2 (Freiburg i. Brsg. 1947); H. Schmieden, *Recht und Staat in den Verlautbarungen der katholischen Kirche* (Bonn 1961); F. M. Schmölz, "Kirche und Demokratie," *Die neue Ordnung* 6 (1963), 401–15; W. A. Purdy, *Die Politik der katholischen Kirche* (Gütersloh 1967); A. Langner, *Die politische Gemeinschaft*

(Cologne 1968); H. Maier, *Der Christ in der Demokratie* (Augsburg 1968); A. Gnägi, *Katholische Kirche und Demokratie* (Zurich, Einsiedeln and Cologne 1970); *Demokratie—Kirche—Politische Ethik* (*Jahrbuch für Christliche Sozialwissenschaften* 10) (Münster 1971); H. Maier, *Kirche und Gesellschaft* (Munich 1973); M. Krämer, *Kirche contra Demokratie? Gesellschaftliche Probleme im gegenwärtigen Katholizismus. Mit einem Geleitwort v. W. Dirks* (Munich 1973); "Aufgaben der Kirche in Staat und Gesellschaft. Arbeitspapier der Sachkommission V der Gemeinsamen Synode der Bistümer in der Bundesrepublik Deutschland," *Synode. Amtliche Mitteilungen der Gemeinsamen Synode der Bistümer in der Bundesrepublik Deutschland* 1 (1973), 45–64.

THE CHURCH AND CONTEMPORARY SOCIAL ERRORS: (a) Socialism—Communism: G. Gundlach, S.J., "Sozialismus," *Staatslexikon* 4 (1931), 1688–95; E. Welty, O.P., "Christlicher Sozialismus," *Die neue Ordnung* 1 (1946/47), 39ff,; G. Gundlach, S.J., "Das Heilige Offizium und der Kommunismus," *StdZ* 144(1948/49), 451ff.; J. Höffner, "Sozialismus und Christentum," *TThZ* 57 (1948), 358ff. (literature); O. v. Nell-Breuning, S.J., "Sozialismus," *Wörterbuch der Politik* 5/2 (1951), 377–430; H. Falk, *Kirche und Kommunismus. Der dialektische Materialismus und seine Verurteilung.* (Düsseldorf 1956); K. Forster, ed., *Christentum und demokratischer Sozialismus* (Munich 1958); *Der Katholik und die SPD,* ed. by the SPD (Bonn 1959); G. E. Kafka, *Der freiheitliche Sozialismus in Deutschland. Das Godesberger Programm der SPD in katholischer Sicht* (Paderborn 1960); *Katholik und Godesberger Programm. Zur Situation nach Mater et Magistra,* ed. by the SPD (Bonn 1962); G. Stavenhagen and J. Höffner, "Sozialismus," *Staatslexikon* 7 (1962), 303–24; M. Stöhr, ed., *Disputation zwischen Christen und Marxisten* (Munich 1966); O. v. Nell-Breuning, S.J., "Sozialismus," *Sacramentum Mundi* IV (1969), 613–19; M. Spieker, *Neomarxismus und Christentum. Zur Problematik des Dialogs* (Paderborn 1974); F. Klüber, *Katholische Soziallehre und demokratischer Sozialismus* (Bonn and Bad Godesberg 1974).

(b) Fascism—National Socialism: E. v. Beckerath, *Wesen und Werden des faschistischen Staates* (Berlin 1927); A. Mirgeler, "Der Faschismus in der Geschichte des modernen Staates. Die Selbstdeutung Mussolinis und seiner Mitarbeiter," *Saeculum* 6 (1955), 84ff.; id., "Faschismus," *Staatslexikon* 3 (1959), 223–31; H. Buchheim, *Totalitäre Herrschaft* (Munich 1962); W. Schieder, "Faschismus," *SDG* 2 (Freiburg 1968), 438–77; E. Nolte, *Die faschistischen Bewegungen,* ed. by M. Broszat and H. Heiler, Vol. 3 (1973); G. Schulz, *Faschismus—Nationalsozialismus. Versionen und theoretische Kontroversen 1922–1972* (Frankfurt 1974); W. Wippermann, *Faschismustheorien. Zum Stand der gegenwärtigen Diskussion* (Darmstadt 1975); D. Albrecht, "Zum Begriff des Totalitarismus," *GWU* 26 (1975), 135–41; H. A. Turner, Jr., ed., *Reappraisals of Fascism* (New York 1975); R. de Felice, *Intervista sul fascismo* (Bari 1975); K. D. Bracher, *Zeitgeschichtliche Kontroversen. Um Faschismus, Totalitarismus, Demokratie* (Munich 1976); H. U. Thamer and W. Wippermann, *Faschistische und neofaschistische Bewegungen. Probleme empirischer Faschismusforschung* (Darmstadt 1977); K. Buchheim, et. al., "Nationalsozialismus," *Staatslexikon* 5 (1960), 905–23; B. Stasiewski, *Akten deutscher Bischöfe über die Lage der Kirche 1933–1945* 1: *1933–1934* (Mainz 1968); 2: *1934–35* (Mainz 1976); 3: *1935–36* (Mainz 1978); K. Gotto, "Katholische Kirche und Nationalsozialismus," *Staatslexikon* 10 (1970); H. Mommsen, "Nationalsozialismus," *SDG* 4 (1971); H. Boberach, *Berichte des SD und der Gestapo über Kirchen und Kirchenvolk in Deutschland 1934–44* (Mainz 1971); K. D. Erdmann, "Nationalsozialismus—Faschismus—Totalitarismus," *GWU* 27 (1976), 457–69; D. Albrecht, ed., *Katholische Kirche im Dritten Reich* (Mainz 1976).

THE FAMILY OF MAN: "WORLD STATE": J. Sonder, *Die Idee der Völkergemeinschaft und die philosophischen Grundlagen des Völkerrechts* (Frankfurt 1955); P. Heintz, ed., *Soziologie der Entwicklungsländer* (Cologne 1962); H. Krauss, S.J., *Die Entwicklungsenzyklika Papst Pauls VI. "Populorum progressio"* (Freiburg i. Brsg. 1967); J. Schmauch, *Herrschen oder Helfen? Kritische Überlegungen zur Entwicklungshilfe* (Freiburg i. Brsg. 1967); E. O. Czempiel, "Die Christen und die Auswärtige Politik. Lehre vom gerechten Krieg oder Praxeologie des Friedens?" *Civitas* 6 (1967), 20ff.; J. Bopp, *Populorum progressio—Aufbruch der Kirche?* (Stuttgart 1968); *Römische Bischofssynode 1971: Gerechtigkeit in der Welt*, ed. by the German Bishops' Conference; *Der priesterliche Dienst—Gerechtigkeit in der Welt* ed. by K. Hemmerle und W. Weber (Trier 1972) 71ff.; A. Weidert, *Elemente einer theologischen Konflikt- und Friedenstheorie. Traditionskritische, biblische und hermeneutische Überlegungen zum Problem des Friedens* (diss., Münster in Westphalia 1973).

8. Main Lines of the Development of Theology between the First World War and the Second Vatican Council

BIBLIOGRAPHY

The works listed below have of necessity been limited to the general line of development. For dates and specific developments see: A. Kolping, *Katholische Theologie gestern und heute. Thematik und Entfaltung deutscher Katholischer Theologie, vom I.Vaticanum bis zur Gegenwart* (Bremen 1964); H. Vorgrimler and R. Vander Gucht eds., *Bilanz der Theologie im 20.Jh.* I–IV (Freiburg, Basel and Vienna 1969–70). For the period immediately before and after the Second Vatican Council see among others: G. Thils, *Orientations de la théologie* (Louvain 1958); A. H. Maltha, *Die neue Theologie* (Munich 1960); E. O. Brien, *Theology in Transition* (New York 1965); E. Menard, *Kirche gestern und morgen* (Frankfurt 1968); M. Schoof, *Der Durchbruch der neuen katholischen Theologie. Ursprünge—Wege—Strukturen* (Vienna, Freiburg and Basel 1969); Y. Congar, *Theology in Service of God's People* (New York 1972); G. A. Gutierrez, *A Theology of Liberation* (New York 1973).

9. Movements within the Church and their Spirituality

LITERATURE

LITURGICAL MOVEMENT: O. Rousseau, *Histoire du mouvement liturgique* (Paris 1945); A. Mayer-Pfannholz, "Das Kirchenbild des 19. Jahrhunderts und seine Ablösung," *Die Besinnung* 3 (1948), 124–44; A. L. Mayer, "Die Stellung der Liturgie von der Zeit der Romantik bis zur Jahrhundertwende," *ALW* III/1 (1953), 1–77; id., "Die geistesgeschichtliche Situation der liturgischen Erneuerung in der Gegenwart," *ALW* IV/1 (1955), 1–51; E. Iserloh, "Die Geschichte der Liturgischen Bewegung," *Hirschberg* 12 (1959), 113–22; B. Fischer, "Das 'Mechelner Ereignis' vom 23.9.1909," *LJ* 9 (1959), 203–19; J. Wagner, *LThK* VI (1961), 1097–1100; F. Kolbe, *Die Liturgische Bewegung* (Aschaffenburg 1964); L. Bouyer, *Don Lambert Beauduin. Un homme d'Église* (Tournai 1964); F. Henrich, *Die Bünde katholischer Jugendbewegung. Ihre Bedeutung für die liturgische und eucharistische Erneuerung* (Munich 1968); T. Maas-Ewerd, *Die Krise der liturgischen Bewegung in Deutschland* (Regensburg 1977).

BIBLIOGRAPHY

CATHOLIC ACTION: E. Schlund, *Die Katholische Aktion, Materialien und Akten* (Munich 1928); F. Magri, *L'Azione Cattolica in Italia,* 2 vols. (Milan 1953); K. Rahner, "Über das Laienapostolat," *Schriften zur Theologie* II (Einsiedeln 1955), 339–73; Y. Congar, *Der Laie* (Stuttgart 1957); L. Tromp, *De laicorum apostolatus fundamento, indole, formis* (Rome 1957); F. Klostermann, *Das christliche Apostolat* (Innsbruck 1962); id., "Katholische Aktion," *Sacramentum Mundi* II, 1070–78.

EUCHARISTIC PIETY: J. A. Jungmann, "Eucharistiefeier und Frömmigkeit," *LJ* 5 (1955), 96–104; id., "Corpus mysticum. Gedanken zum kommenden Eucharistischen Weltkongreß," *StdZ* 164 (1958/59), 401–9; F. Hofmann, "Eucharistie und Frömmigkeit," *LJ* 5 (1955), 105–19; H. Fischer, *Eucharistiekatechese und Liturgische Erneuerung. Rückblick und Wegweisung* (Düsseldorf 1959); *Statio Orbis. Eucharistischer Weltkongreß 1960 in München,* 2 vols. (Munich 1960) J. Ratzinger, "Der Eucharistische Weltkongreß im Spiegel der Kritik," *Statio Orbis* I, 227–42; R. Aubert, "Die Eucharistischen Kongresse von Leo XIII. bis Johannes XXIII.," *Concilium* 1 (1965), 61–66.

DEVOTION TO THE SACRED HEART: A. Hamon, *Histoire de la dévotion au Sacré Cœur,* 5 vols. (Paris 1923–39); H. Rahner, "Grundzüge einer Geschichte der Herz-Jesu-Verehrung," *ZAM* 15 (1943), 61–83; R. Graber, *Das Herz des Erlösers* (Innsbruck 1949); J. Stierli et al., eds., *Cor Salvatoris. Wege zur Herz-Verehrung* (Freiburg 1954); A. Bea and H. Rahner et al., eds., *Cor Jesu,* 2 vols. (Rome 1959); R. Graber, *Die Herz-Jesu-Verehrung in der Krise der Gegenwart* (Eichstätt 1962).

MARIAN DEVOTION: H. M. Köster, *Die Magd des Herrn. Theologische Versuche und Überlegungen* (Limburg 1947); P. Sträter, ed., *Katholische Marienkunde* I–III (Paderborn 1947–51); K. Rahner, "Probleme heutiger Mariologie," *Aus der Theologie der Zeit* (Regensburg 1948); O. Semmelroth, *Urbild der Kirche. Organischer Aufbau des Mariengeheimnisses* (Würzburg 1950); R. Graber, ed., *Die marianischen Weltrundschreiben der Päpste in den letzten hundert Jahren* (Würzburg 1951); O. Semmelroth, *Maria oder Christus?* (Frankfurt 1954); C. Feckes, ed., *Die heilsgeschichtliche Stellvertretung der Menschheit durch Maria* (Paderborn 1954); M. de S. Pierre, *Bernadette. Die wahre Geschichte von Lourdes* (Freiburg 1954); H. Peichl, ed., *Maria im Lichte der Glaubenswissenschaft* (Munich 1955); J. Goubert and L. Cristiani, *Marienerscheinungen* (Recklinghausen 1955); K. Rahner, *Maria. Mutter des Herrn* (Freiburg 1956); P. Sträter, *Maria im Reiche Christi* (Paderborn 1958); A. Müller, "Fragen und Aussichten der heutigen Mariologie," *Fragen der Theologie heute* (Einsiedeln 1958), 301–17; *Mariologische Studien,* ed. by the Deutsche Arbeitsgemeinschaft für Mariologie, I–III, 1962–64; R. Rusch, "Mariologische Wertungen," *ZKTh* 85 (1963), 129–61; H. Graef, *Maria. Eine Geschichte der Lehre und Verehrung* (Freiburg, Basel and Vienna 1964); R. Laurentin, *Die marianische Frage* (Freiburg 1965); W. Beinert, *Heute von Maria reden?* (Freiburg 1973); id., ed., *Maria heute ehren. Eine theologisch-pastorale Handreichung* (Freiburg 1977). M. Schmaus, *Kath. Dogmatik* V (Munich 1961).

SECULAR INSTITUTES: H. U. v. Balthasar, *Der Laie und der Ordensstand* (Freiburg 1949); J. Zürcher, *Päpstliche Dokumente zur Ordensreform* (Einsiedeln 1954); R. Voillaume, *Mitten in der Welt. Das Leben der Kleinen Brüder von Pater de Foucauld* (Freiburg 1956); J. Beyer, ed., *De institutis saecularibus. Documenta* (Rome 1962); J. Kerkhofs, "Aspects sociologiques du sacerdoce," *NRTh* 82 (1960), 289–99; H. A. Timmermann, *Die Weltgemeinschaften im deutschen Sprachraum* (Einsiedeln 1963); J. Beyer, *Als Laie Gott geweiht* (Einsiedeln 1964); A. Wienand, ed., *Das Wirken der Orden und Klöster in Deutschland,* 2 vols. (Cologne 1964); *"Opus Dei"—Für und Wider* (Osnabrück 1967); W. Menges, *Die Ordensmänner in der Bundesrepublik Deutschland* (Cologne 1969); R. Hostie,

Vie et mort des ordres religieux (Paris 1972); A. Menningen, *Christ in welthafter Existenz. Die theol. Grundlagen der Säkularinstitute Schönstatts* (Vallendar 1968).

WORKER-PRIESTS: H. Perrin, *Tagebuch eines Arbeiterpriesters, Journal d'un prêtre ouvrier en Allemagne* (Paris 1945); A. Dansette, *Destin du catholicisme français, 1926–1956* (Paris 1957); A. Collonge, *Le scandale du XXᵉ siècle et le drâme des prêtres ouvriers* (Paris 1957); M. R. (Jacques) Loew, *Journal d'une mission ouvrière 1941–1959* (Paris 1959); G. Siefer, *Die Mission der Arbeiterpriester* (1960); *Les prêtres ouvriers* (Paris 1954).

10. Developments in the Clergy since 1914

SOURCES

Sacerdotis imago. Päpstliche Dokumente über das Priestertum von Pius X. bis Johannes XXIII., ed. by A. Rohrbasser (Fribourg 1962); "Decretum de Institutione Sacerdotali 'Optatam totius' = Dekret über die Ausbildung der Priester," *Das Zweite Vatikanische Konzil. Konstitutionen, Dekrete und Erklärungen* 2 (Freiburg, Basel and Vienna 1967), 309–55; "Decretum de Presbyterorum Ministerio 'Presbyterorum Ordinis' = Dekret über Dienst und Leben der Priester," ibid. 3 (1968), 127–239; "Litterae Encyclicae 'Sacerdotalis Caelibatus' d.d. 24. 6. 1967," *AAS* 59 (1967), 657–97; "Documenta Synodi Episcoporum: De Sacerdotio Ministeriali," *AAS* 63 (1971), 898–922; "Sacra Congregatio pro Institutione Catholica: Ratio Fundamentalis Institutionis Sacerdotalis," *AAS* 62 (1970), 321–84; *Schreiben der deutschen Bischöfe über das priesterliche Amt. Eine biblisch-dogmatische Handreichung* (Trier 1969); "Die pastoralen Dienste in der Gemeinde," *Gemeinsame Synode der Bistümer in der Bundesrepublik Deutschland. Beschlüsse der Vollversammlung* 1 (Freiburg 1976), 581–636; The proceedings: *Protokoll der 5. Vollversammlung, 22–26. Mai 1974*, 136–85; *Protokoll der 7. Vollversammlung, 7.–11. Mai 1975*, 131–51.

LITERATURE

For the role of the priest in the Youth Movement see Youth Movement: A. Klönne, "Eine Literatur-Übersicht zur Geschichte der Jugendbewegung," *Recht der Jugend* 2 (Berlin 1954), 254f.; O. Köhler, *LThK* 5 (1960), 1181f.—On the Worker-Priests in France: H. Perrin, *Journal d'un prêtre ouvrier en Allemagne* (Paris 1945); G. Siefer, *Die Mission der Arbeiterpriester* (Essen 1960); R. Ludmann, *LThK* 1 (1957), 811ff.

For a Discussion of the Role of the Priest since Vatican II: F. Klostermann, *Priester für morgen* (Innsbruck 1970); N. Glatzel, "Die Rolle des Priesters in der Leistungsgesellschaft," *Jahrbuch für christliche Sozialwissenschaften* 12 (1971), 163–83; id., "Soziologische Aspekte der Seelsorgerrolle," *StdZ* 187 (1971), 31–42; H. Küng, *Wozu Priester? Eine Hilfe* (Zurich, Einsiedeln and Cologne 1971); J. Höffner, *Der Priester in der permissiven Gesellschaft* (Cologne 1971): H. Volk, "Priestertum heute," *Internat. Kath. Zeitschrift* 1 (1972), 498–517, 2 (1973), 45–58; H. Schlier, "Grundelemente des priesterlichen Amtes im Neuen Testament," *Theologie und Philosophie* 44 (1969), 161–80; O. Semmelroth, S.J., "Die Präsenz der drei Ämter Christi im gemeinsamen und besonderen Priestertum der Kirche," ibid., 181–95; J. Pieper, "Was unterscheidet den Priester?" *Hochland* 63 (1971), 1–16; *Reform und Anerkennung kirchlicher Ämter. Ein Memorandum der Arbeitsgemeinschaft ökumenischer Universitätsinstitute* (Munich and Mainz 1973); K. H. Schuh, ed., *Amt im Widerstreit* (Berlin 1973); G. Siefer,

Sterben die Priester aus? Soziologische Überlegungen zum Funktionswandel eines Berufs-standes (Essen 1973); F. Luthe, *Berufswechsel der Priester. Eine empirische Studie* (Düsseldorf 1970).

For a Discussion of Priestly Celibacy: E. Schillebeeckx, O.P., *Der Amtszölibat. Eine Kritische Besinnung* (Düsseldorf 1967); K. Rahner, S.J., "Der Zölibat des Weltpriesters im heutigen Gespräch," *Geist und Leben* 40 (1967), 122–38; F. Böckle, ed., *Der Zölibat. Erfahrungen, Meinungen, Vorschläge* (Mainz 1968); K. Kraemer and K. H. Schuh, eds., *Zölibat in der Diskussion. Katholische und evangelische Aspekte* (Essen 1969); J. Coppens, ed., *Sacerdoce et Célibat. Études historiques et théologiques* (Louvain 1971).—On Priest Organizations and Conferences: A. Schilling, ed., *SOG-Papiere. Mitteilungsblatt der Arbeitsgemeinschaft von Priestergruppen in der Bundesrepublik Deutschland und der SOG-Österreich,* (Bochum 1968–73); *Imprimatur. Nachrichten und kritische Meinungen aus der (Trierer) katholischen Kirche* (Trier 1968–75); C. Holenstein, ed., *Churer Dokumente. Bischofs-Symposion 7. bis 10. Juli 1969. Texte der Bischöfe und Priester im Wortlaut* (Zurich 1969); M. Raske, K. Schäfer, and N. Wetzel, eds., *Eine freie Kirche für eine freie Welt. Delegiertenkonferenz europäischer Priestergruppen Rom 10. bis 16. Oktober 1969. Eine Dokumentation* (Düsseldorf 1969); C. Holenstein, *Der Protest der Priester* (Zurich, Einsiedeln and Cologne 1970); K. Schäfer, "Zum Thema Priestergruppen," *StdZ* 185 (1970), 34–46; id., "Nochmals: Zum Thema Priestergruppen," ibid. 185 (1970), 361–78; K. Rahner, S.J., "Chancen der Priestergruppen," ibid. 185 (1970), 172–80; H. Werners, "Priestergruppen—Konzeption und Erfahrung," *Jahrbuch für christliche Sozialwissenschaften* 12 (1971), 185–204.

On Surveys of Priests: O. Schreuder, ed., *Der alarmierende Trend. Ergebnisse einer Umfrage beim gesamten holländischen Klerus* (Munich and Mainz 1970); G. Schmidtchen, *Priester in Deutschland. Forschungsbericht über die im Auftrag der Deutschen Bischofskonferenz durchgeführte Umfrage unter allen Welt- und Ordenspriestern in der Bundesrepublik Deutschland. In Verbindung mit dem Institut für Demoskopie Allensbach* (Freiburg, Basel and Vienna 1973); K. Forster, ed., *Priester zwischen Anpassung und Unterscheidung. Auswertung und Dommentare zu der im Auftrag der Deutschen Bischofskonferenz durchgeführten Umfrage unter allen Welt- und Ordenspriestern in der Bundesrepublik Deutschland* (Freiburg, Basel, and Vienna 1974), esp: O. Simmel, S.J., "Vergleich der deutschen Umfrageergebnisse mit den Ergebnissen der Priesterbefragungen in Österreich, in der Schweiz, in Spanien, in den USA und in Italien," pp. 127–248; P. M. Zulehner and S. R. Graupe, *Wie Priester heute leben. . . . , Ergebnisse der Wiener Priesterbefragung* (Vienna, Freiburg and Basel 1970); P. M. Zulehner, ed., *Kirche und Priester zwischen dem Auftrag Jesu und den Erwartungen der Menschen. Ergebnisse der Umfragen des Instituts für kirchliche Sozialforschung Wien über "Religion und Kirche in Österreich" und "Priester in Österreich"* (Vienna, Freiburg and Basel 1974); A. Müller, *Priester—Randfigur der Gesellschaft? Befund und Deutung der Schweizer Priesterumfrage* (Zurich, Einsiedeln and Cologne 1974).

ON THE REFORM OF PRIESTLY EDUCATION AND THEOLOGICAL STUDIES: L. Waltermann, ed., *Klerus zwischen Wisenschaft und Seelsorge. Zur Reform der Priesterausbildung. Beiträge im Westdeutschen Rundfunk* (Essen 1966); *SKT = Studium Katholische Theologie. Berichte—Analysen—Vorschläge,* ed. by the Kommission "Curricula in Theologie" des Westdeutschen Fakultätentages and E. Feifel, booklets 1–5, (Zurich, Einsiedeln and Cologne 1973–75); A. Arens, "Einleitung und Kommentar zur Ratio Fundamentalis," A. Arens and H. Schmitz, eds., *Priesterausbildung und Theologiestudium* (Trier 1974), 5–67; G. Schmidtchen, *Umfrage unter Priesteramtskandidaten. Studien-und Lebenssituation, Amtsverständnis, Berufsmotive, Einstellung zu Kirche und Gesellschaft. Forschungsbericht des Instituts für Demoskopie Allensbach über eine im Auf-*

trag der Deutschen Bischofskonferenz durchgeführte Erhebung (Freiburg, Basel and Vienna 1975).

11. *Religious Communities and Secular Institutes*

LITERATURE

On papal and episcopal laws concerning the orders, see *Dizionario degli Instituti di Perfezione* (DIP), ed. by G. Pelliccia and G. Rocca, of which three volumes (covering A to Conv.) have appeared (Vol. I, 1974; II, 1975; III, 1976); K. S. Frank, *Grundzüge der Geschichte des christlichen Mönchtums* (Darmstadt 1975), 175-95.

12. *Educational System, Education, and Instruction*

BIBLIOGRAPHY

K. Erlinghagen, *Grundlagen katholischer Erziehung. Die prinzipiellen Erziehungslehren der Enzyklika Pius' XI. "Divini Illius Magistri"* (Freiburg 1963); O. Betz, "Erziehung," H. Fries, ed., *Handbuch theologischer Grundbegriffe* 1 (Munich 1962) 319ff.; A. v. Campenhausen, *Erziehungsauftrag und staatliche Schulträgerschaft* (Göttingen 1967), 115ff.; N.A. Luyten, O.P. *Forschung und Bildung. Aufgaben einer katholischen Universität* (Fribourg 1965).

CATHOLIC EDUCATION IN VARIOUS COUNTRIES: Germany: F. Paulsen, *Geschichte des gelehrten Unterrichts,* 2 vols. (Berlin and Leipzig 1921); E. Weniger, "Bildungswesen," *Die Religion in Geschichte und Gegenwart* 1 (Tübingen 1957), 1281 ff.; F. Pöggeler, ed., *Handbuch der Erwachsenenbildung* 4 (Stuttgart 1975); L. Froese, ed., *Deutsche Schulgesetzgebung (1796–1952)* (Weinheim, n.d.).

Other European States: W. Schultze, ed., *Schulen in Europa,* 3 vols. (Weinheim and Berlin 1968); O. Anweiler, *Geschichte der Schule und Pädagogik in Rußland vom Ende des Zarenreiches bis zum Beginn der Stalin-Ära* (Heidelberg 1964).

General Sources: See *New Catholic Encyclopedia* under education and various universities; F. Laack, *Die amerikanische Bildungswirklichkeit, Idee, Stand und Probleme der Adult Education in den USA* (Cologne 1976); Thomas J. La Belle, ed., *Education and Development: Latin America and the Caribbean* (Los Angeles 1972); William O. Smith, *Education in Great Britain* (New York 1967); Robert Ulich, *Education in Western Culture* (New York 1965); I. Illich, *Education and the Rise of the Corporate State* (New York 1973); Frank P. Graves, *History of Education in Modern Times* (New York 1915); Adolph E. Meyer, *The Development of Education in the Twentieth Century* (New York 1939); G. A. N. Lowndes, *The Silent Social Revolution* (New York 1937); A. Prost, *L'Enseignement en France, 1800–1967* (Paris 1968); Howard C. Barnard, *Short History of English Education* (Great Britain 1947); Raymond Williams, *Culture and Society, 1780–1950* (New York 1958).

Mission Lands: A. Mulders, *Missionsgeschichte. Die Ausbreitung des Glaubens* (Regensburg 1960); S. Delacroix, *Histoire Universelle Des Missions Catholiques* 4 (Paris 1959).

Statistical Aids: UNESCO, *World Survey of Education,* 5 vols. (Paris 1955–71); UNESCO, *Statistical Yearbook* (Paris 1963) (1952–62: *Basic Facts and Figures, International Statistics Relating to Education, Culture and Mass Communication); Bilan du Monde;* CIEO, *The Situation of Catholic Education in the Various Continents* (Brussels 1969).

13. *Information and the Mass Media*

SOURCES

"Inter mirifica, Dekret des Zweiten Vatikanischen Konzils über die Instrumente der sozialen Kommunikation (vom 4. 12. 1963)," *LThK—Das Zweite Vatikanische Konzil* I (Freiburg i. Brsg.), 116–35; *Communio et Progressio. Pastoralinstruktion über die Instrumente der sozialen Kommunikation vom 23. 5. 1971, Nachkonziliare Dokumentation* 11 (Trier 1971); Radio Vaticana, ed., *Documenti Pontifici sulla Radio e sulla Televisione 1929–1962* (Rome and Vatican City 1962); *Documenti Pontifici sulla stampa* (1878–1963) (Rome and Vatican City); *Documenti Pontifici sul Teatro* (341–1966) (Rome and Vatican City 1966).—Bibliographical References to Papal Attitudes toward Publications in Recent History: (1.) Pius XII: W. Hamerski, "Reden Papst Pius' XII. zu Fragen der Publizistik," *Publizistik* 8 (1963), 611–31. (2.) John XXIII: G. Deussen, "Publizistisch relevante Äußerungen Papst Johannes' XXIII. im chronologischen Überblick," *Communicatio Socialis, CS* 6 (1973), 294–96. (3.) Paul VI.: "Die publizistisch relevanten Äußerungen Papst Pauls VI. im chronologischen Überblick," G. Deussen, *Ethik der Massenkommunikation bei Papst Paul VI.* (Paderborn 1973), 328–37.

LITERATURE

International: R. Aguiló, ed., *Catholic Media World Directory* (Rome 1971); Istituto Cattolico per la Stampa, ed., *La Stampa Cattolica nel Mondo* (Milan 1939); K. Richter, ed., *Katholische Presse in Europa* (Osnabrück 1969), "L'opinion publique dan l'Eglise (9e Congrès mondial de l'Union Catholique Internationale de la Presse), Actes du congrès, 1ere–3e partie," *Journalistes Catholiques,* nos. 58–61, July–December 1971 (Paris); G. Ernst and B. Marschall, eds., *Film und Rundfunk. Zweiter internationaler Katholischer Filmkongreß, Erster Internationaler Katholischer Rundfunkkongreß, Gesamtbericht* (Munich 1929); C. Ford, *Le Cinéma au service de la foi* (Paris 1953).

Third World–Missions (Bibliography): W. Herzog, *Church and Communication in Developing Countries* (Paderborn 1973); F. J. Eilers, *Christliche Publizistik in Afrika* (St. Augustin 1964); F. J. Eilers and W. Herzog, *Catholic Press Directory Africa/Asia* (Paderborn 1975); J. Schmidt, *Massenmedien als Instrumente der Mission* (diss., Heidelberg 1974).

Germany: K. Löffler, *Geschichte der katholischen Presse Deutschlands* (Mönchen-Gladbach 1924); W. Kisky, *Der Augustinus-Verein zur Pflege der Katholischen Presse von 1878 bis 1928.* (Düsseldorf 1928); J. W. Naumann, ed., *Die Presse und der Katholik* (Augsburg 1932); M. Hüsgen, *Die Bistumsblätter in Niedersachsen während der nationalsozialistischen Zeit* (Hildesheim 1975), a survey of previous research on the problem of Catholic publications in the Nazi period; M. Schmolke, *Die schlechte Presse. Katholiken und Publizistik zwischen "Katholik" und "Publik" 1821–1968* (Münster in Westphalia 1971); G. Bauer, *Kirchliche Rundfunkarbeit 1924–1939* (Frankfurt am Main 1966).

France: G. Hourdin, *La Presse Catholique* (Paris 1957); J. Godfrin and N. Godfrin, *Une Centrale de la Presse Catholique: La Maison de la Bonne Presse et ses Publications* (Paris 1965).

Netherlands: G. W. Marsman, *De Katholieke Dagbladpers in sociologisch perspectief* (Assen 1967); J. Jemels and M. Schmolke, *Katholische Publizistik in den Niederlanden* (Paderborn 1977).

Austria: K. M. Stepan, *Stückwerk im Spiegel* (Graz and Vienna 1949); F. Funder, *Vom Gestern ins Heute* (Vienna 1952).—Switzerland: F. P. Schaller, *Notstand im christlichen Pressewesen* (Einsiedeln and Zurich 1974).

United States: M. L. Reilly, *A History of The Catholic Press Association 1911–1968* (Metuchen, N.J. 1971). Martin Marty et. al., *The Religious Press in America* (New York 1963).

14. *Charity and Ecclesiastical Works of Assistance*

SOURCES

There is no basic collection of sources. In addition to numerous and often unpublished reports, the following are important: *Zeitschrift Caritas* (Freiburg 1896ff.); *The Catholic Charities Review* (Washington 1916ff.); *Caritas Internationalis. Annuarium* (Rome 1965ff.).

LITERATURE

Jahrbuch des Caritasverbandes 1–11 (Freiburg 1907–17); *Jahrbuch der Caritaswissenschaft* (Freiburg 1925–38): *Jahrbuch für Caritaswissenschaft und Caritasarbeit* (Freiburg 1957–68); *Caritas '68ff. Jahrbuch des DCV* (Freiburg 1968ff.); W. Liese, *Wohlfahrtspflege und Caritas im Deutschen Reich, in Deutsch-Österreich, der Schweiz und Luxemburg* (Mönchen-Gladbach 1914); id., *Lorenz Werthmann und der Deutsche Caritasverband* (Freiburg 1929); A. Foucault, *Histoire de la Société de S. Vincent de Paul* (Paris 1933); *An der Aufgabe gewachsen. Vom Werden und Wirken des Deutschen Caritasverbandes*, ed. by Zentralvorstand (Freiburg 1957); H. H. Havemann and W. Kraus, eds., *Handbuch der Entwicklungshilfe. Fortsetzungswerk in Loseblattform* (Baden-Baden 159ff.); H. Besters and E. E. Boesch, eds., *Entwicklungspolitik. Handbuch und Lexikon* (Stuttgart, Berlin and Mainz 1966); R. Völkl, *Dienende Kirche—Kirche der Liebe* (Freiburg 1969); E. Gatz, *Kirche und Krankenpflege im 19. Jahrhundert* (Paderborn 1971); A. Rinken, *Das Öffentliche als verfassungstheoretisches Problem—dargestellt am Rechtsstatus der Wohlfahrtsverbände* (Berlin 1971); *1897–1972. 75 Jahre Deutscher Caritasverband,* ed. by Deutscher Caritasverband Freiburg (Freiburg 1972); J. Krautscheidt and H. Marré, eds., *Essener Gespräche zum Thema Staat und Kirche* 8 (Münster 1974).

15. *History of the Ecumenical Movement*

LITERATURE

H. L. Althaus, ed., *Ökumenische Dokumente. Quellenstücke über die Einheit der Kirche* (Göttingen 1962); R. Rouse and S. C. Neill, *Geschichte der ökumenischen Bewegung 1517–1948* 1–2 (Göttingen 1957–58); E. Fey and G. Gaßmann, eds., *Geschichte der ökumenischen Bewegung 1948–1968* (Göttingen 1974); F. Biot, *Von der Polemik zum Dialog* (Vienna and Munich 1966); G. H Tavard, *Geschichte der ökumenischen Bewegung* (Mainz 1964); R. Frieling, *Die Bewegung für Glauben und Kirchenverfassung 1910–1937* (Göttingen 1970); A. Deißmann, ed., *Die Stockholmer Weltkirchenkonferenz. Amtlicher deutscher Bericht* (Berlin 1926); F. Lüpsen, ed., *Amsterdamer Dokumente* (Bethel 1948); id., ed., *Evanston—Dokumente* (Witten 1954); id., ed., *Neu Delhi—Dokumente* (Witten 1962); N. Goodall, ed., *Bericht aus Uppsala 1968* (Geneva 1968); R. Groscurth, ed., *Von Uppsala nach Nairobi—Ökumenische Bilanz 1968–1975* (Bielefeld and Frankfurt 1975); H. Krüger and W. Müller-Römheld, eds., *Bericht aus Nairobi. Offizieller Bericht der 5. Vollversammlung des ÖRK 1975* (Frankfurt 1976); A. Boyens, *Kirchenkampf und*

Ökumene 1933–1939 (Munich 1969); id., *Kirchenkampf und Ökumene 1939–1945* (Munich 1973); G. Gloede, ed., *Ökumenische Profile, Brückenbauer der Einheit der Kirche,* 2 vols. (Stuttgart 1961–63); M. Pribilla, *Von der kirchlichen Einheit* (Freiburg 1929); R. Aubert, *Le Saint-Siège et l'Union des Églises* (Brussels 1947); L. Jaeger, *Das Konzilsdekret "Über den Ökumenismus"* (Paderborn 1968); P. Bratsiotis, ed., *Die orthodoxe Kirche in griechischer Sicht* 1–2 (1959–60); S. Harkianakis, "Über die gegenwärtige Situation der orthodoxen Kirche," *Kyrios* 6 (1966), 227–39; J. Meyendorf, *Die orthodoxe Kirche gestern und heute* (Salzburg 1963); S. V. Stavridis, *Geschichte des Ökumenischen Patriarchats* (1967); N. Ehrenström and G. Gaßmann, *Confessions in Dialogue. A Survey of Bilateral Conversations Among World Confessional Families 1959–1974* (Geneva 1975); V. Pfnür, *Kirche und Amt. Neuere Literatur zur ökumenischen Diskussion um die Amtsfrage* (Münster 1975), 22–32; G. Gaßmann, M. Lienhard, H. Meyer and H. V. Herntrich, eds., *Um Amt und Herrenmahl. Dokumentation zum evangelisch römisch-katholischen Gespräch* (Frankfurt 1974).

16. *The Dissident Eastern Churches*

LITERATURE

J. Tyciak, G. Wunderle and P. Werhun, eds., *Der christliche Osten. Geist und Gestalt* (Regensburg 1939); J. Casper, "Die orientalische Christenheit," *Christus und die Religionen der Erde. Hdb. der Religionsgeschichte* III, F. König, ed. (Freiburg 1951), 643–729; W. de Vries, *Der christliche Osten in Geschichte und Gegenwart* (Würzburg 1951); R. Janin, "Les Églises orientales," C. Poulet, *Histoire du christianisme. Époque contemporaine* (Paris 1957), 489–545; J. Gründler, *Lexikon der christlichen Kirchen und Sekten unter Berücksichtigung der Missionsgesellschaften und zwischenkirchlichen Organisationen,* 2 vols. (Vienna, Freiburg and Basel 1961); D. Attwater, *The Christian Churches of the East,* 2 vols. (Milwaukee 1961–62); J. Chrysostomus, "Ostkirche," *Hbd. theologischer Grundbegriffe II,* ed. by H. Fries (Munich 1963), 256–66; B. Stasiewski, "Geschichtliche Überlegungen zur kirchlichen Trennung zwischen Orient und Okzident," *Das Christentum des Ostens und die christliche Einheit* (Würzburg 1965), 13–40; R. Goosmann, *Die Ostkirchen* (Männedorf, Switz. 1966); B. Spuler, *Gegenwartslage der Ostkirchen in ihrer nationalen und staatlichen Umwelt* (Frankfurt am Main 1968); M. Lehmann, *Leitfaden der Ostkirchen* (Vienna 1969); F. Heiler, *Die Ostkirchen* (Munich and Basel 1971); E. v. Ivánka, J. Tyciak and P. Wiertz, eds., *Hbd. der Ostkirchenkunde* (Düsseldorf 1971); J. Madey, *Die Kirchen des Ostens. Eine kleine Einführung* (Freiburg i. Ue. 1972); A. W. Ziegler, *Das Verhältnis von Kirche und Staat in Europa* II (Munich 1972); B. Spuler, "Die morgenländischen Kirchen seit 1965," *Kirche im Osten* 16 (1973), 158–74; *Oriente Cattolico. Cinni storici e statistiche* (Vatican City 1974).

THE ORTHODOX CHURCHES: A. M. Ammann, *Abriß der ostslawischen Kirchengeschichte* (Vienna 1950); G. Zananiri, *Histoire de l'Église byzantine* (Paris 1954); P. Bratsiotis, ed., *Die orthodoxe Kirche in griechischer Sicht,* 2 vols. (Stuttgart 1959–60); A. Attwater, op. cit. II, 6–160; K. Onasch, *Einführung in die Konfessionskunde der orthodoxen Kirchen* (Berlin 1962); B. Spuler, "Die Orthodoxie," *Weltgeschichte der Gegenwart* II (Berne and Munich 1963), 552–67; id., *Gegenwartslage der Ostkirchen,* 17–258; M. Lacko and P. Chrysostomus, "Geschichte und jetziger Stand der orthodoxen Kirchen," K. Algermissen, *Konfessionskunde* (Paderborn 1969), 171–202; F. Heiler, op. cit., 39–301; S. Runciman, *The Orthodox Churches and the Secular State* (Oxford 1971); P. Leisching,

BIBLIOGRAPHY

Kirche und Staat in den Rechtsordnungen Europas. Ein Überblick (Freiburg 1973); P. Meinhold "Das Orthodoxe Christentum," *Saeculum Weltgeschichte* VII (Freiburg, Basel and Vienna 1975), 296–306; N. Thon, ed., "Die orthodoxen Kirchen in Geschichte und Gegenwart," *Königsteiner Studien* (Königstein im Taunus 1975), 129–60; A. Proc, ed., *Jahrbuch der Orthodoxie. Schematismus 1976/77* (Munich 1977).

THE FOUR ANCIENT PATRIARCHATES: *Ekklesia X: Die Orthodoxe Kirche auf dem Balkan und in Vorderasien*, 46: *Die orthodoxen Patriarchate von Konstantinopel, Alexandrien, Antiochien, Jerusalem und das Erzbistum von Cypern* (Leipzig 1941); J. Hajjar, "Le Congrès général du Patriarcat orthodoxe d'Antioche," *PrOrChr* 6 (1956), 128–43; H. Engberding, "Das neue Grundgesetz des griechischen orthodoxen Patriarchats von Jerusalem," *OrChr* 43 (1959), 120–35; Mosconas, "Das griechisch-orthodoxe Patriarchat von Alexandrien," *Kyrios* n.s. 1 (1960/61), 129–39; C. Dahm, *Die Kirche im Osten. Macht und Pracht der Patriarchen* I (Offenburg 1964); F. W. Fernau, *Patriarchen am Goldenen Horn. Gegenwart und Tradition des orthodoxen Orients* (Opladen 1967); I. Doens, "L'Église orthodoxe en Afrique Orientale dans et hors le cadre du patriarcat grec orthodoxe d'Alexandrie," *Revue du Clergé africain* 24 (1969), 543–76; R. Potz, *Patriarch und Synode in Konstantinopel. Das Verfassungsrecht des ökumenischen Patriarchates* (Vienna 1971).

THE ORTHODOX CHURCH IN GEORGIA: M. Tarchnišili, "Die Entstehung und Entwicklung der kirchlichen Autokephalie Georgiens," *Kyrios* 5 (1940/41), 177–93; R. Janin, op. cit., 524–25; D. Attwater, see op. cit. II, 116–18; D. M. Lang, *A Modern History of Georgia* (London 1962); B. Spuler, *Gegenwartslage der Ostkirchen*, 224–28; R. Hotz, "Christen in Stalins Heimat. Die georgisch-orthodoxe Kirche," *Digest des Ostens* 15, no. 12 (Königstein in Taunus 1972), 35–39.

THE MEDIEVAL AND MORE RECENTLY CREATED PATRIARCHATES

THE ORTHODOX PATRIARCHATE OF BULGARIA: M. Bulgarus, "Die heutige Lage der Bulgarischen Orthodoxen Kirche," *Die christlichen Kirchen der Gegenwart* (Munich and Basel 1950), 46–52; D. Slijepčević, *Die bulgarische orthodoxe Kirche 1944–1956* (Munich 1957); S. Zankow, "Die Bulgarische Orthodoxe Kirche in Geschichte und Gegenwart," *IKZ* 48 (1958), 189–208; M. Zambonardi, *La Chiesa autocefala bulgara* (Rome 1960); P. L. Huillier, *La religion en Bulgarie* (Paris 1968); R. Stupperich, ed., *Kirche und Staat in Bulgarien und Jugoslawien. Gesetze und Verordnungen in deutscher Übersetzung* (Witten 1971), 5–15; T. P. Koev, "Patriarch Kiril zum Gedächtnis," *Kirche im Osten* 15 (1972), 11–16; W. Oschlies, "Kirche und Staat in Bulgarien," *Informationsdienst des kath. Arbeitskreises für zeitgeschichtliche Fragen* 72 (Bonn 1975), 63–69; id., "Kirche und Religion in Bulgarien," *Kirche in Not* 24 (Königstein im Taunus 1976), 110–16.

THE ORTHODOX PATRIARCHATE OF SERBIA: D. Geißler, "Die Stellung der serbischen orthodoxen Kirche im Staatskirchenrecht Jugoslawiens," *Jahrbuch des Osteuropainstitus zu Breslau 1940* (Wroclaw 1941), 203–10; T. Spaskij, "Die Lage der serbischen Kirche," *Die christlichen Kirchen der Gegenwart* (Munich and Basel 1950), 42–45; D. Slijepčević, "Die serbische Orthodoxie," *IKZ* 61 (1953), 151–76; B. Spuler, "Die serbisch-orthodoxe Kirche," *Osteuropa-Hdb. Jugoslawien*, ed. W. Markert (Cologne and Graz 1954), 185–87; F. Popan and C. Drašković, *Orthodoxie heute in Rumänien und Jugoslawien. Religiöses Leben und theologische Bewegung* (Vienna 1960); V. Pospischil, *Der Patriarch in der serbisch-orthodoxen Kirche* (Vienna 1966); R. Stupperich, *Kirche und Staat in Bulgarien und Jugoslawien*, 16–54; A. Rauch, "Kirchen- und Religionsgemeinschaften," *Südosteuropa-Hdb.* I, ed. K. D. Grothusen (Göttingen 1975), 345–59.

833

BIBLIOGRAPHY

THE MOSCOW PATRIARCHATE: *Die Russische Orthodoxe Kirche, ihre Einrichtungen, ihre Stellung, ihre Tätigkeit* (Moscow 1958); W. de Vries, *Kirche und Staat in der Sowjetunion* (Munich 1959); A. Kischkowsky, *Die sowjetische Religionspolitik und die Russische Orthodoxe Kirche* (Munich 1960); B. Stasiewski, "Sowjetische Religionspolitik," *Hochland* 52 (1960), 315-24; W. Kolarz, *Religion in the Soviet Union* (London 1961); R. Stupperich, ed., *Kirche und Staat in der Sowjetunion. Gesetze und Verordnungen* (Witten 1962); B. Stasiewski, "Die Lage der christlichen Kirchen in der Sowjetunion," H. Ludat, ed., *Sowjetunion, Werden und Gestalt einer Weltmacht* (Gießen 1963), 259-80; J. Chrysostomus, *Kirchengeschichte Rußlands der neuesten Zeit,* 3 vols. (Munich and Salzburg 1965-68); N. Struve, *Die Christen in der UdSSR* (Mainz 1965); J. Chrysostomus, *Kleine Kirchengeschichte Rußlands nach 1917* (Freiburg i. Brsg. 1968); M. Bordeaux, *Patriarch and Prophets, Persecution of the Russian Orthodox Church Today* (London 1970); W. C. Fletscher, *The Russian Orthodox Church Underground 1917-1970* (London 1971); G. Codevilla, *Stato e Chiesa nell'Unione Sovietica* (Milan 1972); C. Dahm, *Millionen in Rußland glauben an Gott* II (Jestetten 1973); D. Konstantinow, *Die Kirche in der Sowjetunion nach dem Kriege. Entfaltung und Rückschläge* (Munich and Salzburg 1973); J. Chrysostomus, "Die Problematik der heutigen russischen Kirche des Moskauer Patriarchates," *Festschrift für Bernhard Stasiewski. Beiträge zur ostdeutschen und osteuropäischen Kirchengeschichte,* by G. Adriányi and J. Gottschalk (Cologne and Vienna 1975), 203-12; O. Luchterhandt, *Der Sowjetstaat und die Russisch-Orthodoxe Kirche. Eine rechtshistorische und rechtssystematische Untersuchung* (Cologne 1976).

THE RUMANIAN PATRIARCHATE: F. Popan, "Le caractère occidental de la théologie roumaine d'aujourd'hui," *OstkSt* 8 (1959), 169-83; F. Popan and C. Drašković, op. cit.; F. Popan, "Die rumänische Orthodoxe Kirche in ihrer jüngsten Entwicklung 1944-64," *Kirche im Osten* 9 (1965), 67-82; E. C. Suttner, "Ökumenismus in der Rumänischen Orthodoxen Kirche unter Patriarch Justinian," *OrChrP* 41 (1975), 399-448; id., "50 Jahre rumänisches Patriarchat. Seine Geschichte und die Entwicklung seines Kirchenrechts," *OstkSt* 24 (1975), 136-75; 25 (1976), 105-37.

ADDITIONAL ORTHODOX CHURCHES

THE ORTHODOX CHURCH IN GREECE: T. Haramlambides, "Die Kirchenpolitik Griechenlands. Beitrag zur Kulturgeschichte Neugriechenlands von 1821-1935," *ZKG* 55 (1936), 158-92; D. Savramis, "Die griechisch-orthodoxe Kirche und die soziale Frage," *OstkSt* 7 (1958), 66-84; P. Bratsiotis, "Die Theologen-Bruderschaft 'ZOË,'" *ZRGG* 12 (1960), 371-84; P. Poulitsas, "Die Beziehungen zwischen Staat und Kirche in Griechenland," P. Bratsiotis, *Die orthodoxe Kirche* II, 38-48; K. Papapetrou, "Die Säkularisation und die Orthodox-Katholische Kirche Griechenlands," *Kyrios* n.s. 3 (1963), 193-205; H. J. Härtel, "Zur kirchenpolitischen Krise in Griechenland," *OstkSt* 15 (1966), 39-49; G. Podskalsky, "Kirche und Staat in Griechenland," *TThZ* 76 (1967), 298-322; H. M. Biedermann, "Orthodoxe Kirche und Migration im heutigen Griechenland," *OstkSt* 24 (1975), 51-68.

THE ORTHODOX CHURCH IN ALBANIA: "Götzen gegen Gott. 'Die Religion des Albaners ist der Albanismus,'" *Osteuropa* 242 (1974), A 599-A 620; B. Tönnes, "Religionen in Albanien. Enver Hoxha und die 'nationale Eigenart,'" ibid., 661-75; id., "Religion und Kirche in Albanien," *Kirche in Not* 24 (Königstein im Taunus 1976), 101-9.

THE ORTHODOX CHURCH IN MACEDONIA: D. Slijepčević, *Pitanje Makedonske pravoslavne crkve u Jugoslaviji* (Munich 1959); S. K. Pavlowitsch, "The Orthodox Church in Yugoslavia. The Problem of the Macedonian Church," *Eastern Church Review* 1 (1967/68), 374–86; N. Thon, op. cit., 141–42.

THE ORTHODOX CHURCH IN POLAND: I. Grüning, *Die autokephale östlich-orthodoxe Kirche in Polen in den Jahren 1922–1939: Jahrbuch des Osteuropainstituts zu Breslau 1940* (Breslau 1941), 111–26; B. Spuler, "Die Orthodoxe Kirche in Polen," *Osteuropa-Hdb. Polen,* ed. by W. Markert (Cologne and Graz 1959), 114–18; T. Lissek, "Die Heilige Autokephale Orthodoxe Kirche Polens," *Kyrios* n.s. 6 (1966), 43–54; N. Thon, op. cit., 142–46; B. Stasiewski, "Kirchen- und Religionsgemeinschaften," *Länderberichte Osteuropa II Polen,* ed. by the Johann-Gottfried-Herder-Institut (Munich and Vienna 1976), 256–57.

THE ORTHODOX CHURCH IN CZECHOSLOVAKIA: V. Grigorič, *Pravoslavná církev ve státé Československém* (Prague 1928); R. Urban, "Die orthodoxe Kirche des Ostens in der Čechoslovakei," *Kyrios* 3 (1938), 89–97; R. Jakowlewitsch, "Die Orthodoxe Kirche in der Tschechoslowakei," *Stimme der Orthodoxie* (Berlin 1966), 56–62; N. Thon, op. cit., 146–50.

INDEPENDENT EXTRATERRITORIAL ORTHODOX CHURCHES: W. Haugg, "Die orthodoxe Kirche des Ostens in Deutschland. Grundzüge ihres Rechts- und Glaubenslebens," *Kyrios* 4 (1939/40), 57–67; D. Doroschenko, "Die Ukrainische Östlich-Orthodoxe Kirche in Kanada und in den Vereinigten Staaten von Amerika," *Kyrios* 5 (1940/41), 153–57; W. Haugg, "Materialien zur Geschichte der östlich-orthodoxen Kirche in Deutschland," ibid., 288–334; H. M. Biedermann, "Die ostkirchlichen Gemeinschaften in USA und in Kanada," *OstkSt* 3 (1954), 164–78; P. Yuzyk, *Ukrainian Greek-Orthodox Church of Canada 1918 to 1951* (Minneapolis 1958); F. Heyer, "Geschichte der Orthodoxen Kirche in Amerika," *Kirche im Osten* 5 (1962), 9–50; A. A. Bogolepov, *Toward an American Orthodox Church. The Establishment of an Autocephalous Orthodox Church* (New York 1963); *Die Orthodoxen Exilkirchen in der Bundesrepublik Deutschland,* ed. by the Ökumenische Kommission für die Unterstützung Orthodoxer Priester in der Bundesrepublik Deutschland (Munich 1965); J. Madey, "Die Präsenz der Ostkirchen in Westeuropa," *Kyrios* n.s. 10 (1970), 171–73; G. Seide, "Die Russisch-Orthodoxe Kirche in der Bundesrepublik Deutschland," *OstkSt* 20 (1971), 159–84; J. Chrysostomus, "Die dritte Gesamtsynode der russischen Auslandskirche," *OstkSt* 24 (1975), 38–50; N. Thon, op. cit., 130–41; P. Wiertz, "Orthodoxe Kirchen in Deutschland, Anfänge und Entwicklung," *Una Sancta* 30 (1975), 86–87.

THE EASTERN PRE-CHALCEDONIAN NATIONAL CHURCHES: C. Fink, "Die getrennten Kirchen des Morgenlandes," in P. Krüger and J. Tyciak, eds., *Morganländisches Christentum. Wege zu einer ökumenischen Theologie* (Paderborn 1940), 23–48; R. Janin, op. cit. 528–37; D. Attwater, op. cit. II, 170–231; B. Spuler, *Die Morgenländischen Kirchen* (Leiden 1964); A. S. Atiya, *A History of Eastern Christianity* (London 1968); B. Spuler, *Gegenwartslage der Ostkirchen,* 259–320; W. de Vries, "Die getrennten Kirchen des Ostens," K. Algermissen, op. cit., 86–147; F. Heiler, op. cit. 303–405; B. Spuler, *Die morgenländischen Kirchen seit 1965* (1973), 163–74; J. Aßfalg and P. Krüger, eds., *Kleines Wörterbuch des Christlichen Orients* (Wiesbaden 1975).

THE NESTORIAN CHURCH: R. S. Stafford, *The Tragedy of the Assyrians* (London 1935); J. John, *The Nestorians and their Muslim Neighbors. A Study of Western Influence on Their Relations* (New Jersey 1961); H. Anschütz, "Die Gegenwartslage der 'Apostolischen Kirche des Ostens' und ihre Beziehungen zur 'assyrischen' Nationalbewegung," *OstkSt* 18 (1969), 122–45.

BIBLIOGRAPHY

THE MONOPHYSITE CHURCHES

THE WEST-SYRIAN JACOBITE CHURCH: W. de Vries, *Der Kirchenbegriff der von Rom getrennten Syrer* (Rome 1955); H. Anschütz, "Die heutige Situation der westsyrischen Christen (Jakobiten) im Tur 'Abdin im Südosten der Türkei," *OstkSt* 16 (1967), 150–99.

THE SYRIAN ORTHODOX MALABAR CHURCH: E. R. Hambye, "The Syrian Jacobites in India, A Survey of Their Past and Present Position," *ECQ* 11 (1955), 115–29; P. J. Podipara, *Die Thomas-Christen* (Würzburg 1966); N. J. Thomas, *Die Syrisch-Orthodoxe Kirche der Südindischen Thomas-Christen. Geschichte, Kirchenverfassung, Lehre* (Würzburg 1967); P. Verghese, ed., *Die Syrischen Kirchen in Indien* (Stuttgart 1974).

THE COPTIC CHURCH: R. Strothmann, *Die koptische Kirche in der Neuzeit* (Tübingen 1932, reprint Nendeln, Liechtenstein 1966); M. Cramer, *Das Christlich-Koptische Ägypten, einst und heute. Eine Orientierung* (Wiesbaden 1959); S. Chauleur, *Histoire des Coptes d'Égypte* (Paris 1960); E. Wakim, *A Lonely Minority. The Modern Story of Egypt Copts* (New York 1963); P. Verghese, ed., *Koptisches Christentum. Die orthodoxen Kirchen Ägyptens und Äthiopiens* (Stuttgart 1973), 9–129.

THE ETHIOPIAN CHURCH: J. G. Coulbeaux, *Histoire politique et religieuse d'Abyssinie depuis les temps les plus reculés jusqu'à l'avènement de Menelik*, 3 vols. (Paris 1929); E. Hammerschmidt, "Kaisertum, Volkstum und Kirche in Äthiopien," *OstkSt* 6 (1957), 35–45; id., *Äthiopien. Christliches Reich zwischen Gestern und Morgen* (Wiesbaden 1967); *The Church of Ethiopia. A Panorama of History and Spiritual Life, a Publication of the Ethiopian Orthodox Church* (Addis Ababa 1970); F. Heyer, *Die Kirche Äthiopiens. Eine Bestandsaufnahme* (Berlin and New York 1971), continued in: *Ökum. Rundschau* 26 (1977), 196–204; P. Verghese, *Koptisches Christentum*, 133–207.

THE ARMENIAN CHURCHES: M. Ormanian, *The Church of Armenia. Her History, Doctrine, Rule, Discipline, Liturgy, Literature and Existing Condition* (London 1955); J. Mécérian, *Histoire et institutions de l'Église arménienne. Évolution nationale, spiritualité, monachisme* (Beirut 1965); A. K. Sanjian, *The Armenian Communities in Syria under Ottoman Dominion* (Cambridge, Mass. 1965); M. Krikorian and J. Madey, "The Armenian Church. Extension, Hierarchy, Statistics," *OstkSt* 21 (1972), 323–25; B. Brentjes, *Drei Jahrtausende Armenian* (Vienna and Munich 1974); N. Thon, op. cit., 151–60.

SECTION THREE

The Church in the Individual Countries

17. *The Church in Northern, Eastern, and Southern Europe*

LITERATURE

GENERAL: F. LAMA: *Papst und Kurie in ihrer Politik nach dem Weltkrieg* (Illertissen 1925); J. Schmidlin, *Papstgeschichte der neuesten Zeit* 3/4 (Munich 1936–39); A.

Brunello, *La Chiesa del Silenzio* (Rome 1953); Gsovski, ed., *Church and State behind the Iron Curtain. Czechoslovakia, Hungary, Poland, Romania with an Introduction in the Soviet Union* (New York 1955); A. Galter, *Libro rosso della Chiesa perseguitata* (Mailand 1956); W. de Uries, *Kirche und Staat in der Sowjetunion* (Munich 1959); K. Hutten, *Christen hinter dem eisernen Vorhang. Die christliche Gemeinde in der kommunistischen Welt*, 2 vols. (Stuttgart 1962–63); W. Daim, *Der Vatikan und der Osten* (Frankfurt am Main 1967); M. Lehmann, ed., *Die katholischen Donauschwaben in den nachfolge-staaten 1918–1945 im Zeichen des Nationalismus* (Freilassing 1972); T. Beeson, ed., *Discretion and Valour. Religious Conditions in Russia and Eastern Europe* (Glasgow 1974); L. Schöppe, *Konkordate seit 1800. Originaltext und deutsche Übersetzung der geltenden Konkordate* (Frankfurt 1964); *Die Religionsfreiheit in Osteuropa nach Helsinki. Recht und Wirklichkeit. Erfahrungen von Katholiken. Eine Dokumentation*, ed. by the Institut Glaube in der 2. Welt (Küsnacht and Zurich 1977); *Christen unter dem Kreuz. Beiträge zur Information über die gegenwärtige Bedrohung der Kirche in zahlreichen Ländern der Welt*, ed. by the Pressestelle im Sekretariat der Deutschen Bischofskonferenz (Bonn 1976).

SCANDINAVIAN COUNTRIES: J. O. Anderssen, *Survey of the History of the Church in Denmark* (Copenhagen 1930); F. Siegmund-Schultze, ed., *Die skandinavischen Länder* (*Ekklesia. Eine Sammlung von Selbstdarstellungen der christlichen Kirchen*) 2 and 2/8 (Leipzig 1936–38); P. G. Linhardt, *Den nordiske kirken historie* (Copenhagen 1945); K. Harmer, *Bishop Josef Brems* (Copenhagen 1945); H. Holzapfel, *Unter nordischen Fahnen* (Paderborn 1955); H. Holmquist, *Handbok i Svensk kyrkohistoria*, 3 vols. (Stockholm 1948–52); A. V. Palmquist, *Die römisch-katholische Kirche in Schweden nach 1781*, 2 vols. (Uppsala 1954–58); B. Gustafsson, *Svensk kyrkohistoria* (Stockholm 1963); I. Welle, *Norges Kirkehistorie* (Oslo 1948); E. Molland, *Church Life in Norway 1800–1950* (Minneapolis 1957); H. Rieber-Mohn, *Catholicism in Norway* (London 1959); E. D. Vogt, *The Catholic Church in the North* (Bergen 1962); K. R. Brotherus, *Staat und Kirche in Finnland* (Königsberg 1931); G. Sentzke, *Die Kirche Finnlands* (Göttingen 1935); A. Inkinen, *L'Église catholique en Finland* (Bourges 1936); L. Pinomaa, ed., *Finnish Theology, Past and Present* (Helsinki 1963); G. Sentzke, *Finland. Its Church and Its People* (Helsinki 1963).

BALTIC COUNTRIES: J. Mauclère, *La situation de l'Église en Lithuanie* (Le Raincy 1950); R. Wittram, ed., *Baltische Kirchengeschichte* (Göttingen 1956); A. Namsons, "Die Lage der katholischen Kirche in Sowjetlitauen," *Acta Baltica* 1 (1962), 120–30; J. Aunver, "Estlands christliche Kirche der Gegenwart," ibid., 75–92; K. Rukis, "Die Verfolgung der katholischen Kirche in Sowjetlettland," ibid., 93–109; J. Klesment, "Sowjetische Kirchenpolitik in den besetzten baltischen Staaten," *Acta Baltica* 5 (1966), 112–26; E. Dubnaitis, "Der totale Kampf gegen Religion und Geistlichkeit in den besetzten baltischen Ländern," ibid., 127–99; "Chronik der kath. Kirche Litauens," ibid. 14 (1974), 9–123; "Chronik d. Litauischen Kirche," ibid. 15 (1975), 9–101; "Die neuesten Berichte und Dokumente über die Lage der Kirche in den baltischen Ländern," ibid. 16 (1976).

THE SOVIET UNION: A. M. Amman, *Abriß der ostslawischen Kirchengeschichte* (Vienna 1950); C. N. Cianfarra, *The Vatican and the Kremlin* (New York 1950); J. S. Curtiss, *The Russian Church and the Soviet State 1917–1950* (Boston 1953); G. Prokopts-chuk, *Der Metropolit. Leben und Wirken des großen Förderers der Kirchenunion Andreas Scheptytzkyj* (Munich 1955); M. Spinka, *The Church in Soviet Russia* (New York 1956); I. Wlasovsky, *Outline of the History of the Ukrainian Church* (New York 1956); A. Bogolepov, *Zerkov pod vlastin kommunisma* (The Church under Communist

Domination)(Munich 1958); W. de Vries, *Kirch und Staat in der Sowjetunion* (Munich 1959); B. Stasiewski, "Sowjetische Religionspolitik," *Hochland* 52 (1960), 315–24; B. Ivanov, ed., *Religion in the USSR* (Munich 1960); A. Kischkowsky, *Die sowjetische Religionspolitik und die russische orthodoxe Kirche* (Munich 1960); W. Kolarz, *Religion in the Soviet Union* (New York 1961); C. Grunwald, *The Churches and the Soviet Union* (New York 1962); N. Struve, *Les Chrétiens en URSS* (Paris 1963); B. Feron, *Gott in Sowjetrußland* (Essen 1963); B. Stasiewski, "Die Lage der christlichen Kirchen in der Sowjetunion," *Sowjetunion. Werden und Gestalt einer Weltmacht,* ed. by H. Ludat (Gießen 1963), 259–80; C. Korolevskij, *Métropolite André Szeptyckyj 1865–1944* (Rome 1964); K. G. Kindermann, *Rom ruft Moskau* (Baden-Baden 1965); W. Leonhardt, *Kreml und der Vatikan* (Hanover 1965); M. Mourin, *Der Vatikan und die Sowjetunion* (Munich 1967); W. Daim, *Der Vatikan und der Osten* (Vienna 1967); J. Madey, *Kirche zwischen Ost und West. Beiträge zur Geschichte der Ukrainischen und Weißruthenischen Kirche* (Munich 1969); N. Theodorowitsch, *Religion und Atheismus in der UdSSR. Dokumente und Berichte* (Munich 1970); A. Martin, *Die Gläubigen in Rußland. Die offizielle Kirche in Frage gestellt. Dokumentation der Christenverfolgung in der Sowjetunion* (Lucerne and Munich 1971); E. Winter, *Rom und Moskau. Ein halbes Jahrtausend in ökumenischer Sicht* (Vienna 1972); idem, *Die Sowjetunion und der Vatikan, 3. Teil: Rußland und das Papsttum* (Berlin 1972); D. Konstantinow, *Die Kirche in der Sowjetunion nach dem Kriege* (Munich and Salzburg 1973); G. Simon, "Kirchen und Religionsgemeinschaften," *Länderberichte Osteuropa I, Sowjetunion,* ed. by the Koordinationsausschuß deutscher Osteuropa-Institute (Munich 1974), 320–30; *Sowjetunion 1974/75,* ed. by the Bundesinstitut f. ostwissenschaftl. u. internationale Studien (Vienna and Munich 1975), esp. 76–81.

POLAND: W. Meysztowicz, *L'Église catholique en Pologne entre deux guerres 1919–1939* (Vatican City 1944); W. Bieńkowski, *Polityka Watykanu wobec Polski* (Warsaw 1949); E. Ligocki, *Miedzy Watikanem a Polska* (Warsaw 1949); J. Szufdrzyński, "Polozenie Kościóla w Polsce," *Kultura* 5 (1953), 5–49; S. Wielkowski and W. Czarnecki, *Kościól katolicki w Polsce Ludowej* (Warsaw 1953); K. Papée, *Pius XII. a Polska 1939–1949* (Rome 1954); W. Zylinski and B. Wierzbianski, eds., *White Paper on the Persecution of the Church in Poland* (London 1954); C. Naurois, *Dieu contre Dieu? Drames des catholiques progressistes dans une église du silence* (Fribourg and Paris 1956); J. Umiński, *Historia Kościóla* ed. by W. Urban, 2 vols. (Opole 1959–60); B. Stasiewski, "Die Kirchenpolitik der Nationalsozialisten im Warthegau 1939–1945," *Vierteljahrshefte für Zeitgeschichte* 7 (1959), 46–74; B. Stasiewski, "Die römisch-katholische Kirche," *Osteuropa-Handbuch, Polen,* ed. by W. Markert (Cologne and Graz 1959), 103–8; B. Stasiewski, "Die Kirchenpolitik der polnischen Regierung," ibid., 356–66; idem, "Die Jahrtausendfeier Polens in kirchengeschichtlicher Sicht," *Jahrbücher für Geschichte Osteuropas,* n.s. 8 (1960), 313–29; P. Lenert, *L'Église catholique en Pologne* (Paris 1962); F. Manthey, *Polnische Kirchengeschichte* (Hildesheim 1965); H. Holzapfel, *Das katholische Polen heute* (Munich 1967); J. J. Zatko, ed., *The Valley of Silence. Catholic Thought in Contemporary Poland* (Notre Dame and London 1967); B. Stasiewski, "Kirchen und Religionsgemeinschaften," *Länderberichte Osteuropa II, Polen,* ed. by the Koordinationsausschuß deutscher Osteuropa-Institute (Munich and Vienna 1976), 241–261.

CZECHOSLOVAKIA: F. Dvornik, "Évolution de l'église catholique en Tchécoslovaquie depuis la guerre," *Le Monde slave* 7 (1930), 260–75; F. Siegfried-Schultze, ed., *Die Kirchen der Tschechoslowakei* (Leipzig 1937); R. Urban, *Die slavisch-nationalkirchlichen Bestrebungen in der Tschechoslowakei* (Leipzig 1938); L. Němec, *Church and State in*

Czechoslovakia, Historically, Juridically and Theologically Documented (New York 1955);
A. Michel, *Problèmes religieux dans un pays sous régime communiste* (Paris 1955); T. J.
Zubek, *The Church of Silence in Slovakia* (Whinting, Ind. 1956); V. Chalupka,
Situation of the Catholic Church in Czechoslovakia (Chicago 1960); J. Inovecky, *Golgotha ist ganz nahe. Passion der Ordensschwestern in der Tschechoslowakei* (Fribourg 1967);
Kirche, Recht und Land. Festschrift Weihbischof Prof. Dr. Adolf Kindermann ed., K.
Reiß and H. Schütz (Königstein and Munich 1969); J. Hopfner, *Kirche in der ČSSR*
(Munich 1970); R. Urban, *Die tschechoslowakische hussitische Kirche* (Marburg 1973); J.
Mareckova, *Duchovné prudy v našej Republike 2: Prudy cirkevné* (Bratislava 1926); *Tisíc
let pražského biskupstvi 973–1973* ed. by the Ceska Kath. Caritas (Prague 1973); F.
Seibt, ed., *Bohemia Sacra. Das Christentum in Böhmen 973–1973* (Düsseldorf 1974).
In it see especially: H. Slapnicka, *Die Kirchen in der Ersten Republik*, 333–44; B.
Černy, *Die Kirchen im Protektorat 1939–1945*, 345–54; H. Lemberg, *Die Kirche in
unserem Jahrhundert 1918–1973*, 26–32; V. Svoboda, *Die innere Entwicklund des
tschechischen Katholizismus in den letzten hundert Jahren*, 162–74; *Situation der katholischen Kirche in der Tschechoslowakei. Dokumente, Berichte*, ed. by the Schweizerische
National-Kommission Justitia et Pax (Freiburg i. Ue. 1976).

HUNGARY: S. Swift, *The Cardinal's Story: Life and Works of Joseph Cardinal Mindszenty* (New York 1949); Joseph Cardinal Mindszenty, *Memoirs* (New York 1974);
Ambord, *Der Vatikan und die Kirche hinter dem Eisernen Vorhang. Dokumente und
Kommentare zum Budapester Geschehen* (Vatican City 1949); Mindszenty, *Dokumentation*, ed. by J. Vecsey and J. Schwendemann, 3 vols. (St. Pölten 1956–59); Z.
Nyisztor, *Ötven esztendö. Századunk katolikus megujhódása* (Vienna 1962); J. Vecsey,
ed., *Kardinal Mindszenty. Beiträge zu seinem siebzigsten Geburtstag* (Munich 1962); J.
Lévai, *Geheime Reichssache. Papst Pius XII hat nicht geschwiegen. Berichte, Dokumente,
Akten zusammengestellt aufgrund kirchlichen und staatlichen Archivmaterials* (Cologne
and Müngersdorf 1966); E. András and J. Morel, *Bilanz des ungarischen Katholizismus. Kirche und Gesellschaft in Dokumenten, Zahlen und Analysen* (Munich 1969); M.
Beresztóczy. *A katolikus békemozgalom husz éve* (Budapest 1970); A. Meszlényi, *A
magyar hercegprimások arcképsorozata 1707–1945* (Budapest 1970); A. Csizmadia,
Rechtliche Beziehungen von Staat und Kirche in Ungarn vor 1944 (Budapest 1971), and
the review of it by G. Adriányi, *Ungarn-Jahrbuch* 4 (1972), 208–10; J. Staber, "Die
katholische Kirche in Ungarn seit 1918," *Der Donauraum* 18 (1973), 200–219; G.
Salacz, *A magyar katolikus egyház a szomszédos államok uralma alatt* (Munich 1975); J.
Mindszenty, *Erinnerungen* (Frankfurt, Berlin and Vienna 1974); G. Adriányi, *Fünfzig
Jahre ungarischer Kirchengeschichte 1895–1945* (Mainz 1974); *Handbuch des ungarischen Katholizismus*, ed. by the Ungarische Kirchensoziologische Institut (Vienna
1975); J. Közi-Horváth, *Kardinal Mindszenty* (Königstein 1976).

RUMANIA: N. Pop, *Kirche unter Hammer und Sichel. Die Kirchenverfolgung in Rumänien 1945–1951* (Berlin 1953); A. Mircea, *Persecución comunista de la Religión en
Romania* (Madrid 1954); P. Gherman, *L'âme roumaine écartelée. Faits et documents*
(Paris 1955); E. Janin, *Istoria Bisericii Romine*, 2 vols. (Bucharest 1957–58); P.
Tocanel, *Storia della Chiesa cattolica in Romania* (Padua 1960); F. Popan, "Die heutige
Lage der rumänischen Katholiken," *Ostkirchliche Studien* 11 (1962), 183–92; R.
Grulich, "Zur Lage der Kirche in Rumänien," *Informationsdienst des Katholischen
Arbeitskreises für zeitgenössische Fragen e.V.* 76 (1976), 68–77.

YUGOSLAVIA: A. Hudal, *Die serbische-orthodoxe Nationalkirche* (Graz 1922); K. S.
Graganovic, *Le Système général de l'église en Jougoslavie* (Sarajevo 1939); H. Schwalm, J.
Matl, B. Spuler and L. Müller, "Kirchen und Glaubensgemeinschaften in Jugosla-

wien," *Osteuropa-Handbuch, Jugoslawien,* ed. by W. Markert (Cologne and Graz 1954), 173–91; W. de Vries, *Une église du silence. Catholiques de Jougoslavie* (Paris and Bruges 1954); D. M. Slijepčević, *Istoria Srbske Pravoslavne Crkve* (Munich 1962); G. Stadtmüller, "Die Kirchen und Konfessionen Jugoslawiens," *Jugoslawien zwischen West und Ost,* ed. by H. Ludat (Gießen 1963), 37–55; R. Stupperich, ed., *Kirche und Staat in Bulgarien und Jugoslawien* (Witten 1971); J. Buturac and A. Ivandija, *Povijest katolicke crkve medu Hrvatima* (Zagreb 1973); A. Rauch, "Kirchen und Religionsgemeinschaften," *Südosteuropa-Handbuch* 1: *Jusgoslawien,* ed. by K. D. Grothusen (Göttingen 1875), 345–59.

BULGARIA: D. M. Slijepčević, *Die bulgarische orthodoxe Kirche* (Munich 1957); A. Galter, *Rotbuch der verfolgten Kirche* (Recklinghausen 1957), 241–53; M. Zambonardi, *La chiesa autocefala bulgara* (Gorizia 1960); I. Sofranov, *Histoire du mouvement bulgare vers l'église catholique au XIXe siècle* (Rome 1960); R. Stupperich, ed., *Kirche und Staat in Bulgarien und Jugoslawien* (Witten 1971); C. Ognjanoff, *Bulgarien* (Nuremberg 1975), esp. 130–43, 480–82; *Cerkvi i izpovedania v Narodna Republika Bulgaria* ed. by the Sinodalno izdatelstvo (Sofia 1975).

ALBANIA: G. Petrotta, "Il cattolicesimo nei Balcani. L'Albania," *La Tradizione* 1 (1928), 165–203; N. Borgia, *I monaci basiliani d'Italia in Albania,* 2 vols. (Rome 1935–42); W. de Vries, "Die Kirche in Albanien," *StdZ* 149 (1951/52), 467; A. Galter, *Rotbuch der verfolgten Kirche* (Recklinghausen 1957), 221–53; B. Tönnes, "Religionskampf in Albanien," *Informationsdienst des katholischen Arbeitskreises für zeitgeschichtliche Fragen e.V.* 74 (1975), 73–81.

18. *The Church in German-Speaking Countries (Germany, Austria, Switzerland)*

LITERATURE

GERMANY: Bihlmeyer-Tüchle III, 498–503, 514–28; Schmidlin *PG* III, 217–28; IV, 156–67; Maron, 262–70.—To 1945: W. Spael, *Das katholische Deutschland im 20. Jahrhundert* (Würzburg 1964), 176–351. After 1945: F. Spotts, *Kirchen und Politik in Deutschland* (Stuttgart 1976).—Brief Biographies (with literature): R. Morsey, ed., *Zeitgeschichte in Lebensbildern* I (Mainz 1973) (W. Marx, L. Kaas, Cardinal Bertram); 2 (Mainz 1975)(F.v. Papen, K. Adenauer, and the cardinals Faulhaber, Preysing, and Galen).

AUSTRIA: Bihlmeyer-Tüchle III, 503–505, 522ff., 528; Schmidlin *PG* III, 284–86; IV, 125–29; Maron, 271–73; J. Wodka, *Kirche in Österreich* (Vienna 1959), 365–89; E. Weinzierl, ed., *Kirche in Österreich 1918–1965* 1 and 2 (Vienna 1966).—After 1945: E. Weinziere and K. Skalnik, eds, *Österreich-Die Zweite Republik* 1 and 2 (Vienna 1972).

SWITZERLAND: Schmidlin *PG* III, 276ff.; IV, 168ff.; Maron, 270ff.

19. *The Church in the Benelux Countries*

SOURCES

BELGIUM: *Lettres pastorales des évêques de Belgique, 1800–1961* VI: *1906–1926;* VII: *1926–1961; Actes du VIe Congres catholique de Malines,* 8 vols. (Brussels 1937);

Verhandelingen van het VIe Katholiek Kongress van Mechelen, 8 vols. (Brussels 1937); R. Houben and F. Ingham, *Le pacte scolaire et son application* (Brussels 1962); M. A. Walkkiers, *Sources inédites relatives aux débuts de la J.O.C., 1919–1925* (Louvain 1970).

NETHERLANDS: *Analecta* (of the various dioceses in which the official pronouncements, letters, and addresses of the Dutch bishops are published); *Katholiek Archief* (since 1970 *Archief van de kerken*); Reports and memoranda of the Katholiek Sociaal-Kerkeliik Instituut (KASKI); *Pastoral Concilie van de Nederlandse Kerkprovinicie*, 7 parts (Amersfoort 1968–70).

LITERATURE

BELGIUM: J. Bartier, et al., *Histoire de la Belgique contemporaine, 1914–1970* (Brussels 1974); T. Luyckx, *Politieke geschiedenis van België van 1789 tot heden* (Brussels 1973); E. de Moreau, *Le catholicisme en Belgique* (Liège 1928); J. Kerkhofs and J. Van Houtte, eds., *De Kerk in Vlaanderen. Pastoraal-sociologische studie van het leven en de structuur der Kerk* (Tielt 1962); "Structures et évolution du monde catholique en Belgique," *Courrier hebdomadaire du C.R.I.S.P* 252–254 (10 février 1967); K. Dobbelaere and J. Billiet, "Godsdienst in België. Een sociologische verkenning," *De gids op maatschappelijk gebied* 64 (1973), 879–94, 983–98 ; 65 (1974), 39–56; R. Aubert, "L'Église catholique et la vie politique en Belgique depuis la seconde guerre mondiale," *Res publica* 15 (1973), 183–203; R. Boudens, *Kardinaal Mercier en de Vlaamse Beweging* (Louvain 1975); J. Kempeneers, *Le cardinal Van Roey en son temps, 1874–1961* (Brussels 1971); W. Plavsic, *Le cardinal Van Roey* (Brussels 1974); H. Haag, *Rien ne vaut l'honneur. L'Église belge de 1940 à 1945* (Brussels 1946); R. Aubert, "Organisation et caractère des mouvements de jeunesse en Belgique," *Politica e Storia* 28 (1972), 271–323; P. Joye and R. Lewin, *L'Église et le mouvement ouvrier en Belgique* (Brussels 1967); S. H. Scholl, ed., *150 jaar katholieke arbeidersbeweging in België (1789–1939)* I: *De katholieke arbeidersbeweging (1914–1939)* (Brussels 1966); J. Verhoeven, *Joseph Cardijn, prophète de notré temps* (Brussels 1971); A. Dendooven, *Ontstaan, structuur en werking van de Vlaamse K.A.J.* (Antwerp 1967); L. Voyé, *Sociologie du geste religieux. De l'analyse de la pratique dominicale en Belgique à une interprétation théorique* (Brussels 1973); J. Pirotte, *Périodiques missionnaires belges d'expression française. Reflet de cinquante années d'évolution d'une mentalité 1889–1940* (Louvain 1973); P. Debouxhtai, *Antoine le guérisseur et l'Antoinisme* (Liège 1934); id., *L'Antoinisme* (Liège 1945).

LUXEMBURG: G. Trausch, *Un demi siècle d'histoire contemporaine luxembourgeoise, 1914/ 18–1973: Cinquantenaire de la Chambre du Travail* (Luxemburg 1973); A. Heiderscheid, *Aspect de sociologie religieuse du diocèse de Luxembourg* (Luxemburg 1961–62).

NETHERLANDS: L. J. Rogier, *In vrijheid herboren* (The Hague 1953); L. J. Rogier and P. Brachin, *Histoire du catholicisme hollandaise depuis le XVIe siècle* (Paris 1974); S. Stokman, *Het verzet van de Nederlandse bisschoppen tegen nationaal-socialisme en Duitse tyrannie* (Utrecht 1945); H. W. F. Aukes, *Kardinaal de Jong* (Utrecht and Antwerp 1956); J. G. M. Thurlings, *De wankele zuil. Nederlandse katholieken tussen assimilatie en pluralisme* (Nijmegen and Amersfoort 1971); M. Schmaus, J. Scheffczyk and J. Giers, *Exempel Holland* (Berlin 1972); W. Goddijn, *De beheerste kerk. Uitgestelde revolutie in R.K. Nederland* (Amsterdam and Brussels 1973); J. Roes, *Het groote missieuur, 1915–1940. De missiemotivatie van de Nederlandse katholiek* (Bilthoven 1974); J. Lescrauwaet et al., *Bilanz der niederländischen Kirche* (Düsseldorf 1976); *Alfrink en de kerk 1951–1976* (Baarin 1976); *Jaarboeken van het katholiek documentatiecentrum (KDC)* (Nijmegen 1971–75).

841

20. *Catholicism in Italy*

LITERATURE

Publications on Italian Catholicism were until the 1950s lacking in content and originality. Two recent developments have altered this, the rise of an Italian Catholic Party and a new interest in the development of Catholicism following the Second Vatican Council. The results have not always been positive, owing to faulty documentation and the continuing influence of politics.

GENERAL WORKS: F. F. Chabod, *L'Italia contemporanea (1918–1948)* (Turin 1961); F. Catalano, *Dalla crisi del primo dopoguerra alla fondazione della repubblica: Storia d'Italia,* ed. by N. Valeri, V (Turin 1965); G. Mammarella, *L'Italia dopo il fascismo (1943–1968)* (Bologna 1970); R. Romano and C. Vivanti, eds., *Storia d'Italia,* 10 vols. (Turin 1972–76); see also the observations of G. Penco and G. Martina in: *RSCI* 30 (1976), 119–55; L. Cavalli, *Sociologa della storia italiana (1861–1974)* (Bologna 1974).—For Statistics: *Instituto centrale di statistica, Annuario statistico italiano, Annuario statistico dell'istruzione, Sommario di statistiche storiche dell'Italia, 1865–1965;* S. Burgalassi, *Il comportamento religioso degli italiani* (Florence 1968).— On religious problems: *Segreteria di stato. Ufficio centrale di statistica, Raccolta di tavole statistiche* (Vatican City 1971ff.). Indispensable is consultation of such periodicals as *La Civiltà Cattolica, RSCI, AHPont, Storia contemporanea, Rivista di storia contemporanea, Quaderni storici, Bollettino dell'Archivio per la storia del movimento sociale cattolico in Italia, Studi storici.*

WORKS ON CHURCH HISTORY: G. Martina, *La chiesa nell'età dell'assolutismo, del liberalismo e del totalitarismo. Da Lutero ai nostri giorni* (Brescia 1974); id., *La chiesa in Italia negli ultimi trent'anni* (Rome 1977); R. Aubert, "Le demi-siècle qui a préparé Vatican II," *Nouvelle histoire de l'Église* V (Paris 1975), 581–926; A. C. Jemolo, *Chiesa e stato negli ultimi cento anni* (Turin 1963), new ed.: *Chiesa e stato in Italia dall'unificazione a Giovanni XXIII* (Turin 1965); M. Bendiscioli, "Chiesa e società nei secoli XIX e XX," *Nuove questioni di storia contemporanea* I (Milan 1968), 325–447.

FIRST WORLD WAR: AA. VV., *Il trauma dell'intervento (1914–1919)* (Florence 1968); AA. VV., *Benedetto XV, i cattolici e la prima guerra mondiale* (Rome 1963); A. Monticone, *La Germania e la neutralità italiana (1914–1915)* (Bologna 1971); E. Forcella-A. Monticone, *Plotone d'esecuzione. I processi della prima guerra mondiale* (Bari 1972); M. Isnenghi, *Il mito della grande guerra da Marinetti a Malaparte* (Bari 1973).

FASCISM: B. Mussolini, *Opera omnia,* ed. by D. Susmel, 35 vols. (Florence 1951–63); G. Ciano, *Diario,* 2 vols. (Milan 1946); G. Pini and D. Susmel, *Mussolini l'uomo e l'opera,* 4 vols. (Florence 1953–55); R. De Felice, *Mussolini,* 4 vols. (Turin 1965–74); id., *Le interpretazioni del fascismo* (Bari 1969); G. Salvemini, *Scritti sul fascismo* (Milan 1963); F. Deakin, *Storia della repubblica di Salò* (Turin 1963); N. Valeri, *Da Giolitti a Mussolini. Momenti della crisi del liberalismo* (Milan 1967); D. Veneruso, *La vigilia del fascismo* (Bologna 1968); L. Salvatorelli and G. Mira, *Storia d'Italia nel periodo fascista* (Milan 1969); V. Castronuovo, *La stampa italiana dall'unità al fascismo* (Bari 1973); AA. VV., *Fascismo e società italiana,* ed. by G. Quazza (Turin 1973).—The Relationship of the Church to Fascism: R. Webster, *La croce e i fasci* (Milan 1964); P. Mazzolari, *La chiesa, il fascismo e la guerra* (Florence 1966); A. De Gasperi, *Lettere sul concordato* (Brescia 1970); P. Scoppola, *La chiesa e il fascismo* (Bari 1973); F. Molinari and V. Neri, *Olio santo e olio di ricino* (Turin 1976); S. Tramontin, *Cattolici, popolari e fascisti nel Veneto* (Rome 1975); A.

BIBLIOGRAPHY

Fappani, *Giorgio Montini* (Rome 1974). For other controversies on the Catholic Action and the racial laws, see: A. Martini, *Studi sulla questione romana e la Conciliazione* (Rome 1963). Of interest also are the biographies of several bishops: G. Villani, *Il vescovo Elia Dalla Costa. Per una storia da fare* (Florence 1974); AA. VV., *Il cardinale Giovanni Battista Nasalli Rocca di Corneliano, arcivescovo di Bologna (1872–1952)*, ed. by F. Molinari (Rome 1974).

ANTI-FACISM AND RESISTANCE MOVEMENTS: F. Antonicelli, *Dall' antifascismo alla resistenza* (Turin 1961); P. Alatri, *L'antifascismo italiano*, 2 vols. (Rome 1961); AA. VV., *Fascismo e antifascismo* (Milan 1963); M. Bendiscioli, *Antifascismo e resistenza* (Rome 1964); R. Battagha, *Storia della resistenza italiana* (Turin 1970); L. Valiani, G. Bianchi, and E. Ragionieri, *Azionisti e cattolici e comunisti nella resistenza italiana* (Milan 1971); A. Fappani, *La resistenza bresciana* (Brescia 1965); G. Bonfanti, *La resistenza. Documenti e testimonianze di storia contemporanea* (Brescia 1976).

CULTURE: L. Allevi, "Mezzo secolo di teologia dogmatica e apologetica in Italia," *SC* 80 (1952), 365–85; L. Tondelli, "Cinquant' anni di studi biblici in Italia," ibid., 386–98; M. Pellegrino, "Un cinquantennio di studi patristici in Italia," ibid., 424–52; P. Barbaini, "Per la scuola di storia ecclesiastica," ibid. 92 (1964), 211–32, 317–33; 93 (1965), 335–70; B. Ferrari, *La soppressione delle facoltà di teologia nelle università di stato* (Bari 1968); F. Lazzari, "Le facoltà teologiche tra il Sillabo d l'abolizione," AA. VV., *Un secolo da Porta Pia* (Naples 1970), 249–87; M. Guasco, "L'organizzazione delle scuole e dei seminari," *Modernismo, fascismo, comunismo,* ed. by G. Rossini (Bologna 1972), 192–204; G. Rumi, "Padre Gemelli e l'Università Cattolica," ibid., 205–33; V. L. Mangoni, "Aspetti della cultura cattolica sotto il fascismo: la rivista 'Il Frontespizio,' " ibid., 363–417; V. L. Marranzini, "La teologia italiana dal Vaticano I al Vaticano II," *Bilancio della teologia del XX secolo* II (Rome 1972), 95–112; M. L. Crespi, "La storiografia contemporanea ilaliana di fronte a Martin Lutero," *SC* 100 (1972), 134–60; "Gli studi patristici in Italia negli ultimi vent'anni (1951–1970)"; ibid. 101 (1973), 107–39; G. Giavini, "Gli studi biblici in Italia negli anni dal 1950 al 1970," ibid., 9–42; G. Colombo, "La teologia italiana. Dommatica 1950–1970," ibid., 99–191; G. Tassani, *La cultura politica della destra cattolica* (Rome 1976).

SPIRITUALITY: M. Petrocchi, "Schema per una storia della spiritualità italiana negli ultimi cento anni," *Spiritualità e azione del laicato cattolico italiano* I (Padua 1969), 17–58; *Bibliotheca sanctorum*, 13 vols. (Rome 1961–70); Article, "Italy," *Dictionnaire de spiritualité* 7/2 (1971), 2294–2311.—For Religious Orders: *Dizionario degli istituti di perfezione*, 6 vols. (Rome 1973ff.); C. Bellò, *Società ed evangelizzazione nell'Italia contemporanea. Linee di una storia e di una pastorale* (Brescia 1974).—For Individuals: A. Barelli: M. Sticco, *Una donna fra due mondi* (Milan 1967). G. Calabria: Graziano della Madre di Dio, Profilo biografico di don Giovanni Calabria (Venice 1966). G. De Luca: H. Bernard-Maître and R. Guarnieri, *Don Giuseppe De Luca et l'abbé Henri Bremond (1929–1933)* (Rome 1965); R. Guarnieri *Don Giuseppe De Luca tra cronaca e storia (1989–1962)* (Bologna 1975). C. Ferrini: AA. V. V., *Miscellanea Contardo Ferrini* (Rome 1947); AA. VV., *Scritti in onore di Contardo Ferrini*, 4 vols. (Milan 1947). P. G. Frassati: *Lettere,* ed. by L. Frassati (Rome 1950). C. Gnocchi: A. Riccardi, *Don Carlo Gnocchi* (Bologna 1966); R. Lombardi, *Per una mobilitazione generale dei cattolici* (Rome 1948); id., *Squilli di mobilitazione* (Rome 1948); id., *Crociata della bontà* (Rome 1949); id. *Esercitazioni per un mondo migliore* (Rome 1961). B. Longo: M. E. Spreafico, *Il servo di Dio Bartolo Longo* (Pompei 1944). P. Mazzolari: A. Bergamaschi, *Un contestatore per tutte le stagioni* (Bologna 1968); C. Bellò "Primo Mazzolari prete," *Studi cattolici* 13 (1969); 163–68; N. Fabretti, *Don Mazzolari, don Milani. I "disubbidienti"* (Milan 1972); L.

Bedeschi, *Obbedientissimo in Cristo. Lettere di don Mazzolari* (Milan 1974); P. Mazzolari, *Diario (1905–1926) e Lettere,* ed. by A. Bergamaschi (Bologna 1974). L. Milani: Scuola di Barbiana, *Lettera a una professoressa* (Florence 1967); *Lettere di Don Lorenzo Milani* (Milan 1970); *Lettere alla mamma (1943–1967)* (Milan 1973); N. Fallaci, *Dalla parte dell'ultimo, Vita del prete Lorenzo Milani* (Milan 1974). G. Moscati: G. Papasogli, *Vita di Giuseppe Moscati* (Rome 1958). V. Necchi: P. Bondiolo, *Vico Necchi fedele servo di Dio* (Milan 1944); V. Necchi, *Pensieri religiosi,* ed. by P. Bondioli (Milan 1956). G. Salvadori: G. Salvadori, *Lettere,* ed. by P. P. Trompeo and N. Vian (Florence 1945); N. Vian, *La giovinezza di G. Salvadori* (Rome 1960); id., *Amicizie e incontri di Giulio Salvadori* (Rome 1962). G. Papini: G. Cattaneo, *Giovanni Papini prima della conversione e dopo: Modernismo, fascismo, comunismo* (Bologna 1972), 235–47. F. Tognazzi, "Don Milani nell'evoluzione dell'opinione pubblica," *Testimonianze* 18 (1975), 97–128.

FOREIGN MISSIONS: C. Bona, *La rinascita missionaria in Italia. Dalle "Amicizie" all'Opera per la Propagazione della fede* (Turin 1964); S. Beltrami, *L'opera della Propagazione della fede in Italia* (Florence 1961).—G. Allamano and the Missions of the Consolata: B. Bernardi, *Il servo di Dio G. Allamano* (Turin 1960); C. Bona, *Il servo di Dio G. Allamano e un secolo di movimento missionario in Piemonte* (Turin 1960); R. Grazia, *La fisionomia spirituale del servo di Dio Giuseppe Allamano nei suoi scritti* (Turin 1961); C. Pera, *La spiritualità missionaria nel pensiero del servo di Dio Giuseppe Allamano* (Turin 1973).—D. Comboni and the Combonians: C. Fusero, *Daniele Comboni* (Bologna 1961); P. Catrice, *Un audacieux pionnier de l'Église, Mgr. Comboni et l'evangelisation de l'Afrique centrale* (Lyon 1964); P. Chiocchetta, "La Preghiera missionaria di D. Comboni," *La preghiera* II, ed. by R. Boccassino (Milan and Rome 1967), 734–45,—G. M. Conforti and the Saveriani: V. Vanzin, *Guido Maria Conforti* (Parma 1949); L. Ballarin, *L'anima missionaria di Guido Maria Conforti* (Parmi 1962); A. Dagnino, *Dottrina spirituale di Mons. Guido Maria Conforti* (Milan 1966).—On the Pontificio Istituto Missioni Estere (PIME): A. Morelli, *La spiritualità missionaria dal Patriarca Ramazzotti* (Milan 1961); G. B. Tragella, *Le Missioni Estere di Milano,* 2 vols. (Milan 1950–59); P. Manna *Virtù apostoliche* (Milan 1964); *Paolo Manna ieri e oggi* (Naples 1966).

CATHOLIC MOVEMENTS: G. DeRosa, *Storia del movimento cattolico in Italia,* 2 vols. (Bari 1966); P. Scoppola, *Chiesa e stato nella storia d'Italia. Storia documentaria dall'Unità alla repubblica* (Bari 1967); AA. VV., *Spiritualità e azione del laicato cattolico italiano,* 2 vols. (Padua 1969); P. Borzomati, *I giovani cattolici nel mezzogiorno d'Italia dall'Unità al 1948* (Rome 1970); *La "Gioventù Cattolica" dopo l'Unità 1868–1968,* L. Osbat and F. Piva, eds., (Rome 1972); G. Miccoli, "Chiesa e società in Italia dal Concilio Vaticano I (1870) al pontificato di Giovanni XXIII," *Storia d'Italia* V (Turin 1973), 1493–1548; AA. VV., *Modernismo, fascismo, comunismo. Aspetti della politica e della cultura dei cattolici nel '900,* ed. by G. Rossini (Bologna 1972); AA. VV., *I cattolici tra fascismo e democrazia,* ed. by P. Scoppola and F. Traniello (Bologna 1975); P. G. Zunino, *La questione cattolica nella sinistra italiana (1919–1939)* (Bologna 1975); G. Candeloro, *Il movimento cattolico in Italia* (Rome 1974); S. Tramontin, *Sinistra cattolica di ieri e di oggi* (Turin 1974); M. Reineri, *Il movimento cattolico in Italia dall'unità al 1948* (Turin 1975); N. Antonetti, *L'ideologia della sinistra cristiana. I cattolici tra chiesa e comunismo (1937–1945)* (Milan 1976).—On the Renewal of Catholic Action: V. Bachelet, *Il nuovo cammino dell'Azione Cattolica* (Rome 1973).—On Rossi: M. V. Rossi, *I giorni dell'onnipotenza. Memorie di una esperienza cattolica* (Rome 1975).

THE ITALIAN PEOPLE'S PARTY: F. Malgeri, ed., *Atti dei congressi del Partito Popolare Italiano* (Brescia 1969); L. Sturzo, *I discorsi politici* (Rome 1951); id., *La croce di*

Constantino, ed. by G. De Rosa (Rome 1958); id., *Il Partito Popolare Italiano* (Bologna 1956).—On Sturzo: M. Vaussard, *Il Pensiero politico e sociale di Luigi Sturzo* (Brescia 1966); P. Stella, *Don Luigi Sturzo, il prete di Caltagirone* (Catania 1971); G. De Rosa, *L'utopia di Luigi Sturzo* (Brescia 1972); F. Malgeri and F. Piva, *Vita di Luigi Sturzo* (Rome 1972); G. De Rosa, *Storia del movimento cattolico in Italia,* 2 vols. (Bari 1966); id., *Il Partito popolare Italiano* (Bari 1969); id., *Rufo Ruffo della Scalleta e Luigi Sturzo* (Rome 1961); F. L. Ferrari, *Il Domani d'Italia,* ed. by G. P. Dore (Rome 1958); G. M. Rossi, *Francesco Luigi Ferrari. Dalle Leghe bianche al Partito Popolare* (Rome 1965); L. Bedeschi, *I cattolici disobbedienti* (Naples and Rome 1959); id., *Dal movimento di Murri all'appello di Sturzo* (Milan 1969); *I Cattolici e l'attuazione dello stato democratico* (Milan 1966); *Il Partito Popolare. Validità di una esperienza* (Milan 1969); *Il Partito Popolare Italiano. Scritti e saggi nel 50° anniversario della sua fondazione* (Rome 1970); S. Tramontin, *Cattolici, popolari, fascisti nel Veneto* (Rome 1975); C. F. Casula, *Cattolici comunisti e sinistra cristiana* (Bologna 1976); S. Accame, *Gaetano de Sanctis fra cultura e politica. Esperienza di cattolici militanti a Torino 1919–1922* (Florence 1975).

THE CHRISTIAN-DEMOCRATIC PARTY: A. Damilano, ed., *Atti Documenti della Democrazia Cristiana, 1943–1967,* 2 vols. (Rome 1968); M. R. Catti De Gasperi, ed., *De Gasperi scrive,* 2 vols. (Brescia 1974).—Biographies of De Gasperi: M. R. Catti De Gasperi, *De Gasperi uomo solo* (Milan 1964); G. Andreotti, *De Gasperi e il suo tempo* (Milan 1964); id., *De Gasperi e la ricostruzione* (Rome 1974); P. Ottone, *De Gasperi* (Milan 1968).—On the Party: T. Godechot, *Le parti démocrate-chrétien italien* (Paris 1964); G. Baget-Bozzo, *Il partito cristiano al potere. La DC di De Gasperi e di Dossetti,* 2 vols. (Florence 1974).

CRISIS AND POSTCONCILIAR RENEWAL: G. De Rosa, *Cattolici e comunisti oggi in Italia. La via italiana al socialismo e il dialogo coi cattolici* (Rome 1966); id., *Chiesa e comunismo in Italia* (Rome 1970); id., *Il dissenso cattolico* (Rome 1974); C. Falconi, *La contestazione nella chiesa* (Milan 1969); A. Nesti, ed., *L'altra chiesa in Italia* (Milan 1970); R. La Valle, *Dalla parte di Abele* (Milan 1971); R. Sciubba and R. Sciubba Pace, *Le comunità di base in Italia,* 2 vols. (Rome 1976).—On Pastoral Problems and Bishops' Conferences: G. Feliciani, *Le conferenze episcopali* (Bologna 1974).—On Problems of Confession: L. Rossi, ed., *La crisi della confessione* (Bologna 1974).—On the Liturgical Movement: *Rivista liturgica* 61 (1974), 9–179.—Catechesis: "La pastorale catechetica in Italia," *Presenza pastorale* 45 (1975), 1105–89.—On Concordat Revision: AA. VV., *Studi per la revisione del Concordato* (Padua 1970); AA. VV., *Individuo, gruppi, confessioni religiose nello stato democratico* (Milan 1973); C. Pelosi, "La revisione del concordato," *Humanitas* 29 (1974), 894–918; 30 (1975) 24–42.

21. *The Catholic Church of France*

BIBLIOGRAPHY

A Latreille, J. R. Palanque, E. Delaruelle and R. Rémond, *Histoire du Catholicisme en France. La période contemporaine* (Paris 1962); A. Dansette, *Histoire religieuse de la France contemporaine sous la IIIᵉ république* (Paris 1951); id., *Destin du catholicisme français 1926–1936* (Paris 1957); P. Lesourd and C. Paillat, *Dossier secret de l'Église de France* II: *De la révolution à nos jours* (Paris 1968); F. Bouland, "Essor ou déclin du Clergè français?" *Rencontres* 34 (Paris 1950); J. Gadille, "France, VI. La période contemporaine," *Dictionnaire d'Histoire et de Géographie ecclésiastique,* fasc. 102–103, p. 143–57, with biblio.; *Panorama de la France. La documentation francaise* (Paris 1966); P. Gerbod, "Les catholiques et l'enseignement secondaire (1919–1939)," *Revue d'Histoire moderne et contemporaine* 18 (1971), 375–414; "Histoire du catholicisme moderne et contemporain," *Revue Historique* CCXLI (1970), 125–48, 387–440; *Forces religieuses et attitudes politiques dans la France contemporaine sous la direction de René Rémond. Cahiers de la fondation nationale des sciences politiques* 130 (Paris 1965); C. Molette, *L'A.C.J.F. 1886–1907* (Paris 1968); P. Huot-Pleuroux, *Le recrutement sacerdotal dans le diocèse de Besançon de 1801 à 1960* (Paris 1966); J. M. Mayeur, *La séparation de l'Église et de l'État* (Paris 1966); M. Villain, *L'abbé Paul Couturier, apôtre de l'unité chrétienne* (Paris 1957).—Recent bibliography: P. Vigneron, *Histoire des crises du Clergé français contemporain* (Paris 1976), 427–71.

22. The Church in Spain and Portugal

SPAIN: The number of studies on this period is extensive. The *Cuadernos Bibliográficos de la Guerra de España (1936–1939)*, ed. by Vincente Palacio Atard, alone lists more than two thousand titles. Therefore we must limit our selection to what is absolutely necessary. Works mentioned in the footnotes will not be cited. As sources, a great many articles beyond the *Boletines Eclesiásticos* can be found in the periodicals *Razón y Fe, La ciudad de Dios, La Ciencia Tomista, El Mensajero del Corazón de Jesús, Sal Terrae, Ecclesia, Vida Nueva.* Mention must be made of the *Guías de la Iglesia de España*, yearbooks, and statistics for congresses and meetings. S. Azner, *Estudios religiosos-sociales* (Madrid 1949); id., *La revolución española y las vocaciones eclesiásticas* (Madrid 1949); M. Batllori und V. M. Arbeloa, eds., *Archivo Vidal y Barraquer. Iglesia y Estado durante la Segunda República Española 1931–1936* (Montserrat 1971); R. Muntanyola, *Vidal i Barraquer, cardenal de la pau* (Barcelona 1969); J. Lopez and M. B. Isusi, *Las religiosas en España. Situación sociologica y renovación litúrgica* (Bilbao 1969); J. M. Vazquez, F. Medlin, and L. Mendez, *La Iglesia española contemporánea* (Madrid 1973); R. Duocastella, J. Marcos, and J. M. Díaz Mozaz, *Análisis sociológico del Catolicismo español* (Barcelona 1967); J. Rupérez, *Estado confesional y libertad religiosa* (Madrid 1970); A. Alvarez Bolado, *El experimento de Nacional-Catolicismo 1939–1975* (Madrid 1976).

PORTUGAL: *Anuário Católico de Portugal* (Lisbon 1931, 1932, 1933, 1943, 1947, 1953, 1957, 1968); *Portugal e Santa Sé. Concordata e Acordo Missionário* (Lisbon 1943); M. de Oliveira, *História Eclesiástica de Portugal* (Lisbon 1958); *Portugal Missionario* (Cucujães 1928); F. de Almeida, *História da Igreja em Portugal* III (Barcelona 1970); D. Peres, *História de Portugal* (Porto 1954–58); A. H. de Oliveira Marques, *A Iª República Portuguesa* (Lisbon, n.d.); *Boletim de Informação Pastoral* (Lisbon 1959–70); F. Jasmins Pereira, *A Primeira República* (Braga 1972); *Anuário Católico do Ultramar Português* (Lisbon 1960, 1964).

23. The Countries of the English-Speaking Areas

BIBLIOGRAPHY

GREAT BRITAIN: D. Barker, *G. K. Chesterton. A Biography* (New York 1973); G. A. Beck, ed., *The English Catholics, 1850–1950* (London 1950); M. V. Brand, *The Social Catholic Movement in England, 1920–1955* (New York 1963); W. F. Brown, *Through*

Windows of Memory (London 1946); J. M. Cleary, *Catholic Social Action in Britain, 1909–1959. A History of the Catholic Social Guild* (Oxford 1961); J. Crehan, S.J., *Father Thurston. A Memoir with a Bibliography of His Writings* (London 1952); M. Cruickshank, *Church and State in English Education, 1870 to the Present Day* (London and New York 1964); J. Dingle, *Le Catholicisme contemporain en Grande-Bretagne* (Paris 1967); G. P. McEntee, *The Social Catholic Movement in Great Britain* (New York 1927); J. Murphy, *Church, State and Schools in Britain, 1800–1970* (London 1971); E. Oldmeadow, *Francis Cardinal Bourne*, 2 vols. (London 1940–44); G. Scott, *The R.Cs. A Report on Roman Catholics in Britain Today* (London 1967); F. Sheed, *The Church and I* (Garden City, New York, 1974); R. Speaight, *The Life of Eric Gill* (New York 1966); id., *The Life of Hilaire Belloc* (New York 1966); F. Valentine, O.P., *Father Vincent McNabb, O.P., The Portrait of a Great Dominican* (Westminster, Maryland 1955); M. Ward, *Gilbert Keith Chesterton* (New York 1943); id., *Return to Chesterton* (New York 1952); id., *Unfinished Business* (New York 1964); E. Waugh, *Monsignor Ronald Knox* (Boston 1959).

IRELAND: D. H. Akenson, "Education and Enmity," *The Control of Schooling in Northern Ireland, 1920–50* (New York 1973); J. Blanchard, *The Church in Contemporary Ireland* (Dublin 1963); D. Fennell, *The Changing Face of Catholic Ireland* (London 1968); J. Mescal, *Religion in the Irish System of Education* (Dublin 1957); D. W. Miller, *Church, State and Nation in Ireland, 1898–1921* (Pittsburgh 1973); J. H. Whyte, *Church and State in Modern Ireland, 1923 -1970* (Dublin 1971).

UNITED STATES: A. I. Abell, "American Catholicism and Social Action," *A Search for Social Justice, 1865–1950* (Garden City, N.Y. 1960); C. J. Barry, O.S.B., *American Nuncio. Cardinal Aloisius Muench* (Collegeville, Minn. 1969); F. L. Broderick, *Right Reverend New Dealer, John A. Ryan* (New York 1963); H. A. Buetow, *Of Singular Benefit: The Story of Catholic Education in the United States* (New York and London 1970); L. Curry, "Protestant-Catholic Relations in America," *World War I Through Vatican II* (Lexington, Ky. 1972); J. T. Ellis, *American Catholicism* (Chicago 1969); id., *Documents of American Catholic History*, 2 vols. (Chicago 1967); id., *A Guide to American Catholic History* (Milwaukee 1959); id., *The Life of James Cardinal Gibbons, Archbishop of Baltimore, 1834–1921*, 2 vols. (Milwaukee 1952); G. Q. Flynn, *American Catholics and the Roosevelt Presidency, 1932–1936* (Lexington, Ky. 1968); L. H. Fuchs, *John F. Kennedy and American Catholicism* (New York 1967); R. I. Gannon, S.J., *The Cardinal Spellman Story* (Garden City, N.Y. 1962); P. Gleason, *The Conservative Reformers. German-American Catholics and the Social Order* (Notre Dame, Ind. 1968); A. Greely, W. C. McCready and K. McCourt, *Catholic Schools in a Declining Church* (New York 1976); *HK* 31 (1977), 143–47; F. J. Lally, *The Catholic Church in a Changing America* (Boston 1962); T. T. McAvoy, C.S.C., *Father O'Hara of Notre Dame. The Cardinal-Archbishop of Philadelphia* (Notre Dame, Ind. 1967); id., *A History of the Catholic Church in the United States* (Notre Dame, Ind. 1969); S. Marcus, *Father Coughlin. The Tumultuous Life of the Priest of the Little Flower* (Boston 1973); M. A. Marty, "Lutherans and Roman Catholicism," *The Changing Conflict, 1917–1963* (Notre Dame, Ind. 1968); P. Marx, O.S.B., *Virgil Michel and the Liturgical Movement* (Collegeville, Minn. 1957); W. D. Miller, *A Harsh and Dreadful Love. Dorothy Day and the Catholic Worker Movement* (New York 1973); H. J. Nolan, ed., *Pastoral Letters of the American Hierarchy, 1792–1970* (Huntington, Ind. 1971); D. J. O'Brien, *American Catholics and Social Reform. The New Deal Years* (New York 1968); E. J. Power, *Catholic Higher Education in America* (New York 1972); id., *A History of Catholic Higher Education in the United States* (Milwaukee 1958); G. Shaughnessy, *Has the Immigrant Kept the Faith? A Study of Immigration and Catholic Growth in the United States, 1790–1920* (New York 1925, reprinted 1969); J.

G. Shaw, *Edwin Vincent O'Hara, American Prelate* (New York 1957); J. B. Sheerin, C.S.P., *Never Look Back. The Career and Concerns of John J. Burke* (New York 1975); C. J. Tull, *Father Coughlin and the New Deal* (Syracuse, N.Y. 1965); R. Van Allen, *The Commonweal and American Catholicism. The Magazine, the Movement, the Meaning* (Philadelphia 1974); E. R. Vollmar, S.J., "The Catholic Church in America," *An Historical Bibliography* (New York 1963); V. A. Yzermans, ed., *American Participation in the Second Vatican Council* (New York 1967).

CANADA: D. de Saint-Denis, O.F.M. Cap., *L'Église Catholique au Canada. Précis historique et statistique.* The Catholic Church in Canada. Historical and Statistical Summary* (Montreal 1956); S.M.A. of Rome Gaudreau, "The Social Thought of French Canada as Reflected in the Semaine Sociale," *The Catholic University of America Studies in Sociology* XVIII (Washington, D.C. 1946); J. Hulliger, *L'enseignement social des évêques canadiens de 1891 à 1950* (Montreal 1958); L. K. Shook, *College Post-Secondary Education in English-Speaking Canada. A History. Studies in the History of Higher Education in Canada* VI (Toronto 1971); *Vingt-cinq ans de l'École Social Populaire, 1911–1936* (Montreal 1936).

24. The Church in Latin America

LITERATURE

The great national histories of the individual republics treat church relations only down to the turn of the century. On the twentieth century there are only sketches, for the most part in English. The Church is generally regarded from the point of view of the state or politics. Ecclesiastical historiography in its own right does not exist.

For a survey of the individual republics, see: H. Herring, *A History of Latin America from the Beginnings to the Present* (New York 1956) or F. Morales Padrón, "Historia de América," *Manual de Historia Universal* 5–6 (Madrid 1962); Generally reliable are the two editions of J. L. Mecham, *Church and State in Latin America* (Chapel Hill 1934, 1966), to which may be added F. B. Pike, *The Conflict between Church and State in Latin America* (New York 1964) and F. C. Turner, *Catholicism and Political Development in Latin America* (Chapel Hill 1971); an essay-type approach is C. H. Hillekamps, *Religion, Kirche und Staat in Lateinamerika* (Munich 1966).—For Protestantism in Latin America; P. Damboriena, *El protestantismo en América Latina*, 2 secs., (Fribourg and Bogotá 1962–63); E. Willems, "Followers of the New Faith," *Culture, Change and the Rise of Protestantism in Brazil and Chile* (Nashville 1967).—J. Lembke, *Christentum unter den Bedingungen Lateinamerikas. Die katholische Kirche vor den Problemen der Abhängigkeit und Unterentwicklung* (Berne and Frankfurt am Main 1975); J. Thesing, "Die christlichen demokratischen Parteien in Lateinamerika," *HK* 31 (1977), 313–18; H. J. Prien, *Die Geschichte des Christentums in Lateinamerika* (Göttingen 1978); David E. Mutchler, *The Church as a Political Factor in Latin America with Particular Reference to Colombia and Chile* (New York 1971); Karl M. Schmitt, *The Roman Catholic Church in Modern Latin America* (New York 1972); Hugo Latorre Cabal, *The Revolution of the Latin American Church* (Norman 1977).

BRAZIL: M. Barbosa, *A Igreja no Brasil. Notas para a sua história* (Rio de Janeiro 1945); J. M. Bello, *A History of Modern Brazil 1889–1964* (Stanford 1966); E. B. Burns, *A History of Brazil* (New York 1970); P. F. da Silveria Camargo, *História eclesiástica do Brasil* (Petrópolis, Rio de Janeiro and São Paulo 1955); J. Alfredo de Sousa Montenegro, *Evolução do Catolicismo no Brasil* (Petrópolis 1972); T. C. Bruneau, *The Political*

Transformation of the Brazilian Catholic Church (Cambridge 1974); M. Todaro Williams, "Jackson de Figueiredo, Catholic Thinker," *TAM* (*The Americas*) 31 (1974), 139–63; P. A. Ribeiro de Oliveira, *Catholicismo popular no Brasil* (Rio 1970); A. U. Floridi, *Radicalismo cattolico brasiliano* (Rome 1968); H. Fesquet, *Une Église en état de péché mortel* (Paris 1968); E. de Kadt, *Catholic Radicals in Brazil* (London 1970); A. Ghurbant, *L'Église rebelle en Amérique Latine* (Paris 1969); The question of syncretism is treated in R. Bastide, *Les religions africaines au Brésil* (Paris 1960); M. Koch-Weser, *Die Yoruba-Religion in Brasilien* (diss., Bonn 1976); Charles Antoine, *Church and Power in Brazil* (New York 1973).

ARGENTINA: R. Levillier, ed., *Historia argentina* V (Buenos Aires 1968); G. Bleiberg, ed., *Diccionario de Historia de España, Argentina (Época independiente)* I (Madrid 1968), 344–50; J. Vicens Vives, *Historia social y económica de España y América. Burguesiá, industrialización, obrerismo* IV/2 (Barcelona 1959); J. Alameda, *Argentina Católica* (Buenos Aires 1935); G. Furlong, L. M. Baliña, G. Ferrer, J. A. Allenfe, L. M. Ardanaz, C. M. Gelly y Obes, and L. Ayarragaray, *Etapas del catolicismo argentino* (Buenos Aires, n.d.); *Historia argentina contemporánea 1862–1930*, 4 secs. (Buenos Aires 1963–67); J. A. Paita et al., *Argentina 1930–1960* (Buenos Aires 1961); P. Waldmann, *Der Peronismus 1943–1955* (Hamburg 1974); P. Marsal S., *Perón y la iglesia* (Buenos Aires 1955); The position of the Church in the last years is dealt with in. T. T. Evers, *Militärregierung in Argentinien* (Hamburg 1972); J. J. Kennedy, *Catholicism, Nationalism and Democracy in Argentina* (University of Notre Dame Press 1958).

PARAGUAY-URUGUAY: E. Cardozo, *Paraguay independiente* and J. E. Pivel D., *Uruguay independiente-Historia de América* 21 (Barcelona 1949); *Anuario eclesiástico de Paraguay*, ed. by the Centro de estudios socio-religiosos (CESR) in collaboration with the Centro de documentación, estudios y proyectos, pastoral social and the Bishops' Conference of Paraguay (1792); *Diccionario de historia de España. Paraguay (Época independiente)* III, ed. by G. Bleiberg (Madrid 1969), 172–75; *Guí de la Iglesia católica en el Uruguay 1973; Diccionario de historia de España. Uruguay (Época independiente)* III, ed. by G. Bleiberg (Madrid 1969); J. Vicens Vives, *Historia social y económica de España y América. Burguesía, industrialización, obrerismo* II (Barcelona 1959).

CHILE: L. Galdames, *A History of Chile* (Chapel Hill 1941); F. Araneda B., *El arzobispo Errázuriz y la evolución política y social de Chile* (Santiago de Chile 1956); J. Basadre, "Chile, Perú y Bolivia independientes" (Barcelona and Buenos Aires 1948), *Historia de América y de los pueblos americanos*, ed., A. Ballesteros y Beretta; *Estado de la Iglesia en Chile*, ed. by the Oficina Nacional de Estadística de la Acción Católica Chilena (Santiago de Chile 1946); *Guía parroquial y guiá eclesiástica de Chile* (Santiago de Chile 1969); *Diccionario de Historia de España. Chile (Época independiente)* I (Madrid 1968), ed. by G. Bleiberg, 1082–1089; J. Vicens Vives, *Historia social y económica de España y América, Burguesía, industrialización, obrerismo* IV/2 (Barcelona 1959).

BOLIVIA: P. Díaz Machicao, *Historia de Bolivia 1920–1943*, 5 secs. (La Paz 1954–58); H. S. Klein, *Parties and Political Change in Bolivia 1880–1952* (Cambridge 1969); R. J. Alexander, *The Bolivian National Revolution* (New Brunswick 1958); *Anuario eclesiástico de Bolivia para el año del Señor 1960* (La Paz 1960); J. Basadre, "Chile, Perú y Bolivia independiente" (Barcelona and Buenos Aires 1948), *Historia de América y de los pueblos americanos*, ed. by A. Ballesteros y Beretta; G. Bleiber, ed. *Diccionario de historia de Espana. Bolivia (Época independiente)* I (Madrid 1968), 557–66.

PERU: J. Basadre, *Historia de la República del Perú*, 16 secs. (Lima 1968–69); *Historia general de los Peruanos hasta 1973*, sec. 3 (Lima 1973); J. L. Klaiber, "Religion and

Revolution in Peru 1920–1945," *TAM* 31 (1975), 289–312; id., *Religion and Revolution in Peru, 1824–1976*, (Notre Dame 1977). From the extensive literature on the Catholicism of the Indians, J. C. Mariátegui, *Siete ensayos de interpretación de la realidad peruana* (Lima 1974). *Anuario eclesiástico del Perú 1974*, Secretariado del episcopado peruano. Departamento de estadística. Arzobispado de Lima, Perú; J. Basadre, "Chile, Perú y Bolivia independientes," *Historia de América y de los pueblos americanos*, ed. by A. Ballesteros y Beretta (Barcelona and Buenos Aires 1948); *Una universidad que crece. La Pontificia Universidad Católica del Perú recibe un donativo de la Fundación Ford* (Lima 1965).

ECUADOR: A. Pareja Diezcanseco, *Historia del Ecuador*, Sec. 2 (Quito 1958); *Estudio de la viceprovincia del Ecuador III/1, Estudio del personal; Estudio de las residencias y parroquias 2; Estudio de los colegios de la Compañia de Jesús en el Ecuador* (Quito 1969), ed. by the CIAS (Centro de Investigación y Acción Social); J. L. Izurieta S.I., *La Iglesia en el Ecuador, Estudio del personal de 1968 II/1: Análisis; 2: Estadísticas* (Quito 1969), ed. by the CIAS; *La Iglesia en el Ecuador 1949. Sinopsis de la jerarquía ecuatoriana y de las Órdenes y congregaciones religiosas* (Quito 1949); *La Iglesia en el Ecuador 1963. Directorio de la Iglesia católica en el Ecuador*, ed. by the Episcopal Secretariat in cooperation with the Bishops' Conference; J. I. Larrea, *La Iglesia y el Estado en el Ecuador. La personalidad de la Iglesia en el modus vivendi entre la Santa Sede y el Ecuador* (Seville 1954), publication of the School of Spanish-American Studies of Seville, LXXXIII; F. Nuscheler and H. Zwiefelhofer, S.J., *Kirche und Entwicklung in Ekuador und Kolumbien*, ed. by The Political Association at the Munich College of Philosophy (Mannheim and Ludwigshafen 1972); J. Tobar Donoso, *La Iglesia modeladora de la nacionalidad* (Quito 1953).

COLOMBIA: *Historia extensa de Colombia* (Bogotá 1965ff.); G. Guzman et al., *La violencia en Colombia*, Sec. 2 (Bogotá 1962–64); L. Schoultz, "Reform and Reaction in the Colombian Catholic Church," *TAM* 30 (1973), 229–50; *Conferencias episcopales de Colombia 1908–1953* (Bogotá 1956); *Anuario de la Iglesia católica en Colombia* (Bogotá 1951); M. Colón, O.S.A., *Por la Iglesia, Artículos político-religiosos sobre asuntos de actualidad* (Bogotá 1910); *Conferencia episcopal de 1948* (20 June–3 July) (Bogotá 1948); J. M. Fernández, S.J., and R. Granados, S.J., *Obra civilizadora de la Iglesia en Colombia* (Bogotá 1936); R. Gómez Hoyos, *La Iglesia en Colombia. Postura religiosa de López de Mesa en el escrutinio sociológico de la historia colombiana* (Bogotá 1955); G. de Ibarra, O.M.Cap., *La religión católica en el concordato de Colombia* (Assisi 1939); G. Jiménez Cadena, S.J., *Sacerdote y cambio social. Estudio sociológico en los Andes Colombianos* (Bogotá 1967), in the series of the Centro de Investigación Acción Social, *CIAS 2;* F. Nuscheler and H. Zwiefelhofer, S.J., *Kirche und Entwicklung in Ekuador und Kolumbien* (Mannheim and Ludwigshafen 1972); J. Vicens Vives, *Historia social y económica de España y América. Burguesía, industrialización, obrerismo IV/2* (Barcelona 1959).

VENEZUELA: M. Picón Salas et al., *Venezuela independiente 1910–1960* (Caracas 1962); N. E. Navarro, *Anales eclesiásticos venezolanos* (Caracas 1951); *Directorio de la Iglesia católica en Venezuela 1975*, ed. by the Centro de investigaciones en ciencias sociales (CISOR), Departamento de estadísticas y documentación, Secretariado permanente del episcopado venezolano (SPEV), Caracas; V. Iriarte, S.J., *La arquidiócesis de Venezuela 1962*, ed. by the Secretariado permanente del episcopado venezolano, Caracas; R. E., *Venezuela (Época independiente), Diccionario de historia de España*, III, ed. by G. Bleiberg (Madrid 1969), 954–63; J. Vicens Vives, *Historia social y económica de España y América. Burguesía, industrialización, obrerismo II* (Barcelona 1959).

ANTILLES: E. Williams, "From Columbus to Castro," *The History of the Caribbean 1492–1969* (London 1970); R. Guerra Sanchez et al.,*Historia de la nación Cubana,* Secs. 8–10 (Havana 1952); R. W. Logan,*Haiti and the Dominican Republic* (London 1968); under the same title, *The Era of Trujillo,* P. L. Gonzáles Blanco (Santo Domingo 1955) and J. De Galíndez (Santiago de Chile 1956); On Voodooism, A. Métraux, *Voodoo in Haiti* (New York 1959), id., *Religion and Politics in Haiti* (Washington 1966).

CENTRAL AMERICA: F. D. Parker, *The Central American Republics* (London 1964); M. P. Holleran, *Church and State in Guatemala* (New York 1949).

MEXICO: J. Bravo Ugarte, *Historia de México* III. *México* II. *Relaciones internacionales, territorio, sociedad y cultura* (Mexico 1959); D. Olmedo, S.J., "Mexico, Modern" *New Catholic Encyclopedia* IX (1966), 775–83; *México. Diccionario de Historia de España,* ed. by G. Bleiberg, II (1968), 1033–54. "Uber die Zeit der Revolution und ihre Cristero-Phase jetzt," J. Meyer, *La révolution mexicaine 1910–1940* (Paris 1973); H. F. Cline, *Mexico: Revolution to Evolution 1940–1960* (London 1962); J. Meyer, *The Cristero Rebellion 1926–1929* (Cambridge 1976); D. C. Bailey, *Viva Cristo Rey. The Cristero Rebellion and the Church State Conflict in Mexico* (Austin 1974); E. Portes Gil, *The Conflict between the Civil Power and the Clergy* (Mexico 1935) and García Gutiérrez, *Acción anticatólica en Méjico* (Mexico 1959) reflect both parties in the conflict; Robert E. Quirk, *The Mexican Revolution and The Catholic Church 1910–1929* (Bloomington 1973).

For the present situation of the Church in Latin America, the work edited by C. Veliz, *Latin America and the Caribbean: A Handbook* (London 1968) is a good introduction. The documentation for the Second Latin American Bishops' Conferences of Medellín of 1968 is available in *Iglesia y liberacion humana* (Barcelona 1969) and *Revista Javeriana 70* (Bogotá 1968).

In September of 1974 upon the initiative of Padre Dr. Enrique Dussel there was founded in El Salvador the Comisión de Estudios de Historia de la Iglesia en America Latina, *CEHILA.* The History of the Church planned by the commission is to have ten volumes, divided according to regions, and encompass the period from 1492 to the present.

25. *The Young Churches in Asia, Africa and Oceania*

SOURCES AND LITERATURE

Acta Apostolicae Sedis (AAS) 1940–78; A. Reuter, O.M.I.,*Summa Pontificia* (Regensburg 1978); J. Glazik, M.S.C., *Päpstliche Rundschreiben über die Mission von Leo XIII. bis Johannes XXIII.* (Münsterschwarzach 1961); E. Marmy and I. Auf der Maur, *Geht hin in alle Welt. Missionsenzykliken der Päpste Benedikt XV., Pius XI., Pius XII., und Johannes XXIII.* (Fribourg 1961); Streit-Dindinger,*Bibliotheca Missionum (BM),* continued by P. J. Rommerskirchen, O.M.I., and P. M. Metzler, O.M.I., XXII–XXIII; XXVII (Mission Literature of India 1910–46); XXVIII (Mission Literature of South Asia [India, Pakistan, Burma, Ceylon] *1947–68*); XXIX (Mission Literature of South Asia 1910–70): XXX (Mission Literature of Japan and Korea 1910–70); J. Rommerskirchen, O.M.I., *Bibliografia Missionaria* XIII–XLI; *Bibliografia Missionaria* (Supplement): Quaderno n. 1–20,*Documenti e problemi missionari;* J. Beckmann, S.M.B., *Weltkirche und Weltreligionen. Die religiöse Lage der Menschheit* (Freiburg 1960); T. Scalzotto, "I Papi e la

BIBLIOGRAPHY

Sacra Congregazione per l'Evangelizzazione dei Popoli o 'de Propaganda Fide' da Benedetto XV a Paolo VI," *Sacrae Congregationis de Propaganda Fide Memoria Rerum. 350 Jahre im Dienste der Weltmission 1622–1972* III/2 (Freiburg 1976), 253–302; J. Metzler, O.M.I., "Präfekten und Sekretäre der Kongregation in der neuen Missionsära" (1918–1972), loc. cit., 303–53; A. Reuter, O.M.I., "De nova et novissima S. Congregationis de Propaganda Fide ordinatione a Summis Pontificibus S. Pio X et Paulo VI instaurata," loc. cit., 354–81; B. Jacqueline, "L'organisation interne du dicastère missionnaire après 350 ans," loc. cit., 382–412; G. Zampetti, S.D.B., "Le Pontificie Opere Missionare," loc. cit., 413–49; A. Seumois, O.M.I., "La S.C. 'de Propaganda Fide' et les études missionnaires," loc. cit., 450–63; J. Metzler, O.M.I., "Tätigkeit der Kongregation im Dienste der Glaubensverbreitung 1922–1972. Ein Überblick," loc. cit., 464–577; W. Bühlmann, O.F.M.Cap., "Epilogo. Passato e futuro della evangelizzazione," loc. cit., 578–614; J. Metzler, O.M.I., "L'organizzazione dell'attività missionaria," *Via Verità e Vita. Rivista Catechistica* XVI (Rome 1968), 79–88; G. B. Reghezza, *La Cooperazione Missionaria* (Rome 1977); "Sacra Congregazione per l'Evangelizzazione dei Popoli o 'de Propaganda Fide,'" *Annuario* 1976 (Rome 1977); id. *Annuario* 1977 (Rome 1978); T. Scalzotto, ed., *La Sacra Congregazione per l'Evangelizzazione dei Popoli nel Decennio del Decreto "Ad Gentes,"* (Rome 1975).

INDEX

Adam, Karl 265, 306, 468
Adélaïde, Marie 561
Adenauer, Konrad, West German chancellor 535, 548
Adult education 384, 395f, 399–403, 623, 648, 721
Africa 203, 476, 777, 793
—charities 446
—education 405ff
—orders 329, 359f
—radio, Catholic 431ff, 434f
Africanization 778f
Agagianian, Gregorio Pietro XV, cardinal 31, 116, 142
Age limit 120
Albania 530
—orders 375
—Orthodox Church 490
Alberione, Giuseppe 571
Alessandri, president of Chile 697
Alexander III, patriarch of Antioch 477
Alexis, patriarch of Moscow 484, 485, 492ff
Alexius, patriarch of Moscow 104, 116
Alfrink, Bernard, cardinal, archbishop of Utrecht 103, 111, 120, 124, 161, 455, 568
Algeria 230, 782
Allamano, Giuseppe 571
Allende, president of Chile 672, 698
Alphonso XIII, king of Spain 601, 604
Altaner, Berthold 282
Alvarado, Juan Velasco 706
Ambrosios, catholicos 478
Andrej, metropolitan 495
Andrieux, Joseph, cardinal 588
Anglican Church, Anglicans 103, 458f, 469, 472, 615, 619f, 631, 718f, 780, 792f, 796, 800
Angola 230, 788f
Anizan, worker-priest 597
Apartheid policy 781
Arámburu, Juan Carlos, auxiliary bishop of Buenos Aires 688
Arcel, Alfred 334
Argaña, Bogarín, bishop 692
Argentina 685–90
—bishops' conference 689f
—Church and state 219f
—clergy 687f
—orders 330
—postconciliar development 686
Arnold, Franz Xaver 290
Arrupe, Pedro, general S.J. 142
Ascalesi, Alessio, cardinal, archbishop of Naples 576
Asia 150, 203, 446, 794
Associations, Catholic 65f, 69, 71, 401, 536, 540, 547
Athanasius, Greek Church Father 477
Athenagoras, ecumenical patriarch 125, 475, 496
Auer, Alfons 335
Australia 795, 804
—charities 446, 455f
—orders 330
Austria 549–52
—Austrian Marxism 549
—Catholic Action 28
—charity 454
—Church and National Socialism 551
—clergy 337
—clergy, opinion survey 347
—concordat 185, 218f, 551
—diocesan synods 163
—education 402
—press, Catholic 418
—private schools, Catholic 552
—publicity 412
—state and Church 552
—television 428f
—theology 286
Ayala, Ángel, S.J. 611
Aznar, Severino 603

Bacht, Heinrich, S.J. 283
Bailly, Vincent de Paul 419
Balbo, Felice 580
Baldrelli, Ferdinando 451f
Balthasar, Hans Urs von 330, 335, 336, 347
Baltic states 507f
Bangladesh 768, 769
Bantu tribes 781
Barelli, Armida 581
Barnabas, patriarch 480

853

Barone, Domenico 52
Baronio, Cesare, cardinal 97f
Barreto, Vincente, S.J. 692
Barth, Karl 461
Baschir, Anton, exarch 477
Basileios, abuna 501
Basileios, bishop 494
Basileios Paul II, Mar 499
Basileios III George II, Mar, catholicos 498
Basileios IV Eugene I, catholicos 498
Basileios V Matthew I, Mar 499
Batista, Fulgencio, president of Cuba 723
Baudrillart, Henri Marie Alfred, cardinal 42, 584
Bäumker, Clemens 266
Baumstark, Anton 282
Bayer, Karl 451
Bea, Augustin, curial cardinal 33, 101ff, 111ff, 118, 122ff, 127f, 133, 286, 469
Beauduin, Lambert, O.S.B. 300, 560, 657
Belaúnde, president of Peru 706
Belgium 22, 92, 557–60, 783
—Catholic Action 308, 558
—Catholic education 557
—charities 443, 452, 455
—church life 559
—clergy 558
—education 389f, 393, 397
—liturgical movement 299
—Louvain, Catholic university 397, 561
—mariology 318
—organization, social 557
Bell, G. K., bishop 628
Belloc, Hilaire 624
Beloch, historian 30
Bendiscioli, Mario 581
Benedict XV, pope 21f, 35, 153, 584–86
Benoit, P. 285
Beran, Josef, cardinal 136, 519f
Beras-Rojas, Octavio Antonio, cardinal 729
Bergen, Diego von 256
Bergson, Henri 747
Bertram, Adolf, cardinal, archbishop of Breslau (Wrocław) 25, 28, 76, 303, 534f, 537, 544f, 550
Bethmann Hollweg, Theobald von 42f
Bevilacqua, Giulio 577, 581
Biafra 785
Bible (Scriptural studies, Bible movement) 32, 111, 123, 129, 133, 140, 172, 262, 271, 283–88, 294, 305f, 355, 560, 581
Billot, Louis, cardinal 589
Birth control 2f, 135, 144f, 630, 642, 667, 718
Bishops, College of 93f, 113, 117f, 126, 131, 136, 173
Bishops' synods (bishops' councils) 117, 119, 125, 136, 149, 160, 167, 173f, 344f, 347, 688f, 700, 708, 722, 729
Bismarck, Otto von, prince 585
Blake, Eugene Carson 463
Blanco, Rafael Arías, archbishop 719

Blanshard, Paul 659
Blondel, Maurice 277, 284
Bolivia 701–705
Boniface VIII, pope 37
Bonnet, George 592
Bopp, Léon 290
Bormann, Martin, Hitler's secretary 543
Botswana 790
Bouillard, Henri 269
Boulart, Abbé 596, 599
Bourne, Francis, archbishop 616, 624, 629f, 631
Brandts, Max 442
Brazil 673–84
—Catholic Action 675
—Catholic education 680
—Catholic press 681
—church life 675–80
—clergy 674ff, 682, 683
—development, postconciliar 683
—Episcopal Conference 674
—Indian missions 684
—orders 330
—sects 681
—state and Church 204
Bremond, Henri 265, 596
Brent, Charles 459
Breslin, Thomas 256
Breviary 26, 109, 124
Briand, Aristide 229, 585
Brinktrine, Johannes 278
Britten, James 629
Browne, Michael, cardinal 117, 639, 640
Browne, Noel 640
Brown, William Francis 617
Bruce, William George 665
Brüning, Heinrich, German chancellor 301
Buddhism 769f, 775
Bugarini, V. 97
Bukatko, Gabriel, coadjutor archbishop 121
Bulgaria 97, 463, 529f
—orders 375
—Orthodox patriarchate 479f
—persecution of Church 530
—religious policy 201
Bultmann, Rudolf 271f, 285, 287
Buonaiuti, Ernesto 573
Burke, John 644
Burma 774
Burundi 783, 785f
Butler, R. A. 619

Calles, Plutarco Elias, president of Mexico 742
Camacho, Manuel Ávila 744
Câmara, Jaime Barros, cardinal 682
Cameroon 779f, 791
Cambodia 774
Campoamor, José María 713
Canada 667–71, 787
—charity 441, 451, 456f
—education 398, 668ff

—hierarchy, Catholic 668
—population, Catholic 667
—social movements 670f
Canon law 151–77
Canonizations 23, 27, 29, 32, 171, 587, 792
Cape Verde Islands 787
Caraman, Philip, S. J. 631
Caravias, José 693
Carbone, Vincenzo 104
Cárdenas, Lázaro, president of Mexico 743
Cardijn, Joseph 289, 309, 558, 589
Carli, Luigi, bishop 113, 118, 127
Carmona, António de Fragoso, Portuguese
   dictator 186
Caroline Islands 797
Carraro, Giuseppe, bishop 138
Caretto, Carlo 583
Casariego, Mario, archbishop 740
Casel, Odo, O.S.B. 267, 297
Castaña bishop 606
Castelnau, Edouard de, general 587
Castillo, Lucas Guillermo, archbishop 719
Castro, Fidel 698, 700, 723, 724ff
Castro, Juan Bautista, archbishop 719
Cathedral chapter 155, 193, 536
Catholic Action 28, 29, 55–58, 156, 254,
   262, 289, 307ff, 338, 537, 558, 575, 577f,
   589f, 608, 610, 613, 663, 675, 695, 697,
   730, 739, 744f, 766
Cavour, Camillo Benso, count 576
Ceausescu, Nicolae 526
Celibacy, of priests 118, 126, 143, 148, 154,
   171, 337, 341f, 347f, 372, 568, 696, 722
Cento, Fernando, cardinal 112, 124, 141
Central Africa 783
Ceretti, Bonaventura, nuncio 47, 586
Cerfaux, Lucien 560
Cesbron, Gilbert 333
Ceuppens, F. 285
Ceylon 769
Chad 791
Chardin, Teilhard de 269, 399
Charities 436–58
Charles, Raphael 560
Charles I, emperor of Austria 42
Charlotte, grand duchess of Luxemburg 561
Charrière, François, bishop 112
Chesterton, Gilbert Keith 625
Chevrier 329
Chiaudano, Giuseppe 412
Chignoni, Alessandro 573
Chile 697–701
—orders 329f
China 28, 753, 755
—education 398
—Orthodox Church 493
—orders 377
Choren, catholicos 502
Choren, catholicos of Cilicia 504
Christopher, archbishop 490
Christopher II, patriarch 476
Chrysanthius, archbishop 490

Chrysostom I 489f
Chrysostom II, archbishop 490
Church, hierarchical structure 117, 157
Church and state 209–217, 229–59, 371–77,
   693
Churchill, Winston, British prime minister 86
Church music 110, 157, 297, 302ff, 657, 720
Čičerin, Georgij, Russian foreign minister 62
Cicognani, Amleto Giovanni, cardinal 112,
   113, 121
Cieplak, John, archbishop 510
Ciriaci, Pietro, nuncio 102, 158, 518
Clark, Mark 660
Clemenceau, Georges Benjamin, French
   statesman 585f
Colgan, Harold von 319
College of Cardinals 10, 17f, 26, 28, 31f, 35,
   115, 120, 135, 149, 155, 159, 168, 173,
   238, 248, 546, 754, 765, 777ff
Colonialism 773f, 777, 780
Colombia 712–19
—arrangement with Vatican 199
—concordat 219
—state and Church 207
Colombo, Carlo, cardinal 581
Comboni, Daniele 571
Communism (Communist parties) 60, 86,
   124, 128, 144, 200, 202, 207, 231, 248ff,
   375ff, 381 (school system) 415 (press),
   462, 482, 484f, 487, 493, 505, 514, 519f,
   522, 579, 583, 592, 636, 652, 654, 659,
   682, 697, 706, 714ff, 724f, 740, 753f, 761,
   771
Comoro Islands 792
Comte, Auguste 588
Concentration camps 374, 484, 544
Conclave 22, 25, 30, 33, 35, 99, 115, 154,
   159, 173
Concordats 31, 127, 177–228, 372, 380,
   387, 417, 417, 447, 507f, 514, 524f, 527,
   533f, 540, 545, 547f, 583, 586, 591, 609,
   635, 728
—with Italy 52f, 54–59
Confalonieri, Carlo, cardinal 26, 113
Conforti, Guido Maria 571
Confirmation, sacrament of 157, 165
Congar, Yves, O.P. 129, 141, 268, 335,
   468, 596
Congo 778, 783f, 791
Congregation for the Evangelization of
   Peoples 796, 803
Congregation for the Propagation of the Faith
   751ff, 758, 763, 770, 777, 779, 783, 785,
   786, 795
Conzález, Felipe Rincón, archbishop 719
Cook Islands 797
Cort, John 654
Cosgrave, William T. 635f
Couglin, Charles E. 652f, 658f
Crane, Paul, S.J. 626
Crispi, Francesco, Italian minister 576
Crivelli, G., director of Swiss *Caritas* 450

Croce, Benedetto 582
Crowley, Patrick 664
Csernoch, János, cardinal 522
Cuba 723–27
Cullmann, Oscar 108
Curia, Roman
—organization 10–18, 99, 101ff, 108, 116, 153, 155, 302f, 466, 644
—reform of 119, 136, 147f, 167f, 172, 357, 371
Cushing, Richard, cardinal 662
Cyprus 408, 488f
Cyril, abuna in Ethiopia 501
Cyril, patriarch of Bulgaria 479
Cyril III, archbishop of Cyprus 488
Cyril V, patriarch of the Copts 499
Cyril VI, patriarch of the Copts 499
Czechoslovakia 516–20
—celibacy law 154
—charity 450
—Church, national 516f
—Church, Orthodox 493f
—negotiations with Vatican 517f
—orders 375
—religious policy, communist 519
—state and Church 184, 202f
Daem, bishop of Antwerp 139
Damaskinos, archbishop of Athens 490
Damian, archbishop 490
Damianos, patriarch of Jerusalem 477
Dander, Franz 265
Daniel, Yvan 331
Daniélou, Jean, cardinal 268, 335, 596
Dante, Heinrich, archbishop 110
Darmo, Thomas, bishop 497
David V, catholicos of Georgia 478
Dawson, Christopher 628, 631
Day, Dorothy 626, 653
De Gasperi, Alcide 54, 575–80
De Gaulle, Charles, French general and statesman 86, 98, 594
De Hueck, Catherine 650
De la Bédoyère, Michael 632
De Lai, Gaetano, cardinal 644
Delaney, John, S.J. 663
Delehaye, Hippolyte 282
Della Chiesa, Mario 21, 35
Della Torre, Giuseppe 577
Delp, Alfred, S.J. 375
Del Portillo, Alvaro 358
De Luca, Giuseppe 581
Demetrios, metropolitan of Belgrade, patriarch 480
Demetrios I, metropolitan 475
De Montfort, Louis Marie Grignion 640
Denifle, Heinrich, O.P. 282
Denmark 505
Denominational schools 185, 191ff, 193, 218, 225f, 393, 536, 585, 646, 668
—see Religious instruction
Deschanel, French president 585

De Smedt, Emile Joseph, bishop 111, 113, 122, 127, 132, 136
De Valera, Eamon 634ff
Development aid 776, 790, 793, 797, 800, 804
Dey, James, Msgr. 625
Dezza, Paolo, S.J. 351
D'Herbigny, Michel, S.J., bishop 510
Diaconate 119, 126, 134, 171, 703f, 730
Dibelius, Martin 285
Dignan, John, bishop 639
Diekamp, Franz 264
Dilthey, Wilhelm 263
Diocesan synods 99, 103, 159f, 161f (Common Synod of the German bishoprics), 162 (Austria and Switzerland), 338 (Cologne), 556, 582 (Rome)
Dionisij, Polish metropolitan 492
Dionysius VI, Indian metropolitan, catholicos 498
Djibouti 783
Doerner, August, pastor 303
Dölger, Franz-Josef 282f
Dollfuss, Engelbert, Austrian federal chancellor 550f
Döllinger, Joseph Ignaz 261
Dominican Republic 727–30
Doncoeur 587
Donders, Adolf 294
Döpfner, Julius, cardinal, archbishop of Munich-Freising 105, 109f, 113, 116, 130, 137, 143, 345, 549
Dorotej, metropolitan of Czechoslovakia 493
Dositej, Macedonian archbishop 491
Dossetti, Giuseppe 581
Drexel, Katherine 650
Driesch, Hans 263
Dubček, Alexander, Czechoslovakian prime minister 493
Dubois, Louis Ernest, cardinal, archbishop of Paris 589
Duchesne, L. 281
Duff, Frank 319
Dumeige, G. 283
Duschak, bishop, vicar apostolic of Calapan 110

Eastern Churches 102, 112f, 121, 131, 134f, 172, 175, 183f, 201, 459, 461f, 467, 473–531
Eberle, Joseph 412
Ecuador 708–12
Ecumenism, general 27, 100, 102, 111, 121f, 125f, 132, 140, 165, 268f, 319, 402, 458–73, 474, 480, 484, 489, 491, 504, 718, 785, 804
—Secretariat for Promoting Christian Unity 16, 101ff, 112, 128, 133f, 159, 171, 176, 469f
Education 28, 55ff, 139, 180, 181, 220, 264, 378–409, 590, 593f, 601, 602, 616–23,

637, 647, 668, 691, 701, 704f, 709, 713, 721, 772, 774, 794
Egenter, Richard 275f
Egypt 474, 476, 499f, 789f
—education 383, 409
Ehrhard, Albert 24, 26, 281
Ehrle, Franz, cardinal 24, 26, 282
Elchinger, Arthur, bishop 139, 144
Elias IV, patriarch of Antioch 477
Elizabeth I, queen of England 616
Ellard, Gerald, S.J. 657
El Salvador 736–38
England, see Great Britain
Entralgo, Laín 601
Epagneul 597
Ephraem II, catholicos of Georgia 478
Episcopal conferences 24, 73, 76, 108f, 114, 119f, 124, 136f, 138, 150, 160, 163f, 166, 173, 175, 344, 351, 386, 404, 413, 442, 453f, 527, 534, 543f, 548, 550, 553, 569, 583, 594, 609, 635, 643, 645, 673, 677, 679, 682, 684, 689, 692f, 697, 700, 703, 706f, 710, 714, 717, 718, 733, 736, 741, 752, 765, 776, 791, 794, 796, 802
Ermecke, Gustav 275
Erzberger, Matthias, German minister 45
Esch, Ludwig, S.J. 311
Eschweiler, Karl 264, 278
Escrivá de Balaguer, J. M. 328, 357, 610
Ethiopia 499ff, 789f
Eucharistic Congresses 28, 135, 522, 673, 695, 712, 717, 766, 795f
Eugenios, archbishop of Crete 491
Evening Mass 157
Evreinhoff, Alexander, Msgr. 89

Fascism 253f, 308, 559, 574–80, 591
—see Mussolini, Lateran Treaties
Faulhaber, Michael, cardinal 25, 73f, 79, 255, 294, 532, 534, 535
Felici, A., pronuncio 568
Felici, Pericle, cardinal 102, 173
Feltin, Maurice, cardinal 109, 333
Ferrata, Domenico, cardinal 22f
Ferrini, Contardo 24
Figueredo, Sergio, S.J. 729
Fiji Islands 798
Filaret, metropolitan of North America 495
Finland 507
—Orthodox Church 429f
Fisher, Desmond 632
Fisher, Geoffrey Francis, archbishop of Canterbury 103
Fitzsimons, John P. 626
Fliche, Augustin 596
Fonck, Leopold, S.J. 284
Fogarty, Michael P. 624
Ford, John 626
Foucauld, Charles de 326, 355f, 367
France 92, 98, 583–600
—Action Française 589, 592
—bishops' conference 120

—care of souls 588f
—Catholic Action 309
—charities 437
—Church, Protestant 459
—Church and state 178, 185f, 204, 585f
—clergy 344f, 598f
—council participants 109
—ecumenical ideas 468
—education 389f, 393, 397, 591
—nationalism 588
—orders 358
—press, Catholic 419f
—public 413
—schools 595
—situation under Benedict XV 583–86
—situation under Pius XI 586–91
—situation under Pius XII 592–600
—theology 261, 263, 265, 268, 275, 596f
—worker-priests 331–35, 339, 597ff
—world war 584ff, 592ff
Franco, Francisco, Spanish chief of state 86, 199, 217, 373
Franič, Franjo, bishop of Split 113, 126, 129
Franzelin, Johannes Baptist 21
Frascati, Pier Giorgio 572
Freedom of conscience 61, 247
Frings, Josef, Cardinal, archbishop of Cologne 32, 108ff, 117, 120, 124, 127, 128, 142, 453ff, 546, 549
Fröbel, Friedrich 390
Fröhlich, Cyprian 442
Frondizi, Argentine president 686
Funk, Franz Xaver 570

Gabriel V, patriarch of Serbia 480f
Gabon 785, 790
Galen, Clemens August von, bishop of Münster, cardinal 32, 73, 76, 545
Gallagher, Michael James, bishop 652
Gambia 780, 791
Gardeil, A., O.P. 264, 277
Garegin, catholicos of Cilicia 503
Garofalo, Salvatore 581
Garrigou-Lagrange, Réginald 265, 278
Garrone, Gabriel, cardinal 144
Gasparri, Pietro, cardinal, secretary of state 22, 25, 30, 46, 48–52, 62, 151, 154, 254, 291, 526, 574
Gedda, Luigi 583
Geiselmann, Joseph Rupert 111, 271
Gemelli, Agostino 573, 581
Gentile, Giovanni 254, 582
Gentiloni, Italian diplomat 573
Gerlier, Pierre Marie, archbishop 124, 334, 589, 593
German, patriarch of Serbia 481, 491
Germany, Federal Republic of 31, 79ff, 85, 87, 88ff, 251, 253ff, 531–49
—assistance from abroad 545
—bishops' conference 120, 534, 549
—Catholic Action 537f

—charities (*Caritas*) 436ff, 441f, 447f, 451, 453, 457
—Church and National Socialism 62–77
—Church, Protestant 459
—clerical opinion survey 347
—clergy 338, 341, 344, 351
—concordat 540, 551
—concordats (state) 533, 535
—Eastern policy, Vatican 549
—ecumenical movement 460, 463, 468
—education 380, 390f, 394, 397, 400ff
—film 414
—Jews 545f
—liturgical movement 300f
—marriage laws 152
—nunciature 546
—orders 321f, 373f
—organizations 307f
—organizations, Catholic 536
—press, Catholic 416ff, 425ff
—prohibition of party politics for priests 548
—publicity 411ff
—reconstruction 547
—religious policy, National Socialist 540f
—state and Church 190–98, 220–28
—synods 161–66
—television 428f
—theology 260ff, 268, 275, 277f, 284, 285, 290
German Democratic Republic 226f, 556
—charity 450
—Pastoral Synod 162, 557
Gestido, Oscar, president of Uruguay 694
Geyer, Bernhard 266
Ghana 779f
Ghellinck, J. de 266
Gibbons, James, cardinal 660
Gijsen, Johannes Matthijs, bishop 569
Gil, Emilio Portes, Mexican president 743
Gilbert Islands 799
Gill, Eric 624
Gilson, Étienne 263, 596
Giolitti, Giovanni 48, 573
Giordani, Igino 575
Glattfelder, Gyula, bishop 522, 524
Gnocchi, Carlo 580
Godfrey, William, archbishop 616
Godin, H. 289, 331
Goebbels, Joseph, German minister of propaganda 542f
Goettsberger, J. 284
Gomes da Costa, Portuguese general 612
Gomulka, Władysław, Polish prime minister 515
Gonner, Nicholas E. 665
Gosling, Samuel 630
Grabmann, Martin 24, 266
Gracias, Valerian, cardinal 110, 463
Great Britain 86, 88, 614–32
—charities 455
—education 389, 391
—education, Catholic 616–22

—hierarchy, Catholic 615
—instruction, religious 629f
—liturgical movement 630
—population, Catholic 614
—press, Catholic 419, 631f
—publicity 411
—social movement 622–29
—YMCA 458
Gregory (I) the Great, pope 331
Gregory VII, pope 37
Gregory XVI, pope 410
Greece 92, 97, 475
—education 408
—Orthodox Church 489f
Griffin, Bernard, archbishop 616, 629
Gröber, Konrad, archbishop of Freiburg 65f, 303f
Grosche, Robert 468
Grösz, József, archbishop 523
Grundmann, Siegfried 226
Guaggiari, José 690
Guano, Emilio, bishop 130
Guardini, Romano 262, 294f, 298, 301f, 305, 306, 317
Guatemala 739ff
Guérin, Abbé 589
Guevara, Ché 698
Guinea 785
Guinea-Bissau 787f
Gummersbach, J., S.J. 264
Gundlach, Gustav, S.J. 240, 246, 252f, 256
Gunkel, Hermann 285
Gut, Benno, O.S.B., abbot 126
Gutiérrez, Augustín 714
Gwynn, Denis 631

Hadrian VI, pope 117
Haiti 199
Hardt, Feliz 412
Häring, Bernhard 130, 275
Harnack, Adolf von 281
Hartmann, Felix von, cardinal 532
Hartmann, Nicolai 263
Hayes, Carlton J. H. 660
Hayes, John 638
Hayes, Patrick, archbishop 656
Heenan, John, archbishop 112, 128, 132, 616
Heidegger, Martin 263, 266, 608
Heinen, Anton 400
Heinen, Wilhelm 275
Heinisch, Paul 285
Hélder Pessoa Câmara, archbishop 682
Helmsing, Charles Herman, bishop 132
Hengartner, Meinrad 455
Hengsbach, Franz, bishop of Essen 128, 141
Hermaniuk, Maxim, Ukrainian metropolitan 132
Herriot, Édouard 587
Hertling, Georg von, count, imperial chancellor 24
Herwegen, Ildefons, O.S.B., abbot 301

Hess, Rudolf 322
Hessen, Johannes 263
Heydrich, Reinhard, chief of the Gestapo 543
Hilarion, metropolitan of the Ukrainian-Greek Orthodox Church in Canada 496
Hildebrand, Dietrich von 263
Himmler, Heinrich, Nazi politician 543
Hinduism 768
Hinsley, Arthur, archbishop 616, 618, 628f
Hitler, Adolf 63–68, 69, 73, 74ff, 82, 86f, 194, 196, 255, 375, 536, 538–42, 579
Hlond, August, cardinal 514, 546
Hobson, John A. 651
Hochhuth, Rolf 78, 93
Hoeck, abbot 135
Hoffman, Hermann 469
Höffner, Joseph, cardinal, archbishop of Cologne 144, 347
Holland, see Netherlands
Honduras 734–36
Hong Kong 803
Hoover, Herbert, president of the United States 642, 651
Hörle, Georg Heinrich 302
Hornyak, Augustine Eugene O.S.B.M., apostolic exarch 615
Horthy, Miklós, regent of Hungary 521
Hostie, Raymond 323
Howard, Henry 616
Hoxha, secretary general of the Albanian Communist Party 490
Hoyt, Robert 665
Hromadka, Joseph 462
Huidobro, Fernando, S.J. 608
Hume, Basil, cardinal 616
Hummelauer, F. von, S.J. 284
Hungary 520–23
—celibacy law 154
—charities 443
—Church, Orthodox 493
—Jews 94
—marriage laws 152
—orders 376
—relations with the Holy See 214
—religious policy, Communist 522f
—religious revival 521f
—Treaty of Trianon 521
—World War II 81, 91
Husserl, Edmund 267
Huyn, Paul, count, archbishop 517

Ibáñez, president of Chile 697
Ignatius XXXVIII Ephraem, patriarch of Antioch 497
Ignatius XXXIX Jacob III Severus, patriarch of Antioch 498
Illiteracy 793
Imperialism 803
India 497–502, 763, 765
Indochina 771

Indonesia 773f
Innitzer, Theodor, cardinal 550–51
Innokentij, Orthodox archbishop in China 494
Internunciatures 754, 762, 768
Iran 497, 503
Iraq 497
Irenej, Orthodox archbishop of New York 495
Ireland 632–41
—Catholic population 632
—charities 443, 456
—Church and state 217, 635f
—education, Catholic 637f
—hierarchy 635f
—lay apostolate 640f
—political development 633ff
—social movement 638ff
Islam 122, 125, 215, 379, 383, 406, 407f, 499f, 501, 526f, 791
Israel 131, 477, 504
Italy 31, 79f, 84f, 89f, 569–83
—Catholic Action 308, 577
—charities 449, 451
—clerical opinion survey 347
—concordat 217f
—council participants 136
—culture 581
—education 390
—education of priests 569f
—episcopal conferences 120
—Fascism 575–80
—Lateran Treaties 576
—orders 358, 571
—parties, Christian 580
—postconciliar period 583
—press, Catholic 421ff
—religious situation 582
—state and Church 187ff, 204, 254
—theology 99
—university, Catholic 581
Ivory Coast 791

Jacob III, patriarch of the Jacobites 139
Jacobs, Konrad 302
Jaeger, Lorenz, cardinal, archbishop of Paderborn 103, 122, 469
Japan 80f, 757, 761
—education 399
—orders 329
—Orthodox Church 494
—television 429
Jarrett, Bede, O.P. 631
Jaspers, Karl 263, 266
Jedin, Hubert 283
Jelevferij, archbishop and exarch 493
Jerome, archimandrite 490f
Jerzy, metropolitan of Poland 493
Jewish persecution 58, 64, 90–95, 122, 127f, 131, 139, 160, 522, 545, 579, 593, 642, 652, 658
Joann, metropolitan of Prague 493

Joasaph II, patriarch of the Copts 499
John XIX, patriarch of the Copts 499
John XXIII, pope 96–151, 209
Jong, Johannes de, cardinal 562
Joseph, exarch in Bulgaria 479
Jungmann, Josef Andreas, S.J. 265, 292, 294, 315f
Jürgensmeier, Friedrich 274, 306
Justin, patriarch of Rumania 488
Justinian, patriarch of Rumania 488f

Kaas, Ludwig 33, 65, 73, 538
Kallistratos, catholicos of Georgia 478
Kassiepe, Max 303
Keegan, Patrick 129, 626
Kehr, Paul 24, 27
Kennedy, John F., American president 659
Kentenich, Josef 319, 329
Kenya 779, 782, 794
Keough, John W. 649
Keppler, Paul Wilhelm, bishop of Rottenburg 294, 337
Kerby, William J. 443
Kerrl, Hanns, German minister 197, 543
Kevork V, catholicos of Echmiadzin 502
Kevork VI, catholicos of Echmiadzin 502
Kirsch, Johann Peter 282
Klauser, Theodor 282
Koch, Joseph 266
Köhler, Oskar 283
Kolb, Viktor 412
Kolbe, Maximilian 319, 375, 514, 515
König Franz, cardinal, archbishop of Vienna 111, 128, 144, 249
Könn, Joseph 302
Kopp, Georg, cardinal 532, 537
Korea 761f
Kramp, Joseph, S.J. 301
Kraus, Franz Xaver 570
Krestinski, Nicolai, Russian ambassador 62
Kreutz, Benedikt, president of Caritas 447
Krofta, Kamill, Czechoslovak ambassador 517
Kruschev, Nikita 249, 484
Kurth, Godefroid 300
Kuss, Otto 285

Labor unions 67, 562, 588, 589, 603, 622, 627, 640, 651, 654, 670, 697, 702, 705, 707, 712, 714, 744
Lafontaine, Peter, patriarch of Venice 25
LaFarge, John, S.J. 256, 656f
Lagrange, Marie Joseph 284, 286, 306
Lais, Hermann 279
Lakner, F. 265
Lambertini, Prospero, later Benedict XIV, 23f
Landersdorfer, Simon Konrad, O.S.B., bishop 303
Landgraf, Arthur-Michael 266
Landrieux, A., bishop 293
Lang, Albert 278

Langbehn, Julius 262
Lanzoni, Angelo 26
Laos 773
Laros, Matthias 468
Larraona, Arcadio, cardinal 110, 126, 362
Lateran Treaties 27, 30, 47–59, 68, 80, 187, 204, 308, 576f
Latin, as language of the Church 103, 107, 109, 123, 631
Latin America 150, 189, 672–74
—charities 453f
—clergy 345
—council participants 110, 138
—education 378, 387f, 398, 403ff
—lack of priests 121
—orders 358, 360
—radio, Catholic 430ff, 435
—state and Church 189
Latvia 507
—concordat 183
Law books (ecclesiastical) 100, 114, 137, 142, 147, 151f, 154, 158 (Eastern), 158, 173–77, 179f, 353, 412
Lay apostolate 118, 125, 126, 129, 133, 141f, 143, 147, 156, 164, 170, 177, 299, 309, 319, 329, 348, 357, 438, 464, 477, 498, 537, 572, 575, 611, 623, 626f, 630, 635, 637–41, 649, 655, 663f, 665f, 674, 679, 682f, 689, 692, 696, 699, 702, 707, 722, 732, 737, 740, 771, 795
League of Nations 46f
Lebanon 497, 503
Le Bras, Grabriel 596
Lebreton, J. 306
Leclercq, J. 276
Lefebvre, Marcel, bishop 352
Le Fort, Gertrud von 338
Léger, Paul Émile, cardinal 118, 127, 132, 143
Leiber, Robert, S.J. 33, 63, 66
Leme, Sebastião, cardinal 675f
Lemke, William 659
Lemoneyer, A. 285
Lence, Germán 725
Lenin, Vladimir Ilyich 740
Leo XIII, pope 28, 114, 152, 231f, 235, 238, 243, 248, 299, 327, 354, 398, 422
Leontios, bishop of Paphos 489
Lercaro, Giacomo, cardinal 109, 116f, 128, 130
Leslie, Shane 631
Lesotho 781, 785
Lex Ecclesiae Fundamentalis 177
Liberia 790
Lieber, Ernst 412
Liénart, Achille, cardinal 108, 113, 118, 589
Lilje, Hanns, bishop 461
Lithard, V. 289
Lithuania 508f
—clergy 509
—concordat 184, 202
liturgical movement 109, 123, 262, 289,

296f, 299–305, 312, 338, 355, 560, 568, 609, 630, 657, 779, 791
Logue, Michael, cardinal 633
Loisy, Alfred 284
Lokuang, Stanislaus, cardinal 110
Lombardi, Riccardo, S.J. 99, 324, 682
Longo, Bartolo 572
López de Lama, Jesús Agustín, bishop 703
Lortz, Joseph 466, 468
Loew, Père Jacques, worker-priest 334, 597
Lubac, Henri de 268, 270, 596
Lucey, Cornelius, bishop 639
Lutherans 492, 506f, 521, 792
Luxemburg 443, 560

Macarius III, patriarch of the Copts 499
McGowan, Raymond A. 651
McGrath, Marcos Gregorios, archbishop 731
McIntyre, James Francis, cardinal 110
Mackintosh, Donald A., archbishop 627
McNabb, Vincent, O.P. 625
McQuaid, John Charles, archbishop 638, 639
Madagascar 779, 782, 792, 794
Maffi, Peter, cardinal 22, 25
Maglione, Luigi, cardinal, secretary of state 31, 34, 115, 303
Magón, Flores 741
Maier, F. 285
Maier, Hans 212
Majláth, Gusztáv, bishop 582, 524
Makarij, Polish metropolitan 492
Makarios II, archbishop of Cyprus 489
Makarios III, archbishop of Cyprus 489f
Malaku Walda Michael, patriarch of Ethiopia 502
Malaysia 770, 775
Mali 791
Malvy, French minister of the interior 584
Manna, Paolo 571
Manrique, Jorge, archbishop 702
Manton, Martin T., judge 660
Maréchal, Joseph 261
Marella, Paolo, nuncio 119, 333, 597
Marianas 797
Marian devotion (Mariology, Legion of Mary) 27, 34, 127, 134, 269, 309, 318–21, 608, 683, 701, 720, 735, 749, 766, 772
Mariategui, José Carlos 706
Marín Sola, F., O.P. 267
Maritain, Jacques 263, 596, 609
Marmion, Columba, abbot of Maredsous 264
Marquesas 797
Marriage law 53, 58, 130, 152, 156, 157, 171f, 175, 185, 196, 200, 217, 579, 583, 605, 608, 637, 664, 686f, 706, 728
Marriage sacrament 130, 157, 188
Marshall Islands 797
Martil, Germano 351
Martin, Josef Maria, archbishop 121, 132
Marty, François, cardinal 143
Marx, Karl 252, 740, 741

Marx, Wilhelm 538
Mass book 123, 170, 300f
Mass media (television, press, radio) 31, 80, 108, 111, 124, 224, 235f, 410–36, 501, 542, 547, 562, 565, 569, 571, 611, 613, 631f, 652, 663, 665, 666, 681, 687, 705, 731, 733, 735, 739, 766f, 788, 803
Masure, M., 278
Matteotti, Giacomo 576
Maura, Antonio, Spanish politician 604
Maurer, Gheorge 526
Maurer, José Clemente, cardinal 704
Maurin, Peter 626, 653
Maurras, Charles 588f, 592
Mausbach, Joseph 272
Mazzolari, Primo 581
Maximos, patriarch of Bulgaria 480
Maximos IV, patriarch 112, 128
Méchineau, L. 284
Medrano, Luis, S.J. 731
Mehmed V Resad, sultan 39
Meinertz, M. 285
Melchisedek, metropolitan 495
Melchisedek III, catholicos of Georgia 478
Mellos, bishop 497
Melville, Arthur, M.M. 740
Melville, Thomas, M.M. 740
Mena Porta, Juan José Anibal, archbishop 691
Mercati, Giovanni, cardinal 27
Mercier, Désiré, cardinal 22, 25, 300, 397, 532, 557
Merkelbach, B. 273
Merkle, Sebastian 281
Merry del Val, Raphael, cardinal 22, 25, 31, 572
Mersch, E. 274, 306
Merz, Hans-Peter 455
Metzger, Max Joseph 469
Mexico 741–50
—hierarchy, Catholic 745f
—orders 372
—pastoral care 745f, 748–50
—persecution 28, 237, 741–44
—piety, forms of 748f
Meyenberg, A. 272
Meyer, Albert Gregor, cardinal 128, 130, 132
Meyer, Augustinus, O.S.B. 351
Michaelis, Georg, imperial chancellor 42ff
Michel, Virgil, O.S.B. 657
Michoneau, worker-priest 597
Milani, Lorenzo 581
Military chaplains 205, 219, 607, 612
Mindszenty, József, cardinal 249, 523f
Miron, patriarch of Bucharest 487
MISEREOR 803
Mission direction 790
Mission methods 795
Mission patronate 764
Missions 110, 114, 129, 141f, 147f, 154ff, 181, 199, 207, 282, 341, 358f, 379, 380,

405f, 431, 446, 453, 459, 463, 465, 477, 560, 563, 571, 608, 613, 632, 662, 666, 684, 701, 704, 713, 719, 722, 745, 803

Mixed marriages 122, 130, 135, 146f, 171, 721

Modernism 98, 269, 281, 332, 337f, 381, 570

Mohlberg, C., O.S.B. 282

Momme Nissen, B., O.P. 262

Montero, Antonio 605

Montessori, Maria 390

Montini, Giovanni (later Paul VI) 34, 89f, 103, 109, 113, 214, 422, 577

Monzón, Uberfil 692

Mooney, Edward, archbishop 653

Morocco 782

Mörsdorf, Klaus 137

Moscati, Giuseppe 572

Mott, John R. 458

Mounier, Emmanuel 596

Mozambique 787ff

Mstyslav, metropolitan of the Ukranian Orthodox Church in Exile 496

Muench, Aloysius, nuncio 547

Múgica, Mateo, bishop 606

Müller-Simonis, Paul 445

Münckner, Theodor 275

Mundelein, George William, cardinal, archbishop of Chicago 75, 653, 658

Murri, Romolo 337, 572f

Muslims 771, 792, 799, 802f

Mussolini, Benito 49f, 51–58, 81, 85–88, 91, 189, 229, 253, 574–79

Namibia 782

Nasalli-Rocca di Corneliano, Giovanni, cardinal 579

Nasser, Gamal Abdel, Egyptian president 500

National Churches 514f, 526, 755

National Socialism 253ff, 268, 283, 294, 304, 322, 330, 373ff, 416, 447, 468, 514, 522, 538, 541, 545, 551, 591f, 628, 661

—see Hitler, Race theories, Reich, Concordat with the

National synods 770, 788

Natural law 232

Naumann, Johann Wilhelm 425

Necchi, Vico 572

Nell-Breuning, Oswald von, S.J. 251f

Neo-Scholasticism 260

Netherlands 561–69

—Catholic press 423f

—Catholic radio 430

—charities 455, 457

—church crisis 568f

—clergy 344, 566

—clergy, opinion survey 347

—disintegration (1960–70) 564–69

—flowering (1919–60) 561–64

—orders 367

—Pastoral Council 160ff, 567

—rise of Catholicism 564

—teaching and preaching 567

—theology 275

—training of priests 567

Netzhammer, Raimund, O.S.B. 524

Neuss, Wilhelm 283

Neutrality (of the papacy and Church) 23, 35, 37, 79ff

New Caledonia 798, 800

New Guinea 776, 799–803

New Hebrides 799

New Zealand 795f, 804

Nicaragua 733f

Nicholas II, Russian tsar 481

Nicholas V, patriarch 476

Nicholas VI, patriarch 476

Nigeria 779f, 785

Nikel, J. 286

Nikodim, metropolitan of Leningrad and Novgorod 485

Nikodim, metropolitan of Moldavia 487

Nikoly, metropolitan 485

Nikoly, metropolitan of Japan 494

Noldin, H., S.J. 273

Noll, John Francis, bishop 664

Nommesch, bishop of Luxemburg 561

Noppel, C. 289

Norris, James J. 130

North America 388–403

North Korea 377

North Solomon Islands 801

Norway 371, 506

Nunciatures (nuncios, apostolic delegates) 11, 20, 21, 24f, 29, 30, 170, 199, 512, 518f, 522, 526, 528f, 533, 547, 553, 568, 586, 594, 616, 635, 673, 674, 746?, 743, 756, 761f, 766, 768ff, 776f, 784, 801

O'Boyle, Patrick A., archbishop 656

Oceania 795f, 804

O'Connell, William, cardinal 652

O'Dea, Thomas, bishop 634

O'Dwyer, Edward Thomas, bishop 633f

O'Grady, John 443, 451

O'Hara, Edwin, bishop 647, 655

O'Hea, Leo, S.J. 623

Ohm, Thomas, O.S.B. 453

Oldmeadow, Ernest 631

Oliva, Francisco de Paula, S.J. 692

O'Rahilly, Alfred 639

Oraison, Maurice 275

Orders 324, 355–378, 621, 699, 810, 812

Oria, Ángel Herrera, cardinal 611

Orione, Luigi 571

Orlando, Vittorio Emanuele, Italian premier 48f, 576

Ortega y Gasset, José 602f, 747

Osborne, ambassador 81

O'Shaughnessy, Michael 653

Osservatore Romano 41, 72, 81, 85, 100, 422f, 577, 592, 652, 681, 708

Ottaviani, Alfredo, cardinal 102, 109, 111, 113, 117, 120, 127, 140

Otto, Rudolf 264
Ozanam, Frédéric 439

Pacelli, Eugenio (later Pius XII) 29, 31, 42–46, 49, 62, 64f, 75, 533, 535f, 591
Pacelli, Francesco 52
Paganuzzi, Ettore 572
Paisios, archbishop of Albania 490
Pakistan 383, 409, 765, 768
Pallavicino, Pietro S., 146
Panama 730ff
Papal election—see Conclave
Papen, Franz von, German vice-chancellor 64f, 540
Paraguay 690–694
Parecattil, J., archbishop of Ernakulam 175
Parental right 139, 382f, 386, 543, 591, 619f, 645, 659
Parente, Pietro, cardinal 110, 118, 126
Parsch, Pius 286, 302
Pascher, Joseph 290
Pastor, Ludwig von 282
Pastoral theology 288–98
Pasqualina, sister 34
Patriarchate (patriarchs) 19, 98, 104, 107, 112, 116, 125, 135, 145, 473–504, 511, 527
Patronate Church 802
Paul VI, pope 159, 209
Paavali, archbishop of Finland 492
Pázmány, Péter, cardinal 522
Peace efforts (of the pope and others) 39–47, 82–88, 94, 114, 236, 256ff, 591, 660
Peeters, Paul 282
Pellegrino, Michele 581
Pepén y Solimán, Juan Félix, bishop 729
Pérez, Roa, archbishop 722
Perón, Juan Domingo 685f
Perrin, Henri, S.J. 332
Peru 705–8
Pétain, Philippe, French marshal 86, 593, 594
Pfliegler, Michael 292
Philips 126, 128, 133
Phillipines 429, 802
Pichler, J. 292
Piffl, Gustav, cardinal 25, 550
Piłsudski, Józef, Polish president 24
Pimen, patriarch of Moscow 485
Pio, Padre 581
Piontek, Ferdinand, vicar capitular 546
Pius IV, pope 148
Pius IX, pope 299
Pius X, pope 11, 37, 98, 229, 284f, 299f, 312f, 337, 352, 572f, 586, 674, 733
Pius XI, pope 23–29, 47, 59, 155, 586–91
Pius XII, pope 29–34, 77–96, 157, 158, 361, 592–600
Pizzardo, Joseph, cardinal 60
Plater, Charles 623
Pla y Deniel, Enrico, cardinal, archbishop of Toledo 607
Plenary council 765f, 771, 795

Plojhar, Josef 519
Pluralism 211, 235, 242, 246f, 268, 339, 365, 415, 424, 554, 561, 565, 580, 582, 675, 804
Podrecca, journalist 576
Poels, Heinrich 563
Pohlschneider, Johannes, bishop of Aachen 386
Poland 24f, 87, 91, 463, 512–16
—Catholic Action 28
—charities 443, 450
—Church, Orthodox 492
—church life 512f
—church struggle 513f
—clergy 339
—concordat 183, 512
—Eastern policy, Vatican 515
—orders 377
—press, Catholic 427
—relation to Holy See 215
—religious policy 201
—state and Church 197
Portugal 611–14, 764, 787
—Catholic Action 28
—development, postconciliar 613f
—Church and state 186, 204, 217
—church life 613
—Concordat 198f
—film 415
—Marian devotion 318
—press 613
—religious instruction 612f
—revolution, anticlerical 611f
Portuguese patronate 765
Potter, Philip 465
Poucel, V. 335
Prat, Flavian 285
Press, see Mass media
Preysing, Konrad von, cardinal, bishop of Berlin 32, 73, 76, 544f
Pribilla, Max, S.J. 468
Price, Thomas F. 662
Priestly office 129, 143, 149, 155, 165
Priests 674, 688, 693, 704, 771, 780
Priests, seminaries (education of priests) 62, 129, 138, 336, 349ff, 362ff, 477, 483f, 487, 490ff, 495, 497, 502, 507, 513, 567, 569, 597, 612f, 673, 675, 676, 683f, 712f, 727f, 738, 744, 746, 760, 767, 771, 786f, 791, 798, 801
Priests, shortage 121, 127, 339, 481, 520, 673, 712, 720, 729, 737, 800, 802
Primatesta, Francisco Raúl, cardinal 690
Primo de Rivera, Spanish general 604
Pro, Augustinus, S.J. 372
Prohászka, Ottokár, cardinal 522
Prümmer, D. M. 273

Race, theory of (racism) 58, 74, 139, 255, 403, 407, 464f, 471, 535, 577f, 652, 655f, 787

Rademacher, Arnold 468
Radini Tedeschi, Giacomo Maria, bishop 97, 572
Rahner, Hugo, S.J. 265, 311, 320
Rahner, Karl, S.J. 129, 271, 291, 320
Ramazotti, Angelo 571
Ramírez, Pedro P. 685
Rampolla, Mariano, cardinal, secretary of state 21f
Ratti, Achille, nuncio (later Pius XI) 23f, 49, 77, 512
Ratzinger, Joseph 141f, 146, 151
Rauschen, G. 570
Reed-Lewis, William 629
Redwood, Vernon 630
Reich, concordat with the (1933) 63–69, 70f, 191, 195ff, 223
Religious instruction 61f, 183, 187, 188, 190, 198, 206, 227f, 380, 409, 479, 481, 499, 519, 543, 551, 557, 561, 567, 573, 578, 593, 609, 628, 641, 647, 677, 681, 685f, 704, 730, 735
Réunion 792
Révai, József, Hungarian minister 376
Rhodesia 785f
Rimmer, Gerard 626
Rites question 753, 758, 759, 763
Ritter, Joseph Elmer, cardinal 109, 128, 132, 656
Ritter, Xaver, nuncio 519
Roberti, Francesco, cardinal 104
Robinson, Paschal, nuncio 635
Robles, Gil José María 604f
Rodano, Franco 580
Roncalli, Angelo, nuncio (later John XXIII) 96f, 388, 530, 594
Roos, Christian 442
Roosevelt, Franklin D., American president 81, 85, 651, 658, 659f
Ropp, Eduard von, archbishop 510
Rosa, Gabriele de 580
Rosary 98, 594, 684
Rossi, Mario 583
Rotta, Angelo, nuncio 522
Rousselot, P. 261, 278
Rubin, Ladislaus 150
Ruffini, Ernesto, cardinal 127, 138
Rugambwa, Laurean, cardinal 110, 120
Ruíz, Echevarría, archbishop 711
Ruiz y Flores, Leopoldo, apostolic delegate 743
Rumania 93, 94, 463, 523–26
—Eastern policy, Vatican 526
—church life 525
—church policy 201, 524
—church and state 203
—concordat 184, 202, 524
—patriarchate, Orthodox 486ff
Rummel, Joseph F., archbishop 657
Russia, see USSR
Ruanda 783
Ryan, John A. 650ff, 659, 660

Sacred Heart devotion 28, 32, 315
Sacrament of matrimony 130, 157, 188
Salazar, Oliveira, president of Portugal 198, 612
Salcedo, José Joaguín 431
Saliège, Jules Geraud, archbishop 593
Salvadori, Giulio 572
Samoa 798, 800, 804
Samorè, Antonio, cardinal 673
Sandwich Islands 797
Sangier, Marc 337
San Martín, Ramón, Cuban president 723
Santucci, Carlo 50f
São Tomé 787
Sarech I, catholicos of Cilicia 504
Sarpi, Paolo 146
Scandinavia 505
Schachleiter, Alban 373
Scheeben, Matthias Joseph 261, 272
Scheler, Max 263
Schenucha III, patriarch of the Copts 500
Schilling, Otto 273, 274
Schirach, Baldur von, Nazi youth leader 543
Schlink, Edmund 104
Schmaus, Michael 265, 320
Schmidlin, Joseph 282
Schmidt, Karl Ludwig 285
Schmitz Sauerborn, German, auxiliary bishop 708
Schneider, Joseph, archbishop 130
Schöllgen, Werner, 275
Schools, see Education
Schott, Anselm, O.S.B. 300
Schrembs, Joseph, bishop 644
Schulte, Karl Joseph, cardinal, archbishop of Cologne 25
Schulz, A. 286
Schuman, Robert, French foreign minister 301
Schuster, Alfredo Ildefonso, cardinal, archbishop of Milan 56, 116, 577, 579
Schütte, Johannes, S.V.D. 142
Second World War 67–96, 177, 198, 769, 771, 774f, 806f, 797, 799
Secular institutes 33, 158, 326–31, 355–58, 760, 767
Seipel, Ignaz 538, 550
Selassie, Haile, emperor of Ethiopia 501
Semmelroth, Otto, S.J. 320
Senegal 773, 790
Seppelt, Franz Xaver, 282
Seraphim, archbishop 490
Serbia 480f
Serédi, Jusztinián, cardinal 518, 522
Sergius, patriarch of Moscow 483
Sertillanges, Antonia Gilbert, O.P. 263, 585
Seychelles 792
Shahan, Thomas 443f
Sheed, Frank 630
Sickenberger, Joseph 284, 285
Sierra Leone 780

Simeon, bishop of Shanghai 494
Simon XX Paul, patriarch of the Nestorians 496
Simon XXI Jesse, patriarch of the Nestorians 497
Simonis, Adrian, bishop of Rotterdam 569
Siri, Giuseppe, cardinal 118
Sixtus V, pope 10, 11, 18, 115, 148
Slater, Theodor 273
Slipyi, Josyf, metropolitan 512
Smith, Alfred 658
Smith, Matthew J. W., Msgr. 664
Snead-Cox, John George 631
Snoeck, A. 275
Socialism 59, 200, 213, 231, 248–53, 415, 538, 549f, 561f, 573, 576, 603, 624, 688, 699, 714, 741, 743, 791
Society Islands 797
Söderblom, Nathan 458, 460, 467
Soiron, Theodor, O.F.M. 265
Solomon Islands 799ff
Solzhenitsyn, Aleksandr 213
Sotelo, José Calvo, Spanish politician 605
South Africa 779, 781, 785
Southern Rhodesia 782
South Solomons 801
Soviet Union, see USSR
Spain 92, 600–611
—agencies, ecclesiastical 610f
—Alphonso XIII 601–4
—Catholic Action 28, 610
—charities 443, 451, 456
—Church and state 199, 204–8, 211, 216
—Civil War 605ff
—clerical opinion survey 347
—education 218, 393, 397
—episcopal conference 609
—Liturgical movement 305
—orders 357f, 372
—persecution 237, 605f
—press, Catholic 421f
—syndicalism, Christian 603f
Spellman, Francis Joseph, cardinal 81, 105, 111, 113
Spiritual Exercises Movement 310
Sproll, Johann, bishop 544
Staffa, Dino, archbishop 110, 118
Stalin, Joseph 84, 87, 463
Statistics, ecclesiastical 1–21
—Africa 777
—Argentina 685
—Belgium 558
—Brazil 674, 676f
—Buddhism 757
—Canada 667
—charities 439f, 445f, 457
—China 753f
—Colombia 712
—Cuba 723
—Czechoslovakia 516
—Dominican Republic 728

—Eastern Churches 479f
—Eastern Europe 507f, 512f
—Ecuador 708
—education 378
—El Salvador 736
—France 588f
—Gabon 790
—Great Britain 614
—Honduras 734
—Hungary 521
—India 768
—Ireland 632
—Italy 569, 580, 582
—Japan 760
—Kenya 782
—Korea 763
—Madagascar 792
—Mali 791
—Mexico 744f
—Mozambique 788
—Netherlands 563
—Nigeria 780
—Nyasaland 783
—Oceania 799
—orders 479f
—Panama 730
—Paraguay 691
—Peru 705
—Poland 516
—press 415f
—Ruanda 783
—Rumonia 525
—Samoa 798
—schools 393f
—South Korea 762
—Spain 606f
—Uruguay 694
—Venezuela 719
—Yugoslavia 529
State, secretariat of (secretary) 16, 22f, 30, 52, 86, 89, 115, 148, 170, 249, 591
Stefan, metropolitan of Poland 493
Stegmüller, Friedrich 282
Stein, Edith 375
Stelzenberger, Johannes 275
Stepinač, Aloysius, cardinal 249, 528
Stieglitz, Heinrich 293
Stocchiero, G. 289
Stohr, Albert, bishop of Mainz 303
Stojadinović, Milan 528
Stojan, exarch of Bulgaria 483
Stolz, Anselm, O.S.B. 265
Storr, Rupert 310
Stourm, René Louis, archbishop 112, 124
Stresemann, Gustav, German foreign minister 229
Stroessner, Alfredo 691
Sturzo, Don Luigi, Italian politician 50, 54, 574f
Stutz, Ulrich 194
Subercaseaux, Valdés, bishop 700

Subsidiarity, principle of 149, 174, 232, 239, 242–46, 382, 438
Sudan 779, 783ff
Suenens, Josef Léon, cardinal 111, 113f, 116, 118, 130, 137, 455
Suhard, Emmanuel Célestin, cardinal 286, 331f, 596f
Sulu Archipelago 803
Swaziland 781, 790
Sweden 391, 507
Switzerland 81, 552f
—charities 443, 449ff
—clerical opinion survey 347
—diocesan synods 163
—education 389f
—orders 330, 371
—press, Catholic 419f

Tacchi-Venturi, Pietro, S.J. 50, 578
Tahiti 800
Taiwan 755f
Tanganyika 779, 782
Tanzania 792
Tardini, Domenico, cardinal, secretary of state 34, 86f, 100, 113
Taylor, Myron C. 81, 87, 659
Teusch, Josef, vicar general 453
Thailand 774
Theodosius VI, patriarch of Antioch 477
Theological faculty 791
Theophilos I, patriarch of the Copts 501f
Thérèse of Lisieux 336
Thils, Gustave 335
Third world (developing nations) 230, 241, 259, 379, 428, 453, 456, 689
Thomas Aquinas 363
Tien, Thomas, cardinal 31
Tikhon, patriarch of Moscow 482, 492, 494
Tillmann, Fritz 274f, 286, 294, 306
Timoteusz, metropolitan in Poland 493
Timotheos, patriarch of Jerusalem 477
Tiso, Josef, Slovakian statesman 519
Tisserant, Eugène, cardinal 27, 116, 132, 138, 341
Tito, Josip Broz, Yugoslavian chief of state 480f, 528f
Tixeron, J. 266
Togo 779f
Toher, Michael 640
Tonga 800
Tongelen, Josef, president of Caritas 445
Toniolo, Giuseppe, sociologist 572
Torrado, Oswaldo Dorticós, president of Cuba 723
Torres, Camilo 698
Tóth, Tihamér, bishop 582
Trent, Council of 80, 104, 107, 116, 118, 129, 134, 140f, 146f, 151, 152, 313f, 602
Trials, morals charges 75, 374
Tromp, Sebastian, S.J. 110
Trueba, Andrés Martínez 694
Truman, Harry, American president 660

Tunisia 215
Turkey 98, 497, 503
Turner, Thomas W. 655

Uganda 782, 785f, 792f
Unemployment 229, 626, 724
United Nations 629, 756
Universities 23, 25, 100, 139, 156, 206, 283, 380, 384, 389, 395–99, 404, 421, 442, 447, 468, 490, 513, 551, 558, 559f, 562, 570, 578, 581, 596f, 609, 611, 614, 622, 632, 638, 648, 651, 666ff, 669, 680, 686, 691, 699, 701, 706f, 713, 716f, 720f, 726, 733, 739, 747, 757, 766, 772, 786, 803
Upper Volta 779, 791
Urbani, Giovanni, cardinal 136
Uruguay 330, 694ff
Urundi 783
United States of America 86, 498, 503, 642–67, 756, 761, 797
—charities 441f, 449, 451, 456, 659–63
—clergy 348
—clerical opinion survey 347
—council participants 109, 131
—ecclesiastical policy 658–60
—ecumenism 472–73
—education 378, 381, 387ff, 390, 394f, 397, 402
—education, Catholic 645–50
—episcopal sees 154
—film 414
—hierarchy, Catholic 643f
—lay movements 663–64
—liturgical movement 305, 630, 657–58
—orders 367
—Orthodox Church 494f
—population, Catholic 641f
—postconciliar development 667
—press, Catholic 664–67
—publicity 412
—social movement 650–57
—television 429
USSR 28, 80, 86f, 89, 179, 254, 463, 497, 509–12
—catholicate of Echmiadzin 502f
—Church and state, separation of 509
—Eastern policy, Vatican 512
—education 392, 396
—Marian devotion 318
—measures against the clergy 509f
—orders 375
—Orthodox Church in Georgia 478f
—papal assistance mission 510
—patriarchate of Moscow 481–86
—persecution, Catholic 237
—religious freedom, denial of 466
—religious policy 200, 215
—Vatican 59–63

Valeri, Valerio, nuncio 594
Vallainc, Fausto 108
Vanistendael, August 455

Vannutelli, Vincenzo, cardinal 30
Vanrell, Bartolomé, S.J. 692
Van Roey, Joseph Ernst, cardinal 557
Varnava, patriarch 528
Varona, Graciano, O.S.B. 729
Vasgen, catholicos 503
Vassilij, metropolitan of Poland 493
Vatican I (First Vatican Council) 101, 104,
  106f, 116, 118, 122, 126, 131, 133, 146,
  152, 260, 439
Vatican II (Second Vatican Council) 96–151,
  158ff, 209ff, 364–71, 382–88, 553ff, 613,
  696, 752, 755, 760, 767f, 770, 779, 788,
  800
Vaz, Alfonso J. Alfonzo 721
Vélez, José María 721
Venezuela 719–23
Verdier, Johannes, cardinal 589
Vianney, Jean Baptiste Marie 329
Vicent, Antonio, S.J. 603
Victor, exarch of Peking 494
Victor Emmanuel III, king of Italy 49, 88
Vidal y Barraquer, Francisco, cardinal 606
Vietnam 230, 771
—clergy 339
—education 409
Vikentij, patriarch of Serbia 481
Villalba, Leónidas Proaño, bishop 710f
Villalobar, Spanish diplomat 45
Vogels, H. J. 285
Voillaume, René 355
Volk, Hermann, cardinal, bishop of Mainz
  144

Walsh, James A. 662
Walsh, Robert P. 626
Ward, Maisie 630
Ward, Wilfrid 631
Waters, Vincent, bishop 656

Wellhausen, Julius 285
Welte, Bruno 278
Welykyi 112
Wernz, Franz Xaver, S.J. 24
Werthmann, Lorenz, 442f, 444
Willam, Franz-Michel 306
Willebrands, Johannes, cardinal 104, 469
Willmann, Otto 292
Wilpert, Joseph 282
Wilson, Woodrow, American president 45,
  660f
Wojtyla, Karol, archbishop of Cracow (later
  Pope John Paul II) 128
Wolker, Ludwig 301f
Woodruff, Douglas 631
Worker-priests 338, 597f
Wulf, Maurice de 266
Wust, Peter 263, 299
Wyszyński, Stefan, cardinal, archbishop of
  Warsaw 112, 136, 215, 249, 515f

Youth movement 262, 289, 301
Yugoslavia 526–29
—Catholic Action 28
—Catholic press 427
—charities 443
—church persecutions 528
—concordats 185, 527
—orders 376
—situation since 1970 529
—state and church 202, 526
—relations with the Holy See 214
Yuhana Mar Thomas, metropolitan of the
  reformed Jacobites 499

Zaire 779, 783f, 786
Zambia 787
Zamora, Niceto Alcalá, president of Spain
  604